THE ENCYCLOPEDIA OF POLITICAL REVOLUTIONS

THE ENCYCLOPEDIA OF POLITICAL REVOLUTIONS

JACK A. GOLDSTONE, Editor

Congressional Quarterly Inc.
Washington, D.C.

1414 22nd Street, N.W., Washington, D.C. 20037
http://books.cq.com

Book design and production by Naylor Design Inc.,
Upper Marlboro, Maryland

Printed and bound in the United States of America

The paper used in this publication meets the minimum requirements of the American National Standard for Information Sciences—Permanence of Paper for Printed Library Materials, ANSI Z39.48-1984.

Photo credits and permissions for copyrighted material begin on page 545, which is to be considered an extension of the copyright page.

LIBRARY OF CONGRESS CATALOGING-IN-PUBLICATION DATA
The encyclopedia of political revolutions / edited by Jack A. Goldstone
p. cm.
Includes bibliographical references (p.) and index.
ISBN 1-56802-206-9
1. Revolutions—Encyclopedias. I. Goldstone, Jack A.
JC491.E63 1998
903--dc21 98-36771

CONTENTS

PREFACE

Revolutions, with their stunning panorama of violence and change, are an endless source of fascination and debates. Over the past five hundred years, almost every country in the world has been touched by revolutions, either in their own history or through neighboring countries that have spread their influence abroad. The number of individuals—a few of them famous, most of them faceless and unknown—who have participated in revolutions reaches into the millions. Revolutions have stemmed from desires to overcome inequality, from demands for democracy, and from visions of communist or Islamic utopias.

This encyclopedia ranges widely over the globe, across cultures, and across different kinds of events in seeking to describe and explain revolutionary activity since 1500 A.D. We have not insisted on one standard definition of "revolution" for all of the events described herein. Revolutions themselves are enormously varied, and it is notoriously difficult to make a clean separation between revolutions and similar events—revolts and rebellions, civil wars, protest movements, revolutionary coups, reform movements—with which revolutions are often intertwined. Some protest movements, for example, have involved more deaths and violence than some revolutions. This encyclopedia therefore examines those events that share two characteristics: irregular procedures aimed at forcing political change within a society (which may include coups, mass protests, civil war, guerrilla warfare, peasant or urban uprisings, or planned insurrections) *and* lasting effects on the political system of the society in which they occurred. Although this definition excludes a great many events, including routine military coups, civil wars that represent only factional power struggles and do not change the political order, and social reform movements that change only specific policies (for example, abolitionism), our definition embraces many events that one might not expect to find in an encyclopedia of political revolutions, such as the woman's rights and civil rights movements, the Indian and Pakistani independence movements, and slave revolts. Because these latter events involved mass protests and challenged the very definition of who should and should not have political power, we felt they deserve treatment in a volume on the general topic of political revolution.

This encyclopedia features three types of essays, covering revolutionary events, revolutionary leaders, and key concepts. The essays on revolutions generally focus on a specific event. However, in those cases where several events spread across time or across countries are notable mainly for their collective impact (such as Latin American slave revolts or the European revolutions of 1848), we have commissioned survey essays that span those events. And although many revolutionary actors are mentioned in the essays on specific revolutions, we have commissioned a small number of essays on revolutionary leaders and thinkers, particularly those whose influence has spread beyond the boundaries of their own societies.

In addition, we have asked scholars to contribute essays on key concepts and their role in the history of revolution. These include essays on democracy, socialism, gender, Islamic fundamentalism, inequality, injustice, and many more, plus essays that survey the role of revolution in art and in literature. These "key concept" entries are particularly helpful in detailing how revolutions have shaped global history in the realms of politics and culture.

This encyclopedia is, of course, a collective work. But more than that, it has been to an unusual degree the product of genuine teamwork. Members of the Editorial and Advisory Boards have generously given their time to extensive discussions of the form and content of this volume. The authors of individual essays have been patient and flexible in responding to our guidelines. The result is a volume on revolutions that I believe is unique in its intellectual breadth, liveliness, and readability.

The task of choosing particular events, persons, and concepts was difficult. While we could have chosen thousands of entries, doing so would have left little room to address the issues fully or to analyze particular events. We have therefore chosen to feature longer essays, ranging from five hundred to several thousand words, focusing on almost three hundred topics. Readers who do not find a specific event or person in the alphabetical list of articles or list of articles by subject should check the index, which cites many more persons and events. In addition, each entry features a short bibliography to guide interested readers to more detail.

It is a tribute to the efforts of our Editorial and Advisory Boards that the authors of the essays in this book are among the world's leading experts in their fields, and moreover that these authors have taken the time to craft original interpretive essays on their subjects, representing the latest in scholarship. General readers interested in a specific historical event or person, students seeking information and references for a research paper, specialists seeking information in or outside their field, and individuals just curious about the general phenomenon of revolution will find in this volume something new, interesting, and unexpected.

Our Advisory and Editorial Boards helped shape the list of events, topics, and persons covered in the encyclopedia and helped identify and recruit our authors. The Editorial Board members reviewed all the essays and made specific recommendations. For their work, diligently and energetically undertaken, I want to thank these outstanding scholars and colleagues. The entire Editorial Board and myself also owe thanks to our talented sponsoring editor Dave Tarr, who organized and supervised the entire project, and to the superb editorial and production team at Congressional Quarterly: Allison Berland, who handled the essential correspondence and tracking of materials; Jerry Orvedahl, who oversaw the manuscript editing, illustrations, maps, and production of the volume; our copyeditors, Carolyn Goldinger, Steven B. Kennedy, Sabra Bissette Ledent, Madelyn Ross, and Jane Sevier Sánchez; Christopher Karlsten, for ably performing a wide range of editorial services; and Talia Greenberg, who assisted with photo research.

I also wish to thank my family—my wife Gina Saleman-Goldstone and our children Alexander and Simone—for their patience during the many late nights taken for work on this project. It is ironic that without revolutions, my family would not exist. My parents fled Hitler's Nazi Revolution and met in Shanghai, China, during the tumultuous years leading up to the Chinese Communist Revolution. My wife's father left Mussolini's Italy and came to the United States, where he met my wife's mother, whose family had fought in the Russian Revolution of 1917, then later fought in and fled from Stalin's armies and gulags. When I want to see how revolutions have touched lives, I need look no further than my own home. I hope this encyclopedia will help instruct and entertain all those whose lives or imagination have been touched by these most remarkable events.

Jack A. Goldstone
Del Mar, California

September 1998

ALPHABETICAL LIST OF ARTICLES

CONTRIBUTORS

A

ADAS, MICHAEL
Rutgers University
Millenarianism

ADELMAN, HOWARD
York University
Rwandan Civil Wars (1959–1994)

ADELMAN, JEREMY
Princeton University
San Martín, José Francisco de

AFARY, JANET
Purdue University
Iranian Constitutional Revolution (1906)

AHMIDA, ALI ABDULLATIF
University of New England
Libyan Revolution (1969)

ANDERSON, JON LEE
Author and journalist
Guevara, Ernesto "Che"

ARJOMAND, SAÏD AMIR
State University of New York at Stony Brook
Khomeini, Ayatollah Ruhollah

ARMSTRONG, CHARLES
Columbia University
Korean Civil War (1950–1953)
Korean Democracy Movement (1960–1998)

ASPINALL, EDWARD
University of New South Wales
East Timorese Independence Movement (1975–)

AUGUSTINOS, GERASIMOS
University of South Carolina
Greek War of Liberation (1821–1832)

AVERILL, STEPHEN C.
Michigan State University
Chinese Communist Revolution (1921–1949)

B

BANNING, LANCE
University of Kentucky
Jefferson, Thomas

BARRY, KATHLEEN
Pennsylvania State University
Anthony, Susan B.
Woman's Rights Movement

BAXTER, CRAIG
Juniata College
Bangladeshi War of Independence (1971)

BAXTER, STEPHEN B.
University of North Carolina at Chapel Hill
William of Orange (King William III of England)

BEININ, JOEL
Stanford University
Egyptian Muslim Brotherhood Movement (1928–)
Egyptian Revolts (1881–1919)

BELL, J. BOWYER
Columbia University
Irish Revolution (1916–1923)

BERRY, MARY ELIZABETH
University of California, Berkeley
Japanese Tokugawa Shogun Ascendancy (1598–1615)

BLANCHARD, PETER
University of Toronto
Bolívar, Simón
Latin American Revolutions for Independence (1808–1898)

BLUM, CAROL
State University of New York at Stony Brook
Rousseau, Jean-Jacques

BOGGS, CARL
National University
Gramsci, Antonio

BOHR, P. RICHARD
College of Saint Benedict and Saint John's University, Saint Joseph, Minn.
Chinese Taiping Rebellion (1851–1864)
Hong Xiuquan

BRADY, THOMAS A., JR.
University of California, Berkeley
Anabaptism
German Peasant War (1524–1526)
Luther, Martin

BRIC, MAURICE
University College Dublin
Irish Revolts (1790s–1900)

BROERS, MICHAEL
University of Leeds
European Revolutions of 1820
Liberalism
Spanish War of Independence (1808–1813)

BRONNER, STEPHEN ERIC
Rutgers University
Luxemburg, Rosa

BUSTIN, EDOUARD
Boston University
Guinean Independence Movement (1958)

C

CARSON, CLAYBORNE
Stanford University
King, Martin Luther, Jr.

CHILCOTE, RONALD H.
University of California, Riverside
Cabral, Amílcar

CHIROT, DANIEL
University of Washington
Hitler, Adolf
Mussolini, Benito
Stalin, Joseph
Sukarno
Tyranny

CLANCY-SMITH, JULIA
University of Arizona
Islamic Anticolonial Revolts of the 19th Century

CLIFFORD, NICHOLAS R.
Middlebury College
Chinese May Thirtieth Movement (1925)

COBLE, PARKS M.
University of Nebraska at Lincoln
Chiang Kai-shek
Chinese Nationalist Revolution (1919–1927)

COLLINS, RANDALL
University of Pennsylvania
Capitalism

CONROY, DAVID W.
Author
Adams, John
Adams, Samuel

COTMAN, JOHN WALTON
Howard University
Grenada "New Jewel" Revolution (1979–1983)

COVELL, MAUREEN
Simon Fraser University
Madagascar (Malagasy) War of Independence (1947)

CRAWFORD, NETA
University of Massachusetts
South African Antiapartheid Revolts and Reform (1948–1994)

CREED, GERALD W.
Hunter College and the Graduate School of the City University of New York
Bulgarian Anticommunist Revolution (1989–1997)

CROUT, ROBERT RHODES
Charleston Southern University
Lafayette, Gilbert du Motier de

D

DAE-SOOK SUH
University of Hawaii at Manoa
Kim Il Sung

DALY, M. W.
Kettering University
Sudanese Mahdiyya (1881–1898)

DANOPOULOS, CONSTANTINE P.
San Jose State University
Albanian Anticommunist Revolution (1990–1992)

DAVIS, ERIC
Rutgers University
Iraqi Revolution (1958)

DAVIS, JOHN A.
University of Connecticut
Italian Risorgimento (1789–1870)

DeFRONZO, JAMES
University of Connecticut
Films and Video Documentaries

DENG, FRANCIS M.
Brookings Institution, Washington, D.C.
Sudanese Civil War (1955–1972; 1982–)

DIPPEL, HORST
University of Kassel
Constitutions

DOMÍNGUEZ, JORGE I.
Harvard University
Castro, Fidel
Cuban Revolution (1956–1970)

DOVER, PAUL
Yale University
Italian City-State Revolutions of the Renaissance (1494–1534)

DOYLE, WILLIAM
University of Bristol
Buonarroti, Filippo Michele
French Revolution (1789–1815)
Marat, Jean-Paul
Robespierre, Maximilien
Tocqueville, Alexis de

DREYER, JUNE TEUFEL
University of Miami
Tibetan Revolt (1959)

DUBOFSKY, MELVYN
Binghamton University
U.S. Labor Revolts (1890–1932)

DUIKER, WILLIAM J.
Pennsylvania State University
Ho Chi Minh

DUPUY, ALEX
Wesleyan University
Haitian Democratic Revolution (1986–1996)
Haitian Revolution of Independence (1791–1804)
L'Ouverture, François-Dominique Toussaint

E

ESHERICK, JOSEPH W.
University of California, San Diego
Chinese Boxer Uprising (1898–1900)
Chinese Republican Revolution (1911)

EVANS, EMORY G.
University of Maryland at College Park
Henry, Patrick

F

FLAGG, PETER J.
Crocker Art Museum, Sacramento, California
Art and Representation

FORAN, JOHN
University of California, Santa Barbara
Economic Development

FORREST, JOSHUA BERNARD
University of Vermont
Guinea-Bissau Independence Revolt (1962–1974)

FRUCHTMAN, JACK, JR.
Towson University
Paine, Thomas

G

GEORGE, TIMOTHY S.
University of Rhode Island
Japanese Meiji Restoration (1868)

GILDEA, ROBERT
Oxford University
French Student Revolt (1968)

GLEASON, ABBOTT
Brown University
Russian Decembrist Revolt (1825)

GOLDSTONE, JACK A.
University of California, Davis
Democracy
Inequality
Leadership
Population
Radicalism
Reform
Russian-Ukrainian Cossack and Peasant Revolts (1606–1775)
Spanish Conquest, Aztec and Inca Revolts in the Era of (1500–1571)

GOODWIN, JEFF
New York University
Injustice

GORDON, JOEL
University of Nebraska at Omaha
Nasser, Gamal Abdel

GOULD, ROGER V.
University of Chicago
Workers

GRAHAM, HELEN
Royal Holloway, University of London
Spanish Civil War (1936–1939)

GROSS, JAN T.
New York University
Polish Protest Movements and Solidarity Revolution (1956–1991)
Walesa, Lech

GROTH, ALEXANDER J.
University of California, Davis
Dictatorship

GRUNDY, KENNETH W.
Case Western Reserve University
Biko, Stephen
Mandela, Nelson Rolihlahla

GUELZO, ALLEN C.
Eastern College
U.S. Civil War (1861–1865)

GUILMARTIN, JOHN F., JR.
Ohio State University
Armed Forces
Violence

H

HALICZER, STEPHEN
Northern Illinois University
Spanish *Comuneros* Revolt (1520–1521)

HALL, JOHN A.
McGill University
States

HALLIDAY, FRED
London School of Economics
Islamic Fundamentalism
Yemen Revolutions (1962–1990)

HAMILTON, RICHARD F.
Ohio State University
Bourgeoisie
German Revolution (1918)

HANAGAN, MICHAEL
New School for Social Research
British Reform and Emancipation Movement (1820–1833)

HANSON, PAUL R.
Butler University
Parties

HANSON, STEPHEN E.
University of Washington
Lenin, Vladimir Ilyich

HANSON, VICTOR DAVIS
California State University, Fresno
Republics

HARBESON, JOHN W.
City University of New York
Eritrean Revolution (1962–1991)

HARDWICK, JULIE
Texas Christian University
French Frondes (1648–1653)

HIGGINBOTHAM, DON
University of North Carolina at Chapel Hill
Washington, George

HIGLEY, JOHN
University of Texas at Austin
Elites

HOLOMAN, D. KERN
University of California, Davis
Music

HOLT, MACK P.
George Mason University
French Peasant Revolts (1594–1648)
French Wars of Religion (1562–1598)

I

INGLE, STEPHEN
University of Stirling
Orwell, George
Sorel, Georges

J

JANOS, ANDREW C.
University of California, Berkeley
Hungarian Revolutions (1918–1919)

JARAUSCH, KONRAD H.
University of North Carolina at Chapel Hill and Zentrum für Zeithistorische Forschung, Potsdam
East German Revolution and Unification (1989–1990)

JONES, GEORGE HILTON
Eastern Illinois University
British Jacobite Rebellions (1715–1745)

JOSHI, SANJAY
Northern Arizona University
Indian Independence Movement (1885–1947)
Indian Regional Revolts (1947–)

K

KANOGO, TABITHA
University of California, Berkeley
Kenyatta, Jomo

KARL, TERRY
Stanford University
Venezuelan Democratic Revolution (1945–1958)

KATOUZIAN, HOMA
Exeter University
Mosaddeq, Mohammad

KATZ, MARK N.
George Mason University
Cycles, Waves, and Diffusion

KAYALI, HASAN
University of California, San Diego
Turkish Revolution (1908–1922)

KEDDIE, NIKKI R.
University of California, Los Angeles
Islamic Precolonial Revolts of the 18th and 19th Centuries

KELLER, EDMOND J.
University of California, Los Angeles
Ethiopian Revolution (1974–1991)

KERKVLIET, BEN
Australian National University
Philippine Huk and New People's Army Rebellions (1946–mid-1950s; late 1960s–late 1980s)
Philippine "People Power" Revolution (1986)

KETCHAM, RALPH
Syracuse University
Franklin, Benjamin
Madison, James

KICZA, JOHN E.
Washington State University
Latin American Revolts under Colonial Rule (1571–1898)

KIERNAN, BEN
Yale University
Cambodian Khmer Rouge Revolution (1967–1979)

KIRK, JOHN
Dalhousie University
Martí, José

KLEIN, HERBERT S.
Columbia University
Bolivian National Revolution (1952)

KOSTINER, JOSEPH
Tel Aviv University
Arab "Great Revolt" (1916–1918)
Omani Rebellions (1955–1975)
Saudi Arabian Wahhabi Movement (1744–)

KOTKIN, STEPHEN
Princeton University
Gorbachev, Mikhail
USSR Collapse and Dissolution (1989–1991)

KOVRIG, BENNETT
University of Toronto
Hungarian Anticommunist Revolution (1989)
Hungarian Revolution (1956)

KRAMNICK, ISAAC
Cornell University
Burke, Edmund

KRAUS, JON
State University of New York at Fredonia
Ghanaian Independence Movement (1946–1957)
Nkrumah, Kwame

KRIGER, NORMA
Author
Mugabe, Robert Gabriel
Zimbabwe Revolt and Reform (1966–1980)

L

LARKIN, JOHN A.
State University of New York at Buffalo
Philippine Independence Wars (1872–1910)

LAWSON, FRED H.
Mills College
Syrian Revolution (1963)

LAWSON, STEVEN F.
University of North Carolina at Greensboro
U.S. Civil Rights Movement (1954–1968)

LESLIE, WINSOME J.
Embassy of Jamaica, Washington, D.C., and Johns Hopkins University
Congolese/Zairian Upheavals (1960–)

LEVINE, DANIEL H.
University of Michigan
Liberation Theology

LICHBACH, MARK
University of California, Riverside
Rationality

LOCKHART, PAUL DOUGLAS
Wright State University
Swedish Royal Revolution (1523)

LOCKMAN, ZACHARY
New York University
Egyptian Revolution (1952)

LOFCHIE, MICHAEL F.
University of California, Los Angeles
Zanzibar Revolution (1964)

LONG, ROGER D.
Eastern Michigan University
Pakistani Independence Movement (1940–1947)

LONGMAN, TIMOTHY
Vassar College
Burundi Civil Wars (1993–)

LOVEMAN, BRIAN
San Diego State University
Coup d'État

M

MACEOIN, DENIS
University of Durham
Babi Revolts (1844–1852)

MACKEY, THERESA M.
Georgia College and State University
Literature

MARCUM, JOHN A.
Director, Education Abroad Program, University of California
Angolan Revolution (1974–1996)

MARKOFF, JOHN
University of Pittsburgh
Peasants

MARR, DAVID G.
Australian National University
Vietnamese Revolution (1945–1975)

MARSHALL, JOHN
Johns Hopkins University
Locke, John

MAZRUI, ALI A.
State University of New York at Binghamton, University of Jos, and Cornell University
Fanon, Frantz Omar
Nationalism
Nyerere, Julius Kambarage

McCLINTOCK, CYNTHIA
George Washington University
Peruvian "Revolution from Above" (1968–1975)

McCONVILLE, BRENDAN
State University of New York at Binghamton
U.S. Preindependence and Pre-Civil War Rebellions (1675–1850)

McLELLAN, DAVID
Eliot College, University of Kent
Marx, Karl, and Friedrich Engels

MEISNER, MAURICE
University of Wisconsin at Madison
Intellectuals
Socialism

MERRIMAN, JOHN
Yale University
European Revolutions of 1830

MILANI, MOHSEN M.
University of South Florida
Iranian Islamic Revolution (1979)

MORRILL, JOHN
Cambridge University
Cromwell, Oliver

MURRAY, DIAN
University of Notre Dame
Chinese Triad Society Rebellions (18th–20th Centuries)

O

OPELLO, WALTER C., JR.
State University of New York at Oswego
Portuguese Revolution (1974)

OQUIST, PAUL
Author
Colombia's "La Violencia" (1948–1964)

OTTAWAY, MARINA
Carnegie Endowment for International Peace
Mozambican Revolution (1974–1994)

OVERY, R. J.
King's College, London
German Nazi Revolution (1933–1945)

OWNBY, DAVID
University of Montreal
Chinese Late Ming Revolts (1620–1644)
Chinese Sectarian and Secret Society Revolts (1644–)
Chinese White Lotus Rebellions (18th–20th Centuries)

P

PALAIS, JAMES
University of Washington
Korean Rebellions of 1812 and 1862
Korean Tonghak Rebellion (1894)

PALMER, DAVID SCOTT
Boston University
Peruvian "Shining Path" Revolt (1980–)

PAPPE, ILAN
Haifa University
Israeli Independence Revolt (1946–1948)

PAQUETTE, ROBERT L.
Hamilton College
Latin American and Caribbean Slave Revolts (1521–1888)

PARKER, GEOFFREY
Ohio State University
Bohemian Revolt (1618–1648)

PERRY, ELIZABETH
Harvard University
Chinese Cultural Revolution (1966–1969)

PETERS, B. GUY
University of Pittsburgh
Bureaucracy

PINCUS, STEVE
University of Chicago
British "Glorious Revolution" (1688–1689)

PLAKANS, ANDREJS
Iowa State University
Baltic Revolutions of 1991

POLASKY, JANET L.
University of New Hampshire
Belgian Revolutions (1789–1830)

POPKIN, JEREMY D.
University of Kentucky
Media and Communications

PRATT, WILLIAM C.
University of Nebraska at Omaha
U.S. Rural Post-Civil War Rebellions (1865–1940)

PREST, WILFRID
University of Adelaide
British Civil Wars and Revolution (1638–1660)

PRESTON, LAURENCE W.
University of British Columbia
Indian "Great Mutiny" (1857–1859)

PRICE, ROGER
University of Wales, Aberystwyth
European Revolutions of 1848

PYE, LUCIAN W.
Massachusetts Institute of Technology
Deng Xiaoping
Mao Zedong

Q

QUATAERT, DONALD
Binghamton University
Ottoman Jelali and Janissary Revolts (1566–1826)
Ottoman Revolts in the Near and Middle East (1803–1922)

R

REID, ANTHONY
Australian National University
Indonesian National Revolution (1945–1950)
Indonesian Upheaval (1965–1966)

REYNOLDS, CRAIG J.
Australian National University
Thai Revolution (1932)

ROBERTS, ADAM
Balliol College, Oxford University
East European Revolutions of 1989
Rights

RONEN, DOV
Harvard Medical School
Benin Revolutions (1963–1996)

ROTHCHILD, DONALD
University of California, Davis
Ethnic Conflict

ROY, OLIVIER
French National Center for Scientific Research
Afghan Revolution (1978–1995)

RUEDY, JOHN
Georgetown University
Algerian Islamic Revolt (1992–)
Algerian Revolution (1954–1962)

RUSINOW, DENNISON
University of Pittsburgh
Yugoslav Communist Collapse and Dissolution (1987–1992)

RYAN, STEPHEN
Magee College, University of Ulster
Irish Revolt in Northern Ireland (1969–)

S

SABARATNAM, LAKSHMANAN
Davidson College
Sri Lankan (Tamil) Revolt and Civil War (1977–)

SCHMID, A. P.
Erasmus University, Rotterdam, and Leiden University
Terrorism

SCHWARTZ, STUART B.
Yale University
Spanish Struggles against Revolutionary Movements in Southern Europe (1640–1668)

SELBIN, ERIC
Southwestern University
Ideology

SELIGSON, MITCHELL A.
University of Pittsburgh
Costa Rican Revolution (1948)

SHISSLER, A. HOLLY
Indiana University of Pennsylvania
Atatürk, Kemal

SIDBURY, JAMES
University of Texas at Austin
U.S. Slave Revolts (1776–1865)

SIGMUND, PAUL E.
Princeton University
Chilean Socialist Movement and Counterrevolution (1970–1978)

SMITH, CHARLES D.
University of Arizona, Tucson
Palestinian Anticolonial Revolt (1936–1939)
Palestinian "Intifada" Revolt (1987–1996)

STEARNS, PETER N.
Carnegie Mellon University
Anarchism

STOKES, GALE
Rice University
Tito, Josip Broz
Yugoslav Partisans and Communist Revolution (1941–1948)

STONE, JOHN
George Mason University
Race

STORK, JOE
Human Rights Watch
Kurdish Revolts (1958–)

STRANAHAN, PATRICIA
University of Pittsburgh
Propaganda

STRAND, DAVID
Dickinson College
Sun Yat-sen

STREMLAU, JOHN J.
University of the Witwatesrand
Nigerian Civil War (1967–1970)

STUBBS, RICHARD
McMaster University
Malayan Communist Insurgency (1948–1960)

SUNY, RONALD GRIGOR
University of Chicago
Russian Revolution of 1905
Russian Revolution of 1917

T

TARROW, SIDNEY
Cornell University
Symbolism, Ritualism, and Dress

TAYLOR, ROBERT H.
University of Buckingham
Burmese Democratization Movement (1988–)
Burmese Independence Movement (1930s–1948)

TE BRAKE, WAYNE
Purchase College, State University of New York at Purchase
Dutch Revolutions (1780–1800)

THROUP, DAVID W.
Keele University
Kenyan Mau Mau Movement (1952–1960)

TILLY, CHARLES
Columbia University
Counterrevolution

TIRYAKIAN, EDWARD
Duke University
Religion

TISMANEANU, VLADIMIR
University of Maryland at College Park
Romanian Revolution (1989)

TOMBS, ROBERT
St. John's College, Cambridge University
Paris Commune (1871)

TRAUGOTT, MARK
University of California, Santa Cruz
Class

TUTINO, JOHN
Georgetown University
Juárez, Benito
Latin American Popular and Guerrilla Revolts (Independence to 1959)
Mexican Revolution (1910–1940)
Zapata, Emiliano

U

ULTEE, MAARTEN
University of Alabama
Netherlands Revolt (1566–1609)
William the Silent

V

VILAS, CARLOS
National Autonomous University of Mexico
Nicaraguan Revolution (1979)

VOLK, STEVEN S.
Oberlin College
Lechín Oquendo, Juan

VON HAGEN, MARK
Columbia University
Trotsky, Leon

W

WALDER, ANDREW G.
Stanford University
Communism

WALKER, THOMAS W.
Ohio University
Sandino, Augusto César

WALT, STEPHEN
University of Chicago
War

WALTER, BARBARA F.
University of California, San Diego
Civil Wars

WALTER, JOHN
University of Essex
English Kett's Rebellion (1549)

WALTON, JOHN
University of California, Davis
Rebellion and Revolt

WASSERSTROM, JEFFREY N.
Indiana University, Bloomington
Chinese May Fourth Movement (1919)
Chinese Tiananmen Uprising (1989)
Gender
Student Protests and Youth Movements

WHITTAKER, JACOB
University of California, Davis
Chinese Muslim Rebellions (1856–1878)

WHITTAM, JOHN
University of Bristol
Garibaldi, Giuseppe
Italian Fascist Revolution (1919–1945)

WICKHAM-CROWLEY, TIMOTHY P.
Georgetown University
Guerrilla Warfare
Latin American Popular and Guerrilla Revolts (1960–1996)

WOLCHIK, SHARON L.
George Washington University
Czechoslovak "Prague Spring" (1968)
Czechoslovak "Velvet Revolution" and "Divorce" (1989–1993)
Havel, Václav

WOLPERT, STANLEY
University of California, Los Angeles
Gandhi, Mahatma
Jinnah, Mohammad Ali
Nehru, Jawaharlal

WORMALD, JENNY
St. Hilda's College, Oxford University
Scottish Revolution (1559–1568)

Y

YASHAR, DEBORAH, J.
Princeton University
Guatemalan Revolution (1944–1954)
Menchú Tum, Rigoberta

YAZAWA, MELVIN
University of New Mexico
American (U.S.) Revolution (1776–1789)

YOUNG, CRAWFORD
University of Wisconsin at Madison
Colonialism and Anticolonialism
Lumumba, Patrice

LIST OF ARTICLES BY SUBJECT

BIOGRAPHIES

CONCEPTS

EVENTS

INTRODUCTION

Revolutions change everything, or at least they seem to. Revolutions can create new states, produce new institutions of government, rearrange holdings of land and wealth, bring former prisoners and exiles to power, change the basis for social status, and transform the dominant ideology of a society. Yet it is not for nothing that we have the expression, from the French (that land of revolutions), *"plus ça change, plus c'est la même chose"*—the more things change, the more they remain the same. Despite revolutions, prejudices and conflicts remain, governments (albeit new ones) still seek to maintain and extend their power, inequality persists, and the utopias promised by revolutionaries remain forever just out of reach.

Revolutions are not the completely transformative events they promise to be, but neither are they minor or mundane events. Revolutions and revolutionary situations are those rare times when people challenge the very order of things, seeking to re-create the societies in which they live. Not all revolutions succeed, and those that do certainly do not all succeed to the same degree. But even in failure, the challenges and hopes expressed in revolutions ensure that political and social life will never be exactly the same as before.

The puzzles of why revolutions occur and how they alter societies have been central to political philosophy and social science ever since the speculations of Socrates and the analyses of Aristotle. However, revolutions themselves have changed over time. The alternation in Greek city-states of tyrannies, oligarchies, and democracies has given way to the wholesale transformation of societies in the French and Russian Revolutions, to the anticolonial revolutions of the nineteenth and twentieth centuries, and to the anticommunist revolutions of the late twentieth century. In each time and place, the causes, processes, and outcomes of revolutions are somewhat different, presenting new challenges to social scientists seeking to understand them.

THE HISTORY OF REVOLUTIONS

Traditional Revolts and Early Revolutions

From ancient Greece to the Italian Renaissance, city-states experienced conflicts between elitist and populist movements over who should have access to political power. Since these conflicts brought a change from one ruling party to another, the Italians called them "revolutions," because it seemed that power "revolved" from one ruling group to another. For hundreds of years, people thought of revolutions as shifts in fortune that elevated one group or faction to power while felling others.

Traditional monarchies and empires also experienced recurrent popular revolts by rural peasants and urban workers. While most such revolts over taxation, access to land, or the price of bread remained local and were easily suppressed, some grew large enough to strain the resources and legitimacy of the king or emperor. In the sixteenth and seventeenth centuries, the Jelali revolts in the Ottoman Empire, the Late Ming revolts in China, the French peasant revolts, Kett's Rebellion in England, and the German Peasant War challenged the legitimacy of existing authorities.

Moreover, monarchies and empires faced elite-led revolts by groups that believed that their traditional rights or religious beliefs were being trampled by the expanding power of the central government. In the sixteenth and seventeenth centuries, the Spanish *Comuneros* revolt, the French wars of religion, the anti-Spanish revolts in southern Europe, the Bohemian revolt, and the Aztec and Inca revolts in the era of the Spanish conquests are examples of such anti-imperial actions.

The modern idea of revolution, however, is broader. It combines in one sequence of events a change in ruling groups, popular revolts, and elite-led challenges involving issues of "liberty" (such as rights, privileges, or choice of religion), plus the additional element of forging new state institutions. Perhaps the first such modern revolution was the revolt of the Netherlands in 1566, which involved noble elites and Protestant merchants and townsfolk fighting against Spanish taxation and Catholicism, and in the process creating a new Dutch state. Another early modern revolution was the British civil wars and revolution of 1638–1660, in which English, Irish, and Scottish elites, opposing the increasingly harsh taxation and Anglican orthodoxy imposed by the British monarchy and supported by urban and rural rebellions, overthrew the monarchy and erected a parliamentary commonwealth. Yet in the world context of the sixteenth and seventeenth centuries, these were exceptional events. From 1500 to 1789, elite and popular revolts occurred throughout the world, some of them even leading to a change in rulers. But none of these events fundamentally challenged the old Renaissance view that a "revolution" was a circular shift in power among the various groups contending for power in a single society, which could shift again or be reversed. Even the American Revolution of 1776, in which Britain's colonies transformed themselves into the United States, was primarily a contest between colonists who were seeking independence from British taxation, law, and religious constraints and the British authorities. But in 1789 the history of revolutions entered a new phase.

The Birth of the Modern Revolution

Until 1789 in Europe, and until much later elsewhere in the world, the idea of radical change was frightening. Tradition was the only firm foundation for social and political conduct. Thus even the leaders of the Netherlands Revolution and British civil wars appealed to tradition and the defense of "ancient liberties" to justify their revolts against the evil "innovations" of the Spanish and British crowns. But in the eighteenth century, Europeans began to doubt the superiority of ancient and traditional wisdom. The new empirical and analytical philosophy challenged the veracity of the Bible and of the classical texts of Greek astronomy, physics, and chemistry. Essayists such as John Locke; Charles-Louis de Secondat, baron de Montesquieu; and Jean-Jacques Rousseau were seeking new principles for guiding political systems and human behavior. Some of this new thought seeped into the American Revolution of 1776, whose leaders used some of the language and ideas of the new natural rights philosophy to justify their revolt. Nonetheless, they still relied heavily on the models of ancient Greece and Rome and the ancient rights of Englishmen to justify their republican ideals and their opposition to the misdeeds of the British king. It is only with the French Revolution of 1789 that we find "revolution" taking on a new meaning, as a radical attack on all older institutions in the name of creating a wholly new and better society.

The French Revolution began as an elite movement to reform the monarchy and, ironically, started with a call to revive the ancient French Estates-General, which had last met in 1614. Yet the debate over how to constitute the Estates, and how to allocate votes among the clergy, nobility, and commoners, led in unexpected directions. Inspired by the new philosophy, writers such as the abbé Emmanuel-Joseph Sieyès challenged the special rights that had traditionally gone to the nobility and clergy. In the countryside, peasant revolts challenged the traditional prerogatives of noble landlords, and in Paris and other major cities, crowds attacked royal strongholds in support of the Estates. As King Louis XVI came into conflict with the Estates and with its later incarnation, the National Assembly, the actions of the king were challenged, and when other European nations took up arms against France to contain the revolution, the National Assembly declared the monarchy itself incompatible with the interests of the French people.

Although Louis XVI was not the first king to be beheaded in the name of failure to serve his people (that honor goes to Charles I of Britain, who lost his head during the British civil wars and revolution), France was the first nation in which the entire traditional social and political order, based on special privileges for various ranks of nobility, corporations, regions, and municipalities, was fundamentally challenged. By the time Napoleon had completed the work of the Revolution in 1804, France had a new legal code that recognized the legal equality of all citizens; new standards for social and political advance that eschewed family bloodlines; new boundaries and capitals for regional and local government; a new organization of the church; and a new vision for mankind that spoke of universal human rights, not merely those of French citizens.

Of course, the contest between traditional authority and radical innovation was not settled in a single blow, or even a single revolution. With Napoleon's military defeat in 1815, the French monarchy was restored to power, and the champions of French republicanism were forced to fight again—in the revolutions of 1830 and 1848 and in the Paris Commune of 1871—before universal citizenship and republican government were definitively restored. But in the meantime, the ideal of renovating society through revolutionary change spread throughout the world.

In 1830 and 1848 revolutionary efforts were made throughout Europe to challenge the authority of kings and create republics. Most such efforts failed, but nonetheless they led to reforms that curbed the authority of kings and the privileges of hereditary nobles. In a few cases—as in the Greek revolt against the Ottoman Empire (1821–1832) and the Italian Risorgimento (or struggle for unification, which stretched from 1789 to 1870)—new states were forged. Perhaps most striking were the echoes that reached the New World, where republican revolutions in the Spanish colonies transformed Latin America into a set of newly free states. Republican revolutionary aspirations also reached the Middle East and China, in the form of the Iranian Constitutional Revolution (1906), the Turkish Revolution (1908–1922), and the Chinese Republican Revolution

(1911). The period from 1789 to 1911 can thus be seen as a global age of fervor for republican revolution.

The Coming of Marxist Revolutions

In Europe itself, dissatisfaction with mere political change was leading to yet another reconceptualization of revolution. The decades from 1790 to 1860 saw the spread of water- and steam-powered factories and the rapid expansion of industrial cities and centers throughout Europe. Competition from the new industrial centers stripped many traditional workers of their security, while growing populations generally drove down wages and led to demands for state intervention to protect workers from the hardships brought by shifting prices and patterns of employment. Many rural workers also felt left out or threatened by the new industrial society. Meditating on these changes and on the fate of workers in the French Revolution of 1848 (who were cruelly suppressed when their demands for special subsidies and employment exceeded what the French middle classes and notables were willing to pay), Karl Marx and Friedrich Engels determined that a change of the basic economic relationships in society was needed—not just a change of government. They developed a theory of history in which revolutions were necessary and inevitable transitions by which not only ruling groups but also economic relationships were overthrown. In the view of Marx and Engels, the French Revolution may have overthrown the political rule of the nobility and the economic dominance of large landowners, but the resulting society was only a "bourgeois republic": Owners of capital and industry controlled the government and economy, and workers were still effectively dispossessed. Thus, they argued, ahead lay a wave of socialist revolutions in which workers would overthrow the bourgeois republics, end private ownership of capital and industry, and establish communist societies in which workers would control both the state and the economy.

Of course, Marx and Engels were mistaken (at least so far) about the course of history in the "bourgeois republics." Although workers did organize, they did so to obtain bargaining rights and to back political parties that built modern welfare states, with pensions and unemployment support for workers (see the entry, U.S. Labor Revolts, 1890–1932). Private property remained the basis of economic relationships, and modern democratic republics have generally been free of further revolutions.

Yet elsewhere around the world, Marx and Engels's message regarding the superiority of a workers' state provided countries where the industrial economy was just emerging with a compelling alternative to becoming simply an "also ran" in the global industrial economy. Intellectuals in Russia, Asia, Latin America, and Africa were drawn to Marxism as a model for rapidly building a better society in their own countries. Reinterpretations of Marx by Vladimir Ilyich Lenin, then by Mao Zedong, argued that a workers' society could be built even in countries that were still dominated by a rural peasantry if a Marxist vanguard party were to take charge of the revolution, eliminate private property, and guide the new revolutionary state. First in Russia in 1917, then in many countries in eastern Europe in 1948–1949, in North Korea in 1948 and in China in 1949, in Cuba in 1956 and in Nicaragua in 1979, and in a host of African and Southeast Asian countries in the 1960s and 1970s, Marxist-inspired revolutions aimed at leaping directly into the utopian world of workers' societies. In addition, dozens of communist parties and guerrilla movements were active in countries throughout the world. If the heyday of republican revolutions lasted from 1789 to 1911, the years from 1917 to 1979 belonged to the Marxist revolutionary ideal.

The Rise of Nationalism

At the same time that republicanism and Marxism were spreading throughout the world, another revolutionary ideology was also taking hold. This was nationalism—the idea that any people, defined by a common culture, language, and history, should have their own political state. Nationalism aimed at ending the domination of large, multinational empires, such as the Austro-Hungarian Empire in Europe, the Ottoman Empire in the Middle East, and the Russian Empire in Eurasia. It also sought the unification of national peoples who were politically divided, as were the Germans and Italians. As it spread outside Europe, nationalism aimed at ending the many colonial empires that European powers had established, especially in Asia and in Africa, or at toppling regimes that were closely identified with outside powers.

The European revolutions of 1848, in addition to seeking republican governments in France, Germany, and Austria, also sought to unify Germany and Italy and to establish an independent nation of Hungary. Most of these revolutions failed, but their goals were eventually attained, although it took wars—specifically the Franco-Prussian War (1870–1871) and World War I (1914–1918)—to unify Germany and to put an end to the Austro-Hungarian and Ottoman Empires. Nationalist revolutions also occurred in the Balkans in the late nineteenth and early twentieth centuries, and in the Middle East in the aftermath of World Wars I and II. Nationalism sometimes combined with, or was co-opted by, communist revolutions. For example, Russian communists developed an extensive policy for preserving and enhancing national cultures within their new revolutionary state, and communists in Vietnam, North Korea, China, and Cuba often fanned nationalist feelings to gain support for their regimes. But in many other cases in the twentieth century—as in the Algerian Revolution, the Iraqi Revolution, the Egyptian Revolution, the Indonesian National Revolution, the Israeli independence revolt, the Kurdish revolts, the East Timorese independence movement, and the Indian and Pakistani independence movements, among others—nationalism, often incipient and developed by revolutionary leaders, was by itself the main ideological glue of anticolonial or antimonarchical revolutions.

Sometimes nationalism was aligned with democratic movements, but at other times nationalism was combined with authoritarian, militaristic beliefs. The result in the latter case was fascism, as in Italy under Benito Mussolini and in Germany under Adolf Hitler. Their nationalist revolutions helped launch World War II and ushered in a horrific period of international slaughter. The German and Italian fascist revolutions, together with the Russian communist revolution of 1917 and the Chinese communist revolution of 1949, bear the main responsibility for making the twentieth century an era drenched in the blood of tens of millions of innocent people. It is an astonishing paradox of human nature that revolutions have launched some of the most democratic and economically successful countries—Britain, France, Japan, the United States—and some of the most harshly authoritarian, bloody, or destitute states—Sudan, communist China (through the Cultural Revolution), Nazi Germany, Stalinist Russia, Cambodia.

From the end of World War II until the 1980s, the democratic capitalist ideal, as embodied in the United States, and the communist party-state ideal, as embodied in Russia and China, warred for the loyalty of the developing nations of the world. For almost forty years this "cold war" took the form mainly of fomenting revolutions and counterrevolutions around the globe. Yet the luster on Marxism was greatly dimmed in the 1980s when the Soviet Union, Cuba, and eastern Europe became notorious for stagnant economies and horrendous damage to their environments. Marxism faded as a revolutionary ideal, leaving the democratic capitalist model of development as fully dominant.

The end of the cold war did not mean the end of revolutions, for the republican and nationalist ideals remained powerful threats to unpopular authoritarian regimes. The Philippine "People Power" Revolution of 1986 was based on demands to restore democracy to the Philippines and to rid the country of a dictator who was seen as sacrificing Philippine interests to those of the United States. The South African antiapartheid movement, which came to power in 1994, was fueled by both African nationalism and the quest for multiracial democracy. And in Russia, Central Asia, the Baltic states, and eastern Europe, nationalism and the desire for democracy combined in successful movements to overturn communist party-states.

In addition to republicanism and nationalism, a new revolutionary ideology gained prominence in the last quarter of the twentieth century: Islamic fundamentalism. In part a return to traditional values, in part a search for a new path to modernity, Islamic fundamentalist movements have since 1979 overthrown governments in Sudan, Iran, and Afghanistan and have tried to do so in Egypt and Algeria. Islamic fundamentalism has united elites and popular groups against secular rulers and created conflicts between Islamic regimes and Western nations. But it too has often merged with nationalism; in 1998 the two major fundamentalist powers—Iran and Afghanistan—began a conflict over national interests, and in recent regional revolts by Islamic peoples, such as the Kurdish revolts (1958–), nationalism, not Islam, was the main rallying cry for popular revolt.

The Results of Modern Revolutions

In one sense, nationalism, communism, and Islamic fundamentalism all represent variants on the same theme—the search for a path to modernity that will somehow enable developing nations to overcome or break free from the overwhelming economic and political dominance that Western powers have had over the past century. The initial success of the Russian Revolution of 1917 in making Russia into a world superpower helped inspire numerous Third World revolutionaries. Yet no revolutionary path has been found that can ensure attainment of this goal. Communist nations have either foundered or substantially restored private property. Nationalist revolutions have led to greater pride and independence but have fallen far short of giving the peoples of the Middle East, South Asia, Africa, and Southeast Asia the economic gains they sought. Islamic revolutions are recent, but they too seem to have produced more isolation for their societies than triumph in the global economy. As a result of these apparent dead ends, hopes for democratic and capitalist transitions have grown, and in some countries—the Czech Republic, Hungary, Poland, and Slovenia—the democratic revolutions of 1989–1991 that overthrew communism seem to have delivered on their promises.

Yet, in general, the results of revolutions throughout modern history have been mixed. Democratic revolutions, nationalist revolutions, communist revolutions, and Islamic revolutions, along with a host of rebellions, guerrilla movements, and failed revolutions, have moved governments to change policies, expand access to political life, and restructure their economies. They have created new nations, given voice and power to new groups, and changed the balance of power in the world. Where revolutions succeeded, the immediate result was often greater equality, as land was redistributed and the wealth of the elite was seized by the state. Investments in heavy industry also spurred periods of rapid growth in the economies of some revolutionary states, including Russia, China, Mexico, the states of eastern Europe, and the Koreas. However, in many cases, revolutions also brought wholly unexpected and unwanted outcomes. The emergence of a new revolutionary elite often restored inequality, and the authority of revolutionary parties in effect brought back rule by a privileged minority. The massive civil and international wars following the French, Chinese, Russian, Nazi, Iranian, Algerian, and Vietnamese Revolutions killed millions. Tens of millions more were killed in the Stalinist collectivization campaign and purges, in the Chinese "Great Leap Forward," and on the Cambodian "killing fields," all misguided revolutionary efforts to rapidly remodel those societies.

What are the causes of the massive achievements and agonies that revolutions have brought? Since the French Revolution, scholars have fiercely debated whether general principles of history or human action lay behind these varied events. In the next section, we explore their ideas.

THEORIES OF REVOLUTION

Intuitive Accounts

There are many intuitive accounts of revolutions. It may seem that revolutions occur because people are fed up with poverty and injustice and "can't take any more." Yet, sadly, poverty and injustice have been the common lot of most of humankind throughout history, while revolutionary challenges to those ills have been relatively rare. It may appear that revolutions are often the lot of the "losers" in international war, who face humiliation, a distressed population, and a disgruntled army. And indeed, many revolutions have occurred in precisely that situation, as in Russia and Germany after World War I, or the Paris Commune after the Franco-Prussian War. However, most military defeats do not lead to revolutions, and many revolutions—such as the revolutions of 1848 or the Iranian Revolution of 1979—have occurred in states that had enjoyed decades of peace. Finally, it may seem that revolutions are the work of inspirational and heroic leaders who mount a challenge to the established authorities. Yet many revolutionary leaders—such as Lenin in Russia and Václav Havel in Czechoslovakia—spent the bulk of their careers in prison or in exile, only to be astonished when events vaulted them to power in a fashion they hardly expected.

Scholars who have analyzed revolutions have found all of these intuitive explanations helpful but insufficient to explain why revolutions occur only in certain times and places. These explanations also fail to account for the bewildering variety of forms and outcomes that revolutions offer. In addition, scholars differ over precisely which aspects of revolutions are to be explained. Historians of particular revolutions, for example, are most interested in explaining those elements that are unique to that revolution, making it distinct from other similar events. Sociologists are often most interested in identifying those social conditions that seem generally to precede revolutions. And political scientists and psychologists have lately focused on the motivation of individuals, asking why they would take risks to participate in mass events with such uncertain outcomes. Thus efforts to explain revolutions have taken numerous twists and turns and are still moving forward in several directions.

Marxist and Psychological Explanations

In the nineteenth and early twentieth centuries, observers undertook the scientific analysis of revolutions in an effort to distill the phenomenon of revolution down to an essential characteristic that would serve as the ultimate cause of all revolutionary phenomena. In the mid-nineteenth century, Marx and Engels, as we have noted, insisted that the essence of revolution was a struggle between classes over the nature of economic relationships. The rise and fall of political regimes, then, was a reflection of this underlying struggle over the conditions of material life. Revolutions had to occur when one system of economic production was in the process of being displaced by another. For many decades, this Marxist explanation of revolutions was widely accepted, both by scholars and by revolutionaries. But since the late 1970s historical studies have shown that Marx's account of why revolutions occurred was not consistent with the empirical evidence. Even in Marx's classic cases of bourgeois revolution, the British civil wars and revolutions and the French Revolution of 1789, there is no evidence that older systems of economic production were being displaced; that the revolutionary actors who took power were from groups based on new forms of economic production; or that the revolutions contributed to a major change in economic life. It appears that these revolutions were mainly contests over the limits of the power of the state and the church and over such traditional and oft-raised issues as bread prices, dues and rents to landlords, and the rights and privileges of the elites. If we ask what turned contests over these issues into life-and-death struggles over the existence of monarchies, Marxist theories offer little help.

At the turn of the twentieth century, two other theories focused on the emotional aspect of revolutions. Psychologists such as Sigmund Freud and Gustave Le Bon suggested that revolutionary actions were part of the "madness of crowds."

Large assemblies, they argued, provided conditions in which crude emotions were amplified and in which people naturally focused on a leader who appealed to primitive instincts. The sociologist Max Weber, however, suggested that large societies were more likely to run in bureaucratic ruts and that revolution required the emergence of an exceptionally charismatic leader who could inspire people to look beyond their everyday lives. For both kinds of scholars, revolutions were events that arose rarely, but randomly, when either the leader who could inflame crowds or the charismatic leader who inspired movements arrived on the scene. Although these theories helped explain the role of revolutionary leaders and the passions aroused by revolutions, they said little to help us identify where revolutions were likely to arise or how they were likely to unfold.

Analytic and Conjunctural Explanations

A different and more fruitful form of analysis arrived in the second quarter of the twentieth century, with efforts to break revolutions into component parts. The most famous effort in this respect is Crane Brinton's *Anatomy of Revolution* (1938). Brinton, an American historian, sought to divide the course of revolution into discrete stages and to identify a pattern of events that could be found in most major revolutions. Brinton found that revolutions are generally preceded by elite and intellectual opposition to the existing regime and efforts at state reforms; that revolutions generally begin with a fiscal or military crisis of the old regime rather than with action by the revolutionary opposition; and that revolutions move from a moderate phase, to a radical phase, to a terror and military phase, and finally to more pragmatic and routine life. Many of Brinton's findings have been borne out in such recent events as the Iranian Revolution of 1979, which closely followed his model. Yet the later twentieth century has also seen innovations in the making of revolutions that depart from Brinton's scheme. The development of guerrilla warfare, in China, Cuba, Vietnam, and Nicaragua, showed a different route for revolutionary action, and the constant alternation of radicalism and pragmatism in China since 1949 suggests a dynamic of revolutions that is different from that which Brinton had described.

Brinton's focus on elite dissent, state crisis, and radical mobilization as the key elements of revolution led later social scientists to try to explain these various aspects of revolutionary events. In the 1960s and 1970s American social scientists Ted Gurr, Samuel Huntington, and Charles Tilly debated whether elite and popular deprivation or changes in the capacity of governments to make and implement new policies best explained the outbreak of revolutionary events. However, it quickly became clear that only an explanation that joined all of these elements would suffice. In 1979 the sociologist Theda Skocpol presented a *conjunctural* model of revolutionary causation. She argued that major social revolutions occur only in societies that combine three characteristics: a state hampered by military or economic weakness relative to competing states; elites who are seeking to defend their privileges and who have institutional leverage against the central state; and a peasantry that can be easily mobilized against landlords, either through communal village structures or a party organization.

Although Skocpol's analysis was successful in explaining several major historical revolutions, it did not prepare observers for the revolutions of the late 1970s and 1980s. The revolution in Iran, for example, was not a peasant revolution, and the economy and military under Mohammad Reza Shah Pahlavi—reinforced by oil revenues and generous aid from the United States—were by far the strongest in the region. The clerical elites who led the religious revolution against the shah had an esteemed cultural position but no institutional leverage against the shah's regime. Nonetheless, they prevailed, with the help of urban crowds and bazaar merchants in the major cities of Tehran, Qom, and Tabriz. In Russia and eastern Europe, the collapse of communist states did not involve peasant mobilization, and again the elites who led the nationalist and democratic revolts had little if any institutional leverage; they were lesser functionaries in the party and bureaucracy, professors, teachers, engineers and scientists, radio and television broadcasters, writers and intellectuals, and doctors and factory managers. But their support for anticommunist politicians and dissidents brought down the powerful state authorities.

Toward More General Explanations

Partly in response to these events, some scholars have criticized Skocpol's analysis as too mechanical; other scholars have sought to generalize her model or add new elements to it. John Markoff, advancing a line of arguments made earlier by Barrington Moore Jr., has made a powerful case that, aside from whatever conditions existed prior to a revolution, once conflict with the state has begun, the interaction between elites and popular groups can change the course of a revolution and bring unforeseen results. A large number of scholars, such as Lynn Hunt, have pointed out that shifts in the role of gender, and indeed of a host of symbolic social categories, play a crucial and undertheorized role in the dynamics of revolutionary struggles.

I have argued that a theory of revolution should be more general, going beyond the preconditions of a few major historical social revolutions to consider the factors that lead to a wide variety of revolutionary events. I suggested that the state crises that can lead to revolution include not merely economic or political weakness but also a fiscal crisis, a perceived betrayal of national interests, rampant corruption, or any other conditions that create a widespread belief that the current regime is ineffective or unjust. Elites do not need institutional leverage to cripple a regime; they simply need to abandon the state and call for people to oppose it. And popular revolts can take many forms that are effective in overturning a regime: peasant village uprisings, mass urban revolts, or organized urban or rural guerrilla warfare. Regardless of what forms popular uprisings take, their crucial basis is a highly mobilizable group of young men and women with grievances against the state. Putting all of these elements together, I noted that a rise in population, if the economy and state do not expand with it, can simultaneously lead to fiscal problems for the state, heightened competition among the elite and conflicts over elite positions, popular grievances over declining real wages and access to land, and a younger population. In fact, in the history of Europe, the Middle East, and Asia from 1500 to 1850, the timing and spread of revolutions turns out to be far more closely linked to periods of sustained increase in population than to the incidence of wars or economic change.

Further insights have emerged from study of the most recent revolutions in the developing world. The sociologists Jeff Goodwin and John Foran have noted that one particular kind of Third World regime—the dictator who relies on patronage and personal loyalty to control his society—is especially vulnerable to revolution should the sources of patronage suddenly fall short. This was essentially the story behind the collapse of Ferdinand Marcos in the Philippines, Anastasio Somoza in Nicaragua, and the shah's regime in Iran. In addition, Goodwin and Foran have argued that culture and ideology play an essential role in organizing and guiding revolutionary movements and subsequent revolutionary regimes. Without allowing for the effects of individual national cultures, it is difficult to account for the wide variety of outcomes, for example, among the various states that emerged from the anticommunist revolutions of 1989–1991.

Today social scientists stand humbled by their failure to have predicted the collapse of communist regimes in Russia and eastern Europe, or for that matter the fall of the shah in Iran or the Marcos regime in the Philippines. Theorists of revolution now have a much better grasp of the various elements that combine to create a revolutionary situation: some form of state crisis; elite opposition to the regime; urban or rural mobilization; and a culture of opposition that guides and unifies the elite and popular forces against the regime. However, foreseeing exactly when such conditions will arise, in what particular combination, in a specific country still far exceeds our abilities. Perhaps a reader of this encyclopedia will someday make that crucial advance.

Outcomes of Revolutionary Leadership

Analysts of revolution must also confess surprise at the outcomes of recent revolutions. Until recently it seemed that the outcomes of revolutions were fairly clear. Revolutions generally produced states that were stronger and more centralized and had more extensive bureaucracies than the states they had overthrown; they often produced civil and international wars; and they were generally unable to overcome the basic human tendency to inequality that arises from the varying abilities, energies, and fortunes of individuals. Revolutions also produced dictatorship more often than democracy, and economic hardships more often than economic development. Yet in the last two decades of the twentieth century, several events have gone against these general trends. The democratic movements in South Africa and South Korea, and the democratic revolutions in the Czech Republic, Hungary, the Philippines, Poland, and Slovenia, all seem to have produced liberal states, democratic societies, and dynamic economies. The 1979 revolutions in Nicaragua and Iran, some of the 1989–1991 anticommunist revolutions in central Asia and the Balkans, and the 1997 Congo/Zaire revolution all seem to conform to the older historical norm. But it is encouraging that many more revolutions in recent decades have produced economically progressive and politically democratic regimes.

Why have these positive changes occurred in recent years? It appears that we must return to an old and almost discarded factor in the analysis of revolutions—the character of revolutionary leadership. The history of revolutions that produce democracy seems to turn on the choices of leaders who most likely could have taken absolute power but chose not to: George Washington in the American Revolution of 1776, Julius Kambarage Nyerere in Tanzania, Mahatma Gandhi in India, Nelson Mandela in South Africa, and Corazon Aquino in the Philippines. Conversely, the history of revolutions that produce dictatorships shows individuals who promised to create democracy or gained power by manipulating democratic procedures but then overturned them: Napoleon in France, Lenin in Russia, Hitler in Germany, Ayatollah Ruhollah Khomeini in Iran. Where democratic outcomes obtained, it appears that the commitment by individual leaders to democracy was greater than their interests in personal power and that this commitment was crucial as their regimes weathered political storms. No doubt, a well-off and literate society helps in sustaining democracy. But many leaders of democratic revolutions did not have that advantage; their own leadership appears to have been the crucial element in setting the direction of the revolutionary transformations in their nations.

Revolutions to Come?

One of the few general truths about revolutions is that they do not occur in prosperous, democratic societies. Thus one can expect revolutions gradually to be relegated to history as the world advances and more societies join those ranks. But the day when most people live in such societies is still far distant. Several billion people live under regimes that are nondemocratic, economically foundering, or both. In any of these societies, the potential for revolutionary events exists. Given the recent revolutions in Russia and eastern Europe, the Tiananmen revolt in China, the "People Power" Revolution in the Philippines, the Kurdish revolt in the Middle East, the various guerrilla movements active in Latin America, and the Congolese/Zairian upheavals in Africa, it is clear that the age of revolutions is far from over.

We can expect that revolutions will continue to arise in many parts of the world. We can also expect that when revolutions occur, they will occur in states already weakened by economic or other crises. They will have leaders drawn from the elites, and mobilizing popular urban or rural opposition will be a crucial element of the revolutionary process. We can also expect that the direction taken by the revolutions, whether toward dictatorship or democracy, will depend heavily on the character of the revolutions' leadership. But perhaps more than anything else, if the patterns of the past few decades persist, we can expect that revolutions will bring surprises that analysts had not anticipated.

JACK A. GOLDSTONE

BIBLIOGRAPHY

Aminzade, Ron, Jack A. Goldstone, and Elizabeth Perry. "Leadership Dynamics and Dynamics of Contention." In *Voice and Silence in Contentious Politics.* Edited by Ron Aminzade, Jack A. Goldstone, Doug McAdam, Elizabeth Perry, William Sewell Jr., Sidney Tarrow, and Charles Tilly. Cambridge: Cambridge University Press, forthcoming.

Brinton, Crane. *The Anatomy of Revolution.* Rev. and exp. ed. New York: Vintage, 1965 [1938].

Foran, John, ed. *Theorizing Revolutions.* London: Routledge, 1997.

Goldstone, Jack A. *Revolution and Rebellion in the Early Modern World.* Berkeley: University of California Press, 1991.

Goodwin, Jeffrey. *States and Revolutionary Movements, 1945–1991.* Cambridge: Cambridge University Press, forthcoming.

Gurr, Ted Robert. *Why Men Rebel.* Princeton, N.J.: Princeton University Press, 1970.

Hunt, Lynn A. *The Family Romance of the French Revolution.* Berkeley: University of California Press, 1992.

Huntington, Samuel P. *Political Order in Changing Societies.* New Haven, Conn.: Yale University Press, 1968.

Markoff, John. *The Abolition of Feudalism.* University Park: Pennsylvania State University Press, 1996.

Moore, Barrington, Jr. *Social Origins of Dictatorship and Democracy.* Boston: Beacon, 1966.

Skocpol, Theda. *States and Social Revolutions.* Cambridge: Cambridge University Press, 1979.

Tilly, Charles. *European Revolutions, 1492–1992.* Oxford: Blackwell, 1993.

Wickham-Crowley, Timothy P. *Guerrillas and Revolution in Latin America.* Princeton, N.J.: Princeton University Press, 1992.

TIME LINE OF REVOLUTIONARY EVENTS

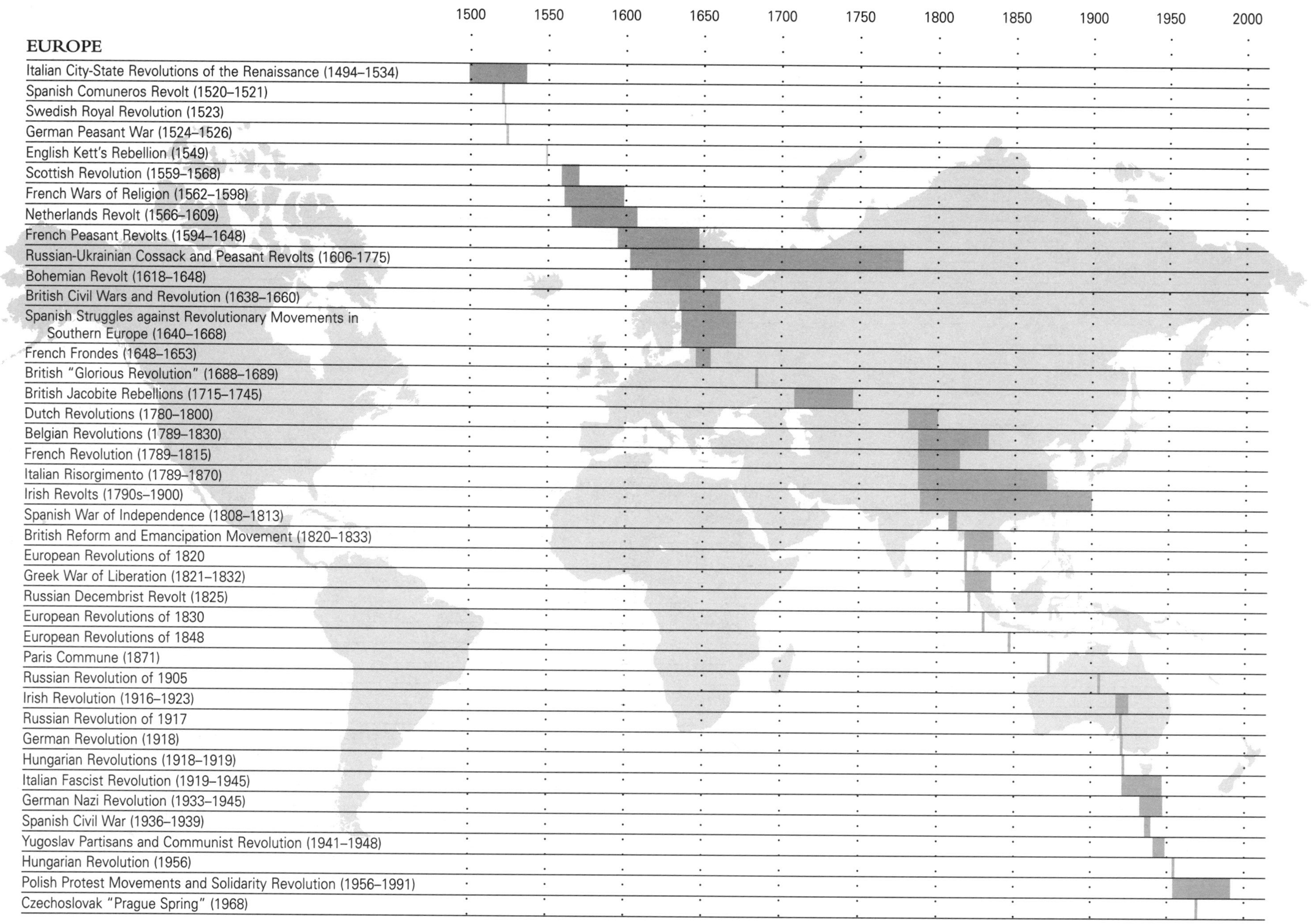

1500 1550 1600 1650 1700 1750 1800 1850 1900 1950 2000

EUROPE

Italian City-State Revolutions of the Renaissance (1494–1534)
Spanish Comuneros Revolt (1520–1521)
Swedish Royal Revolution (1523)
German Peasant War (1524–1526)
English Kett's Rebellion (1549)
Scottish Revolution (1559–1568)
French Wars of Religion (1562–1598)
Netherlands Revolt (1566–1609)
French Peasant Revolts (1594–1648)
Russian-Ukrainian Cossack and Peasant Revolts (1606–1775)
Bohemian Revolt (1618–1648)
British Civil Wars and Revolution (1638–1660)
Spanish Struggles against Revolutionary Movements in Southern Europe (1640–1668)
French Frondes (1648–1653)
British "Glorious Revolution" (1688–1689)
British Jacobite Rebellions (1715–1745)
Dutch Revolutions (1780–1800)
Belgian Revolutions (1789–1830)
French Revolution (1789–1815)
Italian Risorgimento (1789–1870)
Irish Revolts (1790s–1900)
Spanish War of Independence (1808–1813)
British Reform and Emancipation Movement (1820–1833)
European Revolutions of 1820
Greek War of Liberation (1821–1832)
Russian Decembrist Revolt (1825)
European Revolutions of 1830
European Revolutions of 1848
Paris Commune (1871)
Russian Revolution of 1905
Irish Revolution (1916–1923)
Russian Revolution of 1917
German Revolution (1918)
Hungarian Revolutions (1918–1919)
Italian Fascist Revolution (1919–1945)
German Nazi Revolution (1933–1945)
Spanish Civil War (1936–1939)
Yugoslav Partisans and Communist Revolution (1941–1948)
Hungarian Revolution (1956)
Polish Protest Movements and Solidarity Revolution (1956–1991)
Czechoslovak "Prague Spring" (1968)

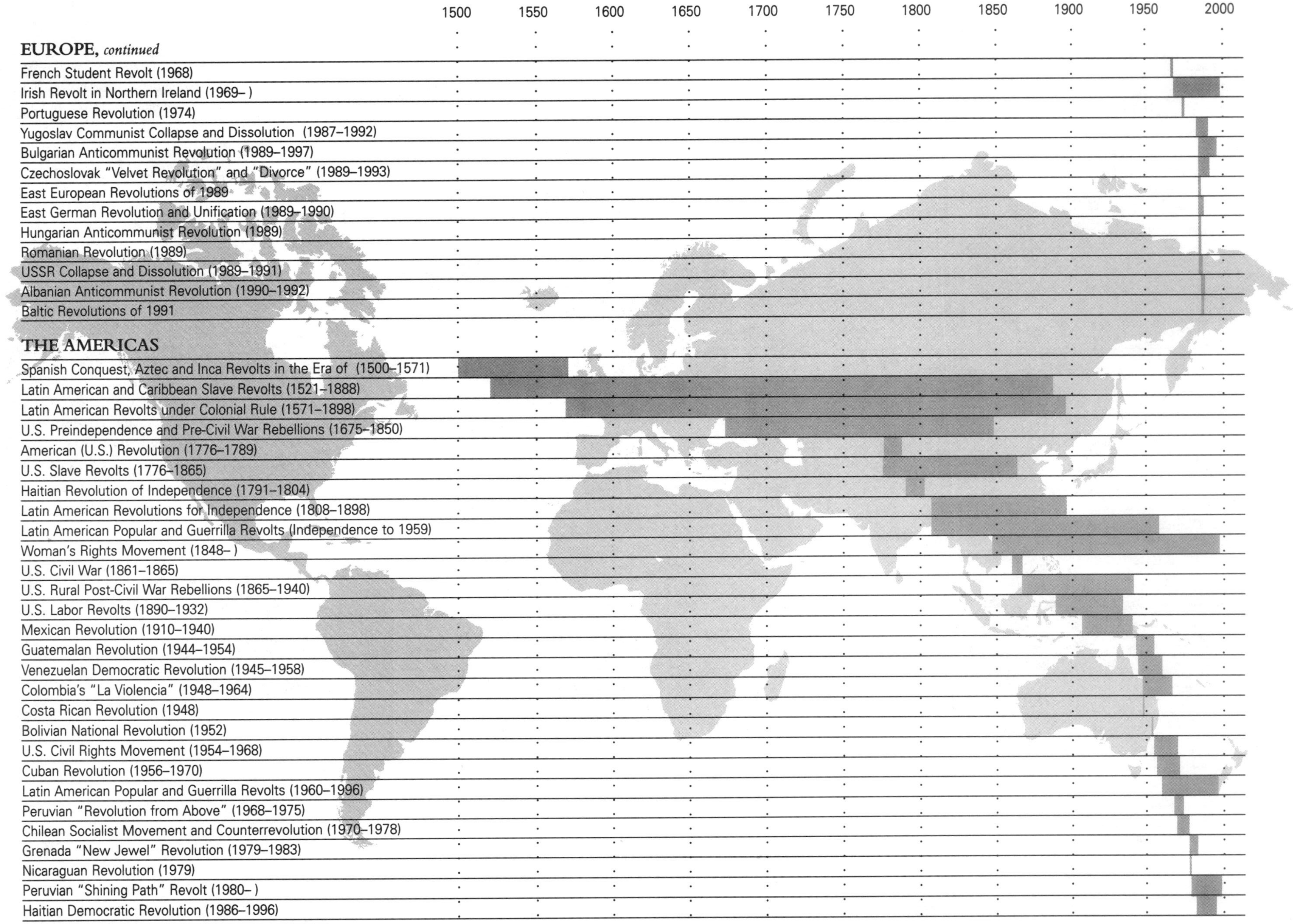

	1500	1550	1600	1650	1700	1750	1800	1850	1900	1950	2000

EUROPE, *continued*

French Student Revolt (1968)
Irish Revolt in Northern Ireland (1969–)
Portuguese Revolution (1974)
Yugoslav Communist Collapse and Dissolution (1987–1992)
Bulgarian Anticommunist Revolution (1989–1997)
Czechoslovak "Velvet Revolution" and "Divorce" (1989–1993)
East European Revolutions of 1989
East German Revolution and Unification (1989–1990)
Hungarian Anticommunist Revolution (1989)
Romanian Revolution (1989)
USSR Collapse and Dissolution (1989–1991)
Albanian Anticommunist Revolution (1990–1992)
Baltic Revolutions of 1991

THE AMERICAS

Spanish Conquest, Aztec and Inca Revolts in the Era of (1500–1571)
Latin American and Caribbean Slave Revolts (1521–1888)
Latin American Revolts under Colonial Rule (1571–1898)
U.S. Preindependence and Pre-Civil War Rebellions (1675–1850)
American (U.S.) Revolution (1776–1789)
U.S. Slave Revolts (1776–1865)
Haitian Revolution of Independence (1791–1804)
Latin American Revolutions for Independence (1808–1898)
Latin American Popular and Guerrilla Revolts (Independence to 1959)
Woman's Rights Movement (1848–)
U.S. Civil War (1861–1865)
U.S. Rural Post-Civil War Rebellions (1865–1940)
U.S. Labor Revolts (1890–1932)
Mexican Revolution (1910–1940)
Guatemalan Revolution (1944–1954)
Venezuelan Democratic Revolution (1945–1958)
Colombia's "La Violencia" (1948–1964)
Costa Rican Revolution (1948)
Bolivian National Revolution (1952)
U.S. Civil Rights Movement (1954–1968)
Cuban Revolution (1956–1970)
Latin American Popular and Guerrilla Revolts (1960–1996)
Peruvian "Revolution from Above" (1968–1975)
Chilean Socialist Movement and Counterrevolution (1970–1978)
Grenada "New Jewel" Revolution (1979–1983)
Nicaraguan Revolution (1979)
Peruvian "Shining Path" Revolt (1980–)
Haitian Democratic Revolution (1986–1996)

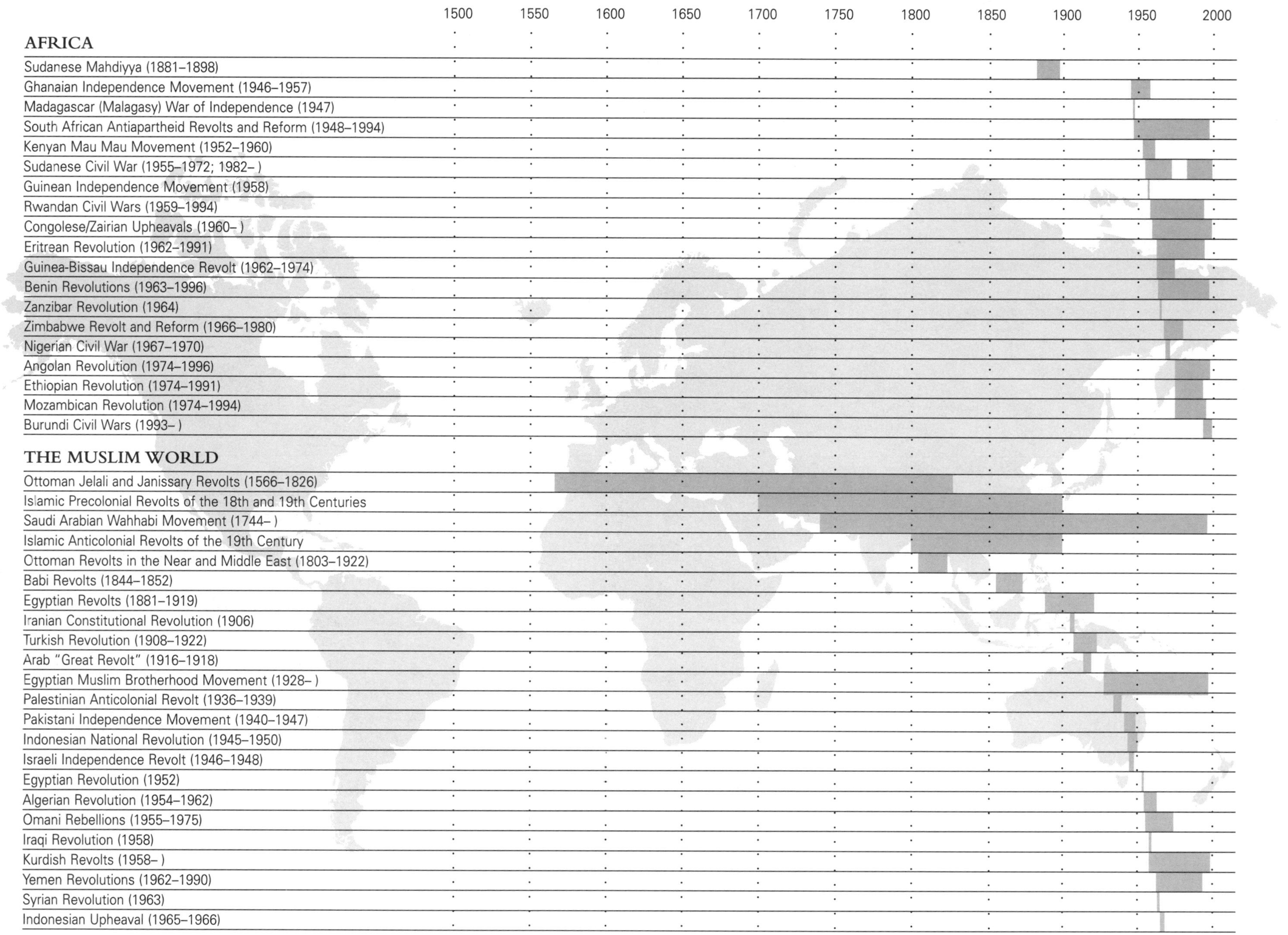

1500 1550 1600 1650 1700 1750 1800 1850 1900 1950 2000

AFRICA

Sudanese Mahdiyya (1881–1898)
Ghanaian Independence Movement (1946–1957)
Madagascar (Malagasy) War of Independence (1947)
South African Antiapartheid Revolts and Reform (1948–1994)
Kenyan Mau Mau Movement (1952–1960)
Sudanese Civil War (1955–1972; 1982–)
Guinean Independence Movement (1958)
Rwandan Civil Wars (1959–1994)
Congolese/Zairian Upheavals (1960–)
Eritrean Revolution (1962–1991)
Guinea-Bissau Independence Revolt (1962–1974)
Benin Revolutions (1963–1996)
Zanzibar Revolution (1964)
Zimbabwe Revolt and Reform (1966–1980)
Nigerian Civil War (1967–1970)
Angolan Revolution (1974–1996)
Ethiopian Revolution (1974–1991)
Mozambican Revolution (1974–1994)
Burundi Civil Wars (1993–)

THE MUSLIM WORLD

Ottoman Jelali and Janissary Revolts (1566–1826)
Islamic Precolonial Revolts of the 18th and 19th Centuries
Saudi Arabian Wahhabi Movement (1744–)
Islamic Anticolonial Revolts of the 19th Century
Ottoman Revolts in the Near and Middle East (1803–1922)
Babi Revolts (1844–1852)
Egyptian Revolts (1881–1919)
Iranian Constitutional Revolution (1906)
Turkish Revolution (1908–1922)
Arab "Great Revolt" (1916–1918)
Egyptian Muslim Brotherhood Movement (1928–)
Palestinian Anticolonial Revolt (1936–1939)
Pakistani Independence Movement (1940–1947)
Indonesian National Revolution (1945–1950)
Israeli Independence Revolt (1946–1948)
Egyptian Revolution (1952)
Algerian Revolution (1954–1962)
Omani Rebellions (1955–1975)
Iraqi Revolution (1958)
Kurdish Revolts (1958–)
Yemen Revolutions (1962–1990)
Syrian Revolution (1963)
Indonesian Upheaval (1965–1966)

1500 1550 1600 1650 1700 1750 1800 1850 1900 1950 2000

THE MUSLIM WORLD, *continued*

Libyan Revolution (1969)
East Timorese Independence Movement (1975–)
Afghan Revolution (1978–1995)
Iranian Islamic Revolution (1979)
Palestinian "Intifada" Revolt (1987–1996)
Algerian Islamic Revolt (1992–)

SOUTH AND EAST ASIA

Japanese Tokugawa Shogun Ascendancy (1598–1615)
Chinese Late Ming Revolts (1620–1644)
Chinese Sectarian and Secret Society Revolts (1644–)
Chinese Triad Society Rebellions (18th–20th Centuries)
Chinese White Lotus Rebellions (18th–20th Centuries)
Korean Rebellions of 1812 and 1862
Chinese Taiping Rebellion (1851–1864)
Chinese Muslim Rebellions (1856–1878)
Indian "Great Mutiny" (1857–1859)
Japanese Meiji Restoration (1868)
Philippine Independence Wars (1872–1910)
Indian Independence Movement (1885–1947)
Korean Tonghak Rebellion (1894)
Chinese Boxer Uprising (1898–1900)
Chinese Republican Revolution (1911)
Chinese May Fourth Movement (1919)
Chinese Nationalist Revolution (1919–1927)
Chinese Communist Revolution (1921–1949)
Chinese May Thirtieth Movement (1925)
Burmese Independence Movement (1930s–1948)
Thai Revolution (1932)
Vietnamese Revolution (1945–1975)
Philippine Huk and New People's Army Rebellions (1946–mid-1950s; late 1960s–late 1980s)
Indian Regional Revolts (1947–)
Malayan Communist Insurgency (1948–1960)
Korean Civil War (1950–1953)
Tibetan Revolt (1959)
Korean Democracy Movement (1960–1998)
Chinese Cultural Revolution (1966–1969)
Cambodian Khmer Rouge Revolution (1967–1979)
Bangladeshi War of Independence (1971)
Sri Lankan (Tamil) Revolt and Civil War (1977–)
Philippine "People Power" Revolution (1986)
Burmese Democratization Movement (1988–)
Chinese Tiananmen Uprising (1989)

THE ENCYCLOPEDIA OF POLITICAL REVOLUTIONS

ADAMS, JOHN

John Adams (1735–1826) was a principal theorist and creator of the American Republic. After graduating from Harvard in 1755, he often despaired over his situation as a young lawyer in Braintree, Massachusetts. It was not just that the area men seemed indifferent to his education and intellect, voters also elevated tavern orators to high office. Vice in government seemed rampant. Adams's experience in local politics was a lesson in the evolving character of colonial society that would haunt him as he became a leader of resistance and revolution.

In 1765 he won renown by composing instructions for Braintree's representative to the Massachusetts Assembly to oppose the Stamp Act. He also published his *Dissertation on Canon and Feudal Law,* which linked parliamentary efforts to tighten control over the colonies with repressive systems of law imposed in Europe in the past. In this "enlightened" age, Adams thought, the legitimacy of governments must be judged by their defense of natural rights. Braintree elected him to the Assembly, which in turn sent him to the First Continental Congress in 1774. As "Novanglus," he argued in a newspaper debate the next year that the internal affairs of the chartered colonies were not subject either to Parliament or even to the king in his "politic capacity." Colonists owed only deference to the king's "person."

In Philadelphia, he agitated to create a new center of governmental gravity for the colonies in Congress and its expanding number of committees. He chaired the Board of Military Ordnance after the outbreak of violence in 1775 and pushed for consideration of independence. In May 1776 he wrote the preamble to resolutions authorizing the colonies to create new governments and helped edit Thomas Jefferson's Declaration of Independence. He explained independence as the mature judgment of not just Congress but of a people mobilized in a descending tier of conventions and committees.

Still, this vocal radical feared that the people at large

John Adams

would fail to maintain the self-effacing virtue that he and many other leaders considered vital to sustaining any republic. Adams insisted in *Thoughts on Government,* published in 1776, that popularly elected legislatures must be checked by a natural social and intellectual elite in control of upper houses and executive authority. In 1778 he drafted such a mixed constitution for Massachusetts, which invested the governor with a veto over legislation.

At the national level, Adams helped consolidate the new nation by winning recognition from the Netherlands in 1782 and securing loans from the Dutch to finance the fledgling republic. With Franklin he helped negotiate the Treaty of Paris, which ended the war in 1783. Congress appointed him ambassador to Britain in 1785, where he continued to press American interests over disputed conditions of the treaty.

Such endeavors never long distracted him from his concern over the stability of the new governments at home. News of Shays's Rebellion in Massachusetts and other unrest stirred him to write *Defence of the Constitutions of the United States* in 1787–1788. Having lost faith that the Revolution had wrought any refinement of American character, he reiterated his conviction that only mixed governments of distinct social orders could check popular passions. Such concerns also influenced the Constitutional Convention's draft of a new national government in 1787.

With his wide experience, Adams won office as George Washington's vice president in 1789 and succeeded him as president in 1796. But Adams's hopes for the consolidation of a natural aristocracy of merit were shattered by the development of popular antipathy toward any such pretensions. Thoroughly disillusioned by his single, turbulent term, he nevertheless helped achieve a constitutionally mandated transition from one political persuasion to another in 1800.

See also *Adams, Samuel; American (U.S.) Revolution (1776–1789).*

DAVID W. CONROY

BIBLIOGRAPHY

Bailyn, Bernard. *Faces of Revolution: Personalities and Themes in the Struggle for American Independence.* New York: Vintage Press, 1992.

Butterfield, Lyman H., ed. *Diary & Autobiography of John Adams.* 4 vols. New York: Atheneum Press, 1964.

Smith, Page. *John Adams.* 2 vols. Garden City, N.Y.: Doubleday Press, 1962.

Wood, Gordon. *The Creation of the American Republic, 1776–1787.* New York: Norton Press, 1972.

ADAMS, SAMUEL

Samuel Adams (1722–1803) was a principal organizer of the American Revolution. When he entered Harvard in 1736, he was ranked according to custom by his family's social status. As the son of a justice, Adams ranked sixth. Such hierarchical distinctions, however, diminished in the political culture to which Adams gravitated after graduation. As Boston's tax collector after 1756, Adams began to construct a base of popular support upon which he drew to resist direct taxation by the Crown after 1765. Indifferent to material enrichment, he personified the republican ideal of self-sacrifice for the commonweal.

Adams acted to thwart the implementation of the Stamp Act tax by helping organize the Sons of Liberty in 1765. The Sons sought to arouse opposition to any parliamentary legislation considered to be a violation of colonial rights under the British constitution. They successfully pressured Stamp Agent Andrew Oliver to resign his office by intimidating him through crowd actions like the hanging of his effigy. Such tactics would be used repeatedly during the next ten years. After Adams's elevation to the colonial legislature (1764–1774), he also acted to influence other colonies. In 1767 his Circular Letter appealed to other assemblies to support Massachusetts's opposition to the Townshend duties. Gradually, Adams became convinced of the existence of a British conspiracy to subvert colonial legislative autonomy.

Adams could never completely control popular protest, as when a crowd provoked British sentries to fire and kill five men in 1770. Characteristically, however, he seized on the event to organize a peaceful protest in the form of elaborate funeral processions uniting Bostonians of all ranks. When in 1772 the Crown tried to make royal officials independent of local institutions by paying their salaries directly, Adams motioned the Boston town meeting to create a committee of correspondence to inform every town in the province of this latest threat. Across the province, towns elected their own committees to write replies in accord with Boston. By this device, Adams elicited an outpouring of popular support for the actions of Boston radicals, but with due respect for formal procedure. In 1773 he condoned the dumping of imported tea liable for tax in Boston harbor only after every means had been exhausted to reach some accord with Governor Thomas Hutchinson. By this breach of respect for property, however, Adams risked alienating leaders in other colonies.

Parliament acted to isolate Massachusetts by a series of punitive acts, including closure of the port of Boston. But Adams's election to the First and Second Continental Congresses in 1774–1775 provided him with a platform to promote colonial solidarity through the adoption of the Continental Association for Nonimportation and the authorization of local committees to enforce it. Techniques of resistance developed and refined in Massachusetts now became devices to construct national unity. Gradually, Adams helped persuade moderates in Congress that petitions to the Crown were pointless and that the colonies must prepare for war in 1775. The next year Adams signed the Declaration of Independence and helped draft the Articles of Confederation, which transformed Congress into a national government.

Along with his cousin, John, Samuel Adams became alarmed over deeper democratization in the 1780s. Now that the people had become sovereign over all branches of government, he saw no need for the creation of popular organizations, such as county conventions advocating reform of the courts, to promote particular political agendas. Shays's Rebellion of desperate debtor farmers in 1786 seemed symptomatic of a general collapse in public virtue. Still, he continued to nurture the infant republican institutions of Massachusetts by presiding as lieutenant governor between 1789 and 1794 and as governor from 1794 to 1797. Under his near unassailable eminence, governing institutions absorbed the new shocks of bitter party divisions by establishing peaceful precedents for the transfer of power from one party to another.

See also *Adams, John; American (U.S.) Revolution (1776–1789).*

DAVID W. CONROY

BIBLIOGRAPHY

Brown, Richard D. *Revolutionary Politics in Massachusetts: The Boston Committee of Correspondence and the Towns, 1772–1774.* Cambridge, Mass.: Harvard University Press, 1970.

Fowler, William M., Jr. *Samuel Adams: Radical Puritan.* New York: Longman Press, 1997.

Maier, Pauline. *From Resistance to Revolution: Colonial Radicals and the Development of American Opposition to Britain, 1765–1776.* New York: Vintage Press, 1972.

AFGHAN REVOLUTION (1978–1995)

The Afghan Revolution, which started on April 27, 1978, with a communist coup against President Daud Khan, was in fact made of two opposed revolutions: the communists tried to implement a socialist state, while the Islamists launched against them a guerrilla movement with the one revolutionary aim of establishing an Islamic state. Nevertheless, both movements lost their ideological dynamic. In the course of the Afghan civil war, which followed the fall of the communist regime on April 26, 1992, ethnic and clan alignments more and more superseded ideological affiliations.

The two trends, communist and Islamist, grew along symmetric patterns. They appeared after 1965 on school campuses of the capital, Kabul, in the wake of a political liberalization initiated by King Zaher. Although their programs were worded in radical, ideological terms (a "socialist" country aligned with the Soviet Union or an Islamic state based on Islamic law), their respective constituencies had from the beginning an ethnic basis. Both movements were divided according to the fabric of the multiethnic Afghan society. The communists were split into two factions: the Khalq ("People"), recruiting mainly among the dominant Pashtun ethnic group, and the Parcham ("Banner"), recruiting among the Persian-speakers, later called Tajiks. The Islamist movement was divided roughly along the same line: the Hizb-i Islami for the Pashtuns and the Jamiat-i Islami for the Persian-speakers. In the summer of 1975 an Islamist uprising was easily crushed by the regime of Daud Khan, which had toppled King Zaher in 1973. The survivors of the 1975 uprising fled to Pakistan, leaving the road open for the communists, who had been infiltrating the state apparatus since King Zaher's overthrow.

The overthrow of Daud Khan on April 27, 1978, was a classic military coup instead of a popular upheaval. But the military immediately turned power over to the civilian leaders of the Khalq faction of the Communist Party. The new president, Nur Mohammad Taraki, was assassinated and succeeded by his deputy, Hafizullah Amin, in September 1979. Between the coup of April 1978 and the Soviet invasion of December 27, 1979, the communist government undertook a truly revolutionary endeavor to change the very traditional Afghan society. An agrarian reform, a compulsory literacy campaign specially aimed at women, a change of all the symbols of the state (including a new red flag), the use of revolutionary Marxist rhetoric, a friendship treaty with the USSR, and an open attack on traditions and even religion antagonized the rural population. Tens of thousands of clerics and traditional leaders were executed in 1979. Popular upheavals broke out in many parts of the country, while the exiled Islamists came back to their native villages to organize the resistance. Thus was born the *Mujahidin* ("fighters for holy war") movement.

Moscow was worried by the growing isolation of the regime and feared that the Iranian Islamic Revolution (February 1979) would strengthen the radical elements of the Afghan resistance. It decided to invade Afghanistan and to replace the ruling faction with one more moderate and acceptable to the Afghan people, hoping that this move would defuse most of the armed opposition. Amin was killed by Soviet commandos. Babrak Karmal, head of the Parcham faction, became the new leader of this second stage of the revolution in the wake of the invasion. He maintained the socialist rhetoric but gave up most of the revolutionary measures, like the agrarian reform, and played the traditional power game in the rural areas to split the *mujahidin*. Traditional local leaders were courted, and tribal groups were supplied with weapons and money. But the Soviet invasion triggered deep opposition among the population. Nationalism, combined with Islamic feelings, rallied most of the population against the regime. Karmal was never able to overcome his image as a Soviet puppet.

The resistance movement emerged along complex pat-

Two Afghanis snipe from horseback at Soviet troops, near Herat, Afghanistan, in January 1980. The raiding party, traveling by motorcycle and horseback, crossed from Iran into Afghanistan's Doab Valley in a three-day raid.

terns. The Islamist parties (Hizb, led by Gulbuddin Hekmatyar, and Jamiat, led by Borhânuddin Rabbani and Commander Ahmed Shah Masud) tried to establish modern political and military structures, but the majority of the *mujahidin* remained traditionalist, even when joining the Islamist parties. In fact the rooting of the resistance movement in rural society reinforced traditional patterns of patronage and loyalty, based on the distribution of weapons and money among clansmen and relatives.

The military supplies provided by the United States beginning in 1984 and channeled through the Pakistani secret services allowed the *mujahidin* to challenge a demoralized Soviet army. In 1986 Moscow decided to find a political solution. The third stage of the revolution saw the replacement in May 1986 of Karmal by Mohammad Najibullah, head of the secret police. Najibullah gave up all of the revolutionary rhetoric, appointed traditional leaders to state positions, offered lip service to Islam, and played a rather successful game in dividing the *mujahidin* and attracting local rural leaders. The rural militias, like that headed by Gen. Abdul Rashid Dustom in the north, became more important than the army in fighting against the *mujahidin*.

After Soviet troops were withdrawn in February 1989, the Najibullah regime survived. From 1989 to 1992 ideological commitments on both sides disappeared in favor of a growing ethnic polarization, pitching the "northerners" (Persian-speakers, or Tajiks, Uzbeks, and Shi'a Hazaras) against the "southerners" (the Pashtuns). When in early 1992 Najibullah promoted Pashtun commanders to most of the key posts in the army, the northern Uzbek militias of General Dustom and most of the Persian-speaking army officers joined Commander Masud. This new alliance took Kabul on May 26, 1992, only to be besieged some months later by the Hizb-i Islami of Hekmatyar and the Pashtun remains of Najibullah's army. The ethnic polarization, opposing a shaky northern alliance against a Pashtun coalition (embodied from 1994 onward by the Taliban movement), has definitively superseded any revolutionary commitment on either side.

Although the communist regime claimed to promote women's rights (by prohibiting expensive dowries and advocating the education of women), most of its reforms in this regard were window-dressing. Urban middle-class educated women, at whom the reforms were aimed, also reacted sharply against the Soviet invasion on nationalist grounds and never provided the regime with a specific female constituency. In rural areas, nothing changed, whatever the political group in charge. When the *mujahidin* took Kabul in 1992, they made the veil compulsory but did not fire women from their jobs (including television anchors and airline stewardesses) and did not close girls' schools. Only when the Taliban took power in 1996 did Afghan women experience a global and systematic effort to expel them from public spaces, including streets and hospitals. But the rise to power of the Taliban, a conservative fundamentalist movement closer to Saudi Arabia than to Iran, embodied the end of any kind of political revolution in Afghanistan.

Olivier Roy

BIBLIOGRAPHY

Arnold, Anthony. *Afghanistan: The Soviet Invasion in Perspective.* 2d ed. Stanford, Calif.: Hoover Institution Press, 1985.

———. *Afghanistan's Two-Party Communism.* Stanford, Calif.: Hoover Institution Press, 1983.

Barnett, Rubin R. *The Fragmentation of Afghanistan.* New Haven, Conn.: Yale University Press, 1995.

Roy, Olivier. *Islam and Resistance in Afghanistan.* 2d ed. Cambridge: Cambridge University Press, 1990.

———. *Afghanistan, From Holy War to Civil War.* Princeton, N.J.: Darwin, 1995.

ALBANIAN ANTICOMMUNIST REVOLUTION (1990–1992)

Albania overthrew its communist regime only in 1991, more than a year after the other East European communist countries overthrew theirs, and only in 1992 was its first fully postcommunist government installed. This delay was due largely to the country's complete economic, ideological, cultural, and political isolation during the period of communist rule. Under its longtime leader, Enver Hoxha, who ruled from 1944 until his death in 1985, Albania had the harshest, bloodiest communist regime in Eastern Europe, and it alienated its one-time communist allies, including the Soviet Union and China, because Hoxha considered them insufficiently Stalinist. But even prior to communism Albania had been a clan-based society, and the lack of trust between the many self-contained groups, combined with a complete absence of democratic tradition, also contributed to the delayed transition.

Nicolae Ceausescu's overthrow in Romania in December 1989 frightened Hoxha's successors and emboldened their opponents, as did the worsening of the country's already dismal economy. The first challenge to the regime came in July 1990, when desperate Albanians stormed foreign embassies seeking visas to leave the country. To rid itself of dissidents, the government of Ramiz Alia allowed these people to leave. This decision exposed the regime's weakness and galvanized others to join efforts for reform.

Students and intellectuals, led by Sali Berisha, Gramoz Pashko, and Azem Hajdari, did not at first challenge the Albania Party of Labor (APL, the communist party) directly, but couched their aims in terms of appeals for greater cultural freedom, economic reform, and the right to travel abroad. Only as the movement gathered momentum did they begin to ask for political pluralism and free elections. Meanwhile, a dramatically falling standard of living led hitherto docile labor unions to stage demonstrations in support of reform.

Divisions between hard-line and reform-minded elements within the ruling APL precluded a forceful response, which might have delayed the collapse of the weakened regime. In December 1990 serious street demonstrations broke out against the government. The army played a crucial role by staying on the sidelines, thus forcing the APL to renounce its exclusive claim on power and allow the reformers to organize the opposition Democratic Party, which was established on December 12, 1990. Other political formations followed shortly thereafter.

Elections were held in March 1991, and the communists managed to defeat their poorly organized opponents; however, the reformed APL (now the Socialist Party) was unable to deal with the severe economic crisis and growing anger of the population. Continuing protests forced the Socialist government to resign in June 1991 and enter into a coalition with opposition forces. With the economy still in decline and thousands of Albanians fleeing the country, new elections were held three years early, in March 1992.

On April 9, 1992, the new Albanian Parliament, dominated by the Democratic Party, elected Sali Berisha as president of the republic. For the first time in its history, Albania had a freely chosen, democratic government. Despite all the tumult, some burning of public buildings (especially in rural areas, where collective farms were dismantled), and the delay in overthrowing communism, there had been surprisingly little bloodshed.

Unfortunately, despite considerable Western financial support and good will, Berisha's regime faced bleak prospects. Albania had always been Europe's poorest country, and the long legacy of communist rule and isolation had only made the situation worse. Democratic procedures were formally instituted, but in practice, governance remained authoritarian, corrupt, and inefficient. Since the fall of communism Albania has suffered periods of virtual anarchy and near civil war, economic mismanagement, and the destruction of some of its few capital assets. It will be a long time before the promise of the revolution of 1990–1992 is fulfilled.

See also *East European Revolutions of 1989; Romanian Revolution (1989).*

CONSTANTINE P. DANOPOULOS

BIBLIOGRAPHY

Austin, Robert. "What Albania Adds to the Balkan Stew." *Orbis* 37 (spring 1993): 259–279.

Biberaj, Elez. *Albania in Transition.* Boulder, Colo.: Westview Press, 1998.

Danopoulos, Constantine P., and Adem Chopani. "Departyizing and Democratizing Civil-Military Relations in Albania." In *To Sheath the Sword: Civil-Military Relations in the Quest for Democracy.* Edited by John P. Lovell and David E. Albright. Westport, Conn.: Greenwood Press, 1997.

Pano, Nicholas. "The Process of Democratization in Albania." In *Politics, Power, and the Struggle for Democracy in South-East Europe.* Edited by Karen Dawisha and Bruce Parrot. Cambridge: Cambridge University Press, 1997.

Schmidt, Fabian. "Albania: The Opposition's Changing Face." *Transition* 1 (June 1995): 44–48.

ALGERIAN ISLAMIC REVOLT (1992–)

The Islamic revolt in Algeria began shortly after the nation's military intervened in January 1992 to depose Chadli Bendjedid, the sitting president, and void an ongoing electoral process, which was on the point of propelling an Islamist political party to a majority position in the parliament. That party, the Islamic Salvation Front, best known by its French acronym FIS, was made up of a broad coalition of Islamists, including populist preachers, educators, disenchanted technocrats, and Muslim intellectual leaders. The military intervention was all the more offensive because the first-round elections of December 1991, which it overturned, were the freest and most open national elections held in Algeria since independence.

The reasons for the breakdown of the Algerian system are not difficult to identify. In 1962 the army came out of Algeria's long, divisive War of Independence against France as the most cohesive institution in a deeply fractured country. The military installed Algeria's first president, and since 1965 every succeeding head of state has been an army officer. The army presided over the creation of a secular, single-party political system and put in place a state capitalist model of economic development, which by the 1980s had proven disastrously ineffective in meeting the needs of Algeria's burgeoning population. As cities began overflowing with unemployed or underemployed young men, and with political speech essentially prohibited, Muslim religious leaders often stepped in to provide for basic needs and to create forums for expressing dissatisfaction with an establishment widely seen as self-serving, corrupt, and out of touch with the everyday lives of Algerians.

Under pressure in the 1980s from the International Monetary Fund and other lenders to liberalize the faltering economy, President Bendjedid (a former colonel) found the road to meaningful reform largely blocked by the existing single party, the National Liberation Front (FLN). In the wake of frightening urban riots in late 1988, he determined that the best way to achieve economic reform was to liberalize the political system, opening the country for the first time to true freedom of expression and association as well as to political pluralism. He took the controversial step of legalizing the FIS for the purpose, most observers believe, of countering tenacious opposition to his liberalization program within the FLN-controlled parliament. He clearly believed he could use the FIS to achieve his ends while keeping it from spinning out of control. In 1990, however, after the FIS swept to victory in a majority of local and

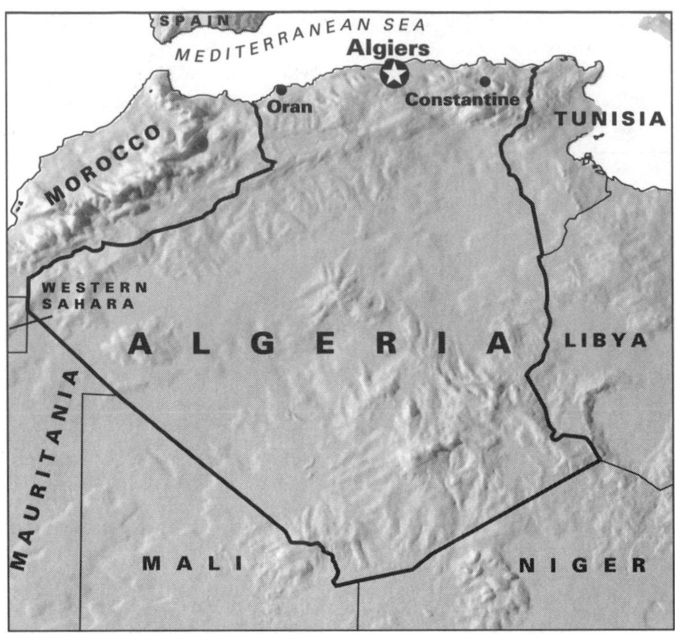

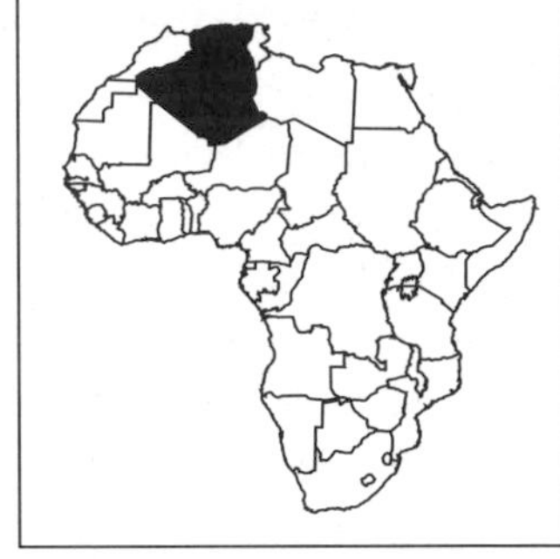

provincial elections, opposition to Bendjedid's initiative grew rapidly, not only within the ruling party but also among the military leadership, which up to then had stayed mainly in the background. In the summer of 1991 security forces imprisoned the two most important leaders of the FIS, Abassi Madani and Ali Belhadj, for allegedly inciting to riot. Then in March 1992, two months after the coup that ousted Benjedid, the new regime outlawed the party itself.

The argument mounted by the military to rationalize its heavy-handed interference with electoral and political processes was that the FIS, were it allowed to come to power, would overturn the secular constitution and replace it with a system dominated by Islamic law. Other observers, noting that the FIS was a coalition ranging from moderates to radicals, argue that it is by no means clear that a majority in the FIS planned to overturn the system, but they certainly wanted to reform it, and many in the military knew such reform would expose decades of mismanagement and corruption in which they had been intimately involved.

To fill out the final two years of Bendjedid's term, the officers appointed a five-man High State Council as a collective executive, which reported essentially to the General Staff. The first violent reactions to the coup by Islamist insurgents occurred in late January 1992. Initially the attacks targeted police, security forces, and government institutions.

But in the succeeding months and years the violence escalated to include assassination of individuals perceived as unsympathetic to Islamist goals and values: writers, artists, journalists, female professionals, a secondary school girl who refused to wear a veil, foreign technicians, and Christian clerics. Then car bombs and other explosive devices were planted in public places, taking lives increasingly at random. In 1996 and 1997 government arming of "patriot defense forces" in the countryside pitted clans and villages against one another in struggles that often seemed only tangentially related to political or ideological issues. At the same time, government repressive tactics became increasingly arbitrary and were responsible for the loss of many innocent lives. After five years of violence, estimates of the death toll ranged from fifty thousand to as high as two hundred thousand.

Violence on the Islamist side was perpetrated by a large array of armed bands. The degree of control exercised by formal Islamist organizations over the bands was often difficult to ascertain. Several broad movements appeared as the insurrection widened over the years, but by 1997 two appeared to have attracted the most followers. The largest was the Armed Islamic Group (GIA), which apparently had little prior link with the FIS but may have been connected with a small guerrilla movement that emerged and was subsequently suppressed in the 1980s. A second group, the Islamic Salvation Army (AIS), appeared more responsive to FIS leadership in exile and also more willing to consider dialogue.

Soon after the insurrection began, the military leaders claimed that they wanted to establish a national dialogue to resolve the political crisis and restore order to the embattled nation. Both secular and Islamist opposition parties expressed interest in negotiation, but dialogue broke down repeatedly. There were several reasons for the lengthy stalemate, including the military's refusal to include the FIS in any settlement plan, its determination never to accede to arrangements that would threaten its ultimate control, and divisions within the army between the conciliatory elements and the intransigents.

In February 1994, after the failure of attempts to build consensus on the way to choose a successor to the High State Council, whose mandate was expiring, the army named Gen. Liamine Zéroual, whom many judged a political moderate, as interim president. In relatively free elections held in November 1995, he was formally elected president by about 61 percent of Algerian voters, a result most observers took as a sign that the great majority of Algerians were not supportive of the continued violence of the radical Islamists. In the succeeding months, however, Zéroual, apparently under pressure from intransigent colleagues, was unable to reach agreement with major opposition parties regarding a constitutional system that would allow genuine sharing of power. In November 1996, supported by only a few parties, he sent to popular referendum a new constitution that formally outlawed religious parties, created a system of proportional representation for a parliament whose functions would be greatly reduced, created an upper house one-third of whose members would be appointed by the executive branch, and greatly enhanced the powers of the executive branch. The constitution was approved on November 28, 1996, in a referendum, which the majority of the opposition as well as outside journalists condemned as highly flawed.

Under the new constitution the regime organized parliamentary elections in June 1997. The elections returned a plurality for a new government party, the National Democratic Rally (RND), which, along with a much diminished but cooperative FLN, commanded a majority in the new body. Spin-offs from two moderate Islamic parties, which had dropped their religious labels, won about one-fourth of the votes. Certain lesser cabinet posts were assigned to representatives of these minority parties, and the government claimed that affairs in Algeria would return to normal. Almost immediately, however, violence erupted again. By the holy month of Ramadan (December 1997–January 1998), violence had reached its bloodiest levels since the beginning of the crisis.

JOHN RUEDY

BIBLIOGRAPHY

Addi, Lahouari. *L'Algérie et la démocratie. Pouvoir et crise du politique dans l'Algérie contemporaine.* Paris: Editions de la Découverte, 1995.

Burgat, François, and William McDowell. *The Islamic Movement in North Africa.* Austin, Tex.: Center for Middle Eastern Studies, University of Texas, 1993.

Fuller, Graham E. *Algeria: The Next Fundamentalist State?* Santa Monica, Calif.: Rand, 1996.

Labat, Séverine. *Les Islamistes algériens. Entre les urnes et le maquis.* Paris: Editions du Seuil, 1995.

Ruedy, John, ed. *Islamism and Secularism in North Africa.* New York: St. Martin's Press, 1994.

ALGERIAN REVOLUTION (1954–1962)

The Algerian Revolution, known within Algeria as the War of Independence, began in the early hours of November 1, 1954. It ended officially on July 3, 1962, when French president Charles de Gaulle, pursuant to agreements reached at Evian the previous March, formally renounced his nation's sovereignty over Algeria and proclaimed its independence.

The French occupation of Algeria, begun in 1830, led to a colonial system in which a minority of European settlers and their descendants dominated the Algerian economy and maintained their domination through monopolies of political power and the means of coercion. During the first half of the twentieth century, a series of initiatives by indigenous leaders sought first to secure meaningful political participation for the Muslim majority within the colonial system and later to negotiate autonomy, confederation, or independence. When these efforts proved fruitless, a group of radical young nationalists founded the Revolutionary Committee for Unity and Action (CRUA), which in 1952 began to plan an insurrection. Six of the CRUA members, together with three political exiles, are considered the "historical leaders" of the Algerian Revolution. The CRUA leaders, led by Mohamed Boudiaf, included Moustapha Ben Boulaid, Mourad Didouche, Belkacem Krim, Rabah Bitat, and Larbi Ben M'hidi. The exiled leaders were Hocine Aït Ahmed, Mohamed Khider, and Ahmed Ben Bella, who later became independent Algeria's first president.

Estimates of the number of militants taking part in the initial insurrection range from nine hundred to about three thousand. It began with attacks on government installations and other targets in several parts of the country, but the most effective actions took place in the Aurès region of the southeast. During the winter of 1954–1955 the French managed to contain the insurrection, limiting its manifestations to the most distant and inaccessible regions. In August 1955 the leadership, concerned that neither the majority of Algerians nor the European community were taking the insurrection seriously, decided to begin targeting European civilians in some twenty-six localities in the eastern part of the country. As many as 123 people, including Europeans and Muslim officials, were killed in what were called the Philippeville massacres. In outraged reaction, French forces took the lives of at least ten times as many Muslims, most of whom were innocent. The massacres and reprisals polarized the two communities in such a way that a narrowly based insurrection became a nationwide revolution; thousands of men took to the back country, while France rapidly built its forces into the hundreds of thousands.

In its initial proclamation, on October 31, 1954, the CRUA had announced the creation of a National Liberation Front (Front de libération nationale, FLN), to which it invited Algerians of all political persuasions to rally. As a result of the polarization following the events of August 1955, Algerian political classes across a broad ideological spectrum—ranging from religious activists to secular democrats, militant socialists, and communists—gradually closed down their independent operations and joined the FLN in revolution. By the summer of 1956 only Messali Hadj, long the leader of the most radical wing of the Algerian nationalist movement but now bypassed by events, remained outside of the FLN.

It is worth noting, however, that while the FLN projected an image of social and political inclusiveness, the dominant leadership, in spite of frequent internal power struggles, remained primarily in the hands of urban males from the middle and lower middle classes. The ideology these men articulated was overwhelmingly secular, leftist, nationalistic, and nonaligned. Such ideology, based in ideas and movements largely European in origin, was filled with contradictions for Algeria. Among the most important of the contradictions were related to issues of religion and gender. In affirming Algerian nationhood, the leadership was affirming an identity one of whose most important components was Islam. Because the majority of the guerrillas who fought the war were rural men and women steeped in various forms of populist Islam, an enormous ideological gap separated leaders and masses from the beginning. One illustration of this gap is found in perceptions of the role of women. Although the leaders were regularly calling for a free Algeria that would not tolerate differences based on class, race, or gender, and although women were playing very active roles in the struggle against the French, equality between male and female was not on the agenda of the majority of Algerians. Thus wartime promises of legislation to guarantee the civil and political rights of women quickly dissipated once independence was won.

In order to accommodate the dramatically broadened movement, the revolutionaries organized a clandestine congress in the Soumamm Valley of the Berber-speaking Kabylie region during August and September 1956. The congress created a broad Conseil national de la révolution algérienne (CNRA) to serve as a proto-parliament, and a Comité de coordination et d'exécution to bear the executive functions. One of the first decisions of the new executive was to initiate, at the end of September 1956, the urban warfare strategy that became known as the Battle of Algiers. A very visible phase of the war that the French had won by the middle of 1957, the urban warfare served the purpose of bringing the war home in a physical way to the majority of *colons* who were urban residents and of attracting serious attention for the first time from the metropolitan French public and the wider world. Another result of the Battle of Algiers was that the severe French repression drove the top FLN leadership out of the country to Tunis. This in turn generated problems in communications and orientation between the external leadership and the internal guerrillas, which caused troublesome divisions within the movement throughout the war and beyond.

Between the fall of 1957 and the spring of 1958 the French army, now grown to roughly 500,000 men, succeeded in bringing most of Algeria under its physical control and was concentrating on limiting cross-border raids by Algerian guerrillas from Morocco and Tunisia. But the military was apprehensive. Fearing that divided political leadership at home, sensitive to the violence involved in pacification and to growing world pressure, might undo its achievements, the army, under the leadership of Gen. Jacques Massu and with the enthusiastic support of the *colons,* proclaimed the creation, on May 13, 1958, of a Committee of Public Safety. The army's challenge to government authority brought down the Fourth Republic and propelled Gen. Charles de Gaulle, who pledged an early resolution of the Algerian conflict, to power as head of the Fifth French Republic. By the autumn of 1958 de Gaulle had offered Algerians the opportunity of total integration as equals into the French Republic, inaugurated a massive plan of economic renewal, and invited the revolutionary troops to join their French compatriots in a "paix des braves."

The CCE and the CNRA rejected these terms and, instead, created a Provisional Government of the Algerian Republic (GPRA) at Tunis, with the democrat Ferhat Abbas at its head. From this point on, even though French forces remained in control of most of Algeria, the GPRA campaigned to win world support for Algerian independence. The campaign centered primarily on developing world and Eastern Bloc countries and on the United Nations. Within a year de Gaulle began speaking of Algerian self-determination. The war of independence might have ended soon after de Gaulle's switch, but there were obstacles. Principal among these was the fate of the Sahara, in which French companies had recently discovered oil. Even more important was the resistance of the *colon* community, which increasingly made common cause with the military. During 1960 they created a Front de l'Algérie française to fight against independence, and in January 1961 they formed the Organisation armée secrète, which led an armed insurrection against French civil authority and launched a campaign of terror against Muslim Algerians.

After several abortive attempts at negotiation, the GPRA and France signed the Evian Agreement on March 18, 1962, which led to unequivocal independence in July. The war had caused the dislocation from their homes of about three million Algerians, the destruction of much social and economic infrastructure, and the deaths of several hundred thousand Algerians. Its conclusion led to the rapid exodus of the overwhelming majority of European residents, whose expertise and capital had been at the heart of most key Algerian systems. The rebuilding tasks faced by independent Algeria would be formidable.

See also *Algerian Islamic Revolt (1992–).*

John Ruedy

BIBLIOGRAPHY

Alleg, Henri, ed. *La guerre d'Algérie.* 3 vols. Paris: Temps actuels, 1981.

Courrière, Yves. *La guerre d'Algérie.* 4 vols. Paris: Fayard, 1968–1971.

Droz, Bernard, and Evelyne Lever. *Histoire de la guerre d'Algérie, 1954–1962.* Paris: Editions du Seuil, 1982.

Horne, Alistair. *A Savage War of Peace. Algeria 1954–1962.* London: Macmillan, 1977.

Ruedy, John. *Modern Algeria. The Origins and Development of a Nation.* Bloomington: Indiana University Press, 1992.

AMERICAN (U.S.) REVOLUTION (1776–1789)

At the close of the French and Indian War in 1763, the British empire in North America was at its zenith. The French and their Spanish allies had been vanquished, and the Paris peace treaty gave Britain control of Canada, Florida, and all land east of the Mississippi River. Nevertheless, in victory, George III and the ministry were faced with two pressing problems. Although revenues from taxes on land, houses, tobacco, sugar, newspapers, linen, brandy, beer, and other items had increased after 1756, those increases were insufficient to offset the elevated levels of military spending the war necessitated. As a result, the national debt had grown by more than 70 percent, from £72 million in 1755 to more than £122.6 million in 1763. Interest on the debt itself was in excess of £4.4 million annually. Furthermore, the British treasury estimated that the cost of defending the new and greatly enlarged empire in North America would add another £200,000 a year to the national budget. Unless new sources of revenue were found, and quickly, there was little hope of containing the national debt, let alone retiring it.

Since the late 1740s, crown and Parliament had also been trying to reform the imperial system to bring the rapidly expanding, increasingly prosperous, strategically important, and substantially self-governed North American colonies under stricter control. The actions the colonists took during the war—especially the grudging responses of the colonial assemblies to imperial requests for men and money, the illegal trade in the French West Indies by colonial merchants in pursuit of windfall profits, and the inability of British commanders to secure compliance to the terms of the navigation acts—seemed only to confirm the pressing need for a stronger centralized administration. With the successful conclusion of the war, imperial authorities were eager to resume their earlier reform efforts.

TAXATION AND THE PUSH FOR INDEPENDENCE

For their part, in 1763 the colonists were ill disposed to entertain any attempt by Parliament to raise imperial revenues by tapping colonial sources. The prosperity of the wartime economy had given way to a postwar depression beginning in 1760 as military expenditures dwindled and demands for the services of merchants, artisans, craftsmen, and a host of ordinary seamen and laborers fell off. Mired in a depressed economy, many colonists were quick to trace the source of their distress to imperial policies instituted since the end of the war. Moreover, the diminution of the French and Spanish threat in eastern North America after 1763 reduced the colonists' dependence on British military protection and may have emboldened them to resist more readily those changes in imperial supervision that signified an end to past policies of permissiveness. With an exaggerated assessment of their contributions toward winning the war, the colonists expected to reap the rewards of their effort. At the very least, they expected to be left as unencumbered as possible in the pursuit of their own economic well-being.

The opposing needs and expectations of the crown and colonists were brought to a head in the dozen years after 1763. For analytical purposes, it is useful to divide the period into two phases, with the Boston Tea Party of 1773 and the resulting Coercive Acts of 1774 as the pivotal point. During the first phase of the imperial crisis, the issue was taxation. Was Parliament empowered legitimately to raise a revenue in the colonies either directly, as in the case of the Stamp Act of 1765, or indirectly as in the case of the Sugar Act of 1764 or the Townshend duties of 1767?

"The Bostonians Paying the Excise Man, or Tarring and Feathering." Copy of a mezzotint attributed to Philip Dawe, 1774.

From the very outset of the imperial crisis, colonial protesters challenged Parliament's right to tax them without their consent. The ministry of British Prime Minister George Grenville tried to convince the colonists that they were virtually represented in Parliament, but the colonists scoffed at the idea. In his *Considerations on the Propriety of Imposing Taxes,* a pamphlet reprinted at least seven times after its first appearance in 1765, Maryland lawyer Daniel Dulany offered the most clearly reasoned rejection of Grenville's argument. Dulany acknowledged that a system of virtual representation might work when the interests of electors and nonelectors were inseparably connected, as they appeared to be for the inhabitants of Britain, because then any act of oppression directed against nonelectors would also affect the electors and the representatives. Such was not the case, however, between electors in England and nonelectors in the colonies. Instead, at times a total *dissimilarity* of interests characterized their relationship, so that actions Parliament took that proved to be harmful to the colonies might benefit inhabitants of Great Britain.

Dulany and most of his fellow protesters in this first phase of the imperial crisis readily admitted that the colonies were dependent on the mother country and that, as the Stamp Act Congress acknowledged, they therefore owed all due subordination to Parliament. But if taxation was not included under the concept of due subordination, what was? What sorts of parliamentary legislation outside the realm of taxation would the colonists accept?

As early as 1765, at least some colonists insisted that Parliament's legislative jurisdiction extended only to the external affairs of the empire—defense, commerce, and navigation—and not to the internal concerns of the individual colonies. Until passage of the Coercive Acts of 1774, however, assertions of this sort tended to be subdued in the interest of conciliation. Parliament's actions in closing the port of Boston, enlarging the powers of the royal governor of Massachusetts, and allowing for changes of venue in capital cases forced the colonists to assert more openly their understanding of the constitutional order of the empire. The Resolves of the First Continental Congress concluded that the recent actions of Parliament compromised American rights because, as radical writers had earlier claimed, the colonists had the right to govern and tax themselves through their own legislatures.

That American radicals by the 1770s had come to believe that Parliament's actions were not merely unconstitutional but maliciously undertaken by men intent on subverting the liberties of the colonists made conciliation even more difficult if not impossible. Based on their understanding of the opposition Whig writers of seventeenth- and eighteenth-century England, colonial radicals thought of themselves as living in a precarious world in which men naturally weak and corruptible were constantly tempted to do wrong. The few who were empowered to enforce the laws needed to protect the property and persons of the many were especially vulnerable, not because they were more inclined to be self-serving than the rest of mankind but because they possessed the means to promote their selfish ends. This they would do not through direct confrontation but through schemes that disguised their true intentions. At the core of the colonial opposition to imperial policy, therefore, was a conviction that corrupt officials in England were engaged in a giant conspiracy against colonial liberty.

Given this fearful perspective, the measures Parliament enacted after 1763 were explosive. Sustained efforts to impose what the colonists perceived to be illegal taxes, the arrival of ever larger numbers of placemen to administer these taxes, the threat of a standing army in peacetime as an instrument of coercion, the curtailment of the right to a trial by jury, and the enlargement of the discretionary powers of the royal governor of Massachusetts were understood by the radicals to be unmistakable signs that men of bad faith were conspiring to defeat the forces of liberty in America. The Declaration of Independence charged George III with having instigated "a design to reduce [the colonists] under absolute despotism" and asked a "candid world" to accept that indictment.

CONFEDERATION AND CONSTITUTION

In June 1776 Richard Henry Lee introduced in Congress resolutions calling not only for American independence but also for a plan of confederation to be submitted to the colonies. Acting on Lee's proposal, Congress appointed a committee headed by John Dickinson to prepare a blueprint for confederation for the states. The Dickinson committee submitted its strategy to Congress on July 12, 1776, and Congress sent a modified version of the plan to the states for ratification in November of 1777. Final approval of the Articles of Confederation was delayed until March of 1781, when Virginia ceded its claims to western lands to satisfy the objections raised by states lacking any claim to western territories, and until Congress pledged to use the ceded lands for the common good of all the states.

The Articles of Confederation reflected the political principles American spokesmen articulated after 1764, the ideological fears the actions of a distant Parliament inflamed especially after 1773, and the diversity of interests and separate identities that had been nurtured in most of the newly independent states for nearly a century. Thus the powers expressly granted to the Confederation Congress were not inconsiderable—it could declare war, conclude treaties, exchange ambassadors, coin money, emit bills of credit, settle state boundary disputes, and raise an army and navy. But in exercising any of these enumerated powers Congress needed the assent of at least nine states. Because each state also retained "every power, jurisdiction, and right" that was not "expressly delegated to the United States," the powers withheld from Congress were at least as important as those granted to it. The power to tax or to coerce obedience, for example, was denied to Congress, and any proposed amendment to the articles required the unanimous consent of the states.

The confederation union was no more than a league of friendship in which Americans recognized the necessity of a central authority but grudgingly allocated power to what they perceived to be a distant congress. The system seemed to work as long as the exigencies of war forced Americans to cooperate with one another. After the British defeat at Yorktown, however, local jealousies asserted themselves with renewed vigor. Only a few months after the articles were finally ratified, Alexander Hamilton was already complaining that a too narrow attachment to state interests had reduced the confederation to a condition of "constitutional imbecility."

Those who favored a stronger central government argued initially for giving Congress the power to set international trade policy to ensure that Americans could command reciprocal advantages. When the Annapolis convention of September 1786 met to consider the commercial regulations of the confederation, however, it attracted only five state delegations and was forced to adjourn without addressing any substantive issues. The attendees expertly managed to avoid further embarrassment by calling for a second convention to meet in Philadelphia the next year and suggesting that this second convention consider all provisions "necessary to render the constitution of the Federal Government adequate to the exigencies of the Union." Within six months, ten states, led by Virginia, had selected delegates to the proposed Federal Convention. When the convention met in May of 1787, only Rhode Island was not represented.

Following the lead provided by the Virginia plan introduced by Edmund Randolph on May 29, most of the delegates in Philadelphia believed that rendering the federal government adequate to the exigencies of the union would require abandoning the Articles of Confederation. After two weeks of sometimes heated exchanges, especially over the allocation of seats in the proposed national legislature, William Paterson, speaking for those who thought the Virginia plan had gone too far, introduced an alternative plan of union. The Paterson, or New Jersey, plan addressed the principal weakness of the confederation by granting Congress the power to impose taxes, regulate trade, and coerce compliance through restrictive penalties. After only four days of deliberation, however, the convention resoundingly rejected the Paterson plan and continued to work for a national legislature, executive, and judiciary.

The convention adjourned on September 17, 1787, and sent the proposed Constitution to Congress with the recommendation that it be forwarded to the states for ratification. The resolution that accompanied the Constitution was purposely silent on whether congressional approval was necessary before the document could be released to the states.

Other strategic decisions made in Philadelphia were aimed at improving the chances of success. Ratification would be handled by delegates elected to state conventions rather than by state legislators because the latter, for self-interested reasons, were likely to be reluctant to surrender power to a stronger central government. Equally important, the approval of only nine states would be sufficient for the new union to take effect under the Constitution. In one fell swoop, the convention avoided the difficulty of meeting the requirement for unanimity established by the Articles of Confederation and ensured that the momentum for ratification would increase with each endorsement. Finally, the convention rejected Edmund Randolph's motion that the states be invited to propose amendments that would then be taken up in a second general convention.

FIGHT AGAINST FEDERALISM

In the debate over ratification, the opponents of the Constitution, or Anti-Federalists, predicted that the Constitution would give rise to a despotic regime amid the ruins of the state governments. Two arguments, in particular, summarized their assorted fears. First, the Anti-Federalists contended that a single consolidated government of the sort projected under the Constitution could not long remain a republic. Republics, the French political philosopher Charles Louis de Secondat Montesquieu had written, must be small geographically. In a large republic, the good of the whole "is sacrificed to a thousand private views," and the resulting turmoil was overcome with the establishment of a monarchy, wherein the sovereign will of the one replaced the chaotic assemblies of the many.

James Madison presented the most cogent reply to this Anti-Federalist objection. In *Federalist* No. 10, he reversed the logic of Montesquieu's argument. The bane of free governments everywhere was selfishness, the impulse to promote one's own interest even when adverse to the interests of the community. This vice was dangerous, however, only when a group of self-interested citizens was large enough to constitute a majority faction because then that group possessed the power to act on its selfish desires. The advantage of a large republic was that it contained such an array of competing factions that the likelihood of a majority faction being formed was slim. Contrary to the position the Anti-Federalists took, therefore, stability and justice were characteristics appropriately associated with an extended republic of the sort established under the Constitution.

The second objection the Anti-Federalists raised was the absence of a bill of rights in the proposed Constitution. Under the various state constitutions individual rights were usually guaranteed by bills of rights that were affixed to the frames of government themselves. But the Constitution—which, as George Mason explained, created a central government more powerful than the state governments—rendered these guarantees precarious. Furthermore, Pennsylvanian John Smilie added, the powers delegated to the federal government were so loosely defined that it would be impossible to fix the limits of authority without an explicit declaration of rights. Worst of all was the dangerous sweeping clause that empowered Congress to "make all laws . . . necessary and proper" for carrying out its enumerated responsibilities.

Supporters of ratification insisted that a federal bill of rights was unnecessary because, as Roger Sherman of Connecticut said in Philadelphia, the several state declarations were sufficient to protect individual rights and because the assumption underlying the proposed Constitution was that the federal government was prohibited from exercising any powers not explicitly delegated to it. Indeed, Hamilton pointed out in *Federalist* No. 84, a bill of rights under these circumstances might prove to be dangerous. James Wilson agreed. A bill of rights might in fact afford men predisposed to abuse their power the excuse to act on their inclination on the pretense that everything not expressly mentioned had been left unprotected.

THE BILL OF RIGHTS

The debate over a federal bill of rights was resumed in the spring of 1789, after eleven states had ratified the Constitution and the first session of the new Congress was convened. Somewhat surprisingly, Madison, who until the fall of 1788 had endorsed the arguments of Hamilton and Wilson, was instrumental in getting the federal bill through Congress. In part, Madison was swayed by his friend

Jefferson's observations on this issue. Writing from Paris, where he was at the time the American minister to France, Jefferson noted that the Constitution already contained clauses that resembled the sort of guarantees ordinarily reserved for a declaration of rights. For example, the federal government was expressly prohibited from suspending the writ of habeas corpus, enacting bills of attainder or *ex post facto* laws, and imposing religious tests for officeholders.

In other words, the logic of the reserved powers argument offered by opponents of a federal bill of rights was violated in the body of the Constitution itself. Madison was further swayed by his belief that the linchpin of the Anti-Federalist opposition to the Constitution had been the absence of a bill of rights. To extinguish any lingering resentment against the system and to remove worry that the Federalists were enemies of republican government, he championed the proposal that covered all ten articles that eventually formed the Bill of Rights.

REPUBLICANISM AND DEMOCRACY

Madison's determination to reassure his former opponents that he and other defenders of the Constitution were not enemies of republican government shows one measure of the radicalism of the American Revolution. Until 1775 most colonists were loyal subjects of George III and no friends of republican governments, which they thought had proven historically to be unstable, short-lived, and imprudent experiments in popular rule. After 1776 independent Americans were proud champions of republicanism and deeply suspicious of anything that smacked of monarchy or aristocracy. This change in self-perception marked the beginning of a fundamental transformation of American society, and, as Gordon S. Wood has observed, makes the American Revolution "as radical and as revolutionary as any in history." Wood is quick to add, however, that the American Revolution was radical "in a very special eighteenth-century sense."

Above all, for most of the leaders of the revolution, republicanism meant something quite different from democracy. A basic tenet of eighteenth-century republicanism was that people were inherently unequal. Some were naturally better—more virtuous, intelligent, talented, and capable—than others. For the republic to work well, it was essential that ordinary citizens recognize these natural aristocrats, defer to their superior judgment, and delegate to them the responsibilities of governing.

Rulership was thus an exclusive realm in the revolutionary republic, but so was citizenship. Participation in public life was restricted to those who were able to prove themselves worthy of being included. All of the revolutionary state constitutions restricted the franchise to adult male property owners or taxpayers. Women, servants, slaves, and men who did not possess the requisite amount of property—in short the vast majority of inhabitants of the new nation—were excluded from voting, let alone holding office, because the revolutionaries believed that these dependent classes were perforce susceptible to all sorts of temptations and impositions from those above them. The ideal republican citizen was autonomous in his personal bearing and independent in the exercise of his will.

Elitism and exclusiveness, the distinguishing characteristics of the revolutionary republic, were anathema to nineteenth-century democrats, and the revolution itself set loose the very forces that made them so. Popular participation in the politics of upheaval convinced otherwise ordinary men and women of their civic competence, and the natural rights rhetoric that justified independence also justified egalitarian aspirations. The rejection of a hereditary aristocracy was followed by a repudiation of the natural aristocracy. What followed was logically consistent: If one opinion is as good as another, then greater wisdom must reside in greater numbers. Majoritarian democracy thus made a shambles of the ideal of exclusivity. In a democratic state, participation ought to be extended to all except those who proved themselves to be unworthy of inclusion. Felons may be excluded without doing harm to democratic ideals, but few others could be.

A REVOLUTIONARY REVOLUTION?

How revolutionary, then, was the American Revolution? There is no simple answer to this question. The revolution did not lead immediately to the abolition of slavery or an expansion of women's rights. And the commitment to republicanism initially entailed certain restrictions on the privileges of the bulk of the inhabitants of the new nation. Nevertheless, the revolution made subsequent improvements in the condition of most Americans almost inevitable by establishing, as Abraham Lincoln said some four score years after independence, standards that American reformers have "constantly looked to, constantly labored for." According to Lincoln, the revolution was ongoing and obligated subsequent generations to live up to the maxims of free government proclaimed but not fulfilled in 1776 or 1789.

See also *Constitutions; Democracy; Jefferson, Thomas; Madison, James; Republics; U.S. Preindependence and Pre-Civil War Rebellions (1675–1850).*

MELVIN YAZAWA

BIBLIOGRAPHY

Bailyn, Bernard. *The Ideological Origins of the American Revolution.* Cambridge: Harvard University Press, 1992.

Countryman, Edward. *The American Revolution.* New York: Hill and Wang, 1985.

Greene, Jack P. *Peripheries and Center: Constitutional Development in the Extended Polities of the British Empire and the United States, 1607–1788.* Athens: University of Georgia Press, 1986.

Jensen, Merrill. *The Founding of a Nation: A History of the American Revolution, 1763–1776.* New York: Oxford University Press, 1968.

Middlekauff, Robert. *The Glorious Cause: The American Revolution, 1763–1776.* New York: Oxford University Press, 1968.

Morgan, Edmund S., and Helen M. Morgan. *The Stamp Act Crisis: Prologue to Revolution.* Chapel Hill: University of North Carolina Press, 1953.

Nash, Gary B. *The Urban Crucible: Social Change, Political Consciousness, and the Origins of the American Revolution.* Cambridge: Harvard University Press, 1979.

Rakove, Jack N. *Original Meanings: Politics and Ideas in the Making of the Constitution.* New York: Alfred A. Knopf, 1996.

Wood, Gordon S. *The Creation of the American Republic, 1776–1787.* Chapel Hill: University of North Carolina Press, 1969.

———. *The Radicalism of the American Revolution.* New York: Alfred A. Knopf, 1992.

ANABAPTISM

Anabaptism was a religious and social movement originally named by its foes and characterized by the rejection of infant baptism in favor of adult or believers' baptism (hence, "re-baptism"). As a movement, Anabaptism emerged in various parts of central and southern Germany just after the Peasants War (1524–1526). In the following decade, its great age, Anabaptism spread across southern Germany and down the Rhine into the Low Countries; those two regions remained its heartland. Its most spectacular phase began in February 1534, when Netherlandish Anabaptists collaborated with local Anabaptists to take over the Westphalian episcopal city of Münster. Their occupation of Münster ended in June 1535 when episcopal and imperial troops stormed the city. Thereafter, pursued and persecuted, the Anabaptists became a splintered, fugitive rural movement. Anabaptism's peak strength probably lay in the tens of thousands of believers.

In the sixteenth century, the movement gained a reputation for subversion of the religious and social order—doubtless justified by the Anabaptists' refusal to bear arms, to swear oaths, to pay taxes, to recognize the principle of the "Christian magistrate," or to conform to the established church, plus their belief in the community of goods, that is, holding all property not individually but in common. But the movement as a whole was not revolutionary in the modern sense of seeking an overthrow or systematic alteration of social relations or an overthrow of the state. An important exception to its nonrevolutionary character, however, was the tradition of radical, apocalyptic spiritualism associated with the "Zwickau Prophets," whose radically disruptive agitation and liturgical reforms at Wittenberg in the winter of 1521–1522 Martin Luther condemned. The prophets' leading figures were the Franconian theologian Andreas Bodenstein von Karlstadt (1480?–1541) and the Thuringian Franciscan Thomas Müntzer (1489?–1525), Luther's two most bitter foes.

Müntzer, who proclaimed the victory of the righteous over the wicked, and coincidentally of the poor over the rich, was a leader of the Peasants War in Thuringia and the main icon of revolution in Reformation Germany. Partly by historical accident, his type of revolutionary spiritual religion became associated with Anabaptism; more typical of the Anabaptists were the peaceful, communitarian biblicists known as the "Swiss Brethren." Yet there were radical spiritualists among the Anabaptist dissenters who converged in 1529–1533 on Strasbourg. One was Karlstadt's leading disciple, Melchior Hoffman (d. 1543), a Swabian furrier who had preached in the Baltic and Scandinavian lands. From Strasbourg his disciples, called "Melchiorites," traveled down the Rhine to the Netherlands, where they merged with Hoffman's earlier Frisian followers. From these circles came those who made revolution at Münster in 1534–1535.

The Anabaptist Kingdom began at Münster in February 1534 after the city's leading Protestant clergyman, Bernhard Rothmann, was baptized by Jan Matthijs, a baker from Haarlem, supported by Jan Beukelsz, a journeyman tailor from Leiden. In February Münster's political elite split, whereupon Rothmann's followers, claiming miraculous and prophetic sanction to prepare for the Last Days, abandoned their pacifism and took up arms. Immediately thereafter the prince-bishop of Münster's army began a sixteen-month siege of the city. About twenty-five hundred supporters streamed into Münster from Westphalia and the Netherlands around Eastertide 1534. They joined the local converts, who, despite the Anabaptists' image as poor and despised, modern research has revealed to have been mostly persons of some substance, much like their fellow Catholic and Protestant burghers.

The turning point in the kingdom's history came with the death of its charismatic leader, Matthijs, in a sortie against the besiegers. His successor, Beukelsz ("Jan of Leiden") proved a much less able and charismatic leader. He retreated from the rule of community of goods, which Matthijs and Rothmann had instituted, and enraged some Anabaptists by proclaiming polygamy. He also inaugurated several successive regimes—the Twelve Elders (April–September 1534) and the Davidic Kingship (September 1534–June 1535)—through all of which the native elite remained powerful. Indeed, as James M. Stayer, the dean of Anabaptist historians today, has written, "behind its radical trappings," the

Anabaptist Kingdom "was a much more traditional society than that created in Anabaptist Moravia."

The kingdom nevertheless shaped Anabaptism's revolutionary image during the sixteenth century and thereafter. It also generated a revolutionary enthusiasm that led, after its fall, to several decades of guerrilla warfare against the temporal and religious authorities in the Netherlands. Until his execution in 1538, Jan van Batenburg led the rebels in a series of church robberies, crop burnings, and murders. Yet by this time the leading figure of Netherlandish Anabaptism was probably David Joris of Delft, who began re-spiritualizing the apocalyptic vision that eventually allowed Menno Simons to lead Netherlandish Anabaptism into peaceful anonymity.

Anabaptism presents no modern or protomodern program or practice of political revolution. Two aspects of the movement nonetheless remain of interest to students of political revolutions. One is that most Anabaptist groups, not just the Melchiorites, rejected the religious and social legitimization of authority, in the absence of which no early modern rulers—kings, princes, or magistrates—could have governed. They justified this from the Bible, particularly models of religious community taken from the New, and eventually also the Old, Testament. Second, in becoming overtly revolutionary, the spiritualist Anabaptists demonstrated the inability of sixteenth-century rulers to constrain completely the apocalyptic and ascetic ideas that have been carried by Christianity from the beginning. Yet the history of Anabaptism also reveals that, in the absence of relatively great political centralization and social mobilization, political revolution could not succeed in sixteenth-century Europe. The Mennonites—Menno Simons's followers—and other modern descendants of the Anabaptists today shun the realm of politics altogether.

See also *German Peasant War (1524–1526); Luther, Martin.*

THOMAS A. BRADY JR.

BIBLIOGRAPHY

Clasen, Claus Peter. *Anabaptism. A Social History, 1525–1618. Switzerland, Austria, Moravia, South and Central Germany.* Ithaca, N.Y.: Cornell University Press, 1972.

Deppermann, Klaus. *Melchior Hoffman: Social Unrest and Apocalyptic Visions in the Age of Reformation.* Translated by M. Wren. Edinburgh: T. & T. Clark, 1987.

Scott, Tom. *Thomas Müntzer. Theology and Revolution in the German Reformation.* Houndmills, Basingstoke: Macmillan, 1989.

Stayer, James M. *Anabaptists and the Sword.* 2d ed. Lawrence, Kan.: Coronado Press, 1976.

Williams, George H. *The Radical Reformation.* 2d ed. rev. Kirksville, Mo.: Sixteenth Century Journal Publishers, 1992.

ANARCHISM

Anarchism as a term is of Greek origin, meaning without a chief or head. Anarchists consistently argue that justice requires abolition of the state and all other authoritarian institutions. Only cooperative agreement among autonomous individuals can create valid organizations. Formal power arrangements, and the state above all, are unnatural and oppressive.

Anarchism has considerable influence in modern protest and revolution, particularly in the decades around 1900. This movement, defined by its hostility to formal organization and power arrangements, is intrinsically difficult to define. As an intellectual current, anarchism dates back to Greek political thinking, particularly the philosopher Zeno of Citium (ca. 335 B.C.–ca. 263 B.C.), and to sectarian strands of Christianity. Bolstered by selective implications of Enlightenment philosophy and by reactions to increased organizational power associated with the industrial revolution and the growth of government, anarchism became a significant protest movement in the second half of the nineteenth century. Anarchist activity trailed off after the 1930s, thanks to government repression and the greater effectiveness of more organized protest movements such as communism and fascism. Anarchist elements persisted, however, particularly in student movements during the 1960s and beyond.

Christian sects such as the Brethren of the Free Spirit (thirteenth century) and the Anabaptists of the sixteenth century frequently attacked formal organizations, including institutional religion, in favor of freely formed religious groupings. Visions of spontaneously operating utopias, without states, figured in other intellectual movements. Enlightenment beliefs in human rationality and perfectibility brought some thinkers like William Goodwin (1756–1836) to contend that people could collaborate voluntarily; Goodwin even argued that orchestras could function without conductors.

Increasing coercion by the factory system and growing effectiveness of political police, not only in western Europe but also in conservative Russia, brought anarchism from doctrine to movement. Theorists who inspired anarchist activity included Pierre-Joseph Proudhon (1809–1865) in France, who envisioned producer cooperatives replacing both factories and the state, and Michael Bakunin (1814–1876) and Pyotr Kropotkin (1842–1921) in Russia.

INDUSTRY AND THE STATE

Anarchists agreed on general goals but differed widely on means. Most early anarchists in the nineteenth century advocated peaceful change. Some hoped that cooperative utopias would persuade people to move away from more formal organizations simply by their existence and success. Bakunin, however, argued that violent destruction of government institutions, including attacks on rulers, was an essential first step that would clear the way for humanity's natural solidarity. Bakunin focused so strongly on terrorist methods that his vision of the future was deliberately vague by contrast.

Anarchists also differed over the nature of protest organizations. None countenanced bureaucratic or top-heavy protest movements. Some, even when drawn from theory into practical action, focused mainly on terrorist cells, kept small out of principle and as a means of avoiding police repression.

But anarchism could also inform major strands of labor unionism that emphasized direct action, such as potentially violent general strikes, for revolutionary rather than bread-and-butter goals in the interests of bringing down the industrial system and the state that was its servant. Anarchism in these cases combined with the syndicalist impulse in movements sometimes dubbed anarcho-syndicalist.

WAR AND ANARCHY

Anarchism exercised an important intellectual influence in many areas, including China and India in the early twentieth century. Its force also prompted important reactions by alternative protest movements, including Bolshevism, eager to beat back what was seen as a disorganized, utopian current doomed to failure. The most potent anarchist movements surfaced in France, parts of Switzerland, Italy, Spain, Russia (including the Ukraine), and several Latin American countries (particularly Argentina and Mexico). It was far less influential in northern Europe.

These patterns defy easy explanation. Very generally, anarchism did best in areas where industrialization advanced—but not too rapidly—and where a strong artisanal or peasant tradition persisted (hence the Jura mountain area of Switzerland more than the major cities; France rather than Germany). Anarchism was also roused by repressive but not fully effective governments. The power of individual leaders and earlier traditions of disaffection—such as peasant Andalusia or urban Barcelona against the central Castilian government in Spain or radical Jewish groups in western and southern parts of the Russian empire—were also influential. Anarchism became more defined after the split with Marxists in the International Workingman's Association in 1872, as Marxists insisted on capturing and using the state in revolution and also on tight organization within the revolutionary movement itself. Even within anarchist ranks, disagreements between advocates of violence and partisans of peaceful change through associative action continued. Anarcho-syndicalist movements gained particular strength in Latin Europe and Latin America. Along with genuinely mass movements, the violent actions of individual anarchists drew attention and repression. Such acts included a self-professed anarchist's assassination of President William McKinley in the United States in 1901. In turn, fears of anarchism frequently led to legal proscriptions that affected the freedom of action of other protest groups.

Anarchist elements in labor union movements, including the American International Workers of the World, remained strong in the first two decades of the twentieth century. Anarchist activity was considerable during the 1905 revolution in Russia, where numerous acts of violence were intended to ignite general insurrection. Increasingly, however, the need for somewhat firmer organization and questions about the utility of terrorist tactics subordinated the purely anarchist element in protest. Anarchism revived in Russia after the outset of the 1917 revolution, particularly in association with peasant-led movements, but it was repressed with increasing success after 1918.

Spanish anarchists, in Andalusia and particularly Catalonia, were important in the Spanish Civil War after 1936, though they were increasingly dominated by more organized groups such as the communists and of course were ultimately defeated by Gen. Francisco Franco's forces. Formal anarchism was by this point largely exhausted, though a spirit of generalized hostility to organization (including any very formal protest organization)—plus some penchant to advocate violence for its own sake—resurfaced in youth movements in the 1960s and successor groups such as the Red Brigades that attacked individual business and political leaders in hopes of toppling the power structure in such countries as Italy and Germany.

See also *Anabaptism; Russian Revolution of 1905; Russian Revolution of 1917; Spanish Civil War (1936–1939).*

Peter N. Stearns

BIBLIOGRAPHY

Avrich, Paul. *The Russian Anarchists.* Princeton, N.J.: Princeton University Press, 1967.

Dirlik, Arif. *Anarchism in the Chinese Revolution.* Berkeley: University of California Press, 1991.

Godway, David, ed. *For Anarchism: History, Theory, and Practice.* London: Routledge, 1989.

Joll, James. *The Anarchists.* New York: Grosset and Dunlap, 1964.

Sonn, Richard David. *Anarchism and Cultural Politics in Fin-de-Siècle France.* Lincoln: University of Nebraska Press, 1989.

Woodcock, George. *Anarchism: A History of Libertarian Ideas and Movements.* Cleveland, Ohio: World Publishing, 1962.

ANGOLAN REVOLUTION (1974–1996)

Preceded by thirteen years of anticolonial insurgency that eroded imperial pretensions, a coup by war-weary military officers in 1974 toppled the Portuguese government in Lisbon and opened the door to Marxist revolution in Angola. Under strongman rule by António de Oliveira Salazar (from 1928 to 1968) and his successor, Marcello Caetano (from 1968 to 1974), the comparatively small and weak state of Portugal had failed to sequester its African colonies from the wave of nationalist sentiment and militancy that Britain, France, and Belgium had reluctantly accommodated by the early 1960s. Their political ambitions frustrated, nationalists in Angola (1961), and subsequently Guinea-Bissau and Mozambique, turned to guerrilla warfare, which persisted despite ethnic, ideological, and personal rivalries within the nationalist movement and repressive counterinsurgency efforts by Portuguese military and police.

Although a decay in Portuguese resolve was manifest in economic stagnancy, massive emigration, and army desertions, the 1974 coup by a disillusioned military caught Lisbon and its American and other NATO allies by surprise. Instead of seeking United Nations or other international intercession to halt an incipient power struggle among three Angolan nationalist movements, the United States and its cold war adversaries mounted or intensified assistance programs for the movements of their choice. Clumsily public "covert" Western support for the "anticommunist" Front for the National Liberation of Angola (FNLA), based among the Bakongo community in the north, and the National Union for the Total Independence of Angola (UNITA), organized principally among the Ovimbundu and other rural communities of central and eastern Angola, unwittingly helped provoke and legitimize audacious Cuban and Soviet intervention, notably by failing to block or strongly oppose South African intervention on behalf of those same forces.

REVOLUTION ASCENDANT

The Popular Movement for the Liberation of Angola (MPLA), with strong support in the capital, Luanda, and the Mbundu population of its hinterland, drew its leadership from urban white and mestizo "leftists." After the intervention of a Cuban expeditionary force in 1975, the MPLA rolled over its adversaries. In November 1975 it proclaimed the independent People's Republic of Angola. By this time, most of the more than 300,000 Portuguese settlers had fled the country, leaving behind much of their oil-, coffee-, and diamond-derived wealth. In military victory, leaders of the MPLA acted with a zealotry and intolerance typical of revolutionaries intoxicated with newly won power. They banned opposition groups and jailed critics, repressed organized religion, barred independent trade unions, and declared the MPLA a Marxist-Leninist party with absolute control over the press, the economy, and the instruments of state. The result was economic ruin, except for an enclave economy based on oil production and export organized, paradoxically, by Western companies.

The victors failed to understand that they would need more than the weapons and personnel of Cuba and the Soviet Union to govern the country. They failed to surmount the limits of their social origins and ideology and reach out to rural communities, which perceived them as a continuation of alien (Portuguese acculturated) rule. The result was governance by draconian force under a revolutionary regime headed by the MPLA's physician and African poet president, Agostinho Neto.

CIVIL WAR: PHASE 1

By 1976 UNITA had regrouped in the remote grasslands and forests of the southeast under the charismatic leadership of its founder, Jonas Savimbi. Exploiting popular grievances against harsh MPLA rule, UNITA sought and received training, materiél, and logistical assistance from South African forces based in neighboring Namibia. The MPLA was providing logistical support to Namibian insurgents of the South West Africa People's Organization, who were seeking independence from South Africa. Operating out of shifting bases in the vast southeastern savannas, UNITA gradually extended its reach northward, forcing the government to build its armed forces to some 300,000 personnel and to spend much of its estimated $3 billion in annual oil revenues on Soviet tanks and aircraft as well as on a Cuban force that numbered 50,000 at its height in 1988. Little money remained for economic reconstruction or development. And by the mid-1980s the United States was again providing "covert" support for the "anticommunist" forces of UNITA, aid that by 1991 totaled some $250 million.

The human tragedy was horrific: between 100,000 and 350,000 battle dead; tens of thousands of land mine amputees; and perhaps half of the country's 10 million people displaced, many of them crowded into burgeoning urban slums. Disease and hunger rampaged within a climate of fear and intolerance that suffused society and political leadership.

Like the colonial phase before it, the cold-war phase of the Angolan conflict ended with a collapse: this time, of the Soviet Union. As cold war motivation waned, so did the incentive for continued Soviet and American support for client forces. This opened a new opportunity for an American-, Russian-, and Portuguese-brokered settlement. Through the medium of the United Nations, a cease-fire and a withdrawal of Cuban forces were engineered, and free elections were held in September 1992. However, faulty, wishful thinking coupled with penny pinching condemned the efforts to failure. The United Nations mounted a winner-take-all election without provision for compensatory provincial or local power for the losers. Even more fatal, it did not, as called for, disarm all parties so as to eliminate the military option for those bested in the zero-sum election. Over-reliance on the mechanism of elections led to disaster. Despite the civic enthusiasm of a war-weary citizenry, which dutifully and peaceably voted with the hope and expectation that "their" party would win and the fighting would end, the election only presaged a period of escalated violence. Political distrust and avarice prevailed.

CIVIL WAR: PHASE 2

The loser, UNITA, rejected the results and reactivated its forces, and Angola hurtled into a third and more devastating phase of seemingly interminable war. The ironies of its torment multiplied as South African mercenaries returned, this time from a politically reformed South Africa that had granted independence to Namibia, to defend an MPLA government that had progressively shed itself of Marxist ideology, and the United States reluctantly accepted the results of the election and distanced itself from UNITA, whose military capacity it had helped construct. Renewed fighting led to massive death and suffering, leveled cities, and added to a lethal legacy of millions of largely uncharted land mines strewn across the country.

Only as exhaustion set in, following more years of inconclusive warfare, were United Nations' efforts to bring the combatants back to the negotiating table successful. By 1996 the Angolan Revolution had run its course. The Russian-educated president, José Eduardo dos Santos, had accepted UNITA participation within the government as well as the legislature. And Jonas Savimbi had purportedly accepted the role of leader of a legal opposition. But UNITA forces continued to occupy much of the country beyond the coastal cities. Only as the decade closed and Savimbi's support from neighboring states—principally the Republic of the Congo and the Democratic Republic of the Congo (formerly Zaire)—dissipated and his control over diamond resources weakened did power seem to shift decisively in favor of a chastened, now market-oriented MPLA government. After three decades of devastating violence, there was renewed hope that Angola's agricultural as well as petroleum and mineral resources might finally be harnessed by a rational and responsible postrevolutionary leadership to create a productive, healthy, educated society—Angola's long denied potential. Yet Savimbi dragged his feet on demobilization, and sporadic fighting continued.

See also *Portuguese Revolution (1974).*

JOHN A. MARCUM

BIBLIOGRAPHY

Birmingham, David. *Frontline Nationalism in Angola and Mozambique.* Lawrenceville, N.J.: Africa World Press, 1993.

Ciment, James. *Angola and Mozambique: Postcolonial Wars in Southern Africa.* New York: Facts on File, 1997.

Guimaraes, Fernando Andresen. *The Origins of the Angolan Civil War: Foreign Intervention and Domestic Political Conflict.* New York: St. Martin's Press, 1998.

Kitchen, Helen, ed. *Angola, Mozambique, and the West.* Westport, Conn.: Praeger, 1987.

Maier, Karl. *Angola: Promises and Lies.* London: Serif, 1996.

Marcum, John A. *The Angolan Revolution.* 2 vols. Cambridge, Mass.: MIT Press, 1969, 1978.

———. "Angola: War Again." *Current History* (May 1993).

Tvedten, Inge, et al. *Angola: Struggle for Peace and Reconstruction.* Boulder, Colo.: Westview Press, 1997.

ANTHONY, SUSAN B.

Anthony (1820–1906), the most controversial and steadfast leader of the woman's rights movement in the nineteenth-century United States, was born in western Massachusetts to a Quaker family and into a generation of women who would reshape the destinies of American women. She grew up during the Industrial Revolution with Quaker egalitarianism as her faith and creed. Her industrious father was one of the first mill owners in the industry that changed the United States from an agrarian to an industrial society.

Although the Industrial Revolution extended the exploitation of labor from the home to the workplace, it also opened a public sphere of work and the potential for an independent economic existence to women. Anthony was among the first to take advantage of these new possibilities. With little advanced education she became a school teacher when the male domination of that field was only beginning to yield. By her late twenties, she found herself in a unique position—economically self-sufficient, employed outside the home, with legal rights that were denied her married sisters, and free to chart her own life. She followed her own interests and turned away from teaching and into social reform movements. Her Quaker family did not discourage her independence, which brought her into the leadership of the antislavery, temperance, and woman's rights movements by mid-century.

During the 1850s Anthony became a leader of the radical

Susan B. Anthony

legislate in their own behalf, they would always be in serfdom. Despite criticism and abuse, she was unwavering in her commitment to women's self-determination. She was equally committed to petitioning Congress and to grassroots organizing of women in village after village that she visited throughout the second half of the nineteenth century.

By the 1870s Anthony, both loved and hated, was the recognized leader of the Woman's Rights Movement throughout the country. She was considered dangerous by many because she could not be made to compromise on women's rights. But for throngs of women she was their charismatic leader. They looked to her for hope. In her lifetime she became a symbol of what was possible for women.

Woman's Rights Movement, having teamed up with feminist reformer Elizabeth Cady Stanton, who had called the 1848 Seneca Falls Convention. Simultaneously, she was a vigorous campaigner against slavery, insisting on the immediate emancipation of all slaves, and she crusaded for women's right to co-education, their entry into the profession of teaching, property rights, the right to divorce for married women, and suffrage. She quickly became known for the courage of her convictions, and as she uncovered wrongs against women, sought the most radical change that would root out the conditions that produced them.

During the Civil War, Anthony organized and led the Women's National Loyal League, petitioning President Abraham Lincoln to emancipate all human beings from slavery. But after the Civil War, when slavery was abolished, the abolitionist men with whom she had worked turned against women by securing a constitutional amendment guaranteeing all *men,* black and white, the right to vote. This dramatic turning point in women's struggle for emancipation found Anthony refusing to compromise. She would not support any law that would exclude one-half of the African American population and all women from the most fundamental right of citizenship. Anthony campaigned for the rest of the century from the conviction that until women had the power to

In 1872 when she was arrested because she voted for president of the United States, her crime—being a woman who voted—was treated as a capital offense. Many other women defied the U.S. Constitution by voting in that election, but Anthony's case became a national issue. When she was arrested, she refused bail and insisted that she be subjected to the full power of the unjust law. Her case took bizarre twists that defy rationality in the history of American jurisprudence. Her friend and lawyer posted her bail because he—chivalrously—could not see her going to jail. But by doing so, he prevented her case from going before the Supreme Court. Then in a jury trial that she condemned as one not of her legal peers as guaranteed to her by the Constitution—in that the jurors were all men with rights denied to her—the judge, who had prepared a decision before the trial began, instructed the jury to read it and convict her. Anthony was fined but refused to pay it, and the court refused to jail her for not paying it. She was more convinced than ever that until women had the power of the ballot, they would be subservient to men's power.

In the 1880s Anthony took the issue of women's rights to Europe and went from one country to the next, building an international woman's rights movement just as she had in the United States. Through the 1890s she solidified the movement for the struggle that she had come to realize would not be won in her lifetime. She was determined to leave a united and well-organized movement behind to carry the struggle to victory. Anthony's radical egalitarianism did not waver, even in her later years, and her charisma was an ongoing force galvanizing the movement, but the movement itself had changed. Women who entered the movement in the 1880s and 1890s no longer appreciated the original reasons for focusing the movement on suffrage. A more-educated generation of women who now for the first time had access to college fought for their suffrage as an individual right, not a claim for self-determination of women.

Anthony's dream of women with full citizenship was not realized in her lifetime. Thirteen years after her death women achieved the right to vote, but it would be eighty-five years and the 1990s before they would begin to vote as a gender block. Anthony's heroic, lifetime commitment to struggle for woman's rights has left her as a symbolic image of women's hoped-for emancipation.

See also *Gender; Inequality; Rights; Woman's Rights Movement*.

Kathleen Barry

BIBLIOGRAPHY

Barry, Kathleen. *Susan B. Anthony: A Biography.* New York: New York University Press, 1988.

Harper, Ida Husted. *The Life and Work of Susan B. Anthony.* 3 vols. Indianapolis: Bowen-Merrill, 1899, 1908.

ARAB "GREAT REVOLT" (1916–1918)

The term *Great Revolt* refers to the rebellion of Arab groups, mainly from the Hijaz in Arabia, led by the Hashimite (in Arabic, *Hashim*) family against the Ottoman Empire during the last two years of the First World War. The family, a well-known clan from Mecca, were descendants of the prophet Muhammad. With British support, the Great Revolt was part of the military campaign leading up to Arab independence from Ottoman rule.

The motives for the revolt were complex and had far-reaching ramifications. On the Arab side, the Hashimite leader Sharif Husayn (Hussein) wished to establish his independence from Ottoman Turkish authority and saw the British as the best guarantor of his aspirations. He also hoped that this achievement would ensure his preeminence in the Arabian peninsula over rival leaders, notably Abd al-Aziz ibn Saud, who was allied with the Wahhabi Muslim reform movement centered in eastern Arabia. Sharif Husayn's son Abdullah had approached British officials in Cairo in February 1914 seeking their support for the independence of the Hijaz from Ottoman rule, but he was rebuffed. Once the war started, however, Britain took the initiative in contacting Husayn to express interest in Abdullah's proposal.

Militarily, an Arab revolt led by Sharif Husayn would divert Turkish troops from Egyptian borders. Politically, it would signify a Muslim revolt in sympathy with the British against the Ottoman Turks, whose leader held the title of Caliph, leader of the worldwide Islamic community. This would mitigate the impact of the Holy War declared by the Ottomans against Britain and reduce the chances of rebellion among Britain's Muslim subjects in India.

Sharif Husayn's goals of regional independence were furthered by his son Faysal's contacts with Arab nationalists centered in Damascus, Syria. The Arab nationalist objective was an independent Arab state after the war that would incorporate the Arabian Peninsula and present-day Israel (former Palestine), Jordan, Lebanon, Syria, and Iraq. Beleaguered by Ottoman Turk military surveillance, these nationalists recognized Husayn as the leader of the Arab cause against the Ottomans subject to his acceptance of their broad territorial demands.

Entrusted with this vision and encouraged by British propaganda that promised Arab independence after the war, Sharif Husayn initiated his correspondence with Sir Henry McMahon, the British high commissioner in Egypt, by demanding Arab independence in precisely those borders defined by the Arab nationalist cause. Official British opinion opposed recognizing those claims, in part because Britain knew of French plans for Lebanon and Syria after the war. These aspirations led the British to plan for control of southern Iraq and a land link from there and the Persian Gulf to the Suez Canal and Egypt, which had been a British protectorate since the outbreak of war. Here, European imperial designs for the postwar period collided with wartime needs to encourage Arab hopes of independence that the British did not intend to fulfill.

After initial hesitation, McMahon promised Arab independence in the areas defined by Husayn, except for the coastal areas north of Beirut and parts of Iraq. Palestine was not mentioned. McMahon's letter of October 24, 1915, was motivated not so much by a commitment to Arab needs as by British desire for a propaganda victory in the Middle East: the Gallipoli campaign had become a disaster and the British invasion of Mesopotamia was threatened. McMahon qualified his promise to Husayn by a reference to areas still subject to the interests of Britain's ally, France, a deliberate qualifier to permit French claims to Syria and Lebanon after the war. With these British commitments, such as they were, Husayn declared his revolt in June 1916, although he explained his goals to his fellow Arabs in Islamic rather than nationalist terms.

The revolt met with limited success initially, capturing the main cities of the Hijaz except Medina, which held out to the end of the war. Lacking modern military equipment or organization, Arab leaders relied on British advisers, including the legendary T. E. Lawrence, and large infusions of British money to retain the loyalty of tribal forces. The revolt's main success came once the British invaded Palestine and Syria in 1917 and then in 1918, carrying out guerrilla operations and cutting Ottoman supply and transportation lines. When the British captured Damascus in October 1918, they permitted Husayn's son Faysal to enter first with his Arab forces to establish a claim to the city and to Syria. By doing so, the British undermined French claims to Syria that Britain had already recognized, another example of the political machinations behind British policy.

Although British officials had conditioned their promises to Sharif Husayn on his undertaking the revolt, they had reached an accord with France, the Sykes-Picot Agreement, to give them Lebanon and Syria as areas of control before the revolt erupted. The agreement recognized British interests in Mesopotamia (Iraq) and designated Palestine as neutral and subject to international concerns. The British were concerned to ensure French cooperation in the war.

Then, with respect to Palestine, the British issued the Balfour Declaration of November 1917, promising that it would become a Jewish national home, a euphemism for an intended Jewish state. This promise likewise reflected wartime interests related to the hope to keep Russia in the war and to encourage greater American involvement on the British/French side.

Thus, the British had entered into several apparently contradictory agreements without consulting their ally, Sharif Husayn, beforehand. When British forces then allowed Faysal to enter Damascus in October 1918, this move symbolized another change of view. London now hoped to establish an Arab government under Faysal, presenting the French with a fait accompli and an excuse for reneging on Britain's promises to them.

In the end, great power needs in the peace settlement overrode British regional designs. London withdrew its support from Faysal to reach agreement with France on other issues, leaving Syria open to French occupation in July 1920. The victorious powers legitimized French claims by awarding Paris mandates for Syria and Lebanon, while Britain assumed responsibility for Palestine and Iraq; the Balfour Declaration was incorporated within the British mandate for Palestine to justify Jewish immigration into that region against the wishes of its Arab inhabitants.

The Arab revolt served British interests politically and militarily, but did not achieve Arab aspirations for independence as supposedly promised. Ultimately, these Arab lands would gain independence, Palestine as a Jewish state. The British compensated the Hashimite family of Sharif Husayn by setting up Faysal, ousted from Syria, as King of Iraq. Abdullah was allowed to establish a shaky emirate in Transjordan buttressed by British gold, ultimately the kingdom of Jordan. Sharif Husayn sought to retain his hold over the Hijaz, but finally succumbed in 1924 and 1925 to the attacks of Ibn Saud, himself backed by British funds to oppose the Turks in eastern Arabia. The result was the kingdom of Saudi Arabia. Husayn went into exile.

The Arab revolt and the political claims surrounding it and opposing it have aroused much political and scholarly controversy. The British-French postwar division of the Arab lands reflected the impulses of imperial design and mutual accommodation regardless of wartime promises. Arab claims of betrayal were met with arguments that the Husayn–McMahon correspondence amounted to promises, not binding agreements, and a scholarly tradition exemplified by the work of the late Elie Kedourie that the British had been fully open and honest with their Arab allies. What is clear is that the Great Revolt set in motion military operations based on certain political expectations that were never achieved, but whose legacy can be found in the contemporary state systems of the central Middle East.

JOSEPH KOSTINER

BIBLIOGRAPHY

Antonius, George. *The Arab Awakening.* London: Hamish Hamilton, 1939.

Baker, Randall. *King Husain and the Kingdom of the Hijaz.* Cambridge: Oleander Press, 1979.

Dawn, C. Ernest. *From Ottomism to Arabism: Essays in the Origins of Arab Nationalism.* Urbana: University of Illinois, 1973.

Kedourie, Elie. *In the Anglo-Arab Labyrinth: The McMahon–Husayn Correspondence and Its Interpretation, 1914–1939.* Cambridge and New York: Cambridge University Press, 1976.

Kostiner, Joseph. *The Making of Saudi Arabia, 1916–1936: From Chieftaincy to Monarchical State.* New York: Oxford University Press, 1993.

Lawrence, T. E. *Seven Pillars of Wisdom: A Triumph.* Dorset: New Orchard, 1986.

ARMED FORCES

Armed forces are a nation's combined military, naval, and air forces. For as long as armed forces have existed, they have played a pivotal role in revolutions, commonly—though by no means always—as an instrument of order acting in support of rulers and governments. Indeed, political traditions in which the armed forces do not participate in revolutionary or counterrevolutionary activity are unusual and comparatively recent. These include the Anglo-American tradition, in which the experience of Oliver Cromwell's military dictatorship produced an enduring distrust of large, standing armies that, in combination with strong democratic traditions, effectively removed the threat of armed military intervention from politics; Japan, where the 1945 Allied terms of surrender and postwar constitution effectively depoliticized the military; and the general tendency since World War II among industrialized democracies toward depoliticized military establishments. A very different pattern of military nonintervention can be seen in Israel, where the external threat is sufficiently great, the burden of military service so widely shared, and the prestige of the armed forces sufficiently high that defense concerns are integral to politics.

Throughout history, armies have played a far more active role in political revolutions than navies because the locus of political power is ashore and navies depend on land-based recruitment and logistical support. Air forces have had even less involvement in revolutions, a function of their highly technocratic nature, limited manpower, and the vulnerability of air bases to ground attack. At the most basic level, armies—or more precisely ground forces—can offer direct political support or opposition to revolutionary activity in ways that naval and air forces cannot. An infantry battalion can occupy the presidential palace or arrest the government, and a squadron of cavalry or tanks can disperse a revolutionary mob. Warships and aircraft may provide vital assistance in either case, providing fire support, preventing the deployment of opposing forces, and so on. They can destroy, they can observe, they can communicate, but they cannot physically control political behavior as ground forces can.

BY SEA AND BY AIR

Examples of significant naval involvement in revolutions include Khaireddin Barbarossa's use of his galley fleet to overthrow local North African dynasties in the early sixteenth century; the pivotal role of the Dutch Sea Beggars in the critical early stages of the Revolt of the Netherlands, 1567–1648; the suppression of Cosinga's Ming loyalist government and seizure of Taiwan by Manchu naval forces in 1681–1683; and the role of postindependence Latin American navies in revolutions and coups. In each of these cases geography was a major factor behind the importance of naval forces because most of what was politically and economically important in the region or nation in question lay near the coast and was readily accessible by sea. Navies can also be crucial in cordoning off revolutionary or counterrevolutionary activity: the Royal Navy helped prevent the intervention of the Holy Alliance of Austria, Prussia, and Russia in the wars of independence in Latin America, 1810–1826, and the U.S. navy, the spread of the Chinese Revolution to Taiwan in the 1950s.

The generally peripheral role of navies in revolutions notwithstanding, politicized sailors have served as flash points of revolutionary activity on a surprising number of occasions, such as the 1905 mutiny of the crew of the Russian battleship *Potemkin* and the adherence of the bulk of the Spanish navy's seamen to the Republic in 1936 in defiance of their officers' orders.

Although air strikes, actual and threatened, have been a common feature of revolutions and coups d'état since World War II, only in Latin America have air forces become institutionally involved regularly in revolutions, and then in partnership with the navy, army, or both. The first and only clear instance of decisive aerial intervention in a revolution came early in the Spanish Civil War, 1936–1939, when regular troops were ferried from Morocco to Spain aboard transport aircraft furnished by Nazi Germany. The neutralization of the Republican navy by Italian bombers sent by Benito Mussolini tipped the balance in favor of the Nationalists at a critical juncture. The only significant example of an air force acting as an independent locus of political power in a revolution is that of the South Vietnamese air force under Marshall Nguyen Cao Ky during 1965–1975.

LOYALTY AND ALLEGIANCE

Historically, military establishments have served to deter or suppress violent revolution, and those establishments that enjoy a monopoly or near-monopoly of armed force are almost always successful in this so long as they retain their cohesion, military effectiveness, and loyalty to the regime. The same point applies in reverse: armed forces seeking to overthrow their government and rule in its place are normally successful, at least in the short term, so long as they exhibit the same traits, even when the government enjoys considerable popular support. The seizure of power by condottieri leaders in Renaissance Italy and the decade and a half of military rule in Chile following the 1973 overthrow of the Salvador Allende government are examples. Wavering loyalty, uncertain motivation, and flagging morale within the armed forces, however, have often been important for revolutionary success, as in the French Revolution, 1789–1791, Chinese Communist success in 1945–1949, and the Cuban Revolution of 1956–1959.

Where the government's legitimacy or effectiveness is challenged by large segments of the body politic, politicized paramilitary forces have often emerged, a development anticipated by the use of militarized customs police to maintain public order in eighteenth-century Europe. These forces may be organized by the government, as with the Spanish Civil Guard raised by the monarchy in the 1840s to suppress rural revolt, and the Assault Guard raised by the Republic in the 1930s to protect it from its enemies. They may arise spontaneously, as in China with the Taipings in the 1850s and the Boxers at the end of the century. They may be raised with the complicity of the army, as with the post-World War I German right-wing paramilitary units called freikorps; or by a ruling communist party, as with the Chinese Red Guards, raised at Mao Zedong's instigation in 1965 to perpetuate his radical vision of revolution. More commonly, they have been political militias of the right, used to intimidate opposition, establish and maintain order at rallies, and project an aura of dynamic intervention in an unsettled political situation. Mussolini's Blackshirts are the prototype of this kind of organization, and the Nazi Storm Troopers, the archetype.

The key to understanding the role of the armed forces is not so much their stated purpose as the social and economic strata from which officers and other ranks are recruited and their relationships with their political superiors. It is worth noting that when military establishments intervene in politics, they almost always do so under the orders of their officers; the only examples of successful military coups led by noncommissioned officers are those of Fulgencio Batista in Cuba in 1932 and Samuel Doe in Liberia in 1980. Armed forces created by an established polity are in some measure organized, trained, and equipped to oppose revolution, and a formal oath of allegiance to the ruler, regime, or state has been a salient feature of military service since antiquity. Such oaths may take many forms: the nation is often invoked, as is religion, though effective oaths generally focus on an organization or individual. The United States is unusual in requiring its military personnel to swear to uphold a legal document, the Constitution.

Although these oaths are taken with greater or lesser degrees of seriousness—today's French officers swear no oath of allegiance at all—they provide useful clues to the behavior of armed forces in revolutions. The oath of personal allegiance that Adolf Hitler required of his officers was more important as an after-the-fact rationalization than as a motivating factor but was an accurate reflection of their political loyalties. Logically, the armed forces' loyalty to their government should vary as a function of the regime's perceived legitimacy or illegitimacy, but the record suggests that cohesion and combat effectiveness are better predictors of adherence to the oath—assuming that it is taken seriously—than legitimacy. The fight to the death of Louis XVI's Swiss Guards in the August 1792 Tuileries massacre is the classic example. But even militarily effective forces can be politically brittle, as the abrupt collapse in 1976 of the Nicaraguan National Guard under the regime of Anastasio Somoza demonstrates.

Such considerations apply to the armed forces of revolutionary movements as well as to those of established, legitimate, polities. Kemal Atatürk's success in transferring the allegiance of the Ottoman forces from the sultanate and Sunni Islam to the Turkish Republic was the keystone of victory in the 1919–1922 revolution and Turco-Greek War. The Irish Republican Army's achievement in 1919–1923 in presenting itself as a national armed force was a major element of victory. The Indonesian army established its legitimacy in revolutionary struggle against Dutch colonial forces and communist rivals during 1945–1949 as a necessary precondition to the emergence of the Indonesian nation.

THE RISE OF MILITARY ELITES

The emerging ascendancy of Western arms in the early modern era led to the adoption of European weaponry, discipline, and training in many non-Western powers, leading in turn to the creation of new military elites. In some cases, traditional elites were successful in rejecting Western military practices and the political destabilization they brought with them, as in nineteenth-century Vietnam, where the emperor's success in preventing importation of Western military practices left the country without effective means of resisting the French conquest. In others, the new elites co-opted and absorbed their traditional rivals, as in Japan, or they suppressed them, as in Russia and the Ottoman Empire, the Ottomans subduing the Janissaries with considerable bloodshed in 1826.

Modern armed forces have wielded great influence in developing nations with weak or uncertain traditions of governance, where the legitimacy and prestige of the armed forces may rival or surpass that of the government, and much of the educated elite is military. This has been the case in Turkey, where the army is charged constitutionally with preserving secular democracy and has intervened militarily to that end on several occasions. Thailand was under direct or indirect military rule from 1932 until 1992, when King Bhumibol endorsed the democratic aspirations of a rising middle class by condemning military suppression of popular protest. The army—far more politically active than the more technocratic and professional navy—was a major force behind economic modernization in Meiji Japan and imposed its militaristic political vision on a succession of increasingly pliant governments from the 1920s until defeat and surrender in 1945.

Military establishments are one of the few generally accepted symbols of national legitimacy in the Arab world, and the 1936 coup in Iraq was the first of many, the most portentous of which was the 1952 overthrow of King

Farouk of Egypt by a group of officers led by Gamal Abdel Nasser and Anwar Sadat. In sub-Saharan Africa the military coup has become the most common means of changing government in the wake of the first generation of postindependence leaders. The Indonesian government of General Suharto, 1966–1998, while technically not a military government, effectively suppressed political activism for thirty years, leaving the armed forces the only corporate entity capable of carrying out a political program.

Marxist-Leninist armed forces have followed a different political trajectory, both as revolutionary forces and as instruments of the state, in that the legitimacy and political authority of the party have gone unchallenged up to the point of political collapse. That this loyalty was more difficult to obtain and more brittle once gained than was commonly supposed was attested to in the Soviet Red Army by the importance of political commissars from beginning to end and by the failure of the 1991 conservative coup aimed at restoring party authority. Although subordinate to the Communist Party, the Chinese Peoples Liberation Army has served as an important focal point of economic development and political influence and as a major political prop, witness the violent suppression of the June 1989 Tiananmen Square demonstrations. No violent uprising against a Marxist-Leninist military has ever succeeded; the only apparent exception, the December 1989 overthrow of the Romanian regime of Nicolae Ceausescu, now appears to have been a preemptive countercoup by elements of the military.

See also *Chilean Socialist Movement and Counterrevolution (1970–1978); Chinese Communist Revolution (1921–1949); Chinese Taiping Rebellion (1851–1864); Coup d'état; Cromwell, Oliver; Cuban Revolution (1956–1970); Egyptian Revolution (1952); French Revolution (1789–1815); German Nazi Revolution (1933–1945); Japanese Meiji Restoration (1868); Latin American Popular and Guerrilla Revolts (1960–1996); Latin American Revolutions for Independence (1808–1898); Netherlands Revolt (1566–1609); Nicaraguan Revolution (1979); Ottoman Jelali and Janissary Revolts (1566–1826); Romanian Revolution (1989); Russian Revolution of 1905; Russian Revolution of 1917; Spanish Civil War (1936–1939); Turkish Revolution (1908–1922); Vietnamese Revolution (1945–1975); War.*

John F. Guilmartin Jr.

BIBLIOGRAPHY

Be'eri, Eliezr. *Army Officers in Arab Politics and Society.* New York: Frederick A. Praeger, 1970.

Chailand, Gerard. *Revolution in the Third World.* Hassocks, England: Harvester Press, 1978.

Downing, Brian M. *The Military Revolution and Political Change: Origins of Democracy and Autocracy in Early Modern Europe.* Princeton, N.J.: Princeton University Press, 1992.

Horne, Alistair. *A Savage War of Peace.* New York: Macmillan, 1977.

Ralston, David B. *Importing the European Army: The Introduction of European Military Techniques and Institutions into the Extra-European World, 1600–1914.* Chicago: University of Chicago Press, 1990.

Wheatcroft, Andrew. *The World Atlas of Revolutions.* New York: Simon and Schuster, 1983.

ART AND REPRESENTATION

Revolution in art is a short story set within the epic narrative of art history. Compared to its major place in philosophy and literature, the subject of revolution appears only sporadically in the representational arts of painting, drawings, prints, and sculpture. It is a subject that has attracted relatively few artists and still fewer of any import. Among the reasons for this are the absence of patronage, a lack of exhibition opportunities, the want of an audience receptive to politically motivated art, and the difficulty of representing an event from the past in a manner appealing to both the intellect and to the eye.

A subgenre of history painting, revolution as a subject in art arose in France in the decade prior to 1789, flourished—if somewhat fitfully—in the nineteenth century during the "age of revolution" in Europe and America, and survived into the twentieth century mostly in the debased form of agitprop. State-sanctioned artists of the post–1945 era in the Soviet Union and China attempted to resuscitate the genre but with predictably uninspired results. In all societies, it has seldom proved possible for the artist to make an individual statement when the state appropriates artistic production for ideological ends. From the 1770s to the 1930s, however, the subject of revolution attracted a number of distinguished artists whose exceptional strength of mind and talent were capable of realizing an art that satisfied personal impulses and public expectations in equal measure.

THE RISE OF REVOLUTIONARY ART IN FRANCE

Prior to the eighteenth century, contemporary history was almost unknown in the representational arts of Europe. Artists typically referred to their own times only indirectly, through allegory—in other words, symbolically—in works portraying episodes from ancient history or classical mythology. After the rediscovery of the writings of Homer and the ruins of Pompeii and Herculaneum in the 1740s, ancient history began to capture the public imagination, and historical subjects in art appealed to a wider audience. In France, the new interest in history painting paralleled the growth of the state-supported Salon and a corresponding expansion of the Salon audience, which included not only the bourgeoisie but also critics from the popular press. Art became a focal point of public discourse, and critics seized upon its ethical content as a central issue of debate. The encyclopedist, Jean-Jacques Diderot, for example, asserted that "art should encourage us to love virtue and hate vice." He also railed against artists who specialized in erotically charged subjects with their love-smitten protagonists, eye-catching colors, and playful atmosphere, inveighing them instead to "paint as they spoke in Sparta," with a minimum of artifice. By the mid-1770s, the rococo was supplanted in the Salon by a new vogue for allegorical scenes from ancient history infused with the patriarchal themes of honor, loyalty, duty, and respect for authority.

The era found its most eloquent and impassioned interpreter in the person and work of Jacques-Louis David (1748–1825), the supreme painter of revolutionary subject matter. David's draftsmanship and manner of painting were radically new, combining linear purity with the restrained use of color and theatrical rhetoric with the suppression of anecdotal detail. David's first work fully conceived in the new style is a single drawing now divided into two sections, *Funeral of a Hero* (Crocker Art Museum, Sacramento) and *Combat of Two Warriors* (Musée de Peinture et de Sculpture, Grenoble), circa 1778. This sequential work announces the artist's main preoccupations during the 1780s: the use of allegory to comment on modern day affairs and the symbolic function of the male corpse as the ultimate repository of republican virtue. The drawings represent a combat of the gods over man's fate, followed by the outcome, the funeral cortege of Patroclus from Homer's *Iliad*. The work is appropriately "Spartan" in its frieze-like format, stylized gestures, meticulous penmanship, and sparing use of highlights, all reflecting the new bourgeois sense of ethics. The heroic figure of Patroclus, at once muscular and inert, is displayed like the dead Christ, a pagan *pietà* in which violence and death are the natural outcome of conflict.

During the 1780s David reworked the theme of self-sacrifice in his allegorical paintings of classical history to the overwhelming approval of critics and public alike. His *Oath of the Horatii* (Louvre, Paris, 1784) created a sensation not only for its content but also because of its late arrival in the Salon and placement high up on a wall, prompting rumors of attempted suppression by the government. This stark and utterly original painting shows three sons receiving the blessing of the family patriarch, Horace, prior to going off to war. While the sons return the father's blessing with arms outstretched in a salute, the women of the family slump in attitudes of grief. David's *Brutus* (Louvre, Paris, 1789) is even bolder in its use of lighting and the Doric column placed off-center to create a dramatic sequence of events. With these devices, David draws the viewer's attention first to a group of weeping women, then to the object of their grief: Roman officers bearing the bodies of their sons and brothers whom Brutus has condemned to death for treason. Only after the eye has taken in the elements does the viewer perceive the figure of Brutus himself brooding in the shadows, an emblem of the triumph of the will over emotion. *Brutus* was exhibited in 1789 after the National Assembly had declared a constitutional monarchy and immediately preceding the public assault on the Bastille. The painting enjoyed a tremendous success and served as a galvanizing force for the pro-revolutionary factions.

Jacques-Louis David, *The Death of Marat* (Musée Royale des Beaux-Arts, Brussels, 1793)

David was elected to the National Assembly in 1792 and took charge of the Committee for Public Instruction, which, among other things, sponsored public pageants in the streets dedicated to Enlightenment ideals. He abolished the Royal Academy of Painting and Sculpture and with it the hierarchy of genres and official bias against the portrayal of contemporary events. By 1794 the revolutionary government under his influence had become the most progressive arts patron in France and had announced a competition in which artists were to depict the momentous events of the revolution in a realistic, straightforward manner. During this period, David executed the unfinished but widely imitated *Oath of the Tennis Court* (Musée National du Chateau, Versailles,

Francisco Goya, *The Third of May, 1808* (Prado, Madrid, 1814)

1791), re-creating the meeting of the National Assembly at the Jeu de Paume with numerous portraits of real individuals who were there. He also made several incomplete studies of martyrs of the revolution, whose effigies were intended to be paraded through the streets to drum up popular support for the cause. His masterpiece of the period, *The Death of Marat* (Musée Royale des Beaux-Arts, Brussels, 1793), is the most perfect fusion of high art and political propaganda imaginable. David portrays the assassinated journalist Jean Paul Marat as a Christ-like figure from an entombment scene, depicting his martyrdom as the ultimate sacrifice for the revolutionary cause.

It was in the person of Napoleon Bonaparte, however, that David was to find his most consistent source of inspiration. His various portraits of the first consul and future emperor represent him working late at night in his study with a volume of Plutarch's *Lives* at his feet (National Gallery of Art, Washington, circa 1798), crossing the Alps above the edifying inscription "Bonaparte, Hannibal, Carolus Magnus" chiseled in the stone (Louvre, Paris, circa 1798), or crowning the Empress Josephine at Notre Dame Cathedral (Louvre, Paris, circa 1807), an artistic and dynastic reference to Peter Paul Rubens's painting, *Coronation of Marie de' Medici.* In every instance, David gave his chosen hero a historical pedigree to lend legitimacy to his rule. His attempts to portray Napoleon as a modern day Roman emperor correspond to Napoleon's efforts to rebuild Paris as an imperial Roman city.

David, however, was not the only artist to portray the revolution and its aftermath. Artists such as Antoine-Jean Gros and Théodore Géricault also captured the spirit of the age, but their works betray an ambivalence about their subjects not found in the more carefully articulated propaganda pieces by David. Gros's *The Pesthouse at Jaffa* (Louvre, Paris, 1804), for example, shows a beatific Napoleon paying a call on a hospital in the Holy Land, but the overt narrative is less compelling to the eye than the color-drenched, minaret-studded locale and the extreme vision of human agony. Similarly, Géricault's *Mounted Officer of the Imperial Guard* (Louvre, Paris, 1812) appears emotionally defeated at the moment when he should be experiencing the elation of victory. Open disillusionment with the promises of the revolution is given fullest expression in Francisco Goya's painting, *The Third of May, 1808* (Prado, Madrid, 1814). The work commemorates the French invasion of Spain in 1808 and the slaughter of political prisoners that ensued. The composition juxtaposes a firing squad with a seemingly endless file of alternately defiant and cowering execution victims. Plainly intended as a response to the *Oath of the Horatii,* Goya's paint-

Eugene Delacroix, *Liberty Leading the People* (Louvre, Paris, 1830)

ing substitutes a line of rifles for Horatian salutes, underscoring with bitter irony the tragic consequences of blind faith and unreflected loyalty.

France's revolutions of 1830, 1848, and 1870–1871 provided artists with a wealth of gripping narratives suitable for depiction, but, with mixed feelings about the efficacy of political action, most of these artists chose to focus instead on the discourse of social upheaval. Eugene Delacroix's seminal work, *Liberty Leading the People* (Louvre, Paris, 1830), represents the bourgeoisie and the working classes united in common cause at the barricades against the tyrannical rule of King Charles X. The artist brushes in the recognizable features of the Pont d'Arcole, the Île de la Cité, and Notre Dame Cathedral in the background for further verisimilitude, but the peasant woman representing Liberty is purely allegorical. There are several sources for this figure, but her resemblance to the heroine in David's *The Sabine Women* (Louvre, Paris, circa 1796) is most telling. Delacroix's *Liberty* leads the way to victory, but it is not clear which of France's social classes stands to benefit. It was the ambiguity of the painting's subtext rather than its overt call to arms that generated controversy when the work was shown at the Salon of 1831. As a result, the French government made the shrewd move of purchasing it for its collections where it languished far from public view for many years thereafter.

During the course of the nineteenth century, disparate artists such as Honoré Daumier (*Rue Transnonain, 15 avril, 1834,* Museum of Fine Arts, Boston, 1834); Gustave Courbet, who assisted in the toppling of the Vendôme column during the Paris Commune of 1870–1871; Jean-François Millet; and Edouard Manet (*The Execution of Emperor Maximilian,* Stadliche Kunsthalle, Mannheim, 1867) occasionally chose to produce works with revolutionary themes. But the goal of these artists was not to portray revolution per se, but rather, in the words of Courbet, "to be able to represent the customs, the ideas, the appearance of my own epoch . . . in short, to create a living art." Courbet and Millet expressed much of their social awareness not in scenes of revolution but in the portrayal of the disenfranchised peasants of the French countryside they knew well from direct experience. Apart from occasional illustrations submitted to support radical publications, most artists in the vanguard did the same. The subject of revolution, by default, became the province of the now-revived Academy, where gifted but more conventional painters like Ernest Meissonier restaged battles they had not witnessed (*1814, The Campaign of France,* Louvre, Paris, 1864) or painted from memory those they had seen (Meissonier's *Souvenirs of the Civil War,* Louvre, Paris, 1849; or *The Siege of Paris,* Musée d'Orsay, Paris, 1870–1884) in naturalistic detail.

REVOLUTIONARY SUBJECTS IN AMERICAN ART

In France, artists had the advantage of a classical education and a long artistic tradition to bring to their work as well as a lively and well-entrenched press to stoke the debate. In America, the situation during the revolutionary years was entirely different due to the absence of a national artistic identity and a lack of government sponsorship. The first artists to address revolutionary themes in their work were, accordingly, journalistic printmakers such as Henry Pelham and Paul Revere, both of whom produced a version of the Boston Massacre, or foreigners such as Jean-Jacques Caffieri and Jean-Antoine Houdon, whose life-size sculptures and portrait-busts of Benjamin Franklin and George Washington continue to astonish with their Old World sense of finish and implied cultural ancestry linking America's early patriots to the rulers of ancient Rome. The famous group of portraits of Washington by Gilbert Stuart, by contrast, seem rather more conventional, skillful depictions of a prominent individual with only marginal references to the historical deeds that made Washington an American hero. Apart from the numerous paintings of the first president, the great history paintings representing the American Revolution come considerably after the fact, lack the immediacy of an eyewitness account, and, with the romanticizing assistance of hindsight, reflect the high-minded principles of federalist rather than revolutionary America.

Paul Revere, *The Boston Massacre* (Library of Congress, Washington, D.C., 1770)

The chief painter of American revolutionary history was John Trumbell, son of the governor of Connecticut, who trained in London and Paris where he consorted with Joshua Reynolds, Benjamin West, and David. Trumbell returned to America enamored with European art and convinced that the nation was in need of a history-painting tradition able to capture for posterity the events that were shaping the new republic. In a letter to Thomas Jefferson (June 11, 1789), Trumbell outlined his goal "to preserve and diffuse the memory of the noblest series of actions which have ever presented themselves to the history of man." With the help of Jefferson and John Adams, Trumbell selected twelve decisive moments from American revolutionary history and spent more than a decade preparing them. Congress eventually commissioned four paintings to adorn the Capitol Rotunda. Among them was *The Declaration of Independence* (Yale University Art Gallery, New Haven, 1786–1797), a modern day epic featuring Jefferson at the compositional apex. Gen. George Washington appears in a number of Trumbell's paintings, including *The Battle of Trenton* (Metropolitan Museum of Art, New York, after 1792), in which he adopts the famous pose of the Hellenistic statue *Apollo Belvedere.* Although his facial expression conveys grim determination, Washington does not appear to be an individual with vital business to attend to.

Trumbell's inability to translate history in exciting visual conceits left the public cold and Congress complaining about the expenditure. Relatively few artists, as a result, attempted to pursue the under-appreciated genre of history painting in the new republic and, beginning with the presidency of Andrew Jackson, there was no further government support for such projects. Thomas Sully's painting, *The Passage of the Delaware* (Museum of Fine Arts, Boston, 1819), shows General Washington on horseback in a wintry landscape filled with the feverish activity of soldiers on the move. The composition of the painting recalls works by David and Gros, but Sully adds his own distinct touches including the rearing horses, the sense of half-perceived activity in the background, and the general's illusive gaze that seems to take in action outside the viewer's range. A more conventional and more famous treatment of the same subject is Emmanuel Leutze's *Washington Crossing the Delaware on Christmas Night* (Metropolitan Museum of Art, New York, 1851) with the general perched heroically if precariously in the prow of a small boat. America's centennial celebration of the Declaration of Independence in 1876 inspired a new round of patriotic subjects, among them Archibald Willer's *The Spirit of '76,* but the Civil War of the previous decade found its visual expression in the work of journalist-illustrators such as Thomas Nast rather than on the canvasses of the nation's leading painters.

Pablo Picasso, *Guernica* (Reina Sofia, Madrid, 1937).

MODERN REVOLUTIONARY ART

French realism and the vogue for depicting revolutionary subjects generated a somewhat delayed response in the art of other European societies, notably Russia where cultural ties with France had remained close and preindustrial social conditions were largely intact throughout the nineteenth century. Individual artists such as Ilya Repin invested paintings such as *Arrest of a Propagandist* (Tretyakov Gallery, Moscow, 1878–1892) with a truthfulness of vision that arises out of the artist's own temperament and individual experience. After the Bolshevik Revolution of 1917, however, the Russian vanguard dissociated itself from realism and narrative art (and the bourgeois materialism to which they were allied), opting instead for the more purified and arcane visual language of international modernism. It was the intention of the Constructivists and Suprematists of the late 1910s and 1920s to create and sustain a new abstract art that reflected the utopian philosophy of the postrevolutionary society, an art that specifically rejected the slavish depiction of actual situations. Under Joseph Stalin, however, modernism was quickly discredited as being useless to the indoctrination of the proletariat, and by 1934 Social Realism—art that was "linked to the task of ideological transformation and education of the workers in the spirit of socialism" (according to the First All-Union Congress of Soviet Writers)—became the sole viable mode of expression for all artists. With the state as their exclusive patron, the Social Realists produced paintings, posters, murals, and other forms of public art depicting the proletariat piloting the twin revolutions of social equality and technological progress under a benign patriarchy. They did not, however, produce riveting narratives in the tradition of the *Oath of the Tennis Court* or *Liberty Leading the People;* nor was their art capable of conferring any distinction on the status quo. The plainness of their pictorial language, the predictably moralizing content, and the absence of allegory, nuance, or humor make for pedestrian work whose quasi-journalistic intent had already been superseded by the more efficient medium of photography.

In Germany, the National Socialist movement of the 1920s and 1930s targeted modernist art as "degenerate" and made an effort in its stead to revive history painting with Adolf Hitler as the central cult hero. *Hitler Putsch, November 9, 1923,* by the obscure painter H. Schmitt (U.S. Army Center of Military History, Washington, D.C., 1933) is conceived in the grand manner of David's Napoleonic subjects with Hitler at the apex of a compositional triangle defying armed troops outside a Munich beer hall. Here, the artist's dutiful attempts to re-create a historic event work against his efforts to make an effective piece of propaganda. Nonetheless, in the interest of public indoctrination, the Third Reich promoted and exhibited native artists willing to depict Nazi heroes, happy peasants, cheerful laborers, and other stock subjects favored by repressive regimes. Hitler purchased thousands of these works to be displayed in the ministries and public buildings throughout Germany with the belief that didactic subjects in art were effective vehicles to convey party ideology and reform society. With this aggressive acquisitions policy, Hitler assured his place numerically as the greatest art patron of the twentieth century.

The last important history painting to successfully capture an unstable society in the moment of crisis is Pablo Picasso's *Guernica* (Reina Sofia, Madrid, 1937). The work commemorates the bombing of a small Basque village on April 26, 1937, by German planes at the behest of the Nationalist opposition. Picasso had earlier that year received a commission from Spain's Republican government to paint a work for the Spanish Pavilion at the Paris World's Fair. The artist began work on the project four days after the bombing and had all but completed the work in three weeks. Picasso builds his composition of terrified individuals perishing in their homes and in the streets around the central figure of an agonized horse representing Republican Spain. The artist eschews the anecdotal detail that trivializes so many paintings of revolutionary activity, but instead concentrates on the overriding atmosphere of slaughter with vividly conceived forms rendered in shades of newsreel gray. In explaining his motives for the painting, Picasso told the *New York Times*, "Artists who live and work with spiritual values cannot and should not remain indifferent to a conflict in which the highest values of humanity and civilization are at stake." *Guernica* appeared before the public while the event was fresh in their minds and with devastating effect. As great as its impact was, however, *Guernica* did not change the course of events in Spain; it was the Nationalist Party under Gen. Francisco Franco (portrayed in the painting in the guise of an angry bull) that eventually won out. Picasso's late masterwork amply demonstrates, however, that a politically conscious art thrives best in the immediacy of the moment when vital issues hang in the balance.

See also *Films and Video Documentaries; Literature; Media and Communications; Music; Propaganda.*

Peter J. Flagg

BIBLIOGRAPHY

Bowlt, John E., ed. *Russian Art of the Avant-garde: Theory and Criticism, 1902-1934.* New York: Viking, 1976.

Clark, Kenneth. The *Romantic Rebellion. Romantic Versus Classic Art.* New York: Harper & Row, 1973.

Crow, Thomas. *Painters and Public Life in 18th Century Paris.* New Haven and London: Yale University Press, 1985.

Leveque, Jean-Jacques. *L 'Art de la Revolution Française.* Neuchatel: Ides et Calendes, 1987.

Rosenberg, Pierre, et al. *French Painting, 1774–1830: The Age of Revolution.* New York: Detroit Institute of Arts and Metropolitan Museum of Art, 1979.

Taylor, Joshua. *America as Art.* Washington, D.C.: Smithsonian Institution, 1976.

ATATÜRK, KEMAL

An Ottoman army officer, Atatürk (1881–1938) emerged as the principal leader of the national resistance movement in Anatolia after World War I. After securing the evacuation of Allied troops and establishing national sovereignty over most territories in Ottoman possession at the time of the October 1918 Armistice of Mudros, he concentrated power in his own hands, abolished the sultanate, and established the Republic of Turkey. As president of the new republic, he carried out wide-ranging reforms aimed at transforming Turkish society and creating a modern nation-state. Although these reforms were not new in their nature or methods but continued efforts at modernization dating from the reign of Sultan Mahmud II (1808–1839), the rapid and uncompromising manner in which Atatürk carried them out was revolutionary.

Born in Salonika, Atatürk was the son of a low-level bureaucrat. He graduated from the General Staff College in 1905, one of the new state-sponsored military high schools and colleges, and, like many officers of his generation influenced by Western ideas encountered during their education, joined the secret Committee for Union and Progress and participated in the Young Turk Revolution of 1908. Though he remained a member of the movement, an uneasy relationship with the committee's most prominent military leader distanced him from the regime after 1913. He was nevertheless active during World War I, serving on the Caucasian and Syrian fronts, as well as at Gallipoli (1915), where he won fame and promotion to the rank of brigadier.

In May 1919, as Greek forces landed at Izmir, Atatürk left Istanbul to join the national resistance then forming in Anatolia. There he forged its disparate elements into a more unified movement and established his own leadership by coalescing support around two fundamental assertions—that sovereignty resided in the nation and that it should be exercised without any limitation in those territories under Ottoman control at the time of the armistice. To give legitimacy to the national movement, he convened a number of congresses (Erzurum, Sivas), culminating in the election of a nationalist majority to parliament in late 1919. That body adopted these principles as the National Pact.

THE SECULAR STATE

The nature of the nation and the future role of the sultan-caliph were matters Atatürk carefully left vague in the early days of the struggle. After the defeat of the Greek forces, however, he no longer needed to compromise with religious conservatives or liberal moderates. The sultanate was abol-

Kemal Atatürk

ished (1922) just before the Lausanne meetings to renegotiate the terms of the peace ending World War I opened, forcing Allied recognition of the Ankara government. In 1923 Atatürk consolidated his political control by dissolving the assembly and calling new elections with carefully prepared lists of candidates. The subsequent founding of the People's Party, encompassing all members of the new assembly, formed the basis of his one-party state, and a republic was declared in October. With a national political organization established and the assembly brought into line, Atatürk set in motion a vast chain of reforms that would change the face of Turkey in a startlingly short time.

First he secularized the state and brought religious institutions under its control. In 1924 Turkey abolished the caliphate, the Office of the Seyhulislam (the chief Muslim jurisconsultant and his staff), the Ministry of Pious Foundations, and remaining religious schools and courts. Religious education and the supervision of pious foundations were severely reduced and brought within the purview of government ministries. The Sheikh Said Rebellion, a Kurdish uprising in the southwest with religious and nationalist overtones (February–April, 1925), provided Atatürk the opportunity to quell political opposition and impose further reforms. These measures were designed to break down religious custom and instill in the populace a secular mentality. Among the more important measures, Sufi orders and sites of pilgrimage were closed; fezzes and turbans were banned and the European brimmed hat imposed (more than six hundred people were executed by special Independence Tribunals for resisting these laws); a secular civil code was adopted; and in 1928 a phonetic Latin alphabet replaced the Arabic-Persian script.

SOCIAL REFORM

The worldwide depression of the 1930s posed new challenges for the Atatürk regime. After a brief flirtation with introducing a second political party, Atatürk responded with the political doctrine of Kemalism, embodied in six points: nationalism, republicanism, populism, statism, secularism, revolution. In practice this amounted to state intervention in the economy in the form of developing industry and supporting agricultural prices—and the creation of a strong Turkish national identity. The regime promoted interpretations of philology and history that emphasized the pre-Islamic past and cast ancient Turkic peoples as the source of most great civilizations. A language reform was attempted, rooting out words of Persian and Arabic origin and replacing them with Turkish neologisms. Even the Qur'an was translated, and mosque prayers were conducted in Turkish. Together with the change in alphabet, these reforms constituted a major break with the past.

Atatürk also worked to expand literacy, and education generally, and to alter radically the position of women. He campaigned for an end to veiling, promoted women's entrance into the workforce and professions, and gradually introduced coeducational classrooms. Monogamous civil marriage was made law in 1926, and women achieved full political rights in 1934.

When Atatürk died, power passed to his long-time associate, Ismet Inonu, who continued to push for Westernization of Turkish society.

See also *Ottoman Revolts in the Near and Middle East (1803–1922); Turkish Revolution (1908–1922).*

A. Holly Shissler

BIBLIOGRAPHY

Berkes, Niyazi. *The Development of Secularism in Turkey.* Montreal: McGill University Press, 1964.

Landau, Jacob M., ed. *Atatürk and the Modernization of Turkey.* Boulder, Colo.: Westview Press, 1984.

Lord Kinross (Patrick Balfour). *Atatürk: The Rebirth of a Nation.* Nicosia and London: K. Rustem and Brother, 1981.

Shaw, Stanford J., and Ezel Kural Shaw. *History of the Ottoman Empire and Modern Turkey.* Cambridge: Cambridge University Press, 1977.

Zürcher, Erik Jan. *The Unionist Factor: The Role of the Committee of Union and Progress in the Turkish National Movement, 1905–1926.* Leiden: E.J. Brill, 1984.

B

BABI REVOLTS (1844–1852)

Babis are followers of Sayyid Ali Muhammad Shirazi (1819–1850), also known as the Bab. This Iranian Shi'ite visionary's claims to divine authority led to civil strife in several regions of Iran and to the creation of a short-lived religious system in which the laws and precepts of Islam were suspended and replaced by new regulations and beliefs.

Some scholars have argued that Babism represents the last of the medieval Islamic movements, rising and expiring on the very brink of modernity, and, indeed, it has many features in common with other militant revivals of Islam in the Sunni world during the eighteenth and nineteenth centuries. But other scholars have pointed out that the Babi movement is a direct response to the modernizing and economic pressures placed on traditional ways of life, even if those pressures are seldom addressed directly. The early Babi modes of discourse and action were thoroughly premodern (holy war, alchemy, astrology, talismans, preaching, minutely detailed laws), and yet in its later phases Babism engendered some of the most progressive thinking in nineteenth- and early twentieth-century Iran. Certainly it was by far the most radical movement of its kind until the Khomeinist revolution of 1979, which also had messianic undertones.

HISTORY OF THE MOVEMENT

The movement can be arbitrarily divided into three main stages: primitive Babism (1844–1850), middle Babism (1850–1870s), and late Babism (1870s–present). Few movements can have gone through so many phases in such a short time. The Bab declared himself to be an inspired interpreter of the Qur'an in 1844, and by 1850 had been executed as Islam's arch-heretic. In a development that had its origins firmly rooted in esoteric trends within contemporary Shi'ism, his first significant religious claim was that he was a precursor, or gateway (Bab), of the Shi'ite messiah, the hidden twelfth imam. By 1848 he had claimed to be the expected imam in person, and by his death to be a new prophet succeeding Muhammad and a representation of the Godhead, whose advent ushered in a new religious dispensation.

The political shift was commensurate. In 1844 the Babis held themselves loyal to church and state and were willing to take up arms to prosecute a holy war for Islam. By 1846 the Islamic legal system had been abrogated by sections of the movement and the Bab was in prison. By 1848 abrogation of Islam was made absolute and Babi *mujahedin* (holy warriors) were fighting state troops in three main centers. By 1850 the state had suppressed the movement and executed the Bab himself.

Two years later, in a last desperate attempt to overthrow the Qajar dynasty, some Babis in Tehran attempted to assassinate the Iranian king Nasir al-Din Shah. Those who survived the spate of executions following the attempt opted for exile in Baghdad. Here another, more ironic shift took place. In Baghdad two brothers came to the fore as leaders of the Babi community: Mirza Yahya Nuri (Subh-i Azal, or the Dawn of Eternity, 1830–1912), who had been appointed the Bab's successor, and his older brother Husayn Ali (Baha Allah, or the Beauty of God, 1817–1892), who had played only a minor role in the movement until then. By the early 1860s, when the exiles were moved to Edirne in western Turkey, Subh-i Azal had lost support and a majority of Babis were accepting Baha Allah as an infallible leader—and in due course as a prophet.

The schism to which this gave rise had profound political significance. The Azali Babis sought to retain intact the laws and theocratic teachings of the Bab—a conservative position that was increasingly at odds with the sentiments of reform and constitutionalism then sweeping the Ottoman Empire and Iran. And yet Azali Babism supplied a large number of the thinkers and activists who took part in the Iranian Constitutional Revolution.

Baha Allah's followers, the Bahais, provided a strange contrast to their Azali rivals. Baha Allah's own writings flipped the original Babi message on its side. He abrogated many of the Bab's laws, abolished holy war, forbade religious intolerance, commanded obedience to the state, and called for constitutional government. But as reformist in its aims as Bahaism was, the injunction not to interfere in politics meant that Bahais remained aloof from the constitutional revolution and the developments it spawned. Nevertheless, Baha Allah does deserve to be studied as an influential writer on constitutionalism, human rights, female emancipation, and related issues.

The Babi uprisings of 1848–1850 have been variously interpreted. The most detailed analysis, a Marxist explanation by Mikhail S. Ivanov, misreads many features of the struggles, not least the social composition of the insurgents. More recently, Moojan Momen has argued, with detailed figures to support his thesis, that the Babis involved in the clashes were drawn from almost all sectors of Iranian life.

The conflicts mainly occurred in three areas: one rural, at a Shi'i shrine called Shaykh Tabarsi in Mazandaran Province, and two urban, in the cities of Zanjan and Nayriz. Between four thousand and five thousand Babis died in these struggles, in the course of which almost all of the movement's leadership was wiped out. At no point did the Babi–state conflict show signs of igniting a general conflagration throughout the country, although there were widespread fears that this might happen at the time.

How much one can interpret Babism as a Shi'i equivalent of other violent revivalist movements elsewhere in Islam during the eighteenth and nineteenth centuries remains an area for investigation. What is important is that the Bab and his most radical followers showed how easily a messianic movement could take up arms against a Shi'ite government.

ROLE OF WOMEN IN BABISM

Bahai writers generally argue that a major plank in the Babi platform of social reform was the emancipation of women. There is little evidence for this, however, in the writings of the Bab or his close followers, and all the signs are that primitive Babism was almost as traditional in this as in other areas. Indeed, what legal changes were made were very minor.

Whatever the theoretical stance on the position of women, however, early Babism provided excellent opportunities for female assertion. Women figured prominently among the defenders of Zanjan and Nayriz, and many women from learned or wealthy families not only converted to Babism but also played definite roles in the spread and defense of their adopted faith.

Prominent among these was a young woman of clerical parentage, Fatima Baraghani, better known as Qurrat al-Ayn, or Tahira (1813?–1832). Well educated and temperamentally volatile, she became one of the Bab's first followers and within a year or so the leader of a core group of believers in Iraq. Her classes and her arguments in favor of abrogating the laws of Islam resulted in serious controversy and her expulsion from the region. Back in Iran, she continued to court controversy, and arguably it was her influence that eventually persuaded the Bab to abandon Islam in favor of a new revelation. She was executed in 1852, in the wake of the attempt on the shah's life.

See also *Iranian Constitutional Revolution (1906).*

DENIS MACEOIN

BIBLIOGRAPHY

Amanat, Abbas. *Resurrection and Renewal: The Making of the Babi Movement in Iran, 1844–1850.* Ithaca, N.Y.: Cornell University Press, 1989.

Bayat, Mangol. *Mysticism and Dissent: Socioreligious Thought in Qajar Iran.* Syracuse, N.Y.: Syracuse University Press, 1982.

Cole, Juan R. *Modernity and the Millennium.* New York: Columbia University Press, 1998.

Ivanov, Mikhail S. *Babidskie vosstaniya v Irane (1848–1852).* Moscow: Instituta Vostokvedeniya, 1939.

MacEoin, Denis M. "Babism." In *Encyclopaedia Iranica.* London: Routledge, 1988, 315–317.

———. "The Babi Concept of Holy War." *Religion* 12 (1982): 93–129.

Momen, Moojan. "The Social Basis of the Babi Upheavals in Iran (1848–53): A Preliminary Analysis." *International Journal of Middle East Studies* 15 (1983): 157–183.

Smith, Peter, and Moojan Momen. "The Babi Movement: A Resource Mobilization Perspective." In *In Iran.* Edited by P. Smith. Los Angeles: Kalimat Press, 1986, 33–93.

BALTIC REVOLUTIONS OF 1991

Though called in the popular press the "Singing Revolution" by analogy with the 1989 "Velvet Revolution" in Czechoslovakia, the 1991 Baltic events that reestablished Estonia, Latvia, and Lithuania as independent countries did not have the characteristics of "revolutions" in the sense of a violent overthrowing of an existing regime. During the failed Moscow coup of August 19–21, 1991, the Supreme Councils (formerly the Supreme Soviets) of the three republics declared that as of that moment they were no longer constituent parts of the Soviet Union and that they were reassuming the standing of independent states they had had before 1940, when they were occupied and annexed by the USSR.

THE POPULAR FRONTS

These declarations in August 1991, however, were the final act of a drama that had begun in 1988, when reformists in the three Baltic societies began seriously to respond to General Secretary Mikhail Gorbachev's call for *perestroika* (restructuring), *glasnost* (openness), and *demokratizaatsia*

(democratization). In Moscow's eyes, this tripartite policy was meant to renew socialism, but in the union republics of the USSR it had ramifications the central government and the Communist Party of the Soviet Union (CPSU) had not counted on and never really understood. Expecting various kinds of "modernization" to have weakened nationalistic sentiments, Moscow and the CPSU seemed bewildered when "renewal" in the western borderlands became increasingly nationalistic and separatist, attitudes fueled in part by Moscow's refusal to come to the aid of beleaguered communist regimes in the East European satellite states in the fall of 1989.

In the Baltic republics, the year 1987 witnessed various protests against local ecological despoliation, believed to have been caused by a central planning apparatus that cared little how Moscow-made industrialization policies affected localities. In 1988, no longer needing the approval of the Communist Party to exist, dozens of other "informal" organizations were created. Among them were the so-called popular fronts (Popular Front of Estonia; Lithuanian Reconstruction Movement, known as Sajudis; Popular Front of Latvia), all three of which announced themselves as organizations meant to help implement Gorbachev's new course. In fact, all three quickly became vehicles for bringing into the public realm a host of accumulated resentments that the Communist Parties of the three countries had deliberately repressed over the years. These included the decades-long, seemingly calculated inflow of Russian and other Slavic populations into the three non-Slavic republics, which diminished the proportion of indigenous Balts; the emergence of Russian as the only language of public affairs; the presence of large contingents of the Soviet army; and, of course, the controls of expression and everyday life exercised by the party with the help of the KGB. These concerns had different weight in the three republics—in Lithuania, for example, the indigenous population by the mid-1980s was 80 percent of the total population, whereas in Estonia the proportion had diminished to 60 percent, and in Latvia to 52 percent. As public debate over these questions became more free and heated, the central question, forbidden for decades, came to the fore: had the Baltic states become part of the USSR by choice or by force?

During 1988 and 1989 the membership of the popular fronts of the three states grew rapidly, as did that of other organizations on the "right" (now demanding immediate independence) and on the "left" (proclaiming continuing allegiance to the USSR). To demonstrate that they were indeed "popular," the fronts organized mass demonstrations and commemorations of historic events that the Communist Parties had trivialized: the independence proclamations of the three states in 1918, their occupation by the USSR in 1940, and the mass deportations of 1941 (meant to cleanse the newly occupied countries of "bourgeois nationalists") and 1949 (meant to rid the countryside of "kulaks" who opposed agricultural collectivization). Each of these events always gathered hundreds of thousands of participants. The three fronts also demonstrated their rapidly increasing strength in the March 1990 elections of the Supreme Soviets, when in all three republics the popular front candidates—running in direct opposition to the candidates put forward by the Communist Parties—scored impressive victories. Soon afterward, the Lithuanian Supreme Soviet (renamed the Supreme Council) proclaimed immediate independence, while its counterparts in Estonia and Lithuania passed resolutions stating independence as the goal to be sought through negotiations with the Moscow government. In all three countries, the Communist Parties split into factions consisting of independence supporters and Moscow loyalists. These changes—though revolutionary in their impact—had been achieved by implementing Gorbachev's policies, using the existing electoral system, and appealing to the clause of the Soviet constitution that granted republics the right to withdraw from the union.

INDEPENDENCE REGAINED

From the summer of 1990 to August 1991, tension between the Moscow government and the front-led governments of the Baltic republics increased. The former sought ways to quash the independence impulse (which was spreading to other union republics), while the Baltic Supreme Councils continued to pass numerous laws predicated on the arrival of independence in the near future. Although in all three states rumors of a coming crackdown (as in Hungary in 1956 and Czechoslovakia in 1968) were rampant, the Moscow government refrained from violent moves, though it did impose an economic blockade on Lithuania and in indirect ways supported the "loyalist" Communists in all three states. Only in January 1991 was brute force used by the Soviet army in Vilnius, Lithuania (resulting in the death of fourteen civilians), and later that month in Riga, Latvia. There, special security forces invaded the Ministry of Interior and in the process killed five people. In both cases the Moscow government pleaded ignorance about who ordered the actions and seemed almost apologetic about them.

The confrontational situation continued during the first half of 1991, but in spite of rumors about the coming imposition of "presidential rule" over the Baltic republics, no such action was taken by Moscow. On their side, the Supreme Councils continued to legislate as if independence were just around the corner: dismantling state enterprises, passing language laws, introducing private property, and reviving the symbols of the interwar period of independence. By August 1991, when the ongoing confrontation was finally resolved, the three Councils were in a strong position to continue as the legitimate governments of renewed states. By September 1991 Baltic independence had been recognized by other countries, including the USSR; the three Baltic republics were seated in the UN as sovereign states. The Soviet Union itself was dissolved by President Gorbachev at the end of 1991. The Supreme Councils remained at the helm of the three Baltic states until the first post-Soviet parliamentary elections, in Lithuania and Estonia in 1992 and in Latvia in 1993.

See also *East European Revolutions of 1989; Gorbachev, Mikhail; USSR Collapse and Dissolution (1989–1991).*

Andrejs Plakans

BIBLIOGRAPHY

Dreifelds, Juris. *Latvia In Transition.* New York: Cambridge University Press, 1996.

Karklins, Rasma. *Ethnopolitics and Transition to Democracy: The Collapse of the USSR and Latvia.* Washington, D.C., and Baltimore: Woodrow Wilson Center Press and Johns Hopkins University Press, 1994.

Lieven, Anatol. *The Baltic Revolution: Estonia, Latvia, Lithuania and the Path to Independence.* 2d ed. New Haven, Conn.: Yale University Press, 1994.

Misiunas, Romuald, and Rein Taagepera. *The Baltic States: Years of Dependence, 1940–1990.* Expanded ed. Berkeley: University of California Press, 1993.

Raun, Toivo U. *Estonia and the Estonians.* 2d ed. Stanford: Hoover Institution Press, 1991.

Senn, Alfred Erich. *Gorbachev's Failure in Lithuania.* New York: St. Martin's Press, 1995.

Taagepera, Rein. *Estonia: Return to Independence.* Boulder, Colo.: Westview Press, 1993.

Vardys, V. Stanley, and Judith B. Sedaitis. *Lithuania: The Rebel Nation.* Boulder, Colo.: Westview Press, 1997.

BANGLADESHI WAR OF INDEPENDENCE (1971)

The civil war in Pakistan that led to the independence of Bangladesh in 1971 had both long-term and immediate causes. The long-term causes were based on a growing feeling in East Pakistan (as Bangladesh was known before its independence) that it was being treated poorly in relation to the larger but less populous West Pakistan (present-day Pakistan). The geographic separation of East and West Pakistan, which were roughly one thousand miles apart, was a legacy of the partition of India in 1947 *(see map, p. 384).*

The first clash concerned the national language of Pakistan, which the West Pakistani-dominated leadership determined would be Urdu. Bengali, the predominant language in the east, would not be accorded equal status even though there were many more speakers of Bengali than Urdu. The language issue was settled in 1954, when both Bengali and Urdu were given the status of a national language. But that decision was reached only after rioting in 1952 in Dhaka, during which a number of Bengali students were killed. The anniversary of the riot is still celebrated in Bangladesh as Martyrs Day.

There were other issues as well. These included parity in parliamentary representation, a concept embedded in the 1956 constitution under which each province had the same number of seats, thereby underrepresenting East Pakistan. Bengalis were also very much underrepresented in the civil and military services. For many years after independence from Great Britain, until the late 1960s, East Pakistan earned more foreign exchange (largely through the sale of jute) than the west, but more capital expenditures were made in the west. The defense policy of Pakistan also was formulated to defend the interests of the west. In the 1965 war with India, East Pakistan was all but defenseless, although India did not attack.

These and other grievances smoldered in East Pakistan and led in 1966 to the Six Points formulated by Sheikh Mujibur Rahman (Mujib), the leader of the Awami League. The Six Points demanded a high degree of autonomy for each of the provinces, with the central government limited basically to foreign policy and defense.

In December 1970, under a martial law regime imposed in 1969 in the wake of the forced resignation of President Ayub Khan, an election was held in which the principle of parity was replaced by representation of the two provinces on the basis of population, meaning more seats would be filled from the east than from the west. The Awami League, under Mujib, won a majority of the seats in Pakistan as a whole, although it won none in the west. Mujib laid claim to the prime ministership and the right to enact a new constitution based on the Six Points. President Agha Muhammad Yahya Khan and his associates were not prepared to accept the full level of autonomy demanded by Mujib. The principal political figure in the west, Zulfikar Ali Bhutto, who opposed autonomy, demanded a share in the governing of Pakistan. No agreement could be reached among the three leaders.

President Yahya reinforced the military in the east as demonstrations for autonomy and then independence began in the east in February 1971. On March 25 the army struck in Dhaka and elsewhere. Mujib was arrested and taken to West Pakistan, charged with treason. The Bangladeshis declared independence and organized a military force to challenge the Pakistan army. An interim government was set up in Calcutta. India provided sanctuary, training, and supplies to the Bangladeshis and invaded East Pakistan in late November. The Pakistan army surrendered on December 16, 1971, and Bangladesh became independent.

The war was very costly to Bangladesh in lives lost and infrastructure destroyed. No exact numbers for casualties are available; one estimate of three million killed is no doubt too high, and about one million may be more accurate. Many of those who fled to the safety of India, especially Hindus, did not return after the war ended.

After the war, Bangladesh found, as all newly independent countries do, that the resources available for development had not changed. However, the independent management of those resources, along with generous official development assistance, has improved the economic conditions of the country significantly. New export industries have been initiated, most notably in readymade garments, that have provided increased employment and foreign exchange. It is questionable whether this development could have taken place if independence had not been gained.

See also *Indian Independence Movement (1885–1947); Pakistani Independence Movement (1940–1947).*

CRAIG BAXTER

BIBLIOGRAPHY

Ahmed, Moudud. *Bangladesh: Constitutional Quest for Autonomy.* Dacca: University Press, 1976.

Baxter, Craig. *Bangladesh: From a Nation to a State.* Boulder, Colo.: Westview Press, 1997.

Muhith, A. M. A. *Bangladesh: Emergence of a Nation.* Dacca: Bangladesh Books International, 1978.

Zaheer, Hasan. *The Separation of East Pakistan: The Rise and Realization of Bengali Muslim Nationalism.* Karachi: Oxford University Press, 1994.

BELGIAN REVOLUTIONS (1789–1830)

The Belgians revolted twice to win their national independence, in 1789 and 1830. The short-lived Brabant Revolution of 1789, named after the central Belgian province, defined a national identity that the Belgians secured in the Belgian Revolution of 1830.

THE BRABANT REVOLUTION

The Belgian provinces prospered under Austrian rule throughout most of the eighteenth century. However, when Joseph II ascended the Austrian throne in 1765, he planned sweeping institutional reforms to modernize and homogenize Austria's territories, including the Belgian provinces. On New Year's Day 1787, Joseph announced sweeping plans to revise the entire Belgian administrative and judicial system. The Austrian emperor also planned to open and control a general seminary.

The estates of the Belgian provinces—the clergy, nobility, and commons—decried the Austrian intrusion into their domestic affairs. Although they welcomed Austrian protection, the Belgians expected to control their internal administration and religious practices. The guilds of artisans and shopkeepers led the protest, charging that the Austrian reforms violated the medieval Belgian constitutions. They threatened to withhold their taxes. The clergy protested Joseph's seminary, which they charged would introduce the godless ideas of the Enlightenment to the Belgian provinces.

In June 1789 Austrian troops barred the doors of the estates' meeting rooms in Brussels. Henri Van der Noot, a counsel to the estates of the central Brabant province, wrote a formal protest. He then set off to negotiate support from the English, the Dutch, and the Prussians. Meanwhile, a secret revolutionary society, For Hearth and Home, under the direction of another Brussels lawyer, Jan Vonck, mobilized a popular campaign. These democrats distributed guns, ammunition, and pamphlets throughout the provinces. In the summer of 1789 their army of volunteers crossed the border to train in the Dutch village of Breda. Van der Noot called on the peasants to arm themselves and take up God's cause.

The followers of Van der Noot and Vonck issued a manifesto of independence in October 1789. They launched their attack on the Austrians on October 24, 1789, the feast day of the archangel Raphael. Much to everyone's surprise, the Belgian army succeeded in driving the Austrian troops from the Belgian provinces in December 1789.

Under Van der Noot, the provincial Belgian estates assumed all of the Austrians' former powers in a new republic, the United Belgian States. The leaders of For Hearth and Home charged the estates with usurping the people's sovereignty. By May 1790 most of these Belgian democrats had been forced by the estates and their supporters to seek refuge across the French border.

Austrian troops returned in October 1790 to defeat the ragged army of the divided Belgian republic. In October 1792 the exiled members of For Hearth and Home supported French general Charles Dumouriez's successful assault on the Austrians. Belgian Jacobins, organized in the Society of the Friends of Liberty and Equality, planted trees of liberty, abolished old tribunals, decreed an end to guild monopolies, and recruited an army for the new Belgian republic. But victorious Austrian troops reentered Belgium in March 1793, greeted by crowds singing parodies of the "Marseillaise." The French reconquered the Belgian provinces in 1794. After the French closed the monasteries and instituted military conscription, peasants rose up in East Flanders. The peasant wars spread throughout the Belgian provinces in October 1798.

The eighteenth-century Belgian revolutionaries coalesced to fight against their foreign enemy. For but a brief moment, the blending of traditional defense of privilege, democratic idealism, and French Jacobinism defined a uniquely Belgian revolution.

THE BELGIAN REVOLUTION OF 1830

When the French empire collapsed in 1815, the Congress of Vienna fused the nine Belgian departments and the Dutch republic into a kingdom ruled by William I *(see map, p. 164)*. Gradually, opposition to Dutch rule grew, among delegates to the Estates-General as well as among the workers. In 1829 Liberal and Catholic leaders from the Belgian provinces coalesced in their call for a free press, religious schools, and the freedom to use French instead of Dutch. The Belgian revolutionary leader Louis De Potter told the Dutch to keep their own customs, religion, and language, but not to impose them on the Belgians.

The second revolution for Belgian independence began with the performance of the opera "La Muette de Portici" in August 1830. The audience emerged from the opera house in the center of Brussels singing tributes to liberty. They were joined by youths in the streets for a night of rioting. They attacked the houses of government leaders and drove the troops back to the Place du Palais. The severe winter and industrial crisis that had caused bankruptcies, low wages, and unemployment fueled the riots, which quickly spread to other Belgian cities. In the industrialized region around Liège, workers attacked factories, smashing machines. The unrest worried the bourgeoisie, who organized a guard to reestablish order and to defend their cities against the Dutch. Commissions of Order took over the city halls.

The leaders of the revolt pressed their demands for freedom of the press and education and for full representation of the Belgians in the government and parliament of the United Netherlands. Deputations from Brussels and Liège traveled to the Hague to meet with William on August 29, 1830. At the same time, William's second son, Prince Frederick, marched his troops south. Prince Frederick met with a deputation in Vilvoorde, just outside of Brussels. After all the negotiations had failed, on September 23 Prince Frederick resolved to enter Brussels with his troops. In the ensuing skirmishes between the Dutch troops and the civic guard, armed workers, and peasants with pitchforks, the Dutch army was driven out of Brussels. The Brabant flag fluttered from rooftops throughout the city. In 1830, as in 1789, the Dutch-speaking Flemish of northern Belgium fought alongside the French-speaking Walloons of the south.

Belgian patriots gathered in Brussels as an enlarged Administrative Commission proclaimed itself the provisional government on October 4, 1830. They appointed a commission to draft a new constitution and organized direct elections for a National Congress.

The new Belgian constitution guaranteed the individual rights for which democrats had struggled in the Brabant Revolution. The responsibilities of the Belgian state were carefully delimited to safeguard the individual freedoms of the press, religion, education, and language.

Meanwhile, William appealed to Great Britain, Prussia, Austria, and Russia to protect the state they had all built in 1815. The London Conference that followed in December 1830 recognized Belgian independence, decreed that

Belgium should be permanently neutral, granted the provinces of Limburg and Luxemburg to the Dutch, and sought a king for the new Belgian nation.

Like the Brabant Revolution, the Belgian Revolution of 1830 was a national revolution. This time, the coalition between Liberals and Catholics proved more stable, endowing the new Belgian nation with a constitution that has survived for more than a century and a half.

JANET L. POLASKY

BIBLIOGRAPHY

Craeybeckx, Jan. "The Brabant Revolution: A Conservative Revolution in a Backward Country?" *Acta Historiae Neerlandica* 9 (1970).

Kossman, Ernst Heinrich. *The Low Countries 1780–1940.* Oxford: Oxford University Press, 1978.

Lijphart, Arend. *Conflict and Coexistence in Belgium. The Dynamics of a Culturally Divided Society.* Berkeley, Calif.: Institute of International Studies, 1981.

Logie, Jacques. *1830. De la régionalisation à l'indépendance.* Paris: Gembloux, 1980.

Palmer, Robert Roswell. *The Age of Democratic Revolution. A Political History of Europe and America 1760–1800.* Princeton, N.J.: Princeton University Press, 1959.

Pirenne, Henri. *Histoire de Belgique.* Vols. V and VI. Brussels: Maurice Lamertin, 1926.

Polasky, Janet L. *Revolution in Brussels 1787–1793.* Brussels: Académie Royale de Belgique, 1986.

Tassier, Suzanne. *Les démocrates belges de 1789.* Brussels: Maurice Lamertin, 1930.

BENIN REVOLUTIONS (1963–1996)

The background to the political revolutions that occurred in Dahomey (renamed Benin in 1975) between 1963 and 1996 was a tripartite cleavage among descendants of the central kingdom of Dahomey (or Abomey), the southeastern kingdom of Porto-Novo, and communities and smaller kingdoms in the north. The regional cleavage was generated in the late nineteenth century, when French colonizers signed treaties of "friendship" with the king of Abomey, made Porto-Novo a French protectorate, and conquered the north. A North-South, mainly religious, cleavage also emerged, beginning in the early 1900s, when the largely Muslim Northerners opposed the presence in the North of Christian "Southerner" administrators and teachers, who had been educated in schools established by the French.

The regional cleavages became political rivalries when in 1951 Dahomey began electing two representatives to the French National Assembly. Sorou Migan Apithy from Porto-Novo, elected in 1945 as the sole representative, was reelected; and Hubert Maga, a Northerner, defeated Justin Ahomadegbe from the Center. North-Center-South regionalism thus was established: Apithy as representative of the South, Maga of the North, and Ahomadegbe of the Center. At independence, achieved in 1960, Maga was the elected president.

MILITARY INTERVENTIONS

The first of four political revolutions, aiming at political stability and economic development, led to five successful interventions by the Dahomey military: in October 1963, November and December 1965, September 1967, and December 1969.

The "October Revolution" of 1963 occurred while President Maga was abroad. Supporters of Ahomadegbe called for a general strike, demanding abolition of a 10 percent austerity tax. In reaction, Col. Christophe Soglo suspended the constitution in an effort to restore order. Following Northern unrest supporting Maga, Soglo appointed a Constitutional Commission, which adopted a new constitution in January 1964 and named Apithy as president and Ahomadegbe as vice president. Maga's exclusion from government produced violent protests in the North between March and October 1964.

A schism between Apithy and Ahomadegbe in May 1965 led labor union supporters of Ahomadegbe to demand Apithy's resignation, while Porto-Novians demonstrated in his support. Colonel Soglo's intervention in November 1965 brought about the resignation of both. A provisional government was formed, new parties were organized, and new elections were planned for January 1966. However, in December 1965 workers striking against a 25 percent salary reduction demanded that the army take power. On December 22, 1965, Soglo, now a general, intervened a third time and formed a "government of technocrats," with himself as president.

In October 1966 the 25 percent public-sector salary reduction was replaced by a 25 percent public- and private-sector "solidarity tax." Strikes followed. In March 1967 junior officers formed a fifteen-member Military Committee of Vigilance to supervise the government and its policies; by May politicians had replaced the government of technocrats, and in November 1967 President Soglo visited France seeking financial assistance. He received insufficient funds to abolish the 25 percent tax. The resulting strikes ended with the fourth military coup, in December 1967 by the junior army officers, who set up a Constitutional Committee.

Elections, called by the Constitutional Committee, were held in May 1968 but were boycotted by most eligible voters, then were nullified by the committee. On July 17, 1968, the military nominated Emil Derlin Zinsou, from the southwest, as president for a five-year term. He was elected, and a

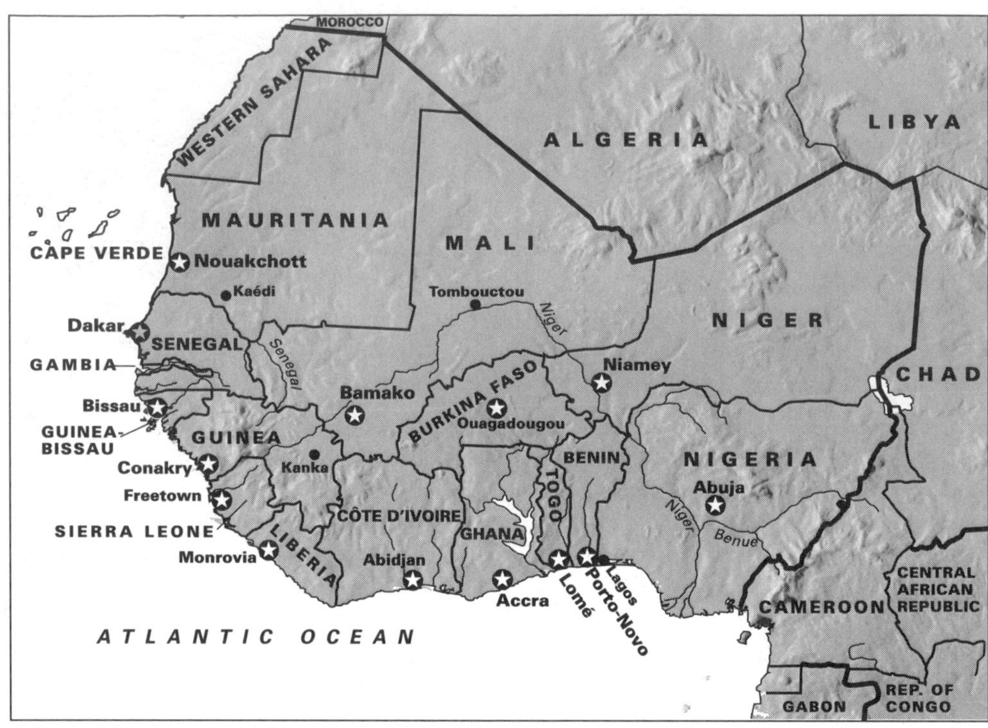

new constitution was adopted on July 28, but in December 1969 junior officers overthrew Zinsou in Dahomey's fifth coup.

In the early 1970 presidential elections all four former presidents participated, each winning in his region. Maga received the most votes and declared that if the Military Directorate, composed of the three highest-ranking officers and serving as the government, did not accept his victory, the North would secede. Apithy, in turn, threatened to attach the Southeast to Nigeria if Maga were ratified as president. Under a threat of civil war the elections were annulled, and a Presidential Council of Maga, Apithy, and Ahomadegbe was formed later in 1970. The presidency was to rotate every two years, with Maga serving first. In May 1972 the presidency was transferred to Ahomadegbe as planned.

THE MARXIST REVOLUTION

The second political revolution began with a sixth coup, in 1972 by another group of four junior army officers. They handed over power to Maj., later Lt. Col., Mathieu Kérekou, a Northerner who, in response to a group of Marxists urging him to try the Marxist option, introduced radical changes in 1974.

The "Beninese Revolution" or "Marxism-Beninism" of Kérekou aimed at restructuring the economy and disengaging from French influence. Most sectors were nationalized, and relations were established with socialist countries and Libya. A single party nominated candidates for elections to a National Revolutionary Assembly. Reforms introduced in schools were intended both to follow Marxist ideology and to abandon the French system.

Popular reactions were negative. Teachers, parents, and students objected to the reforms; and university students and unemployed graduates participated in strikes alongside workers against new economic measures that failed to produce results. In January 1987 President Kérekou switched to "liberalism" and began encouraging private investment, reducing Libyan influence, and accepting French financial assistance. But with no improvements in sight, strikers and demonstrators demanded the president's resignation.

DEMOCRATIC REVOLUTION

The third political revolution ended the Kérekou regime and its Marxist ideology and launched the transition to democracy. In early December 1989 Kérekou organized a provisional government, nominating Nicephore Soglo, nephew of Gen. Soglo and a World Bank official, as prime minister. A National Conference of "all active forces of the nation," including all former presidents, was held in February 1990. A new constitution approved in a December 1990 referendum guaranteed human rights, freedom to organize political parties, and the right to private property. During the February 1991 parliamentary elections, in which 896 candidates ran in 34 political groupings, Southern supporters in the North were attacked by Northerners. Kérekou stopped the attacks. Eleven political parties gained seats in the National Assembly. In March 1991 Nicephore Soglo was elected president, and on April 4 he was sworn in.

Although Soglo's government was persistently accused of nepotism, mismanagement, and failure to erase corruption, there was no political revolution during the five years of his presidency.

Scheduled elections in February and March 1996 produced a fourth political revolution, for they returned Kérekou to the presidency as one committed to democracy and free economy. Criticism of the Kérekou government and the economic situation has been led by Rosine Soglo, wife of Nicephore Soglo, who heads the main opposition party, and the criticism has been aired in a free press. A strike launched in February 1998 was settled, and no new political revolution appears imminent. As the four former civilian presidents are either deceased or retired, political revolutions based on regional cleavages are less likely. A military coup is also less likely. If the economy is consolidated, political stability may prevail.

DOV RONEN

BIBLIOGRAPHY

Adamon, Afize D. *Le renouveau démocratique au Bénin: la Conférence nationale des forces vives et la période de transition.* Paris: Harmattan, 1995.

Bierschenk, Thomas, ed. "Le Benin." *Politique Africaine* 59 (1995): 2-119.

Decalo, Samuel. *Historical Dictionary of Benin.* 3d ed. Lanham, Md.: Scarecrow Press, 1995.

Establet, Jean. *Mathieu Kérekou, 1933 1996: l'inamovible président du Bénin.* Paris: Harmattan, 1997.

Kérckou, Mathieu. *Préparer le Bénin du futur: réflexions d'un citoyen sur le devenir du pays.* 2eme ed. Porto-Novo, Benin: Centre panafricain de prospective sociale, 1996.

Ronen, Dov. *Dahomey: Between Tradition and Modernity.* Ithaca, N.Y.: Cornell University Press, 1975.

———. "People's Republic of Benin: The Military, Marxist Ideology and the Politics of Ethnicity." In *The Military in African Politics,* edited by John W. Harbeson. New York: Praeger, 1987.

BIKO, STEPHEN

Stephen Bantu Biko (1946–1977) was the charismatic leader of the black consciousness movement in South Africa and a founder of and intellectual inspiration behind the South African Student Organization (SASO). Although the Soweto uprising of 1976 was not formally organized by the black consciousness movement, Biko's influence largely triggered the protests and the widespread resistance to apartheid that immediately followed.

Biko, a medical student at the University of Natal (black section), was involved in student politics. Dissatisfied with the way white liberals dominated student politics nationally, he led African and Indian students to quit the National Union of South African Students. In 1968–1969 they organized SASO, with Biko as president. In 1970 they began using the more positive term "black" instead of the negative "nonwhite." The question of race, definitions of South African and African nationalism, and the role of whites in the struggle against apartheid had long been subjects of intense debate among blacks. The Africanist posture of the Pan-Africanist Congress attracted many black intellectuals. The Pan-Africanist Congress had broken away from the African National Congress in 1958, criticizing the ANC's close association with non-Africans and its collaboration with the Communist Party of South Africa.

Biko's arguments against collaboration with whites were more psychological than political. He thought it necessary to liberate blacks from their own attitudes of inferiority and subservience before political rights could be achieved, and thus he sought to exclude whites from the movement in order to encourage black self-reliance. Although he rejected a role for whites in the struggle, his conception of black unity included Indians and coloreds (mixed race) as well as Africans. To Biko, "being black" meant being excluded from power by state-imposed categories of race. But Biko went further to say that once liberation had been won and apartheid ended, race would no longer be the central organizing principle of the polity.

Biko at first maintained that white power would somehow collapse as blacks asserted their unwillingness to abide by it, regardless of the intentions of those in power or the balance of forces. Later he came to see the need for a united front against the state and to realize the likelihood of a protracted struggle. With the black consciousness movement's deemphasis of confrontation, military power, and materialism, the state at first regarded the movement as no threat. But after the Africanist rhetoric of the movement began to appeal to the urban poor and Biko started to reach out successfully to the ANC in exile and to other resistance groups, the state crushed the movement. The authorities feared a unified black opposition.

Biko was detained on August 18, 1977, interrogated, beaten to near death by the police in Port Elizabeth, and then driven to Pretoria, where he died, in a cell, on September 12.

Five weeks after Biko's death, on October 19, the government banned seventeen black consciousness and affiliated organizations. Many of their 14,000 supporters who had fled South Africa during and after the Soweto uprising joined the ANC. Black consciousness was effectively silenced.

An official inquest, conducted in November–December 1977, exonerated the police and state medical officials from responsibility for Biko's death. That inquest has since been totally discredited, and Biko is a martyr in the democratic struggle. In 1997 several police officers, to avoid subsequent prosecution for his murder, sought amnesty from the Truth and Reconciliation Commission, a state body trying to determine the facts about human rights violations under apartheid.

See also *Mandela, Nelson; Race; South African Antiapartheid Revolts and Reform (1948–1994).*

Kenneth W. Grundy

BIBLIOGRAPHY

Arnold, Millard, ed. *Steve Biko: Black Consciousness in South Africa.* New York: Random House, 1978.

Biko, Steve. *I Write What I Like.* San Francisco: Harper and Row, 1986.

Gerhart, Gail M. *Black Power in South Africa: The Evolution of an Ideology.* Berkeley: University of California Press, 1978.

Pityana, Barney, ed. *Bounds of Possibility: The Legacy of Steve Biko and Black Consciousness.* Cape Town: David Philip, 1991.

Woods, Donald. *Biko.* New York: Vintage, 1979.

BOHEMIAN REVOLT (1618–1648)

The outbreak of rebellion in Bohemia in May 1618 initiated a war that lasted thirty years and transformed the political and religious geography of central Europe. "The Holy Roman Empire of the German Nation" contained some one thousand separate, semiautonomous political units, of which the largest comprised the lands of the Austrian Habsburgs: the elective kingdoms of Bohemia and Hungary, as well as Austria, the Tyrol, and Alsace, with (in all) some eight million inhabitants. Although the Habsburg lands constituted a large state by the standards of early modern Europe, three factors caused weakness: the various components did not accept primogeniture (partitions occurred at the death of rulers in 1564 and 1576); they were geographically fragmented; and, above all, many subjects of the Catholic Habsburgs were Protestant. From the 1570s the Protestants of Austria, Bohemia, and Hungary exploited their strength of numbers and control of local representative assemblies ("estates") to secure freedom of worship from their Habsburg rulers. In 1609 the Bohemians forced Emperor Rudolf II to sign a "Letter of Majesty," which granted full toleration to Protestants and created a standing committee of the estates, known as "the Defensors," to ensure that the settlement would be respected.

THE GENESIS OF REVOLT

Rudolf, however, proved fickle. In 1611 he tried to revoke the Letter of Majesty and to depose the Defensors by sending a small Habsburg army into Prague, but the invaders were routed, and the estates deposed Rudolf and offered the crown to his brother Matthias, already ruler of Hungary and most of Austria. Matthias's alliance with the Protestant estates did not long survive his election as king of Bohemia and Holy Roman Emperor in 1612, however. Instead, the new ruler sought to undo the concessions he had made and looked for support to his closest Habsburg relatives: his brother Albert, ruler of the Spanish Netherlands; his cousin Ferdinand, ruler of Inner Austria; and his nephew Philip III, king of Spain. Initially, all three turned him down. Albert had in 1609 concluded a Twelve Years' Truce, which temporarily halted the war between Spain and the Dutch Republic, and wished to allow his lands to recover. Ferdinand, although keen to aid Matthias (not least because he regarded himself as the new emperor's heir presumptive), was at war with Venice. Philip III's forces were engaged in Italy fighting Savoy over the succession to the childless duke of Mantua; Philip could therefore aid neither Matthias nor Ferdinand.

In 1617, however, a temporary settlement to the Mantuan question released Spanish troops to assist Ferdinand, provoking Venice to seek peace. Ferdinand then joined the ailing, childless Matthias, who persuaded the estates of both Bohemia and Hungary to recognize Ferdinand as king-designate and at once worked to halt the concessions made to the Protestants of Bohemia. Over the winter of 1617–1618 an overwhelmingly Catholic council of regency began to censor printed works and to prevent non-Catholics from holding government office. More inflammatory still, the regents ordered Protestant worship to cease in all towns on church lands (which they claimed the Letter of Majesty did not cover).

THE DEFENESTRATION OF PRAGUE

The Defensors strongly objected to these measures and summoned the estates of the realm to meet in Prague in May 1618. When the regents declared the meeting illegal, the estates invaded the council chamber and threw two Catholic regents, together with their secretary, out the window. Next, they created a provisional government, known as "the Directors," and raised a small army.

Superficially, the events in Prague in May 1618 differed little from those in 1609 and 1611. Yet no thirty-year struggle arose from those earlier crises. The crucial difference lay in the involvement of foreign powers. Whereas in 1609 and 1611 the Habsburgs had remained divided, in 1618 they united. Initially, their solidarity achieved nothing because the rebel army expelled loyal troops from almost every part of Bohemia, while Bohemian diplomats secured declarations of support from Silesia, Lusatia, and Upper Austria almost at once, and from Moravia and Lower Austria shortly afterward. In May 1619 Bohemian troops besieged Ferdinand in Vienna. Within a few weeks, however, a large Spanish army, partly financed by the papacy, forced them to withdraw.

The appearance of Spanish troops and papal gold in central Europe immediately awakened the fears of the Protestant rulers of the empire. When in the summer of 1619 the

Bohemians deposed Ferdinand and offered the crown to Frederick V of the Palatinate, who was director of the Union of German Protestant States, he rejoiced. Some of his advisers favored rejecting the offer, since acceptance would surely begin a general religious war; but others pointed out that such a war was unavoidable anyway when the Twelve Years' Truce expired in 1621, and they argued that allowing the Bohemian cause to fail now would merely ensure that the conflict in the Netherlands would also be resolved in Spain's favor, making a concerted Habsburg attack on the Protestants of the empire both inevitable and irresistible.

THE EMPIRE STRIKES BACK

Frederick therefore accepted the Bohemian crown, but in so doing thoroughly alarmed the German Catholics. An earlier Catholic League was revived, and in 1619 its leaders authorized the levy of an army of twenty-five thousand men, to be used as the league's director, Maximilian of Bavaria, thought fit. At much the same time Philip III and Archduke Albert each promised to send a new army into Germany to assist Ferdinand. In the ensuing conflict, the Habsburgs and their German allies defeated the rebels throughout the Habsburg lands (1620–1622) and imposed on them a new constitution that abolished both representative assemblies and Protestant worship (1627). Elsewhere in the empire the Catholic coalition also made remarkable strides in the 1620s, but, thanks to sustained military intervention by Sweden (after 1630) and France (after 1635), in 1648 the Catholic majority had to grant full religious toleration and considerable political autonomy to the Protestant states. The peace of Westphalia, although it sanctioned the permanent submission of Bohemia and its neighbors to the Habsburgs, created a political balance of power in central Europe that lasted for almost a century and a religious settlement that has endured ever since.

GEOFFREY PARKER

BIBLIOGRAPHY

Asch, Ronald G. *The Thirty Years War. The Holy Roman Empire and Europe, 1618–1648.* New York: St. Martin's Press, 1997.

Parker, Geoffrey. *The Thirty Years War.* 2d ed. London and New York: Routledge, 1996.

Polisensky, Josef V. *Tragic Triangle: The Netherlands, Spain, and Bohemia, 1618–21.* Prague: 1991.

BOLÍVAR, SIMÓN

The most famous of the leaders of the Latin American independence struggles, Simón Bolívar (1783–1830) was the "Liberator" of six Latin American countries: Venezuela, Colombia, Panama, Ecuador, Peru, and Bolivia. Born into one of the oldest and wealthiest families in Caracas, Venezuela, he became an adherent to the cause of independence at an early age. His outlook was a result of the influence of his family and teachers, who introduced him to the writers of the European Enlightenment, as well as colonial policies that discriminated against the American-born. His early life was shaped also by travels in Europe and by personal tragedy, particularly the death of his young wife in Venezuela in 1803. After her death, he returned to Europe and while in Rome dedicated himself to his country's freedom.

Bolívar's reputation as well as many of his political ideas were created out of years of military struggle. A skilled but not brilliant general, he succeeded as a result of his passionate belief in the rightness of his cause; his strategy of continuous attack; his appeal to individuals who provided the military skills, recruits, and supplies that kept his armies in the field; and his personal ties with his soldiers. He first came to public attention in 1810 as one member of the group that took over the government in Caracas following the Napoleonic invasion of Spain. He participated in the unsuccessful defense of the first Venezuelan republic, established himself as a military commander in Colombia, and declared the second Venezuelan republic in 1813. Its collapse forced him to reconsider his strategy. He returned to the field in 1816 and led a campaign that secured the independence of Colombia and, eventually, Venezuela. Realizing that success required the freeing of the entire continent, he marched south through Ecuador to Peru and Upper Peru, where his armies had destroyed the remaining royalist forces by 1825. In reward for his accomplishments in Upper Peru, the new republic was named Bolivia in his honor

Bolívar's letters, addresses, and constitutional proposals reveal a man committed to republicanism, centralism, and reformism. His views regarding the nature of the newly independent states gradually changed over time in response to the realities he faced. The chaos and disorder that accompanied his military campaigns and dogged the new states after independence confirmed his belief in the need for strong central authority. Politically conservative, he was socially liberal, introducing measures to improve the conditions of the region's Indian population and to end slavery. Yet his liberalism was tempered by pragmatism and the need to

Simón Bolívar

maintain elite support, a fact that explains the inconsistencies and contradictions in his actions and writings.

Although Bolívar was the most powerful and influential man in Spanish America in the mid-1820s, his desire to create a large, centralized political entity came into conflict with less imaginative, more regionally focused individuals. The target of growing criticism, opposition, and even assassination attempts, Bolívar managed to maintain a position of political importance in Colombia until the late 1820s, when, embittered and disillusioned, he decided to leave South America. However, he died of tuberculosis near Santa Marta, Colombia, on December 17, 1830.

See also *Latin American Revolutions for Independence (1808–1898); San Martín, José Francisco de.*

Peter Blanchard

BIBLIOGRAPHY

Bolívar, Simón. *Selected Writings of Bolívar.* Compiled by Vicente Lecuna. Edited by Harold A. Bierck Jr. 2 vols. New York: Colonial Press, 1951.

Bushnell, David, ed. *The Liberator Simón Bolívar.* New York: Knopf, 1970.

García Márquez, Gabriel. *The General in His Labyrinth.* Harmondsworth, England: Penguin Books, 1990.

Masur, Gerhard. *Simón Bolívar.* Rev. ed. Albuquerque: University of New Mexico Press, 1969.

Salcedo-Bastardo, J. L. *Bolívar: A Continent and Its Destiny.* Edited and translated by Annella McDermott. Atlantic Highlands, N.J.: Humanities Press International, 1977.

BOLIVIAN NATIONAL REVOLUTION (1952)

The Bolivian National Revolution of 1952 was one of the most thorough political and social revolutions in Latin America in the twentieth century. Its origins lie in the disintegration of the established order, which began with the Chaco War (1932–1935).

ORIGINS

In the midst of the Great Depression, a conservative national government provoked a war with Paraguay over lands in the Gran Chaco. The disastrous conduct of the war by the traditional Bolivian elite was to destroy the entire edifice of traditional politics. In 1934 the army ended a civilian oligarchic political structure that had endured since the 1880s. Bolivia also lost large parts of its southern territory to Paraguay and over a quarter of its combatants in the war. Many of the veterans found themselves alienated from the traditional system, and thus was born the "Chaco generation." Marxism and indigenism, the Andean radical movement stressing Indian communal rights, received wide circulation, as traditional liberal thought was rejected. The themes of national control over the economy and liberation of the Indians were well summarized by the slogans of all the new radical groups: "lands to the Indians" and "tin mines to state ownership." Among the emerging radical parties the most important and the most nationalist was the Nationalist Revolutionary Movement (MNR), formally established in the early 1940s but with its roots in groups organized as early as 1936.

The seizure of power by "military socialists" under David Toro and Germán Busch (1936–1939) led to the first nationalization of a foreign oil company, when the government confiscated the Standard Oil Company of Bolivia and gave its properties to the national oil company, the YPFB, in March 1937. Busch nurtured many of the new left-wing parties; enacted a new style "social" constitution in 1938 that replaced the liberal charter of 1880; and created an advanced labor code.

With the progressive radicalization of middle-class whites also came a profound radicalization of the laboring classes, and especially their vanguard, the mine workers. In 1942 a bitter strike at the Catavi mines was suppressed by the army, with many worker deaths. The Catavi massacre became a major rallying cry of the left and of the mine workers, and the event welded the two groups together into a powerful movement. The MNR moved to support the miners and also allied itself with a fascist secret military lodge known as

RADEPA, overturning in 1943 the conservative civilian governments that had been in power since 1939 and ruling with its military allies until a popular uprising in 1946 forced it from power. It worked closely with the mine leader Juan Lechín in creating the Federated Union of Mine Workers of Bolivia in 1944. It also sponsored the first national Indian Congress, in La Paz in 1945.

Although the MNR was badly shaken by the 1946 uprising, it adapted quickly by eliminating its more fascist elements and positioning itself from 1946 to 1952 as a radical and popular party of change. Unable to contain the mine workers or the MNR, the traditional politicians abandoned constitutional government and relied on military power. But the post-World War II decline in international tin prices triggered a severe fiscal crisis, which cost the conservative government support even among previously allied groups. The suppression of workers and the use of fraud to void the electoral victories of the party led the MNR to commit itself to an armed overthrow of the regime. A two-month-long civilian revolt led by the party began in September 1949. In May 1950 the MNR turned a La Paz factory workers strike into an armed insurrection. The MNR made one last attempt at gaining power by democratic means: in May 1951, when it won the presidential elections with 72 percent of the 54,000 votes cast. The officer corps remained loyal to the regime, however, and the army prevented the MNR from taking power.

The MNR was now convinced that only a civil war would win them the government, and thus Víctor Paz Estenssoro and the more conservative leaders of the party finally agreed to an arming of all civilians. (Even in the civil war of 1949 the party had not opened the armories to the public.) The final revolt got under way on April 9, 1952. In three days of intensive fighting, during which the armories were opened to the public and the miners marched on La Paz, the army was defeated. At the cost of more than six hundred lives the MNR returned to power, but the MNR of 1952 was different from the profascist MNR overthrown in 1946. It was now a radical populist movement, and it came to power at the cost of the main institutions of order: the army and the police. By accepting the workers' participation and by arming the populace, it committed itself to a revolutionary outcome despite its traditional reformist ideology. Thus began Latin America's most dynamic social and economic revolution since the Mexican Revolution of 1910.

THE REVOLUTION

To understand the impact of the revolution of 1952, it is necessary to understand that Bolivia was the poorest nation of South America. Despite some increase in literacy and urbanization in the first half of the twentieth century, Bolivians were still predominantly rural, and the majority of them were only marginally integrated into the national economy or polity. Of all economically active persons in 1950, 72 percent were engaged in agriculture, but they produced only a third of the GNP. Land distribution was one of the most unjust and uneconomic in Latin America, and the *latifundia* (large estates) both failed to satisfy traditional food demands and kept a large percentage of the national workforce out of the market by holding down their income in exploitative work and service obligations. There also was little new investment in the previously dynamic mining sector, just when most of the mines began to run out of rich veins. Thus aging plants and declining quality of minerals inexorably forced the costs of mining up to uneconomic levels. By 1950 Bolivia was the highest-cost producer of tin on the world market.

Given the political collapse and economic crisis, the MNR found little opposition to the changes it proposed after 1952. The wholesale distribution of arms to the populace, the creation of urban and rural militias, and the neutralization of the national police and army changed Bolivian political, economic, and social reality beyond even the wildest expectations of the MNR leadership. No matter how limited the aims of the moderate leadership of the party, the "reluctant revolutionaries" were slowly and inexorably forced to propose a basic reorganization of Bolivian society. One of the first acts of the new regime was to establish universal suffrage by eliminating literacy requirements. The Indian peasant masses were enfranchised for the first time, and the voting population jumped from 200,000 to a million persons. It established a national labor federation, the Bolivian Workers Central (COB), which immediately demanded the uncompensated nationalization of the mines, liquidation of the army, and abolition of the *latifundia* system. The MNR leaders tried to restrain basic reforms as much as possible, and it took until early October for the government to nationalize the big three mining companies and merge them to form the state-owned Bolivian Mining Corporation. The workers actually exercised "cogovernment" in mine administration.

Although unenthusiastic about agrarian reform, massive rural violence in late 1952 and early 1953 that resulted from a systematic peasant attack on the entire *hacienda* system forced the government to act. The peasants established armed syndicates. Work records were destroyed and overseers and landlords were killed or expelled and their lands seized. Although the countryside had been relatively indifferent and little affected by the fighting of April 1952, it was the scene of tremendous violence and destruction by the end of that year. Finally, in August 1953 an official agrarian reform was enacted. It granted the *hacienda* lands to the Indian workers through their unions and communities, with the proviso that the lands could not be individually sold. In the predominantly Indian areas, almost all land was seized, and the Indians stopped paying compensation, so the lands in effect were confiscated. The traditional *hacienda* was abolished, the *hacendado* class destroyed, and a new class of communal peasant landowners established. Although often working at odds with one another, and constantly being suborned by the government, the peasants retained control over their own unions and became major actors in national politics, which they remain to the present day.

The appeasement of their land hunger turned the Indians inward, so that for the next two generations the primary concern of the communities and their syndicates was delivering health and education services and guaranteeing their land titles. The genius of Paz Estenssoro was to realize the importance of this new conservative force on the national scene. As his support declined among the middle class and his dependence on the radical COB and workers' groups grew, he created a new power base for the center and right wings of his party among the peasantry. Once created, the alliance of COB, workers' groups, and peasants would survive the temporary destruction of the MNR and even the return of rightist military regimes.

THE POSTREVOLUTIONARY ERA

The collapse of the state, the nationalization of the mines, the destruction of the *hacienda* system, and the shift of government resources into social welfare programs created havoc in the national economy. The agrarian reform also initially reduced agricultural deliveries to the cities, thus necessitating massive food imports. The government responded by printing money, and the result was one of the world's more spectacular records of inflation from 1952 to 1956. The middle classes were forced to pay for part of the revolution. Fixed rents were wiped out, and urban real estate values declined. The MNR lost its traditional civilian middle-class base and was to lose control over the government in 1964. Nevertheless, the party refused to commit itself to a thoroughgoing socialist revolution. Aside from the tin mine nationalization, it did everything to attract foreign capital and protect private property. Even in the agrarian reform it retained Santa Cruz as a rural zone for the expansion of private investment. Finally, the government allied itself with the United States in the cold war. In return for its foreign policy support, Bolivia obtained aid for social programs that the United States did not normally support in other countries. By 1960 Bolivia was the largest single recipient of U.S. foreign aid in Latin America and the highest per capita recipient in the world. The massive aid proved vital in providing economic security and growth in Bolivia, and U.S. food shipments gave Bolivia the crucial foodstuffs needed to pass through the period of severe agricultural dislocation occasioned by the agrarian reform. This aid undoubtedly gave the government the equanimity to deal with the peasants that it might otherwise not have had had there been starvation in the cities.

Although the MNR would be overthrown and would return as only one of several powerful parties in the late twentieth century, the national revolution of 1952 had profound political and social consequences, many of them unintentional. Two post-1952 periods of hyperinflation seriously weakened the white traditional classes and eliminated them from the rural areas. The agrarian reform permitted the *cholos* (people of mixed Indian and white background) to emerge as a powerful economic and political group and even to take over El Alto, the nation's second most populous city. As monolingualism declined with widespread education, Quechua and Aymara become commercial and political languages of national importance. Finally, the denationalization of the state economy that occurred after 1985 did not affect land distribution, and Indians remain one of the most highly mobilized political and economic groups in contemporary Bolivia.

See also *Lechín Oquendo, Juan.*

Herbert S. Klein

BIBLIOGRAPHY

Dunkerley, James. *Rebellion in the Veins: Political Struggle in Bolivia, 1952–1982.* London: Verso, 1984.

Klein, Herbert S. *Parties and Political Change in Bolivia, 1880–1952.* London: Cambridge University Press, 1969.

———. *Bolivia: The Evolution of a Multi-Ethnic Society.* 2d rev. ed. New York: Oxford University Press, 1992.

Lora, Guillermo. *History of the Bolivian Labour Movement, 1848–1971.* Cambridge: Cambridge University Press, 1977.
Malloy, James. *Bolivia, the Uncompleted Revolution.* Pittsburgh, Penn.: University of Pittsburgh Press, 1970.

BOURGEOISIE

The French word *bourgeoisie* originally referred to city dwellers, the citizens of a *bourg.* Later, in a loose usage, commentators applied the term to a "middle class," to those located between the aristocracy and the peasantry. Still later, in industrialized societies, the term was applied to the owners of business enterprises, especially those in manufacturing and trade. To this, commentators added a specification, a crude dichotomy—small and large *(petite* and *grande).* Many descriptions of the bourgeoisie, beginning with the seventeenth-century French dramatist Molière, provide deprecating caricatures of its members, pointing to their avarice, small-mindedness, and poor taste as typical traits.

THE MARXIST VIEW

Historical accounts of nineteenth-century politics focus on the economic and political importance of the class—an importance stemming largely from the influence of the founder of socialism, Karl Marx, and his follower Friedrich Engels. The grande bourgeoisie is treated as the decisive "class" of the modern era. Most historical accounts of the eighteenth and nineteenth centuries refer to the "rising bourgeoisie" and point to its increasing importance in the economy and the polity.

The Marxist literature argues that the bourgeoisie takes power through a revolutionary struggle. It displaces the previous ruling class, the aristocracy, and assumes exclusive management of national affairs, thus initiating the bourgeois (or capitalist) era. Marx and Engels pointed to the struggles in seventeenth-century England, to the English Civil War and the "Glorious Revolution," declaring them to be bourgeois revolutions. The French Revolution (1789–1799), in which the monarchy was overthrown, was announced as the exemplary case. Germany was a deviant case, the bourgeoisie there having failed in its "historic task."

According to the Marxists, in capitalist societies the bourgeoisie would be opposed by the proletariat, or working class. The economic crises inherent in capitalism eventually would generate a revolution in which the bourgeoisie would be overthrown by the working class. Engels defined the bourgeoisie as "the class of modern capitalists, owners of the means of social production and employers of wage-labour." Later that definition was extended to include banks and other financial institutions, transportation and utilities, and privately owned services. One problem never satisfactorily dealt with, however, involved definition of the term *owner.* The major "means of social production" are held by corporations, which in turn are owned by shareholders. The problem: how many shares must one have to qualify as bourgeois? The lack of a satisfactory definition of *owner* and the little relevant ownership information in the public record demonstrate that empirical investigations of this class are rare.

Marxist theory assumes that "class" is a powerful determinant and that the members of a given class have pronounced class-specific outlooks. According to the Marxist scenario, the bourgeoisie initiate the capitalist era by overthrowing the previous ruling class. Then within the bourgeois era they seek to maximize profits and to maintain their political dominance, most especially by blocking the working-class revolution. Rejecting the possibility of competition and fragmented concerns, this view assumes a shared class consciousness and coordinated activity to implement the policies required to maintain bourgeois rule. Classes, however, rarely operate with such single-minded purpose. Problems of divisions within the bourgeoisie have been dealt with through casual arguments about "class fractions," said to be linked to specific economic bases such as industrial versus finance capital.

All of these assumptions are best seen as unsupported hypotheses. The English Civil War and the later Glorious Revolution were not the work of a "rising bourgeoisie." Nor was the French Revolution the result of bourgeois initiatives. The revolutions that swept Europe in 1848 were not the work of industrialists and bankers. Other groups played the decisive roles in all these revolutions—notably, intellectuals, political elites, and the military.

CONTEMPORARY STUDIES

Few studies have been conducted of the bourgeoisie in face of the ultimate crisis—that is, their actions to deal with "the final conflict." Studies of the 1917 Russian Revolution or of the revolutions in Germany and Austria in 1918 have little to say about the bourgeoisie. One exemplary study by Henry A. Turner Jr. of German big business in the early 1930s—faced then by the floundering Weimar democracy, the rise of Hitler, the rise of the left, and the political crisis resulting from the absence of a stable or viable governing coalition—found "the executive committee of the bourgeoisie" befuddled and in disarray.

The petite bourgeoisie (in English usually given as "petty bourgeoisie") is said to be experiencing downward mobility with the proliferation of large-scale industry. The competition of the larger and more efficient firms drives them out of business, forcing their "fall into the proletariat." Marx and Engels claimed that this class is reactionary and that it tries to roll back history. This argument has been used in the twentieth century to explain the rise of fascism. The evidence presently available shows the hypothesis is not supported.

In summary, empirical studies have failed to confirm the two principal Marxist hypotheses for "the bourgeoisie." The grande bourgeoisie does not appear to have played the key role assigned to it. And the claims made about the petite bourgeoisie also do not appear supported.

See also *Class; Communism; Marx, Karl, and Friedrich Engels; Socialism.*

Richard F. Hamilton

BIBLIOGRAPHY

Cobban, Alfred. *The Social Interpretation of the French Revolution.* Cambridge: Cambridge University Press, 1964.

Furet, François. *Interpreting the French Revolution.* Cambridge: Cambridge University Press, 1981.

Goldstone, Jack A. *Revolution and Rebellion in the Early Modern World.* Berkeley: University of California Press, 1991.

Hamilton, Richard F. *The Bourgeois Epoch: Marx and Engels on Britain, France, and Germany.* Chapel Hill: University of North Carolina Press, 1991.

Palmer, Robert R. *Twelve Who Ruled: The Year of the Terror in the French Revolution.* Princeton, N.J.: Princeton University Press, 1969.

Stone, Lawrence. *The Causes of the English Revolution, 1529–1642.* New York: Harper, 1972.

Turner, Henry A., Jr. *German Big Business and the Rise of Hitler.* New York: Oxford University Press, 1985.

BRITISH CIVIL WARS AND REVOLUTION (1638–1660)

During the two middle decades of the seventeenth century the British Isles plunged into prolonged political crisis. Uprisings by the Calvinist Scots (1639–1640) and the Catholic Irish (1641) preceded bitter civil strife in England (1642–1647, 1648), the public trial and execution of the defeated king (1648–1649), and the establishment of a republic (1649) that resisted restoration of the monarchy for eleven more years. Passions and prejudice derived from this tumultuous era still color modern views of the period. Successive generations of historians have failed even to settle on a defining title for its central events, let alone to reach consensus on their causes and consequences. But one point of interpretation endorsed by many recent scholars is that the breakdown of political stability in the late 1630s and early 1640s may be better understood in a British context, even though England, the core kingdom of the Stuart monarchy, was the last to experience its most serious consequences. The accession of James VI of Scotland (1566–1625) to the English throne in 1603 had united these two neighboring if traditionally antagonistic realms under a single ruler, without otherwise modifying their constitutional, ethnic, legal, and religious differences. At the same time, a series of military successes permitted the realization of long-standing English claims to sovereignty over Ireland and enabled English and Scottish colonists to appropriate large tracts of land from the indigenous Catholic population, especially in Ulster. So when the Scottish-born but English-educated Charles I (1600–1649) succeeded his father as king in 1625, this complex, fastidious, insecure, and somewhat naive young man inherited a multiple monarchy of a kind relatively new to British political experience.

Like some European counterparts, Charles's London-based government soon became exasperated by local resistance to initiatives aimed at strengthening the state's authority and increasing its revenues in order to support expanding military commitments. Repeated failures to secure the cooperation of England's national Parliament, a body whose elite membership of landed proprietors, lawyers, and merchants enjoyed a prestigious representative status and somewhat ill-defined veto powers in fiscal and legislative matters, left Charles resolved to rule without parliamentary assistance, or interference. From 1629 his administration embarked on a program of strong government across the overlapping spheres of church and state, funded by extraparliamentary taxes of dubious legality. In Ireland Lord Deputy Thomas Wentworth, an ambitious former parliamentary opponent of royal policies, alienated the Anglo-Irish aristocracy by the ruthlessness with which he advanced both government policies and his own fortunes. Meanwhile, Charles personally encouraged the equally authoritarian Archbishop William Laud to pursue policies aimed at imposing the administrative structures and liturgy of the Episcopal Church of England on the staunchly Presbyterian Scottish Kirk. Within England Laud's support for "Arminianism" clergy, who emphasized free will as opposed to Calvinistic predestination, had earned him, however unjustly, the reputation for covertly favoring Roman Catholicism.

In 1637 attempts to introduce the English prayerbook sparked violent protests in Edinburgh and much of Lowland Scotland, followed by military mobilization on both sides of the border. Charles and his ministers, however, experienced great difficulty recruiting and financing an army with which to subjugate the Scots, despite—and, indeed, partly because of—the widely publicized verdict in the test case *R. v. Hampden* (1638), which narrowly upheld the Crown's legal right to levy ship money (an extraparliamentary tax that had been extended from the coast to the inland, purportedly to finance the Royal Navy). After a first bloodless and inconclusive "Bishops' War" between the Scots and the English in 1639, the "Short Parliament" summoned in April 1640 was dissolved less than a month later because members of the House of Commons (some maintaining close and technically treasonable contact with the rebels) refused to vote funds for war with Scotland while government personnel and policies remained unchanged. Charles now allowed himself to be persuaded by Wentworth that he might employ Catholic Irish troops against his rebellious Protestant subjects. But before they could arrive the Scots swept south in the second Bishops' War, outmaneuvering Charles's scratch forces to occupy the county of Northumberland and the city of Newcastle. To meet Scottish demands the king found himself obliged to summon another Parliament, which met in November 1640 and remained more or less in session for the next thirteen years.

THE LONG PARLIAMENT, 1640–1649

The "Long Parliament" immediately embarked on a vigorous campaign against measures and men identified with Charles's eleven years of nonparliamentary government. "Black Tom Tyrant" Wentworth was impeached for high treason and sentenced to death by parliamentary majority, while Archbishop Laud remained imprisoned in the Tower of London. The ship money tax and similar novel fiscal devices were declared illegal, along with the Court of Star Chamber and other conciliar tribunals. Further legislation provided for the automatic calling of a new Parliament every three years while preventing the dissolution of the present assembly without its own assent. In the face of nearly unanimous parliamentary support, as well as popular backing manifested by mass demonstrations and petitions "out of doors," Charles had little alternative than to go along with this program. He was not slow, however, to exploit an emerging lack of consensus, both within and outside Parliament, on what should happen next.

Religion proved the first and most divisive point of contention. With Laud neutralized and Arminianism on the defensive, some godly Protestant zealots welcomed what they saw as a divinely ordained opportunity to purge the Church of England of its popish relics, including the Crown-appointed bishops, and thereby perhaps smooth the way for Christ's imminent second coming. But other members of Parliament and peers insisted that church and clergy must be upheld against so-called Puritan (radical Protestant) enthusiasts, whose millenarian zeal threatened an institution critical to the maintenance of social and political order, as well as the saving of souls. By presenting himself as the guardian of religious orthodoxy against rabble-rousing preachers and wild-eyed sectaries, Charles sought the support of all who feared that reform, both secular and ecclesiastical, might easily get out of hand.

The question of Charles's own integrity, or lack of it, was a second major cause of division. Through the spring and summer of 1641 revelations of plots against Parliament and royal negotiations with foreign (mainly Catholic) powers brought into question the king's long-term willingness to accept any limitation of his constitutional authority. Such doubts became more pressing in November, with news of a massive and bloody anti-English uprising in Ireland. Despite general agreement that military force was required to subjugate the rebellious Irish papists, those reluctant to place any additional coercive power in Charles's hands had their worst fears confirmed when the king attempted to seize John Pym and four other prominent opposition members from the floor of the House of Commons in January 1642. Although justified by royalists as an act of self-defense, this desperately ill-planned resort to violence initiated an escalating propaganda war between king and Parliament. To validate their respective calls to arms, each claimed to be acting as the true defender of England's ancient constitution and the Protestant religion. Charles then left London and in February sent his family into safety abroad. But the outbreak of the first civil war is conventionally dated from August 1642, when the king formally raised his battle standard at the midlands town of Nottingham.

The first twelve to fifteen months of fighting revealed that each side lacked the military might to overpower the other, and also demonstrated the strength of neutralist sentiment. Vitally important was the Solemn League and Covenant (1643), a treaty pledging armed Scottish assistance to the parliamentary cause in return for commitments to institute reform of the English church along Presbyterian lines. This Anglo–Scots alliance helped bring about the defeat of a royal army commanded by the king's dashing soldier nephew, Prince Rupert, at Marston Moor outside York in 1644. Two consequences flowed from that strategic victory. First, the royalists (or Cavaliers) lost control of the north of England. And, second, among the parliamentarians (or Roundheads), whose main strength still lay in London and the southeastern counties, ascendancy passed to those hawks favoring a military solution over negotiated peace. The next year Parliament's reconstructed New Model Army destroyed the main (if noticeably smaller) royalist force at Naseby in what proved the decisive battle of the first civil war. Yet even as the process of mopping-up royalist strongholds continued, Charles was exploiting divisions among the victors.

Having initially surrendered to the Scots, the king tried to make a separate peace with them. But when negotiations stalled early in 1647 he was handed over to the English Parliament, now dominated by conservatives such as Denzil Holles, who favored some form of limited monarchy, a national Presbyterian church, and no religious toleration. These politicians also wanted to see the victorious army disbanded as quickly as possible, both to save money and to forestall any demand it might make for a role in the settlement. The troops, however, understandably rejected demobilization plans that made no adequate provision for their long-standing arrears of pay. Presbyterian proposals to reimpose religious uniformity also threatened the de facto freedom of belief and worship that had flourished amid wartime disruptions, not least in the cavalry regiments commanded by Lt. Gen. Oliver Cromwell. To safeguard what they came to refer to as "England's Liberties and Soldiers' Rights," the rank and file elected representatives, known as agitators, who in June joined with their officers' delegates to form a General Council of the Army. While this body engaged in increasingly heated exchanges with Parliament, a military detachment seized Charles I from parliamentary custody. The army then entered London in August 1647.

As inconclusive negotiations dragged on with both king and Parliament, the soldiers' representatives produced their own proposals for a settlement. Supporting broadly democratic principles, these schemes revealed the influence of John Lilburne and his fellow London radicals, henceforth known as the Levellers, from their supposed desire to "level" all distinctions of social rank and property. Shorthand transcripts of the army's debate of these and other documents at Putney outside London provide fascinating glimpses of the clash of ideas and interests between critics and upholders of the established political order. Cromwell throughout showed considerable adroitness in seeking to minimize divisions in order to maintain the army's military and political effectiveness. His determination was vindicated by the news that Charles had escaped from London and was again negotiating with the Scots, whose assistance (together with promises of help from the Irish Catholics) precipitated early in 1648 a second English civil war.

It took no more than eight months to crush this ineffective combination of royalist uprisings and ill-coordinated Scottish invasion. Well before that, Parliament was yet again negotiating with "Charles Stuart, that Man of Blood," as the defeated king was now widely referred to by his political and religious enemies, especially in the army. But these parleys were cut short early in December when the military high command forcibly excluded some 140 members from the House of Commons. The remainder, known derisively as "The Rump," hastily established a High Court of Justice, before which Charles was brought to trial. Formally charged with treason to his own people, the convicted king was publicly beheaded on January 30, 1649, before his own palace of Whitehall.

THE ENGLISH REPUBLIC, 1649–1660

Shortly after that dramatic (and for many contemporaries uniquely horrifying) event, the Rump resolved to abolish the monarchy and the House of Lords. But it did not determine what, if anything, would replace them. The new republic, or self-styled "Commonwealth," never quite lost its initial improvisatory character. Beset by enemies, abroad and at home, the regime always depended for survival less on popular support (the extent of which is and was impossible to judge), or even public acquiescence, than on military force. Although the royal martyr attracted more sympathy in death than while he was alive, English royalists and Presbyterians were for the moment largely demoralized and divided. A more urgent threat seemed to come from disaffected radical sectaries and other plebeian opponents of what one hostile pamphleteer now termed "England's New Chains." But Leveller-backed army mutinies were swiftly crushed, while small bands of "Diggers" practicing agrarian communism proved only marginally longer-lived. Despite residual fears of populist unrest and the Levellers' continued ability to mobilize large crowds of civilian supporters in London, by August 1649 the executive Council of State felt more confident about tackling its external opponents. In a whirlwind campaign marked by ruthless (and still remembered) atrocities against civilians, an expeditionary force under Cromwell's command "pacified" papist Ireland. The Scots, whose Parliament had proclaimed Charles's elder son as king, were next invaded and brought under English military rule after suffering major defeats at Cromwell's hand in the battles of Dunbar (1650) and Worcester (1651).

Meanwhile the Rump in London seemed to do little more than sit on and devise schemes to perpetuate its own existence. Such self-seeking inactivity understandably offended all who had believed that the overthrow of monarchy would inaugurate a new era of godly reform. Military frustration with careerist politicians came to a head early in 1653 when Cromwell (still a member of Parliament despite his remarkable rise to military commander in chief) personally foreclosed the Rump's sitting with the aid of a file of soldiers. Having removed this last vestige of legitimate civilian authority by his characteristically forceful action, Cromwell now sought an alternative constitutional structure. His first instinct was to wait upon the Lord, or at least allow the self-professed godly (including the "Fifth Monarchists" led by Maj. Gen. Thomas Harrison) their chance. The resulting Nominated or "Barebones" Parliament, composed of representatives of separatist congregations and other prominent lay activists, dissolved itself in acrimony after less than six months. This failure of millennial optimism was succeeded by an elaborate paper constitution, the "Instrument of Government," which incorporated Ireland and Scotland into a unitary British state ruled by Cromwell as Lord Protector.

The Protectorate worked, after a fashion. The mutual antagonism among "swordsmen," civilian republicans, and Presbyterian crypto-royalists, plus Cromwell's dogged commitment to religious toleration, sabotaged his dealings with successive parliaments. Reform—administrative, ecclesiastical, legal—made barely more progress than the elusive "settlement" for which Cromwell so frequently yearned. Yet the striking triumphs of English arms against the fading Spanish empire in Europe and the New World provided some compensation for these domestic disappointments and the weight of arbitrary government. Unfortunately, the Protector himself remained the one person capable of both controlling the military (on whom the republic ultimately depended) and managing the civilian antiroyalists. His death in September 1658 was followed by an officers' coup six months later, which deposed his ineffective son Richard from the Protectorate. A confused political crisis ensued, as army factions and civilian politicians struggled for ascendancy. Fears of descent into anarchy and social chaos encouraged the intervention of the taciturn English commander in Scotland, Gen. George Monck. His troops entered London early in 1660, encouraging the remnant of the returned Rump, in the final session of a truly Long Parliament, to vote for a general election. The resulting "Convention" formally declared on May 1, 1660, that "according to the ancient and fundamental laws of this Kingdom, the government is, and ought to be, by King, Lords and Commons. . . ." Charles II, and the monarchy, were restored within the month.

HISTORIOGRAPHY

Attempts to chronicle, explain, and understand this complex chain of events begin with contemporaries. Much political argument before and after 1642 took the form of conflicting histories, and the earliest extended accounts of the civil wars were the work of partisan participant-observers. The most accomplished of these, the Earl of Clarendon's *History of the Great Rebellion,* was first published as a Tory polemic at the beginning of the eighteenth century, countering Whiggish celebrations of parliamentarian heroes like Pym and the poet John Milton. Whereas Clarendon emphasized the chance, immediate, and personal causes of the civil war, the great mid-Victorian historian S. R. Gardiner applied new standards of archival research to reconstruct an epic seventeenth-century "Puritan Revolution"—a principled, prolonged, and largely successful struggle for religious and political liberty.

Gardiner's detailed narrative of high politics and diplomacy remains unsurpassed, but his overall interpretation has been substantially modified by subsequent scholarship. For those influenced by various forms of twentieth-century Marxism, the 1640s and 1650s constitute not merely a crucial turning point in English and British history, but the world's first bourgeois revolution. Thus Puritanism has been reconceptualized as the ideology of a rising capitalist class, whose interests and values conflicted with and eventually overturned the economic, political, and social policies of the early Stuart monarchy, together with the ideologies and institutions that supported them.

United only in rejecting such views as excessively determinist, other historians recently have played down both the long-term causes and significance of the British monarchies' temporary collapse. Preferring to explain political events in terms of personalities and the framework of government rather than by invoking deep-seated social-structural forces, they question the existence of any fundamental ideological or social divisions that led to inevitable conflict between royalists and parliamentarians. Indeed, most modern revisionists emphasize continuity and consensus above change and conflict, denying that the 1640s and 1650s brought a decisive victory for constitutional monarchy, capitalism, and modernity over absolutism, feudalism, and tradition. Yet because historical research is a continual, open-ended process, these assertions have inevitably been revised in their turn. One obvious difficulty with the revisionist critique is its narrow chronological and substantive focus. The result is a tendency to discount constraints imposed on the high-political actors by cultural, economic, and social contexts, such as changing demographic pressures, as well as deep-rooted ideological constructions, such as the discourse of antipopery.

In the last analysis, whether mid-seventeenth century Britain experienced revolution, rebellion, or just civil war is more than a merely semantic question. Historians disagree partly because of the complexity of the events themselves, but also because these events involved fundamental conflicts of principle as, for example, between monarchy and republicanism, free will and determinism, egalitarianism and elitism, liberty and righteousness, among others. The fact that contemporary voices on these issues still speak to us, whether through the political writings of Thomas Hobbes, Milton's prose and poetry, Lilburne's pamphlets, or Cromwell's speeches, may be one good reason to regard what happened between 1638 and 1660 as something more than an insignificant local aberration.

See also *Cromwell, Oliver; Millenarianism.*

Wilfrid Prest

BIBLIOGRAPHY

Aylmer, Gerald. *Rebellion or Revolution? England 1640–1660.* Oxford: Oxford University Press, 1987.

Bradshaw, Brendan, and John Morrill, eds. *The British Problem, 1534–1707: State Formation in the Atlantic Archipelago (Problems in Focus).* New York: St. Martin's Press, 1996.

Coward, Barry. *The Stuart Age: England, 1603–1714.* London: Longman, 1994.

Cust, Richard, and Ann Hughes, eds. *Conflict in Early Stuart England: Studies in Religion and Politics, 1603–1642.* London: Longman, 1989.

Hill, Christopher. *God's Englishman: Oliver Cromwell and the English Revolution.* London: Weidenfeld and Nicholson, 1970.

———. *Century of Revolution, 1603–1714.* Wokingham, Berkshire: Van Nostrand Reinhold, 1983.

Morrill, John, ed. *The Oxford Illustrated History of Tudor and Stuart Britain.* Oxford: Oxford University Press, 1996.

Russell, Conrad. *The Causes of the English Civil War: The Ford Lectures Delivered in the University of Oxford, 1987–1988.* Oxford: Clarendon Press, 1990.

———. *The Fall of the British Monarchies, 1637–1642.* Oxford: Clarendon Press, 1991.

Stone, Lawrence. *The Causes of the English Revolution 1529–1642.* London: Longman, 1972.

BRITISH "GLORIOUS REVOLUTION" (1688–1689)

The "Glorious Revolution" of 1688–1689 was a modern nationalist revolution. England in the seventeenth century was a changing and modernizing society. England's domestic and international trade were rapidly expanding. And, since the outbreak of the English Civil War in 1642, the English government was compelled to tap this new mobile—commercial and manufactured as opposed to landed—wealth in order to finance its massively increasing state bureaucracy and infrastructure. The civil war and the ensuing naval conflicts with the Dutch (1652–1654, 1664–1667, 1672–1674) thus brought a broader social and cultural range of Englishmen and women into the political arena.

The expanded political nation was treated to an explosion of political information in the 1640s and 1650s. Although the range and extent of this material was somewhat restricted after the restoration of the English monarchy in 1660, the newfound taste for news and political discussion continued unabated. Englishmen and women from all over the country could visit the newly opened coffeehouses to read the most recent political pamphlets, scurrilous poems, and national newspapers. In the coffeehouses and more traditional locales such as taverns, inns, and alehouses the English in the reign of Charles II (1660–1685) discussed national and international politics, plays, poetry, as well as local scandals. News and gossip quickly traveled the country from end to end. Charles II may well have had many of the political absolutist aspirations of his father and predecessor Charles I, but he understood full well that the social and political nation that he inherited required him to make concessions to public opinion.

Charles II was succeeded in February 1685 by his younger brother James II, who was a man of another ilk. James was a professed and devoted Roman Catholic and a strict and successful military and naval leader. Whereas his elder brother Charles had chosen to adapt to the England he had found upon his return from continental exile in 1660, James II took an activist role. James wanted to resurrect the grandeur and authority of the English monarchy. He did everything he could to limit the intellectual range and social spaces available for political discussion. James was deeply committed to the empire; but for him it was a military, not a commercial, empire. James sought to remake England into a military, agrarian, and deferential society.

Nevertheless, James II's accession was greeted with heartfelt enthusiasm throughout England. The Tories—the party that had been formed to defend James's right to the throne in the Exclusion Crisis (1679–1681)—were initially convinced that he would defend the Church of England and reestablish the prestige of the English monarchy. The Whigs—those who had fought to exclude James—had largely been discredited and smeared with accusations of rebellion. The failed religious rebellion led by James's nephew, the Duke of Monmouth, who was closely associated with the Whig Party, in the summer of 1685 resulted in popular opinion shifting even more firmly in an absolutist direction. Sermons throughout the land, both Anglican and Catholic, insisted that the king's power came directly from God, and that therefore only God, and never the king's subjects, could call the king to account. While James's political philosophy and religious beliefs made many of his subjects wary of him, the English were united in the hope that he would restore England's European status—a status that had suffered under the reign of Charles II. Tories, Whigs, and moderates all hoped that James's well-known military abilities would finally allow the English to curb the growing power of France.

JAMES II'S FRENCH POLITICAL STYLE

Louis XIV's France was widely perceived to be seeking to establish a universal monarchy, a new world empire. French military might, French diplomacy, and French economic prowess had succeeded in cowing most of Europe. Louis XIV, the English felt, was able to develop this great political power only by eliminating the civil and political liberties of the French people. French expansionism and French absolutism went hand in hand. Since the early 1670s English

Parliament offering the Crown to William III and Mary. From a picture by James Northcote (1746–1831).

people of all political stripes and religious convictions had been calling for war against France. Louis XIV, they felt, threatened to destroy the integrity of every European nation, whether Protestant or Catholic, republican or absolutist. The English were deeply concerned that the inroads that French fashion and French literature had made into their culture were but the thin end of the French imperial wedge.

Instead of leading the European struggle against France and in defense of national integrity, however, James II did nothing. In fact, he did less than nothing. He began to build up his navy and model a standing army upon that of Louis XIV. It was soon clear to the international diplomatic community, and to most perceptive Englishmen and women, that instead of attacking France, James II hoped to crush the commercially vibrant and politically pluralist Dutch republic.

Many in England, indeed many lifelong Tories and sympathetic moderates, came to the conclusion that James II sought to appease Louis XIV abroad and mimic him at home. Immediately after the successful suppression of Monmouth's Rebellion, James II set about increasing his power. He insisted that the newly commissioned Catholic military officers—whose very appointments were illegal according to English law—retain their posts. These new officers became the basis for James II's new and ubiquitous standing army. James then set up an Ecclesiastical Commission to regulate church affairs—a commission that many in England felt violated a law Parliament had passed in his father's reign prohibiting a similar commission. One of the commission's first acts was to suspend the bishop of London, Henry Compton, for refusing to discipline a London cleric who had delivered an anti-Catholic sermon. Since the bishop's defense centered around his refusal to recognize the legality of the commission, the constitutional issue of the extent of the king's power was again highlighted. Significantly, Compton came from an old royalist and Tory family, and his new and widely publicized insistence that an Englishman's loyalty was in the first instance to English law rather than his monarch marked a major turning point in English political sentiment. The commission's next highly publicized act, the decision to deprive the fellows of Magdalen College, Oxford, for refusing to appoint as their president the king's nominee, stirred even greater furor.

Many throughout England declared that if Oxford dons could be deprived of their fellowships, legally the equivalent of private property, then no property in England was safe.

The most frequent and most widespread cries that James II was adopting the political style of his French cousin, Louis XIV, arose, however, over his attempts to promote religious toleration in England. The issue was immensely complicated since parliamentary statute required that everyone in England attend Church of England services (the penal laws) and that all officeholders, both civil and military, take communion in the Church of England and forswear the Catholic doctrine of transubstantiation (the Test Act). James adopted a two-pronged strategy. First, he issued two Declarations of Indulgence, which in essence declared that the king would not enforce the penal laws or the Test Acts. Second, he initiated a massive nationwide campaign to pack Parliament, to ensure that the next elected Parliament would repeal those laws. The Declarations of Indulgence infuriated the adherents of the Church of England. James II, they said, was aiming to destroy their national religion, a religion established by law. Although James initially had some support from Protestant nonconformists, most of them turned against the Catholic king as well. They argued that there could be no religious liberty without civil liberty. And nullifying statute law by royal fiat and requiring engagements prior to parliamentary elections vitiated English civil liberty. Indeed, the nationwide canvassing campaign to procure a tolerationist Parliament revealed to the English how committed most of them were to some form of religious toleration and how profoundly opposed they were to James II's methods of achieving those goals. James II, most in England were coming to realize, had no more respect for the law than had Louis XIV.

A POPULAR REVOLUTION

By early 1688 many throughout England had had enough of James II's regime. The regime's perceived Francophilia in both foreign and domestic affairs led a variety of merchants, clerics, gentlemen, and noblemen to begin making tentative approaches to James II's son-in-law, William Prince of Orange, *stadhouder* of the United Provinces of the Netherlands. Not only was William the Protestant husband of James II's eldest daughter, but he was also the European leader in the struggle against Louis XIV. It was clear to William that he had little choice but to act. Louis XIV was preparing his massive army to invade the Rhineland and perhaps the militarily weak Spanish Netherlands, thus potentially encircling and isolating William's Dutch republic, while James II was building up his navy with the full intention of attacking the Dutch by sea. While it was clear that James II was deeply unpopular in England, it was also certain that in a few years the English king's new army would be an extremely formidable force. So, when seven Whig and Tory English politicians formally invited William to invade England, William accepted enthusiastically.

While much has been made of the Dutch invasion of November 1688, the depth of popular support for the revolution should not be underestimated. As William prepared his fleet, vast sums of money poured into his coffers from the English merchant community and the English gentry—sums significantly larger than England's yearly intake from customs revenue. While James II was slow to react to the news of William's preparations, men and women throughout the land eagerly anticipated the arrival of their saviors. When William and his mixed Dutch, English, French, and Scottish forces arrived in the west of England in November 1688, their landing was accompanied by simultaneous uprisings in the north. Volunteers poured into William's army as he marched toward London. James II's army began to desert—many, including Lord Churchill, the future Duke of Marlborough, came over to William's side. After having joined his army at Salisbury, James II lost his nerve and returned to London. When William followed him and entered the capital, he was greeted with wild enthusiasm.

A NATIONALIST REVOLUTION

When James II and his family fled to France a few weeks later, England was left without a king. The hastily elected Convention, which met in February, faced an unprecedented political situation. After much debate the members of the Convention agreed that James II had abdicated and that William and his wife Mary should be crowned king and queen. Although the arguments used to justify this decision were numerous and varied, they were almost all nationalist. They all began with the supposition that each nation created its own government. Those more Whiggishly inclined argued that James II, by breaking a variety of national laws, had destroyed the original contract between the king and his people. As a result the people were justified in resisting James II and could choose their new ruler. Tories and conservative moderates argued, by contrast, that when James had violated English law he had ceased to be king of England and had become merely a tyrant. As a result no resistance against James had taken place, since no allegiance was due him.

Mary and, through a variety of arguments, William were thus said to inherit the throne. Proponents of both views thus agreed that James II had tried to replace an English with a French government. To ensure that this could never happen again, the Convention issued the Declaration of Rights—a statement of English law as the members understood it to be. The members of the Convention were not making new law but were enunciating an understanding of English law—an understanding that insisted that the nation, not the king alone, was sovereign—which the Stuarts had always denied. By 1688–1689 James II had very few adherents to his understanding of the English constitution.

Since the revolution of 1688–1689 was conducted in explicitly nationalist terms, it was inevitable that the revolutionaries would demand a war against France. And so they did. This war, as most knew, could not be fought by traditional means. France was too powerful; warfare had become too expensive. Instead of depending on the English aristocracy to loan or give the king troops and money in order to fight the war, William and his adherents insisted that the war be financed on a national basis. England's increasingly large amounts of mobile, commercial wealth was tapped via new methods of taxation and through new vehicles to service the national debt. The Bank of England was soon created to finance England's war against French attempts to achieve a universal monarchy. The postrevolutionary regime's entire war strategy was predicated on the notion that England was a commercial and not a traditional agrarian society.

Many have denied that the Glorious Revolution was a modern revolution because, they say, it was merely a war of religion, the sort of conflict typical of traditional societies. It is certainly true that James II's Catholicism and his dependence on his Jesuit advisers loomed large in the popular antagonism to his regime. However, it is too simple to reduce the widespread opposition to James to religious prejudice. Most English Catholics were critical of James II's policies. The Papal Nuncio who came to England during James II's reign was well known to be one of the fiercest critics of the king's Jesuit advisers. Most Protestants were happy to live peacefully with their Catholic neighbors. Indeed, when James succeeded to the throne he was greeted enthusiastically despite his known Catholicism. It was instead James II's policies that turned the nation against him. Englishmen and women opposed James for violating the law in his civil and military appointments, not because of his own religious beliefs. The revolution led to no lawless anti-Catholic rioting, only to the lawful destruction of illegally erected Catholic chapels. William was careful to protect the property and lives of Roman Catholics. Significantly, the alliance that William created to fight France was multiconfessional. William's declaration of war and his wartime propaganda were careful to insist that the English were not engaged in a war of religion, but a war to protect the national integrity of every European nation against French universal dominion.

See also *William of Orange (King William III of England).*

STEVE PINCUS

BIBLIOGRAPHY

Harris, Tim. *Politics Under the Later Stuarts.* Harlow, Essex: Longman, 1993.
Israel, Jonathan, ed. *The Anglo-Dutch Moment: Essays on the Glorious Revolution and Its World Impact.* Cambridge: Cambridge University Press, 1991.
Jones, J. R. *The Revolution of 1688 in England.* New York: W.W. Norton, 1972.
Kenyon, J. P. *Revolution Principles.* Cambridge: Cambridge University Press, 1977.
Speck, W. A. *Reluctant Revolutionaries: Englishmen and the Revolution of 1688.* New York: Oxford University Press, 1988.
Trevelyan, G. M. *The English Revolution 1688–89.* New York: Oxford University Press, 1981. First published 1938.

BRITISH JACOBITE REBELLIONS (1715–1745)

The Jacobites, adherents of the exiled Catholic branch of the house of Stuart, took their name from *Jacobus,* the Latin form of the name James. There were three Jacobite uprisings against the Hanoverian kings George I and George II, all unsuccessful. The British "Glorious Revolution" of 1688–1689, which deposed the Catholic monarch James II from the English and Scottish thrones and placed his Protestant daughter, Mary II, and son-in-law, William of Orange (William III), on the throne, left a core of politically important persons and families strongly or vaguely opposed to the postrevolutionary settlement.

For many people, the unbreakable hereditary succession had been broken; to James Butler, duke of Ormond, and other Tories—the most devoted upholders of Anglicanism—that was a great wrong. Many among the Scottish political classes felt cheated by the union of Scotland with England in 1707, which they thought made the northern kingdom dependent on the southern. Other Britons believed the new regime slighted their claims to offices and honors.

The person and position of the devoutly Protestant Queen Anne (reigned 1702–1714) still commanded respect, and her membership in the Stuart house as James II's daughter lent legitimacy to her government, despite the presence abroad of her half-brother, James Stuart, James II's heir under the old rules of succession. In Scotland, however, there was a great wish for separation from England and its political and economic dominance. Several bodies of opinion thus were grouped together as Jacobite. One plotter, though not a fervent one, was John Erskine, earl of Mar.

THE '15 AND AFTER

Mar was one of the important figures (with Ormond and Robert Harley, earl of Oxford) who in the last years of Anne's reign felt menaced by the accession of a new king from Hanover, George I, a great-grandson of James I, who took the throne in 1714. They had been in direct or indirect contact with the court of James Stuart (called "the Pretender" by his enemies). Coldly treated by George I—who suspected Mar's Stuart plots and disliked Anne's Tory ministers for not opposing the French in the War of the Spanish Succession—Mar panicked, secretly went to his own country in northeastern Scotland, and raised a standard for the Pretender, who, previously unwarned, sent the earl a commission empowering him to command other risers for the cause.

Mar was not a general. Ormond was; threatened as was Mar, the duke fled to France, hoping to lead an invasion of England from St. Malo. James was to follow. But Ormond turned back from the English coast when friends ashore did not answer his signals because many of them were under arrest. The Pretender then tried to go to Scotland, at last sailing from Dunkirk and arriving at Peterhead, Aberdeenshire, on December 22, 1715.

Mar had at first secured support from many Scottish Jacobites—both Catholics and Scots Episcopalians who shared national resentments and religious objections to the state-sanctioned Presbyterian Kirk. Some were Highland clansmen, but many were Lowlanders, particularly from the northeast. Their commander may have had 6,000 foot and 800 horse soldiers, but he managed only an indecisive battle at Sheriffmuir in Perthshire (November 13, 1715), and at the Pretender's landing, some of Mar's forces were leaving the army for home.

Thus the young Stuart found that he could only depart, as he did on February 4, 1716, to spare his friends the harsh treatment they would certainly have received had he remained. Indeed, though the Hanoverian government took the rebellions seriously, it was not merciless, and many of the guilty escaped capture. The Pretender himself had to leave France, eventually settling in Italy. "The '15," as this affair was called, did not generate heavy fighting. It roused little zeal in England, where a small body of northern Jacobites were forced to surrender at Preston, Lancashire, on November 14, 1715.

In 1719, during a short war between Britain and Spain, the Spanish planned expeditions against England, to be led by Ormond, and against Scotland, under George Keith, Earl Marischal of Scotland. Ormond's transports were too badly mauled by a storm for him to sail. Spaniards lent to Marischal were too few, and he found little local help when he landed. Keith's forces met defeat at Glenshiel on June 10 and yielded the next day, and the Scottish Jacobites dispersed to safety. The Pretender had gone from Italy to Spain with hopes of returning to Britain. Disappointed, he went back to Italy.

James Stuart married and sired two sons, the elder of whom, Charles ("the Young Pretender"), showed much charm and ability to inspire. Born in 1720, he became the chief hope of Jacobites as his father aged. In 1743, France, on the verge of war with Britain, sent for Charles to head an expedition in his father's name. Circumstances prevented his departure with a French force, but he remained in France, in touch with the Scottish Jacobites.

THE '45

In 1745 Charles embarked with a small group of supporters and landed in the western Highlands of Scotland, setting up his standard at Glenfinnan on August 19. He attracted some of the Highland clans and many Lowlanders, once more Catholics and Episcopalians. This action began "the '45." Although the armies of the two sides were small (Great Britain was then engaged in continental war against France), there was more fighting than in 1715. Unable to prevent Charles Stuart's march to Edinburgh, the Hanoverian forces lost to him at the battle of Prestonpans, East Lothian, on September 21.

Jacobite control of Scotland could not last if George II (reigned 1727–1760) had time to recall his regiments from foreign parts and overwhelm the Young Pretender. Charles advanced his army into England as far as Derby, recruiting but a few Englishmen as he went. Cautious advisers discouraged him from further penetration, and he began a retreat to Scotland on December 6.

France contributed only a small body to help the Jacobites. Nevertheless, the withdrawing force won another battle at Falkirk, Stirlingshire, in January 1746. Desertion plagued it as weeks passed, and enemy maneuvers compelled Charles to move north to near Inverness. On April 16, 1746, George II's son, William Augustus, duke of Cumberland, crushed the Jacobites at Culloden Moor. The French present capitulated, and the Scottish Jacobites scattered after a brief rally.

Cumberland's army wrought a bloody vengeance on the rebels. Many were killed fleeing. Some of the ringleaders left the country, as Charles did after long wandering and many adventures, but the victors took many prisoners. Some leaders died on the scaffold; for the rank and file, transportation was a more common punishment, but many of the transported never returned to Scotland. Great destruction of property in rebellious districts induced famine, and many country people starved or died of exposure. Changes in Scottish law abolished powers clan chiefs and others held over their dependents and were intended to destroy the clan system and feudal holdovers to make future risings almost impossible.

The three rebellions showed that Jacobite strength in Scotland and England was insufficient to overcome regular troops of the British army unless France or Spain sent greater help than either ever did. Proclamations of the Pretenders' intentions made clear that many changes made since 1689 would not have been reversed if the Jacobites had won, though the union of Scotland and England might have been dissolved. But because they lost, claims under the old rules of succession became moot, and the parliament that had changed the rules would win in any contest with the Crown.

While there was a Jacobite threat to the power and perhaps lives of the postrevolutionary settlement government ministers—among them Sir Robert Walpole (in office 1721–1742)—they kept a standing army and avoided war against France or Spain by conciliation and concessions, for those powers might use Jacobites to harm the Hanoverian dynasty and its friends. British foreign policy could never ignore the Stuart menace while it endured.

See also *British "Glorious Revolution" (1688–1689).*

George Hilton Jones

BIBLIOGRAPHY

Jones, George Hilton. *The Main Stream of Jacobitism.* Cambridge, Mass.: Harvard University Press, 1955.

Lenman, Bruce. *The Jacobite Risings in Britain, 1689–1746.* London: Eyre Methuen, 1980.

McLynn, F. J. *France and the Jacobite Rising of 1745.* Edinburgh: Edinburgh University Press, 1981.

Sinclair-Stevenson, Christopher. *Inglorious Rebellion: The Jacobite Risings of 1708, 1715, and 1719.* New York: St. Martin's Press, 1971.

Speck, W. A. *The Butcher, The Duke of Cumberland and the Suppression of the '45.* Oxford: Basil Blackwell, 1981.

BRITISH REFORM AND EMANCIPATION MOVEMENT (1820–1833)

Between 1820 and 1833 the British Parliament enacted a series of reforms that, over the long term, significantly altered the social and political balance of power in Great Britain and Ireland and had profound international implications—all without political revolution. Robert Peel's massive overhaul of the criminal code in 1823 made for a more efficient and less sanguinary legal system, and the repeal of the Combination Acts of 1799 and 1800 (1824) legalized trade unions. Other reforms increased participation in government of the newly emerging middle class and marked the entry of organized Irish Catholics into Parliament; the 1832 Reform Bill was, by far, the most important in the series of reforms that produced twentieth-century British democracy. The struggle for the abolition of slavery in the British Empire, finally achieved in 1833 after a long series of judicial decisions and legal restrictions, led to revolt—but in the Caribbean.

The reform wave that crested in 1832 had begun in 1820 with the accession of the unpopular George IV and popular resistance to his efforts to divorce and depose his wife, Queen Caroline. The defense of a threatened queen allowed the resurfacing of radical popular politics, which had gone underground in the face of government repression after 1795. But radicals of the 1820s differed fundamentally from radicals of the 1790s, shifting their focus from the local to the parliamentary arena, forming open political associations to influence Parliament and pursuing their aims through petitions, rallies, and electoral pressure groups. Born in Britain in the late eighteenth century, social movements had become routine vehicles of protest by 1820.

The shift in political focus was a response to new realities. Twenty-five years of almost continual warfare against foreign enemies and the need for revenues and recruits had led the British government to intervene more directly in everyday life; increased proletarianization, partly a result of wartime taxation but also a product of industrial revolution, helped create workers with less influence at the local level but with new concerns that bound them together across localities. In the 1820s rising prices and declining income for less-skilled laborers in city and countryside increased the popular determination that something must be done, and at the time the power to act politically was visibly more concentrated in the House of Commons.

The reforms themselves were the product of unstable and shifting coalitions of nonconformists and Irish Catholics opposing the power and privilege of the Church of England; Whig magnates challenging the expansion of royal power and fearful of the militarization of British society; London radicals castigating monarchical and aristocratic corruption and especially overtaxation; daylaborers struggling to survive; and artisans defending threatened skills. Among elites, disparate ideological perspectives converged in promoting reform. Optimistic utilitarians who championed economic growth and believed that human reason would bring indefinite progress came to the same political conclusions as nonconformists and Evangelical Anglicans who viewed the world in terms of sin, guilt, retribution, and deliverance.

CATHOLIC EMANCIPATION

Of all the reforms, only two, Catholic emancipation and parliamentary reform, brought the kingdom close to revolution. Catholic emancipation was only one portion of a battle to open government to non-Anglicans, including Protestant nonconformists, Jews, and nonbelievers, but it was particularly volatile because it combined the ever-explosive question of political relations between Great Britain and Ireland with a challenge to a developing English national identity based in part on Protestantism. The Corporation Act of 1661 and the Test Act of 1673 barred all who did not conform to the Church of England, whether Catholic or Protestant, from municipal offices and military, executive, and administrative offices under the Crown, and the Test Act of 1678 denied Catholics the right to sit in Parliament. Disagreement within the nonconformist camp over the desirability and terms of Catholic emancipation prevented unity among reformers. The decision of Protestant nonconformists who supported Catholic emancipation to separate the two issues and to win first the least controversial—relief for Protestant dissenters—enabled the movement to preserve a greater semblance of unity than it in fact possessed.

The repeal of major portions of the Test and Corporation Acts in 1828 was largely symbolic. By the early nineteenth century they were seldom invoked, and important discriminatory bars to Protestant nonconformists remained, such as the obligation to pay Church of England rates, the requirement of marriage by an Anglican minister, and exclusion from Oxford and Cambridge. Yet repeal was a decisive political breakthrough foreshadowing the collapse of discrimination against Protestant nonconformists.

In 1825 Catholic emancipation passed the Commons but failed in the Lords, faced with the outspoken opposition of the Duke of York (the king's brother and presumed successor); the prime minister, Lord Liverpool; and the private lobbying of the king himself. To overcome such opposition, a great deal of pressure was required. The decisive battle was fought in Ireland, where landlords had long sought to increase the voting rights of their tenants as a means of increasing their own political influence. First in the elections of 1826 and then in the sensational Clare election of 1828, Daniel O'Connell's mass-based Catholic Association and the Irish Catholic Church demonstrated their ability to rally Catholic tenant farmers against their landlords. To many observers, including the British prime minister, the Duke of Wellington, unless Catholic emancipation were conceded, Ireland seemed plainly on the road to revolution. Irish mass political action, combined with a reform-minded House of Commons supporting Catholic emancipation and opposing the repression of peaceful protest, forced a recalcitrant Duke of Wellington to concede emancipation. Although the Catholic Association was dissolved (and Irish suffrage restricted), the negotiations between the British government and this mass organization served to establish the legitimacy of mass associations in British politics.

PARLIAMENTARY REFORM

The bitter dissension within Tory ranks brought about by Catholic emancipation led to the collapse of Wellington's ministry in 1830. Its successor, under Earl Charles Grey, the first enduring Whig cabinet in fifty years, took parliamentary reform as its primary responsibility. Whig drafters of reform skillfully developed a reform program that could win moderate supporters without alienating radicals, who had great influence in popular politics. The reform act abolished many electoral districts with small populations and redistributed seats from declining rural agricultural to growing urban industrial districts and areas of Ireland, Scotland, and Wales. The extent of enfranchisement varied regionally; it generally admitted most middle-class males and excluded the mass of working-class males. Women remained unenfranchised. Although the well-known radical Henry Hunt denounced the bill for falling far short of manhood suffrage, such prominent radicals as Francis Place, William Cobbett, and Daniel O'Connell came out in support.

The Whigs' wisdom in conciliating the radicals was demonstrated in the tense and tumultuous months between March and May 1831, which witnessed two dissolutions of parliament as determined Tories first amended the bill to death in the Commons and then rejected it in the Lords by a substantial majority. After the second rejection of the bill, violent demonstrations broke out in Derby, Nottingham, and Bristol. Often intervening to cheer reforms or to intimidate known opponents of reform, crowds, mobilized by such groups as the Birmingham Political Union, thronged the hustings during the electoral campaigns that followed each rejection, demanding "the bill, the whole bill, and nothing but the bill." The rhythm of parliamentary crises and electoral contests coincided very closely with that of popular assemblies and protests, and each election yielded substantial victories for reformers. If there was any moment between 1820 and 1833 when Britain hovered near revolution, it was the months between March and May 1832, when illuminations, petitions, parades, burnings in effigy, and bellringings expressed public discontent with the desperate and unsuccessful efforts of Tories to defeat the bill.

Parliamentary reform has sometimes been depicted as a "missed revolution," a portrayal underlined for contemporaries by the contrast between the *parliamentary* overthrow of the reactionary Wellington ministry in Britain only four months after the *revolutionary* overthrow of the reactionary Polignac ministry in July 1830 in France. But the accomplishments of British reform exceeded those of French revolution. As a result of revolution, suffrage in France expanded at a proportionately greater rate than in England and Wales, but English and Welsh suffrage expansion was three times larger in absolute numbers, with more than five times the proportion of the total population granted suffrage. Both French revolution and British reform removed religious disqualifications for voting without establishing religious equality, but it took another French revolution (1848) to end colonial slavery.

ABOLITION OF SLAVERY

Antislavery, a companion movement of parliamentary reform and religious enfranchisement, did provoke revolt—but outside the United Kingdom. The same years that witnessed the struggle for parliamentary reform saw the renewal of the campaign to outlaw slavery in the British Empire. Outshone by parliamentary reform in 1830–1832, antislavery occupied many of the same platforms and was championed by many of the same speakers. Workers in many of the northern manufacturing cities, through antislavery petitions, powerfully supported the nonconformist and Evangelical leaders who constituted the antislavery movement's most prominent public spokesmen. Antislavery sentiment flourished among artisanal households in mining and manufacturing regions and communities engaged in cottage industry, where the spread of both antislavery sentiment and Evangelicalism marked a break with the eighteenth century. As the antislavery movement demonstrated its popularity, Caribbean slaves in the British colonies became aware of their allies and—in Barbados in 1816, Demerara in 1823, and the "Baptist War" in Jamaica in 1831—adapted the rhetoric of human and constitutional rights to demand their freedom. The reforms of 1833 were an important step in the destruction of slavery.

Slave emancipation in the colonies marked the last of the historic accomplishments of the reform movement that developed between 1820 and 1833. The newly enfranchised middle class was not inclined to use its suffrage as a wedge to give the vote to the lower classes that had supported them so stoutly. The application of coercion to Ireland in 1833 and the passage of the New Poor Law in 1834, which centralized poor relief and attempted to compel all in need to enter spartan workhouses, marked the end of the coalition that had so transformed the British polity.

MICHAEL HANAGAN

BIBLIOGRAPHY

Drescher, Seymour. *Capitalism and Antislavery: British Mobilization in Comparative Perspective.* Oxford: Oxford University Press, 1987.

Hilton, Boyd. *The Age of Atonement, The Influence of Evangelicalism on Social and Economic Thought, 1795–1865.* Oxford: Clarendon Press, 1988.

O'Ferrall, Fergus. *Catholic Emancipation: Daniel O'Connell and the Birth of Irish Democracy, 1820–1830.* Dublin: Gill and Macmillan, 1985.

Rowe, D. J. "London Radicalism in the Era of the Great Reform Bill." In *London in the Age of Reform,* edited by John Stevenson, 149–176. Oxford: Blackwell, 1977.

Temperly, Howard. "The Ideology of Antislavery." In *The Abolition of the Atlantic Slave Trade: Origins and Effects in Europe, Africa, and the Americas,* edited by David Eltis and James Walvin, 21–35. Madison: University of Wisconsin Press, 1981.

Tilly, Charles. *Popular Contention in Great Britain, 1758–1834.* Cambridge, Mass.: Harvard University Press, 1995.

BULGARIAN ANTICOMMUNIST REVOLUTION (1989–1997)

The anticommunist revolution in Bulgaria refers to the protracted process beginning in 1989 through which the political control of the Communist Party was eroded. Anticommunist sentiment existed in Bulgaria throughout the communist era, but open resistance was limited. Dissent began to emerge in the late 1980s as a result of Soviet leader Mikhail Gorbachev's reforms in the Soviet Union and related changes elsewhere in eastern Europe *(see map, p. 141)*. By early 1989 several opposition groups were active in Bulgaria, including the Independent Society for the Defense of Human Rights, the Committee for the Ecological Defense of Ruse, the Club for Glasnost and Perestroika, and a new and independent trade union. Faced with such popular opposition at home, as well as pressure from members of the Bulgarian Communist Party who hoped to dissociate themselves from the former regime, and lacking any potential support from the crumbling Soviet bloc, longtime dictator Todor Zhivkov abdicated on November 10, 1989. That date became the symbolic marker of the democratic revolution. The Bulgarian Parliament abolished the leading role of the Communist Party, and communist leaders joined opposition representatives to negotiate arrangements for a transitional government and democratic elections.

The country emerged from these events politically divided, with continuing support for socialism among the elderly and in the countryside. Consequently, de-communization proceeded erratically as control of the government shifted between socialist and antisocialist parties. The Communist Party, renamed the Bulgarian Socialist Party (BSP), won the first elections, in June 1990. The Union of Democratic Forces (UDF), an umbrella organization of antisocialist parties, emerged as the primary opposition and embarked upon a strategy of noncooperation, which eventually provoked the resignation of the socialist government.

The UDF won the next elections, in October 1991, and ruled in coalition with the political arm of the Turkish minority, the Movement for Rights and Freedoms (MRF). The UDF, however, began to fracture internally, and its alliance with the MRF was strained by economic programs adversely affecting the Turkish population. In late 1992 the UDF government failed a confidence vote and was replaced by a government with an MRF mandate and BSP support. It ruled until December 1994, when new elections officially returned the Socialist Party to power. The Socialist government, however, made little progress toward economic transition, and by the end of 1996 skyrocketing inflation, plummeting currency values, and increasing corruption had forced the prime minister to resign. The BSP initially refused to call new elections and struggled to form a new government. The UDF joined other antisocialist groups in a coalition known as the United Democratic Forces to force new elections. The new year brought daily demonstrations throughout the country, which escalated into street barricades and strike action. Some participants even referred to these events as "our 1989," suggesting that 1997 was the real turning point of the anticommunist revolution. Faced with near civil chaos, the BSP agreed in early February to new elections, which took place in April. The United Democratic Forces won a decisive victory and embarked upon reforms promoting privatization, monetary control, and integration with the European Union and NATO.

In sum, by 1989 international events and local discontent had made a challenge to communist control nearly unavoidable. The reaction of the Communist Party prevented the contest from becoming protracted or violent, which helped sustain the viability of the party's socialist successors and allowed it to tap the continuing socialist sentiment of many Bulgarians. The BSP's stewardship of the country after December 1994, however, significantly eroded socialist support and provided a mandate for more radical decommunization of the polity and economy.

See also *East European Revolutions of 1989; Gorbachev, Mikhail; Socialism; USSR Collapse and Dissolution (1989–1991).*

Gerald W. Creed

BIBLIOGRAPHY

Creed, Gerald W. "The Politics of Agriculture: Identity and Socialist Sentiment in Bulgaria." *Slavic Review* 54 (winter 1995): 843–868.

———. *Domesticating Revolution: From Socialist Reform to Ambivalent Transition in a Bulgarian Village.* University Park: Pennsylvania State University Press, 1998.

Mitsuda, Hisayoshi, and Konstantin Pashev. "Environmentalism as Ends or Means? The Rise and Political Crisis of the Environmental Movement in Bulgaria." *Capitalism, Nature, Socialism* 6, no. 1 (1995): 87–109.

Todorova, Maria N. "Improbable Maverick or Typical Conformist? Seven Thoughts on the New Bulgaria." In *Eastern Europe in Revolution,* edited by Ivo Banac, 148–167. Ithaca, N.Y.: Cornell University Press, 1992.

Troxel, Luan. "Socialist Persistence in the Bulgarian Elections of 1990–1991." *East European Quarterly* 26 (January 1993): 407–430.

BUONARROTI, FILIPPO MICHELE

Participant in, and most authoritative chronicler of, the first attempt in history to bring about a communist revolution, Buonarroti (1761–1837) remained until his death a tireless organizer of revolutionary conspiracies. Despite consistent lack of success, the model of revolution through conspiracy that he promoted had a profound influence on later revolutionaries.

A Tuscan nobleman (from the same family as Michaelangelo), Buonarroti studied law in Florence during the enlightened regime of Grand Duke Leopold. Reading Jean-Jacques Rousseau and other French radical thinkers left him dissatisfied with the limited reforms possible under absolute monarchy, and instead of following the expected administrative career, Buonarroti wrote radical pamphlets and frequented Masonic lodges. Excited by the experimental possibilities offered by the French Revolution, he crossed to Corsica in 1789, where his loud anticlericalism won him appointment as an administrator of confiscated church lands. A conservative uprising, however, forced him back to Tuscany, from where he traveled to Paris and applied for French citizenship. By the time he received it in 1793, he had become a follower of Maximilien Robespierre, and his connections secured him appointment in 1794 as administrator of Oneglia, a tiny north Italian principality occupied by French troops. Here he harassed nobles and clerics and enforced economic controls in the face of a popular hostility that he found inexplicable. Belatedly identified as a Robespierrist, Buonarroti was recalled and imprisoned seven months after Robespierre's fall. During his imprisonment (March–October 1795), he met Gracchus Babeuf (1760–1797) and others who would agitate over the subsequent winter for a restoration of social reforms associated with the memory of Robespierre and for the introduction of the abandoned democratic constitution of 1793.

When in the spring of 1796 the alarmed executive Directory took steps to crush the agitation, Babeuf and Buonarroti went underground and began to plan an uprising whose ultimate aim was the abolition of private property. An initial dictatorship of enlightened leaders would carry out the destruction of the old order before handing over power to the sovereign people. The "Conspiracy for Equality" was betrayed, however, and the leading conspirators were arrested (May 10, 1796). Babeuf was later executed, Buonarroti merely imprisoned. He remained in custody until 1802, and was under some sort of surveillance for much of the rest of his life. But surveillance did not deter him from trying to organize secret revolutionary networks, first against Napoleon, then against the restored Bourbons and the post-Napoleonic fragmentation of Italy. His networks were Masonic in inspiration and ritual and always sought to work through secret, subversive hierarchies. They were repeatedly betrayed and broken up, only to be re-formed under new names.

Buonarroti, however, remained dedicated to the ideals that he thought had come so near to achievement between 1793 and 1796. In 1828 he set them out in his celebrated account, the *Conspiracy for Equality.* Translated into English in 1836 and devoured by the French left for a half century, and not least by Karl Marx and Friedrich Engels, the book received a new lease on life in the twentieth century during the heyday of Soviet communism. A celebration as much of Robespierre's lost "republic of virtue" as of the communistic ideals of the 1796 conspirators, *Conspiracy of Equality* was also a handbook of how (and how not) to bring about an egalitarian revolution and a martyrology of ideological ancestors for all future socialist revolutionaries.

See also *French Revolution (1789–1815); Robespierre, Maximilien; Rousseau, Jean-Jacques.*

WILLIAM DOYLE

BIBLIOGRAPHY

Buonarroti, Filippo Michele. *Buonarroti's History of Babeuf's Conspiracy for Equality.* Translated by Bronterre O'Brien. London: Hetherington, 1836.

Eisenstein, Elizabeth L. *The First Professional Revolutionist. Filippo Michele Buonarroti, 1761–1837.* Cambridge, Mass.: Harvard University Press, 1959.

Rose, Barry. *Gracchus Babeuf. The First Revolutionary Communist.* London: Edward Arnold, 1978.

Talmon, Jacob L. *The Origins of Totalitarian Democracy.* London: Secker and Warburg, 1952.

BUREAUCRACY

Bureaucracies are often considered the embodiment of stability in government and therefore are assumed to be either unrelated or opposed to political revolution. This assumption is usually correct. Bureaucracies serve the existing state and are an elite within the existing society. Therefore they tend inherently to oppose revolutions or other kinds of significant political change. This is the dominant finding in comparative research, and even though individual bureaucrats may favor policy change within their own policy domains, they tend to accept the regime within which they function. Further, bureaucratic elites are often central in the politics of regimes that might be susceptible to revolution or reform. They are also key actors in the clientelistic process that undergirds these systems and hence are generally loathe to undermine the existing sociopolitical relationships.

BUREAUCRACIES AS ADVOCATES OF CHANGE

There are, however, some instances in which the bureaucracy may actually promote, and play leading roles in, political revolutions. This potential role in promoting revolutions results from several features of public bureaucracies. One such feature is that bureaucracies are often the most modern elements of society and may seek to promote modernization against a more traditional political elite. This is especially true when the public sector contains numerous industrial establishments and hence contains many technically and professionally trained employees.

Similarly, bureaucracies may be the natural allies of military groups that promote conservative revolts against more politically liberal existing orders. In a number of cases, the bureaucracy and military have been central in institutionalizing the "bureaucratic-authoritarian" style of governing, especially in Latin American systems. While these changes may in some ways be seen as stabilizing political systems rather than as revolutionary, they also represent real departures from the status quo.

COPING WITH SUCCESSFUL REVOLUTIONS

A second role for the bureaucracy in relationship to revolution is coping with the aftermath of revolutions. After a major change in the political regime, both the bureaucracy and the new political leaders must make decisions about their respective futures. The new political leaders must decide if the existing bureaucrats are sufficiently reliable to be kept in their positions. The answer to that question will depend on the level of the bureaucrat; those in top, "policy-making" positions and in police and security positions are often considered too compromised by their involvement with the former regime to permit them to continue in office. In most revolutionary situations there has been no institutionalized, depoliticized civil service that might be able to continue with little interruption. Further, even if there were such a civil service, a revolutionary elite might not be willing to accept its objectivity and willingness to serve the new regime. This skepticism may be ideological, but there may also be a practical reason for dismissing the existing administration: the people who supported the revolution will want good jobs as a reward for their participation.

For lower-echelon bureaucrats, the new government may have no option but to retain them in office. In many cases they are the only people in society with sufficient training and skills to manage the tasks of government. Any revolutionary elite must find some way of accommodating its goals for governing with the need to utilize the only reservoir of talent in the society. However, if a revolution is based on ethnicity, then the new government may be willing to dispense with the trained personnel in order to ensure the loyalty and commitment of the bureaucracy.

The members of the bureaucracy also must decide how they and their careers will fit in with the intentions of the new regime. In most instances members of the upper echelons of the bureaucracy are likely to believe that they will be unable to cooperate with a regime that is generally antithetical to the ones with which they had become accustomed. Further, especially when the new regime has a strong leftist ideology, it will be unlikely to accord the bureaucracy either the elite position it had enjoyed or the levels of compensation. If the old bureaucratic elite does remain in office, it is likely to be both suspect and uncomfortable.

The more technical and professional members of the bureaucracy may find a new regime compatible, and if the new regime is intent on socioeconomic modernization, they may find it quite congenial. Further, just as the new regime may have few alternative sources of skilled labor, the existing workers may have few other outlets for their skills and education. Similarly, unless an incoming regime is intent on finding as many jobs as possible for its adherents, most of the lower-echelon employees can be retained. Thus, much of the bureaucracy may be kept in place simply because neither the regime nor the bureaucracy has any attractive alternatives.

The concepts of bureaucracy and revolution are rarely thought of together. Despite that, the role of bureaucracy in managing the state requires that the leaders of any new regime consider carefully what to do with the administrators remaining from the previous regime. The new regime will not have a totally free choice, given that the bureaucrats may themselves have views about their continued involvement in government. The simple but compelling demands of making government work mean that any new regime may need the old bureaucracy; if the regime does need the bureaucracy, then it must find some way to accommodate the bureaucracy's values and goals.

B. GUY PETERS

BIBLIOGRAPHY

O'Donnell, G. A. *Modernization and Bureaucratic Authoritarianism.* Berkeley: Institute of International Studies, 1979.

Peters, B. Guy. "The Civil Service in the Consolidation of Democracy." *International Social Science Journal* 143 (1995): 127–140.

BURKE, EDMUND

Edmund Burke (1729–1797) was a British statesman and writer whose book *Reflections on the Revolution in France* (1790) remains to this day the classic antirevolutionary manifesto. Born in Dublin, Burke moved to London to study law and then pursued a literary and political career. He was a member of the House of Commons from 1765 to 1794, and in his speeches and pamphlets he addressed both the American and French Revolutions, defending the former and denouncing the latter.

The Americans were in the right, he argued, because they defended traditional practices and principles, the rights of Englishmen, against the disruptive innovations represented by George III's trade and taxation policies. His conservative preference for the status quo led Burke to see the French Revolution in reverse terms, with bloody revolutionaries recklessly subverting the traditional social and political order that embodied the wisdom and experience of the past.

While most of his British contemporaries applauded the revolutionary developments in France, Burke warned that with the events of 1789 "the age of chivalry is gone . . . and the glory of Europe extinguished forever." What Burke par-

Edmund Burke

ticularly despised about the French revolutionaries was their urge to change social institutions in the name of abstract ideas and ideals. Their mistakes were the direct result of their "faith in the dogmatism of philosophers," he wrote, which led them to place too much confidence in reason and speculation. They sought to remake the world in the name of abstract, a priori principles of natural right, freedom, and equality. He contrasted the French attitude with what he considered a native British antirevolutionary disposition. The English had no illusions of rapid political change; they understood the complexity and fragility of human nature and human institutions. They were "not converts of Rousseau" or "disciples of Voltaire." Their instinct was to repair incrementally the walls of the constitutional edifice, not destroy its very foundations in the name of constructing an ideal new structure.

Revolutionaries, according to Burke, misguidedly assumed that people had the ability to reform society according to rational principles thought up by "learned and speculative men." He was convinced, on the contrary, that the power of human reason was severely limited and that custom, tradition, and habit played a much more important role in politics. Revolutionaries thus wove rational schemes of reform and improvement far beyond the power of a flawed human nature to implement. He believed that people lived less by reason than by "untaught feelings" and "old prejudices;" indeed, they loved their "old prejudices" the longer they lasted. Monarchy, aristocracy, and established religion, ancient ideals and institutions that had stood the test of time, were being uprooted by irreverent revolutionaries.

Burke's *Reflections on the Revolution in France* has inspired legions of antirevolutionaries since 1790 who agree with him that people "are not morally at liberty, at their pleasure, and on their speculations of a contingent improvement" to destroy traditional hierarchical and deferential arrangements in the name of abstractions like freedom, justice, and equality. To do so, Burkeans contend, leads inevitably to "unsocial, uncivil, unconnected chaos."

See also *Constitutions; Counterrevolution.*

ISAAC KRAMNICK

BIBLIOGRAPHY

Burke, Edmund. *Reflections on the Revolution in France.* Harmondsworth, England: Penguin Books, 1968.

Kramnick, Isaac. *The Rage of Edmund Burke.* New York: Basic Books, 1976.

Ritchie, Daniel E., ed. *Edmund Burke, Appraisals and Applications.* New Brunswick, N.J.: Transaction Publishers, 1990.

O'Brien, Conor Cruise. *The Great Melody: A Thematic Biography of Edmund Burke.* Chicago: University of Chicago Press, 1992.

BURMESE DEMOCRATIZATION MOVEMENT (1988–)

In August 1988 Rangoon and other major Burmese cities were engulfed in widespread demonstrations by large segments of the population protesting the conditions in which they were living. The banner they rallied behind was that of democracy, which was seen as the antithesis of the narrow, one-party, military-dominated, socialist order that had governed the country since 1962. These demonstrations, which had begun in March 1988 as a fight between rival groups of students at a tea shop, were finally suppressed brutally by the army in September. A new military government, the State Law and Order Restoration Council, put itself in power at that time and was followed by another military regime, the State Peace and Development Council. Although the democracy movement is not dead, it is very weak in the face of a long-standing military order in Burma.

The conditions for the 1988 mass uprising in Burma were created by twenty-five years of political and economic stagnation. The military government had become increasingly narrow and unadventuresome. The country had grown isolated and lacked the political and social stimulus that comes from interaction with the wider world. The economy, which had been sufficiently strong to allow the population to eat, if not prosper, for many years, was faced by the mid-1980s with a major debt service, which the government could no longer pay. Even the black market was bankrupt, and the population faced no positive prospects.

Even the old regime knew its days were numbered. Gen. Ne Win, the dominant figure in the country for most of the years since independence was regained in 1948, called in August 1987 for a major examination of the country's political and economic order. By then, however, it was too late. The regime was too entrenched and stagnant to think creatively.

The 1988 demonstrators included some in the civil service and even the military. But students played a significant mobilizing role, while veteran politicians from the more democratic, pre-1962 era came forward to reclaim power. Into this confused situation arrived Aung San Suu Kyi, the daughter of Gen. Aung San, the hero of Burma's independence struggle against the British. Assassinated in 1947, Aung San was a hero to almost all Burmese, and his articulate daughter, who had lived abroad most of her life, proved a rallying point for the demonstrators, who were seeking new political leadership.

Recognizing the power of the public mood, the military government promised elections and the creation of a demo-

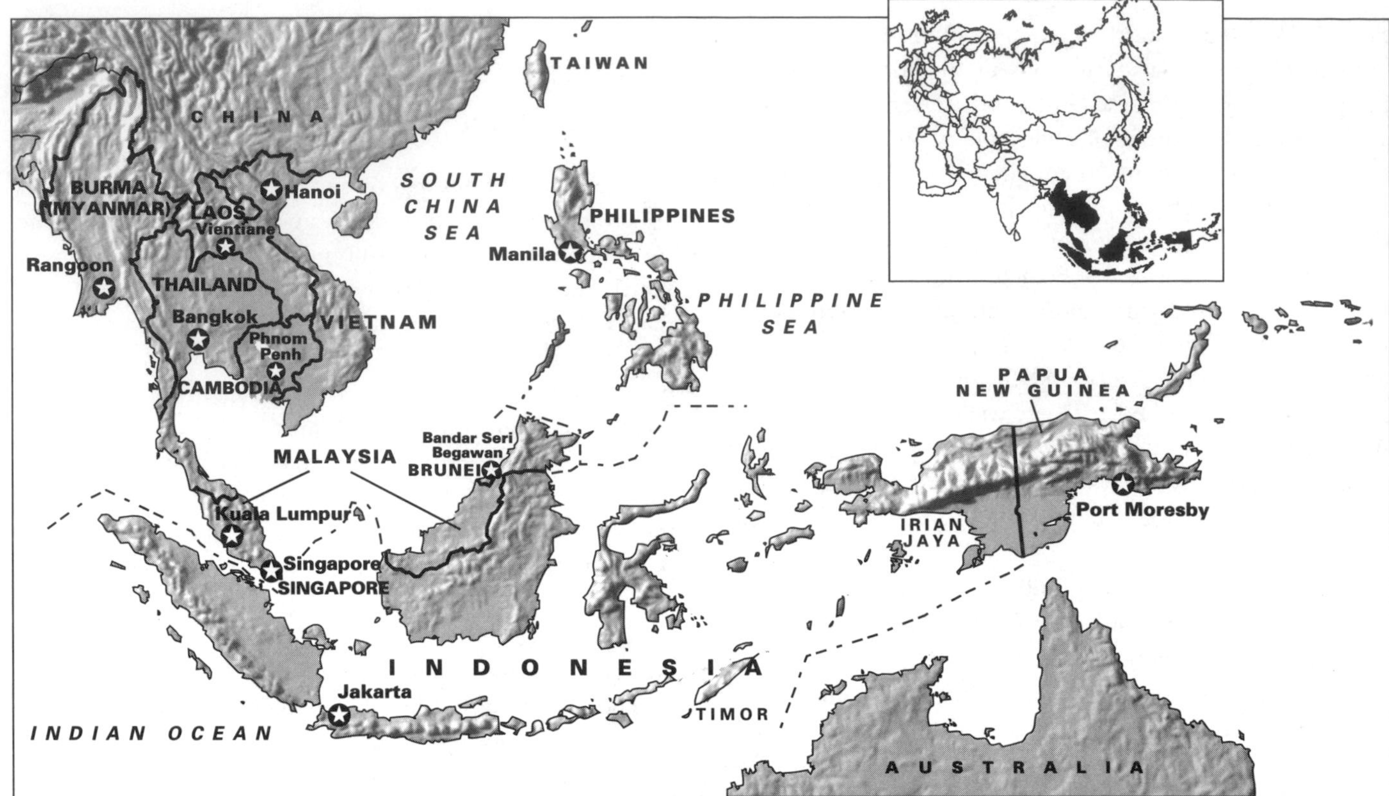

cratic regime. Aung San Suu Kyi, along with students and a number of older leaders, many from the army who had fallen out with Ne Win twenty-five years earlier, formed the National League for Democracy (NLD) to compete in the elections. When these were finally held in 1990, the NLD gained more than 60 percent of the vote and 80 percent of the seats in the promised legislature. However, the army government ignored the results and began a drawn-out process of writing a new constitution for the country. By 1998 the document had yet to appear, and the NLD in the meantime had faced a number of restrictions that effectively destroyed its ability to rule.

The 1988 uprising in Burma, represented by the photogenic and well-spoken Aung San Suu Kyi, gained an international martyr when she was placed under house arrest prior to the 1990 elections. For her highly symbolic role in one of the first post–cold war Asian prodemocracy movements, she received the Nobel Peace Prize in 1991. But the military government was unmoved, and even attempts by Western governments to isolate the country because of its human rights record have done little to weaken the power of the military.

Robert H. Taylor

BIBLIOGRAPHY

Aung San Suu Kyi. *Freedom from Fear and Other Writings.* London: Viking, 1991.

Carey, Peter, ed. *Burma: The Challenge of Change in a Divided Society.* Basingstoke, England: Macmillan, 1997.

Smith, Martin. *Burma: Insurgency and the Politics of Ethnicity.* London: Zed Books, 1991.

BURMESE INDEPENDENCE MOVEMENT (1930s–1948)

Since the early 1920s Burmese opposition to British rule had been deeply connected to student politics. By the early 1930s student opposition to colonial rule had become more militant as ideas borrowed from Irish nationalism and Marxism became integrated into broader culturally based arguments against the legitimacy of foreign rule. The heightened militancy was encapsulated in organizational form through the creation in 1933 of the We Burmans Association, inspired by a leading poet and essayist, Thakin Kodaw Hmaing. Taking the title *thakin* (the Burmese equivalent of the Hindi *sahib,* or "master"), association members symbolically proclaimed their formal equality with their British governors.

Having its social basis initially among urban intellectuals, the We Burmans Association soon expanded as more and more students at Rangoon University joined the movement. As it grew, it also divided into socialist and antisocialist factions. The larger and more popular faction leaned strongly to the left. Led by senior students in the university students' union, including Thakins Aung San and Nu, the movement spread to high school students and eventually throughout the country. They were tapping a stronger anticolonial sentiment than that represented by the more established politicians who had been elected to the colony's legislature. Throughout the country similar student volunteer corps were organized as a demonstration of revolutionary ambition, and many Buddhist monks were active in anticolonial political activities as well.

The opportunity for these anti-imperialist energies to be released came not through the left-wing politics of the We Burmans Association but through the plans of Imperial Japan to gain influence over all of Southeast Asia. In August 1940 Thakin Aung San, soon to be joined by twenty-nine other young men, were received into a Japanese military camp where they were trained as the nucleus of the officer corps of what became the Burma Independence Army (BIA). Entering Burma in early 1942 with the invading Japanese army, the BIA became a rallying institution for young Burmese nationalists. Seeing itself as the new national army of Burma, the BIA, under Aung San's leadership, was betrayed by false Japanese promises of independence but turned against their new rulers only in 1945, as the British reinvaded the country toward the end of World War II.

In the meantime, an extensive network of anti-imperialist socialist and communist organizations had been established across the country. These forces, along with the BIA and other groups, came together to form the Anti-Fascist People's Freedom League (AFPFL) in 1945 to demand independence from the returning British. Always keeping the threat of armed insurrection in their armory of negotiating tactics, the AFPFL, led by Aung San, achieved an agreement for Burma's independence by January 1948. However, Aung San was assassinated by a political rival before that date, and the first prime minister of independent Burma was U (formerly Thakin) Nu. Nu's government immediately faced a divided army, as some units joined with the rebellious Communist Party, which had been expelled from the AFPFL, and other units joined with the separatist Karen National Union. Burmese independence thus resulted in a long series of ideological and ethnic civil wars that have not been fully resolved to this day.

Robert H. Taylor

BIBLIOGRAPHY

Ba Maw. *Breakthrough in Burma: Memoirs of a Revolution, 1939–1946.* New Haven, Conn.: Yale University Press, 1968.

Maung Maung. *Burmese Nationalist Movements, 1940–1948.* Edinburgh: Kiscadale, 1989.

Nu, U. *U Nu, Saturday's Son.* New Haven, Conn.: Yale University Press, 1975.

Taylor, R. H. *The State in Burma.* London: Hurst, 1988.

BURUNDI CIVIL WARS (1993–)

The small East African state of Burundi has been torn by ethnic violence and civil war for much of its modern history. Since the colonial period, the minority Tutsi ethnic group has dominated political, social, and economic power, frequently employing violence to maintain its control. The majority Hutu population has staged periodic revolts, and since 1993 several armed Hutu groups have sought to gain power through combat.

Although the exact meaning of the labels Hutu and Tutsi in precolonial Burundi remains widely contested, most scholars agree that they did not represent ethnic groups in the modern sense. The groups spoke the same language, had common religious practices, and lived together throughout the territory. Intermarriage was common, and identities were flexible. When armed conflicts occurred, they tended to cut across ethnic categories, opposing multiethnic factions against one another. The rulers of Burundi were drawn from a small princely caste, known as the Ganwa, who were considered neither Hutu nor Tutsi. A fourth group, the Twa, constituted less than 1 percent of the population and played an insignificant part in political events.

COLONIAL POLICY AND ETHNIC IDENTITY

Colonial policies served to transform these relatively flexible identities into rigid ethnic categories. German and, after World War I, Belgian colonial administrators and missionaries interpreted Burundian society using European ideas about race. Ignoring important divisions within each group, they regarded the Hutu, Tutsi, and Twa as distinct racial categories. They regarded the Tutsi (including the Ganwa, whom they considered a sub-group of Tutsi) as intelligent and noble, destined to dominate the simple and strong Hutu laborers and the so-called pygmy Twa. The Tutsi, clearly perceiving an opportunity to increase their wealth and power, reinforced European prejudices, helping to craft a mythic history that portrayed them as a foreign tribe, probably of Middle Eastern origin, that had conquered the inferior Hutu several centuries earlier. Colonial policies of indirect rule reserved for Tutsi, who constituted only 15 percent of the population, not only political offices but most educational and business opportunities as well.

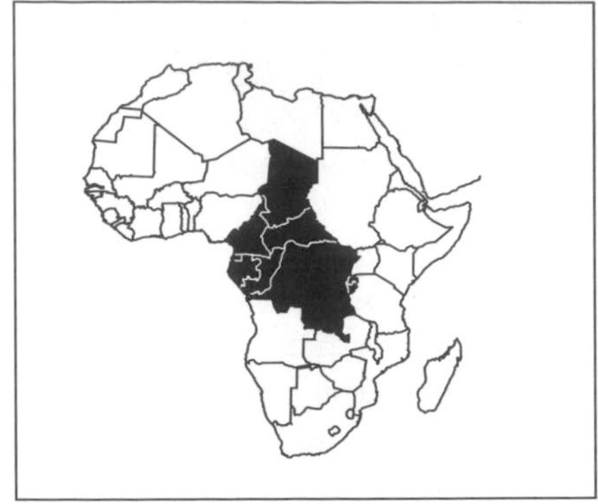

In neighboring Rwanda, where a similar social structure existed, the inequities of the colonial system led Hutu to rise up against their Tutsi chiefs in 1959, killing a small number and driving thousands of Tutsi into exile, beginning a process that led to a complete transfer of power from Tutsi to Hutu by independence in 1962. Although the inequalities between groups in Burundi was never as stark as in Rwanda, the 1959 Hutu revolution in Rwanda became an important symbol for Tutsi in Burundi. Although some Burundian Tutsi believed that a system of ethnic power sharing should be established to prevent revolution, others argued that any compromise with the Hutu would lead inevitably to a complete loss of power and, quite possibly, the wholesale slaughter of Tutsi.

King Mwambutsa named several Hutu to the government, but his son, Prince Rwagasore, leader of the moderate faction, was assassinated in 1961, and in January 1965, the first Hutu named prime minister by Mwambutsa was assassinated after only three days in office by a Tutsi refugee from Rwanda. A few months later, Hutu soldiers and gendarmes attempted a coup in which they killed the Tutsi prime minister and forced Mwambutsa to flee the country. The army then killed hundreds of Hutu military officers and politicians and violently put down a minor Hutu revolt in the interior, killing more than five thousand civilians.

As Burundi polarized along ethnic lines, the radical Tutsi faction gained influence. In November 1966 a group of Tutsi military officers deposed the new king and named Captain Michel Michombero president. Under Michombero, Hutu were systematically excluded from civil and military service. In April 1972 a group of Hutu insurgents attacked and briefly held the southern tip of Burundi. Although the army easily quelled the uprising, the radicals claimed that the attack confirmed the reality of the Hutu threat. In the aftermath of the engagement, the army systematically slaughtered more than 100,000 people, targeting in particular teachers, students, clergy, and other Hutu intellectuals in what has been dubbed a selective genocide intended to eliminate the potential for Hutu rebellion by liquidating all Hutu leaders. Most of the Hutu intellectuals who survived fled into exile.

TUTSI DOMINANCE

Over the next two decades, Tutsi thoroughly dominated social, political, and economic life. In 1988, shortly after Major Pierre Buyoya assumed power in a coup, the army responded to a small Hutu uprising along Burundi's northern border by killing hundreds of Hutu civilians, but rather than using the Hutu uprising as pretext for another general crackdown on Hutu, Buyoya claimed that this incident indicated the need for a new approach. Over the next few years he instituted a number of reforms and brought Hutu into his government. In 1993 he organized multiparty elections, and when he lost to a Hutu candidate, he ceded office peacefully, to the surprise of many.

In July 1993 Melchior Ndadaye thus became Burundi's first Hutu president, over strong Tutsi objections. He was killed in an October 1993 coup attempt. Hutu responded to his assassination by slaughtering thousands of Tutsi civilians in various parts of the country, while the army, which remained overwhelmingly Tutsi, killed thousands of Hutu civilians. At least 50,000 people were killed in this violence, roughly equal numbers of Hutu and Tutsi. Following the coup attempt, another Hutu was named president, but he died a few months later in the Kigali plane crash that also killed Rwandan president Juvénal Habyarimana. A third Hutu then became president but was never able to establish his authority, and with disorder spreading, Buyoya returned to power in a July 1996 coup.

After the July 1996 coup, the countries neighboring Burundi organized an economic embargo to pressure the Buyoya regime to restore democratic rule. Hoping to end sanctions, the government and rebel groups entered talks in mid-1997 sponsored by former Tanzanian president Julius Nyerere. In July 1998 the government and the rebels accepted a cease-fire and announced plans to negotiate a power-sharing agreement. Regardless of the outcome of the talks, the history of violence between Hutu and Tutsi will make any negotiated settlement difficult to carry out.

Although rebel groups do not appear capable of seizing power in the near future, the fact that Hutu outnumber Tutsi by more than six-to-one suggests that rebellion against the government is unlikely to stop unless power sharing can be negotiated.

See also *Nyerere, Julius Kambarage; Rwandan Civil Wars (1959–1994).*

TIMOTHY LONGMAN

BIBLIOGRAPHY

Lemarchand, René. *Rwanda and Burundi.* London: Pall Mall, 1970.

———. *Burundi: Ethnic Conflict and Genocide.* Cambridge: Cambridge University Press, 1994.

Lemarchand, René, and Martin, David. *Selective Genocide in Burundi.* London: Minority Rights Group, 1973.

Longman, Timothy. *Proxy Targets: Civilians in the War in Burundi.* New York: Human Rights Watch, 1998.

Malkki, Lisa H. *Purity and Exile: Violence, Memory, and National Cosmology Among Hutu Refugees in Tanzania.* Chicago: University of Chicago Press, 1995.

Reyntjens, Filip. *L'Afrique des Grand Lacs en Crise: Rwanda, Burundi: 1988–1994.* Paris: Karthala, 1994.

C

CABRAL, AMÍLCAR

From his birth in 1924 in the Portuguese colony of Guinea-Bissau to his tragic death by assassination on January 20, 1973, Cabral achieved recognition as poet, agronomist, theorist, revolutionary, and political organizer. He was one of few Africans to study at a Portuguese university and receive a doctorate, and his work as an agronomist led to agricultural surveys and analyses that served as a foundation for planning the economy of his homeland. As a theorist, he was one of Africa's original, independent Marxist thinkers. As a political organizer, he formed a vanguard party and organized the social and political life of liberated areas as he led a revolutionary guerrilla struggle against Portugal and its imperial and colonial legacy, contributing significantly to the 1974 coup within Portugal that ended a half-century of dictatorship. Most of his life was dedicated to eliminating the Portuguese presence in the colonies and to undermining imperialism in the broader international context.

All evidence depicts Cabral as a mobilizer of people around him. During the late 1940s he participated in student and youth political movements in Lisbon. As an agronomist during the 1950s he was involved in the early political opposition to Portuguese rule in Guinea-Bissau and Cape Verde; founded the African Party for the Independence of Guinea and Cape Verde (PAIGC) on September 19, 1956; encouraged his Angolan comrades to organize a movement to liberate that country from Portuguese control; and helped form a broad anticolonial movement among dissident activists in the Portuguese African colonies.

During the 1960s he was instrumental in the armed struggle. He influenced strategy away from protest in urban areas and toward the organization of the peasant masses in the countryside, and he pushed his movement from political opposition to national insurrection. He was instrumental in launching the guerrilla war in January 1963. Once his movement had succeeded in consolidating control over much of Guinea-Bissau, he began to organize the liberated areas and to build a government independent of the colonial form. A rudimentary administrative structure evolved to perform such tasks as increasing production, ensuring diversification of crops, improving distribution systems, establishing peoples' stores, improving education, building schools, and establishing health-care clinics.

Cabral also envisaged how to deal with the problem of assimilating the new structures in liberated zones with those in the Portuguese colonial enclaves. Village committees, people's courts, people's stores, health clinics, and rural schools founded in the liberated zones were to serve as models for the new integrated society, whereas the land, the Portuguese-controlled trading companies, and the few factories would be brought under national direction. A self-centered development rather than a state bureaucratic model would be emphasized at the outset of independence. The revolutionary party was decisive in establishing in liberated areas a state parallel to the colonial state. At the first PAIGC congress held within Guinea-Bissau, in February 1964, the party was decentralized so that power could devolve to local bodies and special administrative committees in the liberated zones.

As theoretician, disciplined intellectual, and productive scholar, Cabral effectively assimilated old and new ideas and thinking to revolutionary conditions. His thought can be segmented into perspectives on colonialism and imperialism, showing that dominated African peoples are denied their historical process of development under colonialism and that imperialism associates with the expansion of capitalism; revolutionary nationalism and national liberation, with an emphasis on how the armed revolutionary struggle emanates from culture based on history and the successes of resistance and struggle; class and class struggle, in an analysis aware of contradictions everywhere in society, involving races, religions, ethnic groups, and social classes; and a rudimentary theory of state and development.

Cabral showed how a vanguard party in the revolutionary period can govern and provide for basic human needs in liberated areas. His original thinking and independent Marxist analysis demonstrated that success was dependent not on old formulas and revolutionary situations but on unique, particular conditions. Finally, his personal commitment and example as organizer and unifier served to influence and motivate the mass revolutionary movement in achieving independence.

See also *Guinea-Bissau Independence Revolt (1962–1974); Portuguese Revolution (1974).*

RONALD H. CHILCOTE

BIBLIOGRAPHY

Cabral, Amílcar. *Unity and Struggle: Speeches and Writings.* Translated by Michael Wolfers. New York: Monthly Review Press; and London: Heinemann, 1979.

Chabal, Patrick. *Amílcar Cabral: Revolutionary Leadership and People's War.* African Studies Series, no. 37. Cambridge: Cambridge University Press, 1983.

Chilcote, Ronald H. *Amílcar Cabral's Revolutionary Theory and Practice: A Practical Guide.* Boulder, Colo.: Lynne Rienner Publishers, 1991.

Davidson, Basil. *The Liberation of Guiné: Aspects of an African Revolution.* Baltimore, Md.: Penguin Books, 1969.

Rudebeck, Lars. *Guinea-Bissau: A Study of Political Mobilization.* Uppsala: Scandinavian Institute of African Studies, 1974.

CAMBODIAN KHMER ROUGE REVOLUTION (1967–1979)

The Khmer Rouge ("Red Khmer") leaders—Pol Pot, Nuon Chea, Ieng Sary, Son Sen, Chhit Choeun (alias Mok), and Khieu Samphan—ruled Cambodia from 1975 to 1979 in the name of the Communist Party of Kampuchea (CPK). These six leaders of the party "center," who took over the Standing Committee of the CPK Central Committee in the 1960s during its underground phase, continued to control it throughout the party's period in power. They made the major decisions that led to the genocide of 1.7 million people.

Pot was born Saloth Sar in Kompong Thom Province in 1928, into a family with royal connections. His sister and cousin were wives of the Khmer (Cambodian) king, and his brother Suong made a career in the Khmer royal palace. Pol joined him in 1934, at the age of six. A year in a royal monastery was followed by six in an elite Catholic school. The palace compound was closeted, and the old king a French puppet. Outside the compound's walls, the capital Phnom Penh was the home mostly of ethnic Chinese shopkeepers and Vietnamese workers. Cambodians were overwhelmingly rural, and few Cambodian childhoods were as removed as Pot's from the country's vernacular culture.

In 1945 Buddhist monks led Khmer nationalists in common cause with Vietnamese communists, demanding independence from France. Three years later, Pot went to study radioelectricity in Paris. Traveling through Saigon, he felt ill-at-ease in bustling Vietnam, like a "dark monkey from the mountains." This racialist perspective stayed with him and set him apart from the rest of the developing Khmer communist movement.

Not long after his arrival in Paris in 1948, Pot joined the French Communist Party, an organization then in its Stalinist heyday. He kept company with Khieu Ponnary, the first Khmer woman to pass the Baccalaureat. They and other Paris students, including Ieng Sary, Son Sen, and Khieu Samphan, formed a Khmer Marxist circle. But Pot had disagreements with Hou Yuon, later a popular Marxist intellectual in Cambodia, who was to become one of the revolution's first victims upon winning power. Pot also stood out in his choice of an ethnic nom de plume: the "Original Cambodian." Others preferred less racialist, modernist code names like "Free Khmer" or "Khmer Worker." Most members of the Khmer Marxist circle kept their distance from Vietnamese students—nationalist or communist.

After failing his course three times, Pot arrived home in 1953. The country was in turmoil. King Sihanouk had declared martial law, and Cambodia's independence movement was becoming radicalized by French colonial force. With his brother Chhay, Pol Pot joined the Cambodian and Vietnamese communists. Vietnamese cadres began teaching Pot to work with the masses. To him, learning from the Vietnamese was a patronizing slight, like his failure to rise quickly to leadership despite his overseas experience. He decided that Khmers should do everything on their own.

In Pot's view, Cambodia did not need to learn or import anything from its neighbors. Rather, it would recover its pre-Buddhist glory by rebuilding the powerful economy of the medieval Angkor kingdom and regain ancient lost territory from Vietnam and Thailand. Pot treasured his race, not its individual members. National impurities included the foreign-educated (with the exception of his Paris group) and "hereditary enemies"—especially Vietnamese but also other ethnic minorities. To return Cambodians to their imagined origins, Pot needed war and secrecy—the latter he considered the basis of the revolution.

After French and Vietnamese forces left Cambodia in 1954, Pot rose in the Cambodian communist ranks. In 1962, after the disappearance of the Workers' Party leader, Pot took over the organization, renaming it the Communist Party of Kampuchea (CPK) in 1966. Using the code-name "Pol," he consolidated his control during eight years of guerrilla warfare, beginning with the 1967 Samlaut uprising in Battambang Province.

In 1969, embroiled in its war in Vietnam, the United States began a secret B-52 bombardment of Cambodia *(see map, p. 64)*. A year later, Sihanouk was overthrown by the U.S.-backed general Lon Nol. The Vietnam War spilled across

Cambodian children at the "killing fields" memorial, located on the outskirts of Phnom Penh.

the border, and a new war tore Cambodia apart. American planes killed 100,000 Khmer peasants. In 1973 the Central Intelligence Agency reported that Khmer Rouge recruiters were effectively using damage caused by B-52 strikes as the main theme of their propaganda.

The CPK army defeated the Lon Nol regime on April 17, 1975, and began a forced evacuation of the two million inhabitants of Phnom Penh. Yuon, who opposed the evacuation, was shot. Sary and Sen became deputy prime ministers under Pot, while Sen also took charge of the army General Staff and security for the CPK, which operated in secrecy. Samphan became head of the Khmer Rouge State, later renamed Democratic Kampuchea. Chea ran internal party affairs as deputy CPK secretary, and Mok increasingly took over the CPK's armed forces and the Khmer Rouge regional administrations.

In a 1975 victory speech, Pot claimed a victory without any foreign connection. Cambodia cut itself off from the outside world, and foreign and minority languages were banned. Rice and endangered wildlife were exported to China for weapons. Cambodia's Buddhist religion and culture were banned. Peasants were forced into unpaid collective labor. Spouses were separated, and family meals prohibited. In this prison camp state of 8 million inmates, 1.7 million were worked, starved, or beaten to death. Minority and urban groups suffered disproportionately, but half the victims came from the peasant majority.

Pot claimed to be years ahead of other Asian communist states. This claim expressed the regime's racial chauvinism, but it also disguised the influence of Stalinism and Maoism in the Khmer Rouge call for a "Super Great Leap Forward," and even of the French Revolution, which the Khmer Rouge copied when they redesigned Cambodia's month into ten-day weeks.

Pot did not conceive of Cambodia at peace. He shared the traditional Khmer elite's racism against Vietnamese and other minorities and its designs on lost territories. With the help of large-scale Chinese aid, Pot, Sen, and Mok built up the Khmer Rouge army for a new war against Vietnam. Raids on Vietnam, Thailand, and Laos began in 1977. Pot ordered his army to kill the enemy at will. On September 24, 1977, Sen's troops crossed the Vietnamese border and massacred three hundred civilians.

Cambodians who dissented or complained of the burden that war imposed on their country were labeled traitors. Purges multiplied. The CPK's secret police chief, Kaing Khek Iev, alias Deuch, and his chief interrogator, Sen's former student, Mam Nay, ran the notorious Tuol Sleng prison. The prison, known as S-21, was the nerve center of the genocide in Phnom Penh. Of sixteen thousand prisoners held there, seven survived.

Pot's wife Khieu Ponnary formally headed the Women's Association of Democratic Kampuchea. But she was rarely sighted and reportedly suffered from insanity from 1975. Meanwhile, Sen's wife Yun Yat was wiping out Buddhism, considered a reactionary religion incompatible with the revolution. Only two thousand of Cambodia's seventy thousand monks are known to have survived in 1979.

Cambodian communists in the Eastern Zone rebelled in May 1978. Pot's armies were unable to crush them quickly. Of 1.5 million easterners, at least 100,000 were exterminated. In 1979 surviving rebels succeeded Pot after the Vietnamese army drove Pot's army into Thailand.

Mass graves mark every district in the country. So far, more than two hundred "killing field" sites, with a total of 9,500 mass grave pits, have been located. There may be another 10,000 such pits.

Ben Kiernan

BIBLIOGRAPHY

Chanda, Nayan. *Brother Enemy.* New York: Macmillan, 1988.

Chandler, David P. *Brother Number One.* Boulder, Colo.: Westview Press, 1992.

Evans, Grant, and Kelvin Rowley. *Red Brotherhood at War.* Rev. ed. London: Verso, 1990.

Jackson, Karl, ed. *Cambodia 1975–1978.* Princeton, N.J.: Princeton University Press, 1989.

Kiernan, Ben. *How Pol Pot Came to Power.* London: Verso, 1985.

———. *The Pol Pot Regime.* New Haven, Conn.: Yale University Press, 1996.

Vickery, Michael. *Cambodia 1975–1982.* Boston: South End Press, 1984.

CAPITALISM

Capitalism is the system of economic exchange on open markets, based on private property and oriented toward profit. Classic Marxian theory saw capitalism as the ultimate determining force of revolution. Changes in the means of production determine changes in the relations of production, the system of property, law, and the state.

Karl Marx himself was concerned with two great revolutions—one historical and one as yet theoretical—that he regarded as marking the break between the major stages of historical development. The first was the bourgeois revolution, in which capitalism broke through the feudal relations of production; examples are the English revolutions of 1640 and 1689 and the French revolution of 1789. The English and French revolutions convinced Marx that revolutions are made by a rising social class overthrowing the previously dominant class, in these cases the rising bourgeoisie overthrowing the feudal aristocracy. The second great revolutionary transition was to be the future breakdown of capitalist society in the socialist revolution; in this case the rising social class would be the workers. Marx's conception of socialist revolution was purely theoretical, based on his assessment of the dynamics of economic boom and bust cycles, which would culminate in a breakdown of capitalism. But no socialist revolutions have ever come about through Marx's economic crises. Instead, a number of socialist revolutions in the twentieth century came about through dynamics other than the breakdown of capitalism.

Neo-Marxian scholars have taken several different paths in revising Marx's analysis. John Hobson, Vladimir Ilyich Lenin, and Rosa Luxemburg, writing around the time of the First World War, argued that mature capitalist competition was driving the leading capitalist states, such as Britain, France, Germany, and Japan, to struggle for colonies, resulting in turn in war and revolution.

Taking this line further, the American sociologist Immanuel Wallerstein and the world-system school argued that capitalism, since its origins in the late 1400s, has always developed through international and global relations of domination. Core capitalist regions exploit peripheral regions of unskilled labor and raw materials; the entire capitalist world-system goes through cycles of expansion and contraction, bringing about periodic crises on a world scale. At these moments, hegemonic power within the core shifts, as in the historical change in dominance from Spain, to the Netherlands, to England, to the United States.

World-system theory has no clear-cut theory of revolutions. Revolutions have happened from time to time in the core, periphery, and semiperiphery alike, connected in various ways with the strains of transition in the world-system. The most striking theoretical point in the model is that socialist revolution cannot be successful until it happens in the entire system and brings about socialist world government. Premature socialist enclaves like that established by the Russian revolution are inevitably drawn back into capitalist economic relations. Only when the entire globe becomes fully integrated into a single capitalist economy can we expect the final revolutionary crisis of capitalism.

Another line of revision of Marxist theory was formulated by Barrington Moore Jr., a political sociologist writing in the 1960s, who argued that the crucial dynamics of revolution were set in early capitalist agriculture, not capitalist industry. There were three main ways that agriculture became organized for profits on the market, resulting in three different political paths to the modern state. 1) Land-owning aristocrats could push the peasants off the land and themselves become agricultural capitalists; this gave aristocrats an interest in promoting capitalist democracy, as in England. (Moore interpreted the American Civil War as having the same effect since it eliminated slave plantations, which were the main structural obstacle to capitalist democracy.) 2) As landowners began to produce for the market, they could keep the peasants on the land and intensify feudal labor controls in order to increase production; Moore theorized this was the route to fascism, as in eastern Europe and Japan. 3) The aristocratic landowners could become absentee landlords, living in the city and collecting rents from their peasants, who produced directly for the market themselves.

The third route had the greatest potential for revolution, since the peasants were exposed to the ups and downs of market prices, while they were still obligated to pay their rents in good times and bad. The result of this third system was the peasant revolts and attacks on aristocratic property that characterized the French and Chinese revolutions. The extreme result of this third path, Moore argued, was socialist revolution. Further studies of how different kinds of agricultural capitalism have affected socialist revolutions have been made by sociologists Jeffrey Paige and Timothy Wickham-Crowley, in cases ranging from Vietnam to Latin America.

Theda Skocpol extended Moore's model of agricultural revolution and peasant revolt, identifying two other components of the two "great" structurally transformative revolutions. There must also be a state breakdown, brought about by fiscal crisis in state revenues and expenditures; Skocpol argued that the typical source of economic crisis within the state was not capitalism but military strains and expenses.

Skocpol thus began to shift the theory of revolution away from capitalist causes and toward geopolitical causes. Skocpol's other component of revolution is a split within the ruling class, between the state elites concerned with solving the budgetary crisis and the landowning aristocracy, which refuses to pay more to the government and shifts the burden to the already overburdened peasantry.

Jack Goldstone has refined and generalized the Skocpolian model of the three core dynamics of popular distress, state fiscal crisis, and intraelite conflict. In Goldstone's model, the capitalist economy makes a comeback in the form of price inflation, which exacerbates not only the state fiscal crisis but the other components of revolutionary potential. Goldstone shifts the emphasis in the causal chain from geopolitics (as stressed by Skocpol and Randall Collins) to population growth, which he identifies as the main driving force in inflation. The core of the Skocpol/Goldstone model, with its three components of state breakdown, has been widely influential; revolutions are no longer explained by capitalist crisis from below but by breakdown from above.

Although capitalism has been largely discounted as the cause of revolution, it has been resurrected among revolution's consequences. Skocpol argues that great revolutions such as the French Revolution cleared away structural obstacles and unleashed capitalist development. Postrevolutionary economic development can also occur in the form of socialist programs for rapid—even forced—growth, such as took place after the Russian and Chinese revolutions. The anticommunist revolutions of 1989–1991 in the Soviet bloc also unleashed economic transformations, restoring capitalism. But it is too early to tell if the result will be the postrevolutionary spurt of economic growth suggested by Skocpol's model. In general, the theory of the aftermath of revolutions has not been as well developed, and it remains on the agenda for current scholarship.

See also *Luxemburg, Rosa; Marx, Karl, and Friedrich Engels.*

RANDALL COLLINS

BIBLIOGRAPHY

Chase-Dunn, Christopher. *Global Formation. Structures of the World-Economy.* Oxford: Blackwell, 1989.

Goldstone, Jack A. *Revolution and Rebellion in the Early Modern World.* Berkeley: University of California Press, 1991.

Kolakowski, Leszek. *Main Currents of Marxism.* Oxford: Oxford University Press, 1978.

Moore, Barrington, Jr. *Social Origins of Dictatorship and Democracy. Lord and Peasant in the Making of the Modern World.* Boston: Beacon Press, 1966.

Paige, Jeffrey M. *Agrarian Revolution. Social Movements and Export Agriculture in the Underdeveloped World.* New York: Free Press, 1975.

Skocpol, Theda. *States and Social Revolutions.* Cambridge: Cambridge University Press, 1979.

Wickham-Crowley, Timothy. *Guerillas and Revolution in Latin America.* Princeton, N.J.: Princeton University Press, 1992.

CASTRO, FIDEL

Born to a prosperous family in rural eastern Cuba and educated at the country's best Jesuit schools, Fidel Castro (1926–) obtained a law degree from the University of Havana. On March 10, 1952, Fulgencio Batista and some military associates overthrew Cuba's constitutional government. Castro joined the opposition, and on July 26, 1953, he led an unsuccessful attack on the Cuban army's Moncada barracks and soon founded the anti-Batista Twenty-sixth of July Movement. He served two years in prison, went into exile, and, in December 1956, led an expedition from Mexico that landed in eastern Cuba. A guerrilla insurgency followed in the Sierra Maestra Mountains. Batista's ineptly led forces retreated and eventually disintegrated. On December 31, 1958, Batista fled to the Dominican Republic.

Castro emerged from the guerrilla war a hero to many Cubans. A gifted public speaker, he made extensive and nearly continuous use of radio and television to build extraordinary public support. He roamed the country, consolidating his popularity. Between 1959 and 1961 Castro's policies transformed Cuba. His government expropriated all the means of production (except some peasant agricultural plots) and turned all the private schools, hospitals, and charitable entities into state agencies as well. Castro broke with the United States and re-created and mobilized Cuban nationalism, bringing it to a fever pitch. In later years he sought to reduce the role of market forces and the autonomy of civil society. He urged citizens to work for the sake of the nation, not for the rewards of "vile money." In 1961 Castro launched

Fidel Castro

a massive literacy campaign, followed by years of sustained and successful efforts to raise the population's educational level. He instituted free and universal health care, which lengthened life expectancy. Also in 1961, for the first time in his life, Castro proclaimed himself a communist. The Communist Party is the only party legally authorized to operate in Cuba.

During the 1960s Castro ordered the execution of thousands of his opponents and jailed not fewer than tens of thousands of people, many merely for the "crime" of expressing opposition. Relative to its population, Cuba had a rate of political imprisonment in the 1960s among Latin America's highest. More than one million Cubans emigrated between 1959 and 1980.

A U.S.-sponsored brigade of Cuban exiles landed at Cuba's Bay of Pigs in April 1961 but was defeated within three days. The following year Castro secretly requested the deployment of Soviet missiles and nuclear warheads to Cuba as a deterrent to an expected U.S. invasion. In October 1962 he recommended a Soviet first-use of nuclear weapons to respond to a U.S. conventional attack on Cuba, and he subsequently obstructed the missile crisis settlement that the United States and the Soviet Union had negotiated. The Soviet-Cuban alliance strengthened in the 1970s and continued until the collapse of the Soviet Union in 1991. Particularly in the 1970s and 1980s, Cuba received vast economic subsidies from the Soviet Union.

From the 1960s to the early 1990s Castro supported insurgencies in several dozen Latin American and African countries, with few successes. In the 1970s and 1980s, however, he won three international wars. In 1975 he dispatched 36,000 troops to Angola to fight off a South African invasion. In 1977 he sent more than 10,000 troops to defend Ethiopia from a Somali invasion. And in 1987 he raised the number of Cuban troops in Angola to about 50,000 to combat a new South African invasion.

In the 1990s, after the loss of Soviet subsidies, Cuba's economy plunged. Castro enacted some limited market reforms, especially welcoming foreign investment, but sought to prevent extensive political change. Defiant still in his relations with the United States, Castro is one of very few extant communist leaders.

See also *Cuban Revolution (1956–1970); Guevara, Ernesto "Che."*

JORGE I. DOMÍNGUEZ

BIBLIOGRAPHY

Lockwood, Lee. *Castro's Cuba, Cuba's Fidel.* Rev. ed. Boulder, Colo.: Westview, 1990.

Quirk, Robert. *Fidel Castro.* New York: Norton, 1993.

Szulc, Tad. *Fidel Castro: A Critical Portrait.* New York: Morrow, 1986.

CHIANG KAI-SHEK

Chiang Kai-shek (1887–1975) was China's paramount leader from 1927 until 1949. He rose to power in Sun Yat-sen's Kuomintang (Nationalist) movement and was one of the "Big Four" Allied leaders in World War II.

Chiang Kai-shek began training for a military career in China and continued his training in Japan from 1908 until 1911. He joined Sun Yat-sen's movement while in Japan and returned to China to serve in Shanghai during the 1911 revolution. When Sun faced defeat at the hands of the Beijing militarists, Chiang supported his attempts to establish a new revolutionary base in the south.

The turning point in Chiang's career came when Sun established a Kuomintang army with assistance from the Soviet Union. In 1924 Sun appointed Chiang to head the new Whampoa Military Academy near Guangzhou (Canton), in south China. As leader of the academy, Chiang supervised a new generation of officers, who formed the core of the Kuomintang military and the foundation of Chiang's later military and political power. Temporarily allied with the Soviet Union and the Chinese Communists, the Kuomintang prepared to launch a Northern Expedition to unite China.

When Sun Yat-sen died suddenly in 1925, Chiang gained control of the Kuomintang movement. In a deft series of moves he weakened opponents on the right and left. As the Northern Expedition began, Chiang became deeply suspicious of the Communists. In April 1927 Chiang hit the Communists swiftly with a "white terror" in which thousands were executed, gutting their organization and leading to a long civil war. Chiang established his capital at the central city of Nanjing in 1928 and solidified his political claims by marrying the sister of Sun Yat-sen's widow.

In alliance with regional militarists nominally loyal to the Kuomintang, Chiang then completed the Northern Expedition in 1928. Over the next decade Chiang gradually weakened these militarists, but his other rivals, the Communists, proved elusive as they moved into rural base areas. A third force, Japanese imperialism, ultimately proved to be the gravest threat to the Nanjing government. In September 1931 Japanese military forces seized northeast China, creating a puppet state of Manchukuo. Japan gradually encroached on north China over the next several years, forcing a showdown at the Marco Polo Bridge outside Beijing (then known as Beiping) in July 1937.

The war with Japan was a disaster for Chiang. His best forces were destroyed in the battle for the Shanghai area.

Chiang Kai-shek

After retreating to the interior city of Chongqing (Chungking) in 1938, Chiang's position deteriorated under conditions of hyperinflation, corruption, and supply shortages. The Communists, meanwhile, developed a powerful political and military organization in north China.

Ironically, Chiang's domestic weakness coincided with his greatest international prestige. When he met with Franklin Roosevelt and Winston Churchill during the war, he was acknowledged as one of the key leaders of the Allied powers. After World War II ended in August 1945, Chiang was defeated by the Chinese Communists in a bloody civil war. Retreating to Taiwan, he set up a rival Chinese government that received American and United Nations' recognition as the government of China until the 1970s. After his death in 1975, Chiang Kai-shek was succeeded as president of the Republic of China on Taiwan by his son, Chiang Ching-kuo.

See also *Chinese Nationalist Revolution (1919–1927); Sun Yat-sen.*

Parks M. Coble

BIBLIOGRAPHY

Ch'en Chieh-ju. *Chiang Kai-shek's Secret Past: The Memoir of His Second Wife.* Edited by Lloyd E. Eastman. Boulder, Colo.: Westview Press, 1993.

Coble, Parks M. *Facing Japan: Chinese Politics and Japanese Imperialism, 1931–1937.* Cambridge, Mass.: Harvard East Asian Monographs, 1991.

Crozier, Brian. *The Man Who Lost China.* New York: Scribner, 1976.

Eastman, Lloyd E. *The Abortive Revolution: China under Nationalist Rule, 1927–1937.* Cambridge: Harvard University Press, 1974.

Loh, Pinchon P. Y. *The Early Chiang Kai-shek: A Study of His Personality and Politics, 1887–1924.* New York: Columbia University Press, 1971.

CHILEAN SOCIALIST MOVEMENT AND COUNTERREVOLUTION (1970–1978)

In the 1960s and early 1970s the Chilean Socialist Party heightened its revolutionary stance. After the election of party member Salvador Allende to the Chilean presidency in September 1970, the Socialists played a major role in the polarization of Chilean politics, which led to the overthrow of Chilean democracy by a military coup on September 11, 1973.

Since its founding in 1933 by Marmaduque Grove, a former military man, the Chilean Socialist Party has competed for the votes of the left with the Communist Party of Chile, drawing support from workers, intellectuals, and middle-class professionals. Socialist Party members have ranged from social democrats and populists to anti-imperialists and various kinds of Marxists. In 1938 the party moderated the Marxist elements in its program in order to join the Radical Party in the Chilean version of the Popular Front. Following a disappointing experience with the compromises of the Popular Front government, the Socialists split ideologically and organizationally until 1956, when they joined with the Communists in the Front for Popular Action (FRAP). In the 1958 presidential elections the FRAP candidate, Salvador Allende, came close to winning, losing to the conservative candidate, Jorge Alessandri, by only 33,000 votes.

The Communists, outlawed between 1948 and 1956, proclaimed their adherence to the "peaceful way to socialism," but the Socialists, particularly after the triumph of Fidel Castro's revolution in Cuba in 1959, were less enthusiastic about the electoral route to power. After Allende was defeated in the 1964 presidential election by the Christian Democratic candidate, Eduardo Frei, who also had the support of the right, the party began to assume a more revolutionary stance, differing publicly from the Communists on the *via pacifica.* In their 1967 Congress the Socialists described revolutionary violence as "inevitable and necessary" and political action as a prelude to armed struggle. In the late 1960s the Socialists organized a paramilitary group and sent party members to Bolivia to support the failed revolutionary efforts of Argentinian Ernesto "Che" Guevara, an activist in leftist guerrilla movements in Latin America. Allende developed a close friendship with Fidel Castro and was elected president of the Latin American Solidarity Organization, a Cuban-organized support group for the promotion of hemispheric revolution. Yet at the same time he served as a member, and for a time as president, of the

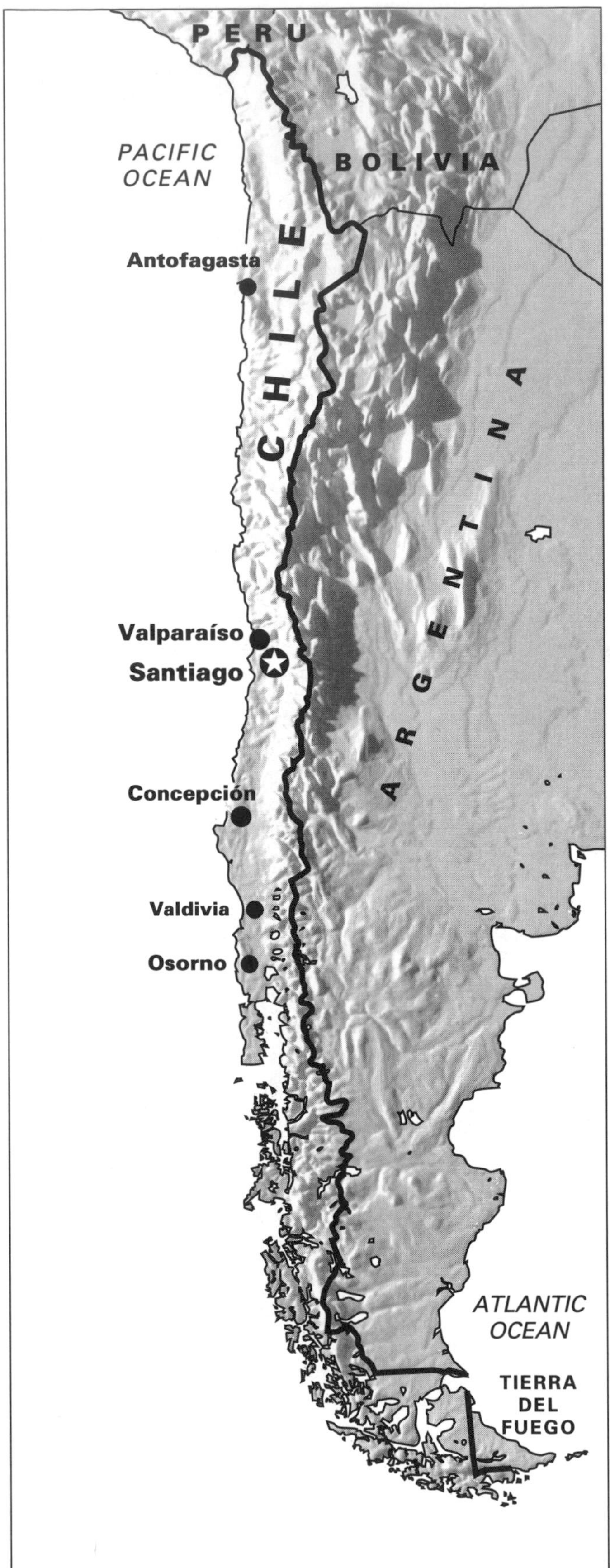

Chilean senate, and the Socialist Party continued to run in Chilean elections, receiving 10–12 percent of the vote.

THE ALLENDE PRESIDENCY (1970–1973)

Despite his admiration for Castro, Allende was more a pragmatic politician than a revolutionary. He was nominated as the Socialist Party candidate for the 1970 presidential election by only one vote and would not have been the candidate of the leftist Popular Unity coalition except for the support of the Communists. He won the election by a 1.3 percent plurality with 36.1 percent of the vote in a three-way race. The congressional runoff that followed was preceded by a failed military conspiracy supported by the U.S. Central Intelligence Agency (CIA) as well as by the assassination of the army commander in chief by rightists who hoped to provoke a coup.

In his inaugural address Allende alluded to the possibility of a peaceful transition to socialism and promised that his government would respect democracy, pluralism, and freedom. Yet two months later at the Socialist Party Congress he supported the election of Carlos Altamirano, the party's most outspoken proponent of revolution, as general secretary. In addition, one-third of the new Socialist Central Committee were members of the paramilitary wing. Together with the supporters of Altamirano they constituted a clear majority of revolutionaries in the party leadership, far outnumbering the moderate Allende faction.

In the first year of Allende's administration, it seemed that the transition could indeed be peaceful. The U.S.-owned copper companies were nationalized by a large congressional majority, and wages rose without an increase in inflation. But after a month-long visit by Fidel Castro in late 1971, opinion became polarized and violence increased, sparked in part by serious production problems in industry and agriculture created by leftist takeovers of factories and farms. The discovery of a disguised shipment of arms from Cuba at the Santiago airport, the onset of food shortages and runaway inflation, and the training of paramilitary groups leading to passage of an arms control law by the opposition-controlled Congress all contributed to an atmosphere of heightened political tension. Several efforts by Allende to negotiate with the opposition broke down because of the intransigence of his own Socialist Party.

THE 1973 COUP AND THE REMAKING OF SOCIALISM

In 1973, after the government announced that a Unified National School would teach all Chilean children the principles of socialism, the generals met to protest the plan. Those who favored a coup were restrained, however, by the constitutionalism of the army commander, Gen. Carlos Prats. After Prats put down a revolt by a tank regiment in June, workers seized several hundred factories. The growth of self-governing shantytowns, seizures of rural lands led by the Movement of the Revolutionary Left (MIR) or the Socialists, and the emergence of autonomous industrial belts and paramilitary training in factories led Altamirano and others to argue for arming the populace in preparation for a coming confrontation with the bourgeois order. Insisting on "advance without compromise," Altamirano also urged enlisted men to disobey their officers in the event of a coup. In turn, the generals stepped up their raids on suspected arms caches and prepared an "anti-insurgency plan," which became the basis of the coup two months later.

In the meantime a general strike led by the truckers' union was paralyzing the Chilean economy, and, over the opposition of his party, Allende appointed a moderate Socialist, Carlos Briones, to negotiate with the opposition. But it was too late. The army generals forced Prats's resignation, and the Chamber of Deputies accused the government of systematically violating the constitution and the laws. On September 11, 1973, the Chilean armed forces seized power and bombed the presidential palace. As the soldiers entered, Allende committed suicide, using a submachine gun given to him by Fidel Castro. Altamirano went into hiding and later escaped to Cuba and then exile in Europe. The military suppressed democracy and instituted a military dictatorship, led by Gen. Augusto Pinochet. At least three thousand Chileans were killed or "disappeared."

International reactions were divided. The left saw the coup as a CIA-promoted fascist plot against an innocent social democrat, while the right hailed the military for saving Chile from Marxism. The truth, as usual, lay somewhere in between. Allende was never able to give up his infatuation with the Cuban Revolution, and his party was increasingly dominated by utopian revolutionaries opposed to any repetition of the experience of the Popular Front. A Marxist takeover, however, was never likely so long as the armed forces insisted on the observance of constitutional legality. The breakdown of legality and the increasing violence on both sides meant that, as seventeenth-century English philosopher Thomas Hobbes once observed, "When no other cards are agreed upon, clubs are trumps."

The exiled Socialist leaders split over the issue of revolution versus "bourgeois" legality. Rethinking his position, Altamirano himself led a faction beginning in 1977 (which eventually prevailed) that argued for a "renovated socialism" that abjured violence and advocated the deepening of democracy and the pursuit of social justice by peaceful means. In the 1980s the Socialists healed their divisions and joined with the Christian Democrats and other parties to form the Coalition for Democracy, which defeated Pinochet in a plebiscite in 1988. The coalition has governed Chile since 1990.

PAUL E. SIGMUND

BIBLIOGRAPHY

Chile-America (Rome), 1974–1983 (monthly).

Drake, Paul. *Socialism and Populism in Chile, 1932–1952.* Urbana: University of Illinois Press, 1978.

Politzer, Patricia. *Altamirano.* Santiago: Ediciones Melquiades, 1989.

Pollack, Benny, and Hernan Rosenkranz. *Revolutionary Social Democracy: The Chilean Socialist Party.* London: Frances Pinter, 1986.

Sigmund, Paul E. *The Overthrow of Allende and the Politics of Chile.* Pittsburgh: University of Pittsburgh Press, 1977.

Walker, Ignacio. *Socialismo y democracia: Chile y Europa en perspectiva comparada.* Santiago: CIEPLAN/Hachette, 1990.

CHINESE BOXER UPRISING (1898–1900)

The Boxer Uprising was a popular movement of peasants in northern China who rose up to attack Chinese Christians, Western missionaries, and other foreigners. Their slogan, "Support the Qing, Exterminate the Foreigners," indicated their loyalty to the Qing, the Manchu dynasty that ruled China from 1644 to 1911. In 1900, with the support of the Qing imperial court, the Boxers besieged the foreign legations in Beijing, bringing on a foreign military expedition which brutally suppressed the uprising. The shock of this defeat and the harsh terms of the Boxer Protocol that ended the incident spurred the Qing to embark on fundamental educational, military, economic, and constitutional reforms during the final decade of its rule.

In the late 1890s, the Boxers United in Righteousness emerged from a series of anti-Christian incidents led by martial arts groups in the villages of Shandong Province on the Yellow River plain. As part of their martial arts rituals, these Boxers practiced a form of spirit possession believed to make them invulnerable. The gods that possessed the young men known as Boxers were all characters from popular operas and storytellers' performances.

Christian missionaries and converts were a new and disruptive presence in the Chinese countryside. Chinese Catholics, in particular, often relied on the intervention of foreign missionaries and their diplomatic protectors to gain advantage in disputes with other villagers. As imperialist aggression against China increased in the 1890s, many Christians took advantage of these assertions of Western power to become even more aggressive, and Chinese resentment grew. The Boxers emerged as a force to rid China of the alien menace.

Incidents between Boxers and Christians escalated in 1899, and sympathetic officials sought to enroll Boxers in local militia forces. Encouraged by mixed signals from the Qing court, the Boxers spread their practices from village to village in the direction of Beijing. The movement lacked an organized leadership, relying on local martial arts masters to transmit its invulnerability rituals and antiforeign message. In the spring and summer of 1900 a prolonged drought left north China peasants desperate, anxious, and inclined to blame the weather on Heaven's anger at Christian irreverence. As a result, the number of Boxers and anti-Christian incidents increased rapidly.

By June 1900, as Boxers streamed into the capital of Beijing, the foreign legations called for protection. Western troops advancing on the capital threatened the Qing court, which declared war and openly supported the Boxers. The Boxers, with this official support, besieged the foreign legations and a Catholic cathedral to which foreigners and Chinese Christians had fled.

Soon a large military force representing eight foreign powers advanced on the capital, relieving the siege on August 14, 1900. The Qing court fled to the interior, then joined the foreigners in suppressing the uprising. Provincial officials in central and southern China opposed the Boxers throughout, defying the Qing court and cooperating with foreign powers to prevent antiforeign incidents.

On September 7, 1901, the Boxer Protocol was signed to end the incident. China was forced to pay an indemnity of $330 million to the foreign powers over a period of thirty years. The defeat and punishment stunned the Qing empire, which immediately embarked on major modernizing reforms.

See also *Chinese Republican Revolution (1911); Chinese Sectarian and Secret Society Revolts (1644-).*

Joseph W. Esherick

BIBLIOGRAPHY

Cohen, Paul A. *History in Three Keys: The Boxers as Event, Experience, and Myth.* New York: Columbia University Press, 1997.

Esherick, Joseph W. *The Origins of the Boxer Uprising.* Berkeley: University of California Press, 1987.

Tan, Chester C. *The Boxer Catastrophe.* New York: W.W. Norton, 1971.

CHINESE COMMUNIST REVOLUTION (1921–1949)

The Chinese Communist Revolution was the extended process of political and social mobilization that took place in a series of interconnected stages, under the general direction of the Chinese Communist Party (CCP), roughly between the time of the party's founding in 1921 and the establishment of the People's Republic of China in 1949. Along with its counterparts in France and Russia, the Chinese revolution is generally considered one of the world's "great revolutions." Even among these classic upheavals, the Chinese case is unprecedented in length, number of people directly affected, and extent of peasant involvement. For some, in fact, the Chinese revolution seems so long, vast, and complex that it is best thought of as a collective term encompassing a series of sometimes overlapping, loosely linked struggles, including the Republican and Nationalist movements, each of which itself may be labeled a revolution.

Regardless of preferences in terminology or periodization, however, virtually all agree that at the heart of China's twentieth century revolutionary experience lies the lengthy and complex political and social mobilization that brought the CCP into power. From its origins in 1921 as a tiny group of young intellectuals, the party expanded by 1949 into an organization of several million members—many of them workers and peasants. Even more impressive was the accompanying growth in the number of nonmembers mobilized to support the party, as soldiers, political activists, and members of mass organizations. This dramatic expansion in adherents and supporters was neither steady nor inevitable; it occurred in a series of waves or stages, a number of which were punctuated by near-fatal setbacks.

EARLY STAGES OF THE REVOLUTION

Though the Communist-led revolution in China is often considered primarily a rural struggle, it began among young urban intellectuals. One of the most important forces encouraging their mobilization was the impact of an intrusive Western presence. Angry at concessions forced from China by Western powers, nationalists began to urge formation of a strong government that could protect China's interests. At the same time, the contrast between China's inherited cultural traditions and those of an attractively "modern" West led many critically to reexamine China's heritage and to begin to explore imported methods of thinking and acting.

Around the turn of the twentieth century, frustrated

nationalists began to use informal study societies and a new system of Western-style schools as venues for political change. After the end of China's last imperial dynasty in 1911, schools and study societies remained focal points for intensified intellectual and political ferment, as political and social philosophies drawn from the West spread and debate continued over how to make China a strong, modern country. Much of this activity was infused by nationalism and energized by the continuing weakness of China's postimperial warlord governments. By 1919–1920, many action-oriented young intellectuals had become convinced that China's problems could best be solved by implementing some sort of radical political ideology.

The central role Marxism accorded to the urban working class—which was then practically nonexistent in China—made Marxism initially much less attractive than anarchism, a doctrine whose dislike of government structure and emphasis on small group projects meshed well with China's existing elite organizations and activities. But anarchist groups were so decentralized and disinclined to cooperate that radicals eventually sought other approaches.

By 1920–1921 some intellectuals turned to Marxist-Leninist organization and, to a lesser extent, ideology, encouraged by developments that made these ideas now seem more applicable to China. The Russian Revolution of 1917 showed that revolution could occur in a relatively backward, rural country; Lenin's thinking on imperialism helped explain how revolution in China might be understood in Marxist terms; and the dispatch to China of representatives from the Third Communist International (Comintern), an organization established in 1919 to help spread revolution around the world, provided critical help in actual party formation.

In mid-1921 a cluster of urban study societies that had become loosely affiliated through personal ties and Comintern coordination formally established the Chinese Communist Party. Early members were attracted primarily by the party's appeal as an organizational device for political action, as Marxist ideology was still only vaguely understood. Most joined in preorganized groups (for example, entire study societies) whose thinking was still rather eclectic, and it took some time and membership turnover before the party became firmly Marxist. Similarly, for several years the party's Central Committee exerted only limited authority over its supposedly subordinate branches in different cities, which retained substantial power to set policy, interpret ideology, and conduct political activity. Only gradually did "democratic centralism" and other aspects of party discipline become embedded in the party's attitudes and practices. Finally, the CCP remained for several years a small group of a few hundred intellectuals. Not until 1925, after the May Thirtieth Movement, did party membership grow rapidly.

By then the CCP, under Comintern pressure, had reluctantly entered into an alliance (the "United Front") with the Nationalist Party (the Kuomintang), headed by the nationalist leader Sun Yat-sen. Between 1924, when the alliance took practical effect, and 1927, when it violently collapsed, both parties fought to establish a strong unified government that could defend China and implement needed social and economic reforms.

During this period, the CCP remained predominantly urban-oriented, because cities housed the working class upon which Marxist theory focused, nurtured intellectual and political ferment that had energized the early revolutionary movement, and contained economic and other resources that made them vital prizes for all groups seeking power. Nevertheless, it was also during this period that the party began to build a rural presence. Though the CCP got its start in cities, its membership included many people of rural origin who joined during their urban sojourns for work or study. After returning to the countryside, they recruited members through study societies and schools, then used familiar forms of factional struggle against rural strongmen to carve out local political space for themselves. Later, as United Front mass movements developed, these nascent rural party organs helped form the numerous peasant associations that proliferated in central and southern China in 1926–1927.

This developing rural presence became vital to the party's survival when the United Front alliance collapsed in mid-1927, accompanied by a violent purge of leftists, known as the "white terror," that hit urban areas particularly hard. Though the countryside was also affected, many rural cadres took advantage of personal ties and a generally weak government presence to escape unscathed. They, along with a few bands of mobilized peasants and small military units under radical commanders, became key elements in the painful but necessary shift in the party's center of gravity from the cities in which it originated to the countryside in which it eventually prospered.

THE GROWTH OF RURAL BASES

Despite the magnitude of the CCP's 1927 defeat, between then and 1930 a dozen or more substantial regions of Communist political and military control grew up in central and southern China. By 1931 these "base areas" (often informally called "soviets" after the Russian-inspired forms of government established in them) covered much of several provinces, and contained somewhere between five and ten million inhabitants.

By late 1927 surviving rural cadres had begun to recruit new followings by allying with armed brotherhoods or bandits and simultaneously mobilizing peasants with appeals for socioeconomic reform. Though most initial uprisings quickly failed, segments of the mobilized forces, often with armed gangs at their core, remained active in rural hinterlands, particularly rugged areas straddling administrative boundaries. New recruits obtained from these poverty-stricken areas strengthened the emerging guerrilla units, which also obtained a steady flow of arms from defeated militia units and army deserters. Gradually, these small regions coalesced into nascent base areas. As they grew in size and security, administrative centralization increased, and it also became possible to implement full-scale land redistribution, local elections, and other reforms. Eventually, at least some bases developed the full range of functions commonly found in modern governments, including elaborate bureaucracies, financial institutions, and judicial systems.

Base area growth was facilitated by lengthy and distracting conflicts between Nationalist government leader Chiang Kai-shek and his various rivals, and more importantly by the emergence of the scattered, semi-independent military units collectively known as the Red Army. Though most of these units (also called "armies") normally operated within well-defined regions, supply limitations and the mobile tactics needed to survive against larger enemy forces kept them in almost constant motion. As they moved, they provided guerrillas and cadres with weapons, training, news, combat aid, and other forms of support, while also linking separate areas of revolutionary activity. At the same time, the armies' strong motivation, determined leadership, and skill in mobile warfare enabled them to protect the emerging bases from the mediocre troops initially arrayed against them.

Despite its dramatic growth, however, the revolutionary movement found itself in severe crisis by late 1930. Within the bases, intensification and consolidation of the revolution led to tensions: some erstwhile supporters objected when their own property was seized; cadres and guerrilla commanders who had built local bases felt their independence and power threatened by centralization efforts; and conservative peasants disliked reforms that provided greater equality to women. The CCP itself was divided by conflicts over strategy and policy. Disputes developed over the proper relationship between military and political organs, the appropriate degree of centralization within the revolutionary movement, and the implementation of reforms such as land redistribution. The most persistent disagreements, however, involved the strategic role and proper defense of the bases. Many (including most Shanghai-based national leaders) thought rural bases should be temporary staging areas for military attacks on major cities, several of which were staged—with spectacularly unsuccessful results—in mid-1930. Others, including future party leader Mao Zedong, saw bases as long-term incubators of revolutionary institutions, methodologies, and practitioners. Mao and some allies preferred to defend the bases by luring enemy units deep within them, where the Red Army could best employ its superior mobility and terrain knowledge. Opponents argued that such tactics led to excessive damage from plundering enemy armies, destroyed security needed for reforms such as land redistribution, and undermined CCP claims to have built a viable alternative government.

These debates were given added urgency by a series of increasingly massive and determined military campaigns that the national government began against the Communist bases at the end of 1930. The first four campaigns were either defeated by the Red Army or broken off due to military tensions elsewhere in China. In 1933, however, a fifth and much more dangerous campaign began. It featured full-scale application of new tactics, in which government units advanced slowly, in coordinated fashion, along a common front, building well-garrisoned fortifications as they went.

These military pressures and the accumulating conflicts within the revolutionary movement gave impetus to waves of intense internal purges—of a scale and impact resembling the Terror in the French Revolution—which erupted in bases throughout China between 1930 and 1934. Known generically as "campaigns to suppress counterrevolutionaries," these purges varied enough in their timing and particulars to suggest that they were manifestations of a widespread evolutionary crisis within the movement rather than a coordinated initiative by CCP leaders. Nevertheless, many party leaders actively participated in the campaigns, and some, including Mao Zedong, gained handsomely from them through the removal of rivals and opponents.

If Mao gained from the purges, however, he suffered from the authority and programs of new party leaders known as the "Returned Students" or the "Twenty-Eight Bolsheviks" (because they met while studying in the Soviet Union). After taking control of the party in early 1931, they launched effective efforts to remove opponents and unify policies, structures, and activities of the isolated, disparate base areas. Mao, who had risen to dominate the largest base, the Central Base Area in Jiangxi Province, was stripped of all military and much political authority in late 1932 and lost further influence after top party leaders relocated from Shanghai to the Central Base Area in early 1933.

As party leaders fought, Nationalist troops continued their fifth encirclement campaign. With most other bases eliminated or reduced, attention focused on the Central

Reprinted by permission of the publisher from *China: A New History* by John Fairbank, Cambridge, Mass.: Harvard University Press, Copyright © 1992 by the President and Fellows of Harvard College. Original map by R. Forget. Alex Tait/EquatorGraphics, Inc.

Base. The enemy's new tactics negated Red Army mobility, and without heavy weapons the Red Army could not oust government troops from their fortifications. After a decisive loss opened the way into the heart of the Jiangxi base, CCP leaders decided to leave. In mid-October 1934, a force of 70,000–80,000 broke out, leaving behind the area's remaining population, along with thousands of guerrillas and local cadres. Within a year or two, most combatants left behind would be dead, with the remnant living a harried, hunted existence.

The fate of those who embarked on the famous retreat known as the Long March was often similar. In constant combat with warlord armies and pursuing government troops, the Long Marchers struggled across thousands of miles of the country's harshest terrain before reaching a small base area in North China's Shaanxi Province in October 1935. By that point, only 10–20 percent of the original force remained. Amid the defeat and hardship, Mao sustained a personal victory and rose a step toward leadership of the CCP. During the journey, at the Zunyi Conference held in Guizhou Province in January 1935, he successfully blamed Returned Student leaders for the recent defeats and resumed a military decision-making role.

Despite the CCP's catastrophic defeat, the era of rural base-building (sometimes called the "Jiangxi Soviet" period after the location of several prominent bases) gave the Communists valuable experience in the complexities of managing a sustained rural revolutionary movement. This hard-won experience in such key areas as mobile warfare, land redistribution, and mass mobilization techniques was to prove invaluable to the party during the next stage of its development.

THE ANTI-JAPANESE WAR PERIOD

In 1937, after years of deepening tensions, China and Japan went to war. The eight-year Sino-Japanese struggle that ensued proved critical for the CCP's revolutionary aspirations. In the short run, the war postponed further combat between the Communists and Nationalists just when the CCP faced total defeat. In the long run, it provided the party with time to digest its past experience and opportunity to build on that experience, in a context where its further political and military expansion could merge with the need to defeat a foreign aggressor.

After Japan occupied much of eastern China and the Nationalist government withdrew deep into the interior, the CCP and the government negotiated an agreement (called the Second United Front) to engage in some cooperative activity during the war. As part of this agreement, Red Army units accepted Nationalist military designations (such as the famous Eighth Route Army) but remained under Communist operational control. Initially with Nationalist consent, the CCP also formed bases in the areas it controlled. The most famous of these, the Shaanxi-Gansu-Ningxia (Shaan-Gan-Ning) Border Region, centered on the town of Yan'an in northern Shaanxi. Eventually, eighteen or more such bases developed during the war. Except for Shaan-Gan-Ning, all were in regions where Japanese troops controlled major towns and communication lines. It was in the numerous scattered interstices between such areas of enemy control that Communist military forces and wartime political institutions developed.

Fierce fighting occurred in these bases, much of it involving vicious cycles of attack–reprisal–counterattack in which civilians as well as soldiers suffered greatly. Eventually, a costly stalemate developed. Japanese troops continued to control major towns and communications lines, crushed overly ambitious Red Army attacks, and made civilian support of local guerrillas very costly through their aptly named "Kill All, Burn All, Loot All" reprisal policy. For their part, Communist forces maintained and even increased their forces, tied down numerous Japanese troops, and used the struggle to enhance their stature as resistors to foreign aggression. United Front constraints and the need for broad wartime support led the CCP to implement moderate measures—such as including nonparty members in border region governments, and advocating rent reduction instead of more radical land redistribution—that generally encouraged even wealthier base area inhabitants to support the war effort.

Conditions in the CCP's Yan'an headquarters and the surrounding Shaan-Gan-Ning base area, neither of which suffered serious Japanese attack, differed somewhat from those in other bases. Yan'an itself was home to most high party leaders and attracted many refugee urban intellectuals who sought to contribute to the war effort. In this relatively secure, talent-rich environment, the CCP constructed an extensive apparatus to make policy, train cadres, and develop propaganda materials. An elaborate network of schools and institutes was set up to meet the voracious demand for cadres. Many new party members were illiterate peasants without administrative experience, for example, while most refugee intellectuals were masters of sophisticated debate but unsympathetic to the disciplined collective effort that the CCP thought necessary for success. Training programs of various types, lengths, and intensities were established to deal with these diverse constituencies.

In addition, party leaders were then debating and distilling the overall policies and interpretations that would guide the CCP on its final drive for power and well beyond. The time in Yan'an gave them an opportunity to evaluate the lessons of the revolution's history to that point. Mao, then consolidating his position as the undisputed leader of the CCP after overcoming Wang Ming, another "Returned Student" rival, early in the war, was centrally involved in this process. One aspect of Mao's consolidation of power involved developing an orthodox interpretation of party history that fixed the meaning of past events and defined Mao's relationship to them in personally advantageous ways. A related aspect was the production of a body of theoretical and practical writings that would both "Sinify" and put Mao's personal stamp on the orientation and policies of the party. These circumstances led Mao to write many of his most important essays during the Yan'an period, outlining in the process what would later be termed "Maoism" or "Mao Zedong Thought."

These processes also had an unattractive side. They led, among other things, to a milder revival of the internal purges of the early 1930s and to occasionally coercive campaigns to "rectify" intraparty deficiencies and reform educated youth through rural work. Writers and other "cultural workers," whether party members or not, were urged to emphasize themes that served the revolution and war effort, rather than reflecting personal feelings and preoccupations. Those who resisted such demands sometimes paid a high price (including reassignment, ostracism, and imprisonment), particularly when they appeared to criticize party leaders such as Mao. Many conceptions formulated or refined during this period—such as the preference for intense, highly mobilized political movements, the notion of the efficacy of reeducation through labor, and the idea that art should serve politics rather than personal needs—would remain integral parts of CCP political culture long after 1949.

Both the CCP and the Nationalists considered the United Front only an expedient, and as the war progressed both sides positioned themselves for renewed postwar struggle. These maneuvers inevitably led to conflicts. One of the most significant of these was the New Fourth Army Incident (or Southern Anhui Incident), a clash that developed when Communist forces operating in the lower Yangzi River valley failed to obey government orders to leave, and in January 1941 were attacked by Nationalist military units.

Though the United Front remained nominally intact, this incident marked the practical end of efforts at tolerance or forbearance by either side. Soon afterward, the Nationalist Army imposed a tight blockade, which lasted throughout the war, on the Shaan-Gan-Ning base. As this was one of the poorest regions in all China, the blockade caused the Communists great hardship. In response, the CCP subsequently abandoned its self-imposed moderation and reimposed more radical socioeconomic policies wherever local conditions made this feasible.

THE COMMUNIST TRIUMPH

When the war ended in 1945, Communist bases were scattered all across North China. Unlike the largely inaccessible prewar base areas, many wartime bases were near densely populated agricultural regions and major cities. Thus, when renewed CCP-Nationalist fighting broke out, the CCP was well positioned to compete for valuable territories and resources. Moreover, the Red Army (by now mustering more than 900,000 experienced and increasingly well-armed soldiers), together with numerous guerrilla bands created during the war, formed a far more formidable force than that available to the CCP in the early 1930s. Finally, the party

Chinese Nationalist infantry on the move near Weishan, Shandong Province, April 27, 1948.

itself was now a far larger, more unified, and sophisticated political organization than it had been when the war began.

By contrast, war had debilitated the Nationalist government. Even after returning to prewar power centers in eastern China, the government's corruption, profiteering, and poor treatment of alleged "collaborators" with the Japanese, combined with its inability to control raging hyperinflation, seriously eroded its support. Students and liberal intellectuals, long sympathetic to left-wing appeals, were especially vocal government critics. To increasing numbers of city people, as well as the peasants to whom the CCP had appealed for years, the Communists—with their image as stalwart anti-Japanese fighters and upright, effective reformers—came to be seen as China's most appealing political alternative.

Under these circumstances, China's civil war unfolded. Although Nationalist armies remained much larger than the Red Army, they were so poorly led and unenthusiastic that CCP leaders soon managed to shift from guerrilla fighting to full-scale conventional warfare. In northern China, Communist forces cut off and forced the surrender of large Nationalist forces in Manchuria. After assimilating much captured equipment, the Communists then pushed south and defeated the bulk of the Nationalist forces in the decisive Huai-Hai campaign. Soon thereafter, the former capital of Beijing surrendered, and Chiang Kai-shek resigned as head of the Nationalist government and fled with many troops and civilians to the island of Taiwan. Though fighting continued for months thereafter, by October 1, 1949, the CCP controlled enough territory to announce the founding of the People's Republic of China.

See also *Chiang Kai-shek; Chinese May Thirtieth Movement (1925); Chinese Nationalist Revolution (1919–1927); Chinese Republican Revolution (1911); Mao Zedong; Sun Yat-sen.*

STEPHEN C. AVERILL

BIBLIOGRAPHY

Chen, Yung-fa. *Making Revolution: The Communist Movement in Eastern and Central China, 1937–1945.* Berkeley: University of California Press, 1986.

Dirlik, Arif. *The Origins of Chinese Communism.* New York: Oxford University Press, 1989.

Gilmartin, Christina. *Engendering the Chinese Revolution.* Berkeley: University of California Press, 1995.

Pepper, Suzanne. *Civil War in China: The Political Struggle, 1945–1949.* Berkeley: University of California Press, 1978.

Saich, Tony, and Hans van de Ven, eds. *New Perspectives on the Chinese Communist Revolution.* Armonk, N.Y.: M.E. Sharpe, 1995.

Schram, Stuart, and Nancy Hodes, eds. *Mao's Road to Power: Revolutionary Writings 1912–1949.* Armonk: M.E. Sharpe, 4 volumes to date: 1992, 1994, 1995, 1997.

Selden, Mark. *China in Revolution: The Yenan Way Revisited.* Armonk: M.E. Sharpe, 1995. (Revised ed. of *The Yenan Way in Revolutionary China.* Cambridge: Harvard University Press, 1974.)

van de Ven, Hans J. *From Friend to Comrade: The Founding of the Chinese Communist Party, 1920–1927.* Berkeley: University of California Press, 1991.

Van Slyke, Lyman. "The Chinese Communist Movement During the Sino-Japanese War, 1937–1945." In *The Cambridge History of China.* Volume 13, *Republican China 1912–1949, Part 2.* Edited by John K. Fairbank and Albert Feuerwerker. Cambridge: Cambridge University Press, 1986.

Wu, Odoric Y. K. *Mobilizing the Masses: Building Revolution in Henan.* Stanford: Stanford University Press, 1994.

CHINESE CULTURAL REVOLUTION (1966–1969)

The Great Proletarian Cultural Revolution was Communist Party chairman Mao Zedong's final effort to keep his Chinese Communist Revolution alive through mass mobilization. Although the Cultural Revolution is now officially said to have lasted a full decade, ending only after Mao's death in 1976, the mass mobilization phase of the movement came to an end in 1969, when the army was called in to suppress the widespread disorder.

Scholars disagree over whether the Cultural Revolution is most appropriately explained as an elite power struggle, an expression of social conflict, or a reflection of Maoist ideology. Indeed, it was all of these things and more. Best remembered for the terror that the student Red Guards inflicted on countless bureaucrats and intellectuals alike, the Cultural Revolution was also a time of political and social experimentation. Torture, suicide, and even vengeful cannibalism were accompanied by a panoply of new programs and institutions. These included the May Seventh Cadre Schools to reeducate bureaucrats, worker-peasant-soldier admissions policies to favor the lower classes in higher education, massive resettlement programs to transfer urban youths from city to countryside, Mao Zedong Thought workers' propaganda teams to enhance the status of the proletariat in political life, revolutionary committees to replace party committees, and many other attempts at social engineering.

ORIGINS

The Cultural Revolution followed in the wake of a series of mass campaigns designed to effect rapid socioeconomic, political, and cultural transformation in communist China. From the land reform efforts of the early 1950s to the Great Leap Forward campaign of the late 1950s to the Socialist Education Movement of the early 1960s, ordinary citizens had become accustomed to frequent participation in frenetic, Maoist-instigated, mass mobilization efforts.

Although the Cultural Revolution can be seen as a continuation or culmination of such earlier initiatives, it also differed from such precedents in significant respects. First, heightened anxieties over Mao Zedong's mortality contributed a special intensity to the Cultural Revolution drama. The exaggerated lengths to which Mao permitted his cult of personality to grow—symbolized by the widespread practice of wearing Mao buttons, reciting from little red books containing "Quotations from Chairman Mao," performing loyalty dances, and even engaging in quasi-religious worship ceremonies in front of portraits of the Chairman—were symptomatic of the general disquiet. Second, the Cultural Revolution invited mass criticism of the Communist Party itself. When Mao penned his "big character poster" calling on the Chinese people to "bombard the headquarters," he was inviting a popular assault on the very institutions of power that he had helped create.

That the masses responded with such alacrity to Mao's clarion call suggests the deep social tensions that had developed during seventeen years of communist rule. People had become disgruntled over university admissions, job conditions, class status, and the like, and their dissatisfaction helped fuel the widespread unrest. Given a chance to express their grievances, many did so with a vehemence that surprised even Chairman Mao.

COURSE OF STRUGGLE

Stimulated by Mao's invitation to rid the Communist Party of "persons in authority taking the capitalist road," the Cultural Revolution quickly turned into a large-scale social upheaval. The expressed goal of the movement was to prevent the Chinese revolution from succumbing to the temptations of "revisionism" that Mao believed had already sapped the Soviet Union of its revolutionary vigor.

On one level, the Cultural Revolution was a giant purge of party leaders who were accused of having fostered capitalist tendencies in China. Often the attacks were motivated by personal grudges as much as by any ideological or policy differences, but the result was nevertheless a massive removal of party leaders from top to bottom. Deng Xiaoping (then head of the Party Secretariat), Liu Shaoqi (head of state), Deng Tuo (editor of *People's Daily),* and Peng Zhen (mayor of Beijing) were among the many celebrated casualties of the campaign. In stark contrast to purges in other totalitarian states, however, Mao's Cultural Revolution relied primarily on the masses—rather than the secret police—to carry out the supreme leader's bidding.

Red Guard student groups were the key vehicle through which Mao initially advanced his campaign. Anxious to ensure "revolutionary successors" who would continue the struggle once Mao and others of his Long March generation had passed on, the Chairman looked to the younger generation for assistance. Red Guard organizations, which sprang up at high school and college campuses across the country, soon split into rival "rebel" and "conservative" factions. Opposing factions differed over the criteria for Red Guard membership and the specific targets of struggle, but all sides claimed to be acting in the name of Chairman Mao and often resorted to violence to press their claims. For a period of time, schools around the country closed down so that the Red Guards might take their campaign out of the classroom and into the streets. In addition to composing political criticisms in the form of big character posters and undertaking "new long marches" to simulate the experiences of their forebears, the Red Guards engaged in a number of less benign activities. In some places, the youngsters unleashed a veritable reign of terror, directed first against academics, artists, intellectuals, and those of "bad class background" (for example, landlords, rich peasants, capitalists, rightists, and so-called "bad elements"), and then broadened to include government and party leaders at all levels. Often the students were egged on from behind the scenes by political patrons determined to discredit their enemies or desperate to save themselves from attack.

Huge mass criticism rallies were convened at which the Red Guards subjected their victims to public humiliation, requiring them to don dunce caps and placards announcing their "capitalist" crimes, to assume the painful "jet-plane" position (with arms forced high behind their backs), and to submit to relentless verbal and physical abuse at the hands of their accusers. Private torture chambers and "cowsheds" provided less public sites for punishment. Many of the victims incurred permanent psychological and physical injuries during their incarceration; some were beaten to death, while others committed suicide.

The "revolutionary" aspects of the Cultural Revolution went beyond raw violence, however. Although Mao was inconsistent in his arguments and policies, his commitment to the continuation of class struggle even after the consolidation of socialism was indeed a revolutionary idea. At the same time that it caused untold suffering for "class enemies," the Cultural Revolution afforded an opportunity for some groups to exercise unprecedented political influence. This was the case not only for student militants, but for many members of the working class as well. When Red Guard factionalism grew too disruptive for Mao's liking, he turned to the workers—through the institution of Mao Zedong Thought Propaganda Teams—to demobilize the students and take charge of schools and workplaces. In several cities, most notably China's industrial capital of Shanghai, workers came to occupy leading political positions as a consequence of the Cultural Revolution turmoil.

In the end, however, perhaps no institution gained more from the mass mobilization phase of the Cultural Revolution than the military. Where factional strife could not be contained by unarmed workers, the People's Liberation Army was called in to do the job. By 1969, Minister of Defense Lin Biao had been named Mao's successor, and the majority of provincial-level governments were controlled by military personnel.

AFTERMATH

Although Defense Minister Lin met his demise in a mysterious plane crash in the fall of 1971, leftist policies remained firmly in place for another five years. Under the so-called Gang of Four (comprising Mao's wife and her three radical colleagues from Shanghai), "capitalist" institutions were subject to tight restriction; markets were repressed, and material incentives in the form of bonuses and profits were virtually eliminated. The Gang of Four also severely limited most forms of artistic and personal expression. Not until Chairman Mao's death in September 1976 and the arrest of the Gang of Four the following month did the repressive tide begin to shift.

The subsequent rehabilitation of Deng and other purged cadres led to a fundamental break with both the ideology and practice of the Cultural Revolution. Committed to leading China down a new post-Maoist path, Deng eliminated class labels and encouraged market incentives of all sorts. Ironically, the searing experience of the Cultural Revolution helped give rise to stunningly successful economic reforms based on repudiation of many of the key tenets of Maoism. Deng's "second revolution" has already converted China into an economic powerhouse by the close of the twentieth century. Although Deng's program did not include major political reforms, popular demands for democratization became more vociferous under his rule. Again, the connection with the Cultural Revolution experience was clear, if ironic. First in the Democracy Wall movement of 1978–1979 and then, more dramatically, during the Tiananmen Uprising of 1989, it was often former Red Guards who took the lead in pressing China's leadership for political reform.

See also *Chinese Communist Revolution (1921–1949); Deng Xiaoping; Mao Zedong.*

ELIZABETH PERRY

BIBLIOGRAPHY

Gao Yuan. *Born Red*. Stanford: Stanford University Press, 1987.

Lee, Hong Yung. *The Politics of the Chinese Cultural Revolution*. Berkeley: University of California Press, 1978.

Liang Heng and Judith Shapiro. *Son of the Revolution*. New York: Random House, 1983.

MacFarquhar, Roderick. *The Origins of the Cultural Revolution*. 3 vols. New York: Columbia University Press, 1974–1997.

Perry, Elizabeth J., and Li Xun. *Proletarian Power: Shanghai in the Cultural Revolution*. Boulder, Colo.: Westview Press, 1997.

Wang, Nianyi. *Da Dongluan de Niandai*. Zhengzhou: Henan People's Press, 1988.

Wang Shaoguang. *Failure of Charisma: The Cultural Revolution in Wuhan*. New York: Oxford University Press, 1995.

White, Lynn T., III. *Policies of Chaos: The Organizational Causes of Violence in China's Cultural Revolution*. Princeton, N.J.: Princeton University Press, 1989.

CHINESE LATE MING REVOLTS (1620–1644)

China's late Ming revolts were a series of popular rebellions that played an important role in the fall of China's Ming dynasty (1368–1644). They culminated in the storming of the capital city of Beijing in April 1644 by hundreds of thousands of rebel forces led by Li Zicheng. Following the suicide of the last Ming emperor, the rebels set up their own short-lived dynasty, which ruled China until the better-organized Manchu forces supplanted the rebels and established the Qing, China's last imperial dynasty (1644–1911).

INSTITUTIONAL DECLINE

A long-term decline in the effectiveness of Ming institutions set the stage for these rebellions, which were sparked by natural disasters. The tax-collection system established at the beginning of the Ming dynasty, for example, assumed an immobile, relatively static peasant population whose land taxes were to provide the bulk of imperial revenues. But demographic increase and regional commercialization soon produced a society of unprecedented mobility, rendering the Ming founder's original vision irrelevant by the sixteenth century. Vast numbers of would-be taxpayers went unregistered, transferring an undue share of the fiscal burden onto those unlucky few who remained on the registers. These people, in turn, often sought protection from the local wealthy by becoming tenants on their estates, which were often undertaxed or not taxed at all. The government was continually strapped for funds as a result, especially from the late sixteenth century onward. When disaster and rural unrest struck, the state had already lost much of its rural bureaucracy due to financial problems.

The military system offers another example of institutional decay. At the beginning of the dynasty, the Ming established a military colony system, wherein hereditary soldiers were to farm state-allotted land in between military training and military engagements. The aim was to furnish a steady supply of recruits at minimal cost to the state. Over time, however, the underpaid farmer-soldiers deserted in droves. The result was that the Ming state, already pressed for revenues by its inadequate fiscal system, found itself without adequate military resources as well, and unable to suppress the organized dissent that poor government often evokes. Beginning in the latter sixteenth century, a series of ineffectual, disengaged emperors added to this unhappy scenario. The lack of imperial attention to administrative duty allowed factionalism to flourish, paralyzing an already weak government as "evil eunuchs" fought "virtuous Confucians" for control of imperial policy. Not surprisingly, China's border peoples, traditional rivals of the dynastic state, were quick to take advantage of Ming weakness; the Manchus from the northeastern border regions were only the most successful of several foreign invaders over the course of the sixteenth and seventeenth centuries. The military expenses incurred to meet the threat of foreign invasion only increased the strain on the faltering institutions of Ming rule.

NORTHERN REBELLIONS

The most famous peasant rebellions, born in the thin soil of China's barren northwest, were nourished by these forces of institutional decline. Rebel armies were overwhelmingly made up of peasant recruits, motivated by poverty and natural disaster (notably the drought of 1628); much of the leadership comprised former military men who had deserted after months of unpaid service, as well as postal attendants dropped from the government payroll in a cost-cutting move. Rebel leader Li Zicheng had been dismissed from just such a post. These desperate men formed bandit gangs in the 1620s, and the state's inability to suppress such violence suggested a weakness that other bands rose to exploit. In the course of the frequent battles between Ming and bandit forces over the next fifteen years, bandit leaders honed their military skills and developed the staying power necessary to effect the transformation from bandits to rebels.

Rebel songs and slogans, circulated by the rebels in an attempt to win the populace to their side, contained numerous references to imperial decline and factionalism, while other rallying cries reflected the age-old yearning for material plenty. Yet while rebel grievances were grounded in imperial malfeasance, rebel ideology, despite its occasional egalitarian overtones, remained securely within the bounds of traditional imperial political culture. Li Zicheng chose for the name of his dynasty "Shun," meaning "obedient to Heaven's will," and one of the few changes he introduced during his brief reign as emperor was to model his government on that of the even more traditional Tang dynasty (589–907). In short, Li at best hoped to revitalize imperial institutions and to realize a genuine paternal, benevolent rule. There is little evidence of a fundamentally new and different social vision emanating from the northern rebels.

SOUTHERN UNREST

Late Ming rebellions, however, were not limited to the forces led by Li Zicheng and Zhang Xianzhong, another famous rebel leader. The riots and uprisings of the southern Yangzi River Valley, or Jiangnan, region are particularly revealing of the social forces at work during this period. Unlike the barren northwest that spawned the northern rebel movement, Jiangnan had grown wealthy and economically sophisticated from late Ming interactions with the world economy. As an economic core, Jiangnan was also much more centrally involved than northwestern China in a number of moral and religious movements that stressed equality, in general terms, as opposed to the hierarchical relationships found in traditional Confucian doctrine. Both of these aspects—commercialization and moral-religious movements—are reflected in the uprisings that shook the region from the early sixteenth century through the dynastic transition. These uprisings took three basic forms: rent resistance, urban riots, and bondservant rebellions.

Rent resistance was most common in the rural areas. As institutional decay and social unrest took root over the course of the early sixteenth century, peasants in Jiangnan and surrounding areas banded together to demand that supplementary rents and labor services, often arbitrarily imposed by landlords, be abolished in favor of strict observance of contractual terms. They also demanded rent reductions and the standardization of grain measures, that is, the physical units of measurement that determined how much grain rent the peasants paid. Although none of these demands was "revolutionary" in and of itself, the willingness of peasants to band together, as well as their attempts to call on the state to intervene in relations between landlords and tenants, suggests a new level of consciousness brought about by changing economic conditions.

Urban riots were often spearheaded by unemployed or underemployed handicraft workers, many of whom had left the farm to work in the booming textile industry. The riots were frequently sparked by the arrival of tax commissioners, often eunuchs, charged with squeezing yet more money out of the wealthy cities of the Jiangnan region. At a deeper level, however, worker dissatisfaction resulted from simultaneous overcompetition, inflation, and cyclical economic downturns of the economy. What might be the beginnings of self-conscious class identification can be seen in the workers' attempts to organize themselves by craft.

Bondservant revolts offer an even more revealing glimpse of the nature of the social changes gripping the region. In China, as elsewhere, bondservants were a hereditary servile group, even if manumission was possible and some bondservants became wealthy and powerful in the service of their masters. During the social chaos unleashed by the Ming decline (especially during the dynastic transition period), bondservants unhappy with their lot rose up against their masters, destroying all evidence of their servile status—together with much of the master's property. Some of the rhetoric employed during these bondservant revolts echoes the emancipatory tone more familiar in the history of Western uprisings.

In the final analysis, although these various forms of popular rebellion contributed to the Ming decline, it was the Manchus that finally succeeded in mounting the sustained military and organizational force necessary to put an end to the chaotic banditry that attended the fall of the Ming and to quell the diehard pro-Ming resistance movement known as the Revolt of the Three Feudatories. Moreover, the Manchus succeeded in refurbishing crumbling Ming institutions so that the late imperial regime, altered only superficially in the change of dynasties, continued to function for another two hundred years, until threats of a rather different order began to bring China's imperial model of government to an end.

DAVID OWNBY

BIBLIOGRAPHY

Parsons, James Bunyan. *The Peasant Rebellions of the Late Ming Dynasty.* Tucson: University of Arizona Press, 1970.

Tanaka Masatoshi. "Popular Uprisings, Rent Resistance, and Bondservant Rebellions in the Late Ming." In *State and Society in China: Japanese Perspectives on Ming-Qing Social and Economic History.* Edited by Linda Grove and Christian Daniels. Tokyo: University of Tokyo Press, 1984.

Tong, James W. *Disorder Under Heaven: Collective Violence in the Ming Dynasty.* Stanford: Stanford University Press, 1991.

Wakeman, Frederic, Jr. *The Great Enterprise: The Manchu Reconstruction of Imperial Order in Seventeenth-Century China.* Berkeley: University of California Press, 1985.

Wiens, Mi-Chu. "Lord and Peasant: The Sixteenth to the Eighteenth Centuries." *Modern China* 6 (1980).

CHINESE MAY FOURTH MOVEMENT (1919)

The May Fourth Movement of 1919 was a multifaceted event involving people motivated by new ideas, patriotic outrage, disgust with official corruption, or a combination of these things. Moreover, new layers of meaning have continually been added to the movement's legacy over the years.

To understand just how complex this legacy has become, consider how the movement's seventieth anniversary was marked. In mainland China, editorials in official newspapers stressed the pivotal role the May Fourth struggle played in inspiring Mao Zedong and other participants to found the Chinese Communist Party (CCP). They also hailed the founding of the People's Republic of China in 1949 as an act that made the May Fourth dream a reality. Also in 1989, however, student activists critical of current CCP leaders gathered in Beijing on May 4 to call for the launching of a "New May Fourth Movement" to further the still unrealized goals of 1919. Meanwhile, some scholars on both sides of the Taiwan Strait expressed a renewed commitment to a less explicitly political May Fourth legacy—the pursuit of enlightenment.

One reason for the elasticity of May Fourth imagery is that the term is routinely applied to two different, overlapping movements. One, the "New Culture Movement," was led by iconoclastic intellectuals who insisted China should embrace "Science and Democracy" and discard "traditional" ideas. Lasting from 1915 until 1923, it was marked by the founding of magazines and lecture campaigns designed to spread the word of new ideas coming from Japan and the West.

The other was a political movement that took place in 1919, led by students influenced by the New Culture Movement. It began with Beijing students marching, on May 4 itself, to protest the Treaty of Versailles, which was to give control of formerly German-run parts of China to Japan. Insisting this made a mockery of the idea that World War I had been fought to defend self-determination rights, the demonstrators clamored for the rewriting of the treaty and punishment of three Chinese officials viewed as pro-Japanese.

The march ended with confrontation. Demonstrators stormed an official's home, police used force, and students were arrested. Support for the movement quickly grew, with the imprisoned students viewed as patriotic heroes and the authorities as despots. The struggle peaked in Shanghai in June when a week-long "triple strike" of students, laborers, and merchants paralyzed the metropolis, then petered out.

In some ways, the political May Fourth Movement was a failure: the Treaty of Versailles went into effect, and the disputed territories were not returned. In other ways, it was surprisingly successful: the hated officials were dismissed, and the arrested students released.

Regardless of its degree of success or failure, the political movement has had a lasting legacy. The movement convinced many young protesters, including Mao Zedong, that mass movements could have great impact on society. Some older revolutionaries such as Sun Yat-sen drew similar conclusions. This helps explain why both the Nationalists on Taiwan and the CCP on the mainland continue to celebrate the May Fourth Movement as a struggle that helped correct the course of a revolution derailed by corrupt, unpatriotic warlords.

See also *Chinese Communist Revolution (1921–1949); Chinese Nationalist Revolution (1919–1927); Chinese Tiananmen Uprising (1989); Mao Zedong; Student Protests and Youth Movements; Sun Yat-sen.*

Jeffrey N. Wasserstrom

BIBLIOGRAPHY

Chow, Tse-tsung. *The May 4th Movement.* Cambridge, Mass.: Harvard University Press, 1963.

Hu, Shih. *The Chinese Renaissance.* New York: Paragon, 1963. Originally published 1933.

Perry, Elizabeth J., and Jeffrey N. Wasserstrom, guest editors. *Shanghai Social Movements, 1919–1949.* Special double-issue of *Chinese Studies in History: A Journal of Translations* (fall–winter 1993–1994).

Schwarcz, Vera. *The Chinese Enlightenment.* Berkeley: University of California Press, 1986.

CHINESE MAY THIRTIETH MOVEMENT (1925)

The May Thirtieth Movement was one of the earliest examples of urban mass mobilization in China and an important catalyst in the unfolding of the Nationalist Revolution. On May 30, 1925, after several months of labor unrest, particularly in the Japanese-owned textile mills of Shanghai, police under the command of a British officer fired into a crowd of demonstrators in Shanghai's Nanking Road in the International Settlement. Eleven or twelve people were killed, and perhaps two dozen more wounded.

Within days, large parts of the city were on strike, the targets mainly Japanese and British enterprises. The May Thirtieth Movement quickly became national in scope, spreading from Shanghai to other major cities such as Beijing, Nanjing, and Hankou. In June the bloodshed worsened when British and French forces opened fire on a Chinese demonstration in Guangzhou, killing more than sixty people. That incident led to a sixteen-month strike aimed against Hong Kong and the British position in South China.

The May thirtieth tragedy provided considerable impetus for both the Communist and Nationalist (Kuomintang) Parties, which had been working together in an uneasy alliance since 1923. Membership in both parties as well as in labor unions soared, and many new united front organizations were formed, cutting across lines of class and region, such as the Federation of Workers, and the Merchants and Students in Shanghai. These developments made the impotence of the official Chinese government in Beijing more apparent than ever. The British bore the brunt of the antiforeign reaction. Other powers such as France, America, and Japan tried to distance themselves, if not always from London's policy, at least from the actions of the more stubborn representatives of Britain in China—particularly those who dominated the Shanghai Municipal Council.

By the late summer and early autumn of 1925, much of the movement's earlier impetus had been lost, due both to a disintegration of the earlier revolutionary unity and the use of repressive force by Chinese and foreign police. Gradually the strikes came to an end everywhere except in Guangzhou, the headquarters of the Kuomintang. One of the movement's more tangible results came in the spring of 1926, when Chinese representatives were admitted to the French Municipal Council and the Shanghai Municipal Council, the two bodies governing foreign Shanghai.

Although the May Thirtieth Movement produced little immediate change, its indirect results were considerable. It revived the faltering alliance between Nationalists and Communists and greatly enlarged the ranks of student and labor unions. Thanks to the movement's propagandists, the movement also made the Chinese people more aware than ever before of the links, real and alleged, between the continuing fact of foreign imperialism and the weakness of the country, cut up as it was between the regimes of competing warlords. In orthodox Chinese historiography, both Nationalist and Communist, the May Thirtieth Movement marks the real beginning of the Nationalist Revolution, which would see the advance of the Nationalists (joined at first by the Communists) and the proclamation of China's reunification (on paper, at least) that came with the fall of Beijing to Chiang Kai-shek's armies in the spring of 1928.

See also *Chinese Communist Revolution (1921–1949); Chinese Nationalist Revolution (1919–1927).*

NICHOLAS R. CLIFFORD

BIBLIOGRAPHY

Chesneaux, Jean. *The Chinese Labor Movement 1919–1927.* Stanford: Stanford University Press, 1976.

Clifford, Nicholas R. *Spoilt Children of Empire: Westerners in Shanghai and the Chinese Revolution of the 1920s.* Hanover: University Press of New England, 1991.

Rigby, Richard W. *The May Thirtieth Movement: Events and Themes.* Canberra: Australian National University Press, 1980.

Wasserstrom, Jeffrey N. *Student Protests in Twentieth-Century China: The View from Shanghai.* Stanford: Stanford University Press, 1991.

CHINESE MUSLIM REBELLIONS (1856–1878)

During the latter half of the nineteenth century, Muslim inhabitants of China rose in rebellion against the Manchu Qing dynasty (1644–1911) in the provinces of Yunnan, Shaanxi, Gansu, and Xinjiang *(see map, p. 97)*. The diverse Muslim populations supporting these rebellions included several Central Asian ethnic groups and large numbers of Hui, culturally assimilated Chinese-speaking Muslims. China's Muslim communities lacked a unified religious hierarchy, and many followed one of several Sufi religious orders, led by charismatic "saints," which connected mosque communities but competed fiercely for members and control of trade. The arrival of the Jahriyya Sufi order in the late eighteenth century sparked a violent confrontation with more established Sufi orders, and the government intervened harshly on behalf of the older Sufi communities. Manchu emperors moved to control Jahriyya's spread through policies that all Muslims found restrictive. Strong anti-Muslim bias in the courts, unfair taxation practices, official corruption, and Han immigration to Muslim-populated frontier areas contributed to Muslim discontent.

THE YUNNAN MUSLIM REBELLION (1856–1873)

The Yunnan Muslim Rebellion (also known as the Panthay Rebellion) grew out of decades of feuding between Hui and Han Chinese over land, employment, and mining rights. A particularly bloody mining feud broke out in 1854, with the Hui gaining the upper hand. In May 1856 provincial officials responded by fomenting anti-Muslim pogroms in Kunming, capital of Yunnan Province, and neighboring areas, with thousands massacred. Disunited Muslims in eastern Yunnan rose in self-defense and were gradually welded into a fractious coalition by Ma Rulong, a leader in the 1854 feud, and Ma Dexin, a revered religious teacher. Another Muslim force seized the strategic center of Dali, in western Yunnan, and installed Du Wenxiu as "Grand Marshal" in October 1856. Du consolidated his rule over western Yunnan and broadened his movement's appeal by appointing some Han officials, confirming the local power of Han landowners and indigenous leaders and issuing laws to combat corruption.

Ma Rulong, unwilling to follow Du and judging a show of loyalty to the Qing advantageous, arranged a "surrender" to the besieged provincial government in 1862, putting Ma effectively in charge of the provincial military apparatus. Du remained steadfastly opposed to Qing rule, hoping to parlay his strong military position into an autonomous state in western Yunnan. Although he used Islamic political symbols, he made little attempt to impose an Islamic vision on his subjects. He preached Han–Hui reconciliation and blamed earlier feuds on Manchu misrule, attempting to restore ethnic peace and solidify support for his regime. Du's forces threatened Kunming in the late 1860s, but the provincial army under new governor Cen Yuying was buoyed by renewed central government support after the suppression of the Taiping and other rebellions. Despite Du's belated attempt to gain British support, by 1873 Cen Yuying had captured Dali, killed the rebel leader, and suppressed the rebellion.

THE TUNGAN REBELLION (1862–1873)

The Tungan Rebellion began as a feud between rival Han and Hui militia, organized to combat a Taiping incursion into Shaanxi Province in 1862. The government intervened against the Hui, who quickly took control of much of Shaanxi and besieged the provincial capital of Xi'an. Ma Hualong and other leaders organized ethnically diverse Muslim communities in neighboring Gansu Province for resistance in anticipation of a Han backlash. Ma himself controlled the Ningxia region from his base at Jinji, using his spiritual power as leader of the Jahriyya order.

Despite a Jahriyya network tying leaders throughout the region to his cause, the rebels lacked effective coordination, and some Muslims fought each other or sided with the government. But with weak forces at their disposal, officials resorted to the expedient of arranging "surrenders" in 1866 that left Ma and others controlling large areas. Ma used this respite to build up his military power, while the Qing court deputed Zuo Zongtang, an eminent scholar-official and general who had played a role in suppressing the Taiping Rebellion, to pacify the region. Organizing a massive logistical effort to sustain his forces in this war-ravaged region, Zuo focused his attack on the Jahriyya adherents, holding out the possibility of pardon to other Muslims who surrendered. Ma's fiercely defended stronghold fell in 1870, and Ma and many of his followers were executed. By 1873 rebel strongholds throughout Gansu had surrendered.

REBELLION IN XINJIANG (1863–1878)

The ethnically diverse Muslim population of Xinjiang, in northwest China, included indigenous Uighurs, Kirghiz, and Kazakh and recent Hui immigrants from Gansu. Xinjiang was also home to several Sufi orders with ties to Central Asia. Added to the Chinese empire only in the 1760s, Xinjiang was frequently troubled by rebellions, as indigenous Muslims chafed under Manchu rule and heavy taxation. In 1863 news of the Tungan Rebellion sparked uprisings in the oasis cities of the Tarim Basin. The following year, Hui troops at Urumqi in northeastern Xinjiang revolted, installing Jahriyya leader Tuo Ming as "Muslim King." As the Qing authority crumbled, an exiled Sufi leader returned to lead his followers in Kashgar, at the western end of the Tarim Basin, but was soon pushed aside by his general, Yaqub Beg. Garnering support and religious sanction as a protector of Islam, he instituted strict adherence to Islamic law and ousted Tuo Ming's forces from eastern Xinjiang. Yaqub established diplomatic relations with Turkey and Britain and traded with the Russians, who had occupied the Ili Valley in 1871. Zuo Zongtang attacked with a large army in 1876 and defeated Yaqub's army the following year. Yaqub died under mysterious circumstances shortly afterward, and his kingdom rapidly disintegrated. Within a year the recovery of Xinjiang was complete, except for Russian-occupied Ili, which was returned in 1881.

As grievances against Manchu rulers and Han neighbors developed into ethnic strife and an adversarial relationship with the government, Muslim groups living in China banded together for self-defense and were occasionally united on a larger scale by capable or charismatic leaders. Although the Islamic idea of *jihad* (holy war) against infidel rule may have influenced Sufi adherents in Xinjiang and the northwestern provinces of Gansu and Shaanxi, many Muslims tried to reconcile loyalty to an infidel emperor with their Islamic faith and were willing to return to the loyalist fold in exchange for personal rewards and protection for their own communities. Opportunism and internecine rivalries prevented Muslim leaders from presenting a united face to the Qing government, while none of the rebel groups succeeded in gaining reliable support from foreign powers. The resurgent Qing state of the 1860s and 1870s was thus ultimately able to thwart the rebels' separatist aims and keep the Chinese empire intact.

See also *Chinese Taiping Rebellion (1851–1864).*

JACOB WHITTAKER

BIBLIOGRAPHY

Broomhall, Marshall. *Islam in China: A Neglected Problem.* London, 1910. Reprinted, New York: Paragon, 1966.

Chan, Wellington K. K. "Ma Ju-lung: From Rebel to Turncoat in the Yunnan Rebellion." *Papers on China* 20 (1966): 86–118.

Chu, Wen-djang. *The Moslem Rebellion in Northwest China, 1862–1878: A Study of Government Minority Policy.* The Hague: Mouton, 1966.

Fields, Lanny B. *Tso Tsung-t'ang and the Muslims: Statecraft in Northwest China, 1868–1880.* Kingston, Ontario: Limestone, 1978.

Gladney, Dru C. *Muslim Chinese: Ethnic Nationalism in the People's Republic.* Cambridge, Mass.: Council on East Asian Studies, Harvard University, 1991.

Lipman, Jonathan N. *Familiar Strangers: A Muslim History in China.* Seattle: University of Washington Press, 1998.

Yuan, Tsing. "Yakub Beg (1820–1877) and the Moslem Rebellion in Chinese Turkestan." *Central Asiatic Journal* 6 (1961): 134–167.

CHINESE NATIONALIST REVOLUTION (1919–1927)

Supporters of China's 1911 Republican Revolution had helped overthrow the Qing dynasty in the belief that, without a monarchy, China would be stronger and better able to reverse the incursions of imperialist powers. Quite the contrary, however, the 1911 revolution ushered in a period of division, warlordism, and weakness. Out of its failure grew the nationalist movement.

Sun Yat-sen, a leader of the 1911 revolution, was forced out of China in 1913 when Yuan Shikai, president of the republic and Beijing military commander, seized complete power. The indefatigable Sun did not give up, however, but returned to China in 1916 and tried to organize a regime based in the southern city of Guangzhou (Canton) to challenge the legitimacy of the Beijing warlord government. Sun's Kuomintang (Nationalist) party was loosely structured and weak, however, and his regime lacked adequate funding and a loyal military. In June 1922 a local militarist, Chen Jiongming, formerly an ally, broke with Sun and forced him to flee anew.

A decade after the 1911 overthrow of the Qing dynasty, Sun's movement thus appeared a spent force. Young Chinese radicals of the May Fourth generation turned toward the budding Marxist and anarchist movements. Sun, disenchanted with the Western parliamentary form of government and getting no assistance from the Western powers, observed the new Bolshevik experiment in Russia with great interest. The success of a small but tightly organized political party led by a charismatic Lenin appeared an attractive model.

NATIONALIST ALLIANCE WITH MOSCOW

Sun Yat-sen began serious discussions with a Comintern representative in December 1921 about the possibility of an alliance with Moscow. Sun did not believe that China needed a communist revolution, however. He saw foreign imperialists, rather than domestic capitalists, as the major exploiters of the Chinese people. If the foreign enclaves and unequal treaties were abolished, China could develop an industrialized economy under Chinese control. Sun's views paralleled Lenin's theory that imperialism was the highest stage of capitalism. From Moscow's vantage, encouraging an anti-imperialist revolution in China would weaken capitalism in the imperialist nations and facilitate socialist revolutions in the West.

In January 1923 Sun Yat-sen reached an agreement with Communist International (Comintern) representative Adolf Joffe. Sun's Kuomintang was completely reorganized as a Leninist-style party, centralized and disciplined. The Soviets supplied financial and military aid, enabling Sun to reestablish his base in Guangzhou and to create a party army under the command of Chiang Kai-shek. The Kuomintang political platform became more radical, stressing the needs of workers and peasants and pledging to eliminate warlords and imperialist privilege in China. Members of the newly established, but still small, Chinese Communist Party were to join the Kuomintang as individuals, in effect becoming a bloc within.

The new alliance with Moscow, cemented when Soviet adviser Michael Borodin arrived later in the year, invigorated the Kuomintang cause. Young radicals enthused by China's May Thirtieth Movement now flocked to the Kuomintang-Communist camp. Party activists began to organize labor, student, and even peasant groups. The movement faced serious opposition, however, from both the warlords and the imperialist powers. Many traditional supporters of Sun with ties to business interests deserted the movement as well. At this pivotal moment, Sun Yat-sen suddenly died in March 1925 in Beijing, creating a succession crisis. In the next few months Chiang Kai-shek seized power and prepared to launch the Northern Expedition to defeat the warlords and unite China under Kuomintang control.

THE NORTHERN EXPEDITION

From July 1926 until April 1927 the Chinese Nationalist Revolution was at its height. Chiang's army moved northward into the Yangzi River Valley of central China, clearing the way for civilian Kuomintang leaders to set up a political regime. The Kuomintang military was outnumbered by the warlords, but its forces were better indoctrinated and motivated than those of the enemy, many of whom were mercenaries. The Kuomintang officer corps included many trained at the party military academy at Whampoa, near Guangzhou. There they had received military training from Soviet advisers and political indoctrination from instructors who included Zhou Enlai, a leading Communist Party member and future premier of the People's Republic of China. The Nationalist officers and soldiers were thus instilled with a sense of fighting for a cause: the salvation of China.

The Northern Expedition was much more than a military campaign. Party activists, both Kuomintang and Communist, organized labor and peasant groups to support the cause. Mao Zedong, future leader of the communist movement, helped organize peasant associations in central China and became convinced of the importance of the peasant movement to the revolution. In Shanghai, China's major industrial center, workers from the Communist-led Shanghai General Labor Union seized control of the city in mid-March. Nearly 600,000 strong, the workers staged a general strike which brought Shanghai to a halt. Anti-imperialist attacks over all of China forced foreigners to flee the interior for the treaty port cities. There the Western powers beefed up security with gunboats and military forces. Forty-two warships anchored at Shanghai alone.

This revolutionary outburst broke the unity of the Kuomintang-Communist alliance. The mushrooming strength of leftist forces alarmed Chiang Kai-shek and conservatives within the Kuomintang. The civilian government that had been established in the central city of Wuhan seemed dominated by Borodin and leftist Kuomintang leader Wang Jingwei. With wealthy Shanghai under his control, Chiang felt confident in breaking the Soviet link. In April 1927 he suddenly launched a violent "white terror" against the left. Turning first against the Shanghai labor movement, Chiang dispatched allies from the criminal underworld into the foreign concessions to target union supporters. Thousands were killed. By the end of 1927 Chiang struck hard at both the Chinese Communists and the leftist elements within his own party. He established his own Kuomintang regime in Nanjing. His rivals in Wuhan saw their political and military position collapse.

Although Chiang would ultimately eliminate the Beijing warlord regime and gain international recognition for his Nanjing government, the radical phase of the Chinese nationalist movement was over. Labor, student, and peasant groups had been suppressed. Chiang's new enemies, the Chinese Communists, would regroup in rural areas to launch a new and very different revolutionary movement.

See also *Chiang Kai-shek; Chinese May Fourth Movement (1919); Chinese May Thirtieth Movement (1925); Chinese Republican Revolution (1911); Mao Zedong; Sun Yat-sen.*

PARKS M. COBLE

BIBLIOGRAPHY

Eastman, Lloyd E. *The Abortive Revolution: China under Nationalist Rule, 1927–1937*. Cambridge: Harvard University Press, 1974.

Sheridan, James E. *China in Disintegration: The Republican Era in Chinese History, 1912–1949*. New York: Free Press, 1975.

Wang, Ke-wen. "The Kuomintang in Transition: Ideology and Factionalism in the National Revolution, 1924–1932." Ph.D. dissertation, Stanford University, 1985.

Wei, Julie Lee, Ramon H. Myers, and Donald G. Gillin, eds. *Prescriptions for Saving China: Selected Writings of Sun Yat-sen*. Stanford: Stanford University Press, 1994.

Wilbur, C. Martin. *The Nationalist Revolution in China, 1923–1928*. Cambridge: Cambridge University Press, 1983.

———*Sun Yat-sen: Frustrated Patriot*. New York: Columbia University Press, 1976.

Yu, George T. *Party Politics in Republican China: The Kuomintang, 1912–1924*. Berkeley: University of California Press, 1966.

CHINESE REPUBLICAN REVOLUTION (1911)

The Chinese Republican Revolution of 1911 ended more than two thousand years of imperial rule and established Asia's first republic. Sparked by an army mutiny in the central Chinese city of Wuchang on October 10, 1911, the revolution was led by officers of the Western-style New Army and members of the gentry and merchant elite in China's southern cities. During the fall and winter of 1911, fourteen provinces declared their independence from the Qing court in Beijing, and on January 1, 1912, they established the Republic of China in Nanjing. Negotiations between revolutionaries in the south and imperial forces in the north soon led to the abdication of the last emperor. But China's new rulers were unable to establish a stable regime, and the nation dissolved into internal division and warlordism.

China's last imperial dynasty, the Qing, was founded in 1644 by Manchu invaders from the northeast. Until the nineteenth century, Manchu rule brought peace and stability, a doubling of China's land area (basically to its present borders), and enough prosperity to spur a fourfold increase in population. Then, beginning with the Opium War of 1839–1842, the dynasty was crippled by bloody internal rebellions and repeated defeats in war with the Western powers. In 1894–1895, China suffered a humiliating defeat by an aggressively modernizing Japan, and in 1900, the capital of Beijing was occupied by an eight-nation expeditionary force that suppressed the Boxer Uprising.

These events convinced the Qing court to embark on a vigorous program of reform. A new school system replaced the civil service examinations based on the Confucian classics. A New Army was formed with modern arms and Western-style organization and drill. The government built railroads and promoted industry in an effort to prevent foreign domination of the modern economy. It also announced a nine-year plan for transition to constitutional government, and in 1909 it allowed a limited electorate of local gentry to select provincial and national assemblies with advisory powers. As autocratic controls weakened, an independent press, chambers of commerce, professional associations, and political groups emerged as a nascent civil society. These groups pressured the government to speed reforms, root out corruption, and defend the nation against imperialism. But the costly reforms also sparked repeated mass protests, especially from the urban and rural poor whose taxes increased while they received few benefits in return.

While the government and domestic elites pursued reforms, a small but vocal group of exiled dissidents called for revolution. For them, national regeneration and resistance to imperialism required overthrowing the Manchus. Beginning in 1895, Sun Yat-sen, a physician educated in Hong Kong and Hawaii, plotted revolutionary uprisings in southern China. In 1905 he allied with radical Chinese intellectuals in Tokyo to form the United League. Through their party paper, pamphlets, and speeches, Sun and other professional revolutionaries promoted anti-Manchu revolution, republican government, and vaguely socialist proposals for "people's livelihood." The party gained significant support from overseas Chinese in America and Southeast Asia, and from the thousands of Chinese students studying in Japan. Some students brought these radical ideas back to China, but revolutionary organization within China was generally weak.

By 1911 the Qing reforms had created a new student class in the urban centers and drawn a substantial number of literate and nationalistic recruits into the New Army. Urban elites in the provinces were empowered by the constitutional reforms and engaged in nationalistic protests to keep railways, vital industries, and mining out of foreign hands. The Qing court, headed by a conservative regent ruling in the name of a five-year-old emperor, blundered fatally in the spring of 1911. Spurning efforts to make the government more representative, it appointed eight Manchus, one Mongol, and only four Han Chinese to China's first responsible cabinet. A month later it nationalized railways then under construction and took out foreign loans to complete the rail lines. Widespread protests followed, heralding a general loss of confidence in the Manchu mandate to rule.

In central China's Hubei Province, small groups of revolutionaries had been organizing within the army for several years. In 1911 discontent with the Manchus led many common soldiers and noncommissioned officers to join their

Yuan Shikai (1859–1916), well-known military leader of the Beiyang Army, became the second president of the new Chinese republic. However, he suspended parliament in 1914 in the face of Japanese aggression and declared himself emperor in 1915. His death in 1916 ushered in the warlord era.

numbers. When the premature explosion of a revolutionary bomb provoked a government dragnet, the army conspirators rose up and captured the provincial capital of Wuchang on October 10, 1911. A military government was established under a popular brigade commander and included the president and other members of the provincial assembly.

From Wuchang the revolution spread to other cities in Hubei, then to the provinces of southern China, and on to the northern provinces of Shanxi and Shaanxi. In each province, some coalition of New Army officers and gentry from the provincial assemblies led a coup in the provincial capital, and from there the revolution spread to other commercial and administrative centers. Although young returned students from Japan, many with revolutionary sympathies acquired abroad, were active in the revolutionary regimes, Sun Yat-sen's United League was a significant force only in Shanghai and Sun's home province of Guangdong.

It was late October before the Qing launched a significant counterattack. After a month of fierce and destructive fighting, imperial forces recaptured Hankou and Hanyang, across the Yangzi River from Wuchang. Pressure from foreign powers, worried that trade would be disrupted, brought a ceasefire on December 3. Later in December, the revolutionary provinces organized a provisional government in Nanjing. Sun Yat-sen, who had heard of the revolution while traveling in the United States, was elected president of the new republic and assumed office on January 1, 1912. Meanwhile, the Qing court had called Yuan Shikai back from forced retirement and made him premier. Yuan was the founder of the imperial army in the north and China's leading reformist official. After a period of intense maneuvering, the last Qing emperor abdicated on February 12, 1912; a month later Sun Yat-sen yielded the presidency of the Republic of China to Yuan Shikai.

China's republican revolution put a definitive end to two millennia of imperial rule. But there was little agreement on the proper shape of the new republic. With military men and local gentry empowered in the provinces, centrifugal forces left the central government weaker than ever. Following Yuan Shikai's death in 1916, the country descended into internal strife and warlordism.

Particularly striking about the 1911 revolution was its uniquely urban nature. More than any other political transition in China, this one was made in the cities. The countryside was largely left out. Indeed, the urban concentration of the reform efforts that led to the revolution and continued under the republican regime probably widened the gap between city and countryside in China—with revolutionary consequences for the years to come.

See also *Chinese Boxer Uprising (1898–1900); Sun Yat-sen.*

JOSEPH W. ESHERICK

BIBLIOGRAPHY

Esherick, Joseph W. *Reform and Revolution in China: The 1911 Revolution in Hunan and Hubei.* 2d ed. Ann Arbor: University of Michigan Center for Chinese Studies, 1998.

Liew, K. S. *Struggle for Democracy: Sung Chiao-jen and the 1911 Chinese Revolution.* Berkeley: University of California Press, 1971.

Rankin, Mary Backus. *Early Chinese Revolutionaries: Radical Intellectuals in Shanghai and Chekiang, 1901–1911.* Cambridge, Mass.: Harvard University Press, 1971.

Rhoads, Edward. *China's Republican Revolution: The Case of Kwangtung, 1895–1913.* Cambridge, Mass.: Harvard University Press, 1975.

Schiffrin, Harold Z. *Sun Yat-sen and the Origins of the Chinese Revolution.* Berkeley: University of California Press, 1968.

Schoppa, R. Keith. *Chinese Elites and Political Change: Zhejiang Province in the Early Twentieth Century.* Cambridge, Mass.: Harvard University Press, 1981.

Wright, Mary C., ed. *China in Revolution: The First Phase, 1900–1913.* New Haven, Conn.: Yale University Press, 1968.

Young, Ernest P. *Liberalism and Dictatorship in Early Republican China: The Politics of the Yuan Shih-k'ai Presidency.* Ann Arbor: University of Michigan Press, 1977.

CHINESE SECTARIAN AND SECRET SOCIETY REVOLTS (1644–)

Sects and secret societies were important forms of popular organization in Qing dynasty China. These groups served on numerous occasions as vehicles of collective violence and rebellion, even if neither sects nor secret societies were established specifically for rebellious purposes.

SECTS VERSUS SECRET SOCIETIES

In the Chinese context, "sect" generally refers to the White Lotus folk Buddhist tradition and its many local variations (even if, strictly speaking, the Christian-inspired Taipings should also be considered "sectarians"). By the late imperial period, folk Buddhism was extremely widespread. Its adherents had spread from their traditional heartland in north central China to establish communities virtually throughout the country. Believers included not only many poor peasants but also city dwellers and mobile groups such as transport workers on the Grand Canal, who supplied the emperor's table with rice from the Jiangnan region. White Lotus doctrine was an appealing mix of popular Buddhism, folk beliefs, and apocalyptic longings for a better world, preserved in scriptures handed down within families of sectarian leaders.

In the Western tradition, sectarians are those who make a conscious decision to dissent from a mainstream religion, and sectarian demands for freedom of religious belief and freedom from persecution have played an important role in the political history of the modern West. By contrast, most Chinese are happily syncretic in their religious beliefs and practices, and few Chinese religions demand exclusive allegiance in the manner that Western faiths often have. Consequently, Chinese White Lotus "sectarians" placed relatively little emphasis on conscious dissent, and many White Lotus Buddhists remained thoroughly Confucian in their attitudes toward their ancestors or indeed toward the emperor. One must therefore be cautious about reading an overly political meaning into White Lotus practices. Whatever the fears of the Chinese state, most White Lotus groups were purely devotional in orientation, and only under extraordinary circumstances—such as the appearance of a charismatic leader or state persecution—did violent revolt become a possibility.

Chinese secret societies were somewhat different. In general, they were made up of young men who had been marginalized by the socioeconomic changes of the late imperial period. Beginning in Southeast China in the seventeenth and particularly eighteenth centuries, such men began to band together in groups that shared certain characteristics. Most employed a blood oath to stress the sanctity of their union as well as to create fictive familial ties, similar to those binding biological families. Most gave themselves a name consisting of three Chinese characters, the last of which meant "society" (Heaven and Earth Society, Three Drops Society, Small Knives Society). They also devised complex initiation rites, borrowing ritual objects and practices from Chinese popular religion, to elevate the power of secret society masters and to suggest that society membership might confer divine protection. Such initiation rites, as well as certain hand gestures and code words, were closely guarded secrets, as was society membership itself, at least in theory.

Some secret societies included in their initiation rituals and slogans explicitly rebellious calls to overthrow the Qing dynasty's Manchu government, although the origin of this stance remains obscure. Nineteenth-century Western observers were quick to identify Chinese secret societies with Freemasons and to see in their "dissent" the echo of such free-thinking Masons as Voltaire and Benjamin Franklin. More recent research discounts both the similarities between Chinese secret societies and Freemasons as well as the notion that secret society dissent can be seen as a plea for the rationalization of politics. Indeed, although many early societies justified their activities in the name of "mutual aid," such assistance often took the form of crime and racketeering, and over time most secret societies seem to have evolved into little more than criminal gangs. With some exceptions, secret society "rebellions" often had their roots in local criminal violence.

THE RECORD OF REVOLT

Even if neither sectarians nor secret societies constituted a self-conscious revolutionary force, there is nonetheless a significant history of rebellions led by groups that claimed to be either sectarians or secret societies, or groups labeled as such by the state. Since 1644 the most significant of these events were concentrated in a wave of rebellions beginning in the late eighteenth century and continuing through much of the nineteenth century.

In 1774 Wang Lun led the first White Lotus rebellion in 150 years, proclaiming himself the "Future Buddha" and leading some one thousand believers to attack three county governments in Shandong Province. Although the rebels seized the important Grand Canal city of Linqing, Qing forces managed to suppress the rebellion handily within three weeks. Some twenty years later, a much larger White Lotus rebellion erupted in the foothills of the middle Yangzi valley, at the confluence of the provinces of Shaanxi, Hubei, and Sichuan. Opened up by desperate, land-hungry men, this internal frontier was controlled neither by traditional social elites nor the local government. In the 1780s and 1790s, White Lotus leaders, driven by government persecution from their homes in central China, found fertile ground for proselytization in the middle Yangzi region. Government orders to investigate White Lotus congregations in the region unleashed a reign of terror, as unscrupulous petty officials and army officers sought to bribe or bully the unfortunate migrant population. The result was a rebellion, beginning in 1796 and continuing for eight long years. By the time it was finally suppressed by the state in 1804, it had nearly emptied state coffers. The rebellion also heightened Qing sensitivities toward other White Lotus groups, even if the "sectarians" of the middle Yangzi region contained many groups that had, at most, only a thin veneer of White Lotus organization or ideology.

Less than a decade later, another uprising erupted, this time in north and central China. In this instance, a clever drifter named Lin Qing took control of a loose sectarian network and organized the Eight Trigrams Rebellion, which coordinated attacks on twelve cities across three provinces in the autumn of 1813 and managed to penetrate, if briefly, the Imperial City in Beijing. More than one hundred thousand participated in the rebellion, which resulted in eighty thousand deaths. Although smaller scale rebellions associated with White Lotus sectarians continued through the 1820s and 1830s, White Lotus rebellions in general seem to have diminished after mid-century. As noted above, however, the massive Taiping Rebellion of the mid-nineteenth century conforms in many ways to our notion of "sectarian" uprisings, and the turn-of-the-century Boxers, if not White Lotus sectarians *per se,* certainly drew on a common base of north China folk religious practices.

Lin Shuangwen's rebellion on Taiwan in the late 1780s marked the first significant Triad (Heaven and Earth Society) uprising and the beginning of several decades of secret society activities. The suppression of this rebellion on both Taiwan and the adjacent mainland areas of Fujian and Guangdong prompted many Triad leaders to flee these base areas and spread the Triad organization elsewhere in South China. In 1802, 1817, and twice in 1837, the Triads staged armed uprisings in Guangdong Province. The surrounding provinces of Guangxi, Jiangxi, Hunan, and Fujian were similarly afflicted. In 1853 the Triads succeeded in putting the provincial capital city of Guangzhou under siege. In 1854 a related secret society, the Small Knives Society, took control of Shanghai as the Qing retreated before the armies of the Taipings. Indeed, brotherhoods throughout south and central China took advantage of the weakness of the imperial state to expand their influence.

Secret society activity subsided in the decades immediately following the suppression of the Taiping and the Nian Rebellions in the 1860s *(see map, p. 97)*. However, as Manchu fortunes fell in the late nineteenth and early twentieth centuries in response to internal unrest and foreign incursion, secret societies resumed their rebellious activities. Indeed, radical and revolutionary intellectuals such as Sun Yat-sen, who, like many of his associates, was exiled from China during this period, attempted to mobilize secret societies in their efforts to overturn the regime. Such cooperation proved difficult, and both the Chinese Republic and the People's Republic of China eventually turned against both sects and secret societies in the process of consolidating their regimes. In the final analysis, even if the wave of sectarian and secret society violence helped weaken China's final dynasty, both sects and secret societies were generally captive to local concerns and incapable of mounting a sustained challenge to the existing order. The decline of the traditional order must rather be attributed to the Western impact and the alienation of China's traditional elites. The revolutionary response required the construction of new political tools: the party and the modern army.

See also *Chinese Boxer Uprising (1898–1900); Chinese Late Ming Revolts (1620–1644); Chinese Taiping Rebellion (1851–1864); Chinese Triad Society Rebellions (18th–20th Centuries); Chinese White Lotus Rebellions (18th–20th Centuries); Sun Yat-sen.*

David Ownby

BIBLIOGRAPHY

Chesneaux, Jean, ed. *Popular Movements and Secret Societies in China, 1840–1950.* Stanford: Stanford University Press, 1972.

Murray, Dian H. *The Origins of the Tiandihui: The Chinese Triads in Legend and History.* Stanford: Stanford University Press, 1994.

Naquin, Susan. *Millenarian Rebellion in China: The Eight Trigrams Uprising of 1813.* New Haven, Conn., and London: Yale University Press, 1976.

Ownby, David. *Brotherhoods and Secret Societies in Early and Mid-Qing China.* Stanford: Stanford University Press, 1996.

Perry, Elizabeth J. *Rebels and Revolutionaries in North China, 1845–1945.* Stanford: Stanford University Press, 1980.

CHINESE TAIPING REBELLION (1851–1864)

The Taiping Rebellion was the most devastating uprising against Confucian China until the twentieth century. Its insurrectionary power emerged from a militant religion which, intersecting with the twin crises of domestic decline and foreign encroachment, inspired a potent ideology, motivation, and organization that nearly toppled China's old order. Taiping efforts to create an egalitarian society, especially along gender lines, anticipated the revolutionary changes of twentieth-century China.

CHINA'S MORAL CRISIS AND THE DEVELOPMENT OF TAIPING RELIGION, 1837–1851

Taiping religion originated with Hong Xiuquan (1814–1864). Raised near Guangzhou, capital of Guangdong Province, Hong belonged to south China's largest ethnic minority group of Hakka Chinese, who had fled invasions of the north centuries earlier. Subsisting as itinerant laborers and tenants of the original settlers, with whom they feuded over land, the Hakka insured survival by sharing property and including their women in agricultural work, buying and selling, and community self-defense.

Hoping to raise his family's status through success in the civil service examinations, Hong memorized the required Confucian texts, which stressed submission to family, hierarchy, and emperor, as well as women's inferiority. But after a series of examination failures and exposure to Protestant missionary writings, Hong had a visionary dream in 1837. In this dream, God denounced Confucius and commissioned Hong (whom He identified as Christ's younger brother) to return China to monotheism.

In his theological writings, Hong blamed the rising economic competition created by shifting trade patterns, population pressures, concentration of landowning, and government corruption following the Opium War (1839–1842) on China's rejection of the universal God revealed in the Bible and in China's own pre-Confucian books. The latter, he argued, proved that God was China's creator and emperor, benevolently ruling an ancient commonwealth of "great peace and equality" *(taiping)*. Tragically, Confucius omitted God from his compilation of the classics, and the emperors usurped God's rule, jettisoned morality for "decadent" Daoism and Buddhism, and polarized Chinese society by abandoning "universal love" for Confucius's hierarchical "partial love." Hong insisted that China could be saved only by restoring God's rule within the framework of the imminent, earth-bound Heavenly Kingdom *(Tianguo)* described in the missionary tracts.

After studying with an American Baptist in Guangzhou early in 1847, Hong railed against the "immoral" consequences of opium smuggling, rising unemployment, confiscation of Hakka land, and theological error in neighboring Guangxi Province. Next, Hong presided over many "God Worshipper" congregations in Guangxi and launched a moral revival there based on a synthesis of Chinese folk religion and Biblical concepts of sin, baptism, veneration of God, and gender equality between God's "daughters" and "sons."

Hong invoked the Ten Commandments to outlaw specific "sins" against God (idolatry and witchcraft), against the community (murder, banditry, and ethnic feuding), and against one's self (promiscuity, gambling, and addiction to alcohol, tobacco, and opium). He generated spiritual anxiety by promising rewards in Heaven and punishments in Hell. During 1848–1850 the ranks of God Worshippers mushroomed as Hong linked New Testament healing miracles with Hakka shamanism and a communal sacred treasury to combat famine and typhus. Through such Hakka mediums as the illiterate charcoal-burner Yang Xiuqing, God, Jesus, and the Holy Ghost daily appeared to comfort the faithful.

MARTIAL DISCIPLINE AND DYNASTIC INSURRECTION, 1851–1853

In the spring of 1850 the Qing (Manchu) government, alarmed by Hong's loyalty to God above dynastic ruler, attacked the God Worshippers. Hong countered by announcing, on January 11, 1851, the inauguration of the "Heavenly Kingdom of Great Peace" *(Taiping Tianguo)*. He invited all Chinese subjects to unite with the twenty thousand Taipings into an army of "Chosen People" whom God, soon to be restored as China's rightful ruler, would deliver, Exodus-like, from "devil Manchu" oppression.

God Himself would reach the individual believer through a religious-military-civilian theocracy capped on earth by Hong (who, as "Heavenly King," was God's vice regent) and his five "brother kings," including Yang Xiuqing, whom Hong made chief of staff. Hong made the Ten Commandments a military code portraying God as a warrior-judge, in whose name summary execution created disciplined soldiers of both sexes. On the march, the Taipings sang hymns and destroyed temples and ancestral shrines. Before battle, they knelt and recited the Lord's Prayer, buoyed by its promise of "Thy kingdom come."

The Taipings swept into the Yangzi River valley at Wuchang with a string of victories, inspired by promises of heavenly bliss and posthumous rank. They were greatly aided by troops of Hakka women, whose unbound feet, capacity for physical exertion, and years of guerrilla combat against the Hakkas' enemies made them formidable battlefield heroines under the generalship of Hong's sister.

Claiming that the creator-God owned the land, Hong decreed that in Taiping China, rents would be abolished and taxes reduced. Moreover, women would receive the same acreage as men. Thousands of China's poorest people sought baptism as Taiping preachers unveiled this "Land System of the Heavenly Dynasty." Designating state power as the vehi-

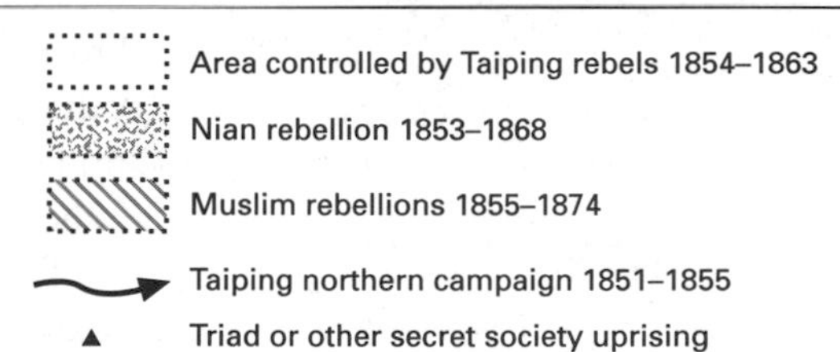

Reprinted by permission of the publisher from *China: A New History* by John Fairbank, Cambridge, Mass.: Harvard University Press, Copyright © 1992 by the President and Fellows of Harvard College. Original map by R. Forget. Alex Tait/EquatorGraphics, Inc.

cle of God's love, Hong ordered its extension to the grassroots "congregation" of twenty-five families. At this, the lowest administrative level ever proposed in China, a God-fearing "sergeant" would administer justice, provide social welfare, insure the equal distribution of the harvest, supervise military training, preach, and extend, for the first time in Chinese history, universal education to boys and girls alike.

THE RISE AND FALL OF TAIPING THEOCRACY, 1853–1864

In March 1853 one million Taipings captured Nanjing, former imperial capital astride the Yangzi River near Shanghai. Hong made Nanjing his Heavenly Capital and revealed himself to be its reincarnated Melchizedek, the messianic priest-king who anticipated David in the Old Testament and Christ in the New. Taiping officials delivered anti-Manchu sermons, offered supplications for victory, and led mass recitations of the Ten Commandments. (Failure to memorize them was a capital offense.)

Guided by the Hakka "old brethren," the Taiping government sought to dismantle Confucianism by nationalizing private property and commerce, prohibiting work on the Sabbath, and democratizing literacy through language simplification. Hong's own writings and the Taiping Bible (which Hong revised, annotated, and amplified with a "True Testament" praising God's saving acts among the Taipings) replaced the Confucian classics as the basis of education and the examinations.

The Taipings' most revolutionary innovations, however, were the reforms on behalf of gender equality. The new government segregated the Nanjing "brothers" and "sisters"—including spouses until 1855—into separate "institutes" to dramatize male-female equality and to enforce puritanism. It also banned footbinding, arranged marriage, wife purchase, widow suicide, and prostitution—traditions already shunned by the Hakka. And it decreed women's equal access to schools, work outside the home (including manual labor), court nobility, the civil service examinations, government appointment, and military service. Those caught violating women were to be summarily executed. Even though the Taiping kings maintained harems (a Chinese institution with Old Testament parallels) and employed the traditional Confucian rhetoric of women's "Three Obediences" to father, husband, and sons (which accorded with Saint Paul's notions of women's inferiority), they imposed monogamy on the rank and file, banned dowries, and encouraged women to marry (and even remarry) of their own free will.

In September 1856 Yang Xiuqing and twenty thousand of his followers were massacred after feuding with Hong over who spoke for God. This fratricidal catastrophe and Hong's retreat into mysticism crippled military coordination at the very moment Qing soldiers were stretched thin fighting other rebels throughout China. Bereft of Yang's strategic genius, Taiping commanders would never control more than the lower Yangzi provinces for any length of time. Unable to muster sufficient administrative resources to implement the communal Land System, the Taipings were forced to rely on the old method of land ownership and tax collection. Over time, moral discipline began to wane among the troops in the field.

In 1859 Hong approved proposals of his cousin Hong Ren'gan, a Christian catechist who had worked for missionaries in Hong Kong and Shanghai, to link Taiping China with the Christian West through adoption of Western-style government, economic development, and philanthropic institutions. But Taiping court factionalism doomed this effort. Nor was support forthcoming from the Christian missionaries, who condemned Hong's religious synthesis as "abominable in the sight of God." In fact, Western governments, fearing that Hong's call for China's global equality would jeopardize their favorable trade arrangements with Manchu China, supplied anti-Taiping forces with mercenaries and matériel. In July 1864 well-trained Chinese troops of the loyalist Zeng Guofan breached Nanjing's wall and leveled "New Jerusalem." Mopping up operations stretched into 1866.

THE TAIPING REBELLION IN PERSPECTIVE

The Taiping Rebellion had much in common with traditional Chinese secret society and sectarian activism. In ethnically complex and anarchic areas like Guangdong and its Guangxi hinterland, where dynastic control was weakest and foreign influence strongest, charismatic leaders often reacted to economic disaster and moral decline by condemning the orthodox order and gathering marginalized converts into salvationist congregations. Sometimes these groups declared insurrection. But the Daoist and Buddhist eschatologies that inspired these rebels lacked a timetable and a plan for a new order. Nor did they envision more than replacing one morally bankrupt dynasty with a virtuous new one.

The Taipings, by contrast, far surpassed this rebel tradition. Hong's interpretation of the Bible connected with and energized Chinese elements to create an explosive religious vision of an entirely new China: a communal, egalitarian Heavenly Kingdom ruled directly by God, the Heavenly Father. Hong's monotheism went beyond even the most heterodox sectarians to inspire a millennial framework that attracted the dispossessed, rationalized the puritanism that disciplined them, and shaped the theocratic organization that propelled them.

Hong's millenarian quest, which took between twenty and forty million lives in sixteen of China's eighteen provinces, was the world's bloodiest civil war. The Taipings held onto their New Jerusalem for eleven years, carrying out unprecedented socioeconomic experiments there. None were more revolutionary than those on behalf of Chinese women. Grounded in Hong's most fundamental theological tenet of universal equality under the common Heavenly Father, the Land System guaranteed women's equality. In addition, state-sanctioned marriage allowed Taiping women to toil in lockstep with men for the common good.

These innovations would be echoed in the Chinese Communists' Marriage Law of 1950, which accorded Chinese women equal rights in marriage, divorce, and property ownership. But the Taiping Rebellion itself was doomed by China's landowning elite, who denounced Hong's heresies and supported, for another half century, the Confucian orthodoxy and its Manchu upholders.

Many scholars depict the Taipings as traditional peasant rebels flawed by Hong's emperor fixation and theocratic despotism. But it must also be acknowledged that Hong's religiously inspired insurrection initiated China's modern history of revolution. Taiping patriotism inspired Sun Yat-sen to call himself "Hong Xiuquan the Second" and to work to destroy the dynastic system in 1911. And the Taipings' social and economic radicalism anticipated China's Nationalist and Communist revolutions, which changed China through strictly secular means.

See also *Chinese Late Ming Revolts (1620–1644); Chinese Sectarian and Secret Society Revolts (1644–); Hong Xiuquan; Millenarianism; Religion; Sun Yat-sen.*

P. RICHARD BOHR

BIBLIOGRAPHY

Boardman, Eugene Powers. *Christian Influence Upon the Ideology of the Taiping Rebellion, 1851–1864.* Madison: University of Wisconsin Press, 1952.

Bohr, P. Richard. "The Heavenly Kingdom in China: Religion and the Taiping Revolution, 1837–1853." *Fides et Historia* 17 (spring-summer 1985).

———. "The Taipings in Chinese Sectarian Perspective." In *Heterodoxy in Modern China.* Edited by Kwang-Ching Liu and Richard Shek. Berkeley: University of California Press, forthcoming.

Jen, Yu-wen. *The Taiping Revolutionary Movement.* New Haven, Conn.: Yale University Press, 1973.

Kuhn, Philip A. "The Taiping Rebellion." In *The Cambridge History of China.* Vol. 10: *Late Ch'ing.* Part I. Edited by John K. Fairbank. Cambridge: Cambridge University Press, 1978.

Michael, Franz, in collaboration with Chung-li Chang. *The Taiping Rebellion: History and Documents.* 3 vols. Seattle: University of Washington Press, 1966–1971.

Shih, Vincent C. Y. *The Taiping Ideology.* Seattle: University of Washington Press, 1967.

Weller, Robert P. *Resistance, Chaos and Control in China.* Seattle: University of Washington Press, 1994.

CHINESE TIANANMEN UPRISING (1989)

The term *Tiananmen* is now synonymous with the Chinese protests of 1989, but it was once just a Beijing place name. Composed of characters meaning "Gate of Heavenly Peace," it referred to a building (containing an archway) and a massive square (across the street). The former opens into the Forbidden City—a cluster of ancient buildings that once housed emperors and is now a museum of prerevolutionary history. The latter was built soon after the 1949 founding of the People's Republic (PRC). It serves as an open-air museum of revolutionary history. The Gate of Heavenly Peace thus divides regimes and epochs.

This is worth remembering when grappling with Tiananmen's political meanings. So, too, are the contrasting uses to which the square has been put—as a site for official commemoration as well as a site for acts of resistance.

OFFICIAL RITUALS, POPULAR PROTESTS

Tiananmen Square contains several structures invested by the Chinese Communist Party (CCP) with sacred significance. One is the Mao Zedong Mausoleum, which is visited by many people—some reverential pilgrims, others curious tourists. Another is a large white obelisk dedicated to martyrs, which contains near its base marble friezes portraying events such as the student-led May Fourth Movement of 1919. Structures such as these make Tiananmen Square a giant shrine, made by and honoring the CCP. Reinforcing this image are buildings that border it: a Museum of Revolutionary History, where the CCP's past is detailed, and a Great Hall of the People, where officials now meet.

The square serves as the site for official celebrations such as annual National Day rallies. Mao held mass audiences with Red Guard contingents here in the 1960s. It was here as well that Hong Kong's transfer to Chinese rule was celebrated in 1997. Many of these supposedly "popular" gatherings are carefully orchestrated affairs, involving only specially selected representatives of the "people." Officials typically do not join the masses but look down on the proceedings from atop the gate.

Twice since 1949, angry citizens have temporarily transformed Tiananmen Square into a counter-hegemonic space—a place for oppositional rituals that articulated a radically different vision of the role that the "people" might play in politics. In each case, the transformation of the square began with the mourning of a political leader and ended with campaigns of repression. This pattern unfolded first in 1976, when the fallen leader was Zhou Enlai, then again in 1989 after the death of Hu Yaobang, a former protégé of Deng Xiaoping, who was removed from office for showing too much leniency toward student protesters in 1986–1987. The first struggle became known within China as the "Tiananmen Incident," but only the second struggle made "Tiananmen" a household word in other lands.

One reason for the contrasting fame of the movements is that the 1989 protests lasted longer and came closer to toppling the regime than those in 1976. Another is that only the 1989 protests were shown live on international television. This was, in part, due to a fluke of timing: even before the protests broke out, many foreign journalists were planning to go to Beijing to cover Mikhail Gorbachev's first trip to China. When the protests upstaged the Gorbachev-Deng summit as a newsworthy event, journalists turned their attention from the leaders to the protesters.

1989: EVENTS AND MISCONCEPTIONS

Because the 1989 movement began with mourning ceremonies, a few words are in order about Hu Yaobang, who died suddenly in April 1989. Like Zhou Enlai, Hu became a symbol for a road toward political openness not taken by the regime. Also like Zhou, he became a symbol of moral courage and selflessness—particularly important in 1989, since official corruption and nepotism were sources of anger for members of all classes.

A desire for greater governmental transparency and less corruption remained key themes throughout the movement. By mid-May, however, the struggle was largely defined as simply a fight for the right to protest.

The movement is sometimes characterized by sympathizers as a nonviolent effort to overthrow the CCP. The Beijing regime describes it as "counterrevolutionary riots" and acts of "turmoil" aimed at destroying communism. In contrast to both of these images, most participants insisted—and not just for strategic reasons—that their aim was not to do away with the CCP but to get the party to live up to its own ideals. They wanted to get the revolution back on track, to *jiuguo* or "save the nation" through patriotic action.

There are good reasons why the 1989 protests have become linked with the word Tiananmen. It was there that some of the struggle's most memorable events occurred—from mid-April ceremonies honoring Hu, to the mid-May launching of the hunger strike, to the late May erecting of the Goddess of Democracy. And it was in the square that the best-known student leaders of what some called the "New May Fourth Movement" of 1989—such as Wang Dan, Wuer Kaixi, and Chai Ling—made their headquarters, near the frieze honoring their spiritual predecessors, the protesters of 1919.

Nevertheless, the tight association of the movement with the square in general and the misleading references in Western works to the June 4 massacre as the "Tiananmen Massacre" have led to some distortions. Beijing was the center of the movement and perhaps the only city in which marches of one million people took place, but it was not the only place protests occurred. A half-million people marched in Shanghai, and smaller protests took place in many cities. Beijing was not even the only place where a massacre occurred; there was one in the southwestern city of Chengdu as well.

Although many Western works on the crackdown continue to refer only to the deaths of "students in Tiananmen Square," most of the people who died on June 4 were workers, not educated youths. In addition, the main killing fields were nearby streets, not the square. Moreover, while some students were punished severely, the harshest sentences tended to go to workers. Remembering this helps explain the severity of the campaign of repression, as the national scope of the struggle and the support it had from workers were major sources of anxiety for the government.

See also *Chinese May Fourth Movement (1919); Deng Xiaoping; Gorbachev, Mikhail; Mao Zedong; Student Protests and Youth Movements.*

Jeffrey N. Wasserstrom

BIBLIOGRAPHY

Barmé, Geremie, and Linda Jaivin, eds. *New Ghosts, Old Dreams: Chinese Rebel Voices.* New York: Times Books, 1992.

Calhoun, Craig. *Neither Gods nor Emperors: Students and the Struggle for Democracy in China.* Berkeley: University of California Press, 1994.

Hicks, George, ed. *The Broken Mirror: China after Tiananmen.* Chicago: Longman's, 1990.

Ogden, Suzanne, et al., eds. *China's Search for Democracy: The Student and Mass Movement of 1989.* Armonk, N.Y.: M.E. Sharpe, 1992.

Unger, Jonathan, ed. *The Pro-Democracy Protests in China: Reports from the Provinces.* Armonk, N.Y.: M.E. Sharpe, 1991.

Wasserstrom, Jeffrey N., and Elizabeth J. Perry, eds. *Popular Protests and Political Culture in Modern China.* 2d ed. Boulder, Colo.: Westview Press, 1994.

CHINESE TRIAD SOCIETY REBELLIONS (18TH–20TH CENTURIES)

The Chinese Triads are a series of multi-surname brotherhoods that emerged in southeast China as a part of the nonelite response to changing social, economic, and demographic circumstances of the late-eighteenth and early-nineteenth centuries. Known in Chinese as the *Tiandihui,* or Heaven and Earth Society, the Triad Society's initiation rituals, which distinguished it from other "secret societies," included an oath of brotherhood sworn before burning incense, the sacrifice of a cock whose blood was mixed with wine and drunk, the act of crawling beneath crossed knives or swords, and the transmission of secret phrases, gestures, and codes.

Originally believed to have been founded exclusively for purposes of political opposition, the Triads are now seen more broadly as an organizational form readily adapted to a variety of ends. The Triads figured in the survival strategies of China's lowest classes in ways that combined both protection and predation. Major functions of the Triads ranged from mutual aid, invoked by Chinese migrants and sojourners to protect themselves from insults and injury on the road or in alien communities, to criminal entrepreneurship, including robbery, the sale of protection and the establishment of brothels, opium parlors, and gambling dens. Triads also played an important role in rebellion, serving as an organizational vehicle for many Chinese uprisings during the eighteenth, nineteenth, and twentieth centuries (*see map, p. 97*).

The Triads first came to the attention of Qing dynasty officials in the aftermath of the Lin Shuangwen uprising (1787–1788). The subsequent criminalization and prohibition of the Triad Society in 1792 forced its member brotherhoods to go underground and adopt new names to avoid detection. Among them were the Hong League, Small Knife Society, and Three Dots Society. Both the Chinese Nationalists and Communists have acknowledged connections between their origins and Triad organizations, and today large Triad syndicates rival those of the Italian mafia in organized crime—especially the narcotics trade.

The origins of the *Tiandihui* are hotly disputed, in part because their politicized nature has caused certain groups to attribute to them characteristics not borne out by the historical record, but ones in which they have a vested interest. During the twentieth century the origins debate has become increasingly intertwined with China's political struggles. Chinese scholars and leaders of the Republican era sought to portray the Triads as a key element in early Chinese resistance against the Manchu Qing dynasty and as a national revolutionary body founded for the purpose of overthrowing the Qing and restoring the Ming. In the end, however, Republican-era scholars were unable to determine the precise time, place, and origin of the Triad Society's founding.

After 1949 political exigency caused Nationalist scholars on Taiwan, who perceived the island as a base from which to reconquer the communist Chinese mainland, to liken their situation to that of the Chinese patriot Zheng Chenggong, whom they believed founded the Triad Society to recover the mainland from the Manchus. Today many Chinese continue to endorse this view despite the fact that archival documents on both Taiwan and the mainland tell a very different story. They indicate that the Triad Society was a nonelite, popular, nonpolitical organization founded by a monk in the Zhangzhou region of Fujian during the 1760s as a mutual aid fraternity whose emergence and spread were closely related to the social and economic circumstances of China's lower classes.

See also *Chinese Sectarian and Secret Society Revolts (1644–).*

Dian Murray

BIBLIOGRAPHY

Murray, Dian H. *The Origins of the Tiandihui: The Chinese Triads in Legend and History.* Stanford: Stanford University Press, 1994.

Ownby, David. *Brotherhood and Secret Societies in Early and Mid-Qing China: The Formation of a Tradition.* Stanford: Stanford University Press, 1996.

Ownby, David, and Mary Somers Heidhues, eds. *Reconsidered: Perspectives on the Social History of Modern South China and Southeast Asia.* Armonk, N.Y.: M.E. Sharpe, 1993.

Schlegel, Gustave. *Thian Ti Hwui: The Hung-League or Heaven-Earth League.* 1866. New York: AMS Press, 1974.

CHINESE WHITE LOTUS REBELLIONS (18TH–20TH CENTURIES)

"White Lotus" is a label given to a variety of folk Buddhist religious groups, extremely widespread in both rural and urban China by the end of the imperial era, some of which were implicated in numerous rebellions. Scholars trace the origins of the White Lotus to a widespread movement during the medieval period to spread Buddhism beyond the confines of monasteries and the religious elite. These efforts succeeded perhaps too well, and as Buddhism became a popular faith, the White Lotus adopted beliefs and practices from other traditions such as Taoism, shamanism, and folk religion.

The White Lotus of the Qing dynasty (1644–1911) took form during the late Ming dynasty (1368–1644), a period of great religious intensity in China. From that point forward, White Lotus doctrine contained the following syncretic mix of elements. The central deity, drawn from Chinese folk beliefs, was the Eternal Venerable Mother, who had created the world and welcomed believers back to the comfort of her paradise in the West. Consistent with the practices of popular Buddhism, believers achieved salvation by chanting mantras that pronounced the name of the Eternal Venerable Mother. Alongside the soothing figure of the central deity were elements drawn from apocalyptic strains of Buddhist doctrine. White Lotus believers adopted the idea of *kalpas,* three great epochs succeeding one another and culminating in the descent of the Maitreya, or future Buddha, who would usher in an eternal reign of peace and harmony for all believers. Folk Taoist elements also figure in many of the meditative, devotional, and dietary aspects of White Lotus practices, thus providing an avenue of entry for traditional Taoist apocalyptic images. At the level of doctrine, it is obvious that such a mixture of beliefs could be explosive.

As befits a folk religion, however, the White Lotus had little in the way of coherent, comprehensive organization. Some leadership came from hereditary "sect leaders," who possessed the White Lotus scriptures ("precious scrolls") and assured their transmission. In other cases, White Lotus organizations were built around a particular occupation, whose members might build lodges, serving both as temples and as housing for those in need. Charismatic leaders who traveled from group to group within loose regional networks occasionally brought out the latent mobilizational potential of the White Lotus. In general, however, the White Lotus was little more than a collection of largely autonomous local devotional groups, dimly aware of other similar groups in their region but feeling little need to interact with them on a regular basis.

Despite this lack of organization, the White Lotus is credited with a number of important rebellions in the Qing period, notably a series of rebellions around the turn of the nineteenth century that are often seen as marking the beginning of the end of China's last dynasty. These rebellions differed in important ways and require different explanations. Some rebellions were the work of charismatic entrepreneurs who sought prestige, power, and perhaps wealth through White Lotus connections, often claiming that the apocalypse was near and that preparation was necessary. Whatever the personal beliefs of these entrepreneurs, such a strategy frequently led to mobilization of large numbers of people, which could easily take the form of rebellion. Another important factor inciting White Lotus rebellions was the heavy hand of the Qing state, which was unusually sensitive to "heterodox" religions and quick to resort to arrest or persecution. Such actions had the double effect of justifying White Lotus uprisings and spreading the influence of the faith, as believers fled the agents of the state and sought converts elsewhere.

See also *Chinese Sectarian and Secret Society Revolts (1644–).*

David Ownby

BIBLIOGRAPHY

Kelley, David E. "Temples and Tribute Fleets: The Luo Sect and Boatmen's Associations in the Eighteenth Century." *Modern China* 8 (1982).

Naquin, Susan. *Millenarian Rebellion in China: The Eight Trigrams Uprising of 1813.* New Haven, Conn., and London: Yale University Press, 1976.

Overmyer, Daniel L. "Messenger, Savior, and Revolutionary: Maitreya in Chinese Popular Religious Literature of the Sixteenth and Seventeenth Centuries." In *Maitreya, The Future Buddha.* Edited by Alan Sponberg and Helen Hardacre. Cambridge, England: Cambridge University Press, 1988.

———. *Folk Buddhist Religion: Dissenting Sects in Late Traditional China.* Cambridge, Mass.: Harvard University Press, 1976.

Ter Haar, B. J. *The White Lotus Teachings in Chinese Religious History.* Leiden: E. J. Brill, 1992.

CIVIL WARS

Civil wars take many forms. They can be fought for a variety of goals, ranging from secession to simple constitutional reform. They can use an assortment of military strategies, from guerrilla warfare to large conventional armies. Some civil wars produce radical social changes; others produce no change at all. They can be long or short, and deadly or relatively benign. They can also have very different causes; the Chinese communists, Bosnian Muslims, American Southerners, and white and black Rhodesians all fought civil wars, but they fought them for very distinct reasons.

This heterogeneous mix makes it difficult to define the term *civil war* and to distinguish a civil war from other types of internal conflicts, such as revolutions, rebellions, insurrections, and internal wars. In fact, these terms are often used interchangeably. Disagreement also extends to specific cases. Some experts would argue that the conflicts in Northern Ireland and Cyprus should be classified as civil wars. Other experts would strongly disagree. Some would include China's Cultural Revolution (1967–1968) and "La Violencia" in Colombia (1948–1958) on the list of civil wars. Others would not. Even Americans disagree on whether their war between 1861 and 1865 was, in fact, a civil war or a war of Northern aggression. And disagreement continues over whether the Korean War was civil or interstate. If civil wars can have different causes, aims, executions, outcomes, and interpretations, how does one delimit what is and what is not a civil war?

DEFINITION

Although scholars and commentators disagree on the definition of *civil war,* they generally agree on the broad characteristics that constitute a civil war. Civil war can be broadly defined as large-scale violence between two or more groups within a recognized state fighting for control of the government or the extent of its jurisdiction.

Four general characteristics, therefore, stand out. First, civil wars are conflicts that occur within the boundaries of a single state. Outside states can be involved in the conflict, but the principal antagonists must be citizens of the same state. Thus, the war fought between Angolan nationals and the colonial state of Portugal between 1962 and 1974 would be classified as a colonial war of independence, whereas the subsequent war between the Popular Movement for the Liberation of Angola (MPLA) and the National Union for the Total Independence of Angola (UNITA) for control of the newly independent government would be considered a civil war. This qualification helps to distinguish civil wars from both interstate and colonial wars.

Second, civil wars must include the government as one of the direct participants in the conflict. This qualification helps distinguish civil wars from regional conflicts or small-scale acts of violence not directed against the government.

Third, civil wars must involve civilians. Violence that is used by one elite group against members of another elite group more aptly characterizes military coups d'état, palace revolutions, purges, and conspiracies. The term *civil war* is used to denote broader-based challenges to the government.

Finally, most people agree that civil wars require at least a minimum level of violence and political organization. This stipulation excludes minor instances of internal violence, such as riots, strikes, and violent demonstrations, and it also excludes violence that tends to be ad hoc and unorganized, such as spontaneous popular insurrections or uprisings. The minimum scale for a conflict to be considered a civil war is generally accepted to be one thousand battle deaths per year.

THE DIFFERENT FORMS OF CIVIL WAR

The working definition of *civil war* sketched above, however, does not tell us all that we really need to know. Where, for example, do revolutionary wars fall? Or ethnic conflicts? Or guerrilla wars? Each of these terms describes what appear to be civil wars, but do they also fall under the definition of civil war? If so, how are they unique?

Civil wars can be broken down into subcategories based on the goals the combatants are pursuing, the type of military strategy they have chosen to use, the characteristics of the different factions, and the outcome. Civil wars in which one faction aims to separate from the original state are sometimes referred to as secessionist wars. Civil wars that are fought using guerrilla tactics and that tend to rely on an attrition strategy rather than conventional strategy are often referred to as guerrilla wars. Civil wars that are fought between different ethnic groups, such as the Tutsis and Hutus in Rwanda or the Serbs and Croats, are often described as ethnic conflicts. And finally, civil wars that aim to change the entire social and political order and that bring about radical change in the government are deemed revolutions. Although each of these conflicts has distinctive characteristics, all still fall under the larger umbrella classification of "civil war."

Are all civil wars revolutions? Absolutely not. That would be the case only if all civil wars succeeded in bringing about radical social and political change. Are all civil wars ethnic conflicts? No. All ethnic conflicts are civil wars if they meet the four criteria outlined above, but many civil wars have no distinctive ethnic features. Colombia's civil war was fought between the Conservative and Liberal Parties. El Salvador's civil war between 1979 and 1992 was fought between Marxist guerrillas and the right-wing government. China's civil war between 1945 and 1949 was fought between Communists and Nationalists.

In short, civil wars can be fought for different reasons, between different groups, with different strategies. They can be as short as the seven-day war between the Jordanian government and the PLO in September 1970 or as long as Vietnam's fifteen-year battle between 1960 and 1975. They can produce hundreds of thousands of battle deaths or as few as a thousand. They can also have different outcomes. Most end in decisive victories, such as the American Civil War, the Vietnam War, and the Chinese civil war. But some end in negotiated settlements (as the recent cases of Nicaragua,

1981–1989; El Salvador, 1979–1992; and Mozambique, 1980–1992, have shown). Civil wars can meet the four prerequisites listed above and still come in many shapes and sizes.

TRENDS

Civil wars received relatively little attention from academics and policy makers until the end of the cold war. Since the early 1990s, interest has increased dramatically, for at least three reasons. First, the number of civil wars has steadily increased over the last fifty years to the point where they now greatly outnumber interstate wars. This is of direct concern to policy makers seeking to limit the spread of war into neighboring states and reduce needless bloodshed.

Second, there has been increasing pressure on the international community to do something to help end these wars, most of which take place in poor countries with weak or collapsing central governments and are fought by relatively unorganized and poorly armed factions. Advanced industrial states have the strength to end these wars but are wary of becoming entangled and are uncertain what types of intervention might help.

Third, observers are beginning to notice disturbing trends that demand explanation. Unlike interstate wars, which tend to end in negotiated settlements, civil wars tend to end in decisive military victories. And even if civil war adversaries negotiate settlements, the settlements tend to break down over time. That so many civil wars seem to defy negotiated settlement poses a striking empirical puzzle for scholars interested in war resolution and an increasingly onerous problem for policy makers interested in ending these wars off the battlefield.

QUESTIONS FOR FUTURE RESEARCH

Studies on civil wars continue to emerge at an increasing rate. Nonetheless, many questions remain to be answered. Most scholars, for example, would agree that civil wars are not the result of historical hatreds between different ethnic groups even if the conflicts break down along ethnic lines. Seemingly ethnic-based civil wars tend to be driven by the same political and economic motivations as non ethnic conflicts. Scholars cannot explain, however, why ethnicity appears to be such a powerful mobilizing force. Why do individuals tend to mobilize along ethnic lines and not along other identifying features such as class or region? This observation leads to a number of related questions. Why do so many recent civil wars appear to be ethnic and not ideological? Are political revolutions a thing of the past? Is ideology dead? Finally, much work needs to be done on the problems of civil war resolution and durability of peace settlements. Only by understanding why civil wars resist settlement and why even signed settlements break down will the international community have a chance to prevent, manage, or resolve these costly wars.

BARBARA F. WALTER

BIBLIOGRAPHY

Eckstein, Harry. *Internal War: Problems and Approaches.* New York: Free Press, 1964.

———. "On the Etiology of Internal Wars." In *History and Theory* 4, no. 2 (1965).

Higham, Robin, ed. *Civil Wars in the Twentieth Century.* Lexington: University of Kentucky Press, 1972.

Licklider, Roy. "The Consequences of Negotiated Settlements in Civil Wars, 1945–1993." *American Political Science Review* 89, no. 3 (September 1995): 681–690.

Licklider, Roy, ed. *Stopping the Killing: How Civil Wars End.* New York: New York University Press, 1993.

Small, Melvin, and J. David Singer. *Resort to Arms: International and Civil Wars, 1816–1980.* Beverly Hills: Sage, 1982.

Wright, Quincy. *A Study of War.* 2d ed. Chicago: University of Chicago Press, 1965.

CLASS

The close causal association between class conflict and revolution has long been considered synonymous with Marxist thought. Earlier varieties of socialism had focused on the exploitation of labor, the unique properties of labor as a source of value, and the organization of labor as the driving force behind social change. In the middle of the nineteenth century, Karl Marx and Friedrich Engels developed an alternative perspective that synthesized the insights of German idealist philosophy, English economic analysis, and French revolutionism. That synthesis emphasized the radical political implications of irreducible class oppositions.

For Marx, a class consisted of all members of society who shared a similar relationship to the mode of production (the system for creating and distributing wealth in society). In certain contexts, Marx distinguished those who passively shared a set of purely economic interests (a "class in itself") from those who possessed, in addition to common economic interests, a strongly felt sense of solidarity with others experiencing the same life conflicts (a "class for itself").

Marxism was materialist at its core, basing its analysis on the forces and relations of economic production, including the class structure of society. The theory pointed to a new constellation of class forces then emerging in the most highly industrialized nations of Europe and predicted that advanced capitalism would bring a series of class-based revolutions led by industrial workers (the proletariat). These violent conflicts would sweep away the existing order and replace it with a new form of communist society. The theory's broad scope and tremendous analytic power allowed it to displace competing versions of socialist thought by the final decades of the nineteenth century.

CLASS AND THE REVOLUTIONS OF THE EIGHTEENTH AND NINETEENTH CENTURIES

The French revolutions of 1789 and 1848 provided important empirical referents for the Marxist view. According to the "social interpretation" of the 1789 revolution, the Old Regime was destroyed by a dynamic, ascendant mercantile class (the bourgeoisie) that cleared away the rubble of feudal society and revoked the special privileges of a decadent aristocracy whose domination of French society had become an obstacle to the growth of capitalism. This view has constituted the orthodox understanding of the French Revolution since the early twentieth century. More recently, it has been challenged on grounds that the Old Regime was not demonstrably feudal, that the bourgeoisie was neither the exclusive nor the primary social force promoting the transformation of French society, and that the net effect of the changes introduced was not clearly procapitalist. This revisionist perspective challenges not only the specific interpretation of 1789 as a bourgeois revolution, but also the class hypothesis more generally by showing that class groups on both sides of the conflict were frequently divided in their political aspirations and actions.

The Communist Manifesto of Marx and Engels was published just a month before the outbreak of the February 1848 revolution in Paris. Though it had no direct impact on those events, it later came to define the model of proletarian or socialist revolution, which some believed the workers' insurrection of June 1848 exemplified. Like the orthodox view of 1789 as a bourgeois revolution, this interpretation of the June Days as a proto-socialist revolution has been challenged, primarily on two grounds: first, members of the declining stratum of artisans, and not a rising stratum of industrial workers, played the leading role in the insurrection; and second, younger members of the same group, organized as the militia force called the Mobile Guard, played the leading role in repressing the insurgents. Thus, critics of the Marxist interpretation point to the existence of "class fractions" with divergent interests and objectives, making it difficult to sustain the strict class hypothesis of social polarization and unified class action.

The 1848 revolution was notable as the most concentrated sequence of revolutionary events the world had ever witnessed. In the weeks following the February Revolution in Paris, more than a score of insurrections brought changes of regime or dramatic reforms to states all across the continent. In most cases, the gains achieved by popular movements were reversed when a wave of reaction spilled across Europe several months later. Although the driving force behind these far-flung incidents appears in retrospect to have been rooted as often in ethnic, nationalist, or local political divisions as in class, this massive upheaval helped define the nineteenth century as the "age of revolution" and gave widespread currency to the class interpretation of history, which had predicted just such an internationalization of revolutionary activity.

CLASS AND SOCIALIST REVOLUTION

It was not until the early twentieth century that a revolutionary movement operating within a class-based frame of reference actually succeeded in capturing state power. The 1917 overthrow of the regime of Russian tsar Nicholas II was led by Vladimir Ilyich Lenin and Leon Trotsky, both brilliant reinterpreters of Marxist revolutionary theory and pragmatic revolutionaries. Among the most influential innovations of the period was the concept of a "vanguard party" of committed activists, capable of leading an as-yet unformed proletarian class to victory. Such an invention was a practical necessity, since Russia in 1917 poorly fit the revolutionary model first advanced by Marx and Engels. Russia was then still in the early stages of industrialization, and although workers from St. Petersburg and Moscow played a crucial part in the revolutionary process, the labor force in both cities consisted mostly of artisans rather than the factory laborers whom Marx believed would compose the revolutionary proletariat.

The second major instance of socialist revolution in the twentieth century proved to be no less momentous and just as full of anomalies. Mao Zedong, after organizing a decades-long guerrilla struggle against both Nationalist Chinese forces and Japanese invaders, succeeded in establishing a socialist regime in China by 1949. The exigencies of the Chinese situation, particularly the importance of rural insurgency, required substantial modification of the original Marxist perspective. The result was a style of class analysis that borrowed from and extended the logic of the original conception but, with its focus on the peasantry as the key revolutionary class, diverged sharply from the theory as originally advanced.

CLASS AND REVOLUTION IN THE CONTEMPORARY WORLD

Marxism can be viewed as an amalgam of two theories of revolution, both class-based, that have tended to become more clearly differentiated over time. The "scientific theory," derived from Marx's analysis of the vulnerability of capitalist societies, has undergone substantial amendment or revision in light of subsequent developments. The emergence of a prosperous middle class as the largest group in modern capitalist societies has forced themes such as the misery of the working classes and class polarization to be downplayed or abandoned. Meanwhile, the vision of a classless society that socialist revolution would make possible, a theme that Marx merely sketched in outline, has remained a powerful lever for mobilizing groups that see themselves as oppressed and exploited classes whose destiny is to overthrow the existing social order.

The high-water mark of class-based perspectives was reached in the immediate post-World War II period. Movements of national liberation among colonized peoples frequently adopted a class logic that was tied to an analysis of the world economy and reinforced by cleavages that, though rooted most obviously in nationality and race, could be portrayed as class divisions. This rash of revolutionary movements in the Third World, combined with the consolidation of socialist regimes in Eastern Europe, was followed by the eruption of insurgent movements on a global scale around 1968, convincing many observers that a modified or "revisionist" class analysis was essential to understanding the political and social developments that could be expected in the late twentieth century. However, over the next two decades, the decline and eventual collapse of socialist regimes in most regions of the world led to the eclipse of Marxist perspectives in many areas of social and political analysis. Such perspectives have had to make room for theories that emphasize political rather than economic determination and that offer a more balanced view of the role that religion, culture, and demography play in the etiology of revolution.

Today, the concept of class is likely to be interpreted more flexibly than it was in the heyday of Marxism and weighed in relationship to other sociological dimensions (such as gender, ethnicity, nationality, religious affiliation, and linguistic differences) that may intensify or diffuse its impact. Classes that seemed less crucial to Marx—such as peasants and intellectuals—loom larger in current analyses of revolution. The meaning of class is also likely to be interpreted within the context of the particular communities or strata in which revolutionary mobilization arises, rather than being considered as fixed by external circumstance. Nonetheless, in this more nuanced form, the concept of class remains an invaluable element in the analysis of revolutionary movements. Reports of the death of class analysis will undoubtedly prove to be greatly exaggerated.

See also *Chinese Communist Revolution (1921–1949); European Revolutions of 1848; French Revolution (1789–1815); Lenin, Vladimir Ilyich; Mao Zedong; Marx, Karl, and Friedrich Engels; Race; Russian Revolution of 1917; Trotsky, Leon.*

MARK TRAUGOTT

BIBLIOGRAPHY

Calhoun, Craig. *The Question of Class Struggle: Social Foundations of Popular Radicalism During the Industrial Revolution.* Chicago: University of Chicago Press, 1982.

Colburn, Forrest D. *The Vogue of Revolution in Poor Countries.* Princeton, N.J.: Princeton University Press, 1994.

Furet, François. *Interpreting the French Revolution.* Cambridge: Cambridge University Press, 1981.

Konrad, George, and Ivan Szelenyi. *The Intellectuals on the Road to Class Power.* New York: Harcourt Brace Jovanovich, 1979.

Lefebvre, Georges. *The Coming of the French Revolution.* Princeton, N.J.: Princeton University Press, 1989.

Marx, Karl. *The Class Struggles in France, 1848 to 1850.* Moscow: Foreign Language Publishing House, 1960.

Marx, Karl, and Friedrich Engels. *The Communist Manifesto.* New York: Oxford University Press, 1992.

Sewell, William H. *Work and Revolution in France: The Language of Labor from the Old Regime to 1848.* Cambridge: Cambridge University Press, 1980.

COLOMBIA'S "LA VIOLENCIA" (1948–1964)

Between 1948 and 1964 the Republic of Colombia was the scene of some of the most intense, protracted, and widespread civilian violence in the twentieth century. Known in Colombia simply as La Violencia, this process took at least 200,000 lives, including 112,000 in the period 1948–1950.

Intense partisan rivalries between the Liberal and Conservative Parties led to political violence after the 1946 presidential elections, in which a victorious Conservative, Laureano Gómez, defeated a Liberal Party divided between two candidates, Gabriel Turbay and Jorge Eliécer Gaitán. Violence at a lesser level had erupted in 1930 when a Liberal candidate had won the presidency over a Conservative Party divided between two candidates. In both cases the partisan violence was related to the postelection construction of political party hegemonies that sought to monopolize power to the total exclusion of the defeated political force. The complete exclusion of the defeated party was a reflection of the prevailing political culture, which had led to numerous civil wars in the nineteenth century.

Partisan conflict had become more intense in the twentieth century as the state had come to play an increasingly important role in national life, to the point that no sector within the dominant groups in society would accept exclusion from state power and its benefits. Control of government was made even more critical owing to the government's role as arbiter of the highly conflictive economic and social relations that had emerged in Colombian life in the course of the twentieth century.

It was in this context that the assassination of Liberal Party leader and ex-presidential candidate Jorge Eliécer Gaitán in 1948 led to the mass insurrection known as the "9 de Abril" (9th of April) in Colombia and as the Bogotazo in the rest of the world. The widespread violence in the capital city and the intense partisan conflict that ensued throughout the country produced a partial collapse of the state. The manifestations of the partial collapse included the breakdown of governing institutions (including the closing of Congress and partisan influence over the police and the judiciary), the loss of state legitimacy for many sectors of the population (including most supporters of the Liberal Party), contradictions within the armed apparatus of the state (including conflicts between the Conservative-dominated police and Liberal army officers), and the physical absence of state officials in extensive regions of the national territory (the eastern plains, most mountain areas, the coffee-growing regions of Antioquia and Caldas, and the valleys of the Valle del Cauca and upper Magdalena).

The partial collapse of the state due to the partisan violence in turn led to full-blown guerrilla civil wars (with both Liberal guerrillas and Communist guerrillas), the violent manifestation of traditional village rivalries, violence for control of local power structures, violence for control of land (parcels lost due to forced evictions has a stronger correlation with the geographical distribution of the violence than do migrations due to the violence), violence over the appropriation of coffee crops, and widespread banditry. In areas where the state maintained relative coherence—the cities, the Caribbean coast, and the southern department of Narino on the Ecuadorian border—violence was not a significant factor.

The armed forces, led by army commander Gen. Gustavo Rojas Pinilla, staged a successful coup d'état on June 13, 1953. The new military government declared a general amnesty for all those involved in the violence except military deserters. The coup enjoyed the support of all political actors except supporters of deposed president Laureano Gómez and the Communists. The combination of coup, amnesty, and removal of the political causes of the conflict led to an immediate and dramatic reduction in the level of violence. The number of fatalities dropped from 13,250 in 1952, to 8,650 in 1953, to 900 in 1954, and 1,013 in 1955.

However, the army's political support and the decline of the violence were short-lived. The fragility of the army's largely psychological influence over the large areas affected by the partial collapse of the state was illustrated by the rapidity with which the violence reignited. By 1956 the violence had returned to a level of 13,000 fatalities, and it was to remain in the 2,000–4,000 deaths-per-year range through 1962, when it began to subside. This second period of La Violencia, or the late violence, corresponded more to socioeconomic conflicts than to traditional partisan rivalries.

Rojas Pinilla's plan to continue in power united the Liberals and Conservatives against what they considered to be the military's usurpation of power. Deprived of party support, the military government attempted to develop its own political base by following largely populist policies. It also repressed the opposition, including a massacre of students in Bogotá in June 1954 and the resumption of violent activities by the paramilitary groups known collectively as the Pájaros ("Birds") in northern Valle and western Caldas. The Pájaros had served the Conservative government before serving the military government politically, as well as promoted their own personal enrichment through land grabs, confiscation of coffee crops, and other forms of banditry. The army also attempted, unsuccessfully, to retake the Communist-controlled areas of eastern Tolima and the Sumapaz in

Cundinamarca. The movement of refugees extended the fighting to all of Tolima and adjacent departments.

The opposition of the traditional parties to the military regime led to negotiations in Spain between Alberto Lleras for the Liberals and Laureano Gómez for the Conservatives. Their talks led to the formation of the Civil Front, which eventually became the National Front. It declared opposition to the military government in November 1956. After a vigorous civil resistance campaign, the Rojas Pinilla regime fell on May 10, 1957. The National Front consisted of a sixteen-year power-sharing arrangement in which the Liberals and Conservatives rotated the presidency and basic policies were negotiated by the directorates of the two parties. Both parties, and every faction within them, were guaranteed equal treatment, access to political decision making, and political posts. None of the powerful groups that controlled Colombia's traditional parties was to fear official discrimination or total exclusion from the benefits of power. Through the National Front, the exclusive, hegemonic political culture that had led to intense partisan rivalries and political violence was overcome.

However, reconstructing state authority over vast reaches of Colombian territory, structuring chronic socioeconomic conflicts, and controlling widespread banditry (especially extortion and kidnapping) proved to be much more daunting tasks. Fatalities attributable to La Violencia fell below the one thousand-per-year level only in 1964, and below the five hundred-per-year level in 1966, without ever disappearing completely. Since the mid-1960s new forms of violence have also made their appearance in Colombia, facilitated in part by the legacy of La Violencia and the partial collapse of the state that it had conditioned.

PAUL OQUIST

BIBLIOGRAPHY

Comision de Estudios sobre La Violencia. *Colombia Violencia y Democracia.* Bogotá: Universidad Nacional, 1996.

Guzmán Campos, Germán, Orlando Fals Borda, and Eduardo Umaña Luna. *La Violencia en Colombia.* Bogotá: Universidad Nacional, 1962.

Montaña Cuellar, Diego. *Colombia: País Formal y País Real.* Buenos Aires: Editorial Platina, 1963.

Oquist, Paul. *Violence, Conflict, and Politics in Colombia.* New York: Academic Press, 1980.

Payne, James L. *Patterns of Conflict in Colombia.* New Haven, Conn.: Yale University Press, 1968.

Pecaut, Daniel. *Orden y Violencia: Colombia 1930–1954.* Bogotá: Cerec Siglo XXI, 1987.

Sanchez, Gonzalo, and Ricardo Penaranda. *Pasado y Presente de la Violencia en Colombia.* Bogotá: Editorial Cerec, 1991.

Santa, Eduardo. *Sociologia Politica de Colombia.* Bogotá: Ediciones Tercer Mundo, 1964.

COLONIALISM AND ANTICOLONIALISM

The term *colonialism,* in contemporary usage, normally refers to the rule by a state over subordinated territories that usually are geographically separated. Colonies had a distinct and separate legal status, and their inhabitants were subjects rather than citizens. Acquisition of territories in the era of global European expansion from the fifteenth to the early twentieth centuries almost always occurred through superior force, whether expressed through military conquest, simple annexation, or treaty.

THE RISE OF THE COLONIAL SYSTEM

The emergence of colonialism, which may be dated from the 1415 establishment of the first Portuguese garrisons at Ceuta and Melilla on the North African coast, was made possible by transformations in navigational technology permitting European ships to venture into the open sea. The initial target was Asia and its high-value trade commodities; Africa had been circumnavigated by 1488. The search for a westward route to Asia led to the European landfall in the Americas in 1492. The race was on for what became a vast territorial partition of much of Asia, almost all of Africa, and the entire Western hemisphere.

The two initial colonizers, Portugal and Spain, sought and received papal blessing for their new claims. In three bulls issued from 1452 to 1456, the papacy, then sole supranational fount of authority, granted Portuguese monarch Prince Henry the Navigator the right to attack, conquer, and subdue all "Saracens" (Muslims) and other "unbelievers" from Morocco to the Indies, to reduce them to slavery, to transfer their lands and properties to the crown, and to enjoy a monopoly of navigation, trade, and fishing. After Spain entered the picture in 1492, Pope Alexander in 1493 extended comparable privileges over the westward domains, in return for a commitment to evangelization. The following year, in the Treaty of Tordesillas, Spain and Portugal divided the extra-European world between them, fixing a boundary one hundred leagues (roughly three hundred miles) west of Cape Verde.

During the sixteenth century three other maritime nations entered the fray. England, France, and the Netherlands gradually began to poach on the rich profits accruing to Portugal and especially Spain from their Asian footholds and American territorial domains: gold, silver, and spices. In the seventeenth and eighteenth centuries competition intensified, as slave-based sugar plantations yielded high returns. After a pause in the first part of the nineteenth century, imperial expansion and rivalry exploded in the last quarter of that century, sweeping within its net nearly all of Africa and Oceania. At this stage, three newly created European states—Belgium, Germany, and Italy—entered the competition. So also did the United States, in the Caribbean and the Asian islands, and Japan. The last phase of expansion of the overland Russian empire, into Central Asia, took an essentially colonial form.

THE IMPACT OF COLONIALISM

The impact of colonialism over the fifteenth to the twentieth centuries was immense and deserves the term revolutionary. Political geography was entirely reconfigured; the territorial legacy of the imperial partition proved enduring. The contemporary map of Asia, Africa, and Latin America essentially reflects the boundaries traced by colonial powers. Massive population changes were set in motion: the European settlement in the Americas and Australasia; the importation of African slaves in the Americas and the importation of South Asian indentured labor in the Caribbean and scattered other locations; and the decimation of indigenous populations through disease, spoliation, or oppression. Colonial powers (apart from Japan) assumed Christian conversion as an integral part of their hegemonical task, except where other universal religious heritages could not be safely uprooted (Islam, Hinduism, Buddhism). Thus Christianity became a world religion. In Africa, paradoxically, the colonial order also permitted a large-scale expansion of Islam. In those areas where the colonial economy depended on labor-intensive plantation crops (tobacco, cotton, especially sugar), the ancient institution of slavery was commercialized, capitalized, racialized, and modernized, surviving until the late nineteenth century. Closely related to slavery and the institutionalized subjugation of racially different populations, pernicious doctrines of racism took root, which continue to cast a large shadow over the Western world. A capitalist economic system progressively permeated the colonized territories, and a globalized international economy took form.

Even before the final paroxysm of colonial expansion in the late nineteenth century, the imperial tide had begun to recede. The revolt of the thirteen British North American colonies from 1775 to 1783 was the first harbinger. Most of the rest of the Americas followed in the early nineteenth century. The people behind this early anticolonialism invariably came to characterize themselves as revolutionary (the American Revolution, various Latin American revolutions), although they were settlers of European descent.

THE EMERGENCE AND TRIUMPH OF ANTICOLONIAL NATIONALISM

The international order began to change after World War I; the reallocation of colonial territories stripped from Germany was accompanied by an explicit obligation to rule them only in the interest of the inhabitants. The doctrine of self-determination received a degree of international sanction and visibility through its dramatic espousal by Woodrow Wilson and Vladimir Ilyich Lenin. Its application, however, was limited at the time to some of the former European possessions of the defunct Austro-Hungarian and Ottoman Empires. Anticolonialism was no longer simply the doctrine of European settlers. In Egypt, the Levant, India, Indonesia, and Indochina a discourse of nationalism took form, and anticolonial movements became a significant political force.

After World War II, anticolonialism became a dominant force. The essence of this creed was the inherent illegitimacy of colonial rule and the inalienable right of all peoples to claim sovereignty and rule themselves. Older doctrines justifying colonial occupation as a benevolent trusteeship exercised by more advanced nations over territories whose populations were incapable of self-rule were repudiated. The only task remaining for the colonizer was organizing, as swiftly as possible, representative political structures to permit dependent territories to accede to independence.

Colonialism was eliminated far more quickly than anyone had anticipated at the end of World War II in 1945. Ideologically, anticolonial movements appropriated the powerful idea of nationalism, which had arisen in Europe in the late eighteenth century. The doctrine was reformulated in important respects: the common bond defining peoplehood was not language or historical statehood but the shared subjugation to a given colonizer. Thus, in a remarkable feat of collective imagination, "India," "Indonesia," and "Nigeria" became nations. The correlate doctrine of self-determination, another potent nineteenth century intellectual innovation, was also central to anticolonial nationalism: a people, thus constituted, enjoyed a sacred right to determine their own destiny and to liberate themselves from alien domination.

Woven into the text of anticolonial nationalism were other contemporary revolutionary doctrines: different strands of socialism, sometimes Marxism-Leninism, always Third-World anti-imperialism. Larger dreams of panterritorial unification—pan-Arabism, pan-Africanism—resonated strongly. Such revolutionary writers and activists as Frantz Fanon of Algeria and Ernesto "Che" Guevara of Cuba integrated anticolonialism into a broader message of a Third World struggle of the rural masses against the domination of the rich industrialized countries. Where colonialism proved intransigent, the idea of wresting independence by armed

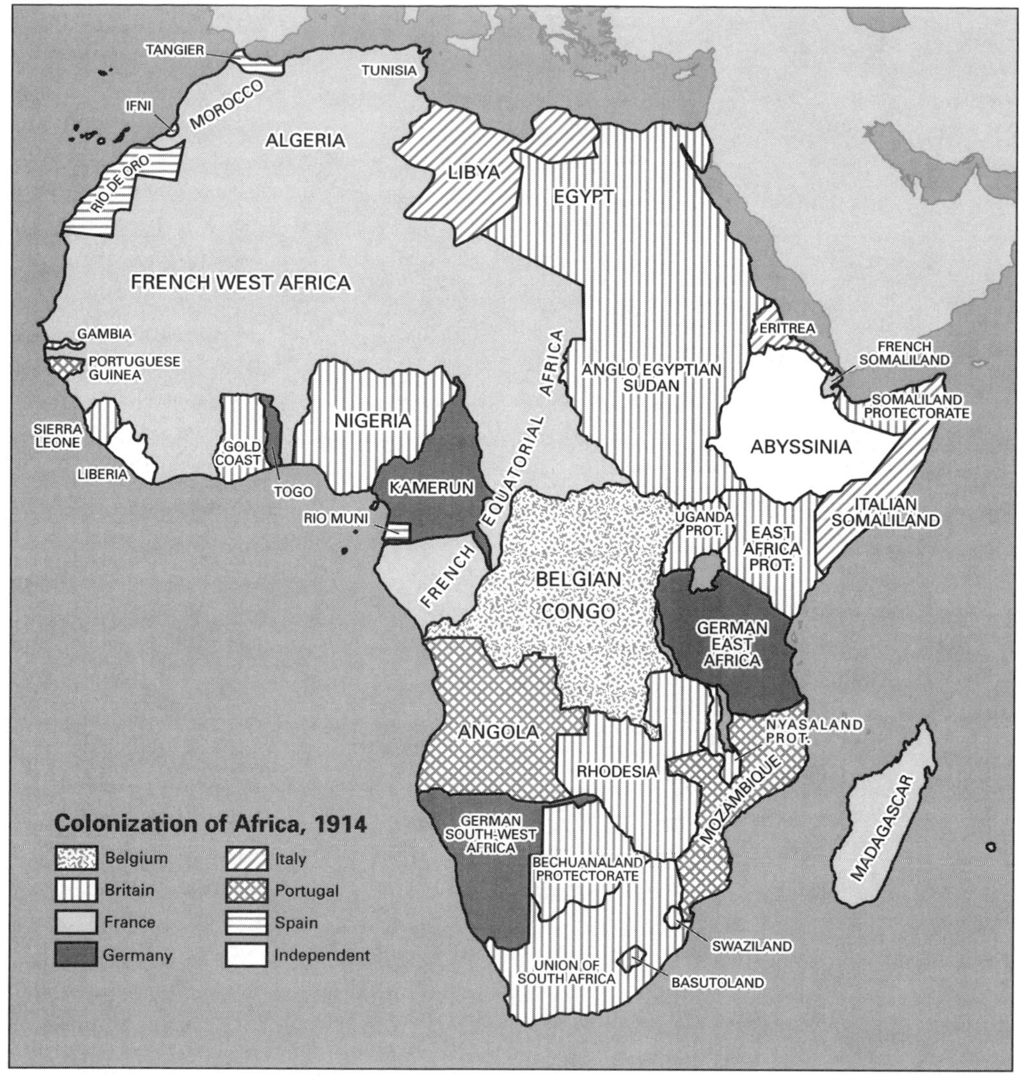

Alex Tait/EquatorGraphics, Inc.

guerrilla struggle drew inspiration from the Chinese, Vietnamese, and Algerian Revolutions.

Anticolonial nationalism had demonstrated its powerful mobilizational force by the 1950s. Although the Netherlands in Indonesia, France in Vietnam and Algeria, and Portugal in Angola, Mozambique, and Guinea-Bissau committed huge resources to combating armed uprisings, they uniformly failed. The lesson was unmistakable, drawn both by colonizers and anticolonial forces: over time, nationalists would succeed in progressively extending their message of liberation to the farthest reaches of the territory. History, all concluded, was on the side of anticolonialism.

Anticolonialism also found a powerful ally in the international normative order. Prior to World War II the international system was dominated by the colonial powers, but they were all greatly weakened by the ravages of the war: Japan and Italy lost the war and their colonies; France, Belgium, and the Netherlands had been under German occupation; and Britain was bled dry by the war effort. In the postwar era the two major powers, the United States and the Soviet Union, were not committed to the colonial order, and both encouraged, in different ways, its dissolution. As newly independent Asian and Middle Eastern states entered the United Nations and other international bodies, they promoted with increasing vigor and effectiveness the anticolonial cause. Latin American states generally rallied to their support, and the Soviet bloc was implacably hostile to colonialism. Thus, by 1960 the dominant voice of the international system called for immediate liquidation of colonialism.

The last major holdout was Portugal; after the collapse of the Portuguese autocracy in 1974, the new regime swiftly abandoned the colonial empire. By 1975 the triumph of the anticolonial revolution was all but complete. Only a handful of territorial morsels remained under the sovereignty of a colonizer. The dependent status of territories such as Puerto Rico, Bermuda, and Martinique, mostly small, economically vulnerable islands, invariably was freely chosen and involved internal self-government. Colonial empires, a central feature of the modern historical era, were dead.

See also *Fanon, Frantz Omar; Guevara, Ernesto "Che."*

Crawford Young

BIBLIOGRAPHY

Bethell, Leslie, ed. *Colonial Latin America.* Volume 2 of *The Cambridge History of Latin America.* Cambridge: Cambridge University Press, 1984.

Dominguez, Jorge I. *Insurrection or Loyalty: The Breakdown of the Spanish Empire.* Cambridge, Mass.: Harvard University Press, 1980.

Emerson, Rupert. *From Empire to Nation: The Rise to Self-Assertion of Asian and African Peoples.* Cambridge, Mass.: Harvard University Press, 1960.

Fanon, Frantz. *The Wretched of the Earth.* London: MacGibbon and Kee, 1965.

Gann, L. H., and Peter Duignan, eds. *Colonialism in Africa 1870-1960.* 5 vols. Cambridge: Cambridge University Press, 1970-1975.

Gifford, Prosser, and William Roger Louis. *Decolonization and African Independence: The Transfers of Power, 1960-1980.* New Haven, Conn.: Yale University Press, 1988.

Nehru, Jawaharlal. *The Discovery of India.* New York: Meridian Books, 1946.

Young, Crawford. *The African Colonial State in Comparative Perspective.* New Haven, Conn.: Yale University Press, 1994.

COMMUNISM

Communism is a doctrine that advocates a revolution to overthrow capitalism and create a socialist society of equality and prosperity. It originated in the nineteenth-century writings of Karl Marx and Friedrich Engels and in the hands of Vladimir Ilyich Lenin was transformed in the early 1900s into an authoritarian doctrine of discipline and obedience to a revolutionary party. Its influence spread widely after Lenin became the leader of the Soviet Union in the Russian Revolution of October 1917. Communism, which became known as Marxism-Leninism, was further modified by such leaders as Joseph Stalin, who led the Soviet Union after Lenin's death in 1924 until his own death in 1953, and Mao Zedong, who led the Chinese Communist Party to political power in 1949 and ruled China until his death in 1976.

DOCTRINE AND REVOLUTIONARY STRATEGY

Marxism-Leninism consists of two fundamental ideas. The first is Marx and Engels's theory of class struggle in which capitalism will inevitably be overthrown by a working class revolution after which private property will be abolished and a socialist economy established. The second was added by Lenin: that a highly disciplined revolutionary party is necessary to seize power on behalf of the working class and to defend the revolution through dictatorial means.

Some early Marxists felt that capitalism could be overthrown gradually by working legally through trade unions and parliaments. Lenin declared this a betrayal of Marxism and the working class. He argued that revolution required a party of a new type—a "vanguard party" made up of highly committed and disciplined full-time revolutionaries. The party would be flexible in its tactics and shift its strategy as opportunities occurred. Within the party, once a decision was made by the leaders, no disagreements could be tolerated, for the same reason that soldiers in an army cannot question their orders in wartime. Once in power, the party would create a "proletarian dictatorship" to eliminate enemies of the revolution, abolish private property, and push for the creation of a socialist system.

Inspired by the Russian Revolution, communist parties and revolutionary movements became an important political force in various parts of the world from the mid-1920s through the early 1980s. Until World War II, however, communists held power only in the Soviet Union and Mongolia. The end of the war brought a rapid expansion in the number of communist regimes and in the size and strength of revolutionary communist movements elsewhere. New communist regimes were created as a result of troop movements at the end of World War II. As the Soviet army advanced on the defeated Germans in eastern Europe, it occupied Poland, Czechoslovakia, eastern Germany, Bulgaria, Romania, and Hungary and soon installed communist governments there. Communist regimes were also created when local communists who had led resistance movements against the Japanese or Germans seized power after their withdrawal, sometimes after fighting a civil war, as in Albania, China, North Korea, Vietnam, and Yugoslavia.

After the early 1950s, the strongest communist movements were very different from the Russian Bolshevik Party led by Lenin in 1917. Lenin's party had been small and secretive; it had connections to urban trade unions but seized power in a coup with limited popular involvement. The new revolutions were inspired by the Chinese model, in which a communist party established support among peasants in rural areas that it controlled, eventually creating a large army that used guerrilla warfare to defeat larger and better-equipped government armies. This strategy led to successful revolutions in Cuba, Vietnam, Cambodia, Laos, Angola, Mozambique, and Nicaragua, and it inspired large communist-led rural movements in southeast Asia, Africa, and Central and South America.

A POLITICAL AND ECONOMIC SYSTEM

Marxism-Leninism declined in the 1980s because of flaws in the political and economic systems installed by ruling communist parties. Communist regimes were ruled by a single party organization designed to permit national leaders' control over national and local organs of government, the military, as well as most factories, offices, and schools. Communist parties also sought strict obedience from their members after their seizure of power just as they had insisted on discipline before; they rewarded the loyal with material privileges and career advancement and punished the disloyal. The pursuit of such discipline sometimes led to damaging purges that in extreme cases involved the imprisonment and death of millions of people in such episodes as the Soviet Union's Great Purges of the 1930s, the Chinese Great Proletarian Cultural Revolution (1966–1969), and the massacres conducted by the Khmer Rouge in Cambodia (1975–1978).

Publications of Karl Marx, including the Communist Manifesto (left).

The economic system of communism, first developed in the Soviet Union under Stalin, was centrally planned and abolished private property, the profit motive, and free markets. Property was nationalized and land was collectivized; families owned only their homes and personal possessions. Government planners set national targets for production, and bureaucracies divided these targets among factories and villages and allocated the products nationwide. Private enterprise was usually very tightly restricted, and trade by individuals strongly discouraged.

The decline of communism, which led to its virtual collapse as an important revolutionary doctrine in the 1990s, is generally attributed to the rigidity and inflexibility of its political and economic systems. Ruling parties aged, became bureaucratic, inefficient, and often corrupt, and were unable to implement new ideas in response to internal problems. The economic system proved too bureaucratic and inefficient to keep up with successive waves of technical and organizational innovation in the world capitalist system. Regimes that were unable to adapt until it was too late, like the Soviet Union, Mongolia, and all of the east European communist regimes, collapsed or became mired in stagnation and poverty, as in Cuba and North Korea. Regimes that have responded by changing their economic system to rely more on family farming, free markets, and the profit motive have so far been able to survive and even prosper (like China and Vietnam), but they have moved far from the doctrines and practices that have defined communism in the twentieth century.

See also *Cambodian Khmer Rouge Revolution (1967–1979); Chinese Communist Revolution (1921–1949); Chinese Cultural Revolution (1966–1969); Kim Il Sung; Korean Civil War (1950–1953); Lenin, Vladimir Ilyich; Malayan Communist Insurgency (1948–1960); Mao Zedong; Marx, Karl, and Friedrich Engels; Mozambican Revolution (1974–1994); Russian Revolution of 1917; Socialism; Stalin, Joseph; Vietnamese Revolution (1945–1975).*

ANDREW G. WALDER

BIBLIOGRAPHY

Kornai, Janos. *The Socialist System: The Political Economy of Communism.* Princeton, N.J.: Princeton University Press, 1992.

Meyer, Alfred G. *Communism.* 5th ed. New York: Random House, 1984.

———. *Leninism.* 2d ed. Boulder, Colo.: Westview, 1986.

Nove, Alec. *The Soviet Economic System.* 3d ed. Boston: Allen and Unwin, 1986.

Schwartz, Benjamin. *Chinese Communism and the Rise of Mao.* 2d ed. New York: Harper and Row, 1967.

Tucker, Robert C. *Stalin in Power: The Revolution from Above, 1928–1941.* New York: Norton, 1990.

CONGOLESE/ZAIRIAN UPHEAVALS (1960–)

The Democratic Republic of the Congo, formerly Zaire, has known violence and political upheaval throughout its existence as an independent nation. After an independence hastily effected by Belgium on June 30, 1960, apparent stability gave way to chaos—the Congo Crisis—within days after the formal ceremonies marking the birth of the new nation. A power vacuum facilitated the take over by Gen. Joseph Mobutu (Mobutu Sese Seko), who ruled as president in Zaire for thirty-two years, using brutal methods to suppress opposition. The ouster of Mobutu by Laurent Kabila, a long-time foe of Mobutu, in 1997 was the culmination of a set of internal and external circumstances, themselves characterized by violence.

In a sense, turbulence is the Congo's historical legacy. At the Berlin Conference partitioning Africa in 1884, King Leopold's de facto control of the Congo was formally recognized with the creation of the Congo Free State. With Leopold's desire to ensure that the Congo was a lucrative venture, the focus was on the extraction of natural resources, more often than not using brutal methods, as well as the destruction of pre-existing African kingdoms through military conquest. Leopold's excesses soon brought heightened international criticism and pressures for Belgian annexation of the Congo. The Free State therefore became a Belgian colony in 1908. In the Belgian Congo the colonial administration was no less brutal. Known as "Bula Matari" (meaning "he who breaks rocks"), the state regulated every aspect of colonial life, working in tandem with the church and the large commercial conglomerates extracting natural resources (rubber and copper). Forced cultivation, forced resettlement, and labor conscription were the norm, and resistance to the system was met with force.

INDEPENDENCE AND DISINTEGRATION OF THE NEW STATE

Independence brought with it a tenuous compromise between the two leading political leaders to emerge during the preindependence elections of May 1960. Patrice Lumumba, head of the National Congolese Movement (MNC) with a base of support in eastern Congo (Orientale Province), won a narrow victory over Joseph Kasavubu, leader of the BaKongo Alliance (ABAKO), with its stronghold in Leopoldville and the surrounding Bas Zaire region. Both leaders not only represented different ethnic groups but also held opposing views of Congolese independence, with Lumumba taking a more "radical" position, calling for genuine political and economic independence and advocating that the Congo should take its place in the Non-Aligned Movement. By contrast, Kasavubu took a more moderate position, and thus enjoyed the support of the Belgians, other Western governments, and the multinational firms operating in the Congo. The outcome of the election led to Lumumba being appointed prime minister and Kasavubu president of the new state, marking the beginning of the First Republic.

Within days of the creation of the Democratic Republic of the Congo, a mutiny of the Congolese army over continued Belgian control and general conditions degenerated after the departure of the Belgian commanders. Soon there were widespread attacks on the European population in the Congo, resulting in a mass exodus of Belgians from the country. Political instability led to Belgian military intervention. Diplomatic relations were severed with Belgium, and the Lumumba government asked the United Nations to secure the withdrawal of Belgian troops. This formal request to the UN Security Council elevated the situation in the Congo to an international crisis. The UN, the United States, Belgium, and the Soviet Union were soon involved in deliberations at the highest levels. From the point of view of the West, the unrest in the Congo, unless controlled, would lead this mineral-rich and strategically important country into the Soviet sphere of influence.

As a further complication, the province of Katanga

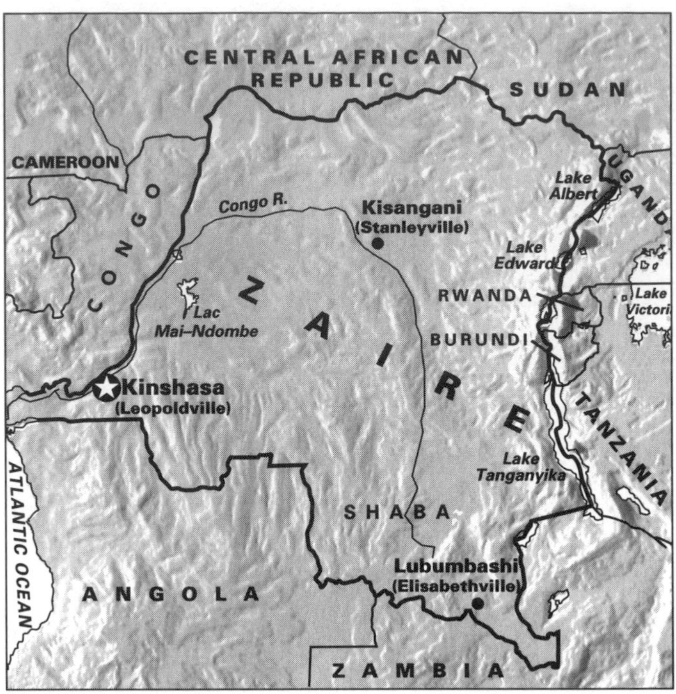

announced its secession, under the leadership of Moise Tshombe, with the unofficial blessing of Belgium. Katanga was the center of copper and cobalt mining operations in the Congo and hence was important to Belgian interests. Belgian support and protection by the Belgian military effectively insulated Tshombe from Lumumba's control. Faced with the loss of jurisdiction over Katanga and critically needed revenues, Lumumba appealed to the Soviets for assistance, thereby alienating not only the West but also President Kasavubu. Plans were therefore put in place to overthrow Lumumba.

By September 1960, three months after independence, the parliamentary regime established as the First Republic had collapsed. With the standoff between Lumumba and Kasavubu, the chief of staff of the Congolese army, Col. Joseph Mobutu, staged a bloodless military coup and appointed a provisional government. Lumumba was subsequently arrested by the army and transported to Katanga, where he was assassinated by Tshombe's forces.

At the time of Lumumba's death in 1961, the Congo seemed irreparably fragmented. Cross-cutting ethnic factionalism and social stratification, previously controlled by the colonial administration, had reemerged. From the point of view of the Congolese, independence had brought an elite to power that retained the same privileges as the Belgians under colonialism, and in similar fashion had appropriated the resources of the state. The regions of Katanga and Kasai, in the center and south of the country, respectively, had seceded, each with its own armed forces. In addition, Stanleyville, in Orientale (the Eastern Province), was claiming to be the legitimate capital of the country in direct defiance of the central government in Leopoldville. Therefore, the Congo Crisis was as much the result of ethnic competition as a call for genuine independence. Political unrest ended in 1965 when Mobutu, assured of Western backing, staged a second coup.

MOBUTU AND THE SECOND REPUBLIC

When Mobutu came to power he quickly implemented several measures to consolidate control over the state and ostensibly reverse the political and ethnic fragmentation that had contributed to the Congo Crisis. He attempted to depoliticize ethnicity and regionalism by transforming provinces in the Congo into purely administrative units. Focusing on restoring law and order, Mobutu reinstituted the authoritarian, centralized state characteristic of the colonial period. Members of the previous government and opposition figures were co-opted, exiled, or eliminated. Political activities were banned, except in the context of a newly created single party, the Popular Movement of the Revolution (MPR). All party posts were intertwined with those of the state to facilitate control. In addition, political mobilization was structured around an artificially created national identity fostered by an "ideology," initially called "authenticity," representing an attempt to recapture the essence of the country destroyed during colonialism. The name of the Congo was changed to Zaire, the Portuguese term for the Congo River, a misspelling of the word *nzadi,* the Kikongo term for river. Colonial names of cities and towns were appropriately changed (for example, Leopoldville became Kinshasa). Finally all citizens were required by law to replace their Christian names with Zairian names, and Mobutu himself relinquished his birth name, Joseph-Désire, to become Mobutu Sese Seko Kuku Ngbendu Wa Za Banga. Authenticity soon gave way to "Mobutuism," essentially the teachings and thoughts of President Mobutu himself.

Running in tandem with this strategy, a "cult of personality" was created, drawing on the notion of the preeminent role of the African chief, in which Mobutu was consistently portrayed as a firm but benevolent "father" of the nation and Zaire's citizens as his "children." It was also implied that Mobutu possessed special supernatural powers as the one chosen by God to lead the nation. This image, embedded in the Zairian psyche, in turn legitimized Mobutu's form of personal rule. Under this system, decision making on all political and economic issues was centralized in the office of the president. All state-party officials were dependent on Mobutu for their selection and maintenance in power, and their vulnerability was maintained through frequent rotations of government and party posts. Personal rule was also strengthened by patron-client politics. Access to the state-party apparatus was the means to personal enrichment, and appropriating the resources of the state was actively pursued, condoned, and encouraged by Mobutu himself. The newly created "political class" was almost exclusively from Equateur, Mobutu's region, which in turn heightened ethnic competition. Continued membership in this elite group depended on loyalty to the president.

The system established by Mobutu ensured that no potential leader could pose a threat to his personal rule. These internal strategies were buttressed by sustained external support from three important allies—the United States, France, and Belgium. Mobutu's support for Jonas Savimbi and UNITA was both profitable to Mobutu and critical to American foreign policy objectives, particularly in Angola in the mid-1980s, after the United States began to channel covert aid to UNITA in its battle against the Soviet-supported MPLA.

POLITICAL CHANGE AND A PARTIAL RETREAT FROM AUTHORITARIANISM

Until the late 1980s protests against Mobutu's authoritarian state, both within the country and by external groups, were intermittent, ad hoc, and largely ineffective, largely due to the president's highly effective strategy of dividing the opposition and to sustained Western support for the regime. Two invasions of the Shaba Province (formerly Katanga) in 1977 and 1978 by the Front for the National Liberation of the Congo (FLNC), first from Angola and then Zambia, were suppressed with external assistance. In 1989, however, the Berlin Wall fell, and subsequently, prodemocracy movements in several east European and African countries were successful in eliminating authoritarian regimes. Internal resistance to the Mobutu regime therefore became more confrontational, violent, and sustained. In addition, the end of the cold war made Zaire less strategically important, and the country's traditional allies began to insist that Mobutu implement democratic reforms. Given this convergence of circumstances, Mobutu felt compelled to initiate a dialogue on political change.

In January 1990 the president undertook a two-month tour of the country, in which Zairians were invited to speak freely. For the first time, there were open criticisms of Mobutu, blatant calls for his resignation, and mass prodemocracy demonstrations. As unrest mounted, the army and civil guard increased repression and intimidation. The president suddenly announced on April 24, 1990, the creation of a multiparty democracy, in effect a major reconstruction of the state, and the beginning of the Third Republic. Effective leadership of the government would be relinquished to a prime minister, and Mobutu, in his capacity as president, would be "above politics" and serve as "referee" in the political process.

Hundreds of parties emerged, each competing for recognition and support. By 1991 the Union for Democracy and Social Progress (UDPS), led by Etienne Tshisekedi from Kasai, emerged as the strongest opposition force. The MPR "reinvented itself" under a new name, the Popular Movement for Renewal. In addition, more than one hundred opposition parties organized into a united front known as the Sacred Union, while Mobutu himself funded the creation of several "opposition" groups that coalesced into the United Democratic Forces. For the first time, there was optimism both inside and outside Zaire that democratic change would put an end to the Mobutu era.

Sustained pressure on Mobutu by the Sacred Union and the international community led to the convening of a National Conference. This model, in which representatives of all political parties would meet to discuss and vote on a new government and constitution, had been pursued successfully elsewhere in Africa. Despite repeated delays and subversive tactics by the president, the conference finally agreed to a series of constitutional changes for the political transition to multiparty politics and adjourned in December 1992. A Transition Charter was formulated to replace the constitution, and provisions were made for a parliament (the High Council of the Republic), which would have control over the government and, ultimately, Mobutu himself. Under the charter, Mobutu would lose control over state finances, foreign affairs, and defense—areas vital to maintaining his political power.

The expected transition to a Third Republic never occurred as the charter stipulated. Instead, Mobutu forced the merger of the High Council and his own Transitional Parliament, creating a new legislature that he could control. Not surprisingly, political instability and violence once again became the norm, with frequent confrontations between the military forces, specifically the elite, well-trained Presidential Guard, and the opposition. As an added complication, the army rank-and-file, poorly paid, if at all, regularly engaged in looting and atrocities against the population. Riots in Kinshasa and Lubumbashi, capital of Shaba Province, in 1991 and 1993 resulted in a limited intervention by Belgian and French paratroopers to evacuate expatriates, rather than, as in the past, to support the Mobutu regime. Clashes occurred between competing ethnic groups in Shaba, North Kivu, and elsewhere in the struggle for political power and, by extension, economic advancement.

In the past, chaos and insecurity had reinforced Mobutu's contention that only he could hold Zaire together. While this had played well with Mobutu's traditional allies during the cold war, by the mid-1990s the deteriorating political and economic situation sparked fears in Western capitals about the collapse of the Zairian state. The pressures for Mobutu to relinquish power increased, as did his international isolation. Foreign aid was withdrawn, even by Belgium, whose government maintained that future assistance would depend on a firm commitment to human rights and good governance.

THE THIRD REPUBLIC

Nevertheless, predictions of Mobutu's political demise proved to be premature. The mass killings of Hutus in Rwanda by Tutsis in 1994, resulting in an unprecedented influx of refugees into eastern Zaire, provided Mobutu with an unexpected opportunity. Cooperation with France on the refugee problem brought him some legitimacy and provided the leverage needed to solidify Franco-Zairian ties once again. Indeed, Mobutu secured an agreement that Belgium, France, and the United States would provide resources to support the electoral process in Zaire. Ironically, however, the presence of more than a million refugees aggravated existing ethnic tensions between the local population and Zairians of Rwandan origin in eastern Zaire (North and South Kivu) and led to Laurent Kabila's rise to power.

First, Hutu militia forces from the former Rwandan government had crossed the border into Zaire to live in the refugee camps, over which they exercised much control. With the acquiescence of the Zairian government and the international community, these forces were allowed to launch attacks against Rwanda from the refugee camps in an attempt to overthrow the Tutsi-led Rwandan government.

Second, in response to this huge influx of population, the Zairian government passed a law in 1995 prohibiting refugees from Rwanda and Burundi from obtaining Zairian citizenship. Zairian authorities also took this opportunity to withdraw Zairian citizenship from Zairian Tutsis known as the Banyamulenge and other Zairians of Rwandan origin (the Banyarwanda) living in eastern Zaire. Even though members of these ethnic groups had been present in the area prior to the colonial period, their relative wealth was a source of resentment. By 1996 the Zairian military and the local population had begun attacks against these groups, and the Banyamulenge fought back, with the help of the Tutsi rebel force, the Rwandan Patriotic Army (RPA). Soon the Banyamulenge were joined by a coalition of several other ethnic groups, with the support of Rwanda, Burundi, Uganda, and Angola, forming a broad-based opposition force known as the Alliance of Democratic Forces for the Liberation of Congo-Zaire. The goal of the alliance was the ouster of Mobutu, and Laurent Kabila, head of a small guerrilla movement opposed to Mobutu for over thirty years, emerged as leader of the alliance. Within weeks, alliance forces were in control of eastern Zaire, and on May 17, 1997, they entered Kinshasa after encountering some resistance from the elite special presidential forces. Mobutu was flown out of the country quietly by helicopter.

Kabila's rapid success was due to popular support from Zairians themselves and the incompetence of the poorly paid and untrained Zairian security forces, who looted in the face of the alliance advance. In addition, Mobutu's poor health, due to prostate cancer, blinded him to the reality of his lack of control over the country. Nevertheless, Mobutu received important diplomatic support from France, which organized an unsuccessful covert operation against the rebels using French, Serbian, and Belgian mercenaries. Even with the rebels on the outskirts of Kinshasa, Mobutu was insisting on a cessation of hostilities and the formation of a consensus government.

The international community, including the United States, cautiously accepted Kabila, stressing the need for a democratic system and free and fair elections in Zaire. Indeed Kabila expressed a commitment to just such a process at his inauguration as president, promising elections in April 1999. Moreover, some symbolic gestures were made to put the country on a new footing, such as renaming Zaire the Democratic Republic of the Congo. However, optimism has all but dissipated. From all indications, little has changed in either the political or economic spheres in the Congo. Corruption and patronage continue as usual, and there are no signs of serious efforts regarding democratic reform. The opposition remains tightly controlled. So far there have been no attempts to restructure and restart the economy. In addition, UN human rights officials maintain that alliance troops committed mass murders and other atrocities in their military campaign to oust Mobutu. The atrocities also involved an element of Tutsi vengeance for the earlier genocide. It is important also to note that Kabila consistently refused the UN team access to refugee sites.

For the majority of Zairians, life under the Third Republic has been disappointing. Although Mobutu is no longer present, the same challenges remain. The reality, however, is that even with the best of intentions, Kabila would face an uphill task if he decided to make meaningful changes. The economy is in shambles, with an external debt of US$15 billion, or more than eight times the value of annual exports. The state apparatus has essentially disappeared, leaving the regions to fend for themselves. In the political sphere, building legitimacy and organizing for elections, whether on the local, regional, or national level, will be a daunting task.

Given current trends, it does not appear that the Kabila regime will be making any major strides with respect to changing the status quo in the Congo in the short term. Furthermore, there is no international consensus at this point to pressure Kabila to make reforms. The French, Belgian, and U.S. governments lack the political will to confront the regime on this issue, as the Congo is no longer vital to their foreign policy interests. This is unfortunate and short-sighted, given the devastating political and economic impact of the Mobutu era, the urgent need to rebuild the country, and the implications that continued instability in the Great Lakes Region has for neighboring countries.

See also *Angolan Revolution (1974–1996); Burundi Civil Wars (1993–); Lumumba, Patrice; Rwandan Civil Wars (1959–1994).*

WINSOME J. LESLIE

The views expressed in this paper are those of the author and not those of the government of Jamaica.

BIBLIOGRAPHY

Callaghy, Thomas. *The State-Society Struggle: Zaire in Comparative Perspective.* New York: Columbia University Press, 1984.

Leslie, Winsome J. *Zaire: Continuity and Political Change in an Oppressive State.* Boulder, Colo.: Westview Press, 1993.

McGaffey, Janet. *Entrepreneurs and Parasites: The Struggle for Indigenous Capitalism in Zaire.* New York: Cambridge University Press, 1988.

Schatzberg, Michael. *Mobutu or Chaos? The United States and Zaire, 1960–1990.* New York: University Press of America, 1991.

U.S. House of Representatives. Committee on International Relations. Subcommittee on Africa. *Zaire: Collapse of an African Giant?* Hearing report, Washington, D.C., April 8, 1997.

Willame, Jean-Claude. *Zaire: Predicament and Prospects.* Washington, D.C.: United States Institute of Peace, 1997.

Young, Crawford, and Thomas Turner. *The Rise and Decline of the Zairian State.* Madison: University of Wisconsin Press, 1985.

CONSTITUTIONS

The Western legal tradition was born of a revolution in the eleventh and twelfth centuries, when legal institutions, a coherent body of law, and a specific legal profession came into being. This revolution, brought about under the auspices of Pope Gregory VII, was a transnational, European event and adapted the Roman law of antiquity to the fundamentally transformed religious, social, political, and economic situation of western Europe. The different legal systems came to secure the individual in his place, which could only be achieved by the supremacy of law over the political authorities. Already by the thirteenth century, the famous English jurist Henry de Bracton claimed that the king could do nothing but what the law allowed him to do, for it was the law that made the king.

PREMODERN CONSTITUTIONS

The fundamental demand that political authority must be firmly controlled by the law gave birth to political constitutions, though only after further western revolutions. However, nowhere in western Europe—not in Tudor England or sixteenth-century France, Spain, Italy, or the Holy Roman Empire—was princely power prepared to yield easily. Instead, royalty relied on Christian dogma, be it Protestant or Catholic, that the authority of magistrates was derived from God and that the laws of God were superior to those made on earth. Secular authors, such as the Italian author and statesman Niccolò Machiavelli (1469–1527) or the French philosopher Jean Bodin (c. 1530–1596), transformed Christian dogma, only to underline the supreme secular authority of the prince.

The tension between law and political authority saw its first major dénouement in seventeenth-century England. When Charles I issued a proclamation forbidding his subjects to obey the Militia Ordinance, Parliament immediately reacted, declaring on June 6, 1642, the royal proclamation "void in law, and of none effect; for that, by the constitution and policy of this kingdom, the king by his proclamation cannot declare the law contrary to the judgment and resolution of any of the inferior courts of justice, much less against the High Court of Parliament."

The term *constitution* increasingly had come into use since around the turn of the seventeenth century, in the context of church, parliament, or the state generally. In 1642, and perhaps for the first time, the term was invoked to repudiate the legitimacy of royal claims in opposition to individual rights. The neologism, however, was still far from being universally accepted, and when late in 1653 a document was proclaimed that may stand for the first English attempt at a written constitution, it was called "The Instrument of Government," without making use of the word *constitution*.

The most important mid-seventeenth-century author focusing on the conflict between law and political authority was James Harrington, who posed the central question: "How does a commonwealth come to be an empire of laws and not of men?" To secure the rule of law against princely arbitrariness, the British Parliament declared the abdication of King James II in the Glorious Revolution of 1688–1689 and issued the Declaration of Rights, soon to become the Bill of Rights. Its purpose was to reduce royal power to actions sanctioned by law as defined by Parliament and in conformity with the essence of English liberties as guaranteed by the English "constitution."

More than any revolution before, the Glorious Revolution was interpreted by contemporaries within the context of "constitution," and they extensively debated whether the Glorious Revolution restored the "ancient constitution" or created a "new constitution." But in both cases, the term represented a premodern notion of constitution, which in the early eighteenth century the British parliamentarian Henry St. John Viscount Bolingbroke defined as an "assemblage of laws" by which the country was ruled. Denis Diderot and Jean le Rond d'Alembert's famous *Encyclopédie* (1751–1772; thirty-five volumes) gave a similar definition and saw it exemplified in the Holy Roman Empire. Old-regime France also claimed to have a constitution, while most European contemporaries looked to the British constitution as a model.

MODERN CONSTITUTIONS

Radical change came with the American Revolution. Those living through it saw that the first step that had to be taken was the formation of a fundamental constitution as the basis of legislation. Constitution was no longer understood as an assemblage of laws to rule the country but as a system of principles to secure individual rights and privileges against any government encroachments. In contrast to their experience with the English constitution, the American colonists believed that a written constitution should secure the individual in his rights and prevent the government from becoming despotic.

This revolutionary redefinition of *constitution* as an instrument for securing individual political liberty became crucial for its modern meaning. Today, we have to remember that *constitution* in its modern understanding is of revolutionary origins, born in the first revolutions that made the modern world—the American and French Revolutions. The modern constitution is a written document, in contrast to the unwritten British constitution, and is created and approved by the people or their representatives. It is founded on generally accepted principles, and as the highest law in the country it is the basis for subsequent legislation. It sets up the different branches of government, more or less separated from one another, and establishes their role and mode of action. Additionally, a constitution may contain a bill of rights—a catalog of the rights and privileges secured by the people.

The first modern constitutions were established during the American Revolution, with Virginia setting the path in June 1776. The idea of the constituent power of the people and the constitution as a guarantee of government by the people was one of the driving forces behind the outbreak of the French Revolution. The first revolutionary step was taken on June 17, 1789, when the third estate of the Estates-General, representing the common people of France, proclaimed itself the Constituent National Assembly. Three days later, the members of the Assembly confirmed by oath not to depart "until the constitution of the kingdom shall be laid and established on a firm basis."

Restoration Europe tried hard to discard or to ignore the revolutionary idea of *constitution,* which the British parliamentarian Edmund Burke called a "monster." But the example set by the American and French Revolutions prevailed and spread over Europe, Latin America, and finally the rest of the world. Hardly any government today is bold enough to rule without at least the formal legitimation confirmed by a constitution.

Despite the triumph of the modern concept of constitution, its meaning varies considerably. Thomas Paine's classical statement—"A constitution is a thing antecedent to a government, and a government is only the creature of a constitution. The constitution of a country is not the act of its government, but of the people constituting a government"—has seldom met with full respect outside the United States. Elsewhere, Paine's separation between government and constitutional convention is not fully accepted; often, normally elected legislative bodies are involved in constitution making. The same is true with regard to the amending power. In some national contexts the people are directly involved in any alteration of or addition to the existing constitution; in others, the people are completely excluded, with a simple majority in the legislature acting in their place.

The basic question, therefore, continues to be that of the difference between constitution and normal statute law. Is constitution a higher law, far beyond the normal reach of a legislature, or is it easily to be altered by the sovereign people? The American and French Revolutions were the origins of the two contrasting models. The American model stresses the supremacy of the constitution beyond the ordinary reach of the sovereign people. The French model rests on the assumption that the constitution receives its legitimation from the sovereign people and, therefore, in case of conflict has always to yield to them. In terms of institutions, the American system will transfer the conflict to a constitutional court whose interpretation of the constitution by way of judicial review will settle it. The French model knows no constitutional court, at best a constitutional council with no power of judicial review and no constitutional remedy, or awkward substitutions at best. In France conflict resolution is transferred to parliament or to the people at large.

Today's ready equation of constitution with democracy disregards, however, the historical origins. When the modern meaning of the term first came into use, the kind of government and political system established by a constitution was open to debate. Americans developed five different types of constitutional government: a moderate, representative republic (the classical example is the Massachusetts constitution of 1780); a radical republic (Pennsylvania constitution of 1776); a unitary state (normal state constitutions); a loose confederation (the Articles of Confederation, 1781); and a federal union as a compound republic (Constitution of 1787). The French adopted only the radical republic (Jacobin constitution of 1793) but added to the list constitutional monarchy (constitution of 1791), antidemocratic republic (constitution of 1795), autocratic republic (constitution of 1799), and autocratic monarchy (constitution of 1804). Almost all later constitutions are more or less variations—or corruptions—of these nine different types.

In contrast to the American and French constitutions, the British constitution remains the last existing premodern constitution. In its basic makeup of laws, custom, and conventions, all of them between several months and several centuries old, it is unwritten. When modern constitutions are said to be written, in contrast to the British constitution, it is true only insofar as their origins are concerned. Every modern constitution develops in the course of time an increasing "unwritten" part. The Constitution of the United States saw the addition of twenty-seven amendments, but it was changed even more so by two hundred years of Supreme Court interpretations, as laid down in more than five hundred volumes of Court decisions. When a constitution is unresponsive to change, it will fail and either become meaningless or open the way to revolution or despotism or both.

See also *American (U.S.) Revolution (1776–1789); Burke, Edmund; French Revolution (1789–1815); Paine, Thomas.*

HORST DIPPEL

BIBLIOGRAPHY

Berman, Harold J. *Law and Revolution. The Formation of the Western Legal Tradition.* Cambridge, Mass.: Harvard University Press, 1983.

Burdeau, Georges. *Le Statut du pouvoir dans l'État.* Vol. 4 of *Traité de science politique.* 3d ed. Paris: Librairie générale de droit et de jurisprudence, 1983.

Handlin, Oscar, and Mary Handlin, eds. *The Popular Sources of Political Authority. Documents on the Massachusetts Constitution of 1780.* Cambridge, Mass.: Belknap Press, 1966.

McIlwain, Charles Howard. *Constitutionalism: Ancient and Modern.* Rev. ed. Ithaca, N.Y.: Cornell University Press, 1947.

Preuss, Ulrich K. "The Political Meaning of Constitutionalism." In *Constitutionalism, Democracy and Sovereignty: American and European Perspectives,* edited by Richard Bellamy, 11–27. Aldershot: Avebury, 1996.

Rosenbaum, Alan S., ed. Constitutionalism: The Philosophical Dimension. Westport, Conn.: Greenwood, 1988.

Rosenfeld, Michel, ed. *Constitutionalism, Identity, Difference, and Legitimacy. Theoretical Perspectives.* Durham, N.C.: Duke University Press, 1994.

Stourzh, Gerald. "Constitution: Changing Meanings of the Term from the Early Seventeenth to the Late Eighteenth Century." In *Conceptual Change and the Constitution,* edited by Terence Ball and J. G. A. Pocock, 35–54. Lawrence, Kan.: University Press of Kansas, 1988.

COSTA RICAN REVOLUTION (1948)

By Central American standards, the insurrection that broke out in Costa Rica in 1948 was unusually brief and limited in its violence, yet it was almost certainly the single most important political event of the century for this country. The outlines of the modern political system emerged out of the "Civil War of 1948," as it is called in Costa Rica, as did a deep respect for the integrity of elections and democratic practices, the contemporary political party system, the elimination of the military as a political force, and leaders who personally and through their heirs have dominated politics to this day. A clash between the traditional oligarchy and modernizing sectors over the social agenda and the influence of communists in government were the major issues creating the conditions for the insurrection. Electoral fraud was the catalyst that set it off.

In the period 1936–1940 the elected government of León Cortés Castro curried popular favor through an extensive public works program but shunned social reform. In 1940 Rafael Angel Calderón Guardia, hand-picked by Cortés and representing the traditional oligarchy, was elected to the presidency by a landslide. To the surprise of many of his conservative supporters, however, he quickly began reforms, eventually implementing a social security system, a labor code, a public housing program, a progressive income tax, and the reopening of the University of Costa Rica.

In order to govern in the light of increasing opposition from the oligarchy, in 1942 Calderón forged an alliance with the Communist Party, which had won 16 percent of the votes in the congressional elections of that year. This alliance alienated an even wider segment of the Costa Rican population, including many small farmers. Nonetheless, in 1944 Teodoro Picado Michalski, hand-picked by Calderón and supported by the Communists, easily defeated Cortés and held the presidency until the 1948 elections. By that time, three groups had formed an alliance to oppose Calderón's bid for reelection. The Social Democratic Party was a fusion of an ostensibly apolitical study group, called the Center for the Study of National Problems, and Democratic Action, led by José Figueres Ferrer. Figueres previously had been exiled to Mexico by Calderón as a result of an inflammatory radio speech that he made in 1942, but he now returned with a plan to overthrow the government by force. The other two opposition groups were the Democratic Party, consisting of supporters of now deceased president Cortés, and the National Union Party, comprising supporters of conservative newspaperman Otilio Ulate Blanco. In July 1947 the opposition alliance supported a strike of businesses in protest against the new income tax law, the strike serving to unify the conservative and reformist members of the opposition.

The February 1948 presidential election was marred by voting fraud on all sides. The opposition, united behind Ulate, appears to have won the popular vote over the Calderón-Communist alliance, but the electoral tribunal declared that the alliance had won a majority in the legislature. The legislature, which had the final authority to ratify the election results, annulled the presidential vote but accepted the results of the legislative election. This drove elements of the opposition to support Figueres's plan for an armed revolt, which broke out on March 12, 1948, and resulted in the loss of between one thousand and two thousand lives, most of them civilian. An end to the war was negotiated on April 19 under the auspices of U.S. diplomats.

The coalition fell apart immediately after the truce was signed but eventually agreed to allow Figueres to lead a revolutionary junta for eighteen months, after which Ulate would take over as president. A new constitution was forged in 1949 abolishing the army and establishing universal suffrage while banning parties such as the Communists. Figueres did step down after eighteen months but was elected president in 1953 as head of the National Liberation Party, which was to become Costa Rica's most cohesive and electorally successful party. The supporters of Calderón formed the major opposition electoral alliance. The social reforms of Calderón, however, were not only maintained but greatly broadened by the National Liberation Party, resulting in exceptionally high levels of social welfare. In the 1990s sons of both Calderón and Figueres succeeded their fathers as presidents of the country.

Mitchell A. Seligson

BIBLIOGRAPHY

Bell, John Patrick. *Crisis in Costa Rica: The Revolution of 1948*. Austin: University of Texas Press, 1971.

Booth, John A. *Costa Rica: Quest for Democracy.* Boulder, Colo.: Westview Press, 1998.

Longley, Kyle. *The Sparrow and the Hawk: Costa Rica and the United States during the Rise of José Figueres.* Tuscaloosa: University of Alabama Press, 1997.

Seligson, Mitchell A. *Peasants of Costa Rica and the Development of Agrarian Capitalism.* Madison and London: University of Wisconsin Press, 1980.

Yashar, Deborah J. *Demanding Democracy: Reform and Reaction in Costa Rica and Guatemala, 1870s–1950s.* Stanford: Stanford University Press, 1997.

COUNTERREVOLUTION

By definition, counterrevolution can occur only when and where a revolutionary transfer of power has already begun. When it happens, counterrevolution provides some of revolution's most vivid scenes, from France's Vendée insurrection of 1793 to the U.S.-backed mobilization against Nicaragua's 1979–1980 Sandinista revolution.

Only rarely does a revolution bring to power a single, unified band of revolutionaries. Instead, the typical successful revolutionary force is a coalition of disparate opponents of the displaced regime. Similarly, revolutionary seizure of power often generates opposition by three rather different clusters of activists: displaced power-holders; allies, clients, and beneficiaries of those power-holders; and other enemies, rivals, and victims of the new rulers. Since the French Revolution of 1789–1799, those who control a revolutionary government have often labeled their domestic opponents as counterrevolutionaries. In those cases, "counterrevolution" has referred to whatever and whomever leaders identified as blocking their own revolutionary programs.

Beyond such polemical uses of the term, counterrevolution also identifies a significant political process. Outside support for counterrevolution (including support from exiles and refugees who have exited from the revolutionary regime) often makes a great difference to its course, but it does not in itself qualify as counterrevolution. Strictly speaking, counterrevolution refers to certain processes arraying domestic opposition against holders of revolutionary power. Once a revolutionary coalition has taken over a state and dislodged its previous rulers, we can speak of a revolutionary regime. If and when domestic opponents of the revolutionary regime then begin to offer concerted public resistance against revolutionary measures and personnel within the regime's own territory, we can reasonably call the process counterrevolutionary. A full-fledged counterrevolution reverses the usual revolutionary situation; it opens a serious, visible split between those who currently control the state (now the revolutionaries) and those who have gathered substantial domestic support for alternative claims to power (now the counterrevolutionaries).

Natural-history theorists of revolution such as the American scholar Crane Brinton have commonly argued that every revolution generates its own counterrevolution, indeed that only successful counterrevolution restores former revolutionary regimes to political equilibrium and domestic peace. Revolutions that have occurred since the eighteenth century, however, suggest different conclusions; the extent, character, and consequences of counterrevolutionary action have varied enormously from region to region and time to time. Revolutionaries, for example, faced fierce, armed domestic opposition through large sections of southern and western France between 1793 and 1795. In contrast, the Cuban revolutionary coalition that came to power in 1959 rapidly cowed, conciliated, or exiled its opposition. Once its forces seized control of Havana, it never faced widespread and open opposition from within its own territory. The Cuban Revolution's many enemies, often supported by the United States, formed almost entirely outside the country, and they attacked from outside as well.

CONDITIONS FOR COUNTERREVOLUTION

Singly and in combination, two main circumstances promote counterrevolution: first, seizure of state power by a group having a narrow social base or many domestic enemies; second, splits in revolutionary coalitions after they have come to power. Relatively pure examples of the first set of circumstances occur when military, religious, or nationalist factions seize state power in the name of revolutionary programs, thereby generating widespread opposition; for example, although Austrian and Russian military forces from outside Hungary ultimately crushed its Magyar nationalist revolution of 1848–1849, the revolution's threat to non-Magyar nationalities had already incited armed opposition from Croats and others before the decisive battles with Austrian and Russian armies began. Great Britain's rapid spiral from parliamentary victory over King Charles I into civil war between 1647 and 1648 combined the first and second circumstances. First, British royalists and opponents of English hegemony retained strong support in parts of Ireland, Scotland, and even England throughout the revolutionary period from 1640 to 1660. Second, the victorious Puritan-dominated revolutionary army began expelling from Parliament its former allies, Presbyterians who enjoyed substantial backing in Scotland and northern England and who after their expulsion joined the military opposition. The Russian revolutions of 1917 provide a somewhat purer example of the second set of circumstances. Between March, when the tsar abdicated, and October, when the Bolsheviks seized power from the Provisional Government, the Bolsheviks split decisively with their revolutionary allies, driving many of them into open counterrevolutionary alliances with a wide variety of dissidents, rebels, and foreign forces; bloody civil wars continued in various parts of the former empire until 1921. Russian revolutionaries later confronted circumstances of the first kind, as independence-seeking rebellions formed in Ukraine, Estonia, Finland, Moldavia, Latvia, Georgia, Azerbaijan, Armenia, and Cossack-dominated regions of the former empire. More recently, the revolution that drove Nicaraguan ruler Anastasio Somoza Debayle from power in 1979–1980 illustrates the second pattern; a broad alliance of Sandinistas, conservatives, and previously unaligned members of agricultural and commercial elites made the revolution then split as the Sandinistas consolidated their hold on the Nicaraguan government and the United States began to back the forces that came to be known appropriately as Contras.

As these cases suggest, external support for counterrevolution significantly affects its strength and success. During the twentieth century, few substantial revolutions have occurred anywhere in the world without provoking some sort of intervention by great powers, and counterrevolutionary forces have prevailed mainly when they have received great power backing.

Like revolution, counterrevolution has produced its own theorists, although they have rarely called themselves counterrevolutionaries. The eighteenth-century French Revolution, for example, inspired Anglo-Irish Edmund Burke and Joseph de Maistre of Savoy to write major antirevolutionary statements. The twentieth-century Bolshevik Revolution likewise stimulated a flood of critical writing. Such counterrevolutionary analysis rarely contributes much to the explanation of revolutionary or counterrevolutionary processes, but it plays a significant part in the ideological combat that accompanies every major revolution.

See also *Burke, Edmund.*

Charles Tilly

BIBLIOGRAPHY

Ashton, Robert. *Counter-Revolution. The Second Civil War and its Origins, 1646–8.* New Haven, Conn.: Yale University Press, 1994.

Brinton, Crane. *The Anatomy of Revolution.* New York: Norton, 1938.

Godechot, Jacques. *La Contre-Révolution. Doctrine et Action.* Paris: Presses Universitaires de France, 1961.

Mayer, Arno J. *Dynamics of Counterrevolution in Europe, 1870–1956: An Analytic Framework.* New York: Harper Torchbooks, 1971.

Petez-Stable, Marifeli. *The Cuban Revolution. Origins, Course, and Legacy.* New York: Oxford University Press, 1993.

Tilly, Charles. *European Revolutions, 1492–1992.* Oxford: Blackwell, 1993.

Woloch, Isser. *The New Regime. Transformations of the French Civic Order, 1789–1820s.* New York: Norton, 1994.

COUP D'ÉTAT

A coup d'état is the unscheduled, extralegal removal and replacement of an incumbent government by a force that is predominantly military. It may involve no violence or high levels of violence, depending on the nature of the incumbent government, the extent of its support, current political conditions, and the relative unity of the armed forces when the coup attempt occurs. Coup d'état as a method of removing and replacing an incumbent government does not imply any particular ideological commitment by the coup makers. Coups may be effected for sundry reasons, for example, as efforts to change government personnel, to modify government policies, to restore political order amid "disorder," or to initiate revolutionary social and political change.

In Spain and Latin America the term *golpe de estado,* sometimes condensed to *golpe,* is the equivalent of coup d'état. The term *pronunciamiento* is often used as a substitute by those supporting the coup d'état to indicate that the coup makers believe that they have a legitimate motive for ousting the government. In Germany and elsewhere, since the Swedish popular revolts of the 1830s, the term *putsch* has become almost synonymous with coup d'état.

HISTORY OF THE COUP D'ÉTAT

The use of armed force and military power to depose incumbent leaders predates recorded human history and the advent of professional military institutions. A common historical benchmark for the institutionalized influence of professional armed forces in politics and the threat of their intervening to control or depose constitutional authorities is the Roman Praetorian Guard. Established as an elite corps to serve the emperor, the Praetorian Guard became an arbiter of Roman politics, manipulating the "election" of emperors and influencing public policy through threats of disobedience, insubordination, or direct intervention in political affairs.

With the gradual emergence of the modern nation-state in Europe, from the European voyages of discovery, conquest, and colonialism after 1492 to the early twentieth century, military leaders and institutions came to play a significant role in national politics. Wars determined the fate of rulers and nations, provoked the growth and specialization of government institutions, and conditioned socioeconomic development. The coincidence of the rise of the modern nation-state and of modern military institutions made the armed forces key political institutions.

What might be considered the first modern military coup occurred in Spain in 1677. Carlos II (1665–1700), last of the

Spanish Habsburgs, inherited the throne at four years of age. His mother, Mariana, served as regent until he reached fourteen. In 1677 the boy-king was challenged by the charismatic bastard son of Felipe IV, Don Juan José of Austria, who invaded Madrid from Aragón with an army of fifteen thousand. His army had been fighting the French in Catalonia. It now became the instrument for altering the central government at Madrid. José's effort was, in a sense, the first Spanish *pronunciamiento,* the term for the commonplace Spanish military coup of the nineteenth century. Like its nineteenth- and twentieth-century analogues, the 1677 movement had a "program," formalized in the 1676 *documento de la grandeza:* good government, removal of "evil" ministers and their followers in the bureaucracy, and an end to "disorder," attributed to the machinations of the queen mother. The demands of the *pronunciamiento* would be echoed by Spanish and Latin American military coup makers for the next three centuries and would be emulated by military coup makers in Asia and Africa after World War II.

The rebels succeeded in forcing the king to remove his principal adviser and to banish the queen to Toledo. Like many later military coups all over the world, José's movement claimed significant civilian support, mobilized diverse social groups against the incumbent government's policies and personalities, and made the army the effective political arbiter of the moment. While the army was the principal element of power, it acted with important support from civilian elites and social groups. Don Juan José made himself the effective ruler of Spain. He ruled in the king's name—just as later coup makers would rule in the name of national interests and constitutions supposedly violated by ousted governments.

With the end of colonialism in Latin America in the nineteenth century and the rise of new states in Africa and Asia, especially after World War II, the role of the military in politics became a core issue around the globe. Military coups were commonplace, and military influence in policy making routine. On the other hand, many military coup attempts fail. A survey of 107 attempted coups between 1945 and 1967 found that 30 percent failed; another study of coups against civilian and military governments found that of 284 coup attempts from 1945 to 1972, approximately 50 percent failed. For example, Syria experienced 13 coup attempts between 1949 and 1972, 7 of them successful.

COUP MOTIVES AND CIVIL-MILITARY RELATIONS

The motives for military coups, both those officially offered by military officers and those unstated, vary greatly, ranging from deterioration in immediate socioeconomic conditions, professional grievances, battles for a bigger military budget, and factional disputes within the armed forces, to fundamental long-term commitments to reorganize government and society according to one or another "revolutionary" blueprint. Sometimes coups are precipitated by ethnic, religious, and social conflicts, sometimes by the election of the "wrong" presidential candidate, sometimes by external influences and the impingement of global changes on national politics, sometimes by idiosyncratic local circumstances, even a president who drinks too much and "embarrasses" the military high command, as in Ecuador in 1963. Some analysts of military coups distinguish between underlying "predispositional conditions" that are endemic and the "triggering events" that activate the predispositional conditions. But whatever the particular conditions in each case, military officers usually proclaim that patriotism motivates their overthrow of governments that they characterize as corrupt, inefficient, antipatriotic, reactionary, or "subversive."

Civil-military relations occur not just between "civilians" and "the military," but among competing civilian interests and military elites divided over policy and their nation's future. Civilians call on the military for expertise, legitimacy, and power to support their own interests; military factions seek civilian allies for their own institutional and policy objectives. Sometimes civilian groups and movements "push" the military to bare their sabers as part of an escalating political "bargaining" process. Sometimes civilians virtually plead for military coups, with the expectation that after the coup the armed forces will allow the civilian "outs" to replace the deposed government. Other times such civil-military alliances lead to military governments, but rarely without some civilian participation. Military governments typically use civilian officials and advisers, and often they come to power with substantial social support. For example, the military coups in Syria (1963), Brazil (1964), Ghana (1966), Peru (1968), Chile (1973), Uruguay (1973), and Argentina (1976) were initially acclaimed by many civilians, although human rights violations and other unpopular policies later caused the governments to lose support.

Thus military coups d'état rarely are strictly military-inspired. The coup is an alternative to legal government succession, an alternative that has been resorted to frequently since 1945 in many countries and a method that remains plausible in most regions of the world.

See also *Counterrevolution.*

Brian Loveman

BIBLIOGRAPHY

Andrews, William G., and Uri Ra'anan, eds. *The Politics of the Coup D'etat: Five Case Studies.* New York: Van Nostrand Reinhold, 1969.

Finer, Samuel. *The Man on Horseback: The Role of the Military in Politics.* New York: Praeger, 1962.

Loveman, Brian. *For* La Patria: *Politics and the Armed Forces in Latin America.* Wilmington, Del.: Scholarly Resources, 1998.

Luttwak, Edward. *Coup d'Etat: A Practical Handbook.* New York: Knopf, 1969.

McWilliams, Wilson, ed. *Garrisons and Government: Politics and the Military in New States.* San Francisco: Chandler Publishing, 1967.

Nordlinger, Eric. *Soliders in Politics: Military Coups and Governments.* Englewood Cliffs, N.J.: Prentice-Hall, 1977.

Solaún, Mauricio, and Michael A. Quinn, eds. *Sinners and Heretics: The Politics of Military Intervention in Latin America.* Urbana: University of Illinois Press, 1973.

CROMWELL, OLIVER

Cromwell (1599–1658) made several distinctive contributions to the British revolutions of 1638–1660 as soldier, religious radical, and Lord Protector, the nonroyal head of the British state. He was a brilliant soldier whose command of cavalry contributed to the parliamentarian defeat of Charles I in the first civil war (1642–1646). He took part in more than thirty battles and in many major sieges and assaults on towns and fortified houses, and he never experienced defeat. In the second civil war he stamped out the royalist uprisings in Wales, and he defeated a Scottish army at the battle of Preston (August 1648); and as Lord General of the forces of the English Commonwealth, he achieved what no English monarch or general had ever achieved—the complete military subjugation of Ireland (1649–1650) and Scotland (1650–1652)—and he defeated Charles II at the battle of Worcester (September 1651).

Oliver Cromwell

Cromwell's conquest of Ireland and Scotland led to the fullest political integration of the islands of Britain and Ireland ever achieved and to a permanent and disastrous transfer of almost half the land mass of Ireland from the established (Catholic) population to English (Protestant) colonists. As a political leader, his late but convinced conversion to the cause of regicide was crucial to stiffening the will of his colleagues in the army and a minority of civilian politicians to put King Charles I on trial for treason against the people of England, for securing his conviction, and for carrying out the public execution (January 30, 1649). As head of the army, Cromwell carried out a series of coups d'état, and he set up a series of constitutional experiments whose common purposes were the establishment of "liberty for all varieties of Protestants" and social justice.

Although in the autumn of 1653 he seems to have avoided taking personal power, by the end of the year he had consented to being made head of state, under the title Lord Protector. He was later to decline a parliamentary offer of the Crown, but his regime increasingly took on the outward trappings of monarchy. He was driven by an absolute conviction that he was God's chosen instrument, called like Gideon or Moses in the Old Testament from a humble background on the fringes of gentry. He once said that he was not "wedded and glued to forms of government," and he clearly believed that all existing political and ecclesiastical structures were infected by the "corruptions of the flesh" and that it was God's will that they be overthrown and replaced by new forms that God would reveal to the "saints," men (and perhaps women) who represented "the various forms of godliness in this nation." As a result, Cromwell was committed to permitting freedom of religious worship and expression. His credentials as one wholly committed to the destruction of ancient constitutionalism and of the principle that membership in the national church was a duty of citizenship are undoubted; the extent to which personal ambition and social conservatism weakened his commitment to the more democratic and egalitarian aspects of the 1649 revolution remains highly contentious.

See also *British Civil Wars and Revolution (1638–1660).*

JOHN MORRILL

BIBLIOGRAPHY

Gaunt, Peter. *Oliver Cromwell.* Oxford: Blackwell, 1995.

Morrill, John S. *Oliver Cromwell and the English Revolution.* Harlow: Addison Wesley Longman, 1990.

Roots, Ivan A. *The Speeches of Oliver Cromwell.* London: Everyman Classics, 1989.

CUBAN REVOLUTION (1956–1970)

The Cuban revolution had four distinct phases between 1956 and 1970. The first (1956–1958) was the insurrectionary phase to take power as the military and the state collapsed. The second (1959) was the struggle within the victorious coalition for leadership and programmatic supremacy. The third (1959–1962) featured the revolutionary state's assertion of its domestic and international power over economy and society and against U.S. intervention. The fourth (1962–1970) entailed the consolidation of revolutionary rule amid severe economic difficulties.

INSURGENCY AND THE COLLAPSE OF THE STATE (1956–1958)

On March 10, 1952, former president and retired general Fulgencio Batista overthrew the constitutional government. For his role in the armed opposition to the Batista government, Fidel Castro served two years in prison and then went into exile. He returned to Cuba at the head of a small insurgent band four years later, on December 2, 1956.

Although Batista ruled as a dictator, the Cuban state lacked the capacity to defeat organized military challenges. Twice before in the twentieth century (1906, 1933), the Cuban armed forces had lost to insurgents. And in the mid-twentieth century, the high command of the Cuban armed forces was staffed largely by unprofessional officers who owed their appointments to political, personal, and family connections. Batista was challenged repeatedly by one military coup attempt after another; several were led by the most professional officers in the army and the navy. Moreover, corruption in state institutions had been rampant both before and during the Batista regime, depriving the state of citizen support.

The army's military campaigns against Castro's guerrillas were inept. When Castro's forces landed in eastern Cuba, they were not pursued for three days, giving them a chance to learn their way about the region. After six days of active pursuit, the army declared victory and withdrew from the mountainous region, leaving the rebels with valuable time to organize and recruit peasants. This pattern of occasional army offensives followed by declarations of victory and military withdrawal was repeated throughout 1957.

In 1958 government military offensives collapsed through defections, desertions, and the simple unwillingness of many field officers and troops to fight on behalf of Batista. Afraid of conspiracies within the military, specifically in the Havana garrisons, Batista kept his most trusted, politically loyal officers and troops in Havana. Thus the officers dispatched to fight the rebellion were those least willing to fight on behalf of the regime.

Much of the violent struggle against Batista was conducted by an urban underground in Havana and other cities; until late 1958 Batista feared the urban underground more than he feared the guerrillas in the mountains of eastern Cuba. In mid-1958 Castro's guerrillas numbered only about three hundred, and his brother Raúl Castro commanded another one hundred. By late 1958, however, the army had begun to retreat in eastern Cuba whenever the rebels attacked. The main constraint to rebel victory became the lack of personnel to occupy the territory the army had yielded.

In November 1958 Batista uncovered a coup attempt led by the chief of army operations. Soon after, another coup attempt was foiled, this one led by the chief of the navy air corps. In December Army Chief of Staff Gen. Francisco Tabernilla visited the U.S. embassy to propose a joint coup against Batista, and then Gen. Eulogio Cantillo, chief of army operations in Oriente Province, the man responsible for conducting the war against the guerrillas, opened direct talks with Fidel Castro.

The insurgent war had featured only one major pitched battle (though there had been many skirmishes). In late December 1958 insurgents led by Ernesto "Che" Guevara defeated the army and captured the city of Santa Clara in central Cuba. At that time no guerrilla forces threatened the capital city of Havana. Nonetheless, on New Year's Eve Batista and his closest civilian and military associates fled the country.

STRUGGLE FOR POWER (1959)

In January 1959 Fidel Castro's Twenty-sixth of July Movement, named for the date of his unsuccessful 1953 attack on a Cuban army installation, was only one of several armed forces that had taken up arms against Batista. In 1958 Eloy Gutiérrez Menoyo had led a force in the Escambray Mountains of central Cuba about as large as Fidel and Raúl Castro's combined guerrillas in the east. The university students' Revolutionary Directorate also had a substantial guerrilla force. The Twenty-sixth of July Movement itself was divided between the urban underground and the mountain insurgents. Many civilian groups had also contributed to Batista's overthrow. Who would prevail in the post-Batista power struggle?

At the outset, the armed forces of the Republic of Cuba were disbanded and replaced by the new Rebel Army, with

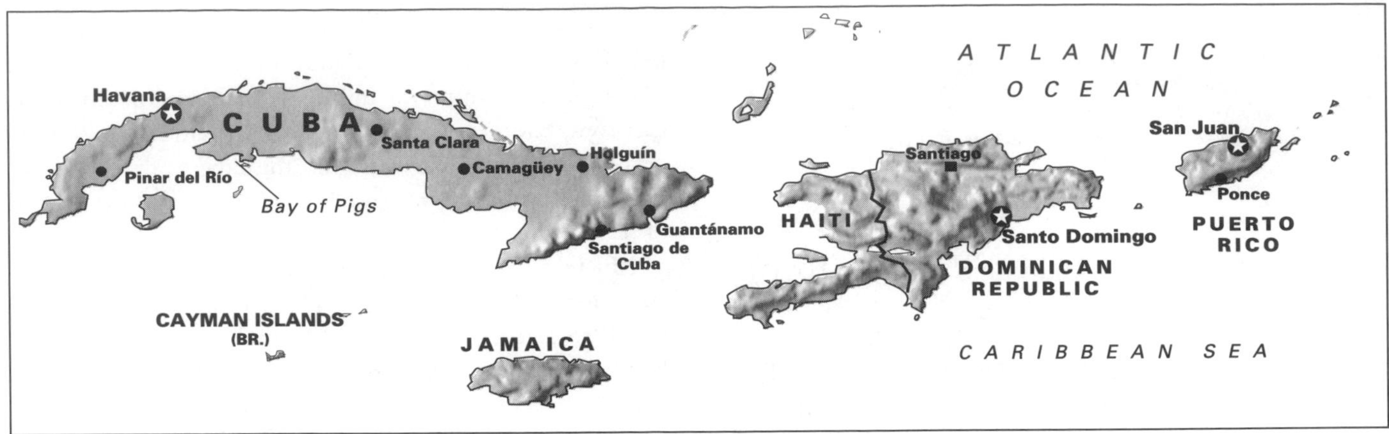

Fidel Castro as its commander in chief. Castro and the Rebel Army soon insisted on disarming other groups to restore order. In so doing, they created a new monopoly of force. In February 1959 Castro became prime minister.

Castro deployed his impressive oratorical skills to build support. Throughout 1959 he gave a public speech on average every other day. These speeches typically lasted several hours and were broadcast nationwide over radio and television. By the late 1950s per capita ownership of radio sets was higher in Cuba than in Italy, Poland, Japan, or Spain; in per capita ownership of television sets Cuba was ahead of most European countries and every country in Latin America. The Cuban revolution was the world's first to be wired for sound and image.

The revolutionary government built support through popular measures. In the first half of 1958 telephone and electricity rates were reduced, as were housing rents. In June 1959 an agrarian reform law promised land titles to peasant smallholders. And, after the civil war the economy recovered quickly, and wages increased.

With a monopoly of force, personal popularity bordering on hero worship, and ample backing for his government's measures, Castro gradually removed from office, or sidelined politically, virtually all other contenders for power. Three-quarters of the cabinet ministers were replaced during 1959. By the end of that year, a new coalition comprising the Twenty-sixth of July Movement, the Revolutionary Directorate, and the prerevolutionary Communist Party had gained power under Castro's undisputed leadership. Elections were postponed indefinitely.

REVOLUTIONARY TRANSFORMATION (1959–1962)

Sometime between March and October 1959 Castro made the fateful decision that no genuine change was possible in Cuba without breaking with the United States. U.S. firms directly owned much of the Cuban economy. Cuban international trade was overwhelmingly tied to the U.S. economy. Tourism from the United States was blamed for casino gambling, prostitution, and cultural degradation. And, if Cuba was to break with the United States, then it had to make an alliance with the Soviet Union. In October 1959 Castro built his first links with the Soviet Union and then launched a series of fierce, public attacks on the U.S. government for seeking to sabotage the Cuban revolution. He called huge public rallies to denounce imperialist aggression, constructing a militant nationalism in a country where such sentiments had been dormant for decades.

The U.S. government responded in kind—and in fury. In early 1960 the U.S. government launched a campaign to weaken the Cuban economy and bring down the Castro government. In March President Dwight D. Eisenhower authorized the Central Intelligence Agency to train Cuban exiles for a possible invasion of their homeland.

Three months later, in June 1960, the Cuban government asked foreign-owned petroleum refineries to refine Soviet crude oil; under instructions from the U.S. government, the firms refused. The Cuban government seized them. The United States cut Cuba's sugar quota, effectively prohibiting Cuban sugar exports to the United States. The Soviet government promised to purchase all the sugar that the United States would not buy and to defend Cuba with its missiles. Cuba expropriated all U.S.-owned firms. Weeks later, all Cuban-owned industries, banks, large plantations, transport, communications, and large commercial enterprises were expropriated as well. The revolutionary government argued that direct control over the economy would better provide for national defense and that central public ownership would allow for more rational economic development.

In early 1961 the U.S. government broke diplomatic relations with Cuba; broadened the sugar quota suspension to encompass a full embargo on trade with Cuba; and, on April

17, 1961, launched the exile invasion that landed at Playa Girón, Bay of Pigs. It was defeated within seventy-two hours. The Cuban government arrested tens of thousands of suspected regime opponents.

Later in 1961 Fidel Castro proclaimed himself, for the first time ever, a Marxist-Leninist and declared the character of the revolution socialist. The revolutionary government soon clashed with the Roman Catholic Church, seizing all private schools, cemeteries, and nearly all charitable institutions; the government deported hundreds of clergy, including many Cuban citizens. Propelled by revolutionary enthusiasm, in 1961 Cuba produced the second-largest sugar harvest in its history and launched a nationwide campaign that virtually eradicated illiteracy. By the end of the year Cubans felt they had accomplished the impossible: defeat the United States, seize the means of production, and transform the society.

Fearful of further U.S. attacks, the Cuban government in 1962 invited the Soviet Union to deploy ballistic missiles and nuclear warheads to Cuba. In October 1962 the United States discovered this secret deployment and forced the Soviet Union to take the weapons out of Cuba. Although Castro opposed this settlement, his government benefited from a parallel U.S.-Soviet understanding that the United States would not invade Cuba. Cuba thereafter sought also to maintain substantial independence from its Soviet ally, even while the Soviet Union supplied Cuba with weapons free of charge and provided significant subsidies to its economy.

REVOLUTIONARY CONSOLIDATION (1962–1970)

In 1962 the Cuban economy collapsed. Rationing of food, clothing, and other basic necessities had to be instituted. Economic hardships would persist for the rest of the decade. In 1963 yet another agrarian reform increased the state's ownership of agriculture; agricultural decline deepened. In 1968 the government expropriated the remaining modest-sized retail and service enterprises, such as barbershops, hot-dog stands, and the like. The economy nosedived thereafter. The government committed its economic resources to produce the largest-ever sugar harvest in 1970; it fell short and, in the process, seriously disorganized the remainder of the economy. The U.S. trade embargo and associated economic penalties injured the Cuban economy severely in the early 1960s, but their impact declined in time. Disorganization, lack of trained personnel, utopianism, and fantasy plans were primarily responsible for poor economic performance.

Hardships, however, rallied a significant proportion of Cubans to sacrifice even more for a revolution that so many called their own. They volunteered their labor in the countryside. They staffed the Committees for the Defense of the Revolution organized in virtually every neighborhood. They joined the official Women's Federation. They served the nation willingly in the armed forces.

The government followed through on the educational revolution, raising schooling standards well beyond literacy. It implemented a nationwide system of health care free of charge. It virtually eradicated prostitution and prohibited gambling. It launched a vigorous program to bring art and other forms of culture to small towns and rural areas. It sought to motivate people to work for the love of the revolution and the homeland, not for individual material incentives.

The government owned and operated all mass media and publishing houses. Only the Communist Party was lawful. In the mid-1960s the government established military camps to turn homosexuals into heterosexuals. By its own count, it held more political prisoners per capita than any other Latin American country. About 10 percent of Cuba's population emigrated.

The government sought also to promote the revolution overseas. In 1963 Cuban troops fought on Algeria's side in a war against Morocco. Cuba gave support, training, weapons, and funding to revolutionary groups in Latin America, Africa, and Indochina. Cubans were sent to join insurgents in Venezuela and Bolivia; in the latter, they were led by Ernesto "Che" Guevara.

In the early 1970s, pressed by economic collapse, widespread "absenteeism" by hundreds of thousands of workers exhausted by massive "volunteer" campaigns, and a cautious Soviet government, the Cuban government adopted more orthodox Soviet-style economic policies and political institutions, attenuated its efforts to effect a cultural revolution in the Cuban psyche, and reduced support for insurgencies in Latin America. The Soviet Union expanded its support, and Cuba's economy recovered. Education and health care expanded greatly. By the mid-1970s Cuba was no longer in revolution, but a new regime had become fully consolidated.

See also *Castro, Fidel; Guevara, Ernesto "Che"; Latin American Popular and Guerrilla Revolts (1960–1996).*

JORGE I. DOMÍNGUEZ

BIBLIOGRAPHY

Domínguez, Jorge I. *Cuba: Order and Revolution.* Cambridge, Mass.: Harvard University Press, 1978.

———. *To Make a World Safe for Revolution: Cuba's Foreign Policy.* Cambridge, Mass.: Harvard University Press, 1989.

Eckstein, Susan Eva. *Back from the Future: Cuba under Castro.* Princeton, N.J.: Princeton University Press, 1994.

Fagen, Richard. *The Transformation of Political Culture in Cuba.* Stanford, Calif.: Stanford University Press, 1969.

Mesa-Lago, Carmelo. *The Economy of Socialist Cuba: A Two-Decade Appraisal.* Albuquerque: University of New Mexico Press, 1981.

Pérez-Stable, Marifeli. *The Cuban Revolution: Origins, Course, and Legacy.* New York: Oxford University Press, 1993.
Thomas, Hugh. *Cuba: The Pursuit of Freedom.* New York: Harper and Row, 1971.
Welch, Richard E., Jr. *Response to Revolution: The United States and the Cuban Revolution, 1959–1961.* Chapel Hill: University of North Carolina Press, 1985.

CYCLES, WAVES, AND DIFFUSION

Revolutions occur in individual countries, but those in different countries can be related to each other, by closeness in time or by their similar goals, forming revolutionary waves. In addition, some scholars see such waves occurring in cycles or having identifiable life spans. *Diffusion* is a general term that can be applied to the various processes whereby revolutionary ideas, revolutionaries, and revolutions spread from country to country and across time. Finally, just as a revolutionary wave might arise in several countries in a given time period, it might later peter out in them more or less simultaneously in a process that can be called *collapse.*

Different scholars have used the term *wave* (or *tide,* or *phase)* in different ways. In the simplest use of the term, scholars have grouped together revolutions occurring close to one another in time and space. Peter Stearns, for example, saw the revolutionary outburst that affected several European countries in 1848 as being part of one revolutionary tide. Others have differentiated among revolutionary waves not by the time period in which they occurred but by the ideology they espoused. Peter Rodman, for example, refers to the decline of the Marxist revolutionary wave as being followed by the Islamic revolutionary wave in the Middle East.

Other scholars have divided revolutions espousing the same or similar ideologies into time period waves in order to analyze their differences. For example, in *Guerrillas and Revolutions in Latin America,* Timothy Wickham-Crowley compared Latin American revolutionary activity during two different waves: 1956–1970 and 1970–1990. Similarly, Nikki Keddie analyzed three distinct phases of revolutionary Islam between 1700 and 1993.

Some scholars have sought to explain how revolutionary waves rise and fall. In *Revolution and Rebellion in the Early Modern World,* Jack Goldstone sought to explain the revolutions that swept across Eurasia from 1560 to 1660 and again from 1760 to 1860. Goldstone theorized that the two intercontinental revolutionary waves resulted from the impact of demographic cycles. He observed that in the two revolutionary centuries, high population growth contributed to dramatic price rises, which led to unmanageable fiscal crises, state breakdown, and increased opportunity for revolutionary activity. By contrast, static population growth in the unrevolutionary century led to stable prices, manageable government finances, strong states, and little opportunity for revolutionary activity. For Goldstone, then, revolutionary waves rose and fell in the early modern world as a result of the impact of exogenous demographic cycles.

In *Revolutions and Revolutionary Waves,* Mark N. Katz viewed individual revolutions as linked less by time or place than by similarities in what they attempted to achieve. Each revolution is seen as having two objectives: to get rid of the existing regime and to replace it with an alternate system. In other words, each revolution is both against something and for something. Revolutions occurring against a similar form of government (for example, antimonarchical revolutions) can be said to belong to the same "against" wave. Similarly, revolutions that establish a similar type of regime (for example, Marxist revolutions) can be said to belong to the same "for" wave.

Katz observed that different types of revolutionary waves have identifiable life spans. For example, the antimonarchical and anticolonial waves (both "against waves") have spread and spread since their inception. By contrast, nondemocratic "for" waves such as the Marxist-Leninist (1917–1991), fascist (1922–1945), and Arab nationalist (1952–1967) expanded dramatically but then collapsed. Katz argues that the Islamic fundamentalist revolutionary wave, which began with the Iranian Revolution in 1979, is similar to these other nondemocratic "for" waves and can thus also be expected to collapse.

The diffusion of revolutionary waves from country to country can take place in different ways. In the case of nondemocratic "for waves," for example, one way is for a revolutionary regime that seeks to be the leader or "central revolution" within an expanding international revolutionary wave to invade one or more other countries and establish satellite or "subordinate" revolutions in them. This was how Joseph Stalin spread the Marxist-Leninist revolutionary wave to several East European countries at the end of World War II.

Revolutionary waves, though, can also spread via "affiliate revolution." Inspired by the central revolution, aspiring revolutionaries elsewhere may seek help from it in bringing about affiliate revolutions in their own countries. Sometimes with much assistance, but more typically with little or no assistance from the central revolution, aspiring revolutionaries may come to power and proclaim themselves to be part of the international revolutionary wave led by the central revolution. For example, after its successful coup d'état in 1958, the Syrian Ba'ath Party insisted that Syria merge with Egypt and that the resulting United Arab Republic be led by the Egyptian revolutionary leader Gamal Abdel Nasser. Similarly, after leading a successful revolution in Cuba in 1959, Fidel Castro quickly affiliated his regime with the Marxist-Leninist revolutionary wave led by the Soviet Union, even though Moscow appears to have played no role in his rise to power.

Nondemocratic "for" waves, however, are inherently unstable. Revolutionary regimes that voluntarily affiliate with a central revolution can often voluntarily "disaffiliate" with it later. For example, the Marxist revolutionary regime led by Mao Zedong voluntarily affiliated with Moscow when it first came to power in 1949 but disaffiliated with it in the late 1950s and early 1960s. Similarly, Syria disaffiliated with Nasser's Egypt by seceding from the United Arab Republic in 1961. A disaffiliate revolution that not only breaks with the central revolution but then vies with it for leadership of the international revolutionary wave can be termed a "rival" revolution—a role played by China vis-à-vis the USSR from the late 1950s to the early 1970s.

The anticommunist revolutionary wave that occurred in 1989–1991 illustrates how similar revolutions can produce different outcomes. All of these revolutions had the same "against" goal: to overthrow Marxist-Leninist regimes. They did not, however, all have the same "for" goal. Some of these revolutions ended up being for democracy (as in Poland, the Czech Republic, and Hungary), others for undemocratic forms of nationalism (as in the Caucasus), and one for Islamic fundamentalism (Afghanistan). For others, the outcome is still uncertain (as in Russia).

MARK N. KATZ

BIBLIOGRAPHY

Goldstone, Jack A. *Revolution and Rebellion in the Early Modern World.* Berkeley: University of California Press, 1991.

Katz, Mark N. *Revolutions and Revolutionary Waves.* New York: St. Martin's, 1997.

Keddie, Nikki R. "The Revolt of Islam, 1700 to 1993: Comparative Considerations and Relations to Imperialism." *Comparative Studies in Society and History* 36 (July 1994): 463–487.

Rodman, Peter W. *More Precious than Peace: The Cold War and the Struggle for the Third World.* New York: Charles Scribner's Sons, 1994.

Stearns, Peter N. *1848: The Revolutionary Tide in Europe.* New York: W.W. Norton, 1974.

Wickham-Crowley, Timothy P. *Guerrillas and Revolution in Latin America: A Comparative Study of Insurgents and Regimes since 1956.* Princeton, N.J.: Princeton University Press, 1992.

CZECHOSLOVAK "PRAGUE SPRING" (1968)

The "Prague Spring" refers to the period of political reform in Czechoslovakia between June and August 1968. The reform was initiated by the Communist Party and was intended to allow Czechoslovakia to develop a form of socialism better suited to its developed, Western-oriented society.

The reform movement emerged into the open in January 1968 when Slovak party leader Alexander Dubček replaced hard-liner Antonín Novotný as head of the Communist Party. However, the reform period itself was preceded by a lengthy period of discussion and theoretical renewal at the elite level that began in the mid-1960s. There were several catalysts for this process, which was initiated by the Communist Party leadership and carried out by loyal party intellectuals.

The most important catalyst was the failure of the Czechoslovak economy. By the early 1960s, Czechoslovakia's economy began to reflect the distortions of the Stalinist model of economic organization. Pushed by the Soviet leadership to reform their ailing economy, Czechoslovak leaders commissioned a team of economists to draft economic reforms. The reforms proposed were the basis of a program of economic change adopted at the thirteenth party congress in 1966. Bureaucratic resistance slowed the implementation of these reforms, and it soon became clear to the reformers that economic reform alone would not work without political changes. Additional teams of specialists were formed to examine other areas of politics and society, including the role of the state in a developed socialist society and the need for different social groups to have political representation.

The broad rethinking of the theoretical basis of socialist society that took place at the elite level was reflected to some degree in the work of the mass organizations. The women's organization, for example, began to question the party's approach to women's issues under socialism. Other groups, including farmers, students, and members of different ethnic groups, also began to organize to pressure political leaders.

Dubček and the other reformers faced what proved to be an unresolvable dilemma. As a result of their effort to develop a new strategy of rule based on genuine legitimacy rather than coercion or material benefits, they were forced to pay attention to mass demands for more radical change. At the same time, they also had to convince the hard-line Soviet, East German, and Polish leaderships that they were in control of the situation. In the end, they proved unable to do both. Newly available archival evidence indicates that Dubček and his colleagues were contemplating steps to rein in the reform in the summer of 1968. However, they did not enact such measures. The growth of more radical calls for change outside the party and the reform leadership's unwillingness to crack down hard on such actions led to the August 21, 1968, Warsaw Pact invasion of Czechoslovakia.

There was little armed resistance to the invasion. However, citizens engaged in numerous forms of passive resistance. There were also sporadic acts of more dramatic defiance, including the self-immolation of Czech student Jan Palach in January 1969. Gustáv Husák's selection to replace Dubček as head of the Communist Party in April 1969 signaled the beginning of an effort to reverse all elements of the reforms. Strict censorship was restored, and a massive purge removed many supporters of the reform from positions of influence in intellectual, cultural, and economic life as well as from political offices.

The most comprehensive effort to reform socialism from above prior to Mikhail Gorbachev's efforts in the Soviet Union, the Prague Spring is often seen as the precursor and, in part, inspiration of Gorbachev's policies. The legacy of 1968 had a dual effect. For reformers elsewhere in the region, the invasion demonstrated the limits of reform the Soviets would tolerate. For many people, the failure of the Prague Spring demonstrated the impossibility of reforming socialism from within. In Czechoslovakia the legacy of 1968 led to the stagnation of the country's political, economic, and cultural life for almost two decades. Afraid that loosening the reins would lead to a repetition of the events of 1968, the hard-line Czechoslovak leadership refused to allow any serious discussion of economic or political reform until the late 1980s.

See also *Czechoslovak "Velvet Revolution" and "Divorce" (1989–1993).*

Sharon L. Wolchik

BIBLIOGRAPHY

Jancar, Barbara. *Czechoslovakia and the Absolute Monopoly of Power: A Study of Political Power in a Communist System.* New York: Praeger Publishers, 1971.

Kusin, Vladimir. *The Intellectual Origins of the Prague Spring: The Development of Reformist Ideas in Czechoslovakia, 1956–1967.* Cambridge: Cambridge University Press, 1971.

Skilling, H. Gordon. *Czechoslovakia's Interrupted Revolution.* Princeton, N.J.: Princeton University Press, 1976.

CZECHOSLOVAK "VELVET REVOLUTION" AND "DIVORCE" (1989–1993)

The terms *Velvet Revolution* and *Divorce* refer, respectively, to the peaceful end of communism in Czechoslovakia in 1989 and the peaceful break-up of the Czechoslovak federation in 1993. The so-called Velvet Revolution was sparked by the police beating of peaceful student demonstrators in Prague on November 17, 1989. Encouraged by the fall of the hard-line East German regime in October 1989, Czech and Slovak citizens took to the streets in mass demonstrations to protest the police actions. Within a few days, hundreds of thousands of Czechs and Slovaks were demonstrating in cities all over the country and calling for the end of communism.

THE VELVET REVOLUTION

Although the demonstrations started spontaneously, opposition leaders soon formed Civic Forum in Prague and Public Against Violence in Bratislava to lead the protests and negotiate with the government. Václav Havel, a playwright who had long been active in the opposition and was a founder of Charter 77, the main dissident group in Czechoslovakia, emerged as the moral voice of the nation and the de facto leader of Civic Forum.

The communist leadership, which was weakened by liberalization elsewhere in the region and by the change in Soviet policy in regard to the area, opened negotiations with opposition leaders in November. Twenty-one days from the start of the mass demonstrations, the communist government resigned. This series of events came to be called the Velvet Revolution because the rigid, hard-line communist system was toppled without violence or the loss of a single life. Havel's election as president of Czechoslovakia in December 1989 capped the victory of the Velvet Revolution.

The successful overthrow of communism in Czechoslovakia was conditioned by outside factors, including changes in Soviet domestic and foreign policies and developments in Poland, Hungary, and East Germany. It is clear that the effort to oust the communist system would not have succeeded without Soviet willingness to let these countries go their own way. However, the rapid success of the revolution also reflected the impact of domestic factors. These included political developments that had occurred in Czechoslovakia since 1987, when Soviet leader Mikhail Gorbachev's policies of *perestroika* ("restructuring") and *glasnost* ("openness") in the Soviet Union began to have echoes in Czechoslovakia.

As the result of these policies, important changes took place at both the mass and elite levels.

Czech and Slovak citizens began to be more active in challenging the regime in the last two years of communist rule. Dissent, which was previously confined to small groups of intellectuals in large cities, began to spread. Independent organizations multiplied, and broader groups of people, including young people, Slovaks, and people who still held positions in the official world, began to participate in the activities organized by the dissidents. In Slovakia nonconformist intellectuals were able to use official organizations such as the Guardians of Nature to engage in independent cultural and other activities. Slovak Catholic activists also began to participate in unauthorized pilgrimages and demonstrations, such as that held in Bratislava in 1988 to call for religious freedom.

There were also important changes at the elite level. After two decades of stagnation, there was a massive turnover of top leaders of the Communist Party between 1987 and 1989. Although they were not reformers, the new leaders were somewhat younger and less committed to upholding the rigid policies of their predecessors at all costs. They were also less experienced and less sure of how to handle the growing challenge from below, particularly in light of Gorbachev's policies in the Soviet Union. Their vacillation between tolerating certain expressions of dissent and cracking down harshly reduced the cost of dissent and allowed participation in nonconformist activities to grow.

Between 1990 and 1993 Czech and Slovak leaders made considerable progress in re-creating democratic institutions and laying the foundations for a market economy. Free elections held in June 1990 legitimized the new government. Political leaders began reforming the bureaucracy, including the military, police, and security forces. The country also experienced a rapid repluralization of political life. In addition to the formation of numerous political parties and voluntary and professional associations, a wide variety of charitable and interest groups was also created. Parliamentary deputies passed new laws to create the legal basis for a private economy and adopted a plan to privatize state enterprises by allowing citizens to buy vouchers that could be redeemed for stock. They also grappled with the question of restitution of property illegally confiscated by the communist authorities.

Czechoslovakia's new leaders also made a good deal of progress in restoring the country to its position as part of Europe and reasserting its sovereignty. They negotiated the withdrawal of Soviet troops and also succeeded in gaining membership in organizations such as the Council of Europe. Originally advocates of the creation of a pan-European security system based on the Council for Security and Cooperation in Europe, Czech leaders came to seek membership in the North Atlantic Treaty Organization as well as in the European Union.

THE VELVET DIVORCE

The country's leaders were less successful in dealing with ethnic issues. In January 1993 the Czechoslovak federation broke up, and two new states, the Czech and Slovak Republics, replaced it. This process, which is sometimes referred to as the Velvet Divorce, also took place peacefully. In contrast to the wars that accompanied the break-up of Yugoslavia, the end of the Czechoslovak state was accomplished without violence.

The break-up of the Czechoslovak state reflected historical, economic, political, psychological, and international factors. Brought together for the first time in a modern state in 1918, Czechs and Slovaks had very different levels of economic development, political and cultural traditions, and opportunities for the development of national movements. Differences between the two groups persisted during the interwar period and were exacerbated by the different experience of the two regions in World War II.

The establishment of a unitary Czechoslovak state after 1945 once again frustrated Slovak aspirations for parity in the joint state with the more numerous Czechs. In contrast to the situation in the interwar period, when the Slovak economy stagnated, communist elites succeeded in narrowing considerably the gap between the development levels of the Czech lands and Slovakia. However, progress in economic development did not quell Slovak desires for a change in the form of the state. Slovak dissatisfaction was one of the forces that led to the reform movement of 1968. The creation of a federal government in 1969 gave symbolic recognition to Slovakia's claims. However, the economy and many other aspects of decision making were soon recentralized.

Slovak dissatisfaction with the joint state was fueled by both political and economic factors after 1989. Despite repeated negotiations, Czech and Slovak leaders proved unable to agree on a division of labor between the federal and republic governments. They also had different views on the kind and pace of economic reform needed. Czech leaders, led by Václav Klaus, favored a rapid move to re-create a market economy; they also favored the use of voucher privatization. Slovak leaders, led by Vladimir Mečiar, on the other hand, were in favor of a more gradual approach to economic reform that would take the special characteristics of Slovakia into account. Because much of Slovakia's industrialization had occurred in the communist era, Slovakia was much more vulnerable to disruption than the Czech lands in

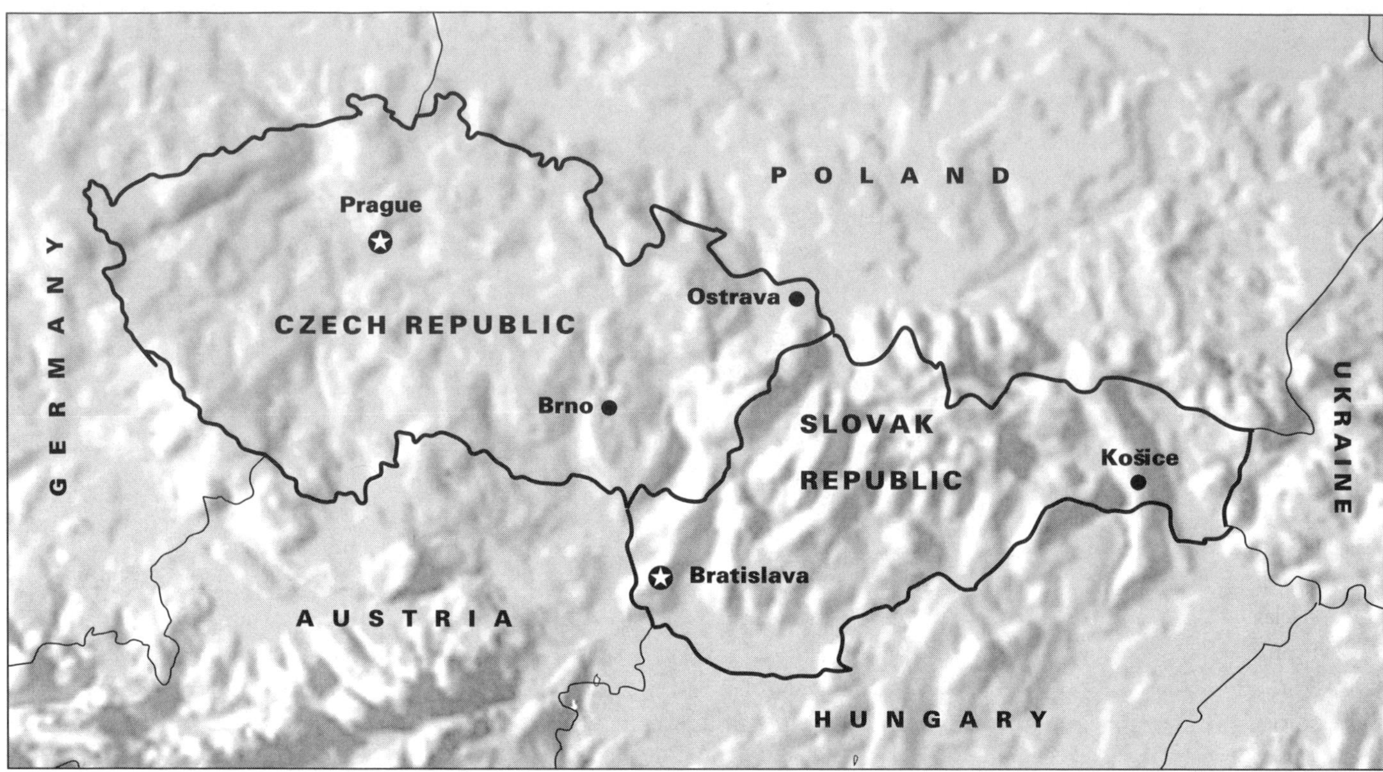

the move to a market economy. Unemployment levels, for example, reached 13 percent in Slovakia in the early 1990s; only 3 percent of citizens in the Czech lands were unemployed during this period.

These differences were reflected in the outcome of the 1992 parliamentary elections. Klaus's right-of-center Civic Democratic Party won the elections in the Czech lands. Mečiar's left-of-center Movement for a Democratic Slovakia won the largest share of the vote in Slovakia. It was clear from these results that the federation would not survive. In the end it was the actions of political leaders, particularly Klaus and Mečiar, that brought about the end of the federation. The majority of citizens in both the Czech lands and Slovakia opposed the break-up prior to 1992 and continued to oppose it even as it was being negotiated by their leaders. However, citizens in the two regions held very different views on many of the most important economic and political issues. Slovak citizens were much less supportive of the privatization of state enterprises; they were also more likely to want the state to retain primary responsibility for the welfare of citizens. Citizens in the Czech lands, on the other hand, were more likely to support a rapid move to the market; they were also more likely to want individuals to take primary responsibility for their own welfare. The election of Klaus and Mečiar was consistent with these differences.

Several factors contributed to the peaceful nature of the Velvet Divorce. These include the fact that discussions about the end of the federation were confined to the elite level, and the fact that the borders between the two regions had been stable for more than one thousand years. Few Czechs and Slovaks lived in the territory of the other ethnic group. The lack of a history of atrocities by members of each group against the other also was important. Finally, the willingness of the larger group, the Czechs, to agree to the break-up and the lack of deep-rooted personal animosity between Czechs and Slovaks also allowed a peaceful dissolution of the joint state.

See also *Czechoslovak "Prague Spring" (1968); East European Revolutions of 1989; Havel, Václav.*

Sharon L. Wolchik

BIBLIOGRAPHY

Butorova, Zora, and Martin Butora. "Political Parties, Value Orientations and Slovakia's Road to Independence." *East European Politics and Societies* 7 (spring 1993): 240–275.

Leff, Carol Skalnik. *National Conflict in Czechoslovakia: The Making and Remaking of a State, 1918–1987.* Princeton, N.J.: Princeton University Press, 1988.

Musil, Jin, ed. *The End of Czechoslovakia.* Budapest: Central European University Press, 1995.

Wolchik, Sharon L. *Czechoslovakia in Transition.* London: Pinter Publishers, 1991.

———. "The Politics of Ethnicity in Post-Communist Czechoslovakia." *East European Politics and Societies* 8 (winter 1994).

DEMOCRACY

Democracy, a form of government in which large numbers of citizens have a say in determining the leaders and policies of their government, dates back to classical Greece, twenty-five hundred years ago. The association between democracy and revolution goes back just as far. In 561 B.C. a popular revolution in Athens overthrew aristocratic rule and placed the populist leader Pisistratus in power. Although Pisistratus ruled as a dictator, the revolution permanently weakened Athens's aristocrats, and his political reforms—building on the laws of Solon—paved the way for the full democracy that emerged shortly after Pisistratus's death.

Athenian democracy involved giving a vote to all adult male citizens, who gathered periodically to debate state policies. But this was practical only for small city-states. Larger political units were generally ruled as monarchies or empires, until a wave of revolutions in the seventeenth and eighteenth centuries helped establish the principle of representative democracy. Representation allowed even large political units to act as democracies, by letting the citizens (whether the citizenry consisted of all adult males, all free adults, or those adults delimited by ethnic or property requirements) vote for a smaller number of representatives who would directly vote for government leaders and policies in national assemblies. In the most important of these revolutions—the American Revolution of 1776 and the French Revolution of 1789—monarchy was attacked as an unfair and unjustifiable form of government that contravened the natural laws of reason. In the name of reason—the principle that people were created capable of judgment, and therefore had the right to exercise that judgment in selecting the people who would lead them—a broad cross-section of Americans and French, including professionals, bureaucrats, aristocrats, farmers, businessmen, housewives, merchants, military reformers, craftsmen, and peasants, overthrew the rule of kings. In its place they supported new governments that started from the principle that government should be composed of representatives of the people of the nation as a whole.

FAILED EFFORTS TO CREATE DEMOCRATIC REVOLUTIONS

This broad principle of representative democracy spread around the world, inspiring revolutions in the name of democracy in Latin America and central and eastern Europe in the nineteenth century, and in the Middle East, Africa, Russia, and China, as well as again in Latin America and eastern Europe, in the twentieth century. Although the imitations often failed to live up to the model of the originals, the ideal of democracy has been the most potent revolutionary ideology of the last two centuries.

The examples of America and France led many people to believe that revolutions are necessary to produce democracy. Yet even in ancient Greece, scholars were often skeptical of the ability of revolutions to produce stable democratic states. Plato, noting that ancient Athens was led to ruin in its war with Sparta by poor decisions of the national assembly, argued that democracies lacked the reason and wisdom to rule well, being too easily swayed by appeals to the vanity or prejudice of citizens. To this day, there are all too many examples of popular assemblies whose poor decisions, or internal conflicts, have paved the way for dictators to seize power.

In fact, for the first two centuries following 1776, few revolutions produced stable democratic regimes. The United States for some time remained the only real democracy with revolutionary origins, and its democracy was limited to property-holding free males, a minority of the adult population. France reverted to dictatorship under Napoleon, and then to monarchy after Napoleon's defeat, not becoming a stable democracy until the 1870s. Almost all the revolutions in the 1830s and 1840s initiated in the name of democracy failed. Great Britain did become a broader democracy in this period, extending the vote to more of its citizens and eliminating various privileges of wealth and religion that distorted its politics, but did so through a series of reforms, rather than through revolution. Latin American states that gained independence through revolutions adopted constitutions modeled on that of the United States or revolutionary France; but more often than not, their democracies gave way to rule by populist dictators or military strongmen.

In the early twentieth century, efforts to create democratic revolutions in Mexico, Russia, and China went awry. Mexico's revolution triggered a ten-year civil war that ended with the authoritarian rule of a single party. Russia's revolution was captured by the Bolshevik party, whose belief in the need for a "dictatorship of the proletariat" to reshape society also led to a one-party regime. China had a republican revolution in 1911 that aimed at democracy, but the new government was too weak to control the nation, and after thirty-eight years of unstable, shifting regimes, the Chinese Communist Party instituted a one-party state. Throughout Africa, the Middle East, eastern Europe, and Asia in the mid-to-late twentieth century, revolutions made in the name of democracy, and producing regimes that styled themselves "Democratic Republics," in fact led to governments that remained under the control of single parties, or of military or civilian dictators. Indeed, from 1800 to 1975, it began to look as if revolutions were incapable of producing democracy.

The failure of these revolutions to create stable democracies had multiple causes. In Russia, China, and Cuba, revolutionary regimes were more concerned to reduce economic inequality, by seizing property and other drastic measures, than to uphold democratic principles. In Africa and Latin America, counterrevolutionary threats, from within and without, led governments to abandon democratic procedures in favor of more authoritarian regimes. And in many cases, leaders cared more about preserving their own power than building the political power of the populace. As a result, despite the proliferation of revolutionary states that called themselves democracies, the number of countries in which leaders were truly under the control of their people remained small through the first three-quarters of the twentieth century.

RECENT DEMOCRATIC REVOLUTIONS

In the last twenty-five years, however, revolutions have once again served as midwives of democracy. In 1974 a revolution in Portugal, caused in part by revolutions against Portuguese rule in Africa, initiated a process that led to the emergence of a democratic regime. A few years later, revolutions in Iran and Nicaragua in 1979 swept away family dictatorships. Although the initial revolutionary republican regimes in both states had limited or questionable democratic credentials, both countries have become considerably more democratic, with Iranians electing a moderate president and Nicaragua now a true multiparty democracy. In 1986, a "people-power" revolution in the Philippines overthrew a populist dictator and replaced his regime with a true democracy. And from 1989 to 1991, revolutionary movements in eastern Europe, Russia, the Baltic states, and central Asia overthrew communist regimes and, in most cases, ushered in Western-style democracies. As a result of these revolutions, the global roster of democracies has grown considerably.

The success of these revolutions in producing democracy also has several causes. The overwhelming economic achievements of Western democracies, compared to one-party regimes and dictatorships, has boosted the prestige of genuine democracy as an ideal to strive for. In addition, the new generation of revolutionary leaders appears far more committed to democracy, seeing it not as a dispensable means to other ends, but as a crucial goal in itself to bring dignity to their nations.

Although these events lend renewed credence to the notion that revolution marks the road to democracy, there is still need for caution in drawing too close a connection between revolutionary and democratic change. Many countries that underwent revolutions decades ago—China, Indonesia, Mexico, Cuba—are still inching their way toward democracy, and are far from having developed competitive political systems with full respect for human and political rights. And many countries that have recently created resurgent democracies—South Africa, Argentina, Chile—did so through consciously *avoiding* revolution, out of fear that the bloodshed and desire for vengeance that a revolutionary change would unleash would make it difficult or impossible to sustain the peaceful political competition that democracy requires.

The transition from a monarchy, empire, one-party state, or dictatorship to democracy clearly requires change. Revolution is one way to create that change. However, it is not the only way; nor is it a sure way to produce a democratic regime. For most of the last two centuries, revolutions have shown a strong tendency to spin out of control, producing more bloody, authoritarian, and erratic results than their leaders or followers had imagined. Nonetheless, from the American Revolution onward, the promise of achieving democracy has inspired more revolutions than any other ideal. Happily, in the last few decades a growing number of revolutions appear to have in fact delivered on that promise.

JACK A. GOLDSTONE

BIBLIOGRAPHY

Diamond, Larry, ed. *The Democratic Revolution: Struggles for Freedom and Pluralism in the Developing World*. New York: Freedom House, 1992.

Dogan, Mattei, and John Higley, eds. *Elites, Crises, and the Origins of Regimes*. Boulder, Colo.: Rowman and Littlefield, 1998.

Lipset, Seymour Martin, ed. *The Encyclopedia of Democracy*. Washington, D.C.: Congressional Quarterly, 1995.

DENG XIAOPING

Deng (1904–1997) was a leading figure in the Chinese communist revolutionary movement for more than fifty years, serving as China's paramount ruler from 1978 to 1997. He introduced pragmatic economic reforms that gave China one of the world's most impressive growth rates and raised the living standards of more people in less time than in all of history. Politically he broke with the radical ideological politics of Mao Zedong's era, although he steadfastly resisted any changes that would have weakened the Communist Party's monopoly on power or challenged China's official ideology of Marxism-Leninism. His resistance to political liberalization culminated in his decision to order the Chinese army to fire on the students and workers demonstrating peacefully in Tiananmen Square on June 4, 1989.

Deng was the eldest son of the leading family of Paifangcun, a rural town in Sichuan Province. His father, who wanted his son to have a modern education, sent Deng when he was only twelve years old to Chongqing for tutoring. Four years later Deng was selected to go to France to participate in a work-study program. There he lived with fellow Chinese students, including Zhou Enlai, who were among the founders of the Chinese Communist Party. As a sixteen-year-old he was by far the youngest among them, but he insisted on assuming adult responsibilities as a working member of their communist cell. Deng's introduction to communism thus differed significantly from that of other first-generation Chinese communists. Many of them came to communism as a consequence of their quests for solutions to China's modernization problems, while for Deng, communism was largely a pragmatic matter of fitting into an established group and skillfully performing one's assigned tasks. Thus, from the outset, Deng adopted a pragmatic, nonideological approach to communism.

After Paris, and a further year of training in Moscow, Deng returned to China to become a full-time party worker, first in the underground organization in Shanghai and then in the guerrilla base camp Mao Zedong had established in the Jiangxi Mountains. During the Long March of 1934–1935, when the Chinese communist armies retreated to their Shaanxi Province stronghold, Mao came to appreciate Deng's quick and practical mind. Deng spent much of the war against Japan as a leading political commissar in the guerrilla headquarters of the communist Eighth Route Army.

After the communists came to power in 1949, Deng quickly demonstrated his administrative skills. During inner-party factional struggles he was purged three times, but each time he was called back because of his recognized administrative abilities. Deng was out of favor when Mao Zedong died in 1976, but he was quickly rehabilitated by Hua Guofeng, Mao's designated successor, and called to Beijing to help run the country. Deng easily superseded Hua and quickly reversed the national course by opening China to the outside world and initiating pragmatic economic policies, which turned out in many respects to be more revolutionary than Mao's ideological politics.

The hallmark of Deng's rule was pragmatism in the economic realm, crystallized in his famous dictum: It doesn't matter whether the cat is white or black as long as it catches mice. The cornerstone of his economic reforms in agriculture was the decision to break up the collective communes and replace them with a "family responsibility system" in which each family worked its own plot of land and was allowed to sell for personal profit any production above a set quota. In industry the major shift was away from the huge state-owned enterprises and toward either privately or collectively owned enterprises and joint ventures with foreigners. Deng also encouraged advances in science and technology, especially by allowing thousands of Chinese students to go abroad to study. He further demonstrated his pragmatism by his formula of "one country, two systems" for the reversion of Hong Kong to Chinese rule, which pledged that the people of Hong Kong could continue their capitalistic system for fifty years.

The secret of Deng's revolutionary reforms was that he allowed the Chinese people to assume greater responsibility for their economic life, while he held to a gradualist approach in policy changes. The elimination of the rural communes was rather abrupt, but in industry he followed a more cautious path. Consequently, at the time of his death the state-owned enterprises had not been fully reformed, leaving questions as to the sustainability of China's economic modernization. On balance, however, Deng's policies, although labeled only as "reforms," transformed China in ways that seem at least as profound as the numerous other revolutions in modern Chinese history.

See also *Chinese Communist Revolution (1921–1949); Mao Zedong.*

LUCIAN W. PYE

BIBLIOGRAPHY

Evans, Richard. *Deng Xiaoping and the Making of Modern China.* London: Hamish Hamilton, 1993.

Franz, Uli. *Deng Xiaoping.* Boston: Harcourt Brace and Jovanovich, 1988.

Goodman, David, S. G. *Deng Xiaoping.* London: Cardinal Press, 1990.

Yang, Benjamin. *Deng, A Political Biography.* Armonk, N.Y.: M.E. Sharpe, 1998.

DICTATORSHIP

Dictatorship and revolution are two frequently linked phenomena of modern political life. Dictatorship in its underlying sense—as arbitrary power concentrated in the hands of one person or a small group of people—frequently results from revolution, when the latter term is used to mean violent change in a country's system of government. Dictatorship is also frequently a prerequisite for revolution, when the term is used in the sense of carrying out far-reaching political, social, economic, or cultural changes. In both instances, either as result or as prerequisite of "revolution," deep divisions within the body politic are critical to the functionality or usefulness of dictatorship. Dictatorship may also be a cause of revolution, when its operation arouses strong resentment and dissatisfaction within a political system.

Revolutions are often followed by dictatorships largely because people in the societies involved are too bitterly opposed to one another to permit less drastic forms of governance to function effectively, and also because the successful revolutionaries may be intent on making highly controversial changes in the social systems they have conquered. Such changes may be possible only with heavy reliance on coercion and arbitrary rule.

Among modern illustrations on the right side of the political spectrum (conservative, traditionalist) was the Spanish Civil War of 1936–1939, in which the military, assisted by various conservative elements and led by Gen. Francisco Franco, overthrew the Republic in a savage, bloody struggle with the loss of several hundred thousand lives. Neither side could have trusted the other in a hypothetical free election in 1939. In any case, Franco and many of his followers sought to banish Communists and other radicals from Spanish political life and to restore the Catholic Church not only to cultural preeminence but even to a censorial role in the intellectual life of the nation. Franco's Nationalists adamantly opposed any attempt to promote separatism and autonomy within Spain, as in the Basque region and in Catalonia. They also generally viewed parliamentary democracy as an invitation to anarchy. Although the specific form of the Spanish dictatorship after 1939 may have been more personally focused on Franco than might have been the case under other conceivable scenarios, the main aims of Franco's followers simply could not have been accommodated within a constitutional republic. Elections with equal suffrage for all citizens regardless of their religious and political convictions would not have "delivered" on their demands.

Analogous considerations prompted a dictatorship from the left in Russia after 1917. Although Vladimir Ilyich Lenin and his Bolshevik colleagues allowed a relatively free election to a Constituent Assembly to take place in Russia at the end of 1917, Lenin dissolved that body as soon as it met because its composition—with the Bolsheviks in the minority—would not have allowed him and his party undisputed power and the realization of suitably radical changes in the social and economic life of Russia. To Lenin, political democracy and rule of law would have meant concessions to class enemies: the bourgeoisie, the petty bourgeoisie, and ultimately landlords and capitalists. A communist society in Russia could not be constructed without first suppressing its allegedly irreconcilable class enemies. The war against class enemies was a matter of "kill or be killed," often quite literally. This notion was an important element of Lenin's "dictatorship of the proletariat" concept.

In Iran, the 1979 overthrow of the regime of the shah was followed both by an election and a constitution, but the constitution paradoxically granted absolute oversight powers to a religious leader, Ayatollah Ruhollah Khomeini. Considering the aspirations of the clerical and proclerical elements in Iran at that time to virtually total religious control over people's lives, and the considerable social opposition to that program, the autocratic outcome of the Iranian revolution was hardly surprising.

Dictatorship enables political actors to obtain from society what a fully sensitive or democratic political system would deny them. Alternately, dictatorship prevents the occurrence of demands, behaviors, or allocations that an open society would likely allow. Illustratively, Hitler's dictatorship in the 1930s shut down German trade unions and the Communist Party. Neither organization could legally

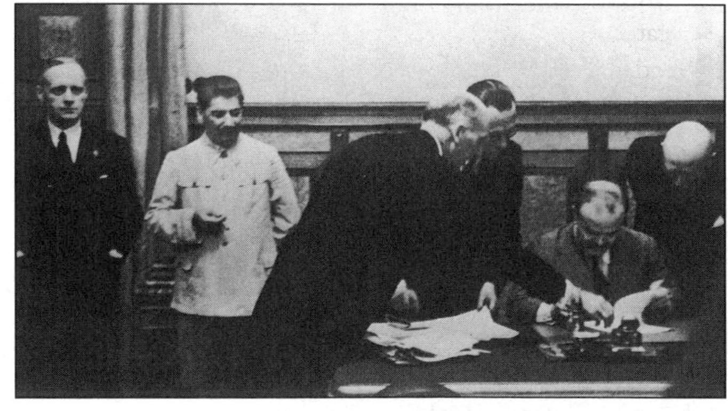

Soviet foreign minister Viacheslav Molotov signs the Nazi-Soviet nonaggression pact in August 1939 while German foreign minister Joachim von Ribbentrop (far left) and Soviet leader Joseph Stalin look on. Dictatorships are capable of pursuing policies that a democratic regime would find unsupportable.

recruit members, engage in strikes, or conduct demonstrations, among many activities that democracy had readily permitted between 1919 and 1933. On the other hand, given our knowledge of the policy positions of all the German political parties that Hitler suppressed, it is clear that such Nazi measures as euthanasia of the physically disabled, the murder of the Jews, and the preparations for military conquests in Europe would not have been sanctioned by a democratically ruled Germany.

Dictatorship's characteristic devices include denial of the rights of free speech, assembly, association, and petition; censorship; at least intermittent use of violence and incarceration without due process of law; secrecy; lack of public access to decision makers; and, above all, the right of the "dictator" to intervene arbitrarily in any sphere of life without regard to law or public opinion, and his or her capacity for arbitrary, idiosyncratic decision making.

The dictator's actions cannot be openly interposed, for example, amended or reversed by any body such as a legislature, court of law, or popular referendum. Nor can the dictator be held openly accountable by removal from office or by public disclosures or criticisms.

Within the above definition of dictatorship, one can recognize a variety of subtypes. One subtype is dictatorships in which power is exercised for relatively limited aims, including individual or family self-enrichment and for the protection of some narrowly defined interests. Examples include the rule of Rafael Leónidas Trujillo Molina (1930–1961) of the Dominican Republic or Fulgencio Batista (1952–1959) in Cuba. Military dictatorships in Chile, Uruguay, and Argentina in the 1970s and 1980s also represented relatively limited types; their main objectives were the maintenance of order and socioeconomic status quo against "communists" and "radicals." Their illegal liquidations of political opponents (the *desaparecidos,* literally "disappeared persons") illustrated—and were, no doubt, intended to illustrate—their dictatorial, interventionist powers. Recent military dictatorships in Nigeria have also conformed to this more limited variety.

At the other extreme, one would find the dictatorships of Adolf Hitler (1933–1945) and Joseph Stalin (1929–1953), who were seeking to restructure profoundly the societies under their control, manipulate the content of people's everyday lives to a very high degree, pursue some innovative, highly controversial policies, or perhaps all of these. The Stalin and Hitler regimes were the quintessential so-called totalitarian dictatorships of the twentieth century. The dictatorships of Fidel Castro in Cuba and Mao Zedong in China corresponded more to this extreme as well, and Deng Xiaoping's corresponded appreciably less so. "Real world" regimes always tend to be hybrids; there are few "perfect" dictatorships, democracies, or any other types.

See also *German Nazi Revolution (1933–1945); Hitler, Adolf; Mao Zedong; Stalin, Joseph.*

ALEXANDER J. GROTH

BIBLIOGRAPHY

Abbott, Gleason. *Totalitarianism.* New York: Oxford University Press, 1995.
Cobban, Alfred. *Dictatorship.* New York: Scribner, 1939.
Friedrich, Carl, and Zbigniew K. Brzezinski. *Totalitarian Dictatorship and Autocracy.* 2d ed. Cambridge: Harvard University Press, 1965.
Irfani, Suroosh. *Iran's Islamic Revolution.* London: Zed Books, 1983.
Linz, Juan, and Alfred Stepan, eds. *The Breakdown of Democratic Regimes.* Baltimore, Md.: Johns Hopkins University Press, 1978.
Rubin, Barry. *Modern Dictators.* New York: McGraw-Hill, 1987.

DUTCH REVOLUTIONS (1780–1800)

The Dutch Republic was transformed by two waves of political revolution in the last decades of the eighteenth century: the Patriot Revolution in the 1780s and the Batavian Revolution in the 1790s.

THE DUTCH REPUBLIC UNDER THE OLD REGIME

The Dutch Republic was born in the course of the Netherlands Revolt (1566–1609) and the Eighty Years' War (1568–1648) against Habsburg Spain. Its political constitution, like that of the Swiss Confederation, was an obvious exception to the rules of princely politics in early modern Europe. The defensive Union of Utrecht (1579) bound its signatories—the provinces of Holland, Zeeland, Utrecht, Gelderland, Overijssel, Friesland, and Groningen—in a perpetual alliance; each sovereign province governed its internal affairs while delegating limited authority over defense and foreign affairs to the central institutions of the republican confederation: the Council of State and the States-General. Within the several provinces, chartered, self-governing cities typically dominated provincial affairs and the provincial delegations to the States-General (with the notable exception of Friesland, where rural freeholders controlled provincial government). At the national level, through the States-General, the urban and commercially dominant province of Holland, which contributed nearly 60 percent of the confederation's budget, often dominated the foreign policy of the nominally equal United Provinces of the Northern Netherlands, as they were formally known.

The republic's formidable military forces were closely linked to the House of Orange/Nassau, which, as a consequence of the charismatic leadership of William "The Silent" (1533–1584) during the early years of the Netherlands Revolt, provided a succession of influential captains-general to the confederation. Traditionally, the princes of Orange/ Nassau combined their appointed military leadership and their ex officio role in the Council of State with an appointment from the provincial estates to the position of *stadhouder*. (During the Habsburg period the stadhouders were provincial governors appointed by the Habsburg overlords.) Though the provincial stadhouders exercised no formal legislative, judicial, or administrative authority, they came over time to exercise considerable authority over the appointment of the republic's powerful regents, who, by virtue of their membership in municipal councils, filled most of the influential offices at the regional and national level. This combination of political patronage and military leadership made the princes of Orange the perennial competitors for national leadership with the official representatives (advocates or regents) of the province of Holland.

Political competition between the princes of Oranges and regents opposed to their political and military influence spilled over into dramatic conflicts on several important occasions during the first two hundred years of the republic's history. For example, after a dispute with Holland over the demobilization of troops in 1650, William II (1626–1650) attempted unsuccessfully to seize power from the regents of Holland. In reaction, the Grand Assembly of 1651 reaffirmed the principle of provincial sovereignty and gave more control over the army to the provincial estates; in addition, five of the seven provinces left the office of stadhouder vacant in a symbolic protest aimed at the federal government.

In 1672 the republic's apparent helplessness in the face of French invasion occasioned the "restoration" of the office of stadhouder and the appointment of William III (1650–1702) as captain-general of the union. In 1702, following the death of William III, the offices of captain-general and stadhouder in several provinces were again left unfilled. In 1747 another French invasion resulted in popular movements on behalf of the prince of Orange and the appointment of Prince William IV (1711–1751) as stadhouder in all seven provinces, the augmentation of the prince's patronage system, and the declaration that the prince's appointments were to be hereditary.

THE PATRIOT REVOLUTION, 1786–1787

The Patriot Revolution, the first popular democratic revolution in Europe, was born of the political and social crisis that resulted from Dutch involvement in the American Revolutionary War. The Dutch were dragged willy-nilly into the war when the British learned of trade negotiations between the rebellious American colonies and representatives of the city of Amsterdam. For the Dutch, the Fourth English War (1780–1784) was a military and economic disaster, and it immediately set forth a torrent of internal bickering and mutual recrimination. On one side, self-styled Patriots attacked Prince William V (1751–1806) for his pro-English proclivities and his conduct of the war as commander in chief of both the army and navy. On the other side, the so-called Orangists attacked the traditional opponents of the princes of Orange—the regents of Holland and the city of Amsterdam, in particular—for provoking an unnecessary war.

In the fall of 1781, this internal debate was crystallized and transformed by a remarkable pamphlet entitled *Aan het Volk van Nederland* (To the People of the Netherlands) in which J. D. van der Capellen, a dissident nobleman from Overijssel, managed to link the disastrous course of the war with a host of domestic issues. Claiming insistently that the current malaise was the consequence of the "tyrannical" policies of William V, van der Capellen concluded that the people of the Netherlands, like the people of America, had to seize control of their own affairs. In 1782 the nascent Patriot movement organized a successful nationwide petition campaign on behalf of recognition of the new United States of America, and in 1783 they began creating burgher committees to coordinate local activities and correspond with Patriots elsewhere, as well as independent militias, to defend the fatherland from external and internal tyranny.

Patriot pamphleteers and journalists seized especially on the alleged abuses of William V's patronage system, and many members of the regent elite, to loud popular acclaim, began chipping away at the formidable influence of William's so-called lieutenants—local allies who in effect controlled access to political office—by flouting the patronage practices that sustained those lieutenants. Eventually the encroachment on William's prerogatives extended to his control of military justice and his military command. In 1785, after he had been relieved of his command of an important garrison in The Hague, a very dejected William abandoned his residence there and retreated to his patrimonial estates in Gelderland.

This early, anti-Orange phase of the Patriot movement was rooted in a variety of local and regional grievances. It allied, however tentatively, a broad range of disgruntled regents with an increasingly organized and confident popular movement. As their incremental successes accumulated, however, the Patriots were faced with the more difficult and divisive issue of who would fill the void left by a much diminished prince of Orange. In the generally familiar eighteenth-century fashion, many Patriot writers argued that to make up for the mistakes of the past, government would henceforth have to proceed from the "sovereignty of the people." Whereas in previous periods of republican history, the "tyranny" of the princes had been replaced by the "true liberty" of a self-perpetuating regent oligarchy, the Patriots now demanded that the citizenry choose its own representatives. The Leiden Plan incorporated many of these ideas, and in the course of 1786, the principle of electoral representation was written into the first draft constitutions for popularly elected municipal governments.

Given the segmented sovereignties of this decentralized republic, the Patriots enjoyed their most meaningful opportunities to institutionalize the principle of popular sovereignty at the local level, within self-governing municipalities where regent elites were clearly vulnerable to the popular pressure of massive petition campaigns and public demonstrations. After a somewhat hesitant start, the Patriots scored their first major success in 1786 in the city of Utrecht, where an escalating series of demonstrations led by a young student named Pieter Ondaatje forced the removal of regents who resisted democratic reform and their replacement by popularly elected city councilors. The events in Utrecht were followed in the spring and summer of 1787 by a rapid-fire series of occasionally violent urban coups in Overijssel and Holland. By this time, the Patriots controlled the provincial estates of three provinces—Holland, Overijssel, and Groningen. The Orangists controlled just two—Zeeland and Gelderland. Rivals vied for control of the remaining two—Utrecht and Friesland.

This more radically democratic and revolutionary phase of the Patriot movement awakened two important forms of opposition. In some places, most ominously in the city of Deventer, in Overijssel, guild-based artisans and shopkeepers who had been the original backbone of the popular movement joined forces instead with Orangist regents when the Patriots' reforms appeared to threaten their economic and political interests. That shift in allegiance gave a new visibility and legitimacy to popular support for the prince of Orange, and the Orangist movement began to imitate the organizational innovations of the Patriots' burgher committees and militias. The revolutionary situation now divided popularly based coalitions against one another, although the Patriots clearly maintained the upper hand in most places. Growing external opposition to the Patriots was rooted in the dynastic ties of William V with both England and Prussia. The British lavishly funded a conspiratorial attempt to buy popular as well as elite support for the prince, and Prussia invaded with twenty thousand troops in September 1787. Although it had pledged to support the Patriot cause with military force, France did not act, and the Patriots' defense preparations proved to be inadequate. Before the year was out, William V had been restored to all his previous functions.

Thus, the Patriot movement came to an abrupt and unsuccessful end: its militias were disarmed, its voluntary associations disbanded, and many of its leaders fled into exile in the Austrian Netherlands and France. Still, the Orangist restoration could not undo certain essential elements of the revolutionary process. First, the conflict had created deep ideological divisions among the regent elite that were merely exacerbated by the political purges that followed the Prussian invasion. Second, the popular politicization and mobilization that attended the Patriot Revolution transformed popular political contention, shifting its organizational base from guilds and patronage networks to voluntary associations and independent militias.

THE BATAVIAN REVOLUTION, 1795–1798

The Batavian Revolution began precisely where the Patriot Revolution left off—in the cities and towns of the sovereign provinces that constituted the old republic. It was precipitated by the northward march in 1794 of French armies under the command of Gen. Jean-Charles Pichegru and Herman Daendels, a Dutch exile in command of the Batavian legion. In January 1795, even before the French troops arrived, revolutionary committees replaced Orangist magistrates in many communities in the Dutch Republic. These local revolutionary governments quickly dispatched delegates to create revolutionary governments at the provincial level, thereby laying the groundwork for a transformation of the institutions of central government clustered around the States-General in The Hague.

The Orangists were immediately and decisively driven from the political stage. William V fled to England with his family and entourage. Thereafter the kind of active counterrevolutionary agitation that had confronted the Patriots in 1787 was conspicuously absent.

Although the Batavian Revolution of 1795, like the Czech Revolution of 1989, has been called a "velvet revolution," it was not without struggle. Under the new, international banner of "liberty, equality, and fraternity," the revolutionary leaders of 1795 moved to replace the last vestiges of old-regime political privilege and patronage with local and provincial institutions of representative democracy. The revolutionary committees that coordinated these initial, essentially piecemeal efforts naturally included many people who had emerged as Patriot leaders in the 1780s, but new, broadly significant patterns of popular mobilization were added to the voluntary associations—the burgher committees and militias—of the 1780s. Under the Orangist restoration, for example, private "reading societies" had often provided a measure of literary cover for the circulation of revolutionary news and opposition political discussion. In 1795 these were supplemented by overtly political clubs intended to mobilize and educate the rank and file of the revolutionary movement. At the same time, neighborhood or district assemblies, much like the French *sections,* were activated to organize the popular election of representatives.

On May 15, 1795, the French Republic and the new Batavian Republic signed the Treaty of The Hague by which, in return for mutual recognition and pledges of noninterference in domestic affairs, the Dutch agreed to pay an indemnity of 100 million guilders as an expression of gratitude for France's "fraternal" support and, in a secret clause, to maintain a French army of 25,000.

Before 1795 was out, a popularly elected National Assembly was called. As the assembly moved to design a new national constitution, however, it divided into factions. Many of the formerly exiled Patriots now favored a French-style centralized state to replace the oligarchic institutions and traditions of the old republican regime. Their opponents, the federalists, also promoted democratization but within a relatively decentralized regime that more clearly replicated the patterns of local self-governance and fiscal independence of the old republican regime. After long and increasingly polarized debate, a compromise constitutional proposal that seemed to satisfy no one was soundly defeated by the electorate in 1797. New elections did little to alter the composition of the National Assembly, and, amid sharpening divisions and conflict, the shape of the Dutch national state remained very much in doubt nearly three years after the defeat of the Orangist regime.

On January 22, 1798, a coup d'état by a small group of unitarists, supported by the French Directory, broke the apparent stalemate and purged the federalists from the National Assembly. In short order, the new Dutch Directory led by Pieter Vreede and Wijbo Fijnje proposed a unitary constitution of national government. On April 23 a purified electorate, which had first to pledge its allegiance to the radical regime, overwhelmingly adopted the new constitution in a national referendum.

The radical unitarists steadily undermined their original support, however, by appearing to consolidate their own personal power. They were removed on June 12 in a counter-coup led by Herman Daendels. The new, more moderate regime, which quickly called new elections, nevertheless retained the centralized national constitution of the unitarists, which thus became a permanent feature of the Dutch state.

Through a succession of French and Dutch regimes after 1795, the costs of French "fraternity" became increasingly evident to the Dutch. The British seizure of Dutch colonial interests and the effective blockade of Dutch shipping destroyed Dutch prosperity, while French demands for Dutch financial support produced friction between the two governments and high levels of Dutch taxation. The continuing presence of French troops aroused popular resentment, as well. French political fraternity under the Directory eventually gave way to domination under the Consulate, and in 1810 the Dutch provinces were formally annexed to France under the Empire. The French were eventually driven out in 1813, and William I (1772–1843), the son of the last stadhouder, became the first king of a new, unitary Kingdom of the Netherlands.

See also *Netherlands Revolt (1566–1609); William of Orange (King William III of England); William the Silent.*

Wayne te Brake

BIBLIOGRAPHY

Jacob, Margaret C., and Wijnand W. Mijnhardt, eds. *The Dutch Republic in the Eighteenth Century: Decline, Enlightenment, and Revolution.* Ithaca, N.Y.: Cornell University Press, 1992.

Leeb, I. Leonard. *The Ideological Origins of the Batavian Revolution: History and Politics in the Dutch Republic, 1747–1800.* The Hague: Martinus Nijhoff, 1973.

Schama, Simon. *Patriots and Liberators: Revolution in the Netherlands 1780–1813.* New York: Alfred A. Knopf, 1977.

Schulte Nordholt, J. W. *The Dutch Republic and American Independence.* Chapel Hill: University of North Carolina Press, 1982.

Te Brake, Wayne P. "How Much in How Little? Dutch Revolution in Comparative Perspective." *Tijdschrift Voor Sociale Geschiedenis* 16 (1990): 349–363.

———. *Regents and Rebels: The Revolutionary World of an Eighteenth Century Dutch City.* Studies in Social Discontinuity. Oxford: Basil Blackwell, 1989.

Te Brake, Wayne P., Rudolf M. Dekker, and Lotte C. van de Pol. "Women and Political Culture in the Dutch Revolutions." In *Women and Politics in the Age of the Democratic Revolutions.* Edited by Darlene Levy and Harriet Applewhite. Ann Arbor: University of Michigan Press, 1990.

EAST EUROPEAN REVOLUTIONS OF 1989

In the last four months of 1989, one-party communist systems that had endured for more than forty years were replaced in six countries: Poland, Hungary, East Germany, Bulgaria, Czechoslovakia, and Romania. These were revolutions of an unusual kind: they were nonviolent in character; they sought not a new future, but rather a type of democracy and economic order already familiar elsewhere on the European continent; and they combined sudden systemic change with ordered transition. The six episodes had many common features: popular pressure, including demonstrations; communist regimes incapable of rallying support; factions within the ruling communist parties favoring reform; attempts at transitional arrangements that failed to satisfy demands for change; abolition of constitutional guarantees of the primacy of the ruling communist parties; and, by 1990 at the latest, the holding of multiparty elections.

These revolutions had great historical importance. They marked the death knell of one-party communist states in Europe and also the end of the cold war between the Soviet bloc and the West, which had been a defining feature of international politics since the 1940s. In the aftermath of the revolutions, and influenced by them, an extraordinary chain of events unfolded. From January 1990 onward cautious moves were made toward multiparty democracy in the two remaining communist-ruled countries in Eastern Europe: Albania and Yugoslavia. On October 3, 1990, Germany was unified for the first time in its history on an entirely consensual basis. On April 1, 1991, the Warsaw Pact, the defense organization to which all six countries plus the Soviet Union belonged, was formally dissolved. In August 1991 an antireform coup in Moscow failed in the face of popular resistance similar to that in Eastern Europe two years earlier. In August–September 1991 the Baltic states, incorporated into the Soviet Union in 1940, regained their independence. In December 1991 the Soviet Union dissolved.

ROLE OF THE SOVIET UNION

Soviet policy was the main factor enabling the transformations of 1989 to happen peacefully. Mikhail Gorbachev, following his accession to the leadership of the Communist Party of the Soviet Union in 1985, legitimized open questioning of aspects of communist rule. This relaxation had a particularly strong impact in countries whose leaders had proclaimed absolute loyalty to the Soviet Union: East Germany, Czechoslovakia, and Bulgaria.

Before 1989 Gorbachev had not formally renounced the Brezhnev Doctrine, a policy articulated by Leonid Brezhnev in 1968 that justified Soviet military intervention in a socialist country where the leading role of the communist party was threatened. However, Gorbachev and Foreign Minister Eduard Shevardnadze had intimated that they were averse to military intervention and that the Soviet Union would not try to inhibit gradual changes in Eastern Europe. They modified but did not completely remove the long-standing Soviet ambiguity between formal support for noninterference and maintenance of an imposed order in Eastern Europe. There was still room for doubt in the spring of 1989 as to whether in an actual crisis the Soviet Union would act in accordance with its recent words or past practice, and whether policy would be made by Gorbachev or by others. Only when the East European revolutions were already under way was the Brezhnev Doctrine renounced. In an interview on October 25 the Soviet Foreign Ministry spokesman announced the "Sinatra Doctrine," referring to Frank Sinatra's "I did it my way." On October 26–27 Warsaw Treaty foreign ministers recognized each country's right to determine its own sociopolitical development.

But in the summer of 1989 it was still doubtful whether the Soviet Union was ready to see communist control in Eastern Europe challenged. Despite his political reforms, Gorbachev remained an advocate of one-party rule. Periods of reforming change in Moscow had presaged tragedy in Eastern Europe in 1953 and 1956. The Soviet Union had reason to remain attached to a security system that had worked for more than forty years. In 1989 Gorbachev had been Soviet leader for only a few years, his reform project was in difficulty, and he was not certain to stay in power.

The abiding visual symbol of the six revolutions of 1989 was the opening of the Berlin Wall on November 9, following huge demonstrations in East German cities. Yet the first decisive shifts away from communist rule in Eastern Europe took place earlier, in Poland and Hungary. In these two countries, the leaders shared some of Gorbachev's reformism; and events in both contained strong evolutionary elements.

POLAND

On January 17–18, 1989, the Central Committee of the Polish United Workers' Party (PUWP, the ruling communist party) accepted proposals for political pluralism articulated by Solidarity, an independent movement founded in 1980. In parliamentary elections in June candidates for Solidarity decisively beat communists. On August 24 the National Assembly elected as prime minister Tadeusz Mazowiecki of Solidarity, and on September 12 it endorsed his proposals for a new coalition government dominated by Solidarity. These events, accepted by the Soviet leadership, suggested that peaceful change to a noncommunist order was possible.

Popular resistance to communist rule had assisted the transition to noncommunist government. For more than twenty years civil resistance had contributed to an evolution in the thinking of the Polish, and indeed Soviet, party leaderships. Strikes in the Baltic ports in the winter of 1970–1971 had shown the capacity of such action to achieve political results even in the face of repression; and many strikes and demonstrations in the next two decades, especially in the summer of 1980, had added to the party's malaise while also providing the pretext for the desperate move in December 1981 of imposing martial law.

Western, especially U.S., policies toward Poland had some impact on the martial law regime. The U.S.-led policy of limited sanctions, introduced by President Ronald Reagan after the imposition of martial law, aimed at forcing the regime to end emergency laws, free political prisoners, and resume dialogue with Solidarity. As these objectives were achieved, the sanctions were progressively lifted. In 1992 there were newspaper reports, arousing much controversy, that during the 1980s Solidarity had received substantial financial support from the West, including from the Vatican bank and the U.S. Central Intelligence Agency. However, the change in Poland was primarily the result of skillfully led pressure from below and changes within the party and government. It occurred because the communist system was recognized as morally and politically bankrupt.

HUNGARY

The changes in Hungary, characterized by a gradual evolution within and beyond the ruling communist party—the Hungarian Socialist Workers' Party (HSWP)—were powerfully influenced by memories of the 1956 Hungarian Revolution and by an awareness of the need to reform the economic system if the country was to be competitive internationally. Although many strikes and demonstrations occurred, there was no dramatic confrontation or sudden transfer of power such as happened in other countries.

During the late 1980s, reformers (including many within the party), influenced in part by events in Poland and the Soviet Union, gradually identified genuine political and economic pluralism as the goals. In May 1988 János Kádár, who as party leader had dominated Hungarian political life since 1956, resigned, freeing the way for reforms. In July 1988 Prime Minister Károly Grósz said that he could "envisage any sort of a system" in Hungary, including a multiparty system. On November 13 a coalition of opposition groups issued a call for democratic elections.

On January 11, 1989, the Hungarian parliament passed a law enabling citizens to establish independent associations. In June various new political parties were set up. On June 21 Imre Pozsgay, the reformist leader of the HSWP, said that the party accepted the principle of a democratic electoral political system based on free elections and rival political parties. In July Kádár died. On September 18 a complex series of talks between the party and opposition organizations resulted in an agreement on new presidential elections, a new constitution, and new electoral laws. On October 7 the HSWP disbanded, re-forming itself as a socialist party purportedly comparable to those in the West. On October 23, 1989, the acting head of state, Mátyás Szürös, formally proclaimed the new Hungarian Republic (no longer the Hungarian People's Republic) and a new constitution.

Disciplined but strong popular pressure within Hungary contributed to the changes by pressing communist reformists to go beyond mere reform. Demands for investigation of the events of 1956, for multiparty elections, and for Soviet troop withdrawals were made in demonstrations in June 1988 (violently dispersed by the police) and in June 1989 (not opposed by the authorities).

The dismantling of fences on Hungary's border with Austria started in May 1989. This bold move, associated with the active reformist policies of Prime Minister Miklós Németh, enabled East German refugees to escape to the West via Hungary and also raised hopes that the whole Iron Curtain could disappear. Hungary's decision to accede to the 1951 UN Refugee Convention buttressed its resolve to permit East German refugees to transit Hungarian territory. On

September 10 Hungary, to the fury of the East German regime, repudiated a secret 1969 bilateral agreement barring unauthorized travel to third states. After a decent interval following its September 10 decision, Hungary received generous state-guaranteed credits from West Germany—an illustration of the role of Western states in assisting change in Eastern Europe.

EAST GERMANY

Unlike in Poland and Hungary, the East German communist regime was against making concessions to its reformist critics. Manifestations of peaceful opposition included demonstrations throughout the summer. Between January 1 and November 9, 1989, some 180,000 refugees fled (mainly via Hungary) to West Germany. In September a nongovernmental body, New Forum, came into existence, calling simply for democratic reform. In October and early November huge demonstrations in East Berlin, Leipzig, and other cities provided further proof that the regime had lost control of its own population and also indicated that the public was more pro-Western than New Forum's leaders. The demonstrations, many led by church officials, were disciplined, and an attempt by Erich Honecker, the head of state and of the ruling Socialist Unity Party (SED), to order the use of force against them on October 9 was foiled by a decision of local party chiefs not to use force.

On October 11 the SED Politburo accepted the need for dialogue with the population; and on October 18 Honecker resigned after eighteen years in power, being succeeded by Egon Krenz, who was not known to be a reformer. Under the leadership of New Forum, the people's demands for more fundamental change continued. On October 30 more than 300,000 people demonstrated in Leipzig, and on November 4 even more demonstrated in East Berlin. The refugee wave continued. On November 8 the new SED leadership indicated that it would accept the idea of free elections. On November 9 travel restrictions were lifted, which meant opening up the Berlin Wall. Subsequent elections led to the meeting of East Germany's first freely elected parliament on April 5, 1990, and to the unification of Germany in October.

The popular pressure on the East German regime benefited not only from Hungary's policy on refugees but also from Soviet noninterventionism. In a speech in East Berlin on October 6 Gorbachev pointedly stressed that "matters affecting the GDR are decided not in Moscow but in Berlin." Gorbachev's memoirs, describing this visit to celebrate the fortieth anniversary of the German Democratic Republic, convey his loathing of Honecker.

BULGARIA

The changes in Bulgaria in 1989 had the character of a "palace coup." On November 10 Todor Zhivkov, who had been first secretary of the Bulgarian Communist Party (BCP) since 1954, was ousted at a meeting of the party's Central Committee. His successor, and the engineer of his removal, was Petar Mladenov, the foreign minister. Popular participation in the leadership transition was limited. The coup's timing and direction were influenced by the domino effect of events elsewhere and by the Bulgarians' conviction that their country's fate is tied to Russia's.

The change in Bulgaria continued in 1990–1991. In June 1990 the Socialist Party (a reincarnation of the BCP) became the first "reformed" East European communist party to win free elections. However, in November a general strike and daily demonstrations in Sofia led to the resignation of the socialist prime minister, thus effectively ending communist rule. In elections in October 1991 the anticommunist Union of Democratic Forces (UDF) came out ahead.

CZECHOSLOVAKIA

The roots of the Velvet Revolution can be traced to the invasion of Czechoslovakia by the armies of five Warsaw Pact states in 1968. Demonstrations and noncooperation after the invasion gave way to resigned acquiescence on the part of the population, but the leadership of the Communist Party of Czechoslovakia (CPCz), installed through foreign pressure, never acquired legitimacy. Charter 77, a movement of peaceful and legal opposition, emerged in 1977 but never gained a mass following.

From the start of 1989 the picture changed. On January 18 five thousand people demonstrated in Prague without interference—a sign that the regime was losing control. Especially after the political changes in neighboring Poland, Hungary, and East Germany, people began to sense that it was safe to oppose openly the decaying system of communist rule.

The actual Velvet Revolution in Czechoslovakia began one week after the breaching of the Berlin Wall (November 9, 1989). On November 17, the anniversary of a Nazi assault on Czech students, Czech police attacked demonstrators in Prague, and for a time it was believed that one student had been killed. On November 19 Civic Forum was formed, linking together various Czech opposition groups. Mass demonstrations and strikes followed, leading to a two-hour general strike on November 27. On December 3 President Gustav Husák swore in a new federal government, and on December 9 he announced his resignation. On December 29 Václav Havel, a playwright and long-standing critic of communist rule, was elected president by unanimous vote of the Federal Assembly, becoming the first noncommunist head of state since 1948.

ROMANIA

The revolution in Romania in December 1989 was the one opposed most violently by the communist regime. President Nicolae Ceausescu, who had led the Romanian Communist Party (RCP) since 1965, had built up a nationalist-cum-communist regime of an essentially Stalinist character, over which Gorbachev's Soviet Union had little influence.

The changes were triggered by events in the ethnically mixed city of Timisoara. On December 15, in response to official orders to move popular Hungarian Protestant pastor László Tökés to a remote village, demonstrations began that became openly hostile to the Ceausescu regime. On December 17 protesters were killed in a slaughter believed at the time to number thousands of victims but that later evidence suggested was nearer one hundred. The reports of killings, far from stopping the protests, made them more widespread.

In Bucharest on December 21, crowds shouting "Down with Ceausescu!" caused the Romanian dictator to panic visibly, in sight of television cameras. The crowd then openly challenged army tanks sent in to restore order. The next day was decisive. Ceausescu made a final disastrous effort to speak to the angry crowds. The army was changing sides. Ceausescu fled from Bucharest, and a former party official, Ion Iliescu, announced the formation of a body called the National Salvation Front.

A murky and violent period ensued. The National Salvation Front's efforts to establish a new government were reportedly opposed by sharpshooters from Ceausescu's hated Securitate forces. On December 25 Ceausescu and his powerful wife Elena, having been captured in their attempt to escape, were tried by a military tribunal and executed. The Romanian Revolution was the only East European revolution of 1989 that involved an element of civil war, and it was the only one in which former leaders were killed.

A major controversy about the authenticity of the Romanian Revolution erupted in 1990. A main focus of the controversy was an interview with former communist dissident Silviu Brucan and former defense minister Nicolae Militaru, published in Bucharest on August 23. They said they had participated in a coup plot, prepared long in advance, that had sealed Ceausescu's fate; and they challenged the National Salvation Front's claim that there had been a serious sharpshooter threat. Despite such criticisms, the popular opposition to Ceausescu in 1989 provided the circumstances in which a change of regime could occur. The revolution, incomplete at the end of 1989 in that there was still no truly democratic government, paved the way for later changes to a more liberal political system.

CONCLUSIONS

These six revolutions, which refuted arguments that communist totalitarian systems were unchangeable, were unusual in their causation, broad class basis, aims and outcomes, nonviolent methods, negotiated transfers of power, and domino effects.

The events of 1989 do not support any simple theory of the economic causes of revolutions. An awareness of the economic failings of socialist systems, and the comparative attractions of Western ones, constituted the background against which events (both reformist and revolutionary) unfolded. However, there was no sudden economic crisis in 1989, and economic issues were not at the top of demands for change. Among the causes of the revolutions were a general sense that communist systems had run out of steam, that they had failed to establish their legitimacy, and that they had lost the right to rule. Such views, which had evolved over several decades, infected all classes, and even some of the top leadership. The revolutions from below in Eastern Europe were in part a response to the failures of Gorbachev's revolution from above.

The modesty of the initial demands made by many of the movements is striking. As events proceeded, demands expanded: in varying ways the demands came to encompass abandoning communist revolutionary ideas and supporting multiparty democracy and basic human rights. Further, they involved coming to terms with the past, not rejecting it. Such aims are untypical of twentieth-century revolutions. Yet the events of 1989 did constitute revolution in the sense of fundamental change: not just in the government of a country but in its whole political, social, and economic system.

The methods of pressing for change were essentially nonviolent. In some countries, especially Hungary, there was relatively more emphasis on evolutionary change; and in others, especially East Germany, more on civil resistance in the form of strikes, protests, and emigration. In all cases the outcome owed much to evolutionary efforts and to pressures from below for radical change; the idea that evolution and pressure from below represent alternative models of how to achieve change is too simple.

The demonstrators, thanks to their restraint, discipline, and emphasis on legality, could not easily be viewed as a security threat and gave no real justification for the use of counterforce. The fact that the pressures for change were nonviolent also facilitated Gorbachev's opposition to any forceful repression. Where force was attempted by beleaguered leaders it did not work. In two of the instances in which force was used against demonstrators, in Prague on November 17 and in Timisoara on December 17, rumors, news reports, and foreign broadcasts exaggerated—whether or not intentionally—the death toll; the effect was to intensify opposition. In at least two other instances, in Leipzig in October and in Bucharest in December, orders from the head of state to use force against demonstrators were left unimplemented by senior officials.

Why, in a highly armed region of the most highly armed continent, did resistance assume a nonviolent form? The many possible explanations include traditions of nonviolent resistance in the region; the influence of churches; ethical rejection of political violence; memories of the miseries of wars and civil wars; and an awareness of the growing vulnerability of the communist system.

These events challenge the view of revolutions as essentially violent acts involving a complete physical sweeping-away of the old order. Some observers coined the term "refolution" to encompass the element of reform, as distinct from revolution, but it has not been widely adopted. Instead, there has been a preference on the part of scholars for keeping ideas about revolution flexible, to encompass developments such as those of 1989.

The events of 1989 also challenge the proposition that a ruling class never capitulates without a fight. Mass demonstrations, strikes, defections from the ranks of their supporters, the collapse of all hope of achieving their political objectives, and the possibility of a "soft landing" induced leaders to abdicate.

A few members of the Soviet leadership subsequently hinted that they had envisaged, or even consciously helped create, the revolutions. Such suggestions are confirmed neither by the documentary record nor by memoirs of the main decision makers, including Gorbachev and Shevardnadze. What does emerge from these sources is the remarkable strength of Gorbachev's conviction that military intervention in Eastern Europe would be a betrayal and a disaster.

The revolutions involved a domino effect as remarkable as that of 1848: events in one country encouraged opposition movements in another and also made the ruling elites and their armed forces aware that change was inevitable. The pace of revolution was also spurred by apprehension that the Soviet reforms might be short-lived. The domino effect of 1989 continued to affect developments in Eastern Europe and the Soviet Union for two more years, especially in Albania, parts of the former Yugoslavia, the Baltic states, and then the Soviet Union itself.

See also *Bulgarian Anticommunist Revolution (1989–1997); Czechoslovak "Velvet Revolution" and "Divorce" (1989–1993); East German Revolution and Unification (1989–1990); Gorbachev, Mikhail; Havel, Václav; Hungarian Anticommunist Revolution (1989); Polish Protest Movements and Solidarity Revolution (1956–1991); Romanian Revolution (1989); USSR Collapse and Dissolution (1989–1991); Walesa, Lech.*

Adam Roberts

BIBLIOGRAPHY

Brown, J. F. *Surge to Freedom: The End of Communist Rule in Eastern Europe.* Twickenham, England: Adamantine Press, 1991.

East, Roger, and Jolyon Pontin. *Revolution and Change in Central and Eastern Europe.* Rev. ed. London: Pinter, 1997.

Garton Ash, Timothy. *We the People: The Revolution of '89 Witnessed in Warsaw, Budapest, Berlin and Prague.* Harmondsworth, England: Penguin Books, 1990.

Gati, Charles. *The Bloc That Failed: Soviet-East European Relations in Transition.* London: Tauris, 1990.

Gorbachev, Mikhail. *Memoirs.* New York: Bantam Books, 1997.

Lévesque, Jacques. *The Enigma of 1989: The USSR and the Liberation of Eastern Europe.* Translated by Keith Martin. Berkeley: University of California Press, 1997.

Nelson, Michael. *War of the Black Heavens: The Battles of Western Broadcasting in the Cold War.* London: Brassey's, 1997.

Pravda, Alex, ed. *The End of the Outer Empire: Soviet-East European Relations in Transition, 1985–90.* London: Sage, 1992.

Stokes, Gale. *The Walls Came Tumbling Down: The Collapse of Communism in Eastern Europe.* New York: Oxford University Press, 1993.

Westad, Odd Arne, Sven Holtsmark, and Iver B. Neumann, eds. *The Soviet Union in Eastern Europe 1945–89.* New York: St. Martin's Press, 1994.

EAST GERMAN REVOLUTION AND UNIFICATION (1989–1990)

The East German Revolution was a crucial part of the collapse of communism in Eastern Europe. Its most dramatic event was the surprising fall of the Berlin Wall on November 9, 1989. Since its construction on August 13, 1961, the fortified border between East and West Germany had symbolized the impenetrability of the "Iron Curtain" that divided the center of Europe during the cold war. When the picture of joyous Berliners dancing on top of the wall flashed around the world, it suggested that ideological and military confrontation between the blocs was coming to an end and the communist dictatorship of the Socialist Unity Party (SED) was about to be overthrown.

Incredulous that the postwar order could crumble so quickly, exhilarated participants in the wall's dismantling talked about witnessing a "peaceful revolution." But when subsequent events went beyond reforming socialism in the German Democratic Republic (GDR) and led to a reunification with the capitalist democracy of the Federal Republic of Germany (FRG), many Eastern intellectuals felt betrayed and taken over by the West. Unsure what to call the drastic changes of their lives, most people resorted to the innocuous term *Wende,* meaning a radical change of direction in sailing. Social scientists and historians started to debate whether the communist system had imploded because of its own inefficiency or had been overturned by revolutionary action from below.

DEMOCRATIC AWAKENING

The uprising of the East German people was precipitated by three sets of events that undermined the gerontocratic leadership. The first was the mass exodus of East Germans in the summer and fall of 1989. Propelled by an elemental demand for mobility, the exodus began when Hungary opened its border with Austria on July 27, raising the prospect of easy transit to the West. The regime responded by restricting travel to Hungary, whereupon thousands of citizens fled to the West German embassy in Czechoslovakia, the only other country to which East Germans could freely travel without a visa. When that avenue was cut off as well, public attacks on the travel restrictions of the SED regime arose. The ailing party leaders had no choice but to promise freer movement, which the restive population turned into the opening of the wall.

A second destabilizing force was the rapid growth of a domestic opposition within the East German state. Since the mid-1970s small groups of pacifist, ecologist, and feminist activists within the Protestant Church had demanded that the state observe the 1975 Helsinki Agreement on human rights. The party responded by criminalizing the activists' challenge, falsifying election results, and creating an elaborate system of secret service (Stasi) informants. When the travel restrictions showed the inflexibility of the rulers, hundreds of thousands of people took to the streets, most notably in the Monday demonstrations at Leipzig, marching with candles in their hands. These nonviolent protests eventually compelled the SED to accept the legalization of an organized opposition to its own dictatorial rule.

Finally, the growing popular unrest also infected the ruling party, leading to calls for the resignation of the rigid party boss, Erich Honecker, who had been in power since 1972. The inspiration for critics within the party was perestroika ("restructuring"), promoted in the Soviet Union by General Secretary Mikhail Gorbachev in an effort to make the communist system economically more competitive. When the old guard refused to liberalize East Germany, a younger and more pragmatic group decided in October 1989 to replace the discredited hard-liners and to select Egon Krenz as the new leader of the GDR. Rebellion within the SED tipped the balance from repression toward a political solution of the problems of mass exodus and demonstrations.

GDR COLLAPSE

Initially, dissidents and liberal communists hoped to save the socialist system by reforming it, but they were forced to abandon the project when the population turned away from the SED regime. During the early winter of 1989–1990 East German intellectuals in the growing opposition and within the ruling party still hoped to use the collapse of the bureaucratic system for the construction of a "third way" between communism and capitalism. Since the SED was daily losing members and authority but various opposition groups such as the New Forum were not yet strong enough to take over the government, both sides cooperated in a roundtable to create a new constitution and solve pressing practical problems.

In midwinter several shocks led to a further psychological distancing of the population from the GDR: first, the bankruptcy of the planned economy, which had lived beyond its means and piled up an unserviceable foreign debt, became public knowledge; second, the storming of Stasi headquarters revealed that ubiquitous secret service surveillance was continuing despite official liberalization; and finally, the Soviet leadership began to reconsider its unconditional guarantee of East German socialism and independence. As a result of these signals, people gave up on reforming the moribund system, and hopes shifted toward joining the West German state.

About one million people celebrated Germany's reunification throughout the night and into the morning of October 3, 1990, in Berlin. The Brandenburg Gate is in the background.

The unambiguous outcome of the first free election, which was held on March 18, 1990, provided a democratic mandate for the end of the GDR as a separate state. The hard-fought campaign was a contest for the loyalty of the population between the reformed communists (PDS), various opposition groups (many of them allied under the Bündnis 90 banner), and the Eastern branches of Western parties (principally the Social Democratic Party, or SPD, and the Christian Democratic Union, or CDU). Due to the promise of economic help by FRG chancellor Helmut Kohl, the electoral alliance led by the CDU scored a surprising victory, redirecting political efforts thereafter toward a rapid unification with the freer and more prosperous West Germany.

GERMAN UNIFICATION

The restoration of national unity took the form of an accession of five new states to the existing federal system of the FRG. The initial step in this process was the establishment of an economic, currency, and social union between the eastern states and the western states on July 1, 1990. Inspired by the positive experience of European integration, this bold initiative was an attempt to stop the flow of refugees from the east by joining the bankrupt planned economy to the more powerful social market economy of the west. Since they received a favorable exchange rate of about 1:1.5 for their currency, eastern Germans could immediately buy consumer goods but thereby destroyed their uncompetitive industries.

The second aspect of the unification process involved gaining the approval of the international community. Strongly supported by the U.S. government, the restoration of Germany was opposed by the Soviet Union, while the leaders of Britain and France had considerable misgivings. A complex negotiation process produced agreement between the two German states and the four victorious powers of World War II. Only through American assurances and West German financial concessions did the Soviet Union ultimately accept German unity and NATO membership.

The final hurdle to unification was codification of the conditions for the accession of the five new states in a Unification Treaty. So as to provide an orderly transition, innumerable questions had to be settled regarding the transformation of laws, the validity of pension claims and educational diplomas, and the fate of institutions like the Academy of Sciences. The most contentious issues proved to be property rights, abortion practices, and the control of Stasi documents. But eventually compromises were worked out and the new East German states joined the Federal Republic on October 3, 1990, amid public celebrations.

CIVIC REVOLUTION

The causes of the self-dissolution of the GDR are to be found in the unexpected interplay of international and domestic developments. First, Soviet perestroika ended the military guarantee of the Brezhnev Doctrine and encouraged citizens, dissidents, and party reformers to seek a liberalization of the Eastern bloc countries. Second, the democratic awakening in the GDR—propelled by exodus, demonstrations, and debates in the SED—led to the appointment of younger pragmatists and the institution of a roundtable bent on reforming socialism. Third, the West German offer to welcome refugees, establish democratic parties, and provide economic support triggered a shift of sentiment toward unification. And fourth, the growth of détente, which spelled the conclusion of the cold war, allowed the international ratification of the restoration of a German national state through Soviet withdrawal from central Europe.

Was the collapse of communism the implosion of a dictatorship, or should it rather be called a revolution? If one looks at the bungling of the SED leadership, the failure of nerve of the Stasi, or the bankruptcy of the planned economy, the metaphor of an imploding system makes sense. Also, the East German rising did not meet Leninist criteria, since it was not based on the workers, failed to involve a cadre party, and lacked large-scale bloodshed. But if one uses the wider definition of a "revolutionary event" and focuses on public unrest and the challenge of the dissidents from below, the concept of revolution seems appropriate. Yet the East German upheaval had a particular civic character, since it started as a citizen movement to restore civil rights, turned into a national demand for unification, and ended in a fundamental socioeconomic transformation.

See also *East European Revolutions of 1989.*

Konrad H. Jarausch

BIBLIOGRAPHY

Fulbrook, Mary. *Anatomy of a Dictatorship: Inside the GDR, 1949–1989.* New York: Oxford University Press, 1995.

Garton Ash, Timothy. *In Europe's Name: Germany and the Divided Continent.* New York: Random House, 1994.

Jarausch, Konrad H. *The Rush to German Unity.* New York: Oxford University Press, 1994.

Jarausch, Konrad H., and Volker Gransow, eds. *Uniting Germany: Documents and Debates, 1944–1993.* Providence, R.I.: Berg Publications, 1994.

Maier, Charles S. *Dissolution: The Crisis of Communism and the End of East Germany.* Princeton, N.J.: Princeton University Press, 1997.

Philipsen, Dirk. *We Were the People: Voices from East Germany's Revolutionary Autumn of 1989.* Durham, N.C.: Duke University Press, 1993.

Zelikow, Philip, and Condoleezza Rice. *Germany Unified and Europe Transformed: A Study in Statecraft.* Cambridge, Mass.: Harvard University Press, 1995.

EAST TIMORESE INDEPENDENCE MOVEMENT (1975–)

Timor, an island lying between Indonesia and Australia, was colonized in the seventeenth century by the Netherlands and Portugal. The western half of the island was controlled by the Netherlands and became independent as part of Indonesia in 1949. Upon the collapse of the Portuguese empire in 1975, Indonesia invaded and laid claim to East Timor. The East Timorese independence movement has survived despite intense Indonesian repression since 1975.

In April 1974 East Timor was entirely unprepared for the collapse of the Portuguese government of Prime Minister Marcello Caetano. Located at the edge of the Indonesian archipelago, East Timor had a predominantly rural population of approximately 650,000, with over 90 percent illiteracy. With the crisis of colonial power, East Timorese society experienced rapid and wrenching politicization. Several political parties were formed. The most important were the Timorese Democratic Union (UDT), which favored a gradual transition to independence in federation with Portugal, and the Revolutionary Front for an Independent East Timor (Fretilin). Fretilin was more radical, advocating mass mobilization and rapid decolonization.

As Portugal, preoccupied by its internal problems, moved clumsily toward disengagement, relations between the UDT and Fretilin deteriorated. Their strained relations led to a brief civil war in August 1975, from which Fretilin emerged victorious.

The Indonesian government of General Suharto, concerned at the prospect of a left-leaning independent East Timor on its border, had been destabilizing the colony for some months. Armed with appeals for assistance from defeated UDT leaders, and with the tacit approval of the major Western powers, Indonesia launched a full-scale invasion of East Timor on December 7, 1975.

In the initial attack, major centers were rapidly occupied, and there were numerous massacres of civilians. Many people fled to the mountainous interior, most of which remained under Fretilin control for the next two years. At first the Indonesian army made little headway in the guerrilla warfare that ensued. In late 1977, however, it launched a series of systematic bombing and encirclement campaigns. Widespread famine resulted, and by early 1979 large-scale armed resistance had been broken.

Although the figures are disputed, it is commonly estimated that between a quarter and a third of the pre-occupation population, approximately 200,000 people, had perished by the early 1980s. The brutality of the Indonesian occupation, however, motivated continued resistance. Through the 1980s and 1990s guerrilla bands continued to operate. Although their effectiveness in military terms declined (underlined by the capture of resistance leader Xanana Gusmao in 1992), they retained symbolic importance.

In the late 1980s a clandestine movement also emerged in the towns. This movement was based on students and youths, raised under Indonesian rule, who were rebelling against educational and cultural policies aimed at securing "integration." They organized a series of violently repressed proinde-

pendence demonstrations during visits by overseas dignitaries—the first at the visit by Pope John Paul II on October 12, 1989. The demonstrations culminated with a mass protest in the capital, Dili, on November 12, 1991, where it is estimated that more than two hundred people were killed by Indonesian troops.

The Catholic Church became increasingly important for the expression of national aspirations, offering protection and speaking out against abuses. Efforts by East Timorese leaders to promote a negotiated solution via the United Nations and other international forums also gained prominence, boosted by the awarding of Nobel Peace Prizes to Bishop Belo of Dili and exiled resistance leader José Ramos-Horta in 1996.

See also *Indonesian National Revolution (1945–1950); Indonesian Upheaval (1965–1966).*

EDWARD ASPINALL

BIBLIOGRAPHY

Carey, Peter, and G. Carter-Bentley, eds. *East Timor at the Crossroads: The Forging of a Nation.* London: Cassell, 1995.

Dunn, James. *Timor: A People Betrayed.* Milton, Queensland: Jacaranda Press, 1983.

Jolliffe, Jill. *East Timor: Nationalism and Colonialism.* St. Lucia, Queensland: University of Queensland Press, 1978.

Taylor, John G. *Indonesia's Forgotten War: The Hidden History of East Timor.* London: Zed Books, 1991.

ECONOMIC DEVELOPMENT

Problems of economic development arguably have been among the root causes of every major social revolution around the world since at least the English Revolution of the 1640s, including the French, Russian, Mexican, Chinese, Cuban, Iranian, and Nicaraguan Revolutions. Scholars have conceptualized the connections between economic development and revolution in many ways; these connections may be central to a comprehensive understanding of the causes and outcomes of the great social revolutions.

ECONOMIC THEORISTS OF REVOLUTION

Classically, economic theories of revolution draw on the Marxist tradition. Karl Marx investigated many aspects of the relationship, including the notions that revolutions occur when modes of production reach the limits of their development; that the economic grievances of social classes explain participation in revolutions; and that revolutions lead to new, more popular and efficient economic arrangements (such as the succession of capitalism from feudalism and socialism from capitalism). Lenin, Rosa Luxemburg, and other Marxist theorists of the early twentieth century took up some of Marx's ideas and cast them in a new framework: the limits to the global expansion of capitalism, leading to its collapse and overthrow by revolutionary movements.

Non-Marxist theorists, classical and modern, have also pursued the economic background of revolutions, beginning with Alexis de Tocqueville's reflections on the French Revolution, in which he noted the paradox that material conditions improved in the decade before the revolution. Tocqueville's observation was followed up in the 1960s by American sociologist James C. Davies, who argued that revolutions break out when a gap arises between popular expectations for continued economic improvement and actual economic decline.

Davies's single-minded and somewhat simplistic economic explanation was refined by a series of social scientists from the late 1960s to the early 1980s, including Eric Wolf, Jeffery Paige, Theda Skocpol, and John Walton. Wolf made a now classic argument about the dislocations caused in peasant societies by the commercialization of agriculture for a capitalist world market, finding this dislocation to be a leading cause of revolutions, from the Mexican to the Vietnamese. Paige nuanced Wolf's thesis by noting that very specific forms of commercial, capitalist agriculture—ones in which large estates are worked by sharecroppers (as in China and Vietnam) or migrant workers (as in European colonies in Algeria, Angola, and Kenya)—tend to produce radical movements for change, especially when coupled with the efforts of urban organizers.

Skocpol shifted the focus of the economic causes of revolutions even further in her 1979 classic, *States and Social Revolutions,* retaining peasant grievances and solidarity as the basis of revolutions but arguing that revolutions break out only when the agrarian state collapses, due to fiscal crisis caused in part by its inability to compete in international markets and in part by the costs of war. Skocpol found this combination of peasant grievances and state collapse in 1789 France, 1917 Russia, and 1949 China. Jack Goldstone's comparative study of early modern Europe and Asia also saw fiscal crisis causing state breakdowns as steady population growth outstripped the productivity of the land, leading to hardship for peasants, declining real wages for urban populations, and tax increases that angered elites.

More recent theories of revolutions in the developing world have also featured economic causes in the mix of factors producing revolutions. Walton's 1984 study of attempted revolutions in the Philippines, Colombia, and Kenya insisted on the domestic consequences of "uneven capitalist development" in the world system. Among these were inflation, the dispossession of agricultural workers by landlords and the exigencies of export production, and insufficient jobs for urban migrants, leading to sharp economic downturns and political crises, relayed by cultural forms such as nationalism to mobilize revolutionary coalitions.

Timothy Wickham-Crowley's even wider survey of successful Latin American revolutions (Cuba in the 1950s and Nicaragua in the 1970s) and two dozen failed revolutions likewise includes an economic component in an otherwise political and state-centered model: the peasants who are at the base of these revolutions come from Paige's background of migrant labor or sharecroppers, supplemented by squatters.

My own theory of revolutions also links economic with cultural and political factors. I argue that it is the contradictory effects of aggregate economic growth and worsening living conditions that generate the grievances that drive broad social forces into revolution. The process that creates this contradiction, called *dependent development,* takes place in the more dynamic developing world economies at particular moments in history. It features both aggregate economic growth—measured by increases in GNP, trade, or industrialization—and the negative effects linked to the dependent relationship of such countries to the world economy and its core powers, including inflation, unemployment, poor housing, poor health, and other hardships for much of the population. I also find, with Davies and Walton, that revolutions in the developing world have been preceded by economic downturns in such places as Mexico (1910), Cuba (1950s), and Iran and Nicaragua (1970s).

Finally, the question of how economic development has shaped the outcomes of revolutions remains a tantalizing puzzle which theorists have yet to fully address. Such efforts might start from the implications of the various causes ascribed by the theorists already mentioned. For example, revolutionary governments in more powerful core economies such as France or post-1917 Russia may have had the latitude that Skocpol posits to restart economic growth in new directions. Smaller, developing states, after their revolutions, have had to contend with the continuing limits of dependency, often combined with economic, political, and military intervention from threatened core states. Few revolutions have come even close to fulfilling the expectations aroused in their making, and the common failure to bring about economic development and well-being must rank high on the list of dashed dreams.

ECONOMIC CAUSES AND OUTCOMES OF THE GREAT REVOLUTIONS

If we take the seventeenth-century English Civil War and the eighteenth-century French Revolution as the first great social revolutions of the modern era, their significance in terms of scholarly debates is as instances of declining feudal systems giving way to emergent capitalist modes of production. Contentious debates exist between advocates and critics of the proposition that these revolutions were "about" capitalism, both as a force that generated contradictions in the prerevolutionary societies and thereby contributed to their revolutions, and as their principal "outcome"—perhaps associated with political democracy. Each generation of social theorists from at least Tocqueville and Marx through the more recent debates among Perry Anderson, Robert Brenner, and Immanuel Wallerstein, among others, has taken up these questions of causation and effect, and there is no resolution yet in sight.

The first great socialist revolution of the twentieth century, in 1917 Russia, also raises the question of causation. Were the contradictions of late-modernizing tsarist capitalism a cause of the revolution that led to the first centrally planned state socialist economy? Leon Trotsky emphasized the uneven development of capitalism amid Russian feudalism as a cause of the revolution; Skocpol saw the revolution as caused in part by Russia's falling behind more advanced capitalist industrial competitors, notably Germany. There is, however, little disagreement over the considerable economic boost the revolution gave to industrialization, military strength, and economic growth generally in the 1920s and after. Yet Soviet economic growth faltered after 1970, and the failure of Soviet socialist economics to meet the cold war challenge of the United States contributed significantly to the overthrow of the Soviet system in the USSR and Eastern Europe between 1989 and 1991 by revolutions that have put the construction of capitalist economies back on the developmental agendas of the region.

Dependent development and conjunctural economic downturns, meanwhile, loom large in the causation of the major social revolutions of the twentieth century in the developing world, starting with Mexico in 1910. There the great economic boost spurred by the openness of Porfirio Díaz's regime to U.S. foreign investment in the decades preceding the revolution undermined the livelihoods of many peasant communities and generated significant worker, artisan, and middle-class grievances in the cities. The boom was followed by a downturn after 1907 owing to a worldwide recession. The post-1907 recession also influenced events in the contemporaneous revolutions in Iran (1905–1911), the Ottoman Empire (1908), and China (1911). Eight decades later in Mexico, a similar pattern emerged. Closer dependence on the United States via the North American Free Trade Agreement—which took effect on January 1, 1994, the day of the Zapatista uprising in Chiapas—was followed later that year by a deepening economic crisis that included a peso devaluation, bankruptcies of Mexican businesses, unemployment, and increased emigration by job-seekers to the United States.

Iran under Mohammad Reza Shah Pahlavi in the 1970s also exhibited this pattern of dependent development and economic recession. With oil revenues growing one thousand times between 1953 and 1977, Iran embarked on a process of industrialization, urbanization, and infrastructural development. Development was attended by extreme income inequality in both countryside and city, malnutrition, and many other ills for a large proportion of the population. In 1977 the oil boom burst, and unemployment and inflation pushed many sectors of Iranian society to active resistance to the Pahlavi state. The lack of a real economic alternative to dependent capitalism has been a major impediment to calling the revolution a success in any terms other than the continued political rule of the clerical party and the somewhat wider legitimacy of the Islamic regime in civil society than that of the shah's.

A final case, the Cuban revolution, provides interesting material for our thesis as well. Like Mexico and Iran, Cuba was closely tied to the rhythms of the U.S. economy in the twentieth century. Economic downturn came about in 1958 due to the rebels' own efforts, however, as they threatened to disrupt the sugar harvest when their armed insurrection gained momentum. The Cuban experience after the revolution is a fascinating case of substantial economic development in the areas of housing, education, health, and provision of significant quality of life gains for the vast majority of the population. These gains were achieved in part due to a large economic subvention from the Soviet Union, whereby the Cubans were paid well above the world market price for their main export, sugar, and paid well below the world price for oil. With the collapse of the Soviet bloc in the 1990s, Cuba experienced a serious and sudden deterioration of its economic indicators and severe hardships for much of the population. The future of the revolution depends in large measure on the regime's ability to reconstruct the economy on new lines in the post–cold war world.

CONCLUSION

This brief survey of the role played by economic development in the making and outcomes of revolution has suggested the centrality as well as complexity of economic development for understanding revolutions. The continuing debates on these issues provide rich materials for students as well as makers of revolutions.

See also *Capitalism; Lenin, Vladimir Ilyich; Luxemburg, Rosa.*

John Foran

BIBLIOGRAPHY

Davies, James C. "Toward a Theory of Revolution." *American Sociological Review* 27 (1962): 5–19

Foran, John. "A Theory of Third World Social Revolutions." *Critical Sociology* 19, no. 2 (1992): 3–27.

Goldstone, Jack A. *Revolution and Rebellion in the Early Modern World.* Berkeley: University of California Press, 1991.

Paige, Jeffery M. *Agrarian Revolution: Social Movements and Export Agriculture in the Underdeveloped World.* New York: Free Press, 1975.

Skocpol, Theda. *States and Social Revolutions: A Comparative Analysis of France, Russia, and China.* Cambridge: Cambridge University Press, 1979.

Tocqueville, Alexis de. *The Old Regime and the French Revolution.* Translated by Stuart Gilbert. Garden City, N.Y.: Doubleday, 1955.

Walton, John. *Reluctant Rebels: Comparative Studies of Revolution and Underdevelopment.* New York: Columbia University Press, 1984.

Wickham-Crowley, Timothy P. *Guerrillas and Revolution in Latin America: A Comparative Study of Insurgents and Regimes Since 1956.* Princeton, N.J.: Princeton University Press, 1992.

Wolf, Eric. *Peasant Wars of the Twentieth Century.* New York: Harper Colophon, 1969.

EGYPTIAN MUSLIM BROTHERHOOD MOVEMENT (1928–)

The Society of Muslim Brothers was established in 1928 by Hasan al-Banna (1906–1949), a primary school teacher influenced by classical Islamic learning and sufism, and six workers employed at the British military base on the Suez Canal. They sought to launch an Islamic renewal to purge Egypt of foreign political, economic, and cultural domination. The Brothers' outlook was inspired by the teachings of the Syrian scholar-activist

Rashid Rida and the Islamic revivalist salafiyya movement. Their organizational methods and style of Islamic political activism were innovative and distinctly modern. Hasan al-Banna's charismatic and authoritarian leadership contributed substantially to the Brothers' strength during his lifetime. After the movement relocated its headquarters from Isma'iliyya to Cairo in 1932, educated, urban, middle-class people became its main activists, although the Brothers also appealed to certain groups of peasants and workers.

The Muslim Brothers became a significant political force in Egypt because of their support for the Arab revolt in Palestine (1936–1939). By 1948 they constituted the most powerful political alternative to the secular nationalism of the Wafd Party and claimed some 500,000 adherents. During the 1948 Arab-Israeli war, the Secret Apparatus of the Brothers was suspected of bombing Jewish neighborhoods and businesses in Cairo. The Egyptian authorities dissolved the society, fearing it was preparing to overthrow the government. It is widely believed that the Brothers assassinated Prime Minister Mahmud al-Nuqrashi in retaliation and that government agents countered by assassinating al-Banna.

Among the Free Officers who carried out the coup of July 23, 1952, in which the monarchy was overthrown, were supporters of the Muslim Brothers, including Anwar al-Sadat. At first, relations between the Brothers and the new regime led by Gamal Abdel Nasser were good, and the Brothers believed they would become the Free Officers' ideological guides. When it became clear that Nasser had his own agenda, the Brothers began to oppose him. In October 1954 they attempted to assassinate Nasser. The society was banned again, and thousands of members were jailed, exiled, or driven underground. Some found refuge in Saudi Arabia, where King Faysal supported their activities against the Nasser regime. During the 1950s the Muslim Brothers established affiliates in Jordan, Palestine, Sudan, Syria, and elsewhere.

In 1964 Nasser released the jailed Muslim Brothers, including Sayyid Qutb, who had joined the Brothers in the early 1950s. In prison, Qutb had written a book variously translated as *Milestones* or *Signposts on the Way* that was widely interpreted as a call for armed jihad against Egypt and other nominally Muslim states. Qutb was executed in 1966 after having been arrested and convicted of plotting to overthrow the Egyptian government. Many of the radical Islamist movements that emerged in Egypt and elsewhere in the 1970s drew inspiration from his writings.

The Islamic resurgence in Egypt was substantially facilitated by al-Sadat's rehabilitation of the Muslim Brothers in the early 1970s. As part of his comprehensive roll-back of Nasserism, al-Sadat released jailed Muslim Brothers and encouraged them to resume their activities. They were permitted to publish magazines and to organize informally but were not permitted to form a political party. The Brothers' collaboration with the Egyptian regime led some young Islamist activists to regard the Muslim Brothers as unacceptably lax. They took up the call for jihad articulated by Sayyid Qutb. Other Islamists have attempted to participate in electoral politics and other forms of legal political action. The Muslim Brothers and those influenced by them remain the most powerful current within the Islamic revivalist movement today.

See also *Egyptian Revolution (1952); Nasser, Gamal Abdel.*

Joel Beinin

BIBLIOGRAPHY

Beinin, Joel. "Islam, Marxism, and the Shubra al-Khaymah Textile Workers: Muslim Brothers and Communists in the Egyptian Trade Union Movement." In *Islam, Politics, and Social Movements,* edited by Edmund Burke, III, and Ira M. Lapidus, 207–227. Berkeley: University of California Press, 1988.

Medani, Khalid. "Funding Fundamentalism: The Political Economy of an Islamist State." In *Political Islam: Essays from Middle East Report,* edited by Joel Beinin and Joe Stork, 166–177. Berkeley: University of California Press, 1997.

Mitchell, Richard P. T*he Society of the Muslim Brothers.* New York: Oxford University Press, 1993.

Wickham, Carrie Rosefsky. "Islamic Mobilization and Political Change: The Islamist Trend in Egypt's Professional Associations." In *Political Islam: Essays from Middle East Report,* edited by Joel Beinin and Joe Stork, 120–135. Berkeley: University of California Press, 1997.

EGYPTIAN REVOLTS (1881–1919)

From the 1870s until nominal independence was attained in 1922, two major popular movements emerged in response to the increasing European military, political, and economic pressures on Egypt. The first, the Urabi revolt of 1881–1882, is often considered to be the formative moment of Egyptian nationalism. But as Egypt was legally a province of the Ottoman Empire until 1914, the activist intellectuals of the 1870s and early 1880s—among them 'Abd Allah al-Nadim, Ya'qub Sannu', Adib Ishaq, Sayyid Jamal al-Din al-Afghani, and Muhammad 'Abduh—expressed an amalgam of nationalist, democratic, Islamic, and Ottoman loyalist sentiments. The 1919 uprising was more clearly nationalist in character and raised the demand for complete independence from Britain.

The development and export of long-staple cotton was a major motive of European involvement in Egypt. European bankers lent large sums of money to Egypt during the cotton boom of the 1860s. When cotton prices collapsed at the conclusion of the American Civil War, Egypt was unable to repay its debts. In 1876 the state declared bankruptcy. Britain and France, in an effort to ensure the recovery of their citizens' capital, imposed a European-dominated cabinet, which reduced the size of the Egyptian army and prescribed other austerity measures. Khedive Tawfiq, legally the governor of the Ottoman province of Egypt despite his exalted title of khedive and aspirations for greater autonomy, collaborated with the Europeans, hoping to secure his own autocratic rule.

The officer corps of the Egyptian army, an Ottoman military unit, was dominated by Turkish speakers who considered themselves superior to Arabic-speaking indigenous Egyptians. In February 1881 Arabophone officers led by Col. Ahmad 'Urabi demonstrated against proposed legislation barring officers of peasant origins from promotion above the rank of colonel. Their protest developed into a movement against European intervention encompassing an unstable coalition of large landowners, government officials, intellectuals, urban guild members, and peasants who looked to 'Urabi to free them from foreign political interference and limit the power of Khedive Tawfiq.

England and France supported Tawfiq's autocracy against the constitutionalist demands of the insurgents, who rallied and forced Tawfiq to appoint 'Urabi minister of war. Fearing that an 'Urabist government would threaten the collection of Egypt's debt and their access to the Suez Canal, the British invaded Egypt in August and defeated 'Urabi's forces at the Battle of Tal al-Kabir on September 13, 1882. 'Urabi and his principal colleagues were exiled. Popular resistance to European domination was crushed by the British military occupation, which lasted until 1956.

Nationalist sentiment reemerged in a more powerful and articulate form after June 1906, when British officers hunting pigeons accidentally shot the wife of the imam of the village of Dinshaway. The outraged villagers who attacked the officers were summarily tried and harshly punished. The intelligentsia launched a press campaign around the Dinshaway incident, contributing to the formation of nationalist political parties and a new political discourse in which previously despised peasants came to be seen as the pure soul of the Egyptian nation. A nascent trade union movement, whose first struggles were directed mainly against foreign employers, was also assimilated into the nationalist movement. The international recession of 1907–1911 drove down the price of cotton and made nationalists out of some large cotton growers. Through press censorship, exile, and other repressive measures, the British dispersed the nationalist movement. Hence there was little resistance when Britain formalized its occupation and declared Egypt a protectorate at the outbreak of World War I.

During the war, many peasants were conscripted to serve in British auxiliary military units, and the government imposed price controls and planting quotas on their crops. Food and fuel shortages were common, and inflation soared during and immediately after the war. Peasants and workers were, therefore, prepared to join the nationalist intelligentsia, large cotton growers, and aspiring industrialists in demanding independence for Egypt. Sa'd Zaghlul, previously a lawyer, judge, cabinet minister, and vice president of the Legislative Assembly, abandoned his earlier gradualist nationalism and cooperation with the British and emerged as the leader of this movement.

In November 1918 Zaghlul and two colleagues called on the British high commissioner and requested permission for an Egyptian delegation to attend the Paris Peace Conference and put Egypt's demand for independence before the international community. The British refused and deported Zaghlul and his colleagues to Malta in March 1919, setting off a popular uprising. Three years of urban street demonstrations, peasant insurrections, strikes and other labor actions, and a boycott of British goods consolidated nationalism as a widespread and popular sentiment and forced the British to grant Egypt nominal independence in 1922.

Joel Beinin

BIBLIOGRAPHY

Cole, Juan. *Colonialism and Revolution in the Middle East: Social and Cultural Origins of Egypt's Urabi Movement.* Princeton, N.J.: Princeton University Press, 1993.

Goldberg, Ellis. "Peasants in Revolt: Egypt 1919." *International Journal of Middle East Studies* 24 (1992): 265–280.

Lockman, Zachary. "The Social Roots of Nationalism: Workers and the National Movement in Egypt." *Middle Eastern Studies* 24 (1988): 445–459.

Schlöch, Alexander. *Egypt for the Egyptians! The Socio-political Crisis in Egypt, 1878–1882.* London: Ithaca Press, 1981.

Schulze, Reinhard. "Colonization and Resistance: The Egyptian Peasant Rebellion, 1919." In *Peasants and Politics in the Modern Middle East,* edited by Farhad Kazemi and John Waterbury, 171–202. Miami: Florida International University Press, 1991.

EGYPTIAN REVOLUTION (1952)

On July 23, 1952, a group of young majors and colonels calling themselves the Free Officers, led by a charismatic thirty-four-year-old colonel named Jamal Abd al-Nasir (Gamal Abdel Nasser), overthrew King Farouk in a virtually bloodless coup and seized control of Egypt. The Free Officers, until then a clandestine group, soon began using the term "revolution" to describe their political and social project. In the following decade and a half

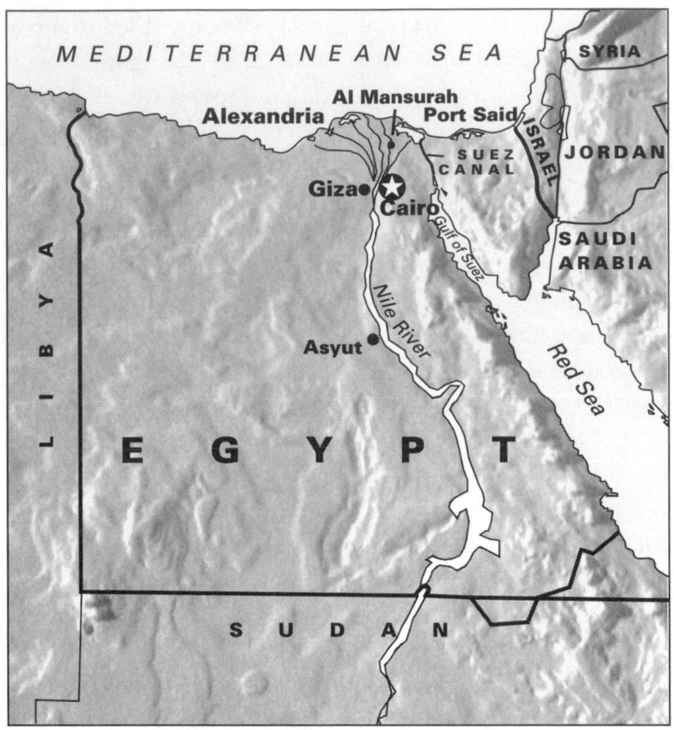

Egypt did indeed experience significant social, political, and economic transformations, largely imposed and controlled from above rather than generated by popular revolutionary activism. Across the Arab world and in many developing countries, the nationalist and reformist—but anticommunist—ideology, politics, and policies of Nasser's Egypt came to be seen as a promising model for achieving national independence, economic development, and social equity.

BACKGROUND TO THE REVOLUTION

The 1952 coup, which Egyptians came to refer to as the July Revolution, and the increasingly radical course that the Nasser regime followed were a response to Egypt's severe political, social, and economic problems. Occupied by Britain in 1882, Egypt had (after a popular anticolonial uprising in 1919) won limited self-rule in 1922 and a fuller measure of independence in 1936. But Egyptians resented continuing foreign political and economic influence, especially the presence of British troops in bases along the Suez Canal, a vital link in Egypt's economy, itself controlled by a European company. The countryside, where most Egyptians lived, was dominated by absentee landowners (including the king and his family), while most of the peasants were desperately poor, illiterate, and disenfranchised. The political system was increasingly discredited by corruption and by the politicians' glaring failure to confront the country's problems adequately.

The defeat in 1948 of the Egyptian army in Palestine, to which forces had been sent to prevent the establishment of a Jewish state, further undermined the monarchical regime and highlighted the need for reform. With radical elements, including communists and Islamists, gaining ground, the Free Officers—most of whom were of middling social origins (Nasser's father was a postal clerk) and for whom a military career had been a path to upward social mobility—resolved to save Egypt by seizing power and implementing essential political and social reforms.

The Free Officers promptly sent the debauched and unpopular King Farouk into exile and later abolished the monarchy altogether. Within months they promulgated an agrarian reform law limiting landownership, thereby striking at the political and social power of the landed elite. Although relatively little land was actually redistributed, many peasants benefited from ceilings on land rents, the establishment of agricultural cooperatives, and improved educational and health services. Over the years Egypt's urban population also benefited from higher wages, subsidies for basic necessities, new social welfare programs, and expanding employment in the public sector.

EGYPT UNDER NASSER

When they first seized power in July 1952, the Free Officers installed a respected older general, Muhammad Najib (Neguib), as Egypt's nominal leader, but behind the scenes Colonel Nasser dominated the new regime. The Free Officers initially promised to withdraw from politics once reforms had been accomplished. Instead they gradually suppressed all opposition, took over important government positions, marginalized those who advocated the restoration of parliamentary democracy (including General Neguib), and established an authoritarian single-party regime led by Nasser.

Nasser, who became Egypt's president in 1955, won growing support at home and across the Arab world by securing the withdrawal of British troops from Egypt, by rejecting the West's political conditions for economic and military aid (instead obtaining support from the Soviet bloc), and by promoting Arab unity and "positive neutralism" in the cold war. His popularity soared when, in 1956, he nationalized the Suez Canal, whose revenues were to pay for Egypt's ambitious development projects, and then went on to snatch political victory from the jaws of military defeat following an attack on Egypt by Britain, France, and Israel. Nasser emerged as the Arab world's preeminent leader and the champion of Arab independence and unity.

In pursuit of economic development (especially industrialization), social justice, and military strength, Nasser's regime moved toward ever greater state control of the economy. By the early 1960s nearly all foreign enterprises in Egypt, and the great bulk of large and medium-sized Egyptian-owned companies and banks, had been nationalized. The regime also emphasized Egypt's Arab identity and engaged in bitter struggles for the leadership of the Arab world. (From 1958 to 1961 Egypt and Syria actually merged into the United Arab Republic, which remained Egypt's official name even after Syria seceded.) Nasser and his colleagues eventually distilled the regime's politics of state-led economic development, authoritarian populism, and pan-Arab nationalism into an official ideology termed "Arab socialism." This ideology, which was depicted as an indigenous alternative to Marxism and to the ideologies promoted by Nasser's Arab rivals, was promoted as the sole path toward unity, independence, development, and social justice for the Arab nation. Egyptian Marxists criticized Nasser for failing to mobilize the masses and carry out a genuinely revolutionary social transformation but eventually came to support his regime, in large part because of Nasser's close ties with the Soviet bloc. Opponents of Nasser denounced him as a dictator who relied on the secret police to maintain control.

The Nasserist model began to run out of steam in the mid-1960s. Despite massive amounts of foreign aid, Egypt could no longer sustain its simultaneous commitment to raising living standards, developing the country's economy, and enhancing its military strength. Egyptian forces got bogged down in a civil war in Yemen, and the Arab world became more fractious than ever. Then, in June 1967, Nasser's gamble that Israel would not resort to war with the Arab states ended in disaster: Egypt, along with Syria and Jordan, suffered a devastating military defeat, underscoring the emptiness of the regime's claims of successful revolutionary transformation. Although Nasser remained in power, his government faced a grave economic crisis and unprecedented popular demands for greater accountability. Nasser died suddenly in 1970 and was succeeded by another former Free Officer, Anwar al-Sadat, who after consolidating power reversed many of his predecessor's policies: he enhanced the role of the private sector, welcomed foreign capital, permitted the Islamist movement to resurface, led Egypt firmly into the U.S. camp, abandoned its commitment to pan-Arabism, and eventually concluded a separate peace agreement with Israel.

The legacy of the Nasser era has been hotly debated. Some Egyptians have interpreted Sadat's policies as a gross betrayal of the July Revolution, others as its logical culmination; some regard the 1952–1970 period as disastrous for their country, but many others view it as an era of hope, pride, and national purpose, Nasser's shortcomings and failures notwithstanding. Although it ultimately failed to reshape Egyptian society fundamentally or to resolve Egypt's grave social and economic problems, the July Revolution nonetheless marked an important turning point in that country's modern history.

See also *Egyptian Muslim Brotherhood Movement (1928–); Egyptian Revolts (1881–1919).*

ZACHARY LOCKMAN

BIBLIOGRAPHY

Abdel-Malek, Anouar. *Egypt, Military Society: The Army Regime, the Left, and Social Change under Nasser.* New York: Random House, 1968.

Gordon, Joel. *Nasser's Blessed Movement: Egypt's Free Officers and the July Revolution.* New York: Oxford University Press, 1992.

Hamrush, Ahmad. *Qissat Thawrat Yulyu* (The Story of the July Revolution). 5 vols. Cairo: Madbuli, 1977–1984.

Hussein, Mahmoud. *Class Conflict in Egypt, 1945–1970.* New York: Monthly Review Press, 1973.

Lacouture, Jean. *Nasser.* New York: Knopf, 1973.

Nasser, Gamal Abdel. *Egypt's Liberation.* Washington, D.C.: Public Affairs Press, 1955.

Waterbury, John. *The Egypt of Nasser and Sadat: The Political Economy of Two Regimes.* Princeton: Princeton University Press, 1983.

ELITES

Elites are small groups of persons who occupy strategic positions in powerful institutions, organizations, and movements and who therefore play a disproportionate and often decisive role in revolutions. It is customary to distinguish between the political elite—a country's senior politicians—and government administrative, military, business, trade union, religious, intellectual, and other elite groups, whose influence on political outcomes is usually more indirect. A distinction is also frequently made between governing or ruling elites and the counterelites who seek to displace them.

There is wide agreement among scholars that elites are pivotal actors in creating, carrying out, and consolidating revolutions. Indeed, early elite theorists like Vilfredo Pareto (1848–1923) thought that revolutions amount to little more than the violent replacement of an increasingly decadent ruling elite by a surging and more vigorous counterelite. In sharp contrast to the Marxist view of revolutions as class struggles, Pareto saw revolutions as merely or mainly "circulations of elites." But while this view correctly identifies a key feature of revolutions, it ignores evidence, which mounted during the twentieth century, that the extent of elite circulation varies greatly from one revolution to another, and that in many revolutions the persistence of elites is at least as marked as their circulation. The relationship between elite circulation and persistence, on the one side, and different kinds of revolutions, on the other, is a question that students of elites regularly address. They also study elite configurations that appear to promote or prevent revolutions, as well as the kinds of elites that revolutions produce.

ELITE CONFLICT AND REVOLUTION

That elites must be in open conflict for revolution to occur is self-evident. Deep and irreconcilable elite divisions and the infighting they spawn undermine states, sometimes to the point of impeding their most routine coercive and administrative functions. Elite divisions may open the door to a class-based social revolution "from below," as did the destructive struggles between aristocratic-monarchist and bourgeois-republican elites prior to the French and Russian Revolutions. Similar elite antagonisms and conflicts preceded and helped trigger the Iranian Revolution at the end of the 1970s. Alternatively, divisions and infighting among the governing elite may lead elites that have been excluded from government power to take over and engineer a sweeping political revolution "from above." Examples are the modernizing revolutions carried out by victorious samurai-bureaucratic elites after Japan's Meiji Restoration in 1868 and by Mustafa Kemal Atatürk's newly dominant faction in Turkey after World War I. Less clearly modernizing but no less consequential political revolutions were launched by Adolf Hitler and the Nazis after gaining power in Germany in 1933, and by a disillusioned, somewhat disaffected, and more youthful Communist Party elite faction led by Mikhail Gorbachev in the Soviet Union starting in 1985.

Elite conflict is thus a necessary condition for revolution; but even a superficial look at history shows that it is not a sufficient condition. Elites in most societies and times have fought one another, yet revolutions have been relatively rare. Much depends on the specific configuration of the conflicting elites and also on the occurrence of domestic or international disasters that help cripple states and open the way to revolution from above or below. Where political and economic power is concentrated in the hands of a despot and his or her corrupt family and military cronies, disaffected business, clerical, intellectual, and professional elites may band together to overthrow the despot in a revolutionary process. This was how revolutions began in Mexico in 1910, Cuba at the end of the 1950s, Nicaragua and Iran at the end of the 1970s, and Romania in 1989. An augmenting circumstance in each case, however, was the sudden withdrawal of foreign financial or political support for the despot. In like fashion, colonies ruled directly and in a strongly authoritarian way by a colonial power have tended to spawn coalitions of elites aimed at both national independence and the society's revolutionary restructuring. Several of the colonies ruled directly by France (Vietnam before 1954, Algeria before 1958) and Portugal (Angola and Mozambique before 1974) produced elite-led liberation movements with such revolutionary thrusts.

ELITES IN REVOLUTIONS

Revolutions always involve much elite circulation. The circulation takes two forms: a "vertical" replacement of existing elite groups by new ones, and a "horizontal" movement of elite persons into and out of the political elite. In social revolutions from below, vertical elite circulation is marked, as persons and groups associated with the old regime are killed, imprisoned, driven into exile, or pushed into nonelite statuses. Their positions or equivalent positions in a succeeding revolutionary regime are filled by persons and groups new to governance and administration. The French, Russian, Mexican, Chinese, Vietnamese, Cuban, and Iranian Revolutions all effected such sweeping vertical changes in elite composition. In political revolutions from above, by contrast, there is a significant sideways movement of elite persons and groups between positions and sectors, with previous state leaders taking top positions in the private sector, military leaders or the leaders of important dissident movements taking top political posts, "deputies" moving up to front-rank political and administrative positions, and so on. Such major reshuffles of existing elites were evident in the Japanese, Turkish, German Nazi, and Soviet political revolutions, and they were a central feature of the political revolutions that occurred in all of the Soviet Union's East European satellite countries during and after 1989.

It is the extent of vertical or horizontal elite circulation that distinguishes a revolution from a coup d'état and other irregular regime changes that pervade modern political history. In most regime changes, elite circulation is limited to the topmost political leaders: the chief executive and cabinet ministers, some party leaders, and parliamentarians. Second-echelon political elites, especially those in regional and local centers beyond the capital city, usually remain in place. Changes in the makeup of administrative, economic, military, professional, and cultural elites are normally insignificant. Even where a regime change is brought about by total defeat in warfare, as in Germany and Japan in 1945, elite circulation tends to be limited to the political, military, and media elites, with only minor changes in the composition of administrative, business, and professional elites. Indeed, it is worth noting that some striking changes from authoritarian to stable democratic regimes have involved hardly any vertical circulation and very little horizontal circulation; instead, the leaders of well-organized but warring elite camps have, in the face of an abrupt crisis, negotiated a "settlement" of their most basic disputes, guaranteed each other continuing elite status and political influence, and "tamed" politics by adopting codes and tacit understandings about their future relations. The settlements negotiated by warring elites in England's "Glorious Revolution" of 1688–1689 and Sweden's "constitutional revolution" of 1809 were classic political turning points that involved little elite circulation and were thus not revolutions in the accepted sense, although some scholars argue that their long-term effects were comparable to those of revolutions.

POSTREVOLUTIONARY ELITES

Exactly because social revolutions from below involve a large vertical circulation of elites, they almost always have unsavory outcomes from a liberal-democratic perspective. Social revolutions usually culminate in the victory of a doctrinaire, previously peripheral elite group, such as the Bolsheviks in Russia, Fidel Castro's small guerrilla force in Cuba, or Ayatollah Ruhollah Khomeini's fundamentalist Islamic faction in Iran. The victorious group is likely to be inexperienced politically, deeply insecure, and committed to a rigid dogma, which served it well during the throes of revolution but which is ill-suited to the complexities of governing a national state. There is, consequently, a strong imperative to concentrate power in one or a few top leaders by means of a far-flung, semiformal elite hierarchy that operates through the group's party or movement. A totalitarian party-state or movement-state requiring utter fidelity to its leaders and the fervent profession of the leaders' beliefs and doctrines by all who hold or aspire to elite positions is the almost inevitable result. Among the social revolutions in modern history, only the English and French Revolutions of 1648 and 1789, respectively, avoided this outcome, when tiny but fanatical elite groups dominated only briefly and were defeated.

The horizontal elite circulation that characterizes political revolutions from above has more varied outcomes. The group or coalition that takes power is usually more experienced politically, somewhat more secure, and probably more skeptical that society's ills have a simple solution. Yet the sweeping reforms that political revolutions involve can seldom be carried out in ways that are fully compatible with liberal-democratic principles. Though some degree of electoral or other political competition may be allowed, as in post-Meiji Japan after 1889 or intermittently in Atatürk's Turkey, the presence of a dominant party or of a strong executive branch that operates beyond the reach of democratic influences ensures that the new political elite's power and program will be largely unchecked. The results range from the German Nazis' abolition of all meaningful democratic procedures, to Gorbachev's significant democratic reforms during the Soviet Union's last years, to the general, albeit uneven, adoption of liberal democracy by the political revolutions that began in Eastern Europe during 1989.

John Higley

BIBLIOGRAPHY

Bottomore, Tom. *Elites and Society.* Rev. ed. London: Routledge, 1993.

Burton, Michael G., and John Higley. "Elite Settlements." *American Sociological Review* 52 (June 1987): 295–307.

Hagopian, Mark N. *The Phenomenon of Revolution.* New York: Dodd, Mead, 1975.

Hough, Jerry F. *Democratization and Revolution in the USSR 1985–1991.* Washington, D.C.: Brookings Institution Press, 1997.

Skocpol, Theda. *Social Revolutions in the Modern World.* New York: Cambridge University Press, 1994.

Trimberger, Ellen Kay. *Revolution from Above.* New Brunswick, N.J.: Transaction Books, 1978.

ENGLISH KETT'S REBELLION (1549)

Kett's Rebellion was one of a number of uprisings occurring in the summer of 1549. They represented the largest single popular movement in England since the Peasants' Revolt of 1381. Kett's Rebellion, taking its name from the leadership of Robert Kett, occurred in eastern England. Some sixteen thousand protesters occupied the regional capital, established a representative council, and sought to negotiate with the royal government over their mainly agrarian grievances. They defeated the first army sent against them, but after two months the rebellion was crushed in a battle that cost the lives of some three thousand rebels. The scale of the uprising reflected the protesters' ability to exploit the weaknesses of central authority, with a minor as king, and a power vacuum in the region created by the monarchy's toppling of the dominant aristocratic powerholders, the Dukes of Norfolk. It also reflected their ability to use the infrastructures of local administration and a developing market economy to organize protest.

Despite its scale, Kett's Rebellion did not pose a direct threat to royal government since the protesters drew justification for their actions from the official transcripts of the state. The government had issued a series of measures attacking the actions of the landlords. The protesters sought to defend the commonwealth—a powerful, if protean, concept at whose core was a model of society as a series of interdependent social groups with mutual rights and obligations—against oppression by the landed class. They shaped their actions to reflect this societal view. They did not march on London but contented themselves with occupying local centers of royal authority. Kett symbolically administered justice to unpopular landlords and (significantly) those in the crowds guilty of looting. As in other early modern rebellions, the protesters sought justice against misgovernment, which they associated not with the (good) king but with local corruption.

Although the rebellion did not threaten royal government, it has been seen as expressing popular hostility against the landed class. The rebels' demands were directed against attempts by the landed class to appropriate a larger share of their tenants' surplus. The famous clause in the rebels' petition—"that all bonde men may be made free for God made all free with his precious bloodshedding"—probably referred to the attempts of the Dukes of Norfolk to exploit this form of serfdom. That the landed class had responded to population growth by seeking to exploit seigneurial privileges helps explain the leadership of prosperous farmers and craftsmen in the rebellion. In 1549 the fault line still lay between the gentry and their tenants. But despite evidence of hostility toward the gentry, it seems likely that the rebels sought to discipline rather than displace them.

Despite Kett's nonrevolutionary aims, the rebellion had major consequences. Its antiseigneurial character helped persuade the English landed class that its interests were best served by an alliance with the rising class of yeoman farmers in pursuit of agrarian capitalism. Ironically, Kett's Rebellion played a major part in robbing later English rural protest of the leadership that could have turned village riot into provincial rebellion.

John Walter

BIBLIOGRAPHY

Beer, Barrett L. "The Commoyson in Norfolk, 1549: A Narrative of Popular Rebellion in Sixteenth-Century England." *Journal of Medieval and Renaissance Studies* 6 (1976): 73–99.

MacCulloch, Diarmaid. "Kett's Rebellion in Context." *Past and Present* 84 (1979): 36–59.

Russell, F. W. *Kett's Rebellion in Norfolk.* London: Longman, 1859.

ERITREAN REVOLUTION (1962–1991)

Eritrea became independent on May 24, 1993, culminating a revolutionary struggle of more than thirty years against forced incorporation within Ethiopia *(see map, p. 159)*. Its creation accomplished the first alteration of imperially established political boundaries in sub-Saharan Africa's independence era. Few other sub-Saharan African states, apart from those of southern Africa, achieved their independence as a result of armed revolutionary insurgency. With the benefit of lengthy, comprehensive processes of public discussion and comment, Eritrea's Constitutional Commission produced a draft document in 1996, which was ratified in mid-1997.

Eritrea is one of Africa's smaller states, with a population of 3.5 million crowded into less than 125,000 square kilometers. It also is one of Africa's poorest states, with an annual per capita income only a little above U.S. $100. Although endowed with a better educated citizenry than its neighbors, Eritrea has limited agricultural potential, and long years of war have weakened its commercial and industrial base. The country's future economic progress rests in the development of its fisheries and tourism and in renewed economic cooperation with Ethiopia. The long revolutionary war gave Eritrea's citizens a high degree of national unity and shared political identity that is singular among African states, leaving understated tensions among its nine component ethnic groups and between its equally large Christian and Muslim communities.

ORIGINS OF ERITREA AND ITS REVOLUTION

Eritrea became administratively separate from Ethiopia when Ethiopia became a colony of Italy late in the nineteenth century. Britain assumed temporary administration of the colony, as a United Nations trust territory, following Italy's defeat in World War II. Ethiopian emperor Haile Selassie I encountered stiff resistance from Eritreans and others to his vigorous campaign for the incorporation of Eritrea into his restored realm, given the postwar African context of European imperial retreat in the face of newly invigorated African nationalism. Tortuous United Nations-sponsored negotiations led in 1951 to a compromise whereby Eritrea was federated with Ethiopia, retaining its own parliament. Haile Selassie, however, set about immediately to undermine the agreement, to cajole, co-opt, and intimidate Eritrea's political leadership, and finally to win the Eritrean parliament's assent to abandon federation for full incorporation into Ethiopia in 1961.

Never extinguished during or prior to federation, Eritrea's independence movement then erupted into armed resistance, first to incorporation and thereafter in support of secession and full independence from Ethiopia. In its initial two phases (described below) it attracted some support from Muslim countries in the Middle East, as it grew from a guerrilla force to a full-scale armed movement. In its third phase, after 1981, the movement became increasingly self-sufficient militarily, rearming itself with captured, rehabilitated Ethiopian army equipment.

In Adi Segdo, Eritrea, women celebrate the UN-supervised referendum of April 1993, in which an overwhelming majority voted for independence.

The movement's ingenuity and resourcefulness were important factors in its growing strength; it established functioning, full-service communities by night and out of sight of the Ethiopian air force. In its third phase the armed movement established a pragmatic, highly effective balance between the central leadership of Issaias Afeworki and inescapable reliance on the tactical initiative of local commanders. It discarded gender inequality as a practical necessity in war time, and the new Eritrean government has sustained the principle of equality in the postwar, postindependence era. Women rose to significant levels of command responsibility during the war and are to be found in high as well as midlevel positions in the new government.

The still uncounted thousands of casualties inflicted by indiscriminate Ethiopian bombing as well as ground-based attacks served only to deepen and broaden the movement's political and military base, to enhance its esprit, and to give it confidence that its cause was not only just but ultimately destined for success. The demoralization plaguing Ethiopian forces from attacking people many regarded as fellow citizens only deepened and broadened as the number of Eritrean casualties grew precipitously. Purges of commanders thought to have gone "soft" on the Eritreans further undermined the vigor and esprit of the Ethiopian armed forces in what many came to see as an endless and ultimately futile misadventure.

COURSE AND OUTCOMES OF THE REVOLUTION

The Eritrean Revolution took place in three phases, each with distinct leadership. Phase one began with the formation of the Eritrean Liberation Movement (ELM) in 1958. Founded by Muslims residing in Sudan, the ELM sought a secular Eritrean state in which Christians, Muslims, and those of all ethnic communities could live together in peace. It undertook to mobilize support among all classes against the patronage politics by which Haile Selassie ruled and controlled those he entrusted to govern Eritrea. The target of intense Ethiopian harassment, the ELM organized itself into clandestine cells with the objective of seizing Eritrean independence through a coup d'état.

Phase two began in 1965 when the Eritrean Liberation Front (ELF) eclipsed the ELM by asserting stronger, more militant leadership of thriving Eritrean national consciousness. More clearly Muslim-led, the ELF's support emanated from a more rural base than its ELM predecessor. The ELF subordinated emergent Marxist-Leninist ideological strains within its ranks to a more inclusive Eritrean nationalism. The ELF was a study in organizational contradictions: an armed guerrilla movement without clearly institutionalized leadership, weakened by the same patronage politics it so despised in Haile Selassie's government, and militantly nationalist yet accentuating the very religious divisions Haile Selassie employed to help sustain his rule over Eritrea. Divisiveness within the ELF led to a civil war among its factions in the mid-1970s. This thwarted a coordinated response both to the conciliatory initiatives of the provisional leader of the armed forces movement that overthrew Haile Selassie's Ethiopian government in 1974 and to the uncompromisingly aggressive military overtures of his eventual successor, Mengistu Haile Mariam.

Phase three commenced with the emergent hegemony, by 1981, of the Eritrean People's Liberation Front (EPLF), led by Afeworki. The EPLF had been one of the warring factions within the ELF. The EPLF rejected the ELF's patronage politics, countered the ELF's pan-Arab orientation with a more pan-African alignment, and rejected the confessional politics perpetuated by the ELF in favor of restoring the ELM's objective of a secular nation-state. The EPLF made a virtue of nonsupport from the Eastern and Western blocs. By building an effective, self-reliant army, it eclipsed the ELF militarily and won independence on the battlefield against a larger but increasingly demoralized Ethiopian army. The EPLF built a disciplined military and political movement by adhering to Marxist-Leninist principles of democratic centralism while exhibiting pragmatic ingenuity in rebuilding Eritrean society behind its lines and remaining flexible regarding the ultimate design of an independent Eritrean state.

Gaining the upper hand militarily and politically within Eritrea against both internal rivals and Mengistu's armies, the EPLF prepared for independence and the post-cold war era. It incorporated the defeated ELF organization, enhancing Eritrean political unity. It collaborated militarily with the Ethiopian People's Revolutionary Liberation Front, which was to overthrow Mengistu in 1991. This collaboration laid the groundwork for postliberation Eritrean-Ethiopian political and economic cooperation.

Reacting to Soviet support for Mengistu and the cold war's end, the EPLF's Second Congress in 1987 endorsed multiparty democracy and a mixed economy. The EPLF has broadly sustained and expanded on these commitments since independence while wrestling with the challenges of rebuilding a war-ravaged society, fashioning viable strategies for achieving equitable development, providing demobilized soldiers economic opportunities, insisting on the continued and extended liberation of women in some communities where traditional gender-based inequalities survived the revolutionary struggle, and sustaining political unity based on a toleration of religious and political diversity.

See also *Ethiopian Revolution (1974–1991).*

JOHN W. HARBESON

BIBLIOGRAPHY

Iyob, Ruth. *The Eritrean Struggle for Independence: Domination, Resistance, Nationalism 1941–1993.* Cambridge: Cambridge University Press, 1995.

Lewis, I. M., ed. *Nationalism and Self-determination in the Horn of Africa.* London: Ithaca Press, 1983.

Markakis, John. *National and Class Conflict on the Horn of Africa.* Cambridge: Cambridge University Press, 1987.

Sherman, Richard. *Eritrea: The Unfinished Revolution.* Westport, Conn.: Praeger, 1980.

Trevaskis, Gerald K. N. *Eritrea: A Colony in Transition 1941–1952.* Oxford: Oxford University Press, 1960.

ETHIOPIAN REVOLUTION (1974–1991)

In September 1974 the imperial regime of Haile Selassie I was deposed by a military coup involving junior officers and enlisted men. Although the coup makers were initially unclear about the ideological direction they would take, in the next year they began to lay the foundation for what would become a Marxist-Leninist regime. The political phase of the revolution was brief, culminating in the removal of the emperor from office. The political revolution was followed by a seventeen-year period in which the new regime, eventually headed by Col. Mengistu Haile Mariam, attempted to consolidate its rule through a social revolution. However, in the end the regime failed, falling victim in 1991 to a revolution within the revolution.

As the social revolution unfolded in the mid-1970s, Ethiopia witnessed more political freedom than at any time in its history, particularly in urban centers, such as the capital city of Addis Ababa. In the rural areas, groups that had been incorporated into Ethiopia in the nineteenth and twentieth centuries—such as the Oromo, Afar, Somali, and Eritreans—began to step up their demands for self-determination. Several of these groups questioned the very legitimacy of the Ethiopian state. They claimed that rather than being a unified multiethnic nation-state, Ethiopia was merely a state cobbled together as a product of the colonial domination of the Amhara ethnic group.

The new government was challenged to devise a survival strategy that would enhance its control over government and politics while creating a basis for popular legitimacy. Various reorganizational and institution-building policies—such as the establishment of the scientific socialist Program for the National Democratic Revolution, the creation of the Worker's Party of Ethiopia (WPE), and the promulgation of the 1987 constitution, creating the People's Democratic Republic of Ethiopia (PDRE)—were designed to achieve these ends.

Initially, with the liberalization of politics, various ideologically based political organizations formed, each with its own view as to the character of the revolution. In an effort to counter civilian opposition groups, the military regime established its own political organization, the military-based Revolutionary Flame. Rather than step aside and leave politics to civilians, the regime attempted to co-opt potential opponents, giving the most significant political organizations voice in a deliberative body, the Politburo.

RISE OF THE SOCIAL REVOLUTION

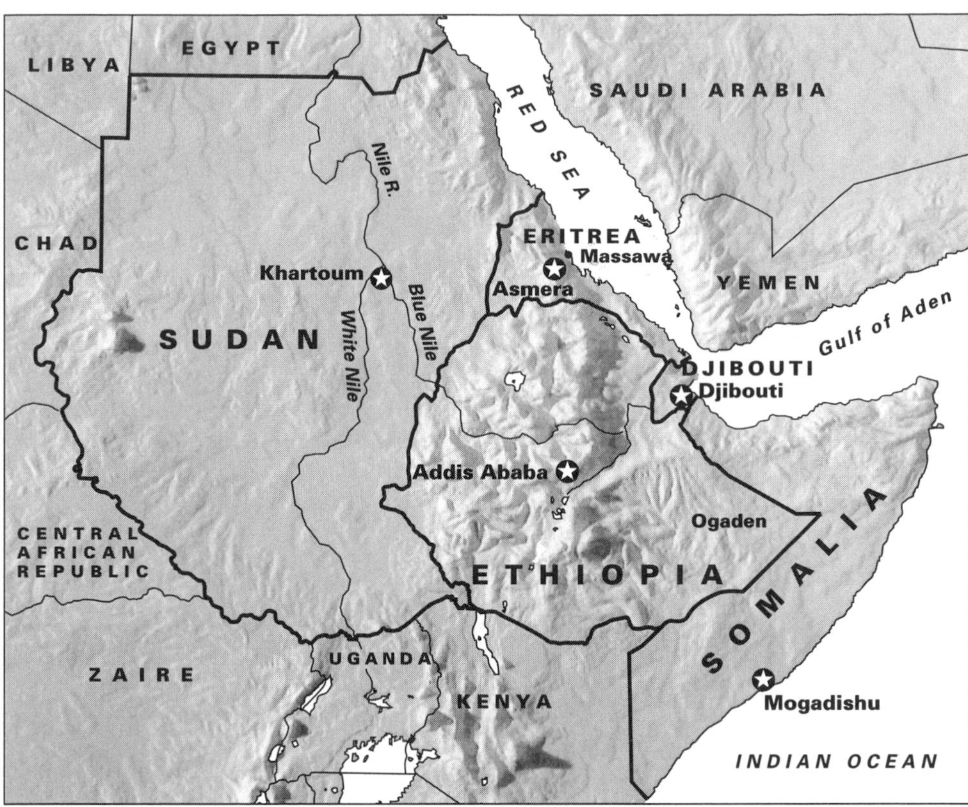

By 1975 it had become clear to observers that the Mengistu regime intended to take the lead role in transforming society. This realization led to criticism from the civilian left, principally from the Ethiopian People's Revolutionary Party, which by the beginning of 1976 had launched a systematic campaign of clandestine urban guerrilla warfare to undermine the military regime. The government viewed the opposition's strategy as "white terror," and later in 1976 it launched its own "red terror" campaign. Peasants, workers, public officials, and even students thought to be loyal to the government were provided with arms to root out the so-called enemies of the revolution. Between 1977 and 1978 roughly 5,000 people suspected to be "enemies" were killed in the name of the red terror.

Growing human rights violations in Ethiopia prompted its superpower ally of more than twenty years, the United States, to counsel moderation. When Jimmy Carter assumed the American presidency in 1977, he targeted Ethiopia as one of a handful of countries that would be denied military assistance because of their deteriorating human rights situation. Tensions between the two countries led to a complete break in relations in the spring of 1977. For a brief period thereafter, the opponents of the regime were able to gain control of vast amounts of territory in the countryside and to destabilize life in the cities. For example, by the summer of 1977 the Eritrean People's Liberation Front (EPLF) had controlled all but the major cities in Eritrea; and Somali irredentists, with the aid of elements of the national army of Somalia, had completely routed the Ethiopian army in the Ogaden region. However, by early 1978 the Mengistu regime was able to secure military assistance from the Soviet Union and several of its allies, including Cuba, which enabled it to regain control of territories that it had lost and to drive its opponents underground.

After regaining its stability, the regime attempted to implement its social revolution and to win popular legitimacy. It set about gaining control of the means of production, distribution, and exchange; creating a vanguard party; implementing a socialist economic development strategy; and improving its control of the central bureaucracy. The regime seemed more interested in statist control than anything else, and concentrated its efforts on developing an administrative apparatus that would allow it to control all aspects of peoples' lives. A good example was the regime's introduction of collectivized agriculture and state farms. Ethiopia's historic semifeudalism was abolished overnight, and peasants were granted use rights to land and commanded to farm collectively. Although primarily interested in statist control, the regime was also highly ideological, seeking to implement a state-led version of scientific socialism. The Marxist-Leninist commitment to collectivized agriculture and politicized education were reflective of the regime's goal.

The Mengistu regime also used its scientific-socialist approach to governance in an effort to negate the demands of ethnic minorities by claiming that ethnic affinities were not an acceptable way of organizing politics. Instead, the populace was forced to join mass organizations such as the Revolutionary Ethiopia Peasants' Association, the Revolutionary Ethiopia Women's Association, the Revolutionary Ethiopia Students' Association, and the Revolutionary Ethiopia Workers' Association. Also, people in all walks of life were commanded to attend regularly political education classes, headed by local political cadres associated with the regime.

An important fact to note is that the Mengistu regime continued to implement its Marxist-Leninist strategy throughout the 1980s even as it experienced civil war and the natural calamities of drought and famine. The international community came to be emotionally affected more by the horrible images of starving and dying people than by the escalating violations of human rights at the hand of the regime. Consequently, humanitarian assistance continued to flow into the country, enabling the government to divert many of its own resources to military purposes and to cling to power despite its political problems.

Another principal aspect of the statist strategy of the military regime was the creation in 1978 of the Committee for the Establishment of the Workers' Party of Ethiopia (COPWE), and in 1984 of its successor, the WPE. The WPE then became the vanguard party leading to the promulgation of the PDRE, which was organized according to principles borrowed from the Soviet model of government.

STATE COLLAPSE

Despite its efforts, the Marxist government continued to be viewed by many as illegitimate, and by 1987 opposition groups that had been driven underground a decade earlier emerged as revitalized and better organized military organizations. Over the next two years the Ethiopian army suffered increasing defeats on the battlefield and demoralization. The army's poor condition was clearly evident in a 1989 attempted coup. Although the coup failed, it severely damaged the regime, as whole units of the Ethiopian military defected, some joining forces with opposition groups.

Between 1987 and 1989 Ethiopia also was losing the support it had enjoyed over the preceding decade from the Soviet Union, and it was clear to the government that it would have to find a political solution to its problems. This realization led the Ethiopian National Assembly in June 1989 to call for unconditional peace talks with the EPLF, and later it agreed to similar talks with the Ethiopian People's Revolutionary Democratic Front (EPRDF), an umbrella organization formed in 1989, headed by the Tigre People's Liberation Front and including the Ethiopian People's Democratic Movement (mostly Amhara-based), the Oromo People's Democratic Organization, and the Ethiopian Democratic Officers' Movement. The officers' movement was made up of defectors from the Ethiopian army.

By mid-1989 the Soviet Union was in the midst of its own transformation, from communism to capitalist democracy, and it served notice to Ethiopia that it would soon cease to provide military and economic assistance to that country. The Mengistu regime continued to pursue its statist development strategy, but it was forced to introduce some cosmetic changes in its political and economic policies. The regime declared the door open to market capitalism as well as to multiparty democracy. However, this turn of events had no positive effect on the regime's rapidly declining fortunes.

Even as talks proceeded, opposition forces acquired more and more territory. In February 1990 the EPLF mounted a major drive aimed at capturing the port city of Massawa, the entry point for much of the food and military supplies for Ethiopia. By the middle of the month it had overrun the city, dealing a decisive blow to the Ethiopian army. A year later the EPRDF encircled the capital, in the heartland of Ethiopia. And in May 1991 the EPLF took complete control of Eritrea.

Between 1989 and 1991 the United States had attempted to broker peace in Ethiopia through negotiations held in continental Europe and London. However, the negotiations were for naught. The Ethiopian army had lost its will to fight, and its political leaders conceded defeat. Mengistu in May 1991 took flight into exile in Zimbabwe, and those leaders left behind agreed to allow the EPRDF virtually without bloodshed to take control of Addis Ababa. Thus ended Ethiopia's experiment with Marxism-Leninism. The EPRDF, promising not only to restore political order but to create a government based on the principles of pluralist democracy, moved quickly to fill the power vacuum by establishing a transitional government with a four-year mandate.

See also *Eritrean Revolution (1962–1991).*

EDMOND J. KELLER

BIBLIOGRAPHY

Clapham, Christopher. *Transformation and Continuity in Revolutionary Ethiopia.* Cambridge: Cambridge University Press, 1988.

Harbeson, John. *The Ethiopian Transition.* Boulder, Colo.: Westview Press, 1988.

Holcomb, Bonnie, and Sisai Ibssa. *The Invention of Ethiopia: The Making of a Dependent Colonial State in Northeast Africa.* Trenton, N.J.: Red Sea Press, 1990.

Keller, Edmond J. *Revolutionary Ethiopia: From Empire to People's Republic.* Bloomington: Indiana University Press, 1988.

Korn, David. *Ethiopia, the United States and the Soviet Union.* London: Croom Helm, 1986.

Library of Congress. *Ethiopia: A Country Profile.* Washington, D.C.: Library of Congress, 1993.

Markakis, John. *National and Class Conflict in the Horn of Africa.* London: Zed Press, 1990.

Tiruneh, Andargachew. *The Ethiopian Revolution 1974–1987.* Cambridge: Cambridge University Press, 1993.

ETHNIC CONFLICT

The interaction between state and society normally assumes a constant engagement of rival interests in the contemporary political arena, an interaction among various groups that have mobilized to secure public resources from those in authority at the political center. In many societies, ethnic conflict has played a role in revolutionary movements or outcomes, such as the Greek revolt of 1821; the Irish revolts and revolution; the Malay communist insurgency; the Sudanese civil war; the South African settlement; the Sri Lankan civil war; the Oromo and Tigrean revolutions in Ethiopia; the Kurdish insurgencies in Turkey, Iraq, and Iran; the Chechnyan civil war; and the Bosnian civil war. Ethnic identity groups may have distinct origins and appeals, but they do share common features: They are socially constructed identities that advance demands upon the state, encountering one another in a dynamic interplay of interest-inspired conflict and collaboration. In worst-case situations, where groups feel physically or culturally threatened by a state dominated by an ethnic adversary, the pattern of competition changes significantly, and intense conflict or revolutionary activity can emerge. In particular, uncertainty over the intentions of others may lead to a dangerous shift in the ethnic balance of power, creating an incentive on the part of the leaders of the threatened group to launch a preemptive strike to establish a new balance or to divide the country into semiautonomous or fully autonomous units. Identity group members, fearing exclusion from their community more than the risks of violent action, coalesce around their ethnic leaders to struggle as necessary to achieve their group's collective goals.

ETHNICITY AND ETHNIC GROUP

To understand how ethnic leaders can activate an ethnic group to make demands on the state or launch revolutionary activities, it is necessary first to examine the characteristics of that ethnic group and then to analyze the role that such groups play in the political process. The term *ethnicity,* as used in this context, refers to a subjective perception of common origins, historical memories, ties, and aspirations; this sense of peoplehood, by stimulating awareness and a sense of belonging among the potential members of a group, spurs group formation and provides psychological support for interest-oriented social action.

The term *ethnic group* suggests organized activities by people who are linked by a consciousness of a special identity, who jointly seek to maximize their corporate political, economic, and social interests within or outside the state. Ethnic groups are, in essence, culturally based social organizations that join the subjective dimension of peoplehood with the articulation of objective interests. For the most part, the leaders of ethnic groups act as do other political interests, using influence, concessions, alliances, threats, and at times even force to attain the ends of collective action. Nevertheless, it is important not to overlook an important difference between ethnic groups and other interest groups: whereas most political interest groups can end their existence by passing an appropriate resolution to that effect, ethnic groups, which seek to advance the common (or indivisible) purposes of their membership, cannot terminate their existence in such a straightforward manner. Ironically, even though many ethnic groups are of relatively recent origins and lack homogeneity and cohesiveness, they gain a life of their own because they represent poles around which peoples can mobilize to compete for scarce resources and to ensure group security in an uncertain political environment.

REVOLUTIONARY INFLUENCES

Although a wide range of conflict-producing influences is apparent in multiethnic societies, we will begin by distinguishing between those conflicts that lend themselves to negotiable (and hence nonrevolutionary) outcomes and those that are not easily reconciled within the political system. To the extent that ethnic rivalries take place over material interests, there is a greater possibility that bargaining will resolve the conflict in a mutually acceptable manner. Negotiable demands tend to be elastic and realistic in terms of collective expectations; they tend to accept the legitimacy of the political order and therefore to be amenable to divisible outcomes. Because they involve the participation of ethnic intermediaries in the channeling of group demands to those in power, they give ethnic spokespersons an opportunity to work within the political system to effect change.

However, nonnegotiable (or uncompromising) demands are expressive of a political environment of unclear and inhospitable channels for the expression of group claims on the state. Nonnegotiable demands, which are often presented in an unyielding manner, tend to involve such high stakes issues as group status, identity, territory, and, above all, security—issues that do not lend themselves to divisible outcomes. These nonnegotiable demands, often evident in highly authoritarian regime contexts, can have the effect of limiting and modifying group perceptions and therefore becoming the source of revolutionary actions.

Other, more general conflict-producing influences also contribute to revolutionary movements. Sharp differences in ethnoregional rates of modernization, negative memories and a history of collective disrespect and low status, and the repression and exclusion of important ethnic interests from key decision-making positions by an ethnic-dominated state can all create a revolutionary situation. In these cases, ethnic-related interests may feel unfairly deprived of material or non-material opportunities and rewards, creating intense inter-ethnic resentments that can precipitate violence. If these conflict-creating conditions are a backdrop to a revolutionary situation, the likelihood of intense violence is made more immediate when ethnic leaders and group members have (or feel they have) reason to fear for their future physical safety. In a situation of state weakness and unreliable information about the intentions of their adversaries, ethnic leaders, recognizing the existence of a diffuse fear among the elite and membership for group survival, may decide on a preventive attack aimed at catching enemies off balance—before their adversaries are prepared to take offensive action. The fear-inspired assault by hard-line Hutu leaders upon the Tutsi and moderate Hutu in Rwanda in 1994 conformed to this scenario.

REVOLUTIONARY MOBILIZATION

Although popular revolutionary actions born of group deprivation have been launched spontaneously from time to time, sustained revolutions have generally required the existence of well-established groups and dedicated leaders prepared to take substantial risks to achieve social goals. The tasks of mobilizing an ethnic-based support group to achieve common purposes are inevitably complex ones. Because an ethnic group is heterogeneous and often of recent origins, it includes many marginal members who may have strong loyalties to other political, economic, and social associations. Consequently, for the elite to mobilize marginal group members for collective action, it must be able to make effective appeals for common purposes, manipulate collective historical memories (whether accurate or not) of past injustices, or utilize pressures or incentives to encourage otherwise reluctant members to commit themselves to group objectives.

Ethnic negotiation with state elites or ethnic leaders can be likened to a two-level game: An ethnic leadership builds solidarity within the group before attempting to engage competing leadership coalitions at the second level. Only after the marginal members of a group become convinced that their common ethnic obligations demand their primary loyalty will the leadership be able to make effective demands both upon their membership and their rivals to advance the interests of their group as a whole. In manipulating the sentiments of the membership, the leaders may gain the support of external interests (both ethnic kinsmen living abroad and other states) in strengthening their claims for support among their marginal members at home.

REVOLUTIONARY OUTCOMES

Once the conditions are propitious for collective action and the ethnic leadership becomes determined to use group power to demand change or the preservation of the status quo, it can negotiate with rival interests; alternatively, it can use the power of the state to repress or terrorize opponents or to oppose the authoritative state by means of limited rebellions, civil wars, or terrorism.

During the twentieth century, aggregate data have shown that most civil wars have been settled by military victory or capitulation—not through political bargaining. About one-fourth of the time, however, state and ethnic leaders have been able to agree upon some form of negotiated settlement. Normally, this happens when both sides become exhausted and see little possibility of winning an outright victory in the foreseeable future. However, because many civil wars fail to weaken the state's grip on society, ethnic leaders, unflagging in their determination to shift the structure of relations to their advantage and the benefit of their group, may continue their struggle through revolutionary action, including various forms of political violence. Renewed civil wars (for example, in Sri Lanka, Angola, Rwanda, or Sudan) have tended to be fiercer and more destructive of life and property than they had been prior to the negotiated agreement, largely because the adversaries feel that they were deceived by the earlier agreement. Thus, rebellions and revolutions add to hostile political memories and make the negotiation of new contracts between ethnic and state leaders more difficult over time.

The consequences of these actions are varied in terms of new regimes and new political system outcomes. Whereas the hegemonic scenario and repression can prolong the status quo or lead to military victory, ethnic and cultural cleansing, or partition and secession, negotiations can result in various measures of accommodation (balanced recruitment, proportionality formulas in allocations, power sharing, regional or local autonomy, mutual vetoes, rotating presidents) or to peaceful separation, as exemplified by Czechoslovakia's "velvet divorce." What we find is an interlinked and reinforcing system of relations in which revolutionary outcomes usually follow logically from revolutionary influences. Democracy and respect for the self-determination of ethnic peoples tend to facilitate state-society and interethnic negotiation, providing a favorable environment in which open, reliable information will be available and a great measure of security will exist for all actors. The result will likely be to encourage commitment to the peaceful settlement of differences within the state.

At the same time, it is important to note that the quest of

revolutions for unity and regime security can prove quite hostile to the aspirations of minority groups for equality, or even for open expression of identity and even existence. As shown by the examples of the Ismailis in Iran, Miskito Indians in Nicaragua, Tibetans in China, and Armenians in Turkey, fierce persecutions of ethnic minorities often follow from revolution, due in part to the insecurity of the new regimes.

Ethnic groups can thus become the focus, or the target, of revolutionary mobilization against regimes. In coping with the powerful revolutionary influences in the environment, then, it is necessary for those intent on securing peaceful relations to move quickly to prevent the basic causes of revolution from arising and, if they do emerge, to accommodate different values and preferences.

Donald Rothchild

BIBLIOGRAPHY

Eisenstadt, S. N. *Revolution and the Transformation of Societies: A Comparative Study of Civilizations.* New York: Free Press, 1978.

Goldstone, Jack A. "Theories of Revolution: The Third Generation." *World Politics* 32, no. 3 (April 1980): 425–453.

Gurr, Ted Robert, and Barbara Harff. *Ethnic Conflict in World Politics.* Boulder, Colo.: Westview, 1994.

Lake, David A., and Donald Rothchild, eds. *The International Spread of Ethnic Conflict: Fear, Diffusion, and Escalation.* Princeton, N.J.: Princeton University Press, 1998.

Licklider, Roy. "The Consequences of Negotiated Settlements in Civil Wars, 1945–1993." *American Political Science Review* 89, no. 3 (September 1995): 681–690.

Oberschall, Anthony. *Social Conflict and Social Movements.* Englewood Cliffs, N.J.: Prentice-Hall, 1973.

Rothchild, Donald. *Managing Ethnic Conflict in Africa: Pressure and Incentives for Cooperation.* Washington, D.C.: Brookings Institution, 1997.

EUROPEAN REVOLUTIONS OF 1820

The revolutions of 1820 in Spain, Portugal, and Naples, and that in Piedmont in 1821, form a coherent, interrelated political phenomenon. They had the common aims of overthrowing the absolutist regimes in their states, which had been restored by the Congress of Vienna in 1814–1815 after the defeat of Napoleon. Although they are often neglected by scholars, these revolutions shook the confidence of newly restored regimes throughout Europe.

ORIGINS OF THE REVOLUTIONS

These four revolutions illustrate almost perfectly the "domino effect" in action. The first revolution broke out in Spain in January 1820; the other three were genuine "copycat" revolts. They are bound together on several different levels, and their common origins reveal them to stem from the unfinished business of the revolutionary Napoleonic period. They all took place in regions that had been deeply affected by the long period of Napoleonic rule and the Napoleonic Wars between 1800 and 1814. The kingdoms of Naples and Piedmont had become accustomed to French-style rule, whereas Spain and Portugal had been greatly transformed by the traumas of the Peninsular War (1808–1814); Spain had been occupied by the French, and Portugal by the British between 1808 and 1813. The end of the war left Spain and Portugal with economic dislocation, little law and order, and discontented, underpaid armies. By 1820 the restored rulers could not cope with these problems. The postwar conditions produced discontent throughout Spain and Portugal, but the revolutions owed their coherence more to political and ideological factors.

The revolutions in the western Mediterranean were the work of discontented, usually young army officers who were members of revolutionary secret societies, called the Carbonari in Italy and the Carbonares in Spain (meaning "the charcoal burners," so-called because they met in secret, just as charcoal burners worked deep in the woods). There were many other, similar societies, such as the Adelfi in northern Italy and the Comuneros in Spain, but all had the same goal of establishing the Spanish constitution of 1812, which was democratic in character but allowed for a constitutional monarchy.

COURSE OF THE REVOLUTIONS

The revolutions followed very similar patterns; in Spain, Portugal, and Naples they were almost identical; in Piedmont the course of events was similar to the others but differed somewhat because it was the last to revolt. In all four cases, the uprising began when young, revolutionary officers in a large provincial garrison "proclaimed" the Spanish constitution of 1812, were followed by the garrisons of other large cities, and then took the capital. The Spanish revolt began in the coastal city of Cadiz in January 1820, among troops who had been waiting to sail to quell the revolts in Latin America and whose ships had been allowed to rot in harbor by government inefficiency. Portuguese officers in Porto, the second largest town in the country, followed the Spanish example in February; the Neapolitan revolt began in the city of Nola, in July; the Piedmontese army rose in January 1821, in Alessandria, the second city of Piedmont.

In Spain, Portugal, and Naples the initial victory came quickly, and the capital cities were seized within weeks with little resistance. Ferdinand VII in Spain and Ferdinand I in Naples gave in to the demands for the constitution and

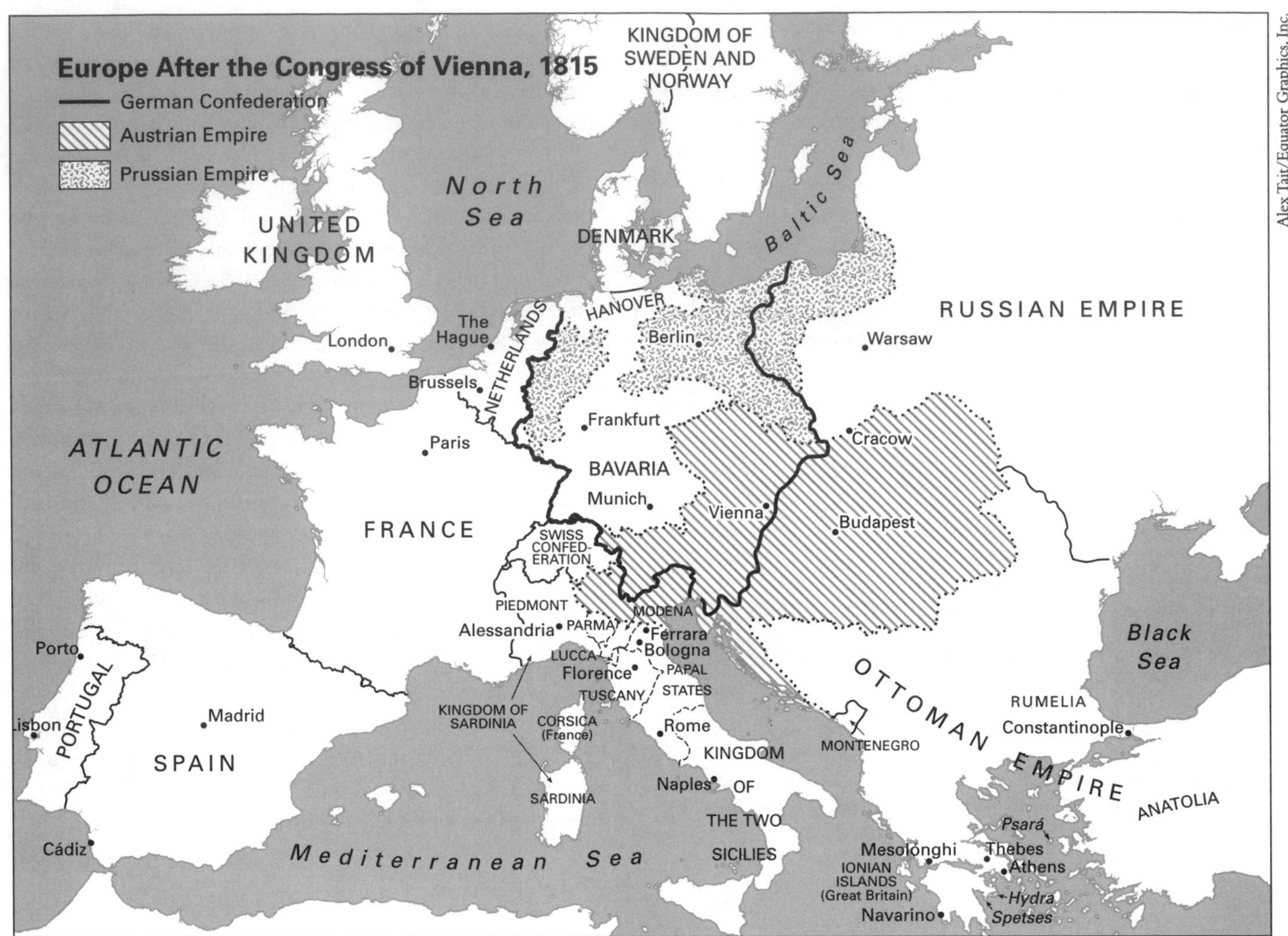

Alex Tait/Equator Graphics, Inc.

allowed elections. While King John VI of Portugal was in Brazil, his English regent, Lord Beresford, was driven from power. When the new revolutionary assemblies met, the young, radical officers found their position challenged by older reformers, many of whom had served Napoleon in Naples or, in Spain, had been in the anti-French government of the resistance Cortez of Cadiz; in Portugal, the older reformers had often worked with the English occupiers. Members of the older generation were better versed in parliamentary tactics than the radicals and were able to curb the radicals' plans for democratic reforms, causing bitter internal divisions within the revolutionary camp. In Piedmont the officers did not get as far as the other revolutionaries. King Victor Emanuel I abdicated rather than give in to them, and several large garrisons remained loyal to his successor, Charles Felix, who was out of the country; few older reformers joined the rebels, either.

Charles Felix initiated the process that ended the revolutions. He called successfully for military intervention by the great powers to restore him. An Austrian army entered Piedmont, and the revolt collapsed. By December 1821 the Austrians had also dealt with Naples. Spain proved harder to quell, but by 1823 a French army had defeated the rebels, with much help from Spanish counterrevolutionaries. In the final military crises, the radical soldiers retook power from the moderates in a last attempt to save the revolution. In Spain, the hub of the revolutions, their ruthless policies of mass conscription and "war government" alienated the moderates still further, as did their calls to help their fellow revolutionaries in Italy. The Portuguese revolt collapsed without foreign intervention when King John VI returned to Portugal and rallied popular, conservative forces to him. Although foreign intervention was decisive, the collapse of the revolutions also shows them to have been elitist in character, if not in aims. The peasantry and most of the urban workers remained loyal to the old regimes, as did the nobility and clergy. With so little support, the revolutions had little chance of real success. They seized power from weak governments but could not assert their own authority over most of the country.

CHARACTER AND RESULTS OF THE REVOLTS

The revolutions of 1820 revealed the weakness of both the restored governments and the revolutionaries. Conservative statesmen, influenced by Klemens von Metternich, the Austrian foreign minister, drew the first lesson and embarked on repressive policies. France, Russia, Prussia, and Austria supported a policy of direct intervention to help conservative regimes threatened by revolution; Britain rejected this approach, and the revolutions of 1820 led to Britain's withdrawal from European politics for the remainder of the nineteenth century.

Michael Broers

BIBLIOGRAPHY

Bernstein, Harry. *The Lord Mayor of Lisbon. The Portuguese Tribune of the People and His 24 Guilds.* Lanham, Md.: University Press of America, 1989.

Broers, Michael. *Europe after Napoleon. Revolution, Reaction and Romanticism, 1814–1848.* Manchester, England: Manchester University Press, 1996.

———. *Napoleonic Imperialism and the Savoyard Monarchy, 1773–1821.* Lampeter and Queenston, U.K.: Edwin Mellen Press, 1997.

Callahan, William. *Church, Politics and Society in Spain, 1750–1874.* Ithaca, N.Y.: Cornell University Press, 1984.

Woolf, Stuart J. *A History of Italy 1700–1860.* London: Methuen, 1979.

EUROPEAN REVOLUTIONS OF 1830

The European revolutions of 1830 began in France, where the Bourbon monarchy was overthrown in the streets of Paris. An insurrection that began in Brussels brought Belgian independence from the Dutch monarchy. Insurrections in behalf of reform occurred in several Italian and German states; in Poland military cadets launched a revolt that aimed at independence from Russia. Although the revolutions were not really interdependent, and the influence of the French Revolution of 1789 was largely indirect, the revolutions of 1830 were a culmination of the clash in a number of states between political liberals (and, in some places, precocious nationalists) and conservative regimes that had dominated Europe since Napoleon's final defeat in 1815 *(see map, p. 164)*.

After 1815 the victorious allies—Austria, Prussia, Great Britain, and Russia—led by the Habsburg chancellor Prince Klemens von Metternich, hoped to prevent liberal and national movements from challenging monarchical legitimacy. However, Great Britain made clear that it would maintain an independent foreign policy, and in any case, the constitutional nature of the British monarchy seemed out of step with the monarchical principles espoused by the other three major powers that had helped defeat Napoleon. France returned to the good graces of the allies, and a French army put down a liberal uprising in Spain in 1823. However, once the powers supported the cause of Greek independence against the Turks, a major crack occurred in the unqualified acceptance of the principle of monarchical legitimacy. The demands of liberals generated a sense of political crisis in many European states in the late 1820s, one that was accentuated by a general economic downturn that had begun in 1826. In May 1829 students demanding constitutional government battled troops in the "Battle of the Market-Place" in Oslo, Norway.

THE JULY REVOLUTION

Although the fall of the French Bourbons in 1830 was by no means inevitable, provocative policies carried out by King Charles X following his advent to the throne in 1824 generated increasing liberal political opposition. Yet the restored Bourbon monarchy had demonstrated some surprising accommodation with changes that had been brought by the revolutionary and imperial epochs. Indeed, many returning noble émigrés were outraged that their lands sold by the revolutionary government would not be returned, that the bureaucracy that emerged out of the revolutionary and imperial periods would be essentially maintained, and that the charter Louis XVIII had promulgated upon his return to the throne had created a Chamber of Deputies, which would be elected, albeit by an extremely narrow franchise (allowing about 100,000 men to vote) based on wealth as measured by taxes paid. The very conservative "Ultras" provided opposition from the far right during the first years of the Restoration; the assassination of the heir to the Bourbon throne, the Duc de Berry, in 1820 revived their influence on the monarchy and led to another period of reaction.

Political liberals (some of them vaguely Napoleonic in their allegiance) found the electoral franchise too restrictive and tilted in favor of traditional landed interests. Liberals who objected to the alliance of "altar and throne" were outraged when the Chamber of Deputies passed a law making sacrilege a capital crime (although the law was never used). As rumors spread that the monarchy was going to restore the tithe, the government financed a law in 1825 indemnifying those who had lost land during the Revolution by lowering the interest paid to holders of the national debt, most of whom considered themselves middle class. The economic crisis in 1826–1827 helped generate further discontent, as some businessmen blamed the government for not being sufficiently attentive to their interests. In rural France, grain riots pitted poor peasants against wealthy property-owners, grain merchants, and state authorities. In 1828 liberals formed an association to refuse to pay taxes and worked to register all property-owners eligible to vote.

In 1829 Charles X named the reactionary Prince Jules de Polignac to be premier. This shot across the bow convinced liberals that the king ultimately sought to end constraints on his authority. Some 221 deputies responded with defiance to a provocative speech by the king opening the Chamber of Deputies' session in March 1830. Charles dissolved the Chamber, but new elections returned an even more liberal Chamber. Determined to end the crisis by a bold, devastating stroke, Charles X promulgated the July Ordinances. These dissolved the newly elected Chamber; disenfranchised three-fourths of the electorate; announced new elections in which only the wealthiest men in France, most of them owners of vast landed wealth, would be eligible; and imposed even harsher press censorship. Demonstrators took to the streets in protest on July 26. The following day, protesters battled troops sent in to restore order. Protest turned into revolution. Barricades blocked the narrow streets of Paris, and soldiers faced bullets as well as rocks and tiles thrown from rooftops.

After first naming Louis-Philippe, the duc d'Orléans, to be lieutenant-general of the realm, Charles abdicated on August 2. Victorious liberals offered Louis-Philippe the throne as king of the French, a title intended to reflect that his power stemmed from the people and thus represented accommodation with the French Revolution. The tricolor once again became the flag of France, and a law in April 1831 doubled the number of eligible voters by lowering the property qualification. The latest French revolution brought a considerably more liberal monarchy, one that removed Catholicism as the nation's official religion. Furthermore, during the July Monarchy—as the regime came to be called—lawyers and other middle-class men played a greater role in French political life than they had before the Bourbons had been toppled. And while the representation of businessmen in the new Chamber of Deputies was not particularly marked, the broadened electoral suffrage greatly increased middle-class representation. The July Monarchy proved conducive to business interests, reducing the impact of bankruptcy, liberalizing credit policies, and implementing beneficial tariff policies. To be sure, land remained the basis of most wealth in France. However, contemporary images associating the July Monarchy with the triumphant middle classes are accurate.

In France the greatest significance of the revolution of 1830, a political revolution with social consequences, stems from its aftermath. As the Orléanist monarchy consolidated power, liberals who had expected an even more expanded suffrage became increasingly dissatisfied. "Liberty," the watchword of the revolution, had different meanings to different groups. To peasants living a precarious existence in the mountains, liberty encompassed their hope that the revolution might bring a return of collective rights they or their ancestors had once enjoyed. To left-liberals, the revolution had fallen short of fulfilling their demands for an even more expanded electoral suffrage, and a nascent republican movement emerged in France, based in new voluntary associations. At the same time, skilled workers put forward demands for higher piece-rates and wages and better working conditions. For wine producers and consumers, liberty meant freedom from the high tax on beverages. But their sense of liberty conflicted with that of many masters and employers, for whom "freedom of work" meant the continued illegality of strikes and the state not becoming involved in work-related disputes. Class-consciousness gradually took shape among some workers.

With remarkable speed, the July Monarchy lost popularity and found determined opponents whose ideologies would help shape political contention in France. The July Monarchy sought to hold the line, as troops broke up demonstrations. Ordinary people rioted in Paris during the trial of the ministers of Charles X in December 1830. The next year, workers sacked the archbishop's palace in Paris, and silkworkers in Lyon battled their employers and would rise up again in 1834. The revolution of 1830 served as a catalyst for social, political, and ideological evolution despite repressive laws passed in 1834 and 1835 that severely restricted, respectively, the right to form associations and the freedom of the press. French republicanism and socialism developed rapidly.

REVOLUTIONARY SUCCESSES AND FAILURES ELSEWHERE IN EUROPE

The news that the Bourbons had fallen to another revolution in France encouraged liberal and nationalist movements in a number of other countries. The second successful revolution occurred in Belgium. The Congress of Vienna had left the southern Netherlands, which had belonged to Habsburg Austria before being conquered by French armies during the French Revolution, attached to the Dutch monarchy. But Belgium was underrepresented in the Dutch Estates General. Furthermore, Catholics, comprising the vast majority of the population, paid a disproportionate amount of taxes.

Shortly after news of the revolution in France was received, the Brussels opera presented the story of a revolt in Naples in 1648 against Spanish rule. A demonstration against Dutch rule followed, leading to an insurrection in which bourgeois joined workers angered by unemployment. In the Netherlands, the Estates General called for Belgian independence. However, William I vowed to put the revolt down, even as it spread to other Belgian cities. A Dutch army moved against Brussels but then hesitated, fearing that military action would swell the revolt and believing that people of means in Brussels still supported the Dutch monarchy. After three days of intermittent fighting, the army retreated to the north, where the bombardment of Antwerp angered many Flemings in northern Belgium, leading them to join the revolt. In early October a provisional government declared Belgium's independence. After British pressure forced one of Louis-Philippe's sons to turn down the throne, the Belgian Congress offered the crown to Leopold of Saxe-Coburg, who became King Leopold I in July 1831. The European powers then guaranteed Belgium's independence, and French troops forced the end of a Dutch invasion in August and the return of Antwerp to the new Belgian state, in which Flemish was spoken in the north, and French in Wallonia in the south.

The settlement imposed on Europe by the Congress of Vienna in 1815 suffered another political defeat in Switzerland, where Metternich had supported the domination of the federation of semiautonomous cantons by the three most powerful: Bern, Lucerne, and Zurich. Bending to a mobilization by artisans, shopkeepers, intellectuals, and prosperous peasants, the federal Diet granted constitutional reforms guaranteeing greater freedom and curtailing some of the influence of the Catholic and Protestant clergy. Among the most important gains, this period of "regeneration" gave all adult men the right to vote, which made Switzerland unique at the time, and, in the canton of Zurich, made education obligatory (and free for poor children) up to sixteen years of age. Thus, Switzerland retained its decentralized cantonal structure and precociously liberal character.

In central and eastern Europe the revolutions of 1830 encouraged nationalist movements. In Poland an uprising against Russian authority began in November of that year when military cadets seized an arsenal in Warsaw. When Russian troops withdrew from the city, the ranks of insurgents swelled in number, some of them, primarily artisans, demanding Polish independence from Russia. In January 1831 a crowd surrounded the Polish Sejm (Diet) and forced it to proclaim independence, establishing a provisional government. However, Polish nobles hesitated to mobilize peasants against Russian rule, fearing the peasants would attack them instead. In August Russian troops surrounded Warsaw, where disagreements between moderates and radicals had compromised the defense. When the British and French governments refused to aid the cause of Polish independence, Warsaw fell. The insurrection led not to independence, but rather to Poland losing even its special status within the Russian Empire. A wave of Polish exiles left for freer environments, above all, Paris.

In the Italian states, beset by economic stagnation, protests against inefficiency and corruption occurred in Bologna and the Duchy of Modena. In Parma insurgents evicted the Duchesse Marie-Louise from the city; she was restored by an Austrian army in March 1831. Several cities in central Italy, angered by what they considered to be misgovernment, proclaimed their independence from the Papal States, trying to create a "United Provinces of Italy." The pope's army was defeated by a ragtag army of Italian opponents, but, in the meantime, Austrian forces had captured Ferrara, Parma, and Modena and then took Rome. The revolution of 1830 lasted only about a month in the Italian states. However, what had begun as a series of only vaguely connected movements essentially for reform encouraged Italian nationalists, notably Guiseppe Mazzini, who desired Italian unification.

In the German states disturbances forced concessions by rulers in Hanover and Hesse-Kassel; more serious uprisings won constitutions in Saxony and Brunswick. The failed Polish uprising encouraged nationalist agitation at the University of Heidelberg, leading to an attempt by students to capture Frankfurt. In response, the Federal Diet of the German Confederation decreed the "Ten Articles," which made it easier for the police to watch and encumber liberals, whose strength grew in the 1830s and 1840s.

That there was no insurrection or revolution in Great Britain is revealing of differences between Britain and the continent. Popular protest during the previous fifteen years had included grain riots; machine-breaking; and demands for an expanded suffrage, the end of electoral corruption, and Catholic emancipation. Following the arrival of news of the events in France, more constables and troops poured into the streets than protesters. Nonetheless, the British upper classes wondered if Britain might yet be next. In 1832 a Whig government passed the Reform Bill, expanding the electoral franchise. In doing so, the British landed elite demonstrated its capacity for compromise when faced with the political mobilization of ordinary people. The Reform Bill of 1832, a turning point in the history of modern Britain, was indicative of the influence of the continental revolutions of 1830, for the latter reflected more than just short-term political tensions between conservative monarchies and liberal and national principles. Although there are flaws in the old Marxist interpretations of the revolutions of 1830 playing the role of a "bourgeois revolution," certainly the role of economic crisis and of the development of bourgeois public opinion—represented, for example, by a marked expansion of middle-class print culture—played an important part in the mobilization of opposition to the post-Napoleonic settlement.

In 1848 another, much larger wave of revolutions would sweep Europe, bringing a considerably greater level of popular mobilization. Republicans, socialists, and nationalists, their ideologies honed by years of political opposition, exile, and repression, would prove more difficult to turn back. By challenging and, in the cases of France and Belgium, overturning the old order, the revolutions of 1830—whether liberal (France, Switzerland, and several of the Italian states), nationalist (Poland and Belgium, with the twist in the latter case that Walloons and Flemings found common cause), or something of both (some of the German and Italian states, at least in consequences)—encouraged political contention and the development of mass political life in modern Europe.

See also *European Revolutions of 1848; French Revolution (1789–1815).*

JOHN MERRIMAN

BIBLIOGRAPHY

Church, Clive. *Europe in 1830: Revolution and Political Change.* London: Allen and Unwin, 1983.

Craig, Gordon. *The Triumph of Liberalism: Zurich in the Golden Age 1830–1869.* New York: Scribner, 1988.

Merriman, John M., ed. *1830 in France.* New York: Franklin, 1975.

Pilbeam, Pamela. *The 1830 Revolution in France.* London: Macmillan, 1991.

Pinkney, David H. *The French Revolution of 1830.* Princeton, N.J.: Princeton University Press, 1972.

Sheehan, James J. *German History, 1770–1866.* New York: Oxford University Press, 1989.

EUROPEAN REVOLUTIONS OF 1848

The French Revolution of 1789; the assault upon monarchy, the nobility, and church; and the long wars between 1792 and 1815 promoted a polarization of opinion between conservative social and political elites and those groups, largely excluded from power, that wanted political liberalization and social reform. Two major waves of revolution occurred in Europe in the first half of the nineteenth century that threatened the internal and international order agreed on by the powers at the Congress of Vienna in 1815 *(see map p. 164).* The first came in 1830–1832, most notably in France and the Netherlands. In France the Bourbon monarchy, closely associated with aristocratic political predominance, was replaced by a monarchical regime that extended political rights to wider groups of property owners and increased the authority of parliament; in the Low Countries the independence of Belgium was recognized. Elsewhere, and especially in Britain and some German states, varying degrees of political liberalization were conceded. In 1848 the second wave of revolution arose, on a much greater scale both geographically and in terms of the demands made for political and also social reform.

THE ONSET OF CRISIS

In an influential article published in 1948 the French historian Ernest Labrousse insisted on the importance of economic crisis as a cause of social unrest but insisted equally that not all economic crises led to revolution. Differing levels of economic development among countries and regional variations within them render hazardous generalizations about the impact of economic difficulties. Nevertheless, the revolutions of 1789, 1830, and 1848 were all preceded by major crises. In many respects, and in spite of rising agricultural productivity, these were typical preindustrial crises, caused by two or three successive poor harvests. The poor harvests greatly intensified the social problems caused by population growth and by the transition to capitalistic production in both agriculture and industry. As prices rose, consumers were forced to spend increasing portions of their incomes on basic foodstuffs and correspondingly less on manufactured goods. As a result, the crisis spread to industry, leading to widespread unemployment and underemployment just as the cost of living was dramatically rising. Economic contraction, together with the disorders caused by protests about high prices, led to a widespread loss of confidence, which further reduced demand for industrial products and for services and resulted in a generalized economic and social crisis.

Additionally, by the 1840s the economic cycle was beginning to be transformed by the accelerating development of a more modern industrial and commercial economy and of international financial markets. In this transitional stage many regions suffered the impact of both a preindustrial crisis caused by poor harvests and a modern crisis caused by a loss of confidence in major financial centers, industrial overproduction and underconsumption, and commercial glut. Significantly, however, the most advanced country (Britain) and some of the more backward ones, least integrated into international trade, like Russia, were less severely affected by crisis than those economies undergoing the initial stages of structural change. The most advanced and least advanced areas, for structural and other reasons, did not experience revolution.

Where revolution did occur, it appears that economic and political crises coincided. To a degree the two obviously were interrelated, with governments blamed for the misery and anxiety that afflicted most of the population. Popular disaffection with governmental responses to economic pressures reinforced demands for constitutional reform, reawakening throughout western and central Europe the liberal and democratic aspirations created in the aftermath of 1789. The disparate character of the political opposition should, however, be noted. The opposition included liberals interested in limited constitutional change and the rule of law and radicals committed to manhood suffrage and to vague measures of social reform. In France following the 1846 elections, the government's refusal to extend the property-based franchise that had been established following the 1830 revolution encouraged those politicians who despaired of electoral victory to seek the support of the unenfranchised. They organized protests in the form of banquets in order to evade laws regulating public meetings, and they were able to mobilize substantial public support. They were certainly not revolutionaries but by arousing political passions helped create a situation in which violent conflict became possible.

In the German states and the Austrian Empire reform was further complicated by the emergence of nationalist sentiment. In relatively homogeneous Germany nationalist sentiment was expressed by demands for greater unity, and in multiethnic Austria by a growing will to question the decisions of a largely Germanic bureaucracy and to assert claims to linguistic and cultural equality, most notably in Bohemia, Hungary, and Italy.

The impact of growing political discontent depended to a large extent on the ways in which governments responded. Revolutions occurred where governments failed to make concessions that might have satisfied at least some of their opponents. The inherent weakness of monarchical government, dependent on the qualities of those individuals born to power, was once again revealed by the inept crisis management of French king Louis-Philippe and his prime minister, François Pierre Guillaume Guizot, and the paralysis that affected both the Austrian and Prussian regimes as news of the February Revolution in Paris encouraged internal protest. Monarchs such as Prussian king Friedrich Wilhelm IV, convinced of their divine right to rule and dependent on the advice of a narrow circle of court nobles, were not likely to make timely concessions. Austrian chancellor Klemens von Metternich had been determined since 1815 to preserve monarchical absolutism and aristocratic power against further revolution. The effectiveness of the imperial regime, however, had been considerably weakened by its own lack of cohesion. Weak emperors had been unable to impose a spirit of cooperation on squabbling ministers. Constant financial difficulties made it impossible to sustain an efficient bureaucracy and army. Governmental inertia in the various countries undoubtedly had the effect of undermining the legitimacy of existing regimes and reducing the strength of support for the status quo.

Discontent in itself, however, was not sufficient to lead to revolution, particularly where almost no one, at least initially, was planning revolt. Secret revolutionary societies existed, but they were small, internally divided, and usually penetrated by the police. There was certainly considerable potential for violence where opponents of a government demonstrated on the streets and were confronted by police and troops. The revolutionary overthrow of a regime will occur, however, only if its military forces are defeated, and that depends on mass participation.

REVOLUTION AS AN EVENT

Revolts began in capital cities—Paris, Vienna, Berlin, and Milan—the foci for political activity but also urban centers experiencing rapid economic change and population growth. The revolts only subsequently affected other towns and rural areas. Violence began with clashes between the military and demonstrators, after which the latter erected barricades both as a form of protection and to secure control of the cities. In Paris the government's decision to ban a demonstration in support of electoral reform planned for February 22, 1848, its failure to disperse protesting crowds, and its inability to prevent the upward cycle of violence that resulted from the deployment of the army led to a crisis of confidence within the political leadership and to a rapid loss of authority. News of events in Paris between February 22 and 24 stimulated protest in Vienna on March 13, and this in its turn encouraged revolt in Milan and Venice, and in Berlin on March 18. The Austrian and Prussian monarchs, their confidence shattered, felt obliged to promise constitutional reform, afraid of otherwise being dragged into an uncontrollable, continentwide crisis. The concessions made in Berlin and Vienna inevitably weakened the resistance to reforms of the monarchs in the smaller German states.

The two essential components of revolution were thus the rise of opposition and the collapse of government. At the onset the call for protest was made largely by men already engaged in politics and drawn mainly from the professional middle classes. Given that they had not wanted revolution, it is hardly surprising that they were rarely among those killed on the barricades. Those who fought in the streets were not, as the conservative press of the day so often claimed, the unemployed, semicriminal elements common in the preindustrial city, but mainly representatives of the lower middle classes (small businessmen) and especially skilled workers from the small workshops and building trades. They were motivated by a desire for greater material security and enhanced social status and by resentment of those (employers, wholesale merchants, landlords, and politicians) who exploited them and excluded them from political debate.

These were men politicized at work, in the tavern, at meetings of friendly societies, and, given their high literacy rates, by pamphlets and the press. They were attracted by simple slogans in favor of "liberty," producers' cooperatives, and democratic rights.

POSTREVOLUTIONARY DILEMMAS

Unplanned revolution created a power vacuum into which those groups with at least a modicum of organization and authority might step. In France, with monarchy apparently discredited, a small body of mainly moderate middle-class republicans formed a Provisional Government. The new ministers included the aristocratic poet Alphonse de Lamartine and more radical figures like Alexandre Ledru-Rollin, the socialist theoretician Louis Blanc, and the worker Albert, well known to the Parisian public because of their political and journalistic activities. To retain mass support they immediately introduced manhood suffrage for the election of a constituent assembly, which would draft a republican constitution. In a major radicalizing move, popular sovereignty was thus recognized. Nevertheless, in France, and to an even greater extent in Austria and Prussia where monarchs simply invited liberal politicians to participate in government, substantial elements of the old regime remained intact. Although they accepted the principle of constitutional reform, Emperor Ferdinand and King Friedrich Wilhelm retained considerable authority and control of the bureaucracy and army. The old elites retained their property and much of their influence. They were certainly frightened and initially willing to accept liberal or moderate republican ministers in the hope of avoiding something worse, but in the longer term they were committed to political reaction. Moreover, the moderates who had acceded to power were anxious to avoid further violence and sought compromises acceptable to existing social elites.

In the meantime, the new governments faced major problems, notably those of securing recognition for their authority and achieving a constitutional settlement. In Germany surmounting this problem involved not only instituting liberal reforms but responding to the demand for greater national unity articulated by those liberals who, meeting in late March as a Preparliament in Frankfurt, pressed for the election of an assembly to prepare a federal constitution. The new governments also needed to respond to the demands made by a variety of groups sharing in the almost utopian sense of expectancy created by the revolutions. Among the most expectant were the many people thrown out of work by the renewed crisis of business confidence caused by political upheaval. They wanted immediate assistance and the eventual restoration of prosperity. A small but growing minority proved susceptible to socialist calls for a permanent reorganization of work on the basis of producers' cooperatives.

In the cities politics was transformed in the first few months of the revolution by the political mobilization of the masses, sustained by a newly free press; by numerous political clubs, meetings, and demonstrations; and by the extension of the franchise and preparation for elections. Foremost in advocating producers' cooperatives were skilled artisans already organized at the level of their trades and facing changing economic conditions that threatened not only their livelihoods but their entire way of life. They were anxious to assert their status both as creators of wealth and members of the political community. In many regions peasants reacted against the growing commercialization of agriculture by demanding the restoration of customary rights of usage in forests and on common land. In eastern Germany and the Austrian Empire they demanded abolition of the last vestiges of serfdom. An additional problem was posed by the demands for greater autonomy articulated by Italian, Polish, Czech, Hungarian, and Romanian landowners and intellectuals. The instability caused by competition for power within governments constituted by informal coalitions was thus reinforced by the efforts of a variety of social and political groups to put pressure on political leaders. As the new governments sought to impose their authority, disorder spread and inexperienced ministers relied increasingly on the bureaucratic and military machines inherited from the old regimes.

Initially, the French government felt obliged to make concessions. Its decree of February 25 proclaimed the right to work but appeared to promise far more than was intended. The national workshops established in Paris and in many other towns were merely an extension of the charity workshops traditionally created in periods of high unemployment to provide poorly paid relief through public works projects. The decree was not intended to establish the producers' cooperatives that militants believed would bring an end to "the exploitation of man by man." The government of moderate republicans was primarily concerned with promoting economic recovery and the restoration of order through the reestablishment of business confidence. Restoring confidence required the avoidance of any socialistic measures. Indeed, the French government was so determined to balance its budget that it introduced a 45 percent surcharge on the land tax, hardly an effective means of winning over the rural population. In much of Germany and in the Austrian Empire rural discontent was calmed by the attenuation or abolition of surviving feudal rights. These measures had the effect of isolating urban revolutionaries.

The appointment of liberal ministers in the German states

and Austria, most notably Ludolf Camphausen and David Hansemann in Prussia, although it appeared to herald constitutional change, did not reduce the absolute commitment in government circles to the preservation of the existing social order. Liberals had wanted nothing more than limited political reform. The threat to order posed by crowds demonstrating for social change transformed liberals into ardent defenders of private property and Christian civilization. Significantly, German and Austro-German liberals were unable to accept that to non-Germans "freedom" and "unity" might suggest the end of German dominance. Efforts by the Poles in Prussian Posen and by the Czechs in Prague to claim greater autonomy were suppressed with relative ease. Far more serious for the Austrian regime were events in Italy and Hungary, where the opposition was composed of regular troops as well as civilian insurgents and where, following the initial revolution, full-scale wars of national liberation would be fought.

COUNTERREVOLUTION

The year 1830 had confirmed for conservatives that the revolutionary monster hatched in 1789 had not been slain. The year 1848 represented a much greater threat. However, once concessions had been made to liberal demands, a political realignment occurred as the more moderate liberals, especially among the better off, affirmed their fundamental determination to avoid social change. In France this was evident as early as April. The first mass elections, to the Constituent Assembly, had the potential to pose a major threat to social stability. But the results were reassuring. Traditional elites, including the clergy, were able to exert considerable influence on an inexperienced electorate. Of nearly nine hundred deputies elected, only some three hundred appear to have been republicans before 1848, and only seventy to eighty of these would reveal any sympathy for social reform. The remainder were monarchists, most of whom temporarily adopted a republican label. Socially the Assembly was a gathering of wealthy provincial notables.

In Prussia, where liberals enjoyed some success in the May local elections, conservative landowners responded by organizing an Association for the Protection of Property and the Advancement of the Welfare of all Classes. In Prussia and in German Austria landowners combined concessions to "their" peasants with an exaggeration of the threat posed by the left to property, religion, the family, and the nation. Where this appeal failed, intimidation was usually possible.

The return to military repression was indeed surprisingly rapid. In France a mass insurrection occurred in June following the government's announcement of its intention to close the Paris national workshops. The decision not only threatened the existence of the large number of unemployed workers and their families but also had considerable symbolic significance. The workshops had appeared to represent the first step in a program of social reform, all hope of which disappeared with the workshops. Thus, many insurgents felt justified in resorting to violence in spite of the existence of a democratically elected Constituent Assembly. Against them the moderate republican general Louis-Eugène Cavaignac deployed the army, civilian National Guards—drawn mainly from middle-class districts but including many workers—and the Mobile Guard, recruited from among young unemployed workers. Given the determined leadership and ruthless tactics of the forces of order, their success was inevitable. The revolt, however, impressed the whole of Europe. It was described by the aristocrat Alexis de Tocqueville as a "brutal, blind but powerful attempt by the workers to escape from the necessities of their condition" and by Karl Marx as "the first great battle . . . between the two classes that split modern society." The insurgents were in fact drawn overwhelmingly from the small workshops and building sites of the capital. In terms of their social profile, they had more in common with the sans-culottes of 1789 than with a modern factory workforce. In any case, the victory of the "forces of order" was acclaimed by conservatives everywhere.

Also in June the Austrian general Alfred, Prince zu Windischgrätz regained control of Prague. September saw the return of the army to Berlin; October the deaths of between two thousand and five thousand insurgents in Vienna. In 1849 the Austrians deployed substantial forces, first in northern Italy and subsequently in Hungary, where with Russian help resistance was finally crushed between August and October, with an estimated fifty thousand dead on both sides. Uprisings in southwest Germany, in the Rhineland and Saxony, that arose in May–June 1849 in protest against Friedrich Wilhelm's refusal to recognize the imperial constitution prepared by the elected German assembly at Frankfurt were easily crushed.

In spite of their successes, conservatives remained anxious. Even as governments regained control of the major cities, democratic groups like Republican Solidarity in France and the Central March Association in Germany continued to organize in provincial towns and villages. It seemed to conservatives that radicals might one day win an election. There was an urgent need, therefore, to change the electoral rules and to reduce the new-found powers of parliamentary institutions. The June insurrection in Paris had confirmed their worst fears about the revolutionary threat. As a result, radicals were forced to give up politics or were reduced to clandestine and less effective activity. In France the election of Louis Napoleon Bonaparte, nephew and heir of the great

Emperor, as president of the Republic in December 1848 was part of the drive to restore social order. His election additionally represented a widespread desire for prosperity and security. Bonaparte would launch a coup d'état in December 1851 as a prelude to establishing the Second Empire. Thus, military repression was accompanied by a return to absolutist government, and even where manhood suffrage was retained, as in France, its impact was reduced through electoral manipulation and police intimidation.

In seeking to ensure long-term stability, governments were assisted by the more prosperous economic circumstances of the 1850 and 1860s. They also engaged in social engineering, through educational systems that more deliberately than ever before sought to persuade the poor and unprivileged to accept the place in society that God had ordained for them.

CONCLUSIONS

This short essay can do only partial justice to the complexity of political behavior. It would be a gross oversimplification to read the history of the revolutions of 1848 simply in terms of class conflict. Diverse communities and social and cultural groups responded to complex crises in order to protect their particular interests; their political behavior was suggested both by tradition and the rapid diffusion of new, more modern political forms. Initially, members of the middle classes were particularly interested in political representation; workers and peasants sought, above all, economic security. Subsequently, when political disorder disrupted economic life and it appeared as if the entire social system, with its hierarchy based on the ownership of property, was under threat, there arose a widespread desire for a return to "normalcy." Their recoil strengthened the powerful capacity for resistance of established elite groups, which were entrenched in state bureaucracies and the military. German historians have tended to dwell on the failure of the middle classes in 1848 to press for the creation of a liberal state and have seen this as a sign of the uniqueness of German history. However, it would seem that the middle classes' "treachery against the people" and willingness to "compromise with the crowned representatives of the old society" (Marx) was a characteristic of the property-owning classes throughout Europe.

In the decades following 1848 the capacity of established ruling elites to respond to discontent was substantially increased. The construction of telegraph and railway systems allowed the swift diffusion of information and movement of military forces. More significantly, larger and better organized civilian police forces reduced dependence on the often provocative employment of the army for crowd control. Moreover, mass discontent was reduced by improvements in living standards. The communications revolution ensured the disappearance of the subsistence crises, which had been such a prominent feature of the prerevolutionary situations in 1789, 1830, and 1848. Furthermore, major steps were taken toward the institutionalization of protest and the development of mass education and of the media as fundamentally conservative agencies of socialization. For as long as existing state and social systems preserved an aura of legitimacy by protecting order and prosperity and retained their capacity for occasional repression, revolution was unlikely. War, as the collapse of the French Second Empire in 1870 revealed, was the primary threat to internal stability. Significantly, growing nationalist discontent in central and eastern Europe, which was another legacy of 1848, would be a major cause of the internal and international tensions that led in 1914 to the war that destroyed the political order created in 1848.

Roger Price

BIBLIOGRAPHY

Agulhon, M. *The Republican Experiment, 1848–1852.* Cambridge: Cambridge University Press, 1983.

Deak, I. *The Lawful Revolution: Louis Kossuth and the Hungarians, 1848–49.* New York: Columbia University Press, 1979.

Pech, S. *The Czech Revolution of 1848.* Chapel Hill: University of North Carolina Press, 1969.

Price, R. *The Revolutions of 1848.* Atlantic Highlands: Humanities Press, 1989.

———*The French Second Republic: A Social History.* Ithaca, N.Y.: Cornell University Press, 1972.

———*Documents on the French Revolution of 1848.* New York: St. Martin's Press, 1996.

Rath, J. *The Viennese Revolution of 1848.* Austin: University of Texas, 1957.

Sked, A. *The Survival of the Habsburg Empire: Radetzky, the Imperial Army and the Class War 1848.* London: Longman, 1979.

Sperber, J. *The European Revolutions, 1848–1851.* Cambridge: Cambridge University Press, 1994.

Sperber, J. *Rhineland Radicals: The Democratic Movement and the Revolution of 1848–49.* Princeton, N.J.: Princeton University Press, 1991.

FANON, FRANTZ OMAR

Fanon (1925–1961) is regarded by many as the most original black political thinker of the twentieth century. Born in Martinique, a Caribbean island that was already becoming part of metropolitan France, he was destined to fight one day to prevent Algeria from being similarly absorbed into metropolitan France.

Fanon was educated in Martinique and France, finally qualifying in medicine and psychiatry at the University of Lyon. From 1953 to 1956 he served as head of the psychiatry department of Blida-Joinville Hospital in Algeria, which was then officially regarded as part of France. Yet he was from 1954 secretly committed to a movement in favor of Algeria's independence.

He joined the National Liberation Front (FLN) of Algeria in opposition to French rule. In 1956 he became editor of the FLN newspaper, *El-Moudjahid,* which was published in Tunis. In 1960 the FLN's Provisional Government appointed Fanon its ambassador to the recently independent Republic of Ghana. There is some speculation that Fanon's exposure to Kwame Nkrumah's Ghana three years after Ghana's independence deepened Fanon's understanding of the temptations of power for the postcolonial elite, and the resulting malaise of aggrandizement and alienation.

Fanon's main contributions to political thought are in the role of violence, the impact of cultural alienation and dependency, the nature of anticolonial nationalism, and the malaise of the postcolonial elites.

On the role of violence as redemption, Fanon's views need to be studied alongside the Christian concept of the crucifixion. Fanon was convinced that anticolonial violence was a healing experience for the colonial freedom fighter. "At the level of individuals, violence is a cleansing force. It frees the native from his inferiority complex, from his despair and inaction" *(The Wretched of the Earth,* 94). Although the crucifixion of Jesus was an act of violence, it was also doctrinally an act of atonement and redemption. There is a convergence between Fanon's thought and Christian doctrine in this respect.

Although he died a few months before Algeria gained independence, Fanon had acted out some of his ideas by participating in the Algerian anticolonial war (1954–1962) on the side of the Algerian revolutionaries. Fanon studied at close quarters the psychology of violence generated by a clash of nationalisms—French and Algerian. As a psychiatrist he also studied trauma cases of the brutal war, which in the end cost more than a million lives.

And yet Fanon was among the first to identify the dual malaise of postcolonial elites. One part of the dual malaise is externally oriented—a constant effort to imitate the bourgeoisie of the former colonial power, thus manifesting acute cultural dependency (the "Black Skin, White Mask" syndrome). As a psychiatrist Fanon prefers to see this cultural dependency as a neurosis and a form of alienation. The second part of the dual malaise is self-oriented—the pursuit of self-aggrandizement and elite-promotion. The old anticolonial fighters become what Fanon calls "that company of profiteers impatient for the returns."

Cultural dependence and cultural alienation may also take the form of excessive reliance on the language of the imperial power. Fanon lamented the supreme status accorded the French language in Algeria by France. But he lamented even more the Algerian elite's complicity in this linguistic servitude. Fanon regarded the imperial language as an index of power. He himself was a child of Martinique, and was therefore a product of such a configuration between language and power. Fanon was sensitive to the positive role that women often play in revolutions. By being underestimated by the enemy, women can penetrate enemy ranks more easily. A woman can turn her own weakness into a weapon. Fanon draws attention to how Algerian Muslim women used the veil as camouflage for grenades.

Fanon's most influential book, *Les Damne's de la terre* (1961), was published in English as *The Wretched of the Earth* (1965). This book established Fanon not only as a social thinker but also as a prophetic figure. He was widely interpreted as urging colonized peoples to submit themselves to "collective catharsis" through revolutionary violence against colonialism.

See also *Algerian Revolution (1954–1962); Nationalism.*

Ali A. Mazrui

BIBLIOGRAPHY

Fanon, Frantz. *Black Skin, White Masks.* New York: Grove Press, 1967.
———. *A Dying Colonialism.* New York: Grove Press, 1967.
———. *Toward the African Revolution.* New York: Grove Press, 1969.
———. *The Wretched of the Earth.* New York: Grove Press, 1968.

FILMS AND VIDEO DOCUMENTARIES

The depiction of revolutions in video documentaries and popular films contributes immensely to the public's understanding and interpretation of these events. Ideally, documentaries on revolutions should cover important aspects of the history and culture of the relevant society. In particular, it is important to present and describe factors critical for the growth or success of a revolutionary movement, such as the development of mass discontent and a divided and at least partially radicalized elite, a motivation for revolution capable of unifying otherwise diverse social groups or classes in an effective prorevolution alliance, a severe weakening of prerevolution government legitimacy and coercive capacity, and a permissive or favorable orientation toward the revolution on the part of other states, if any, with the power to intervene and block the triumph of a revolutionary movement.

CHARACTERISTICS OF DOCUMENTARIES

In reality, the ideal documentary on revolution is nearly impossible to achieve. Occasionally, members of a political group or movement with a particular point of view produce a documentary biased in favor of their orientation, either by oversimplifying or dehumanizing the side in the revolutionary conflict they oppose and inordinately glorifying the side they support, or by selectively omitting important factors or events. In addition to political motives, the organization, presentation, and distortion of documentary material may be driven by "market" considerations. That is, a documentary may be biased to correspond to the prejudices of the prospective audience. In other cases, documentaries on complex revolutionary situations may omit significant material due to the inexperience or limited knowledge of the producers or due to time constraints imposed by the documentary's length.

Students of revolution would love to be able to view documentary footage of the great pre-twentieth century revolutions, such as those that ousted the French monarchy or freed the thirteen colonies from British rule. A passion to experience and present to the public a visual account of the development and victory of a major social revolution motivated a young filmmaker in New York City, Russian immigrant Herman Axelbank, to spend years of his life and much of his profits from films on journeys to Europe and the Soviet Union, searching out and buying scraps of black and white film on tsarist Russia and the 1917 February and October Revolutions. The result was "The Russian Revolution: Czar to Lenin," a stirring documentary of the 1917 revolutions and the resulting civil war, which was shown in American movie theaters in the 1930s. This thirty-minute film was apparently the first documentary of a sweeping social revolution.

In recent years there has been a great increase in the number of documentaries dealing with revolutions, particularly the major communist revolutions—Lenin and Stalin in Russia, Mao Zedong in China, Vietnam during the revolutionary struggle against the U.S.-supported South Vietnamese regime, and Castro in Cuba. For each of these revolutionary episodes, a number of good-quality documentaries—many of them made for public television—are available from major video libraries. There are also valuable documentaries dealing with the struggle to end apartheid in South Africa and with the U.S. involvement in the Iranian and Nicaraguan Revolutions, which tend to focus more on the U.S. role than on longer-term local issues.

REVOLUTION IN POPULAR FILMS

Popular films dealing with revolutionary movements and related conflicts seem generally to provide incomplete coverage. Popular films appear to be even more affected by factors such as political bias and audience prejudices and expectations than documentaries. Consequently, films with positive treatments of revolution are relatively rare. Apart from "Revolution," a film about the American Revolution, and a few other exceptions, films available in the United States with favorable orientations toward revolution pertain to situations in which there was no direct U.S. involvement. Examples include "Spartacus," the saga of the famous slave rebellion against the cruelties of the Roman Empire; "Biko," a film concerning the Black Consciousness leader murdered by South African police; and "Braveheart," the story of William Wallace's Scottish rebellion against British tyranny. Another film, "The Battle of Algiers," dealt with the brutal efforts of French soldiers to destroy the Algerian independence movement as well as the violent methods used by the Algerian revolutionaries, including the bombing of facilities frequented by Europeans. Other movies with a somewhat positive view of revolution and that helped the audience comprehend the causes of revolutionary movements included "Underfire," which dealt with aspects of the Nicaraguan Revolution, and "Salvador," which depicted brutal characteristics of the El Salvadoran civil war. The movie "Gandhi" presented the leader of India's independence movement in a favorable light. "Michael Collins" portrayed the leaders of the Irish Revolution positively but shied away neither from the brutal tactics used by all participants nor from the hatreds, violence, and tragedies within the revolutionary alliance.

Some movies such as "Nicholas and Alexandra" (Russia) and "The Last Emperor" (China) focus on the flawed and tragic lives of prerevolutionary rulers. These films appear crafted to evoke sympathy for the deposed rulers but provide little understanding of or sympathy for the relevant revolutionary movements or revolutionary leaders and supporters. Similarly, films such as "Reds" or "Doctor Zhivago" primarily portray the lives and romantic involvements of particular characters whose fates were affected by revolutions.

The key to comprehending the limitations of popular films concerning revolutions is the adjective "popular." Many filmmakers evidently have perceived that there is not much of a market for works that depict the reality of revolution, especially where the United States played a primarily counterrevolutionary role. This orientation appears well demonstrated in regard to the subject of Vietnam. Almost all popular films on Vietnam virtually ignore treatment of the Vietnamese Revolution. (Could there ever be an American film on the life of Ho Chi Minh?) Films such as "Platoon," "Casualties of War," and "Full Metal Jacket" show U.S. troops battling a determined foe but focus more on the horrifying, perverting, and tragic impacts of revolutionary warfare on American soldiers.

Other films such as "Apocalypse Now" and "The Deer Hunter" present the Vietnam War not only as tragic and dehumanizing but also, in some ways, as bizarre. Certain films, such as "Ballad of the Green Berets," portray American forces in an extremely favorable light compared with their opposition. In some films the forces opposing the United States in Vietnam are described so negatively as to create an awesome mystery in the minds of any thinking viewer. Namely, how could such "evil" revolutionaries win the war? They obviously were no match for the Americans in weapons, and they had no air support over much of Vietnam. But since they are presented as vicious and wicked in their behavior, they must also have lacked popular support. Therefore, the United States must have won the war! Obviously, something is very distorted in these films.

One of the better popular films related to Vietnam is "The Killing Fields," which deals with the brutality of the Khmer Rouge regime and its attempt to purge certain elements of the population and to restructure Cambodian society along a rural collectivist model. But although it suggests some reasons why many Cambodians joined the Khmer Rouge, such as American bombing of Cambodian villages, the film does not present much of an explanation for the revolution or the Khmer Rouge victory.

In summary, many useful documentaries are available on twentieth century revolutions and related conflicts. Few, however, adequately explain the revolutionary movements they depict, and many concentrate more on certain aspects of a revolutionary conflict, such as the U.S. role in Vietnam. Popular films seldom deal with the causes of revolution, but rather with elements of revolutionary conflict that are emotionally appealing to the audience. For example, a film that adequately explained the causes of the Vietnam Revolution might provoke unpleasant emotions from an American audience and quickly fail financially. But films that focus on the excitement and violence of war and the heroism of American soldiers or on a love story with the drama of a revolutionary setting in the background often appeal to audiences and are likely to be financially successful.

James DeFronzo

BIBLIOGRAPHY AND SELECTED FILM/VIDEO SOURCES

American Friends Service Committee, 2161 Massachusetts Ave., Cambridge, Mass. 02140

Consortium of College and University Media Centers and R. R. Bowker. Educational Film and Video Locator. 2 vols. New York: R. R. Bowker, 1990–1991.

DeFronzo, James. *Revolution and Revolutionary Movements.* Boulder, Colo.: Westview, 1996.

Filmmakers Library, 124 East 40th St., New York, N.Y. 10016

Films Incorporated Education, 5547 N. Ravenswood, Chicago, Ill. 60640

Public Broadcasting Service, 1320 Braddock Pl., Alexandria, Va. 22314

www.aetv.com

www.biography.com

www.historychannel.com

FRANKLIN, BENJAMIN

Benjamin Franklin (1706–1790), printer, postmaster, scientist, essayist, politician, and diplomat, led the movement to defend the rights of the British colonies in North America, 1757–1775, and then signed the Declaration of American Independence, 1776; the French Alliance, 1778; the peace treaty with Great Britain, 1783; and the Constitution of 1787. He was the only American to sign all four basic documents.

The first fifty years of Franklin's life, described in his

Benjamin Franklin

famous autobiography, though suffused with apparent loyalty to the British Empire in which he lived, in fact placed him firmly on the road to revolution. As a youth growing up in Puritan Boston and then as a rising tradesman in Philadelphia, he was a self-made, independent-minded man used to managing his own life and accustomed to the opportunity available in what was for its day an unusually open society. Reading such writings as Plutarch's *Lives,* John Locke's works, the *Cato's Letters* of John Trenchard and Thomas Gordon placed Franklin's thinking squarely in the civic republican and radical Whig outlooks well-known in Boston and Philadelphia. Thus in thought and lifestyle he was ill-prepared to be a contented resident of a colony of a distant and increasingly controlling mother country.

His active life as a foe of tyranny began in Pennsylvania in the 1750s, when he led opposition to the efforts by the proprietary Penn family to impose its will on the colonial legislature of which he was a member. There he recruited and led militia forces that were unsanctioned by the Penns' executive authority in Pennsylvania. Thomas Penn wrote from London that Franklin was "a dangerous man . . . I should be very glad he inhabited another country, as I believe him a very uneasy spirit, . . . a sort of Tribune of the People." When Franklin left for London in 1757 to explain his dispute with the proprietors to British authorities, he was already in a rebellious frame of mind.

Living in London, 1757–1775, Franklin opposed first proprietary tyranny in Pennsylvania (ironically trying to substitute for it Royal government of the province) and then the measures of the British government that from the Stamp Act (1765) to the so-called Coercive Acts (1774) increasingly and forcefully imposed British authority from New England to Georgia. Franklin at first sought relief from Parliament and from the king's ministers, but, ignored and humiliated by those in power, by 1775 he had become so disgusted with "the extreme corruption prevalent among all orders of men in this old rotten state" that he feared "more Mischief than Benefit from a closer Union" with the realm of George III. He left England in 1775 ready for independence.

Back in America, in his seventies, Franklin busied himself with the affairs of what he hoped would be an independent nation. He helped plan details of supply and training for Pennsylvania's militia regiments, took part in debates in the Continental Congress, made a winter journey to Canada to seek (without success) its participation in the Revolution, drafted articles of confederation for the colonies, drew guidelines for revolutionary diplomacy in Europe, and served on the Committee to Draft the Declaration of Independence, which he signed in July 1776. Declared a traitor with a price on his head by George III, Franklin remained steadfast in his revolutionary stance, asserting, in accord with Thomas Paine's *Common Sense,* that the cause of the new United States was "the cause of all Mankind." Along with Thomas Jefferson, Paine, and John Adams, Franklin's was the authentic voice of the American Revolution.

A perilous sea voyage across the North Atlantic in December 1776 brought Franklin to France, where for nine years he sustained the Revolution. As minister to France, he negotiated the important French alliance of 1778 and managed repeatedly, with great tact, to persuade Foreign Minister Charles Gravier Vergennes of France to loan the vital cash that kept George Washington's armies in the field. Then with John Adams and John Jay, he negotiated the favorable 1783 treaty of peace with Great Britain, granting the United States standing as a fully independent nation whose western border was the Mississippi River. Heralded on both sides of the Atlantic as, along with Washington, the foremost hero of the Revolution, he had completed the most successful diplomatic mission in American history.

Home in Philadelphia, eighty years old and suffering from a painful bladder stone, Franklin nonetheless concluded his revolutionary career by taking an active part in nation-building. He was elected president of Pennsylvania, attended every day of the Constitutional Convention of 1787, making crucial conciliatory proposals, took part in the ratification contest, and spent his last public energies opposing slavery. He died in April 1790, a few months after having congratulated a French friend on the beginning of their revolution in favor of the principles of the American Revolution.

See also *Adams, John; American (U.S.) Revolution (1776–1789); Jefferson, Thomas; Locke, John; Paine, Thomas.*

Ralph Ketcham

BIBLIOGRAPHY

Ketcham, Ralph, ed. *The Political Thought of Benjamin Franklin.* Indianapolis, Ind.: Bobbs-Merrill, 1965.

Labaree, Leonard, et al., eds. *The Papers of Benjamin Franklin.* New Haven, Conn.: Yale University Press, 1959. 31 vols. to date (papers of 1708–1780).

Van Doren, Carl. *Benjamin Franklin.* New York: Viking Press, 1938.

Wright, Esmond. *Franklin of Philadelphia.* Cambridge, Mass.: Harvard University Press, 1986.

FRENCH FRONDES (1648–1653)

In the annals of political revolution, the French civil wars of the mid-seventeenth century that became known as the Frondes hold an ambiguous place. While as early as 1655 a Venetian author entitled his account of the tumultuous events *The History of the Revolution in France,* his contemporaries were more cautious in their assessment. Contemporary French men and women named the crises as "frondes," borrowing the term they used for slingshots that children and pranksters used to dispatch stones at their targets. For participants, observers, and pamphleteers, "fronde" became a shorthand for the wide variety of illegal behaviors that occurred during the years of crisis, from formal military struggles between armies to informal local disturbances between crowds.

THE COURSE OF EVENTS

The Frondes began in the summer of 1648. The judges who were members of the Paris *parlement* (the supreme law court for half of France) refused a royal order to continue their legal work. Instead, in an act of solidarity with lower court justices, they protested what they perceived as the Crown's increasing encroachments on their revenues and competencies. When the government responded by arresting one of the leading judges, Parisians erupted in outrage, filling city streets with hundreds of barricades. France's leading nobles also joined the revolt, ostensibly to force the resignation of the king's chief minister, but with the larger goal of enhancing their own power while the monarchy appeared weak.

In many ways these actions marked less the start of a new phase than the climax of years of rising tensions caused by various issues: opposition to relentless tax increases, hostility to the Crown's efforts to centralize government, food shortages, and epidemic diseases. In the preceding decades, France had experienced what prominent historian Roland Mousnier described as "the permanent crisis of the seventeenth century." The high cost of France's civil wars and prolonged involvement in the Thirty Years War had sparked extraordinary increases in direct taxation—up to 300 percent in twenty years in some places. Even then the Crown could not meet its expenses and sought other means to enhance its revenues, like creating and selling new positions (known as offices). Louis XIII (reigned 1610–1643) and his chief ministers, first Cardinal Richelieu and then Cardinal Mazarin, also sought to use royal officials called *intendants* in new ways to enhance the efficiency of tax collection and provincial administration. These measures quickly led to widespread opposition from the 1630s onward. Ordinary French men and women stopped paying their taxes, and many of the Crown's own officials, protesting the impact of royal policies on their own income and property (because they had to buy their positions, whose value thus depended in part on the revenues they might expect to generate), ceased their work too. These civil disobediences were accompanied in many areas by overt rebellions and acts of violence. The death of Louis XIII in 1643 exacerbated the gathering crisis, as the Crown passed to his five-year-old son (Louis XIV), creating an enormous power vacuum in a political system where royal authority and patronage networks relied on the person of the king.

Thus the events in Paris of the summer of 1648, which culminated in the flight of the king and the royal family from Paris, highlighted nationwide disorders in which many different groups pursued their own grievances. After a winter of conflict, the Parisian *parlement* settled its dispute with the Crown in the spring of 1649 in the Peace of Reuil. The judges gained some notable concessions—particularly the abolition of the *intendants,* whose rising prominence had become an emblem of the growth of the central state, and a lowering of direct taxes. But the mobilization of the nobles, who were not parties to the agreement, meant that civil war continued.

The next three years, 1649–1652, saw violent armed conflicts, political unrest, and ultimately stalemate across France. Although this phase has traditionally been described as "the Fronde of the Princes" to demarcate it from the earlier "Fronde of the Judges," in fact both nobles and judges were involved throughout, albeit the provincial rather than Parisian judges after 1649.

A turning point came in 1651 when Louis XIV declared his majority, thereby ending the opportunities for rebels to claim that they were rebelling not against the king but against the regent and ministers who governed during a royal minority. By the summer of 1652, when the judges gave up virtually all of the concessions they had secured in the early months of the Fronde and conceded that they had no right to interfere in matters of state, large-scale unrest had ended.

Although many French men and women experienced the conditions that sparked revolt in the tumultuous years of mid-century, not all of them rose up. The unpredictability of who rebelled and where rebellion took place highlights the importance of local conditions in shaping Fronde disturbances. Only four of the ten *parlements* rebelled, and while cities like Aix and Bordeaux were at the forefront of rebellion, other French cities stayed calm. The incidence of revolt or the lack thereof seems to have been determined by a variety of factors, including the character of regional elite clientage and kinship networks, through which resistance could be mobilized.

Moreover, apart from the initial Parisian street blockades of August 1648, only in Bordeaux did the Fronde appear to take on a truly popular character. As the Fronde struggles wound to an exhausted standstill elsewhere, in this city on France's Atlantic coast a movement named the Ormée (after the elm trees, *ormes,* under which participants met) gained control of the city in 1652–1653. The Ormistes seem to have been drawn from the middling urban ranks—lawyers, merchants, and master artisans—who had considerable standing in their own neighborhoods and yet no real influence in seventeenth-century government. They gained control of the city by allying with the nobles and proposing an agenda that pivoted around their rights to participate in city government and to expect accountability in the handling of city finances. In the summer of 1653, however, with the royal army outside the city successfully seducing the noble allies of the Ormistes, Bordeaux's experiment with citizen government ended with the expulsion of three hundred or so participants and the execution of one of their leaders.

ASSESSING THE FRONDES

Historians have conducted a lively debate over the origins of the Frondes, but they concur about the limits of the immediate challenge the revolutions presented. Various explanations of the widespread political revolts that climaxed with the Frondes have been proposed. Were they responses to the expansion of royal administrative initiatives with the new uses of the *intendants,* the result of state efforts to co-opt an emerging bourgeoisie in ways that undermined the power base of the traditional nobility, or the consequence of a power vacuum that resulted from a royal minority, which in turn allowed local conflicts to erupt?

In no case did the participants in the many uprisings that comprised the Fronde make demands that can be construed as revolutionary. Not even the Ormistes challenged the fundamental authority of the monarchy or proposed an alternative program of their own to match the republicanism of the contemporary British civil wars. Many historians have seen the participants as motivated primarily by their own personal political and economic interests. Even those historians who have seen the actions of the Crown's opponents as principled have argued that the judges, for instance, tried to check the power of the Crown rather than undermine it. Although an alliance of all disgruntled groups might have held the potential for a revolutionary remaking of the structures of state authority, no such alliance coalesced beyond the demands of immediate contingency.

Yet the long-term implications of the Frondes may have been more potent than the goals of its participants. Many historians have argued that the Crown learned the dangers of alienating its nobles and its lesser subjects and point to the myriad ways in which Louis XIV and his chief minister, Jean-Baptiste Colbert, sought to pacify the realm in the 1660s. Their policies—of lowering taxes, rebuilding national client networks, and co-opting the nobles—seem to suggest well-taken lessons. In the 1670s, moreover, the king displayed both his distaste for the turbulent Parisian politics of his childhood and his newly enhanced power by building a new palace outside of the city, at Versailles. Taking a longer perspective still, other historians have seen in the Frondes the creation of a basis for elite civic activism and the accentuation of patterns of popular urban protest that laid foundations for the momentous years of the late eighteenth century, when France truly found itself in the grip of an unprecedented revolution.

Julie Hardwick

BIBLIOGRAPHY

Beik, William. *Urban Protest in Seventeenth-century France: The Culture of Retribution.* Cambridge: Cambridge University Press, 1997.

Kettering, Sharon. *Judicial Politics and Urban Revolt in Seventeenth-century France: The Parlement of Aix, 1629–1659.* Princeton, N.J.: Princeton University Press, 1978.

Moote, A. Lloyd. *The Revolt of the Judges: the Parlement of Paris and the Fronde, 1643–1652.* Princeton, N.J.: Princeton University Press, 1971.

Ranum, Orest. *The Fronde: A French Revolution, 1648–1652.* New York: W.W. Norton, 1993.

Westrich, Sal. *The Ormée of Bordeaux: A Revolution during the Fronde.* Baltimore, Md.: Johns Hopkins University Press, 1972.

FRENCH PEASANT REVOLTS (1594–1648)

The series of popular uprisings and insurrections against the French crown between the French wars of religion (1562–1598) and the Fronde (1648–1653) was a legacy of the religious wars, whose tax burdens left a widening rift between haves and have-nots, as well as a reaction to the fiscal policies of Louis XIII (1610–1643) and his chief minister, Cardinal Richelieu. The religious wars had established a pattern that was to be repeated in the period 1620–1648: whenever the crown was involved in an extended period of warfare, the need for revenues forced the government to undermine different groups' tax exemptions as well as to force disastrously large loans on royal officers, who were coerced to lend money to the crown at very unfavorable terms. The result was an unwieldy fiscal system that peacetime revenues could never sustain. The inevitable consequence was that the government ended each cycle of war and peace in bankruptcy, as happened in 1602, 1634, and 1648. It was to counter such structural weaknesses in the French state that first Henry IV, then Louis XIII and Richelieu, made efforts to strengthen royal authority, especially in those regions of France where local elites had traditionally held the power to assess and collect taxes. The crown's efforts to bypass local elites in favor of royal tax officials, and after 1630 the appointment of royal *intendants* to implement the royal will, at least in theory, inevitably led to opposition. Thus, ironically, popular revolts were destined to become the handmaiden of the absolutist state.

HISTORIOGRAPHY OF THE REVOLTS

Since those who were least able to pay were most liable to be taxed, it is nearly impossible to separate bread riots from tax revolts in the period 1594–1648. Indeed, the historiography of the revolts reflects this inherent problem. The Russian historian Boris Porshnev used a Marxian analysis in 1948 to explain the popular revolts in terms of socioeconomic conflict. He saw the French peasant revolts as instigated, organized, and led from below by peasants and other members of the popular classes, as an essentially feudal reaction against their exploitation by landlords in league with the French crown. Thus, for Porshnev the peasant revolts were motivated primarily by class conflict and the inherent social tensions within a feudal society.

Porshnev's explanation was roundly criticized by the French historian Roland Mousnier, who denied the existence of class altogether before the eighteenth century. For Mousnier the revolts were more the result of local or regional antagonisms against the crown's encroachment on local privileges. Thus, he insisted that they were composed of members of all social groups, who banded together to oppose royal fiscal policies. And in contrast to Porshnev, Mousnier stressed the leadership of local elites and the collaboration between local magistrates and crowds. The views of both Porshnev and Mousnier proved ultimately to rely on a superficial and overly simplistic framework, which did not fully account for the complexity of the revolts themselves. Indeed, recent research has shown that elements of both models were often vital ingredients of many of the popular uprisings of the period.

RURAL AND URBAN REVOLTS

Of the scores of popular uprisings that took place between 1594 and 1648, by far the majority were rural in nature and scattered widely over many villages and towns of a particular province. The most intense and widespread of the uprisings occurred in the southwest, in the region around Bordeaux and along the Dordogne and Garonne river valleys. The southwest had a tradition of popular unrest; in 1548 the introduction of a salt tax had resulted in rioting and disturbances that lasted for weeks. In 1594, however, it was the draining legacy of warfare that caused peasants in dozens of villages to revolt against a doubling of the personal income tax and against the forced billeting of soldiers in their homes. Pillaging soldiers and billeting troops had been the norm in the region, off and on, since the mid-sixteenth century. The peasants, called *croquants* by their critics, meaning "country bumpkins," sought an end to the civil wars as well as a return to normal tax levels. Large numbers of peasants—between twelve thousand and twenty thousand in some instances—organized themselves to petition local seigneurs and even sent a petition to King Henry IV. In 1635 a second peasant revolt broke out in the southwest, this time over the issues of forced loans and the raising of the rations tax, the latter a thinly disguised attempt to avoid troop billeting, but a tax that still forced the local populations to feed and house an army in the field. Other similar widespread peasant revolts occurred in Provence in the autumn of 1630 and in Normandy in 1639. The cities and towns were not exempt from popular insurrection either. The revolts that occurred in Dijon (1630), Aix (1631), Lyon (1632), Bordeaux (1635), Moulins (1640), Châlons-sur-Marne (1641), Marseilles (1644), and Montpellier (1645) are the most well known, though there were dozens of other minor urban disturbances during the period.

IMPACT OF THE REVOLTS

What is striking is the scale of the revolts in such a concentrated period. According to Yves-Marie Bercé, a specialist on the revolts, in the southwest, where the revolts were the most intense, 459 separate peasant uprisings can be identified in the 125 years between 1590 and 1715, of which 47 occurred before 1635, 282 between 1635 and 1660, coinciding with the French war against the Habsburgs, and 130 after 1660. Whereas in 1600 only one uprising occurred per year on average, by 1635 there were ten; over the same period, taxes rose between four- and fivefold.

What did the revolts accomplish? Although they rarely managed any military successes against professional troops or even local militias, the peasants got the crown's attention. Moreover, many of them managed to win at least temporary tax concessions from the crown. Ultimately, they were fighting a long-term battle against the French crown's systematic efforts to centralize tax collection, a goal necessitated above all by war. Inevitably, the crown's efforts clashed with local privileges, traditions, and autonomy. This is not to suggest, however, that the absolutist state was entirely successful. The growth in monarchical power in the seventeenth century was achieved only because Louis XIII and Richelieu found ways to accommodate the twin engines of the peasant revolts: local solidarities and socioeconomic tensions.

See also *French Frondes (1648–1653); French Wars of Religion (1562–1598).*

Mack P. Holt

BIBLIOGRAPHY

Beik, William. *Urban Protest in Seventeenth-Century France: The Culture of Retribution.* Cambridge: Cambridge University Press, 1997.

Bercé, Yves-Marie. *History of Peasant Revolts: The Social Origins of Rebellion in Early Modern France.* Translated by Amanda Whitmore. Ithaca, N.Y.: Cornell University Press, 1990.

Coveney, P. J., ed. and trans. *France in Crisis, 1620–1675.* London: Macmillan Press, 1977.

Mousnier, Roland. *Peasant Uprisings in Seventeenth-Century France, Russia and China.* Translated by Brian Pearce. London: George Allen and Unwin, 1971.

Porshnev, Boris. *Les soulèvements populaires en France de 1623 à 1648.* Translated by Robert Mandrou. Paris: S.E.V.P.E.N., 1963.

Salmon, J. H. M. "Venality of Office and Popular Sedition in Seventeenth-Century France." *Past & Present* 37 (1967): 21–43.

FRENCH REVOLUTION (1789–1815)

The social and political upheavals in France, spreading subsequently to most of Europe over the generation after 1789, constitute the classic revolution of modern times. Matched in world historical importance only by the Russian and Chinese communist revolutions of the twentieth century, the French Revolution was the founding episode of modern political culture, setting the agenda for public life throughout the nineteenth century over much of the world populated or controlled by Europeans.

ORIGINS

The trigger for the French Revolution was a financial crisis. The government of King Louis XVI, already burdened by substantial debts incurred to finance midcentury wars, intervened between 1778 and 1783 in the American War of Independence in the hope of destroying the power of Great Britain. Taxing too little and borrowing too much on disadvantageous terms, the king found himself by 1786 facing bankruptcy. To avoid it, an ambitious plan of reform was formulated, but when the plan was laid before a handpicked Assembly of Notables in 1787, members claimed, after much detailed criticism, that the only body competent to approve such far-reaching changes was the elected Estates-General, which had not met since 1614. From the dissolution of the Notables (May 1787) until August 1788 the government struggled to avoid convening a body that seemed bound to diminish hitherto absolute royal power. Financial paralysis, however, forced Louis XVI to convoke the Estates for 1789.

The question then was their composition. Precedent dictated three houses representing the orders of clergy, nobility, and third estate (comprising everyone else in the kingdom), numerically equal in membership but voting by order. Thus the first two "privileged orders" could outvote the third estate, even though it represented the vast majority of the nation. By the time of the elections in spring 1789, in response to a massive publicity campaign, double representation had been conceded to the third estate, but it remained undecided whether votes would be counted by order, preserving the dominance of the clergy and nobility, or by head, which would give the third estate—now doubled—an equal vote. The issue, unresolved until six weeks after the Estates convened, dominated the elections, producing a groundswell of hostility toward the nobility.

Precedent also dictated that electors draw up grievance lists *(cahiers)* to guide the legislative activities of elected deputies. The effect was to articulate widespread demands for social as well as political reform and to raise expectations. All this took place against a background of acute economic crisis, with soaring bread prices, a collapse in consumer demand for manufactures, and rising unemployment. Hopes that the Estates might resolve all problems, however, were dashed by deadlock among the Estates over the issue of how to count votes. Frustrated by noble resistance, on June 17 the third estate, reinforced by a few renegade clergy, declared itself the National Assembly, with full sovereign powers. Attempts by the king and certain nobles to resist the claims of the third estate, ultimately with the threat of military force, produced rising popular alarm, which culminated on July 14 with a revolt in Paris as a terrified, hungry populace scoured the city for arms. With the help of military mutineers, the people stormed the main state prison, the Bastille. Unsure of his troops' reliability, the king abandoned his resistance to the seizure of sovereignty by the French nation's elected representatives.

OBJECTIVES

Steeped in the rationalistic, utilitarian thought of the Enlightenment, the men of education who made up the National Assembly sought to endow France with a written constitution enshrining regular election of public officials, separation of powers, decentralization of authority, and uniformity of institutions. The constitution, adopted August 26, 1789, was prefaced (on the model of certain American states) by a Declaration of the Rights of Man and the Citizen, whose seventeen points included the sovereignty of the nation, civil equality before the law, freedom from arbitrary arrest, freedom of thought and speech, and the inviolability of property.

Resulting from a struggle against noble privilege, the Revolution was made even more antiaristocratic as a result of rural unrest in the latter half of July 1789. As panic swept the countryside, there were widespread attacks on the residences of landlords and the symbols and records of their manorial rights. A move by the Assembly on August 4 to defuse the situation by abolishing certain "feudal" burdens accelerated overnight into an orgy of renunciation in which manifestations of feudalism or privilege of any sort—ecclesiastical tithes and venality of public offices—all disappeared, condemned as abuses of the *ancien régime*. Hostility to privilege and feudal rights formed the core of a liberal agenda that would be pursued by revolutionaries everywhere for more than a century.

The French Revolution was not initially antimonarchical. It sought to turn an absolute monarchy into a constitutional one; and despite the struggles of 1787–1789, goodwill toward Louis XVI survived almost undented until he seemed to resist sanctioning the reforms of August 4 and measures designed to limit his legislative powers in the future. The suspicion that he aroused led to a march of Parisian women to Versailles on October 5–6 (the "October Days"), which forced king and Assembly alike to move to the capital, where they would be under constant popular scrutiny. Thus began five years in which the people of Paris saw themselves as the watchdogs and guarantors of revolutionary achievements.

Brought together in consequence of a financial crisis, the men of 1789 regarded the state's debt as a sacrosanct "national treasure" to be honored at all costs. But, by decreeing compensation for abolished property rights (notably in venal offices) they immeasurably increased its volume. They sought to defray the burden by nationalizing the properties of the church (perhaps one-tenth of the kingdom's landed wealth) and selling them off. Bonds redeemable in "national goods" were also issued, and these *assignats* rapidly acquired the status of paper currency. But the abolition of tithes and the confiscation of ecclesiastical lands left the problem of how to finance the church, and with this problem began the Revolution's most serious difficulties.

AGAINST RELIGION

A remarkable nationwide consensus underlay the Revolution's early reforms. Only a handful of nobles, who began to leave the country after July 14, refused to accept them. But when the National Assembly turned its rationalizing zeal to the church it proved impossible to maintain unity. Loss of tithes and lands was followed by the abolition of monasticism and a refusal to declare Catholicism the national religion. Even so, many clergy in 1790 were prepared to accept salaries under the civil constitution of the clergy (with its new ecclesiastical boundaries, lay election of clergy, and denial of papal jurisdiction) until the pope denounced it. An attempt to enforce compliance by imposing a loyalty oath on all clergy backfired when half refused it. Those who resisted ("Refractories") were ejected from their living quarters and placed under increasingly close surveillance. They became rallying points for all who opposed the Revolution, and suspicion of them rubbed off onto all religious denominations, including the "Constitutionals" who had taken the oath.

When a counterrevolutionary rebellion broke out in the Vendée region of the west in 1793, priests were widely blamed, and later that year anticlerical sentiments culminated in several months of semispontaneous "de-Christianization," which witnessed massive vandalism—a word coined then—and brought public worship throughout the country to a standstill. Many conservative observers, at the time and long afterward, saw this assault on religion as the logical, and intended, consequence of a century of Enlightenment atheism.

After a fleeting attempt by Maximilien Robespierre in June 1794 to set up a rationalist "Cult of the Supreme Being," the state withdrew support and funding from all religious organizations. Nevertheless, the late 1790s saw a religious revival, even as French armies overthrew the Papal States in Italy and captured the pope. Ever the realist, Napoleon Bonaparte, as soon as he came to power in 1799, resolved to capitalize on the revival of religion in France by reaching a settlement with Rome. By the Concordat of 1801

Lafayette is shown in this period etching ordering his soldiers to fire on members of the Cordeliers Club. They were gathering signatures on the Champ de Mars for a petition to abolish the monarchy.

Catholicism was recognized as the majority religion, and the Catholic Church was to be funded by the state in return for recognition of the loss of its prerevolutionary property and privileges. Despite later quarrels with the pope, Napoleon always supported the state church, as did successive French regimes until 1905. The left, however, always regarded the restoration of the church as a betrayal of the Revolution's achievements and consistently worked throughout the nineteenth century to sever the link afresh.

AGAINST MONARCHY

The split in the church from 1791 between Refractories and Constitutionals both reflected and encouraged a split in the laity. The most significant lay person to be alienated was the king himself, who between October 1789 and June 1791 had grudgingly accepted all revolutionary reforms. Unwilling, however, to receive the sacraments from a constitutional priest, the king and his family attempted to leave the country in the flight to Varennes (June 21, 1791).

The king's capture and return to the capital unleashed a wave of republicanism not seen previously. Declining popular support for the constitutional monarchy alarmed the Assembly, which sought to reinstate the king and appease him by last-minute conservative amendments to the near-complete constitution, while Parisian authorities shot down republican petitioners (Massacre of the Champ de Mars, July 17, 1791). Meanwhile, the king's recapture prompted the emigration of thousands of noble army officers who believed his captivity absolved them from their oaths of loyalty. It also evoked threats of armed intervention from foreign rulers to protect the king (Declaration of Pillnitz, August 27, 1791). When the new Legislative Assembly, meeting in October 1791, passed punitive decrees against émigrés and refractory priests, the king used his powers under the constitution to veto them. His continued refusal to give his sanction even after the outbreak of war led to his being mobbed in his palace (June 20, 1792) and ultimately to the overthrow of the monarchy itself by popular action (August 10, 1792).

A new, republican constitution was needed after the monarchy's fall, and a freshly elected Convention met on September 22 to begin drafting it. The Convention's first task, however, was to settle the fate of the former king, and after long debates it decided to try him for betraying his engagements to the nation. He was found guilty, condemned to death, and, despite maneuvers to reprieve him, executed on January 21, 1793. His unpopular Austrian queen, Marie Antoinette, followed him to the scaffold in October, and his sickly son, Louis Charles, remained a prisoner until his premature death in May 1795. Upon Louis Charles's death, Louis XVI's younger brother, who had made good his own emigration in June 1791, proclaimed himself Louis XVIII, and in the Declaration of Verona (July 1795) committed himself, when restored, to bringing back the entire *ancien régime.* The Verona declaration made a monarchical restoration politically impossible, and a new republican constitution was adopted the following autumn, with the executive vested in a five-man Directory.

Although support for a monarchy as a focus for order remained strong, much of this monarchical constituency was captured by Napoleon after 1799. Napoleon's religious settlement of 1801 also broke the link between church and king, which had sustained counterrevolution for almost a decade. Napoleon politely told Louis XVIII that he could never return; and he did so only after the emperor's military defeat. And although the charter issued by Louis XVIII upon his return in 1814 made a number of concessions to representative government and subjects' rights, those loyal to the memory of the Revolution regarded its legacy as quintessentially republican, and regarded the monarchy as a natural obstacle to the fulfillment of the promise of 1789.

AGAINST EUROPE

The revolutionaries of 1789 wished to live at peace with their neighbors and declared that France would go to war only if attacked. But the threats uttered by foreign monarchs after the flight to Varennes and their support for bellicose émigrés began a drift toward war, which won increasing support in France from politicians anxious to expose domestic enemies. Others, including the king and queen, hoped that the debilitated state of the French army would allow the forces of their fellow monarchs to rescue them after easy victories.

France declared war against the Austrian Empire on April 20, 1792, to almost unanimous enthusiasm, but a disastrous start was the essential background to the fall of the monarchy. The French victory at Valmy (September 21, 1792) then inaugurated six months of stunning success, during which the Austrian Netherlands were overrun and the French republic offered fraternity and help to all peoples wishing to recover their liberty, and offered "peace to the cottages, war on the castles" in the path of its armies. It was the first war of liberation; but by invading the Netherlands, France brought a hitherto isolationist Great Britain into the conflict. Soon the young republic was on the defensive again. Without allies and wracked for much of 1793–1794 by internal rebellion and civil war, France survived only by marshaling the entire resources of the country behind a mass conscript army of unprecedented size. By the end of 1794, French mobilization was finally bringing a consistent string of victories. Both northern and southern Netherlands were overrun, and in 1796 France invaded Italy so as to strike at Austria in the rear. General Bonaparte's victories in Italy had brought peace with all countries except Great Britain by 1797. France had expanded to her self-proclaimed "natural frontier" along the Rhine and was protected beyond by "sister republics" in Holland and northern Italy, ruled by France with the collaboration of native sympathizers. The next year, the absence of Bonaparte, who was in Egypt where he hoped to sever British links with India, facilitated the formation of a new anti-French coalition, which drove the French out of many of their conquests. But the unexpected return of the hero of Italy, who had seized power in October 1799, led within two years to victory over the coalition and the end of the revolutionary wars.

Although even the British had made peace, Napoleon's restless ambition soon provoked a new series of conflicts, more properly termed Napoleonic, which eventually carried French forces as far as Portugal in the west and Moscow in the east. By 1806 the shock of French armies had destroyed the Holy Roman Empire, the oldest political entity in Europe, and a number of smaller states in Germany and Italy. If the Revolution overthrew the French *ancien régime,* it was Napoleon who ended the old order in much of the rest of Europe, replacing it with a French empire and a number of more or less compliant client states. Even states that fought against Napoleon had to reform their own institutions extensively. But he never subdued Spain, or Russia, or Great Britain, and in the end the "Spanish ulcer," the Russian winter, and the British fleet combined to defeat Napoleon and ensure the return of Louis XVIII, though hardly the full *ancien régime* he had promised twenty years earlier.

JACOBINISM AND TERROR

For the first six years of the French Revolution, political life outside the assemblies was largely conducted in clubs, of which the most famous, at the center of a nationwide network, was the Jacobin Club. Eventually, it eclipsed all rivals, and outside France "Jacobin" became a general term for sympathizers with French aims and aspirations. Throughout the nineteenth century the term would be used, whether with pride or opprobrium, for a wide range of republican radicals, reformers or revolutionaries, both within France and as far afield as Russia and Brazil.

Until June 1791 the Jacobins never moved ahead of the revolutionary mainstream, but mobilization to support clerical oathtaking began to radicalize them, and after Varennes they split over how to deal with the king. While conservatives seceded to form the short-lived Feuillant Club, Robespierre held more radical and populist elements together under the old name. They appealed more and more for support to poorer artisans, whom they called *sansculottes* (no knee-breeches). The Parisian Club was active in preparing the overthrow of the monarchy and muted in condemnation of the popular attack on the inmates of the capital's prisons, the September massacres (September 2–5, 1792). Subsequently, it expelled the Girondins, members of the Convention who opposed the power of the *sansculottes,* and connived at their ultimate expulsion under popular pressure from the Convention itself (June 2, 1793). The period between June 2 and the fall of Robespierre (July 28, 1794) is often called the Jacobin Republic. It is also the period of the most notorious episode of the Revolution: the Terror.

To terrorize enemies with violence had been a reflex response among the people of Paris ever since the fall of the Bastille. Though often advocated by populist journalists like Jean-Paul Marat, violence was never a course favored by those in power, until the spring of 1793, when successively the Vendée and a number of provincial capitals revolted against the Convention. When, over the last few months of 1793, central control was gradually reestablished, convicted rebels were executed en masse under the supervision of Jacobin deputies sent out with plenary powers. In the spring of 1794 trial for political crimes was centralized in the Revolutionary Tribunal in Paris, and more than a quarter of the Terror's 15,000 official victims were guillotined then (the total number of unrecorded victims was probably several times greater).

The liberal dawn of 1789 had led to a regime of arbitrary and brutal political justice for the first but certainly not the last time in the history of revolutions. Criticism of the policy of Terror was at first silenced by the execution of the popular Georges Jacques Danton and his allies (April 5, 1794); but, as safeguards for accused persons were progressively abrogated, deputies became alarmed that no end to the killing was in sight. The overthrow and execution of the Terror's main defender, Robespierre (July 28, 1794), led, however, to a rapid dismantling of the terroristic apparatus. The Thermidorean period (so called from the revolutionary name for the month of Robespierre's fall) that followed proved chaotic, and in many regions witnessed a "White Terror" of conservative revenge.

The Terror has always besmirched the historical reputation of the French Revolution. Commentators have been divided between those who see the Terror as an integral and inevitable part of the whole episode, and those who regard it as an unplanned and unforeseen consequence of a war emergency in a politically divided country. A further complication was that the Terror accompanied the most socially radical phase of the Revolution, which saw the adoption of egalitarian styles of dress and speech, a command economy, and punitive taxation on the rich; the beginnings of property redistribution; the proclamation of social welfare policies; the abolition of slavery; and a commitment to implementation once the war was won of a constitution far more democratic than that of 1791.

All of these policies, adopted by many subsequent social revolutions, were rapidly abandoned after the fall of Robespierre. Popular revolts in Paris seeking their restoration after a catastrophic winter in 1795 were crushed. So was the similarly motivated plot of Gracchus Babeuf in 1796, the first attempt at communist revolution in history. The regime of the Directory between 1795 and 1799 was committed above all to the defense of property, and particularly that redistributed by the Revolution from the church and noble émigrés. Unable, however, to guarantee property rights without repeated political purges, the Directory found itself ousted in 1799 by Napoleon. In abandoning representative government, restoring the church and the nobility, and finally making himself a hereditary monarch, Napoleon turned his back on much of the Revolution's achievement. But in his commitment to rational, uniform administration, and above all the unconditional guarantee he offered to property owners, he was the Revolution's authentic heir.

THE LEGACY

Apart from the initial liberal program of liberty and equality (fraternity was added to the famous slogan only in 1793), the history of the Revolution bequeathed a pattern that has been endlessly studied for lessons since by revolutionaries and conservatives alike. Not only did it destroy or traumatize the *ancien régime* throughout Europe, but by loosening the grip of old governments on their colonial empires it also helped to precipitate the independence of Latin America and the greatest slave revolt in history, which culminated in the first modern black republic in Haiti. The Revolution pointed the way toward building states and armed forces of unprecedented power, and its conduct of warfare transformed military practice. With the French Revolution the People, as a self-conscious political entity, made its modern debut, as did the nation-state pursuing nonnegotiable sovereign claims. The Revolution lies at the root of both nationalism and international socialism. Unprecedented in scale, impact, and ramifications, the French Revolution changed the very meaning of the word *revolution* and provided the touchstone against which the significance of all political upheavals, before it and after, must be judged.

See also *Buonarroti, Filippo Michele; Burke, Edmund; European Revolutions of 1820; European Revolutions of 1830; European Revolutions of 1848; Lafayette, Gilbert du Motier de; Marat, Jean-Paul; Media and Communications; Music; Paine, Thomas; Robespierre, Maximilien; Rousseau, Jean-Jacques; Terrorism; Tocqueville, Alexis de.*

William Doyle

BIBLIOGRAPHY

Best, Geoffrey, ed. *The Permanent Revolution. The French Revolution and Its Legacy 1789–1989.* London: Fontana, 1989.

Blanning, Timothy C. W. *The French Revolutionary Wars, 1787–1802.* London: Arnold, 1996.

———. *The French Revolution. Class Conflict or Cultural Clash?* London: Macmillan, 1997.

Broers, Michael G. *Europe under Napoleon 1799–1815.* London: Arnold, 1996.

Doyle, William. *Origins of the French Revolution.* 3d ed. Oxford: Oxford University Press, 1999, forthcoming.

———. *The Oxford History of the French Revolution.* Oxford: Oxford University Press, 1989.

Furet, Francois. *Revolutionary France 1770–1880.* Oxford: Blackwell, 1992.

Scott, Samuel F., and Barry Rothaus. *Historical Dictionary of the French Revolution.* 2 vols. Westport, Conn.: Greenwood Press, 1985.

Sutherland, Donald M. G. *France 1789–1815. Revolution and Counterrevolution.* London: Fontana, 1986.

FRENCH STUDENT REVOLT (1968)

In May 1968 a movement of students and workers, taking the form of strikes and demonstrations, shook the French state headed by Gen. Charles de Gaulle to its foundations. The crisis had been precipitated by three factors. First, the rapid modernization of France after the Second World War had created a new working class in new industrial centers, which was obliged to increase productivity massively without being consulted in the workplace. Creation of a new working class was paralleled by a huge increase in students attending high schools and universities, who were suffering overcrowding and rigid discipline and were facing the prospect of employment in low-grade jobs. Second, the Fifth Republic, founded in 1958 by de Gaulle after twelve years of political bickering, had become progressively more authoritarian. The established politicians were discredited, deeply divided, and unable to challenge de Gaulle and his governmental party. By the same token, however, they were unable to channel the discontent and frustration that was building in French society. Third, the outside world was exploding, with the Vietnam War, the Cultural Revolution in China, the revolutions of Fidel Castro and Che Guevara in Latin America, the Civil Rights movement in the United States, and the "Prague Spring" in Czechoslovakia. There was a ferment of new ideas attacking dominant thought systems from Catholicism to orthodox Marxism. All three underlying factors produced echoes among the angry and highly politicized student population, led by the Trotskyist Alain Krivine and the anarchist Danny Cohn-Bendit.

A SPONTANEOUS REVOLT

The cradle of the student revolt was the University of Nanterre, which had been set up in 1964 outside Paris on the bulldozed site of a former shantytown to take the excess of students in Paris. The number of students there grew from 4,000 in 1964 to 15,000 in 1967. The authorities reacted harshly to increasing discontent at the university, arresting student militants on March 20–21, 1968. Their arrest provoked the occupation of the university's administrative block on March 22, and teaching was suspended two days later. On May 2 the whole campus was closed, with the result that student agitation spread to the Sorbonne in central Paris. On May 3 the police were ordered into the Sorbonne to arrest student leaders, and the university was shut down. Police brutality was entirely counterproductive. The students' union, backed by that of the lecturers, organized a strike. Demonstrations against the police spread to the surrounding Latin Quarter, and during the night of May 10–11, barricades were once again thrown up in the streets of Paris.

The government hesitated. President de Gaulle was in favor of sending in the army. The prime minister, Georges Pompidou, subordinate to de Gaulle but demonstrating greater political acumen, favored reopening the university and had his way. Violence gave way to debate. The Sorbonne became a student commune, a libertarian utopia in which the students held endless meetings, daubed graffiti, and questioned everything and anything about contemporary society. In previous French revolutions the link between students and workers had been crucial, and in May 1968 the trade unions lent their support. They called a general strike on Monday, May 13, and in Paris 800,000 demonstrators turned out to declare the solidarity of students, teachers, and workers and to demand the resignation of de Gaulle. The strike spread to many branches of industry and the services, affecting 10 million workers, who demanded not only better wages and conditions but adequate representation and industrial democracy.

CRISIS AND CONTAINMENT

A successful revolution requires not only a mass movement but paralysis of the state and the division of the governing class. France in 1968 experienced all three, but not in sufficient degree to destroy the system.

Despite the mass movement of students and workers, the most powerful opposition party, the Communists, and the Communist-led trade union, the Confédération Générale du Travail (CGT), had a mortal fear of spontaneous revolution. Although resolutely hostile to de Gaulle's republic, the Communists saw the revolution as stirred up by anarchists, Trotskyists, and Maoists, not as controlled by themselves. Far from putting themselves at the head of the movement, therefore, the Communists were desperate to bring it to an end and effectively betrayed it by not embracing it.

Paralysis of the state was exemplified when de Gaulle flew off to Romania on a state visit on May 14. He returned four days later but did not address the nation until May 24, when he proposed to defuse the crisis by holding a referendum on greater representation of students in universities and of workers in industry. On May 29 he boarded a helicopter and disappeared, not even alerting Prime Minister Pompidou. He went to visit French troops stationed in Germany, although it is more likely that he wanted to stage a comeback on the waves of political panic than on that of airborne forces. Fortunately, Pompidou retained a cool head. He invited trade unions and employers to talks at the Ministry of Labour and hammered out a compromise that satisfied the CGT bosses if not the rank-and-file workers. Then he persuaded de Gaulle to abandon the referendum, which had only provoked opposition leaders to take part in rallies and demonstrations in Paris between May 27 and 29, in which they postured as future leaders should the general lose the vote. Instead of a referendum, Pompidou won the case for general elections, which restored the initiative to the established political parties and required the politicians to return to their constituencies.

With the announcement of general elections, the unity of the governing classes was shown. Those loyal to de Gaulle, 500,000 strong, paraded triumphantly down the Champs-Elysées on May 30, and in the general elections, fought over two rounds on June 23 and 30, 1968, the Gaullist party won an absolute majority in the National Assembly.

CONSEQUENCES

The Gaullist regime survived, but de Gaulle, who had mismanaged the crisis, was doomed. French conservatives learned that they could have a strong regime without the general. On April 27, 1969, many of them voted alongside the center and left against de Gaulle's referendum on constitutional reform. De Gaulle resigned, and Pompidou, architect of the regime's survival in 1968, was elected president of the republic.

The left learned the lessons of division. A new socialist party was formed in 1971 and negotiated a union of the left with the Communist Party, not least to control and displace it as the principal party of the left. Ten years later, the Socialist Party came to power under François Mitterrand. However, it was unable to contain all the radical ideas that bubbled from the cauldron of 1968 and developed in the 1970s as feminism, gay liberation, anticolonialism, the antinuclear movement, regionalism, and ecologism. These manifold currents of opposition were the most durable legacy of 1968.

See also *Student Protests and Youth Movements.*

Robert Gildea

BIBLIOGRAPHY

Berstein, Serge. *The Republic of de Gaulle, 1958–1969.* Cambridge: Cambridge University Press, 1993.

Brown, Bernard J. *Protest in Paris: Anatomy of a Revolt.* Morristown, N.J.: General Learning Press, 1974.

Caute, David. *Nineteen Sixty Eight. The Year of the Barricades.* London: Hamish Hamilton, 1988.

Fraser, Ronald, ed. *1968. A Student Generation in Revolt.* London: Chatto and Windus, 1988.

Hirsch, Arthur. *The French New Left. An Intellectual History from Sartre to Gorz.* Boston: South End Press, 1981.

Schnapp, Alain, and Pierre Vidal-Naquet. *Journal de la Commune étudiante: textes et documents, novembre 1967–juin 1968.* Paris: Seuil, 1968.

FRENCH WARS OF RELIGION (1562–1598)

The series of eight civil wars known as the French wars of religion divided France for more than thirty-five years and threatened to overthrow the Crown in the second half of the sixteenth century. The legacy of religious division of the Reformation combined with a series of weak French kings to produce the most serious political crisis in French history prior to the Revolution of 1789. The slow advent of Protestantism in the 1540s in various French towns and cities, including Paris, spurred King Henry II to suppress and persecute the minority Calvinist sect. Not only did his policy prove to be inefficacious, but the systematic effort by John Calvin in Geneva to send a series of Calvinist pastors into France to start new congregations, coupled with the accidental death of Henry II in a jousting accident in 1559, led to a spurt of Protestant growth in France. The new Geneva-trained pastors served as a catalyst to an already growing movement, while the young son of Henry II, Francis II (1559–1560), died after a year on the throne and left an even younger son, Charles IX (1560–1574), as the titular head of a regency government ruled by Henry's widow, Catherine de Medici. During the power vacuum at court many French nobles converted to Protestantism and opposed the ultra-Catholic faction—led by the Guise family—that had dominated the reigns of both Henry II and Francis II. By the early 1560s perhaps 10 percent of the people of France had converted to Protestantism.

THE EARLY WARS OF RELIGION

Although Catherine de Medici was a devout Catholic, she recognized that the systematic persecution initiated by her husband had failed. Moreover, the last thing she wanted was to see the kingdom of her son Charles disintegrate into a civil war over religion. Thus, along with the chancellor, Michel de l'Hôpital, she decided on a policy of limited toleration of the Protestants, called Huguenots in France. She issued the Edict of Toleration, limiting their right to worship to only a few places, in January 1562, believing it to be the only way to avoid civil war. Catherine's policy was as unproductive as her husband's, however, as the Huguenots opposed it as too restrictive and the Catholics refused to honor it as too lenient. Within two months civil war had broken out.

Although both sides won victories on the battlefield in the early wars (1562–1570), neither was able to secure a complete victory because there were far too many towns for either army to occupy. One turning point came in 1572, when Catherine de Medici and Charles IX rashly ordered the murder of several dozen Huguenot nobles who had come to Paris to attend the wedding of the king's sister to a leading Huguenot nobleman, Henry of Navarre. This bloody maneuver accomplished the goal of eliminating the Huguenot leadership, but it set off a frenzy of popular violence as French Catholics mistakenly believed the king had ordered all Huguenots to be killed. The St. Bartholomew's massacres resulted in maybe two thousand Protestant deaths in Paris, and perhaps as many as four thousand in the provinces. Although the massacres ended the spurt of Protestant growth and resulted in hundreds of abjurations and reconversions to Catholicism, they did not bring outright victory. Moreover, they led Huguenot political thinkers to condone resistance to the monarchy. Initially opposed by Calvin, ideas of resistance to the king had emerged even before the St. Bartholomew's massacres. These ideas were based on the notion that kings had a contract with their subjects to protect and defend them; and when kings abrogated these duties, then "lesser magistrates" such as nobles had a duty to oppose them.

THE HOLY LEAGUE AND THE EDICT OF NANTES

A second turning point came in 1584, when the fourth and youngest son of Henry II and Catherine de Medici died, leaving the childless third son, Henry III (1574–1589), without a direct heir. It was a supreme irony that the next in line to the throne was the Protestant Henry of Navarre, still married to the king's sister. The line of succession gave the Protestants hope once more for full political rights, especially after Henry III's assassination in 1589 left Navarre as the rightful heir to the throne. Militant Catholics, however, formed the Holy League to prevent Navarre's coronation, claiming that a Protestant could not inherit the throne. They also adopted the Huguenots' ideas of resistance but went even further to advocate regicide as well as revolution. They were now arguing that a heretical king not only could be opposed but could be murdered. The result was the bloodiest and deadliest of the civil wars (1588–1589), the last of the eight. This one, too, was unwinnable by either side, until Navarre recognized that peace was impossible unless he converted to Catholicism. His abjuration and conversion in July 1593 turned the popular tide in his favor, as one by one the Holy League-supported towns surrendered to him. The Edict of Nantes (1598), like all earlier peace edicts, was attacked by some Huguenots as too harsh and by some Catholics as too conciliatory, although it did initiate the first extended period of peace in France since 1562.

Although France was still publicly a Catholic state, and the edict guaranteed that all French institutions would remain Catholic, two generations of civil war had left it a very changed kingdom, with the Huguenots (probably less than 5 percent of the population after 1598) forced to survive in a distinctly minority status. After the death of Henry IV in 1610, a small faction of Huguenots, composed largely of nobles, refused to accept this diminished status and rebelled against Henry's son, Louis XIII. A series of military campaigns in the 1620s quelled the rebellions, concluding with the siege of La Rochelle in 1628.

The small Huguenot minority struggled to survive in an overwhelmingly Catholic France until 1685, when Louis XIV unwittingly gave the movement new life by revoking the Edict of Nantes altogether, forcing the Protestants to go underground or abroad for survival and beginning a period of Huguenot resurgence. An additional legacy of the French religious wars was the political idea of resistance to the Crown, which was adopted by the enemies of Charles I in seventeenth-century England. The revolutionary rhetoric of both the Huguenots and the militant Catholic Holy League of the 1570s, 1580s, and 1590s was resurrected by radical Puritans in the 1640s to serve a different revolutionary cause.

Mack P. Holt

BIBLIOGRAPHY

Benedict, Philip. *Rouen during the Wars of Religion.* Cambridge: Cambridge University Press, 1981.

Davis, Natalie Zemon. *Society and Culture in Early Modern France.* Stanford: Stanford University Press, 1975.

Diefendorf, Barbara B. *Beneath the Cross: Catholics and Huguenots in Sixteenth-Century Paris.* New York: Oxford University Press, 1991.

Greengrass, Mark. *France in the Age of Henri IV.* 2d ed. London: Longman, 1995.

Holt, Mack P. *The French Wars of Religion, 1562–1629.* Cambridge: Cambridge University Press, 1995.

Kelley, Donald R. *The Beginning of Ideology: Consciousness and Society in the French Reformation.* Cambridge: Cambridge University Press, 1981.

Salmon, J. H. M. *Society in Crisis: France in the Sixteenth Century.* New York: St. Martin's Press, 1975.

GANDHI, MAHATMA

Gandhi (1869–1948) was the greatest leader of India's national movement and one of the great world revolutionaries of the twentieth century. Born in Gujarat, Mahatma ("Great Soul") Mohandas Karamchand Gandhi went to London to study law at the Inner Temple and was called to the bar in 1891. After returning home he accepted a job in South Africa, representing a Muslim firm there. He suffered harsh racial discrimination, including being thrown out of a first-class train carriage by an English officer. That violent act transformed him into a revolutionary leader of the entire South African Indian community. Gandhi spent two decades in South Africa, where he developed and tested his *satyagraha* ("hold onto the truth") technique of nonviolent noncooperation, later used with great success against the British in India.

Satya means "truth," and to Gandhi, "truth is God." He also asked his followers in every struggle to accept *ahimsa* ("nonviolence"), arguing that if *satya* is joined to *ahimsa,* "we can move the world," for the positive side of *ahimsa* is "love." Gandhi's other important Yogic method of struggle, also harking back to ancient India's Vedic and Upanishadic times, was *tapas* ("self-imposed suffering"). Yoga is the oldest form of religious and philosophic thought in India. Great soul and yogi that he was, Gandhi pitted his powers of truth, love, and suffering against those of the mightiest empire on earth at the time, and he won.

His first nationwide *satyagraha* movement was launched against British India's "Black" Acts, imposing extensions of martial law after World War I upon the land that had done so much to help the British win that war. The Punjab, scene of a massacre by British troops in April 1919, became the crucible of revolutionary Indian nationalism, and Mahatma Gandhi its new national hero and revered leader. The cold-blooded killing of hundreds of unarmed Indians and the gross atrocities that followed British imposition of martial law throughout Punjab Province convinced Gandhi of the

Mahatma Gandhi (center)

"satanic" nature of British rule and modern Western industrial society, which were built on violence and oppression. He called for a return to ancient rural Indian values, to India's village communities, *ashrams,* several of which he started and which survive to this day as exemplars of Gandhian communism, where each contributes what he or she does best for the benefit of all.

Sarvodaya ("the uplift of all") was the name Gandhi gave to his method of social reform. He helped revive interest in and use of Indian handicrafts and made daily spinning and weaving of cotton an integral part of his life and the lives of his followers. He was also determined to put an end to Hindu "untouchability" and struggled against orthodox upper-caste Hindu Brahman leaders to get them to open temples to "untouchables" and to open their homes as well, as he always did. Gandhi's crusade against untouchability bore fruit; it was abolished by law in India's constitution after 1950, and in 1997 India's first ex-untouchable was inaugurated as the country's tenth president. Gandhi never called for the abolition of India's caste system, however, insisting that people were born with differing strengths and weaknesses, some to preach and teach, others to engage in business, and still others to perform hard physical labor.

Gandhi's most famous *satyagraha* movement was his campaign against the British tax on salt, which he led in 1930. His last campaign was his call on the British to "quit India" in 1942, which resulted in his last long incarceration. Gandhi never accepted the idea of partition between Pakistan and India, calling it "vivisection of the mother," and his last years of life were mostly bitter, ending in his tragic assassination at the hands of a hate-crazed Brahman, who called the saintly Father of India "Mohammad," instead of Mahatma, since he read passages from the Quran at several of his evening prayer meetings. But to Mahatma Gandhi, all great religions taught much the same truth, for each appealed to God, as he did, trying to make the world a safer, saner, more loving place in which all peoples could work together helping one another survive and enjoy longer life.

See also *Indian Independence Movement (1885–1947); Jinnah, Mohammad Ali; Nehru, Jawaharlal.*

Stanley Wolpert

BIBLIOGRAPHY

Brown, Judith M. *Gandhi: Prisoner of Hope.* New Haven, Conn.: Yale University Press, 1993.

Erikson, Erik H. *Gandhi's Truth: On the Origins of Militant Nonviolence.* New York: Putnam, 1969.

Gandhi, M. K. *An Autobiography: The Story of My Experiments with Truth.* Boston: Beacon Press, 1993.

Tendulkar, D. G. *Mahatma: Life of Mohandas Karamchand Gandhi.* 8 vols. Bombay: Jhaveri and Tendulkar, 1952–1954.

GARIBALDI, GIUSEPPE

During his lifetime (1807–1882) Garibaldi, a guerrilla fighter and revolutionary, became a popular, almost legendary figure because of his heroic exploits in South America and his leading role in the unification of Italy.

Born in Nice, then part of the Italian kingdom of Sardinia and Piedmont, Garibaldi led the adventurous life of a merchant seaman as a young man. In 1833, however, he met Giuseppe Mazzini, leader of the republican organization Young Italy, and dedicated himself to the creation of a united Italy. Implicated in a republican conspiracy against the king, he fled to South America and was sentenced to death in his absence. From 1836 to 1848 he led a contingent of Italians fighting for liberty for Brazil and Uruguay. The poncho he wore in Montevideo (and later the red shirt) became his distinctive style of clothing and an integral part of his personality cult.

He returned to Italy to participate in the revolutions that swept Europe in 1848. Despite his republicanism, he was prepared to support the king of Piedmont against a threat from Austria, which controlled northeastern Italy. Garibaldi was never a rigid idealist like Mazzini but a man of action. Rebuffed by the royalists, he fought with his volunteers until the king signed an armistice with Austria. He then went to Rome to defend Mazzini's short-lived Roman republic. Although Garibaldi was defeated in the summer of 1849, his heroism and epic retreat won him lasting fame.

Exiled again, he worked briefly in a New York candle factory before resuming his career as a merchant captain. Disillusioned with Mazzini, he returned to Italy in 1858, where he began an uneasy relationship with Camillo Cavour, the Piedmontese premier. When war with Austria broke out in 1859, he led his volunteers in a successful guerrilla campaign in the Alps. Cavour's surrender of Nice to France, Piedmont's ally, embittered Garibaldi.

In May 1860, with most of central and northern Italy liberated, Garibaldi launched a famous expedition of his redshirted volunteers, known as "The Thousand," rapidly conquering Sicily and Naples. Proclaiming himself temporary dictator, he promised social reforms that led millions of southern peasants to revere him as a savior. Fearful of Garibaldi's radicalism and his plan to seize Rome, which was defended by a French garrison, Cavour sent Victor Emmanuel II and the royal army south to confront him. Civil war was avoided when Garibaldi agreed to surrender his conquests to Victor Emmanuel, now king of an almost unified Italy. Garibaldi then retired to the island of Caprera, which he had purchased, declining President Abraham Lincoln's offer of a command in the American Civil War.

He made abortive attempts to capture Rome in 1862 and 1867. Ironically, these failures only enhanced his prestige. In 1866 he again fought against Austria and in 1870 supported republican France against Prussia. That same year Rome was finally captured by the new Italian state but, like Mazzini, Garibaldi could only deplore the methods used to create the new Italy. The people had been largely marginalized by politicians, generals, and diplomats.

See also *European Revolutions of 1848; Italian Risorgimento (1789–1870).*

John Whittam

BIBLIOGRAPHY

Hearder, Harry. *Italy in the Age of the Risorgimento, 1790–1870.* London: Longman, 1983.

Hibbert, Christopher. *Garibaldi and His Enemies.* London: Penguin, 1987.

Mack Smith, Denis, ed. *Garibaldi: A Portrait in Documents.* Florence: Passigli Editori, 1982.

———. *The Making of Italy, 1796–1870.* New York: Harper and Row, 1968.

GENDER

To think about the gendered dimensions of the revolutionary experience and the ways in which scholars have analyzed or ignored those dimensions is to wrestle with a series of conundrums. Thanks to the complex and contradictory nature of the sexual politics of revolt and the various trajectories of the scholarship on the role and position of women in times of revolution, it is perhaps more useful at present to frame questions than to attempt answers.

SIX CONUNDRUMS

A first conundrum concerns the commonplace images of revolutions as upheavals that radically change the way power is exercised. How do we account for the fact that many revolutions have done little to alter the balance of power between men and women? In some cases, just after a revolution takes place, positions of high authority seem even less accessible to women than was the case before the previous regime fell. No French woman was as powerful in 1795 as Marie Antoinette had been before 1789, and no Russian woman was as powerful in the 1920s as Alexandra once was. Islamic revolutions, such as those of Algeria and Iran, provide more dramatic examples still of how revolutionary upheavals, while improving the positions of some formerly powerless groups, can leave women with less room to maneuver in the public sphere, although some scholars and activists have claimed that the social and cultural—as opposed to explicitly political—implications of these upheavals have been ambiguous, or perhaps even beneficial for women.

A second conundrum has to do with using ideology to estimate how a revolution will affect women. Revolutionary leaders' and parties' expressions of commitment to gender equality turn out to be at best a problematic predictive tool. Some successful revolutions have been led by organizations and individuals critical of patriarchy (the Bolsheviks, for example, and Sun Yat-sen to an extent). Others have been led by people uninterested in the status of women (George Washington, for instance). Why is it that the personal beliefs of revolutionary leaders seem to have so little effect on the patriarchal tendencies of the nations created or reshaped by revolutions?

A third conundrum, closely related to the last, has to do with levels of female participation and the way new regimes end up handling issues of gender equality. From Mexico in 1910 to Nicaragua and El Salvador since the 1970s, women have played key parts in many Latin American revolutions, as nonviolent petitioners or armed guerrillas. Yet it is hard to correlate varying levels of such participation with the policies of Latin American revolutionary regimes. Those that have directed a relatively large amount of energy toward changing gender-based distributions of economic and political power (as in Cuba) have not necessarily been those in which female participation was most crucial in bringing down the old order, and the inverse is also true (as in Mexico). Similar points could be made about various African revolutions in which women have played key roles.

A fourth conundrum, with links to the previous three, has to do with the vilification of old regimes. Why should the corruption and weakness of prerevolutionary regimes dominated by males so often be personified in revolutionary mythology by individual women such as China's Empress Dowager or by men imagined to have been dominated by dangerous women, such as Russia's last tsar? Why, moreover, are femininity and conservatism so often linked in this same mythology? For example, why is it that in France and Mexico, in the immediate aftermath of 1789 and 1910, the counterrevolutionary pull of Catholicism—a religion in which men hold the positions of formal power—was linked primarily to women?

A fifth conundrum has to do with revolutionary symbols, and it is only a conundrum because of the last one: Why do revolutionaries who feminize the orders they seek to overturn often end up using female imagery to represent the causes they support? The French experience is the quintessential example of this curious phenomenon. Revolutionary tracts used a wide range of strategies to make Marie Antoinette stand for all of the evils of the monarchy. She was vilified for her supposed sexual immorality, ties to foreign powers, and alleged emasculation of Louis XVI. Nonetheless, in French revolutionary discourse, the principal virtues of the revolution (liberty, equality, and even the seemingly masculine virtue of fraternity) were represented by women—or, more accurately, by goddesses. Similarly, in China's abortive revolution of 1989, students mocked Deng Xiaoping as a new "Empress Dowager" yet rallied around the "Goddess of Democracy" as a symbol for their struggle.

A final conundrum has to do with disjunctures in scholarly trends relating to revolutions. Why is it that even though many of the most interesting recent case studies of revolutionary activism have focused on topics related to gender (for example, the policies toward women of Turkish nationalists, the role of feminine and masculine symbols in various west European upheavals of the eighteenth and nineteenth centuries, and the sexual politics of the east European upheavals of 1989), the most influential works that put forth grand comparative paradigms continue to give short shrift to such topics? Part of the explanation for this last conundrum lies in the time-lag factor: comparativists tend to build on the case studies of the previous decade. This kind of argument can be used to account for the relatively little attention paid to gender in a synthetic work published in the late 1970s, which appeared just as serious analysis of the sexual politics of the events of 1789, 1917, and 1949 was beginning.

BEYOND CONUNDRUMS

Some of the conundrums alluded to above reflect broader trends that affect topics other than gender. For example, the failure of revolutionary regimes to live up to their promises to women are similar to the failures of these same regimes to come through with promises they make to other disadvantaged groups. Not only gender hierarchies but also class and ethnic divisions are often reproduced after a change in power has taken place. Similarly, the split between case studies of individual revolutions that have a great deal to say about gender symbolism and general comparative works that ignore this subject can be linked to a more general divide relating to cultural as opposed to material factors. Perhaps because they are easier to quantify, the latter tend to get much more attention than the former from social scientists interested in building models.

When taken together, however, the conundrums suggest that the gendered dimensions of revolutionary processes are a subject that remains undertheorized, despite the richness of the case study material brought to light by recent scholarship. We now know much more than we once did about specific revolutionary demonstrations involving large numbers of women, the gendered aspects of linguistic struggles set in motion by revolutionaries, and a host of other issues rooted in or with ramifications for sexual politics. What remains less clear is what can be done with this new knowledge—how it can be integrated into or used to transform models of revolutionary processes.

Several hints about how such integration and transformation might be encouraged can be gleaned from reading across national and topical boundaries, hints that may also place in novel perspective some of the conundrums spelled out above. One hint, drawn from feminist scholarship in general, as opposed to the literature on revolutions in particular, relates to patriarchy as a concept. The more we learn about the varying ways that societies with clear-cut gender hierarchies can be structured, the less satisfying becomes the idea of patriarchy as a singular term and the clearer it becomes that there are multiple patriarchies to be found in the contemporary world and the historical record.

The importance of this insight lies in its ability to help us break free of the "revolutions change everything" and "revolutions change nothing" dichotomy. The debate over the gender implications of Islamic revolutions, for example, is worth attention. Feminist scholars have staked out a range of contrasting positions on specific aspects of this question, such as the meaning one should attach to requirements by revolutionary regimes that women wear veils. Some argue that to treat these injunctions simply as signs of female disempowerment is to distort the cultural complexities of the situation; others dispute this notion. All seem to agree, however, that the symbolic meaning of the veil as a marker of gender is different today than it was before revolutions transformed nations such as Iran and Algeria.

An appreciation of the multiple forms that patriarchy can take encourages one to ask how a revolutionary event may have altered gender relations, even if women seem to be just as oppressed after the event as they were before it. We should, in short, make room for the possibility that the superficially similar patriarchal structures of an old regime and the revolutionary one that replaces it may actually be fundamentally different, and also that within the revolutionary moment itself roads not taken that could have led to something other than partriarchy may have been followed briefly and then abandoned. The persistence of patriarchy need not imply simple continuity—just as class relations are reconfigured even when a new ruling class that looks much like the old one emerges after an upheaval.

A second and related hint about how to move beyond conundrums comes from work on specific revolutions that stresses the need to look beyond the particular things upheavals accomplish (or fail to accomplish) in the short run, and focus instead on changes in visions of the politically possible. The best example relating to gender comes from the French Revolution. In the short run, the move from monarchical patriarchy to republican patriarchy may seem to have done little for women. Some have even argued that women ended up much worse off after 1789, both in political and economic terms. Women did not secure political rights, which were defined by the revolutionary leadership as those embodied in "The Declaration of the Rights of Man and the Citizen," and despite largely female crowds playing key roles early in the struggle against the monarchy, in the end the notion that women should be allowed to participate in public actions was largely discredited.

What this sort of pessimistic analysis misses is that, in the debates that followed on the heels of the adoption of the aforementioned declaration and the debates over female participation in various kinds of public politics, issues that had not been part of mainstream discourse in earlier eras were explicitly put on the table, including the notion that women might be entitled to be full-fledged citizens. The French Revolution gave rise to a potent language of rights that did not initially include women, to be sure, but that language could and would be drawn on by later generations of feminist activists.

A final hint is that students of revolutionary processes would do well to look for inspiration at developments in the study of nationalism, in which attention to gendered categories, narratives, and symbols has lately been the subject of much interesting discussion. A bridge between general studies of nationalism and case studies of individual revolutions can be found in some recent case studies that analyze revolutions as "family romances" or that place nearer the center of the picture the most obviously gendered but least studied of 1789's famous triumvirate: fraternity. Besides providing valuable links between the problems faced by scholars working on nationalism and those working on revolutions, studies of this sort also suggest strategies for moving beyond the tendency to treat "gender" as shorthand for "women," since they highlight the extent to which masculine images and identities are reconfigured during the same upheavals. The challenge now is both to produce more case studies of this sort (for example, to trace the impact on gender relations in Vietnam from a mythology of patriotism that celebrated early female rebels against Chinese domination to one in which "Uncle Ho" looms large), and also to move across time and space looking for patterns in the way femininity and masculinity are reconfigured as revolutions unfold.

See also *Anthony, Susan B.; Inequality; Woman's Rights Movement.*

JEFFREY N. WASSERSTROM

BIBLIOGRAPHY

Applewhite, Harriet, and Darline G. Levy, eds. *Women and Politics in the Age of the Democratic Revolution.* Ann Arbor: University of Michigan Press, 1990.

Hunt, Lynn. *The Family Romance of the French Revolution.* Berkeley: University of California Press, 1994.

Kruks, Sonia, Rayna Rapp, and Marilyn B. Young, eds. *Promissory Notes: Women in the Transition to Socialism.* New York: Monthly Review Press, 1989.

Moghadam, Valentine M. "Gender and Revolutions." In *Theorizing Revolutions.* Edited by John Foran. New York: Routledge, 1997.

Rowbotham, Sheila. *Women in Movement: Feminism and Social Action.* New York: Routledge, 1992.

Tétrault, Mary Ann, ed. *Women and Revolution in Africa, Asia, and the New World.* Columbia: University of South Carolina Press, 1994.

Wasserstrom, Jeffrey N. "Gender and Revolution in Europe and Asia." *Journal of Women's History* 5 (winter 1994): 170–183; and 6 (spring 1994): 109–120.

GERMAN NAZI REVOLUTION (1933–1945)

The German Nazi revolution refers to the political revolution in Germany brought about by Adolf Hitler's National Socialist Party between 1933 and 1945. The National Socialist German Workers' Party, founded in 1920, was one of many small radical nationalist organizations that flourished in Germany in the aftermath of German defeat in World War I. Its leaders promised national renewal and social transformation. When Hitler was appointed chancellor of Germany on January 30, 1933, his followers declared a national revolution. Germany was turned into a one-party state, society was made to conform with National Socialist values, and the regime embarked on a course of state-led racial discrimination and territorial expansion. The National Socialist revolution was exported to the rest of Europe during World War II, as the regime tried to establish a Germanic empire across the continent. German capitulation in May 1945 ended the National Socialist revolution.

THE RISE TO POWER

The rise of the National Socialist Party was a direct consequence of the deep national crisis experienced by German society following German defeat in November 1918. A period of revolutionary turmoil ensued, during which, in January 1919, the young German Communist Party (KPD) tried to stage a coup in imitation of Lenin's Bolsheviks. The communist movement was violently suppressed by the new democratic regime. Then came the peace treaty, signed at Versailles in June 1919, which called for Germany to disarm and to pay reparations and stripped Germany of colonies, fleet, and extensive territory and raw material resources. Four years of rising inflation and social conflict followed Versailles, culminating in November 1923 in the collapse of the German currency. That same month the National Socialists launched an abortive coup d'état in Munich, the German city where the movement had been founded.

In 1924 the currency was revalued and the National Socialists were banned by the democratic Weimar government. Hitler was imprisoned. But two years later the movement revived when Hitler was released, and a network of party branches was rapidly established across Germany. When the fragile economic recovery and political stabilization of Germany was undermined by the onset of a severe economic slump early in 1929, social conflict was renewed and millions of Germans began to move to the political extremes. The Communist Party doubled its number of seats in the

German parliament between 1928 and 1932, and political violence on the streets of Germany's major cities took a mounting toll. Fearful of communism, millions of Germans began to look for some radical alternative. The National Socialist Party was the main beneficiary. The moderate parties of the center and left found their appeal fading in a climate of economic desperation and social confrontation. The National Socialist share of the vote increased from 2.6 percent in 1928 to 37.4 percent in the election of July 1932.

The National Socialists benefited from the radicalization of German society for a number of reasons. Their ideology was both nationalist and social revolutionary. The party promised a new, classless society, a program of moral renewal and racial development, and an end to parliamentary decadence and Marxist agitation. It also promised to revive Germany as a great power by rejecting the peace settlement of 1919 and stimulating a sense of national pride and assertiveness. Above all, the party and its leader, Hitler, were not tainted by association with the old political order. Hitler promised a revolutionary transformation of Germany under his messianic leadership, an appeal that was skillfully exploited by the party's propaganda machine run by Joseph Goebbels.

The appeal of the movement crossed the social divisions. Support came from millions of impoverished German farmers, disillusioned intellectuals who rejected Westernism and democracy, small traders ruined by economic modernization, and millions of German manual workers. The revolutionary appeal of the party and its fierce anti-Marxism attracted workers who disliked socialist militancy but wanted a new kind of society. Manual workers made up 39 percent of the National Socialist electorate in 1932, which was little less than the 42 percent composed of farmers, small businessmen, and professionals. The party failed to win the support of a majority of workers, however, and made fewer inroads in Catholic areas of Germany. The party created a social alliance of those bourgeois and working-class groups hostile to the left but profoundly disillusioned with liberal democracy. When Hitler was appointed chancellor in 1933, he lacked a parliamentary majority, but he was unquestionably the most popular politician in Germany.

THE NATIONAL SOCIALISTS IN POWER

In power, Hitler insisted on a legal road to revolution rather than a crude seizure of the state. On February 27, 1933, the German parliament passed an emergency decree giving the regime extraordinary powers to use against the Marxist parties. Thousands of National Socialist opponents were rounded up by the party's paramilitary wing, the SA (Sturmabteilung), and put in makeshift prisons or camps. On March 26, 1933, a more comprehensive enabling law was passed that gave Hitler's government unlimited powers to suspend civil rights and rule by terror. On July 14 parliament passed the Law against the Establishment of Parties (the socialist parties were already banned from parliament), and Germany became formally a one-party state. The following year the death of President Paul von Hindenburg, first elected in 1925, allowed Hitler to fuse the offices of chancellor and president and become the leader *(fuehrer)* of Germany, armed with absolute authority.

There were elements in the party that wanted Hitler to speed up the revolutionary process by removing or transforming the old institutions and social elites; some wanted German capitalism to be brought under state control. Hitler wanted to move more cautiously, relying at first on conservative allies in the military, big business, and the bureaucracy. On June 30, 1934 (the "Night of the Long Knives"), Hitler ordered the murder of Ernst Roehm, head of the SA and the leading spokesman for a "second revolution." Other opponents were killed as well, and Hitler's authority in the party was finally secured. Heinrich Himmler, leader of the SS (Schutzstaffel), the party's elite paramilitary force, took over responsibility for all internal security affairs and on June 17, 1936, was appointed national leader of all German police and security forces. Political opposition was ruthlessly stamped out. Dissidents were forced into exile or were imprisoned in a network of concentration camps set up across Germany. Between 1933 and 1939, 225,000 Germans were imprisoned for political offenses.

By the mid-1930s Hitler was secure enough in power to end his alliance with conservative politicians. The main areas of state administration were brought under the control of party leaders. Hermann Goering, head of the Luftwaffe and veteran of the party, was given responsibility for economic affairs under a four-year plan established in October 1936; in February 1938 the party's foreign affairs spokesman, Joachim von Ribbentrop, became foreign minister; finally, in February 1938 Hitler appointed himself supreme commander of the armed forces. From 1938 onward the party began to encroach on all the major areas of state administration, and Hitler's dictatorial powers reached their fullest extent.

GERMAN SOCIETY AND NATIONAL SOCIALISM

The National Socialist revolution was introduced piecemeal in Germany after 1933. No area of social or cultural life was free of its influence. The party organized German society on corporate lines. Corporations were established representing labor and management, craft workers, farmers, women, artists and writers, and the many professions. Women were encour-

At a mass rally, Adolf Hitler (left) greets Heinrich Himmler, who served as chief of the Gestapo from 1936 to 1945.

aged to stay at home raising sons for the fatherland and were excluded from most professions and from politics, which were seen as the preserve of the male. The regime dictated what could be produced culturally and banned hundreds of authors and artists. The press was controlled. Youth movements were closed down, and all young Germans were compelled to join the Hitler Youth or the League of German Maidens. Compulsory labor service was introduced for young men and women. Everywhere the party supervised the conduct of public affairs. The uplifted arm of the Hitler salute came to symbolize the individual's commitment to the new cause. Membership of the party expanded substantially, while active dissent declined. There were 849,000 members in 1933, but an estimated 8 million by 1945.

The party sought to impose a revolution of values as much as a social revolution. The structure of society changed little during the period of National Socialist rule. The economy remained largely in private hands, though subject to such close state regulation that by 1939 business independence had been almost entirely eroded. National Socialist economists developed the concept of the "managed economy," an economy private in form but responsible for carrying out national tasks as set by the leaders of the state. The change in values was more important to National Socialism than was the transformation of economic ownership. The party sought a classless society, one in which the individual was willing to merge with the national community, rejecting selfish materialist interests for the sake of the development of the nation as a whole. The new society was to emphasize the martial virtues of obedience, loyalty, and honor.

Above all, the new society was to be developed on clear biological lines. The most revolutionary element in National Socialist ideology was the commitment to racial engineering and racial cleansing. On July 26, 1933, the Law for the Prevention of Hereditarily Diseased Progeny was announced, giving the state the right to enforce compulsory sterilization. In the 1936 penal code, crimes against the race were defined to include prostitution, abortion, and homosexuality. At least 50,000 homosexuals were prosecuted, and 5,000 were sent to concentration camps. In the spring of 1939 Hitler ordered the state murder of all those with mental or physical disabilities, who had come to be seen as a threat to the survival of the pure racial stock. The chief enemy of racial hygiene was deemed to be the Jew, and from the announcement of the Nuremberg Laws in September 1935 the Jews were singled out for legal discrimination. They lost citizenship rights and the right to marry non-Jews, and they were driven out of the professions, economic life, and education. Some 247,000 emigrated in the 1930s. Those who remained suffered persistent persecution. The regime was committed to racial cleansing and a program of raising German "race-consciousness" as a necessary precondition for building the new Germanic community.

WAR AND GENOCIDE

The remilitarization of Germany was also a major priority for the regime. By the late 1930s extensive rearmament and economic preparations were under way to turn the new Germany into a military superpower. Hitler's object was to extend German domination over eastern and central Europe and to create a racial empire in the east ruled by the new National Socialist elites. When war broke out in September 1939, a series of rapid German victories paved the way for the establishment of what was called the New Order in Europe. The object of the New Order was to transform Germany into the prosperous, industrialized heartland of an economic region kept in permanent subordination to German needs. In June 1941 German armies invaded the Soviet Union to complete the process of empire building.

The war against the Soviet Union was seen as a war against the Marxist enemy, led by Jewish Bolsheviks who dominated the mass of racially inferior Slavs. The war in the east was an attempt to export the revolution that had been introduced into Germany eight years before. The German invaders destroyed the political elites and cultural life of the areas they conquered and imposed a policy of racial cleansing, which led to the deaths of an estimated six million Jews and perhaps as many as seventeen million Poles, Russians, Ukrainians, and Belorussians. Much of the Jewish population of the rest of occupied Europe was also rounded up and exterminated between 1942 and 1945.

The revolution of values under National Socialism made possible the transformation of the ethnic geography and political complexion of eastern Europe through programs of extraordinary barbarity. The fantastic vision of a Germanic empire based on racial hierarchy and the permanent militarization of German society—a latter-day Roman Empire—was under construction even while German forces fought to maintain the momentum of German victory. Only comprehensive defeat by the Allied powers of America, Britain, and the Soviet Union prevented that vision from becoming reality.

The National Socialist revolution was a failure. Its consequences were almost all negative. Following Hitler's suicide on April 30, 1945, the movement disintegrated. Allied de-Nazification programs were set up inside occupied Germany, but the majority of National Socialists abandoned their ideology and their revolutionary zeal overnight. Those leaders who had not been killed or committed suicide were put on trial at Nuremberg in 1946, and the nature of the regime was fully exposed to the view of the German public. Small parties embracing elements of National Socialism were established in the years after 1945, but they recruited only a tiny number of right-wing radicals. In most other respects the legacy of National Socialism failed to endure beyond defeat.

See also *Dictatorship; Hitler, Adolf; Italian Fascist Revolution (1919–1945).*

R. J. Overy

BIBLIOGRAPHY

Bartov, Omer. *Hitler's Army: Soldiers, Nazis and War in the Third Reich.* Oxford: Oxford University Press, 1991.

Burleigh, Michael, and Wolfgang Wippermann. *The Racial State: Germany, 1933–1945.* Cambridge, England: Cambridge University Press, 1991.

Cesarani, David, ed. *The Final Solution: Origins and Implementation.* London: Routledge, 1994.

Crew, David, ed. *Nazism and German Society, 1933–1945.* London: Routledge, 1994.

Fischer, Conan. *The Rise of the Nazis.* Manchester, England: Manchester University Press, 1997.

Frei, Norbert. *National Socialist Rule in Germany: The Fuehrer State, 1933–1945.* Oxford: Oxford University Press, 1993.

Kater, Michael H. *The Nazi Party, 1933–1945: A Social Profile of Members and Leaders, 1919–1945.* Oxford: Basil Blackwell, 1983.

Kershaw, Ian. *The "Hitler Myth": Image and Reality in the Third Reich.* Oxford: Oxford University Press, 1987.

Overy, Richard J. *War and Economy in the Third Reich.* Oxford: Oxford University Press, 1994.

Schoenbaum, David. *Hitler's Social Revolution: Class and Status in Nazi Germany 1933–1939.* New York: W.W. Norton, 1980.

GERMAN PEASANT WAR (1524–1526)

The greatest rural insurrection in premodern European history occurred between mid-1524 and 1526 in the central and southern parts of the Holy Roman Empire (corresponding to present-day Alsace, France; parts of Switzerland; the Austrian lands of Vorarlberg, Tyrol, Styria, Carinthia, and Upper Austria; and the German states of Baden-Württemberg, Bavaria, Rhineland-Pfalz, and Thuringia). Its causes have been variously located in rising rents and servile dues to replace lost seigneurial incomes, social tensions created by population increases in the villages, and new tax burdens imposed by the princely states. The Peasant War, the peak of a long wave of rural revolts, began in the southern Black Forest and spread eastward across Swabia and westward across the Rhine, engulfing Alsace, Franconia, Thuringia, and the Austrian lands. The high point came when the Upper Swabian rebels formed the Christian Union at Memmingen on March 7, 1525, and issued the movement's programmatic "Twelve Articles of the Swabian Peasantry." The movement was crushed by the Swabian League, a regional federation of rulers, in a series of military actions, the last in Tyrol in 1526.

The Twelve Articles are held to be an archetypal statement of the rebels' grievances. The rebels demanded an end to serfdom and servile dues; restoration of the common pastures, woods, and waters as the basis of communal agriculture; and recognition of the villages' right to nominate and depose pastors and collect and distribute the church taxes (tithe). The grievance list displays a developed sense of village needs and the desire for peasants' representation in a more responsive and effective state. The insurrection's more comprehensive programs reveal a general consciousness of the state and show that the German Peasant War was by no means simply a reaction to local economic grievances.

ACHIEVEMENTS

There is little disagreement among scholars about the insurrection's course or the reasons for its defeat. Although peasants attracted support from burghers, miners, priests, and even some nobles, the movement's military weaknesses were insuperable. The rotation of men from the villages into regionally organized bands diluted the effects of drilling them with weapons, and the armies were woefully weak in experienced military leadership. The decisive tactical weakness, however, was the rebels' lack of cavalry and artillery. They won only one battle, at Schladming in Styria (July 3, 1525).

The Peasant War ended partly in military defeats, partly in negotiated truces followed by treaties. Leaders, where captured, were commonly executed. There are no reliable figures for casualties, though the traditional figure for the rebel dead, men and women, is 100,000; almost nothing is known about the participants in the rebel armies, including women and some clergy.

The rebels' defeat in the Peasant War by no means ended rural resistance in the Holy Roman Empire, though the tempo of rural revolt slackened by the mid-eighteenth century. The chief post-1525 changes were a geographical shift in the revolt from the southwest, including Switzerland, to the eastern lands of Austria, Saxony, Silesia, and Lusatia and a shift in targets from feudal dues and serfdom to state taxes. Furthermore, the post-1525 "judicialization" of resistance shows that peasants learned to employ the courts against their seigneurs.

PEASANTS' WAR AS REVOLUTION

The Peasant War's revolutionary character has been much debated. Following the line taken by Friedrich Engels, Max Steinmetz, the leading expert in the German Democratic Republic (d. 1990), identified the war as the high point of a movement from 1476 to 1535 that he called "the early bourgeois revolution," the historical task of which was to promote the transition to capitalism and the creation of a unified national state. Peter Blickle, currently the principal German authority on this subject, holds that the Peasant War marked the culmination of a communal movement, which since its rise among peasants (and burghers) around 1300 represented an alternative to absolutism in German political development.

These arguments, especially Blickle's, are supported by the programmatic documents from the movement itself. In the larger states, rebels demanded an end to political privilege based on the ownership of land and the command of servile labor and parliamentary representation of the common people through their local communes; in the highly fragmented regions, they proposed whole new states based on their own federations, roughly on the model of the Swiss rural states. The most sophisticated program, Michael Gaismair's (d. 1528) "Tyrolean Constitution," proposed to reorganize the Tyrolean state according to the common good of the whole territory. He wanted to abolish feudal and urban privileges; eliminate the clergy's temporal jurisdiction; reorganize weights, measures, and money; and manage trade through centrally located markets.

The Peasant War's connection to the Protestant Reformation is a major theme of modern research. The most important link was the idea of a "godly law," which was related to, although it preceded, Martin Luther's biblicism *(sola scriptura,* meaning "by the Bible alone"). The rebels' appeal to "godly law" aimed to neutralize the local fragmentation of peasant consciousness and to legitimize nontraditional appeals to justice. Article 3 of the Twelve Articles, for example, argues against serfdom: because Jesus shed His blood for all, the shepherd as well as the king, no man should own another. The Peasant War's leading theorist, the theologian Thomas Müntzer (d. 1525), identified the movement with an apocalyptic struggle of the righteous common people against their unchristian rulers.

Luther both encouraged and condemned the Peasant War. His early vernacular writings may fairly be said to have contained calls for direct action by the authorities in behalf of reform, and the village communes and federations certainly thought of themselves as authorities. The rebels of 1525 undoubtedly regarded Luther as one of their spokesmen. Luther, however, had already *(On Temporal Authority,* 1523) decided that Christians were bound to obey the temporal ruler, whose authority came directly from God, and while he recognized the cause of the 1525 rebels in terms of temporal justice, he condemned them for employing religious arguments to justify direct action for temporal ends. His decision sealed the antirevolutionary character of Lutheran policy, though Calvinist revolutionary doctrine grew partly out of German Lutheran roots. The widely believed proposition that Luther's condemnation of the Peasant War gave rise to an especially German propensity for political quietism is a legend.

Finally, it is worth mentioning that for four hundred years the Peasant War has served as a point of historical reference for German liberalism and socialism. In 1945 Thomas Mann, the most famous German writer, then in American exile, called it Germany's lost chance at a libertarian revolution, while the German Democratic Republic chose the Peasant War as its chief positive point of reference in the premodern past and adopted the revolutionary Müntzer as one of its heroes. Müntzer's stature as a sixteenth-century revolutionary rests to a great degree on his participation and death in the Peasant War; though many have tried to derive from his difficult writings a revolutionary doctrine relevant to modern revolutionism, no one has ever succeeded.

See also *Anabaptism; Luther, Martin.*

Thomas Brady Jr.

BIBLIOGRAPHY

Blickle, Peter. *The Revolution of 1525: The German Peasant War from a New Perspective.* Translated by Thomas A. Brady Jr. and H. C. Erik Midelfort. Baltimore, Md.: Johns Hopkins University Press, 1981.

Blickle, Peter, Hans-Christoph Rublack, and Winfried Schulze. *Religion, Politics, and Social Protest: Three Studies on Early Modern Germany,* edited by Kaspar von Greyerz, 61–98. London: George Allen and Unwin, 1984.

Scott, Tom. "The Peasant War: A Historiographical Review." *Historical Journal* 22 (1979): 693–720, 953–974.

Scott, Tom, and Bob Scribner, eds. *The German Peasant War: A History in Documents.* Atlantic Highlands, N.J.: Humanities Press International, 1991.

Scribner, Bob, and Gerhard Benecke, eds. *The German Peasant War: New Viewpoints.* London and Atlantic Highlands, N.J.: Humanities Press International, 1979.

GERMAN REVOLUTION (1918)

After four years of war and with defeat imminent, Germans saw a complex series of events lead in 1918 to revolution in Germany's major cities. The emperor abdicated and fled to the Netherlands. A new government led by the Social Democrats (SPD) proclaimed a republic and, hard-pressed on all sides, oversaw the ending of the war.

BEGINNING OF THE END OF WAR

The regime change in Germany was closely linked to the collapse of the military effort. The 1918 spring offensive had brought German troops to within thirty-five miles of Paris, but by mid-July the forward movement had been stopped. On August 8 an Allied tank attack broke the German lines. In the weeks of retreat that followed, Germany's political and military leaders, recognizing the unavoidable, named new leaders and created more representative institutions in order to improve the likelihood of favorable peace terms.

In early October 1918, Prince Maximilian of Baden was named to replace Chancellor Georg Hertling. Ministers, for the first time, were drawn from Germany's parliament, the Reichstag, including representatives of the moderate centrist parties and Social Democrats. Prince Max, as he was called, announced a series of reforms. Constitutional changes provided for ministerial responsibility to parliament and civilian control over the military. Reform of the discriminatory Prussian three-class system was promised but not carried through.

Although of far-reaching importance, the changes had limited impact because public attention was focused on the collapse of the military and its implications. With losses continuing on all fronts and with serious privations at home, the regime faced a general loss of legitimacy. Both the armed forces and the civilian population wished an immediate end to hostilities.

In late October an "admirals' rebellion" occurred. Rather than surrendering the fleet, the commanders, acting without authorization from the new government, planned a last final engagement—a manifestly futile North Sea battle against the British. This event brought about a sailors' rebellion, which was followed by takeovers of important north German cities. The army garrisons there gave little or no opposition, the soldiers refusing to fight or in some instances joining the insurgents. Workers' and soldiers' councils were formed which called for an end to the war and for democratization.

Austria too was facing imminent collapse, and on November 4 Emperor Charles I agreed with the Allies to an armistice. The Austrian armed forces collapsed and a republic was declared. In neighboring Bavaria, Kurt Eisner, an Independent Social Democrat, called for an end to the war and for a regime change. On November 8 insurgents took over in Munich, expelled the monarchy, and announced a Bavarian republic. The next day the revolutionary activity spilled over into Berlin and into all German capitals.

The developments in Bavaria and Berlin led Prince Max to urge the most decisive personal change, the removal of the emperor. Within a few hours, William II was en route to exile in the Netherlands. Prince Max then resigned and passed the chancellorship to Friedrich Ebert, the moderate SPD leader.

Although a republic was not specified in these hasty arrangements, at a giant rally on November 9, Philipp Scheidemann, the second-ranking Social Democrat, announced that the Hohenzollerns had abdicated and added, "Long live the German Republic." The enthusiastic response to that statement foreclosed one option, that of a constitutional monarchy. That declaration was challenged the same day by Karl Liebknecht, leader of the Spartacus League (later the German Communist Party), who called for a German socialist republic.

The armistice was signed and took effect on November 11, 1918. The war was over. But the new government faced enormous problems. Most pressing of all: food had to be supplied for both the civilian and military populations. Moreover, because the armistice required the immediate withdrawal of the armies from all fronts, millions of men had to be transported home and demobilized. Interim governing arrangements were needed in cities where authority was in dispute.

In the meantime, groups on the left were presenting demands and soon posed serious challenges. The election for the Constituent Assembly, which would write a new constitution, was set for January 19, 1919. Thus a framework, party organization, and campaign effort were needed, as well as consideration of new forms of government.

The new regime soon faced legitimation problems. Ignoring facts he well knew, army chief of staff general Erich Ludendorff declared the army had been "stabbed in the back." Used also by Gen. Paul von Hindenburg, who along with Ludendorff directed the German war effort, the image soon became a staple for nationalist demagogues. Ebert added to the problem by telling returning troops they were "undefeated in the field." The leaders of the new regime were soon denounced as the "November criminals." The Treaty of Versailles, setting the terms of the peace, would not be signed until June 1919. From the outset, however, it was clear that the costs for Germany would be very heavy.

Ebert's government initially was "socialist," consisting of the SPD and the Independent Social Democrats, a group that had broken away from the SPD in 1917 over the question of war aims. But "socialism" was not an immediate concern for either party. The Independent Social Democrats left the government before Christmas. In early 1919 the Constituent Assembly met in Weimar to write a constitution that gave direct governing power to the Reichstag. In February Ebert was named president of the new Weimar Republic. For several weeks the SPD ruled alone until Social Democrat Philipp Scheidemann formed a coalition government that included the Center (Catholic) Party and the left-liberal Democrats. Given the immediate concerns, the lack of a specific mandate, and the constraints provided by the coalition partners, no serious efforts toward socialism were undertaken.

A THREAT FROM THE LEFT

From the outset of the new regime, Ebert and the moderate SPD leaders had faced a threat from the left, some of whose members took as a model the new revolutionary government in Russia with its local soviets (councils). Given the presence of council governments in many cities, some conflict was anticipated. But at a meeting of the Congress of Councils in mid-December 1918, with representatives from across the nation, it was clear the moderates were in complete control.

Early on, Ebert had made an alliance with Gen. Wilhelm Groener, General Ludendorff's successor, providing for mutual guarantees of protection. The new government would see to the orderly retreat of troops still on foreign soil, guarantee the integrity of the army, and ensure respect for its commanders. In exchange, some new and "reliable" paramilitary units, *Freikorps* (Free Corps), would be formed to maintain order against revolutionary threats. The *Freikorps* soon did fight in German cities and later in a series of border struggles—characterized by exceptional brutality—on the much-disputed new eastern frontier.

The leftist forces, led by the Berlin-based group Spartacus, formed the Communist Party (KPD) in the last days of 1918. On January 5, 1919, the party leaders called for a revolution to begin the next day. Social Democratic leaders called out Berlin workers to defend the new government, a task largely completed before intervention by the *Freikorps* toward the end of the week.

A second KPD action that began in Berlin in March with a general strike also was put down by *Freikorps* units. In mid-April a leftist insurgency took over in Munich. In the first week of May the *Freikorps* "liberated" the city, killing some six hundred persons, most of them workers. These units were active in many cities.

Early in 1920 the government, as mandated by the Versailles Treaty, ordered the dissolution of the *Freikorps*. The response was the Kapp Putsch, an attempted takeover of the government by *Freikorps* units facing dissolution, in mid-March. The government was forced out of Berlin. A general strike followed, and the insurgent units withdrew from Berlin a week later. The government used the *Freikorps* to defeat a KPD-inspired response to the putsch in Ruhr cities. But then the units were dissolved.

The first Reichstag election followed on June 6, 1920. In the election the coalition parties all suffered serious losses.

One major consequence: the Social Democrats withdrew from the government. For the next decade Germany was governed by a shifting coalition of "bourgeois" parties.

The events of 1919–1920 do not fit well within any standard social science theory. One observer, Walther Rathenau, commented that the general strike of a defeated army was called the German Revolution, but it was, he said, a *Revolution aus versehen*—an inadvertent revolution.

See also *German Nazi Revolution (1933–1945); Hungarian Revolutions (1918–1919); Italian Fascist Revolution (1919–1945); Russian Revolution of 1917.*

RICHARD F. HAMILTON

BIBLIOGRAPHY

Comfort, Richard A. *Revolutionary Hamburg: Labor Politics in the Early Weimar Republic.* Stanford, Calif.: Stanford University Press, 1966.

Horn, Daniel. *The German Naval Mutinies of World War I.* New Brunswick, N.J.: Rutgers University Press, 1969.

MacDonald, Stephen C. *A German Revolution: Local Change and Continuity in Prussia, 1918–1920.* New York: Garland, 1991.

Mitchell, Allen. *Revolution in Bavaria, 1918–1919: The Eisner Regime and the Soviet Republic.* Princeton, N.J.: Princeton University Press, 1965.

Waite, Robert G. L. *Vanguard of Nazism: The Free Corps Movement in Postwar Germany 1918–1923.* New York: Norton, 1969 (original, 1952).

GHANAIAN INDEPENDENCE MOVEMENT (1946–1957)

The political movement that brought independence to Ghana in 1957, the Convention People's Party (CPP), made a revolutionary impact on Ghanaian political life, the social location of power in Ghanaian politics thereafter, the structure and dominant ideological ethos of future Ghanaian politics, the pace of African decolonization, and the movement for African unity. A revolution involves a rapid and basic change in the domestic political system, its dominant values, the dominant social class, leadership, government institutions, and types of political activity. The CPP under Kwame Nkrumah's leadership generated a political revolution in Ghana and stimulated political change elsewhere in Africa by its behavior, single-party structure, and impact on decolonization and African unity.

RADICAL POPULIST ANTICOLONIALISM

The CPP was born of a split in the first postwar nationalist movement in the (then) Gold Coast, the United Gold Coast Convention (UGCC). The UGCC was a loosely organized movement founded in 1946 by the tiny bourgeois-professional class. Its members were closely allied with the major traditional leaders (chiefs) and assumed that they and their class would succeed the British in power. These lawyers and merchants, part-time politicians, recruited from England in late 1947 a young Ghanaian, Kwame Nkrumah (then thirty-eight), to run the UGCC full-time. Nkrumah had left Ghana in 1935 to study in the United States, where he spent a decade and attended college and graduate school; from the United States he moved to England, where he engaged in political organizing of West Africans.

Postwar political and economic conditions and Nkrumah's leadership turned a series of somewhat sedate UGCC protests in 1947–1949 into a mass movement. Ghanaians were outraged by high postwar inflation and import scarcities, impatient with the slow pace of constitutional change, and mobilized by general wartime promises of self-determination and successful independence movements in Asia. Briefly jailed after the 1948 riots, the bourgeois UGCC leaders opted for law and order and joined a new constitutional committee.

Nkrumah and the nationalist movement animated a wide range of urban and rural groups with intense economic grievances: trade unionists, cocoa farmers, small traders, ex-servicemen, and the unemployed. Radical populist protest had two sources within the commoner class: an increasingly educated stratum of "youngmen" struggling for power against their British-controlled chiefs; and elementary school graduates fighting against the obstacles to education and jobs posed by the colonial social order composed of chiefs, colonial economy, and British rule. Nkrumah appealed broadly to the commoner class, which was already organized in youth societies in many towns and villages throughout the colony and Ashanti areas (southern Ghana). Nkrumah's militant demand for "Self-Government Now," his egalitarianism, and his rapport with the discontented youth made him the commoners' champion. The CPP was founded on June 12, 1949.

Militant nationalism between 1948 and 1954 transformed Ghanaian political life: the mass movement delegitimated and undermined British rule and commenced the creation of a nation from a multiethnic territory; the populist movement altered the social class location of power, shifting it from the British and chiefs to the CPP, led by elementary school graduates and teachers. In the 1951 elections the CPP won a majority of the elective Legislative Assembly seats. Nkrumah, who had been jailed in early 1950, was freed to head a new internal self-rule government, which was re-elected in 1954 and 1956. A new Local Government Act passed in 1952 ended the power of "indirect rule" chiefs and put local power in the hands of largely elective local councils, dominated by commoners. Rear-guard struggles by chiefs and elders led to some local violence and helped generate support for most of the ethnic and regional opposition

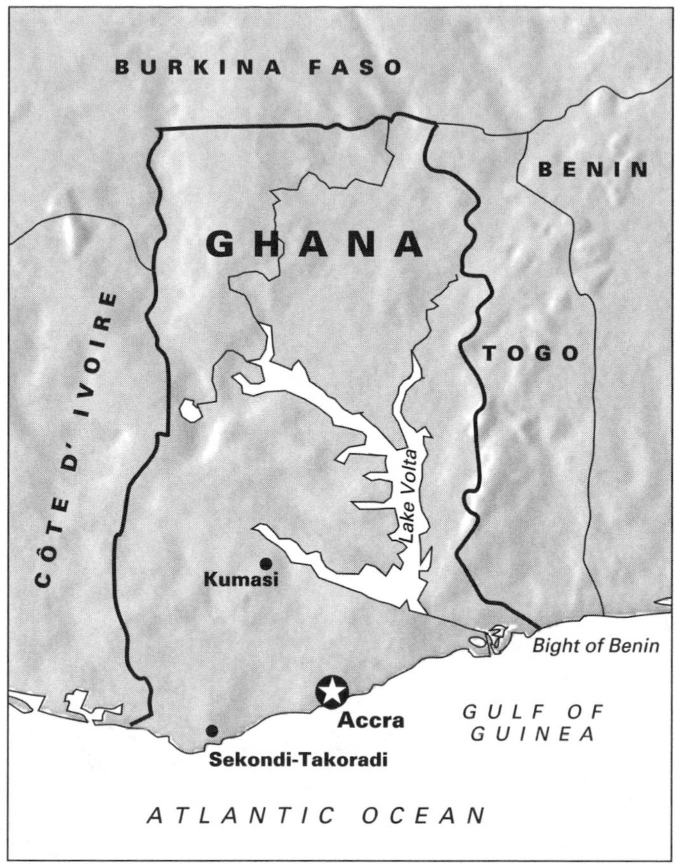

movements that developed in 1953–1956, the most important and violent in the cocoa- and gold-rich Ashanti region. But the rule (not the influence) of the chiefs was fundamentally undermined, and a democratic and egalitarian ethos was spread by the CPP commoners and their allies.

STATE SOCIALISM AND RADICAL CHANGE

Practical political compromises and the need for electoral success made the CPP into a nationalist omnibus in the 1950s, on which all were encouraged to climb in order to defeat the British and regional-, ethnic-, and religious-based parties. Public policies were mildly populist; economic policy was capitalist. But foreign capital still dominated cocoa marketing, mining, wholesale- and retail-level import-export trade, commerce, transport, and industry.

After independence Nkrumah sought to develop a new socialist political base to support more nationalist economic policies. Nkrumah had ambitious plans to industrialize, which required state initiatives given the low levels of investment by foreign and local capital. During 1959–1960 Nkrumah promoted younger, militant lieutenants in new organizations at the expense of the CPP "old guard" cabinet ministers who had led the independence struggle. CPP factional conflicts became intense; old guard "capitalists" were drummed out of the CPP. Cocoa trade was nationalized; many state corporations were started in industry and commerce; and new state secretariats were created. But debilitating factional conflicts and several assassination attempts against Nkrumah led him to jettison the young radicals. Nkrumah continued to promote the state sector as the engine of growth and Marxist-Leninist language as appropriate political speech. But Nkrumah never sought to build an ideological cadre party to replace the local-based mass party.

THE CPP POLITICAL LEGACY

The military overthrew the Nkrumah government in February 1966, banning the CPP and all its party wings. The party had become amorphous, its leaders often corrupt, and its elections fraudulent. Although many CPP members of parliament voiced public complaints, Nkrumah was highly dictatorial and nonaccountable. Despite this authoritarianism, the CPP and the government's populist policies and statist development strategy had an enduring impact in defining future boundaries of morally rightful public policies and visions. Its populist ideological ethos, legitimation of state power, and organizational networks created a CPP legacy that has persisted in Ghanaian political life for more than thirty years. New CPP/Nkrumahist parties are reborn with each period of civilian rule, struggling to claim the CPP legacy. A CPP-based party won the elections in 1979, but its leaders were corrupt and cynical. Flight Lieutenant Jerry Rawlings also called on populist sentiment during his authoritarian rule (1982–1992). Despite new CPP-based parties in the Fourth Republic (1993–), Rawlings was elected twice as president by capturing much of the old CPP constituencies and articulating populist visions.

See also *Nkrumah, Kwame.*

Jon Kraus

BIBLIOGRAPHY

Apter, David. *Ghana in Transition.* 2d ed. rev. Princeton, N.J.: Princeton University Press, 1972.

Austin, Dennis. *Politics in Ghana.* London: Oxford University Press, 1964.

Bing, Geoffrey. *Reap the Whirlwind.* London: Macgibbon and Kee, 1968.

Bretton, Henry. *The Rise and Fall of Kwame Nkrumah.* New York: Praeger, 1966.

Ikoku, Samuel G. *Le Ghana de Nkrumah.* Translated by Yves Benot. Paris: Frances Maspero, 1971.

James, C. L. R. *Nkrumah and the Ghana Revolution.* London: Allison and Busby, 1977.

Jones, Trevor. *Ghana's First Republic, 1960–1966.* London: Methuen, 1976.

Owusu, Maxwell. *Uses and Abuses of Political Power.* Chicago: University of Chicago Press, 1970.

GORBACHEV, MIKHAIL

Gorbachev (1931–), born in the village of Privolnoye in Stavropol Province, a fertile land of the north Caucasus, inadvertently helped bring the 1917 Russian Revolution to an early close. The father of Soviet *perestroika,* or restructuring, he experienced a life trajectory resembling that of millions of his compatriots: a middling-peasant family background; the somersault of the rural social order with collectivization; the arrest (and release) in the Terror of his collective-farm-chairman grandfather; the (brief) deportation to Siberia of his other grandfather; the World War II front for his father (who somehow survived); the Nazi occupation for the women and children left behind in the village; and Communist Youth League (Komsomol) service, migration to the city, and Communist Party membership for Mikhail. He rose, and despite the devastating hardships the country rose along with him—he just got further than most, only to bring everything down.

Like his father and grandfather, Gorbachev might have become a farmer, but Stalin's upheavals of the 1930s brought—besides death and destruction—expanded educational opportunities. Mikhail completed eight grades in the village, two more in the district center twenty kilometers away, and set his sights on a university education, aiming not for the local ones but for Moscow. With a peasant-worker background, a pupil's silver medal, a high state award for helping bring in the harvest, and precocious candidate membership in the party, Gorbachev was accepted, and in 1950 made the leap to the Soviet capital. During his five years at Moscow State University's law faculty, the Stavropol hayseed came into contact with a handful of erudite professors as well as members of the Moscow cultural elite, met and married Raisa Titorenko, mourned the death of Stalin, and wrote a thesis setting out socialism's superiority to capitalism. Posted upon graduation to the Stavropol procuracy, Gorbachev switched almost immediately to a position in the Komsomol bureaucracy and set about organizing discussion groups in remote settlements in order, as he explains in his autobiography, to "fling open a window to the world." As he climbed the Komsomol ladder, Nikita Khrushchev's de-Stalinization provided a boost. But Gorbachev writes that survivalist functionaries sabotaged the Moscow-instigated reforms. In 1964 the top party elite removed Khrushchev in a conspiracy.

Khrushchev became a memory, local officials advanced higher, and Gorbachev was shifted in 1966 to the party bureaucracy. By 1970 he had climbed to first secretary for Stavropol Province. Because his fief happened to be a southern region where the central elite maintained sanatoria, he played host to many top figures in the leadership, including KGB chief Yuri Andropov. It was Andropov who in 1978 arranged Gorbachev's transfer to Moscow as the new chief of the Central Committee agricultural department. This assignment was followed in 1980 by promotion to full membership in the Politburo. Andropov, who succeeded Leonid Brezhnev in 1982, placed Gorbachev in charge of new appointments, allowing his protégé to congratulate personally those marked for elevation. Andropov was ill, however, and upon his death in 1984 the old guard blocked Gorbachev's path. Yet once the invalid Konstantin Chernenko also passed away, in 1985, the surviving septua- and octogenarians had little choice but to anoint the one relative youth in their midst. With the support of the KGB (Andropov's old power base) as well as officials in the Central Committee and economic ministries whose appointments he had overseen, the fifty-four-year-old Gorbachev became general secretary for what looked like a very long time.

Mikhail Gorbachev

As head of the party, and later Soviet president, Gorbachev led the country on a quest for reformed socialism, but his program of *perestroika* culminated in the autoliquidation of both socialism and the USSR. Unable to control or counter the forces he had helped set in motion, he officially disbanded the USSR and stepped down in December

1991. However, Gorbachev left the deepest of impressions on his times, above all, in the area of disarmament.

See also *USSR Collapse and Dissolution (1989–1991).*

STEPHEN KOTKIN

BIBLIOGRAPHY

Brown, Archie, ed. *The Soviet Union: A Biographical Dictionary.* London: Weidenfeld and Nicholson, 1990.

Gorbachev, Mikhail. *Memoirs.* New York: Doubleday, 1995.

Medvedev, Zhores. *Gorbachev.* New York: Norton, 1986.

Wieczynski, Joseph, ed. *The Gorbachev Bibliography, 1985–1991.* New York: Norman Ross, 1996.

GRAMSCI, ANTONIO

Gramsci (1891–1937), one of the greatest Marxist theorists, labor activists, and political journalists of the twentieth century, was born in the small town of Ales in Sardinia. Influenced by Karl Marx, Benedetto Croce, and the Italian Marxist Antonio Labriola, he joined the Italian Socialist Party in 1913.

During World War I he became deeply radicalized, investing the bulk of his energies in the militant Turin working-class movement associated with both the emergent council formations and the Italian Socialist Party. As a party journalist, Gramsci hoped to articulate the theories of the spontaneous popular movements of Turin. Sharply disillusioned when party leadership failed to take advantage of revolutionary opportunities during 1916–1919, Gramsci and other leading Italian radicals founded the Italian Communist Party in 1921, with Gramsci as one of its guiding intellectual and political figures.

In 1922 Gramsci went to Moscow to serve as the Italian Communist Party representative to the Comintern. He returned to Italy just as fascism was consolidating power, and in May 1924 he was elected to parliament as a party delegate. With the right on the ascendancy, Gramsci was arrested by the regime of Benito Mussolini in November 1926. From late 1926 until just before his death in April 1937 Gramsci was confined to prison, often kept in isolation, where he suffered mounting ill health, loneliness, and detachment from the world of everyday politics.

Despite the ordeal of prison, Gramsci was able to read and write—and he indeed wrote prolifically. It was during these years that Gramsci compiled his various notes, which were eventually smuggled out by his sister-in-law, Tatiana Schucht. Systematically assembled only after World War II, these notes would come to be known as the *Prison Notebooks,* a collection of treatises that would soon be famous around the world. International pressure mounted for Gramsci's release, and he was finally given his freedom in Rome in April 1937. But by this time he was so physically and mentally broken that he died just five days after his release.

The body of Gramsci's intellectual contribution includes his early writings from the Italian Socialist Party and the journal *The New Order* (1914–1920), his prolific interventions during the Italian Communist Party years (1921–1926), and above all the *Prison Notebooks.* The *Notebooks,* which have been translated into every major language, covered amazingly diverse topics—Italian history, political affairs, education, culture, philosophy, theory of the state, and his illuminating discourses into the realm of (Marxist) political strategy. A major theme underlying his otherwise fragmented notes was the task of forging a Marxist theory and strategy adequate to the requirements of socialist transformation in the advanced industrial setting.

In the late twentieth century Gramsci became probably the most widely known of the Western Marxists who sought to free classical Marxism of its economism and determinism and who looked to a more democratic, egalitarian revolutionary process than was typical of the Soviet and other Leninist experiences. Gramsci's most famous concept was that of ideological hegemony, which pointed toward the complex forms of ideological and cultural domination that helped reproduce capitalism, especially in highly industrialized societies. To combat the spread of capitalism, Gramsci insisted on the necessity of a broad cultural war of position designed to renew civil society—that would join the more conventional war of position associated with the struggle for political and economic power. Gramsci expected influential critical thinkers immersed in the everyday life of workers to lead the struggle.

Gramsci's legacy is a powerful and multifaceted one that lives on within and without the Marxist tradition. Throughout the 1980s and 1990s Gramscian discourse entered into and helped shape a number of modern academic disciplines, including sociology, history, film studies, literature, urban planning, and anthropology. Gramsci's ideas have spread throughout the world, far outlasting the regime that sought to silence him.

See also *Communism; Italian Fascist Revolution (1919–1945); Marx, Karl, and Friedrich Engels.*

CARL BOGGS

BIBLIOGRAPHY

Adamson, Walter. *Hegemony and Revolution.* Berkeley: University of California Press, 1980.

Boggs, Carl. *The Two Revolutions: Antonio Gramsci and the Dilemmas of Western Marxism.* Boston: South End Press, 1984.

Fiori, Giuseppe. *Antonio Gramsci: Life of a Revolutionary.* New York: E. R. Dutton, 1971.

GREEK WAR OF LIBERATION (1821–1832)

In the early nineteenth century, Greek subjects of the Ottoman Empire undertook a multiyear struggle that resulted in the creation of a small, independent national state under European protection.

By 1500 A.D. Ottoman armies had conquered Asia Minor (Anatolia) and most of the Balkans. Ottoman rule initially brought significant political, social, economic, and demographic change to the mostly Christian Orthodox subject peoples. Ottoman rule effected social leveling as the local aristocracy was eliminated, subordination to imperial authority, demographic change from migrations and the settlement of new peoples, and the elaboration of an agrarian-based economic system which supplied the needs of the imperial capital, Istanbul (Constantinople), and the military.

Once Ottoman rule was established, the subject people were organized into and recognized by communities of faith. Greeks and eventually other Eastern Orthodox Christians were part of the *Rum millet,* whose leader was the Greek Orthodox patriarch. The Greeks' situation differed from that of the other Christian subjects in the Balkans in that Greek communities were widely scattered in the empire and in many cities in Europe. In time their geographic separation helped the Greeks create a socially diverse world. Among the Greeks, economic and intellectual elites developed which took advantage of contacts outside the empire and opportunities within to serve the Ottoman state. A commercial elite grew in the trading centers, local notables in the countryside established clientage relationships with the peasantry, the Greek ecclesiastical hierarchy asserted its preeminence over other Orthodox communities in the Balkans, and educational centers were established.

By the second half of the seventeenth century imperial Ottoman political and military authority was eroding in the provinces. This erosion benefited local lords and encouraged the interference of European great powers.

A SENSE OF NATION

By the early nineteenth century many Greeks who had benefited from Ottoman rule believed that it was best to maintain things as they were. This outlook prevailed among many in the ecclesiastical hierarchy, prosperous merchants, and local notables. But other Greeks felt that political change was needed to gain the full measure of progress. More important, a more defined sense of identity, beyond the traditional culture of Greek-speaking Orthodox subjects *(reaya),* crystallized among those conscious of changing times. Greeks were a distinct people, a nation *(ethnos)* whose patrimony was classical Greece and who ought to be free of foreign rule. Such ideas marked the writings of Rhigas Velestinlis (ca 1757–1798) and Adamantios Korais (1748–1833), who devoted themselves to literary work in behalf of their nation. The former envisioned a war of liberation of all the peoples in the Balkans and the creation of a federal but culturally Hellenized state, replacing the Ottomans. Korais, enamored of Western classicism, sought a nation revived by recovering its ancient legacy.

Ideas became a project with the founding of the Filiki Etairia (the Friendly Society) in 1814 in the Russian Black Sea port of Odessa by a few Greek merchants. Neither socially broad nor unified, the society recruited several thousand members, including Greeks and other Balkan Orthodox, who desired political change. Its goal was to replace the Ottoman state with one led by Greeks. To lend credibility to such a venture, the leadership purported to have support from the Russian government and managed to enlist Alexandros Ypsilantis, a Greek in the military service of the tsar, as leader.

Although the international climate at the time was against revolutionary movements, the society took action on March 6, 1821, when Ypsilantis led Etairist forces into the Danubian Principalities, hoping for a general uprising in the Balkans. Revolts broke out in the region as local leaders fought to gain or maintain political control against Sultan Mahmud II, who was seeking to recentralize imperial authority. Uprisings by Greeks in the Peloponnesos and western Greece (Rumeli) in April were as much an opportunistic response to a revolt by a local lord in Epiros, Ali Pasha, against the sultan's authority as a response to the call from the Etairists.

WAR, POLITICS, AND INTERNATIONAL DIPLOMACY

Ypsilantis's volunteers were quickly defeated by Ottoman forces, as was Ali Pasha. But in other places the Greeks were successful, and by 1822 they held much of the Peloponnesos, nearby islands (Hydra, Spetses, and Psará), and some areas north of the gulf of Corinth, including Athens, Thebes, and Mesolónghi *(see map, p. 164)*. However, they were militarily unprepared on land and sea in materiel and organization, and they were politically too disunited to make more headway. Military leaders Theodore Kolokotronis, Yannis Makriyannis, and Odysseas Androutsos favored the traditional tactics of armed bands. But like many civilian figures, such as Ioannis Kolettis, they had localized political interests.

These individuals, along with others such as Alexandros Mavrokordatos from the Danubian Principalities, did attempt to form a national, centralized government, bringing together islanders, landed notables, and armed chieftains. A national assembly was created early in 1822, but regional assemblies existed as well. Sharp rivalry within and between the various groups soon resulted in civil war. The Greek revolt survived, however, due in part to the difficulties the sultan's forces encountered in campaigning and the influx of financial aid, supplies, and volunteers from philhellenes like Lord Byron.

To defeat the Greek rebellion, Mahmud II allied with his Egyptian vassal Muhammad Ali. The latter provided his seasoned naval and land forces, under the command of his son Ibrahim, which landed in the southern Peloponnesos in February 1825. Mesolónghi fell to Ibrahim in April 1826, and Athens to the Turkish commander in June 1827.

When the Greek revolt began, the European powers reacted negatively. They feared that if the Ottoman Empire collapsed, rivalry among the great powers for territory would ensue. Many Greeks, however, looked to Britain or France for support. When they appealed to Britain for protection, under an "Act of Submission" in 1825, George Canning, the foreign secretary, sought Russia's cooperation. By the St. Petersburg Protocol (April 4, 1826), the two powers offered to mediate between the Greeks and Ottomans with an autonomous Greece as the basis. The Ottoman government eventually bowed to Russian demands on other issues in the Balkans but continued to pursue a military victory against the Greeks. This first attempt at mediation was followed by the Treaty of London (July 6, 1827), which included France in a three-power effort to bring an end to the fighting. When the Ottoman sultan refused mediation, an allied fleet was dispatched to the Mediterranean to induce a cessation of hostilities. When the fleet entered the bay of Navarino in the southern Peloponnesos to compel the Egyptian forces to stop their operations, a battle ensued which Ibrahim's navy decisively lost.

THE MAKING OF THE GREEK STATE (1827–1832)

The sultan, however, did not cease hostilities, and war with Russia commenced in April 1828, which ended in Ottoman defeat. By the Treaty of Adrianople (September 14, 1829), the sultan accepted the Treaty of London regarding Greece. Meanwhile, the Greeks, in an effort at unity, had elected Count John Kapodistrias president of their nascent state in April 1827. Doing his best in a chaotic situation and combining a fervent belief in the nation with a paternalistic attitude to governance, Kapodistrias tried to reorganize the government to limit factionalism and centralize authority.

At a conference in London (February 3, 1830), Britain, France, and Russia agreed to an independent, monarchical Greek state with limited territory and offered the crown to Prince Leopold of Saxe-Coburg. The prince refused the offer, concerned over the Greeks' reaction to the proposed frontiers. In February 1832 the crown was offered to Prince Otho, son of King Ludwig of Bavaria. In July the sultan, in return for an indemnity, recognized Greece as an independent kingdom with a slightly larger frontier than had been proposed in London. In the meantime, Kapodistrias had been assassinated (October 9, 1831) by members of the Mavromichalis clan of Mani. Order was finally restored in January 1833 with the arrival of Otho.

A Greek state independent of Ottoman authority had been created. The struggle had caused social upheaval and economic distress but had not ameliorated the condition of the peasant majority. Moreover, Greece was dependent for its national survival on the protecting powers. Political life revolved around the interventionist role of the bureaucratic state and factions based on personalities and clientage. The war for independence validated the idea of a national struggle. But the new kingdom included only a portion of the nation. To liberate the entire nation from Ottoman rule became the legitimizing principle of the state for nearly a century.

See also *European Revolutions of 1820; European Revolutions of 1830; Ottoman Revolts in the Near and Middle East (1803–1922).*

GERASIMOS AUGUSTINOS

BIBLIOGRAPHY

Clogg, Richard, ed. *The Struggle for Greek Independence.* London: Macmillan, 1973.

Dakin, Douglas. *The Greek Struggle for Independence.* Berkeley: University of California Press, 1973.

Diamandouros, Nikiforos P., John P. Anton, John A. Petropulos, and Peter Topping, eds. *Hellenism and the First Greek War of Liberation (1821–1830): Continuity and Change.* Thessaloniki: Institute for Balkan Studies, 1976.

Woodhouse, C. M. *The Battle of Navarino.* London: Hodder and Stoughton, 1965.

———. *Capodistria.* London: Oxford University Press, 1973.

———. *The Philhellenes.* Rutherford, N.J.: Fairleigh Dickinson University Press, 1971.

GRENADA "NEW JEWEL" REVOLUTION (1979–1983)

The short-lived Grenada Revolution of 1979, openly aligned with socialist Cuba and Sandinista Nicaragua, was a bold attempt to remake a newly independent British Caribbean isle. Grenada sits one hundred miles north of Venezuela *(see map, p. 217)*. It was ruled by Britain until 1974, and five years later experienced a radical break from the legacy of British colonial rule.

ORIGINS OF THE REVOLUTION

The roots of Grenada's revolution were fourfold. First, government policies pursued following World War II did nothing to ameliorate the socioeconomic inequities associated with uneven economic growth. Second, inflation and economic contraction, prompted by global recession in the 1970s, led to falling real wages, pushed small farmers into wage labor and a growing informal economy, and made it impossible to counteract chronic unemployment and poverty-induced emigration.

Third, the failure of the Eric Gairy regime (1961–1962 and 1967–1979) to meet demands for democracy and better living conditions fueled an opposition movement that challenged his government's legitimacy. Political grievances flowed from growing inequality, falling real income, economic crises, state corruption, authoritarianism, lack of accommodation to competing elite interests, and a desire to secure independence from Britain under a democratic government. By 1974 disenchantment with Gairy had fomented a broad political movement of youth, peasants, workers, entrepreneurs, large landowners, women, trade unions, community self-help groups, political parties, and opposition members of parliament.

Finally, heightened regime repression in response to peaceful demands led the left to arm itself in self-defense, inciting armed rebellion. The increasingly tyrannical rule of former trade union leader and charismatic black populist Gairy closed existing channels for reform. Gairy's personal security force tortured and murdered opponents, yet the opposition's organization, mobilization, and resource base mushroomed. The leftist New Jewel Movement (NJM) built a military capability to resist state and paramilitary violence and unexpectedly took power in 1979.

The NJM originated from the 1973 fusion of Joint Endeavour for Welfare, Education, and Liberation (JEWEL), led by educator Unison Whiteman, and the Movement for the Assemblies of the People, led by lawyers Maurice Bishop and Kenrick Radix, Whiteman, trade union organizer Vincent Noel, and educator Jacqueline Creft. The NJM comprised three political currents. One was a social-democratic, populist current led by a group of professionals, intellectuals, and entrepreneurs. The second tendency, led by Bishop, Radix, Whiteman, Noel, and Creft, had won widespread respect and popularity. Their anticolonial, Black-Power politics had transformed them into revolutionary Marxists who created a vanguard party to topple Gairy. They were firm believers in mass-based participatory democracy. Third was a pro-Moscow, Stalinist tendency, led by economics professor Bernard Coard.

THE REVOLUTION

On March 10, 1979, NJM leaders—aware of Gairy's order to murder them while he was abroad—were in hiding. The March 13 insurrection began with a successful attack on the main army base. Bishop asked islanders in a radio broadcast to disarm the police. By afternoon the fifty-member NJM military had toppled the government with three deaths and minor casualties. The Grenada Revolution was championed by the people.

The NJM-led People's Revolutionary Government (PRG) adopted a "basic needs" development approach. State economic policy aimed to improve human capabilities as the basis for economic growth and social equity. The promotion of literacy, technical and scientific proficiency for all adults, and improved health and living conditions would enhance economic productivity and social well-being.

The revolution was not socialist, although the NJM hoped to lay the foundations for a socialist future. The goals of the government included transforming rural areas to ben-

A New Jewel Movement political meeting is conducted before portraits of (left to right) Maurice Bishop, Nicaraguan leader Daniel Ortega, and Cuban leader Fidel Castro.

efit small farmers and increase food self-sufficiency and agricultural productivity; industrializing, based on agroindustries using local crops; building a modern airport crucial to tourism; achieving full employment and implementing state social service programs; diversifying and expanding international relations, with emphasis on Caribbean and developing world states, Europe, and the Soviet bloc, especially Cuba; creating participatory politics based on elected assemblies and voluntary mass organizations of workers, farmers, women, and youth; consolidating a domestic political alliance dominated by workers and peasants and aligned with the capitalist class; and expanding and professionalizing the armed forces while launching a popular militia.

Prime Minister Bishop's government rescinded Gairy's repressive laws, advanced women's equality, instituted free, high-quality medical care, built new schools and health clinics, established free public education and adult literacy programs, lowered prices of food and other necessities, increased food self-sufficiency, improved housing, reduced unemployment and infant mortality, launched a public transit service, aided small farmers and farm workers, adopted and enforced prolabor laws, secured significant amounts of foreign aid, acted initially to deepen popular political participation, and brought a new airport close to completion. And by 1983 the government was drafting a constitution as the basis for national elections.

COUNTERREVOLUTION AND U.S. INVASION

Political shortcomings of the NJM precipitated the revolution's collapse. After March 1979 the party grew more distant from working people. While Bishop actively engaged citizens in the revolution and built the legitimacy of the government, Deputy Prime Minister Coard's secret clique blocked admittance into the party. By fall 1982 it had grown to only 350 members. NJM membership policy discriminated against small farmers; they were excluded (as property owners) since the NJM was a "workers party." Discrimination against property owners excluded most islanders from party membership.

Despite justified government efforts to bring to justice those responsible for terrorist acts against the Bishop regime, state policy violated civil liberties and damaged the regime's political prestige. Detention and torture of opponents was the most potent source of the revolution's declining legitimacy. Those directly implicated in these heinous acts were members of the hidden Coard faction. The NJM's failure to institutionalize popular democracy in the party, state, and mass organizations made it impossible for Bishop and his allies to counteract authoritarian policies—led primarily by Coard—within the party and regime.

On October 13, 1983, the revolution was toppled by a Coard-led coup. Bishop was arrested. His allies who escaped detention resisted the counterrevolution and were joined by outraged citizens. The second Grenada Revolution occurred on October 19, when at least fifteen thousand islanders defied army troops and freed Bishop, who led a popular rebellion to restore the revolutionary regime. Before sunset on the 19th, soldiers loyal to Coard had killed dozens of unarmed civilians—including NJM founder Noel—and wounded scores more. On the orders of the Coard putschists, government ministers Bishop, Whiteman, Creft, Norris Bain, and Fitzroy Bain were executed by firing squad. Grenadians were shocked and demoralized and feared for their lives. Coard's dictatorship set the stage for the U.S. invasion of October 25, 1983, which sought the revolution's permanent defeat.

See also *Castro, Fidel; Counterrevolution; Cuban Revolution (1956–1970); Latin American Popular and Guerrilla Revolts (1960–1996); Nicaraguan Revolution (1979).*

John Walton Cotman

BIBLIOGRAPHY

Clark, Steve. "The Second Assassination of Maurice Bishop." *New International* 6 (1987): 11–96.

Cotman, John Walton. *The Gorrión Tree: Cuba and the Grenada Revolution.* New York: Peter Lang Publishing, 1993.

Heine, Jorge, ed. *A Revolution Aborted: The Lessons of Grenada.* Pittsburgh, Penn.: University of Pittsburgh Press, 1991.

Lewis, Gordon K. *Grenada: The Jewel Despoiled.* Baltimore, Md.: Johns Hopkins University Press, 1987.

Marcus, Bruce, and Michael Taber, eds. *Maurice Bishop Speaks: The Grenada Revolution 1979–83.* New York: Pathfinder Press, 1983.

Pryor, Frederic L. *Revolutionary Grenada: A Study in Political Economy.* New York: Praeger Publishers, 1986.

Thorndike, Tony. *Grenada: Politics, Economics, and Society.* Boulder, Colo.: Lynne Rienner Publishers, 1985.

Williams, Gary. "Prelude to an Intervention: Grenada 1983." *Journal of Latin American Studies* 29, no. 1 (February 1997): 131–169.

GUATEMALAN REVOLUTION (1944–1954)

The Guatemalan Revolution defined a decade of democratic rule and social reforms that contrasted sharply with the harsh authoritarian regimes that preceded and followed it. The revolution began with a multiclass movement that toppled the dictator, Gen. Jorge Ubico y Castañeda, and oversaw the country's first democratic elections. It ended with a multiclass movement that overthrew the second democratically elected president and reinstalled military rule. The Guatemalan Revolution is colloquially referred to as Guatemala's "Ten Years of Spring."

THE OCTOBER REVOLUTION

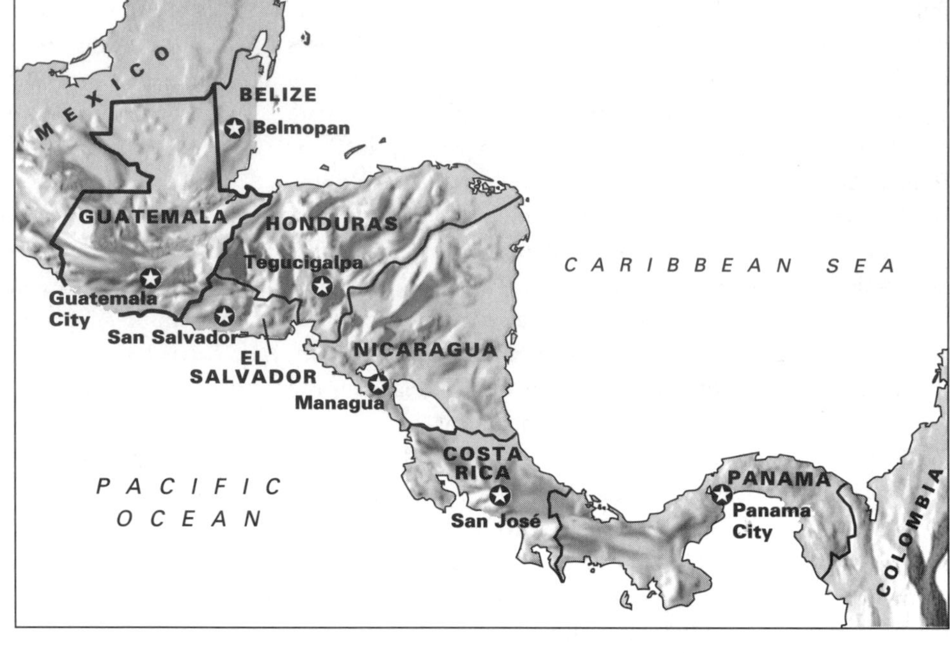

In May 1944 a small group of university students contested General Ubico's administrative appointments at the national university. This act constituted an unprecedented challenge to Ubico's dictatorship (1931–1944), which had banned civic associations and freedom of expression. The students' public demands unleashed an unexpected surge in multiclass protests that ended with Ubico's resignation. Ubico did not effectively lose control, however, until dissident military officers and civilians staged an armed overthrow on October 20, 1944, commonly referred to as the "October Revolution."

The revolutionary junta, headed by former military officer Jacobo Arbenz Guzmán, Maj. Francisco Arana, and civilian Guillermo Toriello, governed for five months and effected Guatemala's first democratic transition. The junta oversaw a popularly elected constituent assembly that recognized citizenship rights, expanded suffrage, legalized the right to form political parties and civic associations, and demilitarized the country. It also oversaw democratic elections in 1944, which favored Juan José Arévalo Bermejo for the presidency. National elections in 1950 selected Arbenz as president. During both administrations, loosely formed left and left-of-center coalitions governed, attempting to democratize politics and promote social reforms.

These political changes engendered and were supported by a surge in civic organizing. By 1951 workers had developed a largely united labor movement, the General Confederation of Workers of Guatemala. At its height the labor movement claimed 100,000 members and significantly improved labor's collective bargaining power in the workplace. Between 1945 and 1954, thirteen labor leaders were elected to Congress. Organized labor also began to mobilize in the countryside, where Ubico and landlords had exercised their most repressive and exploitative control. In this context, peasants founded the autonomous National Peasant Confederation of Guatemala (CNCG) in May 1950. The CNCG worked to increase access to land, credit, and literacy programs and developed a voice in rural politics. By 1954 the peasant confederation claimed between 200,000 and 240,000 members, 37 percent of the economically active rural population.

Presidents Arévalo and Arbenz came to rely increasingly on organized labor and the peasantry for support, and each president legislated landmark social reforms that responded to labor and peasant demands. Arévalo primarily targeted urban sectors and advanced entitlement and regulatory reforms, including a national health system and a labor code. The latter established collective bargaining rights, minimum wages, and maximum working hours and overturned Ubico's rural vagrancy laws. The Arbenz administration introduced redistributive reforms that brought the revolution to the countryside. A 1950 national census had revealed that 2 percent of all agricultural units claimed 72 percent of arable land. Amidst vitriolic debates, the Arbenz administration legislated land reform in 1952. By 1954 an estimated 100,000 peasant families had benefited from the land reform, which redistributed state lands, idle land on large estates, and some municipal lands. Organized peasants and rural workers participated in the implementation of the land reform, and rural mobilization increased.

THE COUNTERREVOLUTION

The administrations of Arévalo and Arbenz confronted printed protests from landed elites and unsuccessful coup attempts from dissident military officers. The land reform, however, provoked a more vocal and violent multiclass opposition that also included the Catholic Church, professionals, middle-class students, and market women. The United Fruit Company, which had been a casualty of Arbenz's commitment to economic nationalism, also joined the opposition. Arbenz had initiated infrastructure projects that challenged the monopoly of U.S. subsidiaries affiliated with United Fruit. The land reform, however, most directly challenged United Fruit by expropriating two-thirds of the company's lands. United Fruit had been Guatemala's largest private landowner and had maintained significant idle lands in reserve. The company actively opposed Arbenz and drew on its ties to the administration of President Dwight D. Eisenhower to secure U.S. support for the Guatemalan opposition.

The opposition launched a violent media campaign against the regime and warned of a communist takeover. They denounced the role of communist leaders in the legislature, labor unions, and peasant movement and charged that Arbenz and his wife were loyal to the communist cause. Indeed, the newly founded but small communist party, the Guatemalan Workers Party, had fielded important leaders in all of these areas. The communists, however, were reformers and democrats who were immediately interested, like Arbenz, in promoting capitalist development. They had played a key role in drafting the land reform, for example, but drew on World Bank recommendations when doing so. Nevertheless, the land reform appeared radical to some as it constituted the first time that the state had simultaneously challenged landed elite interests and encouraged peasant mobilization.

The opposition forces sought to reverse the reforms yet had limited electoral appeal, no serious political parties, and no viable presidential candidate. Therefore, they turned once again to arms. Carlos Castillo Armas, an ex-military officer, launched an attack on June 17, 1954. While militarily weak, Castillo Armas used U.S. government arms, funds, and propaganda techniques to create an image of strength. Citizens loyal to the government formed civilian militias and asked for arms to defend the regime, as they had done in the aftermath of Francisco Arana's failed 1949 coup attempt. Arbenz refused. He rightfully believed that the attack was small in scale but wrongfully concluded that the military would defend him. On June 27, 1954, he was forced to resign as his own military command—fearful of communism and the loss of control over the countryside—betrayed him.

In the immediate aftermath of the coup, Castillo Armas tried to reverse the legacy of the October Revolution: dismantling many state institutions; repressing unions and reform parties; and undermining most of the social reforms, including the labor codes and land reforms. For the next thirty years, the Guatemalan military asserted control over the state and oversaw one of Latin America's most brutal and enduring periods of authoritarian rule.

DEBORAH J. YASHAR

BIBLIOGRAPHY

Cardoza y Aragón, Luis. *La revolución guatemalteca.* Mexico City: Cuadernos Americanos, 1955.

Galich, Manuel. *Del pánico al ataque.* Guatemala City: Editorial Universitaria, 1977.

Gleijeses, Piero. *Shattered Hope: The Guatemalan Revolution and the United States, 1944–1954.* Princeton, N.J.: Princeton University Press, 1991.

Handy, Jim. *Revolution in the Countryside: Rural Conflict and Agrarian Reform in Guatemala, 1944–1954.* Chapel Hill: University of North Carolina Press, 1994.

Immerman, Richard. *The CIA in Guatemala: The Foreign Policy of Intervention.* Austin: University of Texas Press, 1982.

Jonas, Susanne. *The Battle for Guatemala: Rebels, Death Squads, and U.S. Power.* Boulder, Colo.: Westview Press, 1991.

Schlesinger, Stephen, and Stephen Kinzer. *Bitter Fruit: The Untold Story of the American Coup in Guatemala.* Garden City: Anchor Press, 1982.

Yashar, Deborah J. *Demanding Democracy: Reform and Reaction in Costa Rica and Guatemala, 1870s–1950s.* Stanford: Stanford University Press, 1997.

GUERRILLA WARFARE

So closely do we generally connect guerrilla warfare (also known as partisan warfare or insurgency) with the writings of twentieth-century revolutionaries like T. E. Lawrence, Mao Zedong, Võ Nguyên Giáp, and Ernesto "Che" Guevara that we have developed historical tunnel-vision about the phenomenon. In fact, guerrilla warfare was not often connected, either factually or theoretically, with social-revolutionary conflicts until the twentieth century.

Instead, the *guerrilla* (meaning "little war") is surely the earliest form of warrior and warfare, and we should define its basic form in strictly military terms. A Hittite king referred ruefully thirty-five hundred years ago to elusive enemies who preferred to launch nighttime attacks on his own sleeping, unprepared, and unaware people. If one's enemies are superior in numbers or weaponry, the best way to minimize risk is to avoid open, pitched battles with full-size armies in favor of selected engagements with small enemy contingents. Surprise, elusiveness, and deception recur regularly as the central themes of partisan warfare. Typical guerrilla tactics include wide-ranging mobility and quick dispersal; ambushes; lightning attack-and-withdraw tactics against columns and supply lines; waylaying messengers and denying the enemy intelligence about one's own forces; and securing more and better weapons from defeated opponents. These tactics are very likely to increase frustration and depress morale in one's opponents, as military theorists have noted.

The usual larger-scale tactic is the surprise attack launched from excellent cover against a small (usually), isolated, and perhaps tactically crippled contingent of enemy soldiers. When such an attack is launched by an unusually large or united contingent of guerrillas against an enemy weakened by dispersal and isolation and by difficulties of terrain or weather, they can inflict defeats of near-epic dimensions on "clearly" superior foes. The classic example is probably Vercingetorix's defeat of Julius Caesar's legions in the Teutoberg Forest (in today's Germany). Vercingetorix, however, also supplies a negative object lesson for guerrillas who seek to move too early toward conventional tactics like (1) provoking more conventional, massed battlefield engagements or (2) taking refuge in hill-forts, towns, or stockades. The former tactic allows superior numbers, weapons, or battlefield organization (such as the ancient Greek phalanx or medieval Swiss infantry) to carry the day; the latter allows well-supplied armies to lay siege to enclosed and isolated opponents. A siege at Alesia (in modern-day France) disastrously ended Vercingetorix's campaign, centuries later prompting the famous sculpture, "The Dying Gaul."

In most historical instances guerrilla warfare emerged as a by-product of invasion, and therefore the guerrilla forces could usually rely on local knowledge and the support of the people to foster effective resistance against ethnic outsiders. The true innovation of twentieth-century, revolutionary guerrilla warfare is the systematic transfer of guerrilla tactics to internal, civil wars. The modern revolutionary insurgency is, or intends to become, a civil war in which the populace will eventually be forced to side with either the guerrillas or the government in power. That choice is *not* an obvious one, given the often common ethnicity of all parties. With support problematic—and "support" for guerrillas can mean anything from failing to report armed insurgents in the vicinity to vigorous participation in the guerrillas' forces—it is not surprising that twentieth-century revolutionary writing (and many nineteenth-century military theories) about guerrilla warfare has always focused on securing and maintaining popular support and denying the same to the incumbent regime (and occasionally to other, competing revolutionary organizations as well).

Thus the writings of Mao, Giáp, and Guevara are all centered on the relationship between the population through which the guerrilla army moves—like a "fish in water," in Mao's famous aphorism—and the guerrillas themselves. In Mao's writings, insurgents are instructed to be proper and disciplined in civilian encounters. Giáp's coinage, "people's war," aptly expressed the goal of an intensely interdependent, symbiotic relationship between the guerrilla army and civilians, now virtually a signature of twentieth-century guerrilla theorizing. (The anticolonial context of the Vietnamese Revolution certainly made that symbiosis an easier goal to achieve.) Professional soldiers regard Giáp as a better military theoretician than either Mao or Guevara.

The writings of both Mao and Giáp provided as well the theoretical inspiration for the Latin American guerrillas' strategic switch in the 1970s and 1980s to "prolonged popular war" from the *foco* strategy. Guevara, with parallel contributions by Régis Debray—a French theorist on the subject and author of *Revolution in the Revolution?* who also visited several guerrilla sites—had developed the *foco* strategy. The *foco* strategy was widely deemed a failure by the late 1960s, especially in the wake of Che's 1967 failure and death in Bolivia. The *foco* theory argued that a small rural guerrilla nucleus could grow quickly via military victories and consequent recruitment successes until it was eventually large enough to confront and defeat a conventional army. But both of those Latin American guerrilla theories—the "quick-fix" *foco* theory and the later "prolonged popular war" strategy—are fundamentally similar in their insistence on support and recruitment from the civilian population.

It is hard to find novel strategies or tactics of a purely military sort in the writings of these revolutionaries, again partially excepting Giáp. Yet another type of "military" issue is novel and often becomes central. Precisely because popular support and obedience—for either the insurgents or the regime—become problematic in modern, revolutionary guerrilla warfare, terror often is used against civilians. But careful scholarship must reject the casual and common conflation of the terms *guerrilla* and *terrorist*. (By contrast, the zone between guerrilla and brigand has often been gray and easily crossed.) Guerrilla warfare is a *strategy,* but terror is a *tactic,* and *terrorist* should be used mainly as an adjective to describe systematic or indiscriminate violence against unarmed civilian populations. When the terms are defined in this way, governments are usually more likely to use terror than their insurgent opponents, or at least their terror is likely to be more indiscriminate than focused. Both groups, however, use terror more when the support and obedience of civilians are withheld or suspect, especially when they are instead given to one's opponents.

See also *Chinese Communist Revolution (1921–1949); Cuban Revolution (1956–1970); Guevara, Ernesto "Che"; Latin American Popular and Guerrilla Revolts (1960–1996); Latin American Popular and Guerrilla Revolts (Independence to 1959); Malayan Communist Insurgency (1948–1960); Mao Zedong; Sandino, Augusto César; Terrorism; Vietnamese Revolution (1945–1975); War.*

TIMOTHY P. WICKHAM-CROWLEY

BIBLIOGRAPHY

Asprey, Robert B. *War in the Shadows: The Guerrilla in History.* New York: W. Morrow, 1994. (Originally 2 vols. New York: Doubleday, 1975.)

Guevara, Ernesto "Che." *Guerrilla Warfare.* 3d ed. rev. and updated. Introduction and case studies by Brian Loveman and Thomas M. Davies Jr. Wilmington, Del.: Scholarly Resources, 1997.

Laqueur, Walter. *Guerrilla: A Historical and Critical Study.* Boston: Little, Brown, 1976.

Mao Zedong. *Mao Tse-tung on Guerrilla Warfare.* Translated and with an introduction by Samuel B. Griffith. New York: Frederick A. Praeger, 1961.

Võ Nguyên Giáp. *The Military Art of People's War: Selected Writings of Võ Nguyên Giáp.* Edited and with an introduction by Russell Stetler. New York: Monthly Review Press, 1970.

Wickham-Crowley, Timothy P. "Terror and Guerrilla Warfare in Latin America, 1956–1970." In *Exploring Revolution.* Edited by Timothy P. Wickham-Crowley. Armonk, N.Y.: M. E. Sharpe, 1991.

GUEVARA, ERNESTO "CHE"

Ernesto "Che" Guevara (1928–1967) was born in Rosario, Argentina. A charismatic Marxist revolutionary, he was instrumental in helping Fidel Castro seize power and install a socialist system in Cuba. As a radical minister in Castro's government, he advocated the spread of socialism and sponsored numerous armed guerrilla campaigns against U.S.-backed governments in Latin America before leaving Cuba to spearhead efforts himself in Bolivia, where at the age of thirty-nine he was killed by his military captors.

The eldest of five children born to a middle-class Argentine family, Ernesto Guevara de la Serna studied medicine and obtained a medical degree in 1953, but after leaving Argentina and witnessing the 1954 U.S.-backed military overthrow of Guatemala's leftist president, Jacobo Arbenz Guzmán, he was drawn to radical politics. He joined the 1956–1958 revolutionary war led by Castro against Cuba's dictator, Fulgencio Batista, became one of Castro's closest aides, and earned renown as the guerrilla commander known as "Che."

Following the rebel victory in January 1959, Guevara helped consolidate Castro's power by presiding over revolutionary purge trials of the defeated security forces and organizing Cuba's new Revolutionary Armed Forces, civilian National Militias, and state security apparatus. He also played a leading role in brokering Castro's eventual political alliance with the Cuban Communist Party and in drafting the agrarian reform that nationalized large private landholdings and foreign-owned properties, paving the way for a state-run Cuban economy.

An early advocate of Castro's confrontation with the United States, which wielded sweeping economic and political influence in Cuba, Guevara was also a principal catalyst of the new links forged between Havana and Moscow. He traveled widely as Castro's emissary, seeking trade and diplomatic ties in meetings with such leaders as Nikita Khrushchev, Mao Zedong, Gamal Abdel Nasser, and Jawaharlal Nehru. As Cuba's national bank president Guevara increased state control of the economy, and as minister of industries he lobbied for the island's rapid industrialization in order to reduce its reliance on sugar exports.

By the mid-1960s, however, faced with Cuba's increasing dependency on the Soviet Union and thwarted in his ambitious industrialization campaign, Guevara had soured on the Soviet model of socialism. In a February 1965 speech he accused the Kremlin of engaging in "exploitative" relationships with developing nations and called for a new socialist "solidarity" in the common struggle against the capitalist West. In his essay, *Socialism and the New Man in Cuba,* published after his personal break with the USSR, Guevara extolled the notion of "heroic" self-sacrifice as a means of creating a true socialist consciousness. During this time he also developed the *foco* theory of guerrilla warfare and revolution, based on his reading of the Cuban events of 1956–1958.

In April 1965 Guevara left Cuba to assist Marxist-led revolutionaries fighting for power in the former Belgian Congo, but his forces were quickly routed. In 1966 he traveled to Bolivia to spark what he hoped would become a "continental revolution" in Latin America. Instead, after an abortive eleven-month guerrilla campaign, he was wounded, captured, and on October 9, 1967, executed on the orders of the Bolivian president, Gen. René Barrientos, in the tiny mountain hamlet of La Higuera.

See also *Castro, Fidel; Cuban Revolution (1956–1970); Guerrilla Warfare.*

Jon Lee Anderson

BIBLIOGRAPHY

Anderson, Jon Lee. *Che Guevara: A Revolutionary Life.* New York: Grove Press, 1997.

Castaneda, Jorge G. *Companero: The Life and Death of Che Guevara.* Translated by Marina Castaneda. New York: Alfred A. Knopf, 1997.

Guevara, Ernesto Che. *The Bolivian Diary of Ernesto Che Guevara.* Edited by Mary-Alice Waters. New York: Pathfinder Press, 1994.

———. *Episodes of the Cuban Revolutionary War, 1956–1958.* Edited by Mary-Alice Waters. New York: Pathfinder Press, 1996.

Taibo, Paco Ignacio, II. *Ernesto Guevara: Also Known as Che.* New York: St. Martin's Press, 1997.

GUINEA-BISSAU INDEPENDENCE REVOLT (1962–1974)

From 1962 to 1974 a nationalist political party, the African Party for the Independence of Guinea and Cape Verde (PAIGC), staged an armed revolt against the colonial authorities in Portuguese Guinea (later renamed Guinea-Bissau).

In the 1950s and 1960s Portugal made clear its unshaking commitment to retain direct control over its African colonies, while France and England were granting independence to their respective African colonies. Portuguese intransigence proved especially frustrating for those Guineans and Cape Verdeans who aspired to the national liberation of their countries. Moreover, colonial rule in Portuguese Africa had proved particularly harsh, and Portuguese colonialists retained such practices as forced labor into the 1950s, long after they had been abolished elsewhere in Africa. The character of Portuguese rule created social discontent in Guinea's rural areas that accentuated the Guinean peasantry's long-held resentments against Lusitanian imperial rule.

Also, many indigenous groups, particularly those located in geographically dense terrain in the south (Tombali, Quinara) and northwest of the colony (Cacheu, Oio), had successfully countered Portuguese armed incursions for several hundred years—until well into the twentieth century. Thus, for many Guineans the revolt represented an opportunity to rekindle long-standing indigenous traditions of armed resistance.

ORGANIZATION OF THE INDEPENDENCE REVOLT

The idea of a nationalist revolt against colonial rule in Portugal's African colonies originated with intellectuals from Guinea, Cape Verde, Angola, and Mozambique who had been studying together in Lisbon and in Paris in the 1940s. In the early 1950s Amílcar Cabral and a handful of other Guinean and Cape Verdean educated urban workers and civil servants began clandestinely to organize a nationalist movement in the capital cities of Bissau, Praia, and Lisbon. Their efforts led to the creation of the PAIGC in Bissau in 1956.

The PAIGC was distinctive both for seeking to incorporate all ethnic groups in Portuguese Guinea and for insisting on the simultaneous, "binationalist" independence of Portuguese Guinea and Cape Verde. The party was in fact created as a single unit whose members and leaders consisted of both Cape Verdeans and Guineans. Initially, the PAIGC competed with a number of other nationalist political parties in Bissau and in Lisbon. However, many of these parties aimed for the independence of Guinea separately from that of Cape Verde or were based on a single ethnic group, and so they received less popular support than the PAIGC.

In its first major action, in 1959, the PAIGC helped organize a dockworkers' strike in Bissau. However, just as Mao Zedong had discovered in 1927, when working-class communists in urban Shanghai were easily repressed, the PAIGC learned how vulnerable it was in urban areas when the dockworkers were raked with gunfire by Portuguese police. In 1960 Cabral and most of the PAIGC leaders relocated to Guinea-Conakry (which borders Guinea-Bissau to the south), from which they launched a rural-based campaign within Portuguese Guinea to galvanize supporters. Thousands of peasants, especially in the south and northwest, responded favorably, providing food, supplies, and young men to serve as PAIGC soldiers. By 1962 the PAIGC was ready to carry out military attacks on Portuguese army garrisons.

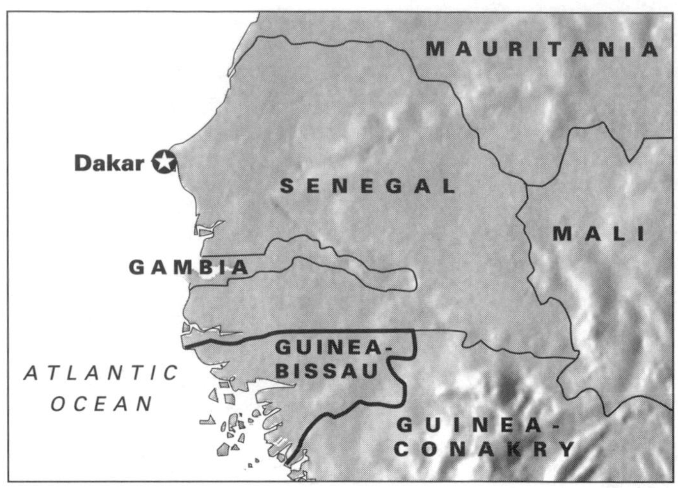

AMÍLCAR CABRAL AND PAIGC MILITARY SUCCESSES

The nationalist struggle in Guinea-Bissau was principally organized and directed by Amílcar Cabral. Cabral's leadership was crucial to overcoming internal divisions within the PAIGC during the period of the independence revolt. However, Cabral also spent an extraordinary amount of time abroad, making more than eighty visits to twenty different countries to promote internationally the political legitimacy of the anticolonial revolt and to raise funds and obtain supplies for the PAIGC.

Cabral's diplomatic skills enabled him to co-opt most other Guinean nationalist political leaders or to out-finesse them in lobbying for the support of potential allies, including the Organization of African Unity, the United Nations, and the presidents of neighboring Senegal (Léopold Sédar Senghor) and Guinea-Conakry (Ahmed Sékou Touré). Senghor and Touré then, from the mid-to-late 1960s, allowed the PAIGC to operate out of military bases in their respective countries.

On the ground, PAIGC commanders consistently proved strategically superior to their Portuguese counterparts. In 1964 the PAIGC soldiers were organized into the Revolutionary Armed Forces of the People (FARP), eventually comprising some 5,000 guerrilla fighters and another 10,000 logistical supporters. The FARP proved able to seize control of approximately half the territory of Portuguese Guinea by 1966 and three-quarters by 1969. (No fighting would take place on the Cape Verde Islands, where the relatively open terrain was not conducive to guerrilla warfare.)

The FARP's military accomplishments in Portuguese Guinea in large part reflected the success of their field commanders' guerrilla hit-and-run strategy, which was based on more than thirty highly mobile groups of FARP soldiers that had been dispersed throughout the countryside. In addition, the FARP benefited immensely from the provision of modern antiaircraft weapons and other supplies from Eastern Bloc countries. By 1973 the Portuguese armed forces in Guinea—25,000 regular soldiers supported by modern fighter jets—had been pushed by the FARP out of more than thirty rural military garrisons into a handful of fortified urban areas.

In September 1973 the PAIGC declared the independent state of Guinea-Bissau in the regions it controlled. In April 1974 the revolution in Portugal led to Lisbon's decision to withdraw its troops and to recognize Guinea-Bissau. Six months later, in October 1974, the PAIGC marched triumphantly into Bissau and assumed national political power.

PROBLEMS INTERNAL TO THE PAIGC

Despite its military and political successes, the PAIGC suffered three major internal problems throughout the 1960s. First, many Guinean party members and FARP commanders rejected the party's binationalism and frequently complained that the PAIGC ruling circle was dominated by Cape Verdeans rather than Guineans. Second, repeatedly during the armed struggle (1962–1974), some soldiers from the Balanta ethnic group (the Balanta comprised most of the FARP soldiers) were accused by PAIGC leaders of acting too independently of the PAIGC's central party structure. This criticism in part reflected a long-held custom on the part of young Balanta men to demonstrate their independent military qualities. In 1964 a third problem emerged: the authoritarian tendency of PAIGC leaders to overreact violently against these independent military men. Several dozen Balanta soldiers were executed by the PAIGC leaders in 1964 and 1967, and others were executed on an individual basis throughout the remainder of the revolt.

Rising internal party centralism exacerbated the dissent among some PAIGC and FARP members. The binationalist controversy was never fully resolved and would lead to the PAIGC's biggest loss: the killing of Amílcar Cabral in Guinea-Conakry by an anti-Cape Verde Guinean nationalist in the course of a failed kidnapping of PAIGC leaders by party dissidents. The antagonism caused by the binational issue, as well as the PAIGC's tendencies toward authoritarian internal practices, reemerged after independence. In 1980 a violent coup d'état ended the regime of Guinea-Bissau's first president, Luíz Cabral (Amílcar's half-brother), and ended the party's direct link to Cape Verde. Guinea-Bissau's newly installed president, João Bernardo Vieira, a FARP commander during the independence revolt, then proceeded to consolidate his control over the country's political system.

See also *Angolan Revolution (1974–1996); Cabral, Amílcar; Chinese Communist Revolution (1921–1949); Mozambican Revolution (1974–1994); Nationalism; Peasants; Portuguese Revolution (1974).*

JOSHUA BERNARD FORREST

BIBLIOGRAPHY

Chabal, Patrick. *Amílcar Cabral. Revolutionary Leadership and People's War.* Cambridge: Cambridge University Press, 1983.

Chaliand, Gérard. *Armed Struggle in Africa. With the Guerrillas in 'Portuguese' Guinea.* New York: Monthly Review Press, 1969.

Davidson, Basil. *No Fist Is Big Enough to Hide the Sky: The Liberation of Guinea-Bissau and Cape Verde.* London: Zed Press, 1981.

Dhada, Mustafah. *Warriors at Work. How Guinea Was Really Set Free.* Niwot: University Press of Colorado, 1993.

Forrest, Joshua B. *Guinea-Bissau. Power, Conflict and Renewal in a West African Nation.* Boulder, Colo.: Westview Press, 1992.

Galli, Rosemary E., and Jocelyn Jones. *Guinea-Bissau: Politics, Economics and Society.* Boulder, Colo.: Lynne Rienner, 1987.

Lopes, Carlos. *Guinea-Bissau: From Liberation Struggle to Independent Statehood.* Boulder, Colo.: Westview Press, 1987.

Rudebeck, Lars. *Guinea-Bissau: A Study of Political Mobilization.* Uppsala: Scandinavian Institute of African Studies, 1974.

GUINEAN INDEPENDENCE MOVEMENT (1958)

The former French West African colony of Guinea, sometimes known as Guinea-Conakry to distinguish it from neighboring Guinea-Bissau or from Equatorial Guinea in Central Africa *(see maps, pp. 40, 212)*, appeared on the world scene September 25, 1958, when alone among France's sub-Saharan territories, it refused to join the Franco-African community proposed by Charles de Gaulle. Instead, it voted twenty to one (1,136,324 to 56,981) for immediate independence. Responding to de Gaulle's warnings, Guinean leader Ahmed Sékou Touré uttered the famous, if partly apocryphal, cry of defiance: "We prefer independence in poverty to servitude in comfort."

France reacted by abruptly pulling out all its administrative personnel, cutting off all financial transfers, and excluding Guinea from the French currency zone. France also attempted to ensure the diplomatic isolation of the newly independent state. The purpose was to make an example of Guinea; indeed, it did so, but not in the way de Gaulle had intended. Guinea became a symbol of defiance and freedom to the whole African continent and to the developing world at large. The West Indian poet and politician Aimé Césaire, the champion of *négritude,* wrote in 1961, "What is at stake today in Guinea is not only Guinea's fate, but the fate of Africa."

Much of the international visibility Guinea gained at that time came from the way the country seized its independence, but in truth De Gaulle, however reluctantly, had made independence an option when he set the terms for the 1958 referendum. It continued to remain available for other African territories that elected to remain part of a French-dominated community as self-governing entities, a status all of them, including Guinea, had enjoyed since 1956. Guinea's bold option for immediate independence, however, soon made the more accommodating position of the other leaders of "Francophone" Africa untenable. Within less than two years, all of them—even those who, like Côte d'Ivoire's Félix Houphouët-Boigny, had referred to independence as "nonsense"—had yielded to popular pressure and requested France to let them acquire international sovereignty. Some even declared it unilaterally to avoid being stigmatized as French puppets. The main difference between Guinea and those latecomers, however, was that all of them negotiated bilateral agreements with France that created the conditions for enduring French influence. They also enjoyed the economic advantages of continued association with France, whereas Guinea suffered the penalties that de Gaulle had prescribed against those who declined to join the Franco-African community.

The name of Sékou Touré (1922–1984) remains durably and legitimately linked not only with Guinea's independence movement, but with the heady years of Africa's quest for dignity and unity—including its failures, frustrations, and betrayals. Touré was one of the youngest members of the cohort of postwar nationalist leaders in French sub-Saharan Africa. Unlike some of his elders, such as Léopold Sedar Senghor or Houphouët-Boigny, Touré lacked the prestige attached to advanced education or to wealth and traditional status, even if he could claim distant kinship with Samory Touré (1830–1900), the hero of anti-French resistance in nineteenth-century Upper Guinea. Touré took a minor part in the 1946 launching of the African Democratic Rally (RDA) at Bamako and soon became the leading figure of its Guinean branch, the Democratic Party of Guinea (PDG). His real strength and following, however, stemmed from his earlier work, starting during World War II, as a labor organizer among Conakry's white-collar workers. This put him in touch with the French left-wing, including communist union activists affiliated with the General Labor Confederacy (CGT), who contributed to his ideological training a deep strain of Marxist orthodoxy that he never truly renounced. Accordingly, he tended to shrink from the various brands of African socialism proclaimed by diverse leaders such as Senghor, Julius Nyerere, Tom Mboya, or even Kwame Nkrumah.

Touré's labor base grew nearly tenfold in two years with the postwar development of the iron and bauxite mining industry in Guinea: the number of registered union members went from 4,600 in 1953 to 44,000 in 1955. The PDG's mobilization of popular support, however, took many other forms. In his native area of Upper Guinea, Touré took full advantage of regional/ethnic solidarity; he also cultivated those Muslim authorities not beholden to the French. In the Futa Jalon region, where the French had developed a working arrangement for governance with the local Fulbe aristocrats, the PDG used a populist, egalitarian approach to reach for the support of the commoners. Expanding the franchise—the number of registered voters rose from 131,309 in 1946 to 1,376,048 in 1957—also worked to the advantage of the PDG, whose image as the "people's party" was enhanced by the blatant persecution it suffered through 1955 at the hands of the French administration.

When self-government was granted to France's overseas territories under the 1956 Deferre Act, the PDG easily gained control of the legislature, and Touré became vice president (and de facto head) of Guinea's Government Council. He immediately used his position to revamp the local administration system in a way that stripped power from the traditional chiefs who remained the backbone of anti-PDG forces, particularly in Futa Jalon. Touré also distanced himself from Houphouët, his erstwhile mentor, over the issue of "balkanization," which had resulted from the deliberate breakup of French West Africa and French Equatorial Africa, the federations of colonial territories set up by the French. Instead, he came out in favor of African unity, along with Senghor or Nkrumah. The May 1958 fall of the French Fourth Republic and de Gaulle's rise to power, however, forced all Francophone African leaders to put off the issue of regional integration and to respond to France's offer of an ostensible "new deal."

Once these leaders had been reassured that the option of subsequent independence would remain open, all of them agreed to go along with de Gaulle's scheme. Touré insisted that full independence should be compatible with the continuation of close Franco-African ties, but in view of de Gaulle's stubborn opposition on that point (which, however, he came to accept by late 1959), the Guinean leader opted for an immediate break. Aside from the nationalistic pride and anticolonial militancy that he shared with other African leaders, two domestic considerations may have been crucial in Touré's fateful decision. One was his ability to paint his remaining opponents into the untenable corner of campaigning *against* independence—a trap from which they extracted themselves only through a last-minute climb on the PDG bandwagon, thereby implicitly endorsing Guinea's transformation into a single-party state. The other consideration was Guinea's apparent potential for rapid development of its impressive mineral resources, which already had attracted the interest of major aluminum firms and led Guineans to believe that new foreign capital would easily compensate for the loss of the French connection.

In this expectation, Guinea was partly mistaken. Its postindependence isolation forced it to make unprofitable deals with foreign corporations as well as with the USSR, which moved in to fill the vacuum left by France's departure, but offered aid only in exchange for substantial mining concessions. (Relations with the USSR soured after 1961 but were never fully broken.) Touré's visions of African unity were hamstrung by his estrangement from most of his Francophone neighbors and by the successive falls of the two partners—Ghana's Nkrumah (given asylum in Conakry after his 1966 overthrow) and Mali's Modibo Keita (toppled in 1968)—with whom Guinea had set up a rather tentative federation. Guinea actively supported the anti-Portuguese liberation movement in neighboring Guinea-Bissau, prompting Portugal to attempt a covert destabilization in 1970 and orchestrate the 1973 assassination of nationalist leader Amílcar Cabral in Conakry. Guinea also developed functional, if not ideological, ties with two other neighbors, Liberia and Sierra Leone, but it was never able to be anything more than a small, subregional power.

The moral, ideological, or exemplary influence of Guinea, however, was for almost two decades quite out of proportion to the country's objective importance. Having refused to let his country become part of the Soviet bloc, despite his Marxist orientation, Touré became a leading figure in the nonaligned movement. Although his regime became increasingly repressive, paranoid, and nepotistic, he remained a source of inspiration, especially among the disgruntled intellectual elites of Francophone Africa, thanks to his ceaseless output of political writings and speeches, which add up to the most massive and articulate body of ideological thought produced in Africa.

Touré's political thought was always informed by his experience as a militant practitioner. Rejecting the temptation to add to the Marxist creed or to "Africanize" it and disdaining personalistic labels such as "Nkrumahism," "Nasserism," or "Mobutism," he was content to leave both theory and practice under the catch-all label of *Révolution Guinéenne,* which serves as the general heading of his collected works. In practice, the revolutionary mystique consisted primarily of self-reliance—a necessary response to Guinea's self-righteous isolation—and of the consciously pursued emergence of a "new Guinean man"—incorruptible, selfless, and vigilant against any counterrevolutionary movements. Touré's 1968 call for a Cultural Revolution—echoing voices coming from Paris as much as from Beijing—was lost in a succession of bloody domestic plots and purges. In 1984 the regime fell within a week of the death of its founder, leaving behind a confused legacy. To the outside world the Guinean Revolution had been solely identified with Touré's 1958 defiance of French neocolonialism, but to the Guineans it was associated with the earlier and more protracted process whereby a "new class" displaced the established African *notables,* who had developed a symbiotic relationship with the colonial power. The fruits of that latter revolution are still alive in Guinea.

See also *Cabral, Amílcar; Guinea-Bissau Independence Revolt (1962–1974); Nkrumah, Kwame; Nyerere, Julius Kambarage.*

EDOUARD BUSTIN

BIBLIOGRAPHY

Ameillon, B. *La Guinée: Bilan d'une indépendance.* Paris: Maspero, 1964.

Chaffard, Georges. *Les Carnets secrets de la décolonisation.* 2 vols. Paris: Calmann-Lévy, 1965–1967.

Diane, Charles. *Sékou Touré: L'Homme et son régime.* 2d ed. Paris: Berger-Levrault, 1984.

Morgenthau, Ruth Schachter. *Political Parties in French-Speaking West Africa.* Oxford: Clarendon Press, 1964.

O'Toole, Thomas, and Ibrahima Bah-Lalya. *Historical Dictionary of Guinea.* London and Lanham, Md.: Scarecrow Press, 1995.

Rivière, Claude. *Guinea: The Mobilization of a People.* Ithaca, N.Y., and London: Cornell University Press, 1977.

Touré, Ahmed Sékou. *L'Action politique du Parti Démocratique de Guinée.* 18 vols. Conakry: Imprimerie Nationale, 1958–1972.

HAITIAN DEMOCRATIC REVOLUTION (1986–1996)

The democratic revolution in Haiti began in the early 1980s and culminated in the election of liberation theologian Father Jean-Bertrand Aristide to the presidency in December 1990, the first truly democratic polling in Haiti since it gained independence in 1804. The major turning point occurred in February 1986, when popular opposition forced "President-for-Life" Jean-Claude "Baby Doc" Duvalier to flee Haiti for exile in France. His departure ended thirty years of dictatorial rule by the Duvalier family, which had begun when François "Papa Doc" Duvalier came to power in 1957; François transferred power to his son before his death in 1971.

The fall of Jean-Claude in 1986 unleashed a power struggle among the Duvalierists and the military. Four military-dominated governments exchanged power between February 1986 and March 1990, but thanks to relentless pressure from the democratic movement, none of them was able to consolidate power. The democratic movement represented a broad cross-section of Haitian society, including professional and political organizations, workers' associations and trade unions, women's organizations, religious and lay community organizations, neighborhood committees, youth groups, and peasant organizations. Finally, a civilian government was formed, and that government organized the internationally supervised elections that resulted in a landslide victory for Aristide.

After a failed coup d'état against the president-elect in January 1991, Aristide became president in February. The democratic movement fought to rid the country of dictatorship, democratize the government, eliminate corruption in public office, reform the military and police, and create a more just and equitable society. Vowing to carry out this mandate, Aristide earned the enmity of the Duvalierists, the military, the tiny Haitian bourgeoisie, and the United States, which branded him a "radical firebrand." It was not at all surprising, therefore, that he lasted a mere seven months in office. Threatened by Aristide's proposed reforms and his continuing encouragement of his popular supporters to agitate for change, the military hierarchy, supported by the wealthy business elite, overthrew Aristide on September 30, 1991, and sent him into exile, first to Venezuela and later to the United States.

In the context of the post-cold war "New World Order," the United States adopted a dual policy toward the coup leaders. On the one hand, President George Bush condemned the coup and demanded that the military junta in

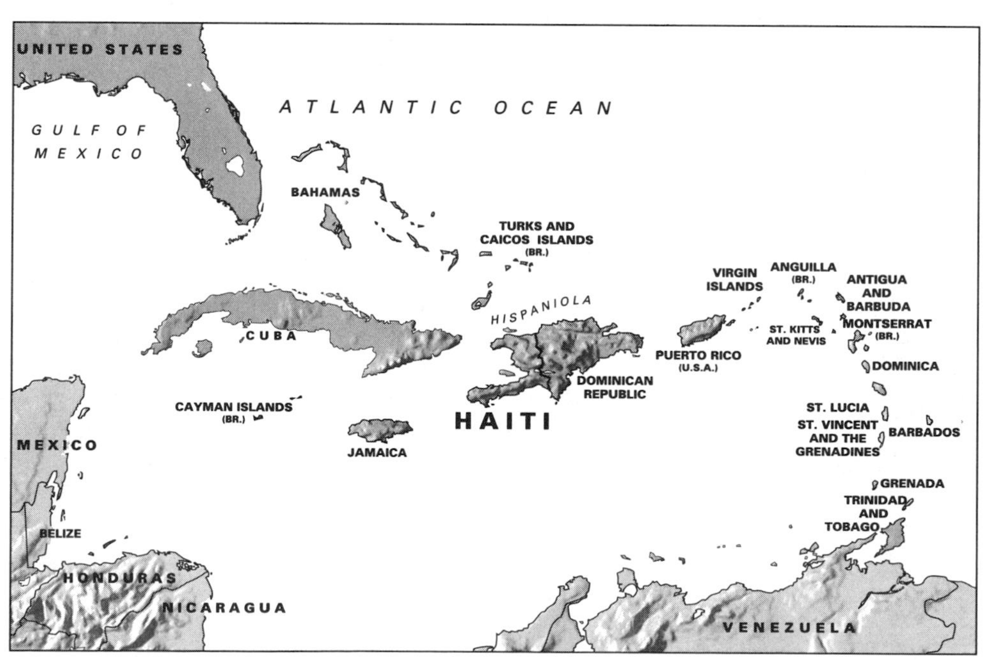

Haiti step down and allow Aristide to return to office; and the administration joined the Organization of American States (OAS), and later the United Nations (UN), in adopting sanctions against the military junta. On the other hand, the Bush administration stalled in enforcing the sanctions and in compelling the coup leaders to leave office.

Taking office in January 1993, President Bill Clinton followed the same dual policies as his predecessor, until an increasing flow of refugees from Haiti, combined with domestic criticism of his policies, convinced him to change course. In October 1994, with the approval of the UN Security Council, Clinton sent a U.S.-led multinational peacekeeping force into Haiti to remove the junta and return Aristide to power.

Yet Aristide returned as a weakened president. As conditions for his return, the United States insisted that he agree not to reclaim the three years he had spent in exile, but to serve out the remaining eighteen months of his original five-year mandate; and that he accept the neoliberal economic policies advocated by the International Monetary Fund and the World Bank. New elections were held in December 1995, and Aristide's former prime minister, René Préval, became Haiti's new president. The democratic revolution succeeded in establishing a formal democracy in Haiti, but it did not change the class system that made Haiti the poorest country in the Western Hemisphere.

ALEX DUPUY

BIBLIOGRAPHY

Aristide, Jean-Bertrand. *Dignity.* Translated by Carrol F. Coates. Charlottesville: University Press of Virginia, 1996.

Dupuy, Alex. *Haiti in the New World Order: The Limits of the Democratic Revolution.* Boulder, Colo.: Westview Press, 1997.

North American Congress for Latin America (NACLA). *Haiti: Dangerous Crossroads.* Boston: South End Press, 1995.

HAITIAN REVOLUTION OF INDEPENDENCE (1791–1804)

Haiti is the only country to have won its independence through a simultaneous slave and anticolonial revolution in modern times. The revolution began in August 1791 and ended in January 1804 when the revolutionary leaders declared their independence from France and changed the name of the former colony from Saint-Domingue to its ancient Taino Arawak name of Haiti.

Before it became a French colony in 1697, Saint-Domingue was part of the colony that Spain established on the island it named Hispaniola after conquering the island in 1492 and destroying the indigenous Taino Arawak population. Once it passed under French control, Saint-Domingue, which occupied the western third of Hispaniola, grew to become the wealthiest and most productive of all Caribbean colonies. As with all other slave colonies, Saint-Domingue's population was classified and segmented racially. In 1791 it comprised whites (numbering about 40,000); *affranchis* (freed people of color, numbering around 28,000, including mulattos); and black slaves (numbering about 455,000).

A class system compounded the racial hierarchy. The dominant class consisted of the *grands blancs,* or large planters, who owned most of the slaves and the sugar plantations; the merchant bourgeoisie or their representatives in the colony; and the French colonial administrators and high-ranking army officers. Mulattos also figured among the slave- and property-owning class, but they owned mostly smaller coffee plantations rather than large sugar plantations. Still, by 1790 mulattos owned about one-fourth of the slaves and one-third of the colony's productive properties. Mulattos, however, were denied equal social and political rights with whites, hence they remained subordinated to, and could not exercise equal political power with, whites.

Below the class of slave and property owners were a middle class of professionals and plantation overseers and a working class of skilled craftsmen and unskilled manual wage-laborers. The majority of whites, known as the *petits blancs,* or small whites, belonged to these two classes, as did most of the *affranchis* population. Below the dominant slave and property owners and the middle and working classes, which together constituted the free population, were the black slaves, who made up the majority of the population.

The slave-labor system of Saint-Domingue was particularly harsh. Slaves were overexploited to the point of exhaustion. Extreme labor practices, combined with an inadequate diet and health care, resulted in a higher death rate than birth rate among slaves. Had it not been for the constant supply of new slaves from the African slave trade, the slave population of Saint-Domingue would have died out. Thus, when the slave revolt began in 1791, the majority of the slave population had been recently imported from Africa.

THE SAINT-DOMINGUE REVOLUTION

The French Revolution of 1789 had a profound influence in Saint-Domingue. All the free classes in the colony sought to exploit the Revolution to their own advantage, but all were united in wanting to maintain the slave system. The resident planter class, allied with the *petits blancs,* pushed for greater self-government in Saint-Domingue and representation in the French National Assembly. The mulattos pressed for full equality with whites. The absentee proprietors in France and the merchant bourgeoisie favored the status quo and opposed the demands of the resident planters, the *petits blancs,* and the mulattos. In the midst of this political turmoil, the decisive revolt of the slaves in 1791 forever altered the balance of power in and the future of Saint-Domingue. By 1800 the revolutionary army of ex-slaves led by François-Dominique Toussaint L'Ouverture had gained control over the colony after deporting the principal French colonial and military officers and suppressing a civil war led by the mulattos against L'Ouverture.

After 1800 the Saint-Domingue revolution proceeded in two phases. In the first phase, between 1800 and 1802, L'Ouverture insisted on self-government for the colony and liberty and equal rights for all. But he also understood that Saint-Domingue could not go it alone, and that ties with France and the capital and know-how of the planter class would have to be maintained. Consequently, he did not declare the independence of Saint-Domingue, and he encouraged the planter class to remain in the colony, invest in their plantations, and employ their former slaves as wage-laborers.

L'Ouverture's strategy failed because all other major interests in the colony opposed it. The French government under Napoleon Bonaparte, the merchant bourgeoisie, and the colonial planter class viscerally opposed black rule in the colony and freedom for the slaves. The mulattos also opposed freedom and equal rights for the slaves but benefited from the flight of whites by extending their control over the properties the whites had left behind. In the meantime, the revolutionary leaders in control of the colony had transformed themselves into a new property-owning class by appropriating the property of the French planters who had fled the colony. Consequently, a faction of the revolutionary leadership opposed L'Ouverture's policy of conciliation with the whites and desired full independence instead. For their part, the former slaves, who equated freedom with landownership, escaped to the hills to become independent farmers.

FROM SAINT-DOMINGUE TO HAITI

The second phase of the Saint-Domingue revolution began when Bonaparte sent a military expedition in February 1802 to regain control of the rebellious colony and reimpose the slave regime. At that point, Jean-Jacques Dessalines and his proindependence supporters broke with L'Ouverture and allowed him to be captured and deported to France. Dessalines and his forces then joined ranks with the mulattos, who feared the return of the French and the loss of their rights, to organize the revolts that led to the defeat and expulsion of the French forces from Saint-Domingue and the declaration of Haiti's independence.

The unity achieved between the black and mulatto leaders to expel the French from Haiti was only temporary, however. Soon after independence, these two factions of the dominant class engaged in open and continuous struggles to determine who would dominate economically and politically and extract the maximum amount of wealth from the slave-turned-peasant producers. Conflict between blacks and mulattos would characterize Haiti well into the twentieth century and give the state its unique characteristics among its Caribbean neighbors.

Haiti's revolution of independence, then, was the first to pose the fundamental question that applied to all subsequent revolutions in the developing world but that still remains unresolved: How to break with imperial domination and create a viable alternative socio-politico-economic system that benefits the majority and guarantees freedom and equal rights for all?

See also *L'Ouverture, François-Dominique Toussaint.*

ALEX DUPUY

BIBLIOGRAPHY

Dupuy, Alex. *Haiti in the World Economy: Class, Race, and Underdevelopment since 1700.* Boulder, Colo.: Westview Press, 1989.

Fick, Carolyn E. *The Making of Haiti: The Saint Domingue Revolution from Below.* Knoxville: University of Tennessee Press, 1990.

James, C. L. R. *The Black Jacobins: Toussaint L'Ouverture and the San Domingo Revolution.* New York: Vintage Books, 1963.

HAVEL, VÁCLAV

Havel (1936–), playwright and former dissident, became president of Czechoslovakia following the fall of communism and of the Czech Republic after the dissolution of Czechoslovakia. A long-term advocate of human rights, Havel played a key role in bringing about the end of communism in Czechoslovakia in 1989.

Havel was born to a wealthy family in Prague. After the establishment of communist rule in Czechoslovakia in 1948, however, this was a stigma. Due to his family background he was forced to take night courses while working to finish high school. He studied briefly at a technical university and completed his education as an external student in the Theatre Department of the Academy of Fine Arts. He worked as a stage hand at the ABC Theatre in Prague and later at the Theatre on the Balustrade. There his plays, including *The Garden Party, The Memorandum,* and *The Increased Difficulty of Concentration,* were an important part of Prague's developing theater of the absurd. In the mid-to-late 1960s Havel was active in trying to liberalize the official Writers Union.

Václav Havel

After the Warsaw Pact invasion of Czechoslovakia in August 1968, Havel could no longer work as a playwright. His plays were banned in Czechoslovakia. However, some of his plays gained acclaim abroad. Havel also wrote several politically oriented books, including *Living in Truth* and *Letters to Olga*.

In 1977 Havel became one of the founders of the human rights movement Charter 77 and the Committee for the Defense of the Unjustly Persecuted. He continued to be a leading figure in the opposition in Czechoslovakia in the 1970s and 1980s. Havel was arrested numerous times and served several jail terms. Sentenced to four and a half years in jail in 1979, he was released in March 1983. He was again jailed for several months in the spring of 1989 for participating in a peaceful demonstration in January 1989 in honor of the Czechoslovak student, Jan Palach, who burned himself to death in January 1969 in protest against the Soviet invasion.

When mass demonstrations developed in Czechoslovakia after the November 17, 1989, beating of peaceful student demonstrators, Havel and other dissidents took the lead in founding Civic Forum, the organization that led mass protests and negotiated the end of communist rule with the regime. Havel quickly emerged as the main symbol of the so-called Velvet Revolution that peacefully ousted the communist system. Seen as the moral voice of his country, he was elected president of Czechoslovakia in December 1989 by the parliament, which still had a majority of Communist deputies.

As a political leader, Havel attempted to put his ideals into practice. The effort was noticeable in his support of Czechoslovakia's return to Europe and focus on regional cooperation with other central European countries. Under his leadership, Czechoslovakia became a member of the Council of Europe and signed an association agreement with the European Union. Havel negotiated the withdrawal of Soviet troops from Czechoslovak territory and worked to restore good relations with the United States. Originally an advocate of a pan-European security structure, he became an ardent supporter of NATO membership.

Havel was unable to prevent the break-up of Czechoslovakia. Unwilling to preside over the break-up of the Czechoslovakian federation, he resigned as president of Czechoslovakia after the Slovak government declared Slovakia's sovereignty in July 1992.

Havel was elected president of the Czech Republic in February 1993 and was reelected in January 1998. Although the powers of the Czech presidency are not as great as those of his previous position, Havel's stature as a world figure has allowed him to have more influence in Czech affairs than the formal powers of the Czech presidency alone would suggest.

See also *Czechoslovak "Prague Spring" (1968); Czechoslovak "Velvet Revolution" and "Divorce" (1989–1993); East European Revolutions of 1989.*

Sharon L. Wolchik

BIBLIOGRAPHY

Havel, Václav. *Disturbing the Peace.* New York: Vintage Books, 1990.

Kriseová, Eda. *Václav Havel: The Authorized Biography.* New York: Pharos Books, 1993.

HENRY, PATRICK

Henry (1736–1799), revolutionary leader, lawyer, and orator, was born in Hanover County, Virginia, the son of John Henry, a planter and middle-level member of the Virginia gentry. His schooling was limited, and in the 1750s he failed at storekeeping and farming. He then pursued a career in the law, and in 1760, after brief study, he was authorized to practice law in the county courts. Henry was almost immediately successful.

In 1763 he took on a case that later was called the "Parsons' Cause." He appeared for the defense and invoked compact theory, asserting that the original compact between the king and people, protection on the one hand and obedience on the other, had been broken when George III, by disallowing a good law, the Two Penny Act, had forfeited the right to his subjects' compliance. The argument was popular, and it was enhanced by the young lawyer's oratorical gifts.

The Parsons' Cause brought him recognition and was, no doubt, crucial in his 1765 election to the House of Burgesses in the midst of the Stamp Act controversy. Parliament was levying for the first time a direct tax on its American colonies. The tax was widely opposed on the grounds that Parliament could regulate trade but not impose internal taxes—a view expressed strongly when the House of Burgesses adopted Henry's Stamp Act Resolves. In supporting the resolves he declared that Caesar had his Brutus, Charles I his Cromwell, and George III might profit by their example. Only four of the original seven resolutions were approved, but all were published widely in colonial newspapers, and Henry emerged as an unremitting opponent of British policies.

In 1773 Henry was one of those who worked to establish intercolonial committees of correspondence. He was elected in 1774 and 1775 as one of Virginia's delegates to the Continental Congress. Thereafter he held no continental or national offices, but in Virginia he remained active. In March 1775 he pushed through the second Virginia Convention resolutions providing for military preparedness and reportedly concluded one speech with his famous remark "give me liberty or give me death." In May 1776 his version of a resolution proposing independence was approved by the fifth Virginia Convention, and soon thereafter he was elected the new state's first governor, a post he held from 1776 to 1779 and from 1784 to 1786. He was Virginia's most popular politician.

Henry was a localist. Unlike Thomas Jefferson and James Madison, Henry had no national vision. He resisted measures to strengthen the Articles of Confederation; declined to serve in the Constitutional Convention of 1787; and opposed the new constitution. Henry feared a powerful, centralized government, which he believed would be too far removed from its citizens. In his last years he became a Federalist, expressing a desire for "order" in government, but he declined offers of national posts. He died in 1799 at his estate in Charlotte County, Virginia.

Henry's role in the American Revolution was substantial. An unmatched orator who closely identified with the people, he contributed to making the Revolution a more popular movement. And his opposition to strong central government still resonates in American political culture.

See also *Adams, Samuel; American (U.S.) Revolution (1776–1789)*.

EMORY G. EVANS

BIBLIOGRAPHY

Beeman, Richard R. *Patrick Henry: A Biography.* New York: McGraw Hill, 1974.

Henry, William Wirt, ed. *Patrick Henry, Life Correspondence and Speeches.* 3 vols. New York: Charles Scribner's Sons, 1891.

Mayer, Henry. *A Son of Thunder: Patrick Henry and the American Republic.* Charlottesville: University Press of Virginia, 1991.

Meade, Robert D. *Patrick Henry.* 2 vols. Philadelphia: Lippincott, 1957–1969.

HITLER, ADOLF

Hitler (1889–1945) was guided in his political life by his pseudo-scientific understanding of race. His goal was to create a biologically pure, strong Germanic race that would use the rest of the world's races as its servants and slaves. Undesirable and inferior people would be exterminated. The Jews, in his view, were the most dangerous and polluting of all races because the Jews could infiltrate and mix with other races to weaken and destroy them.

Hitler was born in Austria and had an ordinary childhood. In 1907 he went to Vienna to become an artist but failed to get into the Academy of Fine Arts. Reduced to poverty, he picked up the anti-Semitic, German nationalist views then current in Vienna and came to blame Jews, who occupied many prominent positions in Vienna's high cultural life, for his failure. In 1913 he moved to Munich, Germany. When World War I broke out in 1914, he joined the German army. He was an exceptionally courageous, highly decorated soldier. After the defeat of 1918, he joined a small ultranationalist movement in Munich, the Nationalist Socialist German Workers' (Nazi) Party. His extraordinarily persuasive speeches and ability to attract followers quickly gained him the party's leadership.

The Nazis wanted to end the democracy imposed on Germany by the victorious allies and to regain German greatness. To do this it was necessary to rid Germany of those whom German rightists viewed as the traitors who had ruined it in 1918, particularly Jews and social democrats. The party organized uniformed gangs of street fighters, the Brown Shirts, to demonstrate and rally support for their cause. The unsettled political conditions in Germany and economic instability that led to ruinous inflation in 1923 swelled the ranks of the malcontent and fearful, and the Nazis benefited.

In 1923 Hitler attempted a coup, but the authorities in Munich held firm, and he was jailed. While in prison in 1924, he wrote his autobiographical political program, *Mein Kampf* (My Struggle). Along with ridding Germany of Jews, he called for expansion of German territory to provide living space and resources. He proposed to create a more youthful, dynamic, and warlike Germany where opportunity would be open to all pure Germans, no matter what their class origins. His vision (except for the anti-Semitism) resembled Benito Mussolini's Italian fascism in that it promised to end the alienation, class-based disputes, and corruption of modern capitalist democracy. The fascist future would be more wholesome, vigorous, and natural.

Out of jail, from 1925 to 1929 he slowly built up Nazi Party membership throughout all of Germany. The Great Depression, which began in 1929, gave him his chance. With over a quarter of the German work force unemployed, Nazi strength rose rapidly. In 1928 the Nazi Party won 3 percent of the vote in parliamentary elections; in 1930, 18 percent; and in July 1932, 37 percent, to become Germany's largest single party. Though the party's vote fell in a second election in 1932, to 32 percent of the electorate, Hitler, allied to other nationalist parties, became chancellor (prime minister) in January 1933. The combination of continuing street violence carried out by both his Brown Shirts and by communist thugs, the demand for economic and political stability, and the inability of the other parties to unite convinced German conservatives that they had no alternative to Nazi control of government.

Hitler quickly banned all opposition, ended democracy, and turned Germany into a totalitarian police state with himself as *fürher,* or leader. State and party control was gradually imposed on industries and all key social institutions. Rearmament and a huge road-building project ended the depression. Once Hitler had stabilized Germany, Jews, the feeble minded, and homosexuals (all deemed "racially inferior") began to be herded into concentration camps, and some were killed.

But it was only in 1939, when Hitler launched World War II, that his nightmarish plan was fully implemented. His armies conquered and enslaved most of Europe: six million Jews and hundreds of thousands of Gypsies were exterminated. More than ten million Slavic (and therefore, according to Nazi doctrine, also "racially inferior") Poles, Russians, Ukrainians, and others in Eastern Europe were slaughtered or died of starvation and disease. Millions more died elsewhere in Europe.

By the end of 1941, only the Soviet Union and Great Britain held out against him. But the entry of the Americans into the war against him in 1942 and the Soviet victory at Stalingrad in the winter of 1943 turned the tide. In June 1944 the Americans and British landed in France and began to push toward Germany. Dissident German army officers tried to assassinate Hitler in July 1944 but failed.

The allies invaded Germany from east and west in 1945. On April 30, 1945, with the Soviet army a few blocks from his Berlin bunker, Hitler committed suicide after urging the world to continue the struggle against "international Jewry" and calling for Germany to "win territory in the East."

Adolf Hitler (far right), who became chancellor of Germany in 1933 through legal means, transformed Germany into a fascist dictatorship.

The totalitarian Nazi Germany that Hitler created had much in common with Josef Stalin's communist state. Both leaders were guided by a revolutionary vision for a new world based on what we know to have been false science. Both deified the leader, created police states, and militarized their societies. Both exterminated their enemies by the millions. Hitler's particular legacy was at least thirty-five million civilian and military deaths and a ruined Europe.

See also *Dictatorship; German Nazi Revolution (1933–1945); Mussolini, Benito.*

DANIEL CHIROT

BIBLIOGRAPHY

Arendt, Hannah. *The Origins of Totalitarianism.* New York: Meridian, 1958.

Bullock, Alan. *Hitler: A Study in Tyranny.* Rev. ed. New York: Harper Torchbooks, 1964.

Burleigh, Michael, and Wolfgang Wippermann. *The Racial State: Germany 1933–1945.* Cambridge: Cambridge University Press, 1991.

Fest, Joachim C. *Hitler.* New York: Vintage Books, 1975.

Kershaw, Ian. *Hitler.* London: Longman, 1991.

HO CHI MINH

Few political figures have had as much influence on the twentieth century as the Vietnamese revolutionary Ho Chi Minh (1890–1969). Born in a small village in central Vietnam at a time when his homeland was under French colonial rule, Ho became a member of the French Communist Party in the early 1920s. After studying in Moscow, he founded the first communist party in Vietnam and became the chief agent of the Comintern, an organization established in Moscow in 1919 to promote the cause of world revolution, in Southeast Asia. After World War II he led the Communist-dominated Vietminh Front (the popular name for the League for the Independence of Vietnam) in a long struggle that led to the withdrawal of the French in 1954 as a result of the Geneva Conference.

The Geneva Conference temporarily divided Vietnam into two zones—a Communist North and a non-Communist South. Ho was elected president of the Democratic Republic of Vietnam in the North, with its capital in Hanoi. The Geneva agreement called for national elections to reunify the country in 1956, but the government in the South, with U.S. backing, refused to carry them out. In response, Ho and his colleagues launched an insurgent movement in South Vietnam, which won wide popular support from the local population. In 1965 President Lyndon B. Johnson ordered the dispatch of U.S. combat troops to prevent a total Communist victory. Ho died in 1969 while the war was still under way.

By his own admission, Ho (whose real name was Nguyen Tat Thanh) was initially attracted to communism by Vladimir Ilyich Lenin's famous "Theses on the National and Colonial Questions" (1920), which urged support by Soviet Russia for anticolonialist movements around the world against the common enemy of Western imperialism. Like his Chinese contemporary Mao Zedong, Ho rejected the Marxist orthodoxy assigning primacy to urban insurrections and argued that revolutionary movements in Asia could not succeed without support from the oppressed rural masses in the region. Ho's distinctive approach to waging revolution—using a combination of nationalism and populism while downplaying issues related to class struggle and proletarian internationalism—was often criticized by European Marxists. But it became the foundation of Vietnamese revolutionary strategy and is widely viewed as the key to the party's final victory over the South in 1975. His personal charisma (because of his avuncular and self-effacing style, he was widely revered by many Vietnamese as "Uncle Ho") was also a major contributing factor in that victory.

In addition to his role as the guiding force behind the Vietnamese revolution, Ho Chi Minh was a leading figure in the international communist movement. He gave vocal support to the revolutionary cause throughout Asia, Africa, and Latin America, and he worked tirelessly to prevent, or minimize the impact of, the Sino-Soviet dispute, which split the communist world into contending factions during the last decade of his life.

See also *Vietnamese Revolution (1945–1975).*

WILLIAM J. DUIKER

BIBLIOGRAPHY

Duiker, William J. *The Communist Road to Power in Vietnam.* 2d ed. Boulder, Colo.: Westview Press, 1996.
Halberstam, David. *Ho.* New York: Knopf, 1987.
Hémery, Daniel. *Ho Chi Minh: De l'Indochine au Vietnam.* Paris: Gallimard, 1990.
Lacouture, Jean. *Ho Chi Minh: A Political Biography.* Translated by Peter Wiles. New York: Vintage, 1968.

HONG XIUQUAN

Hong (1814–1864) envisioned and led China's millenarian Taiping Rebellion (1851–1864). A member of south China's oppressed Hakka ethnic minority, Hong aspired to upward mobility through government service. Instead, his repeated failures in the state examinations and exposure to missionary Christianity in Guangzhou (Guangdong's provincial capital) precipitated, in 1837, a powerful dream. In Hong's dream, God identified Hong as Christ's younger brother and commissioned him to replace Confucian China with an egalitarian "Heavenly Kingdom of Great Peace" *(Taiping Tianguo).*

In subsequent sermons and essays, Hong claimed that the biblical God was also China's creator and emperor, who had reigned over an ancient utopia of "great peace and equality" *(taiping).* As "brothers" and "sisters," God's worshipful children had shared equally in the fruits of His creation. But, Hong lamented, Confucius left God out of his compilation of China's classical texts. And China's emperors usurped God's rule, attributed His sustaining powers to "lifeless" Daoist and Buddhist idols, and abandoned universal love for Confucius's "partial love," which exalted emperor over subject, family over individual, and male over female.

Hong concluded that the result of China's apostasy was social conflict, which he blamed for the Hakka's suffering. Indeed, following the Opium War (1839–1842), population pressures and foreign encroachment intensified unemployment, landlord greed, banditry, opium smuggling, ethnic polarization, famine, and plague throughout south China's

Guangzhou delta and neighboring Guangxi Province. During the late 1840s Hong preached moral revival among his "God Worshipper" congregations, which honeycombed throughout southeastern Guangxi. He insisted that these congregations were the vanguard of the biblically promised Heavenly Kingdom *(Tianguo)* come to earth. To prepare for the new dispensation, Hong wove Christian baptism, the Ten Commandments, and Chinese sectarian ideals into compelling ritual, an ascetic, universalist morality, and a communal "Sacred Treasury," which incorporated Hakka customs of property-sharing and gender equality.

Alarmed by the God Worshippers' loyalty to a transcendent God, the Qing (Manchu) emperor unleashed troops against Hong's flock in the summer of 1850. On January 11, 1851, Hong announced the inauguration of the Taiping Heavenly Kingdom. He invited all Chinese to unite as one "Chosen People," whom God, now restored as China's legitimate ruler, would deliver from Manchu despotism and Confucian injustice. Militant faith and an all-embracing theocratic leadership enabled one million Taipings to capture Nanjing, the former imperial capital near the mouth of the Yangzi River, in March 1853.

Christening the city "New Jerusalem," Hong made Nanjing his Heavenly Capital. Proclaiming himself the reincarnated Melchizedek (the Bible's messianic priest-king) as well as China's Heavenly King (God's earthly vice regent), Hong used ceaseless worship and a strict moral code to maintain discipline. He assaulted Confucianism by abolishing female footbinding, concubinage, arranged marriage, and prostitution, and by decreeing women's equal access to schooling, the examinations, public office, military service, and landholding. Hong also substituted the Bible and his own writings for Confucian texts as the basis of universal public education and the examinations and guaranteed economic security and social welfare through property-sharing at a level of government never before proposed in China: the "congregation" of twenty-five families.

A fratricidal power struggle in 1856 between Hong and his chief deputy crippled theocratic control. After that, Hong's plans to link Taiping China with the Christian West were sabotaged by the missionaries' condemnation of his "heretical" religion and by Western military support of Qing forces, who crushed "New Jerusalem" in the summer of 1864.

Hong was a leader without parallel in Chinese history. Believing that China could be saved by fusing Chinese and biblical ideals, he developed a bold millennial blueprint that far surpassed the aims and scope of traditional rebels, especially in its efforts to make Chinese women equal partners of men in carrying out the Heavenly Father's mandate to transform China. In fact, Hong's religious vision presaged China's twentieth-century revolutions, which—while also inspired by a unique synthesis of Chinese and foreign sources—succeeded through exclusively human means.

See also *Chinese Taiping Rebellion (1851–1864); Millenarianism; Religion.*

P. RICHARD BOHR

BIBLIOGRAPHY

Bohr, P. Richard. "The Politics of Eschatology: Hung Hsiu-ch'üan and the Rise of the Taipings, 1837–1853." Ph.D. dissertation, University of California, Davis, 1978.

———. "The Theologian as Revolutionary: Hung Hsiu-ch'üan's Religious Vision of the Taiping Heavenly Kingdom." In *Tradition and Metamorphosis in Modern Chinese History: Essays in Honor of Professor Kwang-Ching Liu's Seventy-fifth Birthday.* 2 vols. Edited by Yen-p'ing Hao and Hsiu-mei Wei. Taipei: Institute of Modern History, Academia Sinica, 1998.

Spence, Jonathan D. *God's Chinese Son: The Taiping Heavenly Kingdom of Hong Xiuquan.* New York: W.W. Norton, 1996.

Wagner, Rudolph G. *Reenacting the Heavenly Vision: The Role of Religion in the Taiping Rebellion.* Berkeley: University of California, Institute of East Asian Studies, 1982.

HUNGARIAN ANTICOMMUNIST REVOLUTION (1989)

The process that brought communist dictatorship to an end in Hungary and restored democracy has been aptly called a "negotiated revolution," for it was incremental, nonviolent, and legalistic. The principal actors included some communist party leaders, many intellectuals and technocrats, and the Soviet reformer Mikhail Gorbachev.

That the revolution was peaceful owed something to the policies of Hungarian party leader János Kádár, who, after consolidating communist rule in the wake of the 1956 revolution, had adopted a conciliatory approach symbolized by the slogan "those who are not against us are with us." The implicit bargain was that if Hungarians acknowledged the inevitability of party dominance and Soviet overlordship, the regime could become less repressive and pursue economic modernization. The New Economic Mechanism, inaugurated in 1968, introduced some elements of the market and promoted a measure of consumerism. Cultural and travel restrictions were eased. But the middle classes and farmers benefited more from these changes than did the industrial working class, and a conservative backlash, backed by the Soviet Union, brought the reform to a halt in 1972. Market-oriented reforms were again introduced in the late 1970s. Nonetheless, Hungary's economy continued to suffer from the communist system's inherent inefficiency as well as from the effects of the oil crisis.

Although Hungary was by some standards the most liberal and prosperous country in the Soviet sphere, by the early 1980s Kádár's popularity and the credibility of the regime's reforms were plummeting. Inflation rose, and many people had to resort to second or third jobs to maintain their living standard. Social inequality increased, as many people fell below the poverty line while a few others, mainly in the tiny private sector, became comparatively affluent. The regime borrowed heavily, more to buy social peace than to modernize production, and as a result Hungary became saddled with the world's highest per capita debt in hard currency. The social consensus that underpinned the conciliatory approach of Kádárism was gradually eroded by economic discontent, but the government's palliative economic measures, its marginal concessions to political participation, and memories of the ill-fated 1956 revolution all helped forestall overt challenge to its legitimacy. The regime also courted popularity by making concessions to national sentiments, notably in criticizing Romania over its treatment of the Hungarian minority in Transylvania.

THE EMERGENCE OF POLITICAL OPPOSITION

The 1989 revolution was the outcome of an elite process that began to emerge in the early years of the decade. Driven by the failure of Kádárism and the necessity for more radical reforms in the economic and political realm, critics emerged both within the party hierarchy and among the noncommunist intelligentsia. The various reform-oriented groups shared the belief that Leninism should give way to pluralism, and state socialism to a market economy, but they were divided over the pace of change and the role that a socialist party would play in the new order.

In the party, reformers coalesced around Imre Pozsgay, who had been demoted for his liberal views, and Rezsó Nyers, one of the architects of the New Economic Mechanism. At lower levels of the party, so-called reform circles gradually came to play the role of an opposition, testing Kádár's tolerance for intraparty democracy. Outside the party, several distinct clusters of intellectual dissidents emerged. One important group, which drew some inspiration from the prewar "populist" movement, professed liberal Christian democratic and nationalistic values and showed some disposition to collaborate with party reformers to bring about gradual change. Members of the group invited Pozsgay to the meeting in September 1987 at which the Hungarian Democratic Forum was established. A second important group, sharply delineated from the first and sometimes known as the "urbanists," included prominent intellectuals who had converted from Marxism to liberalism and antiregime activists, some of them Jewish. They formed the Alliance of Free Democrats, shared a cosmopolitan outlook, and championed rapid and sweeping political transformation. Similar goals inspired the youthful members of the Federation of Young Democrats. Many economists contributed to the burgeoning opposition movement with their constructive criticism. Eventually the opposition came to include groups that had broken away from the official trade union organization to form the Democratic League of Independent Trade Unions, as well as reconstituted elements of postwar parties such as the Smallholders.

The opposition movement was spurred by external factors as well. The ongoing Conference on Security and Cooperation in Europe had put civil rights on the European agenda. Easier travel and communication reinforced the belief among many Hungarians that only association with Western Europe could bring democracy and prosperity. The new Soviet leader, Mikhail Gorbachev, who had come to power in March 1985, seemed intent on reforming the Leninist system and on rapprochement with the West. In July 1989, on a visit to Budapest, President George Bush indicated that a democratic Hungary would benefit from Western economic aid.

THE SHIFT TO DEMOCRACY

One obstacle to change disappeared when, at a party conference in May 1988, the aging Kádár was summarily retired. His successor, Kàroly Grósz, tried to restrain the momentum of reform and preserve the party's supremacy, but he was soon eclipsed by the leaders of the reform wing: Pozsgay, Nyers, and Prime Minister Miklós Németh. Reform received further impetus from developments in Poland, where roundtable discussions between the government and opposition representatives—approved by Gorbachev—led to parliamentary elections in June 1989 and the sweeping victory of Solidarity. A similar roundtable conference opened in Budapest on June 14, 1989. Two days later, Imre Nagy, the leading figure of the 1956 revolution, who was executed in 1958, was ceremonially reburied; the 1956 revolution itself was officially acknowledged to have been a legitimate and popular challenge to despotism.

The roundtable talks, which were marked by sharp discord not only between regime and dissidents but also within the diverse opposition, ended in mid-September with a compromise agreement that provided for direct election of a president, to be followed by free parliamentary elections, as well as for a reformed legal system and depoliticization of the armed forces. The first point was a victory for the government: if Pozsgay, whose popularity had soared, won the presidency, he and a reformed party could supervise the transition. Meanwhile, the government earned Western plaudits by

Austrian foreign minister Alois Mock and Hungarian foreign minister Gyula Horn cut the wires at the Austrian-Hungarian border, July 27, 1989.

breaking its treaty obligations to the German Democratic Republic and opening Hungary's border with Austria to allow thousands of East German "tourists" to leave for West Germany.

At a party congress on October 10, the majority of delegates voted to dissolve the Hungarian Socialist Workers' Party and, opting for democratic socialism, formed the Hungarian Socialist Party, led by Nyers. But freedom was in the air, and the tide of public opinion was turning against the reformed communists. Parliament passed laws disbanding the party-controlled Workers' Militia and banning party cells in workplaces. The Free Democrats and Young Democrats (who, along with the independent trade union group, had refused to sign the roundtable agreement) organized a petition campaign that led to a referendum on the timing of the presidential election. As a result of the referendum, the presidential election was postponed until after the parliamentary elections. In those elections, held in March 1990, the conservative Hungarian Democratic Forum emerged as the strongest party and formed a government led by József Antall; the Hungarian Socialist Party won only slightly over 10 percent of the vote. The negotiated revolution had given Hungary its first democratically elected government in forty-five years, and communism ended.

See also *East European Revolutions of 1989; East German Revolution and Unification (1989–1990).*

Bennett Kovrig

BIBLIOGRAPHY

Ash, Timothy Garton. *The Magic Lantern: The Revolution of '89 Witnessed in Warsaw, Budapest, Berlin, and Prague.* New York: Random House, 1990.

Bozóki, Andràs, et al., eds. *Post-Communist Transition: Emerging Pluralism in Hungary.* New York: St. Martin's Press, 1992.

Brown, J. F. *Surge to Freedom: The End of Communist Rule in Eastern Europe.* Durham, N.C.: Duke University Press, 1991.

Gati, Charles. *The Bloc that Failed.* Bloomington: Indiana University Press, 1990.

Kis, Jànos. *Politics in Hungary: For a Democratic Alternative.* Highland Lakes, N.J.: Atlantic Research, 1989.

Tókés, Rudolf L. *Hungary's Negotiated Revolution.* New York: Cambridge University Press, 1996.

HUNGARIAN REVOLUTIONS (1918–1919)

The Hungarian Revolutions of 1918–1919 were part of the political upheavals on the European continent following the Russian Revolution of 1917 and the defeat of the Central Powers in the First World War. Propelled by war-weariness, impending military defeat, and material deprivation, spontaneous demonstrations broke out in Budapest on October 31, 1918. Former prime minister Count István Tisza was assassinated on that day, and the left-leaning Count Mihàily Károlyi, leader of Hungary's liberal-democratic opposition, was appointed premier as one of the last acts of state by Emperor-King Karl IV. Under Károlyi's premiership, and later, presidency, Hungary declared its independence from Austria, signed an armistice with the Entente powers, and proclaimed a republican form of government.

The liberal-democratic government of Károlyi faced grave external and internal pressures. Externally, the Entente powers demanded the piecemeal surrender and evacuation of some territory of the historical Hungarian state. Internally, the government faced the disgruntlement of conservatives and the relentless agitation of the newly formed Communist Party, which was capitalizing on rising popular discontent. Indeed, the agitation of the Communists undermined the government's authority and paralyzed its foreign policy. When the Entente presented its last set of territorial demands on March 21, 1919, Károlyi resigned and handed the helm of government to a coalition of left socialists and Communists. The coalition proclaimed a Soviet Republic on the country's remaining territory.

This second, Soviet, republic followed closely the Leninist model. On April 6 an election was held, one of the first in modern history to use a single list of candidates. Nominally, local legislative and administrative authority was vested in local councils, and national authority in a Congress of Councils. But the Congress met only once, for a brief period of four days (June 24–28), and real power was in the hands of a Revolutionary Governing Council. It was this body that ordered all land and means of production socialized, that suspended civil rights, and that repressed the opponents of the regime through self-styled terrorists under Tibor Szamuely, Otto Korvin, and József Cserny.

In foreign affairs, Béla Kun, the most forceful and conspicuous figure of the republic, rejected the ultimatum of the Entente and took the lead in organizing a Red Army to defend Hungarian territory in the name of proletarian internationalism. Shortly after proclamation of the republic, the armies of Czechoslovakia and Romania invaded the territories under its control. Under its commander, Vilmos Böhm, an erstwhile printer, and its chief of staff, Aurel Stromfeld, the Hungarian Red Army rolled back Czech advances and, in the process, was instrumental in proclaiming a Slovak Soviet Republic in Eperjes (Prešov). On the eastern front, however, the Hungarian army was overpowered by the advancing Romanians.

On July 30 the eastern front collapsed. Kun and most members of the Revolutionary Council escaped to Vienna, and the Romanian army entered Budapest on August 1, putting an end to the first communist state outside the Soviet Union. After a brief Romanian occupation, and under French auspices, Adm. Miklós Horthy's national army and assorted white detachments entered the Hungarian capital. The national army and its allies inflicted their own terror on the left and proceeded to restore the prerevolutionary social and political order in what was to be the territory of interwar Hungary.

ANDREW C. JANOS

BBLIOGRAPHY

Borsanyi, György. *The Life of a Communist Revolutionary: Bela Kun.* New York: East European Monographs, 1993.

Janos, Andrew, and William B. C.-Slottman. *Revolution in Perspective: Essays on the Hungarian Soviet Republic.* Berkeley, Calif.: University of California Press, 1971.

HUNGARIAN REVOLUTION (1956)

The Hungarian Revolution of 1956 was a watershed in the history of communism and of the cold war. It revealed broad and deep popular opposition to communist dictatorship and Soviet domination. At the same time, it tested the will of the Great Powers and served to confirm that, at least provisionally, the division of Europe could not be overcome.

The revolution's roots lay in the inadequacies of a socialist system imposed by domestic and external coercion. The stability of the system, personified by Soviet leader Joseph Stalin, was shaken by Stalin's death in March 1953 and by his successors' experiment with a so-called New Course. In Hungary, the Stalinist party leader Màtyàs Ràkosi was compelled to share power with a new, reform-minded prime minister, Imre Nagy, who tried to address consumer needs, mitigate police terror, reconsider agricultural collectivization, and investigate the case of communists purged on charges that they supported the independent course followed by the Yugoslav communist leader Josip Broz Tito. Although Ràkosi managed to have Nagy dismissed in early 1955, he could not halt the process of political decompression. The Hungarian party's self-confidence and unity were shaken by the Kremlin's reconciliation with Tito, which implied that there could be various paths to socialism, as well as by Soviet leader Nikita Khrushchev's "secret speech," in February 1956, denouncing the crimes of Stalin.

Much of the party's intelligentsia had rallied to Nagy, and by 1956 they and students were openly criticizing political oppression, a falling standard of living, and Russian domination. The ceremonial reinterment on October 6 of Làszló Rajk, a purged communist leader, drew a huge crowd, and student manifestos soon appeared demanding national independence and sweeping changes in the system. At the Kremlin's command, Ràkosi was replaced in July 1956 by Ernó Geró, who proved to be as inflexible as his predecessor, and the divided and demoralized party was unable to replicate its Polish counterpart's determined defense of national autonomy in the face of Soviet demands.

On October 23 students in Budapest demonstrated in solidarity with the Polish "quiet revolution"; later that day, police guarding the radio building fired into a crowd. On Soviet advice, Nagy was named prime minister again, and he eventually included representatives of noncommunist parties in his government. The reformist communist intellectuals were soon overshadowed, as all social strata joined the revolution. Insurgent groups organized throughout the country and impelled Nagy to promise restoration of an autonomous, democratic system and a mixed economy. The new communist party leader, János Kádár, who had replaced Geró on October 24, endorsed the revolution's goals.

The Soviet leadership was initially conciliatory, but the increasingly anticommunist thrust of the revolution and the coincidence of the Suez crisis, which divided the West and diverted Western attention from Eastern Europe, tilted the balance in favor of repression. Alarmed at Soviet military preparations, Nagy proclaimed Hungary's neutrality and withdrawal from the Warsaw Pact. On November 4 the Red Army moved to crush the revolution, ostensibly at the invitation of Kádár, who had been persuaded to change sides. Spontaneously formed workers' councils engaged in passive resistance for several weeks, but Soviet-communist domi-

nance was restored. The revolution had claimed some 2,700 Hungarian lives, in battle or by subsequent execution, and 20,000 people were imprisoned or deported; more than 200,000 fled the country.

What had been a profoundly patriotic and popular uprising was officially denounced as a "counterrevolution." Over time, the experience nevertheless induced Kádár to introduce a less repressive variant of communist dictatorship.

BENNETT KOVRIG

BIBLIOGRAPHY

Fehér, Ferenc, and Agnes Heller. *Hungary 1956 Revisited.* London: Allen and Unwin, 1983.

Gati, Charles. *Hungary and the Soviet Bloc.* Durham, N.C.: Duke University Press, 1986.

Kovrig, Bennett. *Communism in Hungary from Kun to Kàdàr.* Stanford, Calif.: Hoover Institution Press, 1979.

Lomax, Bill. *Budapest 1956.* London: Allison and Busby, 1976.

Nagy, Imre. *On Communism: In Defense of the New Course.* London: Thames and Hudson, 1957.

I

IDEOLOGY

Ideology generally refers to the realm of thoughts and ideas in circulation in any society; a specific ideology may be thought of as a package of relatively consistent ideas that people draw on to make sense of their place in society and the world around them. Many ideologies include a vision of what society and the world should be like and how that vision might be obtained. No ideology is so monolithic as to be exempt from internal contradictions or disagreements among its adherents; in times of revolution, in particular, such disagreements can develop into deadly confrontations.

Since several competing ideologies coexist in any society, with different sets of values and beliefs held as truth by different groups, the issue of ideology is often a central one in the various stages of revolutionary processes. The relative weight of ideology, ideas, and conscious, intentional action—as opposed to so-called objective or material circumstances and forces—in determining the outcome of any given situation remains the subject of a lively debate among students of revolution; few subscribe wholeheartedly to one extreme or the other anymore.

IDEOLOGY AND REVOLUTION: AN INTERTWINED HISTORY

Modern conceptions of revolution date from the convulsions in France after 1789, so it is fitting that the term "ideology" was born in France shortly thereafter. Introduced by the French scholar Antoine Destutt de Tracy shortly after the French Revolution, "ideology" was meant to become the scientific study of ideas. This initial conceptualization of ideology, like that of the revolution that formed its matrix, was firmly rooted in Enlightenment thinking and the attendant presumption that people could understand and control their world through systematic, scientific analysis and rational action. As the French Revolution began to wane, overcome by its enemies' successes and its own excesses, the Catholic Church and French nobility sought to construe "ideology" and its students—"ideologues"—in negative terms. These efforts were rewarded when Emperor Napoleon Bonaparte, in trouble at home and abroad and seeking to destroy the remnants of the changes wrought by the Revolution, condemned the nascent study of ideology and its "sinister metaphysics" for confusing people and undermining authority.

Thus emerged the most familiar notion of ideology, one that referred to ideas and specifically to a coherent body of ideas. The connotation was entirely negative and remained so, as amplified by Karl Marx (1818–1883). Although some of Marx's later writings would serve as the basis for redefining the nature and scope of ideology, his early work disdained ideology not only for confusing and "mystifying" people but also because it ostensibly served those in power by justifying and legitimating the rule of the dominant class in society. As Marx and Friedrich Engels, his frequent coauthor, made clear in *The German Ideology* (1845–1846; first published in 1932), it is imperative for those classes not in power to see through the ideology of the ruling class and thereby empower themselves to change their lives and, by extension, the world around them. Marx later recognized the role of ideas in shaping the ways people perceive their lives and the world around them and conceded that such ideas influence the decisions people make and the actions they choose; this thinking is perhaps most apparent in Marx's *The Eighteenth Brumaire of Louis Bonaparte* (1852).

Although the twentieth century has witnessed many interpretations of ideology, two broad approaches stand out. The first—ideology as a consistent body of ideas—is most readily apparent in the "isms" generally associated with the term: anarchism, capitalism, conservatism, communism, fascism, liberalism, socialism. This approach to ideology is, in essence, a theoretical one in which ideas exist almost on their own, as more or less monolithic bodies of thought independent of those who produce and transmit them. In this conceptualization, people embrace a formal ideology, which provides them with a theory about the world and their place in it and suggests actions they may take. While this remains the dominant conception of ideology, it is not necessarily the most useful, particularly with regard to the study of revolution.

Other conceptualizations draw on the later Marx and Marxists such as Vladimir Ilyich Lenin, Antonio Gramsci, and Ernesto "Che" Guevara. Here ideology has less to do with a comprehensive set of beliefs summed by any one "ism" than with a consistent set of actions from which theory follows. The key to such conceptions is "praxis," a term that in general refers to human action. In this view, people are conscious actors who create their own reality and therefore can change themselves and their world. Practice comes first; theory follows. Talk is less important than action. Guevara, for example, reportedly liked to quote the maxim of Cuban independence hero José Martí: "The best way to speak is to act." Guevara emphasized revolutionary attitudes and the new sensibilities that would develop as the social revolutionary process unfolded.

Viewed in this way, ideology is a social *process*. Its "isms" are idealism, pragmatism, and voluntarism, in contrast to the dogmatism and scholasticism implicit in the first approach. Ideology is a popular idea system that reflects the conditions of people's everyday lives and provides a resource upon which they may draw as they confront a world that is often hostile to their interests and desires. Ideas, which neither exist in a vacuum nor appear out of thin air, emerge from people's actual experiences, from the lessons passed on to them orally as part of their collective memory, and from "grand" ideas such as the Declaration of the Rights of Man and the Citizen, the right to property, evolving concepts of social justice, and so on. Such an ideology provides the believer with a picture of the world both as it is and as it should be. In so doing, it organizes the tremendous complexity of the world into something fairly simple and understandable and guides behavior on a daily basis. So equipped, ordinary people, seeking to realize their desires and change their world, sometimes create extraordinary situations.

REVOLUTION AND IDEOLOGY: A DIALECTICAL RELATIONSHIP

The French Revolution provided the paradigm for future revolutionaries, offering the world the powerful ideals of liberty, equality, and fraternity; the Declaration of the Rights of Man and the Citizen; and the notion of the sovereignty of the people, which implies their right to self-determination. Those principles have underpinned the revolutionary movements of the twentieth century, often paired with a grand myth such as international revolution, the classless society, freedom from foreign domination, or the return of a moral, indigenous, or religious tradition. Some twentieth century examples include Russia (1917), China (1949), Cuba (1959), and Iran (1979).

Almost two hundred years after the French Revolution, the Iranian Islamic Revolution (1979) brought the role of ideology sharply back into focus. Several of the ideas noted above, most notably the desire for freedom from foreign domination and the resurgence of a religious tradition, united an array of groups to overthrow a repressive monarchy. After obtaining political power, the Islamic fundamentalists were able to consolidate their hold on power and create an Islamic Republic that has inspired a generation of ideologically driven Islamic revolutionaries across Asia and North Africa, while raising issues about religious freedom, women's rights, and justice.

What all revolutionary ideologies share is a strong critique of the previous regime and society. That critique provides a framework for the articulation of social ills and obstacles and a vision of a new society. As a result, it rationalizes, legitimizes, justifies, and ennobles people's demands and their actions. A vision of a new society and a better world promotes a sense of unity, solidarity, cohesion, commitment, devotion, and sacrifice among the people. This rallying cry for the population is vital to the revolutionaries' critical task of mobilization before and after obtaining power.

Although social revolutionary leaders may articulate an often elaborate ideology, they are rarely able simply to impose a new political and cultural system upon the population. Individuals have their own sets of feelings, ideas, and expectations, some of which are distinctly antisystemic and even perhaps revolutionary, but which do not necessarily correspond to the vision of the revolutionary leadership. Such divergent and nonconformist popular attitudes have played roles both in limiting and in pushing decisions made by revolutionary leaders. As a result, social revolutionary ideologies, which already may be cobbled together from various factions, inevitably either blend with elements of the preexisting culture to produce a new ideology or produce clashes as the revolutionaries attempt to impose a new ideology from above.

Such popular views represent a belief system, albeit one less formal and less rigid than those generally associated with the term ideology. Composed as it is of many factors, it is best understood as a collection of the ways in which people marry the practical ideology they use to judge events and the practical knowledge they bring to bear in their day-to-day lives.

The timeless ideals of justice, liberty, equality, democracy, opportunity, and freedom (from fear, from hunger, from disease; of assembly, of speech, of religion) remain powerful and compelling in a world where many people's daily lives reflect none of these. Well aware of the risks of seeking to topple those in power, people around the world, at different times and under various circumstances, have shown their capacity and willingness to rebel; the ideology that emerges within and from this process carries the revolutionaries and the population through their struggle.

IDEAS, IDEALS, AND LEARNING: THE END OF IDEOLOGY?

Historically, the achievement of political victory has not been sufficient to guarantee that the visions of the revolutionaries or the population—which are not necessarily the same—will be realized. Nonetheless, ideas—transmitted and transmuted via people—travel across time and space. The most important ideas are powerful, pervasive, and timeless. As they propagate, people learn, taking into account past experiences and factoring in new information. It would be disingenuous to suggest that social revolutions somehow constitute an unbroken process, but it is evident that strong historical and contemporary connections exist among revolutions and their attendant ideologies. This is not to ignore that in practice many, perhaps most, of the ideals invoked may be betrayed once political victory has been achieved.

Late twentieth century contentions that both ideology and revolution have lost their relevance for scholars and the immense majority of humanity seem questionable, especially in view of the second approach delineated above, in which ideology is a social process rather than an abstract set of values and belief structures. Dominant ideologies continue to play an enormous role in how the powerful construct reality and shape popular discourse.

Claims of the end of ideology have been advanced at various points in history, for example, by the Roman Catholic Church, their Protestant usurpers, the early liberals, and those in the post-World War II era who argued that with fascism defeated and communism failing, ideological struggle was over. All such claims have been premature. As people seek to rework and reform their living conditions, there is every reason to expect that they will continue to generate ideologies and make revolutions, perhaps in forms we have yet to consider.

See also *Anarchism; Capitalism; Communism; French Revolution (1789–1815); Gramsci, Antonio; Guevara, Ernesto "Che"; Iranian Islamic Revolution (1979); Liberalism; Marx, Karl, and Friedrich Engels; Socialism.*

ERIC SELBIN

BIBLIOGRAPHY

Guevara, Ernesto "Che." "Notes for the Study of the Ideology of the Cuban Revolution" and "Socialism and Man in Cuba." In *Che Guevara Reader: Writings on Guerrilla Strategy, Politics and Revolution*. Edited by David Deutschmann. Melbourne and New York: Ocean Press, 1997.

Marx, Karl. "The Eighteenth Brumaire of Louis Bonaparte." In *The Marx-Engels Reader*. 2d ed. Edited by Robert Tucker. New York: Norton, 1978.

Marx, Karl, and Friedrich Engels. "The German Ideology." In *The Marx-Engels Reader*. 2d ed. Edited by Robert Tucker. New York: Norton, 1978.

Moaddel, Mansour. *Class, Politics, and Ideology in the Iranian Revolution*. New York: Columbia University Press, 1993.

Rudé, George. *Ideology and Popular Protest*. New York: Pantheon Books, 1980.

Selbin, Eric. "Revolution in the Real World: Bringing Agency Back In." In *Theorizing Revolutions*. Edited by John Foran. London: Routledge, 1997.

INDIAN "GREAT MUTINY" (1857–1859)

The Indian "Great Mutiny" was a series of military rebellions and peasant insurrections against the rule of the British East India Company that occurred in northern India from mid-1857 to 1858 and continued as a protracted guerrilla war in central India until 1859. The cause of the mutiny was debated when it occurred and subsequently in historical scholarship and political discourse.

Often seen as a traditionalist reaction to social change instituted in India under British rule, the mutiny nevertheless had elements of an anti-imperial war of liberation. Contemporary observers, such as Karl Marx, recognized these parallel aspects. During the Indian nationalist movement after 1900, the mutiny was interpreted as the first war of Indian independence. Moving away from overarching causal explanations, current historiography emphasizes specific issues of locality and social change to explain the great variety of rebellious outbreaks during the mutiny.

The Indian troops of the East India Company rebelled, apparently over the issuing of cartridges greased with the fat of forbidden animals, in May 1857 at the major army base at Meerut, north-east of Delhi. The mutineers marched on Delhi, the old imperial capital of the Mughal dynasty and still the residence of the powerless and elderly Bahadur Shah II, the last of the Mughal emperors. Bahadur Shah was urged to reassert his authority over India and the East India Company, which still remained, at least technically, his subject. Delhi was held by the mutineers until September 1857, when the British retook the city after several days of street fighting.

Concurrently, numerous further rebellions took place in the mid-Gangetic valley. The mutineers seized the strategic city and military base of Kanpur in June 1857, which led to a massacre of British captives. The killing of British women being held hostage became, for the British, proof of the brutality of the Indians, which the British returned in kind. Rebels also took the important city of Lucknow, capital of a former Indian state. The British were besieged in the residency of the former British embassy. The residency was once reinforced (September 1857) before being reinvested, only finally being relieved in March 1858.

The inability to hold strategic points such as Lucknow and Delhi prevented the rebels from creating a unity of command or a clear plan of campaign. Moreover, there is no evidence that the rebels had a clear objective once the British were defeated. The mutiny was more a series of local rebellions, some at major locations such as Delhi, Kanpur, and Lucknow, but many more in small towns and villages. These latter were often sites of peasant insurrection.

The events of 1857–1859 led to the end of the East India Company and to direct British rule in India. Various conservative reforms were instituted to prevent another mutiny, but the British would never again completely trust their Indian subjects. For Indians, the Great Mutiny must stand as the beginning of the end of British imperialism in India.

See also *Indian Independence Movement (1885–1947).*

LAURENCE W. PRESTON

BIBLIOGRAPHY

Hibbert, Christopher. *The Great Mutiny: India 1857.* New York: Penguin, 1980.

Stokes, Eric. *The Peasant Armed: The Indian Revolt of 1857.* Edited by C. A. Bayly. New York: Oxford University Press, 1986.

Taylor, P. J., ed. *The Oxford India Companion to the "Indian Mutiny" of 1857.* New York: Oxford University Press, 1996.

Ward, Andrew. *Our Bones Are Scattered; The Cawnpore Massacres and the Indian Mutiny of 1857.* New York: Henry Holt, 1996.

INDIAN INDEPENDENCE MOVEMENT (1885–1947)

The story of Indian nationalism can be divided into three phases. Beginning in the last third of the nineteenth century, middle-class activists sought to fashion themselves as the representatives of an Indian nation by critically scrutinizing the colonial state, as well as indigenous social and cultural practices.

Around the end of the First World War (1914–1918), this movement widened its social base under the leadership of Mohandas Karamchand Gandhi. Broadening the movement also brought to fore latent social discords, and the growing success of nationalist politics in India in the third and fourth decades of the twentieth century accentuated these disagreements.

Party politics and electoral concerns were paramount in the third phase of Indian nationalism starting in the 1930s. Political developments of the 1930s and 1940s ultimately determined India's political landscape in 1947 and resulted in not one but two independent nation-states.

Early nationalists were middle-class Indians, mostly the products of Western-style educational institutions established by the British. Such institutions were founded to realize the goals of the nineteenth-century English administrator and historian Thomas Babington Macaulay, who thought that the British should work to produce a class of men "Indian in blood and color, but English in taste, in opinions, in morals, and in intellect." Instead, Western-educated Indians began public associations and newspapers critical of the colonial state and demanded greater Indian participation in the government and administration of the country. In 1885 men from different associations came together to form the Indian National Congress (INC). Though not a significant political force, early nationalists did succeed in establishing the middle class as the recognized voice of Indian nationalism.

Early nationalists represented many points of view and competing agendas. Moderates believing in the benevolence of British rule competed with extremists convinced that only compulsion would make the British grant political concessions. Reformers advocating changes in social practices confronted committed religious revivalists. Some Muslim leaders labeled the INC a Hindu-dominated organization and in 1906 established the Muslim League as a separate political party. Yet in this phase, nationalist politics of any hue seldom reached beyond the ranks of educated professionals. Even the small band of revolutionaries outside the INC were a part of the middle-class elite.

GANDHI AND POPULAR NATIONALISM

Gandhi's ideas, charisma, organizational abilities, and strategic vision transformed the INC from an elite debating club to a mass political party. Gandhi had spent several years practicing law in South Africa, where he had fought for the rights of that country's Indian population. Using techniques he developed in South Africa, Gandhi proposed *ahimsa* (nonviolence) and *satyagraha* (soul-force) as the basis of his unique political strategy in India. He urged people to disobey unjust laws and advocated peaceful but complete noncooperation with the colonial state. Starting with small, local protests, Gandhi moved on to large all-India campaigns of noncooperation in 1921–1922 and a civil disobedience movement in 1930–1931, both involving millions of Indians.

Though an idealist, Gandhi was far from an otherworldly visionary. Civil disobedience and peaceful noncooperation attracted more followers than calls for directly confronting a well-armed colonial state ever could. Moreover, his *satyagrahas* were meticulously planned, and Gandhi paid equal attention to organizing the INC, revamping its administrative structure and playing an important role as its major fund raiser.

The Salt March: Mohandas Karamchand Gandhi and his followers walk two hundred miles to the sea to collect salt in symbolic defiance of the government monopoly.

Indian nationalism's success was based on Gandhi's ability to reach out to the humblest members of Indian society. His ascetic lifestyle, his use of religious imagery, and the apparently miraculous nature of his political successes all contributed to Gandhi's popularity among India's peasants, who before had been left out of nationalist politics. Gandhi criticized modern industrial society and thus appealed to people who had seen none of the benefits of modernization but suffered many of its negative consequences.

Gandhi's most significant contribution to Indian nationalism, however, was his ability to control mass movements and to choose issues that did not divide Indian people. Gandhi quickly withdrew the noncooperation movement in 1922 when popular violence threatened loss of control over mass activity. For the next major agitation in 1930, Gandhi chose the seemingly trivial issue of the colonial government's monopoly on salt production. This issue not only resonated with the lived experience of almost the entire population, it also focused all resentment against the colonial regime and away from internal differences of class, caste, or gender.

The relationship of mainstream nationalism with the politics of subordinated groups was paradoxical. Although nationalism allowed such groups a chance to participate in organized politics, it also suppressed, marginalized, or coopted the demands of women and lower-class groups by insisting on primacy of the anticolonial struggle led by middle-class men. Once nationalism politicized subordinated groups, however, it became impossible to ignore their demands. Despite Gandhi's opposition to class struggle, peasant and working-class organizations did develop, and their presence ensured the INC was committed to a more equitable economic and social agenda. Though Gandhian nationalism initiated Indian women into politics in large numbers, male nationalists stoutly opposed more radical demands for gender equality proposed by early feminists. Many middle-class feminists succumbed to this pressure and often reinforced women's roles as "mothers of the nation." Yet their presence in the party ensured that the INC could never entirely neglect women's issues either.

THE RISE OF POLITICAL CONFLICT

The 1920s, however, also saw the proliferation of political conflicts the INC could not manage. The most visible of these was a dramatic increase in riots between Hindus and

Muslims. Long before the British arrived, Hindus and Muslims had occasionally quarreled over religious and more mundane issues, but colonial policies derived from assumptions about primordial antagonisms between the two groups created new political constituencies based on religion in India. The British introduced electoral politics in India, albeit in a limited way and with a very restricted franchise. Their electoral system, however, was premised on the necessity of separate representation of religious communities and thus promoted construction of Hindu and Muslim political communities.

Perceiving a threat to their traditional privileges as lower classes became involved in politics, some upper-caste Hindus began in the 1920s to advocate a narrow Hindu nationalism. The INC's successes, as well as global developments, made the Muslim League more vociferous in championing the rights of Indian Muslims. Many Muslims recognized the sultan of Turkey as the temporal leader of the Islamic community. By incorporating Muslims' concern over the fate of the Turkish caliphate after World War I as an integral part of the first noncooperation movement, Gandhi secured their support for the movement. But Gandhi's unilateral withdrawal of the movement in 1922 and the abolition of the caliphate by Turkish revolutionary nationalists in 1924 fractured the fragile alliance between the INC and Muslim leaders.

In the 1930s party and electoral politics predominated. Political reforms of 1935 allowed for elected majority governments in provincial assemblies. Led by Jawaharlal Nehru, who would go on to become India's first prime minister, the INC swept elections held in 1937, but the Muslim League fared disastrously, failing even in provinces with Muslim majorities. The INC governments resigned in 1939 over Britain's unilateral decision to declare India's participation in World War II.

The 1937–1939 period was crucial, however, in shaping the political future of the subcontinent. The INC saw electoral success as the vindication of its claim to represent the entire nation. The league, under Mohammad Ali Jinnah's leadership, excoriated INC governments as pro-Hindu and for the first time demanded a separate Muslim homeland where they could safeguard Muslim interests. Popular involvement returned only when the British arrested the entire top leadership of the INC as it prepared to launch a movement demanding the British "Quit India" in 1942. Without a moderating leadership, the movement turned violent, and only the massive presence of war-ready troops allowed the British to suppress the most serious popular rebellion in the history of colonial India. But the Quit India movement did make British leadership realize the impossibility of holding onto India by force.

DECOLONIZATION AND INDEPENDENCE

After the war it was simply a question of when and how decolonization was to take place. Elections held for central and provincial assemblies in 1945–1946 saw the INC retain its strength, but this time the league won all the Muslim seats in the center and most Muslim majority provinces. But the INC was not prepared to share power with its opponents, and the Muslim League reiterated its commitment to a separate Muslim homeland. Attempts at reaching a negotiated settlement failed. Riots between Muslim and Hindu groups in most urban centers of northern India made political agreement between the two parties imperative. Finally the INC leadership, over Gandhi's opposition, accepted the league's demand for separation rather than share power with it.

In August 1947 Pakistan was created out of Muslim-majority areas in the east and northwest of the subcontinent *(see map, p. 384)*. The human implications of the decision were momentous. More than 10 million people were forcibly dislocated, and more than a million people died in the riots and organized massacres that accompanied independence and partition. After civil war between East and West Pakistan, the East won independence as Bangladesh in 1971. Independence came at a tremendous cost for millions of South Asians.

See also *Bangladeshi War of Independence (1971); Gandhi, Mahatma; Jinnah, Mohammad Ali; Nehru, Jawaharlal; Pakistani Independence Movement (1940–1947).*

SANJAY JOSHI

BIBLIOGRAPHY

Chandra, Bipan, et al. *India's Struggle for Independence.* Delhi: Penguin Books, 1989.

Chatterjee, Partha. *Nationalist Thought in a Colonial World: A Derivative Discourse?* Delhi: Oxford University Press, 1986.

Forbes, Geraldine H. *Women in Modern India.* Cambridge: Cambridge University Press, 1996.

Gandhi, Mohandas Karamchand. *Hind Swaraj and Other Writings.* Edited by Anthony J. Parel. Cambridge: Cambridge University Press, 1997.

Mushirul, Hasan, ed. *India's Partition: Process, Strategy and Mobilization.* Delhi: Oxford University Press, 1993.

Omvedt, Gail. *Dalits and the Democratic Revolution: Dr. Ambedkar and the Dalit Movement in Colonial India.* Thousand Oaks, Calif.: Sage Publications, 1994.

Sarkar, Sumit. *Modern India, 1885–1947.* Madras: Macmillan India, 1983.

INDIAN REGIONAL REVOLTS (1947–)

India has the potential for more regional revolts than it has faced since independence in 1947. More than twenty-five languages are spoken by a million or more people each. India also has large religious minorities, significant ethnic and cultural diversities in the population, and imbalances in regional economic development. But regional, linguistic, or ethnic identities become politically important only in specific circumstances.

Regional revolts in India have emerged from the workings of a democratic political system and have, for the most part, been accommodated within that system. India's federal political system has a historically determined bias favoring the central federal government at the expense of the states. A single political party, the Indian National Congress (INC), controlled the central government from independence until 1996, with only two short breaks. This domination, and the manner in which the INC has responded to challenges to its political authority, have been crucial in creating and resolving regional revolts in India *(see map, p. 384)*.

THE CARROT AND THE STICK

Early leaders like India's first prime minister, Jawaharlal Nehru, negotiated with moderate factions within separatist groups and usually managed to co-opt movements and their leaders. Nehru agreed to reorganize Indian states on linguistic lines in 1956, despite having reservations about the policy. The demand for a separate Tamil-speaking nation in southern India catalyzed this change in policy. A separate Tamil-speaking state of Madras (later renamed Tamilnadu—home of the Tamils) was created to inhibit Tamil separatism. In the new state, the Tamil nationalist party, the Dravida Munnetra Kazagham (DMK), defeated the INC in elections in 1967. Once in power, the DMK dropped its separatist demands.

Nehru similarly co-opted revolts by tribal groups in northeastern India. In response to secessionist demands by Naga leaders at the time of independence, Nehru used the army to quell violent extremists among the Nagas. He then negotiated with moderate Naga organizations to create the state of Nagaland in 1960. Separatist demands from Mizo tribals in 1959 also led to the suppression of violent Mizo separatism by the army. Later, Mizo lands were made centrally administered territories, which became the separate state of Mizoram in 1986.

ASSAM

Later INC leaders like prime ministers Indira Gandhi and her son, Rajiv, led central governments to take a more parochial and short-sighted approach to regional revolts. Political upheavals leading to the creation of Bangladesh in 1971 brought a huge influx of Bengali Muslim immigrants into India's neighboring Assam Province. Assamese, particularly educated youth, demanded expulsion of illegal immigrants, but the INC-led state government saw immigrants as a potential vote-block. A massive popular movement against the state and central governments emerged in Assam. The Asom Gana Parishad (AGP), a political party floated by the agitators, won the 1985 elections convincingly. The central government did not, however, extend its cooperation to the AGP, making the party's leaders unable to live up to their electoral promises.

The United Liberation Front of Assam (ULFA) emerged in response to AGP failures, formed of dissidents among the Assam agitators who now demanded complete secession from India. Hitting industrial and political targets, the liberation front became a major embarrassment for the government. The INC defeated the AGP in the 1993 elections but has had to continue resorting to a mix of financial incentives, political intrigues, and a massive military operation to crush the movement, without complete success.

SIKH SEPARATISM

Groups claiming a separate nation for the Sikh religious community spearheaded the revolt in Punjab in the 1980s. The demand for a Punjabi-speaking state was conceded only in 1966, but Punjab had a wafer-thin Sikh majority. Political control fluctuated between the Akali Dal, a Sikh party, and the INC. In the 1980s the INC decided to divide Akalis by encouraging an extremist faction, but the move backfired, with Sikh extremists gaining control of Sikh politics and demanding a separate Sikh state of Khalistan. The central government refused to make any concessions, even to moderate Akalis.

Sikh activism continued, culminating in the assassination of Indira Gandhi in 1984. When Rajiv Gandhi could not carry out the terms of an accord he reached with moderate Akalis in 1985, Sikh militancy escalated. Using a classic mix of coercion and compromise, Narasimha Rao's government finally brought moderate Akalis to the negotiating table in the 1990s and persuaded them to return to electoral politics. With the Akalis in power and militancy waning, the central government's willingness to share powers with regional elites subdued another regional revolt and brought the rebels into the system.

KASHMIR

The ongoing insurgency in Kashmir presented the most serious challenge to Indian politics. A Hindu king ruled Kashmir, a Muslim-majority province, until 1947. Because of Kashmir's Muslim majority, Pakistan believed that Kashmir should be a part of the new Muslim state. Though preferring independence, the Hindu ruler finally chose to join India, leading to a brief military conflict between the newly independent states of India and Pakistan. The National Conference dominated politics in Kashmir after independence. Conference leaders adopted an approach that demanded greater autonomy for Kashmir but not outright secession. Wanting control over Kashmir, the INC encouraged factionalism in the National Council and managed to topple the government in 1985.

Many Kashmiris believed that the elections of 1987 were rigged in favor of the INC, sparking great disaffection among Kashmiri youth, many of whom turned to Pakistan for help. Moral and material help from Pakistan has since helped nurture the separatist movement in Kashmir. Despite extensive use of the army, the Indian state has been unable to crush the revolt. In the late 1990s the militarization of Kashmir, both by Kashmiri militants and the Indian state, made a democratic solution to the conflict appear impossible.

See also *Bangladeshi War of Independence (1971); Civil Wars; Ethnic Conflict; Indian Independence Movement (1885–1947); Nehru, Jawaharlal; Pakistani Independence Movement (1940–1947); Sri Lankan (Tamil) Revolt and Civil War (1977–).*

SANJAY JOSHI

BIBLIOGRAPHY

Brass, Paul. *The Politics of India since Independence.* 2d ed. Cambridge: Cambridge University Press, 1994.

Dasgupta, Jyotindra. "Community, Authenticity, and Autonomy: Insurgence and Institutional Development in India's Northeast." *Journal of Asian Studies* 56 (May 1997): 345–370.

Hazarika, Sanjoy. *Strangers of the Mist: Tales of War and Peace from India's Northeast.* New Delhi: Viking, 1994.

Kapur, Rajiv A. *Sikh Separatism: The Politics of Faith.* Boston: Allen and Unwin, 1986.

Kohli, Atul. "Can Democracies Accommodate Ethnic Nationalism: The Rise and Decline of Self-Determination Movements." *Journal of Asian Studies* 56 (May 1997): 325–344.

Puri, Balraj. *Kashmir: Towards Insurgency.* New Delhi: Orient Longman, 1993.

Tully, Mark, and Satish Jacob. *Amritsar: Mrs. Gandhi's Last Battle.* London: J. Cape, 1985.

INDONESIAN NATIONAL REVOLUTION (1945–1950)

The revolutionary character of the period in which the Indonesian Republic was born has been played down by the military-backed Suharto government, in power since 1966, which has sought to characterize it as a "physical struggle" or "war of independence." Nevertheless the label *revolution* was already well established both in Indonesia and in the foreign literature. The period 1945–1950 invites comparative analysis as revolution by its spontaneous progression to the left until curbed by a military-led reaction as well as its remaking of Indonesian society and memory.

The movement for independence from the Netherlands contained a very strong Marxist component until 1926, when disorganized uprisings by the Indonesian Communist Party (PKI) were crushed and revolutionary parties banned by the colonial government. Subsequently, underground or exiled communist leaders such as Tan Malaka and Musso, and sometimes-legal nationalists like Sukarno and Mohammad Hatta, argued that independence could come only through revolution. However, when the opportunity came with the Japanese occupation (1942–1945) and subsequent surrender (August 14, 1945) to Allied forces, which took several months to arrive in Indonesia, Sukarno and Hatta were on the nonrevolutionary side of a fierce debate.

As the Indonesian political leaders already accepted by the Japanese, the charismatic Sukarno and more programmatic socialist Hatta sought to ensure that whatever move they made was acceptable to the Japanese, who still controlled their territory. Younger militants led by Sutan Sjahrir, one of the few prewar politicians not to have cooperated with the Japanese, demanded a revolutionary proclamation of independence. After the militants kidnapped Sukarno and Hatta on August 16, a tense compromise was arranged through the mediation of the Navy's Admiral Tadashi Maeda, a gadfly in the Japanese army administration who had cultivated links with the nationalists. Outside Maeda's house at dawn on August 17, Sukarno read a hastily drafted two-sentence proclamation of independence, which he and Hatta had signed.

Despite Allied instructions to preserve the status quo, the Japanese army on the island of Java allowed the kind of puppet government that had been prepared under their auspices to take ever more power, in the hope this would prevent violent anti-Japanese outbreaks. Young activists throughout Indonesia, including about 150,000 who had received some military training from the Japanese, nevertheless acted on their own to raise the Indonesian flag over public buildings, seize large quantities of arms from the demoralized Japanese, and bully Japanese-sanctioned Indonesian officials into either taking more vigorous action in support of independence or stepping aside.

Violence escalated in October as armed Indonesian bands fought losing battles with Japanese troops who had been ordered by the Allies to put down revolutionary uprisings, skirmished with the Dutch and pro-Dutch units being formed in the cities, and took out their frustrations on isolated Europeans released from the prison camps. The heaviest fighting took place in the city of Surabaya, which a British Indian brigade under Gen. A.W. S. Mallaby attempted to occupy on October 25. The unexpected, spontaneous attack on this brigade was halted by appeals from Sukarno, Hatta, and Sjahrir, but the peace broke down when Mallaby was murdered on October 30. The British reacted savagely, and the armed Indonesian groups united in a frenzied

defense against a British division backed by air strikes and naval bombardment. The Battle of Surabaya began on November 10, 1945, since commemorated as Heroes' Day. Thousands of Indonesians died in a resistance their leaders had neither sought nor sanctioned.

In Jakarta, meanwhile, a new government was gradually taking over from the Japanese-sanctioned leaders, who were compromised in the eyes of both Allies and the young militants. The "antifascist" intellectuals Sjahrir and Amir Sjarifuddin became prime minister and defense minister, respectively, on November 14, sidelining Sukarno but retaining him as president, since the socialists needed his mass appeal. The constitutional arrangements that had been sanctioned by the Japanese were ignored in proclamations declaring a multiparty system in which the cabinet ministers would be responsible to a Parliament comprising all the new movements sustained by a variety of armed groups. By this means, contact, if not control, was reestablished between a diplomatically necessary government and an insurgent population.

The new government needed the support of the increasingly disciplined parties of the left to gain control of a revolutionary process that was following its own path in each locality. Many villages acted on their own to overthrow headmen blamed for the terrible exactions of the Japanese period. In large areas of Java and Sumatra the whole governing system was swept away between November 1945 and March 1946. Many aristocrats and elite figures were killed, but still more were arrested and publicly humiliated in a variety of violent reversals of colonial norms. In Aceh, Banten, and elsewhere the leaders and beneficiaries of this movement were the local Islamic counterelite, who were embittered by Dutch and Japanese preference for their aristocratic rivals. In eastern Sumatra and the north coast of Java, where home-grown communists played a large role, attempts were made to establish redistributive bodies, cooperatives, and soviets, and the movements called themselves "social revolutions." Of the national leaders, only Tan Malaka, who had broken with the Leninists and been denounced by them as a Trotskyist, sought to ride this radical wave to power, and he was outmaneuvered in bidding for armed support. By the middle of 1946 the unruly "social revolutions" had been curbed by their own disorganization and the opposition of orthodox Leninists and the progovernment section of the Republican army.

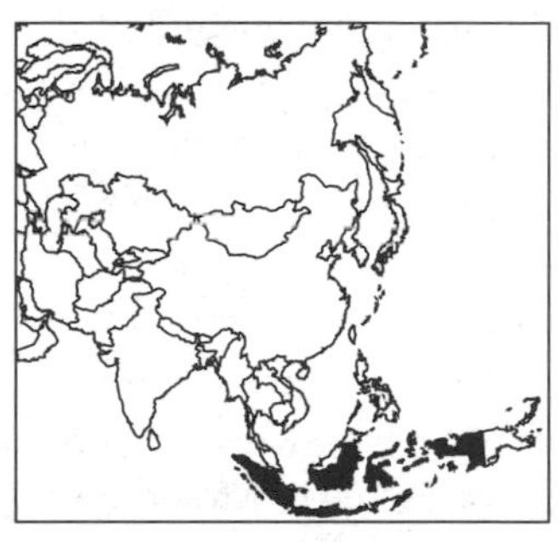

The British commander of allied forces in Southeast Asia, Lord Mountbatten, was reluctant to hand over his responsibilities in Java and Sumatra to the Dutch without some agreement between them and the Republican leaders. The Dutch fared better in underpopulated Borneo and the eastern islands, where they took over from Australian forces in January 1946 and by the end of that year had suppressed armed opposition and set up a federal system of Dutch-dependent states. Finally, on November 14, 1946, at Linggajati, an agreement was reached between the Indonesian Republic and the Dutch for de facto Republican authority over Java and Sumatra and Dutch authority over Borneo and the eastern islands, with the two sides to cooperate in establishing a "United States of Indonesia." Neither the Dutch nor the Indonesian Republic could command much support for this compromise, however, and Dutch conservatives believed that the Republic would collapse under military pressure. In July 1947 this was disproved when Dutch forces unilaterally occupied the most lucrative plantation and oil-bearing areas of Java and Sumatra.

In the areas remaining under its control, the central Republican government gradually established some authority over the autonomous revolutions that had occurred in each locality. But the growing strength of overt and covert Leninists within the government increasingly isolated Sjahrir, whose government was replaced in June 1947 by one led by Amir Sjarifuddin, a complex mixture of Christian, westernizer, and Marxist. When his government in turn fell in January 1948 on the issue of excessive compromises with the Dutch, Sukarno outmaneuvered the left by appointing a presidential emergency cabinet of national unity led by Hatta. The increasingly monolithic left, minus Sjahrir's small group of democratic socialists, preferred to go into opposition, where they adopted a radical program opposing negotiation with the Dutch and supporting an agrarian revolution.

Cold war ideology exacerbated the Indonesian left's radicalism when Musso returned in August 1948 from a twenty-year exile in Moscow. He promoted the "two-camp" doctrine and the need for communist leadership of the anti-imperial revolutions, and he took the lead of a new, expanded PKI. His influence encouraged strikes on the oil fields and sugar estates and the distribution to poor peasants of "official land," which had been the mainstay of elite authority in the villages of Java. In the increasingly bloody military polarization in the Republic between left and right, PKI forces lost badly in Surakarta and responded by taking local power in Madiun on September 18.

Sukarno denounced the PKI as traitors who must be wiped out. Although the PKI leaders had been surprised by the coup in Madiun, Musso embraced it in a bid for leadership of the revolution, and he denounced Sukarno in turn. The issue was resolved on the battlefield, with some 35,000 communist supporters arrested by the end of November, and all of its leaders executed. Although probably the worst blood-letting of the whole revolutionary period, the "Madiun affair" strengthened the Republican government's deteriorating position internally and won it the admiration of a U.S. government becoming alarmed by cold war setbacks elsewhere in Asia. The revolution had been jolted sharply to the right.

When the Dutch sought to eliminate the Republic by a lightning attack on December 19, 1948, the Republican cabinet allowed itself to be captured in Yogyakarta, trusting in international support through the involvement of the United States and the United Nations. The Republican military leadership, which commenced a guerrilla war against the overstretched Dutch, saw the cabinet's arrest as its justification for national leadership. The UN Security Council insisted that the Netherlands restore Republican power in Yogyakarta, and moderate Indonesian opinion moved radically against the Dutch as a result of the military action.

After UN-supervised negotiations, the Netherlands transferred full sovereignty on December 27, 1949, to a Federal Indonesian Republic (RSI) in which the Republic would be a constituent with one-third of the parliamentary seats. Once Dutch backing was removed, however, the federal states collapsed one by one. On August 17, 1950, Indonesia became a unitary republic in which only those who had been on the Republican side since 1945 held legitimacy.

Ending the revolution took longer. Discontent from the pro-Dutch right was dealt with quickly in a late 1950 military expedition against the "Republic of the South Moluccas." Islamic revolutionaries who had fought on the basis that the goal was a Muslim state did not put down their arms until the early 1960s. Although Tan Malaka had been killed by a Republican unit in 1949, some groups aligned in his direction fought on for a few years in southern Banten and the mountains of central Java. The revived PKI of the 1950s made common cause with Sukarno to bury parliamentary democracy under the slogan that the revolution was unfinished, and in that sense only the destruction of the PKI in 1965 marked the definitive end of the revolution. In its denial of legitimacy to prerevolutionary authority, its sharp break with the colorful variety of Indonesian pasts, and its construction of heroic new myths of unity, Indonesia was from 1950 undoubtedly a postrevolutionary state, profoundly different on that count from its neighbor Malaysia.

See also *Indonesian Upheaval (1965–1966); Sukarno.*

Anthony Reid

BIBLIOGRAPHY

Anderson, Benedict. *Java in a Time of Revolution, Occupation and Resistance, 1944–1946.* Ithaca, N.Y.: Cornell University Press, 1972.

Kahin, Audrey, ed. *Regional Dynamics of the Indonesian Revolution: Unity from Diversity.* Honolulu: University of Hawaii Press, 1985.

Kahin, G. McT. *Nationalism and Revolution in Indonesia.* Ithaca, N.Y.: Cornell University Press, 1952.

Reid, Anthony. *The Indonesian National Revolution.* Australia: Longman, 1974. Reprinted Westport, Conn.: Greenwood Press, 1986.

INDONESIAN UPHEAVAL (1965–1966)

The presidential transition from Sukarno to Suharto in 1966 constituted a dramatic reversal of policy accompanied by great violence. The revolutionary changes involved, however, were disguised by the gradual nature of Sukarno's removal from power and the Suharto regime's embargo on internal discussion of the regime change and accompanying massacres.

THE COUP

Indonesia under the "Guided Democracy" of President Sukarno became steadily more polarized between 1963 and 1965 *(see map, p. 237)*. The Communist Party of Indonesia (PKI) and allied left-wing nationalists supported the "confrontation" of newly formed Malaysia and an ever closer alliance with communist China, North Korea, and North Vietnam externally and a campaign against landlords and the rural elite internally. As Sukarno appeared ever more sympathetic with this orientation, anticommunist elements both in Indonesia and externally looked to the army to stem the trend. Tension increased when Sukarno, suffering from kidney problems, collapsed at a rally on August 4, 1965, and both sides may have begun contingency planning to act against their key rivals in the event of his demise.

In the early hours of October 1, 1965, the 30th September Movement, led by Lt. Col. Untung of the Cakrabirawa palace guard, seized and killed six leading generals, including army commander Ahmad Yani. They failed to seize Defense Minister Abdul Haris Nasution, the most senior Indonesian general, making off by mistake with his adjutant. The movement broadcast statements that it had seized power to prevent the machinations of a CIA-influenced "council of generals." The PKI and the air force command issued statements of support, while Sukarno appeared vacillating and ambivalent. His failure publicly to endorse the coup, perhaps because he disapproved of the bloodshed or thought it might not succeed once Nasution had escaped, was fatal to the hopes of the coup leaders.

Major-General Suharto, commander of the army strategic reserve, had not been targeted by the coup, evidently because his previous stance had been nonpolitical and army-centered. He rallied the army against the 30th September Movement, and he had regained control of the central city facilities by the evening of October 1. Suharto, with the backing of Nasution, remained respectful of Sukarno's position but insisted on retaining authority to "restore security and order." The recovery of the bodies of the murdered generals from a well near Halim Air Force Base was given maximum publicity, and the army placed primary responsibility for the coup attempt on the PKI. Anticommunist youth fronts were mobilized with army backing to demand the banning of the PKI and punishment of its leaders. Despite futile appeals by Sukarno for a "political solution" rather than vengeful killings, a massive purge of the Communist Party and its supporters began.

Even if a few communist leaders knew of and encouraged the coup attempt, the party as a whole was unprepared and ill-equipped for resistance. Only in Central and East Java were left-aligned military forces strong enough to take temporary control of towns and kill some hundreds of their opponents. Elite commandos were sent there from Jakarta on October 18, and they quickly tipped the balance toward the Suharto forces in the towns. To destroy the party in the villages, however, local army commanders recruited and briefly trained Muslim youth, who went through the countryside in bands strong enough to seize and usually kill their opponents.

Throughout the remainder of 1965 hundreds of thousands of rural Javanese were killed, beginning with PKI activists but often extending to members of front organizations or others who had supported local communist land campaigns. These rural campaigns were rooted in deep antagonisms, going back to the 1940s, between *santri* (Muslim-educated) and *abangan* (syncretic Javanist-Muslim) villagers supporting rival political parties. The long-standing feud now found resolution in horrific violence.

The killing of communist supporters reached its highest level as a proportion of population in Bali. In early December, tens of thousands of Balinese leftists were slaughtered, seemingly without resistance, by supporters of the locally dominant nationalist party. In other islands, communists were a small minority, but their small numbers did not save them from a fierce massacre in strongly Muslim Aceh. North Sumatra and Lombok each also suffered more than ten thousand dead, with killings continuing into early 1966.

Although the only official Indonesian commission to investigate the massacres, late in 1965, produced a figure of 87,000 deaths, the number was clearly an underestimate even at the time. There is no firm evidence of the death toll, but most students of the atrocities now presume that it must have been between 300,000 and 500,000. In addition, 1.5 million people were detained, most of them only briefly. PKI leader D. N. Aidit was summarily shot when captured in November, and some other Central Committee members were given show trials in special military courts in 1966.

About 10,000 detainees, categorized as neither to be tried nor released, were confined from 1969 to 1979 on the little-populated eastern island of Buru. All detainees suffered permanently from many civil disabilities, their suspect status being noted on their identity cards.

Sukarno had proved unable to protect the PKI from total destruction. Without its mobilized mass support, he was ultimately defenseless against the military, now united around Suharto. After several months of maneuvering over cabinet appointments, refusing military demands to ban the PKI, and reiterating his Marxist and revolutionary goals, Sukarno suffered a "disguised coup" on March 11, 1966. Army troops surrounded the palace and intimidated the president into signing a letter authorizing General Suharto "to take all measures considered necessary to guarantee security." Suharto used this authority immediately to ban the PKI, to arrest such Sukarno confidantes as Foreign Minister Subandrio, and to turn Indonesia toward a moderate, pro-Western market economy, which proved remarkably successful. March 11, 1966, is considered the birthdate of the "New Order" of army-dominated government, although Suharto did not become acting president until March 1967, and substantive president until a year later.

See also *Indonesian National Revolution (1945–1949); Sukarno.*

ANTHONY REID

BIBLIOGRAPHY

Cribb, Robert, ed. *The Indonesian Killings of 1965–1966: Studies from Java and Bali.* Clayton, Victoria: Monash University Centre for Southeast Asian Studies, 1990.

Crouch, Harold. *The Army and Politics in Indonesia.* Ithaca, N.Y.: Cornell University Press, 1978.

Hughes, John. *The End of Sukarno.* London: Angus and Robertson, 1968.

INEQUALITY

Inequality is one of the most often cited grievances of revolutionaries, and alleviating or eliminating inequality is one of the most cherished goals of revolutionary governments. People or groups can seek several kinds of equality: political equality or equal rights; economic equality, including equality of income, wealth, or land; gender equality, allotting equal rewards and access to position and careers; and equality of opportunity. In addition to these forms of internal inequality, revolutions have also aimed at ending international inequality—that is, a weak or subservient position of a society in the international arena. Various revolutions have aimed for various types of equality, with very different results.

INEQUALITY AS A CAUSE OF REVOLUTIONS

Inequality is a normal social condition. Every known society has some form of stratification, whether by seniority, wealth, informal leadership, social rank, or achievement. Most societies have several overlapping forms of hierarchy. Generally, people do not question these hierarchies but seek to make the best of their lives or improve their positions within them.

In certain conditions, however, people question not merely their own fate but challenge the entire system of inequality embodied in social institutions and practices. This situation occurs mainly when people—whether elites, workers, or peasants—come to believe that the prevailing system is unfair, that it rewards the undeserving while ignoring or penalizing those who deserve more. Peasants who find they cannot keep their lands from grasping landlords; workers who face chronic unemployment or declining real wages; aristocrats who are in danger of losing their lands or positions to new groups of well-to-do seeking their share of power; and educated men and women who are denied positions because they lack some arbitrary qualifications—all these groups are inclined to see their social system as no longer fair or just.

The degree of inequality is generally not the issue that produces grievances. Alexis de Tocqueville, a nineteenth-century French social theorist, observed that it is small inequalities, if they seem unnecessary or unjust, that rankle deepest, while great inequality is something that people tend to accept. Many highly unequal societies can last through centuries of political stability, while revolutions can occur even when inequality is modest and decreasing if the remaining degree of inequality is seen as unjustified.

In many cases, concerns about internal inequality are joined, or even superseded, by concerns about a society's unequal position compared with other nations. Elites, in particular, often grow concerned if they perceive their own society as being technologically or militarily outpaced by other nations, or if they see their own government as subservient to or dependent on more advanced nations. In Japan's Meiji Restoration in the mid-nineteenth century, in China's republican revolution in 1911 and May Fourth Movement in 1919, in Turkey's revolution of 1921, in the Afghan revolution of 1978, and in Iran's Islamic revolution of 1979, the main thrust of revolutionary action was to seek a new regime to strengthen the nation against foreign domination.

INEQUALITY AS AN OBJECT OF REVOLUTIONARY POLICY

Most people accept that some forms of inequality of economic outcomes are inevitable. It is reasonable to reward those who work harder or who accomplish more than those who do not. Most revolutions then have focused on political or social equality as their goal. That is, they have sought to recognize an equality among all those who are recognized as citizens, such that all can have a chance to obtain office and cast equal votes. Most revolutions have also extended opportunities for public education or literacy, to help make good on their promise of equal opportunities for all to advance. One of the slogans of the French Revolution of 1789 was to create careers "open to talent," instead of reserving high civil and military positions for members of the nobility.

In the late twentieth century, many revolutions have aimed further, seeking to create actual equality of economic conditions and equality for women. In some cases (in Mexico, Nicaragua, and Cuba, for example), the efforts to create equality focused on land reform, distributing major land holdings to landless peasants. In other cases, however, the efforts to create equality were quite brutal. Joseph Stalin forced independent farmers into large, egalitarian collective farms in Russia in the 1930s, causing tens of millions of deaths. The Chinese Communists under Mao Zedong sought to create equality in the workplace. Wages, housing allowances, even clothing were designed to maintain as much economic equality as possible. But the Chinese went further, punishing those who had previous bureaucratic or professional experience with loss of their positions and often exile to the countryside.

Despite these efforts, inequality in many guises has been difficult, if not impossible, to eliminate. As the sociologists Jonathan Kelley and Herbert Klein have pointed out, even if a revolution were to redistribute all land and physical assets, people would still retain their differences in talent, previous level of education, ambition, and energy. Eventually, such differences would re-create a new pattern of inequality. Because revolutionary regimes tend to create stronger, more centralized regimes, they lead to an expansion of the state bureaucracy, with the attendant growth of a privileged leadership stratum ranked in an official hierarchy. This structure too becomes a source of inequality, even in revolutionary societies.

Similarly, if an agricultural society underwent a revolution that redistributed land but then began to industrialize, the workers and capitalists in the industrial society would eventually grow richer than the peasants tilling their family-sized plots, thereby creating a new dimension of inequality. In fact, in all societies, even those that have experienced revolutions, urban populations have considerably higher incomes than rural residents. By the end of the twentieth century the differences between urban and rural incomes in China may once again be as high as they were before the communist revolution.

Most socialist revolutions have sought to legislate equality for women and have opened the professions to women to an unprecedented degree. Yet gender inequality has been remarkably persistent. Although many professions in socialist nations were opened to women, those professions (especially law and medicine) lacked the advantages of income and prestige they had in the West and thus provided no basis for elevating the position of women in society. In addition, whatever the public proclamations of revolutionary regimes, men continued to insist on subservient roles for their wives and daughters in the home—especially in Latin America. And in countries with Islamic revolutions, even where women took an active role in seeking to end subservience to Western powers, the revolutionary regimes sought to reduce the visibility and opportunities of women outside the home.

Finally, the record of revolutionary regimes is also mixed in regard to alleviating international inequality. Russia was able to fend off the German onslaught during World War II, a marked advance on its weakness in World War I. Japan after the Meiji Restoration in the mid-nineteenth century, and China since its communist revolution in 1949, have been independent, even becoming competitors of Western powers. But most small nations—Ethiopia, Iran, Nicaragua, Bolivia, the Philippines, and many others—have seen no significant gain in their international stature after revolutions.

Inequality of income in itself is rarely if ever a major cause of revolutions. But perceived injustice, as evidenced through unfairly unequal income, access to power, or chances for success, is perhaps the major cause of revolutionary mobilization. Revolutions often try to create equality, but some types are far easier to achieve than others. Revolutions often create their own kinds of inequality through economic development policies and the growth of state bureaucracies.

See also *Capitalism; Class; Colonialism and Anticolonialism; Communism; Economic Development; Elites; Gender; Ideology; Injustice; Intellectuals; Liberalism; Peasants; Workers.*

JACK A. GOLDSTONE

BIBLIOGRAPHY

Eckstein, Susan. "The Impact of Revolution on Social Welfare in Latin America." In *Revolutions.* 2d ed. Edited by Jack A. Goldstone. Fort Worth, Texas: Harcourt Brace, 1994.

Kelley, Jonathan, and Herbert S. Klein. "Revolution and the Rebirth of Inequality: Stratification in Post-Revolutionary Society." In *Revolutions.* 2d ed. Edited by Jack A. Goldstone. Fort Worth, Texas: Harcourt Brace, 1994.

Tocqueville, Alexis de. *The Old Regime and the French Revolution.* Translated by Stuart Gilbert. New York: Anchor, 1955.

Whyte, Martin King. "Inequality and Stratification in China." In *Revolutions.* 2d ed. Edited by Jack A. Goldstone. Fort Worth, Texas: Harcourt Brace, 1994.

INJUSTICE

Feelings of injustice are a primary motive behind most if not all revolutions and rebellions. The belief that one belongs to a group that has been wronged by others, or that suffers from unjust social or political arrangements, is an important ingredient in the complex of causes that lie behind any particular instance of revolution or rebellion. Such beliefs, however, never arise automatically from structural or objective conditions but spring from people's perceptions and interpretations of such conditions. Structural arrangements that one group may consider unjust, undeserved, and subject to redress may appear to another group as natural, normal, and inevitable. Group beliefs about injustice, furthermore, are probably effective in spurring members to take action only when they are associated with or elicit strong collective emotions, such as shame, anger, indignation, and vengefulness. A group may view or label a situation as unjust but not feel strongly enough about it to protest, let alone to take up arms. So to say that injustice is one causal component of revolution, therefore, is to point to a contingent cognitive and emotional reaction to structural conditions.

INJUSTICE AND THE STATE

Feelings of injustice can also motivate other forms of political action, of course, not just revolution. Why, then, are groups with a specifically revolutionary ideology—and who perhaps employ such risky strategies as armed struggle—sometimes able to attract support from people who feel wronged or able to create such feelings among large numbers of people? Why, in other words, do people who feel they have been treated unfairly sometimes attempt to overthrow the state? Much depends, clearly, on the nature of the state that potential rebels or revolutionaries confront, as well as on whether the subjects or citizens of that state understand or interpret its actions as legitimate or not. It helps revolutionaries, for example, if the state sponsors or protects economic and social arrangements that are widely regarded as unjust. In certain societies, economic and social arrangements may be widely viewed as unjust (that is, as not simply unfortunate or inevitable), yet unless state officials are seen to sponsor or protect those arrangements—through legal codes, taxation, conscription, and, ultimately, force—revolutionary collective action aimed at overthrowing the state is unlikely. People may angrily blame their particular superiors or employers for their plight, for example, or even whole classes of superiors, yet the state itself may not be challenged unless there exists a widely shared perception that it stands behind those elites and the injustices for which they are held responsible.

Revolutionaries also fare well, other things being equal, when the state legally or forcibly excludes aggrieved groups from state power or resources. Even if such groups do direct their claims at the state, they are unlikely to seek its overthrow if they attain—or believe they can attain—some fair or significant share of state power or influence. Indeed, even if such groups view their political influence as unjustly limited, their access to state resources or inclusion in policymaking deliberations—unless it is clearly only for show—will likely prevent them from becoming radicalized. In fact, involving mobilized groups—including the putatively revolutionary proletariat—in parliamentary and other political institutions (by extending the suffrage, for example) has typically served to deradicalize them. Such groups often view this sort of inclusion as the first step in the accumulation of greater influence and resources; as a result, they are unlikely to jeopardize their relatively low-cost access to the state—unless that state itself is in deep crisis—by engaging in disloyal or illegal revolutionary activities. For this reason, among others, no popular revolutionary movement has ever violently overthrown a consolidated democratic regime.

Exclusionary authoritarian regimes, by contrast, tend to incubate radical forms of political contention. Revolutionaries tend to prosper under such regimes because many people come to view radicals as more realistic and potentially effective than political moderates and reformists. These moderates and reformers, meanwhile, come to be viewed as hopelessly ineffectual and even utopian—an exact reversal of how people in democratic societies normally perceive these groups. Virtually every powerful revolutionary movement, not surprisingly, has mobilized popular support against an authoritarian exclusionary regime, including the Bolsheviks in Russia, the Communists in China and Vietnam, Fidel Castro's Twenty-sixth of July Movement in Cuba, the broad coalition that opposed the shah in Iran, and the guerrilla movements of Central America, among many others.

STATE VIOLENCE

Indiscriminate, but not overwhelming, state violence against mobilized groups and opposition political figures also unintentionally helps revolutionaries. For reasons of simple self-defense, people who are physically threatened by the state may arm themselves or join groups that have access to arms. People whose families or friends have been victimized by the state may also join or support revolutionaries to seek revenge against the perpetrators. The general population is also likely to view indiscriminate state violence as illegitimate or unjust, especially if the targets of this violence are making demands or claims that are widely perceived to be just or at least worthy of recognition.

Unless state violence is directed at unpopular groups or is simply overwhelming, then, indiscriminate coercion usually backfires, producing an ever-growing popular mobilization, typically led by armed movements, and an even larger body of indignant sympathizers. Revolutionary groups may thus prosper not so much because of their ideology as such but simply because they can offer people some sort of protection from violent authoritarian states. Generally speaking, groups have turned to militant strategies or armed struggle only after their previous efforts to secure change through legal means were violently repressed. Under repressive conditions, ordinary people are likely to view armed struggle as a legitimate means of political action.

Finally, like political exclusion, indiscriminate state violence also reinforces the plausibility and legitimacy of specifically revolutionary ideologies—that is, ideologies that interpret the existing order as fundamentally unjust and envisage a radical reorganization not only of the state but of society as well. After all, a society in which aggrieved people are routinely denied an opportunity to redress perceived injustices—and may even be murdered on the mere suspicion of political disloyalty—is unlikely to be viewed as requiring just a few minor reforms; such people are more likely to view their society as in need of a fundamental reorganization. In other words, violent, exclusionary regimes often unintentionally bolster the popularity of their most radical social critics—religious zealots, socialist militants, and radical nationalists, for example—who view society as more or less totally corrupt, incapable of reform, and thus requiring a thorough and (if need be) violent reconstruction.

Certain types of states or state policies thus unintentionally promote powerful revolutionary movements by contributing to widespread feelings of injustice, focusing those feelings on the state, foreclosing possibilities for peaceful reform, compelling people to take up arms to defend themselves and enhancing the plausibility and legitimacy of revolutionary ideologies.

See also *Castro, Fidel; Chinese Communist Revolution (1921–1949); Guerrilla Warfare; Inequality; Iranian Islamic Revolution (1979); Latin American Popular and Guerrilla Revolts (1960–1996); Liberation Theology; Rationality; Tyranny; Vietnamese Revolution (1945–1975).*

JEFF GOODWIN

BIBLIOGRAPHY

Brockett, Charles D. "A Protest-Cycle Resolution of the Repression/Popular-Protest Paradox." In *Repertoires and Cycles of Collective Action.* Edited by Mark Traugott. Durham, N.C.: Duke University Press, 1995.

Gamson, William A. *Talking Politics.* Cambridge: Cambridge University Press, 1992.

Goodwin, Jeff. *States and Revolutionary Movements, 1945–1991.* Cambridge: Cambridge University Press, forthcoming.

Gurr, Ted Robert. "Persisting Patterns of Repression and Rebellion: Foundations for a General Theory of Political Coercion." In *Persistent Patterns and Emergent Structures in a Waning Century.* Edited by Margaret P. Karns. New York: Praeger, 1986.

Lichbach, Mark Irving. "Deterrence or Escalation? The Puzzle of Aggregate Studies of Repression and Dissent." *Journal of Conflict Resolution* 31 (1987): 266–297.

Mason, T. David, and Dale A. Krane. "The Political Economy of Death Squads: Toward a Theory of the Impact of State-Sanctioned Terror." *International Studies Quarterly* 33 (1989): 175–198.

Wickham-Crowley, Timothy P. *Guerrillas and Revolutions in Latin America: A Comparative Study of Insurgents and Regimes Since 1956.* Princeton, N.J.: Princeton University Press, 1992.

INTELLECTUALS

Intellectuals have played a most prominent role in modern revolutions. From the French Revolution of 1789 through all the upheavals of the nineteenth and twentieth centuries, in both Western and non-Western lands, it is difficult to think of a major revolution that was not prepared ideologically by intellectuals, nor one whose leadership was not drawn significantly from an intelligentsia. Whether intellectuals have been the beneficiaries of the revolutions they did so much to inspire, and often led, is, however, quite another matter.

Yet "revolutionary intellectuals" are the exception, not the norm, in modern history—just as revolutions themselves are very exceptional historical events. Most intellectuals at most times and places are more likely to be conservative ideological defenders of the existing sociopolitical order, or politically passive professionals who support (at least implicitly) the prevailing order of things. In ordinary times, even most politically radical intellectuals banally tend to accommodate themselves to the regime in power.

The term *intellectual* is not amenable to easy definition. It is in fact maddeningly imprecise, assuming very different meanings in different historical situations. In the most general sense, the term *intellectuals* sometimes refers simply to those primarily engaged in mental rather than physical labor. In some historical cases, the term has been applied to those who have attained a certain level of education, usually an advanced university degree but sometimes merely the equivalent of a secondary-school education. Or it might mean simply the cultured stratum of society, however "culture" might be variously defined in different times and places. Somewhat more precisely, *intellectuals* often is confined to the educated and cultured members of society who are vitally concerned with the "larger" social, political, and philosophical issues of the day.

The more important distinction, for the purposes of considering the revolutionary role of intellectuals, is between "intellectuals" in general (however defined) and the members of the intellectual class who form an *intelligentsia.* The latter term, derived from nineteenth-century Russian historical experience, suggests a stratum of intellectuals whose crucial characteristic is their alienation from existing state and society—and who feel a burning moral need, overwhelming all other needs and considerations, to totally transform society and to do so by revolutionary means if necessary. It is in this sense that the term *intellectuals* is employed here. Other characteristic features of the nineteenth-century Russian intelligentsia—an orientation to messianic beliefs, an aversion to professionalism and occupational specialization, a populist conception of "the people" as a single organic entity, and a hostility to capitalism in favor of some sort of socialist vision—may or may not be present.

THE PHENOMENON "DESERTION OF THE INTELLECTUALS"

The critical role of intellectuals (in the sense of "intelligentsia") in the making of revolutions often has been noted. Crane Brinton, in his classic study *The Anatomy of Revolution*—a comparison of the English, American, French, and Russian Revolutions—finds in all four cases "the transfer of allegiance of the intellectuals" to be a common symptom of a "pre-revolutionary situation" foreshadowing the breakdown of the old regime. Suggested here is not mere dissatisfaction with existing conditions, but rather a desertion by intellectuals from the established sociopolitical order with which they have been a part and their moral-political commitment to a revolutionary cause promising a new and presumably better society. The intellectuals who desert the old regime are commonly the younger members of the ruling class—they are, in effect, traitors to their class. As Brinton observes, "the existence of rebellious radicals in the upper classes" is a sign of the decadence of a ruling class, especially one "in a pre-revolutionary society [that] fails to act as a ruling class should act to preserve its power."

The phenomenon of "the desertion of the intellectuals" is the first of the three sets of "mutations" that Barrington Moore, in his analysis of patterns of revolutionary change, has identified as occurring within the dominant classes prior to the outbreak of serious revolutionary violence. Moore, however, finds it to be something more profound than desertion. Rather it is a challenge to the prevailing modes of thought and "to the whole perception of the possible causes of and remedies for human suffering."

In the original Marxist conception of socialist revolution, the desertion of the intellectuals is given considerable weight in the making of revolution, although neither the word "desertion" nor "intellectuals" is used by radical socialist theorist Karl Marx and his colleague Friedrich Engels. In the *Communist Manifesto,* Marx and Engels note (foreshadowing Crane Brinton's notion of "the transfer of allegiance of the intellectuals") that just as "at an earlier period, a section of the nobility went over to the bourgeoisie" during the era of capitalist revolutions, so now in the era of socialist revolutions a portion of the "bourgeois ideologists" will join the proletariat.

The version of Marxism espoused in the early twentieth century by Russian revolutionary Vladimir Ilyich Lenin greatly elaborated and expanded on this notion, so much so that Lenin (unlike Marx) assigned intellectuals the decisive role in the revolutionary process. According to Lenin, the carrier of a true socialist consciousness is an elite group of "bourgeois intellectuals" who must impose that consciousness on the spontaneous movement of the masses in order to guide the revolutionary movement along its proper course. This notion is the intellectual rationale for the Leninist concept of a tightly organized and highly disciplined "vanguard" communist party. The appeals of the Leninist scheme of party organization, offering intellectual elites both the decisive historical initiative and an efficient method of political organization, have extended well beyond socialist and communist circles. For example, in 1924 the Chinese Nationalist Party of Sun Yat-sen and Chiang Kai-shek adopted Leninist methods of political organization and retained its Leninist organizational character for many decades after its brief alliance with Russian and Chinese communism ended in 1927.

ROLE OF INTELLECTUALS IN MODERN REVOLUTIONARY HISTORY

Even the most cursory review of the great social revolutions reveals the prominence of intellectuals (and the phenomenon of the desertion of the intellectuals) in modern world history. Although the French Revolution of 1789 is commonly referred to as a "bourgeois revolution," its democratic and egalitarian ideology was largely articulated by younger members of the aristocracy who had turned to intellectual and political pursuits—in effect, young intellectuals who became defectors from their class. And while the bourgeoisie (and capitalist development) eventually were the principal beneficiaries of the revolution, few merchants and industrialists climbed the barricades in 1789. Rather, the dramatic events that brought down the *ancien régime* were performed by the urban poor under the leadership of radical intellectuals and professionals, especially doctors and lawyers.

The leaders of the Russian Bolshevik revolution of 1917 were intellectuals turned professional revolutionaries, much as Lenin had anticipated. They could not have succeeded without the active support of the urban working class and the spontaneous radicalism of the peasantry, to be sure, but in the end an elite of revolutionary intellectuals was thrust into power.

The events leading to the Chinese communist victory of 1949 illustrate with particular clarity the crucial place of intellectuals in modern revolutionary history. The origins of the modern Chinese intelligentsia are found in the 1890s when younger members of the gentry–official ruling class lost faith in the old imperial order and attempted unsuccessfully to transform it radically from within on the basis of models drawn from the West and Meiji Japan. The failure of their reformist efforts hastened the emergence of a revolutionary intelligentsia—alienated from the state and in many cases from traditional culture as well—in the early decades of the twentieth century. From the ranks of that intelligentsia, inspired by the nationalistic and politically activistic impulses of the May Fourth movement of 1919, emerged the organizers and leaders of the Chinese Communist Party (CCP), who eventually proved victorious by harnessing the forces of peasant revolt in China's vast countryside. While the CCP's social base resided in the peasantry (even though it formally claimed to be the party of the urban proletariat), the 1949 revolution gave power to neither peasants nor workers but rather to a revolutionary elite largely drawn from the May Fourth generation of intellectuals.

It is tempting to conclude from the history of modern revolutions, especially twentieth-century communist revolutions, that the ultimate victors and beneficiaries of successful upheavals have been intellectual elites, perhaps evidence in support of Vilfredo Pareto's theory of "the circulation of elites" (the late nineteenth-century social thinker maintained that innovative and conservative elites tend to alternate over different historical periods). But this would be too hasty a judgment. For even where revolutionary intellectuals have become dominant in a postrevolutionary regime, they have been transformed into bureaucrats in the process, no longer intellectuals as intellectuals but rather rulers often suppressing new generations of intellectuals. A longer-term historical perspective reveals it has been the role of revolutionary intellectuals to prepare the way for the dominance of new economically based social classes. In the French Revolution, this class was clearly the bourgeoisie, although the French bourgeoisie required the better part of a century to consolidate fully its political ascendancy. In the Russian and Chinese revolutions, the ultimate victors appeared to be new (and different) types of bureaucratically generated capitalist classes.

See also *Leadership; Rationality.*

MAURICE MEISNER

BIBLIOGRAPHY

Brinton, Clarence Crane. *The Anatomy of Revolution.* Rev. ed. New York: Random House, 1966.

Daedalus 89 (summer 1960)—issue on the Russian intelligentsia.

Haimson, Leopold. *The Russian Marxists and the Origins of Bolshevism.* Cambridge: Harvard University Press, 1955.

Levenson, Joseph. *Confucian China and Its Modern Fate: A Trilogy.* Berkeley: University of California Press, 1968.

Moore, Barrington. "Revolution in America?" *New York Review of Books,* January 30, 1969, 6–12.

Schwartz, Benjamin. *Chinese Communism and the Rise of Mao.* Cambridge: Harvard University Press, 1952.

Shils, Edward. *The Intellectuals and the Powers and Other Essays.* Chicago: University of Chicago Press, 1972.

IRANIAN CONSTITUTIONAL REVOLUTION (1906)

The Iranian Constitutional Revolution was the first democratic political movement of modern Iran and had significant social and cultural dimensions. The revolution brought about a parliament (Majlis) and a constitution that curtailed the authority of both the monarchy and the clerical establishment *(ulama)* and gained much international support before it was put down through Russian intervention.

BACKGROUND TO THE REVOLUTION

The establishment of new transportation systems between Europe and the Middle East in the late nineteenth century led to an unprecedented increase in trade with the West that changed a way of life for millions of people. As with many other developing countries of this era, Iran became a source of cheap raw materials and a market for the more industrialized European countries. Soon, the two Great Powers, Britain and Russia, came to play a more aggressive role in the region. With the treaties of 1813 and 1828, Russia had ended Iran's control of Transcaucasia, and Britain had forced Iran to give up its claim to Afghanistan in 1857. By 1891–1892 greater contact with Western concepts such as modern nationalism and democracy as well as reaction to Iran's losses in the north and east had helped bring about a coalition of merchants, politicians, the *ulama* and theology students, shopkeepers and trade guilds, and religious reformers that demanded commercial protection, revocation of tobacco concessions that had been granted to a British firm, and judicial reforms. Religious reformers included Freemasons, freethinkers, and affiliates of the persecuted Babi religious movement, whose political clubs and associations helped pave the way for the constitutional movement.

Alex Tait/Equator Graphics, Inc.

To generate funds for the government, Minister of Finance Nasir al-Mulk brought Belgian administrators to Iran to reform the customs bureau. Although government revenue from the reform increased substantially by 1904, the reforms that were proposed by the Belgian adviser Joseph Naus created much anxiety among the local merchants. The reforms had favored foreign imports and exposed local merchants to strong competition from abroad. The Russo-Japanese War of 1904–1905, and especially the Russian Revolution of 1905, accelerated and contributed to the national demands for political change. In the spring of 1905 a series of protests against the customs reforms of Naus brought the two leading clerics, Sayyid Muhammad Tabataba'i and Sayyid 'Abdullah Bihbahani, into a close alliance in the nationalist movement. In December 1905, when governor 'Ala al-Dawlah had two Tehran merchants beaten, the opposition gained greater momentum. In July 1906 protesters moved to the garden of the British Legation and the religious city of Qom. With permission from the acting chargé d'affaires, E. Grant Duff, fourteen thousand protesters, including many guild members, took sanctuary in the garden. Several leading reformers, including Sani' al-Dawlah, the shah's son-in-law, formed a committee to discuss the principles of a constitutional government with those who had taken sanctuary in the garden. Soon, the earlier, vague demands for a house of justice were replaced with calls for a house of representatives. As the strikes escalated throughout the city, Muzaffar al-Din Shah was forced to recognize these demands. On August 6, 1906, he agreed to the formation of a National Consultative Majlis.

THE FIRST CONSTITUTIONAL PERIOD (1906–1908)

The electoral laws of September 9, 1906, created a limited male franchise and brought about a Majlis drawn from the ruling Qajar family, the *ulama* and theology students, nobles, landowners and small holders, and merchants and guild members. As in most countries at the time, women were excluded from voting, and property and language qualifications excluded most others from representation in the first Majlis. The heavy representation given guilds and Tehran and Tabriz resulted in a more radical Majlis than would have been elected through universal suffrage. The inclusion of trade guilds, as well as the contributions of liberal and social democratic delegates, made the first Majlis into one of the most respected political institutions of twentieth-century Iran. The constitution of December 30, 1906, effectively limited the authority of the shah, the ministers, and the foreign powers. Deputies gained and practiced the right to ratify major financial transactions, to ban foreign loans, to remove irresponsible ministers and government officials, and to cut the salaries of court employees and the shah. The first Majlis also abolished land allotments (similar to European fiefs), gave administrative autonomy to the provinces, established a free press, and introduced secular laws and judicial codes that reduced the powers of the *ulama*.

Many of these reforms were initiated by radical deputies, such as Hasan Taqizadah, who had been influenced by the ideas of social democracy from Russian-controlled Transcaucasia. The Organization of Iranian Social Democrats, whose headquarters remained in Baku, opened branches inside Iran and followed a modified social democratic agenda. The Social Democrats, as well as other liberal supporters of the movement, helped create modern schools, published newspapers, and encouraged multiethnic participation, especially in the northern provincial councils. Some councils encouraged rent and tax strikes by peasants in the Caspian region in Azerbaijan. Activist women of Tehran took the initiative in organizing societies, schools, and orphanages and also wrote for leading newspapers of the period. There was also a burst of literary creativity centered around journals such as *Sur-i Israfil* ("The Trumpet Call of Angel Gabriel"), in which the writings of 'Ali Akbar Dihkhuda appeared. The new monarch, Muhammad 'Ali Shah (1907–1909), detested the limits that the Majlis and the constitution placed on the previously unbridled power of the monarchy, and he openly began to undermine the new order.

The monarch was encouraged by the leading conservative cleric, Shaikh Fazlullah Nuri, and many wealthy landowners. They backed the shah and stated that the constitution was incompatible with Shi'ite religious laws. This conservative coalition tried to block new laws that guaranteed civil rights for both individuals and newly formed associations. In the protests that ensued, several leading clerics, including Nuri, were forced out of the cities of Tehran, Tabriz, and Rasht by constitutionalist supporters. A compromise was announced in the fall of 1907. The new Supplementary Constitutional Law of 1907, a much larger and more important document than the 1906 constitution, guaranteed some basic civil rights for citizens, including equal rights for all Iranian male citizens. But most of the new rights were burdened with the added stipulation that they conform to Islamic Shariat laws. Furthermore, the new laws gave unprecedented powers to the *ulama,* through a council of clerics whose authority superseded that of the Majlis. Although this council did not function during the constitutional era, as it was ostensibly aimed at placating the hostile clerics, the existence of such an article in the constitution marked the delegates' inability to establish the principle of separation of religion and state in a parliamentary democracy and would have important political and ideological ramifications for twentieth-century Iran. The Anglo-Russian Convention of 1907, which divided Iran between a northern Russian zone of influence and a southern British one, coincided with the growing hostility of the two powers toward the councils and the Majlis, since the new democratic institutions were determined to reduce foreign domination of Iran. On June 23, 1908, Muhammad 'Ali Shah, with the aid of his Russian Cossack adviser, Col. Vladimir Liakhoff, bombarded the Majlis building and brought the first Majlis to an end.

THE MINOR AUTOCRACY OF 1908–1909

The revolutionary center now moved to Tabriz. Royalist forces surrounded the city, but Tabriz mounted a fierce resistance. More than five hundred armed revolutionaries from Transcaucasia, including many Iranian migrant workers, Armenians, Georgians, and Russian socialists, poured into the region. A similar volunteer army gained control of the city of Rasht (in Gilan Province of northern Iran) in February 1909. The struggle to reestablish constitutional rule included an impressive international component. Supporters in Turkey and Central Asia joined those of Transcaucasia in sending volunteers and arms to Iran. Prominent members of the British Parliament, European intellectuals, and Russian social democrats wrote articles exposing the imperialist policies of European governments in Iran. The revolutionary army of the north, known as the *mujahidin,* joined by the Bakhtiari tribesmen from the south, marched toward Tehran and reconquered it on July 16, 1909.

THE SECOND CONSTITUTIONAL PERIOD (1909–1911)

In the summer of 1909 Muhammad 'Ali Shah was deposed, and his young son Ahmad Shah (1909–1925) was named the new shah. Nuri was tried by a revolutionary tribunal and executed. In Tehran elections were held, and new political parties were formed. The Democrat Party, which formed a vocal minority in the new Majlis, espoused a social democratic agenda and included several Armenian and Azeri social democrats in its ranks. The party called for separation of religion and state and a new definition of nationalism that transcended religious and ethnic affiliations. The Democrats were opposed by the more conservative Moderate Party, whose leadership included the ranking cleric, Sayyid 'Abdullah Bihbahani.

Soon the conflict between the Democrat and Moderate Parties escalated into a series of political assassinations, followed by the forcible disarmament of most of the *mujahidin* and the exile of prominent social democrats. These internal conflicts made it easier for Britain and Russia to increase their pressure on the Majlis. On October 14, 1910, Britain handed an ultimatum to Tehran. If the southern trade routes, which were within the British zone of influence, were not recovered from the Qashqa'i tribes who controlled them, Britain would establish its own security force in the south, similar to the Russian Cossack Brigade in the north. Meanwhile, Germany wanted to nullify some of the advantages that Britain had gained through the 1907 Anglo-Russian Convention in the Middle East and Asia. At the November 1910 Russo-German Potsdam meeting, Germany recognized the political influence of Russia in northern Iran in return for economic concessions in that region. A new railroad, financed jointly by Russia and Germany, was planned in order to facilitate the two countries' transportation of goods into northern Iran. Taxes had not been collected for a few years, and the country was in the midst of a fiscal crisis. Britain and Russia did not permit Iran to hire a financial adviser from a major European country to reform its treasury. The Majlis therefore turned to the United States and hired Morgan Shuster and his team to reorganize the national treasury. It was hoped that a financial adviser from the States would have significant political standing, enabling him to withstand the pressure of both Britain and Russia. At the initiative of the Democrat Party a series of progressive laws were passed that established free and compulsory elementary education and universal male suffrage. After Shuster published a letter in the *Times* of London (November 10–11, 1911) in which he exposed the politics of Russia and Britain in Iran, the two powers decided they had had enough of him. In November 1911 the Russian government, with British support, demanded the dismissal of Shuster. Additionally, Russia demanded a guarantee by the Iranian government that it would not hire foreign advisers without consent of the two powers. Soon, Russian troops began to move toward Tehran. The Russian ultimatum was resisted by the Majlis almost to the end. But the cabinet, faced with the impending occupation of Tehran, closed down the Majlis on December 24, 1911, thereby bringing the Constitutional Revolution to an end.

See also *Iranian Islamic Revolution (1979).*

Janet Afary

BIBLIOGRAPHY

Afary, Janet. *The Iranian Constitutional Revolution, 1906–1911: Grassroots Democracy, Social Democracy, and the Origins of Feminism.* New York: Columbia University Press, 1996.

Amanat, Abbas. *Resurrection and Renewal: The Making of the Babi Movement in Iran, 1844–1850.* Ithaca, N.Y.: Cornell University Press, 1989.

Bayat, Mangol. *Iran's First Revolution: Shi'ism and the Constitutional Revolution of 1905–1909.* New York: Oxford University Press, 1991.

Browne, Edward G. *The Persian Revolution of 1905–1909.* Cambridge: Cambridge University Press, 1910.

Keddie, Nikki. *Religion and Rebellion in Iran; The Tobacco Protest of 1891–1892.* London: Frank Cass, 1966.

Martin, Vanessa. *Islam and Modernism: The Iranian Revolution of 1906.* London: I. B. Tauris, 1989.

Shuster, William Morgan. *The Strangling of Persia.* New York: Century Press, 1912.

IRANIAN ISLAMIC REVOLUTION (1979)

Iran's Islamic Revolution of 1979 is arguably the most popular revolution of the modern time. Paradoxically, Mohammad Reza Shah Pahlavi lost the Peacock Throne at the pinnacle of his power and glory despite the full support of the United States; SAVAK, his feared secret police; and the imperial army, the world's fifth largest. Equally surprising was the subsequent establishment of the Islamic Republic by Ayatollah Ruhollah Mussavi Khomeini in a land with more than twenty-five hundred years of monarchical tradition *(see map, p. 246).*

THE LONG-TERM REASONS FOR THE REVOLUTION

The main long-term reason behind the revolution was that, during the reign of Mohammad Reza Shah (1941–1979), the economy grew considerably and was somewhat modernized whereas the state remained traditional. The shah's policies alienated the nationalists, the *ulama* (experts on Islamic law and Islam), the *bazaaris* (merchants and shopkeepers), and others. He suppressed his opponents, denied political participation to the masses, and failed to rely on a popular ideology to legitimize his modernizing reforms. While appearing strong, the Pahlavi state was in fact fragile, infected with the virus of autocracy, devoid of much popular support, and insufficiently disciplined to withstand the tensions the king's policies had generated.

When Mohammad Reza became king in 1941, he hoped to emulate his father's autocratic ways but could not. He lacked Reza Shah's iron will and charisma, and the armed forces, upon whose might his father had ruled, were in disarray. The crisis that transformed his rule to autocracy was created by the National Front, an alliance of nationalists formed by Mohammad Mosaddeq in 1949. Mosaddeq became prime minister in 1951, nationalized the British-controlled Anglo-Iranian Oil Company, and reduced the king's powers. In retaliation, the British and American intelligence agencies, with the support from the Iranian military and the shah, staged a coup d'état and overthrew the popular prime minister in August 1953.

The coup that saved the shah was the first major step toward the revolution that ended his dynasty. The shah lost legitimacy and was tainted as "America's shah," irrevocably damaged his relationship with nationalists and intellectuals, and formed a new alliance with the United States that facilitated his ascendance as a powerful autocrat. He appointed Gen. Fazlolah Zahedi, a major player in the coup, as Mosaddeq's replacement. The general, in effect, denationalized the oil industry by making an agreement with a new consortium consisting of British and, for the first time, American oil companies, and he unleashed a campaign of terror, killing hundreds and arresting thousands of people, including Mosaddeq. In 1957 the shah, with CIA support, created SAVAK, which he personally controlled.

In the early 1960s the emboldened king launched the White Revolution, the linchpin of which was the distribution of land to the landless peasants. Supported by Washington as a deterrent against a peasant revolution, land reform created a rift between the shah and the two traditional pillars of monarchical support: the landed upper class and the *ulama,* who were landowners and administrators of some forty thousand charitable religious endowments. Without ever mentioning land reform, Ayatollah Khomeini opposed the White Revolution as a conspiracy against Islam and Iran. (Ayatollah is a revered title in Shi'i Islam conferred on an individual recognized for his piety, expertise in Islamic jurisprudence, and the ability to make independent judgment on all kinds of issues that his followers are obligated to follow.) Khomeini's arrest by the government precipitated the June Uprising of 1963, in which the police killed and injured hundreds of his supporters. Upon his release, Khomeini warned that Prime Minister Hassan Ali Mansur's proposed bill before the parliament in 1964, granting legal immunity to U.S. military personnel, would make Iran a U.S. colony. After the passage of the controversial legislation, Khomeini, the uncompromising nemesis of the shah, was exiled to Turkey and then to Iraq in November 1964. Two months later, Mansur was assassinated by the United Islamic Societies, whose creation Khomeini had blessed before his exile.

After Khomeini's exile, the already tense relations between the *ulama* and the shah deteriorated further. Cognizant that Shi'ism, the major minority sect in Islam and Iran's state religion since 1501, provided legitimacy to the monarchy, the shah sought to bring it under his command. He brought many religious schools under the state's control and created the Religious Corps. The corpsmen, graduates of the state-administered universities and not of the seminaries the *ulama* controlled, were to spread the "Pahlavi" version of Shi'ism. This frontal attack on the *ulama,* the spread of Western culture, and the glorification of the pre-Islamic Persia unified some of the *ulama* against the regime.

ECONOMIC GROWTH, REPRESSION, AND RESISTANCE

Prerevolutionary Iran experienced impressive economic growth. While it raised the standard of living of most Iranians, this oil-induced growth increased the gap between the rich and poor, Iran's dependence on the West, and corruption. Industrialization and the proliferation of supermarkets and financial institutions outside the *bazaari* also decreased the power of the *bazaaris.*

As the economy grew, the population became more urban, literate, and educated, the size of the middle and working classes increased, and the society became vibrant. Consequently, the demand for political participation intensified. Instead of gradually incorporating people into the political process, the shah pursued a four-pronged strategy that ultimately undermined him. First, he built royal parties that lacked independence and could not enlarge his popular support. In 1975 he ordered everyone to join his new Rastakhiz Party or face arrest and exile. Second, he sought to buy loyalty. But most of the loyalty he purchased with oil money evaporated in the mid-1970s when the economy entered a mild recession and the government reduced social welfare expenditures. Third, he relied on the generous support of Washington, which considered Iran, with its oil riches and its more than fourteen hundred miles of common borders with the Soviet Union, a valuable strategic asset for containing communist expansion. Finally, he relied on his armed forces and especially SAVAK, which used atrocious methods of torture, killed many dissidents, and created the myth of his invincibility.

This strategy and the increasing reliance on oil export as the state's principal source of revenue made the state increasingly autonomous from the population. The more autonomy the state enjoyed, the more dictatorial the shah became. He blatantly ignored the 1906 constitution, which had limited the king's powers; made all the critical decisions; turned the parliament and the judiciary into extensions of his will; imposed censorship; banned all independent parties, associations, and guilds; and failed to develop a popular ideology to legitimize his initiatives.

Repression, however, could not obliterate the opposition to the shah, but only pushed it underground. Although the National Front, Iran's Liberation Movement (an Islamic/nationalist organization that Mehdi Bazargan had created in the early 1960s), and the pro-Moscow Tudeh Party had lost their effectiveness in Iran, they were still active in the anti-shah student movement in Europe and North America. Two guerrilla organizations, the Mojahedin-e Khalq and Fada'iyun-e Khalq, assassinated some Iranian officials and a few Americans in Iran in the mid-1970s. The United Islamic Societies organized small gatherings for Khomeini's disciples, like Ali Akbar Hashemi Rafsanjani and Seyyed Ali Khameini, both of whom later became president of the Islamic Republic.

Most important were the ideas of Ali Shariati and Khomeini, the two ideologues of the revolution. Shariati offered a revolutionary interpretation of Shi'ism, energized a generation of Islamic activists, and built a bridge with secularists who came to respect Shi'ism as a doctrine of liberation. In 1969 Khomeini declared Islam to be diametrically opposed to monarchy and argued that the *ulama* have a divine mission to govern directly over an Islamic government whose characteristics he did not discuss. Thus, he legitimized rebellion against the monarchy and became the first to offer an Islamic alternative to it.

THE IMMEDIATE REASONS FOR THE ISLAMIC REVOLUTION

The shah's liberalization policy in 1977, implemented after the government's economic policies had generated popular discontent, provided an opportunity for those suppressed by the regime to start the protest movement. As the protest movement unfolded, the shah made faulty assumptions about its nature, was reluctant to put to work all the repressive resources at his disposal, and failed to forestall the alliance between the secular and Islamic forces. Once the apex of the highly centralized system he had created was overcome by a paralysis of will, the entire system crumbled quickly. The revolutionaries did not win the revolution, the shah lost it. He was innately weak. The 1953 coup had been organized for him by his foreign allies, and the decision to crush the June Uprising was made by his prime minister, Asadollah Alam. The side-effects of treatment of his cancer accentuated his innate indecisiveness during the protest movement.

The government's difficulties began in the mid-1970s when oil prices fell, the economic boom ended, and inflation became rampant. To fight inflation, the government imposed a price stabilization and antiprofiteering program, arresting and convicting between 8,000 and 17,000 so-called price gougers, most of them *bazaari* and a few industrialists. Then in 1977 the government lifted the price controls, imposed a freeze on wages and salaries, and increased taxes, angering the salaried middle class. Government expenditures were reduced, and the pace of economic growth was slowed. Thus, the many who were dependent on government assistance and subsidies were adversely affected. When these policies generated popular discontent, the shah began to liberalize his rule.

President Jimmy Carter's human rights policy was the impetus behind liberalization. In trying to enhance human rights without offending the shah and without damaging Washington's lucrative economic and military ties with Iran, Carter pursued an inconsistent and self-defeating policy. He sometimes pressured the shah to liberalize, and he sometimes urged the king to pursue an iron-fist approach. This inconsistency increased the shah's suspicion that Washington's intention was to undermine him, and it almost paralyzed his decision-making capability; it also generated a widespread perception that Washington was no longer supporting the shah unconditionally, giving the shah's opponents a new lease on life.

The protest movement began in 1977 when the shah promised to create a free political atmosphere and stop torturing dissidents. In the new environment, the leaders of the National Front and some intellectuals circulated open letters to him, complaining about corruption and autocracy. Gradually, dozens of professional and student associations were reactivated and created. In this phase, the protest movement was reformist and nonviolent, with nationalists and intellectuals its most vocal components.

The publication of a provocative article in government newspapers attacking Khomeini as an agent of colonialism in January 1978 transformed the protest movement. When a few hundred people organized a pro-Khomeini rally in Qom, center of Iran's Shi'i seminaries, the police killed a dozen people. Many of the *ulama*, including Ayatollah Seyyed Kazim Shariatmadari, castigated the government for its harsh reaction. When the police stopped the people in Tabriz, Shariatmadari's stronghold, from entering the mosques to commemorate the fortieth day of the death of the martyrs of the Qom uprising, the protesters became violent, and the police killed a few and arrested hundreds of protesters. Thereafter, the *ulama*'s network of thousands of mosques and small Islamic associations was used to mobilize the masses across the country. No other group had such an effective network, and because of its overtly religious nature, the regime could not easily destroy it. As more protesters were killed by the police, the subsequent forty-day commemorations to honor the dead became larger. Gradually, the protest movement became more coordinated and national, with Shariatmadari in Iran and Khomeini in Iraq assuming its leadership.

In August 1978 some 370 people were burned to death when a theater in Abadan was mysteriously set ablaze by arsonists. The opposition blamed SAVAK. Iran was on the brink of revolution: martial law was imposed in a few cities, the king replaced SAVAK's chief, and the protest movement became more violent. To weather the storm, the shah either had to use brute force and crush the movement or to strike a deal with the moderate camp of the protest movement, which included the sagacious Shariatmadari and the National Front. He chose neither option and ordered his obedient servant Jafar Sharif Imami to form a government of "national unity" in September 1978, and thereby he strengthened the radical, pro-Khomeini faction and facilitated the eventual unity of the moderate and radical factions of the protest movement. The problem was that the king wanted to be a "democratic autocrat," to take away with one hand what symbolic little he had given by the other hand. Therefore, every reform he championed and every concession he granted was perceived as a sign of weakness.

To appease the *ulama,* Imami released some political prisoners, reinstated the Islamic calendar the shah had changed in 1975, and dissolved the Rastakhiz Party, the last organized source of civilian support for the shah. Although Shariatmadari was prepared to collaborate with Imami, the Black Friday massacre in September 1978, in which the police killed hundreds of protesters, ended that possibility. The cantankerous Ayatollah Khomeini in Iraq was also in no mood to compromise, urging the people to continue the struggle against the shah. In retaliation, the shah asked the Iraqi government to expel Khomeini, who left for France. Khomeini's unyielding stance toward the shah forced Shariatmadari to repudiate the possibility of compromise with the regime.

With every passing day, the shah's chances of survival were declining, a fact Washington was slow to accept. In late September 1978 the Defense Intelligence Agency had concluded that the shah would remain actively in power for the next ten years. Shortly after that assessment, the nationwide strikes, including the oil workers', began in the fall of 1978, and the nationalists formed a de facto alliance with Khomeini. Supported by the financial contributions of the *bazaari,* the strikes paralyzed the country. To defuse the crisis, the shah belatedly approached Karim Sanjabi, the leader of the National Front, to form a government. Sanjabi asked to meet with Khomeini first. After the meeting, Sanjabi, who like many others believed mistakenly that Khomeini would cease to intervene in politics once the shah was out of power, joined Khomeini and declared the monarchy illegitimate. The new alliance consolidated Khomeini's leadership, weakened Shariatmadari, and increased Khomeini's appeal among the nationalists, leftists, and the educated. Henceforth, Khomeini, surrounded by some Western-educated intellectuals, championed such popular themes as independence, freedom, and democracy to unify the protesters. His sermons were now widely distributed among the population on cassette tapes.

The shah responded to this alliance by turning to his trusted armed forces. In November 1978 he appointed Gen. Gholam Reza Azhari, an ailing old man, to form a military government but ordered him to avoid bloodshed. One day after the appointment, the shah recognized the legitimacy of the revolutionary movement in a nationally televised speech. The speech, the obituary of the Pahlavis read by the shah himself, was perceived as another sign of his weakness. Khomeini recognized the paralysis of the shah's will and for the first time spoke explicitly of creating an Islamic government.

Azhari's reforms, including the release of Khomeini supporters Ayatollah Hossein Ali Montazeri and Hashemi Rafsanjani and the arrest of former prime minister Amir Abbas Hoveyda, only diminished the confidence of the ruling class in his ability to handle the crisis. The impotence of his government became visible when millions of people participated in street demonstrations that reaffirmed Khomeini's leadership and advocated the creation of a government based on Islamic precepts. The hapless and helpless shah turned to the National Front's Shahpur Bakhtiar, who agreed to form a government contingent on the shah's departure from Iran. Although Washington and the armed forces supported Bakhtiar, he had no chance of success: the National Front expelled him, and Khomeini, who controlled the streets and the crowds, opposed him. Khomeini called Bakhtiar's major reforms, including the dissolution of SAVAK, shams and demanded his resignation.

With SAVAK's dissolution, all major players focused on the armed forces. Carter sent Gen. Robert E. Huyser to Tehran on January 5, 1979, one day after the convening of the Guadeloupe Conference, at which the leaders of the major Western nations asked the shah to leave Iran. Whatever his real mission, which some analysts insist was to prevent a proshah coup and others believe was to protect sensitive American military equipment in Iran, Huyser arrived when the tidal wave of revolution had reached irreversible heights. Further, the Iranian generals were better trained to deal with external aggression than internal rebellions and were more qualified to execute the shah's order than solve political equations. They melted like snow when the shah left Iran on January 13, 1979.

As soon as the shah announced his departure, Khomeini established the secret Council of the Islamic Revolution as a shadow government. Six days after his triumphant return to Iran on February 1, 1979, he formed a provisional revolutionary government, headed by Mehdi Bazargan. Iran briefly had two governments. While Bazargan was negotiating with the armed forces, the air force technicians became the first to hail Khomeini as their new leader. Angered by the defection, the "Immortals," the shah's most trusted soldiers, attacked the technicians, and a mini-civil war started. The revolutionaries, including the leftists, joined the technicians, defeated the Immortals, and attacked the Evin prison, Iran's Bastille. On February 11, 1979, the demoralized armed forces declared their neutrality, Bakhtiar went into hiding, the Islamic Revolution became a reality, and the postrevolutionary power struggle began. Khomeini first created a state within the state and then used that ministate to defeat his rivals and consolidate the infant republic. In April 1979 the Islamic Republic was officially established through a national referendum, and six months later the new Islamic constitution was approved in another national referendum.

In July 1980 Mohammad Reza Shah, like his father, died in exile in grief. And in June 1988 Khomeini became the first ruler since the Constitutional Movement of 1906 not to be exiled and to die while still ruling Iran.

See also *Iranian Constitutional Revolution (1906); Islamic Fundamentalism; Khomeini, Ayatollah Ruhollah; Mosaddeq, Mohammad.*

Mohsen M. Milani

BIBLIOGRAPHY

Abrahamian, Ervand. *Iran Between Two Revolutions.* Princeton, N.J.: Princeton University Press, 1982.

Amirahmadi, Hooshang. *Revolution and Economic Transition.* Albany: State University of New York Press, 1990.

Arjomand, Said Amir. *The Turban for the Crown.* New York: Oxford University Press, 1988.

Bill, James. *The Eagle and the Lion: America and Iran.* New Haven: Yale University Press, 1988.

Cottam, Richard. *Nationalism in Iran.* Pittsburgh, Penn.: University of Pittsburgh Press, 1988.

Debashi, Hamid. *Ideology and Discontent: The Ideological Foundation of the Islamic Revolution in Iran.* New York: New York University Press, 1985.

Keddie, Nikki, with Yann Richards. *Roots of Revolution: An Interpretative History of Modern Iran.* New Haven, Conn.: Yale University Press, 1981.

Khomeini, Ruhollah. *Islam and Revolution: Writings and Declarations of Imam Khomeini.* Translated and annotated by Hamid Algar. Berkeley: Mizan Press, 1981.

Milani, Mohsen. *The Making of Iran's Islamic Revolution: From Monarchy to Islamic Republic.* 2d ed. Boulder, Colo.: Westview Press, 1994.

Ramazani, R. K. *The United States and Iran: Pattern of Influence.* New York: Praeger, 1982.

Zonis, Marvin. *The Majestic Failure: The Fall of the Shah.* Chicago: University of Chicago Press, 1991.

IRAQI REVOLUTION (1958)

On the morning of July 14, 1958, Iraqi army units entered Baghdad and, with almost no resistance, overthrew the Hashimite monarchy that had ruled modern Iraq since its founding in 1921. After the royal family was captured at the Rihab Palace, it was machine-gunned by a junior army officer not associated with the conspirators, the Free Officers organization. Among the dead were King Faysal II and the former regent, Prince 'Abd il-Ilahi. The next day, the hated prime minister, Nuri al-Sa'id, was shot while trying to escape the capital. After a short period of urban mob violence, the Free Officers organization restored order and installed Staff Brigadier 'Abd al-Karim Qasim as prime minister of the newly declared Iraqi republic *(see map, p. 474)*.

The 1958 Iraqi Revolution had profound consequences for Iraq and the entire Middle East. Iraq withdrew from the U.S.-sponsored Baghdad Pact that had been created three years earlier. The influence of the large Iraqi Communist Party in the new government alarmed not only the United States but also Egypt's leader, Gamal Abdel Nasser, and other Pan-Arabists both inside and outside Iraq. The uprising also influenced U.S. president Dwight Eisenhower's decision to send American marines into Lebanon in July 1958.

The 1958 revolution received widespread support throughout Iraq. The populace saw the monarchy as corrupt and under the control of Great Britain and the United States. There was a tremendous disparity of income between a few large landowners, merchants, and industrialists and the impoverished peasantry and urban poor, and the oil economy that developed after World War I only increased the gap between rich and poor. The middle classes and peasantry welcomed the Qasim regime's emphasis on land reform and ridding the country of the political and economic elites that had supported the monarchy and foreign interests.

THE QUESTION OF PAN-ARABISM

Among the Free Officers, however, a rivalry quickly developed between Qasim and one of the central conspirators, Col. 'Abd al-Salam 'Arif. Qasim resisted efforts by 'Arif and other Pan-Arabist Free Officers to declare immediate political unity with Egypt. Iraqi Pan-Arabists supported the idea that developed after World War II of uniting all the Arabic-speaking people in a single Arab state and wanted Iraq to join the United Arab Republic that Egypt and Syria formed in 1958. Although supportive of inter-Arab cooperation, Qasim felt that Iraq needed to set its own political and economic house in order before joining any Pan-Arab state. Consequently Qasim laid himself open to the accusation of being a local nationalist unconcerned with Pan-Arabism, especially creating a unitary Arab state and helping the Palestinians resist Zionism.

The tension between Pan-Arabism and local Iraqi nationalism bedeviled Qasim throughout his rule. Many Iraqis, especially Sunni Arabs, looked to Pan-Arab unity to counter the social and political fragmentation that had beset the new Iraqi state formed from three Ottoman provinces after the empire's collapse in 1918. Sunnis viewed Pan-Arab unity as a means to offset their minority status in light of a Shi'i majority and a large Kurdish minority. Many Iraqis, both Shi'i and Sunni, truly believed that only through such unity could Iraq confront what was seen as excessive Western influence in the Middle East. More perniciously, Pan-Arabists tarred Qasim and other local nationalist as *'ajam,* connoting foreigners but especially Persians who were accused of being responsible for the decline of the 'Abbasid Empire (749–1258). Viewed as consciously having promoted Persian at the expense of Arab interests, the 'ajam were seen as undermining the empire's Arab character and strength and hence its internal unity. Qasim was labeled with the derogatory term, *al-shuayn ubiya,* associated with the movement through which Persian influence spread in 'Abbasid society. In the modern Arab world, the term refers to the divisive introduction of sectarian identities into a society and political system. In a society in which historical symbols carried great weight, Pan-Arabists attempted to manipulate the past to undermine the legitimacy of the Qasim regime.

The struggle between a Pan-Arabist as opposed to a local nationalist definition of the Iraqi political community intensified. It came to a head during a March 1959 uprising by Pan-Arabist forces in the northern city of Mosul led by Col. 'Abd al-Wahhab al-Shawwaf. The ill-prepared coup d'état brought fierce clashes between Pan-Arabists and communists. The abortive coup led Qasim to give the Iraqi Communist Party even greater influence in his government and latitude to organize. After the collapse of the al-Shawwaf revolt, both Qasim and the party were at the peak of their popularity and influence.

The Qasim regime, however, lacked financial resources and technical personnel to carry out the ambitious plans for land reform and economic development formulated soon after the revolution. Qasim grew concerned as the Iraqi Communist Party expanded its political influence, especially through the creation of militia units. The wealthy, Pan-Arabists, and sectors of the middle classes became alarmed at what they saw as the spread of communist, and potentially Soviet, influence in Iraqi society. Fearing the increased power of the left, Qasim began to swing toward the right, reining in the communists and strengthening forces opposed to them. He thereby initiated a pattern of supporting one faction until it became too strong only to empower its opponents afterwards in an ever more tenuous balancing act designed to maintain his control over political power—a policy that would pave the way for his downfall.

THE BA'TH THREAT

The Ba'th (Renaissance) Party was formed in Syria in the early 1940s, and in Iraq, in the late 1940s. The party ardently supports Pan-Arab unity as a means of recreating the glories of the early Arabo-Islamic empires, the Umayyad Empire (661–750) and the 'Abbasid Empire (749–1258). Although it has supported mild forms of socialism, the party has always violently opposed communist groups as divisive in their emphasis on class struggle.

The unsuccessful October 1959 assassination attempt against Qasim by a squad of Ba'th Party members that included the future Iraqi leader, Saddam Husayn al-Takriti, was a symptom of Iraq's sharp political divisions. Having little ideological background or political experience, Qasim was ill-equipped to respond to the intense political currents that swirled around him. Rather than working to build a political base—for example, among the democratically oriented political parties such as the National Democratic Party—he instead chose to isolate himself and assume the role of dictator. Qasim ruled under the illusion of widespread political support that was created, in part, by the unswerving support of the Iraqi Communist Party for him under the title of sole leader.

Qasim's support began to wane gradually. Many among the intelligentsia and professional classes became disenchanted by Qasim's failure to hold elections, his press censorship, and the trying of political opponents in a People's Court presided over by his cousin, Fadil al-Mahdawi, in which due process was neglected. Rather than negotiating a serious autonomy agreement with Iraq's Kurds in the north, Qasim decided to respond to their demands with force, thereby drawing the army into a futile and unpopular military campaign. In an effort to divert attention away from the deterioration of domestic politics, Qasim fabricated a conflict with Kuwait after it received independence from Great Britain in 1961 by threatening to annex the country. Only British warnings that such action would be countered by force led him to back down. The result was a thorough foreign policy humiliation.

With help from sympathetic military units, on February 8, 1963, the Ba'th Party began an insurrection in Baghdad. Qasim rushed to the Ministry of Defense to mount a counterattack. After a day of fighting around the ministry, few army units remained loyal to Qasim, and he surrendered with his main advisers on February 9. 'Arif tried to force Qasim to agree that 'Arif had been responsible for planning the July 1958 overthrow of the monarchy. Qasim refused and, after a rump trial, was summarily executed, his body later exhibited on Iraqi state television to show all, especially the urban poor, that he was in fact dead.

The Ba'th Party regime that came to power after Qasim's ouster proved to be a brutal one. Communists and leftist sympathizers were rounded up and imprisoned. Torture and executions became the order of the day. The violence of the Ba'thist militia, the National Guard, was so excessive that even some Ba'thist leaders such as party founder Michel 'Aflaq called for reining in these gangs of largely uneducated and unemployed youth. The violence of the Ba'thist regime finally led 'Arif to intervene once again to oust the party from power in November 1963. The violence, torture, and complete disregard for human rights of the 1963 Ba'thist regime was a taste of much worse things to come under the second Ba'thist regime that seized power in July 1968 under the control of Saddam Husayn.

THE REVOLUTIONARY LEGACY

Despite its problems, the 1958 revolution left an important legacy for Iraqi society and the larger Arab world. Although authoritarian, Qasim's regime was characterized by little extrajudicial violence. Indeed, Qasim himself was too quick to forgive enemies like 'Arif, who would later be responsible for his demise. Among modern Arab leaders, Qasim was one of a small group of social reformers who won the hearts of the peasantry, workers, and urban poor, whom he truly sought to help. Qasim refused to embrace a nationalism based on chauvinism and sectarian identity. As such his regime provided a model for the entire Arab world by reconciling Iraq's status as a multiethnic and multiconfessional society rich in cultural heritage with its singular position as a society that made great contributions to Arab civilization and Arabism. This more open definition of political community contrasts sharply with the repression and xenophobia practiced by the Ba'thist regimes that followed. The Ba'th Party's response to cultural difference was to repress it by force or to manipulate history to fit its own ideological definition of the past.

In Iraq, the years between 1958 and 1963 represented far more than revolutionary change. They also constituted a period of struggle between a definition of Arab politics based on a romantic and nostalgic definition of Arabism and a more tolerant definition of political community based on a recognition of the Arab world's cultural and ethnic diversity. Today the effort to resolve this tension remains at the heart of Arab politics.

See also *Egyptian Revolution (1952); Ethnic Conflict; Kurdish Revolts (1958–); Nasser, Gamal Abdel.*

ERIC DAVIS

BIBLIOGRAPHY

Batatu, Hanna. *The Old Social Classes and Revolutionary Movements in Iraq: A Study of Iraq's Old Landed and Commercial Classes, and of its Communists, Ba'thists and Free Officers.* Princeton, N.J.: Princeton University Press, 1978.

Dann, Uriel. *Iraq Under Qassem: A Political History, 1958–1963.* New York: Frederick A. Praeger and the Reuven Shiloh Research Center, Tel Aviv University, 1969.

Farouk-Sluglett, Marion, and Peter Sluglett. *Iraq Since 1958: From Revolution to Dictatorship.* London: I.B. Tauris, 1990.

Fernea, Robert A., and William Roger Louis, eds. *The Iraqi Revolution of 1958: The Old Social Classes Revisited.* London: I.B. Tauris and the Center for Middle Eastern Studies, University of Texas, 1990.

Khadduri, Majid. *Republican Iraq: A Study in Iraqi Politics Since the Revolution of 1958.* London: Oxford University Press, 1969.

IRISH REVOLT IN NORTHERN IRELAND (1969–)

In August 1969 serious conflict erupted between the Protestant and Catholic communities in Northern Ireland, leading to British army intervention and nearly three decades of violence. The speed with which a peaceful civil rights movement led to serious intercommunal strife reveals the depth of divisions in postpartition Northern Ireland.

THE SITUATION BEFORE 1969

The partition of Ireland in 1920 established a fractured province in Northern Ireland, dominated by Protestants (also called unionists or loyalists). Descendants of settlers who had expropriated the land of the indigenous population in the sixteenth and seventeenth centuries, they constitute approximately 60 percent of the population and define themselves as British. The province remained part of the United Kingdom after 1920 but was granted home rule with its own parliament and prime minister. These political institutions remained firmly in unionist hands.

Although the vast majority of unionists are united in opposition to the incorporation of Northern Ireland into the Republic of Ireland, they are divided about what would be the best constitutional arrangement for their province. The minority community, Irish and Catholic, is not predisposed to confer any legitimacy on the state in which it lives. Two main groups make up this community. The "constitutional nationalists" are the more moderate and have been more willing to seek accommodation with the Protestant state. "Republicans," who are fewer in number, have been more uncompromising. Sinn Fein, the political party that best represents this tradition, is much more willing to support violent action in support of the goals of Irish nationalism.

Given the history of antagonism between settler and native it was not surprising that as late as 1969, four decades after the partition, mutual suspicion and occasional acts of intercommunal violence plagued the province. Few interests cut across the divide to moderate the polarization. Intermarriage remained low, there were no significant cross-community political parties, and education remained segregated. Yet by the start of the 1960s it seemed that mutual accommodation was possible. In 1962 a demoralized Irish Republican Army (IRA) abandoned its "border campaign" for lack of support. This seemed to indicate that violent republicanism had lost its appeal. In 1965 Terence O'Neill, the prime minister of Northern Ireland, met his counterpart in the Republic of Ireland, Sean Lemass. Some hoped that their meeting could be the start of a more fruitful cross-border relationship. The decade was also a time of economic progress, and although a gap in living standards between Catholics and Protestants remained, the O'Neill government believed that growth could improve the lot of Catholics and make Protestant rule more acceptable to them.

To the contrary, rising expectations among Catholics, living in a province where they experienced systematic discrimination, led to growing opposition. The Northern Ireland Civil Rights Association (NICRA), established in 1967, used nonviolent techniques to focus on a number of grievances: the administration of justice; the actions of the Protestant-dominated police force; discrimination in the workplace and in the allocation of public housing; the weighted voting system that worked against Catholics; and gerrymandering.

The unionist government, under pressure from London, attempted limited reform, but many Protestants remained suspicious of NICRA. They feared that major concessions would weaken their own position within the United Kingdom. They were also concerned about latent irreden-

tism in the Republic of Ireland, where Articles 2 and 3 of the 1937 constitution claimed the whole of the island. Protestant leaders knew that if they were too accommodating, they were open to attack from their own community.

THE ONSET OF VIOLENCE AND ITS CONSEQUENCES

In August 1969 serious rioting began after a Protestant march in Derry. The riots spread to Belfast, prompting the British government to dispatch the army to the province, but since the Northern Ireland parliament remained in place, nationalist fears about its role persisted. At the start of 1970 the Provisional IRA (PIRA) broke away from the more socialist official IRA. Its militant nationalism, drawing on the Irish republican tradition of armed struggle, quickly won support in besieged Catholic communities. The British government also alienated many Catholics through tough security measures taken in response to PIRA violence. These included curfews and house searches. In August 1971 several hundred Catholics were jailed without trial, and in January 1972 British soldiers killed thirteen civil rights marchers in Derry. In the face of these incidents PIRA activities increased. It used the language of anticolonialism and self-determination, encapsulated in the phrase "Brits out." However, this attitude blinded republicans to unionist values and interests. Inevitably, the growth of PIRA violence contributed to the rise of loyalist paramilitaries. The most important of these was the Ulster Defence Association, which emerged in September 1971.

More than thirty-five hundred people were killed between 1969 and 1996 on the island of Ireland and in Great Britain and continental Europe. Many more were injured. Residential segregation increased. The Northern Irish economy was kept afloat only through massive subsidies from the British taxpayer. Yet the violence has not been uniform in time or space. Violence peaked in 1972–1974 and then fell to fewer than one hundred deaths a year. Geographically, the violence has been concentrated in working-class areas of the larger towns or in border areas close to the Republic. Many people have therefore been able to lead relatively normal lives, which may explain the longevity of the violence: costs have not been high enough to force the competing parties to compromise.

THE SEARCH FOR A SETTLEMENT

The "Troubles" swept away the old government in Northern Ireland. In 1972 the British Parliament adopted direct rule from London through a secretary of state. This was meant to be a temporary measure, but all subsequent proposals for the political future of Northern Ireland have been rejected because they threatened the goals of one or other of the parties. The proposals included a power sharing executive (1973–1974); a constitutional convention (1975–1976); three devolution proposals between 1977 and 1984; and interparty talks organized by two secretaries of state, Peter Brooke and Patrick Mayhew (1991–1992).

At the end of August 1994 the IRA declared a cease-fire in response to the joint British-Irish Downing Street Declaration of December 1993. The declaration envisaged Sinn Fein participation in political talks in return for an IRA cease-fire. It also stated that Northern Ireland would remain part of the UK only as long as the majority wanted it to. This recognition of the right of self-determination seemed to weaken Northern Ireland's bonds with the rest of the UK. Despite unease in Protestant areas, the loyalist paramilitaries announced their own cease-fire in October 1994. In February 1996 PIRA resumed its attacks, accusing the British government of bad faith. A major disagreement had arisen over the issue of weapons' decommissioning. The British government and unionists insisted that PIRA surrender their arms before talks with Sinn Fein could begin. This the IRA refused to do. However, in May 1997 a new Labour

Party government was elected in the UK, which adopted a more flexible approach. The IRA reestablished the cease-fire in July 1997, and Sinn Fein was invited to participate in political talks that started in September 1997. In April 1998 the parties agreed to a comprehensive settlement package, which was approved in separate referenda by over 70 percent of the population in Northern Ireland and over 90 percent in the Republic.

See also *Irish Revolts (1790s–1900); Irish Revolution (1916–1923).*

Stephen Ryan

BIBLIOGRAPHY

Arthur, Paul. *Government and Politics of Northern Ireland.* Harlow: Longman, 1980.

Bew, Paul, and Gordon Gillespie. *Northern Ireland: A Chronology of the Troubles 1968–1993.* Dublin: Gill and Macmillan, 1993.

Bew, Paul, and Henry Patterson. *The British State and the Ulster Crisis.* London: Verso, 1985.

Darby, John, ed. *Northern Ireland: The Background to the Conflict.* Belfast: Appletree Press, 1983.

McCann, Eamonn. *War in an Irish Town.* Harmondsworth: Penguin, 1974.

O'Leary, Brendan, and John McGarry. *The Politics of Antagonism: Understanding Northern Ireland.* London: Athlone Press, 1993.

Ruane, Joseph, and Jennifer Todd. *The Dynamics of Conflict in Northern Ireland.* Cambridge: Cambridge University Press, 1996.

Whyte, John. *Interpreting Northern Ireland.* Oxford: Clarendon Press, 1990.

IRISH REVOLTS (1790s–1900)

By 1790 agrarian protest movements such as the Whiteboys (from 1761) and Rightboys (1785–1788) had highlighted the main targets of Irish popular revolt: the increased tithes that were due to the established Church of Ireland and the higher rents and shorter leases that were being fixed by landlords. However, they did not outlaw these payments *per se.* Instead, they identified "what the house can afford," and, toward this end, they published schedules of payments, above which the locality was sworn not to pay.

Such mobilization led contemporaries to speak of "popular combinations," which gave the peasantry both the self-confidence and the means to ameliorate its lot. The priest and landlord were not eclipsed as mediators of public grievances. However, the peasantry had discovered its own power to present and redress public grievances, and this influenced both the direction and character of subsequent revolt in Ireland.

During the 1790s the tradition of popular protest in Ireland was influenced by the American and French Revolutions. After 1791 the United Irishmen pursued a republican polity, but as the movement spread, its middle-class leaders came into contact with the more agrarian-minded Defenders, the decade's successor to the Whiteboys. In 1796 the two organizations agreed on a common platform that gave a social as well as political dimension to the putative republican revolution in Ireland. Accordingly, the so-called United Irish Rebellion of 1798 was fought in the name of both the "rights of man" and agrarian change.

This rebellion unfolded with great violence on both sides. In its aftermath, the Insurrection Act passed by the Irish Parliament was used to suspend habeas corpus and to replace civil with military courts. Parliament interpreted the rebellion as a threat to the state and, as such, different from Whiteboyism. No doubt, France's two (failed) attempts to assist the United Irishmen colored this view. However, French assistance also blurred the distinction between the social and political aspects of the revolt, even after the legislative union of Britain and Ireland (1800) had generated a nationalist reaction that overarched both.

THE CHALLENGE OF CONSTITUTIONAL PROTEST

During the 1840s Daniel O'Connell directed the movement to repeal the union. Despite the continuing prevalence and violence of agrarian protest, he insisted on campaigning within the law. In 1829 his system of regional, county, and parochial committees had forced the British government to seat Catholics in the imperial Parliament at Westminster. During the 1820s and 1830s O'Connell also brokered a number of social reforms and convinced many followers that constitutional agitation and social progress were not mutually exclusive. In 1843, however, the British government made it clear that the union would be preserved, by force if necessary. This policy checked O'Connell's leadership and highlighted the limits of constitutional revolt in Ireland, however widely and well-organized its popular support was.

In 1848 disillusionment with O'Connell led to the quickly suppressed rising of the Young Ireland movement. However, it was also inspired by a belief that the inaction of the British government had contributed to the deaths of some one million people during the Great Famine (1845–1850).

Anglophobia was particularly strong among the two million Irish who emigrated to America between 1845 and 1860. It was also central to the Fenian movement that after 1860 blossomed in the United States with the aim of achieving Irish independence by force. In cities such as New York and Chicago, U.S. Civil War veterans offered their military experience and services to "free Ireland," while others collected money and arms to stage the rebellion of 1867. Although the so-called Fenian rising failed, it left an enduring influence on Irish nationalism and ensured an enhanced role for Irish-Americans in subsequent Irish revolts.

CULTURAL ASSERTION

Fenianism also inspired the foundation of the Gaelic Athletic Association (GAA) in 1884 and the Gaelic League nine years later. These organizations drew on networks of local and county clubs to promote traditional Irish games and the Irish language, respectively. As a result, nationalist revolt developed a cultural as well as political vocabulary, the power of which was implied in the lines of William Butler Yeats: "Did that play of mine send out / Certain men the English shot? . . . Could my spoken words have checked / That whereby a house lay wrecked?"

Social revolt also continued, especially after the Land League was formed in 1879 to pursue agrarian reform. Like the GAA, branches of the Land League were established in many parishes. Although it preached the need for peaceful collective action, such as boycotts, it contributed to the rise of agrarian crime, including arson and the assault and assassination of landlords and others who broke the "combination." In 1880 alone some twenty-eight hundred such agrarian incidents were recorded.

Despite this violence, Irish nationalist leader and member of Parliament Charles Stewart Parnell revived O'Connell's legacy of constitutional agitation during the 1880s. By 1891, however, his citation in divorce proceedings had brought his parliamentary career to an inglorious end. Deprived of their "uncrowned king," many Irish nationalists turned from the corridors of Westminster to the halls of the Gaelic League and the pitches of the GAA. Between 1886 and 1906 Irish Unionists could count on an almost uninterrupted succession of Conservative governments to keep the union intact. Parliamentary debate seemed to Irish nationalists to be ineffective, and the GAA and the Gaelic League helped revive the more militant tradition of separatist revolt.

By 1900 Irish revolt had developed a multifaceted character that over time and space meant different things to different people. People also differed on the priority of social over political revolt and whether the military strike was more effective than constitutional agitation. Whatever the focus of protest, however, or the path to redress, all questioned the nature of the relationship with Britain. The most extreme proclaimed Irish independence on Easter Monday 1916.

See also *Irish Revolt in Northern Ireland (1969–); Irish Revolution (1916–1923).*

MAURICE BRIC

BIBLIOGRAPHY

Dickson, David, et al. *The United Irishmen.* Dublin: Lilliput Press, 1993.

Garvin, Thomas. *Nationalist Revolutionaries in Ireland, 1858–1928.* Oxford: Clarendon Press, 1987.

Grada, Cormac O. *Ireland: A New Economic History, 1780–1939.* Oxford: Oxford University Press, 1995.

Townshend, Charles. *Political Violence in Ireland.* Oxford: Oxford University Press, 1983.

IRISH REVOLUTION (1916–1923)

In 1916 Ireland was on the margins of world events, an offshore island far from the great battlefields of World War I where millions were being slaughtered, empires were at risk, and the future of the world was being determined. Ireland was no longer a strategic liability to England but merely a rural, underdeveloped backwater where home rule in some form after the war would assure further tranquillity. But the failed Easter Rising of 1916 by a small, dedicated group of Irish nationalists would serve as a catalyst to a broader-based movement to achieve an Irish republic. The Irish political and military struggle in pursuit of national independence would become a model for later twentieth century liberation struggles, not only in terms of strategy and tactics but also in limitations and liabilities.

THE EASTER RISING

By 1912 a renewal of Irish cultural nationalism was under way, as illustrated by a Gaelic Athletic Association, an Irish language movement of the Gaelic League, and the literary revival of William Butler Yeats, John Synge, and others. Catholic demands for home rule had led Protestant unionists, who had the allegiance of some in the British army, to threaten rebellion and to form the Ulster Volunteers. To counter the unionists, the Irish nationalists had established their own Irish Volunteers, but when World War I intervened in 1914, most unionists and nationalists rallied to the Crown. The nationalist Irish Republican Brotherhood—the Fenians, or IRB, founded in 1858 on ideals and examples arising from the French Revolution and agrarian discontent—was all but forgotten. John Redmond and his Home Rule Party supported the war effort, and even the eleven thousand nationalists who stayed with the Irish Volunteers seemed unlikely revolutionaries. Most Irish social and economic grievances had been accommodated, and home rule in some form would assure future stability, since most of the Irish aspired only to devolved, regional government.

Those who sought to use force to achieve the Irish republic were an odd lot: language freaks, old felons, poets, and

Marxist radicals. The IRB dispatched a number of members to secure German aid: Thomas Clarke, an old Fenian; James Connolly, a radical socialist who had seen Irish labor savaged by the loss of the great dock strike of 1913; Padraig Pearse, headmaster of a small Irish-Irish school; Eamon De Valera, a Brooklyn-born mathematics teacher; Maj. Seán MacBride, who had fought for the Boers; Countess Constant Markievicz, a militant feminist who had founded the Irish boy scouts; Fianna Éireann; and the reformer Sir Roger Casement. German assistance would be necessary because the IRB had decided that with the British Empire engaged in a world war, an insurrection could lead to the Irish republic.

In all revolutions, those committed are criminally optimistic, and the IRB assumed that the Irish people, energized by the example of the volunteers, would rise as well. It also assumed that the British, stunned by events, would compromise rather than pursue a second war against a risen people. The insurrection, planned for April 1916, failed like all previous Irish rebellions; it failed even before the shooting began. An expected shipment of 20,000 rifles secured from Germany went down when the *Aud* had to be scuttled off the Irish coast. Then the leader of the Irish Volunteers, Eoin MacNeill, unaware of the IRB plans, canceled his mobilization order on the evening of April 22. Pearse, Connolly, and others decided the next day to go ahead: the rising would take place at 1 p.m. on Easter Monday, April 24. Not all the Irish Volunteers received word; central command and control was lacking. But the will was there, and in Dublin at noon in front of the General Post Office Pearse, as president, proclaimed the Irish Republic.

The British were caught by surprise, but that advantage was short-lived. The country did not rise, and those volunteers who did were ineffectual. In Dublin the local Irish commanders, mostly innocent of war, seized some key points and ignored others. The British regrouped, dispatched reinforcements, sent in artillery and gunboats, and took a week to batter down the resistance in central Dublin. Only sixteen hundred volunteers were involved, most of them in the capital, and by Friday, April 28, the center of the city was in ruins. Resistance was futile, and the survivors surrendered—460 had been killed, but not the key commanders, and 2,600 wounded. The British were outraged, the Irish people appalled, and the rising over.

The survivors were marched off to detention amid hostile crowds. The commanders were tried, convicted, and executed. The same crowds were again appalled at what was seen as British brutality. Irish discontent in the spring of 1916 did not matter much in London. The real war was in France, Ireland was again pacified, and the Easter insurrection had been but a futile and failed gesture of zealots. Except as a blood sacrifice, which had never been the intention of the IRB, the Irish insurrection had been a disaster. But the Easter Rising offered to the next and more pragmatic generation of Irish rebels lessons that they would apply.

NATIONALISM INVIGORATED

In December 1916, when the prisoners began to return from the internment camp at Frongoch in Wales, Ireland was changing. Sinn Féin successfully ran two candidates for Parliament, who refused to take their seats. And by the time the last prisoners arrived in June 1917, Irish national sentiment was sweeping the island—de Valera soon won a Clare by-election with a large majority for Sinn Féin. Michael Collins and others, convinced of the need for physical force, reorganized the Irish Volunteers. They attracted recruits to the new Irish Republican Army (IRA). The movement toward national resistance increasingly led to strains among the IRA, Sinn Féin, national organizations, newspapers, societies and clubs, the core of the Irish Republican Brotherhood, and Clann na Gael in America.

Nationalist momentum grew when the British government under David Lloyd George tried to introduce conscription into Ireland, a highly provocative act that produced not insurrection but intense Irish organization for confrontation. The British had already arrested most known agitators: de Valera; Arthur Griffith, who had founded Sinn Féin; Countess Markievicz; the new widow Maud Gonne MacBride, the love of William Butler Yeats; and Thomas Clarke's widow. Women had always been among the most militant Irish republicans. The arrests missed Collins and the new generation. Lloyd George then called a snap election that was used by Sinn Féin as a means to elect an Irish parliament, the Dáil Éireann. On December 14, 1918, Sinn Féin received a huge majority of the vote and seventy-three seats; the old Irish parliamentary party of Redmond was wiped out, taking only seven seats, and four of those in largely Protestant Ulster; and the unionists won twenty-one seats in the north-east, along with the four of Trinity College. Everything was utterly changed. The Sinn Féin candidates not imprisoned met in Dublin on January 21, 1919, to form the first independent Dáil Éireann. All who voted Sinn Féin might not have wanted a republic, but all wanted a nation once again.

The more zealous republicans wanted action. The new Irish Volunteers, the IRA, had enlisted 100,000 members. Few were trained or armed, but all were committed to resisting British coercion and to pursuing an irregular war. On January 21, the same day the First Dáil met, IRA volunteers attacked a Royal Ulster Constabulary patrol at Soloheadbeg, Tipperary, and killed two constables to open hostilities in the

A Sinn Féin member is arrested at gunpoint in November 1920.

Tan War. The IRB was transmuted in part into the leadership of the IRA, and in turn the IRA evolved into the archetype national liberation struggle. Collins managed de Valera's escape from a prison on the Isle of Wight so that he might become president of the republic. The nation could be established only by imposing Irish will and skill over British assets, legitimacy, and persistence.

The British found an independent Ireland difficult to imagine, the anguish of the Irish unionists easy to understand, and coercion congenial. For the Irish, the struggle for an independent republic was legitimized by history and by the 1918 elections. But the IRA's armed campaign was only one means to its goal. The Irish also attempted to influence world opinion, especially during the negotiations at Versailles and in America, while establishing a functioning government in Ireland. The British in turn frustrated Irish diplomacy and sought to close down Irish nationalist institutions. So the island moved toward irregular war, a guerrilla insurrection deploying the IRA against the British army, police, and auxiliary units—against the power and reputation of the Crown.

GUERRILLA WARFARE

The IRA guerrillas, farmers or clerks when not on operations, focused first on the police—the means of control in the countryside. Then they turned to the reinforced army and special units, including the notorious counterterror Black and Tan auxiliaries. Their campaign made much of the country ungovernable but did not achieve liberated zones or greatly penalize the British: total losses by the 1921 truce would be three hundred killed. All actions were small in scale, for at best the IRA had two thousand volunteers, most of them badly trained and poorly armed. In addition to ambushes, the guerrillas burned security facilities and intimidated loyalists. Deeply frustrated, the auxiliaries often retaliated with arson and murder. The war in the countryside was often one of murder by ambush and authorized murder in response.

Gunmen in the cities, especially Collins's squad in Dublin, sought out particular British targets. Collins, Chief of Staff of the IRA Richard Mulcahy, and Dublin commander Dick McKee (who was murdered on the eve of the operation), authorized an attack for Sunday morning, November 21, 1921, on a group of British officers engaged in counterespionage. All over Dublin, the squad killed fourteen British agents, devastating the intelligence apparatus and morale. That afternoon a group of auxiliaries opened fire on a crowd at Croke Park in Dublin, killing twelve and wounding seventy. Bloody Sunday, as the massacre came to be called, was an indicator that the only tactic the British had left was counterterror.

The cycle of provocation and retaliation hardened Irish resolve—and raised the fears of the Protestant unionists that they might be abandoned by the Crown to Catholic rule, not just home rule. Every effort by the nationalists focused on eroding British power and escalating Irish national aspirations: there were ritual funerals and banned meetings; new martyrs who generated new ballads; and the support of all the old poets and artists. Sinn Féin, with Griffith as acting president, by 1921 had established a parallel governance: a republic, an elected Dáil, national bond drives, ambassadors and legates, courts and ministerial initiatives, all the pretensions of independence. All facets of propaganda were initiated: radio broadcasts, books, pamphlets, tours, appeals, and press releases. The nationalists appealed to the new League of Nations and to old friends in the United States and elsewhere, and they orchestrated rallies within the Irish diaspora. The issue was internationalized and politicized, while the vicious irregular war continued. The model for all future armed struggles was fashioned from Irish needs and British vulnerabilities.

BRITISH ACCOMMODATION AND IRISH CIVIL WAR

By early spring 1921 Prime Minister Lloyd George and the British establishment felt the material and morale drain of Ireland too great to continue. On June 7, 1921, a parliament that had been authorized by the Government Ireland Act of 1920 met in Belfast to administer the province of Northern Ireland and so protect the unionists of at least six counties *(see map, p. 255)*. On July 11, 1921, a truce came into effect. The Irish Dáil sent a delegation to London in October 1921, led by Collins. A treaty was negotiated and signed on December 6—the alternative, Lloyd George insisted, was renewed war. Collins said the treaty guaranteed more than had been gained in eight hundred years and could lead in time to full independence and even the republic. His was not a compelling case for a document few Irish nationalists viewed with enthusiasm.

The settlement would mean dominion status for Ireland in the Commonwealth. The six counties of Northern Ireland, even if apparently not viable, would for the time being be a province of the United Kingdom, and the British would keep several military bases. Members in the new Irish parliament would take an oath to the Crown upon election to make clear there was no republic. There would be for the first time a free Irish state. The Second Dáil approved the treaty on January 7, 1923, after intense and emotional debate, by a sixty-four to fifty-seven vote.

Many republicans felt the Dáil had no right to do wrong. The republic had not been achieved. The partition, oath to the Crown for members of the Dáil, and British bases were accommodations that the militant Irish republicans could not accept, and the country drifted into civil war. The new government of the Irish Free State pursued the militants—the IRA—by conventional tactics and troops. The war was bitter and vicious, and nearly one thousand people were killed as the regulars gradually imposed order. Fighting against IRA "irregulars," the Free State won when the IRA gave up, dumped its arms, and waited for another day. By then Collins had been killed in an ambush in Cork, Griffith had died of a heart attack, more martyrs had been made and atrocities committed, most of the irregulars were in prisoner camps, and the country was divided and devastated.

Once peace came, the republicans split into those who would follow de Valera and the new Fianna Fail into the Free State Dáil in 1925 and then power in 1932, and the Sinn Féin and covert IRA, which gradually eroded. The country, however, was so divided that two generations would pass before other issues would determine party membership.

The new Irish Free State was a small, underdeveloped rural country, partitioned, war-wracked, divided, without great natural resources or encouraging prospects, and marginal to Europe; but many of the great ideological and strategic battles of the century were first played out in Ireland. In the years after 1918, the Irish not only fashioned the model for armed struggle but also indicated the dangers of national liberation and the limitations of revolution.

See also *Irish Revolt in Northern Ireland (1969–); Irish Revolts (1790s–1900).*

J. Bowyer Bell

BIBLIOGRAPHY

Coogan, Tim Pat. *Michael Collins.* London: Arrow, 1990.

Dhonnchadha, Máirín Ní, and Teo Drogan, eds. *Revising the Rising.* Derry, Northern Ireland: Field Day, 1991.

Edwards, Owen Dudley, and Fergus Pyle, eds. *1916: The Easter Rising.* London: Macgibbon and Kee, 1968.

Hopkinson, Michael. *Green Against Green, The Irish Civil War.* Dublin: Gill and Macmillan, 1988.

Neeson, Eoin. *The Civil War in Ireland 1921–1923.* Cork: Mercier, 1986.

O'Neill, Thomas P., and the Earl of Longford. *Eamon de Valera.* Dublin: Gill and Macmillan, 1970.

Thompson, William Irwin. *The Imagination of an Insurrection: Dublin Easter 1916.* New York: Oxford University Press, 1967.

Townshend, Charles. *The British Campaign in Ireland, 1919–1921.* London: Oxford University Press, 1975.

ISLAMIC ANTICOLONIAL REVOLTS OF THE 19TH CENTURY

Throughout the nineteenth century various forms of European imperialism, particularly settler colonialism, posed acute challenges to Muslim societies in the vast area stretching from Morocco and sub-Saharan western Africa to Indonesia. The leading European colonial powers—the British, French, Dutch, and Russian—expanded through political, military, and economic means into territories where Islamic regimes had traditionally held sway or Muslims formed a majority. This raised the specter of living under infidel rule, particularly in places of white settler colonization, as happened in French North Africa and parts of the Dutch East Indies. Already in the eighteenth century Russian expansion into adjacent regions formerly controlled by Muslim states elicited revolt, especially in the ethnically and religiously complex area of the Caucasus (between the Black and Caspian Seas). There Russian expansion from 1723 on sparked a number of Islamic-based movements among peasants and notables recently converted to Islam; both conversion and anti-Russian resistance were mainly the work of the Naqshbandi Sufi Order (an Islamic mystical organization or religious association), one of many Islamic brotherhoods. In the Caucasus anti-Russian revolts by Muslim peoples persisted well into the nineteenth century and, in some cases, into the twentieth.

ISLAMIC RESPONSES TO EUROPEAN COLONIAL RULE

Muslim responses to their increasing loss of independence or outright foreign control varied immensely. Militant anticolonial activities represented only one of several solutions to the disruptions of Western economic penetration or domination. Others ranged from emigration, evasion, or withdrawal from contact with the invaders to accommodation or even collaboration. Collective or individual resistance also assumed a number of guises: from refusal to pay taxes or provide labor to the colonizers to the dissemination of anti-European propaganda or the mobilization of armed followers in the defense of Islam. In many parts of the Muslim world, sufi brotherhoods provided the organizational matrix for united action on the micro level. It should also be noted that local rebellions or uprisings whose causes lay principally in the internal arrangement of power in a particular Muslim community might ultimately be directed outward to challenge foreign or colonial rulers.

Frequently, concerted efforts to repel the invaders or limit their harmful influence also included attempts by local Muslim figures to impose a "purified" form of Islam upon fellow Muslims regarded as lax in their faith, in order to better oppose the foreigners. The Shi'ite Persian Safavid lands in the Caucasus (in Daghestan) that fell under Russian domination from the 1700s on provide an excellent case study of these interrelationships. Between 1834 and 1859 a sufi and imam (local religious leader) of the Naqshbandi Order named Shamyl (or Shamil) assumed the leadership of free peasants opposed both to the Russians and to the Muslim lords who had thrown in their lot with the infidels. Shamyl proclaimed the Sharia (Islamic law) as the only law of the land and prohibited smoking, dancing, and all other activities deemed in violation of Islamic principles. By 1844 Shamyl and his followers had defeated many Muslim elites in Daghestan viewed as Russian collaborators; this particular jacquerie, however, was defeated by superior Russian forces in 1859. Yet Islamic protest in the Caucasus was not ended. Another great revolt broke out in 1877–1878; once again sufi orders and sufi leaders played a major role in the rebellion, their participation representing both a cause and effect of the spread of sufism among the region's inhabitants. A similar process emerged in Inner Asia at the end of the century; there the Chinese state began to absorb forcibly non-Chinese Muslim Turkic-speaking peoples, like the Uighurs and Kazakhs in Sinkiang Province north of Tibet, thus sparking a number of rebellions. These militant forms of resistance were often aided by sufi networks, and brutal suppression by the Chinese state only enhanced the attraction of Islam and sufism.

Recent scholarship emphasizes the complexity and diversity of Islamic-inspired revolts against occupying European/Christian powers or their local agents. Islam in its many manifestations played a double role: conferring legitimacy upon the leaders of a particular movement; and providing the ideological and symbolic bases for uncommon forms of political cooperation, since the forces working against unified, long-term militant action were often as strong as those working for it. Given the wide array of Muslim peoples, societies, and states in the nineteenth-century Islamic world, the local interplay between religion as lived and politics could be extraordinarily complicated. Nevertheless, the resistance of Muslim populations to European hegemony tended to display patterns. First, the micropolitics of anticolonial activity were shaped by older forms of political cooperation, conflict, and contestation predating the Europeans' arrival or the rise to power of their coopted indigenous representatives. For example, ancient alliances or rivalries among pastoral nomadic communities in places like Iran and northern Africa might determine whether or not their tribal chiefs would actively oppose European influence or rule. Second, the unfolding of collective action invariably reveals the importance of popular or populist forms of religion and its communal representatives: sufi orders and venerated sufis; charismatic local big men or women; and living saints, male and female, and their clienteles.

Several kinds of revolts characterized the nineteenth century—jihads, millenarian or mahdist movements, and tribal rebellions against invading European armies or settlers. However, these should not be construed as distinct forms of Islamic religio-political action since they often in practice merged into one another. In addition, tribally organized rebellions in mountains or deserts frequently offered more scope for women to participate as warriors; for example, in Algeria during the conquest era, from 1830 until the 1850s, women from aristocratic warrior clans sometimes fought in armed combat against the French army.

JIHADS, MAHDIST MOVEMENTS, AND ANTICOLONIAL PROTEST

A complicated notion in Islamic theory, *jihad* in practice is holy war declared against the enemies of Islam—whether infidels or lapsed Muslims. Jihads frequently were initiated by Muslim scholars or clerics seeking to return a "corrupted" Muslim community to the purified practices of the Prophet Muhammad's era (that is, the seventh century) while protecting an Islamic state or community from outside, non-Islamic forces or influences. Jihad and mahdism intersected when the recognized leader of a holy war was regarded by mobilized followers as possessing those signs and traits expected of the Muslim redeemer within the larger context of unusual socio-moral crisis. In addition, mahdism (collective political action organized around belief in the Mahdi) and holy war, operating in tandem, might combine militant resistance to Western inroads with various kinds of state-building; this was frequently the case in Africa, both sub-Saharan and Mediterranean.

Since the disruptions introduced by European colonialism in Muslim communities across the globe were associated in the minds of many people with the redeemer's advent and the world turned upside down, millenarian protest movements under the Mahdi's guidance loomed large in the repertoire of nineteenth-century Muslim political action, especially prior to the emergence of urban-based nationalist protest. As the Islamic world increasingly fell under European hegemony in the nineteenth century, many Muslims began actively to await the redeemer's advent, although the circumstances surrounding his appearance varied from place to place.

One of the most spectacular millenarian revolts of the late nineteenth century occurred in British-occupied Sudan, where a local religious figure, Muhammad Ahmad ibn Abdallah, proclaimed himself the Mahdi in 1881 and went on to erect a viable state structure. This triggered a series of Islamic-inspired revolts against foreign rule that lasted until 1899. In northern Nigeria and the northern Cameroons during the early nineteenth century, a religious scholar from Hausaland, Uthman Dan Fodio (1754–1817), declared jihad against the non-Islamic behavior and customs that had crept into the practices of West African Muslim states. In 1804 he declared holy war against the nearby pagan rulers of Gobir. By this time Dan Fodio's followers viewed him as the Mahdi sent in fulfillment of the prophecies. Drawing upon these two strands of religio-political legitimacy and action—jihad and mahdism—Dan Fodio went on to create an enduring Islamic state known as the Caliphate of Sokoto. Dan Fodio's activities sparked other jihads, the founding of yet more Islamic states in West Africa, and mass conversions to Islam among nonelites. The existence of these Muslim state formations by the end of the nineteenth century signaled the spread of Islam to ordinary people in a huge swatch of the African continent but also alarmed French and British imperialists obsessed by pan-Islamic movements worldwide; in 1903 the British defeated the Sokoto Caliphate.

Mahdist-led revolts were also prevalent in Mediterranean Africa between 1830, when France invaded Algeria, and 1912, when Morocco was forcibly incorporated into the French empire. Indeed, movements led and organized by self-proclaimed messianic leaders often pulled France deeper into the Sahara in the course of the nineteenth century; thus, Western imperial expansion was, at times, the consequence of Islamic movements rather than the result. This process was also at work in other parts of the globe where European colonial powers were unwittingly drawn into regions as direct rulers, replacing an older system of indirect domination through co-opted local elites. For example, in the Dutch East Indies, in the Banten area of Java, an Islamic religious revival of the 1840s and 1850s was combined with widespread popular expectations of the Mahdi's advent and collective distress at European inroads into the economy. This ultimately produced the great insurrection of 1888, which, while brutally suppressed by Dutch colonial forces, compelled the Netherlands to reexamine the nature of its rule in Indonesia. One of the greatest ironies is that the suppression of anticolonial upheavals by European powers invariably spread Islam into new areas through conversions.

Finally, rebellions and revolts, whatever guise they assumed, in the countryside or in provinces removed from the centers of colonial rule sometimes gave way to rural banditry or later moved into cities in the form of riots or urban labor protest. By the nineteenth century's end, anticolonial movements in many places had begun to display the characteristics of urban nationalist agitation. Nevertheless, anticolonial resistance inspired by Islamic principles should not be seen as an expression of some sort of irrational religious impulse. Rather, it was informed by rational calculations and choices and infused by a deeply felt desire to defend faith and homeland against foreign incursions with the moral, material, and ideological means available at the time. That these movements failed due to cruel repression does not mean that they left no enduring legacy. Collective memories of local resistors and their brave followers and of unified forms of political action lived on in Muslim communities in Asia and Africa, later providing twentieth-century nationalists with a pool of heroic ancestors and with patterns of politics upon which to build visions of independent nation-states.

See also *Colonialism and Anticolonialism; Egyptian Revolts (1881–1919); Indian "Great Mutiny" (1857–1859); Islamic Precolonial Revolts of the 18th and 19th Centuries; Millenarianism; Sudanese Mahdiyya (1881–1898).*

JULIA CLANCY-SMITH

BIBLIOGRAPHY

Adas, Michael. *Prophets of Rebellion: Millenarian Protest Movements against the European Colonial Order.* Chapel Hill, N.C.: University of North Carolina Press, 1979.

Burke, Edmund. *Prelude to Protectorate in Morocco: Precolonial Protest and Resistance, 1860–1912.* Chicago: University of Chicago Press, 1977.

Burke, Edmund, and Ira M. Lapidus, eds. *Islam, Politics, and Social Movements.* Berkeley: University of California Press, 1988.

Clancy-Smith, Julia. *Rebel and Saint: Muslim Notables, Populist Protest, Colonial Encounters (Algeria and Tunisia, 1800–1904).* Berkeley: University of California Press, 1994.

Martin, Bradford G. *Muslim Brotherhoods in Nineteenth-Century Africa.* Cambridge: Cambridge University Press, 1976.

Mukherjee, Rudrangshu. *Awadh in Revolt, 1857–1858: A Study of Popular Resistance.* New York: Oxford University Press, 1984.

Robinson, David. *The Holy War of Umar Tal: The Western Sudan in the Mid-Nineteenth Century.* Cambridge: Clarendon Press, 1985.

Zenkovsky, S. A. *Pan-Turkism and Islam in Russia.* Cambridge, Mass.: Harvard University Press, 1960.

ISLAMIC FUNDAMENTALISM

From the 1920s onward, and particularly since the 1970s, movements have developed in a number of Muslim countries calling for Islamic revolution and the constitution of an Islamic state. While not all Islamist movements have involved "revolution," they have in many cases involved wide levels of mass mobilization and political activity comparable to that of revolutionary movements elsewhere.

FUNDAMENTALISM: ESSENCE AND VARIETY

The term *Islamic fundamentalism* has been applied to a range of movements that have sought to challenge secular regimes in the Muslim world and establish some kind of Islamic state. Although the term *fundamentalist* originated in the United States in the 1920s, referring to Christian groups that denied evolutionary theory, it has come to be used more widely of tendencies in other religions—Judaism, Hinduism, Buddhism as well as Islam—that combine the original Christian claim of a return to holy text with a program of political and social action. By *fundamentalism* one may, therefore, denote movements that display two general characteristics. The first is a selective, instrumental reading of texts, which is presented as either a call for the return to a literal reading of these texts or, as in the case of Hinduism, the modernist attempt to select certain existing texts for special canonical status. Second, fundamentalism involves the mobilization of popular or other support in order to implement at the political and social levels a model of the ideal state and of social practice supposedly derived from those texts. Particular attention is paid to those aspects of the social order deemed to be under threat—the position of women, clothing, and, where this is relevant to the religion, orthodox practices such as ritual purification and correct diet. Most Islamic fundamentalists also demand a return to shari'a, the corpus of Muslim law, which they present, inaccurately, as a body of jurisprudence and legislation applicable to contemporary society.

Islamic fundamentalists share a view of Muslims as oppressed by an alliance of corrupt rulers and foreign exploiters and call for a return to the model of the seventh century. All stress the need for women to conform to, and participate in, the redefinition of society—as secular revolutionaries had also done. The term *revolution* was used by some Islamist movements, just as they appropriated other terms from the vocabulary of twentieth-century radicalism and populism. The reality was, however, that only in the case of the Iranian Islamic Revolution of 1979 could the movement be termed "revolutionary" in a full sense; elsewhere, political elites, in or out of power, were deploying the term for their own purposes. In one respect none of these movements, the Iranian included, could be termed revolutionary since, for all their rhetoric on political and social issues, they had no distinctive economic program.

Movements calling for a return to the core texts of Islam—the Qur'an, or word of God, the *hadith,* or sayings of the Prophet, and the shari'a—have recurred throughout the fourteen centuries of the Muslim religion. In the eighteenth century the Wahhabi movement in the Arabian Peninsula, which was to triumph with the creation of Saudi Arabia in the 1920s, proposed such a return. In the twentieth century a number of thinkers began to call for such a policy—Hassan al-Banna, who founded the Muslim Brotherhood in Egypt in 1928, the Egyptian theorist Sayyid Qutb, and the Pakistani Sayyid Abu'l-'Ala Maududi. They appealed across state and ethnic boundaries for a mobilization of the community of Muslims, the *umma,* against corrupt rulers and foreign domination and called for the establishment of an Islamic state. Equally, they denounced the corruption of women by alien forces and the mixing of men and women.

A MASS ISLAMIC REVOLUTION: IRAN

These nineteenth- and early-twentieth-century fundamentalists were in the main of the Sunni branch of Islam, by far the majority of Muslims. In the 1970s a fundamentalist trend also developed among the Iranian population, of Shi'ite confession. A growing movement of opposition within Iran to the regime of the shah in the latter part of 1978 culminated in the revolutionary overthrow of his regime and the establishment in February 1979 of the Islamic Republic of Iran. The leader of that revolution, Ayatollah Ruhollah Khomeini, argued, in contrast to many other Shi'ite thinkers, that it was possible to establish an Islamic government. In a combination of secular and religious legitimations, Khomeini himself was proclaimed both *rahbar,* leader of the Islamic revolution, and *faqih,* supreme authority in Islamic jurisprudence. Khomeini established a regime in which the Islamic clergy played a central role and implemented a wide-ranging Islamization of society—evident in the enforcement of a restrictive dress code on women and in the transformation of the legal system to rid it of secular elements. Women were mobilized into the economy and into public political activity but in a form, as well as a garb, determined by the fundamentalist movement itself. At the same time he called for the unity of all Muslims at the international level and for a common struggle by the "oppressed" against what he termed "global arrogance," meaning in part Western domination.

ARAB WORLD, AFGHANISTAN, PAKISTAN, TURKEY

The Iranian Revolution appeared to inspire movements in other countries moved by similar or analogous views. In southern Lebanon Shi'ite movements opposed to Israeli occupation were both inspired and armed by Iran. In neighboring Afghanistan a wide-ranging guerrilla resistance to the communist regime established in 1978 drew its inspiration from Islamic ideas. Some of the Afghan currents, such as the Hizb-i Islami of Gulbuddin Hekmatyar, were fundamentalist in the sense of combining traditional and modern ideas, while others, such as the Taliban, who emerged in 1994 and captured Kabul in 1996, were of a more conservative orientation, based on the *madrases* or religious schools. In Arab states such as Egypt, Jordan, Iraq, and Algeria and among the Palestinians, movements calling for a return to an Islamic social order developed: the Algerian fundamentalists combined a critique of foreign economic and cultural influence with the demand for a society like that of the Prophet and the full implementation of shari'a. Faced with an authoritarian military regime, the Algerian Islamists turned increasingly to bombing and massacre of civilians, abandoning any pretense of being guided by the traditional legal or cultural constraints of orthodox Islam.

In Egypt fundamentalism developed in the 1970s in protest at the dictatorial nature of the military regime and at that state's improvement of relations with Israel. The response of the regime was two-sided, repression at the political level, and appropriation of Islamist ideas at the cultural and social levels. In Sudan a military regime allied to fundamentalists came to power in 1989. It set out to Islamize the legal and political systems, using force to suppress opponents in the Arab north and non-Muslim south. In Pakistan, by contrast, the established military regime of Gen. Zia al-Haq, which came to power in 1977, used Islamization and the support of certain Islamist parties, such as Jama'at al-Islami, to isolate its political opponents. In Turkey Islamist currents became stronger after the coup of 1980. Initially encouraged by a military regime keen to isolate the secular left, they acquired a political and economic life of their own, and in 1995 the Islamists came to power in a coalition government. The Rifah Party, in seeking a "just society," invoked Qur'anic principles, as well as those of the Ottoman Empire, and sought to segregate men and women and reintroduce Islamic law. But, as elsewhere, the Islamic program lacked a distinctive economic policy.

COMPARATIVE PERSPECTIVES: PROGRAM AND PRACTICE

Despite the apparently religious element of these movements, they had several features in common with other movements of protest in Third World states. Thus they drew support from social groups that were disadvantaged or marginalized by secular states. The irony of the Iranian Revolution was that, while its ideological goal was a return to the theocratic rule of the seventh century, its means of achieving this goal were those conventionally associated with revolution in a developed society—the mass urban demonstration (the largest in human history) and the political general strike.

Although they developed in contexts where the more established forms of secular protest, nationalist and left-wing, had lost some of their appeal, fundamentalists borrowed heavily from the language and organizational practices of these movements. The model of the state was derived from Jacobin France, their international theory was a diluted version of Marxist views of imperialism and of dependency theory, and their appeal to the masses and oppressed and their denunciations of corrupt rulers echoed those of Third World populists. The very goal they set for themselves, "revolution," was taken from the vocabulary of left-wing movements.

Islamic fundamentalism, once in power, also behaved in a manner similar to that of other postrevolutionary regimes. Authoritarian political systems, based on state control and directed forms of mass mobilization, were created in Iran and Sudan. In Iran education was transformed by a "cultural revolution." In their foreign policies these regimes combined conventional diplomacy with unorthodox methods, be these the detention of Western diplomats or the export of revolution through political and military means. There were also differences: the Iranian Revolution created no party, relying instead on the network of mosques and mass organizations created in the revolution and the subsequent war with Iraq. While the Iranian regime prevented opposition groups from organizing, it allowed a degree of pluralism of opinion in the press and parliament uncharacteristic of most dictatorial postrevolutionary systems.

As with other revolutionary movements, fundamentalists exhibited the tension between their transnational aspirations, evident in ideology and practice, and their location in specific social and political contexts. From the 1920s and even more so from the late 1970s there was a community of ideas, sentiment, and, to some degree, organization between different Muslim countries. Yet no Islamic "international" comparable to that of the communist movement ever emerged, and each of these movements was located in a specific state and had distinctive social, national, and, in the case of Iran, confessional characteristics. Islamic revolutionaries, like their secular counterparts, divided the peoples they appealed to as much as they united them. They were able to come to power in only a few of the countries they aspired to control.

See also *Afghan Revolution (1978–1995); Algerian Islamic Revolt (1992–); Egyptian Muslim Brotherhood Movement (1928–); Iranian Islamic Revolution (1979); Islamic Anticolonial Revolts of the 19th Century; Islamic Precolonial Revolts of the 18th and 19th Centuries; Saudi Arabian Wahhabi Movement (1744–); Sudanese Civil War (1955–1972; 1982–); Sudanese Mahdiyya (1881–1898).*

FRED HALLIDAY

BIBLIOGRAPHY

Abrahamian, Ervand. *Khomeinism, Essays on the Islamic Republic.* Berkeley: University of California Press, 1993.

Ayubi, Nazih N. M. *Political Islam: Religion and Politics in the Arab World.* London: Routledge, 1991.

al-Azmeh, Aziz. *Islam and Modernities.* London: Verso, 1993.

Eickelman, Dale, and Piscatori, James. *Muslim Politics.* Princeton, N.J.: Princeton University Press, 1996.

Halliday, Fred. *Islam and the Myth of Confrontation.* London: I. B. Tauris, 1995.

Marty, Martin, and Scott Appleby, eds. *Fundamentalisms and the State.* Chicago: University of Chicago Press, 1993.

Roy, Olivier. *The Failure of Political Islam.* Cambridge, Mass: Harvard University Press, 1994.

Zubaida, Sami. *Islam, the People and the State: Essays in Political Ideas and Movements in the Middle East.* London: I. B. Tauris, 1989.

ISLAMIC PRECOLONIAL REVOLTS OF THE 18TH AND 19TH CENTURIES

In the Muslim world, a number of revolts and *jihads* ("holy wars") occurred between 1700 and the rise of Western colonial rule that aimed at the creation of states that would be more Islamic and more just. These events were concentrated in West Africa and in South and Southeast Asia, though the Wahhabis of Arabia may be considered part of this group. Despite the great geographical distances between the movements, they share some common features that may indicate similar causes as well as common Islamic traditions. From Senegal to Sumatra the Muslim revolts expressed many of the same themes: mahdism (belief in a messianic figure who would save the world); jihad; and a turn to stricter Qur'anic and Islamic laws and practices, including those affecting women, than were being followed by the governments against which the revolts were directed. They expressed a desire for a clear common law and an Islamically oriented state, which were seen as benefiting many societal groups, including the growing trading classes.

THE ARABIAN WAHHABIS

The most ideologically influential of the eighteenth-century movements was that of the Arabian Wahhabis, who insisted on what they saw as pure early Islam and who were very hostile to what they saw as innovations, including Shi'ism, shrine- and icon-worship, and sufism and its practices. The Wahhabis stressed the Islamic law of the strictest legal school. At the turn of the nineteenth century the Wahhabis conquered Mecca from its hereditary *sharifs,* and pilgrims who came from abroad, including leaders of Sumatran and West African movements, were influenced by them. However, later Western and local sources often exaggerated the "Wahhabi" nature and influence of movements outside Arabia.

WEST AFRICAN MOVEMENTS

Jihad movements in West Africa moved over time from the coast to the interior, the same path that was followed by Western trade, especially but not exclusively the slave trade. Western trade not only brought widespread suffering but also led to the rise of groups and classes newly involved in long-distance trade that had an interest in setting up more centralized and law-based governments. The traders, as well as the partly nomadic Fulani ethnic group, were important in several West African jihad movements. The jihads began among the Fulani of the Senegambian area called Futa Jalon in the seventeenth century and then spread to the Mauritanian-Senegalese area under a Nasir al-Din in the late seventeenth century. Further jihad movements in the Senegambian area in the eighteenth and nineteenth centuries, like the earlier ones, failed to set up strong and lasting states, but they did increase the long-term influence of Muslim scholars and law and the clear identity of Muslim communities. The original jihad leaders tended to favor egalitarianism but later abandoned it to privilege a few powerful families and to discourage popular participation in politics.

The most important West African jihad was that in Nigeria under Usman Dan Fodio. Reflecting socioeconomic tensions arising from the slave trade and from government policies, Usman and his followers referred to the fifteenth century Maghrebi writer al-Maghili, who wrote strongly against rulers' mixing un-Islamic customs with Islam. Maghili said that rulers who imposed unjust taxes were unbelievers, and he reiterated the Islamic belief that every century would see a renewer of Islam. He added that jihad against false Muslims was more meritorious than against unbelievers. Usman first built up his own orthodox community in the state of Gobir, and his jihad began when his community was attacked from Gobir in 1804, after he insisted on changes. Usman's 1804 manifesto said that jihad was incumbent against both non-Muslims and against rulers who abandoned Islam or combined it with un-Islamic observances. Jihad was said to be a duty against oppressors and those who, like the current rulers, imposed illegal taxes, took bribes, and did not observe Islamic law. The movement was militarily successful and created in the Sokoto caliphate (in present-day northern Nigeria) a long-lived state unmatched by other movements. How revolutionary the state was after its initial victories is another question, as old dynastic and hierarchical structures were soon reinstalled, with some change in personnel to benefit the largely Fulani conquering classes.

Some other African movements extended into the colonial period and took on an anticolonial aspect; examples include later movements in Senegal and Mali, the Sudanese Mahdiyya, and the Senussi movements in Libya. A number of these African movements shared not only similar backgrounds of socioeconomic disruption and change and a desire for stronger government and law, but also a similar stress on certain features of Islam, including jihad, messianic and charismatic leadership, and adherence to law (such as Islamic taxes and the veiling and other treatment of women).

SUMATRA

The Padri movement in Minangkabao, Sumatra, occurred simultaneously with the Usman Dan Fodio movement, thousands of miles away. In Sumatra, as in West Africa, Islam had been spread primarily by traders and sufis; states were weak; and rulers, though nominally Muslim, did not follow strict Islamic law or practice. Also as in West Africa, trade with the West had been very important in recent centuries and had created economic changes and trading classes that would benefit from more unified government and law. A late eighteenth century Islamic reformer who advocated better application of Islamic law was known as "the patron of traders." The new trade wealth and interest in Islam led to a rise in pilgrimage to Mecca, and in 1803 three pilgrims from Minangkabao witnessed Wahhabi rule in Mecca and returned determined to force the application of Islamic law. These militant Muslims, operating in the apparently inhospitable territory of a matrilineally structured society, launched a jihad. For almost three decades their influence spread through violent and peaceful means. They were defeated only in the 1830s, by the Dutch, allied with local opponents. Their last leader, Imam Jonbal, has been memorialized as an Indonesian national hero.

Padri doctrines were puritanical and strict, and they included greater veiling and seclusion of women. Over time the Padris, however, had to compromise with local matrilineal practices and also lessened their strictness regarding alcohol and gambling. The militant movements in both West Africa and Sumatra marked a phase in the growing Islamization and unification of the respective societies.

India and Pakistan also saw some militant movements for stricter Islam that began in certain areas before the British conquest but became known especially after that conquest. The most important was that of the so-called Indian "Wahhabis," who grew out of an Islamic reform movement and fought for a stricter Islam.

The simultaneity and common features of these movements are explained in part by the increase in Western trade, the resultant strengthening of local trading classes who favored unified law, and a similarly resultant increase in socioeconomic tensions and conflicts that made people open to messianic or radical religious appeals. In several areas these movements, like the original rise of Islam, also marked a major stage in the transition from pre-state (tribal, or as in Minangkabao, local) societies to state organizations of society and from less formalized, varied religious structures to more formal and more unified religion and law.

See also *Islamic Anticolonial Revolts of the 19th Century.*

Nikki R. Keddie

BIBLIOGRAPHY

Clarke, Peter B. *West Africa and Islam.* London: Edward Arnold, 1982.

Dobbin, Christine. *Islamic Revivalism in a Changing Peasant Economy: Central Sumatra, 1784–1847.* London: Curzon Press, 1983.

Hiskett, Mervyn. *The Sword of Truth: The Life and Times of Shehu Usuman Dan Fodio.* New York: Oxford University Press, 1973.

Keddie, Nikki R. *Iran and the Muslim World: Resistance and Revolution.* New York: New York University Press; London: Macmillan, 1995.

Last, D. M. *The Sokoto Caliphate.* London: Humanities Press, 1967.

Levtzion, Nehemia, and John Voll. *Eighteenth Century Renewal and Reform in Islam.* Syracuse, N.Y.: Syracuse University Press, 1987.

Robinson, David. *The Holy War of Umar Tal.* Oxford: Clarendon Press, 1985.

ISRAELI INDEPENDENCE REVOLT (1946–1948)

In February 1947, after ruling Palestine for almost thirty years under League of Nations and United Nations (UN) mandates, Britain referred the Palestine question to the UN. The British left without settling the ongoing conflict between the Zionist and Palestinian national movements. The UN faced two very different communities. The indigenous Arab community was already well defined as the Palestinian nation but was guided by a traditional and fragmented leadership. The Jewish community, on the other hand, since its arrival in Palestine in 1882 had been energetically and systematically building an infrastructure for a future state. It successfully competed with the local Palestinian population over land and markets, using the British mandate system to its advantage. After the Second World War, the Zionist position was enhanced even further by pro-Jewish world public opinion in the wake of the Holocaust in Europe. Furthermore, it enjoyed the support of both the United States and the Soviet Union, a rare coincidence during those years of the emerging cold war.

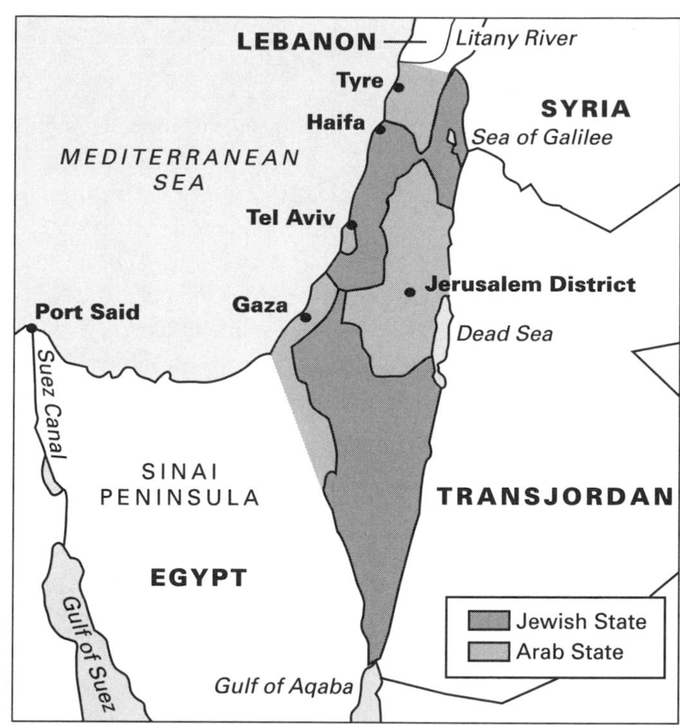

UN partition of 1947

ISRAEL'S WAR OF INDEPENDENCE AND THE PALESTINIAN CATASTROPHE

International backing for the Jewish community also stemmed from its readiness to cooperate with the UN in its attempts to solve the conflict. The Arab Higher Committee, the supreme representative body of the Palestinian community during the mandatory period, and the Arab states as a whole rejected the UN peace plan and efforts. In November 1947 the UN General Assembly suggested terminating the British mandate and partitioning Palestine into two states: Arab and Jewish. The plan recommended the internationalization of Jerusalem and called upon the two sides to construct an economic union between themselves.

Parallel to the UN effort, the Hashemite Kingdom of Transjordan and the Jewish Agency, the executive and representative body of the Jewish community in Palestine, tried to reach an understanding on Palestine's future. They did not sign an official agreement but reached a tacit understanding on the principle of partition—not between the Palestinians and the Jews, as had been proposed by the UN, but between Transjordan and the future Jewish state. They failed to agree, however, on the future of Jerusalem. The unwritten agreement was that the Transjordanian army, the strongest Arab army at the time, would not invade the areas allocated to the Jewish state by the UN in return for Jewish consent to the Transjordanian annexation of the state allocated by the UN to Palestinians.

The Transjordanian ruler, King Abdullah, while privately colluding with the Zionist movement over the future of Palestine, publicly toed the general Arab line. This line was formulated by the regional pan-Arab organization, the Arab League. The Arab states rejected the UN proposal and regarded the partition as capitulation to the Zionist movement, which in their eyes had no right whatsoever to the land of Palestine.

At first the League recommended that the Arab states dispatch arms and volunteers to resist the implementation of the UN partition plan, and particularly the establishment of the Jewish state. When it transpired that volunteers and materiel were not enough, the Arab League obliged the Arab states to take military action against the nascent Jewish state. King Abdullah skillfully navigated between his commitment to the Jewish Agency and his wish to play a major role in the Arab war preparations, as British rule in Palestine neared its end.

Immediately after the partition plan had been accepted by a majority of the UN General Assembly, a civil war broke out in Palestine between the Jewish and Arab communities, lasting from November 1947 to May 1948. An ill-prepared and outnumbered Palestinian paramilitary force tried in vain to oppose a more efficient and stronger Jewish military organization from capturing anything left behind by the withdrawing British government of Palestine. The bloody clash resulted in a Jewish takeover of strategic routes and junctures in Palestine and occupation of the four mixed Arab-Jewish towns of Palestine.

The urban Palestinian elite fled Palestine at the beginning of the war. Most of those who had stayed behind were expelled by the Jewish forces. The Jewish forces committed several massacres, the most notorious of which was the April 1948 massacre of Dir Yasin, where about 150 Arabs were killed, but by no means was it the worst of them.

The developing civil war in Palestine generated second thoughts among American policy makers. They toyed with the idea of establishing an international trusteeship over Palestine but abandoned the idea in the wake of strong Zionist lobbying. Nothing could stop an overall military confrontation. On May 15, 1948, the British mandate was terminated, and the state of Israel was declared. Israel was immediately recognized by both the United States and the Soviet Union.

Israel after 1948–1949 war

THE 1948 WAR

The strong verbal commitment of the Arab states to the Palestinians did not translate into impressive deeds on the ground. Five Arab states sent to the battlefield an army of 20,000 troops, half of which were volunteers with no military training. They faced a Jewish military force of comparable size and similar inexperience. The Arab armies, for a short while, enjoyed superiority in equipment and armament, which contributed to successes in the first week of fighting. The Transjordanians, loyal to their tacit understanding with the Jewish Agency, limited their military effort to the Jerusalem area, where they occupied the Jewish Quarter in the Old City but lost control of the Arab neighborhoods in the western part of the city. In the north, Syrian, Iraqi, and Lebanese troops made their way into Palestine but lost the initiative and gained few victories on the battlefield.

A truce was reached with the help of a UN mediator, Count Folke Bernadotte. After the truce had expired, the balance tipped in Israel's favor. While Britain, the main arms supplier of the Arab countries, imposed an embargo on weapons to the Arab world, Israel found ready suppliers in the Eastern Bloc (with Moscow's blessing). A victorious Israeli army swept over Palestine, reaching the Gulf of Aqaba in the south and the Litany River in the north by the end of 1948. Two areas of Palestine remained under Arab control: the Egyptians had the Gaza Strip, where they imposed military rule, and the Jordanians took the area known today as the West Bank, which Jordan officially annexed in April 1950.

The Israelis expelled hundreds of thousands of Palestinians from their homes during the fighting and wiped out their villages, turning them into farmland for existing Jewish settlements or building new settlements on their ruins. New Jewish immigrants from the Arab world and Europe were allowed to claim houses in the abandoned Arab towns.

The fate of the refugees had become a major concern of the UN even before the war ended. The organization demanded the repatriation of the refugees, but Israel refused, thereby preventing any substantial dialogue with the Arab world. After the fighting ended, the only agreements concluded were armistice pacts, which delineated Israel's borders with Egypt, Jordan, and Lebanon. The refugees would remain in camps run by the UN, as many do to this day.

The refugee question was discussed at a peace conference convened by the UN in Lusanne in April 1949. The conference was run by the UN Palestine Conciliation Commission. This body replaced Bernadotte, who had been assassinated in September 1948 by Jewish extremists who opposed his peace plan for Palestine. Like Bernadotte, the commission tried to base a solution to the Palestine problem on three tiers: the partitioning of the country into two states, the internationalization of Jerusalem, and the repatriation of the refugees. Although the Arab states were more willing to compromise than they had been before, an intransigent Israeli prime minister, David Ben-Gurion, foiled this last chance for peace. He was satisfied with the status quo. Seven years later, the second Arab-Israeli war took place, followed by three more rounds of fighting.

See also *Palestinian Anticolonial Revolt (1936–1939).*

ILAN PAPPE

BIBLIOGRAPHY

Khalidi, Walid. *Palestine Reborn.* London: I.B. Tauris, 1992.

Masalha, Nur. *Expulsion of the Palestinians: The Concept of "Transfer" in Zionist Political Thought, 1882–1948.* Washington, D.C.: Institute for Palestine Studies, 1992.

Morris, Benny. *The Birth of the Palestinian Refugee Problem, 1947-1949.* Cambridge: Cambridge University Press, 1988.

Pappe, Ilan. *The Making of the Arab-Israeli Conflict, 1947-1951.* London: I.B. Tauris, 1994.

Segev, Tom. *The First Israelis.* New York: Free Press, 1986.

Shlaim, Avi. *Collusion Across the Jordan.* Oxford: Oxford University Press, 1988.

ITALIAN CITY-STATE REVOLUTIONS OF THE RENAISSANCE (1494–1534)

In 1500 the map of the Italian peninsula was a patchwork of hundreds of political units, most of them in the hands of several dozen families. Some of these fiefs were scarcely larger than a village, but others were states in their own right. Endless disputes over borders and jurisdictions in this crowded political landscape added to the various inter- and intrastate rivalries that plagued Italy, many of them left over from the Guelf-Ghibelline conflicts that had pitted the supporters of the papacy and the Holy Roman Empire against each other in the twelfth and thirteenth centuries. Competing factions were only too willing to exploit any weaknesses their rivals and neighbors displayed. Violent change was the norm.

Violence and upheaval were crucial constituents of the major political contest of the Middle Ages in Italy, the struggle between republican and seigniorial forms of government. The twelfth and thirteenth centuries saw the advent of broadly based republican regimes in many northern and central Italian communes, as power was wrested from bishops or the local aristocracy. In these republics, the middle class and members of the major guilds, and occasionally even artisans and petty tradesmen, enjoyed access to communal offices and legislative councils. By 1500, however—under the pressures of war and economic strife, factional conflict, and a hostile and powerful nobility—nearly all of the Italian popular communes had become despotisms, with power concentrated in the hands of a single ruler or ruling house.

In Florence, a city of perhaps 50,000 souls—with another 140,000 or so in its dependent territories in north-central Italy—the contest between republicanism and despotism came to a head in the years 1494–1532. Since 1434, although there remained at least a facade of republican government, de facto leadership in Florence had been in the hands of a select patrician oligarchy led by the Medici family. For sixty years, most notably under Cosimo (1434–1464) and his son Lorenzo "the Magnificent" (1469–1492), the Medici carefully orchestrated elections to state offices and skillfully manipulated patronage networks to control the government of Florence. But Lorenzo's heir, Piero di Lorenzo, faced with the threat of a French invasion of Italy, showed himself to be a weak and ineffectual leader, and in 1494 the Medici regime collapsed. The central figure in the overthrow was the charismatic Dominican monk Girolamo Savonarola, who brazenly branded the Medici as tyrants and prophesied their downfall and the arrival of a "new Cyrus" who would sanctify Florence as a "City of God." Savonarola assumed an overtly political role after the exile of the Medici, urging the passage of strict moral legislation and the adoption of institutional and spiritual reform.

REPUBLICAN INTERLUDE

Spurred by the exhortations of Savonarola and by deep anti-Medicean enmity, the new republican government introduced a democratized constitution and a new Great Council, membership to which was granted to all men over the age of twenty-nine whose fathers and grandfathers had previously been eligible to hold office in the city of Florence. The council became known by Florentine republicans as the "soul of the city." Unfortunately for the new regime, the advent of this open constitution coincided with the onset of the Wars of Italy, which made the peninsula the chief battleground for the armies of France and Spain.

The republic suffered for its inability to subdue the rebellious city of Pisa, and it had to repel at least five attempts by Piero di Lorenzo and the Medici to force their way back into the city. Florence's political isolation increased when Pope Alexander VI excommunicated Savonarola in 1497 in retaliation for the steady stream of vitriol the friar had directed at the pontiff and also threatened Florence and her merchants with a papal interdict. By 1498 many in Florence had tired of the Dominican's moral harangues and the political ostracism he brought on the city. Savonarola's torture-induced confession was promptly followed by his hanging and public immolation in the Piazza della Signoria.

A second French invasion of Italy, in 1499, heightened the external pressure on Florence and forced vital foreign policy decisions into emergency committees called *pratiche,* the members of which were almost always the wealthiest and most experienced patricians in Florentine society. The city began a drift back toward oligarchy, evidenced in the creation in 1502 of a lifetime chief executive position, the *gonfaloniere a vita,* occupied by the able patrician Piero Soderini.

But despite the renewed presence of patricians, the government repeatedly displayed its commitment to republican ideology. It placed Donatello's statue *Judith*—the biblical heroine who saved her city by lopping off the head of King Holofernes—in front of the Medici Palace and added an inscription warning against would-be tyrants. Figurines of famous Florentines such as Dante, Boccaccio, and Leonardo Bruno were placed above the city gates as expressions of republican sentiment. In 1506 the Great Council signaled a return to the military system of the early Florentine republic by approving the establishment of a civic militia, the pet project of one of Soderini's chief advisers, Niccolò Machiavelli. These moves assured the opposition of the *ottimati,* the aristocratic elites of Florence, as well as the continued hostility of pro-Medici conspirators.

The republican regime and its challenges also engendered a lively political debate over the ideal constitutional and institutional make-up of Florentine government. Much of the discussion centered around the extent to which Florence should emulate the twin models of early republican Rome and the Republic of Venice. This rational investigation and comparison of different polities, past and present, represented a new approach to political thinking, embodied in the writings of Machiavelli and his contemporary, the political theorist and historian Francesco Guicciardini.

THE RETURN OF THE MEDICI

The Soderini regime, remarkably, lasted ten years, in large part because the gravest external pressures on Florence lapsed. In 1512, though, external danger once again made for internal threat. When Soderini refused to join the anti-French league proposed by Pope Julius II, the pontiff, with a sizable Spanish army backing him up, forced Soderini to flee and reinstalled the Medici in Florence.

The return of the Medici was marked by the dissolution of all the trappings of the previous regime. The Great Council was eliminated, as was Machiavelli's militia. Machiavelli began an extended period in the political wilderness, during which he composed his famed tracts *The Discourses* and *The Prince.* The Medici introduced a new constitution written to assure that they would once again control political life. With the election of two popes from the Medici family, Leo X (1513–1521) and Clement VII (1524–1537), the affairs of Florence and the papacy became closely intertwined, with real control of Florentine government resting with the pope in Rome.

But republicanism in Florence was not yet dead. After troops of the Holy Roman Emperor savagely sacked Rome in 1527, taking Clement VII prisoner, republican revolutionaries in Florence, many still inspired by the example of Savonarola, rose and ejected the Medici once more. The Great Council was restored and hosts of Medici supporters driven out or imprisoned. The revolution was deeply influenced by Christian millenarian ideas, and in 1528 legislation was carried electing Christ king of Florence. The conclusion of peace between pope and emperor in 1529, however, spelled the end for this last republic. Despite the heroic resistance of the populace and the best efforts of the governor of fortifications, Michelangelo Buonarotti, the city fell to an imperial army after plague and starvation had killed nearly a third of the population.

Restored once more, the Medici this time made no mistake. Under the oversight of Pope Clement, in 1532 the Medici were written into the constitution as hereditary rulers of Florence, and Alessandro de Medici became the first duke of Florence. In 1534 Alessandro hired the famed architect Antonio da Sangallo (the younger) to commence construction on a state-of-the-art fortified citadel known as the Fortezza da Basso. Built as much for political reasons as for any military purpose, this structure was a potent symbol of the authority of the Medici dukes and served as a stark warning to any would-be revolutionaries. Florence had joined the ranks of the despotisms.

The close association of internal politics and the exigencies of foreign policy suggest a critical weakness of the Florentine republics—and perhaps a reason for the ultimate demise of republicanism. Open factional squabbling and class tension proved crippling to the republican regimes. The government was never able to content the voices of opposition. The rapid turnover in offices, the inexperience of many of the office-holders, and the reluctance of the middle classes to consent to further taxation undermined responsibility and decision making precisely at the time when institutional stability and prompt action were needed. The new realities of the Italian peninsula demanded, as Machiavelli observed in *The Prince,* that force take pride of place in Italian politics. For better or worse, by the fourth decade of the sixteenth century the princes of the Medici house were best equipped to employ this force. The future of Florence lay with them.

See also *Millenarianism*.

PAUL DOVER

BIBLIOGRAPHY

Butters, Humfrey. *Governors and Government in Early Sixteenth-Century Florence, 1502–1519.* Oxford: Clarendon Press, 1985.

Guicciardini, Francesco. *The History of Florence.* Translated by Mario Domandi. New York: Harper and Row, 1970.

Hale, John. *Florence and the Medici: The Pattern of Control.* New York: Thames and Hudson, 1978.

Herlihy, David, and Christiane Klapisch-Zuber. *Tuscans and Their Families.* Translated from the French. New Haven, Conn.: Yale University Press, 1985.

Machiavelli, Niccolò. *Florentine Histories.* Translated by Laura Banfield and Harvey Mansfield Jr. Princeton, N.J.: Princeton University Press, 1988.

Martines, Lauro. *Power and Imagination: City-States in Renaissance Italy.* New York: Knopf, 1979.

Roth, Cecil. *The Last Florentine Republic.* Methuen: London, 1925.

Stephens, J. N. *The Fall of the Florentine Republic, 1512–1530.* Oxford: Clarendon Press, 1983.

ITALIAN FASCIST REVOLUTION (1919–1945)

After his Blackshirt troops marched into Rome in October 1922, Benito Mussolini, newly appointed premier of Italy, announced the triumph of the Fascist revolution. The regime he established did not produce the radical transformation of Italy that many anticipated, however, and historians have presented widely divergent interpretations of the nature of Italian Fascism.

Although defining Fascism and estimating its revolutionary impact on Italian society have always proved difficult and controversial, there is general agreement among historians about the origins of the movement. They have examined three time periods, all hinging on World War I, in which Italy joined with the Allies against Germany and the Central Powers.

The first period is the decades of intellectual ferment before war broke out in 1914, when many of the established beliefs of the nineteenth century were condemned. Liberalism, rationalism, the concept of peaceful progress, and parliamentarianism were attacked, and new theories emerged such as social Darwinism, integral nationalism, and syndicalism. Industrialization and rapid technological change, combined with a new focus on the masses, required new ideas and techniques. Friedrich Nietzsche, a German philosopher, called for a superman to resolve the contradictions of the modern world, while others placed emphasis on violence and war to solve all problems. Young men like Mussolini and Adolf Hitler absorbed many of these doctrines and later built the ideologies of Fascism and National Socialism around them.

Second is the experience of the war itself, when advocates of violence, war, blood sacrifice, and heroism witnessed the realization of their aims. The destruction and mass slaughter were greater than anyone anticipated, and the degree to which warfare unified the nation was decidedly less than expected. Advocates of the war drew comfort, however, from the comradeship of the trenches and the creation of a battle-hardened elite who would construct a new order from the ruins of the old. Both Mussolini and Hitler were combatants who exalted the discipline and leadership qualities that would be required in peacetime as well as in war.

Third are the immediate postwar years of 1919–1922, which left Italy in political disarray. Economic distress and dismay at the peace settlement, which failed to grant Italy many of the country's territorial claims, produced disillusionment and widespread fear and anger. The Bolshevik revolution of 1917 in Russia raised the specter of communism in Italy, spreading panic among propertied classes in town and countryside. The paralysis of the government, confronted by left-wing parties and trade unions, prompted many bourgeois elements to look elsewhere for protection. They found it in Fascism.

THE RISE OF FASCISM, 1919–1926

Mussolini began his political career as a socialist agitator, becoming a leader of the revolutionary extremists by 1912 and the editor of the party newspaper. He parted company with the socialists in the autumn of 1914, when they opposed his campaign to force Italy into the war. Establishing his own newspaper, he joined Gabriele D'Annunzio, a popular writer, and other interventionists. They triumphed in May 1915 ("Radiant May") when street demonstrations forced parliament to sanction Italy's entry into the war. Mussolini fought at the front before being invalided out of the army. Like many others, he hoped the war would unify and revolutionize the country.

Angered by the "mutilated victory," the rise of socialism, and governmental incompetence, Mussolini founded his Fascist movement in Milan, in March 1919. (The term is derived from the Latin *fasces,* a bundle of rods and an ax carried by lictors, or guards, before important officials as a symbol of authority.) This radical program, which was republican, anticlerical, and hostile toward capitalism, pressed for sweeping social reforms. The Fascists performed disastrously in the November 1919 elections. The future seemed to belong to D'Annunzio, who seized and held the disputed seaport of Fiume, which Italy had failed to acquire in the peace settlement. This flamboyant war hero and "poet as superman" introduced all the choreography later associated with Fascism—the Blackshirts, the balcony speeches, mass parades, and corporative ideas. His defeat in December 1920 was welcome news for Mussolini.

The Fascist breakthrough came in 1920–1921, after socialists had occupied the northern factories and left-wing leagues had seized land in the countryside. Fascist bosses, or *ras,* formed armed squads to protect capitalists and landowners; they rapidly destroyed most left-wing strongholds, while the state prefects, police, and army looked on approvingly, as did the church. By this time, Fascism was abandoning its republican, anticlerical, and anticapitalist origins. Opponents saw it as the "agent of capitalism." The movement became a party in November 1921, and Mussolini, who had become a parliamentary deputy in May, began to intrigue with top politicians while his squads terrorized towns and villages. The march on Rome in October 1922 was the result of this dual approach.

The Duce, as he was now called, used the threat of violence to secure his legal appointment as premier. For four years, to the dismay of radical Fascists, there were few signs of a Fascist revolution. An influx of nationalists and conservatives changed the social composition of the party. The squads were incorporated into a national militia, soon to be commanded by safe, regular army officers. The king, the armed forces, the judiciary, big business, and the church remained largely untouched, and there was no drastic purge of the civil service. It was only a parliamentary crisis in 1924 that forced Mussolini to make a clean break with the liberal past. The murder of Giacomo Matteotti, a socialist member of parliament and leader of the opposition to Fascism, precipitated the crisis. Mussolini disclaimed the murder but tightened police control. Even then, the main framework of the old parliamentary system was retained.

In January 1925 Mussolini announced the formation of an authoritarian state. By 1926 the Fascists were the sole, legal party; censorship was tightened and repressive legislation increased police powers. The party itself became subordinate to state authorities, while Mussolini's personal power grew steadily, as did his popularity—especially after he signed the Lateran pacts with the pope in 1929, resolving a long-standing dispute between the Italian government and the Vatican, and waged a successful colonial war in Ethiopia in 1935. The cult of the Duce and the attempt to convert Fascism into a secular religion dominated the 1930s. For Mussolini, this was the revolution.

THE CULT OF THE LEADER

Pope Pius XI praised Mussolini as a man sent by Providence for reconciling church and state. It was a great achievement, but the pope in an independent Vatican was clearly a rival leader with an alternative ideology. The Duce's aim to create a new Fascist man and woman, which was the core concept of his "Fascist revolution," became an impossible task. The continued presence of King Victor Emmanuel III as head of state also limited Mussolini's totalitarian pretensions, particularly as the armed forces owed allegiance to the monarch. Big business, represented by Confindustria (an employers' association), was more powerful than ever after the elimination of the left. It could largely ignore Mussolini's much vaunted corporations, which represented employers and employees for each branch of the economy, and let propagandists portray them as crucial innovations that proved the existence of a distinct "Fascist economic policy."

It was, in fact, the regime's propaganda apparatus that created the illusion of a Fascist revolution. It could claim that, for the first time, the masses were participating in national life. Millions joined the party, the youth movements, the recreational clubs, and organizations for women and students. Above all, it could refer to the mass demonstrations increasingly centered on the cult of the Duce. Mussolini's

In Messina, Italy, a mutilated portrait of Benito Mussolini hangs from a tree, speared by a bayonet. Italian Fascism did not long survive Mussolini.

revival of the grandeur of the Roman Empire became another propagandist theme, which naturally involved praise for the regime's foreign policy.

After the war Mussolini proclaimed his intention to make Italy great, feared, and respected, to turn the Mediterranean into an Italian lake. Fascism emphasized violence and martial qualities; war would unify and strengthen the nation. Because of the cowardice of the old ruling class, he claimed, this goal had not been achieved in World War I. The Ethiopian war and defiance of the League of Nations revealed Italy's new, belligerent style. In 1936 Mussolini intervened in the Spanish Civil War on the side of Gen. Francisco Franco. This interference alienated Britain and France, forcing the Duce to turn to Hitler. In late 1936 he announced the Rome-Berlin Axis, beginning the fateful and unequal partnership between the two dictators. Anti-German sentiment and the passing of anti-Semitic laws in 1938 gradually eroded Mussolini's popularity. His Pact of Steel with Germany in May 1939 alarmed the business world and the military; they were relieved when Italy declared neutrality in September. The relief was short lived. Mussolini declared war on Britain and France in June 1940, on the Soviet Union in June 1941, and on the United States in December 1941.

The illusory nature of the Fascist revolution was brutally exposed by the series of military and naval disasters suffered between 1940 and 1943. Even more revealing was the reaction to the news in July 1943 that Fascists in Mussolini's inner circle had challenged his leadership and that the king and his generals had arrested and imprisoned the Duce. The party simply disintegrated, with Italian Fascists making no serious attempt to rescue him. A rescue was left to the Germans, who freed Mussolini and reestablished him as head of a small republic in northern Italy dominated by the Nazis. It was too late to attempt to launch a second Fascist revolution. Mussolini's capture and execution by partisans in April 1945 ended the Fascist era. Neo-Fascism was its feeble successor.

See also *German Nazi Revolution (1933–1945); Hitler, Adolf; Mussolini, Benito.*

JOHN WHITTAM

BIBLIOGRAPHY

De Grand, Alexander. *Italian Fascism.* 2d ed. Lincoln: University of Nebraska Press, 1989.

Lyttelton, Adrian. *The Seizure of Power.* New York: Scribner, 1973.

Mack Smith, Denis. *Mussolini.* New York: Knopf, 1982.

Tannenbaum, Edward. *The Fascist Experience: Society and Culture, 1922–1945.* New York: Basic Books, 1972.

Weiss, John. *The Fascist Tradition.* New York: Harper and Row, 1967.

Whittam, John. *Fascist Italy.* Manchester: Manchester University Press, 1995.

ITALIAN RISORGIMENTO (1789–1870)

The term *Risorgimento* means "resurrection" and describes the struggle for independence from Austria that in 1860 resulted in the creation of an independent Italian constitutional monarchy ruled by the former king of Sardinia, Victor Emanuel II (1849–1878). Since the fifteenth century the Italian states had been controlled by the great European dynasties. In 1800 Napoleon invaded the peninsula, and the Italian states were drawn into the French empire until the Congress of Vienna restored the legitimist rulers in 1814 and placed them under Austrian protection. Austria ruled directly only in Lombardy and Venetia but was nonetheless the power behind every Italian throne. When revolutions occurred in Naples and Turin in 1820–1821, in the Papal States in 1831, and throughout Italy in 1848, the rulers were restored by Austrian bayonets.

Austria was the common enemy for the opponents of the autocratic Italian rulers, but for as long as the European powers supported the system of alliances established in 1814, Austrian power was unassailable. The revolutions of 1848 weakened the Habsburg Empire, but the most dangerous threat to Austrian hegemony came from Napoleon III's desire to restore French influence in Italy, and in 1859 France became the Italian nationalists' powerful ally. Yet hostility to Austria divided Italians more than united them. The sense of cultural unity that was powerfully expressed in the operas of Giuseppe Verdi and the art and literature of the period was not enough to create a common political front, and the struggle for independence brought moderates, radicals, monarchists, republicans, and federalists into often violent confrontation. Unification, always the least likely outcome of the struggle for independence, was the result of conflict, not unity.

ORIGINS OF THE REFORM MOVEMENT

Demands for independence grew out of the struggle for political reform that began after the French Revolution. Revolutionary France first invaded Italy in 1796, setting up republics where Italian unity and representative government were openly debated for the first time. The divisions that would later separate democrats and moderates were also exposed. When in 1799 the French withdrew, the republics they had sustained collapsed, but after Napoleon's victory over the Austrians at Marengo (1800), in northwest Italy, the political climate of the new empire was more authoritarian.

The political geography of the Italian states was redrawn, and some states disappeared, but Napoleon deliberately kept those that remained divided. French rule brought modernization but no space for political debate and much disaffection. For the mass of the population, French reforms that abolished feudalism and encouraged enclosures and the disappearance of common lands aggravated land-hunger and threatened the survival of many rural communities, while conscription and taxation provoked frequent revolts. The propertied and educated classes at first rallied enthusiastically to Napoleon's regime, but their ruthless subordination to the military and financial needs of the empire and the denial of political freedom fueled demands for political representation. Censorship and police controls forced the opponents of French rule to work through secret societies, such as the Carbonari.

THE RESTORATION, 1814–1848

With the Catholic Church as their ally, the restored rulers declared war on liberalism and all forms of religious, cultural, and intellectual freedom. Opposition continued to center on the secret societies, which attracted many young professionals, intellectuals, army officers, and aristocrats. The secret societies played an important part in the revolutions of 1820–1821 and 1831, but neither revolution had effective leadership or coherent goals. To provide those ingredients, Giuseppe Mazzini in 1831 founded Young Italy, an openly revolutionary movement dedicated to achieving clearly defined objectives. Influenced by the ideas of Claude-Henri de Rouvroy Saint-Simon—and like him deeply hostile to the French Jacobin tradition whose principal advocate in Italy was Filippo Michele Buonarroti—Mazzini argued that independence would only be achieved through a popular and national revolution that overthrew the pope, the church, and the existing rulers to create a single democratic republic.

Mazzini's belief that insurrection was the principal form of political education and propaganda horrified conservatives and moderates. But while sharing Mazzini's republicanism, many democrats preferred the federalist projects of Carlo Cattaneo or Giuseppe Ferrari and believed that constitutions on the Swiss and American model were more suited to Italy's political, cultural, and economic diversity.

REVOLUTIONS OF 1848–1849

In a climate of growing tension prior to the revolutions of 1848, political debate became more open. As in the rest of Europe, popular unrest in Italy was driven by commercial recession and harvest failures. Alarmed by the insurrectionary rhetoric of the radicals, conservative nationalists urged the Italian rulers to take the political initiative. Vincenzo Gioberti's proposal in 1843 that the pope lead an independent confederation of Italian princes won enthusiastic support, and in 1844 a distinguished Piedmontese nobleman, Cesare Balbo, called on the rulers to negotiate independence from Austria. As popular unrest grew and new insurrections occurred in southern and central Italy, another Piedmontese aristocrat, Massimo Taparelli d'Azeglio, begged the revolutionaries to trust the force of respectable public opinion and moral persuasion—"a conspiracy in open daylight"—rather than violence.

The conservatives' hopes were heightened by the election in 1846 of Pope Pius IX. Apparently sympathetic to the liberal cause, the new pope seemed uniquely qualified to reconcile independence and the preservation of the existing political order. But the conservatives' hopes proved short-lived. Beginning in Sicily in January 1848, the Italian states were overwhelmed by revolutions driven by popular unrest, and by March every ruler, including the pope, had granted limited constitutions. By now the crisis had developed a continental momentum, as in February Paris and then in March Vienna succumbed to revolution, and the Austrians were forced to abandon Venice and Milan, although only after the aged Field Marshal Joseph Radetzky had tried to bombard the city into submission.

The revolution in Vienna deepened the crisis in Italy, where rival political forces contended for power. On March 23 Charles Albert, the king of Piedmont-Sardinia (reigned 1831–1849), declared war on Austria and sent an army to support the revolution in Milan, but the Lombard democrats suspected that he was using the nationalist cause to further his own territorial ambitions. The position of the conservative nationalists was greatly weakened, however, when on April 29 Pius IX denounced the war against Austria, followed by the king of Naples, who suspended the provisional constitutional government (May 15) and also withdrew from the war.

On July 24 Charles Albert's army was routed by the Austrians at Custoza. Mazzini now called for the war of the princes to become the war of the people, and radicals took power in Turin and Florence. In November the pope and his cardinals fled after the leader of the provisional government was assassinated, and on February 9, 1849, a republic was proclaimed in Rome. Among its leaders was Mazzini, but Austrian armies were marching south, and the Republican government in Paris also sent a French army to restore the pope. On March 23 Charles Albert was again defeated by the Austrians, at Novara, and abdicated in favor of his son Victor Emanuel II. Despite Giuseppe Garibaldi's heroic defense of Rome, early in August French troops entered the city, and after Venice surrendered to the Austrians, the revolutions were over.

CAVOUR AND PIEDMONT, 1849–1860

The revolutions of 1848–1849 failed because European powers had continued to support Austria and because the nationalists lacked resources and unity. The radicals suffered worst. They had been divided and had failed to win popular support, and throughout Italy disillusioned peasants had turned against the revolutions. Failure brought exile and recriminations, many radicals arguing that Mazzini's insurrectionary tactics were irresponsible and counterproductive.

Among the propertied classes the violence of 1848–1849 strengthened the desire for political change without revolution, and increasingly they looked to Piedmont and its monarchy for leadership. After 1849 Piedmont was the only constitutional monarchy in Italy, and its appeal was greatly enhanced by the liberal reforms of the prime minister, Count Camillo Benso di Cavour (1810–1861), who in the 1850s promoted commercial expansion, drew foreign investment, and strengthened parliamentary government. Turin became a haven for political exiles from all over Italy, although radicals were treated with suspicion, and the death sentence that had been passed on Mazzini in 1834 was not lifted.

Cavour's position was still precarious. Challenged by the democrats, he was also bitterly opposed by conservatives and the church. Victor Emanuel II was no liberal, but he discovered that only the liberals were willing to support his expansionist ambitions. Their support in 1854 enabled Victor Emanuel to enter the Crimean War (1854–1856) as an ally of Britain and France against Russia, while Austria maintained an awkward neutrality.

This realignment of the great powers and Austria's new diplomatic isolation at once aroused nationalist expectations in Italy. The democrats moved first, and in July 1857 Carlo Pisacane attempted to raise a major revolt in the south. The revolt ended in disaster, but it mobilized Cavour's supporters in central Italy, who in August founded the Italian National Association to organize support for the Piedmontese monarchy and to keep the radicals in check when war with Austria resumed.

Alex Tait/Equator Graphics, Inc.

THE WAR OF INDEPENDENCE, 1859

The war that broke out in 1859 was the result of careful diplomacy. Cavour and Victor Emanuel believed that Piedmont needed a powerful ally in order to confront Austria without incurring the political risks of mobilizing volunteers, and they believed that Napoleon III might be willing to support Piedmont. An attempt on his life by an Italian nationalist, Felice Orsini, in January 1858 seems to have persuaded Napoleon III that the "Italian problem" was becoming a threat to European peace, while offering France an opportunity to restore its political influence on the peninsula.

In January 1859 France and Piedmont made a secret defensive alliance. Piedmont mobilized, on April 23 Austria issued an ultimatum to Piedmont, and a French army came to Piedmont's defense. After three bloody engagements that France won (at Magenta, June 4; and San Martino and Solferino, June 24), the war ended on July 8 when Napoleon III negotiated an armistice with Austria at Villafranca. Cavour, who had not been consulted by Napoleon III, resigned.

The unilateral French withdrawal left its ally in an extremely dangerous situation. Under the terms of its armistice with France, Austria had withdrawn from Lombardy but retained the Veneto, while the rulers of the central Italian states remained in power. The radicals demanded an immediate resumption of the war, but Cavour's supporters staged faked revolutions in Tuscany, Emilia, and the Romagna in favor of annexation to Piedmont, thereby subverting the terms of the armistice. Annexation of these regions by Piedmont was legitimated by carefully supervised plebiscites, which blocked French hopes of acquiring Tuscany. The propertied classes of central Italy had rallied to Piedmont, and after Cavour returned to office in January the moderates won an easy victory in the first elections for the enlarged kingdom of Sardinia (March 25).

GARIBALDI'S EXPEDITION TO THE SOUTH, 1860

In April news broke that Nice and Savoy were to be ceded to France. The nationalists were outraged. Garibaldi began preparations to liberate Nice, his birthplace, but abandoned the project when news arrived of a revolution in Sicily, which offered an opportunity to extend the war to the whole of Italy. With one thousand volunteers Garibaldi landed at Marsala in western Sicily on May 11 and joined forces with the revolution in Palermo. On September 7 he entered Naples.

The rapid and quite unexpected collapse of the Bourbon monarchy in the south reopened the peninsula's political future. But Garibaldi and his radical followers had no clear program other than to liberate Rome. Cavour knew that an attack on Rome would give France a pretext to intervene to protect the pope, even though Britain (which was extremely suspicious of the Franco-Piedmontese alliance and determined that no other power should gain a footing in Italy if Austria withdrew) had threatened war if this happened. To cut off Garibaldi's advance, Cavour in September sent a Piedmontese army through the Papal States. The outcome might have been civil war, but on October 26 Garibaldi loyally surrendered his command to Victor Emanuel.

UNIFICATION, 1861–1870

The radicals had extended the geography of the revolution, but the moderates had retained control of its form. Yet when on March 17, 1861, Victor Emanuel II was proclaimed king of Italy in the first Italian parliament, the new nation was incomplete. Austria would retain the Veneto until it was defeated by Prussia in 1866. Despite two unsuccessful attempts (in 1862 and 1867) by Garibaldi and the radicals, Italian troops were unable to enter Rome until Napoleon III had been defeated by the Prussians at the battle of Sedan in 1870.

The battle for unification also left many lesions. The rift between church and state was irreparable, and on October 2, 1870, Pius IX excommunicated Victor Emanuel. In the south, violent peasant rebellion broke out, which the government tried to disguise as brigandage. The southern provinces were placed under military law, and plans for regional autonomy, favored by Cavour (who died suddenly in 1861), were shelved.

The new state had many critics. Mazzini dismissed it as the mere corpse of the nation he had hoped to create, and in the twentieth century the Italian communist Antonio Gramsci argued that unification was the product of an incomplete bourgeois revolution that created a narrow and flawed democracy. But Gramsci's view owes too much to hindsight. The new state inherited huge problems from the past—great internal diversity and social inequality; a relatively small propertied and educated elite; deep political, religious, and cultural differences; and enormous debts. The liberal revolution did not resolve these problems, but by setting them in a national context it created the premise for Italy's rapid political, economic, and social development in the second half of the nineteenth century.

See also *Buonarroti, Filippo Michele; Garibaldi, Giuseppe; Gramsci, Antonio.*

JOHN A. DAVIS

BIBLIOGRAPHY

Beales, Derek D. *The Risorgimento and the Unification of Italy.* London: Barnes and Noble, 1981.

Duggan, Christopher. *A Concise History of Italy.* Cambridge: Cambridge University Press, 1994.

Holmes, George, ed. *The Oxford Illustrated History of Italy.* Oxford: Oxford University Press, 1997.

Lovett, Clara. *The Democratic Movement in Italy 1830–76.* Cambridge, Mass.: Harvard University Press, 1982.

Mack Smith, D. *The Making of Italy 1796–1866.* 2d ed. London: Macmillan Press, 1988.

———. *Mazzini.* London: Yale University Press, 1994.

Riall, L.J. *The Italian Risorgimento: State, Society and National Unification.* London: Routledge, 1994.

Sarti, Roland. *Mazzini: A Life for Religion and Politics.* Westport, Conn.: Praeger, 1997.

Woolf, S.J. *A History of Italy 1700–1860: Social Constraints of Political Change.* 2d ed. London: Routledge, 1991.

JAPANESE MEIJI RESTORATION (1868)

The Meiji Restoration was a palace coup in which loyalist *samurai* (warriors) of powerful southwestern domains seized control of the emperor's palace in Kyoto on January 3, 1868, and declared the restoration of power to the throne after seven centuries of warrior rule. In a broader sense, the Restoration was the revolutionary political, economic, and social transformation of Japan—from the 1850s through the 1880s—from a peripheral country with a centralized feudal system to a modernizing imperial nation-state.

THE END OF THE TOKUGAWA PERIOD

The domestic and foreign pressures Japan faced late in the Tokugawa period (1600–1868) were less serious and began slightly later than those that threatened Qing China, but the revolution that replaced the old order with a modernizing regime came more quickly in Japan. This rapid change was possible because of Tokugawa Japan's multipolar political order, its economic and social development, its diverse intellectual world, and its ability to learn from China's experience. The Tokugawa period began in 1600 with a victory in the battle of Sekigahara by a coalition of feudal lords *(daimyo)* allied with Tokugawa Ieyasu, who was named *shogun* (national military leader) by the emperor in Kyoto. For two and a half centuries the Tokugawa shogunate dominated Japan's roughly 260 *daimyo* domains from its capital in Edo (now Tokyo). It directly controlled 25 percent of Japan's land, as well as its major roads, ports, and mines, and its foreign relations. This system of control, often described as centralized feudalism, was based on the threat of force, and the shogunate fell when it lost the power to make this threat real.

Samurai staffed the domain and shogunal governments. They were at the top of the official ranking of society, followed by peasants, artisans, and merchants. Yet economic development, with its accompanying social changes, made the reality of Tokugawa society increasingly distant from this ideal. After two centuries of peace, by the mid-nineteenth century Japan's literacy rate was comparable to those of industrializing Western nations, and its standard of living was high for a preindustrial society, but the fruits of this development were by no means evenly distributed.

Warriors were partially transformed into bureaucrats, and some turned to scholarship to justify their claims to social prestige. Many in the lower ranks sought by-employment to supplement their stipends. Townspeople developed a vibrant urban culture and economy, and commoners traveled for business and pleasure and on religious pilgrimages. The expansion of domestic commerce affected rural Japan as well as the towns and cities, and by late Tokugawa many farmers could no longer be called peasants. Villages were largely self-governing and were increasingly diversified economically and socially as tenancy developed and cash crops became common. Income disparities and awareness of class differences increased, as did rural uprisings, especially in the wake of famines in the 1830s.

Responses by the shogunate and domains to these famines both drew on and further inspired a broad range of thought and provided models for further reforms. The Neo-Confucianism promoted by the shogunate was never a rigidly enforced orthodoxy. "Dutch learning" was fueled by the information received about Europe, both directly through the Dutch trading post in Nagasaki and indirectly through Chinese translations of Western works. Nativist thinkers sought the pure essence of Japan in works written before Chinese influence and emphasized the importance of the emperor and of Shinto, Japan's indigenous religion. All of these schools of thought could be used to challenge the shogunate's authority and ideology and to channel loyalty in other directions.

Japan's fear of losing control of the terms of its relations with foreign countries was justified by China's defeat in the first Opium War (1839–1842). A U.S. naval squadron forced the shogunate to sign a treaty establishing relations in 1854. In 1858, during a second war between China and Western powers, commercial Japanese treaties with the United States and major European nations opened ports to trade, gave foreigners extraterritorial protection, and limited tariffs. Revision of the unequal treaties remained a major policy goal and a rallying cry for nationalists until extraterritoriality was ended in 1899 and tariff autonomy was regained in 1911.

The treaties brought criticism of the shogunate, as well as economic disruptions such as inflation and an outflow of gold. Popular unrest and calls for "world renewal" were reflected in peasant rebellions, boisterous mass pilgrimages, and urban riots, but the occasional actions of the crowd did not bring down the Tokugawa. Activist samurai, though their numbers were far smaller, were more important. Under the slogan *sonno joi* ("revere the emperor and expel the barbarians"), they attacked foreigners and attempted to gain control of their domain governments.

By 1866 the shogunate was competing with the leading *daimyo* as little more than first among equals, but its military and diplomatic initiatives showed some chance of success. The anti-Tokugawa southwestern domains of Satsuma and Choshu allied to prevent this, and the shogun agreed in the fall of 1867 to resign and be replaced by a council dominated by *daimyo.* But when Satsuma loyalists gained control of the young emperor on January 3, 1868, and secured an edict ordering the shogun to give up his lands, a civil war ensued between the Tokugawa army and the new Imperial Army of Satsuma and Choshu forces. Long before the war ended in June 1869, Japan's new rulers had declared the beginning of a new era, Meiji (1868–1912), and the restoration of the emperor, who was moved to Edo, now renamed Tokyo.

MAKING JAPAN MODERN

Modern Japan was born in the Restoration. Politically, economically, and socially, the revolution was secure by the mid-1880s.

In April 1868 a Charter Oath issued in the name of the emperor promised that an assembly would decide policy by open discussion, that "evil practices of the past shall be abandoned," and that "knowledge shall be sought all over the world." The immediate purpose was to gain support for the new government, particularly from the *daimyo,* who expected to comprise the assembly. Had the new leaders stopped here, the Restoration would not have been a revolution. Instead, they set in motion a rapid transformation of Japan—and within two decades after assuming power they were no longer revolutionaries but conservative guardians of the new order they had created. During this period the people came to identify themselves as Japanese rather than merely people of a certain region, and the word for "country," *kuni,* came to mean the "nation" of Japan more often than it meant domain or prefecture.

The new government at first controlled little more than the former Tokugawa lands. The *daimyo* were induced to return their lands to the emperor in 1869, and the domains were made prefectures with appointed governors. Direct control of the entire nation by the central government became a reality when these changes were followed by a land survey giving individual farmers title to their land and enabling the collection of the land tax in cash and the establishment in 1873 of a Home Ministry to govern the prefectures and operate a police system.

Formal political participation of local notables in the new system began with prefectural and local assemblies. In 1881 an imperial decree promised a national constitution and parliament by 1890. The year 1881 was also the peak of the Movement for Liberty and Popular Rights, which demanded a constitution and produced a number of drafts. Newspapers informed Japan's literate population about politics, political discussion groups sent speakers throughout the country, and national political parties were established in 1881 and 1882. By the early 1880s Japan had for the first time a government whose effective influence and control reached every part of the country and all levels of society, and an active and informed civil society expressing opinions and attempting to influence policy.

For the economy, as in politics, an initial period of possibilities and uncertainty ended by the early 1880s, though Japan did not begin its takeoff into modern economic growth until the 1890s. The land tax in cash tied farmers more closely to the national economy and provided the government with an income that did not fluctuate with the harvest and the price of rice. Silk, whose production was easily mechanized, provided foreign exchange for the purchase of weapons and technology and helped the nation achieve a favorable balance of trade by the mid-1880s.

The government built a number of model factories and then sold them to private interests in 1881 and 1882. In the early 1880s retrenchment policies demonstrated the government's new power to affect the economy and the people's livelihood. They restored the yen to a sound footing, but the resulting deflation squeezed farmers and increased tenancy. The Bank of Japan, created in 1882, gave the nation a centralized financial system.

Samurai in the new government disestablished their class, though not without opposition. Conscription created a commoner army, and the sword-carrying policeman replaced the samurai as the personification of government authority. The former warriors were given government bonds in place of their stipends. The 1877 Satsuma Rebellion by dissatisfied samurai in the southwest was put down at great cost by the new army and was the last domestic military challenge to the new government.

By 1880 Japan had replaced the informal and decentralized education system of the Tokugawa period with one of elementary and middle schools, normal schools to produce teachers, and a Western-style university, all controlled by the Ministry of Education. The military and schools gave their soldiers and students an awareness of being Japanese and taught them how to act in groups, at fixed times and according to written regulations, subject to a clear hierarchy of authorities appointed according to merit rather than inherited status. Similarly, young farm women working in silk mills learned that they were part of something bigger than their village, and that efficiency and competence were required for individual and national success.

WAS IT A REVOLUTION?

No other event is as central to interpretations of modern Japanese history as the Meiji Restoration, and none has provoked such controversy over its causes and meaning. Only the period from the 1930s to the 1950s—when the institutions established by the Restoration leaders were first changed significantly—approaches the Restoration in its effects on the course of Japan's modern history.

The question of why the Restoration occurred may be broken down into two parts: what made change necessary, and what made it possible. Domestic pressures certainly made some sort of change inevitable, but Japan could have retained a shogunate-domain arrangement for some time, even with capitalist development, had it been able to continue to limit its relations with the outside world. But in the age of industrialization and imperialism, isolation was no longer possible.

Marxist scholars have argued that the Restoration was carried out by an alliance of lower samurai and merchants. Most Restoration leaders were in fact from the lower samurai ranks, frustrated that their abilities were not reflected in higher incomes and positions of greater responsibility, but the importance of this in motivating their actions is difficult to judge. Merchants, due to both practical concerns and coercion, provided support to both sides. Popular discontent, though by no means a determining factor, certainly contributed to the nationwide mood of uncertainty and desire for change.

One thing making change possible was the fact that it could be couched in terms of a return to old values and symbols, as the very term "restoration" implies. Traditional loyalty could be transferred from domain to emperor and nation. Also important were the decentralized nature of the Tokugawa polity and the variety of Tokugawa thought, which gave Restoration leaders familiarity with a broad range of government models and an openness to alternatives. In addition, a long tradition of knowledge from abroad made it easier for Japan to learn from China's problems and recognize the strengths of the West, as the call by Sakuma Shozan, a late Tokugawa intellectual, for blending of "Eastern ethics and Western science" exemplified.

Interpretations of the Restoration, both positive and negative, have tended to parallel views of the course of modern Japan and of the Tokugawa period. By the twentieth century the Meiji Restoration was seen as a successful response to the foreign threat, enabling Japan to compete with the Western powers. In the 1920s Japanese Marxist historians debated whether it had been a bourgeois capitalist revolution or an incomplete revolution leading to an intermediate stage of absolutism between feudalism and capitalism. Since the end of World War II, the Restoration has been viewed as either setting Japan on the proper path to modernization, from which the militarism of the 1930s and 1940s was a deviation, or as containing within itself the seeds of fascism and aggression. Observances of the centennial of the Restoration in 1968—the year in which Japan's gross national product passed West Germany's—highlighted these differences over the modernity that traces its beginnings to the defensive revolution that was the Meiji Restoration.

See also *Japanese Tokugawa Shogun Ascendancy (1598–1615).*

Timothy S. George

BIBLIOGRAPHY

Beasley, W. G. *The Meiji Restoration.* Stanford: Stanford University Press, 1972.

Craig, Albert M. *Choshu in the Meiji Restoration.* Cambridge, Mass.: Harvard University Press, 1961.

———"The Meiji Restoration: A Historiographical Overview." In *The Postwar Development of Japanese Studies in the United States.* Edited by Helen Hardacre. Leiden: E. J. Brill, 1998.

Huber, Thomas M. *The Revolutionary Origins of Modern Japan.* Stanford: Stanford University Press, 1981.

Jansen, Marius B. *Sakamoto Ryoma and the Meiji Restoration.* Princeton, N.J.: Princeton University Press, 1961.

Jansen, Marius B., and Gilbert Rozman, eds. *Japan in Transition: From Tokugawa to Meiji.* Princeton, N.J.: Princeton University Press, 1986.

Smith, Thomas C. "Japan's Aristocratic Revolution." In *Native Sources of Japanese Industrialization, 1750–1920.* Edited by Thomas C. Smith. Berkeley: University of California Press, 1988.

Totman, Conrad D. *The Collapse of the Tokugawa Bakufu, 1862–1868.* Honolulu: University Press of Hawaii, 1980.

JAPANESE TOKUGAWA SHOGUN ASCENDANCY (1598–1615)

The final victor of prolonged civil wars, Tokugawa Ieyasu (1542–1616) used the title of *shogun* to construct an early modern state that would survive, under fifteen successive Tokugawa heads, from 1603 until 1868. The changes accompanying state formation were revolutionary in scope but counterrevolutionary in intention.

THE BACKGROUND OF WAR

Ieyasu was a product of the "Era of the Country at War," which began in 1467 with local rebellions against the national governing organs of the Ashikaga shogunate (1336–1573) and the proprietary authority of absentee landholders in both the civil and martial elites. Rebellion sought multiple purposes defined by multiple players—including leagues of peasants, townspeople, religious sectarians, and debtors of all stations. Conflict increasingly centered, however, on scores of martial houses (some led by high-placed deputies of the Ashikaga, but most by lower-ranking functionaries and land managers) seeking autonomous control of territories secured by violence. By the 1560s, contests over local hegemony gave way to contests over regional, and ultimately national, hegemony within a group of roughly fifteen exceptionally powerful *daimyo* (great lords).

The unification stage of civil war is associated with three particular *daimyo.* Oda Nobunaga captured the capital of Kyoto, where he ousted the last defenders of the Ashikaga shogunate (1573), and staged campaigns that delivered one-third of the country to Oda troops by the time of his death (under attack by an embittered vassal) in 1582. Toyotomi Hideyoshi, a peasant adventurer who became one of Nobunaga's most brilliant generals, completed national pacification by 1590—in part through conquest, in greater part through alliance and conciliation. Departing from the Oda pattern of total war and annihilation of rivals, Hideyoshi confirmed the territorial claims of competing *daimyo* (and even of some defeated enemies) in exchange for fealty. He died in 1598, leaving a child heir in the custody of five *daimyo* deputies.

One custodian, Tokugawa Ieyasu, had parlayed a small lordship over Mikawa Province into Japan's largest domain (extending into eight provinces around his major castle in Edo, modern Tokyo) through unusual alliances with both the Oda and the Toyotomi. Ieyasu moved against Hideyoshi's heir, defeating Toyotomi loyalists in two major battles (Sekigahara in 1600 and Osaka in 1615). He elicited the title of *shogun* from a largely symbolic emperor as early as 1603 and transferred that title to a mature son in 1605. Originally a temporary martial commission awarded to leaders of frontier wars, *sei-i-tai-shogun* (barbarian-subduing generalissimo) had denoted since 1192 the heads of martial administrations responsible, under the wavering authority of the imperial court, for practical national governance. (Oda Nobunaga had eschewed titles; Toyotomi Hideyoshi had ruled under the title of imperial regent, *kampaku).*

THE POLICIES OF PACIFICATION

The Tokugawa polity, derived in good measure from Toyotomi initiatives and the practices of other leading *daimyo,* was federal in form. As a condition of political union, most local power remained in the hands of roughly 250 *daimyo* (including a substantial number of Tokugawa vassals promoted to lordship over lands confiscated or redistributed after battle), who retained control over their own samurai armies, fiscal resources, and governing institutions. The Tokugawa claimed direct authority over lands that produced roughly 25 percent of Japan's registered resources. They also claimed certain national governing prerogatives that focused on peacekeeping. After a century and more of war—which saw almost universal male conscription, the marshaling of armies as large as 300,000 troops, and the catastrophic casualties resulting from musket and cannon fire (introduced after 1550 by European traders)—the "Tokugawa Peace" sought a stable framework to protect *daimyo* allies from each other and ambitious subordinates.

The central prerogatives of the Tokugawa can be divided into three categories. First, the shogun exercised over the *daimyo* a lordly authority encompassing the rights to vest and inspect domains, punish insubordination, recruit martial and civil labor, and restrain capacities for aggression (by limiting fortifications, transferring dangerous rivals to new domains, and prohibiting private alliances and suspicious marital unions). Second, the shogun assumed jurisdiction over a "public province" that included resources too valuable to entrust to any single *daimyo* (such as mines, highways, and major ports and cities) and policies too integral to permit local latitude (such as foreign relations, the standardization of measures, and the regulation of coinage). Third, the shogun enforced public order through acts of social engineering.

This last category saw the boldest initiatives. Peasants, townspeople, and monks were disarmed; most samurai were removed from agrarian villages to the castle towns of their *daimyo;* changes of residence and class (broadly those of samurai, peasants, artisans, and merchants) were forbidden. Surveillance of the *daimyo* escalated by 1635 to requirements that each lord spend half of each year in the shogunal capital of Edo. Controls on foreign contact, which began with injunctions against Christian proselytism, eventuated by 1639 in the confinement of foreign trade (solely by the Chinese and the Dutch) to the port of Nagasaki and the proscription of foreign travel by Japanese.

UNFORESEEN DIRECTIONS FOR CHANGE

These profoundly conservative policies, which were intended to secure the ascendancy of the Tokugawa and their confederates, provoked radical change. Once hegemonic conquerors, the *daimyo* became hereditary, often honorary administrators of domains they occupied sporadically. Once enfeoffed warriors, the samurai became urban salary men and overeducated (often underemployed) public officials. The relocation of military men and their retinues to cities transformed an agrarian nation into a highly urbanized one, where huge numbers of townspeople (up to 20 percent of the population) produced a centralized commercial economy and a literate commoner culture. And in the wake of the martial exodus from the countryside, village peasants assumed practical rights of land ownership and a fair degree of self-governance.

No less paradoxically, a feudal order of personal alliance and contracts in land became an increasingly bureaucratic order of universalistic principles. Wartime demands for recruitment had led (by the 1580s) to systematic cadastral surveys and standardized land valuations, which led in peacetime to national cartographic and demographic surveys as well as the coordination of measures, monetary exchange and banking, and communications. The pressures of integrated rule provoked administrative routine, institutional development, and even meritocratic leanings in the well-trained, competitive officialdom that staffed shogunal and domainal bureaucracies.

Thus a clearly authoritarian and regularly repressive system, which confined power to *daimyo* and samurai, contained fissures. As landholders and village headmen, prosperous peasants emerged as self-respecting participants in the polity. So, too, did the prominent townsmen who administered their neighborhoods and supervised commerce under generally remote supervision. An emphasis among samurai officials on training and performance—combined with mounting expertise throughout the commoner elite—imperiled the axiomatic equation between status and power.

MARY ELIZABETH BERRY

BIBLIOGRAPHY

Berry, Mary Elizabeth. *Hideyoshi.* Cambridge, Mass., and London: Harvard University Press, 1982.

Bolitho, Harold. *Treasures among Men: The Fudai Daimyo in Tokugawa Japan.* New Haven, Conn.: Yale University Press, 1974.

Brown, Philip C. *Central Authority and Local Autonomy in the Formation of Early Modern Japan.* Stanford: Stanford University Press, 1993.

Hall, John Whitney, and Nagahara Keiji, eds. *Japan before Tokugawa: Political Consolidation and Economic Growth, 1500–1650.* Princeton, N.J.: Princeton University Press, 1981.

Totman, Conrad D. *Early Modern Japan.* Berkeley and Los Angeles: University of California Press, 1993.

JEFFERSON, THOMAS

Jefferson (1743–1826) was a central figure in two democratic revolutions: the American and the French. A member of the Virginia House of Burgesses by 1769, he soon identified himself with the colony's resistance to recent British measures. When illness prevented his own election to the First Continental Congress, he drafted "A Summary View of the Rights of British America" (1774) as a proposed set of instructions for Virginia's delegates. It was one of the earliest revolutionary pamphlets to maintain that the colonies were connected to Great Britain only by way of a compact with the king. In 1776 his reputation as a theorist and penman led to his selection to draft the Declaration of Independence, after which he returned to Virginia to serve two terms as wartime governor and to lead the infant state in an ambitious republican revisal of its laws. His *Statute for Securing Religious Freedom,* one of the great landmarks in the American separation of church and state, was a leading feature of the revision.

Jefferson returned to Congress in 1783, serving long enough to draft the Land Ordinance of 1784, thus pioneering the concept of a gradual extension of a union of equal, self-governing states across the North American continent. In 1785 he succeeded Benjamin Franklin as U.S. minister to France and strengthened his reputation as a philosopher as well as a revolutionary statesman by publishing his *Notes on the State of Virginia,* which powerfully condemned both slavery and the insufficiently democratic, poorly balanced early revolutionary constitutions. Jefferson continued in Paris through the early stages of the French Revolution and participated, with Gilbert du Motier de Lafayette and other friends among the liberal nobility, in discussions leading to a constitutional revision and the drafting of the Declaration of the Rights of Man. He returned to the United States in October 1789 and reluctantly accepted an appointment as secretary of state in the new administration of George Washington.

As minister to France, Jefferson had been unable to participate in framing the new American Constitution, although he filled his correspondence with influential appeals for the addition of a bill of rights. By 1792, however, he was moving to the head of an emerging opposition to the financial

Thomas Jefferson

program, foreign policy, and broad interpretation of the Constitution promoted by Alexander Hamilton, the secretary of the Treasury. Jefferson resigned from Washington's administration at the end of 1793 but continued to lead the first organized political party. Elected vice president in 1796, he nevertheless secretly drafted the Kentucky Resolutions of 1798, which laid a groundwork for later claims that the states, as parties to the compact that had created the Constitution, retained a right to interpose against "unconstitutional" measures such as the Alien and Sedition Acts of that year. Jefferson considered his defeat of John Adams in the presidential election of 1800 to be "as real a revolution in the principles of our government as that of 1776 was in its form." As Jefferson perceived it, his victory permitted the Jeffersonian Republicans to correct the pro-British slant of Federalist foreign policy, to end the danger of a close and corrupt connection between the federal government and a moneyed few, and to withdraw that government within the bounds originally envisioned by the framers and ratifiers of the Constitution.

As a proponent of limited government, a skeptic about urbanization and industrialization, a lifelong slaveholder, and a philosopher who expressed a strong suspicion that blacks might be inferior to whites, Jefferson has recently become a favorite target for critics of the limitations of American revolutionary thought. For much of American history, however, he has seemed perhaps the best exemplar of the American democratic spirit and the most eloquent spokesman for the democratic and libertarian ideals enunciated in the Declaration of Independence and developed in his messages, writings, and correspondence. During the age of democratic revolutions, certainly, he had few peers as an effective champion of popular rule within the confines of respect for constitutional charters, civil liberties, and inherent natural rights.

See also *American (U.S.) Revolution (1776–1789); French Revolution (1789–1815); Lafayette, Gilbert du Motier de.*

LANCE BANNING

BIBLIOGRAPHY

Malone, Dumas. *Jefferson and His Time.* 6 vols. Boston: Little, Brown, 1951–1981.

Onuf, Peter S., ed. *Jeffersonian Legacies.* Charlottesville: University Press of Virginia, 1993.

Peterson, Merrill D. *Thomas Jefferson and the New Nation: A Biography.* New York: Oxford University Press, 1970.

JINNAH, MOHAMMAD ALI

Jinnah (1876–1948) was the "Great Leader" who founded Pakistan ("Land of the Pure") and served as its first governor general from August 14, 1947, until his death. Born in Karachi, Jinnah went to London, where he studied law at Lincoln's Inn, and became one of the most successful barristers of British India by the eve of World War I.

Jinnah launched his political career as a member of India's National Congress Party. A liberal Anglophile leader who worked for Hindu-Muslim unity, Jinnah initially brought the Congress and the Muslim League together in their nationalist demands, which he drafted in 1916. After 1919, however, when Mahatma Gandhi revolutionized the hitherto moderate Congress's program, Jinnah was driven out of that party. He turned more to his legal practice but also helped build up the Muslim League, demanding greater electoral representation for India's Muslim minority on all newly expanded legislative councils.

In 1935 Jinnah was chosen to serve as permanent president of the Muslim League by his disciples and admirers, and five years later he presided over the party's most famous session, in Lahore. "The Musalmans are a nation," Jinnah told his cheering followers that March of 1940, insisting that the problem of India was not intercommunal but international. The next day, the Muslim League adopted its famous Pakistan Resolution, calling for the creation of autonomous and sov-

Mohammad Ali Jinnah

ereign Pakistan, to be carved out of British India's northwest and northeast zones, in which the Muslims were a majority. Despite his tenacious insistence on his League's Pakistan demand, however, Jinnah was wise enough to accept the British cabinet mission's confederal plan of 1946, by which the British would transfer their imperial power to a single confederal Indian Dominion. Congress also agreed to that plan, but then Nehru took back the position of Congress president, which he had turned over to Maulana Azad throughout World War II, and at his first press conference Nehru insisted that India's Constituent Assembly would not be bound by any prior formula or agreement, since it would be a sovereign body. Jinnah considered that a betrayal and immediately called on the Muslim nation to prepare for direct action, saying for the first time in his life, "good-bye to constitutionalism." In his last years, conservative, legalist Jinnah became the leader of a Muslim revolution in South Asia, and the response to his call was mass violence over the next year throughout British India, slaughter that started in Calcutta and spread swiftly to the northwest frontier. By April 1947 the British saw no other solution to their greatest imperial headache than to transfer power to two dominions, India and Pakistan, rather than one, and that summer the partition lines were drawn through Punjab and Bengal, which turned into rivers of blood in late August and September.

Though Great Leader Jinnah presided over the birth of South Asia's first Muslim nation, he never totally abandoned his own admiration for British law and the secular ideals of parliamentary government. In early August 1947 he addressed Pakistan's first Constituent Assembly in Karachi, advising his countrymen to forget the past and concentrate on the well-being of the people, especially the poor. He urged all Pakistani citizens to abjure the poisons of bribery, corruption, black-marketing, and nepotism. He was, however, fatally afflicted by that time with both tuberculosis and cancer of the lungs, and he lacked the strength to enforce his will on less enlightened followers. Instead of prospering and developing its economy and polity, Pakistan fell victim to all the divisive forces within its tribal and provincial society and could not long retain the allegiance of its eastern half, which in 1971 gained independence as Bangladesh, with Indian military assistance.

See also *Gandhi, Mahatma; Indian Independence Movement (1885–1947); Nehru, Jawaharlal; Pakistani Independence Movement (1940–1947).*

STANLEY WOLPERT

BIBLIOGRAPHY

Ahmad, Riaz. *The Works of Quaid-i-Azam Mohammad Ali Jinnah.* 2 vols. Islamabad: National Institute of Pakistan Studies, 1996–1997.

Allana, G. *Quaid-E-Azam Jinnah: The Story of a Nation.* Lahore: Ferozsons, 1967.

Mujahid, Sharif al. *Quaid-i-Azam Jinnah: Studies in Interpretation.* Karachi: Quaid-i-Azam Academy, 1978.

Wolpert, Stanley. *Jinnah of Pakistan.* New York: Oxford University Press, 1984.

JUÁREZ, BENITO

Preeminent leader of Mexico's liberal reforms, Juárez (1806–1872) remains a symbol of Mexican nationalism. Born a Zapotec Indian, he moved at age twelve to the city of Oaxaca. Educated first at a seminary, in 1828 he entered the Oaxaca Institute of Sciences and Arts and took up liberal politics. After completing his legal studies, Juárez held office as Oaxaca city councilman in 1832, Oaxacan state legislator in 1833, and judicial magistrate in 1834. With the end of liberal rule in 1835, Juárez turned to legal work, often aiding Oaxaca's immigrant merchant community.

In 1846, as war with the United States began, liberals reclaimed power and Juárez became a deputy in the national congress. He returned to Oaxaca in 1847 as the elected state governor. He aimed to support the war effort but faced rebellion among the Zapotecs of the Isthmus of Tehuantepec, who demanded political autonomy and opposed liberal laws that privatized community lands and coastal salt beds. Juárez defended the liberal state, private property, and commercial production, sending troops to defeat the rebels in a conflict that consumed much of his term as governor.

The conservative regime of Antonio López de Santa Anna forced Juárez into exile in New Orleans in 1853. He was there when Juan Alvarez led the revolt of Ayutla, bringing the liberals to national power in 1855. Juárez became minister of justice in Alvarez's cabinet. In November 1855 they issued the Ley Juárez ending the separate legal jurisdictions enjoyed by the clergy and the military. Early in 1856 Juárez was again elected governor of Oaxaca.

In October 1857 Juárez became president of the Supreme Court, which also made him successor to the presidency. After President Ignacio Comonfort defected to the conservative opposition, Juárez became president of a beleaguered liberal regime in January 1858. For three years he roamed Mexico, finally leading liberal forces to victory over the conservatives late in 1860. In 1861 he was elected president, but conservatives had asked Napoleon III of France to support their fading cause. A French force landed in 1862, only to be defeated by Juárez's liberal armies on May 5, the celebrated Cinco de Mayo. French reinforcements forced Juárez into a nomadic, five-year defense of the liberal regime, culminating in the capture and execution in 1867 of the imposed emperor, Maximilian of Habsburg.

Juárez, elected president a second time in the fall of 1867, asserted national power, completed the nationalization of church properties begun in 1856, and pressed forward the privatization of community lands. The power of conservatives and the church was broken, but regional elites and peasant villagers rebelled repeatedly in the late 1860s. Juárez's troops slowly defeated the fragmented opposition and consolidated the liberal regime, allowing his reelection in 1871.

President Juárez died in July 1872. He had led Mexico's liberals in defeating conservatives, dispossessing the church, and ending the French intervention. His regime had challenged the landed, political, and cultural autonomy of peasant communities and the central role of Catholicism in Mexican culture. The conflicts that defined Juárez's liberal era persisted into the revolutionary confrontations of the early twentieth century. For his political achievements, and as a symbol of nationalism, the Zapotec president holds a pivotal place in Mexican history.

JOHN TUTINO

BIBLIOGRAPHY

Bazant, Jan. *Alienation of Church Wealth in Mexico: Social and Economic Aspects of the Liberal Revolution, 1856–1875.* Cambridge: Cambridge University Press, 1971.

Hale, Charles. *Mexican Liberalism in the Age of Mora, 1821–1853.* New Haven, Conn.: Yale University Press, 1968.

Hamnett, Brian. *Juárez.* London: Longman, 1994.

Sinkin, Richard. *The Mexican Reform, 1855–1876: A Study in Liberal Nation-Building.* Austin: University of Texas Press, 1979.

Weeks, Charles. *The Juárez Myth in Mexico.* Tuscaloosa: University of Alabama Press, 1987.

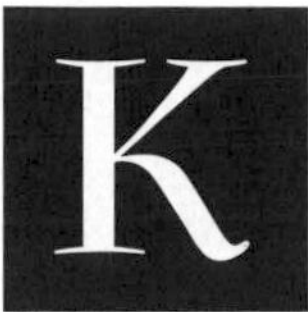

KENYAN MAU MAU MOVEMENT (1952–1960)

The Mau Mau movement was a revolt against British colonial rule primarily by the Kikuyu people of central Kenya. Violent attacks on British settler farms and Africans associated with the colonial regime, such as agricultural instructors and policemen, grew gradually from early 1950. Mau Mau drew support from several sectors within the Kikuyu community, most notably dispossessed sharecroppers on European farms in the Rift Valley, the urban unemployed in Nairobi, and the landless in the Kikuyu homelands. The movement always lacked cohesion, since it drew upon the different grievances of the various Kikuyu groups, and whatever cohesion was provided by the Mau Mau central committee, or Muhimu, in Nairobi was first dislocated and then completely broken by two British countermeasures—the declaration of a state of emergency on October 20, 1952, and Operation *Anvil* in early 1954, which broke Mau Mau influence in Nairobi. The name *Mau Mau* was invented by the British; its origins have been variously, but never definitively, explained. Kikuyu fighters in the forests always referred to themselves as the Land and Freedom Army. The Mau Mau movement came into the open in late 1952, following the declaration of emergency after the assassination of Senior Chief Waruhiu wa Kungu of Kiambu on October 9, 1952.

HISTORIOGRAPHY OF THE MOVEMENT

Historians of the Mau Mau movement can be divided into those who emphasize the protonationalist aspects of the struggle against British colonial rule in the 1950s and those who are more interested in the movement's distinctive social causes, the political ambitions of ordinary Africans cultivating their maize crops, the motives of the forest fighters, or the aims of the Muhimu, not to mention the aims of Kenya's constitutional African politicians. Interpretations of Mau Mau have changed over time. The atavistic primitivism of the movement, denounced by colonial rulers, British settlers, and local missionaries in the 1950s, gave way in the 1960s among European and American political scientists and historians—and African novelists, the first Kenyans to analyze the movement—to a new nation-building Mau Mau in which the forest fighters were seen as radical nationalist heroes, fighting with home-made guns and knives for "the Kenya we want." Then in the 1970s, the heyday of neo-Marxist underdevelopment theory, Mau Mau fighters became the true heroes of the nationalist struggle who were sold out by the *comprador* elite, which had inherited the political kingdom at independence in December 1963. With the waning of Marxism in the 1980s, conservative historians began to question whether Mau Mau had really been a nationalist movement. William Ochieng', the Kenyan scholar, even went so far as to wonder if Mau Mau was an embarrassment, a primitive "tribal" movement dominated by the Kikuyu people of Central Province (who despite being the largest ethnic group in Kenya form only 22 percent of the population) rather than a true struggle for national freedom.

Continuing research in the archives and by oral historians and anthropologists has not resolved these issues, especially the question as to whether Mau Mau was a single, political movement, a social protest, or a combination of several protests with different followers and aims. Certainly, very different factors lay behind the development of Kikuyu protests in the 1940s and early 1950s in the Rift Valley, Nairobi, and Central Province.

MAU MAU IN THE RIFT VALLEY

Kikuyu squatters, sharecroppers on European settler farms in the dairy-farming and beef-ranching districts in the eastern Rift Valley, had been seriously hit after 1945 by new restrictions on African stock-holding and cultivation. Squatter household incomes had plummeted, and thousands had refused to accept the new labor contracts imposed after World War II by the settlers, who had the money to expand production and replace Kikuyu laborers with imported machinery. Local leaders of the Kikuyu Central Association directed the squatters' protests and introduced new oaths to unite the Kikuyu, who formed the vast majority of farm workers in the eastern Rift Valley. As early as 1948, reports of a new subversive movement—Mau Mau—reached British administrators in the settler farming area in the Rift Valley known as the "White Highlands," where only European farmers could buy land. Despite widespread protests in 1945–1947, Kikuyu opposition seemed to have been effectively broken by 1948.

MAU MAU IN NAIROBI

Nairobi, Kenya's rapidly expanding capital, was another center of Mau Mau activity. During World War II (1939–1945), the city's population had more than doubled, to over 100,000 Africans. Rents were high, housing conditions were appalling, and wages had fallen far behind the rate of inflation. As people found it impossible to survive on their small plots in Central Province or were dispossessed by settler farmers in the White Highlands, more and more moved to the capital, creating an additional problem—unemployment. Kikuyu residents from neighboring Central Province formed over half the capital's population and dominated all aspects of urban African life, including the better paid jobs, the provision of food and accommodation, politics, the fledgling trade union movement, and organized crime and prostitution. Thus, while life in Nairobi radicalized many Africans, it also divided the city's Kikuyu inhabitants from other Africans whom they competed with for jobs and exploited. The failure of general strikes in September 1947 and May–June 1950 highlighted the ethnic tensions among Nairobi Africans, with many non-Kikuyu refusing to support the strike call. Thus, when Kikuyu radical trade unionists, led by Fred Kubai and Bildad Kaggia, seized control of the Nairobi branch of the Kenya African Union (KAU) and began to introduce a new oath of unity, support for the campaign was largely restricted to Kikuyu workers and unemployed. This oath, later regarded as the first Mau Mau oath, was administered to all those Kikuyu whom radicals in the Rift Valley and the trade unionists in Nairobi believed could be trusted.

MAU MAU IN CENTRAL PROVINCE

Even in Central Province, the Kikuyu homeland, support for violence was initially confined to a relatively small group. Most peasants with sufficient land sided with the British, considering that they would gain more from the introduction of individual title deeds and the cultivation of high-value cash crops, such as coffee, a "privilege" that had recently been extended to Africans who owned more than four acres. Kikuyu Christians also found the new oaths repugnant and refused to support Mau Mau, as did many old-style traditionalists who resented the politicization of oath taking. Mau Mau, however, found many recruits in the three Kikuyu districts of Central Province—Kiambu, Fort Hall (now Murang'a), and Nyeri, on the slopes of Mount Kenya. Kikuyu tenants and poor relations, whose support had been a valuable resource in the nineteenth century when smallholdings had to be carved out of the forest and defended from marauding Maasai and Kamba, had long since become a liability, begging land to grow subsistence crops that Kikuyu senior lineages wanted to use to farm commercially. As a result, Mau Mau's fight with the British in Central Province soon became a Kikuyu civil war between the landless (including many who had returned after working as squatters for a generation in the White Highlands) and established *mbari,* or sub-clan leaders, with sufficient land; between those who rejected mission Christianity and those who had found personal salvation; and between the young and the old.

Recent research has further illuminated the complexity of the Kikuyu responses to Mau Mau, emphasizing the importance of the differing experiences of the Kikuyu to colonialism. Some *mbari,* for example, had resisted the British conquest and had been punished; others had remained quiescent; while still others had actively collaborated with the colonialists and their Maasai auxiliaries. Some *mbari* had lost a lot of land, alienated to European settlers; others had maintained control over most of their cultivated land and grazing grounds and had prospered by expanding production. Some areas, close to the main roads and bus routes, were easily accessible to Nairobi and had been oathed months before the declaration of the emergency on October 20, 1952, which placed draconian restrictions on African freedom of assembly and movement. More remote areas remained isolated from market forces and politically inactive.

NATIONALIST POLITICS AND MAU MAU: THE AMBIGUOUS ROLE OF JOMO KENYATTA

The Kikuyu, even those politicians the British believed directed the movement, were deeply divided in their attitudes to Mau Mau, while the other 80 percent of Kenya's African population were hostile. Jomo Kenyatta, who had returned in 1946 from fifteen years' exile in Britain to reorganize the KAU, was detained on October 20, 1952. Although he was accused of masterminding Mau Mau since early 1950, he had, in fact, attempted to resist the militants' takeover first of KAU's Nairobi branch and then of key positions in the national organization. The trade union leaders Kubai and Kaggia had led the challenge to Kenyatta's authority and knew that he was opposed to violence and had

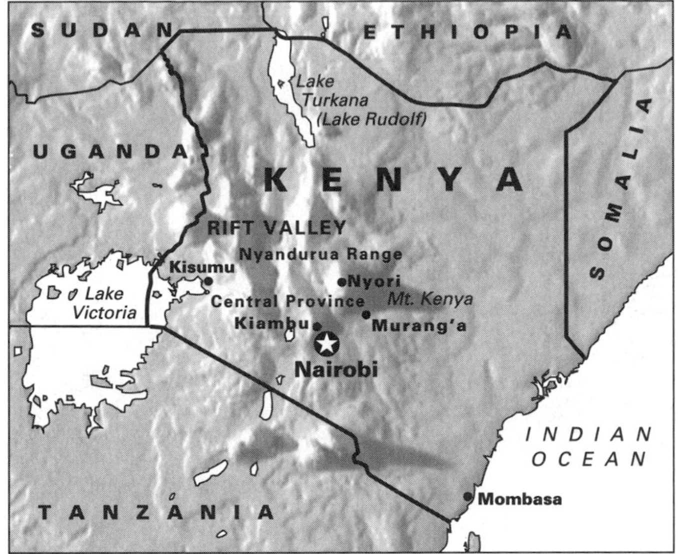

denounced Mau Mau. But most ordinary Kikuyu, including the vast majority of those who had taken the first Mau Mau oath of unity, like the British colonialists, considered Kenyatta to be the movement's leader. Certainly, most of the young recruits who went into the Aberdare (now the Nyandurua range) and Mount Kenya forests to fight for "land and freedom" did so only after Kenyatta's arrest and knew little about the political goals of the Nairobi radicals or of their conflict with the nationalist movement's established leadership.

THE ARMED STRUGGLE, OCTOBER 1952 TO OCTOBER 1956

It took some months after Kenyatta's detention—and those of Kubai and Kaggia—for armed resistance to British rule to grow into a serious threat. Following the declaration of the emergency, thousands of Kikuyu sharecroppers in the Rift Valley were dismissed and compelled to return to Central Province or Nairobi, further exacerbating social tensions. By early 1953 many Kikuyu youths had secretly gone into the forests and begun to attack government-nominated chiefs, prominent Christian opponents of the movement, local agricultural instructors and tribal policemen, and a few isolated settler farms. British troops were rushed to the colony, local settlers were enlisted into the Kenya Regiment, and the police and security forces were dramatically expanded. Despite a few conspicuous Mau Mau successes, draconian measures by the British gradually defeated the movement. First, the British successfully broke the back of Mau Mau in the capital, destroying the lines of communication between the remaining members of the Muhimu and the forests. Following Operation *Anvil* in 1954, when all Kikuyu living in Nairobi were interrogated, 80,000 adult male Kikuyu were held in detention, approximately one-third of the community's adult male population. In another measure to undermine the Mau Mau "gangs," peasants throughout Central Province were herded in 1954–1955 into "protected villages" where twenty-three-hour curfews were imposed to prevent them from providing information or supplies to fighters operating in the Reserves. Then a fifty-mile-long bamboo barrier was erected around the foothills of the Mount Kenya forest and a shoot-on-sight policy was implemented throughout the Reserves. By December 1955 most of the large Mau Mau "gangs" had disintegrated into small groups of only two or three fighters. Exhausted, hungry, and with only hand-made weapons, they posed little challenge to the security forces. The capture of "Field Marshal" Dedan Kimathi, the Mau Mau commander in the Aberdare forest and a former dairy cooperative clerk, in October 1956 marked the end of military operations. Official figures reveal the brutality of the colonial forces: An estimated 12,000 Mau Mau fighters or passive-wing supporters were killed during the emergency, compared to 2,000 African "loyalists" who opposed Mau Mau, 120 members of the security forces, and 20 European settlers. Despite British propaganda about Mau Mau bestiality, the terror tactics of the colonial state were far more effective.

THE POLITICAL LEGACIES OF MAU MAU AND THE "TRANSFER OF POWER"

The state of emergency formally ended only in January 1960, on the eve of the first Lancaster House conference. These negotiations in London marked Britain's final abandonment of its settlers and the beginning of the transfer of power to a new generation of African constitutional politicians. Less than four years later, Kenyatta led Kenya to independence with the message, "we all fought for freedom." Kenyatta attempted to heal the bitter wounds of civil war among his own Kikuyu people and to gain the confidence of those Africans, Europeans, and Asians who had fought against Mau Mau. Largely confined to the Kikuyu and regarded by many of them as a civil war rather than a struggle for freedom, the Mau Mau movement provided a dubious symbol for the newly independent nation. The struggle certainly speeded Britain's departure from East Africa, ending the attempts of the 1940s and early 1950s to create a multiracial political structure in which the European settlers were to have a key role. The violence also enabled the colonial state drastically to reconstruct landholding throughout Central Province, introducing individual titles and creating "yeoman" farmers who were to provide the bedrock of Kenya's political stability and economic success in the 1960s and 1970s, stigmatizing poor peasant opposition as Mau Mau subversion. But it did little to create a sense of national unity or to reduce the rivalries of Kenya's various ethnic communities. Although the few fighters remaining in the forests surrendered to Kenyatta's new government, Mau Mau's legacy was fraught with ambiguity, and the new state faced unresolved animosities and social problems. Kenya's future in 1963 seemed likely to be as conflict-ridden as its past.

See also *Kenyatta, Jomo.*

DAVID W. THROUP

BIBLIOGRAPHY

Berman, Bruce J., and John M. Lonsdale. *Unhappy Valley.* Oxford: James Currey; and Athens, Ohio: Ohio University Press, 1992.

Furedi, Frank. *The Mau Mau War in Perspective.* Oxford: James Currey; and Athens, Ohio: Ohio University Press, 1989.

Kanogo, Tabitha. *Squatters and the Roots of Mau Mau.* Oxford: James Currey; and Athens, Ohio: Ohio University Press, 1987.

Kershaw, Greet. *Mau Mau from Below.* Oxford: James Currey; and Athens, Ohio: Ohio University Press, 1997.

Rosberg, Carl G., Jr., and John Nottingham. *The Myth of Mau Mau: Nationalism in Kenya.* London: Stanford Praeger, 1966.

Throup, David W. *The Economic and Social Origins of Mau Mau.* Oxford: James Currey; and Athens, Ohio: Ohio University Press, 1987.

KENYATTA, JOMO

Founder and first president of independent Kenya, and popularly referred to as *Mzee* ("wise elder"), Kenyatta (ca 1888–1978) was born Kamau Muigai in Ngenda, Central Province, Kenya. He received his early education at Thogoto Mission, Kikuyu, between 1909 and 1914. Baptized Johnstone, he dropped all three names and adopted Jomo Kenyatta upon leaving school.

Kenyatta launched his political career in 1928, when he became secretary general of the Kikuyu Central Association (KCA), a regional political party established in 1924, and editor of *The Reconciler,* a journal that articulated African grievances. In 1929 and again in 1931 Kenyatta was sent to London by the KCA to represent African grievances, especially the conveyance of "White Highlands" (the "stolen lands") by the colonial government to European settlers; lack of political representation; forced labor and low wages; racial discrimination; and inadequate social amenities, including schools and hospitals. His second visit lasted until 1946 and included studies at the London School of Economics, where

Jomo Kenyatta

he completed a diploma in Anthropology. His dissertation was published in 1937 under the title *Facing Mount Kenya.*

In 1946 Kenyatta returned to Kenya and assumed the presidency of the Kenya African Union (KAU), a party established in 1944 that transcended ethnic groups. Steering national politics, Kenyatta focused on dismantling colonialism. Extensive impoverishment among peasants and urban workers, deplorable working conditions, and land hunger precipitated widespread agitation. Although he was not privy to the rapid radicalization of the KAU and trade union movement, which by 1951 was administering the "Batuni" platoon oath committing the partakers to violence against the colonial state, Kenyatta himself adopted an openly radical political stance in his public pronouncements between 1948 and 1952.

On October 19, 1952, Kenyatta and more than 150 other African leaders were arrested. The colonial state accused Kenyatta of leading the clandestine Mau Mau movement. The Mau Mau were associated with sporadic violence in rural Central Province, among Kikuyu squatter laborers on settler plantations, and in such urban areas as Nakuru and Nairobi. At his trial at Kapenguria, Kenyatta denied the charge. Nonetheless, he was detained at Lokitaung Prison in Lodwar until 1961. To the extent that the Mau Mau idealized and idolized Kenyatta and anticipated independence under his leadership, he was guilty of managing the Mau Mau movement. By 1955 the guerrillas had been militarily defeated.

Although Kenyatta was in detention while crucial constitutional changes were introduced between 1954 and 1960, his name was constantly evoked. Released in August 1961, Kenyatta accepted the presidency of the Kenya African National Union (KANU), the stronger and more militant of the two major parties contending for leadership at independence. Overcoming ethnic tension and suspicion, KANU emerged victorious to lead an independent Kenya in December 1963.

Under the *harambee* ("self-help") concept that Kenyatta created, the Kenyatta era (1963–1978) ushered in a phenomenal expansion of health services and primary and secondary schools. The White Highlands and civil service were Africanized. Despite these changes, issues of ethnicity and socioeconomic and regional inequality continued to plague the country. As practiced under Kenyatta, African socialism was capitalist. Kenyatta pursued a conservative political strategy, and in 1969 Kenya became a single-party state. He died in office on August 22, 1978.

See also *Kenyan Mau Mau Movement (1952–1960).*

TABITHA KANOGO

BIBLIOGRAPHY

Arnold, Guy. *Kenyatta and the Politics of Kenya.* London: Dent, 1974.
Aseka, Eric Masinde. *Jomo Kenyatta: A Biography.* Nairobi: East African Educational Publishers, 1992.
Kenyatta, Jomo. *Facing Mount Kenya: The Tribal Life of the Kikuyu.* New York: Vintage Books, 1965.
———. *Suffering Without Bitterness: The Founding of the Kenya Nation.* Nairobi: East African Publishing House, 1968.
Murray-Brown, Jeremy. *Kenyatta.* 2d ed. Boston: George Allen and Unwin, 1979.

KHOMEINI, AYATOLLAH RUHOLLAH

The charismatic leader of the Islamic revolution of 1979 in Iran, Khomeini (1902–1989) began his career as a revolutionary leader quite late in life, after he had attained the clerical rank of grand ayatollah (literally "sign of God"), the highest Shi'ite honorific title. His political campaign culminated in the overthrow of the monarchy of Mohammad Reza Shah Pahlavi on February 11, 1979. Although the rhetoric of his Islamic revolution was directed against the shah and the United States, Khomeini's formation predated both the last shah and the appearance of the United States on the Iranian scene. It can be argued that Khomeini was taking on no less than the twentieth-century ideas of modernization.

PREREVOLUTIONARY CAREER

Khomeini was a child during the Constitutional Revolution (1906–1911), which ushered in the era of modern politics in Iran. Shi'ite religious leaders appeared in the forefront of the first popular protests but were divided during that revolution, and one of them, Shaikh Fazlullah Nuri, led a traditionalist movement against the constitution in 1907–1908. The policies of centralization and secularization under Reza Khan (Reza Shah Pahlavi after 1925), the builder of Iran's modern state, were opposed by a few clerics in the 1920s and 1930s, but this opposition remained ineffective.

The reign of Reza Shah (1925–1941) encompassed Khomeini's formative years. Khomeini chose to specialize in mystical philosophy, which was highly suspect in the legalistic scholarly community of Qom. In the 1930s, while teaching mystical philosophy to a small number of students, he also began teaching courses in ethics for a much larger audience, which first brought him to the attention of the police.

Khomeini never forgot the loss of clerical power that resulted from secularization and the modernization of the state and the humiliation of clerics by Reza Shah. He transferred his hostility to the latter's son, Mohammad Reza Shah (1941–1979), whom he contemptuously referred to as "the son of Reza Khan" throughout the revolutionary struggle.

Although Khomeini had frequented the clerical activists in the 1920s and 1930s, his public career began in the 1940s with a tract against an anticlerical pamphleteer and a clerical advocate of reform of Shi'ism. Khomeini first appeared on the national political scene in 1963 as an outspoken critic of the shah and his reform program. He was imprisoned and, after demonstrations by his supporters were violently suppressed in June, exiled to Iraq. It was during his decade and a half of exile in Iraq that Khomeini began to prepare a beleaguered Shi'ite hierarchy to take over a secularizing state. By the late 1970s he had enlisted the loyalty of many of the ablest and most energetic Shi'ite clerics. The militant clerics rallied behind him in opposition to Western cultural domination and to the shah's policies, which they considered a threat to the integrity of Islamic religious institutions.

To launch the revolutionary movement for the establishment of Islamic government, Khomeini assumed the title of *imam*—a title hitherto reserved in Iranian shi'ism for the Twelve Holy Imams. The leading militant clerics, who later came to occupy the highest positions of power in the Islamic Republic, were mostly his former students. Khomeini also mobilized many younger clerics from humbler rural and small-town backgrounds who preached his revolutionary message in mosques and religious gatherings. Other groups, too, became vocal in their opposition to the shah when he tried to liberalize his regime in 1977. As massive demonstrations and strikes paralyzed the government in 1978, all of the political groups that formed the revolutionary coalition against the shah accepted the leadership of Khomeini.

Khomeini's themes of American imperialism and U.S. control of the shah were already popular with nationalists and leftists, including youth and students. Khomeini was also helped by a popular reaction to changes that had hurt or uprooted various segments of Iranian society, and by the prior work of Islamic ideologues and groups such as Ali Shariati, Al-e Ahmad, the Liberation Movement of Iran, and even the leftist Mojahedin-e Khalq.

LEADERSHIP OF THE ISLAMIC REVOLUTION

While in exile, Khomeini had formulated a new theory of theocratic government. The Shi'ites believe that their Twelfth Imam went into hiding in the ninth century and will remain there until the end of time. Khomeini had argued that, during the "Occultation of the Twelfth Imam," the right to rule belonged to clerical jurists.

Upon the victory of the Islamic revolution, Khomeini treated the property confiscated from the Pahlavi family and other industrialists of the old regime as war booty according to religious law and used it to endow several foundations, including the Foundation for the Disinherited. Most of the foundations were put under the direction of clerics. Khomeini also appointed Mehdi Bazargan, the leading member of the liberal and nationalist elements in the revolutionary coalition, as prime minister of a provisional government. A clerically dominated Assembly of Experts, elected in place of a constituent assembly at Khomeini's behest, rejected the draft constitution that had been prepared by the provisional government and proposed a theocratic government, as advocated by Khomeini, with an elected parliament and president. The theocratic constitution was approved by a referendum in December 1979, shortly after the occupation of the American embassy and the taking of its staff as hostages, which resulted in the toppling of Bazargan's government. By backing the taking of hostages, Khomeini caused a major international crisis.

In the course of the ensuing power struggle among the partners in the revolutionary coalition, Khomeini sanctioned the violent suppression of the leftist and secular elements in Iranian politics. After the revolutionary power struggle ended with the complete victory of his supporters, Khomeini sought to maintain unity between the conservative and the radical clerics.

Khomeini opposed ending the increasingly unpopular war with Iraq (1980–1988) but was finally persuaded to accept a ceasefire in view of the gravity of the military situation. In the last year of his life, Khomeini caused another international crisis by issuing, on February 14, 1989, an injunction sanctioning the death of Salman Rushdie, a non-Iranian writer who lived in England.

Khomeini died on June 3, 1989, a charismatic leader of immense popularity. Millions of Iranians had massed to welcome him when he returned from exile in 1979, and a million or more joined his funeral procession.

See also *Iranian Constitutional Revolution (1906); Iranian Islamic Revolution (1979); Islamic Fundamentalism; Religion.*

Saïd Amir Arjomand

BIBLIOGRAPHY

Algar, H. "Imam Khomeini: The Pre-Revolutionary Years." In *Islam, Politics and Social Movements.* Edited by E. Burke III and I. M. Lapidus. Berkeley: University of California Press, 1988.

Arjomand, S. A. *The Turban for the Crown: The Islamic Revolution in Iran.* New York: Oxford University Press, 1988.

Khomeini, Ruhollah. *Islam and Revolution.* Translated by H. Algar. Berkeley, Calif.: Mizan Press, 1981.

KIM IL SUNG

Kim Il Sung (1912–1994) was a revolutionary who ruled the northern half of Korea for nearly a half century. He was general secretary of the Workers' Party of Korea and president of the Democratic People's Republic of Korea. Born the eldest of three sons of a poor peasant in Pyongyang, Korea, Kim Il Sung fought for his country's liberation from Japanese colonialism and for a socialist system of government in Korea.

As a young man in colonial Korea, Kim Il Sung fled his home and attended Korean and Chinese secondary schools in northeastern China. He left school after being jailed for participating in underground communist activity, and he joined the Chinese communist guerrilla force known as the Northeast Anti-Japanese United Army to fight for Korean independence from Japan and for the cause of communism in Korea. He fought well against the Japanese, but when the United Army was defeated by a Japanese expeditionary force, he fled to the Russian Maritime Province and joined a special military unit of the Soviet Far Eastern Command. When Japan was defeated at the end of World War II, he became the leader of North Korea at the age of thirty-three.

The United States and the Soviet Union withdrew their occupation forces after creating separate governments, each claiming legitimacy across the entire Korean Peninsula. In his effort to unify the divided country, Kim Il Sung launched a military attack from the north in June 1950, thus starting the Korean War. It ended in 1953 a stalemate. Kim consolidated

Kim Il Sung

his political power after the war by eliminating his political rivals. By the time of the Fourth Party Congress in 1961, he had recovered economically and politically from the war.

North Korea encountered trouble in the 1960s when its closest allies, the Soviet Union and China, split. Because of the historical ties that Kim Il Sung and his revolutionaries had with the Chinese communist movement, North Korea sided with the Chinese, straining Soviet-North Korean relations. During the Chinese Cultural Revolution (1966–1969), however, the Chinese Red Guards criticized Kim Il Sung and his leadership in North Korea. Kim decided to become independent of both the Soviet Union and China and declared a self-reliance policy. North Korea established diplomatic relations with more than one hundred developing countries and joined the nonaligned movement.

Kim Il Sung created his own political ideology for North Korea, the idea of self-reliance called *chuch'e.* He advocated that North Korea become politically self-reliant, economically self-sustaining, and militarily self-defending. Armed with this idea, he began to promote his own cult of personality, which easily surpassed those of Joseph Stalin in the Soviet Union and Mao Zedong in China. He revised the constitution to justify his rule, and his rule was so absolute that the socialist republic he had labored so long to build looked more like his kingdom than a haven for the workers and peasants. His indoctrination of the people was so complete that when he appointed his son to succeed him, the people accepted it without question. He claimed that he had built a socialist system that the people could enjoy for generations, but his "self-sustaining" economic system collapsed after his death, and his once proud political system was reduced to the status of international mendicant.

See also *Korean Civil War (1950–1953); War.*

Dae-Sook Suh

BIBLIOGRAPHY

Party History Research Institute. *History of Revolutionary Activities of the Great Leader Comrade Kim Il Sung.* Pyongyang: Foreign Languages Publishing House, 1983.

Suh, Dae-Sook. *Kim Il Sung: The North Korean Leader.* Rev. ed. New York: Columbia University Press, 1995.

KING, MARTIN LUTHER, JR.

King (1929–1968), a Baptist minister and proponent of Gandhian concepts of nonviolent social change, became the most widely known leader of the African-American civil rights movement. He was also a consistent and outspoken supporter of anticolonial revolutionary movements throughout the world.

King was born in Atlanta, Georgia, the son of the Reverend Martin Luther King Sr. and Alberta Williams King. From his childhood during the Great Depression, King was influenced by the African-American social gospel tradition, which combined Christian egalitarianism with political activism. In addition to his father and grandfather, King's role models for politically engaged religious leadership included educator Benjamin E. Mays, who served as president of Morehouse College during King's undergraduate years (1944–1948). During his senior year at Morehouse, King was ordained as a minister and decided to attend Crozer Theological Seminary (1948–1951) in Pennsylvania, where he deepened his understanding of liberal theology. He then undertook graduate studies in systematic theology at Boston University (1951–1955), where he received his doctorate.

In December 1955, soon after King accepted his first pastorate at Dexter Avenue Baptist Church in Montgomery, Alabama, Rosa Parks, secretary of the local chapter of the National Association for the Advancement of Colored People (NAACP), was jailed for refusing to obey racial segregation laws. When black residents formed the Montgomery Improvement Association (MIA) to coordinate a bus boycott movement, King became president and main spokesman for the new organization. After the U.S. Supreme Court overturned Alabama's bus segregation laws late in 1956, he assumed the presidency of a new regional group, the Southern Christian Leadership Conference (SCLC). King emerged as a major spokesperson for an expanding African-American civil rights movement. His speeches often linked that movement to anticolonial movements in Africa and Asia and, more generally, to worldwide struggles against racism and oppression. King attended the 1957 independence celebration of Ghana. In 1959 he increased his understanding of Gandhian precepts of nonviolence during a month-long visit to India as a guest of Prime Minister Jawaharlal Nehru.

After leaving Montgomery to return to Atlanta early in 1960, King participated in numerous major protest movements, most notably civil rights campaigns in Albany, Georgia (1961–1962); Birmingham, Alabama (1963), St. Augustine, Florida (1963–1964); and Selma, Alabama (1965). These campaigns spurred passage of the 1964 Civil Rights Act and the 1965 Voting Rights Act. After achieving these civil rights reforms, King sought to confront economic issues in a major series of protests in Chicago (1966–1967) and in the Poor People's Campaign (1968), which intended to bring large numbers of protesters to Washington, D.C. During this period, he became more outspoken in his insistence that major economic reforms were necessary to achieve social justice in the United States.

Although King was reluctant to risk his prestige as a civil rights leader by opposing the Vietnam War, he publicly criticized President Lyndon Johnson's war policies as immoral and as a harmful diversion of funds from antipoverty programs. On April 4, 1967, in his first major public statement against the war, King told an audience at New York's Riverside Church "that if we are to get on the right side of the world revolution, we as a nation must undergo a radical revolution of values." King's advocacy of conscientious objection to military service and his call for a unilateral cease-fire in Vietnam decreased his political influence in the United States, but he nonetheless remained an internationally recognized advocate of world peace and militant nonviolence until his assassination on April 4, 1968.

See also *Inequality; Injustice; Race; U.S. Civil Rights Movement (1954–1968).*

Clayborne Carson

BIBLIOGRAPHY

King, Martin Luther, Jr. *Stride toward Freedom: The Montgomery Story.* New York: Harper and Row, 1958.

———. *Where Do We Go from Here? Chaos or Community?* New York: Harper and Row, 1967.

———. *Why We Can't Wait.* New York: Harper and Row, 1964.

KOREAN CIVIL WAR (1950–1953)

The Korean Civil War ranks as one of the most devastating international conflicts in the history of the cold war. Although the Korean War has most often been seen as a conflict between great powers, especially the United States and China, it was also a clash between two social systems: one a self-styled "revolutionary" regime under the patronage of the Soviet Union, and the other more conservative and pro-American. The struggle over the political orientation of the postcolonial Korean government became enmeshed in the emerging strategic rivalry of the cold war, resulting in a civil war that quickly became internationalized.

THE PATH TO CIVIL WAR

With the sudden collapse of colonial rule in Korea after Japan surrendered to the Allies on August 15, 1945, most Koreans expected an independent, Korean-led government quickly to assume authority over the peninsula. Prior to the Japanese surrender, however, the United States and the Soviet Union had quietly agreed to a temporary division of Korea into zones of Allied occupation, with the USSR overseeing the area north of the thirty-eighth parallel, and the United States in control of the south.

The Soviet occupation recognized and worked through a network of "people's committees," ad hoc organizations to keep local order, which had emerged across Korea when colonial rule ended. In February 1946 a North Korean Provisional People's Committee was established in Pyongyang, under Soviet auspices, as the de facto central government of North Korea. In the spring and summer the Provisional People's Committee instituted far-reaching social reforms, including a thoroughgoing redistribution of land to poor farmers. In the south the United States abolished the people's committees, ruled directly as a military occupation government, and allied with landed elites.

By early 1946 separate and mutually antagonistic pro-Soviet and pro-American regimes had begun to take distinctive shape on opposite sides of the thirty-eighth parallel, with their capitals in Pyongyang and Seoul, respectively. Despite several attempts at forging a Koreawide coalition government, Soviet-American disagreements, contradictory policies of the occupation forces on the ground, and the development of separate power centers in Seoul and Pyongyang made a single Korean government increasingly unlikely. In 1947 the United States handed over the Korean question to the United Nations, which created a United Nations Temporary Commission on Korea (UNTCOK) to oversee general elections in Korea. The North refused to cooperate with UNTCOK, and elections were held only in the South in May 1948.

The Republic of Korea (ROK) was declared in Seoul on August 15, the third anniversary of liberation from Japanese colonial rule, and American-educated Syngman Rhee became president. On September 9 Pyongyang announced the establishment of the Democratic People's Republic of Korea (DPRK) under premier Kim Il Sung, a veteran of the guerrilla war against Japan in Manchuria, who had spent the last years of World War II as an officer in the Soviet Far Eastern Army.

With two states both claiming to be the legitimate government of the whole of the Korean Peninsula, civil war was virtually inevitable. By the summer of 1949, after the departure of Soviet and American military forces, the situation across the thirty-eighth parallel had become extremely tense. Syngman Rhee spoke belligerently of a "march north" to take the rest of the peninsula for the ROK, both sides amassed troops at the parallel, and border skirmishes occurred frequently.

This stalemate was breached when the North launched an all-out attack on the South in the early morning of June 25, 1950. At the time, many in the West believed that the invasion had been masterminded by Joseph Stalin as part of a global strategy of Soviet expansion. Evidence from Soviet and Chinese sources made available in the 1990s suggests that the invasion of the South was largely initiated by Kim Il Sung, with the knowledge and support of the Soviet and Chinese leaderships. It appears that Stalin agreed to support North Korea in "liberating" the South after Kim convinced him that the war would be won quickly and decisively, before the United States had time to intervene. Mao Zedong apparently agreed to deploy Chinese troops in North Korea's defense should the need arise.

FIERCE FIGHTING, HEAVY LOSSES

The war initially went well for the North. The North Korean People's Army overwhelmed South Korean forces, taking Seoul in three days; by August the North Koreans had taken all but a small corner of the southeastern part of the peninsula, the so-called Pusan perimeter. The North Koreans revived the people's committees and instituted land reform and other social reforms in liberated areas. A permanent communist reunification of the entire peninsula seemed a foregone conclusion.

In mid-September the tide was reversed, after U.S. general Douglas MacArthur's landing at the port of Inchon near Seoul. Under the flag of the United Nations, U.S., ROK, and other Allied troops retook Seoul and crossed the thirty-eighth parallel into North Korea on September 30. Just as the North had done in the South, ROK forces imposed the Southern system on North Korea—returning land to landlords, reversing social reforms, and executing communists.

With her brother on her back, a Korean girl passes by a stalled tank at Haengju, Korea, June 9, 1951.

Despite warnings of a Chinese counterattack, UN forces continued to move toward the Yalu River dividing North Korea from China. In November thousands of Chinese People's Volunteers crossed into Korea, pushing UN forces back across the parallel. Throughout the war, China sent hundreds of thousands of troops and suffered immense casualties. The USSR also came to North Korea's assistance, albeit much more discreetly. The Soviet Union contributed fighter pilots into combat over the northern part of North Korea and prepared as many as five divisions of Red Army soldiers to enter the war, although they were never sent. What began as a civil war thus became a major international conflict involving the main protagonists in the emerging cold war between the West and the communist bloc.

After the Chinese entry into the war and the UN counteroffensive, UN and communist forces fought for another two-and-a-half years while attempting to negotiate a peace agreement. Massive armies clashed up and down the peninsula, causing enormous human and material destruction. Overall the North suffered the greater devastation, largely due to the tactics and technological superiority of the UN forces, especially the United States Air Force. The United States used massive and prolonged aerial bombardment as a means of breaking the morale of the North Korean population; Pyongyang and virtually every other city in North Korea was leveled. Toward the end of the war, dams and hydroelectric plants were bombed, devastating vast areas of North Korea's farmland. Napalm was deployed on a wide scale for the first time, and in the spring of 1951 the United States considered the use of the atomic bomb.

Some three million Koreans were killed in the war, two-thirds of them in the North. China suffered about one million casualties, while the United States lost 54,000, and other UN forces lost several thousand troops. An armistice was signed by the military commanders of the United States, China, and North Korea on July 27, 1953, in the Korean village of Panmunjom. A ceasefire line cutting across the middle of the peninsula, not far from the original thirty-eighth parallel division, established a new boundary between North and South Korea, who were to remain in a state of mutual hostility and military stand-off for decades to come.

See also *Civil Wars; Kim Il Sung; War.*

CHARLES ARMSTRONG

BIBLIOGRAPHY

Chen, Jian. *China's Road to the Korean War: The Making of the Sino-American Confrontation.* New York: Columbia University Press, 1994.

Cumings, Bruce. *The Origins of the Korean War.* Volume one: *Liberation and the Emergence of Separate Regimes, 1945-1947.* Princeton, N.J.: Princeton University Press, 1981.

———. *The Origins of the Korean War.* Volume two: *The Roaring of the Cataract.* Princeton, N.J.: Princeton University Press, 1990.

Goncharov, Sergei N., John W. Lewis, and Litai Xue. *Uncertain Partners: Stalin, Mao and the Korean War.* Stanford, Calif.: Stanford University Press, 1993.

Stueck, William. *The Korean War: An International History.* Princeton, N.J.: Princeton University Press, 1995.

Zhang, Shuguang. *Mao's Military Romanticism: China and the Korean War, 1950–1953.* Lawrence: University Press of Kansas, 1995.

KOREAN DEMOCRACY MOVEMENT (1960–1998)

Popular protest against authoritarian government has been a perennial occurrence in South Korea, growing into a wide-ranging movement for democracy between the 1960s and the 1990s. From the founding of the Republic of Korea (South Korea) in 1948 to the emergence of a democratically elected civilian government in the 1990s, much of South Korea's political history has been characterized by highly authoritarian and repressive forms of government, including more than twenty-five years of military rule (1961–1988). Antigovernment protests, often led by students and laborers, emerged periodically throughout this time. Protests and agitation for democracy peaked during three periods when the authoritarian government weakened and collapsed: 1960–1961, 1979–1980, and 1987. By the 1980s the South Korean democracy movement had become a large and diverse coalition of students, urban workers, farmers, religious groups, and middle-class professionals. The democratic "opening" of the late 1980s seems to have broken the cycle of resistance and repression and led to a permanent, if still incomplete, democratization of South Korean politics.

ANTIGOVERNMENT PROTESTS OF THE 1960S AND 1970S

Antigovernment protests by workers and students can be traced back to the period of Japanese colonial rule (1910–1945) and to the demonstrations against the U.S. military government and the Syngman Rhee regime during the American military occupation (1945–1948). But the contemporary South Korean democracy movement did not really begin until the "April Student Revolution" that led to the downfall of President Syngman Rhee in 1960. On April 19, 1960, tens of thousands of university and high school students marched toward the presidential palace to protest Rhee's corrupt reelection campaign of the previous month and his regime's heavy-handed treatment of political dissent. A violent confrontation between the protesters and police ensued, leading to riots in Seoul and other South Korean cities. Under pressure from his own government and the United States, Rhee resigned and went into exile in Hawaii.

He was replaced by his former vice president, Chang Myon, who was overthrown the following year in a military coup masterminded by Maj. Gen. Park Chung Hee and Lt. Col. Kim Jong Pil. Park became president in 1963 and remained in power until his death in 1979, and Kim Jong Pil went on to found and direct the Korean Central Intelligence Agency (KCIA), a notorious instrument of domestic surveillance and political control under Park and his successors.

The democratic movement exploded on the scene again after Park Chung Hee was assassinated by his own chief of security in October 1979. After a brief period of civilian rule under President Choi Kyu-hwa, a new military junta took command of the government in December 1980, led by Maj. Gens. Chun Doo Hwan and Roh Tae Woo. Chun took control of the KCIA in April 1980 and declared martial law in May, touching off a wave of student protests across the country. A brutal clampdown on protesters in the southwestern city of Kwangju, home of leading dissident Kim Dae Jung, led to an armed insurrection by the citizens of the city, which was met in turn with regular army forces and resulted in the deaths of as many as two thousand Kwangju residents. The legacy of Kwangju haunted Chun throughout his presidency, and the May 18 anniversary of the Kwangju massacre became an annual event marked by large protests on student campuses throughout South Korea.

Meanwhile, the industrial workforce, having grown rapidly under Park Chung Hee's economic development programs of the 1960s and 1970s, was becoming an increasingly critical and outspoken element in the movement for democracy and workers' rights. The Rhee, Park, and Chun governments had all severely curtailed the rights of workers to form independent labor unions, and working conditions remained poor. In November 1970 a young garment worker named Chun Tae-il publicly burned himself to death in protest against the abysmal state of factory workers. This event sparked a new awareness of labor issues among the South Korean population; in particular, student groups and the progressive wings of the Protestant and Catholic Churches became major allies of the working-class opposition movement of the 1970s and 1980s.

CULMINATION OF THE DEMOCRACY MOVEMENT

The third and most lasting democratic opening began in the summer of 1987, with the largest outburst of popular demonstrations in South Korean history. These protests were sparked by Chun Doo Hwan's choice of his right-hand man, Roh Tae Woo, as his successor as president, as well as by Chun's opposition to constitutional reform and direct presidential elections, and the revelation that a student had died as a result of police torture. In June 1987 up to one million people in Seoul alone marched in protest against the Chun government. Prodemocracy demonstrations merged with workers' demands for improved working conditions and the right to form unions; in 1987 there were some 3,500 labor disputes in South Korea, more than in the previous twenty-five years combined.

Faced with such an enormous public outcry on the eve of the 1988 Seoul Olympics, when the world's media would be focused on South Korea, President Chun stepped down and announced a new election for December 1987. Longtime opposition leaders Kim Dae Jung and Kim Young Sam both ran as presidential candidates, and Roh Tae Woo won the election with 36 percent of the vote. Under President Roh, South Korean politics became considerably more open, particularly in the areas of freedom of speech, freedom of the press, and human rights. Workers, however, remained prohibited from funding political candidates or forming a prolabor party, although workers' material conditions improved considerably.

In January 1990 Kim Young Sam merged his party with Roh's ruling Democratic Justice Party and formed the Democratic Liberal Party (DLP), a name not coincidentally much like Japan's conservative and long-ruling Liberal Democratic Party. In 1992 Kim Young Sam won the presidency over Kim Dae Jung and his isolated Democratic Party. The DLP soon faltered, however, losing badly in the 1995 local government elections. Kim Young Sam's own popularity plummeted in the latter half of his presidency, as he was beset by corruption scandals that included a jail sentence for his own son on charges of bribery. Adding to Kim's troubles, shortly before the presidential election scheduled for December 1997, South Korea was caught up in the Asiawide financial crisis that had already devastated Southeast Asia. In part because of the blame Kim's administration took for the financial disaster in Korea, the ruling party candidate lost the election. Kim Dae Jung, running as a presidential candidate for the fourth time, won the election in a bizarre alliance with his longtime nemesis, former KCIA head Kim Jong Pil, whose agency had attempted to have Kim Dae Jung killed more than once.

Kim's election marked the first time in the history of the Republic of Korea that an opposition candidate and prodemocracy activist had won a presidential election. Kim Dae Jung assumed the presidency at a time of acute economic uncertainty with unforeseeable social and political consequences. His attempts to create a consultative alliance among the government, big business, and organized labor would be severely tested by the economic reforms required to ease the financial crisis. South Korean democracy still remained constrained, especially by the National Security Law that restricted any activity deemed pro-North Korean, and by the modified but still powerful Agency for National Security Planning (as the KCIA was renamed). Nevertheless, the election of Kim Dae Jung in late 1997 signified, at least in part, the success of a long and tenacious struggle for democracy, of which Kim had been one of the best-known leaders.

Charles Armstrong

BIBLIOGRAPHY

Abelmann, Nancy. *Echoes of the Past, Epics of Dissent: A South Korean Social Movement.* Berkeley: University of California Press, 1996.

Choi, Jang-jip. *Labor and the Authoritarian State: Labor Unions in South Korean Manufacturing Industries.* Honolulu: University of Hawaii Press, 1990.

Clark, Donald N., ed. *The Kwangju Uprising: Shadows over the Regime in South Korea.* Boulder, Colo.: Westview Press, 1988.

Ogle, George E. *South Korea: Dissent within the Economic Miracle.* London: Zed Books, 1990.

Soon, Cho Wha. *Let the Weak be Strong: A Woman's Struggle for Justice.* New York: Crossroads, 1988.

Wells, Kenneth M., ed. *South Korea's Minjung Movement: The Culture and Politics of Dissidence.* Honolulu: University of Hawaii Press, 1995.

KOREAN REBELLIONS OF 1812 AND 1862

The rebellions of 1812 and 1862 were large-scale uprisings that signaled the decline of the Chosòn dynasty's fortunes because of the government's inability to maintain at least minimal probity in the conduct of officials and clerks and fairness in the administration of taxes, credit, and relief. The rebellion of 1812 in the northwest tapped into grievances about discrimination against the region and the discontent of private merchants, as well as the hardships of mine workers and sharecroppers, but its threat to establish a new dynasty was quickly repressed by government forces. The widespread 1862 rebellions, by contrast, were much more serious—if less well organized and coordinated—because they occurred mainly in the country's southern rice basket and illustrated the morbidity of government institutions.

THE HONG KYÒNGNAE REBELLION OF 1812

On January 31, 1812, Hong Kyòngnae, a professional geomancer from a poor peasant family, launched an armed rebellion against the Chosòn dynasty with about two hundred men, from his base in Taboktong in Pyòng'an Province in the northwest corner of the Korean Peninsula. The rebels increased their force to two or three thousand and captured seven major districts in the first couple of weeks, but government forces blocked the rebel advance before it reached either Anju to the east or Üiju on the Yalu River to the west and recaptured all but one of the lost districts within a month. More than 8,000 government troops besieged 2,000 rebels in the walled town of Chòngju for four months and then massacred the 1,900 survivors en masse.

When the rebellion broke out, most of the participants were gold miners, but they were joined by several thousand sharecroppers, landless farm laborers, handicraft and factory workers, slaves, bandits, vagrants, and starving peasants suffering from the natural disasters and famine of recent years. Men with military experience or natural fighting talent took command of the troops and became garrison commanders over captured towns. Hong had also gained the support of many merchants, local influentials, rich landlords, local clerks, military guards, and officers. Merchants who chafed at the extortion of district magistrates and the restrictions by government-licensed monopoly shops handled logistical support, and local clerks and influential rich men acted as fifth columnists in undermining district magistrates. Since there were few *yangban* (hereditary aristocrats) in the northwest, landlords, local clerks, and military officials who constituted the local elite resented the contempt shown them by the capital *yangban* and the district magistrates, all of whom were dispatched from other provinces.

Hong denounced not only the court of the young King Sunjo but also the most powerful man in the country, Kim Chosun of the Andong Kim lineage, the father-in-law of King Sunjo and the de facto regent, for corruption and discrimination against the northwest. He also appealed to the millenarian belief that recent natural disasters and omens had signaled dynastic collapse and a new age of prosperity. He used the well-known prophecy about the replacement of the Chònju Yi royal house by a "genuine man" *(chin'in)* from the Chòng lineage, claiming that such a man born in the province was in China preparing an army to invade and purify Korea. Reluctant to trample his own place of birth, however, this man had instead commissioned Hong's band of brave men to rise in rebellion and save the people.

Since Hong never mentioned a plan to redress peasant grievances, abolish slavery, nationalize private property, redistribute land to the peasants, end merchant monopolies, or establish a new system of government, it would appear that he aimed primarily at establishing a new dynasty.

THE IMSUL REBELLION OF 1862

By the mid-nineteenth century the district magistrates and their hereditary clerks had depleted district treasuries and created perpetual shortages for the central government through embezzlement. They were best known for their corruption in the administration of the famous three evil institutions: the land tax, the military service support tax, and the official grain loan and relief funds. Arrears caused by clerk embezzlements could only be made up by ad hoc and arbitrary levies on rich and poor alike, but these extra levies provided the spark for a series of local and mainly uncoordinated uprisings in 1862 and 1863.

Clerks with lifetime tenure had become more powerful because of the rapid turnover of district magistrates. Local *yangban* had become vulnerable to these magistrates and clerks because they had lost the opportunity for officeholding in the face of intense competition for posts. Since the mid-eighteenth century, district magistrates had begun convening local councils to recommend a commutation rate from grain or cotton to cash for the new comprehensive land tax *(togyòl)*. This tax had been devised to replace the land tax, military cloth tax, and grain loan interest revenues. In a reflection of the local *yangban*'s loss of prestige, all members of the community typically participated in local council meetings, but *yangban* still opposed commoner peasant interests when discussing the method of paying for extra taxes to make up for shortages in the district's comprehensive tax quota.

The majority of protests and violence against corrupt clerks was directed by commoner peasants, especially those who supplemented their income as woodcutters, because they had gained experience over the years resisting *yangban,* rich landlords, and clerks who had tried to ban woodcutting. In Tansòng, Kyòongsang Province, where the first uprising took place, *yangban* leaders took over and ran the district through village meetings for three months, until a pacification commissioner arrived on June 4, 1862. Otherwise, local *yangban* functioned mainly in drawing up petitions and negotiating with magistrates, withdrawing from action whenever the peasants turned violent. In Ch'ungch'òng Province, where many capital *yangban* lived in retirement, peasant rebels attacked and destroyed the homes of local *yangban,* lenders and mortgage holders, magistrates, and clerks.

Violence began in March 1862 in Tansòng and Chinju, to the west of the Naktong River, and then spread to 79 of the approximately 330 districts in the country, focusing primarily on the southern three provinces of Chòlla, Kyòngsang, and Ch'ungch'òng. A major rebellion broke out on Cheju Island against Kaesòng merchants, who took away peasant income from the horsehair market for traditional Korean hats, and officials who increased taxes on swidden cultivation, but most of the risings elsewhere were brief paroxysms of rage against the maladministration of the "three institutions." There was very little coordination among the villages: no accumulation of a large army, no declaration to overthrow the dynasty, no coordinated attack against the *yangban* as a class, and no program for land redistribution.

King Ch'òlchong's initial response to the uprisings was to dismiss magistrates and clerks accused of corruption, punish only rebel leaders, and dispatch pacification commissioners and secret censors to investigate. When rebellions continued, he shifted to military repression and execution of rebel leaders on June 11. Although he established a bureau to carry out institutional reforms of the nefarious three institutions, enthusiasm flagged and reform was abandoned by the end of December. When the next king, Kojong, ascended the throne as a minor in 1864, his father, the Taewongun (Grand Prince, a title reserved for fathers of kings who had not themselves been kings), engineered a program of institutional reform that lasted ten years and provided a generation's respite from uprisings for the dynasty.

Despite the prevalence of aristocratic *yangban* landlords in the south, they not only were unable to help the government maintain control, but often led challenges to corrupt administration because many had lost their contacts with the capital bureaucrats and their ability to restrain local magistrates and clerks. Rebellious peasants outstripped them in attacking clerks and magistrates and even *yangban* landlords who were themselves the cause of sharecropping rack rents.

The wildfire of peasant unrest spent itself quickly in a series of individual outbursts because peasant leaders lacked both the ideology and organization necessary to pose a major challenge to the dynasty's legitimacy and viability. Perhaps only by chance, however, the Tonghak (Eastern or National Learning) religious movement began at the same time even without direct connection to the 1862 risings themselves. That movement was to provide the ideology and organization that made the Tonghak Rebellion of 1894 and 1895 the most serious threat to the dynasty in its long history.

See also *Korean Tonghak Rebellion (1894).*

James Palais

BIBLIOGRAPHY

Lee, Ki-baik. *A New History of Korea.* Translated by Edward W. Wagner with Edward J. Shultz. Cambridge: Harvard University Press, 1984.

Mangwòn Han'guksa yòn'gusil, 19 segi nongmin hangjaeng pun'kwa, ed. *1862 nyòn nongmin hangjaeng: Chungse malgi ch'ònguk nongmindòl ùi panbonggòn t'ujaeng.* Seoul: Tongnyòok, 1988.

Yu Hongnyòl, ed. *Han'guksa taesajòn.* Seoul: Koryò ch'ulp'ansa, 1996.

KOREAN TONGHAK REBELLION (1894)

The Tonghak Rebellion of 1894 was the largest rebellion in Korean history, inspired by a new syncretic religious movement designed to protect Korean culture against the West, eliminate hereditary status and social hierarchy on behalf of the common peasant, and eliminate corruption from the Korean bureaucracy. Unfortunately the rebellion brought on the Sino-Japanese War of 1894–1895 and led to a suppression of the rebellion by Japanese forces on Korean soil, but it left a legacy that stimulated a new era of modern nationalism, social egalitarianism, and non-Confucian religious belief.

The Tonghak movement had its origin in a new religion begun by Ch'oe Cheu of North Kyòngsang Province, the son of a *yangban* (aristocrat) and his concubine. After a decade selling cotton textiles and Chinese medicine, he experienced an epiphany in 1860 in which the Lord of Heaven *(Ch'ònju)* commanded him to teach the Way of Heaven *(Ch'òndo)* to the people. Since he believed that orthodox Neo-Confucianism had failed to provide the Korean people with either a strong spiritual base or national spirit with which to combat the Christianity and science of the West introduced into Korea from China since the late eighteenth century, he created a new national religion called *Tònghak* (Eastern or Korean Learning) by combining virtually every element of belief found in Korea—Confucianism, Buddhism, Taoism, animism, prophecy, and the use of elixirs and talismans. He also aimed his new faith at the masses, not just the educated *yangban* elite.

Ch'oe Cheu was arrested in 1862 and executed in 1863 for propagating heterodoxy. After his death, the Tonghak religion was led by the second patriarch, Ch'oe Sihyòng, who created a strong organizational base of custodians (Chòpchu) for the religion. He then became northern custodian for North Kyòngsang Province but moved his headquarters to Po'un in Ch'ungch'òng Province after 1872. After two more decades in the underground, in 1892 the Tonghak unsuccessfully petitioned the governor of Ch'ungch'òng Province to stop the persecution of their religion and take steps against corrupt local officials. Ch'oe Sihyòng then petitioned King Kojong in 1893 to clear the martyred Ch'oe Cheu and grant toleration of the religion. But at the same time, a militant Tonghak wing of the southern custodians from Chòlla Province under Chòn Pongjun, a local *yangban* from Kobu district, posted anti-Japanese, anti-Manchu, and anti-Western bills and secretly supported the king's father, the *Taewongun,* in his unsuccessful attempt to depose the king. King Kojong persuaded the Tonghak demonstrators to return home by promising toleration, but then immediately betrayed his word by ordering an official crackdown.

Chòn Pongjun responded by leading a brief local peasant rising against the corrupt magistrate of Kobu in Chòlla Province in February 1894. He then raised a peasant army of a thousand men that took over Kobu on April 25. He issued a manifesto demanding that the king purge his incompetent ministers and expel the Japanese diplomats and merchants allowed in Korea under the terms of the Kanghwa Treaty of 1876. Chòn also declared his loyalty to the king at the same time that he conspired secretly with the Taewongun to return him to power.

Chòn went on to capture Chònju, the capital of Chòlla Province, on May 30. This shocked the timorous King Kojong into making a fateful decision to ask China to send military reinforcements, even though Korean government forces had already surrounded Chònju and forced Chòn to agree to an armistice on June 11. The unnecessary 2,500 Chinese troops that landed on June 8 were more than matched by 6,000 Japanese troops on June 9. The Japanese government purposely violated the terms of the Tientsin Agreement of 1885 with China, which only allowed either side to match any increase in the size of its legation guard. It did so in order to start an undeclared war with China, which began on July 23, and drive China out of the Korean Peninsula. Japanese troops also invaded the Korean palace, detained the king and queen, forced the king to appoint a new reform cabinet, and brought in the Taewongun to act as regent. On September 16 Japanese forces defeated the Chinese at Pyongyang and drove them completely out of Korea.

Under the armistice, the Tonghak rebels were permitted to take over the administration of fifty-three district governments under the rebels' own units of local control, called Netrope Control Centers. This arrangement lasted four months, during which time the rebels banned grain loans, reduced rents and taxes, and administered justice, but without waging class war or confiscating land. The rebels were enraged, however, at the reforms of the Kabo cabinet and the Japanese dismissal of the Taewongun for conspiring with the Chinese. Chòn Pongjun thus began a second Tonghak rebellion on October 11, 1894, with a force of 227,000 men. His troops held their own against regular Japanese and Korean troops for two months, but Chòn's march to Seoul was blocked when he suffered defeat at Kongju because of overwhelming Japanese firepower. Chòn fought his last battle on December 23 and was executed on April 23, 1895.

The Tonghak Rebellion was significant because its syncretic theology reflected a protonationalist reaction to foreign imperialism, its religious organization provided the basis for large-scale rebellion, its egalitarian social message contributed to the breakdown of Korea's social hierarchy, and its brief experience in local government brought the masses into organized politics for the first time. The rebellion probably would have overthrown the dynasty had it not been for the Japanese military presence in Korea. Had they succeeded, the Tonghak rebels would probably have overturned the rigid social legacy of hereditary *yangban* aristocracy and slavery more thoroughly and opened up greater opportunities for some of the peasant masses to rise to power in a new government. Although its antiforeignism and defense of Confucianism and Buddhism would have obstructed a progressive move toward new scientific and technical knowledge, continuing pressures would have brought changes in attitudes.

The Tonghak movement spawned the Ch'òndogyo religion (of the Heavenly Way) in 1906, which remains strong to this day. After Japan annexed Korea as a colony in 1910, the Tonghak movement's third patriarch, Son Pyònghùi, was one of the thirty-three signers of the Declaration of Independence on March 1, 1919. Soon surpassed by more radical political forces to the left and right, the Tonghak movement nonetheless made a major contribution to both national consciousness and social egalitarianism in Korean society.

See also *Korean Rebellions of 1812 and 1862.*

JAMES PALAIS

BIBLIOGRAPHY

Conroy, Hilary. *The Japanese Seizure of Korea, 1868–1910.* Philadelphia: University of Pennsylvania Press, 1960.

Lew, Young-ick. "The Conservative Character of the 1894 Tonghak Peasants Uprising." *Journal of Korean Studies* 7 (1990).

Weems, Benjamin B. *Reform, Rebellion and the Heavenly Way.* Tucson: University of Arizona Press, 1964.

KURDISH REVOLTS (1958–)

The Kurds—a culturally and linguistically distinct people whose homeland lies mostly within present-day Turkey, Iraq, and Iran—have engaged in frequent insurrections against the central governments of those three states. Kurds today number 25–27 million. At least half live in Turkey, where they constitute more than 20 percent of the population; between 5 million and 6 million live in Iran, comprising about 10 percent of the population; and Iraqi Kurds probably number 4.2 million and make up about 23 percent of that country's population *(see map, p. 474).*

In the decades after World War I, as the newly independent governments attempted to impose Turkish, Arab, and Persian political and cultural hegemony throughout the territories they controlled, resistance by Kurds reflected dominant tribal solidarities more than a broader Kurdish nationalism. In Turkey and Iran, the earliest revolts also displayed an Islamic resistance to the counterreligious secularist agendas of Kemal Atatürk and Reza Shah.

IRAN

Although it controlled only a portion of Iranian Kurdistan, the brief appearance in 1946 of the Mahabad Republic based in the Iranian city of that name enlisted the active support of Iraqi as well as Iranian Kurds—and urban nationalists as well as rural chiefs and tribes people—and thus marked a watershed in the emergence of Kurdish nationalist consciousness and direct political action. The republic appeared at the end of World War II, when northern Iran was within an explicit sphere of Soviet influence; the project foundered when the Soviets withdrew and Tehran reestablished its control. Kurdish nationalist opposition in Iran remained embodied in the Democratic Party of Iranian Kurdistan and several other nationalist organizations. Kurdish political and military control of territory in Iran surfaced again, for a time, with the breakdown of central authority accompanying the revolution of 1978–1979 that established the Islamic Republic.

IRAQ

The defeat of Mahabad coincided with the reassertion of military control of Iraqi Kurdistan by the authorities in Baghdad, leading to the forced exile to the Soviet Union of Mullah Mustafa Barzani, the traditional leader from northern Iraq whose charisma and military skills gave him an authority beyond his status as a tribal chief and among Kurds outside Iraq as well. The July 1958 revolution led by Iraqi military officers against the British-installed monarchy allowed Barzani to return to Iraq and take control of the Kurdish Democratic Party (KDP). Autonomy negotiations soon broke down, however, and for almost two decades the face of Kurdish nationalism visible to the outside world was a series of Iraqi Kurdish revolts under Barzani's leadership against Arab nationalist regimes in Baghdad. In the most serious of these, from 1972 to 1975, Iran, Israel, and the United States—for their own strategic aims—pressured Baghdad by supporting Barzani and supplying arms and material. When in 1975 Iraq agreed to Iranian terms in a major border dispute, this support ended, and the Kurdish revolt collapsed.

In the wake of this disaster, which crystallized long-standing disaffection with Barzani's leadership, the Patriotic Union of Kurdistan (PUK)—led by a former Barzani lieutenant, Jalal Talabani—initiated guerrilla activities and eventually contested the Kurdish Democratic Party's hegemony in Iraqi Kurdistan. The KDP remained strongest among those Kurds in the more rural northwestern part of Iraqi Kurdistan who speak the Kurmanji dialect, but the PUK predominates among those in the more urban southeast who speak the Sorani dialect.

The 1981–1988 war between Iraq and Iran saw the resumption of armed struggle led by the Iranian and Iraqi Kurdish parties and supported by the rival regimes. In the final months of that war, the Iraqi government responded to what it regarded as the treasonous behavior of the Kurdish Democratic Party and the Patriotic Union of Kurdistan by launching a military campaign of genocide in which an estimated 150,000–200,000 perished, some 4,000 villages and hamlets were destroyed, and at least 1.5 million persons were forcibly resettled. In March 1991, in the aftermath of the allied rout of Baghdad's forces from Kuwait, popular uprisings in the south of Iraq quickly spread to the Kurdish north. The two Kurdish parties, initially hesitant under the shadow of the earlier genocide campaign, soon established political and military leadership. Within weeks, however, an Iraqi military campaign of reconquest led to a wholesale flight of the Kurdish population toward the Turkish and Iranian borders. When Turkey refused them entry, the magnitude of the humanitarian crisis compelled the Western allies to establish an aerial military umbrella against Iraqi military intrusion.

Inside this protected area, May 1992 local legislative elections saw the Kurdish Democratic Party and the Patriotic Union of Kurdistan nearly evenly split the popular vote and the resulting autonomy administration. Several factors—the scarcity of resources, the hostility of all regional governments, the paralyzing rivalry of the two parties—contributed to extensive bouts of armed conflict between party militias beginning in May 1994. In August 1996 the KDP "invited" Iraqi government forces to assist it in vanquishing the PUK, but this victory was fleeting. A military and political standoff between the two parties and widespread popular disillusionment with their leaders characterized Iraqi Kurdistan in the subsequent period.

TURKEY

In Turkey, self-consciously Kurdish political activism developed in the late 1960s and 1970s in an intensely polarized political environment, initially through activism in leftist Turkish political parties and groups. The hesitancy of Turkish leftists to support publicly Kurdish demands, along with a fierce official repression, especially after the military coups of 1970 and 1980, led to the formation of more radical groups. The most notable of these, the Kurdistan Workers' Party, launched a guerrilla war in 1984 that continued unabated in the late 1990s. The fierce and often brutal struggle between the party and the Turkish army has thoroughly politicized that country's Kurdish population and has forcibly dispersed much of that population out of traditionally Kurdish areas to the major cities and towns to the west.

LIMITED AUTONOMY

Contemporary regional and global geopolitics have compelled the dominant Kurdish parties to seek arrangements for political and cultural autonomy rather than independence. Kurdish struggles have mainly been confined within national borders, but campaigns in one country have increasingly traversed those borders. Social and economic forces, as well as political struggles and repression, have drastically reconfigured Kurdish communities, making them increasingly urban and stratified by class rather than tribal categories, though traditional loyalties still persist. Kurdish autonomy has been formally conceded only in Iraq, where the Kurdish proportion of the population is the largest, but the parochial and clan-rooted Kurdish leadership there and the totalitarian character of the present Iraqi government provide little basis for optimism. In Turkey—where Kurdish numbers are largest—although the military and political establishment remains largely unbending, the long and costly stalemate has persuaded many Turks that the Kurdish question requires a political rather than a military solution.

See also *Iraqi Revolution (1958).*

Joe Stork

BIBLIOGRAPHY

Bruinessen, Martin van. *Agha, Shaikh and State: The Social and Political Structures of Kurdistan.* London: Zed Press, 1992.

———. "The Kurds Between Iran and Iraq." *Middle East Report* 141 (July–August 1986): 14–27.

Human Rights Watch. *Genocide in Iraq: The Anfal Campaign Against the Kurds.* New York: Human Rights Watch, 1993.

Kutschera, Chris. "Mad Dreams of Independence: The Kurds of Turkey and the PKK." *Middle East Report* 189 (July–August 1994):12–15.

McDowall, David. *A Modern History of the Kurds.* Rev. ed. London: I.B. Tauris, 1997.

Meseilas, Susan. *Kurdistan: In the Shadow of History.* New York: Random House, 1997.

LAFAYETTE, GILBERT DU MOTIER DE

Lafayette (1757–1834), though remembered today mostly as a prominent military figure in the American and French Revolutions, served in the late eighteenth and early nineteenth centuries as a symbol of the military and political struggles for liberal republicanism and constitutionalism in North America, Europe, and Latin America. He was the descendant of a noble family that had served France since the Middle Ages. The deaths of his parents early in his life left Lafayette a young man of independent means. A chance encounter in 1775 at Metz with British king George III's brother, the Duke of Gloucester, stirred his interest in the American cause. He purchased a ship in the spring of 1777 and sailed for America despite family and governmental opposition. Though the Continental Congress usually rejected applications from foreign officers, Lafayette received the rank of brigadier general. George Washington took an interest in the young nobleman and rewarded him with a field command. Lafayette served through the final campaign of the war and developed a strong following among most Americans.

After his return to France in 1782, Lafayette supported greater political, economic, and religious liberty and the reduction of governmental regulation on trade. In March 1789 the nobility of Riom chose him to serve in the Estates-General. In the new National Assembly, he proposed a declaration of rights as a preamble for a forthcoming written constitution. After the fall of the Bastille in July, the Paris municipal government named him commander of its bourgeois militia, which he renamed the Paris National Guard and reorganized to maintain order. After 1790 Lafayette found his efforts around Paris increasingly challenged by radical Jacobins and royalist reactionaries. With the completion of the new constitution in August, he resigned his command on October 8, 1791, to retire to his farm—much as his republican idols Washington and Cincinnatus had.

In this period drawing, Lafayette is depicted as assisting the French nation (Marie) in trampling feudal rule just as it had trampled the people.

Lafayette's retirement was short-lived. He was named commander of one of three armies formed in December 1791 to defend the Revolution against neighboring absolutist monarchies. He led his army into battle against Austria in May 1792. As a result of Paris violence in June, Lafayette briefly returned to the city to criticize political factionalism in time of national crisis. This caused him to be attacked by

Jacobins in the Assembly and in the press. The fall of the constitutional monarchy on August 10 to radical republicans led Lafayette to rally his troops to continue supporting the constitution, which brought about his removal from command; on August 19 he was declared a rebel. That day, Lafayette and his staff crossed the border to flee to America. Austrian authorities intercepted him and imprisoned him until October 1797.

Lafayette returned to France in December 1799. In 1802 he opposed Napoleon's bid for lifetime consulship and requested his retirement from the army. During the remainder of Napoleon's regime, Lafayette found himself under surveillance. With the restoration of the Bourbon monarchy in France, Lafayette continued under close government scrutiny. Nonetheless, he remained publicly active, serving in the Chamber of Deputies from 1818 to 1824 and from 1827 until his death. He served as an icon for republican and revolutionary movements and liberal causes and was the frequent recipient of visits from reformers tied to the movements in Italy, Spain, Great Britain, the Austrian and Russian empires, and Latin America. His American tour of 1824–1825 was partially an effort to urge Americans to support the struggles for republicanism and liberal causes elsewhere in the world. By the time of the revolution of July 1830, he was the most widely recognized symbol of reform in France. Assured of his commitment to liberal principles, Lafayette publicly endorsed Louis-Philippe, Duke of Orleans, to be constitutional monarch and accepted the rank of commander of the French National Guard. Soon disappointed by the new king's violation of his promises, Lafayette bitterly resigned in December 1830 and became a leading opposition figure in the Chamber of Deputies.

Lafayette continued during his last years to support such causes as Greek and Polish independence, public education and libraries, the abolition of slavery, prison reform, and women's rights—all outgrowths of the ideas he had espoused from youth.

See also *American (U.S.) Revolution (1776–1789); French Revolution (1789–1815).*

ROBERT RHODES CROUT

BIBLIOGRAPHY

Idzerda, Stanley J., et al., eds. *Lafayette in the Age of the American Revolution. Selected Letters and Papers, 1776–1790.* 5 vols. to date. Ithaca, N.Y.: Cornell University Press, 1977– .

Idzerda, Stanley J., Anne C. Loveland, and Marc H. Miller. *Lafayette, Hero of Two Worlds: The Art and Pageantry of His Farewell Tour of America.* Hanover, N.H.: Queen's Museum, 1989.

Kramer, Lloyd S. *Lafayette in Two Worlds: Public Cultures and Personal Identities in an Age of Revolutions.* Chapel Hill: University of North Carolina Press, 1996.

Neely, Sylvia. *Lafayette and the Liberal Ideal, 1814–1824: Politics and Conspiracy in an Age of Reaction.* Carbondale: Southern Illinois University Press, 1991.

LATIN AMERICAN AND CARIBBEAN SLAVE REVOLTS (1521–1888)

On first contact Columbus thought that the indigenous people of the New World would make excellent servants. They proved him mistaken. Before their rapid devastation by imported European pathogens during the sixteenth century, enslaved Indians in Hispaniola, Cuba, Mexico, and other areas of Spanish settlement had rebelled against the brutal labor to which they were subjected in mines and on estates, often by fleeing into the bush. By the end of the century both the Spanish and Portuguese crowns had legislated prohibitions of indigene enslavement, but the loosely interpreted exception of the just war continued the practice for centuries, most notably in the Portuguese colony of Brazil. Indian slaves in the southeastern grain-producing captaincy of São Vicente, for example, came to outnumber whites eight to one by the mid-seventeenth century, when they took advantage of their numbers and white factionalization to erupt in an extraordinary series of revolts. Five revolts by enslaved Indians broke out in 1660 alone; the largest appears to have embraced hundreds of slaves.

ETHNIC AFRICAN INFLUENCE

Yet well before the mid-seventeenth century, slave revolt in the Americas would be more generally identified with Africans and persons of African descent. During the four-hundred-year history of the Atlantic slave trade (c. 1450–c. 1870), Latin America and the Caribbean received more than three quarters of the 11 million or so enslaved Africans who survived the middle passage. Spanish, Portuguese, French, English, Dutch, and other West European buyers tended to concentrate these Africans and their progeny in gangs in large-scale commercial agriculture, especially on sugar plantations, which gave rise, however sporadically, to various forms of collective resistance: riot, demonstration, outlawry, strike, conspiracy, mass desertion, as well as bloody revolt.

From the time of Columbus to 1888, when Brazil became the last country in the Americas to abolish slavery, Latin America and the Caribbean experienced scores of slave conspiracies and revolts that embraced at least dozens of slaves. The first documented revolt of African slaves in the Americas broke out around Christmas 1521 in southeastern Hispaniola on a sugar estate owned by the eldest son of Christopher Columbus. At peak, the rebels probably numbered fewer than fifty, most of them ethnic Wolofs from the Senegambian region of West Africa. Like most subsequent Latin American and Caribbean slave revolts, this one was quickly crushed by the authorities, who suspected shortages of food as the precipitant.

Despite sophisticated methods of control and brutal punishment and repression, masters in every Latin American and Caribbean slave society contended with much larger revolts whose causes, content, timing, and goals varied significantly according to local conditions or a much larger circle of influences. The great slave revolt in the French colony of Saint-Domingue began in 1791 when the colony was the world's leading producer of sugar and coffee. The revolt stands out not only because it eventually mobilized tens of thousands of slaves and led to the 1804 creation of the independent country of Haiti but because it also marked a turning point in the pattern of slave resistance in the Americas. Slave revolt with a strong restorationist, African ethnic dimension did not end after 1791, however, and even during the revolt in Saint-Domingue, the ranks of Congos and other African-born rebels had aims that differed from more visible Creole (American-born) chiefs such as François-Dominique Toussaint L'Ouverture, a freed person of color and, before 1791, a slaveholder himself.

The character of slave revolt in Latin America and the Caribbean clearly had much to do with the operation of the Atlantic slave trade: the sources of supply, their magnitude, and the location and strength of demand. The intensification of the sugar plantation system in Jamaica during the eighteenth century brought from the Gold Coast waves of imported Coromantee (Akan-speaking) slaves. In 1673 they initiated Jamaica's first revolt of hundreds of slaves and predominated among the thousands involved in Tacky's revolt (1760), one of the largest essentially ethnic slave revolts in the history of the Americas. Before Tacky, the spread of slavery and sugar cultivation on the island of St. Thomas almost made its Danish owners the first Europeans to lose an American colony to slave revolt when hundreds of Mina (also Akan-speaking) slaves erupted in 1733.

Cuba's sugar boom during the first half of the nineteenth century led to several serious ethnic revolts by recently imported Yoruba-speaking slaves. The sugar-producing region of Bahia in northeastern Brazil yielded more slave plots and revolts than any other region of the country, around twenty during the first three decades of the nineteenth century. The most famous uprising took place in the city of Salvador in 1835. It united hundreds of African-born Hausa and Yoruba-speaking Muslims and was headed by religious figures.

The largest revolts, with thousands of enslaved insurgents, surfaced on islands or in regions with a very high proportion of slaves. At the outbreak of the three largest slave revolts in the British Caribbean (Barbados, 1816; Demerara, 1823; Jamaica, 1831), slaves amounted in each island to more than 80 percent of the total population. Shortly before the outbreak in 1791 of the Saint-Domingue revolt, the slave population reached almost 90 percent of the total and a higher proportion in the sugar zones of the northern province where the revolt began. During Cuba's nineteenth-century sugar boom, the island's whites almost always outnumbered the slaves, but in the western districts—which featured revolutionary plots in 1812 and 1843–1844, a major slave revolt in 1825, and scattered African ethnic uprisings—slaves formed a substantial majority of the population.

A noteworthy number of plots and revolts began on estates with absentee masters (for example, Surinam, 1757; Tortola, 1790; Santo Domingo, 1796). Most rebel leaders initiated movements at moments of real or perceived weakening of the internal forces of control, taking advantage of imperial rivalries (for example, St. Kitts, 1778; Curaçao, 1800; Cuba, 1843–1844), redeployed troops and decaying garrisons (for example, Berbice, 1763; Jamaica, 1776; Grenada, 1795), and divisions within the ruling elite or among other social groups (for example, Venezuela, 1731–1733; Grenada, 1795; Brazil, 1798).

DESERTION AND THE MORAL ECONOMY

Throughout Latin America and the Caribbean, masters (or their surrogates) and slaves established relations with a pronounced ethical dimension, a kind of moral economy. Provisioning crises and abrupt violations or reversals of the unwritten ground rules on a plantation—whether triggered by warfare, natural disaster, or human idiosyncrasy—occasionally sharpened the slaves' sense of injustice to the point of rebellion (for example, Barbados, 1649; St. Croix, 1759; Brazil, 1822). Favorable terrain better prepared slave leaders to open lines of communication with other rebel slaves, mobilize followers, and conduct subversive activity, although access to inhospitable frontiers could also siphon off discontented slaves to such an extent that it undercut more ambitious projects of resistance. With vast hinterlands to the south and west, respectively, Surinam and Brazil became more noted for the size and activity of their communities of runaway slaves than for the magnitude of their open slave revolts. An extensive revolutionary conspiracy that joined African and Creole slaves in Antigua in 1736 formed only after the planting elite had diminished opportunities for slave desertion by clearing almost all of the island for cultivation.

Masters tried to maintain order by using divide-and-rule techniques. But in differentiating slaves by privilege and status, masters also created space within their society for the emergence of rebel leaders. In most major slave revolts in Latin America and the Caribbean, privileged slaves assumed leadership. From their advantaged position, they enjoyed more freedom of movement with which to meet and recruit their fellow slaves, to detect white weaknesses, and to obtain information about events in the wider world. Enslaved agricultural foremen (drivers) figured prominently as leaders in many of the largest slave revolts of the eighteenth and nineteenth centuries (for example, Saint-Domingue, 1791; Barbados, 1816; Cuba, 1825). That many African slaves came from warrior cultures contributed to revolt in the Americas, and generations of resistance by African and Creole slaves created in certain zones and districts what even white contemporaries saw as a kind of tradition of rebellion.

Large-scale revolts embraced different kinds of slaves: privileged and unprivileged, African and Creole, male and female, mulattos and blacks, rural and urban. Female slaves fought and died in slave revolts but rarely led them. Internal divisions, including rivalries between African ethnicities, help explain why the number of betrayed revolts probably exceeded the number of those that got off the ground. Big revolts developed multiple lines of authorities and often appear less as a homogenous mass than as loose coalitions of enslaved groups that might also attach themselves to disaffected nonslaves. In an ambiguous position, Indians and free people of color served as both allies of rebel slaves and as agents of their repression.

Slaves usually planned their revolts to begin under the cover of darkness and at time of white distraction, such as Sundays and holidays. All Latin American and Caribbean masters learned to keep up their guards during the Christmas season. In Catholic countries, Epiphany, Holy Week, and saints' days also became favored moments of slave revolt. Easter and Whitsuntide proved to be popular for slave rebels in the British Caribbean. Slave revolts often suffered from a lack of coordination, and nowhere, it appears, did clock time enter into the calculations of slave leaders. Information passed at funerals, on the docks, in churches, taverns, and social clubs, and along waterways. Before, during, and after the revolt in Saint-Domingue rumors of an impending or suppressed metropolitan decree of emancipation mobilized slaves to revolt in a number of Latin American and Caribbean colonies (for example, Mexico, 1735; Venezuela, 1749; Curaçao, 1795).

ACCOMMODATION AND THE END OF SLAVERY

Given the grisly outcome of virtually all slave revolts and the class bias of the available documentary evidence, the specific goals of the insurgents remain difficult to discern. To be sure, at one level, most slaves revolted to escape their enslavement, although numerous cases exist of insurgencies that started as attempts by slaves to extract concessions from masters or redress perceived violations of the unwritten rules on an estate rather than as a fundamental challenge to the institution of slavery as such. How masters responded to challenges from below often proved to be as important in the course of slave revolt as what the rebel slaves accomplished themselves. In any given slave revolt, individual rebels could have multiple goals, including personal liberation, plunder, access to land, extermination of whites, return to Africa, legal rights, or the creation of a new society with varying degrees of African influences. Leaders could have goals that differed from those of the soldiers; African-born rebels did not necessarily have the same aims as their Creole counterparts.

Slave revolt, like all forms of slave resistance, countered the dehumanizing logic of an ancient institution rooted in the notion of enslavement as a living death that substituted for actual death in warfare. Throughout Latin America and the Caribbean, both the fear and reality of slave revolt and the toll of lives and property drove masters into tense negotiations with their slaves. Everywhere slaves achieved incremental gains, qualifying their dependency in ways that enhanced their dignity, improved their material well-being, and better prepared them for further struggles ahead. In this process, accommodation served not as an alternative to revolt but as a prerequisite to it. Some of the more enduring slave codes, passed in the aftermath of slave revolt, contain articles intended to tighten controls and deter prospective rebels. But more often than not, these codes also conceded a carrot in attempting to guarantee slaves a minimal standard of living.

Much debate has focused on the role of slave revolt in ending slavery in the Americas. Although at one level the decisive forces in the destruction of slavery as a social system lay outside Latin America and the Caribbean, the discrete paths to freedom cannot be understood apart from the collective violence and other initiatives of the slaves themselves, as the events of 1848 in Martinique and the Danish Virgin Islands or those of the 1880s in Cuba and Brazil attest.

See also *Haitian Revolution of Independence (1791–1804); Inequality; Injustice; L'Ouverture, François-Dominique Toussaint; Race; Rights; U.S. Slave Revolts (1776–1865).*

ROBERT L. PAQUETTE

BIBLIOGRAPHY

Craton, Michael. *Testing the Chains: Resistance to Slavery in the British West Indies.* Ithaca, N.Y.: Cornell University Press, 1983.

Fick, Carolyn E. *The Making of Haiti: The Saint Domingue Revolution from Below.* Knoxville: University of Tennessee Press, 1990.

Gaspar, David Barry. *Bondmen and Rebels: A Study of Master-Slave Relations in Antigua.* Baltimore, Md.: Johns Hopkins University Press, 1985.

Geggus, David Patrick, and David Barry Gaspar, eds. *A Turbulent Time: The French Revolution and the Greater Caribbean.* Bloomington: Indiana University Press, 1997.

Genovese, Eugene D. *From Rebellion to Revolution: The Afro-American Slave Revolts in the Making of the Modern World.* Baton Rouge: Louisiana State University Press, 1979.

Paquette, Robert L. *Sugar Is Made with Blood: The Conspiracy of La Escalera and the Conflict between Empires over Slavery in Cuba.* Middletown, Conn.: Wesleyan University Press, 1988.

Reis, João José. *Slave Rebellion in Brazil: The Muslim Uprising of 1835 in Bahia.* Baltimore, Md.: Johns Hopkins University Press, 1993.

Viotti da Costa, Emilia. *Crowns of Glory, Tears of Blood: The Demerara Slave Rebellion of 1823.* New York: Oxford University Press, 1994.

LATIN AMERICAN POPULAR AND GUERRILLA REVOLTS (INDEPENDENCE TO 1959)

Popular revolts and guerrilla resistance have marked Latin American history since independence. In response to the Napoleonic takeover of Spain in 1808, Latin American elites mobilized to create and control national states. Long conflicts against forces loyal to Spain, however, led to diverse forms of popular mobilization. From the 1810 Hidalgo revolt in Mexico's Bajío region, to the rise of Afro-Venezuelan *llanero* guerrillas, to the activities of indigenous *montoneras* in the Andes, between 1810 and 1825 popular forces at times joined the armies of independence, at times opposed them, and at times took advantage of them to pursue independent agendas.

POPULAR PARTICIPATION IN NATION BUILDING, 1810–1900

From the 1820s on, elites struggled to rule emerging national states. Promises of popular sovereignty justified independence and led to republican institutions. Simultaneously, elite fears of popular power led to limits on effective popular participation via property and literacy requirements for voting and indirect elections. Popular forces, however, had refused to demobilize after independence. In the Mexican Bajío, heartland of the Hidalgo revolt, the mass insurrection in 1810 gave way to a decade of agrarian resistance that ended commercial-estate production and created a society of *rancheros*—tenant families controlling production on estate lands through the mid-nineteenth century. The participation of slaves and their descendants in the wars for independence also forced emerging nations to address the institution of slavery. Most abolished it in the first decades of national life.

Postcolonial nations proved to be difficult and long-contested creations. The decades from the 1820s to the 1870s brought persistent wars over the dimensions of new nations and over the definition and control of state powers. Elite factions repeatedly mobilized popular groups in battles to define national boundaries, political institutions, and ideological visions, while the popular forces demanded concessions in exchange for their armed participation. When popular concerns were ignored, political warfare often gave way to independent popular resistance.

In Mexico the conflicts of the 1820s over provincial autonomy and central power evolved in the 1830s into confrontations between liberalism and conservatism. Vicente Guerrero, who had led guerrillas fighting for independence between 1811 and 1821, in the 1820s demanded provincial autonomy and effective popular participation in national affairs. He became president in 1829, only to be ousted and killed. The popular movement continued from the 1830s under Juan Alvárez, who defended local autonomy, community land rights, and popular government. He led Mexican liberals to national power in the 1850s. In victory, however, the liberal movement became dominated by more urban, ideological forces. Provincial autonomy was attacked, and church and community landholding abolished. Liberal consolidation was delayed for decades as peasant village resistance and revolts for provincial autonomy mixed with conservative opposition and French intervention. The liberals' return to state power in 1867 ended clerical and conservative opposition, but peasant and provincial resistance challenged the liberal hegemony via numerous regional insurrections through the 1870s.

In Yucatán, Mayan leaders mobilized popular groups after 1812, claiming local autonomy under the Spanish liberal constitution. During the decades that followed, Yucatecan elites negotiated their place within the Mexican nation, while Mayan communities negotiated places in Yucatán. They demanded the political participation promised by liberalism while opposing the commercialism and land privatization promoted by Yucatecan liberals. Decades of participation in local politics brought Mayan villagers promises repeatedly broken. Recruited to fight in armed factions led by elites, Maya emerged armed and disillusioned. When Mexico faced war against the United States in 1847, Mayan communities rose in arms against the Yucatecan state, its taxes, and land privatization. In a war for Mayan independence, labeled a "caste war" by elite opponents, the rebels all but ruled the region for several years, remained in the field for over a decade, and, once state power was reestablished, maintained a Maya state of resistance in the interior into the early twentieth century.

Central American independence brought labyrinthine conflicts over whether to become one nation or five.

Simultaneously, liberals challenged traditional Hispanic culture and politics. In 1838 Rafael Carrera led an insurrection insisting that Guatemala become a separate nation, opposing liberal attacks on the church, and defending community lands from privatization. Indigenous villagers joined him in defense of the church and their community lands. Guatemala's one export product, cochineal dye, was produced by landed villagers. In a new nation dependent on village production, the Conservative Carrera mobilized villagers in defense of local autonomy, village landholding, and traditional colonial culture. Their success consolidated Guatemala as a nation and delayed liberal state building and plantation development for decades.

Brazilian independence emerged from the machinations of Portuguese monarchs transported to Rio de Janeiro amid the Napoleonic conflicts. The decades after the proclamation of the Brazilian Empire in 1822 brought revolts against centralizing power in northeastern sugar regions and in the southern pastoral zone of Rio Grande do Sul. Amid these conflicts over imperial power, numerous slave revolts developed, notably the Muslim uprising of 1835 in the northeastern state of Bahía. Imperial consolidation inhibited regional resistance after 1840, and slave resistance was increasingly contained. But when a national abolition movement developed in the 1870s, slaves used work disruptions, flight, and local conflicts to help force formal emancipation in 1888.

In Andean regions of South America, the slow consolidation of national states brought local conflicts and international wars. In the War of the Pacific of 1879–1883, Chile and Peru disputed control of valuable coastal nitrate zones. Peruvian elites mobilized indigenous guerrillas in defense of the nation. Simultaneously fighting Chilean armies and negotiating with Andean peasant communities, Peruvian elites came to fear popular mobilization more than defeat by Chile. They negotiated a peace favorable to Chile and turned to containing popular insurrections. Yet popular resistance continued, often in pursuit of land and local autonomy, as in the Atusparia uprising of 1885.

Conflicts over nation building also brought popular mobilization in Cuba, a Spanish colony throughout the nineteenth century. The Escalera conspiracy of 1843 united British abolitionists, Cuban slaves, and free people of color demanding an end to slavery. Dissident planters and intellectuals rebelled in 1868 seeking independence and offering freedom to slaves who joined them. Slaves came to the cause in large numbers, making slavery a key issue. The planter elites divided, many refusing to consider abolition, thus facilitating a Spanish victory in 1878. Spain announced slavery's abolition in 1880, a process completed in 1886. Cuban planters, angered by Spain's turn against slavery, again divided in the face of a second war for independence, this one led by José Martí in 1895. Martí recruited among former slaves, many frustrated with the limited gains allowed them by a very restricted emancipation. Their roles made Afro-Cuban political power and land-rights central to the war for independence, leading many planters to accept the U.S. invasion, which imposed a limited independence in 1898 and blocked Afro-Cuban rights. Conflicts over U.S. power, planter dominance, and Afro-Cuban rights would persist well into the new century.

GUERRILLA RESISTANCE AND WORKERS MOBILIZATIONS, 1900–1959

Fundamental social, cultural, and political conflicts continued across Latin America in the twentieth century. They became national revolutions in Mexico in 1910, Bolivia in 1952, and Cuba in 1959; a nationalist reform in Guatemala from 1944 to 1954; and the persistent *violencia* of twentieth-century Colombia.

Less transforming conflicts developed elsewhere. Rising U.S. power and repeated interventions, especially in small nations, led to adamant resistance. From 1917 to 1922, popular guerrillas fought U.S. forces occupying the Dominican Republic. In Nicaragua, Augusto César Sandino led guerrillas against U.S. marines and their Nicaraguan allies in the late 1920s. Elsewhere, popular resistance challenged local elites and exclusionary state powers. In El Salvador, Agustin Farabundo Martí led communist organizers, including many artisans, in proselytizing among rural families expropriated by the coffee-export economy. When that economy collapsed in the depression amid political conflicts, peasant insurrection began in Salvadoran coffee zones early in 1932—only to face the repression known as the *matanza* ("slaughter"). That brutality consolidated the rule of Gen. Maximiliano Martinez Hernandez, who fell in 1944 to the nonviolent mobilization of urban protesters.

The twentieth century also brought rapid industrialization and urbanization across Latin America, along with labor mobilization and urban resistance. Union organization and strikes peaked after World War II in Argentina, Brazil, Chile, and Mexico. As labor power increased, it often met violent repression. Yet organized workers found ways to promote labor agendas, often in the face of authoritarian regimes, but at times amid national mobilizations that allowed them to act more openly. The populist experiments of Getúlio Vargas in Brazil (1930–1945 and 1950–1954), Lázaro Cárdenas in Mexico (1934–1940), and Juan Domingo Perón in Argentina (1944–1955), along with the contemporary popular front governments of Chile, all responded to rising labor power by attempting to meet workers' demands while also capturing their organized power to reinforce industrialization. Workers' gains were real, yet limited. Populist rulers gave way to more conservative, often military, authoritarian regimes. But populist experiments demonstrated that mobilized urban workers had become major participants in national developments.

Since independence, popular groups have promoted alternative visions of work, family, community, politics, and culture across Latin America. Some worked within movements for independence and national consolidation, whereas others became forces of opposition—turning to insurrection when grievances peaked and opportunities emerged. In the twentieth century, some popular groups joined national revolutions. Others negotiated limited changes within established regimes. By diverse means, popular groups ranging from slaves to peasants to urban workers have adapted to changing circumstances and participated in movements of incorporation and of resistance in Latin American nations.

See also *Guatemalan Revolution (1944–1954); Guerrilla Warfare; Júarez, Benito; Latin American Revolutions for Independence (1808–1898); Martí, José; Mexican Revolution (1910–1940); Sandino, Augusto César; Zapata, Emiliano.*

JOHN TUTINO

BIBLIOGRAPHY

Bergquist, Charles. *Labor in Latin America: Comparative Essays on Chile, Argentina, Venezuela, and Colombia.* Stanford: Stanford University Press, 1986.

Guardino, Peter. *Peasants, Politics, and the Formation of Mexico's National State: Guerrero, 1800–1857.* Stanford: Stanford University Press, 1997.

Mallon, Florencia. *Peasant and Nation: The Making of Postcolonial Mexico and Peru.* Berkeley: University of California Press, 1993.

Paquette, Robert. *Sugar Is Made with Blood: The Conspiracy of la Escalera and the Conflict between Empires over Slavery in Cuba.* Middletown, Conn.: Wesleyan University Press, 1988.

Reis, João José. *Slave Rebellion in Brazil: The Muslim Uprising of 1835.* Baltimore, Md.: Johns Hopkins University Press, 1993.

Rugeley, Terry. *Yucatan's Maya Peasants and the Origins of the Caste War.* Austin: University of Texas Press, 1996.

Tutino, John. *From Insurrection to Revolution in Mexico: Social Bases of Agrarian Violence, 1750–1940.* Princeton, N.J.: Princeton University Press, 1986.

LATIN AMERICAN POPULAR AND GUERRILLA REVOLTS (1960–1996)

The Cuban Revolution (in part) gave rise to many popular revolts, mainly by ideological inspiration but less regularly via direct aid and training. Régis Debray's famous *Revolution in the Revolution?* described how older, often reformist communist-party activity gave way by the 1960s to a newly inspired, energetic, and violent turn toward rural guerrilla warfare and sometimes its urban counterpart. Most guerrilla groups either splintered from left-wing parties, including the communists, or were direct creations of the communists. The leader-organizers of these new movements were overwhelmingly young, highly educated men from the urban middle and upper classes and from rural elites. After 1970 the main change in the membership was the greater participation of women as leaders and regulars (some organizations later containing one-third or more women) and more ethnic minorities in the rank and file.

THE ORIGINS AND SHIFTING FORTUNES OF RURAL AND URBAN REVOLUTIONARY MOVEMENTS

Albeit less frequently than is often claimed, the Cuban revolutionary regime gave substantial aid, most commonly in the form of training, to some guerrilla groups in the 1960s. Cuba aided the Armed Forces of National Liberation (FALN; here and elsewhere using the Spanish acronyms) in Venezuela, the Rebel Armed Forces (FAR) in Guatemala, the Army of National Liberation (ELN) in Colombia, the Movement of the Revolutionary Left (MIR) in Peru, and, of course, Che Guevara's own 1966–1967 Bolivian adventure, where his death led to a short-term ebb tide in new regional insurgencies. The clear exception was Colombia, where rural upheavals ranging from pure revolutionism to outright and violent banditry both predated and postdated Cuban influences. Clearly, that nation was a special case, especially in the decades-long actions of groups like the Colombian Revolutionary Armed Forces (FARC) and the ELN.

In the mid-1960s Guevara and Debray outlined a strategy, which Che put into practice, of building from a small rural nucleus (or *foco)* a guerrilla army that could confront and eventually defeat a regular army. The "*foco*" theory of revolution came under both ideological and practical critique, including a roughly decade-long impetus toward forming, instead, "urban guerrilla" movements. Their leadership was strikingly similar to that of the rural groups, save for an earlier trend toward female membership. They were also, appropriately, far more active and newsworthy in the more urbanized and developed nations, especially Argentina, Brazil, Chile, and Uruguay. Notably, their actions resembled those of the Red-Brigades in Germany and Italy.

The partial, if short-lived, successes and the memberships of the European and the Latin American urban guerrillas were remarkably alike and are probably best understood in similar terms. Their urban "terrorist" (a sometimes accurate term) activities, and later the substantial urban uprisings during the Nicaraguan Revolution and the Salvadoran insurgency, often led analysts to perceive a major shift from rural guerrilla war toward urban insurrection in Latin America. In fact, rural guerrillas usually had substantial urban support networks and activities; these were exceptionally visible in Havana and Caracas at the height of events in Cuba and Venezuela. The left's new optimism about urban guerrillas' prospects often ignored just how often and regularly governments—whose military and infrastructural strength is greatest in the towns, not the countryside—crushed the urban revolutionaries. Governments scored major victories in urban areas over the Tupamaros of Uruguay; the MIR in Chile (following the 1973 overthrow of Salvador Allende); the Brazilian National Liberating Action (ALN), led by urban-guerrilla theoretician Carlos Marighella; and the strongest urban group of all, the left-Peronist Montoneros of Argentina.

The supposed "end" of revolutionary upheavals with Guevara's 1967 death was greatly exaggerated. Multiple and major revolutionary groups took hold or grew stronger after the early 1970s. Several different guerrilla organizations in El Salvador united as the Farabundo Martí Front for National Liberation (FMLN). In Guatemala, a parallel, Salvador-inspired process led multiple guerrilla groups to come together in the 1980s and 1990s in an umbrella organization known as the Guatemalan National Revolutionary Unity (URNG). Cuban aid was never decisive in the movements' fortunes in the 1970s and 1980s, even though in this period it often came in the form of direct or indirect arms shipments and not just training of combatants. It was probably greatest for the FMLN, less for the Sandinistas, and much less for the URNG. Cuban aid had little bearing on the long-term insurgency in Colombia, which was periodically fractured by electoral openings then reinvigorated, with the ELN taking the more decisive role that the FARC had exercised earlier. Last, Cuban aid was utterly irrelevant in the extreme case of Peru's Shining Path guerrillas, whose origins lay in multiple and ever-more Maoist splinterings from the Peruvian Communist Party. Along with Guevara's Bolivian disaster, the Shining Path is also one of the few movements whose strength and fortunes were deeply damaged by the capture or death of a leader, in this case that of Abimael Guzmán Reynoso in 1992.

WHY SOME REVOLUTIONARY MOVEMENTS FARED BETTER THAN OTHERS

If "foreign aid" was at best only a secondary contributor to the growth, staying power, or occasional successes (Cuba, Nicaragua) of the many rural revolutionary movements, the real keys to their successes and failures lay largely in the (non)support of the peasantry and in national political contexts.

Peasants came to constitute a majority of most rural guerrilla movements. John Booth, Cynthia McClintock, and Timothy Wickham-Crowley, among others, have made roughly similar cases for economic grievances as underlying the growth of some, but not all, of these revolutionary movements. They sometimes also studied nations and cases without substantial rural guerrilla activity for contrast. Booth focused on income levels and distribution in five Central American nations after 1970, McClintock on El Salvador and Peru 1980–1992, and Wickham-Crowley on different rural class structures and shifts in land-tenure for a dozen different national movements from 1956 to 1991. Wickham-Crowley found that areas with disproportionate numbers of squatters, sharecroppers, or recently displaced cultivators were more likely to support insurgencies than were neighboring regions with fewer such people. While the more recent Chiapas rebellion in Mexico is often claimed to be a highly novel, even "postmodern" rural insurrection, the historically and relatively severe *and* worsening patterns of income and land-tenure in Chiapas make that uprising mostly intelligible in the same terms as previous guerrilla movements: peasant economic grievances conjoining with nonpeasant mobilizers in armed insurrection.

Yet not all features associated with greater popular support for, or membership in, insurgent movements are economic in any neat sense. Wickham-Crowley also found stronger insurgencies where the incipient guerrilla movements could take hold of preexisting linkages in the countryside, where guerrilla leaders could approach and recruit peasants, not as strangers, but as members of the same groups (such as unions or left-wing parties) or even as community members. Such structured access to the peasantry was especially visible in the early expansion and success of Peru's Shining Path, which was deeply rooted in a provincial, highlands university attended by the descendants of Quechua-speaking peasants; the relations established there were the foundation of the Shining Path's link to a lower-class, Andean rank and file. Wickham-Crowley and others have also tried to make a case that long-term peasant "cultures of resistance" vary from region to region and from nation to nation, also conducing (or not) different peasantries toward support of rural revolutionaries. The Colombian interior and far eastern Cuba both clearly showed this more supportive pattern.

Unsurprisingly, since revolutions involve the overthrow of state power, analysts have also focused on those states whose structures or actions tend to "push" the populace toward or away from support for revolutionaries. While Booth, McClintock, and others often emphasize the distributional effects of state policies on peasant living standards, other scholars focus on states as repressive agents and on state-based regimes that permit effective popular political participation or exclude it. Democratically elected governments have consistently been able to sap the strength from insurgencies by providing the populace with political choices and alternatives: witness the 1990s peace accords in El Salvador and Guatemala. Although exclusionary dictatorial regimes are sometimes able to repress insurgents, they rarely can induce lasting peace. Jeff Goodwin has directly traced the growth of many large-scale insurgencies to the terroristic actions of state actors (especially the military), including cases where the growing insurgency later seizes power (Nicaragua) where governments can terrorize certain populaces and regions but cannot effectively govern them (as in certain northern regions of El Salvador or western regions of Guatemala during the 1980s). He and other scholars have drawn attention to one regime-type with a unique vulnerability to revolutionary overthrow: the dictatorial, highly personalized and privatized control of the state, government, and armed forces known as the "patrimonial praetorian regime." Such dictators have fallen to revolutionary upheavals (Fulgencio Batista in Cuba, Anastasio Somoza in Nicaragua) but also to cross-class, populist upheavals without clear revolutionary traits (the Haitians' ouster of Jean-Claude "Baby Doc" Duvalier and the Filipinos' ouster of Ferdinand Marcos). Such overthrows in Latin America and elsewhere have typically been carried out by a massive, antidictatorial, cross-class coalition, with guerrilla revolutionaries in the forefront of the opposition but far from alone.

See also *Cuban Revolution (1956–1970); Grenada "New Jewel" Revolution (1979–1983); Guerrilla Warfare; Guevara, Ernesto "Che"; Nicaraguan Revolution (1979); Peruvian "Shining Path" Revolt (1980–).*

TIMOTHY P. WICKHAM-CROWLEY

BIBLIOGRAPHY

Allemann, Fritz René. *Macht und Ohnmacht der Guerilla.* Munich: R. Piper, 1974.

Berardo, João Batista. *Guerrilhas e guerrilheiros no drama da América Latina.* São Paulo, Brazil: Edições Populares, 1981.

Booth, John. "Socioeconomic and Political Roots of National Revolts in Central America." *Latin American Research Review* 26, no. 1 (1991): 33–73.

Goodwin, Jeff. *State and Revolution, 1945–1991.* Cambridge: Cambridge University Press, 1998.

Gott, Richard. *Guerrilla Movements in Latin America.* London: Nelson and Sons, 1970.

Gross, Liza. *Handbook of Leftist Guerrilla Groups in Latin America and the Caribbean.* Boulder, Colo.: Westview, 1995.

Kohl, James, and John Litt, eds. *Urban Guerrilla Warfare in Latin America.* Cambridge, Mass.: M.I.T. Press, 1974.

McClintock, Cynthia. *Revolutionary Movements in Latin America: El Salvador's FMLN and Peru's Shining Path.* Washington, D.C. : United States Institute of Peace Press, 1998.

Wickham-Crowley, Timothy P. *Guerrillas and Revolution in Latin America: A Comparative Study of Insurgents and Regimes since 1956.* Princeton, N.J.: Princeton University Press, 1992.

LATIN AMERICAN REVOLTS UNDER COLONIAL RULE (1571–1898)

For much of its colonial history Latin America experienced few revolts in its core areas of central Mexico and the Andean zone, but this peacefulness disappeared in the late eighteenth century. The uprisings fall into five categories: native revolts, slave uprisings, urban riots, frontier uprisings, and regional rebellions involving several groups at a time.

RELATIVE TRANQUILLITY IN CORE AREAS BEFORE 1700

Native communities decimated by epidemics following the Spanish conquest did not compete for land or water until the end of the seventeenth century. Because many communities had previously been subjects of indigenous empires and found much familiar in the Spanish system, they often bargained effectively with the colonial administration in matters involving tribute and labor service, selection of leaders, censuses, and the setting of boundaries.

Resistance was rampant among the black slaves brought to America by the Spanish, but that resistance generally consisted of work slowdowns, property destruction, and flight. Slave rebellions were recorded in Mexico in 1546, 1570, 1608, and 1670; in Colombia in 1550; and in Venezuela in 1552, the 1730s, and 1789. Overall, these were spontaneous events that expressed local grievances. The historical record contains no evidence of a revolt aimed at overthrowing the institution of slavery until close to 1800.

Several factors account for the quiescence of the growing urban centers. The lower classes were divided along ethnic lines, and business and property owners commonly maintained patron-client relationships with their workers. Cities contained social welfare institutions, such as hospitals and orphanages, and price controls generally kept staples affordable. Finally, cities contained civic patrols and militias as repressive instruments. As a result, urban riots in Mexico City in 1624 and 1692 were exceptional occurrences that were not repeated until the late eighteenth century.

NATIVE REVOLTS ALONG THE FRONTIERS

Frontier uprisings by tribal societies were quite frequent throughout the colonial period. Many took place in northern Mexico, where colonial authorities pursued an aggressive policy of relocating tribes onto remote missions, using military force as needed. South American tribes rarely faced comparable relocation efforts, and frontier uprisings were rarer. One exception was the insurgency led by Juan Santos Atahualpa, a Jesuit-educated highland Indian, in the tropical lowlands of eastern Peru in 1742–1752. Santos repeatedly raided the densely populated central highlands bordering his jungle base, elicited some support among native communities there, and was never defeated. The colonial authorities finally curtailed his attacks by constructing fortresses along the eastern edge of the highlands.

Frontier uprisings typically occurred several decades after a mission's establishment. By then epidemics had greatly reduced the native population, weakening the indigenous culture. In such circumstances, some peoples attempted nativist revolts to purge themselves of European culture and return to traditional ways. In northern Mexico the Tepehuanes rebelled in 1616, the Conchos in 1640, the Tarahumaras in 1648 and the 1690s, and the Yaquis in 1740. The insurgents typically killed all Spaniards in the vicinity, including missionaries, and razed buildings before fleeing. They believed their traditional gods rendered them impervious to harm.

Nativist revolts typically involved only a single people, but the Pueblo Revolt in New Mexico in 1680 united native communities behind the shaman Popé. By the time a Spanish expedition reentered Pueblo territory in 1692, the alliance had collapsed, and colonists resettled the area.

Southern Mexico, lightly settled by Spaniards, experienced one notable frontier uprising, the Tzeltal Revolt of 1712. A maiden in Cancuc, who claimed to be in communication with the Virgin Mary, became the center of a cult that incorporated many elements of traditional native belief and practice and sought to eliminate all who were not Tzeltal. The Catholic Church denounced the cult, sparking a violent protest. Some priests were among those killed. After several months, a Spanish military force destroyed the cult with considerable loss of life.

EIGHTEENTH-CENTURY REVOLTS

Dramatic changes in Latin America in the eighteenth century engendered a wave of revolts that continued even after the nations of the region achieved independence from Spain. Growing numbers of colonists and Indians raised demands for land and water resources. As colonial economies grew in size and importance, Spain and Portugal sought to tighten political control over their possessions, increase tax revenue, and direct their economies in ways that would benefit the mother countries. Ideas of balanced government, political equality, and civil liberties, derived from the European Enlightenment, penetrated the colonies widely.

Informed by Western political thought, slaves revolted with increasing frequency, beginning with the Haitian Revolution of 1791–1804. Rebels now sought to overthrow slavery rather than escape it. From 1807 to 1835, uprisings led by Hausa and Yoruba slaves of the Muslim faith swept Bahia, Brazil. Cuba experienced numerous slave rebellions after 1840.

Native groups in Mexico and the Andes rebelled against the Spanish authorities and the successor governments throughout the eighteenth century and into the nineteenth, protesting disruptions of established local patterns by censuses or boundary surveys, increased taxes, labor service requirements, and proposed changes in religious personnel, practices, or beliefs. Most such uprisings were local affairs, spontaneous and short-lived, involving entire village populations without spreading to adjacent communities. Participants rarely used weapons, resorting instead to farming tools and household implements. Violence and property destruction were targeted and limited. An exception occurred in 1750, when Indians from Lima and the adjacent province of Huarochirí plotted to exterminate the Spanish. They were denounced and the plot suppressed before the revolt could begin.

Urban riots proliferated in the late colonial period. Disturbances occurred in Quito, Ecuador, in 1765; Guanajuato, San Luis de la Paz, and San Luis Potosí, Mexico, in 1767; Arequipa, Peru, in 1780; and Pasto, Colombia, in 1780 and 1800. The Mexican uprisings protested the expulsion of the Jesuit order. The others targeted revised tax structures; new royal monopolies on tobacco, liquor, and playing cards; and the exclusion of local people from colonial posts. In these uprisings, which lasted for periods ranging from a few days to several months, the Creole elite allied with the lower classes—including urban Indians—although each group had distinct interests. Because local militias were headed by the Creoles spearheading the uprisings, the colonial government had few means of suppression available and often agreed initially to the rioters' demands. Once the movements had lost their impetus, however, authorities would arrest some of the ringleaders and reimpose the taxes or monopolies that had occasioned the protest. The second imposition typically did not engender further protest.

Beginning in the 1780s regional rebellions staged by multiple groups struck the empire. The most notable were the Tupac Amaru Revolt of 1780–1783 in highland Peru and the 1781 Comunero Revolt in Socorro, Colombia. As with urban riots, popular animosity against new economic and political policies engendered these insurgencies. The Tupac Amaru Revolt was led by a provincial native headman whose claim to Incan lineage and denunciation of the government's labor and tribute demands drew support from the highland

Indians. Some Creoles, mixed bloods, and blacks responded to other issues. The rebellion resulted in about 100,000 fatalities but never expanded beyond the highlands. Subsequent uprisings, especially in Bolivia, were more narrowly indigenous in composition.

The Comunero Revolt began as an urban protest against increased taxes, restrictions on tobacco cultivation, and the strict government liquor monopoly. The disturbance spread quickly through the province of Socorro, and affiliated uprisings sprang up some distance away. Inept efforts at suppression enhanced its popularity, and when the rebels threatened the capital of Bogotá, colonial administrators became conciliatory, renounced the detested policies, and granted a broad pardon.

In 1789 some elite residents of Minas Gerais, Brazil, conspired to seek independence for Brazil, but the movement was discovered before it got started. In 1798 members of the urban working class in Bahia, many of mixed-race ancestry, plotted to gain independence for Brazil and to abolish slavery, but their movement, too, was suppressed before it began.

Between 1868 and 1878 eastern Cuba was racked by the Ten Years War, in which some forty thousand Creoles, mixed bloods, and free blacks fought unsuccessfully for independence. This poor part of the island suffered disproportionately from restrictive trade policies, a regressive tax structure, and increasing political repression. The refusal of the revolt's white leadership to move the war into the vulnerable sugar-plantation zone and to denounce slavery limited its range and appeal. The Pact of Zanjón, which ended the revolt in 1878, promised political reforms, a general amnesty, and freedom to slaves and indentured workers in the insurgent army. Thus, like the regional revolts on the Latin American mainland in the late eighteenth century, the Ten Years War served as a prelude to the independence movement that followed some twenty years later.

See also *Haitian Revolution of Independence (1791–1804); Latin American and Caribbean Slave Revolts (1521–1888); Latin American Revolutions for Independence (1808–1898); L'Ouverture, François-Dominique Toussaint.*

JOHN E. KICZA

BIBLIOGRAPHY

Deeds, Susan M. "Indigenous Rebellions on the Northern Mexican Mission Frontier: From First-Generation to Later Colonial Responses." In *Contested Ground: Comparative Frontiers on the Northern and Southern Edges of the Spanish Empire.* Edited by Donna J. Guy and Thomas E. Sheridan. Tucson: University of Arizona Press, 1998.

Genovese, Eugene D. *From Rebellion to Revolution: Afro-American Slave Revolts in the Making of the New World.* Baton Rouge: Louisiana State University Press, 1979.

Godoy, Scarlett O'Phelan. *Rebellion and Revolts in Eighteenth Century Peru and Upper Peru.* Cologne: Böhlau Verlag, 1985.

Gosner, Kevin. *Soldiers of the Virgin: The Moral Economy of a Colonial Maya Rebellion.* Tucson: University of Arizona Press, 1992.

Katz, Friedrich. "Rural Uprisings in Preconquest and Colonial Mexico." In *Riot, Rebellion, and Revolution: Rural Social Conflict in Mexico.* Edited by Friedrich Katz. Princeton, N.J.: Princeton University Press, 1988.

McFarlane, Anthony. "Civil Disorders and Popular Protests in Late Colonial New Granada." *Hispanic American Historical Review* 64 (February 1984): 17–54.

Maxwell, Kenneth R. *Conflicts and Conspiracies: Brazil and Portugal, 1750–1808.* Cambridge: Cambridge University Press, 1973.

Phelan, John Leddy. *The People and the King: The Comunero Revolution in Colombia, 1781.* Madison: University of Wisconsin Press, 1978.

Taylor, William B. *Drinking, Homicide, and Rebellion in Colonial Mexican Villages.* Stanford: Stanford University Press, 1979.

LATIN AMERICAN REVOLUTIONS FOR INDEPENDENCE (1808–1898)

The revolutions for Latin American independence broke out in the early nineteenth century and had freed most of the American colonies of Spain and Portugal by 1825. Cuban independence, achieved in 1898, marked the end of Iberian colonial rule in the Western Hemisphere.

The struggles for independence were triggered by the Napoleonic invasion of the Iberian Peninsula in 1807–1808, which ruptured the ties between metropolises and colonies, led to declarations of self-government throughout the colonies, and created opportunities for individuals committed to independence to press their case. However, much of the colonial population remained lukewarm, even strongly opposed, to separation. As a result, force was required to end European dominance, with the ensuing wars lasting fifteen years. Yet, in some areas, notably Brazil, independence was secured relatively peacefully, underlining the differing experiences of the colonies and their varying responses to the internal and external pressures that were pushing toward separation.

Social factors played a central role in what occurred. Throughout Latin America a white minority ruled a nonwhite majority. Society was stratified by color; color served as an entrance or a barrier to wealth, social position, office, occupation, choice of marriage partner, even the clothes one might wear. In much of Latin America the nonwhite sector was composed of the descendants of the original inhabitants, with natives comprising 60 percent of the Mexican population in the late colonial period and almost as much in Peru. In addition, a substantial mixed-blood, or *mestizo,* population had emerged over the generations. In many areas blacks, imported as slaves from Africa, constituted another important nonwhite sector of the population. Peru, Venezuela,

Colombia, the Rio de la Plata, and Cuba had large populations of slaves, free blacks, and mulattos, or *pardos.* The most significant concentration of blacks was in Brazil, where in 1810 nearly two-thirds of the population was of African origin, of whom close to one million were slaves. They, along with other nonwhites, constituted much of the colony's labor force, an exploited, oppressed, and abused group at the bottom of the social ladder.

The white population in Spanish America, which in the early 1800s numbered only about three million, may have enjoyed a position of prominence over almost 14 million nonwhites, but it, too, was stratified, split between American-born whites, or creoles, and Spaniards, or *peninsulares.* There were at most only 40,000 of the latter, but their link to the metropolis produced a sense of superiority that was much resented by the creoles. The whites were also divided according to wealth, class, and position. Their different interests meant their response to crown policies often varied and led to frequent complaints, yet they were united in their determination to maintain their position atop the social ladder against the pressures of the masses below. Consequently, the whites remained loyal to Spain and Portugal, whose military might could be called on at times of unrest. Some whites may have favored political change and even separation, but most opposed and feared anything that might lead to social revolution. Their racial fears, regionalism, and class and group interests hindered the growth of a national identity.

LATE COLONIAL REFORMS

Tensions rose in the late eighteenth century as a result of changes in the relations between the metropolises and the colonies. The Iberian crowns, in an attempt to impose greater royal absolutism and more centralized administration throughout their empires, introduced various "reforms." In the case of Spain, the desire to reestablish its faded imperial glory and to impose greater efficiency and control in the colonies involved the creation of new administrative units and the appointment of new officials to replace those who were considered corrupt and inefficient. The reforms were intended in part to address a perceived threat to the colonies from Spain's European enemies—and to this end military fortifications were constructed and local militias trained—but the aim was also to take local power out of the hands of the creoles who had come to dominate in many areas. The new officials, as a result, were largely *peninsulares,* reversing a previous trend and denying creoles the opportunity to rule their own areas. The centralizing trends also led to changes in the relationship between the crown and one of its strongest supporters—and one of the colonies' most influential institutions—the Roman Catholic Church, in particular the wealthy and powerful Jesuit order. Distrusted for their wealth, independence, and influence, the Jesuits were expelled from Portugal and its dependencies in 1759 and from Spanish territory in 1767. The church in Spanish America suffered further in the early years of the nineteenth century as the cash-strapped crown sequestered church funds that had served to meet the needs of local priests.

Accompanying the administrative changes were various economic reforms also designed to benefit the Iberian nations at the expense of the colonies. In America this involved the establishment of economic monopolies, the imposition of new taxes, the improved collection of old taxes, and, in the case of the Spanish colonies, the introduction of a policy known as *comercio libre* (free trade), which was designed to stimulate the Spanish economy and extract greater quantities of American bullion by permitting more Spaniards to trade directly with America. The reforms also saw the establishment of economic societies, the application of modern technology, and the appointment of experts who were sent to the colonies to improve production, particularly in the all-important mining sector. Efficiency and higher returns lay behind these changes, but they also reflected the impact of enlightened ideas that were gradually spreading to the colonies, if only in their scientific application.

ANIMOSITY AND REBELLION

The reforms produced economic growth in parts of the colonies to the benefit of some of the population, but they also aroused widespread animosity. The imposition of a more absolutist and centralizing system challenged the traditional relationship between metropolis and colony. Spanish American elites who considered their territories equal in status to the kingdoms of Spain found their political, religious, and economic positions threatened by the appointment of Spaniards to high administrative and ecclesiastical offices and the arrival of large numbers of Spanish merchants who undercut the old monopolies. The new taxes alienated many sectors of the population, as did the removal of the Jesuits who were the sons, nephews, and grandsons of prominent creoles, the protectors of the indigenous communities, and the educators of all. Sequestration of church funds removed money from the colonial economies and added to the alienation, particularly among lower clergy.

Smoldering and widespread resentment burst into flames in various parts of Latin America during the eighteenth century. Higher taxes combined with age-old animosities, especially among the exploited groups, as well as economic distress tied to bad harvests and food shortages fomented unrest, riots, and rebellions. The most serious were the Túpac Amaru rebellion (1780–1783) in highland Peru and Upper Peru

(Bolivia), the Comunero revolt (1781) in New Granada (Colombia), and a slave revolt in Venezuela in 1795.

Although the violence indicated the depth of colonial antagonism, these revolts were not precursor movements. Few of the rebels called for independence. Rather, as in the case of the Comunero movement, the participants expressed loyalty to the crown while condemning "bad government." They wanted reform, not separation. Indeed, the unrest of the era may have reinforced loyalty, for the rebels' appeal to the Indians, slaves, and mixed-bloods for support and their call for improvements for the downtrodden renewed racial fears among the creole elite. Creole fears were intensified further by the slave uprising in the French colony of Saint-Domingue that broke out in 1791 and led to the destruction of the colony's slavery system and the creation of the independent black republic of Haiti in 1804.

Although racial fears remained a constant factor in the unfolding events, they could not prevent the growth of separatist ideas and the activities of individuals committed to independence. Radicals were few in number, but they benefited from the growing dissatisfaction with Spain. They criticized Spain for its obvious military weakness, as indicated by its various defeats at the hands of England. Spain's military failures were contrasted with the creoles' own successes against the same enemy, as in 1806 and 1807 when local militias beat off English invasions of Buenos Aires. Critics found justification for separation in the enlightened philosophies that questioned the citizens' relationship with the monarch. They also had a concrete example of these ideas in the United States, whose revolution provided a model. The French Revolution was of less importance in the conservative colonies of Latin America, although its republican features had some appeal among creoles. Prominent among them was the Venezuelan Francisco de Miranda. Miranda's life became an unending odyssey to win foreign support for his plans to free Spanish America, but his appeals and his efforts, like those of other radicals, aroused little enthusiasm until Napoleon's 1807–1808 invasion of the Iberian Peninsula.

THE OUTBREAK OF VIOLENCE

The Napoleonic invasion brought to a head the tensions of the previous decades. In the case of Portugal, the royal family fled to Rio de Janeiro, where it reestablished the court and eventually raised Brazil to equal status with Portugal. The royal presence and continuity helped prevent serious discord. In Spanish America, on the other hand, the abdication of the king created a political crisis. Since all authority came from the king, who had the right to rule? In Spain local juntas loyal to the king appeared, followed by the establishment of a Central Junta, a Regency Council, and eventually a *córtez* (or parliament) centered in Cádiz, which introduced a liberal constitution. However, their authority over the colonies was not at all clear. In the colonies the local elites responded to the shifting political reality of the metropolis in various ways that proved to be the first faltering steps in the movement toward self-government. In Peru the viceroy remained in power in the name of the king, and royalism triumphed. Elsewhere, differences between creoles and *peninsulares* and even within these groups led to competition over who should rule. In Buenos Aires the creoles, with the support of the local militia, succeeded in gaining control of the governing junta in 1810, while in Mexico City it was the *peninsulares* who dominated.

Frustration, disagreement, and ambition led quickly to violence as those claiming authority sought to impose their control over neighboring regions and towns, even though virtually all were ruling in the name of the king. In Buenos Aires the new rulers sought to dominate the entire viceroyalty, but the elites in the interior, particularly in Paraguay, forcefully rejected this domination and set up their own administration, which soon developed into de facto, if undeclared, independence. Elsewhere formal independence was declared. In July 1809 creoles in La Paz declared separation not only from Buenos Aires but also from Spain. In Caracas a group of radical creoles declared independence in July 1811.

These movements, however, failed to win widespread support as the majority of people continued to fear social unrest, and all were soon crushed. Racial fears had been sparked once again by indigenous and slave movements that accompanied the political jostling. The most violent of the early republican movements occurred in Mexico, where a conspiracy of creoles who had been antagonized by the peninsular takeover of the government erupted in September 1810, led by a disaffected priest, Father Miguel Hidalgo y Costillo. This movement differed from others in its unswerving call for independence and its appeal to the masses. The involvement of the masses threatened a real social revolution. The radicalism and violence of the movement alienated large numbers of people, leading to its eventual defeat and Hidalgo's capture and execution in July 1811. The movement continued under another priest, José María Morelos, who proved a more effective military leader, but he, too, was eventually captured and executed. Subsequently, the cause of Mexican independence remained alive only in small guerrilla bands that fought valiantly but unsuccessfully against royalist counterinsurgency measures.

The restoration of Ferdinand VII of Spain in 1814 reinvigorated the royalist cause everywhere. Absolutism was reimposed, and armies were mobilized to suppress the colonial unrest. As a result a second republic in Venezuela was crushed, largely by a royalist guerrilla force composed of interior plainsmen, or *llaneros,* and disaffected blacks. In New Granada the Spanish army destroyed local patriot-led governments. By 1815 the royalists seemed on the verge of eliminating the remaining vestiges of independent rule.

However, the independence cause survived. In Buenos Aires the creoles remained self-ruling, as did other provinces in the region. Realizing the need to solidify their position, the local elites in July 1816 declared the independence of the United Provinces of the Rio de la Plata (Argentina). To protect that independence, they recognized that royalism everywhere in the continent had to be destroyed. Argentine armies had already tried to free Montevideo, but Portuguese and later Brazilian claims to the area, as well as local demands for self-rule, led to a prolonged struggle that ended only in 1828 with the creation of Uruguay as a buffer between Argentina and Brazil. Armies also invaded Upper Peru, trying to join with local guerrilla groups committed to independence, but they were resoundingly defeated. These failures prompted an alternative strategy, to invade the royalist stronghold of Peru, via Chile, where there was strong patriot support and an unpopular Lima-imposed administration. An army led by the Argentine José Francisco de San Martín crossed the Andes in 1817, defeated the royalist armies in Chile, and declared Chilean independence in February 1818. San Martín then prepared to invade Peru.

Simultaneously, a similar movement was approaching from the north, led by the other great independence leader, the Venezuelan Simón Bolívar. Despite earlier defeats, Bolívar remained committed to the idea of independence, and, bolstered by supplies from the Haitian government, he invaded Venezuela in 1816. He brought together a number of the patriot forces, prominent among them the *llaneros,* who now supported independence, and large numbers of British and other foreign mercenaries. He neutralized black opposition by introducing antislavery legislation and freeing slaves who joined his army. In 1819 Bolívar crossed the Andes into Colombia and surprised and defeated a royalist army, permitting him to focus once more on Venezuela.

In January 1820 developments in Spain intervened again to affect the wars. Troops in Cádiz mutinied, leading to the reintroduction of liberal rule. The Spanish government ordered its generals to negotiate with the American rebels, giving the latter time to bolster their strength and causing some of the royalist generals to return to Spain. In Mexico the events provoked creole concern. They questioned whether Spain was any longer capable of protecting their interests or prepared to do so. A royalist commander, Agustín de Iturbide, with the backing of other like-minded individuals opened negotiations with the guerrillas, paving the way for a declaration of independence in September 1821. In Venezuela, Bolívar's troops defeated the remaining royalist armies, securing the country's freedom. He then turned his attention to Peru, first invading Ecuador, where his army was successful in 1822, and from there prepared to move south.

Peru remained a royalist bastion. While the events in Spain weakened royalist support and permitted San Martín to invade, a royalist army continued to function with significant local backing. San Martín's declaration of Peruvian independence in July 1821 failed to alter the situation, and, seeking assistance, he traveled north to Guayaquil, where he met Bolívar in July 1822. San Martín bowed out before the younger and more dynamic Bolívar, who took charge of the Peruvian struggle the following year. Even though the return of absolutism in Spain once more divided royalist support in Spanish America, a powerful royalist army remained in the field. Bolívar's army defeated it first at Junín in August 1824 and then definitively at Ayacucho in December. A remaining royalist army in Upper Peru was defeated the following year, freeing the region that would become known as Bolivia after its liberator.

Events in Brazil had also been affected by developments in Europe. Liberals took over the Portuguese government following the defeat of Napoleon and forced the return of the emperor in 1821. Determined to reestablish Portuguese dominance over Brazil, the legislators introduced various restrictive laws and mobilized Portuguese troops. In 1822 the son of the emperor, who had been left in Brazil as regent, declared Brazil's independence. With the backing of the nation's conservative, Catholic, slaveholding landowners, who had been antagonized by the latest demands from Lisbon, he was named Pedro I, Emperor of Brazil.

RESULTS

Throughout Latin America, the confrontations and struggles of 1808–1825 left a heritage of divisions that led to many more years of conflict. Separation from Spain unleashed centrifugal forces, with the new leaders squabbling over the nature of the new governments. Conservatives confronted liberals, while centralists opposed federalists. The result was continuing civil strife and instability. Central to the postindependence developments were the military heroes who claimed leadership of the new countries. These military strongmen, or *caudillos,* with their regional, provincial, and national support, kept much of Latin America in flames in the early nineteenth century and made the military the arbiter of political affairs. The unsettled conditions were tied also to the economic weakness of the new states as they tried to restore economies severely damaged during the wars. Funds were not available to buy either peace or order. Continuing racial fears also produced support for *caudillo* rule, as the long period of warfare had created opportunities for the masses to vent their hostility and to challenge the status quo.

The conflicts and antagonisms that emerged during the independence wars help explain the political divisions that occurred subsequently. Venezuela and Ecuador eventually broke away from Colombia. Central America separated from Mexico in 1823 and then divided into the states of Guatemala, El Salvador, Nicaragua, Honduras, and Costa Rica in 1838.

The remaining Spanish American states achieved their independence later in the century, largely in response to external developments. Santo Domingo declared its independence in 1821, but it was absorbed by Haiti in 1822, separated in 1844, sought readmission into the Spanish empire in 1861, and then definitively established itself as the Dominican Republic in 1865. Cuba had remained loyal to Spain in response to racial fears as well as economic benefits, but pressures for independence grew during the nineteenth century, leading to a number of rebellions and wars that gradually weakened Spanish resolve and strengthened the independence movement. A new rebellion in the 1890s was on the point of victory for the rebels when war between Spain and the United States broke out, and American military success in 1898 was followed by Cuban independence. Thus 1898 marked the end of Spanish and Portuguese colonial administration in the Western Hemisphere.

The events of the early nineteenth century had freed most of Latin America, but much of the colonial heritage remained. New problems emerged with the growing absorption of Latin America into the world economy at the end of the century. Within twelve years of Cuba securing its independence, the first "modern" revolution in Latin America erupted in Mexico. It proved to be a harbinger of similar revolutions that were to occur throughout the area during the twentieth century. They pointed to the fact that the revolutions for independence had not resolved many fundamental issues and that further struggles were required.

See also *Bolívar, Simón; Haitian Revolution of Independence (1791–1804); Latin American Revolts under Colonial Rule (1571–1898); San Martín, José Francisco de.*

PETER BLANCHARD

BIBLIOGRAPHY

Anna, Timothy E. *The Fall of the Royal Government in Lima.* Lincoln: University of Nebraska Press, 1979.

———. *The Fall of the Royal Government in Mexico City.* Lincoln: University of Nebraska Press, 1978.

Bethell, Leslie, ed. *The Independence of Latin America.* Cambridge: Cambridge University Press, 1987.

Graham, Richard. *Independence in Latin America: A Comparative Approach.* 2d ed. New York: McGraw-Hill, 1994.

Hamnett, Brian. "Process and Pattern: A Re-examination of the Ibero-American Independence Movements, 1808–1826." *Journal of Latin American Studies* 29 (May 1997): 279–328.

Kinsbruner, Jay. *Independence in Spanish America: Civil Wars, Revolution, and Underdevelopment.* 2d ed. Albuquerque: University of New Mexico Press, 1994.

Lynch, John. *The Spanish American Revolutions, 1808–1826.* 2d ed. New York: W.W. Norton, 1986.

Lynch, John, ed. *Latin American Revolutions, 1808–1826: Old and New World Origins.* Norman: University of Oklahoma Press, 1994.

Rodriguez O., Jaime, ed. *The Independence of Mexico and the Creation of the New Nation.* Los Angeles: UCLA Latin American Center Publications, 1989.

Russell-Wood, A. J. R., ed. *From Colony to Nation: Essays on the Independence of Brazil.* Baltimore, Md.: Johns Hopkins University Press, 1975.

LEADERSHIP

In "great man" theories of history, revolutions are presented as the triumph of one or a few individuals, whose ideas and devoted efforts changed the course of history. This view was most famously expressed by the German sociologist Max Weber in his depiction of the "charismatic" leader as an exceptional presence who moves people to break free from the normal course of events. This view is often presented in popular histories and biographies and reaches its most profound expression in those revolutionary states that developed "cults" around their leaders. Vladimir Ilyich Lenin in Russia, Mao Zedong in China, Fidel Castro in Cuba, and Ayatollah Ruhollah Khomeini in Iran are just a few of the individuals who have been given heroic, if not divine, attributes as revolutionary leaders.

In contrast, most social scientific analyses of revolutions give much less credit to individual leaders for making revolutions. Focusing instead on the weakness of old regimes, the impact of international conflicts, and the struggles between classes or political factions, social scientific analyses often give leaders the much more limited role of opportunists who step forward to act in a situation that invites, or even impels, revolutionary actions. "Structuralist" social scientists, such as the American scholar Theda Skocpol, hardly mention revolutionary leaders in their analyses. For the structuralists, social-structural factors lead to the rise and fall of regimes, and revolutionary "leaders" are often frustrated, surprised, or confounded by their inability to control events, as they too are swept along by the forces of history.

THE NATURE OF REVOLUTIONARY LEADERS

Studies of revolutionary leaders, such as those by the American political scientists Mostafa Rejai and Kay Phillips, reveal that they are surprisingly diverse and have more in common with conventional political leaders than one might guess. Whereas some leaders, like Castro and Leon Trotsky, are dashing and daring, others are quietly noble, such as George Washington and Václav Havel; still others, like Lenin and Maximilien Robespierre, are puritanical ascetics. In their education (above average for their societies) and family background (professional and middle class), revolutionaries are mostly like conventional political leaders. Drawn to politics from an early age, many of them envisioned careers in conventional politics, only to have a personal crisis wrench them onto a radical path.

Revolutionary leadership, like leadership in general, takes two major forms. Scholars identify these as "people-oriented" leadership, the ability to communicate an ideological vision that will inspire loyalty and persuade people to work for a common cause, and "task-oriented" or organizational leadership, the ability to mobilize people and resources to achieve specific goals. Successful revolutions require both kinds of leadership, whether combined in a single dominant leader or, much more commonly, spread among a key elite of primary leaders. Where leadership groups fail to combine and mesh these skills, revolutionary movements fail. And where both types of leadership are present but divided among different leaders who come into conflict, revolutionary regimes are thrown into turmoil. Examples of the former are Ernesto "Che" Guevara's efforts to create a revolution in Bolivia, which foundered on lack of organizational skills, or the efforts of the liberal Kadets under Alexander Kerensky to create a revolutionary regime in Russia, which collapsed in part through the inability of Kerensky to match Lenin's popular appeal. Examples of the latter are communist China, where recurring conflicts between ideologically devoted Maoists and more pragmatic technocrats periodically disrupted China and led to the tragedies of the Cultural Revolution; and the short-lived New Jewel revolution in Grenada, which extinguished itself through the homicidal conflict between its ideological and organizational leaders.

THE CONTRIBUTION OF LEADERSHIP TO REVOLUTION

The tendency of structuralist social scientists to minimize the role of revolutionary leaders in making revolutions arises in part because what successful revolutionary leaders do best is take advantage of structural weaknesses in an existing regime. Thus successful leadership and structural vulnerability are almost always found together and are easily confounded. It is probably true that revolutionary leaders cannot "will" the destruction of a strong, united, existing regime. But that does not mean that their role is modest or incidental. Without outstanding revolutionary leadership, the fall of an old regime can simply lead to chaos, civil war, or a series of unstable regimes. In France from the fall of Napoleon in 1815 until 1870, in many African and Latin American societies, and in several modern countries in eastern Europe and central Asia, such as Yugoslavia and Tajikistan, vulnerable and collapsing regimes were followed by long and distressing waves of dictatorship, violence, and instability. Revolutionary leadership is crucial to consolidate a new regime, unite various revolutionary factions, and create a new political, economic, and social structure that can endure.

Moreover, the goals and character of revolutionary leaders can place an indelible stamp upon the new regime. India, the Philippines, Nicaragua, and South Africa are democracies today, despite high rates of poverty, inequality, and racial and ethnic conflict, because the leaders who founded their regimes (Mahatma Gandhi in India's independence movement, Corazon Aquino in the Philippines' "People Power" Revolution, the Ortegas in the Nicaraguan Revolution, and Nelson Mandela in South Africa's reform movement) were devoted to the ideal of democracy. In contrast, autocratic leaders—such as Lenin in Russia, Mao in China, or Castro in Cuba—tend to establish autocratic regimes, whatever their expressed plans for future democracy. Similarly, the choice of a socialist or capitalist path among revolutionary regimes depended greatly on the experience and ideology of revolutionary leaders, not just the disposition of foreign powers or the structure of their prerevolutionary economies.

Revolutionary leaders, then, are indispensable to revolutions. Without talented, balanced, and united revolutionary leadership, even the collapse of states does not automatically bring forth a new regime. And when a new regime is constructed, the choices and vision of revolutionary leaders are crucial to shaping its future.

JACK A. GOLDSTONE

BIBLIOGRAPHY

Aminzade, Ron, Jack A. Goldstone, and Elizabeth Perry. "Leadership Dynamics and Dynamics of Contention." In *Voice and Silence in Contentious Politics.* Edited by Ron Aminzade, Jack A. Goldstone, Doug McAdam, Elizabeth Perry, William Sewell Jr., Sidney Tarrow, and Charles Tilly. Cambridge: Cambridge University Press, forthcoming.

Rejai, Mostafa, and Kay Phillips. *Leaders of Revolution.* Beverly Hills: Sage Publications, 1979.

Selbin, Eric. *Modern Latin American Revolutions.* Boulder, Colo.: Westview Press, 1993.

Skocpol, Theda. *States and Social Revolutions.* New York: Cambridge University Press, 1979.

Weber, Max. *The Theory of Social and Economic Organization.* Edited by Talcott Parsons. New York: Free Press, 1954.

Wilson, Edmund. *To the Finland Station: A Study in the Acting and Writing of History.* New York: Harcourt Brace, 1940.

LECHÍN OQUENDO, JUAN

Lechín (1914–) led the powerful Bolivian tin miners and Bolivia's central labor confederation for most of their existence. The tin miners, in particular, stood at the center of the Bolivian Revolution of 1952, one of the most radical proletarian-peasant-nationalist revolutions in Latin American history.

Bolivia's trade unionists, particularly the miners in this country long dependent on tin, developed a militant theory and practice. The Bolivian Federation of Miners (FSTMB), founded in 1944, was shaped ideologically by Trotskyist and Leninist thought; the Bolivian Workers Central (COB), founded shortly after the successful revolution of 1952, was long influenced by Communists, Trotskyists, and left-wing nationalists. Juan Lechín stood at the center of these organizations, as executive secretary of the FSTMB from its founding until his resignation in June 1986, and as general secretary of the COB from its founding until July 1987.

Lechín, of Lebanese ancestry, was born in the mining town of Corocoro. He attended the American Institute run by the Methodist Church, but family debts prevented him from pursuing his studies. He was hired as a clerk in the Catavi tin mines in 1929. After service in the Chaco War (1932–1935) against neighboring Paraguay, he was appointed to a municipal government post in a mining district, and he quickly became involved in local union affairs.

Lechín's ideological flexibility (alternatively interpreted as a lack of theoretical discernment or, more likely, a keen sense of political pragmatism) allowed him to serve as a key intermediary among the parties that worked intensively in the politically crucial mining sector. Influenced by the Trotskyist Revolutionary Labor Party (POR), he provided early backing for militant miners, supporting their frequent occupation of the mines and calls for general strikes. Yet Lechín was never fully comfortable with socialist ideology, and in the late 1940s he broke with the POR and moved over to the Nationalist Revolutionary Movement (MNR), the populist party that won power in April 1952.

Representing the MNR's left flank, Lechín influenced the new government's adherence to a number of radical measures including nationalization of the mining industry, worker cogovernment (with a specified number of COB-nominated ministry seats), and comanagement of the new state mining corporation. But if Lechín helped nudge the MNR to the left, he also acted to prevent more radical forces from gaining control of national policy. Thus, he called for the nationalization of the mines, but also for payment of compensation. He supported worker control in the mines, but not the election of delegates subject to recall by the workers they represented. He prevented Hernán Siles Zuazo (president from 1956 to 1960) from turning the COB into a state-controlled institution, but he also won the COB's support of Siles's stabilization plan, which was detrimental to the workers.

Often promised the presidency on the MNR ticket, Lechín had to settle for the vice presidency under Víctor Paz Estenssoro in 1960, only to be forced out soon after the election on a trumped-up cocaine charge. Long uneasy with both Trotskyists and communists and abandoned by the MNR, Lechín founded the Revolutionary Party of the Nationalist Left, which served as his base for a number of unsuccessful presidential runs. His support of strike calls during numerous military governments after 1964 and his near legendary stature as Bolivia's top labor leader led him to jail and exile on dozens of occasions.

Lechín's advancing age and inability to halt the neoliberal reforms of the mid-1980s finally marginalized him from the labor movement, and, since 1987, he has had little influence either in labor or national politics.

See also *Bolivian National Revolution (1952).*

STEVEN S. VOLK

BIBLIOGRAPHY

Cajias, Lupe. *Juan Lechín: Historia de una leyenda.* 3d ed. La Paz: Editorial Los Amigos del Libro, 1994.

Dunkerley, James. *Rebellion in the Veins. Political Struggle in Bolivia, 1952–82.* London: Verso, 1984.

Klein, Herbert S. *Bolivia: The Evolution of a Multi-Ethnic Society.* 2d ed. New York: Oxford University Press, 1992.

Malloy, James M., and Eduardo Gamarra. *Revolution and Reaction: Bolivia, 1964–1985.* New Brunswick, N.J.: Transaction Books, 1988.

LENIN, VLADIMIR ILYICH

Lenin (1870–1924) was the founder of the Bolshevik Party and one of the most influential revolutionary theorists of the twentieth century. Vladimir I. Ulyanov was born in Simbirsk, Russia; his father was a provincial official. In 1887 Vladimir's older brother Alexander was executed after being found guilty of taking part in a terrorist conspiracy to murder the tsar. As a result, the entire Ulyanov family began to be treated with suspicion by the authorities, and Vladimir was expelled from law school after taking part in a student demonstration. While continuing his legal studies through correspondence courses, he began to study Marxism. In 1895 he was arrested for attempting to publish a socialist newspaper and spent the next five years in prison and in Siberian exile.

Vladimir Ilyich Lenin

In Siberia Ulyanov devoted himself to developing Marxist theory and revolutionary strategy in the context of Russian social conditions. His first book, *The Development of Capitalism in Russia* (1899), endeavored to show that the traditional Russian agrarian economy, based upon the peasant commune, had already been irreversibly undermined by the increasing marketization of agricultural production. In 1900 he left Russia to join the leading Russian Marxists, Georgii Plekhanov, Pavel Axelrod, and Vera Zasulich, in Switzerland, where, along with Leon Trotsky, they founded the newspaper *Iskra* ("Spark"). In 1901 Ulyanov began to sign his articles "Lenin."

Throughout the prewar period Lenin considered himself an orthodox Marxist in the mold of Karl Kautsky, the chief theoretician of the German Social Democratic Party. Indeed, Lenin's famous treatise *What is to be Done?* (1902) was built upon Kautsky's argument that the proletariat could never create a revolution without leadership by committed Marxist intellectuals. However, Lenin went beyond Kautsky in asserting that the working class could be successfully organized only by a strictly disciplined party of professional revolutionaries. Lenin's insistence on this model of organization at the second congress of the Russian Social Democratic Party (held in 1903) played an important part in the subsequent split between the Bolsheviks, or "those in the majority"—so named because of Lenin's success in getting a bare majority of delegates present to vote to prohibit part-time party membership—and the Mensheviks, or "those in the minority," who resisted Lenin's leadership. By 1904 Plekhanov and his followers had also left Lenin's group to protest what they saw as the latter's dictatorial tendencies—ironically leaving the Bolsheviks very much a minority among Russian Marxists before 1917.

All of this infighting left both the Bolsheviks and Mensheviks almost totally unprepared for the Russian Revolution of 1905—an event that nevertheless demonstrated the increasing instability of Nicholas II's autocracy and the genuinely revolutionary orientation of the Russian working class. Lenin returned to Russia to help promote the Bolshevik cause but arrived a month after Nicholas II had succeeded in stabilizing his regime through the introduction of a limited constitutional order. In 1907 Lenin was again forced into exile in western Europe. The years 1907–1914 were bleak for him, as the Russian economy experienced steady growth and his own movement fragmented into warring splinter groups.

However, the outbreak of World War I in 1914, which both discredited global capitalism and rapidly undermined the legitimacy of the tsarist regime, revived the Bolsheviks' fortunes. As Lenin argued in his essay *Imperialism* (1916), the support by European socialist parties for their governments' participation in the war appeared to demonstrate that even supposedly "orthodox" European Marxists had been hopelessly corrupted by payoffs from capitalist imperial expansion. The proletarian revolution, he concluded, was therefore more likely to begin in Russia, the periphery of what had become a truly global capitalist system, than in the developed countries of the West, despite the weakness of Russian capitalism and the relatively small size of the Russian working class.

The opportunity to act on this theory arose when Nicholas II's sudden abdication in March 1917 left Russia in near anarchy. A Provisional Government made up of former Duma deputies tried, with Allied support, to continue the war against Germany, but in the cities actual power devolved, as in 1905, to local soviets (councils) of workers and soldiers. In the countryside, peasant revolts spread. Lenin returned to Petrograd (now St. Petersburg) in April, advocating the overthrow of the Provisional Government, the establishment of a socialist republic based upon the soviets, and the immediate cessation of the war. While the radicalism of these proposals at first stunned many of his own closest supporters, by the summer mounting war casualties and the disintegrating economy had turned the tide of opinion among workers and soldiers in the Bolsheviks' favor. On November 7 Lenin and his supporters successfully seized state power and quickly subordinated all other organized political forces within the territory they controlled.

However, Lenin's theoretical expectation that Bolshevik victory would spark socialist revolutions throughout the imperialist world turned out to be unfounded. From 1918 to 1920 Lenin and Trotsky directed an enormously destructive and bloody civil war against various supporters of tsarism, liberalism, anarchism, and anti-Bolshevik socialism. But after having reconquered most of the territory of the former Russian Empire, Lenin began to realize that the final global proletarian victory might be delayed indefinitely. In March 1921, in an attempt to revitalize the ruined Russian economy, Lenin introduced the New Economic Policy, which freed grain prices from state control and allowed small-scale capitalist trade in the cities; simultaneously, however, he further strengthened one-party rule through a ban on "factions," meaning open dissent within the party would no longer be tolerated. In 1922 he promoted Joseph Stalin to the new position of general secretary of the Communist Party, entrusted with the task of ensuring party discipline through control over personnel decisions.

Shortly thereafter Lenin suffered the first in a series of strokes that ultimately left him incapacitated. During brief periods of activity during the last two years of his life he wrote a series of articles in which he struggled—sincerely if rather unsuccessfully—to make Marxist theoretical sense of the dictatorial semicapitalist Soviet state he had founded. He also bitterly denounced Stalin, whom he began to see as a dangerously powerful "great Russian chauvinist" prone to abusive treatment of non-Russian communists and as a man "too rude" to be entrusted with the position of general secretary. Lenin died in January 1924, having failed to dislodge Stalin from the institutional position he was to occupy for the next three decades.

See also *Russian Revolution of 1917; Stalin, Joseph.*

STEPHEN E. HANSON

BIBLIOGRAPHY

Hanson, Stephen E. *Time and Revolution: Marxism and the Design of Soviet Institutions.* Chapel Hill: University of North Carolina Press, 1997.

Harding, Neil. *Lenin's Political Thought.* 2 vols. New York: St. Martin's Press, 1977.

Lewin, Moshe. *Lenin's Last Struggle.* New York: Pantheon, 1968.

Ulam, Adam. *The Bolsheviks: The Intellectual and Political History of the Triumph of Communism in Russia.* New York: Macmillan, 1965.

Williams, Robert C. *The Other Bolsheviks: Lenin and His Critics, 1904–1914.* Bloomington: Indiana University Press, 1986.

LIBERALISM

Liberalism is a slippery, diffuse political term, but in the context of the political revolutions of the nineteenth and early twentieth centuries, liberalism acquired considerable coherence. The term was first used directly to describe the proreform deputies in the Cortez of Cádiz (1810–1813) during the Spanish War of Independence, but liberalism really had emerged in the French Revolution of 1789–1799, and it did so in the context of revolutionary politics. Until 1848 the French constitution of 1791 was a hallmark of liberal principles, which centered on elected, accountable government, a rational centralized administration, a codified body of law, freedom of religion and the press, public trials, laissez-faire economics, and the protection of private property. Liberals believed that voting rights should be confined to men with property, the clearest issue separating them from radicals, who held that universal manhood suffrage was the only acceptable basis for a constitution.

The essence of liberalism, however, was a belief that the only legitimate government was constitutional government. Revolutionary liberalism meant opposing and, if necessary, overthrowing existing regimes to establish constitutional rule. What made liberals into revolutionaries was their belief that they had a right to attack any unconstitutional regime, which often led them into alliance with more radical elements. Once their basic objective of constitutional rule had been achieved, however, liberals sought to stop the revolutionary process, especially to protect private property. They could be ambivalent about the role of the popular classes in political life despite their belief in civil or human rights for all, as first evidenced by the distinction drawn between "active" citizens and others by French liberals in 1791. The liberals' less ambitious agenda made their relationship with radical and popular movements very fragile once the common enemy of absolutist rule was absent. Liberals were also usually, but not invariably, committed to uniformity in law, language, and administrative practices within states, something that could lead them into conflict with reactionaries, "to their right," as well as radicals, "to their left." Their belief in restricted electorates and a centralized state made liberalism into an elitist political doctrine, but its contribution to many political revolutions was all the more vital for its elitism.

LIBERALS AND POLITICAL REVOLUTION

The political geography of where liberals became revolutionaries follows a clear pattern after the French Revolution: Where governments refused to grant constitutions, liberals were in opposition to them; where those governments also refused a degree of freedom of the press, liberals turned to violent resistance. Thus, in early nineteenth century Europe, liberals were inside the political system in Britain, France, the Netherlands, and the south German states but outside it in Spain, Portugal, Russia, and most of the Italian and north German states; the pattern of revolution in Europe follows closely this division between constitutional and absolutist states, except in France.

Revolutionary activity by liberals seldom meant popular revolts, however; rather, it reflected liberalism's elitist character. The conspiratorial movements of early nineteenth century Europe, such as the Carbonari in Italy and the Comuneros in Spain, contained many liberals, as well as radicals, who played a leading part in the revolutions of 1820–1821 and 1830. The Russian Decembrists were wholly liberal in their political demands and middle class in composition. Conspiracy was their preferred method of violent resistance, which often led to conflict with radicals, who wanted wider popular involvement. Nevertheless, liberal politicians could become great popular leaders. Daniel O'Connell in Ireland during the campaign for Catholic emancipation in the late 1820s, Louis Kossuth in Hungary in 1848, and Benito Juárez in Mexico in the 1860s are classic examples. In such cases, however, liberal leaders either led nonviolent mass movements—like O'Connell—or emerged as national leaders following foreign invasion and the destruction of preexisting parliamentary institutions, as with Kossuth and Juárez. In each case, once parliamentary rule was secured, the leader sought to end the revolutionary process. Liberals are linked by their behavior when faced with a threat to constitutionalism and by their commitment to parliamentary institutions. Indeed, all three leaders—and others less famous—were lawyers by profession. After the start of the French Revolution, lawyers and legal training shaped many future liberal revolutionaries.

Between 1827 and 1831 liberal regimes emerged in western Europe, some by violent revolutions, as in France and Belgium in 1830–1831, others through bloodless constitutional agitation, as in Britain and Spain. But, aware of their common commitment to parliamentary rule based on narrow propertied electorates, Britain and France supported the liberal governments of Spain and Portugal against reactionary rebellions throughout the 1830s.

The revolutions of 1848 marked a turning point in the relationship between liberalism and revolution. In France and most of Germany liberals abandoned their objections to universal manhood suffrage, but then they abandoned their radical allies in fear of "socialism" and popular disorder. By 1849 many liberals had rejected popular revolution. Only in true autocracies did liberals continue to participate in revolutionary risings after 1848, as in Russia in 1905 and in the October Revolution of 1917, where the Kadet Party played the major role in overthrowing the monarchy. In western Europe and South America, liberalism became more associated with right-wing ideology than with that of the left in the course of the nineteenth century.

LIBERALS AND REVOLUTIONARY POLITICS

When revolutionary movements produced parliamentary institutions, liberals were usually quick to dominate them, driving radicals and socialists to the fringes of official government and back into extraparliamentary clubs and societies, as happened in France between 1789 and 1792 and throughout Europe in 1820–1821, 1830–1831, and 1848–1849. Usually more experienced in public debating than radical leaders, the liberals dominated revolutionary assemblies, thus usurping leadership of the revolution and causing the fragile alliances between liberals and radicals to fall apart. Unless reunited by the renewed threat of reactionary resistance—as in the later phases of the revolutions of 1820–1821 and 1848, or in Spain throughout the 1830s—these splits hardened as liberals sought to halt the revolution at the point where constitutional government had been achieved. Liberals steered revolutions but seldom provoked them.

See also *European Revolutions of 1820; European Revolutions of 1830; European Revolutions of 1848; French Revolution (1789–1815); Juárez, Benito; Russian Decembrist Revolt (1825); Spanish War of Independence (1808–1813).*

MICHAEL BROERS

BIBLIOGRAPHY

Broers, Michael. *Europe after Napoleon. Revolution, Reaction and Romanticism, 1814–1848.* Manchester: Manchester University Press, 1996.

Church, Clive. *Europe in 1830.* London: Longman, 1983.

Furet, Francois. *Revolutionary France 1770–1880.* Oxford: Blackwell, 1992.

Hamnett, Brian. *Juárez.* London and New York: Longman, 1997.

MacDongah, Oliver. *O'Connell. The Life of Daniel O'Connell 1775–1847.* London: Weidenfeld and Nicolson, 1991.

Rosenberg, William G. *Liberals in the Russian Revolution. The Constitutional Democratic Party, 1917–1921.* Princeton, N.J.: Princeton University Press, 1974.

Sheehan, James J. *German Liberalism in the 19th Century.* Chicago: University of Chicago Press, 1987.

Sperber, Jonathan. *The European Revolutions of 1848–1851.* Cambridge: Cambridge University Press, 1994.

LIBERATION THEOLOGY

Liberation theology emerged in Latin America in the late 1960s as part of a general effort in Roman Catholicism to rethink religion's role in society and politics and to rework religious and political structures to make room for participation by the poor and powerless. The writers and thinkers who created liberation theology constitute a distinct generation in the Latin American church. Highly educated (often in Europe) and with experience far beyond the norm for ecclesiastical careers, these young men began holding seminars, writing and publishing, advising movements, forming leaders, and, after a while, entering into contact with one another. These interchanges were reinforced by local and regional initiatives that joined elements from the churches with professionals, activists, and organizers in pursuit of common goals: medical students and doctors worked with local clergy and community leaders to promote health committees; educators joined together in alternative schools; cooperatives formed as communities called on clergy for assistance; and clergy helped communities find new sources of aid.

Liberation theologians were concerned with historical change, insisted on the necessity and primacy of action to promote justice, and underscored the importance of everyday experience as a source of religiously valid values. Their commitment was socially specific: not to the poor in spirit but rather to the materially poor. A new audience was present. By the mid-1960s economic and political transformations were producing new kinds of poor people in Latin America. In contrast to their mostly peasant ancestors, poor people were by then likely to be more physically mobile, to have access to communications media, and even to be literate. They were more available for organization, more capable of organizing themselves. In these circumstances, the message of liberation theology—with its characteristic stress on justice and activism in the pursuit of justice—resonated strongly.

A POLITICAL THEOLOGY

Liberationist insistence on going to the people spurred efforts to promote organization among the poor. Extensive networks of groups were established: base communities (small groups originally formed for religious study), peasant and urban unions, cooperatives, neighborhood associations, self-help groups, and communal kitchens, as well as centers for research and publication. Church-sponsored institutions provided these groups with shelter, protection, and invaluable human and material resources. Such institutions have been particularly active in human rights groups, peasant unions, and urban subsistence groups.

Central to the innovative character and impact of liberation theology was a radical shift in religion's view of itself and the world. Experience, above all the experience of the poor, became a source of new and religiously valid insight. In the effort to understand this experience—to make sense of why Latin American societies were the way they were—theologians drew heavily on the new Marxist sociology being created about this time in Latin America. Concepts of class, exploitation, and dependence began to appear in religious discourse. Working with notions of class, and using a sociological understanding of the world, meant that generalities about the common good, charity, avoidance of violence, and promotion of peace yielded precedence to powerful and specific critiques of injustice.

Practical consequences soon followed. Initial encounters with Marxist theory were reinforced and carried forward by alliances forged from the ground up between Catholic and Marxist groups from Chile and Peru to Central America and Brazil. Looking at their own societies, this generation saw unjust social structures marked by inequalities of class and power and held together by force. Insisting on the social specifics of poverty put liberationists and those who espoused their ideas at the heart of regional conflicts. Pivotal among these conflicts were the civil wars in Central America and resistance to arbitrary government and military rule throughout the continent. Activists were also deeply involved in the organization of peasant movements and urban neighborhood groups and in promoting and defending human rights throughout the region.

THE NEW FACE OF LIBERATION

Liberation theology's early impact was magnified by a factor of surprise. That change should arise in the Catholic Church took many observers unawares. Wedded to theories of secularization, scholars had little room in their analytical schemes for vigorous moves by religious groups to reclaim the public stage, much less in the name of change. Elites and activists were also surprised and challenged by the energetic surge of the new ideas and groups that religion began to push and pull onto the public scene. Liberation theology drew strength by combining the power of religious speech with the legitimacy of religious institutions and the space for action that they marked out. New issues were placed before the public eye and on the agendas of governments and major institutions.

Liberationists were influential in writing the documents produced at the 1968 Second General Conference of Latin American Bishops in Medellín, Colombia, as well as the countless pastoral letters and other communications in which bishops' conferences and individual prelates set out an agenda critical of the "established disorder." In the movement's early days, working within the institutional structure of the churches clearly empowered liberationists, giving them access to important material and symbolic resources.

The collapse of socialism, the defeat of the Sandinista revolution in Nicaragua in 1990, and the failure of many groups in which liberationists placed their hopes have combined to prompt a new look at incremental change and political democracy. For some time theologians have also been slowly shifting their agendas away from class and politics to new issues such as developing a distinctively liberationist spirituality; exploring the teachings of historical precursors such as Bartolomé de Las Casas, the sixteenth-century bishop famous as the defender of the indigenous peoples; and crafting a liberationist understanding of ecological issues. The search for new political strategies was spurred by loss of grassroots support and the growing realization that most members of liberationist groups came not from the poorest of the poor but rather from lower-middle-class and stable working-class populations, including peasants with some land. Most groups are less ambitious, more localized, less explicitly political, and much more conventionally religious than originally supposed.

PROBLEMS AND PROSPECTS

In recent years notices of the decay and death of liberation theology have abounded. Reading the signs of contemporary events, scholars and journalists have joined religious and political activists in writing obituaries for liberation theology as a vision of faith and action able to inspire and carry change. Sustained opposition from the Vatican, the fall of socialism in Europe, the defeat of the Sandinista regime in Nicaragua, and the growth of evangelical Protestantism among groups that liberationists had seen as their core constituency have reinforced a sense that the promise of liberation theology is at best played out, at worst, an illusion that never was.

Despite these difficulties, it is too early to write obituaries for liberation theology. It is more useful rather to specify its long-term impact on religion, on politics, and on the relation between the two. A clear distinction should be drawn between the resonance of ideas and the fate of specific movements or alliances. Liberation theology has undergirded a practical theory of rights grounded in presumptions of equality and access. Liberationist ideas have clearly entered the mainstream of both religion and politics. Issues like human rights, accountability, and the legitimacy of active participation by ordinary people have been put on the agendas of crucial institutions and attracted national and world attention.

Movements have fared less well, and many have foundered on a deadly combination of repressive violence (above all in Central America), the gap between radical visions of activists and the more modest goals most members espouse, and, finally, on the impact of democracy itself. The return of civilian rule and political democracy opened new channels for activism and led to splits as members divided among available alternatives. The practical legacy of liberationist movements will depend on whether the generation that came to maturity in liberationist movements remains activist, and in what specific ways.

See also *Class; Inequality; Injustice; Latin American Popular and Guerrilla Revolts (1960–1996); Nicaraguan Revolution (1979); Religion.*

DANIEL H. LEVINE

BIBLIOGRAPHY

Berryman, Phillip. *Liberation Theology.* New York: Pantheon, 1989.
Boff, Leonardo. *Ecology and Liberation.* Maryknoll, N.Y.: Orbis, 1995.
Gutiérrez, Gustavo. *A Theology of Liberation: History, Politics, and Salvation.* Maryknoll: Orbis, 1973.
McGovern, Arthur. *Liberation Theology and Its Critics.* Maryknoll, N.Y.: Orbis, 1989.
Smith, Christian. *The Emergence of Liberation Theology.* Chicago: University of Chicago Press, 1993.

LIBYAN REVOLUTION (1969)

The Libyan Arab Popular and Socialist Jamahiriyya, the official name of Libya, is a self-declared revolutionary state. This regime originated on September 1, 1969, when a group of young, pan-Arab officers in the Libyan Royal Army, led by a charismatic twenty-seven-year-old officer named Mu'ammar Abu-Minyar al-Qadhafi, overthrew the monarchy of King Idriss I in a bloodless coup d'état while the king was vacationing in Turkey. The twelve junior officers were the central committee of a clandestine organization within the Libyan army called the Libyan Free Unionist Officers' movement. The central committee renamed itself the Revolutionary Command Council (RCC) and declared the birth of the Libyan Arab Republic.

A 1969 constitutional proclamation gave the RCC all executive, legislative, and judicial powers. The RCC began to refer to its political and social policies as a "revolution." Yet, aside from anticolonialism, anticommunism, Arab nationalism, Islam, and anticorruption, the RCC did not have a clear program and looked to the 1952 Egyptian Revolution as a model, at least in the early years. In the last three decades, Libyan society indeed underwent major social, political, and economic experiments and transformations. The new government initiated and imposed its social, political, and economic programs from above in the absence of popular participation from below. After Qadhafi consolidated power in 1975, he began to experiment with creating a "precapitalist socialist society," using oil revenues and a large measure of non-Libyan expatriate labor, ironically the products of Libyan integration in the world capitalist economy.

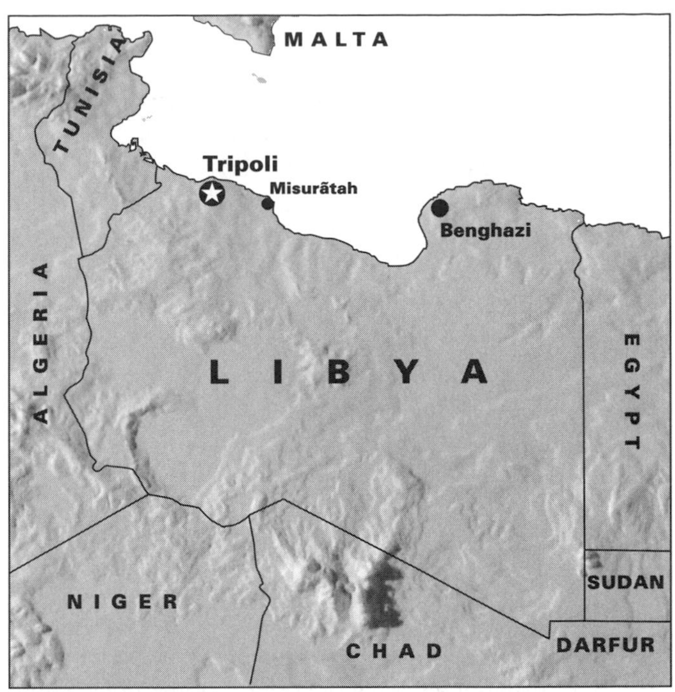

BACKGROUND TO THE REVOLUTION

The radical and nationalist ideology of the Libyan Revolution is a reaction to the crisis of the Sanusi monarchy (1951–1969) and regional and international politics in the last three decades.

Libyan independence in 1951 was engineered by Britain and France in alliance with the defeated and exiled Sanusi leaders in Egypt. Britain wanted to isolate Libya, a key to Britain's security in the Middle East, from Arab nationalism by supporting the tribal structure of the Sanusiyya in eastern Libya over the urban nationalist movement in Tripolitania. The exiled leader of the Sanusiyya, Amir Muhammad Idriss al-Sanusi, agreed to support British interests in exchange for political independence. And on December 24, 1951, Amir Idriss was crowned King Idriss I of the United Libyan Kingdom. The new government consisted of upper class urban families and tribal leaders, mainly from Barqa, the home base for King Idriss and the Sanusiyya. One of the poorest states in the world, the new kingdom was in dire need of revenues to balance its budget. It granted military base rights to Britain and the United States in exchange for yearly rent and economic aid.

After the discovery of oil in 1961, the monarchy initiated various programs in education, health, transportation, and housing. By the late 1960s the educational policies had led to the rise of a salaried middle class, student movement, small working class, trade unions, and intellectuals. The Sanusi monarchy depended on Arab teachers from Egypt, Palestine, and Sudan, who brought Arab nationalist ideas to their young Libyan students. In addition, most of the first postindependence generation of university students had gone to Egyptian universities, and the first class of Libyan military officers had graduated from the Baghdad military academy in Iraq.

Many young Libyans became involved in Arab nationalist politics of the Nasserite or Ba'athist branches. To aggravate the crisis of the monarchy, the king was a very aloof man. And despite the discovery and production of oil, many rural Libyans remained poor. The monarchy became a victim when it did not adjust institutionally to its own economic and educational programs, as some educated but marginalized middle- and lower-middle-class Libyans found themselves outside of the political patronage of the old tribal leaders and the influential notable families. The military, staffed largely by members of the emerging middle class, was the most organized of all the groups opposed to the monarchy.

DOMESTIC POLITICS UNDER THE REVOLUTION

The social base of the RCC was predominantly the lower middle class created by the monarchy's postindependence social and economic programs. Of the twelve members of the RCC, only two came from majority tribes, the Magharba and Awagir, and one from a prominent coastal family. The rest came from poor and minor tribes of the interior or the poor social strata in the coastal towns. It could be argued that the revolution pitted the lower middle class from the interior and the oases against the large towns' notable families and the dominant tribal leaders. A very peculiar policy of the monarchy was its reliance on the police force for its security rather than the army. The police force was recruited from loyal tribes and was well equipped, whereas the small Libyan army remained open to nonelite students.

RCC ideology stressed Arab nationalism, Islam, self-determination, and social justice, and it denounced the corruption of the old regime. The officers were also anticommunist, which brought them international recognition from U.S. president Richard Nixon. Despite its claims to radical change, the new regime continued many of the economic and social polices of the monarchy. The RCC continued to develop the country's infrastructure. Most Libyans began to benefit from the expanded welfare state—for example, new hospitals, roads, and schools—thanks to the increased oil revenues of the state. The regime received national popular support after it successfully negotiated the return of military bases from Britain and the United States. Furthermore, the regime asserted Libyan control over its oil resources, raising prices and achieving Libyan participation in foreign-owned oil production in 1973.

Following the policy of the monarchy, the RCC banned political parties and independent trade unions in 1970, and the council adopted the Egyptian model of a one-party system in 1971. This model was abandoned two years later when the party, the Arab Socialist Union, failed to mobilize the Libyan masses. Facing the opposition of the old elite, an apathetic bureaucracy, and the failure of the Arab Socialist Union, Qadhafi declared his own popular revolution in a famous speech in Zuwara, in western Libya, on July 15, 1973. In this speech he asked the people to remove the old bureaucracy and replace it with popular committees of employees in their places of work. Qadhafi's new initiative led to a split within the RCC over the role and authority of the popular committees. The disagreement reflected major ideological differences inside the RCC over the direction of the revolution. A technocratic faction led by Umar al-Muhashi, the minister of planning, argued the need for expertise and professional competence, while Qadhafi insisted on ideological mobilization and political loyalty. When the two factions could not reconcile their differences, al-Muhashi led a coup against Qadhafi on August 13, 1975. The coup failed when Abdulsalam Jalud—a key figure in the council—sided with Qadhafi. Umar al-Muhashi escaped into exile in Tunisia and then Egypt. The failed coup ended the RCC, and Qadhafi consolidated his power with the help of four other RCC members.

Qadhafi began to advocate what he called the Third Universal Theory, a third way between capitalism and Marxism based in direct democracy of popular congresses and committees. At the same time, he sought to undermine existing social and political institutions and organizations, including independent trade unions, students' organizations, and the army. Finally, in March 1977 the People's General Congress, meeting in the southern city of Sabha, proclaimed the people's power and renamed Libya the Libyan Arab Popular and Socialist Jamahiriyya.

By May 1976 Qadhafi had become impatient with the opposition within the popular committees and the People's General Congress, and he called for the formation of a new layer of organization, "revolutionary committees," which would instruct and mobilize the popular committees. In reality, the new committees were made of Qadhafi loyalists. In the late 1970s an estimated 100,000 of the best educated Libyans lived outside the country. Still, most Libyans continued to enjoy the benefits of the welfare state and supported the government.

FOREIGN POLICY UNDER THE REVOLUTION

In the early 1980s the revolutionary government pursued an independent foreign policy, buying arms from the USSR, supporting liberation movements in Africa and the Middle East, such as the Palestinian resistance, and opposing the American-sponsored peace process between Egypt and Israel. When Ronald Reagan came to the White House in March 1981, he targeted Qadhafi's regime as a sponsor of terrorism. The Reagan administration attempted to overthrow or weaken the Libyan government by assisting Qadhafi's enemies inside and outside Libya. A major American covert action in Chad was initiated in 1981 and led to the defeat of the Libyan army and its Chadian allies.

On April 14, 1986, after a terrorist bomb exploded in a night club frequented by American soldiers in Berlin, Germany, the Reagan administration accused the Libyan government of participating in the bombing and authorized an air strike against Libya. Despite the fact that the accusation turned out to be false, American jets hit the Libyan cities of Tripoli and Benghazi, killing fifty civilians on April 14, 1986.

The Libyan government faced a hostile regional and international environment and new challenges. The regime became isolated in the Arab world and was targeted by American economic sanctions. A number of opposition groups were formed in exile, and oil prices declined drastically in 1986. In 1988 Qadhafi blamed the revolutionary committees for being overzealous and abusing their power. He released political prisoners and abandoned many of his experiments with precapitalist collective markets and bartering.

The administration of President Bill Clinton kept the old economic sanctions on Libya in place and in 1992 accused two Libyan nationals of planting the bomb that brought down a Pan-Am plane over Lockerbie, Scotland, in 1988. When the Qadhafi government refused to turn over the two suspects, the United States sponsored a UN Security Council resolution imposing new sanctions, banning direct flights to Libya and reducing Libyan diplomatic missions abroad.

The Qadhafi government began to institutionalize power by forming a Ministry of Social Mobilization to replace the revolutionary committees. Furthermore, a charter of human rights was adopted in June 1988. These measures brought the government back to the Arab regional system, and diplomatic ties resumed with other Arab states.

The Libyan Revolution brought many changes to ordinary Libyans, such as free medical care, a modern infrastructure, and free education, especially for Libyan women. At the same time, the Libyan government is currently more dependent on oil for its revenues than it had been under the old regime, and agriculture continues to decline despite all the large and expensive projects. The once vibrant civil associations that made Libyan society appear to be ahead of many gulf states in the 1970s are either weakened or destroyed. Despite these mixed legacies, the Libyan Revolution transformed Libyan society and was a turning point in the making of modern Libya in the twentieth century.

See also *Egyptian Revolution (1952); Iraqi Revolution (1958).*

ALI ABDULLATIF AHMIDA

BIBLIOGRAPHY

Ahmida, Ali Abdullatif. *The Making of Modern Libya: State Formation, Colonialization, and Resistance, 1830–1932.* Albany: State University of New York Press, 1994.

Anderson, Lisa S. *The State and Social Transformation in Tunisia and Libya, 1830–1980.* Princeton, N.J.: Princeton University Press, 1986.

Davis, John. *Libyan Politics: Tribe and Revolution.* Berkeley: University of California Press, 1987.

El Fathaly, Omar, and Monte Palmer. *Political Development and Social Change in Libya.* Lexington, Mass.: Lexington Books, 1980.

First, Ruth. *Libya: The Elusive Revolution.* Harmondsworth, England: Penguin, 1974.

Vandewalle, Dirk, ed. *Qadhafi's Libya, 1969 to 1994.* New York: St. Martin's Press, 1995.

LITERATURE

In virtually every culture literary writers have described, justified, or criticized the political realities in which they live. Literature's role in revolution is not just descriptive, however. Literature has also helped motivate, support, or suppress revolution.

THE LITERARY FOUNDATIONS OF REVOLUTION

The earliest literatures were primarily descriptive. Writers described immediate events, recounted history and legend, and described and praised deities. Literary writers approach revolutions and wars differently from historians—comprehensive coverage is rarely a goal—but their works provide insights that historical and political writings cannot. A literary text allows readers to step into a created world that reflects or records the historical moment. Homer's great epic poem the *Iliad* describes only a few weeks in the ten-year Trojan War, which probably took place sometime between the fourteenth and twelfth centuries B.C., but it presents historical figures as three-dimensional humans. In a sense the created world becomes more real than the historical because identifications with characters are more possible.

Identifications do more than allow readers to understand revolution. They can also inspire revolution. When a revolutionary figure is presented as a hero, even as an especially interesting character, readers may be inspired to imitate that figure or further his or her goals. This power was realized as early as the fifth century B.C. in ancient Athens. In Plato's *Republic* the philosopher Socrates warns of literature's dangers: certain tales, particularly those with great "poetical charm," may render people excitable, too fearful of death to defend a state, or admiring of people with views threatening to the state. Socrates recommended strict censorship of literary works to ensure political stability, advice followed by many later heads of state.

Literatures of the European Renaissance set the foundation for politically revolutionary thought, though relatively little of political revolution was directly described. Renaissance literature was human centered, emphasizing the potential within individuals. Belief in human potential underlies the human desire to better political situations, and the revival of human-centered texts from classical Greece and Rome (as opposed to medieval God-centered texts) was important in forging new political realities. Humanists from the fourteenth century forward made later political revolutions possible.

Ideas for completely new political states had been considered by such ancient writers as Plato and Cicero, but in the sixteenth century Thomas More, an English statesman, churchman, and humanist, introduced ideas central to modern revolution. More's *Utopia* is permeated by a strong spirit of democratic republicanism, with the idea that the true function of government is to serve the people and promote their well-being. It also anticipated socialism in its proscription of private property. William Shakespeare, in the next century, showed the fallibility of nobility and argued that individuals must be themselves, though he also demonstrated the firmness of sociopolitical structures and the price of opposing traditional or legal standards (for example, in *Macbeth, King Lear,* and *Romeo and Juliet*). In Spain, Félix Lope de Vega's play *Fuenteovejuna* (c.1619) showed that the upper classes could err, that the masses were entitled to oppose them when they went against established law, though he also affirmed the rightness of structures of power and law.

MODERN LITERATURES OF REVOLUTION

In the eighteenth century, an age of revolution politically and otherwise, writers questioned political authority more directly. Writings of the French *philosophes,* or philosopher-writers, inspired many political revolutionists. John Locke, an English political philosopher, had already argued that humans are born free (in *Two Treatises of Government,* 1689), but Jean-Jacques Rousseau added the rousing "yet we see him everywhere in chains" in *The Social Contract* (1762). From Rousseau came several ideas essential to later revolutions: the will of the people must be recognized, the majority is generally right, sometimes the minority is more representative than the majority, and freedom must sometimes be imposed on a population. Both the French and American Revolutions were inspired by Rousseau's writings as well as by those of other writers such as François Voltaire.

The nineteenth century, an age of literary nationalism, produced many powerful revolutionary works. Because nationalist revolution requires not only a sense of nation but pride in nation, literatures celebrating national identity were important. The writer's intent was not essential; where a ruling power tries to suppress a people's worth, a work may express as mild a sentiment as "what a beautiful country we have" and still be regarded as revolutionary, especially if these sentiments are expressed in a language that has been banned.

In certain regions, literature has been particularly important in revolution. The Irish cultural renaissance, which began in the nineteenth century, was an essential precursor to the Easter Rebellion of 1916. As pride in being Irish was reinstilled, the Irish independence movement was strengthened. The poet Thomas Davis founded the Young Ireland movement to further Irish culture, language, and political nationalism. Padraic Pearse, leader of the Easter Rebellion, was a poet and story writer. During the 1919–1921 war of independence, such works as William Butler Yeats's "Caitlin ni Houlihan," a play in which the title character represents Mother Ireland, were essential to motivating revolutionary participation. Today the Irish Republican Army supports Irish language and literature as a means of fostering revolutionary sentiment.

A conflict in which literature and literary figures were particularly important was the Spanish Civil War of the late 1930s, which attracted the participation of literary writers throughout the world. Most writers opposed the insurgent government led by Gen. Francisco Franco; these included Stephen Spender, W. H. Auden, John Cornford, and C. Day Lewis. Among Franco's supporters were Hilaire Belloc and Roy Campbell. Others recounted the revolution: George Orwell, in the essay "Looking Back on the Spanish War," and Wyndham Lewis, in the novel *The Revenge for Love.* Franco's victory and the defeat of republicans had a great effect on many writers. Orwell wrote that every line he wrote after that time was written against totalitarianism and for democratic socialism.

In Latin America, belief in the nation was also strengthened by literature. The beginning of nationalism in that region came with José Hernández's *Martín Fierro* (1872), an epic poem that swept his native Argentina and then the continent. It was the first work to glorify a common Latin American—the gaucho, essentially an Argentinean cowboy—and criticize the Europeanization of America. It was memorized and recited throughout the country. Later Latin American works also promoted or described revolution. In *Canto General* (1943), an epic verse history of Latin America, the Chilean poet Pablo Neruda describes the need for class struggle, the problem of dictators, and the evolution of a socialist consciousness. An insightful analysis of the Mexican Revolution is Carlos Fuentes's *The Death of Artemio Cruz* (1962), which uses three points of view to describe a dying participant in that revolution.

The degree to which politics and literature are intertwined in Latin America is evidenced by the large number of politicians and revolutionaries who are also writers. Ernesto Cardenal, revolutionary poet-mystic, was a revolutionist, then a minister in Nicaragua's Sandinista government in the 1980s. Argentine-born Ernesto "Che" Guevara, active in the 1950s and 1960s and possibly the most famous Latin American revolutionary, was a poet as well as a physician.

In much of eastern Europe, writers have been important to revolutions. In Russia, activism was long an essential role of the intelligentsia. Much of Russian literature grew from opposition to political or social realities, from the liberal nobility in Aleksandr Sergeyevich Pushkin's time in the early nineteenth century to the disgruntled aristocratic officers in the later tsarist period to the new literary vanguard after the 1917 revolution. After the October Revolution, when literature was required to support the new order, many writers continued the tradition of protest, openly when possible, covertly or in exile when not. With good reason, Soviet authorities took writers seriously. Writers known for their political writings include Vladimir Maiakovsky, Osip Mandelstam, and Alexandr Solzhenitsyn. Literature was also important to Soviet satellite republics. Political playwright and dissident Václav Havel was elected president of Czechoslovakia in 1989.

Much of Middle Eastern literature was apolitical until the twentieth century, when it changed to accommodate revolutionary needs. The great revolutionary and reformer Kemal Atatürk, who in 1905 joined the Young Turk movement that sought to reform the Ottoman Empire, understood the importance of separating Turkish identity from that of the Ottoman rulers. One of Atatürk's reforms, when he became president of Turkey, was to "purify" the language and to replace Arabic script with the Roman alphabet. The populist literary movement, which began in 1911, supported these reforms in the name of nationalism. In the 1910–1922 nationalist revolution against the Ottomans, Turkish poets reached a wide audience.

The success of the 1952 army revolution in Egypt and the rise of Gamal Abdel Nasser inspired an Arabic pride that encouraged Arab theater and cultural forms. The Arabic word for commitment, *iltizam,* became essential in literary criticism after 1950. The need for literature to promote socialist values was reiterated by the radical Egyptian thinker Salama Musa (1887–1958). Most nationalist revolutions in the Middle East were supported by literary writers. The Palestine Liberation Organization supports many cultural institutions and programs, recognizing that cultural pride is essential to national pride.

EFFECTS OF REVOLUTION ON LITERATURE

In most parts of the world, revolution has strengthened literature. In times of revolution, people read serious literature and attend the theater more than during times of stability. Sometimes this interest is a reaction against censorship. The Russian poet Mandelstam once commented, "Only in our country is poetry respected—they'll kill you for it."

Revolution also affects literature's styles and forms. Writers seeking revolutionary effect must be clear and straightforward. Avant-garde literature, which is often not accessible to general readers, is generally less attractive to revolutionary elites as well as to revolutionary masses. Changes are not always conscious: instability motivates a return to traditional styles and forms, whereas stability encourages innovation.

Literature and revolution, then, have maintained a close, symbiotic relationship throughout history, each nourishing the other.

See also *Art and Representation; Atatürk, Kemal; Havel, Václav; Irish Revolution (1916–1923); Music; Orwell, George.*

THERESA M. MACKEY

BIBLIOGRAPHY

Harlow, Barbara. *Resistance Literature.* New York: Methuen, 1987.

Hauser, Arnold. *The Social History of Art.* Vols. 1–4. New York: Vintage Books, 1985.

Mackey, Theresa. "Literature and Revolution in the Mediterranean World." In *Mediterranean Perspectives: Literature, Social Studies, and Philosophy.* Edited by James E. Caraway. New York: Dowling College Press, 1996.

Parkhurst, Priscilla. *The Making of a Culture.* Berkeley: University of California Press, 1987.

Ruhle, Jurgen. *A Critical Study of the Writer and Communism in the Twentieth Century.* Translated and edited by Jean Steinberg. London: Praeger, 1969.

Strauss, Leo, and Joseph Cropsey, eds. *History of Political Philosophy.* 3d ed. Chicago: University of Chicago Press, 1987.

Wilkinson, James D. *The Intellectual Resistance in Europe.* Cambridge: Harvard University Press, 1981.

LOCKE, JOHN

Locke (1632–1704) was an English gentleman, philosopher, and political theorist who defended rights of resistance to absolute government in his *Two Treatises of Government* (1689). His ideas later became influential in American revolutionary arguments.

Locke argued that in terms of political rights all men are born naturally free and equal. Government is created to secure individuals' property, meaning their rights to life, liberty, and estate, and individuals consent to join political society for that purpose. According to Locke, each individual possesses a natural right to self-defense by using force against unjust force; any individual can use that right against a government that threatens his and others' life, liberty, and estate. Resistance is justified against a government or any part of a government that violates its "trust," for instance, by altering the forms of government established by the people to secure their rights; by preventing part of the government—such as Parliament—from meeting when it is needed to ensure the safety of the people; and by failing to act as an impartial umpire between individuals but instead establishing its own will under color of forms of law.

Locke, who believed these violations of trust had all been committed by the English king, Charles II, during 1679–1683, was probably composing these arguments in the midst of plans for armed resistance against the king. By late 1681 Charles was ruling without Parliament and had prevented parliamentary attempts to exclude his brother James, Duke of York, from the succession: Many parliamentarians held that James, because he was a Roman Catholic, would not protect the Protestant religion and the liberties and property of Englishmen. Charles had then instigated trials and executions of parliamentary supporters by questionable legal means, though using the forms of law.

In 1681 Charles attempted to have the Earl of Shaftesbury, Locke's patron, indicted for treason, but a Middlesex (London) Grand Jury refused. The Crown then forced surrender of various charters and franchises and gained control of the appointment of grand juries. Shaftesbury and others planned armed resistance in 1682–1683, and perhaps earlier. It did not materialize, and Locke fled into exile in Holland. After Charles's death, the Duke of York succeeded his brother in 1685, as James II.

John Locke

In 1688–1689 William of Orange and his wife, Mary (daughter of James), gained the English throne after leading an invasion against James that was supported by much of the English political nation. Locke's *Two Treatises* were largely ignored as immoderately radical when they were first published as an interpretation of this "revolution." Locke's contemporaries generally agreed that James had "abdicated" in an essentially unchanged "ancient constitution," not that the government had been dissolved and reconstituted in a way that involved Lockeian natural rights of resistance.

Locke's ideas, however, circulated in England, the Netherlands, and the American colonies. In the late eighteenth century some of his arguments became important to justify American resistance to the "tyranny" of the British Crown. Thomas Jefferson, author of the Declaration of Independence (1776), cited Locke's work as among the books expressing the sentiments that were harmonized in the declaration.

See also *British "Glorious Revolution" (1688–1689); William of Orange (King William III of England).*

JOHN MARSHALL

BIBLIOGRAPHY

Ashcraft, Richard. *Revolutionary Politics and Locke's Two Treatises of Government.* Princeton, N.J.: Princeton University Press, 1986.

Dunn, John. *The Political Thought of John Locke.* Cambridge: Cambridge University Press, 1969.

Goldie, Mark A., ed. *Two Treatises of Government by John Locke.* New York: Everyman, 1993.

Marshall, John W. *John Locke: Resistance, Religion, and Responsibility.* Cambridge: Cambridge University Press, 1994.

Wootton, David, ed. *Locke: Political Writings.* New York: Penguin, 1993.

L'OUVERTURE, FRANÇOIS-DOMINIQUE TOUSSAINT

L'Ouverture, originally known as Toussaint Bréda, was born a slave in 1743, or 1746 depending on the source, on the Bréda plantation (hence his original name) in the north of the French colony of Saint-Domingue (present-day Haiti). He died imprisoned at Fort de Joux, near Paris, France, in April 1803, where he had been sent after his capture in Saint-Domingue by Gen. Victor Emmanuel Leclerc in June 1802.

L'Ouverture belonged to that relatively privileged group of slaves whose occupations distinguished them from field hands. In addition to receiving a rudimentary education in French and Latin, he initially took care of flocks and herds, then became a coachman to the plantation's overseer, and ultimately a manager of all the livestock on the plantation.

L'Ouverture was not among the original leaders of the slave revolution that erupted in August 1791. Around November 1791, however, he joined the rebellious slaves who had defected to the Spanish army in neighboring Spanish San Domingo, which, along with the English, was fighting the French in Saint-Domingue. L'Ouverture never intended to remain in the Spanish army. He agreed to join the French army to help it expel the Spanish and English from Saint-Domingue only after the French government decreed the emancipation of the slaves in 1794. He took with him a force of 4,000 experienced fighters, all former slaves, and was promoted to the rank of brigadier general.

By mid-1800 L'Ouverture and his army of ex-slaves had emerged as the dominant force in Saint-Domingue. Once he consolidated his power, L'Ouverture proceeded to reorganize the colony without declaring its independence from France. This would prove to be his greatest mistake. L'Ouverture believed in self-government for Saint-Domingue, but he wanted it to remain a French possession and the former slaves to become French citizens because he did not believe that the colony could prosper without maintaining its economic, political, and cultural ties with France. Therefore, L'Ouverture sought to preserve the plantation

François-Dominique Toussaint L'Ouverture

system established by the French in the seventeenth century, and he encouraged the former slave-owning planter class to remain in the colony, to invest in their plantations, and to employ their former slaves as wage-laborers.

L'Ouverture's solution was 146 years too early. The status he sought for Saint-Domingue in 1800 was implemented by the remaining French Caribbean colonies of Guadeloupe, French Guiana, and Martinique in 1946, when their General Councils voted to become overseas departments of France. But in 1800 all major social interests in Saint-Domingue opposed L'Ouverture's policies for different reasons, and they sought to undermine him. Consequently, when Napoleon Bonaparte sent a military force to recapture the colony and reimpose slavery in 1802, L'Ouverture's most trusted general officers abandoned him and allowed General Leclerc to capture and deport him. Jean-Jacques Dessalines then took over the leadership of the revolutionary forces and continued the war that won Haiti its independence in January 1804.

See also *Hatian Revolution of Independence (1791–1804); Latin American and Caribbean Slave Revolts (1521–1888); Latin American Revolts under Colonial Rule (1571–1898); U.S. Slave Revolts (1776–1865).*

Alex Dupuy

BIBLIOGRAPHY

Dupuy, Alex. *Haiti in the World Economy: Class, Race, and Underdevelopment since 1700.* Boulder, Colo.: Westview Press, 1989.

James, C. L. R. *The Black Jacobins: Toussaint L'Ouverture and the San Domingo Revolution.* New York: Vintage Books, 1963.

Pluchon, Pierre. *Toussaint Louverture: de l'esclavage au pouvoir.* Paris: Éditions de l'École; Port-au-Prince: Éditions Caraïbes, 1979.

Schoelcher, Victor. *Vie de Toussaint-Louverture.* Deuxième Édition. Paris: Paul Ollendorff, 1889.

LUMUMBA, PATRICE

Lumumba (1925–1961) was a leading Congolese nationalist at the time of independence and, through his assassination, a martyr to African liberation. He enjoyed only the briefest moment on the political stage in the Congo, but the flamboyant aggressiveness of his nationalist commitment, and the international complicities in his overthrow and assassination, made his short life a symbol of the struggle for African liberation. (The Congo was renamed Zaire in 1971 and became the Democratic Republic of the Congo in 1997.) In his martyrdom, he became a figure much larger than life.

He was born in a small village in east central Congo. After checkered experiences in mission schools, where he reached the secondary level, he became a postal clerk in Stanleyville (now Kisangani). By the early 1950s he was making a mark as an organizer and leader in the welter of urban associations, which engaged the energies of the emerging elite. He also attracted Belgian notice as a talented and able young subject; he had two audiences with King Baudouin during the king's 1955 tour of the colony.

Nationalism, virtually absent in Congo until 1956, spread rapidly in the years following. Lumumba, who moved to the capital city of Leopoldville (now Kinshasa) in 1957 as sales agent for a brewery, emerged as the leader of a major political party, the Congolese National Movement (MNC). In 1959 the party split, and Lumumba retained control of the larger faction, now renamed MNC-Lumumba. At the end of 1958 he attended a pan-African conference in Accra, Ghana, where he came into contact with such leading African nationalists as Kwame Nkrumah and Ahmed Sekou Touré. He rapidly absorbed the doctrine of radical anticolonial nationalism, dedicated to a unitary, centralized, strong state.

Belgium in January 1960 agreed to immediate independence for its colony; a short but intense process of extending party mobilization from the towns into the countryside followed. Lumumba, fluent in several Congolese languages, proved a superb tribune. In the elections of May 1960, his party and its allies, though far from achieving a parliamentary majority, demonstrated more widespread national support than any other party. Lumumba became prime minister.

Impulsive and intolerant of opposition, he quickly found himself embattled. Within a fortnight of independence, the army mutinied against its Belgian officers; the Belgian functionaries who occupied nearly all the top government posts fled; the richest province, Katanga, seceded; and the country became the cockpit of international influences and cold war rivalry.

Lumumba's conflict with his political rival, President Joseph Kasavubu, deepened, and Western powers became increasingly distrustful of what they saw as Lumumba's erratic behavior and disposition to seek Soviet support. On September 5, 1960, Lumumba was ousted from office with Western support, and soon thereafter he was arrested. Even in prison he was feared by the West, and the American Central Intelligence Agency in fall 1960 plotted his assassination. Its schemes failed, but in January 1961 Lumumba was transferred to the secessionist province of Katanga and at once assassinated.

A huge international wave of indignation followed. The memory of Lumumba served as a mobilizing symbol in a rebellion that swept the country in 1964–1965. Throughout Africa the name Lumumba remains an evocative symbol, representing the dream of total African liberation.

See also *Congolese/Zairean Upheavals (1960–); Nkrumah, Kwame.*

CRAWFORD YOUNG

BIBLIOGRAPHY

Kanza, Thomas. *Conflict in the Congo: The Rise and Fall of Lumumba.* London: Rex Collings, 1978.

Lumumba, Patrice. *Le Congo terre d'avenir est-il menacé.* Brussels: Office de Publicité, 1961.

van Lierde, Jean. *La pensée politique de Patrice Lumumba.* Paris: Présence Africaine, 1963.

Willame, Jean-Claude. *Patrice Lumumba: la crise congolaise revisitée.* Paris: Karthala, 1990.

Young, Crawford. *Politics in the Congo.* Princeton, N.J.: Princeton University Press, 1965.

LUTHER, MARTIN

The leading figure in the Protestant Reformation in Germany, Luther (1489–1546) was the founding theologian of the Lutheran confession and, indirectly, of all forms of Protestant religion. Born into a prosperous family at Eisleben in Thuringia, he attended the University of Erfurt, entered the Order of the Augustinian Hermits there, and became professor of theology in the University of Wittenberg in Saxony. After 1517 he became antagonistic toward local church authorities, the papacy at Rome, and the Holy Roman Empire. Protected by the electors of Saxony, Luther presided over the defining of German Protestantism and influenced, through the unprecedented explosion of his works in print, movements against Rome in Germany and in other countries of transalpine Europe.

Luther's relationship to political revolution is twofold. In the first place, he encouraged the German princes to revolt against the Catholic Church's authority *(Address to the Christian Nobility,* 1520) and stimulated Christian individuals to take the interpretation of the Bible and the organization of congregations into their own hands. He nonetheless decided even before the Peasant War (1524–1526) that Christians must obey the legitimate temporal ruler *(On Temporal Authority,* 1523), and in 1525 he condemned the rebels for appealing to religion to justify their demands. He never admitted an individual's right to resist authority, and in 1530 he deferred to the jurists the question of the prince's right to resist the emperor. It is widely held, and not only by Marxist historians, that Luther, having early encouraged private judgment and spontaneous church organization, had turned against them (and, some would say, against the common people) by the mid-1520s. In the German Democratic Republic he was long officially regarded as a traitor to the cause of revolution.

Second, Luther has long been regarded as a deeply conservative force for political passivity in the German-speaking world. The definitive form of this charge was framed by the theologian Ernst Troeltsch (1865–1923), who considered Luther's social and political thinking to have been trapped in the conservative, aristocratic, feudal world of Saxony. In the twentieth century Luther has been portrayed as one of the major counterrevolutionary figures in German history, an image Thomas Mann, Germany's best-known twentieth-century author, did much to encourage. Probably, his counterrevolutionary image owes a great deal more to Allied propaganda in the two world wars, which portrayed the reformer as the source of German authoritarianism, than it does to Luther's actual influence in German history. It is worth mentioning that his movement was successful, in the sense that it came to dominate the religious life, in only about one-third of the Holy Roman Empire, and also that Lutheranism produced its own versions of apocalypticism as well as the basic elements of the Protestant resistance theory, chiefly that subordinate magistrates—but not individuals—may resist a ruler whose commands contradict God's laws. The Prussian Lutheran philosopher Johann Gottlieb Fichte (1762–1814) cited Luther and Jesus as patron saints of revolution.

See also *Anabaptism; German Peasant War (1524–1526); Religion.*

THOMAS BRADY JR.

BIBLIOGRAPHY

Cargill Thompson, W. D. J. *The Political Thought of Martin Luther.* Totowa, N.J.: Barnes and Noble, 1984.

Troeltsch, Ernst. *Protestantism and Progress: A Historical Study of the Relation of Protestantism to the Modern World.* 2d ed. Boston: Beacon Press, 1958. (1st ed., 1912)

Wolgast, Eike. *Die Wittenberger Theologie und die Politik der evangelischen Stände.* Gütersloh: Gerd Mohn Verlag, 1977.

LUXEMBURG, ROSA

Luxemburg (1871–1919), a Polish-born German revolutionary leader, advocated a militantly libertarian Marxism opposed to both bureaucratic reformism and communist authoritarianism. Luxemburg based her conception of democracy on a refusal to identify freedom with any set of institutions and a concern with furthering the self-administrative capacities of working people. Thus her influence has largely been confined to movements and thinkers critical of both the socialist and communist mainstream.

Born in Russian Poland, Luxemburg became involved in antitsarist politics as a teenager. Forced into exile, she entered the University of Zurich, where in 1898 she completed a dissertation on the industrial development of Poland. The internationalism evident in this work became her trademark.

Luxemburg feared that nationalism would divide workers, foster militarism, generate class compromise, and threaten the values of socialist democracy. Her most important work, *The Accumulation of Capital* (1913), attempts to demonstrate how capitalism generates militarism, nationalism, and imperialism. Because of these views, she remained a pacifist during World War I, spending much of the war in prison.

Luxemburg gained notoriety with her contribution to the revisionism debate. The chief advocate of revisionism, Eduard Bernstein, sought to replace the revolutionary ideology of the labor movement with evolutionary reform. He aimed to substitute a politics of class compromise for visions of a future capitalist collapse. Luxemburg, in *Social Reform or Revolution* (1899), insisted that reform is limited, that a systemic breakdown is unavoidable, and that a policy of class compromise will only empower party bureaucrats.

Luxemburg's *Organizational Questions of Social Democracy* (1904), in the same vein, criticized Vladimir Ilyich Lenin's concept of the "vanguard party." During the following year

Rosa Luxemburg

she participated in the Russian revolution of 1905. The experience inspired perhaps her finest theoretical work. *Mass Strike, Party, and Trade Unions* (1906) emphasized the spontaneity of revolutionary uprisings and the ability of the working class to rule society in a democratic fashion. The pamphlet anticipates her most famous work, *The Russian Revolution,* written in 1918, while she was in jail. In this work Luxemburg criticized Lenin's dictatorship by claiming that political democracy with full civil rights must serve as the precondition for socialism.

When Luxemburg was released from prison in 1918, proletarian uprisings were sweeping Europe. She became president of the new German Communist Party and participated in the attempt to bring a new regime of soviets, or workers' councils, into being. In 1919 she was murdered by the right-wing militia employed by the first government of the Weimar Republic.

See also *Communism; German Revolution (1918); Marx, Karl, and Friedrich Engels.*

STEPHEN ERIC BRONNER

BIBLIOGRAPHY

Bronner, Stephen Eric. *Rosa Luxemburg: A Revolutionary for Our Times.* University Park: Pennsylvania State University Press, 1997.

Frolich, Paul. *Rosa Luxemburg: Her Life and Work.* Translated by Johanna Hoornweg. New York: Monthly Review Press, 1972.

Nettl, J. P. *Rosa Luxemburg.* 2 vols. New York: Oxford University Press, 1966.

Waters, Mary-Alice, ed. *Rosa Luxemburg Speaks.* New York: Pathfinder, 1970.

MADAGASCAR (MALAGASY) WAR OF INDEPENDENCE (1947)

The Malagasy rebellion against French colonial rule that broke out during the night of March 29, 1947, was the first postwar revolt in the French colonies, although it is less well known (and was less successful) than subsequent revolts in Vietnam and Algeria. The rebellion resulted in the deaths of more than 90,000 people, all but approximately 550 of whom were Malagasy, and it was not completely subdued until December 1948. The roots of the revolt lay in the French annexation of the island of Madagascar in 1896, the colonial system established by the French, and the reactions of the inhabitants of the islands, the Malagasy, to the annexation and the colonial economic and social system.

The French colonial system had been established only after considerable resistance from the various "kingdoms" that constituted Madagascar at the end of the nineteenth century. The largest and most centralized was the Merina monarchy, centered on what was to become the colonial capital and then the capital of an independent Madagascar, Antananarivo. Only after the capture of the city and the abolition of the monarchy did the 1896 Law of Annexation formally add the island to France's African colonies. Resistance to French rule continued throughout the colonial period and was vigorously repressed through a legal system that limited the rights of Malagasy to form political parties and unions and to operate newspapers. In several areas of the island, particularly along the east coast and in the central highlands, land was confiscated and turned into plantations run by French settlers and companies.

The Second World War laid the immediate grounds for the 1947 rebellion. In 1940, after initial hesitation, the colonial government in Madagascar sided with the French Vichy regime, which was collaborating with the Germans. The British, fearing German occupation of the island, which lay between South Africa and India, invaded and occupied Madagascar. They then handed the island over to the Free French, who reimposed the colonial system with even more rigor, using the island as a source of personnel and raw materials for their war effort. To the usual rules were added an increased demand for labor and rationing of the island's main foodstuff, rice. With the rationing came a black market, and shortages were induced by both the rationing and the underground market.

The end of the war set the scene for the rebellion in several different ways. The relaxation of rules governing indigenous political activity, and the creation of a second electoral college with a Malagasy electorate, gave the nationalist movement an arena in which to communicate its goals. The United Nations Charter and wartime declarations of the Allies had raised hopes among the Malagasy that the postwar era would mean the end of the colonial system. Members of the Malagasy nationalist movement were well aware of the demands for autonomy that were being made in French Indochina and of the progress of India toward independence from Britain.

The organizational efforts of the nationalist movement were spurred by the series of elections that took place after the war, in October 1945 and June 1946, to the two Constituent Assemblies that met in Paris to draft the constitution of the Fourth French Republic and to the French legislature. The elections to the first Constituent Assembly returned two well-known nationalist leaders, Raseta and Ravoahangy. Once in Paris, they recruited Jacques Rabemananjara, a poet from the east coast. The three founded a political party, the Democratic Movement for Malagasy Renewal (MDRM), with the goal of winning the three seats in the French legislature that were to be elected by the Malagasy second college. Their ultimate goal was independence.

The MDRM was an amalgamation of various currents of the nationalist movement. Malagasy soldiers returning from the war often formed the middle level leadership of the movement, between the urbanized deputies and the largely rural electorate, and they also extended the geographical reach of the movement beyond the area around the capital

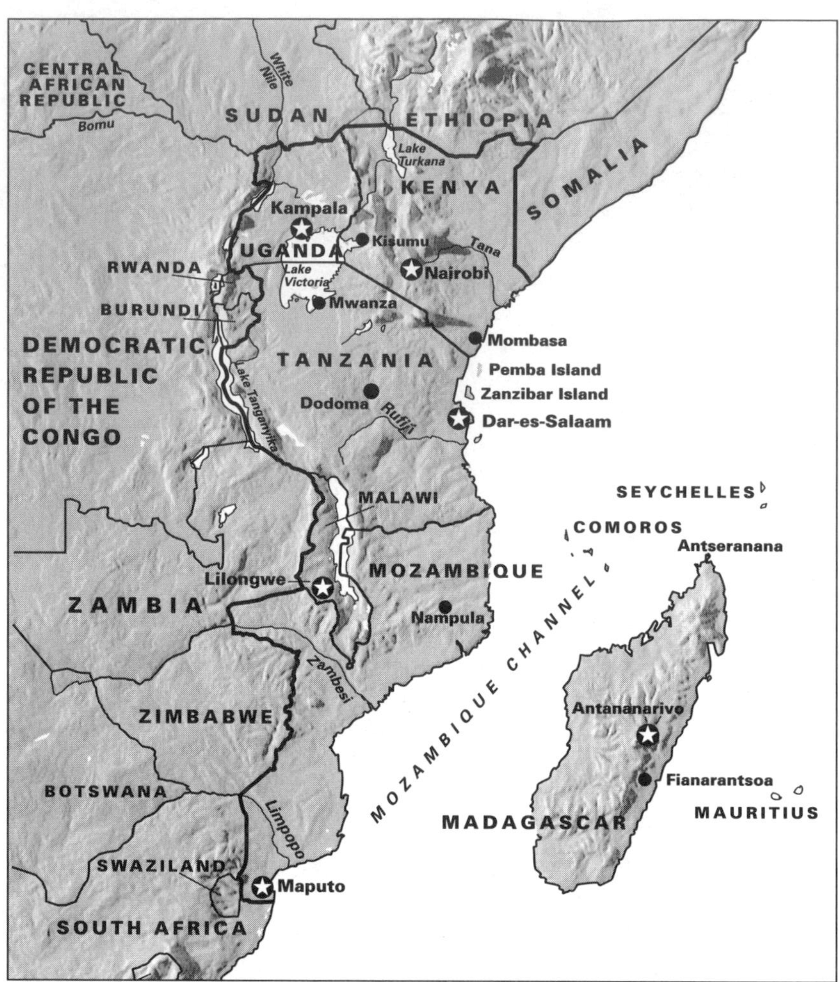

city. In addition, two "secret societies," the Malagasy Nationalist Party (PANAMA) and the Nationalist Youth League (JINA), which had formed during the war to resist the reimposition of the colonial system, sent members to the MDRM and its associated organizations. These societies had adherents throughout the island but were particularly strong on the east coast.

The three founders of the MDRM tried to get the Constituent Assemblies to revise the status of Madagascar, but they were not successful. The French Union created by the constitution of the Fourth French Republic was a modernized version of the old empire, and Madagascar's status remained that of a colony; it did not gain the semiautonomy granted to Syria and Algeria. Attempts to have the 1896 annexation law repealed were no more successful.

The rebellion broke out in part in reaction to the failure to move toward autonomy. It was most effective on the east coast and in the central highlands. These had traditionally been areas of nationalist activity, had been the most affected by the imposition of the colonial regime, and were connected by the island's rail lines. The western part of the island remained quiescent. Its quiescence and the failure of the rebels to capture the French military camps in Antananarivo and Fianarantsoa and the naval base at Diego Suarez (now Antseranana) led to the failure of the uprising. However, the rebels retreated to guerrilla warfare, particularly along the east coast and its hinterland, and the revolt could not be considered over until December 1948, by which time the French had worn the guerrillas down.

The French colonial authorities blamed the MDRM, and in particular its three deputies, for the rebellion. The party was dissolved in May 1947, and the deputies, along with others accused of complicity in the uprising, were tried in 1948. Raseta, Ravoahangy, and four others were condemned to death, while Rabemananjara was sentenced to life at hard labor. (The sentences were later commuted to life imprisonment, and the deputies were freed at the time of Malagasy independence.) Most of the actual leaders of the fighting had died by the time of the trial, either in battle or by execution.

The degree of involvement of the MDRM and its deputies in the rebellion is still a matter of debate. It seems probable that they had some idea of what was going on, without being the actual instigators. The probable organizers were the members of the secret societies, many of whom had joined the MDRM before the rebellion.

The rebellion was in part a civil war between Malagasy opposed to the colonial regime and those whom they considered to be its collaborators. The First Malagasy Republic, which was established in 1958 and became fully independent in 1960, was led by people from groups that either had been targeted by the rebels or that had not participated. Its attitude toward the revolt was ambiguous. The Second Malagasy Republic, established in 1975 as the Democratic Republic of Madagascar, claimed as part of its inspiration "the martyrs of

1947." It declared the anniversary of the uprising a national holiday and erected a monument to the martyrs in Antananarivo.

MAUREEN COVELL

BIBLIOGRAPHY

Brown, Mervyn. *Madagascar Rediscovered: From Early Days to Independence.* Hamden, Conn.: Archon Books, 1979.

Covell, Maureen. *Historical Dictionary of Madagascar.* Lanham, Md.: Scarecrow Press, 1995.

———. *Madagascar: Politics, Economics, Society.* London: Frances Pinter, 1987.

Heseltine, Nigel. *Madagascar.* New York: Praeger, 1971.

Tronchon, J. *L'Insurrection malgache de 1947: Essai d'interpretation historique.* Paris: Maspero, 1974.

MADISON, JAMES

James Madison (1751–1836), planter, writer, and political leader, participated in the American revolutionary and nation-building movement from his resistance to the Townshend Acts in 1769 to his politically active retirement in the 1830s. As a member of Virginia revolutionary, constitutional, and legislative assemblies, as a member of the Continental Congress, the Constitutional Convention of 1787, and the Federal House of Representatives, as secretary of state and president, and as sage and public affairs adviser in twenty years of retirement, he took part in every phase of the long American revolutions in loyalty, purpose, and character that extended throughout his lifetime.

As a schoolboy in the 1760s Madison seems to have had access to such civic republican, liberal, revolution-sustaining works as those of Cicero, Joseph Addison, Montesquieu, and John Locke, doubtless along with early revolutionary pamphlets of John Dickinson, Richard Bland, and others. We know, too, that his father corresponded about and took part in the boycotts of and resistances to the Stamp Act (1765), the Townshend duties, and other British measures. Then, during his years at the College of New Jersey in Princeton, 1769–1772, Madison studied in a hotbed of radical Whiggery presided over by a fervent opponent of "lordly domination and sacerdotal tyranny," Presbyterian John Witherspoon (later a signer of the Declaration of Independence). Reading more Locke as well as John Trenchard and Thomas Gordon, John Milton, Algernon Sidney, Adam Ferguson, and other Whiggish writers, participating in student protests against the Townshend duties, and then listening to graduation orations by his classmates on such subjects as "Omnes Homines, Jura Naturae, liberti sunt" (all men, under natural law, are free), Madison was imbued with revolutionary ideals long before 1776.

His participation in revolutionary activity began formally when at age twenty-three, in December 1774, he was elected to the Orange County, Virginia, Committee of Safety, of which his father was chair. He practiced marksmanship and took part in some militia forays in 1775, but his sickliness then and later kept him from entering the army. Instead, he mustered local soldiers, collected arms and supplies, and harassed Tories—he gloated that "one Scotch parson. . . [was] ducked in a coat of tar and surplice of feathers. . . [for] his insolence."

Elected at age twenty-five to the Virginia Convention of 1776 that voted for independence and drafted a new, republican constitution for the state, Madison wrote the clause that declared that "all men are equally entitled to the free exercise of religion, according to the dictates of conscience," language substituted for the more invidious concept of "fullest toleration" in matters of religion. In this and other extensions of freedoms and civil rights, Madison remained a front-running revolutionary all his life. Service in the legislative session of 1776 that undertook Jefferson's "republicanizing" of the laws of Virginia began the fifty-year-long collaboration of the two men in fashioning the meaning of the American Revolution. Membership on the Virginia Council of State, 1777–1779, where he took day-to-day part in sustaining Virginia's war effort, completed his revolutionary activity in the state.

Elected to the Continental Congress in 1780, he began more than three years of steady service there doing all he could to support Washington's army, rescue disastrously inflationary finances, defend the French alliance, and otherwise bring the Revolutionary War to the successful conclusion secured by the Treaty of Paris in 1783, which Madison voted to ratify. Independence, though, for Madison was not the end, but the beginning of the revolution. He worked to further revise the laws of Virginia, 1784–1786, but paid greatest attention to strengthening and making more republican the union of the states. As chief proposer of the Federal Convention of 1787, as a leading advocate there of measures to strengthen the national government, as explainer of the new Constitution in the *Federalist Papers,* and as its profound and stalwart defender at the Virginia ratifying convention of 1788, Madison more than any other person defined the frame, nature, and future of American revolutionary government. His service as one of President Washington's chief advisers and as a member of the Federal Congress, 1789–1797, completed his primary revolutionary career begun a quarter-century earlier. He had no career other than revolutionary and nation-builder.

In sixteen years as secretary of state and president, 1801–1817, Madison worked out what he saw as the foreign policy implications of the American Revolution and the domestic postures in government appropriate to it. He supported and sympathized with the ideals of the French Revolution ("republics should draw near to each other," he thought), resisted unlawful depredations (mainly by Great Britain) on American high seas commerce, and led the nation in 1812 into what he saw as a "Second War for American Independence," at once defeating Britain's renewed attempt to dominate the United States and assuring republican survival. For Madison, victory in the War of 1812 completed the American Revolution.

See also *American (U.S.) Revolution (1776–1789).*

Ralph Ketcham

BIBLIOGRAPHY

Hutchinson, William T., et al., eds. *The Papers of James Madison.* Chicago: University of Chicago Press; and Charlottesville: University Press of Virginia, 1962. Three series, 23 vols. to date.

Brant, Irving. *James Madison, the Virginia Revolutionist.* Indianapolis, Ind.: Bobbs Merrill, 1941.

Ketcham, Ralph. *James Madison: A Biography.* New York: Macmillan, 1971; Charlottesville: University Press of Virginia, 1991.

Miller, William Lee. *The Business of May Next: James Madison and the Founding.* Charlottesville, Va.: University Press of Virginia, 1992.

MALAYAN COMMUNIST INSURGENCY (1948–1960)

The "Malayan Emergency," which broke out in June 1948, pitted the British colonial government of Malaya against the Malayan Communist Party, its rural-based guerrilla army, and their supporters. The guerrilla war resulted from the turmoil of the Japanese occupation during World War II, from 1942 to 1945, and the decision of the Communist Party to take advantage of the chaotic situation to wage an armed struggle aimed at ousting the British administration. The party was made up almost entirely of Malayan Chinese and initially relied heavily on the support of rural Malayan Chinese squatters who lived along the jungle fringes. Overall, Malayan Chinese constituted 38.5 percent of Malaya's population of five million, while the Malays, the other major ethnic group, made up 44 percent. Malays tended to be overtly anticommunist because of past tensions between the two ethnic groups.

Despite being disorganized and able to count on only a minority of the population for recruits, funds, supplies, and information, the Malayan Communist Party gained ground in the first few years of the emergency. The primary reason for its success was the government's misguided strategy. The indiscriminate way in which the security forces shot anyone vaguely suspected of being a guerrilla or burned the homes of those thought to be communist sympathizers drove many ethnic Chinese to support the communists. At the same time, the basic grievances of the population, which included rice shortages, high prices for most foodstuffs, and low wages, turned people against the government.

Rising demand for Malaya's two major commodities, rubber and tin, during the Korean War (1950–1953) gave the government the respite it desperately needed. The government's revenue doubled, allowing for the resettlement of nearly a half million rural Chinese into enclosed "new villages." The plan was to cut off the guerrillas from their base of support. However, the communist guerrillas waged an increasingly violent campaign, and by late 1951 there was widespread pessimism that they would ever be defeated.

Two events in 1952 started to turn the tide. First, the Communist Party, fearing that its violent campaign was alienating supporters, began to put greater emphasis on political mobilization. Guerrilla-instigated violent incidents dropped dramatically, and, ironically, the government was given credit for this. Second, a new high commissioner, Gen. Sir Gerald Templer, revised and energized the government's counterinsurgency campaign. He introduced a "hearts and minds" approach, which sought to win over the Malayan, and especially the Malayan Chinese, population. New vil-

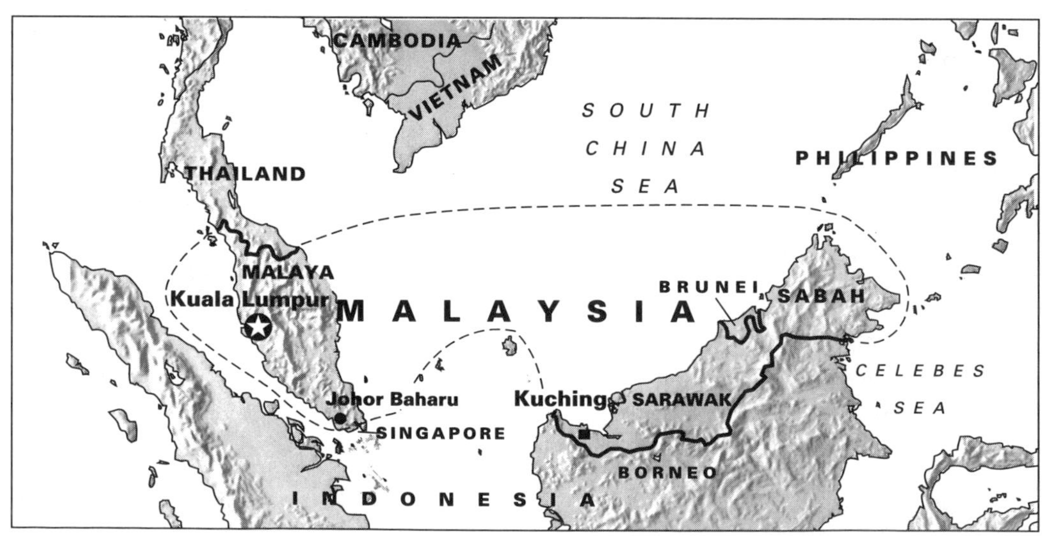

lages were supplied with clean water, schools, community centers, basic medical care, and other amenities; elections were introduced at the village level and later, in 1955, were extended to the federal level; strict controls were placed on foodstuffs and other supplies vital to the guerrillas' existence; the military and police were retrained, with the emphasis put on helping Malayans rather than abusing them; and the intelligence and propaganda units were made more effective.

Gradually, the momentum swung away from the Malayan Communist Party. The government gained administrative control of the country, and the population saw the guerrillas as increasingly irrelevant to their daily needs. Most Malayans were not so much won over as neutralized. The communists had to retreat to the Thai border region as their base of support evaporated. After Malaya declared independence in 1957, the Malayan Communist Party became marginalized, and the guerrilla war officially came to an end on July 31, 1960.

RICHARD STUBBS

BIBLIOGRAPHY

Short, Anthony. *The Communist Insurrection in Malaya 1948–1960.* New York: Crane Russak, 1975.

Stubbs, Richard. *Hearts and Minds in Guerrilla Warfare: The Malayan Emergency 1948–1960.* Singapore: Oxford University Press, 1989.

Thompson, Robert. *Defeating Communist Insurgency: Experiences from Malaya and Vietnam.* London: Chatto and Windus, 1966.

MANDELA, NELSON ROLIHLAHLA

Mandela (1918–) is the president of South Africa and the internationally venerated voice of all South Africans. As a young leader of the African National Congress, Mandela, together with Walter Sisulu and Oliver Tambo, founded the ANC Youth League (ANCYL) in 1944. In 1948 he was named its national secretary, and in 1950 its president. They radicalized the ANCYL and later the ANC itself, moving it from an essentially bourgeois reformist body to one aggressively seeking sociopolitical revolution.

In the 1950s Mandela was arrested and convicted under the Suppression of Communism Act and was banned for nine years, yet he continued his work. He developed the "M Plan" (named after him), by which the ANC branches prepared for underground activity. Arrested again in 1956 for high treason, he was acquitted more than four years later.

In March 1960, panicky police fired on demonstrators at a police station in a township south of Johannesburg, killing sixty-nine people. After the Sharpeville massacre, the ANC and the Pan-Africanist Congress were outlawed, and during the subsequent state of emergency Mandela was detained without charge, although he was allowed to practice law in Johannesburg on weekends. In March 1961, after his acquittal in the treason trial, he defied his banning order and went underground, remaining an active ANC organizer and fugitive for seventeen months. During that time he helped organize Umkhonto we Sizwe (March 1961), the ANC's military wing, and served as its commander in chief from December 1961.

Mandela fled South Africa, received guerrilla training in Algeria, and traveled throughout Africa and to London. On his return he was captured in August 1962 and sentenced to five years' imprisonment. He was tried again with seven other ANC leaders in the Rivonia trial of 1963–1964. Mandela's four-hour statement from the dock received worldwide publicity. All eight defendants were sentenced to life imprisonment, beginning in 1964, at the notorious Robben Island prison. In 1982 Mandela was transferred to Pollsmoor prison outside of Cape Town, and in 1988 to Victor Verster prison.

From July 1986 onward, Mandela met government representatives secretly and eventually met with Presidents P. W. Botha (July 1989) and F. W. de Klerk (December 1989). He also met with senior members of various antiapartheid groups in his final months in prison. His position on the issues for negotiation was straightforward. Mandela demanded his and others' unconditional release, amnesty for returning exiles, the legalization of the ANC and other resistance groups, and the commencement of a process of negotiations leading to a transfer of power. Upon his dramatic release from prison on February 11, 1990, Mandela traveled to Zambia to meet the ANC executive committee in exile and to Sweden to meet ANC president Tambo. Mandela was appointed the ANC's deputy president and served in that capacity until Tambo's death in 1993.

The discussions about the transfer of power, which began with the government in May 1990, culminated with the general elections of April 1994, in which the ANC carried 62 percent of the vote. The resulting Government of National Unity included the ANC, the National Party, and the Inkatha Freedom Party. These three parties also hammered out the outlines of a constitution. On May 9, 1994, Mandela was elected by the National Assembly unopposed as president.

In 1993 Mandela shared the Nobel Peace Prize with de Klerk. Mandela's unchallenged leadership comes by virtue of his personal qualities, particularly his energy, integrity, negotiating skills, dignity, and courtesy. He is a superb strategist and tactician. Mandela is respected for his unbending opposition to minority rule and his loyalty to ANC principles and discipline, but he is not especially at home with ideas. His

Newly elected president Nelson Mandela addresses the crowd from a balcony of the town hall in 1994.

leanings toward reconciliation with the whites, a multicultural, ecumenical "rainbow" nation, rights for all, respect for tradition and personal loyalty, and a flexible approach to economic development provide the nation with a model of tolerant, mature leadership. He has quietly abandoned the ANC's earlier attraction to socialism and nationalization and now seems inclined toward a social democratic approach to "unbundling" large corporations and to attracting foreign investments and creating economic opportunities for all. Thus Mandela's revolutionary appeal as president is moderated by his image as a dignified, wise, and steadfast leader, one prepared to compromise only on strategy and tactics, not principle. Mandela's activist reputation had been forged during the early resistance years. His twenty-seven years out of the limelight allowed the metamorphosis to occur and be accepted by the people.

See also *South African Antiapartheid Revolts and Reform (1948–1994).*

KENNETH W. GRUNDY

BIBLIOGRAPHY

Benson, Mary. *Nelson Mandela: The Man and the Movement.* Harmondsworth: Penguin, 1994.

Johns, Sheridan, and R. Hunt Davis Jr., eds. *Mandela, Tambo and the African National Congress: The Struggle against Apartheid, 1948–1990.* New York: Oxford University Press, 1991.

Lewis, Anthony. "Mandela the Pol." *New York Times Magazine.* (March 23, 1997): 40–79.

Mandela, Nelson. *The Struggle Is My Life: His Speeches and His Writings.* London: International Defence and Aid, 1990.

———. *Long Walk to Freedom: The Autobiography of Nelson Mandela.* Boston: Little, Brown, 1994.

MAO ZEDONG

Mao Zedong (1893–1976) was arguably the most outstanding revolutionary figure of the twentieth century. Indeed, his name has become the universally recognized label for radical revolutionary extremism, as in *Maoism* and *Maoist.* He was the embodiment of the Chinese communist revolution. His military skills brought the party to power in 1949. His passion for ideological purity and revolutionary commitment stirred the Chinese people to make great sacrifices. His policies advanced but also seriously set back China's progress. Mao himself believed that he rightfully belonged in the apostolic succession of communism's great leaders as the next in line after Marx, Engels, Lenin, and Stalin. The Chinese people treated his "Thoughts" as sacred words, and his *Little Red Book* of quotations as a guide for all manner of actions. His rule made China probably among the most ideologically saturated and politically disciplined societies in world history.

Mao was born in the small town of Shaoshan in Hunan Province, where his father was a successful farmer and landlord. At the age of sixteen he left home in search of more education, and subsequently attended the First Teacher's Training School in the provincial capital of Changsha. When his professor moved to Peking University, Mao went with him and became an assistant librarian. It was there during the excitement of the May Fourth Movement of 1919 that Mao became a Marxist.

Mao was one of a small band of student-intellectuals who founded the Chinese Communist Party in Shanghai in 1921. Whereas others went on to France or Russia to learn more about revolutionary work, Mao remained in China, first working as a union organizer and then most successfully as a guerrilla leader. Driven into the mountains of Jiangxi Province by the encircling Nationalist armies of Chiang Kai-shek, Mao built up a military force that would in time make the Long March up to Yan'an. There, Mao transformed the Chinese Communist Party from a leftist intellectual move-

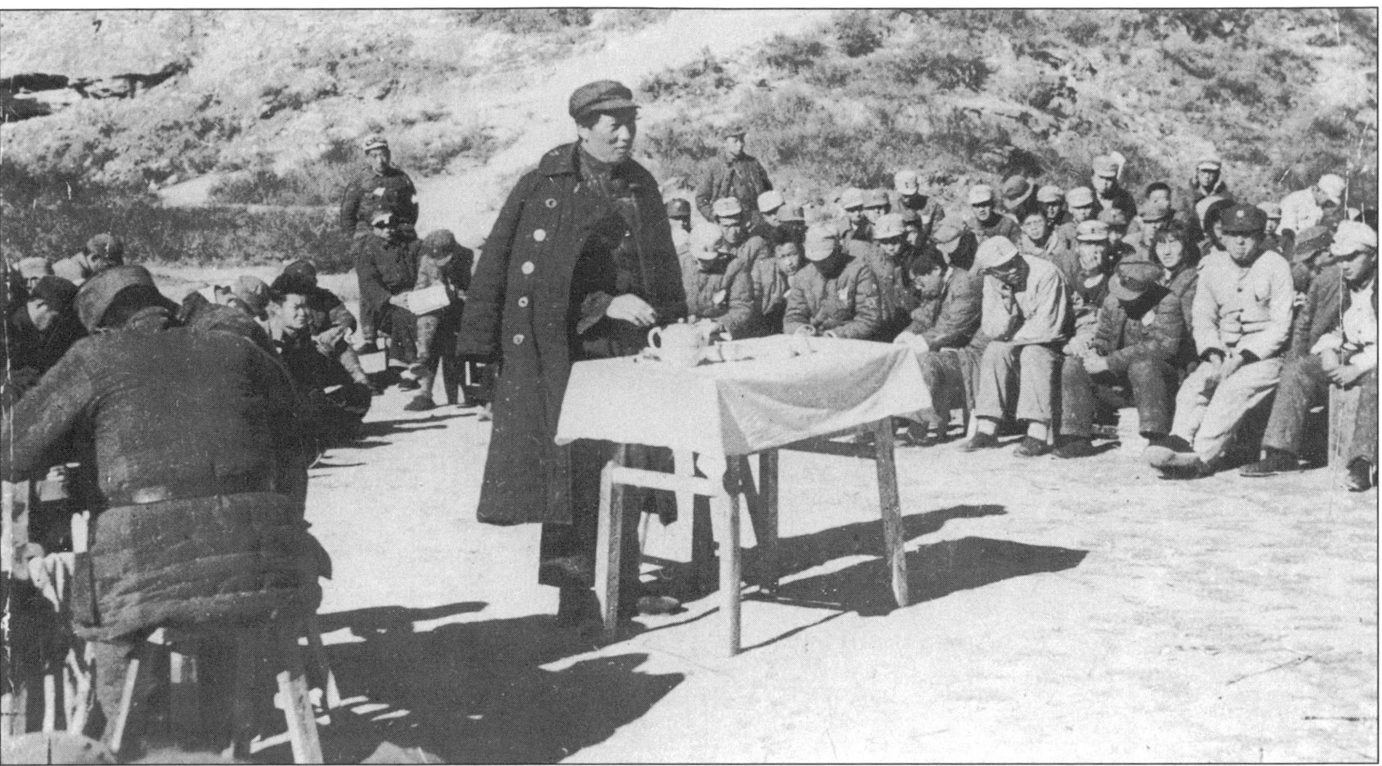

Mao Zedong addresses a group of his followers at the Communist base in Yan'an.

ment into a disciplined Leninist party. When the Japanese army began conquering China in 1937, Mao's guerrilla fighters expanded the communists' political power base into the territories occupied by Japan.

After the defeat of Japan, the communists mounted their successful campaign against the far stronger Nationalist forces under Chiang Kai-shek. Mao's dependence on military force, codified by his dictum that "Power grows out of the barrel of the gun," meant that the Chinese revolution depended on rural peasants, who made up the guerrilla armies, and not the orthodox Marxist revolutionary base of urban workers.

On October 1, 1949, Mao proclaimed the establishment of the People's Republic of China from the reviewing stand in Tiananmen Square. The immediate task of the party was to revive the economy and indoctrinate the entire population with communist ideology. Just as he had done in relying on peasants rather than workers to gain victory, Mao did not follow orthodox Marxism in meeting these new challenges. Mao made class distinctions in China depend, not on objective economic criteria, but on people's subjective orientations and thoughts.

During the first years of Mao's rule the Chinese communists relied heavily on economic assistance from their "big brother," the Soviet Union. The Moscow–Beijing alliance became even more intense after China entered the Korean War and came to view the United States as its mortal enemy. However, strains in relations with Moscow began to surface after Stalin's death. Mao was critical of Stalin's successors and felt that he should become the acknowledged leader of the world communist movement.

By 1958 Mao's impatience to make China a modern power drove him to some serious policy mistakes. Although the Chinese economy was growing at a respectable rate in the early 1950s, Mao decided to mobilize the entire country in a great effort to increase output, which became the disastrous campaign known as the Great Leap Forward. The focus was on rapid collectivization in the countryside, where the existing cooperatives were consolidated into large communes run like huge factories. Agricultural decisions were made by party officials and not by knowledgeable farmers. People were also encouraged to operate small "backyard furnaces" to increase steel production, diverting labor and resources from other necessary economic pursuits. The end result was the worst famine in known history, and the deaths of 25 to 40 million Chinese.

By 1961 Mao had to accept the failure of the Great Leap, and for a brief period he pulled back from day-to-day involvement in government. However, as the Chinese economy recovered, Mao became increasingly concerned about the loss of revolutionary fervor and the danger of revisionism, that is, a return to bourgeois thinking and practices. He was convinced that the Soviet Union had become a revisionist state. In 1965, to revive the people's revolutionary spirit and regain full control of the party, Mao launched the Great Proletarian Cultural Revolution. This was another disastrous campaign, which tore the party apart, closed schools and universities, disrupted government administration, set back all forms of science and technology, and eventually sent a whole generation of young people to the countryside to "learn" the presumed "revolutionary spirit" of the peasants. For much of the world it seemed as though China had gone mad.

Although the country had by 1969 reached a perilous state, it took the shock of a border conflict with Soviet troops to end the excesses of the Cultural Revolution. The danger of war with the Soviet Union now occupied the attention of Chairman Mao, and he was quick to pick up on President Richard Nixon's offer of better relations with the United States. During the last years of his rule, Mao had to accept the idea of a gradual opening to the outside world, although he still insisted on upholding his vision of a China totally under the control of an all-powerful Communist Party. Until his death Mao still believed that China's development called for ideological dedication, national self-reliance, economic autarky, and the intellectual leadership of ordinary workers and peasants.

Mao's successor, Deng Xiaoping, succeeded in putting China on the path of rapid economic growth and fuller integration with the world economy. With the hindsight of the post–Mao era, most Chinese came to accept that Mao's leadership had been seriously flawed, especially in the economic realm. However, in spite of his manifest failures, Mao also had many notable achievements. He unquestionably consolidated the unity of China as a modern nation; he broke down the iron grip of traditional thinking and practices that had held Chinese progress back; even his call for China's youth to challenge authority during the Cultural Revolution had the quite unintended effect of making a generation of Chinese more skeptical of their government and more open to new ideas. Thus, although no longer worshipped by the Chinese people as a god-figure, Mao is still seen in China as a great revolutionary hero.

See also *Chiang Kai-shek; Chinese Communist Revolution (1921–1949); Chinese Cultural Revolution (1966–1969); Chinese May Fourth Movement (1919).*

LUCIAN W. PYE

BIBLIOGRAPHY

Karnow, Stanley. *Mao on China: A Legacy of Turmoil.* New York: Penguin Books, 1990.

Li, Zhisui. *The Private Life of Chairman Mao.* London: Chatto and Windus, 1994.

Pye, Lucian W. *Mao Tse-tung: The Man in the Leader.* New York: Basic Books, 1976.

Salisbury, Harrison E. *The New Emperors: China in the Era of Mao and Deng.* Boston: Little, Brown, 1992.

Schram, Stuart R. *The Political Thought of Mao Tse-tung.* New York: Praeger, 1969.

———. *Chairman Mao Talks to the People: Talks and Letters, 1961–71.* New York: Pantheon, 1974.

Terrill, Ross. *Mao: A Biography.* Stanford: Stanford University Press, 1998.

Wilson, Dick. *Mao Tse-tung in the Scales of History.* New York: Cambridge University Press, 1977.

MARAT, JEAN-PAUL

Between 1789 and 1793 Marat (1743–1793) was the most notorious of French revolutionary journalists. His assassination, commemorated by Jacques-Louis David in one of the best-known images ever painted, made him a martyr to the revolutionary republican cause.

Born a Prussian subject at Boudry near Neuchatel into a family of modest means, Marat left school at sixteen to spend six years in France, where he became interested in medicine. From 1765 to 1776 he lived in England. Here his medical expertise was accepted, making him enough money to buy a doctorate. He also began to write works of speculative philosophy and in 1774 produced *The Chains of Slavery,* in which he denounced government as a violent usurpation against which insurrection was a legitimate recourse. (Written in English, the book became well known only when he published a French translation in 1792.) Back in France by 1777, Marat lived from medicine and sought to make his name as a

A period etching (1793) shows Jean-Paul Marat and others celebrating his acquittal by the Revolutionary Tribunal.

writer on science. Rejection of his discoveries by the Academy of Sciences left him convinced that he was a victim of a conspiracy of envious but well-connected mediocrities.

During the political excitement of the spring of 1789 Marat wrote a number of unmemorable pamphlets, but in September he found his vocation when he began to publish a regular newspaper of comment. After the first few issues he called it *The People's Friend,* a title by which he soon became known himself. Though not an outright republican until the fall of the monarchy in 1792, Marat was a consistent populist. The people, he claimed, were forever being duped and betrayed by those in power. Their salvation lay either in choosing a selfless dictator or in massacre of the guilty. On several occasions he was forced into hiding or fled abroad after inciting his readers to kill public officials or deputies. When suspected counterrevolutionaries were massacred in September 1792, Marat was widely blamed, and he reveled in the fact.

Marat was popular enough in Paris to win election to the Convention in the fall of 1792, where he voted for the king's death and denounced a number of fellow deputies as counterrevolutionaries. Prosecuted in the newly established Revolutionary Tribunal for his denouncements in the Convention, he was triumphantly acquitted and had the satisfaction six weeks later of seeing those he had denounced purged from the Convention under popular pressure (June 2, 1793). But by now he was seriously ill with a skin disease for which the only relief came from constant hot baths. He was in his bath when the royalist Charlotte Corday stabbed him to death on July 13, 1793.

The government capitalized on the genuine popular grief in Paris to make Marat's memory into a political cult. He became a sort of patron saint for the policy of Terror, which dominated the twelve months after his death. His cult culminated in September 1794 with the installation of his remains in the Pantheon, but after the retreat from Terror they were removed in February 1795. Since then his memory has never been entirely rehabilitated, and scholarly research has largely confirmed his enemies' charges of prerevolutionary charlatanism. Left-wing historians, however, stress his pioneering commitment to popular democracy.

See also *French Revolution (1789–1815); Media and Communications.*

William Doyle

BIBLIOGRAPHY

Gottschalk, Louis R. *Jean Paul Marat. A Study in Radicalism.* New York: Greenberg, 1927.

Hampson, Norman. *Will and Circumstance. Montesquieu, Rousseau and the French Revolution.* London: Duckworth, 1983.

MARTÍ, JOSÉ

In 1953, following an abortive attack on the Moncada garrison in Santiago, Cuba, Fidel Castro announced that the inspiration for his uprising was José Martí (1853–1895), a poet-revolutionary who had been killed nearly sixty years earlier. Martí, a hero of the Cuban fight against Spanish colonial rule, continues to be a symbol for all Cubans, regardless of their political ideology. In Havana he is particularly revered, with his bust featured in front of every school; the national library, revolutionary square, and Havana's major airport are named after him, his picture appears on one-peso bills, and President Castro has often cited his influence.

Martí was born of lower-middle-class Spanish parents in Havana. His father was a member of the occupying military forces, determined to prevent Cuba from securing independence, as mainland Latin America had done several decades earlier. Martí was educated by a well-known poet and supporter of Cuban independence, Rafael Maria de Mendive. Throughout his adult life, Martí would struggle for Cuban independence. Indeed, from the age of sixteen, his life

José Martí

revolved around the goal of winning political freedom for his country, and he paid dearly for his revolutionary vocation: he was jailed for treason by the Spanish authorities from 1869 to 1871, deported in 1871, returned to Cuba in 1878, was deported again in 1879, saw his family life fall apart, and traveled feverishly among groups of Cuban exiles in the United States to organize a rebellion against Spain. On May 19, 1895, he was shot by Spanish forces, just a month after returning to Cuba to lead the revolution.

Martí is important for several reasons. First, he was the leader of the independence struggle of Cuba, which would win political liberation from Spain in 1898. Second, he was a superb writer. Although he dabbled in a variety of literary genres, he was best known for his poetry and journalism, both of which were internationally recognized in the 1880s. If his fame had not rested upon his political activities, he would have been remembered as one of the leading Spanish American letters of the nineteenth century. Third, Martí was a superb political thinker and organizer, uniting diverse Cuban exile groups living in the United States in a movement to overthrow Spanish control of the island.

Debates have arisen in Miami and Havana about the nature of Martí's political thought. For some, his work was inspired by socialist goals; others have seen him as a classical liberal; and a minority have emphasized his adventurism. It is clear, however, that Martí was a radical and an anti-imperialist (he denounced the Spanish, French, and British Empires). He was also extremely suspicious of U.S. goals in Latin America, and particularly in Cuba, and tried to alert the people of what he called "Nuestra (Our) América" about the nature of Washington's interests in Latin America. Martí was also a revolutionary, who struggled all his adult life to win independence of his country from Spain and introduce a variety of radical sociopolitical policies in Cuba.

Martí will be remembered for his progressive political thought and his superb literature (his *Complete Works* consist of some twenty-seven hefty volumes). A man of action who paid the ultimate price for his political goals, he espoused a moral approach to politics. It was necessary to educate Cubans about the need to sacrifice everything for the country and to inculcate in them a sense of duty, he believed. His untimely death at the hands of Spanish marksmen denied him the opportunity to introduce his well-developed political ideas.

See also *Latin American Popular and Guerrilla Revolts (Independence to 1959); Latin American Revolts under Colonial Rule (1571–1898).*

John Kirk

BIBLIOGRAPHY

Fernández Retamar, Roberto. *Lectura de Martí.* Mexico: Editorial Nuestro Tiempo, 1972.

González, Manuel Pedro. *José Martí, Epic Chronicler of the U.S. in the Eighties.* Chapel Hill: University of North Carolina Press, 1953.

Kirk, John M. *José Martí, Mentor of the Cuban Nation.* Gainesville: University Press of Florida, 1983.

Mañach, Jorge. *Martí Apostle of Freedom.* New York: Devin-Adan, 1950.

Martínez Estrada, Ezequiel. *Martí revolucionario.* Havana: Casa de las Americas, 1967.

MARX, KARL, AND FRIEDRICH ENGELS

The ideas of Marx (1818–1883) and Engels (1820–1895) on revolution are a direct consequence of their general materialist views on historical development, that is, that the development of society is determined by changes in its economic basis, in the tools and implements that people have at their disposal at any given time (the forces of production, in Marx's terminology), and the corresponding way in which people organize themselves to make use of their tools (the relations of production). They wrote: "At a certain stage of their development the material forces of production in society come into conflict with the existing relations of production, or—what is but a legal expression for the same thing—with the property relations within which they had been at work before. From forms of development of the forces of production these relations turn into their fetters. Then comes the period of social revolution." Thus Marx could call the revolution "the driving force of history," and all of his and Engels's studies in other fields were devoted to uncovering the springs of that driving force.

The most important characteristic of the next revolution was that it would be social and not merely political: it would not only proclaim abstract rights such as freedom of the press, which in fact only a few could enjoy, but achieve a general emancipation by penetrating to the real life of humanity—socioeconomic life. The next revolution would be the first to involve the whole of society:

> All previous historical movements were movements of minorities, or in the interest of minorities. The proletarian movement is the self-conscious, independent movement of the immense majority, in the interests of the immense majority. The proletariat, the lowest stratum of our present society, cannot stir, cannot raise itself up, without the whole superincumbent strata of official society being exploded into the air.

Thus the radicalism of the revolution depended on the class that was carrying it out: the proletariat could represent the

Karl Marx

Friedrich Engels

interests of society as a whole, a society in which class antagonisms were sharpened and simplified to an extent that permitted their abolition. Marx returned to this distinction between the political and the social in his discussion of the Paris Commune (1871), which he claimed was "the political form of social emancipation."

Because they were no prophets, Marx and Engels did not go into great detail concerning the exact nature and circumstances of the revolution they believed to be imminent. They did, however, say something about when a revolution might occur, where it would break out, and whether it would be violent.

Concerning the conditions necessary to produce a successful revolution, Marx and Engels were more or less sanguine depending on the historical situation in which they found themselves. Their expectations were strongest during the 1848 revolutions and faded gradually thereafter, except for a brief renascence during the Paris Commune.

Linked to the necessary conditions was the question of where the revolution would break out first. The materialist view of history of Marx and Engels seemed to indicate that the most advanced industrial countries were most ripe for revolution. Yet they realized that European revolutions were becoming more dependent on the general world situation. In a letter to Engels in 1859 Marx mentioned the opening up of California, Australia, and the Far East and continued: "Revolution is imminent on the Continent and will also immediately assume a socialist character. Can it avoid being crushed in this small corner, because the movement of bourgeois society is in the ascendant over much larger areas of the earth?" But Marx also thought that in some underdeveloped countries (for example, Germany) a bourgeois revolution could spark a subsequent proletarian revolution. Later in his life Marx came to believe that Russia might prove the starting-point of the revolution, which "begins this time in the East, hitherto the invulnerable bulwark and reinforcement of the counterrevolution." Of Russia he said a year before his death: "If the Russian revolution becomes the signal for a proletarian revolution in the West, so that both complete each other, then the present Russian system of community ownership of land could serve as the starting point for a communist development."

Marx was certainly well aware of the importance of colonial exploitation for hastening the coming revolution. After describing the influence of English industry on India, he outlined the prospects that colonialism afforded for a worldwide revolution: Colonial exploitation has globalized the world, but only egalitarian social revolution will enable all of humanity to enjoy the fruits of this globalization.

One of the reasons why Marx and Engels did not think that violent revolution would automatically occur in the most advanced countries was that in some of the advanced countries communism could come about by peaceful means. In 1872 Marx spoke of his belief in the possibility of a peaceful revolution in America, England, and Holland. He took the same line in 1879 when he wrote:

> A historical development can only remain "peaceful" so long as it is not opposed by the violence of those who wield power in society at that time. If in England or the United States, for example, the working class were to gain a majority in Parliament or Congress, then it could by legal means set aside the laws and structures that stood in its way.

Were the proletariat to gain a voting majority, Marx continued, any violence would come from the other side. However, in 1871 he blamed the Paris Commune for not being willing to start a civil war, and declared at the Congress of the International in the same year: "We must make clear to the governments, we know that you are the armed power that is directed against the proletariat; we will proceed against you by peaceful means where that is possible and with arms when it is necessary." But however much both Marx and Engels may have thought that force was sometimes the midwife of revolution, they never (except briefly in 1848 and under tsarist conditions in Russia) approved of the use of revolutionary terror. They strongly criticized the use of terror by the Jacobins in the French Revolution; its use was for Marx and Engels a sign of the weakness and immaturity of that revolution, which had tried to impose by sheer force what was not yet inherent in society. Marx believed that a revolution, if the socioeconomic conditions are not appropriate, inevitably leads to a reign of terror during which the revolutionary powers attempt to reorganize society from above.

Physical force, however, as opposed to terror, was to Marx and Engels a perfectly acceptable revolutionary weapon provided that the economic, social, and political conditions were such as to make its use successful. In their view the form of government that would follow a successful revolution was a "dictatorship of the proletariat." The expression was seldom used by Marx, and never in documents for publication, though Engels did later cite the Paris Commune as a good example. In a letter to his friend Joseph Weydemeyer Marx claims as one of his contributions to socialist theory the idea that "the class struggle necessarily leads to the dictatorship of the proletariat; that this dictatorship itself is only a transitional stage toward the abolition of all classes." And in the *Critique of the Gotha Program* Marx wrote that when capitalist society was being transformed into communist society, there would be "a political transition period during which the state can be nothing but the revolutionary dictatorship of the proletariat." It should be noted that the word *dictatorship* did not have quite the same connotation for Marx and Engels that it does for us. They associated it principally with the Roman office of *dictatura,* where all power was legally concentrated in the hands of a single man during a limited period in a time of crisis. Although Marx and Engels seldom discuss the measures that such a government would enact, the fullest account is the ten-point program outlined in the *Communist Manifesto,* which is in many respects a fairly moderate program.

It was also Marx's view that a successful revolution—at least in the long run—was impossible if confined to one country. In *The Class Struggles in France* Marx criticized the leaders of the French proletariat for thinking that they could consummate a proletarian revolution within a France surrounded by bourgeois nations. But Marx believed equally that the degree of working-class organization necessary to produce an international revolution could only be achieved by building up working-class parties within existing nations. Marx was strongly in favor of the unification of Germany and Italy and of the resurgence of Polish nationalism.

Engels survived Marx by thirteen years, and toward the end of his life the growing electoral success of the Social Democrats in Germany led him to stress the evolutionary rather than the revolutionary side of Marxism and to declare the tactics of 1848 to be outmoded in every respect. This view is encapsulated in the preface to a reprint of Marx's *Class Struggles in France,* written by Engels in 1895 shortly before he died, where he portrays the growth of social democracy as a natural, organic process that could be endangered by revolutionary hotheads.

See also *Communism; European Revolutions of 1848; Paris Commune (1871).*

David McLellan

BIBLIOGRAPHY

Berlin, Isaiah. *Karl Marx.* 3d ed. Oxford: Oxford University Press, 1963.

Draper, Hal. *Karl Marx's Theory of Revolution.* New York: Monthly Review Press, 1986.

Hunt, Richard. *The Political Ideas of Marx and Engels.* Pittsburgh: University of Pittsburgh Press, 1974.

Marx, Karl. *Selected Writings.* Edited by David McLellan. Oxford: Oxford University Press, 1977.

Tucker, Robert. *The Marxian Revolutionary Idea.* New York: Norton, 1970.

MEDIA AND COMMUNICATIONS

From Martin Luther's pamphlets during the Protestant Reformation to Radio Venceremos ("Rebel Radio"), the symbol of El Salvador's insurrectionary movement in the 1980s, communications media have played a central role in all revolutionary crises in the modern Western world. Indeed, some communications theorists, notably Marshall McLuhan, have argued that significant changes in the media, such as the invention of printing, constitute in and of themselves genuine revolutions in society and culture, and that these changes are more fundamental than the political and social movements normally labeled as revolutions. Even if one does not embrace McLuhan's redefinition of what constitutes a revolution, it is difficult to conceive of a revolutionary movement of more than local scope developing without some medium of communication to spread its ideological message and news of its successes and failures.

Communications media are not merely conduits for information, however. The creation of new media and the discrediting or transforming of old ones are integral parts of the revolutionary process, symbolic evidence of the existence of a crisis situation and of its evolution. The "media revolution" that invariably constitutes part of a revolutionary crisis usually produces a communications system that transmits information more quickly, reaches a larger audience, and gives a more urgent and emotional tone to the messages it carries than the media system it replaces. As revolutionary regimes consolidate themselves, the media may be toned down and subjected to renewed controls, but media revolutions, like revolutions in general, usually generate lasting effects.

By providing a means of disseminating the same message to a large population in a short period, the invention of the printing press in the 1400s made the era of modern Western revolutions possible. The Protestant Reformation was the first mass movement to demonstrate the power of printed propaganda in spreading radical ideas for change over a broad geographic area. Coupled with an oral medium of great power—the sermon—printed pamphlets and woodcuts were essential in the dissemination of new religious and social ideas.

The English Revolution of the 1640s was the first movement to exhibit the full characteristics of a modern media revolution, as a new medium, the periodical newsweekly, supplanted irregularly published pamphlets. These periodicals, called "mercuries," created a regular communications network that reached the whole country, and editors such as Marchamont Needham were the first true revolutionary journalists.

Newspapers and journalists were equally important in the American Revolution. Benjamin Franklin, Thomas Paine, and Benjamin Franklin Bache played principal roles in promoting independence, while the loyalist editors such as James Rivington demonstrated that a revolution creates opportunities for media opposing the movement as well as for those supporting it. The Alien and Sedition Acts, passed by the Federalists to stifle opposition in 1789, were a typical, although unsuccessful, example of the process by which postrevolutionary governments often try to reverse the broadening of the public sphere that usually results from a media revolution.

1789: A CLASSIC MEDIA REVOLUTION

The French Revolution of 1789 provides the classic model of a media revolution. The critical events of June and July 1789 were foreshadowed by a deluge of pamphlets that had started with the announcement of the monarchy's fiscal crisis in 1787. When the Estates-General convened in May 1789, printed bulletins enabled the population to follow its proceedings. The storming of the Bastille (July 14, 1789) swept away the last vestiges of prerevolutionary press controls and unleashed a wave of new periodicals. Daily newspapers, almost unknown before 1789, quickly came to dominate the market, and entrepreneurs competed to get their publications to even the most distant provinces as rapidly as possible. Previously unknown writers such as Camille Desmoulins and Jean-Paul Marat used vehement rhetoric to transform the tone of public debate and elevate themselves to the status of revolutionary leaders. Jacques-René Hébert, a writer and political agitator who disguised himself as a plain-spoken man of the people under the pseudonym Père Duchesne, introduced popular vocabulary into the political arena. The existence of the revolutionary press allowed citizens to follow legislative debates and events in the streets of Paris, and the conviction that their words were being broadcast to the whole nation gave revolutionary leaders a basis for their claim to speak for the citizenry. Newspapers set the agenda for discussions in the streets, cafés, and revolutionary clubs; the clubs often timed their meetings to coincide with the arrival of the latest issues, and they made public reading of their favored sheets one of their major activities.

Visitors to revolutionary France regularly commented on the large number of newspapers for sale, which struck them as one of the most tangible signs of the radical change affecting the country. French citizens demonstrated their loyalty to particular revolutionary factions by the newspaper they read, and burning or destroying enemy newspapers was a common form of symbolic protest. A host of other media—caricatures, illustrated broadsheets, songs, plays, and objects of all kinds decorated with revolutionary motifs—supplemented the press in transmitting the revolutionary message and popularizing revolutionary symbols and slogans. But the newspapers, because of their regular appearance, their pervasiveness, and their close links to the leaders of revolutionary assemblies and clubs, had the greatest impact.

As the effervescence of the Revolution's early stage dissipated, the new rulers gradually tamed the press and the other media. Censorship, imposed during the Reign of Terror then lifted after the fall of Maximilien Robespierre, was effectively reinstated when Napoleon seized power. The French press never returned to its prerevolutionary condition, however. Daily publication remained the norm; Napoleon's dream of limiting the press to a single, government-directed title never became reality; and the citizenry no longer regarded a censored press as legitimate. Memories of the dynamic and aggressive free press of the revolutionary era became an integral part of the revolutionary myth. The examples of Marat and the fictional Père Duchesne continued to inspire radical journalists into the twentieth century.

The French Revolution demonstrates with unusual clarity the major ways in which media structure revolutionary crises. The media, particularly the press, were critical in redefining group identities. Pamphlets such as the abbé Emmanuel-Joseph Sieyès's famous tract *What is the Third Estate?* led many people to see themselves for the first time as a new kind of "imagined community," a "nation," and to consider themselves as the bearers of political sovereignty. The realization that other citizens throughout the country were reading the same news at the same time helped give concreteness to the notion of a unified nation. Readers of the counterrevolutionary newspaper *Friend of the King,* on the other hand, learned to recognize themselves as a different kind of group, avowed opponents of the new order. The divergent views of the competing newspapers that flourished until the Reign of Terror demonstrated convincingly to readers of all opinions that the country was far from having reached a consensus about the shape of its new institutions.

From the outset of the Revolution, newspapers served as models of a new kind of active citizenship. The celebrated epigraph of the *Revolutions of Paris,* one of the most important revolutionary periodicals, compressed the revolutionary message into two pithy sentences: "Those above us only look big to us because we are on our knees. Rise up!" The newspaper's radical content exemplified the new attitude that it urged on its readers.

MEDIA AND REVOLUTIONARIES AFTER 1800

In the wake of the French Revolution, the publication of newspapers and journals became the principal activity of its would-be emulators throughout the world. Whereas the revolution of 1789 had preceded the appearance of new revolutionary media, in the nineteenth century, the creation of avowedly revolutionary periodicals often preceded other manifestations of crisis. The innumerable revolutionary exiles of the period often had no other way of serving their causes. Almost all of the important revolutionary theorists of the period, including Karl Marx, Pierre-Joseph Proudhon, and Giuseppe Mazzini, were active as journalists both in the long intervals between actual insurrectionary events and during such crises as the revolutions of 1848. The phenomenon was not limited to Europe: exiled opponents of Mexican dictator Porfirio Diaz's regime published newspapers in Texas prior to the revolution of 1910. Vladimir Ilyich Lenin, a classic product of the revolutionary milieu, fully shared its faith in the power of the media. In one of his earliest articles, he argued that producing a revolutionary newspaper not only served to spread radical ideas to its readers but taught its collaborators the discipline and organization they would need to take power when the opportunity came. Whether in or out of power, communist movements after 1917 followed Lenin's teaching and invested great energy in the production of newspapers, magazines, films, and other propaganda media, as did such radical right-wing movements as Benito Mussolini's Fascists and Hitler's Nazi Party.

The development of modern electronic media offered revolutionary movements new possibilities for spreading their messages, but the complexity of the required equipment and its vulnerability to police countermeasures have often kept insurrectionary movements from creating their own broadcasting systems or making their own films, unless political conditions have allowed them to operate from secure bases in other countries. After 1917 the Soviet regime successfully employed films such as Sergei Eisenstein's classic "Ten Days That Shook the World" to propagandize its own population and to spread abroad the myth of a victorious people's revolution. "Battle of Algiers" was made some years after the triumph of the Algerian independence movement whose struggles it celebrated.

In countries with centralized, state-operated broadcasting systems, the media themselves have become potential arenas for revolutionary contestation. A strike by French broadcast journalists during the quasi-revolutionary "May events" of 1968 deprived the government of Charles de Gaulle of one of its most important tools for influencing public opinion; de Gaulle himself gave higher priority to ending the strike than to almost any other aspect of the crisis. A popular movement's success in taking over the broadcast media has become one of the key signs that a revolution has triumphed. When television systems in the Soviet satellite countries of Eastern Europe suddenly began to broadcast scenes of mass demonstrations against their regimes in 1989, viewers realized that the communist order had disintegrated.

The development of global media networks transmitting from satellites has opened new possibilities for revolutionary groups to capture the attention of journalists and broadcasters. The Mexican Zapatistas and the Peruvian Tupac Amaru guerrillas are two examples of groups that have employed the global media to gain a worldwide audience for their causes. Computer networks and fax transmissions now allow revolutionary groups to contact supporters and journalists around the world in "real time." Revolutionary groups have also made imaginative use of the "small media" that technology has generated. Underground resistance movements in Nazi-occupied Europe printed tracts on the mimeograph machines that had become ubiquitous in the first half of the twentieth century, and followers of Iran's exiled Ayatollah Ruhollah Khomeini listened to his messages on tape cassettes smuggled into the country during the 1970s.

Newspapers may no longer play the same decisive role in revolutionary crises that they did from the time of the English Revolution to the first half of the twentieth century, but media continue to be vitally involved in every revolutionary upheaval. Media organs are still essential in formulating and disseminating revolutionary messages, and the transformation of the media remains one of the most important symbolic aspects of such upheavals. The ongoing globalization of the media is making it increasingly difficult for revolutionary movements and regimes to create media systems under their own control; they now have to collaborate with outside journalists and broadcasters to get the attention they desire. At the same time, however, the global media's intense interest in revolutionary phenomena has permitted revolutionaries to project their images and messages on a worldwide scale with unprecedented speed. In new forms, the symbiosis between media and revolution remains as intimate as ever.

See also *Films and Video Documentaries; Franklin, Benjamin; Literature; Marat, Jean-Paul; Music; Paine, Thomas.*

JEREMY D. POPKIN

BIBLIOGRAPHY

Darnton, Robert, and Daniel Roche, eds. *Revolution in Print: The Press in France, 1775–1800.* Berkeley: University of California Press, 1989.

Gitlin, Todd. *The Whole World Is Watching: Mass Media in the Making and Unmaking of the New Left.* Berkeley: University of California Press, 1980.

Labrosse, Claude, and Pierre Rétat. *Naissance du journal révolutionnaire 1789.* Lyon: Presses Universitaires de Lyon, 1989.

Lenin, V. I. "Where to Begin" (1901). In *Collected Works.* Vol. 5. Translated by Joe Fineberg and George Hanna. Moscow: Progress Publishers, 1964, 17–24.

Lopez Vigil, José Ignacio. *Rebel Radio: The Story of El Salvador's Radio Venceremos.* Translated by Mark Fried. Willmantic, Conn.: Curbstone Press, 1994.

Popkin, Jeremy D., ed. *Media and Revolution.* Lexington: University Press of Kentucky, 1995.

———. *Revolutionary News: The Press in France, 1789–1799.* Durham, N.C.: Duke University Press, 1990.

Smith, Jeffrey A. *Printers and Press Freedom: The Ideology of Early American Journalism.* New York: Oxford University Press, 1988.

MENCHÚ TUM, RIGOBERTA

Menchú's name has become synonymous with the fight for economic justice, human rights, and democracy in Guatemala. As a Nobel laureate, she has also become a spokersperson and activist for indigenous peoples throughout the world.

Menchú (1959–) was born in the village of Chimel, El Quiché, Guatemala, and grew up in a context of extreme poverty, inequitable land distribution, inhuman labor conditions, and repressive authoritarian rule. These pervasive socioeconomic conditions, shared by the majority indigenous population, gave rise in the 1960s and 1970s to popular movements, revolutionary organizations, and civil war.

Menchú and her family played an active role in popular movement organizing in the 1970s. Her father, Vicente Menchú, a prominent Mayan peasant and catechist leader, cofounded the Committee for Peasant Unity (CUC). The CUC mobilized indigenous and nonindigenous peasants throughout the countryside and soon became one of the country's most significant legal opposition movements. Rigoberta Menchú officially joined the CUC in 1979, at a time of heightening civil war that resulted in an estimated 100,000–140,000 killed, 40,000 disappeared, 440 villages razed, and 1,000,000 internal and external refugees.

Following the political assassination of her brother, mother, and father, Menchú went into political exile in Mexico in 1981. There she joined the exile community in its international campaign to denounce atrocities committed by the Guatemalan government and to garner support for the popular movements. As a member of the CUC and of the Unitary Representation of the Guatemalan Opposition (RUOG), she repeatedly traveled to the United States and Europe and demonstrated her capacity to generate support from audiences moved by her experiences. With backing from the exile community, she collaborated in 1982 with Elisabeth Burgos-Debray to produce her testimonial, *I, Rigoberta Menchú: An Indian Women in Guatemala.* The book was awarded the Casa de las Américas prize for the best testimonial work in 1983. With the book's publication, Menchú gained international recognition and a platform to denounce the Guatemalan government's repression. She simultaneously gained a more prominent voice in the United Nations, where she had been participating regularly at the UN Subcommittee for Ethnic Issues.

Menchú's work, however, was not widely known within Guatemala until 1988, when she returned for a meeting with the National Reconciliation Committee. Upon arrival, the government arrested her and another RUOG member. Protests mounted, newspapers wrote front-page articles, and television stations prepared interviews. The military's actions and her powerful comments following the arrest catapulted her to center stage. Within Guatemala, she subsequently became a symbol and interlocutor of the Guatemalan opposition movement—speaking for peasant, labor, indigenous, and women's organizations.

Menchú received the Nobel Peace Prize in 1992. With the prize money, Menchú founded the Rigoberta Menchú Tum Foundation. The foundation supports education, health, and human rights projects and has played an active role in the return and resettlement of Guatemalan refugees. Menchú has since returned to Guatemala to live and has played a prominent role in defending democratic institutions and promoting the peace accords, which were signed in December 1996 by the government and the revolutionary forces.

She continues to maintain a high international profile and participates in various UN- and indigenous-sponsored conferences. In 1993 she was the UN goodwill ambassador for the International Year of Indigenous Peoples, and, among other things, she is currently a promoter for the UN's Decade of Indigenous Peoples.

See also *Inequality; Injustice; Liberation Theology.*

DEBORAH J. YASHAR

BIBLIOGRAPHY

Arias, Arturo. "From Peasant to National Symbol." In *Teaching and Testimony: Rigoberta Menchú and the North American Classroom.* Edited by Allen Carey-Webb and Stephen Benz. Albany: State University of New York Press, 1996.

Brittin, Alice. "Close Encounters of the Third World Kind: Rigoberta Menchú and Elisabeth Burgos's *Me llamo Rigoberta Menchú." Latin American Perspectives* 22 (fall 1992): 100–115.

Carmack, R. ed. *Harvest of Violence.* Norman: University of Oklahoma Press, 1988.

Menchú, Rigoberta. *I, Rigoberta Menchú: An Indian Women in Guatemala.* Edited and introduced by Elisabeth Burgos-Debray. Translated by Ann Wright. London: 1984. First published as *Me llamo Rigoberta Menchú y así me nació la conciencia.*

Menchú, Rigoberta, y Comité de Unidad Campesina. *Trenzando el futuro: luchas campesinas en la historia receinte de Guatemala.* Guatemala City: Tercera Prensa, 1992.

MEXICAN REVOLUTION (1910–1940)

The Mexican Revolution began in 1910 with a disputed presidential election. It ended in the 1930s with radical land reform, the expropriation of foreign oil companies, and the consolidation of a new national state and political system. During three decades of conflict, Mexicans fought over social, economic, cultural, and political questions that had divided them since the wars of independence a century earlier. The postrevolutionary regime brought political stability, promises of prosperity and justice for the rural majority, and a turn toward urban and industrial development that created new conflicts and patterns of inequality.

By 1910 eighty-year-old Porfirio Díaz had ruled Mexico for more than three decades. Prior to the 1876 inception of his regime, Mexicans and foreigners had fought for decades over power and policies to define the nation. Since independence in 1821, federalists promoting regional autonomy had fought centralists proclaiming rule from Mexico City. Since the early 1830s liberals had challenged the temporal and cultural power of the Catholic Church, demanded the privatization of the peasant community lands, and promoted the incorporation of Mexico into the Atlantic economy via export development. By the late 1830s a conservative opposition was calling for the preservation of Catholic culture, negotiation with indigenous communities, and the industrialization of Mexico.

Amid escalating Mexican political and social conflicts, the United States claimed the northern half of Mexico in 1847. Another decade of internal conflict led to a new liberal constitution in 1857, war between liberals and conservatives, liberal victory in 1860, and French occupation from 1862 to 1867. Consolidation of liberal power in 1867 brought conflicts with regional elites that resisted state centralization and with peasant villagers who opposed land privatization into the 1870s.

When General Díaz, hero of the war against the French, took power in 1876, he consolidated liberal rule by compromising with conservatives and the church. He centralized state power by negotiating with regional elites and promoted railroad development, export production, and industrialization. He continued the liberal program of privatizing community lands yet tried to mediate the inevitable conflicts. He engineered his repeated reelection as president. The Díaz era, from 1876 to 1910, did not resolve the conflicts that had divided Mexicans since the Hidalgo revolt of 1810. It brought a respite of political stability by delicately balancing conflicts that persisted—even deepened—as the population grew and commercial development accelerated in the late nineteenth century. After 1900 rural Mexicans resented escalating landlessness caused by growing population, legal land privatizations, and illegal land grabs. Emerging middle sectors and working classes, created by industrialization and urban development, resented their exclusion from Díaz's political regime.

REVOLUTIONARY CONFRONTATIONS, 1910–1915

As elections neared in 1910, the aging Díaz encouraged talk of democracy while refusing to name a successor. In the campaign he faced opposition from Francisco Madero, son of one of the wealthiest landed, mining, and banking families of northern Mexico. Demanding "effective suffrage and no reelection," Madero drew crowds. Díaz proclaimed his own reelection, whereupon Madero fled to Texas and called for insurrection. He found support among northern farmers, cowboys, and mineworkers, especially in the state of Chihuahua; they accepted Madero's call for democracy and resented recent Díaz policies of land taking and strike breaking. Madero also allied with Emiliano Zapata, leader of rebel villagers in the sugar region of Morelos, south of Mexico City. Already outlawed for their rebellion over local land disputes, Zapata and his followers saw the return of lost lands in Madero's call for democracy and justice.

In 1910 and early 1911 Madero's alliance of upper- and middle-class, mostly urban political reformers committed to electoral democracy joined with rural insurgents from the northern borderlands and the peasant south to challenge Díaz. Unsure of U.S. backing and unable to claim a decisive victory, Díaz resigned and left for Paris. A negotiated transfer of power maintained the federal army and congress. An interim president oversaw elections that brought Madero to the presidency in 1911.

Madero's victory proved divisive: the federal army pressed conservative interests; Zapata demanded immediate land reform. Madero called for time to allow democracy to work, but instead great political mobilization followed and conflicts escalated. Zapata rebelled against Madero in the fall of 1911, promoting his Plan of Ayala, which especially demanded the immediate return of lands to villagers. The federal army, led by Gen. Victoriano Huerta, turned on Madero in February 1913, denouncing his inability to pacify the nation. Aided by the U.S. embassy, Huerta ousted Madero, who was shot and made a martyr.

While Zapata remained in rebellion, Pancho Villa rose to lead rebellious ranchers and workers in Chihuahua and other

Rural Mexicans took up arms in the second decade of the twentieth century largely over land issues: escalating landlessness, legal land privatizations, and illegal land grabs.

northern regions. Venustiano Carranza, the landowner who was governor of Madero's home state of Coahuila, proclaimed himself "first chief" of the Constitutionalist forces. He found support among Sonoran forces led by Alvaro Obregón. From early 1913 to the summer of 1914, Zapata, Villa, Carranza, and Obregón allied to fight General Huerta and the forces of military reaction. The United States, under new president Woodrow Wilson, now opposed Huerta and invaded the port of Veracruz in April 1914. The occupation allowed Huerta to claim the mantle of nationalist resistance against Yankee intervention.

In the summer of 1914 Villa won a series of victories that ousted Huerta. An autumn convention at Aguascalientes revealed that popular forces led by Zapata and Villa threatened the elite and middle-class reformers who looked to Carranza, to whom Obregón remained loyal. Late 1914 brought war among the divergent revolutionaries, and by December Villa and Zapata claimed Mexico City and ruled nearly all of Mexico. Thus an alliance based on popular mobilization and the promise of land reform appeared ready to consolidate national power, while Carranza was isolated at the port of Veracruz.

In November 1914 the United States had evacuated that port to Carranza, leaving him arms and ammunition. His allies took control of the oil fields of coastal Tampico and the henequen zone of Yucatán, thus bringing to the Constitutionalists substantial export earnings from an Atlantic economy moving into World War I. Such revenues were not available to the popular alliance occupying the capital and the central plateau. In January 1915 Carranza called for the restitution of land to rural villagers, thus usurping the program that defined Zapata's appeal across the rural regions of the center and south. Through the spring and summer of 1915, Carranza and Obregón used export earnings to rebuild their armies, garnered support by promoting land reform, and then defeated Villa in key battles in the north-central Bajío. By fall Carranza, Obregón, and the Constitutionalists held state power, while Zapata and Villa were reduced to local resistance in their home regions of Morelos and Chihuahua.

STATE POWER, AGRARIAN MOBILIZATIONS, AND CULTURAL CONFLICTS, 1915–1929

Once he ruled the national state, Carranza retreated from his promise of land reform and returned estates to wealthy landlords. He called a constitutional convention in 1916—seeking only limited changes to the liberal charter of 1857. Obregón, however, recognized that compromise on popular issues had brought the Constitutionalists to power, even if they had later defeated popular leaders. He assembled a reformist coalition that inserted land reform, labor rights, and national control of subsoil resources into the constitution of 1917.

Carranza remained president until 1920, consolidating state power and limiting reform to the end of his term. His loyalists assassinated Zapata in 1919. When Carranza tried to impose a puppet successor in 1920, Obregón rebelled. He allied with Zapata's remaining followers and other reformers to oust Carranza. The coalition that brought Obregón to power in 1920 demonstrated that land reform remained a key to political mobilization and a necessity for pacification. Once president, Obregón delivered land to the Zapatistas and to others essential to his coalition. Yet where his supporters were landed elites, he protected the large estates; for Obregón, land reform was a political tool, not an ideological commitment. Meanwhile, the United States denied him recognition. The coup of 1920 served as a pretext for the United States to pressure Mexico regarding its constitutional assertion of national control of oil resources.

President from 1920 to 1924, Obregón struggled to contain regional forces, juggle agrarian demands, and promote export development while negotiating with the United States over oil and recognition. With the Bucareli accords of 1923, he backed away from oil nationalization and gained recognition. Obregón also began a national cultural campaign celebrating Mexico's indigenous past in art and literature while promoting education to Mexicanize the nation's diverse peoples through Spanish language and literacy. He attacked as superstition and fanaticism the religious beliefs cherished by many rural villagers and traditional urban families. Political consolidation thus brought with it escalating cultural conflict.

Obregón's decision to promote Sonoran ally Plutarco Elías Calles to the presidency provoked rebellion by much of the army and many regional leaders in 1923. To sustain the regime and his chosen successor, Obregón mobilized a coalition of reformers and beneficiaries of agrarian reform, and Calles took power in 1924. Calles continued to seek rapprochement with the United States and to resist further agrarian reform. He promoted industry, export development, and those labor organizations that supported his regime. And he accelerated the assault on the church, imposing limits on the clergy and state control of the curriculum in church schools.

When Mexican bishops responded by halting public worship in 1926, a massive popular uprising exploded in the west-central regions of Michoacán and Jalisco. Communities committed to traditional beliefs and festivals, to their priests, and to autonomy from revolutionary state intervention rose to fight against the regime that claimed to represent the revolution. Church leaders were little involved in mobilizing the rebellion. The Cristero War contested the postrevolutionary state and its cultural project throughout the late 1920s. This three-year civil war saw peasant fighting peasant: agrarians fought for the state in defense of land reform; others, proudly Cristeros, fought for religion and local autonomy—against a state forcing them to choose between land reform and cultural autonomy.

That conflict proved a deadly stalemate until bishops and government negotiated a return of public worship in 1929. Cristero resistance declined, while government repression eased. Amid the Cristero conflict, Obregón won reelection to succeed Calles in 1928, only to be assassinated before taking office by an angry supporter of the church. Calles used the power vacuum to make a new attempt to consolidate the postrevolutionary state.

From 1928 through 1934 Calles retained political dominance as "maximum chief," while Emilio Portes Gil, Pascual Ortíz Rubio, and Abelardo Rodríguez each sat as president for two years. In 1929 Calles founded the National Revolutionary Party (PNR), wherein he aimed for a single party coordinating regional forces loyal to his rule; that is, he sought to consolidate his power without the need for personal reelection. Once agrarians were no longer needed to fight Cristeros, he called again for an end to land reform. Instead, he promoted commercial and export production—policies that brought support from surviving landed elites and emerging entrepreneurs.

REVOLUTIONARY CONSOLIDATION, 1929–1940

The year 1929 brought the end of the Cristero War, the creation of the revolutionary party, and the move to curtail land reform. It also brought depression to the world economy. Calles's attempt to consolidate a postrevolutionary state through compromise with landed elites and the promotion of exports collapsed as an option. During the early 1930s thousands of Mexicans returned from the United States. Their labor no longer in demand, they found relief reserved for U.S. citizens. The migrants' return amid international depression increased pressures for land reform and for economic development that would emphasize production for Mexican markets. While Calles worked to consolidate the postrevolutionary state, new pressures developed for land reform and more inclusive models of production and politics. A 1933 convention of the PNR called for popular politics, renewed land reform, and more equitable national development. A growing segment of Calles's party challenged his vision for Mexico.

In 1934 he designated Gen. Lázaro Cárdenas to be president. Cárdenas had fought Cristeros and served as governor in his home state of Michoacán. He had joined Calles in promoting secular education. The maximum chief expected Cárdenas to serve as another malleable president, perhaps adding a populist touch. Indeed, when Cárdenas took office late in 1934, Calles named the cabinet.

Cárdenas had another vision. During the 1934 campaign he toured Mexico as if the election was in doubt. In cities, towns, and isolated villages he asked people's concerns and offered to help once president. He took office understanding popular demands for land reform, labor rights, and a government and development program that would serve popular needs. He solicited petitions for land and responded favorably. He encouraged workers to demand better pay and working conditions; when they struck, he intervened in their favor. Rapidly mobilizing popular support, Cárdenas, after six months in office, moved against Calles—forcing the once maximum chief into exile and removing his men from the cabinet. During his first three years in office, Cárdenas used the state to favor peasants and workers. He built the power of the state, expropriated landed elites, and forced businessmen to negotiate with workers. By the end of his term, he had distributed more land to villagers than all his predecessors combined. Nearly half of Mexico's arable land in 1940 was in *ejidos*—community-owned properties given villagers by the revolutionary state. Urban workers had joined powerful unions and made real gains in wages, benefits, and the negotiation of working conditions.

In 1938 one labor dispute became first an international conflict and then a nationalist triumph. Petroleum workers employed by British and North American companies struck, and a Mexican arbitration board determined that the workers deserved higher wages and that the companies could pay. The companies refused, denying the jurisdiction of Mexican courts. Cárdenas activated Article 27 of the 1917 constitution and expropriated the companies' Mexican operations. The companies, backed by the U.S. and British governments, demanded compensation, to which Cárdenas agreed—basing values on the companies' previous tax declarations to Mexico. The companies argued that those tax valuations were low, so Cárdenas demanded back taxes based on the values sought as compensation. The Mexican state and union workers occupied oil installations, and international conflict escalated.

The expropriation dominated Cárdenas's last years in office. He backed away from land reform and labor mobilization, aiming to hold Mexican landowners and employers within a nationalist coalition against U.S. pressure. He reorganized the National Revolutionary Party into the Party of the Mexican Revolution (PRM): a peasant sector included land reform beneficiaries; the labor sector incorporated government-backed unions; a popular sector was built around government bureaucrats; and the military sector was dominated by Cárdenas loyalists. The reconstituted party asked the beneficiaries of Cárdenas's reforms to become the political foundation of a consolidated regime. The reforms, the party, and the state all held up. The oil expropriation was eventually accepted by the United States and Britain; the strategic need for petroleum for World War II overshadowed the defense of corporate property.

LEGACIES: STABILITY, DEVELOPMENT, CONFLICT

The institutional legacies of those events echo throughout Mexico today. Cárdenas is remembered across Mexico as the president who delivered land to peasant villagers. The government-led coalition of unions continues to rule Mexican labor. The PRM later became the Institutional Revolutionary Party (PRI), with the military removed, leaving peasant, labor, and popular sectors as the bases of a one-party regime that brought remarkable stability to Mexican politics through the middle of the twentieth century.

Since 1940 Cárdenas's reforms and the Mexican Revolution have occasioned continuing debates. Did Cárdenas aim to benefit peasants and workers, building a powerful state apparatus only to fend off opposition? Or did he aim primarily to consolidate an enduring national state, while understanding the political necessity of providing gains to peasants and workers? Cárdenas's motivation will remain an enigma. His programs did bring basic gains to peasants and workers. And in the end he consolidated a newly powerful state. After 1938, under Cárdenas and his more conservative successors, that state turned to limiting the power of popular groups. From the 1940s the state forged in revolution increasingly served to control the peasants, workers, and others who had promoted the revolution.

Recently, many scholars and political observers have questioned the gains of the Mexican Revolution. After 1940 the policies of the institutionalized "revolutionary" state limited popular participation and promoted development models—first state-directed, now market-oriented—that have concentrated wealth and limited the gains of urban workers and peasant villagers.

Yet the revolution brought substantial change, not from utopian visions but from negotiations forced on the powerful by mobilized peasants, workers, and others. The landlords who dominated rural Mexico were expropriated and destroyed as a landed elite, though many survived to rule other endeavors. Peasant villagers received nearly half of the nation's arable land in *ejido* grants but faced a newly powerful state. Mexico claimed control of its petroleum resources. And Mexicans consolidated the most stable political system of twentieth-century Latin America. Yet the stability was forged by the inclusionary regime of Cárdenas in the 1930s; later regimes became ever more exclusionary and authoritarian as the century progressed.

In revolution, Mexicans fought over basic issues of national life: Madero demanding democracy; Villa and Zapata demanding land for rural families and communities; Obregón promoting political consolidation and nationalist education; Cristeros fighting for religion and cultural autonomy; and Cárdenas distributing land, building unions, promoting industry, expropriating oil, and consolidating the state. In the 1930s Mexicans forged a compromise between the demands of peasants and workers and the interests of elites seeking a nationalist model of commercial development. Through the 1940s and 1950s rapid urban and industrial development combined with irrigation projects and the "green revolution" to produce an economic boom alongside political stability.

Yet by the late 1960s Mexicans faced new crises of political participation, economic uncertainty, and social inequity. Do late twentieth-century crises indicate a "failure" of the revolution of 1910 to 1940? Or are they results of the turn against popular participation since 1940? The revolution was a time of complex conflicts; it was never a program, an ideology, or a state. As such, the revolution could neither succeed nor fail. It revealed the profound aspirations of Mexico's people and the deep conflicts in Mexican society and culture. Recent economic crises, escalating inequities, and rising demands—once again—for effective democracy emerge from new concentrations of power in the state and among economic elites. They emerge from the end of land reform, the shift of agriculture toward production for export, assaults on union power and labor rights, the political exclusion of popular forces, and the rapid incorporation of Mexico into a global economy. Yet at the same time, most Mexicans are pressed to supply cheap food, cheap oil, and cheap labor (at home and in the United States). The conflicts that drove the revolution of 1910 to 1940 have not vanished. They continue to define Mexican life.

See also *Latin American Popular and Guerrilla Revolts (Independence to 1959); Zapata, Emiliano.*

JOHN TUTINO

BIBLIOGRAPHY

Benjamin, Thomas, and Mark Wasserman, eds. *Provinces of the Revolution: Essays on Regional Mexican History, 1910–1929.* Albuquerque: University of New Mexico Press, 1990.

Hamilton, Nora. *The Limits of State Autonomy: Post-Revolutionary Mexico.* Princeton, N.J.: Princeton University Press, 1982.

Joseph, Gilbert, and Daniel Nugent, eds. *Everyday Forms of State Formation: Revolution and the Negotiation of Rule in Modern Mexico.* Durham, N.C.: Duke University Press, 1994.

Katz, Friedrich. *The Secret War in Mexico: Europe, the United States, and the Mexican Revolution.* Chicago: University of Chicago Press, 1981.

Knight, Alan. *The Mexican Revolution.* 2 vols. Cambridge: Cambridge University Press, 1986.

Meyer, Jean. *The Cristero Rebellion: The Mexican People between Church and State, 1926–1929.* Cambridge: Cambridge University Press, 1976.

Tutino, John. *From Insurrection to Revolution in Mexico: Social Bases of Agrarian Violence, 1750–1940.* Princeton, N.J.: Princeton University Press, 1986.

Vaughan, Mary Kay. *Cultural Politics in Revolution: Teachers, Peasants, and Schools in Mexico, 1930–1940.* Tucson: University of Arizona Press, 1997.

Wells, Allen, and Gilbert Joseph. *Summer of Discontent, Seasons of Upheaval: Elite Politics and Rural Insurgency in Yucatan, 1876–1915.* Stanford, Calif.: Stanford University Press, 1997.

Womack, John, Jr. *Zapata and the Mexican Revolution.* New York: Alfred A. Knopf, 1968.

MILLENARIANISM

Although many historians have insisted that revolutions have been phenomena largely confined to the early modern and modern epochs of history, millenarian movements with decidedly revolutionary attributes are among the most ancient forms of collective protest known to humankind. The profound social transformations that most scholars view as defining for revolutionary upheavals have long been associated with millenarian visions, which have very often launched sustained efforts to destroy an existing political *and* socioeconomic order and replace it with one usually configured in utopian terms. Almost all of the millenarian movements that occurred before the industrial epoch were grounded in religious beliefs and rituals and involved expectations on the part of their adherents of interventions by supernatural forces on their behalf. But the participants saw themselves as critical agents in the profound social and political transformations the movements were to generate. Thus, though they have often been depicted as tradition-oriented, even reactionary, millenarian movements frequently provided, or at least were intended to provide, the impetus for profound change and for the construction of radically new ways of organizing societies and of structuring human interaction, both within the terrestrial realm and in relation to the supernatural.

As the foregoing suggests, though historically embedded in preexisting religious traditions, millenarianism is oriented toward abrupt, imminent, and substantial adjustments in the earthly realm rather than the promise of heavenly rewards in some distant future for the obedient and long-suffering. Those who articulate millenarian ideologies, such as the Taiping leader Hong Xiuquan and the Sudanese mahdi, often build on what are perceived by religious and political authorities as peripheral and heterodox elements of established belief systems or ideas that are utterly heretical. They emphasize that retribution for their followers will come in the here and now and that salvation lies in the establishment of a new and just order that they will enjoy collectively in this world. Although once thought to be mainly associated with the pronounced messianic and apocalyptic strains of the great Semitic religious traditions—Judaism, Christianity, and Islam—millenarian phenomena have occurred from early times in diverse cultures over much of the globe, from highly stratified civilizations, such as those that flourished in China, India, sub-Saharan Africa, and the Americas, to more isolated, decentralized societies, such as those found in the Pacific islands or the rain forests of Brazil.

Nonetheless, as research in recent decades has made clear, the spread of civilizations and the proselytization of religious systems have frequently generated millenarian responses in the zones where they led to cross-cultural contacts. This has been particularly evident in the global expansion of Islam and Christianity. But millenarianism can also be detected as a recurring response to the periodic extension of Chinese hegemony in East and Central Asia, the spread of Buddhism in its various formulations throughout Southeast and East Asia, or the proliferation of the so-called mystery religions in the Mediterranean region in the last centuries B.C.E. and early centuries C.E. Though improvements in record keeping may be partly responsible, there appears to have been a sharp increase in the incidence of millenarian sectarianism and rebellion in the early modern and modern eras. Many of these movements were directly connected to the overseas expansion and colonial dominance of the states of Western Europe, which were responsible for deeply unsettling changes and the establishment of alien and highly exploitative regimes over much of the non-Western world.

In some instances, severe natural disasters or the sudden intrusion of inexplicable phenomena into previously isolated societies, such as airplane flights over the interior of New Guinea, appear to have been sufficient to evoke millenarian responses. But most of the millenarian movements for which we have substantial historical or ethnographic evidence have been caused by severe social disruptions, economic and legal inequities, and exorbitant state demands comparable to those that contributed to more mundane and familiar upheavals, such as the French and Russian Revolutions. Frequently, millenarian responses to these sorts of material, psychic, and status deprivations have involved withdrawal into sectarian communities and attempts to avoid overt conflict with those seen to be responsible for the dislocations and oppression. When challenged by the forces of the established order, millenarians have either resorted to other modes of nonconfrontational protest, such as flight, or risen in violent rebellion. In a substantial number of instances, particularly involving alien, European colonial regimes, millenarian movements have from their inception been committed to violent revolts aimed at overthrowing the existing order and ushering in religious utopias.

Some millenarian revolts have been organized around displaced religious and political leaders invoking prophecies and signs deeply rooted in the cultures of the peoples involved. But most millenarian rebellions of any scale and duration have been centered on prophetic or messianic figures, whose visions and prognostications both articulate the grievances of their followers and help define the organizational and ritual contours of the utopian society they seek to establish. Very often, prophetic leaders provide their followers with talismans and other magical devices to offset the superior weapons that their adversaries employ to crush them. Incantations, rituals, and the threat of ostracism are also enlisted to compel obedience and instill discipline on the part of those who rally to prophetic calls to rebellion. Strict ethical codes and puritanical injunctions against such perceived vices as alcoholism, gambling, and sexual promiscuity are frequently associated with millenarian risings. Often little or no quarter is given to adversaries, who are depicted as the agents of evil, and whose destruction is a prerequisite for the inauguration of the new order.

Because prophecies and talismans have failed, many millenarian revolts have been short-lived. Most eventually have ended in defeat or been institutionalized in religious states, such as that which ruled in the Sudan in the late nineteenth century or that which currently governs in Iran. However, millenarian elements have also played a subsidiary role in major revolutions, such as the English Revolution of the seventeenth century and the American Revolution. Millenarian expectations can also be discerned in avowedly secular, even determinedly antireligious, revolutions, such as those in Russia and China in the twentieth century.

See also *Chinese Taiping Rebellion (1851–1864); Egyptian Muslim Brotherhood Movement (1928–); Hong Xiuquan; Islamic Precolonial Revolt of the 18th and 19th Centuries; Sudanese Mahdiyya (1881–1898).*

MICHAEL ADAS

BIBLIOGRAPHY

Adas, Michael. *Prophets of Rebellion: Millenarian Protest Movements against the European Colonial Order.* New York: Cambridge University Press, 1987.

Barkun, Michael. *Disaster and the Millennium.* New Haven, Conn.: Yale University Press, 1974.

Burridge, Kenelm. *New Heaven, New Earth.* New York: Schocken, 1969.

Cohn, Norman. *The Pursuit of the Millennium.* New York: Harper and Row, 1961.

Thrupp, Silvia L., ed. *Millennial Dreams in Action.* New York: Schocken, 1970.

Wilson, Bryan. *Magic and the Millennium.* New York: Harper and Row, 1973.

MOSADDEQ, MOHAMMAD

Mosaddeq (1882–1967), liberal, democrat, parliamentarian, and prime minister, was a leader in the struggle for Iranian democracy and national sovereignty, known as the Popular Movement of Iran. His father was a notable and a high state official, his mother, a first cousin of the reigning monarch.

He became active—as a vice president of the Society for Humanity—in the Constitutional Revolution of 1905, and in 1906 he was elected to the first Majlis, but Mosaddeq was not summoned because he did not meet the minimum age qualification. Between 1909 and 1914 he studied in Paris and Switzerland, and he obtained his doctorate in law from the University of Neuchâtel, being the first Iranian to obtain such a degree from a European institution. On return, he taught at Tehran's School of Law and Politics and became deputy minister of finance.

In 1919 he went back to Switzerland and became so depressed by the news of the 1919 Anglo-Iranian agreement that he decided to become a Swiss citizen. The agreement had been almost universally interpreted as turning Iran into a British protectorate. But the climate in Iran quickly changed, and Mossadeq was named minister of justice in the new cabinet, though he ended up as the governor general of Fars. While in that post he opposed the 1921 coup by Reza Khan and Sayyed Zia, and he had to go into hiding until the fall of Zia's cabinet three months later.

In the next two years Mosaddeq served in various cabinets as finance minister, governor general of Azerbaijan, and foreign minister, but when in 1923 Reza Khan became prime minister, Mossadeq became a Majlis deputy, where he joined the "independents" who sometimes voted with the government and sometimes with the opposition. In 1925 he was one of five deputies to reject openly the change of dynasty in favor of Reza Shah, saying in a most effective speech that it would result in dictatorship.

He withdrew from politics after 1928. Then in 1940 he was imprisoned without charge. A year later he was allowed to return to his farm under house arrest. Reza Shah abdicated in 1941—in the wake of the Allied invasion of Iran—and in 1943 Mosaddeq again became a Majlis deputy, where he campaigned for democracy and clean government. But he was most effective in his opposition to the Soviet demand for an oil concession. He also passed a bill prohibiting the grant of any foreign oil concession without prior Majlis approval.

In 1949 Mosaddeq founded the Popular (commonly known as "National") Front, and after an intense parliamentary struggle he managed to nationalize Iranian oil shortly before becoming prime minister in May 1951. The Tudeh (communist) Party saw Mossadeq as an agent of American imperialism, and his insistence that the shah reign, not rule, angered the shah and worried the religious establishment that the country would go communist. The American government became convinced of the same danger.

Mosaddeq's government was overthrown in an August 1953 coup in which his domestic opposition (including a splinter group of the Popular Front) was financed and organized by the American and British governments. He was put in solitary confinement for three years after a military trial, and afterward he was banished to his farm without further legal proceedings.

His last involvement in politics was between 1963 and 1965. Upon the failure of the second Popular Front, which he had had no hand in forming or leading, Mossadeq organized via secret correspondence the third Popular Front. This front was very short lived because of the regime's onslaught against it.

Mosaddeq died in March 1967 and was mourned by most of the politically aware public as a symbol of the struggle for democracy within their country and for its full sovereignty and independence.

See also *Iranian Constitutional Revolution (1906).*

HOMA KATOUZIAN

BIBLIOGRAPHY

Abrahamian, Eravand. *Iran between Two Revolutions.* Princeton, N.J.: Princeton University Press, 1982.

Azimi, Fakhr al-Din. "The Reconciliation of Politics and Ethics, Nationalism and Democracy: An Overview of the Political Career of Dr. Muhammad Musaddiq." In *Musaddiq, Iranian Nationalism and Oil.* Edited by James A. Bill and William Roger Louis. London: I. B. Tauris, 1988.

Katouzian, Homa. *Musaddiq and the Struggle for Power in Iran.* London: I. B. Tauris, 1990.

Keddie, Nikki. *Roots of Revolution.* New Haven, Conn.: Yale University Press, 1981.

Musaddiq, Mohammad. *Musaddiq's Memoirs.* Edited and introduced by Homa Katouzian. Translated by S. H. Amin and Homa Katouzian. London: Jebhe, 1988.

MOZAMBICAN REVOLUTION (1974–1994)

The Mozambican Revolution was a natural continuation of the war for national liberation waged since 1964 against Portuguese colonial domination. The Front for the Liberation of Mozambique (Frelimo) aspired not only to independence but also to a complete transformation of society and economy. After achieving independence in 1975, Frelimo pursued a far-reaching socialist program. In 1984 the revolutionary phase came to an end. Under the onslaught of the Mozambican National Resistance (Renamo), a South Africa-backed armed movement, the Mozambican government signed a nonaggression agreement with South Africa and turned to Western countries and international financial institutions for assistance. By 1994, when the first multiparty elections in the history of the country were held, Mozambique had embraced economic liberalization and democratic transformation *(see map, p. 334)*.

Like all Portuguese colonies, Mozambique was desperately poor. Portuguese colonialism had been particularly exploitative, relying on forced labor to increase production, developing little physical infrastructure except where the Portuguese lived, and providing little education. Jobs in the small urban sector—even menial ones—were reserved for whites. Most of the African population lived off subsistence farming, supplemented by the remittances from migrants working in the South African mines. The experience of poverty and exploitation, coupled with the exposure to socialist ideals of the few Mozambicans allowed to study abroad, had a strong influence on Frelimo's leaders. Formed in 1964, the movement was openly socialist by 1969, when an internal power struggle led to the rise of the radical wing under the leadership of Samora Machel.

CONTRADICTIONS OF MOZAMBICAN SOCIALISM

In 1975 Mozambique became independent. Portuguese settlers, panicked by Frelimo's radical image, left en masse. After their departure the commercial farm sector, the trading networks, and the little existing industry disintegrated. Frelimo struggled to govern the collapsing country with few cadres, little experience, and no resources. Nevertheless, it moved ahead with its ambitious and ultimately disastrous socialist program.

Major contradictions plagued the revolution from the beginning. Ideologically, the party had serious problems reconciling its commitment to improving the lives of the peasants with a vision of socialism that included a Soviet-style fascination with large collective farms, huge agroindustrial "complexes," and economic planning. In the attempt to reconcile the contradiction, Frelimo alienated a considerable segment of the population and failed to generate economic growth.

Frelimo tried to implement its socialist program in rural areas both by promoting the formation of communal villages, where the population would produce collectively, and by developing state farms on the abandoned Portuguese land. Ideologically, Frelimo was strongly committed to the communal villages. In reality, the state farms absorbed most of the money and attention. Neither was successful.

Communal villages reached only a small percentage of the population and failed to increase production, although they did improve access to education and health services for the peasants. However, they also created resentment, particularly since Frelimo systematically excluded traditional authorities from positions of leadership. The state farms also failed to increase production, turning instead into inefficient, money-losing giants, heavily supplied with Soviet bloc machinery that was chronically in disrepair. Mozambique as a result became increasingly dependent on imports and eventually on international assistance.

Mozambicans queue to vote in the multiparty elections of October 1994, which marked the end of the socialist revolution in Mozambique.

Similar contradictions existed in the political realm. Frelimo had a tradition of grassroots participation, developed first to administer the liberated zones during the war and then used successfully after independence by "dynamizing groups" of Frelimo members and supporters to organize the population while Frelimo struggled to set up a government. But at its third congress, in 1977, Frelimo officially embraced Marxism-Leninism and decided to transform itself into a tightly organized vanguard party. In the ensuing reorganization, many old-time Frelimo supporters were excluded from the party, which became increasingly isolated from the population.

The Frelimo leadership recognized these economic and political weaknesses, freely admitting at its fourth congress, held in April 1983, that it had made many mistakes. But the problems were never corrected, in part because by 1983 Mozambique was again in the midst of war, this time with Renamo.

ABANDONING THE SOCIALIST PROJECT

Renamo started as a tool of the white regime in Rhodesia, and after 1980 it became a tool of the apartheid regime in South Africa, which used it to destabilize Mozambique in order to keep the African National Congress from operating there. Its foreign connection made Renamo into a particularly destructive movement, more interested in obliterating any accomplishment by Frelimo—schools and rural clinics were favorite targets—than in building a strong following and an alternative program. Despite its brutal tactics and lack of political program, Renamo enjoyed some support among people resentful of Frelimo's policies, as well as from ethnic groups, particularly in the central part of the country, that perceived Frelimo as a movement dominated by southerners.

The destruction caused by Renamo, the problems resulting from Frelimo's own policies, and the decreasing willingness of the Soviet Union to provide support for Marxist-Leninist African countries forced the government to seek accommodation with South Africa and a rapprochement with Western countries and international institutions. In March 1984 Mozambique and South Africa signed the Nkomati Agreement, pledging to withdraw support, respectively, from the ANC and Renamo. Within a few months Mozambique also joined the World Bank, opening the way for a rapid increase in international assistance. These decisions practically ended the socialist revolution in Mozambique.

It took several more years, however, to complete the process of abandoning socialism. In 1989 the Frelimo party congress rejected socialism, and in 1992 the constitution was amended to allow the formation of political parties other than Frelimo. In October of the same year, after a long period of intense international mediation, Renamo and Frelimo signed a peace agreement. Under the supervision of the United Nations and with the technical and financial assistance of bilateral donors and multilateral financial institutions, the Frelimo army and the Renamo guerrillas were demobilized and a new army formed, making it possible to hold multiparty elections in October 1994. The elections, and the continuing process of economic reform, concluded the short-lived attempt to carry out a socialist revolution in Mozambique.

See also *Angolan Revolution (1974–1996); Portuguese Revolution (1974).*

Marina Ottaway

BIBLIOGRAPHY

Abrahamsson, Hans, and Anders Nilsson. *Mozambique: The Troubled Transition.* London: Zed Books, 1995.

Hanlon, Joseph. *Mozambique: The Revolution Under Fire.* London: Zed Press, 1984.

Isaacman, Allen. *A Luta Continua: Creating a New Society in Mozambique.* Binghamton, N.Y.: Fernand Braudel Center, State University of New York, 1978.

Isaacman, Allen, and Barbara Isaacman. *Mozambique: From Colonialism to Revolution, 1900–1982.* Boulder, Colo.: Westview Press, 1983.

Munslow, Barry. *Mozambique: The Revolution and Its Origins.* London: Longman, 1983.

Saul, John, ed. *A Difficult Road: The Transition to Socialism in Mozambique.* New York: Monthly Review Press, 1985.

Vines, Alex. *Renamo: Terrorism in Mozambique.* London: James Currey, 1991; and Bloomington: Indiana University Press, 1991.

MUGABE, ROBERT GABRIEL

Mugabe (1924–), Zimbabwean nationalist and political leader, was considered the most committed of his fellow revolutionaries to scientific socialist ideology, but he was also a pragmatist. He believed in a one-party Marxist state but promised to introduce it only if it had the people's support. He envisaged a gradual state takeover of all land, private investment, and banks.

He was born in Kutama, Rhodesia (now Zimbabwe), some eighty miles west of the capital, Salisbury (now Harare). He received a Jesuit education. After teaching primary school, he won a scholarship to the University of Fort Hare in South Africa, where he obtained a B.A. in 1951. Mugabe then taught in Rhodesia, Northern Rhodesia, and Ghana.

In 1960 he returned from Ghana and began his political career in the National Democratic Party. Joining those who broke from Joshua Nkomo and the Zimbabwe African People's Union (ZAPU) to form the Zimbabwe African National Union (ZANU), he became secretary general, and Ndabaningi Sithole became president.

Mugabe was among the nationalist leaders imprisoned in 1964 by the white regime of Ian Smith. While in prison, Mugabe obtained a law degree and a B.A. (administration) through the University of London. Imprisoned ZANU central committee members removed Sithole as president of the party in 1970 because he had renounced the armed struggle while on trial for his alleged attempt to assassinate Prime Minister Smith, and they installed Mugabe as leader.

In November 1974 Mugabe was released from prison to represent ZANU at unity talks among the nationalists in Lusaka, Zambia. But the front-line states refused to recognize his leadership over Sithole's. In March 1975 ZANU was thrown into turmoil by the assassination in Zambia of ZANU's acting president, Herbert Chitepo. The Zambian government jailed ZANU's military and political leaders, whom it blamed for Chitepo's death. Sent to fill the vacuum in political leadership, Mugabe and Edgar Tekere clandestinely crossed into Mozambique in April 1975.

Fearing that Mugabe did not control the guerrillas in Mozambique, President Samora Machel restricted the two men to Quelimane, away from the guerrilla camps. In September 1975 imprisoned members of ZANU's War Council made it known that they wanted Mugabe to replace Sithole. Commanders at Mgagao, the most important camp in Tanzania, signed a declaration, later accepted at other camps, that Mugabe was the only political leader they would accept. Mugabe represented ZANU at British-sponsored settlement talks in Geneva. On his return to Mozambique, leaders who had controlled the war effort from late 1975 and who opposed his leadership were imprisoned. Mugabe was formally elected president and commander-in-chief at ZANU's September 1977 congress in Chimoio, Mozambique. Mugabe's remaining opponents on the ZANU central committee were imprisoned in Mozambique in 1978. Mugabe thus established his leadership of ZANU late in the struggle for independence.

Mugabe's reign as prime minister (1980–1987) and as president (1988–) has been marked by the consolidation of the renamed ZANU-PF's power. Mugabe presided over a vicious campaign against a small band once loyal to ZAPU. The conflict ended only in December 1987 when ZAPU agreed to merge with the ruling party. In practice, ZANU-PF enjoys the advantages of a one-party system, and its radicalism—it abandoned Marxism–Leninism in 1991—has been chiefly rhetorical. Mugabe is confronting unprecedented criticism for the rapidly deteriorating economy, and many are calling for him to step down.

See also *Zimbabwe Revolt and Reform (1966–1980).*

NORMA KRIGER

BIBLIOGRAPHY

Mugabe, Robert Gabriel. *Our War of Liberation. Speeches, Articles, Interviews 1976–1979.* Gweru, Zimbabwe: Mambo Press, 1983.

Rake, Alan. "Man Behind the Mask: Robert Mugabe." In *100 Great Africans,* edited by Alan Rake, 408–412. Metuchen, N.J.: Scarecrow Press, 1994.

Smith, David, and Colin Simpson, with Ian Davies. *Mugabe.* Salisbury, Zimbabwe: Sphere, 1981.

MUSIC

The capacity of music to inflame the passions—"to make men march," as the French put it in the 1790s—has been understood by philosophers of the arts since the beginning of written musical discourse. Perhaps the earliest poetry in the Old Testament (thought to be an eyewitness account) is a song celebrating revolutionary victory. Miriam, the prophetess and sister of Aaron, takes a timbrel in her hand, dances, and exultantly cries: "Sing to the Lord, for he has triumphed gloriously; / the horse and his rider he has thrown into the sea" (Exodus 16:21). Handel set this text for the climactic choruses of the oratorio *Israel in Egypt* (1739).

Mozart's *The Marriage of Figaro* (1786), with its subtext of decaying nobility confronted by a vibrant working class, overtly challenges the political and social order. The same is true of Rossini's *William Tell* (1826), which tells of Swiss peasants rising against Austrian oppression, and the dozens of "rescue operas" that culminate in Beethoven's *Fidelio* (1805), in which Leonore disguises herself as a young man to arrange the escape of her husband, Florestan, a political prisoner. Beethoven also tapped the French revolutionary idiom in the funeral march (movt. II) of the "Eroica" symphony, op. 55 (1803). In addition, the best republican songs of the 1790s were sung lustily again in 1830 and 1848.

Yearnings for national identity shared many affinities with musical romanticism, and the more engaged composers of that era willingly joined in the formulation of political agendas and wrote music for their own particular cause. The national anthems adopted in the nineteenth century often celebrate revolutionary victory, and even less provocative works, such as Sibelius's *Finlandia* (1899), came to be understood as rallying points by the oppressed and as sedition by governments under attack. The music of revolution and nationhood merges naturally with military music in general, but all these types share a fundamental goal: to stir the spirit to resolve and the body to action—often to arms.

The first major composer in American history was William Billings (1746–1800), Yankee jack-of-all-trades and dabbler in the revolutionary movement. Included in his first published collection, *The New-England Psalm-Singer* (1770), is "Chester," whose tune and inflammatory text served as a kind of battle hymn of the American Revolution:

> Let tyrants shake their iron rod,
> And slav'ry clank her galling chains.
> We fear them not, we trust in God;
> New England's God forever reigns.

In his next publication, *The Singing Master's Assistant* (1778), an anthem, "Lamentation over Boston," paraphrases Psalm 137 and Jeremiah: "By the Rivers of Watertown we sat down and wept when we remember'd thee, O Boston." It justifies the taking up of arms against brothers and implores the Lord to forbid "that those who have sucked Bostonian Breasts should thirst for American Blood."

FRENCH REVOLUTION

The central musical repertoire of the French Revolution is that of the great public manifestations meant to unite the citizenry in republicanism—the spectacles in the Champ de Mars, grand funereal progresses to the Panthéon, and the like—which began as early as the first anniversary of the fall of the Bastille. From the beginning, these Fêtes Nationales had a strong musical component. Composers of merit—first François-Joseph Gossec, and through him Étienne Méhul, Simon Catel (bandmaster of the National Guard from the age of eighteen), and Jean-François Le Sueur—amassed a sizable body of revolutionary work. They kept their songs and marches purposefully simple, of memorable lyric and hummable tune, the better to reach their countrymen at arms. (By contrast, the big ceremonial cantatas, like Méhul's superb *Chant national du 14 Juillet 1800,* are works of high art.) The numbers of people involved in the Fêtes Nationales were immense: hundreds of musicians, thousands of soldiers, and tens of thousands of spectators.

For instance, a short *Marche lugubre* (1791) by Gossec (1734–1829), dean of the French revolutionary composers, commemorates victims of the so-called Nancy affair, in which dozens had been killed in a skirmish with counterrevolutionaries. In April and July 1791 it was heard during the processions to remove the ashes of Mirabeau and then Voltaire to the Panthéon. The *Marche lugubre* uses novel instrumentation to make its point: in addition to the usual band instruments of the era, it calls for trombones, what may be the first notated strokes of the tam-tam, and ranks of players of the *tuba curva*—a long, looped tube of brass meant to replicate something of Roman antiquity and said to have made as much noise as five serpents. The effect of the slow tattoo of muffled drums, the strokes of the tam tam alternating with the eerie homophonic progress of the massed winds, and the harmonic idiom that is, for its time and place, progressive must have mesmerized the citizenry with its heroic *pompe funèbre.* There are both stylistic and historical reasons to imagine that the *Marche lugubre* served Beethoven as a model for the funeral march in the "Eroica" Symphony.

Rouget de Lisle, composer of the *Marseillaise* (1792), was an army engineer described by a superior as "almost incapable of serious reflection." His famous marching hymn, composed in Strasbourg on the evening of April 24, 1792, commemorates a battalion of volunteers called Les Enfants de la Patrie and adopts the wording of a poster affixed to doors and kiosks announcing the imminent invasion of the allied armies of Prussia and Austria to restore Louis XVI to the throne: *"aux armes, Citoyens."* It was published as a *Chant de guerre pour l'armée du Rhin* shortly afterward, then sung by the Marseilles volunteers as they marched to Paris in August. In 1795 it was proclaimed appropriate for singing at all official events. During the Restoration and Second Empire its popularity was officially discouraged, but the *Marseillaise* never fell from the public affection. It was proclaimed the national anthem of the Republic of France in 1879.

The Magasin de Musique, a music publishing bureau and one of the chief propaganda wings of the National Convention, was formed in early 1794 and mandated to procure and publish the hymns and patriotic songs necessary for the Fêtes Nationales of the French Republican calendar and for events such as military victories and state funerals. The Committee of Public Safety ordered more than twelve thousand subscriptions for students at the military academy in Paris as well as troops in the field.

The monumental task of assembling and transcribing the revolutionary repertoire fell to Constant Pierre (1844–1918) and was undertaken—like the Eiffel Tower—in conjunction with the 1889 centennial of the French Republic. Contained in his work are more than 150 compositions as well as a catalogue of more than 2,300 works.

What might be considered the revolutionary or Napoleonic idiom was woven into high romanticism by Hector Berlioz (1803–1869). Following the revolution of July 1830, he prepared stirring orchestrations of the *Marseillaise* and a *Chant du 9 Thermidor,* commemorating the day Robespierre was assassinated (though he had been obliged to sit out the July Days while locked into a lodging at the Institute, just across the river, for a composer's competition). Berlioz's setting of the *Marseillaise* has become more or less the standard for great ceremonial events of the present. For example, it was sung in the Champs-Elysées on July 14, 1989, by Jessye Norman, swathed in a tricolor garment. Rouget and Berlioz met, and it was the old poet who first used the term "volcanic" to describe the petulant young composer. An integral part of Berlioz's work perpetuates the ideals of 1789: the famous Requiem Mass (1837), a *Hymne à la France* (1844), the Napoleonic cantata *L'Impériale* (1854), and the great Te Deum (1855). Yet Berlioz sat out his second revolution, too, finding himself in London in February 1848 when demonstrations began anew in Paris. His closest brush with political uprising was a near riot that broke out at the performances of his setting of the Hungarian *Rákóczy March,* in Prague in February 1846. Shortly thereafter he adopted it as the *Hungarian March* in *The Damnation of Faust* (1846).

1848 AND AFTER

The short-lived revolutionary fervor of 1848–1849 fostered less new music than did concurrent nationalist and unification movements. Nationalist composers invariably sought to embrace folk dance patterns, the native lore, and their own language in their composition. National groups venerated composers as cultural icons: Liszt, with his Hungarian Rhapsodies and gypsy-band idioms; Chopin, with his Polish-based mazurkas, polonaises, and "Revolutionary" Etude; Smetana, with his references to Hussite chorales and frequent citation of a musical motif representing Vyšehrad castle, legendary stronghold of the Bohemian kings. At the time, this manner of musical expression was meant more in support of a people's artistic soul than for practical purposes (but surely contributing to the general cultural unrest that eventually sought resolution in world war); and it was noted and lamented that both Liszt and Chopin were expatriates. But the resulting nationalistic repertoire, extending as it did throughout Austria-Hungary and north through Russia and Scandinavia, still stands as the core of nineteenth-century postromanticism. More politically successful was the thinly veiled revolutionary sentiment to be found in the works of Verdi. In *Nabucco* (1842), for example, the chorus of captive Babylonians was deemed to express the sentiments of Italians under the Austrian yoke. *Viva VERDI!,* as shouted at La Scala and elsewhere, was widely understood as a call for unity under *V*ittorio *E*mmanuele, *R*e d'*I*talia. And *Un Ballo in Maschera* (*A Masked Ball,* 1859), with its call for the overthrow of a king, was made to take place in the governor's palace in Boston—the irony of a setting at that birthplace of revolution presumably lost on the censors.

D. KERN HOLOMAN

BIBLIOGRAPHY

Berlioz, Hector. *Mémoires.* Edited and translated by David Cairns. London: Gollancz, 1969, and subsequent editions. Chapter 29.

Boyd, Malcolm. *Music and the French Revolution.* New York: Cambridge University Press, 1992.

Charlton, David. "Revolutionary Hymn." In *The New Grove Dictionary of Music and Musicians.* 6th ed. Edited by Stanley Sadie. London: Macmillan, 1980, 15:776–778.

Pierre, Constant, ed. *Musique des fêtes et cérémonies de la Révolution française.* Paris: Imprimérie Nationale, 1899. (Collection of 148 works of Gossec, Cherubini, Le Sueur, Méhul, Catel, and others from 1789 through 1800.)

———. *Les Hymnes et chansons de la Révolution.* Paris: Imprimérie Nationale, 1904. (A catalogue, with commentary and bibliography, of the entire revolutionary repertoire: some 2,300 works from 1789 through 1802.)

Wagner, Richard. "Die Revolution" (1849), "Die Kunst und die Revolution" (1849). In *Gesammelte Schriften.* Leipzig: E.W. Fritzsch, 1871–1883. Edited and translated by William Ashton Ellis. New York: Broude Brothers, 1966.

MUSSOLINI, BENITO

Mussolini (1883–1945) was one of the great revolutionary figures of the twentieth century, but he is rarely recognized as such because his foreign policies led Italy to ruinous defeat and his revolutionary ideals were fatally compromised by his alliance with conservative interests in Italy. His goal was to end free-market capitalism, parliamentary democracy, and bourgeois values in order to replace them with a tightly controlled, state-run economy, a totalitarian (he was the first to use this term) dictatorship, and a new set of heroic values. His new form of social organization, corporatism, was supposed to end the class conflict and alienation that marked the modern industrial world.

His ideas were much admired and inspired revolutionaries from South America to East Asia. Among those he influenced was Juan Domingo Perón of Argentina. The Iron Guard in Romania, a nationalist and antidemocratic organization founded in 1924, also took many of its ideas from Mussolini, as did the Thai generals who came to power in 1932. The combination of nationalism and corporatism was appealing, as well, to the Falange in Spain and to Francisco Franco, who came to power in 1939 in the wake of the Spanish Civil War. The idea of a centrally coordinated economy and society survived Mussolini and in a milder form led to many of the reforms made throughout western Europe after World War II.

Mussolini's bombastic style also inspired Adolf Hitler, who always thought of Mussolini as a kind of spiritual father figure. Mussolini saw Italy as being in the vanguard of the poorer, developing nations, those he called "proletarian," in the struggle against the established great powers, which he called "plutocratic." This world view was also admired in the 1920s and 1930s by the leaders of non-Western nations, and many of the anti-Western leaders of newly independent states after World War II adopted his style, rhetoric, and belief in militant, aggressive nationalism.

Born into a fervently socialist family, Mussolini became a leading socialist himself and a prominent journalist. He broke with socialists during World War I, when he turned to extreme nationalism, and after the war he organized disgruntled veterans into a militaristic, violent revolutionary movement that came to be called "fascism." (This, also, was a term that he originated.) In the chaos and disillusionment that enveloped Italy after the war, he offered a promise of order and renewed grandeur. Conservative forces, including leading intellectuals, businessmen, and the king of Italy,

Benito Mussolini (far right) inspired Adolf Hitler (far left), who visited Mussolini in Venice in June 1934, less than a year after coming to power in Germany.

turned to him as a savior and conferred executive power on him in 1922. He established a police state and had some of his key opponents murdered or imprisoned, though compared with his contemporaries, Hitler and Joseph Stalin, his rule was fairly mild. In order to keep his conservative and business allies, he had to tone down the revolutionary side of his program, so that corporatism became, in effect, little more than a way of repressing unions. To make up for this, he turned increasingly to foreign adventures.

Mussolini used the Italian army to establish control over the rebellious colony of Libya, in North Africa, from 1923 to 1931. In the process, he killed close to half its population. In 1935 he shocked world opinion by invading Ethiopia and using modern weapons, including poison gas, to subdue this technologically backward African country. In 1936 he sent an Italian army to Spain to help the rebellious fascist General Franco.

When World War II began, Il Duce ("the leader," as he liked to be called) remained neutral until 1940, when he saw that Hitler was defeating France. Then he joined the Germans. He invaded Greece, and then British-held Egypt, but in both instances his armies were routed and saved only by massive German intervention. As the war turned against Germany, and Italy was invaded by the Americans and British in 1943, he was overthrown by the Fascist Party and imprisoned. Mussolini was rescued by commandos sent by Hitler, who set him up as leader of a puppet Italian fascist state in northern Italy. In 1945, with the Germans on the verge of surrender, he was captured by Italian communist resistance fighters as he was trying to flee to Switzerland. He and his mistress were shot, and their bodies were hung up for public viewing in the streets of Milan.

See also *German Nazi Revolution (1933–1945); Hitler, Adolf; Italian Fascist Revolution (1919–1945).*

DANIEL CHIROT

BIBLIOGRAPHY

Mack Smith, Dennis. *Mussolini.* New York: Vintage, 1983.

Sternhell, Zeev. *The Birth of Fascist Ideology.* Princeton, N.J.: Princeton University Press, 1994.

NASSER, GAMAL ABDEL

Popularly known as the first Egyptian to rule his country since the pharaohs, Nasser (1918–1970) led the Free Officers coup of July 23, 1952, which toppled a discredited monarchy, secured full independence from Great Britain, instituted sweeping social reforms, and defined an era in the Arab world. The son of a junior postal official, Nasser grew up in the tumultuous aftermath of the 1919 rebellion against British rule. In secondary school he participated in anti-British demonstrations, once receiving a slight bullet wound. He enrolled in the Military Academy in 1937, a year after the officer corps was opened to middle-class sons, and soon became involved in secret nationalist activities. The core of the Free Officers movement coalesced within cells organized by the Muslim Brotherhood in 1943–1944; movement leaders later determined to maintain their independence from all civilian forces. During the 1948 Palestine war, Nasser and his comrades resolved upon military intervention within Egypt to enforce political reform, then acted in July 1952, well ahead of their schedule, when they feared arrest.

Initially a reform movement led by a joint command of junior officers, the Free Officers consolidated power over a two-year period, abrogating the existing constitution, abolishing political parties, outlawing radical movements, and proclaiming a republic. Nasser increasingly assumed individual power. After an attempt on his life in October 1954, reputedly organized by the Muslim Brotherhood, the regime eliminated its greatest internal threat. Elected president in January 1956, Nasser governed virtually uncontested until his death.

In 1955 escalating tensions on the Egyptian-Israeli border, Egyptian support for nonalignment and Afro-Asian liberation struggles, and the purchase of Eastern Bloc arms put Egypt on a collision course with the West. Nationalization of the Suez Canal in July 1956 precipitated the Suez War in October against British-French-Israeli forces. Egyptian troops and civilians suffered grave setbacks, but the "tripartite" invasion stalled in the face of Soviet and American opposition, and Nasser emerged triumphant throughout the region.

Nasser's multiple legacies remain controversial. Nasserism comprised a variety of sociopolitical elements: authoritarian single-party rule; land and health reform; public education; nationalization of heavy industry, finance, mass media, and the arts; and pan-Arabism. In the late 1950s the regime espoused a radical program of Arab socialism, which was formally proclaimed in the 1962 National Charter. In 1965 Egyptian communists, many imprisoned for over a decade, agreed to dissolve their organizations and join Nasser's mass party, the Arab Socialist Union. Nasserist foreign policy led Egypt into an ill-fated union with Syria (1958–1961), debilitating involvement in the Yemeni civil war (1962–1968), and, finally, the crushing defeat of the June 1967 Arab-Israeli war. The financial cost of foreign involvement undercut many of Nasser's domestic reforms.

In his last years Nasser struggled to rebuild a shattered country, materially and morally, and to unite a divided Arab world. He died of heart failure on September 28, 1970, after negotiating a cease-fire between Jordanian troops and Palestinian guerrillas: perhaps his greatest diplomatic achievement. Nasser's sudden death stunned Egyptians, who mourned openly in the streets. But his successor, Anwar al-Sadat, downplayed his achievements, highlighting Nasser's authoritarian rule and corrupt associates. In recent years Egyptians increasingly recall Nasser as a populist hero, and the Nasser era as one of national pride and unity, aspirations for social justice, and a golden age of cultural production.

See also *Egyptian Muslim Brotherhood Movement (1928–); Egyptian Revolution (1952).*

JOEL GORDON

BIBLIOGRAPHY

Gordon, Joel. *Nasser's Blessed Movement: Egypt's Free Officers and the July Revolution.* 2d ed. Cairo: American University in Cairo Press, 1996.

Lacouture, Jean. *Nasser.* New York: Knopf, 1973.

Magid Farid, Abdel. *Nasser: The Final Years.* Reading, U.K.: Ithaca Press, 1994.

Nasser, Gamal Abdel. *Egypt's Liberation.* Washington, D.C.: Public Affairs Press, 1955.

NATIONALISM

Nationalism can be an ideology with specific constituent ideas or a set of sentiments, loyalties, and emotional predispositions. In the European context, nationalism emerged in the course of the development and maturation of the nation-state. Many European nationalists made no distinction between loyalty to the state as a system of authority and loyalty to the nation as a fellowship of community.

In Europe nationalism emerged with the decline of two earlier paramount allegiances—to localized feudal fiefdoms and to the church in Christendom. De-feudalization and the beginnings of secularization left a fertile ground for new foci of fidelity. The Treaty of Westphalia of 1648 was the midwife of the new nation-state. By the eighteenth century nationalism had become one of the ideological forces of Europe.

The political thought of Jean-Jacques Rousseau, French philosopher of the late eighteenth century, included a nationalist tendency. His distinction between the "general will" and "will of all" was a distinction between the inviolate will of the nation and the will of all the citizens at any particular moment in time. The general will was superior to the will of all. The nation was more enduring than its citizens.

In the eighteenth and early nineteenth centuries nationalism was often combined with liberal values. Prince Otto von Bismarck, chancellor of Germany from 1871 to 1890, was among the first great conservative nationalists and authoritarian unifiers. A much worse example of right-wing nationalism combined with militant unification was, of course, Adolf Hitler in the twentieth century. A more humane nationalist unifier was Giuseppe Garibaldi in the struggle for the unification of Italy in the 1860s.

In Africa the anticolonial struggle gave birth to both localized nationalisms and pan-African movements. In the Arab world nationalism was often combined with transnational pan-Arabism. In the years between the two world wars, Japanese nationalism attempted to rally the rest of Asia with slogans like "Co-Prosperity" and demands for Western imperialists and colonizers to "Quit Asia." Pan-movements are usually cases of *transnational nationalism*.

Japanese nationalism at that time was combined with imperialism. A desire to build an empire can itself be a goal of nationalism. Rudyard Kipling, British poet of the early twentieth century, was an imperial nationalist who glorified empire building by the white man. One of his best known poems, "Take up the White Man's Burden," was an appeal to American nationalism, encouraging white Americans to accept the burdens of imperial power in the Philippines. Kipling and Cecil Rhodes, British colonizer of Rhodesia, also often appealed to that side of British pride, which was in effect *imperial nationalism*.

Nationalism can sometimes be preoccupied with the defense or revival of culture, rather than with fidelity to the state. Among the major European powers, the French are preeminent cultural nationalists. Cultural nationalism in France profoundly affected its colonial policies and gave rise to such goals as the assimilation of the colonized. The defense of French cultural influence has also affected French foreign policy more broadly, complete with a readiness to invest considerable resources in the propagation and teaching of the French language from Senegal to Saigon. When the nationalism and the language are substantially fused, the result is *linguistic nationalism*. The focus of the nationalism is substantially pride in one's language. The foreign policy of France in Rwanda in the 1990s was partly a defense of the French language in the Great Lakes area of Africa. But one may have to distinguish between direct linguistic nationalism and derivative linguistic nationalism. Direct linguistic nationalism is when the central focus of the nationalism is the issue of language in relation to identity. Separatism in Quebec is a case of direct linguistic nationalism. Derivative linguistic nationalism is when the pride in language is part of a wider cultural pride. It is arguable that the French are primarily cultural nationalists—and their linguistic nationalism is part of the wider cultural patriotism, which covers pride in French literature, role in history, cuisine, and civilization.

The Arabs are also great linguistic nationalists, but in the derivative sense. They are proud of the Arabic language partly because they are proud of the Arab role in world history, the Arab impact on world religion, Arab civilization through time, and the Arabs as the ultimate custodians of the Islamic heritage.

Turkish linguistic nationalism has sought to impose the language on the Kurdish minority. The Kurdish language has often been denied legitimacy in the Turkish state. Inevitably, such policies provoke Kurdish nationalism, both linguistic and otherwise. Turkey may be the most striking illustration of nationalism wearing the garb of secularism. In Turkey secularism is not just an attitude of mind; it is a militant ideology often linked to nationalism. In its cultural nationalism Turkey has faced one dilemma: how to dis-Arabize without risking dis-Islamization? Can Turkey be secular and Muslim at the same time?

This brings us to nationalism and orthography. The nationalist revolution of Kemal Atatürk dis-Arabized the alphabet (and adopted the Latin) and dis-Arabized dress culture (and adopted Western dress). Nationalist Turkey also dis-Arabized much of the vocabulary of the Turkish language.

Whereas nationalism in Turkey has been linked to militant secularism, in the Islamic Republic of Iran since 1979 it has often been linked to militant Islam. Iranian nationalism has been in rebellion, especially against American power and presence in the Gulf.

Nationalism may be sustained by religion, such as Sikh nationalism in India; by race, as in movements like Negritude, Black Power, and certain schools of pan-Africanism; or by an idealized memory of the past and a desire to revive it, such as the Zionist movement. Nationalism can also be sustained by negative memories of the past—especially a sense of martyrdom from a specific experience. Armenian nationalism has been partly sustained by the Armenian massacres under the Ottoman Empire in 1915. And nationalism can be sustained by rivalry for territory and by disputes over borders. Nationalism in both India and Pakistan has been influenced by the dispute over the fate of Kashmir. This is quite apart from the nationalism of the Kashmiri people themselves, in rebellion against forced integration with India.

Nationalism may seek to reunite those who have been divided by history and imperialism—such as the Somalis and Kurds. On the other hand, nationalism may lead a people to want to pull out of an enforced territorial marriage—such as the Tamils of Sri Lanka or the Chechens of the Russian Federation.

The word "nationalism" has transcended its etymology. Nationalism is now much wider and more diverse than the unit of the "nation." As we have indicated, it is possible to have transnational nationalism (like that of the Arabs) or subnational nationalism (like that of the Kurds). The term *nationalism* has come to be associated with certain forms of militant patriotism and with allegiance to units that are more diverse than merely the nation-state.

ALI A. MAZRUI

BIBLIOGRAPHY

Alter, Peter. *Nationalism.* London: Edward Arnold, 1989.

Bendix, Reinhard. *Nation-Building and Citizenship.* New York: John Wiley, 1964.

Kohn, Hans. *Nationalism: Its Meaning and History.* Princeton, N.J.: Van Nostrand, 1955.

Rotberg, Robert, and Ali Mazrui, eds. *Protest and Power in Black Africa.* New York: Oxford University Press, 1970.

Shafer, Boyd. *Nationalism: Myth and Reality.* New York: Harcourt Brace, 1955.

Smith, Anthony D. *The Ethnic Origins of Nations.* Oxford: Blackwell, 1986.

Snyder, Louis, ed. *The Dynamics of Nationalism: A Reader.* Princeton, N.J.: Van Nostrand, 1955.

NEHRU, JAWAHARLAL

Nehru (1889–1964), India's first prime minister, was born in Allahabad, the only son of Kashmiri Brahman Pandit Motilal Nehru, an upper caste Brahman from Kashmir and one of the wealthiest lawyers in India. Motilal enrolled Jawaharlal at the prestigious boarding school, Harrow, in 1905, and "Master Joe" went from there to Trinity College at Cambridge, in 1907. After graduating from Cambridge, Nehru studied law at London's Inner Temple. He hoped to remain in London, but his father was eager to bring him home to his legal practice after Jawaharlal was admitted to the bar in 1912. Motilal also found a suitable Kashmiri bride for his son and arranged Nehru's marriage to young Kamala Kaul in Delhi in 1916. Their only child, Indira, was born the following year.

Young Nehru was as bored by the provincialism of Allahabad as he was by family life and his uneducated child bride. He had heard Sinn Fein revolutionary thunder in Dublin and was attracted to George Bernard Shaw's Fabian socialist rhetoric at Cambridge, but it was Mahatma Gandhi's revolutionary *satyagraha* ("hold fast to the truth") movement that changed his life, transforming him into an ardent Indian nationalist revolutionary. Thanks to Gandhi, Nehru discovered India's peasant village poverty and became a passionately brilliant opponent of British paternalistic imperial rule in the aftermath of World War I. He was first imprisoned in 1921; between 1921 and the end of World War II, Nehru was locked behind British Indian bars for almost nine years, during which time he wrote his autobiography and *Discovery of India.*

In 1927 Nehru returned to Europe and visited Moscow for the tenth anniversary of the Russian Revolution. He became an ardent admirer of the Soviet Union, especially its state planning, which he tried to adopt for India. From this time forward he remained an intellectual Marxist-Leninist, though he did not join the Communist Party. Despite growing ideological differences with Gandhi, Nehru never broke with him, remaining his heir to leadership of India's National Congress Party. Nehru's socialist predisposition attracted Britain's Labour Party leadership, and Prime Minister Clement Attlee's viceroy, Lord Mountbatten, invited him to serve as the Dominion of India's first prime minister in 1947. Mountbatten became governor general. Nehru remained prime minister for seventeen years, from mid-August 1947 until his death on May 27, 1964. His popularity was second only to Gandhi's, and he led their Congress Party to victory in every election, enjoying more power over democratic India than any Mughal emperor or British viceroy.

Nehru's nonaligned foreign policy helped win substantial

Jawaharlal Nehru

foreign economic support for India's five-year plans, over which he personally presided. He aspired to lead a pan-Asian-African Third World as a counter to cold war superpower confrontation, but he failed to win either Chinese or Pakistani support for that movement. Nehru's excessive faith in socialism and the Soviet Union ultimately weakened India's economic development. His inability to work with Mohammad Ali Jinnah proved a fatal blow to Hindu-Muslim cooperation before British India's partition and to Indo-Pakistani cooperation after it. His domestic policy of secular and democratic ideals, however, helped liberate India's ancient polity from many of its caste-related prejudices and deep-rooted authoritarian weaknesses. Despite his revolutionary socialist rhetoric, Nehru groomed his daughter Indira to inherit his premier power, thus founding a "democratic" dynasty.

See also *Gandhi, Mahatma; Indian Independence Movement (1885–1947); Jinnah, Mohammad Ali.*

STANLEY WOLPERT

BIBLIOGRAPHY

Brecher, Michael. *Nehru: A Political Biography.* London: Oxford University Press, 1959.

Nanda, B. R. *The Nehrus: Motilal and Jawaharlal.* New York: John Day, 1963.

Nehru, Jawaharlal. *Toward Freedom.* New York: John Day, 1941.

Sar Desai, D. R., and Anand Mohan, eds. *The Legacy of Nehru: A Centennial Assessment.* Springfield, Mass.: Nataraj Books, 1992.

Wolpert, Stanley. *Nehru: A Tryst With Destiny.* New York: Oxford University Press, 1996.

NETHERLANDS REVOLT (1566–1609)

The revolt of the Netherlands against Spanish rule stands out among early modern European uprisings because of its success. The uprising had diverse political, religious, and economic causes and joined together unlikely allies such as wealthy nobles, Protestant reformers, urban merchants, common people, northern and southern provinces, and the rulers of England and France. The rebellion and subsequent wars also shaped the flourishing Golden Age economy and culture of the seventeenth-century Dutch Republic. Influencing political theory and revolutionary practice by establishing modern concepts of federalism, freedom of speech, and freedom of conscience, the federation of diverse provinces, independent towns, and dependent rural areas provided an alternative to monarchy.

In medieval times the Netherlands consisted of a patchwork of local jurisdictions jealously maintaining their privileges. Their nominal overlords included kings of France and dukes of Burgundy, the prince-bishop of Liège, and the Holy Roman Emperor. By the mid-sixteenth century Emperor Charles V (ruled 1519–1558) had established his authority over most of the Seventeen Provinces, roughly the present-day Netherlands, Belgium, and Luxembourg. Individual provinces had deliberative bodies called States, to which clergy and towns sent delegates. The States-General combined delegates from all provinces and generally met when summoned to hear the fiscal demands of the government at Brussels. Troubles arose when Protestant Reformers won converts in the prosperous provinces of Brabant and Flanders. To solve the problems of religious discord, Charles V ordered persecutions of heretics, such as those in 1544–1545.

SPANISH DOMINION

Charles's son and successor Philip II, king of Spain (1555–1598), took a harsher attitude toward religious dissent and rebellion. Persecution increased dramatically—in Flanders prosecutions for heresy rose from 187 in 1551 to 1,322 in 1565. Local authorities who had tolerated religious diversity were overruled. A wealthy noble loyal to the king, Prince William of Orange, declared that heresy laws were unenforceable because princes could not control the faith of their subjects. Nonetheless, Philip II proceeded with a scheme to create new bishoprics congruent with the political boundaries of his lands, to impose the Inquisition, and to increase royal authority over the church at the expense of local interests.

Fearing the loss of their liberties, the Netherlanders protested. In 1565 four hundred nobles conspired against the government and formed a league for compromise. As grain prices and misery increased in 1566, they presented a petition to the regent in Brussels, Margaret of Parma (Philip's half-sister), urging her to stop the persecutions and make a religious settlement with the States-General. While Margaret referred the matter to her brother in Spain for a decision, militant Calvinists destroyed images in Catholic churches. Some towns declared themselves for the Protestants and against the government. Margaret raised troops and moved against the rebels in the field, and Philip began to mobilize the resources of the rest of his monarchy. He entrusted overall command to his most experienced military commander, the Duke of Alva.

When Alva arrived in August 1567, he made many crucial changes. Spanish troops, quartered in loyal as well as rebel towns, acted with brutality toward the people. Alva appointed the Council of Troubles, also known as the Council of Blood, a secret court to punish rebels with death and confiscation of property. Heretical books were burned. The court inspired terror, and opponents fled into exile. In 1568 William of Orange led the exiles and their foreign supporters in multiple invasions of the Netherlands from Germany, France, and England. Despite some rebel successes, Alva's forces emerged triumphant, and he imposed a harsh peace, reorganizing the bishoprics, the laws, and the tax system.

INTERNATIONAL REPERCUSSIONS

The Spanish government was determined that the Netherlands should pay the costs of suppressing the revolt. In 1569 Alva asked the estates to approve new sales and capital taxes, the Tenth, Twentieth, and Hundredth Pennies. Only the last, a one-time levy of 1 percent on property, was approved and collected. The duke's demands for more were strongly resisted; by 1571 he lost patience with customary forms and resolved to collect taxes by force, touching off another revolt.

Conditions were more favorable for revolt in 1572. A bad winter and the merchants' strike against Alva's taxes had made life more difficult for the people. William of Orange found supporters among Calvinists in exile and those chafing under Spanish rule. His fleet of *Watergeuzen* (Sea Beggars or buccaneers) attacked Spanish shipping and raided the coasts. On April 1, 1572, they captured the strategic port of Brill in Holland and went on to other towns.

The revolt took on larger European significance. Spain was fighting against the Turks in the Mediterranean, and Philip's resources were inadequate to achieve his goals. William planned more invasions and sought military support from England and France. Queen Elizabeth I of England was consolidating her power against Catholic and Spanish plots. In France the princely marriage of the Protestant Henry of Navarre and the Catholic Marguerite de Valois was supposed to settle the civil wars between Protestants and Catholics, but in the ensuing St. Bartholomew's Massacres (August 23–24, 1572) thousands of Protestants were killed.

By July 1572 many towns in Holland and Zealand had joined the revolt, sometimes against the wishes of conservative magistrates and town councils. The States of Holland offered William of Orange their military command, and he prudently joined the Calvinist church. Orange was fighting for popular causes: freedom of conscience and traditional liberties. Alva launched counterattacks and allowed his troops to commit exemplary atrocities. This policy may have quelled the revolt in the south, but in the north resistance to Spanish sieges stiffened. The Sea Beggars kept up their attacks on Spanish shipping and blockade of ports. Seeing that Alva's hard-line approach had failed, Philip decided in 1573 to recall him.

Alva's more conciliatory successor, Don Luis de Requesens, abolished the Council of Troubles and abandoned the Tenth Penny (10 percent sales tax). In the spring of 1574 the military situation was mixed: the Spaniards lost Middelburg and failed to capture Leiden. When they were not paid, Spanish troops went on the rampage, and with no money, Requesens was under duress to settle. He announced a general pardon and opened negotiations with the States of Holland and Zealand. Requesens was willing to agree to constitutional guarantees and Spanish troop withdrawals from the Netherlands, but he could not tolerate Protestantism. By July 1575 talks were deadlocked, and the parties resumed fighting. Although Requesens did well militarily, Philip II's declaration of bankruptcy made it impossible to pay his troops. Requesens died in March 1576, believing the Spanish cause was lost.

PACIFICATION AND UNION

As mutinous Spanish soldiers again threatened public order, in September 1576 William of Orange called the States-General without the king's consent. The time appeared right for a solution involving all the provinces of the Netherlands. In November they were horrified by the "Spanish fury" at Antwerp, days of killing and looting by unpaid troops who slaughtered thousands of citizens. On November 8, 1576, the States and Orange's agents approved the Pacification of Ghent. Rebel and loyal provinces agreed to stop fighting each other and joined together to oust the Spaniards. Provinces would choose their religion and work toward toleration.

The States-General boldly asserted its independence from the monarch and assumed the functions of government. It was an unwieldy body, requiring all delegations to agree on binding decisions, and it could not bridge all the differences between north and south, urban and rural, Catholic and Protestant. By the Perpetual Edict of February 1577, the new governor general, Don Juan of Austria (Philip's half-brother), accepted the Pacification of Ghent and ordered a troop withdrawal. With good reason, William of Orange and militant Protestants did not believe Spanish promises. They refused to cooperate with Don Juan, who brought back the hated Spanish troops. The States-General repeatedly humiliated Don Juan, forcing him to send away the troops, surrender his authority, and even ask Philip for his own recall.

As they would do again, the States then looked for a foreign prince to act in Philip's place in the Netherlands. In October they asked the young Habsburg archduke Matthias (Philip's nephew), who was pliable and worked with Orange. In 1578 Catholic nobles in the south sought support from François, duke of Anjou and brother of the French king. With Orange's agreement, Anjou received the title of "defender of the liberties of the Netherlands."

For five years Orange tried to preserve a tenuous unity. Two groups of provinces formed "closer unions" in January 1579. First came the Union of Arras among the southern provinces of Artois, Hainault, and Walloon Flanders; then the Union of Utrecht, mostly Dutch-speaking areas of the north. The southern provinces reconciled with Philip II, but their northern neighbors eventually formed a new state, the United Provinces of the Netherlands, or Dutch Republic. Scholars differ as to whether the separation resulted from the revolt or reflected deeper social and cultural differences. Hopes for reunion remained alive well into the seventeenth century, and reappeared in Greater Netherlands schemes of the twentieth century.

RELIGIOUS AND CULTURAL DIVISIONS

Spanish influence revived after 1578 when the capable Alexander Farnese, duke of Parma, became commander of the army of Flanders. Farnese was also Philip's nephew, the son of Margaret of Parma, who returned as regent. He understood that Spain's best hopes lay with the largely Catholic south. Many Calvinists fled northward, and the southern population could reconvert to Catholicism. With Philip's finances on sounder footing, military victories reestablished Spanish power.

When further negotiations failed, the Spaniards declared William of Orange an outlaw in 1580 and offered a reward for his murder. This move increased his popularity and prompted the publication of his *Apology,* a potent propaganda text that fostered the "black legend of Spain." The States were ready to break permanently with Philip II and transfer their allegiance to a foreign prince. Since Archduke Matthias could not defend them, they chose Anjou as "prince and lord of the Netherlands" in January 1581. On July 26, 1581, the States deposed Philip in the Act of Abjuration. The contractual theory of lordship advocated by medieval writers and Huguenots was put into revolutionary practice.

It was uncertain whether the new regime would last. Anjou had limited authority and less talent for government: in 1583 he tried to seize power in Antwerp and failed miserably. When Anjou returned to France and died in 1584, Orange's policy was a failure and the war was going badly. Orange, "father of the fatherland," might have assumed sovereign powers himself, but on July 10, 1584, he was assassinated by a Catholic fanatic. After his death, the rebel state offered its sovereignty to the rulers of France and England, but both declined. Open support of the Dutch was tantamount to declaring war on Spain.

By the Treaty of Nonsuch (1585), however, Elizabeth took that risk, agreeing to provide money and English troops commanded by Robert Dudley, earl of Leicester. In 1586 the States-General made Leicester their governor general, though his service was brief—he too plotted a coup. Meanwhile, Farnese recaptured much of the south, including Ghent, Brussels, and Antwerp. Philip II felt more confident about the Netherlands and made plans to punish England with his great Armada of 1588. Yet when that misbegotten enterprise and renewed civil wars in France took precedence over Farnese's reconquest of the Netherlands, Spanish good fortune ended. The Dutch profited from the diversion of Spanish power, and even generals as good as Farnese and Ambrogio Spinola could not prevail.

THE DUTCH REPUBLIC

The survival of the new Dutch Republic owed much to its leaders. Maurice of Nassau, a younger son of William of Orange, reorganized the States' army. Johan van Oldenbarnevelt, the hard-working advocate of the States of Holland, led the Republic's domestic and foreign policy. In the annual ebb and flow of warfare, the Dutch were gaining ground by the late 1590s. Philip II again declared bankruptcy in 1596, and his generals again faced mutinies. When Philip III became king in 1598, he lacked resources to reassert Spanish power. Spain recognized Dutch independence by agreeing to the Twelve Years Truce of 1609.

The Dutch were embarking on their glorious Golden Age. The new republic practiced political and religious toleration. Although the Calvinist Reformed Church was officially recognized, it was not a state church—membership was voluntary and strictly limited. Freedom of conscience in a decentralized, pluralistic society prevailed, and its prosperity became a model for Europe and America.

See also *William the Silent*.

MAARTEN ULTEE

BIBLIOGRAPHY

Duke, Alastair C. *Reformation and Revolt in the Low Countries*. London: Hambledon Press, 1990.

Gelderen, Martin van. *The Political Thought of the Dutch Revolt, 1555–1590*. Cambridge: Cambridge University Press, 1992.

———, ed. *The Dutch Revolt*. Cambridge: Cambridge University Press, 1993.

Geyl, Pieter. *The Revolt of the Netherlands (1555–1609)*. New York: Barnes and Noble, 1958. Based on a work first published in Dutch, 1931.

Israel, Jonathan I. *The Dutch Republic: Its Rise, Greatness, and Fall 1477–1806*. Oxford: Clarendon Press, 1995.

Kossmann, Ernst H., and A. F. Mellink, eds. *Texts Concerning the Revolt of the Netherlands*. Cambridge: Cambridge University Press, 1974.

Nierop, H. F. K. van. *The Nobility of Holland: From Knights to Regents*. Translated by Maarten Ultee. Cambridge: Cambridge University Press, 1993.

Parker, Geoffrey. *The Dutch Revolt*. London: Allen Lane, 1977.

Smit, J. W. "The Netherlands Revolution." In *Preconditions of Revolution in Early Modern Europe*. Edited by Robert Forster and Jack P. Greene. Baltimore, Md.: Johns Hopkins University Press, 1970.

NICARAGUAN REVOLUTION (1979)

On July 19, 1979, the Sandinista Front for National Liberation (known by its Spanish-language acronym, FSLN) entered Managua, Nicaragua's capital city, in triumph. Two days before, Gen. Anastasio Somoza Debayle had fled the country in defeat after five decades of dictatorial rule by the Somoza family. The Sandinista victory was the culmination of almost two decades of guerrilla warfare against a regime inaugurated in the early 1930s by Somoza's father, Gen. Anastasio Somoza García *(see map, p. 208)*.

BACKGROUND TO THE REVOLUTION

Somocismo merged dictatorial rule and rampant corruption with subordination to U.S. foreign policy. Each of these factors contributed to the ideology of the Nicaraguan Revolution, which called for democracy, electoral representation, and popular mobilization; socioeconomic reform, including agrarian reform and nationalization of Somoza family properties deemed to have been obtained through corruption; and national self-determination.

Like other Latin American revolutionary organizations at that time, the FSLN was influenced by the Cuban Revolution. Above all, however, it owed its character to the nationalist heritage of Augusto César Sandino, an oil worker turned soldier who gained prominence in the 1920s as a liberal leader in the civil wars between the Liberal and the Conservative Parties, and in the struggle against the U.S. invasion of Nicaragua in 1926. Before leaving Nicaragua, the U.S. Marines created a constabulary (the National Guard), appointing General Somoza García as its head. Somoza turned the guard into an instrument of his own political ambitions. Because Sandino was an obstacle to those ambitions, Somoza first attempted to exclude him from public affairs and then ordered his assassination.

Somoza ran Nicaragua until he was killed in 1956 by a politically motivated university student. His sons Luis and Anastasio inherited political and military power, which devolved upon Anastasio after Luis's death. The sons managed to preserve U.S. support, retain strong personal control over the National Guard, and accumulate huge amounts of money through the manipulation of government budgets. A web of agreements with the Conservative Party enabled the brothers to weather several political crises. The Somozas' system combined intraelite electoral manipulation, military repression of the opposition, and alignment with U.S. cold war policies, including territorial support for U.S.-backed military invasions of Guatemala (1954) and Cuba (1961).

By the 1950s, members of the middle and even upper classes understood that only through some kind of direct, armed confrontation could Nicaraguans rid themselves of *Somocismo*. In 1958–1959, disenchanted members of both the Conservative and the Liberal Parties made several attempts at starting guerrilla warfare. Although supported by remnants of Sandino's army and students inspired by socialism, the initiatives failed due to infiltration and lack of resources.

The FSLN emerged around 1962 from the melding of several groups: students at the National University campus in León, Nicaragua's traditional stronghold of progressive ideas (many of whom had previously been involved with the Nicaraguan Socialist Party or were influenced by what later came to be known as liberation theology); peasant and worker organizers; shopkeepers and artisans from both the Liberal and the Socialist Parties; and veterans of previous guerrilla initiatives.

With opposition to Somoza and anti-imperialism as its unifying forces, *Sandinismo* combined nationalism, popular sovereignty, and armed struggle against state power to achieve broad revolutionary appeal. Cuba gave the FSLN initial support because of its apparent sympathies for Cuba's revolution, but also because Nicaragua proved under the Somozas to be a handy tool of Washington's anti-Cuba policy.

During a September 1984 military parade in Managua, a Sandinista howitzer passes in front of a billboard with the likenesses of Nicaraguan leaders.

THE REVOLUTION'S SOCIAL SETTING

It took the FSLN almost two decades to defeat the Somoza regime, losing in the process more than thirty of its highest ranking leaders as combat casualties and experiencing several internal divisions before reunifying. During the struggle, Nicaragua's economy and society underwent decisive transformations, which the FSLN was able to turn to its advantage.

The expansion of export agriculture (cotton, sugarcane, cattle) accelerated after 1950 and fostered social differentiation. Changes in legal patterns of land tenure and ownership led to massive peasant eviction, swelling the ranks of rural wage earners and forcing migration to towns and to the rural frontier in the mountains. Meanwhile, new fortunes were built through access to state subsidies and military repression of peasant resistance. By 1970 almost 39 percent of peasant families were landless. Even before the earthquake that left Managua in ruins in December 1972, urban poverty had exploded as a combined product of migration and the inability of a weak industrial sector to offer employment to the growing population. The few unions were weak.

In the wake of the earthquake, 57 percent of Managua's population lost their jobs, and 60 percent of the city's people were forced to move elsewhere. Urban life was dismembered and remained in that condition for years. The impact of the overlapping of oligarchic accumulation and geological catastrophe on the everyday life of the people was compounded by the National Guard's pillaging and the misappropriation of foreign relief aid by officials of the Somoza government. Segments of the business elite began to separate themselves from the Somoza family, whom they accused of indulging in "unfaithful competition"—corruption, illegal privatization of government-owned assets, manipulation of information and credit, and the like. The tight alliance between Somoza and the traditional elites began to crumble.

GUERRILLA WARFARE AND INSURRECTION

The FSLN spent the 1960s as a rural guerrilla front in the mountains. The movement was able to gather the support of frontier peasants fleeing from rural capitalism, although the relative isolation of these regions prevented further political growth. After the earthquake, internal discussions started over whether to continue fighting in the mountains or move down to the towns, where signs of popular distress and opposition were growing. Doing so would mean shifting emphasis from the peasantry to industrial workers and the urban poor. While most founders of the FSLN remained attached to the *Guerra Popular Prolongada* (protracted people's warfare), a faction that became known as the Proletarian Tendency reoriented its activity to towns and export-agriculture areas, where it targeted workers, students, city dwellers, and landless peasants as the strategic agents of revolution. Shortly afterwards, some former adherents of the Guerra Popular Prolongada attempted to forge a third path. The *Tercerista* faction combined guerrilla warfare in economically dynamic areas with urban mobilization, together with an approach to the middle and upper classes already disenchanted with the dictatorship. The strategy of national unity to confront dictatorship enabled the Terceristas to gain international support from governments such as those of Costa Rica, Panama, and Mexico, and eventually to neutralize the distrust of the U.S. government.

From 1974 to 1977 a state of siege aimed at smashing the FSLN enabled the government to conduct a harsh attack on peasants, students, workers, and poor city dwellers suspected of sympathizing with the revolution. However, Sandinista diplomacy mobilized international pressure, forcing Somoza to lift the state of siege in mid-1977. By then the Terceristas had successfully approached anti-Somoza segments of the bourgeoisie, many of whose sons and daughters were FSLN members or supporters. The Group of Twelve (G-12), composed of prominent businessmen and intellectuals, played a role in the FSLN's strategy of enhancing domestic and international support. That October the Terceristas launched an armed offensive against military targets in several southern towns, which increased people's enthusiasm for the revolution despite the ensuing repression by the National Guard.

The FSLN's struggle was accelerated by the assassination of Pedro Joaquín Chamorro in January 1978. An internationally known journalist and member of an upper-class family, Chamorro was an early opponent of Somoza and a participant in failed guerrilla attempts in the 1950s. Through his family-owned newspaper, *La Prensa,* he had denounced Somoza's abuses of human rights and the regime's perks and privileges, including illegal dealings in which the dictator's elder son, Anastasio Somoza Portocarrero ("Chigüin"), was involved. Chamorro's assassination on Chigüin's orders prompted the final rupture with the business elite. Business associations called for two national strikes to force Somoza to step down and demanded that the U.S. government withdraw its support for the dictatorship. The strikes failed, however, and the U.S. government adopted an ambiguous stance, oscillating between acceptance of Somoza's increasing domestic isolation and fears of "another Cuba" if the revolutionaries triumphed.

The Sandinistas took advantage of the massive outburst of anger that surfaced in reaction to Chamorro's assassination. People crowded the streets in Managua and burned down buildings and firms owned by the Somozas or their relatives. The FSLN launched attacks on military barracks, increased rank-and-file organization, and strengthened relations with democratic governments in Latin America and Europe, which provided both diplomatic support and supplies. Young people from poor and middle-class neighborhoods poured into Sandinista groups without much concern for the FSLN's internal factionalism.

Both the Terceristas and the proletarian factions reinforced their organizational work in Managua and in provincial capitals, while the Guerra Popular Prolongada succeeded in temporarily seizing some provincial towns. The weakness of reformist political parties such as the Social Christian Party, or their ambivalence toward Somoza, increased the FSLN's revolutionary appeal and people's perception that the FSLN was the only effective opposition to dictatorship. The regime's military response to insurgency, which included bombing of civil populations, reinforced the growing perception of an open confrontation between state and society.

In May 1978 the FSLN-backed G-12 invited most of the opposition political parties and unions into a broad oppositionist front known by its Spanish-language acronym, FAO. The hesitation of most of its allies soon prompted the G-12 to withdraw from the FAO, but not before issuing a "democratic government program" that included a broad range of institutional, military, and judicial reforms. Shortly afterwards the FSLN started the Movement for People's Unity (MPU), an amalgam of political, workers', women's, and student organizations with an openly revolutionary stance. Whereas the FAO was a failed Sandinista attempt at consolidating bourgeois and well-to-do opposition, the MPU bore witness to the FSLN's success in strengthening people's unity as a central ingredient of revolutionary struggle. The MPU demanded the abolition of the National Guard; nationalization of Somoza's properties and of foreign-owned firms operating those properties; agrarian reform; free labor organization and progressive reform of labor laws; and observance of civil rights.

As people's involvement in the Sandinista struggle grew, the FSLN's internal factions moved toward reunification. In March 1979 a joint national directorate was created. Coordination increased insurgent actions and efficacy. In June 1979 the joint directorate launched what turned out to be the final stage of insurrection, combining definitive attacks on military targets with widespread popular seizures of cities. As the revolution advanced, the business elites moved their capital and their families abroad. Workers and landless peasants occupied abandoned estates and factories and assumed control of production. Capital flight, combined with the breakdown of the agricultural cycle, fostered economic disarray and accelerated economic and financial crisis. Governance was finally reduced to failed military attempts to delay the revolutionary victory.

In May 1979 the U.S. government attempted to build a multinational military force under the umbrella of the Organization of American States to prevent a Sandinista victory. The FSLN's massive insurrection, overwhelming rejection of Somoza throughout the hemisphere (in response to the FSLN's diplomacy), withdrawal of business support for Somoza, and the dictator's stubborn hold on power combined to render the U.S. initiative a failure. The National Guard surrendered to the FSLN on July 17, as Somoza and his family abandoned Nicaragua. On July 19 a five-member board for national reconstruction inaugurated revolutionary government under the FSLN's leadership.

See also *Cuban Revolution (1956–1970); Liberation Theology; Sandino, Augusto César.*

Carlos Vilas

BIBLIOGRAPHY

Booth, John. *The End and the Beginning: The Nicaraguan Revolution.* Boulder Colo.: Westview Press, 1982.

Close, David. *Nicaragua: Politics, Economy and Society.* London: Pinter Publishers, 1988.

Diederich, Burt. *Somoza.* New York: Dutton, 1981.

Gould, Jeffrey. *To Lead as Equals: Rural Protest and Political Consciousness in Chinandega, 1912–1979.* Chapel Hill: North Carolina University Press, 1990.

Spalding, Rose, ed. *The Political Economy of Revolutionary Nicaragua.* Boston: Allen and Unwin, 1987.

Vilas, Carlos M. *The Sandinista Revolution: National Liberation and Social Transformation in Central America.* New York: Monthly Review Press, 1986.

———. *Between Earthquakes and Volcanoes: Market, State, and the Revolutions in Central America.* New York: Monthly Review Press, 1995.

NIGERIAN CIVIL WAR (1967–1970)

War between the Federal Republic of Nigeria and its eastern region, the secessionist state of Biafra, was the violent extension of a political struggle among ethnic elites to govern a polyglot state. Leaders of the three main ethnic groups—the Muslim Hausa/Fulani in the north and the Christian Igbos and Yorubas in the southeast and southwest, respectively—had long sought to dominate Africa's most populous and potentially wealthiest country. Political disputes have prevented an accurate census, but approximately 65 percent of Nigerians belong to the three major ethnic groups, while the rest are members of 250 linguistically distinct ethnic communities. Today, some thirty years after the outbreak of civil war, the nondemocratic ethnic power struggle for control of the oil-rich Nigerian state continues by less violent means.

The causes of the civil war were complex. They were deeply rooted in the ethnic-based divide-and-rule policies of British colonialism from 1861 until 1960, when Nigeria suddenly became the UN's tenth-largest country. The proximate causes of the war, however, were clear cut. Five years of bitter rivalry among the dominant ethnic groups to control the newly independent state's central organs resulted in a series of political crises capped by a military coup on January 15, 1966. An Igbo, Gen. J. T. U. Aguiyi-Ironsi, emerged briefly as Nigeria's first military head of state. His attempt to impose a unitary government precipitated a series of deadly pogroms against the privileged Igbo minority that ran much of the economy and civil service in the predominantly Hausa/Fulani Muslim north. Thousands of Igbos sought refuge in their ancestral villages of eastern Nigeria. A second coup deposed Ironsi in July 1966; for nearly three days Nigeria drifted without a leader until a consensus finally formed around a thirty-two-year-old Christian from one of the north's ethnic minorities, Lt. Col. Yakubu Gowon.

Gowon sought to contain the threat of secession by consolidating the support of the northern elite and appealing successfully for the allegiance of the Yorubas, who dominate the southwest. (A shaky Hausa/Fulani-Igbo alliance during the first five years of independence had excluded the Yorubas from most of the spoils of the central government. The alliance further limited Yoruba influence when in 1964 it split the Yoruba region in two: west and midwest.) In June 1967 Gowon boldly decreed that Nigeria's four regions be subdivided into twelve states: six northern and six southern. It was a blatant appeal to the east's ethnic minorities, who were restive under Igbo domination and who occupied the territory that contained most of Nigeria's newly discovered oil reserves. Over the longer term, the breakup of the four big regions might have led to cross-ethnic coalitions, which, with skillful political leadership, might have become the foundation for liberal democracy.

PROPAGANDA AND INTERNATIONAL HUMANITARIAN INTERVENTION

The war over Biafran secession acquired international significance not as a result of any revolutionary political, economic, or social forces or its status-quo outcome but because of the unprecedented nature and scale of the foreign intervention that it generated. In their campaign for Biafran independence, secessionist leaders tried to overturn the principles of nonintervention and respect for territorial integrity that are the basis for modern international order and are especially prized in intra-African relations. Biafran leaders argued with remarkable success that the moral imperative for foreign intervention to save the lives of their suffering civilians must take precedence over Nigeria's territorial integrity; the survival of the Biafran state, they claimed, was the only way to prevent a genocide of the Igbo people. Most governments balked, but the appeal attracted sufficient assistance from privately and publicly funded humanitarian organizations—including small contributions from millions of concerned individuals—primarily in North America and western Europe to sustain the rebellion from mid-1968 to January 1997.

Biafra began the war with few advantages. It controlled

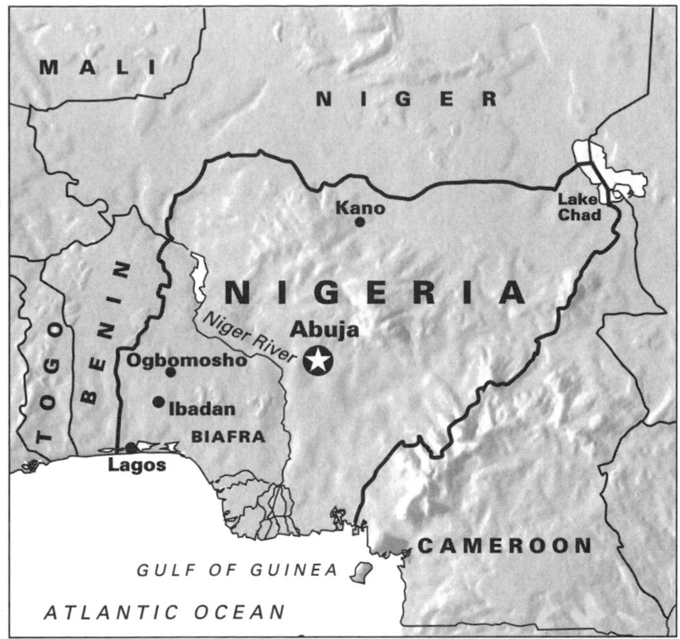

barely one-sixth of Nigeria's territory, had no army, and faced a blockade that virtually all governments were prepared to respect. By mid-1968 it was a tiny, landlocked, overcrowded enclave of several million starving people with no discernible prospects of military victory or sovereign statehood. But an unparalleled humanitarian intervention suddenly transformed and fueled Biafra's campaign for independence. (Biafra was a precursor of the numerous political disasters and humanitarian efforts in the 1990s in Bosnia, Somalia, Rwanda, the Caucasus, and elsewhere.)

During the most desperate years of the war, Biafra's leaders, in partnership with an extraordinary coalition of private charities and religious organizations, raised sufficient financial and material support—much of it from Western governments—to defy Nigeria's embargo with nightly flights of food and other essential material that exceeded the scale and duration of the 1948–1949 Berlin airlift. This intervention was devoid of cold war strategic implications and was not as overtly political as the private assistance given to antifascists in the Spanish Civil War. But it also showed the impossibility of humanitarian agencies remaining politically impartial.

When Biafran leader Col. C. Odumegwu Ojukwu became the first black African to appear on the cover of *Time* magazine, elites on both sides of the conflict recognized that the strategy to internationalize the conflict by humanitarian means was working. Nigerian leaders began showing greater diplomatic flexibility, joining Commonwealth-sponsored peace talks, allowing international observers to verify their military behavior, cooperating with intergovernmental consultative groups, and mounting their own public relations campaign. Biafra's campaign for political self-determination collapsed only when federal troops overran the enclave on January 15, 1970.

Despite the extraordinary humanitarian intervention, Biafra was never able to compete diplomatically, as Western governments made a somewhat artificial but expedient distinction between providing indirect humanitarian assistance and withholding political recognition of Biafra. By prolonging the war, however, the outside assistance contributed to the death of thousands of Biafra's poor from hunger and disease.

Foreign governments and regional and international organizations had made no overt efforts to prevent the civil war and held to the traditional diplomatic principle of nonintervention in a purely domestic affair. Washington and Moscow did not want this conflict to become another cold war problem, so soon after the Six-Day War in the Middle East and with the Vietnam War raging. The Nigerians wisely purchased arms from the Soviet Union as well as from their traditional British suppliers. Meanwhile, most African governments, fearing that the breakup of the continent's biggest state could spark demands for self-determination by ethnic minorities elsewhere, lined up solidly behind the federal government. Intervention by the United Nations under these circumstances was politically impossible.

No one denied that the 1966 pogroms in the cities of northern Nigeria had forced the Igbos to become refugees in their own country. But there was no validity to the charges of genocide that became the centerpiece of the Biafran propaganda campaign for international assistance and recognition. Moreover, Biafra's leaders did not believe their own propaganda, as Ojukwu and others informed the author from the safety of exile shortly after the war. They knew from intelligence reports that as the federal army moved forward that there would be no reprisals against civilians. At least from mid-1968 onward, when most of the million or more civilian causalities occurred as a result of the humanitarian disaster in Biafra, it was clear to the secession's leaders that in the absence of substantial foreign intervention the rebellion would suffer a certain military defeat.

OUTCOME AND AFTERMATH

Upon receiving news of Biafra's surrender, Gowon immediately granted a general amnesty, and there were almost no war-related detentions for the vanquished and no military honors for the victors. Senior Biafran officers reverted to their prewar rank in the Nigerian army, were placed on indefinite leave, and then retired. The author met with numerous former Biafran leaders, including the director of propaganda, when they returned to the federal capital of Lagos within days of the military collapse to collect back rents on abandoned properties, seek or reclaim jobs, and visit relatives. Compared with the aftermath of the American, French, Russian, Spanish, and other civil wars, there was an extraordinary lack of enduring bitterness. But if the civil war ended with civility, many profoundly troubling issues persisted.

The military salvation of the Nigerian state contributed little to the politics of building a Nigerian nation. No postwar democratic revolution occurred. Instead, a succession of increasingly repressive and corrupt military dictatorships ruled Nigeria, with the exception of a four-year interlude from October 1979 to December 1983 of inept but democratically elected leadership. By the 1990s the number of states had grown from twelve to thirty; to some extent, the division did lead to cross-ethnic coalitions, but without any discernible democratic effects. Instead, the proliferation of state budgets and bureaucrats allowed the military government to use its power and as much as $12 billion in annual oil revenues to pursue a debilitating neocolonial policy of divide and rule.

A survey of global humanitarian emergencies, published by the U.S. government in 1996, placed Nigeria at the top of a "watch list" of potential crises, noting that if widespread ethnic- or religious-based violence were to erupt, the conflict would be a huge catastrophe for Nigeria and all of West Africa. In contrast to 1967–1970, the Nigeria army, police, civil service, and judiciary have lost most of the professionalism and integrity that helped discipline the war effort. The battle lines also would not be as sharply drawn as they were by Biafra. And there would not be as clear a consensus among governments about how to manage a new Nigerian crisis. It would be tragic in the extreme if military rule, which precipitated the last civil war, is setting the stage for another one. This time there would be no underlying political logic to the conflict and its grammar would be anarchy.

JOHN J. STREMLAU

BIBLIOGRAPHY

De St. Jorre, John. *The Nigerian Civil War.* London: Hodder and Stoughton, 1972.

Kirk-Greene, A. M. H. *Crisis and Conflict in Nigeria: A Documentary Sourcebook 1966–1970.* 2 vols. London: Oxford University Press, 1971.

Stremlau, John J. *The International Politics of the Nigerian Civil War, 1967–1970.* Princeton, N.J.: Princeton University Press, 1974.

NKRUMAH, KWAME

Nkrumah (1909–1972) led Ghana to become in 1957 the first black African colony to win independence and was the foremost Pan-African leader of his era. He was Ghana's first prime minister (1951–1957, 1957–1960) and president (1960–1966).

Born of poor parents in rural Ghana, Nkrumah was an exceptional student and was educated as a teacher at Achimota Teachers College. After teaching briefly, Nkrumah went to the United States (1935–1945), where he successfully pursued a university education. He engaged in African nationalist organizing in England from 1945 to 1947, when he was invited home to be secretary to Ghana's new, bourgeois-led nationalist movement.

By 1949 Nkrumah had organized a more radical populist Convention People's Party (CPP), whose militant protests and strikes demanding independence forced the British to accelerate constitutional reforms. The CPP drew heavily for its activists and leaders on commoners in the traditional order, many of whom were elementary school graduates or teachers whose rising aspirations and nationalism Nkrumah articulated and embodied. The CPP became the dominant nationalist movement, winning repeated elections and independence in 1957, with Nkrumah as prime minister. Nkrumah's leadership was highly charismatic and populist. It was also autocratic after 1959, when a one-party system was consolidated. Nkrumah's personal authority dominated. More positively, Nkrumah was crucial to the CPP's role in integrating a multiethnic society and creating a Ghanaian national, rather than ethnic, identity.

Nkrumah was the architect in 1959–1966 of a serious, if unsuccessful, state socialist effort to restructure the Ghanaian economy through industrialization and agricultural mechanization. Despite many failures, Nkrumah's program was the only sustained effort in Ghana up through the 1990s. Nkrumah personally pushed construction of the massive Volta Dam and electrification project and the associated alumina operation. Nkrumah's government was overthrown by military coup in 1966. He spent his last years in exile in Guinea. Nkrumah's life was politics. He married late, an Egyptian, Fathia, and had three children by her and a son by a prior relationship.

Despite criticism of Nkrumah's dictatorship and CPP corruption, the Nkrumah/CPP legacy became an enduring political tradition in Ghana owing to successful policies in education and employment, the populist egalitarian ethos, economic nationalism, and the CPP's extensive organization. Nkrumahist/CPP-based parties reappeared as one of two

Kwame Nkrumah

dominant political orientations for voters in subsequent democratic regimes.

One of Nkrumah's most lasting contributions was his powerful commitment to pan-African unity among Africa's new, weak states, so that Africa could escape imperial domination, develop bargaining power with multinational corporations, and prevent great power interventions. Nkrumah was insistent on the need for continental political union, which proved unrealistic. Nkrumah devoted enormous resources to pushing for African unity, from his student days on, at the level of governments and of political parties. Nkrumah's efforts involved both personal ambition and genuine ideals for Africa. He provided intellectual and political support for African unity efforts, with some major impacts: he made the intellectual case for unified policies and strategies to overcome structural dependence; he organized many Pan-African conferences and several political unions, forcing Africa's reluctant states to concede at least to creating the Organization of African Unity in 1963; and he successfully delegitimated great power interventions through forceful Pan-African diplomacy against such intrusions in Africa.

See also *Ghanaian Independence Movement (1946–1957).*

JON KRAUS

BIBLIOGRAPHY

Apter, David. *Ghana in Transition.* 2d ed. rev. Princeton, N.J.: Princeton University Press, 1972.

Arhin, Kwame, ed. *The Life and Times of Kwame Nkrumah.* Accra: Sedco Publishing, 1991.

Davidson, Basil. *Black Star: A View of the Life and Times of Kwame Nkrumah.* New York: Praeger, 1973.

Nkrumah, Kwame. *The Autobiography of Kwame Nkrumah.* London: Thomas Nelson, 1957.

Thompson, Scott. *Ghana's Foreign Policy, 1957–1966.* Princeton, N.J.: Princeton University Press, 1969.

NYERERE, JULIUS KAMBARAGE

Nyerere (1922–) was an anticolonial African nationalist who after World War II sought the independence of Tanganyika, which was at the time a United Nations trusteeship under British administration. In pursuit of self-government and independence, Nyerere helped form the Tanganyika African National Union on July 7, 1954. The movement was successful, and the country became independent on December 9, 1961, with Nyerere as prime minister. Nyerere became president on December 9, 1962.

Linked to Nyerere's nationalism was his pan-Africanism, a commitment to the pursuit of African unity. Sometimes he put his pan-Africanism ahead of his nationalism, as when in 1960 he offered to delay Tanganyika's independence if this would help achieve the creation of an East African federation of Tanganyika, Kenya, and Uganda. In the end there was not enough political will in the other two countries to achieve such a union. On the other hand, Nyerere's Tanganyika did form a union with Zanzibar, in 1964, to form the United Republic of Tanzania. This remains the only case in Africa of previously sovereign states uniting into a new country.

Tanganyika played host to other major Pan-African activities. It became a frontline state for the liberation of Mozambique and Angola from Portuguese rule, and Rhodesia and South Africa from white minority government. Tanganyika established major training camps for southern African liberation fighters.

Nyerere's credentials as official host to liberation movements were put into question in 1964 when he was forced to invite British troops to put down a mutiny of his own army. More radical African heads of state, like Ghana's Kwame Nkrumah, regarded Nyerere's use of British troops as "neocolonial." Nyerere defended himself and continued his liberation role, successfully most of the time.

Domestically, Nyerere inaugurated three areas of reform—a political system based on the principle of the

Julius Kambarage Nyerere

one-party state; an economic system based on an African approach to socialism (what he called *ujamaa,* or familyhood); and a cultural policy based on the Swahili language.

The cultural policy was the earliest and the most durable. Tanganyika (and later Tanzania) became one of the few African countries to use an indigenous language in parliament and as the primary language of national business. Kiswahili was promoted increasingly in politics, administration, education, and the media. It became a major instrument of nation-building, and nation-building became the most lasting of Nyerere's legacies.

Nyerere's one-party state produced good political theory but bad political practice. The theory that the one-party state could be as democratic as the multiparty system and was more culturally suited to Africa was intellectually stimulating, but it failed the test in practice. Tanzania became a multiparty state not long after Nyerere left office. He personally accepted the transition to multiparty rule.

The economic experiment of *ujamaa,* which was launched dramatically by the Arusha Declaration on Socialism and Self-Reliance in 1967, captured the imagination of millions of reform-minded Africans. It was also greatly admired by Western liberals, intellectuals, and some governments. By 1987, however, disenchantment with *ujamaa* was widespread. Far from being self-reliant, Tanzania was more dependent on foreign aid than ever. And *ujamaa* had left the country poorer than it might otherwise have been. Liberalization, privatization, and marketization were not far behind.

Nyerere's regional East African legacy is also mixed. Although he was once committed to creating an East African federation, his socialist ideals clashed with his East African ideals. As he struggled to create socialism in his own country, he had to create barriers against free movement of capital, labor, and resources in and out of Kenya and Uganda. Socialist planning in one country proved to be incompatible with an open-door, pan-East-African policy.

Nyerere was raised as a Roman Catholic. Some believe that his recognition of the secessionist Biafra in 1968 was a form of solidarity with fellow Catholics, the Igbos, against a federal Nigeria which was potentially dominated by Muslims. Less convincing is the assertion that Nyerere's military intervention in Uganda in 1979 was motivated by a sectarian calculation to defend a mainly Christian Uganda from the Muslim dictator Idi Amin. In reality, Nyerere might have been motivated by a wider sense of humanitarianism and universal ethics. He was also defending Tanzania from Idi Amin's territorial appetite.

See also *Angolan Revolution (1974–1996); Mozambican Revolution (1974–1994); Nkrumah, Kwame; Zanzibar Revolution (1964).*

ALI A. MAZRUI

BIBLIOGRAPHY

Nyerere, Julius Kambarage. *Freedom and Development: Uhuru na Maerdeleo* Oxford: Oxford University Press, 1973.

———. *Freedom and Socialism: Uhuru na Ujamaa.* Oxford: Oxford University Press, 1969.

———. *Freedom and Unity: Uhuru na Umoja.* Oxford: Oxford University Press, 1969.

———. *Ujamaa: Essays on Socialism.* Oxford: Oxford University Press, 1968.

OMANI REBELLIONS (1955–1975)

Tribal groups in the lower Persian Gulf area for centuries have attempted to retain their autonomy from central governments. Isolated by their mountainous habitat and occupying a minority position in the Arab world (as followers of the Ibadi sect), the tribes of the interior periodically have rebelled against the sultans of Oman, centered in Muscat, now the capital city of this oil-rich state *(see map, p. 474)*.

Revolts in the provinces of Jabal al-Akhdar, in 1955–1958, and in Dhufar (Zufar), in 1965–1975, reflect the traditional themes of rebellion set against the new contexts of state building, Arab nationalism, and Marxist revolution. The Jabal al-Akhdar rebellion was spurred by the election of Ghalib bin Ali as *imam,* or religious-political leader, of the tribes in the interior of Oman. Resenting centralization and change, including oil exploration in the region, Ghalib bin Ali led efforts to prevent the Omani central government from subduing the tribes of the interior. The sultan, Said, dispatched military expeditions in December 1954; recaptured the main regional town, Nizwah; and quelled some of the tribes. However, Said made no serious attempts to develop or improve services in the area, and rebellion broke out again in the summer of 1957. The imam's brother, Talib, led a tribal force, which he had organized while in exile in Saudi Arabia, and with the help of local tribes overpowered the sultan's regiment in the region. This act heightened tensions. Various tribes joined the rebels, while radical Arab nationalist leaders, mainly from Egypt, criticized Oman's "blind following" of its patron state, Britain.

Saudi Arabia, then involved with Oman and Britain in a territorial dispute, was also interested in advancing subversive actions against Oman. When the rebel groups entered the main towns of the region, the sultan formally asked for Britain's help. Beginning in the fall of 1957, in two stages, British infantry and air forces, aided by the sultan's forces, pushed the rebels back into the mountains. By early 1959 (with the help of British commandos) they had dislodged the rebels. Later Said and the British met with rebel leaders to discuss the "Oman question," including British protection and the autonomy of the interior.

During this cold war period, a majority of states in the United Nations questioned the legality of British colonialist protection, the sultan's rule over the interior, and suppression of the rebellion. In 1965, when the sultan refused to allow a UN fact-finding committee to enter Oman, the UN declared the country to be an international problem, although no action was taken. Yet the legitimacy of Omani, British-backed rule was widely questioned.

The regional and international dimensions of the Jabal al-Akhdar rebellion were once more evident in the Dhufar (located in eastern Oman) rebellion. The cause of the rebellion was the negligence with which the local population was treated by the Omani government, in addition to harsh taxes, lack of jobs, and restrictions on movement. Feeling estranged from the Omani government, the local population (of approximately 60,000 people in the 1970s) started a rebellion in 1963. The original rebellious groups included development-oriented patriots and pan-Arabists, who in June 1965 formed the Dhufar Liberation Front (DLF). With the encouragement and support of a quasi-Marxist, pro-Soviet regime in South Yemen, the DLF was re-formed in September 1968 as the Popular Front for the Liberation of the Occupied Arabian Gulf (PFLOAG). It relied on Iraqi, Chinese, and Palestinian support and guidance from South Yemen. Styling itself a guerrilla movement, it aimed to liberate Oman and ultimately the entire Persian Gulf area from "exploitative" regimes. By late 1969 most of Dhufar's mountain ranges and the few main roads had been captured by the rebels. They established a revolutionary organization among the local population, focusing on communal cooperation, women's education, and anti-imperialist and socialist indoctrination. New rebellious groups joined the PFLOAG. They launched bombing attacks on Omani cities in 1970–1971 and established branches in neighboring Kuwait and Bahrain.

The Omani government went on the offensive against the rebellion only in late 1970, when a new sultan rose to power: Qabus deposed his father, Said, in a coup in July 1970 that was coordinated by the British. Educated in a British military academy, the new sultan brought a message of modernization and tolerant rule. Dhufar was his first testing ground. With income from oil revenues, Qabus initiated a "hearts and minds" campaign, improving education and health services, lifting restrictions, and initiating construction projects in Dhufar. He also began a massive recruitment and training campaign for a new army. Because the struggle against the PFLOAG was portrayed in Western and pro-Western states as a stand against Marxist subversion, motivated by the survival of the oil states in the Gulf region, states committed to stopping the "domino effect" of Marxist expansion came to Oman's help. Iran, whose shah assumed the role of pro-Western policeman of the Gulf, sent combat units that engaged the rebels in the mountain strongholds. Jordan and Britain each sent instructors and commando units, as well as air force units.

As a result, the rebels lost popular support. Qabus's new initiatives influenced some of the original, non-Marxist rebel leaders to come to his side, thereby narrowing the rebel ranks. Between 1971 and 1973 the rebels were pushed back from some mountain ridges. The military campaigns focused on the establishment of lines of strongholds in the fighting areas.

In May 1974, during a PFLOAG conference, a schism broke out between the militants, who sought to continue guerrilla warfare at all costs, and more pragmatic elements, who were prepared to carry on a political, nonviolent struggle. Reflecting the difficulties, the conference decided to rename the organization the Popular Front for the Liberation of Oman, focusing only on Oman. This change was paralleled by growing victories of the progovernment forces, which led to the rebels' defeat in December 1975.

The Dhufar rebellion was the most serious attempt by a radical, Marxist movement to exploit tribal discontent and revolutionize the Gulf population. It shows how a vigorous, internal modernization campaign, launched by Qabus and drawing on oil income, was able to undermine the rebels' purpose for being. Moreover, the suppression of the revolt also shows how pro-Western forces, both Middle Eastern and British, were alarmed by the Marxist threat and combined to thwart it.

See also *Yemen Revolutions (1962–1990)*.

JOSEPH KOSTINER

BIBLIOGRAPHY

Bierschenk, Thomas. *Weltmarkt, Stammesgesellschaft, und Staatsformation in Sudostarabian (Sultanat Oman)*. Fort Lauderdale: Breitenback, 1984.

Fiennes, Ranulph. *Where Soldiers Fear to Tread*. London: Hodder and Stoughton, 1975.

Halliday, Fred. *Arabia without Sultans*. London: Penguin, 1974.

Peterson, John. *Oman in the Twentieth Century*. London: Croom Helm, 1978.

Skeet, Ian. *Oman: Politics and Development*. New York: St. Martin's, 1992.

Townsend, John. *Oman: The Making of a Modern State*. New York: St. Martin's, 1977.

Wilkinson, John. *The Imamate of Oman*. New York: Cambridge University Press, 1987.

ORWELL, GEORGE

Orwell (1903–1951) attempted, in his writing, to confront the paradox of socialist revolution: that a successful socialist revolution could only grow out of a politically conscious proletariat and that a politically conscious proletariat could only grow out of a successful socialist revolution. A believer in the innate virtue of the proletariat, Orwell was led by his experience to conclude that these virtues would be undermined by the very process of revolution. Orwell was born Eric Arthur Blair in Motihari, Bengal, the son of an Indian civil servant. He joined the Imperial Police in 1922, serving in Burma. Almost from the beginning Orwell hated his work and left the service upon his return to Britain on leave in 1927.

While in Burma Orwell had worked on a novel, *Burmese Days* (1935), and also developed an ideology based upon the nexus of imperialism. Orwell came to see the inevitably corrupting nature of power, and his subsequent association of power with capital turned him into a socialist. He spent a period of time on a commission from the Left Book Club, living with working-class families in the north of England, and subsequently published these experiences in *Road to Wigan Pier* (1937), in which he extolled the values of ordinary workers and contrasted these with the self-seeking and patronizing values of middle-class socialists and communists. Orwell went to Spain in 1936; joined one of the pro-Republican militias, POUM (the Marxist Workers Party), which had Trotskyist affiliations; and fought on the front. He came to believe that the Republican forces had been betrayed by the USSR and its communist allies. As a consequence of his service in Spain, Orwell redefined his socialism, becoming profoundly anti-Soviet. He published a record of his war experiences, *Homage to Catalonia* (1938), which did even less to endear him to the orthodox left than his previous work.

As a writer Orwell spent a great deal of time living with and writing about the working class in Britain, and he became a champion of what he took to be working-class socialism. Nonideological—maybe anti-ideological—and certainly anti-intellectual, Orwell emphasized the importance of common decency; institutions should reflect structures that enable ordinary people to participate in their decisions. He saw the USSR as embodying the opposite set of values and wrote a devastating critique of the Russian Revolution and its consequences in the form of a fable, *Animal Farm* (1945), and a bitter, even bilious, characterization of life in a centralized, technocratic—and socialist—state, *Nineteen Eighty-Four* (1949).

Orwell could claim to have been a man of action. He craved for the "barricades to go up" and for the workers to confront their "natural enemy" the police, so that he could stand shoulder to shoulder with the proletariat. Orwell experienced what he took to be a truly socialist revolution in civil war Barcelona and was intoxicated by the atmosphere of equality and solidarity. If Barcelona fired his imagination about the possibilities of revolution, however, subsequent events, particularly the systematic harrying of Trotskyist and anarchist groups by the Spanish communists, made him pessimistic.

Although many critics have understood Orwell's work to offer an indictment of revolution as a process, he himself made no such claim, and there is overwhelming evidence that he both hoped for and expected a revolution in Britain in the early years of the Second World War. When this showed no signs of happening, and when indeed the government felt able to arm its citizens (the Home Guard), Orwell's own patriotism overcame his revolutionary fervor. Although he continued to believe that a working-class revolution would transform society hugely for the better—and that if there were any hope it lay with the "proles" (proletariat)—he came to accept that revolutions are likely to be dominated by intellectuals and to result in no tangible benefits for the working class. He became profoundly pessimistic about the prospects for socialist revolution as his health deteriorated, and he died in London in 1951 from his longstanding tuberculosis.

See also *Literature; Socialism.*

STEPHEN INGLE

BIBLIOGRAPHY

Crick, Bernard. *George Orwell: A Life.* Harmondsworth, England: Penguin, 1992.

Ingle, Stephen. *George Orwell: A Political Life.* Manchester, England: Manchester University Press, 1993.

Rodden, John. *The Politics of Literary Reputation.* Oxford: Oxford University Press, 1989.

Shelden, Michael. *Orwell: The Authorised Biography.* London: Heinemann, 1991.

OTTOMAN JELALI AND JANISSARY REVOLTS (1566–1826)

There is considerable uncertainty over the definition of "Jelali" revolts, the political unrest that occurred in various provincial areas of the Ottoman Empire from roughly the 1580s to the 1650s. The term *Jelali* originated with the Ottoman state, which used it to denote those who sought to overthrow the government by force. The interpretation of the Jelali rebellions as peasant revolts against the state has been largely abandoned. Some scholars present the Jelali rebellions as the actions of Muslim subjects who were seeking to avoid taxes by seeking entry to tax-exempt elite status. Others see the revolts as by-products of state centralization, in which the state consolidated its power by bargaining with the Jelali bandits who sought to profit from, rather than challenge, the state.

Ottoman historians now agree that the Jelali rebellions, and the deteriorating economic and social conditions and state violence of the same era, did not permanently damage the Ottoman economy and body politic. Society and state recovered and continued to evolve in directions quite different from the preceding era. Thus, the period was one of change, not disintegration.

The revolts of the Janissaries, the elite soldiers of the Ottoman armies, took place over the broader span of Ottoman history, from the fifteenth century (and perhaps even earlier) until the annihilation of the Janissary Corps in 1826. The Janissaries entered history as the firearm-carrying infantry elite, the terror of their Balkan and Iranian foes, who fought in the center of the Ottoman armies of conquest during the fourteenth to the sixteenth centuries. Exhaustively trained and severely disciplined, these Ottoman praetorians, nearly from their earliest days, exercised the power granted by their proximity to the monarch and frequently acted as sultan-maker.

Whereas the Jelalis have been seen as standing fully outside the state apparatus, specialists have presented the Janissaries as fallen angels—elements of the state apparatus run amok. Neither group, but the Janissaries in particular, is credited for the positive roles it played in the Ottoman social formation. Their denigration is part of a general tendency in Ottoman historical writing in which specialists have stressed the power of the state and given it primacy of place in historical research. Those outside of or challenging the state have been either ignored or treated derisively.

Most present-day scholarship portrays the Janissaries in more or less the same way that they appear in the court-sponsored chronicles written in previous centuries. During the fifteenth and sixteenth centuries, they are noted for their military valor and for their role in intraelite domestic politics and in the deposing of sultans and high state officials. They then become a debased and depraved institution of the classical age—a vulgar, crude, reactionary, and unreasoning mob. When, in this view, they deservedly were destroyed in 1826, it was said that their barracks had been cleansed, that scorpions had been removed.

The reality is more interesting, if still not well understood. Although their military successes became mere memory, the Janissaries continued to go off on campaign. Their arms and their training declined in quality, and others took their place as the actual fighting core of the army. Garrisoned in cities and serving as the guardians of the streets and markets while awaiting the next campaign to the frontiers, they merged with the populations they originally were intended to police and protect. By the eighteenth century, many Janissaries earned livelihoods as artisans, transporters, and laborers in the capital city of Istanbul/Constantinople and a number of other important Ottoman cities, including Cairo, Belgrade, Damascus, and points in between. In combining their former guardian functions with these new occupational activities, they came to represent the interests of the urban productive classes—including the maintenance of guild corporation privilege and economic protectionist policies. Thus, their political role had shifted out of the arena of elite politics, and during the eighteenth century they often fought for the interests of these urban workers. Through their commander, the Janissary aga, whose position entitled him to a place in the inner circles of power, the Janissaries' voice could be heard at the highest level, and, when ignored, they mobilized the larger urban population in support.

The eighteenth century, when the power of the central state was least apparent, was a golden age of Ottoman street politics. During the period 1730–1826 the popular classes, through their Janissary spokesmen, exercised a greater voice in Ottoman politics than at any point before or since. Even at its peak, however, their voice was one among many contesting for power. And, throughout the period, the Janissaries' position remained vulnerable because of their continued poor military performance on the battlefield.

In the early nineteenth century the Janissaries stood in the way of the state's goals of recentralized political power and the employment of laissez-faire economic policies. Thus, after carefully isolating his Janissary rivals, Sultan Mahmud II militarily moved against them in a series of actions, killed thousands of them in Istanbul and the provinces, and then abolished the corps.

See also *Ottoman Revolts in the Near and Middle East (1803–1922).*

DONALD QUATAERT

BIBLIOGRAPHY

Barkey, Karen. *Bandits and Bureaucrats. The Ottoman Route to State Centralization.* Ithaca, N.Y.: Cornell University Press, 1994.

Bodman, Herbert. *Political Factions in Aleppo, 1760–1826.* Chapel Hill: University of North Carolina Press, 1963.

Inalcik, Halil, with Donald Quataert, eds. *An Economic and Social History of the Ottoman Empire, 1300–1914.* Cambridge: Cambridge University Press, 1994.

Islamoglu-Inan, Huri, ed. *The Ottoman Empire and the World Economy.* Cambridge: Cambridge University Press, 1987.

Quataert, Donald. *Workers, Peasants and Economic Change in the Ottoman Empire. 1730–1914.* Istanbul: Isis Press, 1993.

OTTOMAN REVOLTS IN THE NEAR AND MIDDLE EAST (1803–1922)

At the beginning of the nineteenth century, the Ottoman Empire was a formidable territorial state. In its Near Eastern portion—the Ottoman provinces located in the Balkan Peninsula—Istanbul ruled over lands occupied by the modern-day states of Serbia, Bosnia, Albania, Bulgaria, Greece, and Romania. Its Middle Eastern provinces included most of the lands that are today's Turkey, Syria, Lebanon, Jordan, Israel, Iraq, and Egypt, as well as parts of Saudi Arabia and several other Arabian peninsula states. In 1922, after more than six hundred years of existence, the last sultan went into exile and the empire disappeared from the face of the earth.

The list of revolts against the Ottomans during the nineteenth and twentieth centuries is long. It begins in 1803 with eruptions in the Serbian lands to the north and Arabia to the south. The 1820s revolt among Ottoman Greeks in the southern Balkan Peninsula ended with a Greek state, at about the time that peasants in Palestine and in Lebanon revolted to redress their grievances. In the 1850s, as unrest in the Lebanon region continued, major uprisings occurred among the populations of the eastern Danubian basin, around Vidin in modern Bulgaria, which endured until the late 1870s. Famed in the Arab lands was a massive peasant rising in the Kisrawan region of Lebanon in 1858–1861. During the mid-1870s, Herzegovinian and then Bosnian peasants rose in revolt. During the final decade of the century, as Armenians revolted in Anatolia, the Lebanon region again was wracked by unrest.

In the twentieth century, a massive insurrection occurred in Macedonia. Further west in the Balkan Peninsula, there was a revolt among Albanians, a Muslim group that had been providing the Ottoman state with a disproportionate number of loyal soldiers and bureaucrats. Subsequent to this

Alex Tait, Equator Graphics, Inc.

crushingly steady sequence of revolts, the Arab provinces fell under British and French colonial rule (after 1917), and the Anatolian areas evolved into Turkey, beginning in 1923.

TRADITIONAL INTERPRETATIONS

Although the facts are clear about the numerous domestic revolts and the Ottoman imperial collapse, the connection between the revolts and collapse is not. Most of the scholarly debate to date has taken place within the framework of imperialism and nationalism, that is, the policies of the Great Powers on the one hand and the ideological and economic grievances of the subject populations on the other. Within these sets of explanations, different authors give varying measures of blame or praise (depending on their views of the Ottoman Empire) to international interference and the nationalist fervor of the subject peoples.

Briefly, scholars have focused on the ambitions of the Great Powers, particularly the Austrian Habsburgs and the Russian Romanovs, in the Balkan lands and Britain and France in the Arab provinces. In southeastern Europe, centuries of interimperial warfare among the Habsburgs, Romanovs, and Ottomans eroded the Ottoman frontiers. Within the Balkans emerged various native bourgeoisies which, during the nineteenth century, rediscovered their national glories and sought to seize control of political and economic life. One scholarly view holds that, sickened by the political tyranny and economic devastation brought by the "Turkish yoke" of corruption and maladministration, the subject peoples rebelled, often aided by one or another Great Power, and gained independence. In the Anatolian provinces, Greek and Armenian nationalist movements were the first to emerge, followed by Arab nationalism and, last of all, Turkish nationalism. In this scenario, the economically more advanced Ottoman Greeks and Armenians sought economic and political freedom. Arab nationalism, to the contrary, has been presented by some scholars in a curiously unbourgeois manner as a movement of intellectuals of indeterminate class, whereas Turkish nationalism often is seen as a last-minute movement to save a state being ripped apart from within and without. Much of this type of analysis has been presented by European diplomatic historians, on the one hand, and apologists for the newly founded nation-states on the other.

Standing somewhat to the side of, and yet linked to, these imperialist/nationalist interpretations are the writings of some Ottoman specialists who try to make the Ottoman state the central explanatory factor of the revolts. For them, the reform efforts of the Ottoman state—well-intentioned but insufficient—take center stage, and the argument is as follows. The Ottoman regime during the nineteenth century sought to assert its power in an unprecedented manner, in the process moving against the power of local notables in order to gain control over the peasants and their surplus production. The reforms included equality of all subjects before the law; more equitable tax burdens; and land rights and other legal protections for actual cultivators, including an end to their compulsory labor for the notables. Once-privileged elites were being undermined at precisely the same time as expectations were rising among the peasants. In this interpretation is the implicit argument that, if only the state had lived up to its promises more fully and its subjects had been properly grateful, the empire could have been saved.

At least two large-scale revolts seem to defy the traditional imperialist/nationalist interpretations: those of Mohammad Ali Pasha in Egypt and the Wahhabi movement in Arabia. In the chaos following Napoleon Bonaparte's 1798 invasion of Egypt, the charismatic Mohammad Ali Pasha maneuvered successfully and established himself as de facto ruler of the region. During his leadership in Egypt, 1805–1848, he sought to win independence from the Ottomans (while at one point he seemed ready to overthrow the Ottoman state and replace it with his own). In the end, his career meant subsequent de facto Egyptian independence from Ottoman control, and his family ruled Egypt until 1952. In this example, dynastic ambition and the geopolitical peculiarities of Egypt seem to explain the revolt and its success. The Wahhabi movement is similarly idiosyncratic. Here, descendants of a religious reformer, Mohammad ibn Abdul Wahhab, erupted out of central Arabia and sought to overthrow the Ottoman regime as godless and corrupt. To prove the point, the Wahhabis, led by members of the Saudi dynasty who eventually formed the modern Saudi Arabian state, captured the holy city of Mecca in 1803, thus challenging the Ottomans' role as protector of the Muslim holy places and ultimately their legitimacy as Muslim rulers.

RECENT REINTERPRETATIONS

In recent years, a number of works have appeared that offer a different understanding of conditions within the empire, economic as well as political and ideological. While the works are quite different in content and approach, together they suggest the need for a radical reassessment of the links among imperialism, nationalism, the Ottoman revolts, and the final decades of territorial contraction. Evocative for a new understanding of revolts in the whole empire are Benedict Anderson's arguments that the state preceded the nation, a position antithetical to that of nearly all Balkanist/Ottomanists, who have argued for the nation as the creator of the state. Michael Palairet has demonstrated that the Balkan provinces were prospering economically, not declining, in the final years of Ottoman rule. His work provides a new context—one of overall economic vitality—in the midst of political separation, and these findings need to be placed against the matrix of Anderson's views on the emergence of the state before the nation.

Moreover, a number of recent works on the Arab provinces have convincingly argued against nationalism as a cause for the revolts and the Ottoman demise in that region. Ottoman state policies are shown to have remained multireligious and multiethnic well into the World War I era, while evidence exists of considerable satisfaction among most Ottoman subjects with the sultan's rule, even during the final years of the empire. In this view, the empire was dismantled from without, and its subject population was cast adrift to find and form new identities.

At the least, the new scholarship seems to demand a reassessment of the role of nationalism among the subject peoples and a more careful examination of the actors and the events that led to the breakaways. In sum, these new findings hold out hope for a fresh and vital reinterpretation of the Ottoman revolts in the Near and Middle East between 1803 and 1922.

See also *Egyptian Revolts (1881–1919); Islamic Precolonial Revolts of the 18th and 19th Centuries; Ottoman Jelali and Janissary Revolts (1566–1826).*

Donald Quataert

BIBLIOGRAPHY

Anderson, Benedict. *Imagined Communities.* London: Verso Editions, 1983.

Anderson, M. S. *The Eastern Question, 1774–1923.* New York: St. Martin's Press, 1966.

Inalcik, Halil, with Donald Quataert, eds. *An Economic and Social History of the Ottoman Empire, 1300–1914.* Cambridge: Cambridge University Press, 1994.

Kayali, Hasan. *Arabs and Young Turks. Ottomanism, Arabism and Islamism in the Ottoman Empire. 1908–1918.* Berkeley: University of California Press, 1997.

Palairet, Michael. *The Balkan Economies; c. 1800–1914. Evolution without Development.* Cambridge: Cambridge University Press, 1997.

Stavrianos, L. S. *The Balkans since 1453.* New York: Holt, Rinehart and Winston, 1958.

Todorova, Maria. *Imagining the Balkans.* New York: Oxford University Press, 1997.

PAINE, THOMAS

A writer and activist, Thomas Paine (1737–1809) participated in the two most significant political revolutions of the early modern period: first in America, then in France. Born in Thetford, England, he spent his first thirty-seven years working in a variety of occupations until, in 1774, he emigrated to America, which was in ferment over acts of Parliament that the Americans thought were specifically designed to subjugate them. These acts, which placed high taxes on the American colonists without their consent, inspired Paine to write the first public pronouncement of why America must separate from Britain.

With the support of Benjamin Franklin, John Adams, and Benjamin Rush, in January 1776 Paine published *Common Sense,* an immediate bestseller in America and England. The pamphlet focused on British mistreatment of their American cousins by denying to them the historic rights of English citizens. Six months later, the Continental Congress, having revised Thomas Jefferson's draft, issued the Declaration of Independence. Paine thereafter was fully engaged in the Revolutionary War as a soldier (serving for a time as an aide-de-camp for Gen. Nathanael Greene) and more importantly as a writer. Between 1776 and the end of the war in 1781, he published several newspaper pieces, known collectively as *The American Crisis Series,* to rally the Continental Army to the American cause. George Washington read the first in the series, with its heartstopping first line, "These are the times that try men's souls," to his troops on Christmas Day, just before they crossed the Delaware in a successful attack against the sleeping Hessian mercenaries whom King George III had hired from his German dominions.

In 1787, four years after the formal end of the war, Paine returned to England, but he eventually settled in France to sell his design for a pierless iron bridge, which he wanted to construct over the Seine. Although this effort failed, he was soon caught up in the French Revolution. He published his second-greatest work, the two-volume *Rights of Man*

Thomas Paine

(1791–1792), which set forth the rationale for political revolution against tyranny and social revolution against inequality. Elected in 1792 to serve in the French National Convention, Paine helped draft a new constitution. France, the previous year, had become a constitutional monarchy, but it became a republic after Louis XVI was overthrown in August 1792. The constitution of 1793, although adopted by the Convention, was never implemented, because Maximilien Robespierre, the leader of the Committee of Public Safety, abolished it during the Reign of Terror (1793–1794) while eliminating his principal opposition, the Girondins, and anyone else whom he suspected of harboring antirevolutionary sentiments. Paine was imprisoned for eleven months in the Luxembourg Prison.

In 1802 Paine returned to America, which he considered his true home, and seven years later died in New York City, largely alone, forgotten, and despised by his Federalist enemies, mainly John Adams, and others who never forgave him for his attack on organized religion in *The Age of Reason* (1793–1794). As a writer and activist for the freedom of all people everywhere, Thomas Paine inspired later generations to follow his example to transform the world from tyranny and privilege to liberty and equality.

See also *Adams, John; American (U.S.) Revolution (1776–1789); French Revolution (1789–1815); Jefferson, Thomas; Robespierre, Maximilien; Washington, George.*

Jack Fruchtman Jr.

BIBLIOGRAPHY

Foner, Eric. *Tom Paine and Revolutionary America.* Oxford: Oxford University Press, 1976.

Fruchtman, Jack, Jr. *Thomas Paine and the Religion of Nature.* Baltimore, Md.: Johns Hopkins University Press, 1993.

———. *Thomas Paine: Apostle of Freedom.* New York: Four Walls Eight Windows, 1994.

Keane, John. *Tom Paine: A Political Life.* Boston: Little, Brown, 1994.

Kramnick, Isaac, and Michael Foot, eds. *The Thomas Paine Reader.* Harmondsworth: Penguin, 1987.

PAKISTANI INDEPENDENCE MOVEMENT (1940–1947)

The Pakistani independence movement was a campaign by the All-India Muslim League to create a separate nation-state for the Muslims of British India. The league feared that in an independent India, Muslims would be a minority subject to the political and economic control of the overwhelming Hindu majority. On March 23, 1940, at its annual session, held in Lahore, the All-India Muslim League (founded in 1906) moved the Pakistan Resolution, demanding independent Muslim states in the northeastern and northwestern parts of India. Adoption of the resolution officially launched the Pakistani independence movement.

The idea of an autonomous homeland in northwestern India for the Muslims of South Asia was first publicly advocated by the poet and philosopher Mohammad Iqbal in 1930, when he served as chair of the All-India Muslim League annual session in Allahabad. In 1933 an Indian student at Cambridge, Choudhary Rahmat Ali, coined the word Pakistan: "P" for Punjab, "A" for Afghan (North-West Frontier Province), "K" for Kashmir, "S" for Sind, and "Tan" for Baluchistan. The word also means "land of the pure" in the Urdu language.

In the years before 1940 a number of constitutions were devised by several Muslim politicians for an independent India that would safeguard the language, way of life, law, educational institutions, and political influence of the Muslims. These were studied by the league, and parts of them were incorporated into the Pakistan Resolution. From 1936 the league was under the leadership of Mohammad Ali Jinnah. He had been a leading figure of the All-India National Congress (founded in 1885) prior to and during World War I, but he had become alienated from the National Congress, which was increasingly seen as a Hindu organization, during the 1920s.

The key to the league's success in achieving Pakistani statehood was winning the Muslim seats in the provincial and central legislative assemblies in the general elections of 1945–1946, especially in the Punjab region, the "cornerstone of Pakistan." They did so in overwhelming fashion, winning 100 percent of the Muslim seats in New Delhi and 80 percent in the provinces. Their electoral success was achieved by mobilizing Muslims through raising their group consciousness: by discussing their rights in the pages of the league's newspaper, *Dawn* (founded as a weekly in 1941 and converted into a daily in 1942), and in conferences held all over the country; by claiming that Islam was in danger from the Hindu majority; by encouraging activism among students and intellectuals in the major Muslim universities, especially Aligarh Muslim University; and by demanding nothing less than equality with the National Congress in negotiations with the British. Muslim success in the electoral arena, along with obstruction in constitutional negotiations with the weary British and tired National Congress leaders, forced the Congress to agree to the British proposal to partition India in 1947. The sovereign dominion of Pakistan was created on August 14, 1947, with Mohammad Ali Jinnah as the nation's first governor general.

See also *Bangladeshi War of Independence (1971); Gandhi, Mahatma; Indian Independence Movement (1885–1947); Jinnah, Mohammad Ali; Nehru, Jawaharlal.*

ROGER D. LONG

BIBLIOGRAPHY

Low, D. A., ed. *The Political Inheritance of Pakistan.* New York: St. Martin's Press, 1991.

Talbot, Ian. *Freedom's Call: The Popular Dimension in the Pakistan Movement and Partition Experience in North-West India.* Karachi: Oxford University Press, 1996.

———. *Provincial Politics and the Pakistan Resolution: The Growth of the Muslim League in North-West and North-East India 1937–47.* Karachi: Oxford University Press, 1988.

———. *Punjab and the Raj: 1849–1947.* Riverdale, Md.: Riverdale, 1988.

Wolpert, Stanley. *Jinnah of Pakistan.* New York: Oxford University Press, 1984.

PALESTINIAN ANTICOLONIAL REVOLT (1936–1939)

The Palestinian Arab revolt of 1936–1939 sprang from multiple causes linked to claims to Palestine advanced before World War I by the worldwide Jewish movement known as Zionism. The British mandate for Palestine of 1922, issued under the authority of the newly formed League of Nations, included the 1917 Balfour Declaration, which promised a national home for the Jewish people in Palestine. British and Zionist leaders intended Palestine to become a Jewish state once Jews became a majority of the population.

That intent altered a key principle of mandates at the time. Conceived by Britain and France as a device for taking over the colonial lands of their defeated enemies without violating the call of U.S. president Woodrow Wilson for self-determination, mandates required a commitment to develop a region's population to self-governing status. Under the Balfour Declaration, Britain was obliged to suppress the indigenous Arab population and encourage Jewish immigration to ensure the future political dominance of Jews, who were 12 percent of the population in 1918.

British sponsorship of Jewish efforts to gain control of their ancient land in the face of resistance from the Arabs who had inhabited that land for centuries was complicated in the 1930s by events in Germany. Adolf Hitler's assumption of power in 1933 brought swift implementation of anti-Jewish regulations. The Jewish population of Palestine quadrupled between 1933 and 1936 as German Jews emigrated to Palestine, bringing with them wealth and investment capital.

The influx of Jewish immigrants intensified Arab fears of Zionist success, already exacerbated by Jewish purchases of Arab lands and subsequent displacement of tenant farmers. Rival Arab political factions agreed in November 1935 to consider participation in a legislative council based on proportional representation, a concept rejected in the 1920s when backed by the Zionists. Now the Zionists opposed the idea and called for the transfer of Palestinian Arabs to the kingdom of Transjordan. The British parliament scuttled the council initiative in February 1936. These events, and the killing by British police of Muslim sheikh Izz al-Din al-Qassam, who had been suspected of murdering two Jews, incited the Arab revolt.

Frustration at the British refusal to entertain Arab hopes of political representation fanned resentment. By 1936 fellow Arabs under other mandates either had already gained independence (as had Iraq in 1932) or had been promised greater political participation (as France promised Syria and Lebanon that year).

The first stage of the revolt lasted from April to November 1936 and was marked by attacks on Jewish settlements, a general strike, and a boycott of Jewish goods. A British commission, formed to investigate the revolt's causes and headed by Lord Peel, concluded in July 1937 that British obligations under the mandate were impossible to fulfill given rival Arab and Jewish claims for independence. The Peel Commission's report called for the partition of Palestine into two states—one Jewish, one Arab—with the Arab state in central and eastern Palestine to be absorbed into Transjordan, which was ruled by King Abdullah of the Hijaz (the region containing Mecca and Medina). Palestinian Arab identity would be erased.

The report incited the second, more violent stage of the Arab revolt, which lasted from September 1937 to early 1939. Although they lacked political or military coordination, Arab bands controlled much of the countryside until British reinforcements arrived in late 1938 to crush resistance. Once it had quelled the revolt, Britain reversed its policy toward Palestine. On the eve of war, Britain was acting to appease Arab anger outside Palestine. In May 1939 London restricted Jewish immigration and land purchases and announced its intention to see a Palestinian Arab government with a Jewish minority within five years.

Arabs and Jews alike rejected the new British policies. The Arab leadership in exile refused to accept a substantial Jewish minority. The Zionists, facing potential loss of self-rule, began to prepare for violent resistance to British control of Palestine that would ultimately result in the creation of Israel in 1948. Yet the revolt retained a hold on Palestinian national consciousness, recalled in the Palestinian intifada and the creation of the al-Qassam brigade of Hamas, the Islamic organization that has resisted Israeli rule in the West Bank and Gaza Strip.

See also *Israeli Independence Revolt (1946–1948); Palestinian "Intifada" Revolt (1987–1996).*

CHARLES D. SMITH

BIBLIOGRAPHY

Abboushi, W. F. "The Road to Rebellion: Arab Palestine in the 1930s." *Journal of Palestine Studies* 6 (spring 1977): 23–46.

Bowden, Tom. "The Politics of Arab Rebellion in Palestine, 1936–1939." *Middle Eastern Studies* 11 (May 1975): 147–174.

Cohen, Michael. *Palestine, Retreat from Mandate: The Making of British Policy, 1936–1945.* London: P. Elek, 1978.

Swedenburg, Ted. "The Role of the Palestinian Peasantry in the Great Revolt." In *Islam, Politics, and Social Movements.* Edited by Edmund Burke III and Ira Lapidus. Berkeley: University of California Press, 1988.

———. *Memories of Revolt: The 1936–1939 Rebellion and the Palestinian National Past.* Minneapolis: University of Minnesota Press, 1996.

PALESTINIAN "INTIFADA" REVOLT (1987–1996)

The word *intifada* means to throw off something that oppresses. Palestinian Arabs used the word to depict their revolt against Israeli rule in the occupied territories of the West Bank and the Gaza Strip. Those lands, along with the Golan Heights and the Sinai Peninsula, had been taken by Israel during its victory in the 1967 war against Egypt, Jordan, and Syria; Israel returned the Sinai to Egypt in stages following the peace treaty negotiated between Egypt and Israel in 1979. Israel withdrew fully from the Sinai in April 1982.

As a spontaneous, popular revolt, the intifada ultimately changed the negotiating stances of the Palestine Liberation Organization (PLO), Israel, and Israel's ally, the United States. Iraq's invasion of Kuwait in 1990, at the lowest point in the Palestinians' fortunes, ultimately proved a boon: To secure the cooperation of Egypt and Syria in resisting Iraq, U.S. president George Bush agreed to reopen Middle East peace talks, this time with Palestinian participation.

THE ROOTS OF THE INTIFADA

The roots and inspiration of the intifada illustrate the dilemma of peoples seeking to escape occupation and achieve self-rule while caught up in regional conflicts with global implications, in this case the conflict between Arab states and Israel in the context of the cold war.

In November 1967 United Nations Security Council Resolution (SCR) 242 established the principle of land returned in exchange for peace as a basis of an Arab-Israeli settlement of territorial issues stemming from the 1967 war. But the same resolution defined the Palestinian question as one of refugees made homeless at the time of the creation of the state of Israel in 1948. From the mid-1970s, the PLO strove unsuccessfully to alter that clause to include the political question of Palestinian self-government, an issue the United States would consider only after the PLO had accepted Israel's existence based on SCR 242 and renounced terrorism. From the Palestinian perspective, to accept SCR 242 as it stood meant accepting the definition of the Palestinian question solely in terms of refugees, nullifying their quest for political recognition.

Within this broader context was a narrower one. The intifada forced a direct confrontation between competing nationalist aspirations. For most Arabs in the occupied territories, Palestinian statehood meant gaining control over the West Bank and Gaza while abandoning the goals of destroying Israel and regaining all of Arab Palestine (as stated in the 1968 PLO charter). The latter objective remained the official stance of the PLO, whose leadership moved to Tunis after the Israeli invasion of Lebanon in June 1982.

For right-wing Israelis of the Likud and minority religious parties, Jewish nationalism required absorption of the territories, especially the West Bank, to ensure sovereignty over all of what had been ancient Israel. For them, even Palestinian Arab moderation was unacceptable to the extent the moderates embraced SCR 242, which most Israeli politicians opposed because of its implications for the West Bank.

ISRAELI SETTLEMENTS IN THE OCCUPIED TERRITORIES

The Camp David Agreement of 1978 and the Egyptian-Israeli peace treaty of 1979 had envisioned procedures, never implemented, to resolve the fate of Gaza and the West Bank, presumably through an arrangement between Israel and Jordan. Likud governments of Israel, under Menachem Begin and Yitzhak Shamir, strove from 1978 onward to retain the West Bank regardless of the intent of these pacts. Begin asserted after the 1979 treaty that SCR 242 did not apply to the West Bank.

Whereas an average of 770 Israelis settled in the West Bank annually from 1967 to 1977, the annual influx rose to 5,960 in the years between 1978, when Likud assumed power, and 1987, the year the intifada began. This officially sponsored influx, backed by an Israeli takeover of Arab lands by government decree and regardless of title, infuriated Palestinians in the territories. At the same time, Israeli security organizations tolerated the growth of Islamic groups, especially in Gaza, to counter Palestinian secular nationalism loyal to Arafat and the PLO. That policy backfired once Yitzhak Rabin of the Israeli Labor Party became defense minister in a coalition government headed by Shamir. The new government intensified Israeli pressure on Arab opposition in the territories and instituted an "iron fist" policy that accelerated arrests of young Palestinians, actions that had the effect of fostering greater militancy among the emerging Islamic groups as well as the existing secular groups.

Combined with these developments was the gradual decline of economic standards in the territories. Palestinians had been part of the labor force in Israel since the 1967 war, assuming menial jobs formerly allotted to Jews from Arab lands. Wages were relatively high during the 1970s, as Israel experienced an economic expansion. At the same time, higher oil prices after the 1973 Arab-Israeli War enabled Palestinians in the Persian Gulf sheikhdoms to increase remittances to relatives in the territories, and expanded job opportunities in the Gulf encouraged younger Palestinians to leave the territories, a safety valve for political frustration. During the 1980s, however, these circumstances changed. Lower oil prices meant fewer jobs and reduced remittances at a time when the Israeli economy's momentum declined, limiting access to additional employment. Palestinians in the territories depended on Israel's economy for jobs, and resistance to Israeli takeovers of land could mean denial of work permits, a practice that particularly affected Gaza, with its poverty and extraordinary population density.

OUTBREAK OF THE INTIFADA

The intifada erupted in Gaza in December 1987 following a road accident in which an Israeli truck killed several Palestinians. Totally spontaneous, it spread rapidly to the West Bank. It was a popular rebellion of the youth and lower classes that the leadership and elites, in the territories and in Tunis, strove to control. Undertaken without firearms, the revolt established a battle zone where Palestinian stones met Israeli bullets with great effect in the international media. Heretofore rival Arab groups cooperated in a unified campaign. The political program announced in January 1988 called for an independent Palestinian state in the West Bank and Gaza to coexist with Israel.

In reaction, Israel sought to crush the revolt by force in the territories and abroad, in part because the call for peaceful coexistence threatened Likud's determination to retain the West Bank. In April 1988 the Israeli cabinet authorized the murder of Khalil al-Wazir (Abu Jihad), the PLO official in Tunis believed to be directing the resistance. By the end of 1989, nearly 700 Arabs and 50 Israelis had been killed, more than 37,000 Arabs wounded, and 40,000 imprisoned. The Palestinians made some political gains in the process. In December 1988 the United States, over Israeli objections, agreed to talk with the PLO on the grounds that the organization had renounced terrorism and accepted SCR 242. This decision permitted American diplomats to meet PLO representatives on an official basis.

Israel suppressed the intifada as a sustained revolt by early 1990. Resistance continued but with less direction and more intentional armed violence as new groups, primarily Islamic, came to the fore. In June the United States suspended talks with the PLO, charging it with complicity in a terrorist attack on Israel by groups stationed in Baghdad.

Fate intervened in the form of Saddam Husayn's occupation of Kuwait in August 1990 and Iraq's apparent threat to Saudi oil fields. Determined to respond with force, the administration of U.S. president Bush created a military coalition that included Egypt and Syria. In exchange for the participation of its Arab partners, the United States promised to pursue peace talks after the crisis. Those talks would include the Palestinians. The end of the Gulf War in February 1991 led to the Madrid talks (1991–1993), in which delegates of the Arab states and Israel negotiated directly with the Palestinians, who were part of the Jordanian delegation.

PEACE TALKS IN MADRID AND OSLO

Despite their historic significance, the Madrid discussions offered little hope of concrete achievements. The stalemate, coupled with Arafat's waning fortunes among his constituents, raised the specter of an Islamic takeover of the

Palestinian leadership, a prospect that led the new Israeli prime minister, Yitzhak Rabin, to allow private talks between PLO and Israeli delegates in Oslo, separate from the Madrid forum. Those talks resulted in the Oslo accords and the Israeli-Palestinian agreements of September 1993, in which the PLO recognized Israel's right to exist, while Israel agreed to talk to the PLO as representative of the Palestinian people. No comparable recognition of a Palestinian right to a state was given.

The intifada did not throw off Israeli rule, but, coupled with international developments, it did serve to create negotiating opportunities heretofore unattainable. In addition to the agreements of 1993, the consequences of the intifada include the assassination of Rabin in November 1995 by a right-wing Israeli opposed to the progress achieved in PLO-Israeli negotiations over withdrawals from the occupied territories. The subsequent election of a Likud prime minister, Benyamin Natanyahu, who proclaimed his determination to retain as much of the West Bank as possible, left peace talks stalled in the midst of Palestinian anger and Israeli settler militancy, with Islamic groups commanding a significant reservoir of political as well as military allegiance.

See also *Israeli Independence Revolt (1946–1948); Palestinian Anticolonial Revolt (1936–1939).*

CHARLES D. SMITH

BIBLIOGRAPHY

Hunter, F. Robert. *The Palestinian Uprising: A War by Other Means.* Berkeley: University of California Press, 1991.

Lockman, Zachary, and Joel Beinin, eds. *The Palestinian Uprising Against Israeli Occupation.* Boston: South End Press, 1989.

Nassar, Jamal, and Roger Heacock, eds. *Intifada: Palestine at the Crossroads.* New York: Praeger, 1990.

Robinson, Glenn. *Building a Palestinian State: The Incomplete Revolution.* Bloomington: Indiana University Press, 1997.

Schiff, Ze'ev, and Ehud Ya'ari. *Intifada: The Palestinian Uprising—Israel's Third Front.* New York: Simon and Schuster, 1990.

Smith, Charles D. *Palestine and the Arab-Israeli Conflict.* 3d ed. New York: St. Martin's, 1995.

Sprinzak, Ehud. *The Ascendance of Israel's Radical Right.* New York: Oxford University Press, 1991.

PARIS COMMUNE (1871)

The Paris Commune, the seventy-two-day insurrection that took control of Paris on March 18, 1871, and was finally crushed two months later after a long, bloody, and destructive battle with government troops, was the last of the long series of Parisian uprisings that began in 1789. It stands as perhaps the biggest spontaneous urban revolt in modern Western history.

ORIGINS OF THE PARIS COMMUNE

The origins of the Commune lie in the Parisian revolutionary tradition. Parisians had overthrown conservative regimes in 1830 and 1848 and aspired to an egalitarian "democratic and social republic." In the late 1860s republicanism was revived by campaigns against Emperor Napoleon III and radicalized by the effects of the disastrous Franco-Prussian War (1870–1871). The defeated French emperor was overthrown in a republican revolution on September 4, 1870. With German invaders besieging Paris from September 1870 to January 1871, citizens were armed and enrolled in a mass-based National Guard, which later created its own Republican Federation (hence the name *Fédérés* given to the insurgents). Starved into surrender, Parisians were both armed and angry, blaming the government for defeat. The election of a royalist-dominated National Assembly in February 1871 increased the danger of conflict between Paris and the national government, now led by Adolphe Thiers. The situation detonated when Thiers ordered an attempt to disarm the National Guard by seizing its artillery, much of which was parked on the hill of Montmartre. Spontaneous and largely peaceful resistance by crowds of men, women, and children caused the government to retreat to the nearby town of Versailles, hence their usual nickname, the *Versaillais.*

The improvised leaders of the Republican Federation called elections for a city council on March 26. The new council adopted the title, Paris Commune. *Commune,* the French term for the basic unit of local government, signified grass-roots democracy and recalled the first revolutionary Paris Commune of 1792; it did not imply communism. The red flag and (at least officially) the 1793 revolutionary calendar were also adopted, placing Paris in Year 79. The proclamation of the Commune was a joyous popular ceremony, described by the writer Jules Vallès (a member of the Commune) as "calm and beautiful as a blue river."

THE PEOPLE OF THE COMMUNE AND THEIR PURPOSE

Some 230,000 had voted—a majority of the electorate. They chose a body representative of the left wing of Parisian politics, especially socialists and neo-Jacobin radicals, descendants of the Jacobin revolutionaries of the 1790s. About half were middle class (journalists, lawyers, small businessmen, master craftsmen), and the other half white-collar workers or skilled manual workers, often labor leaders, from the main Paris trades. In contrast to earlier revolutions, the leaders of the Commune were not national politicians; few had more than a local reputation. The better known include the elderly neo-Jacobin journalist Charles Delescluze, the socialist bookbinder Eugène Varlin, and the painter Gustave Courbet.

The aims of the Commune leaders were above all to defend the republic against a monarchist restoration and to assert the autonomy of Paris as the republican capital. Their immediate acts were aimed at those they saw as the republic's enemies: the Catholic Church (which they disestablished), the regular army (which they abolished, at least for Paris), and the police and bureaucracy, which were to be democratized and turned over to ordinary citizens—a project that barely got off the ground. In the free and somewhat anarchic atmosphere, grass-roots initiatives in education and the arts were permitted and even encouraged.

Economic reforms were far less sweeping. Initiatives included encouraging workers' cooperatives, forbidding night work in bakeries, canceling wartime rent arrears, and returning small items free from the municipal pawnshops. There was never any question of seizing private business or financial institutions, such as the Bank of France. Karl Marx criticized this as timidity, but few French socialists favored state control of an economy still dominated by small business. The Commune's only clear political split, on May 1, was over whether to hand emergency dictatorial powers to a five-man Committee of Public Safety (another reference to the 1790s). The majority, mainly neo-Jacobins and followers of the authoritarian revolutionary Auguste Blanqui, voted in favor, against a minority, mainly socialists, who opposed the move on grounds of democratic principle.

The Commune's supporters, usually known as *Communards* or *Communeux,* were broadly representative of the people: the manual and white-collar wage-earners, self-employed craft workers, and small business people who composed the majority of Parisians. They were comparable with participants in earlier revolutions in 1848, 1830, and even the 1790s. For reasons of political organization, community solidarity, and economic need, support was concentrated in the populous working-class districts on the city's outskirts.

Women played a much-remarked role in the Commune. They were prominent in the streets when the insurrection began. Later, activists such as Nathalie Le Mel, Louise Michel (subsequently a well-known anarchist), and the Russian Elisveta Tomanovskaya were a few of the many public speakers, organizers of cooperatives and schools, military nurses, and—so conservatives alleged—wielders of rifles and firebombs. There is debate as to how extensive and how new such activity really was, but some argue that the Commune marked a new stage in women's political assertiveness.

CIVIL WAR AND DEFEAT

The life of the Commune was dominated not by ideology or legislation but by civil war. Skirmishes began on April 1. A Parisian march on Versailles on April 3 failed. The Versaillais regular army began full siege operations a week later. For the rest of April and May, the Commune faced the huge task of organizing, arming, equipping, feeding, paying, and leading its part-time democratic citizen army in continuous fighting in the suburbs against ever-increasing numbers of Versaillais, who eventually totaled 130,000 men. Most contemporaries and historians have emphasized the disorganization and indiscipline of the Fédérés, who were about 170,000 strong on paper. Given the improvised and largely voluntary character of their effort, a balanced picture would give more credit to their two-month defense. The Fédérés were aided by Paris's massive fortifications and the huge stock of weaponry built up during the German siege. Nevertheless, chances of survival were slim: they could not defeat the regular army in battle; they had no significant help from the rest of France (sympathetic uprisings in Marseilles, Lyons, Toulouse, and other cities were quickly extinguished); and the German army was camped at their rear, ready to intervene if required.

From early May, the war turned against the Commune. Outlying defenses fell one by one. On May 21, regular troops poured through the city's ramparts, and a week of street fighting began, notorious as *La Semaine Sanglante* (Bloody Week). Several thousand diehards built hundreds of street barricades. The Versaillais troops, in overwhelming number, used cannon fire in an inexorable advance across the city from west to east. Some Fédérés began to set fire to buildings, first as a defensive measure, later as a reaction to defeat. Symbolic monuments were gutted, badly damaged, or narrowly rescued from the flames, including the Tuileries Palace, the City Hall, the Palace of Justice, the Finance Ministry, the Louvre, and Notre Dame. The last flickers of resistance, in the working-class eastern quarters, were stamped out on May 28.

The Versaillais army slaughtered prisoners by the hundreds. The number of Communards, or suspected Communards, killed in the street fighting, shot down summarily, or executed after hasty court-martial will probably never be certain: about ten thousand bodies are known to have been buried in Paris as a result, but most historians assume the full number to have been around twenty thousand. Many conservatives applauded the carnage as the way to guarantee a generation of peace. Angry Fédérés shot several dozen hostages in retaliation, including the archbishop of Paris, although without the approval of most of the Commune. The intensity of the civil violence was unique in Europe between the French and Russian Revolutions, and it left deep scars. To this day an annual commemoration is held by French socialists at a wall in Père Lachaise Cemetery where hundreds of prisoners were executed and buried.

THE LEGACY OF THE COMMUNE

The Commune has been variously interpreted. Most famously, Karl Marx and his followers hailed it as the dawn of the age of proletarian revolution and the precursor of a new form of popular revolutionary government, the dictatorship of the proletariat. They praised the courage of its "martyrs," and the song *L'Internationale,* written by Commune member Eugène Pottier, became a lasting revolutionary anthem. Marx and especially Vladimir Ilyich Lenin argued that the Commune's failure proved the need for less decency, more ruthlessness, and more disciplined leadership in the future. The Soviet Union later claimed to have fulfilled the Commune's aims: as a symbolic gesture, Lenin's body was wrapped in a red Fédéré flag. Later historians have broken away from the Marxist interpretation, stressing the specifically French, republican, and Parisian nature of the Commune. It was, writes Jacques Rougerie, the end of an era, "dusk not dawn." François Furet concludes that "in this Paris in flames, the French Revolution bade farewell to history." However, some historians and sociologists, especially in America and Britain, have suggested that in certain other ways—as a specifically urban revolution, for example, in which women played such a prominent part—the Commune can be seen as dawn as well as dusk.

See also *European Revolutions of 1848; Marx, Karl, and Friedrich Engels.*

Robert Tombs

BIBLIOGRAPHY

Barry, David. *Women and Political Insurgency: France in the Mid-Nineteenth Century.* New York: St. Martin's Press, 1996.

Furet, François. *Revolutionary France, 1770–1880.* Oxford: Blackwell, 1992.

Gould, Roger V. *Insurgent Identities: Class, Community, and Protest in Paris from 1848 to the Commune.* Chicago: University of Chicago Press, 1995.

Lissagaray, Prosper-Olivier. *Histoire de la Commune de 1871.* Paris: Dentu, 1896.

Marx, Karl. *The Civil War in France.* Beijing: Foreign Languages Press, 1966.

Rougerie, Jacques. *Paris libre 1871.* Paris: Seuil, 1971.

Serman, William. *La Commune de Paris (1871).* Paris: Fayard, 1986.

Tombs, Robert. *The Paris Commune 1871.* New York: Longman, 1999.

PARTIES

"A revolution is not a dinner party," wrote Mao Zedong in 1927, yet at the time it was axiomatic that a *revolutionary party* was essential to the success of revolution. Six years earlier Mao had participated in the founding of the Chinese Communist Party at a moment when the revolutionary movement was in disarray in China and there were very few communists in the country. Just twenty years later, in 1948, on the eve of Communist victory in China, Mao would write, "If there is to be revolution, there must be a revolutionary party."

THE JACOBINS: PROTOTYPE OF THE REVOLUTIONARY PARTY

It is one of the ironies of history that the prototype of the revolutionary party, the Jacobins of the French Revolution, did not think of themselves as a revolutionary party at all. Inspired as they were by the political writings of Jean-Jacques Rousseau, the Jacobins viewed parties as "factions," more likely to fragment the "general will" than to assist in its formation. The Jacobin Club, founded in 1789 as the Breton Club, soon called itself the Society of Friends of the Constitution and functioned at first more as a reading and debating society than as a political club. It came to be known as the Jacobins because its members met in a hall of the Jacobin monastic order. Most early members were committed to the ideal of a constitutional monarchy and saw the club as a vehicle for the enlightenment of the citizenry under such a system. Affiliated clubs soon formed in provincial French cities and towns. By March 1791, 426 clubs existed; four months later the number exceeded 900.

By 1793 the Paris club, known as the "mother society," stood at the center of an impressive national network, corresponding on a regular basis with clubs in virtually every town and major village of France. The Paris club counted among its members nearly every radical deputy in the National Convention and functioned as a sort of shadow parliament. Important issues of the day were discussed first in the Jacobin Club. The will of the club was then carried to the National Convention and communicated to affiliated clubs in the provinces. No true party discipline existed. For example, some provincial clubs disagreed with the Paris club and broke their affiliation in the winter and spring of 1793. But there certainly was a revolutionary élan, and Jacobins thought of themselves as a revolutionary elite. In the Year II, the year of the Terror, the Jacobin network functioned as an informal arm of the Montagnard government, carrying out policies dictated from Paris. With the fall of Maximilien Robespierre in July 1794 the Jacobin clubs went into decline, and in November the government ordered them closed. Thus, the ascendancy of the Jacobin Club was coterminous with the radical phase of the French Revolution, and the ideals of the Revolution, as well as its excesses, came to be explicitly associated with Jacobinism.

The collapse of the Napoleonic empire in 1814 left the ideals of the French Revolution still flickering in Europe, particularly in those regions in which Napoleon's armies had awakened nationalist aspirations. In Italy and other parts of southern Europe, a secret society known as the Carbonari kept the Jacobin tradition alive. Among the Carbonari's leaders was Filippo Michele Buonarroti, who had been a member of the Jacobin Club in the 1790s. Buonarroti's writings inspired August Blanqui, a Frenchman who remained committed throughout the nineteenth century to the idea that a dedicated group of revolutionary conspirators, championing the ideals of social and political equality, could seize control of the state by launching a successful coup. Blanqui attempted many such coups, all failures, for which he spent many years in prison. His heroic failures served both to sustain the revolutionary tradition in Europe and to convince those who followed that an organized party was necessary.

THE ROAD TO THE BOLSHEVIK REVOLUTION

Most of the revolutionary upheavals that occurred in Europe in the nineteenth century were led by underground parties, and nearly all of them were unsuccessful. Most notable was the wave of revolutions that swept across Europe in 1848. In that same year, Karl Marx and Friedrich Engels published *The Communist Manifesto,* which offered both a theory of revolution and a call for the creation of a communist party to lead a proletarian revolution against bourgeois, capitalist society. Marx himself played a leading role in the First Workingman's International, founded in 1864, the first effort to create such a party. But revolutions remained essentially national, not international, affairs, and the failure of the Paris Commune in 1871 seemed to provide conclusive evidence that a proletarian revolution could not succeed without a disciplined revolutionary party in the lead.

That lesson was most cogently applied by Vladimir Ilyich Lenin, the founder and leader of the Russian Bolsheviks, initially rivals to the Mensheviks within the Social Democratic Party. Lenin argued that a successful revolutionary party must base its policies and actions on revolutionary theory, must be led by a narrow elite of disciplined and committed activists who were linked to the masses, and must be prepared to overthrow the existing political order by violent means. Although leadership was to be centralized, decisions were to be collective, a practice described as "democratic centralism." The Mensheviks favored a broader-based party and were open to the possibility of gaining power through parliamentary elections. It was Lenin and the Bolsheviks who prevailed, however, seizing power in October 1917 by violent revolution.

Lenin and the Bolsheviks exported their blueprint for revolution, to be led by a disciplined, tightly organized party, through the creation of the Communist International (Comintern) in 1919. Communist parties sprang up throughout western Europe, but the most dramatic developments occurred in China, where in 1905 Sun Yat-sen had founded a loosely structured party known as the Revolutionary Alliance. Comintern advisers urged Sun, and later Chiang Kai-shek, to form a more disciplined party, which became the Kuomintang. Thereafter, China's revolutionary history was a struggle between the Kuomintang, a nationalist party, and the Chinese Communist Party, led by Mao Zedong. Mao built on Lenin's ideas but insisted that the dynamic force in a Chinese revolution would be the peasantry, not the proletariat. Mao introduced the concept of the "mass line," by which party cadres would draw upon and cultivate the revolutionary potential of the peasantry.

Most revolutions in the twentieth century have followed the Russian or Chinese model, with a revolutionary party taking the lead. Examples are the Institutional Revolutionary Party (PRI), which still dominates Mexican politics; the National Liberation Front (FLN) in Algeria; the Sandinistas (FSLN) in Nicaragua; and the Farabundo Martí National Liberation Front (FMLN) in El Salvador. Some revolutions, however, have not been led by a tightly organized party. The Iranian Revolution of 1979 was led by Islamic clerics, and organized parties played little role in the wave of revolutions in Eastern Europe in 1989. Solidarity, in Poland, for example, could more properly be described as a social movement than as a revolutionary party.

Just as the increased repressive power of the modern state once made a disciplined, revolutionary party essential to a successful revolution, the advent of the computer age may render the idea of a revolutionary party obsolete, given the capacity of computer networks to disseminate information around the world almost instantaneously and therefore to generate and sustain social movements with revolutionary potential.

See also *Buonarroti, Filippo Michele; Chinese Communist Revolution (1921–1949); European Revolutions of 1820; European Revolutions of 1848; French Revolution (1789–1815); Italian Risorgimento (1789–1870); Lenin, Vladimir Ilyich; Marx, Karl, and Friedrich Engels; Paris Commune (1871); Russian Revolution of 1917.*

PAUL R. HANSON

BIBLIOGRAPHY

Goldstone, Jack A., ed. *Revolutions: Theoretical, Comparative, and Historical Studies.* New York: Harcourt Brace Jovanovich, 1986.

Gross, Feliks. *The Revolutionary Party: Essays in the Sociology of Politics.* Westport, Conn.: Greenwood, 1974.

Kennedy, Michael L. *The Jacobin Clubs in the French Revolution.* 2 vols. Princeton, N.J.: Princeton University Press, 1982 and 1988.

Lenin, V. I. *State and Revolution.* New York: International Publishers, 1943.

Mao Zedong. *Selected Works.* Beijing: Foreign Languages Press, 1975.

Mason, David S. *Revolution and Transition in East-Central Europe.* Boulder, Colo.: Westview Press, 1996.

Rabinowitch, Alexander. *The Bolsheviks Come to Power.* New York: Norton, 1976.

Schwartz, Benjamin I. *Chinese Communism and the Rise of Mao.* New York: Harper and Row, 1951.

PEASANTS

Rural people have played major roles in many revolutionary upheavals, yet generalizations about their actions have proved elusive. At times peasants have participated in overthrowing old regimes; at other times they have opposed revolutionary claimants to power. In some places they have organized for local action within their own communities; elsewhere they have enlisted in armies organized by revolutionary parties of urban origin and have engaged in combat far from home. They have participated in movements claiming to fight for land, for socialism, for the rightful king, for the true religion, and for expelling the foreign enemy, as well as against governments and movements making such claims. They have also fought each other. Their specific targets have included agents of state authority (such as tax collectors and military recruiters), local landowners (and their rent-collectors and financial supporters), and the agents or allies of foreign powers.

Contemporary writers and historians sometimes see peasants as concerned only with immediate, practical, and material objectives such as acquiring land or securing food, and sometimes as caught up in visionary struggles for a just society, or even for the establishment of God's rule on earth. Educated, urban revolutionaries have seen them variously as hopelessly hostile supporters of reaction, as natural supporters of revolution, and as potential cannon fodder in a cause that is not really their own. Even in a single instance of revolution, country people may play many different parts. During the French Revolution of 1789, for example, peasants in some areas were very active in revolt in the early months, thereby helping bring down the Old Regime, but later became much less prone to insurrection. In other places peasants who did not accept the new legislation were so difficult for the new regime to deal with that they became a major cause of the Revolution's radicalization. In still other places peasants who opposed the new authorities seriously threatened the very survival of the Revolution.

CAUSES OF THE VARIETY IN PEASANT POLITICAL ACTION

The cause of so much variety in peasant political action lies in the variety of social relations in the countryside and in the variety of ways rural people are connected to distant centers of wealth and power. Peasant action in revolutions is best considered not on its own, therefore, but in relation to a mosaic of other participants who are variously allies or enemies, whose actions variously enable, complement, discourage, or suppress autonomous peasant actors.

Rural people gain their livelihood in many ways. Land may be worked by resident families who either own the land or rent it. It may be worked by temporary laborers hired for the planting and harvesting seasons or by a permanent labor force understood to be legally bound to a master or to the land. Some production may be for self-consumption; some may be for a local or distant marketplace. The technology of planting and protecting the crops (from weeds, drought, and animal or human predators) may be primitive or relatively advanced. Nonagricultural sources of income may exist; for example, rural weaving, spinning, and metallurgy. The hand of the state may be more or less heavy: peasants may or may not be taxed or conscripted by national governments. Local elites may build and maintain roads, run local courts, employ local police, and support religious practice—or the state may perform these activities. In one time and place cultural horizons may be bounded by the village world, but in others country people may have worked in towns, traveled as seasonal laborers, served in foreign wars, absorbed new ideas through literacy, and kept in touch with current politics through television. All of these factors affect patterns of cooperation and rivalry among peasants, and between the peasantry and local elites.

COLLECTIVE ACTION

It can be dangerous openly, directly, and collectively to challenge the claims of local landowners and the agents of governments. In the face of that danger, peasants have developed a wide repertoire of methods of individual self-protection, including concealing their earnings from tax and rent collectors, falsifying the ages of their sons when dealing with recruiting sergeants, and avoiding visible criticism of the powerful, all without proceeding to open collective action. In some places and times, however, the rhythms of social life facilitated the forging of collective action. In western Europe before the nineteenth century, for example, market days became occasions for country people not only to come together, but also to join with town residents in coercing local authorities to provide flour or bread at affordable prices. A local tavern could be a place where the chiefs of work-gangs of seasonal laborers could plan action for better wages. Sunday churchgoing provided an occasion to bring an entire community together and was therefore likely to be the favored day for concerted action.

Such traditions of collective action could escalate into major challenges to authority. Local powerholders and the agents of central states were often in bitter conflict, and their quarrels could provide opportunities for peasants. As the central administrations of Europe's more powerful states grew stronger at the expense of local elites from the fifteenth through the eighteenth centuries, many opportunities for rural insurrection were created, often involving broad alliances of local peasants and those elites. The demands of colonial administrations outside Europe in the twentieth century often had similar consequences.

Interstate warfare has sometimes been a source of favorable opportunity for several reasons. The coercive forces of states, when engaged in fighting each other, were less readily available for suppressing rebellion. Increased demands for tax revenues, productive labor, and military manpower increased the political leverage of contentious peasant forces and provoked the long-standing antipathy to conscription. Peasants in military service returned home with military experience, and sometimes with weapons. Finally, battlefield defeat powerfully delegitimates political authority. In France in the early 1790s, for example, rebellious peasants pushed the new revolutionary legislature to abolish definitively the claims of France's lords, while the threat of conscription triggered an enormous revolt. Following the abdication of Russia's tsar in 1917, military discipline eroded; peasants abandoned the carnage of World War I and returned to their villages, sometimes with weapons, to join in widespread land seizures.

The integration of local economies into national and international markets has generated many forms of rural conflict by creating important differences of interest between those with and those without surpluses to sell; between consuming town and producing country; between elites whose power was enhanced and elites whose power was diminished by the marketplace; and among wage-earners, smallholders, and large landowners.

PEASANT PARTICIPATION IN REVOLUTIONS

Actions by rural people have been major components of the prerevolutionary breakdown of numerous states. They have contributed to the collapse of old regimes by attacking local elites, denying resources to central authorities, and adding to a climate of disorder that exacerbates conflict among elites. They have sometimes prodded new revolutionary authorities into concessions (and thereby radicalized those new authorities). At other times, they have triggered repressive violence by the new state. After the Mexican Revolution of 1910 the new claimants to national authority were doggedly defied for years of bloody struggle by land-seizing peasants in the state of Morelos, a situation that was a major source of instability in Mexico City until the government accepted the land claims.

Peasant participation in revolutions is by no means limited to actions by more or less autonomous rural social networks. Before the twentieth century, much rural political action was carried out by local elites mobilizing peasant clienteles. (It is not always easy for a historian to distinguish autonomous peasant actions from those directed by others.) In the twentieth century the mobilization of rural armies for guerrilla campaigns has been a major strategy of revolutionary parties in China, Yugoslavia, Malaya, Vietnam, the Philippines, Guatemala, and El Salvador. Although such processes have sometimes been called "peasant wars," that label can be doubly misleading. First of all, the rural location of combat tells us something about tactics and strategy, but not necessarily about recruitment. Substantial numbers of fighters might well be of town origin. Second, the leadership stratum is usually made up of members of radical parties, radicalized military officers, and radicalized students and intellectuals, few of whom are peasants.

A revolutionary party's recruiters may have to offer something in return for peasant support. In studying peasant communities in situations of long-term guerrilla warfare, it is important to try to understand the capacity of those communities to negotiate their relationships with the government and its armed forces, on the one hand, and the revolutionary parties and their armed forces, on the other. Peasants may provide information, supplies, and combatants to one or another side. The revolutionary forces may provide protection or legitimation for peasant goals such as land seizures. On the other hand, the presence of revolutionary forces may bring down shells and bombs on peasant communities. A long tradition of peasant self-organization and resistance to the claims of local elites and state agents probably gave Colombia's peasants a considerable say in relation to revolutionary movements attempting to implant themselves in the countryside beginning in the late 1940s, but this has not been the case everywhere. The revolutionary movement that fought in rural El Salvador in the 1970s and 1980s, for example, was far more completely led by urban intellectuals of the left.

By the late twentieth century a declining proportion of the population and wealth in most countries was to be found in the countryside, thereby lessening the revolutionary role of peasants vis-à-vis urban workers, radicalized intellectuals, dissident army officers, and activists in leftist political parties. Now more than ever, therefore, whether or not the setting for warfare is rural, the fate of revolution depends not on peasant action or allegiances alone, but on the mosaic of actions of peasants and other political participants.

See also *Chinese Communist Revolution (1921–1949); Colombia's "La Violencia" (1948–1964); French Peasant Revolts (1594–1648); French Revolution (1789–1815); German Peasant War (1524–1526); Guerrilla Warfare; Latin American Popular and Guerrilla Revolts (1960–1996); Mexican Revolution (1910–1940); Nicaraguan Revolution (1979); Philippine Huk and New People's Army Rebellions (1946–mid-1950s; late 1960s–late 1980s); Russian Revolution of 1917; Vietnamese Revolution (1945–1975); Yugoslav Partisans and Communist Revolution (1941–1948); Zapata, Emiliano.*

JOHN MARKOFF

BIBLIOGRAPHY

Markoff, John. *The Abolition of Feudalism: Peasants, Lords, and Legislators in the French Revolution.* University Park: Pennsylvania State University Press, 1997.

Moore, Barrington, Jr. *Social Origins of Dictatorship and Democracy: Lord and Peasant in the Making of the Modern World.* Boston: Beacon Press, 1966.

Paige, Jeffery M. *Agrarian Revolution: Social Movements and Export Agriculture in the Underdeveloped World.* New York: Free Press, 1975.

Scott, James C. *The Moral Economy of the Peasant: Rebellion and Subsistence in Southeast Asia.* New Haven, Conn.: Yale University Press, 1976.

Skocpol, Theda. "What Makes Peasants Revolutionary?" In *Social Revolutions in the Modern World.* Edited by Theda Skocpol. Cambridge: Cambridge University Press, 1994.

Stinchcombe, Arthur L. "Agricultural Enterprise and Rural Class Relations." *American Journal of Sociology* 67 (September 1961): 165–176.

Wickham-Crowley, Timothy P. *Guerrillas and Revolution in Latin America: A Comparative Study of Insurgents and Regimes Since 1956.* Princeton, N.J.: Princeton University Press, 1992.

Wolf, Eric R. *Peasant Wars of the Twentieth Century.* New York: Harper and Row, 1969.

PERUVIAN "REVOLUTION FROM ABOVE" (1968–1975)

The revolution in Peru, under the auspices of the nation's military, led by Gen. Juan Velasco Alvarado, brought about enormous social and economic changes. Implemented by the military between 1968 and 1975, these changes were the most dramatic in a leftist direction made by a Latin American military in the twentieth century.

ORIGINS OF THE REVOLUTION

In contrast to some military institutions in Latin America, the Peruvian armed forces were not closely allied to landowning elites, and their concern was not internal but external war. In the War of the Pacific (1879–1883), Peru was badly defeated by Chile. One reason for the defeat was that Peru's elites feared that peasants mobilized against the Chileans might turn against the Peruvian government. After this defeat, one of the military's goals was to enhance the sense of national identity among Peru's peasants.

During the 1960s, in the wake of the Cuban Revolution and the possibility of similar uprisings elsewhere, agrarian reform became a priority for many Latin American governments. After the Peruvian military was asked to quell guerrilla uprisings in the Andean highlands and officers became aware of the peasants' conditions, they more adamantly sought agrarian reform. As a candidate, Fernando Belaúnde pledged significant agrarian reform during his campaign, but as president (1963–1968) he did not carry it out. One of the reasons was that Peru's civilian political parties were engaged in opportunistic partisan maneuvers, gradually convincing most officers that a civilian government could not implement the changes that were necessary for the country.

Also in the late 1960s the Peruvian military became critical of the U.S. government. Officers were angry at U.S. support for the International Petroleum Company (IPC), a subsidiary of U.S. Standard Oil, in a dispute with the Belaúnde government, as well as at a U.S. decision to hold up a sale of Northrop F-5 jets to Peru.

The military's rejection of civilian elites and the U.S. government was in part a result of officers' socioeconomic backgrounds and education. To an unusual degree among Latin American nations, Peru's officers were drawn from lower-middle-class, provincial backgrounds. They were also unusually well educated. At the pinnacle of Peru's military educational system was the Center for Advanced Military Studies, where critical analysis of the nation's social and political problems was a full-year course.

CHARACTER OF THE REVOLUTION

On October 3, 1968, President Belaúnde was sent into exile, and, with considerable popular support, General Velasco proclaimed the "Revolutionary Government of the Armed Forces." Velasco, whose background was, like that of many army officers, provincial lower-middle-class and who had risen within the army by merit, was one of the most progressive officers in the coup coalition. Gradually over the next few years, Velasco sidelined his political opponents, many of whom were in Peru's navy.

Velasco proclaimed that his goal was a bloodless revolution that would ultimately make democracy viable in Peru. As he said in his memoirs, he sought a "fully participatory social democracy, in which the people whose work generates wealth control the means of production and direct the social, economic, and political institutions." The Velasco government considered dramatic new social designs, such as workers' self-management, adapted from the Yugoslav experience and the Chile of Salvador-Allende Gossens.

The government's highest priorities were to eclipse the power of the Peruvian oligarchy and of the U.S. government. Its agrarian reform devastated large landowners more than any other in Latin America, except for Cuba's. Peru's haciendas were transformed into agrarian cooperatives, providing major benefits to the roughly 10 percent of all Peruvian farm

families who became cooperative members. The government also expropriated oligarchic fishing, mining, and banking companies, as well as the IPC and other U.S. enterprises.

The government spearheaded other changes as well. For a period, teaching of the indigenous language, Quechua, was required, and access to higher education was made easier. Industrial development was promoted through tariff, exchange, and other policies. Overall, income distribution became less skewed, although the primary effect was a redistribution from the richest 1 percent of families to the next 20 percent, rather than toward the poorest. In the international arena, the Peruvian military ended most collaborative activities with the U.S. military and made major arms purchases from the Soviet Union.

However, the political agenda of the Velasco government was unclear. Officers were undecided whether their government was to last a few years, a decade, or longer. While they claimed to seek a "fully participatory social democracy," they made most important decisions without input from civilian groups. There were no national elections. Although the government was not repressive by Latin American standards—there was no pattern of torture or disappearances—numerous opposition political leaders and intellectuals were deported. The country's major daily newspapers were expropriated in 1974 and gradually became mouthpieces for the regime.

The government created a political agency, the National System for the Support of Social Mobilization. Although some officials hoped that it would control citizens' political activities, it did not. On the contrary, worker and peasant organizations under leftist banners expanded dramatically.

RESULTS OF THE REVOLUTION

After 1973 the Velasco government faltered. Velasco fell ill, and intense struggles emerged among different factions of the military. In addition, the economy began to falter. In early 1975 riots demonstrated the paucity of support for the government. In September Velasco was replaced by Gen. Francisco Morales Bermúdez. But the economy worsened, and popular protest mounted. In July 1977 Morales Bermúdez promised a return to constitutional government and kept his promise.

The results of the Peruvian Revolution were mixed. Vast power and wealth were no longer wielded by the approximately forty oligarchic families, but the reforms failed to benefit the vast majority of Peruvians, especially the poorest. Many of the poor were highlands peasants, a group that in the 1980s provided some support for the Shining Path guerrillas. Peasants' and workers' organizations became much stronger, but political parties and other civilian institutions did not. A "fully participatory social democracy" probably could not have been attained by any Peruvian government. Whether the goal was closer or farther away as a result of the revolution is a controversial question.

See also *Latin American Popular and Guerrilla Revolts (1960–1996); Peruvian "Shining Path" Revolt (1980–).*

Cynthia McClintock

BIBLIOGRAPHY

Booth, David, and Bernardo Sorj, eds. *Military Reformism and Social Classes: The Peruvian Experience, 1968–80.* London: Macmillan, 1983.

Lowenthal, Abraham F., ed. *The Peruvian Experiment: Continuity and Change under Military Rule.* Princeton, N.J.: Princeton University Press, 1975.

McClintock, Cynthia, and Abraham F. Lowenthal, eds. *The Peruvian Experiment Reconsidered.* Princeton, N.J.: Princeton University Press, 1983.

Philip, George D. *The Rise and Fall of the Peruvian Military Radicals, 1968–1976.* London: The Athlone Press of the University of London, 1978.

PERUVIAN "SHINING PATH" REVOLT (1980–)

The Shining Path is a Peruvian guerrilla organization that follows extreme Maoist Cultural Revolution principles of peasant mobilization, permanent revolution, and constant internal purification. It began as a Communist Party student organization in 1963 at the University of San Cristóbal de Huamanga in Ayacucho, an isolated south-central highland city *(see map, p. 395)*. Its leader was Abimael Guzmán Reynoso, a professor in the university's education program beginning in 1962. Following the 1963 Sino-Soviet split, Guzmán allied his group with the faction supporting China, known as Red Flag. He broke away from Red Flag between 1968 and 1970 to form his own Maoist party, which he called the "Communist Party of Peru in the Shining Path of Mariátegui." (José Carlos Mariátegui was the Marxist founder of Peru's original Socialist Party in 1928.) Between 1969 and 1976 Guzmán and other members of his party's central committee traveled on several occasions to China, where they received training and witnessed the Cultural Revolution (1966–1976). Guzmán sided with the so-called Gang of Four, which represented the more extreme elements in that tumultuous period, and, with their defeat, his party was cut off from further support from China. Back in Peru, Guzmán concluded that the only true course of communist revolution lay with the pursuit of Gang of Four principles, and he prepared to launch a "people's war" in his homeland.

The Shining Path campaign began inauspiciously on May 17, 1980, the eve of Peru's first presidential elections in seventeen years, when a few armed militants burned ballot boxes in the remote Indian market town of Chuschi, Ayacucho Department. Over the course of the decade, Shining Path relentlessly pursued a strategy of selective killings of police officers, local officials, political leaders, and community activists. Its goal was to cut off the rural periphery from the urban center and build its own grassroots "popular" organizations. By the early 1990s the movement had brought the government of Peru perilously close to collapse. In a drive that started September 13, 1992, however, Peru's police intelligence service turned the tables on Shining Path by capturing Guzmán, other top officials, and the organization's master files. From its peak armed strength of 5,000 to 8,000 in the early 1990s, Shining Path was reduced to a cadre of less than 1,000 by 1998. Incidents of political violence declined correspondingly, from more than 4,000 casualties in 1990 to less than 200 in 1997. Even so, Peru suffered great losses: more than 30,000 killed since 1980, some 5,000 disappeared, and more than $26 billion in lost production and property damage. Although diminished, Shining Path continued in 1998 to recruit and carry out operations in various parts of Peru.

How did the Shining Path guerrilla movement begin and grow in a democratic country? There are many reasons for its development and initial success. Shining Path had a charismatic and committed leader whose message conveyed a powerful ideological appeal. It enjoyed an extended period of preparation and organizing. As with many guerrilla movements, Shining Path began in a poor, remote area; in this case a department with a large Indian population. In addition, it was established within a provincial university with unique extension services to the area's population. The guerrilla movement benefited from a significant agrarian reform by a military central government in the 1970s that left most peasants in the Ayacucho area worse off and more susceptible to Shining Path appeals. Finally, the Peruvian government did not respond in a timely fashion to the growth of Shining Path. In the 1980s the central government sent the military to control the guerrillas, but the soldiers often abused the peasants they were supposed to protect.

Conditions on the national level also contributed to the success of the Shining Path. Serious national economic mismanagement over the decade produced hyperinflation, significant economic decline, and widespread disillusionment with party politics. An inefficient judicial system could not cope with bringing to trial, jailing, and keeping in prison the large numbers of accused terrorists.

Various factors enabled the government to gain the upper hand slowly in the early 1990s. For example, in 1990 a population disgusted with the failure of traditional parties to deal with the country's problems elected a no-nonsense president, Alberto Fujimori, who had no ties to these parties. Fujimori implemented some drastic measures that stabilized the economy. The government changed its military strategy to include economic measures, with incentives to appeal to local populations. It assisted in the establishment of 3,000 to 4,000 local peasant self-defense groups. The Fujimori government carried on a new counterintelligence strategy to track Shining Path leaders and a military justice system to secure rapid trials. During this period Fujimori suspended his country's constitution in a self-imposed coup, a move that threatened the legitimacy of the government. But he also had the good fortune to capture Guzmán and his files after the coup. Finally, Peru was able to restore economic growth and reduce somewhat the peasants' extreme poverty after 1994.

See also *Peruvian "Revolution from Above" (1968–1975).*

David Scott Palmer

BIBLIOGRAPHY

Palmer, David Scott. "The Revolutionary Terrorism of Peru's Shining Path." In *Terrorism in Context*. Edited by Martha Crenshaw. University Park: Pennsylvania State University Press, 1995.

———, ed. *Shining Path of Peru*. 2d ed. New York: St. Martin's Press, 1994.

Stern, Steve, ed. *Shining and Other Paths: War and Society in Peru, 1980–1995*. Madison: University of Wisconsin Press, 1998.

PHILIPPINE HUK AND NEW PEOPLE'S ARMY REBELLIONS (1946–MID-1950S; LATE 1960S–LATE 1980S)

During its first fifty years (1946–1996), the Republic of the Philippines had three major armed uprisings. The Huk and the New People's Army rebellions (discussed here) were primarily agrarian based but also had urban supporters and participants. Both had communist party involvement, and both eventually receded, for some of the same reasons. The New People's Army rebellion was the larger of the two.

The Huk rebellion was concentrated in central Luzon. This national "rice basket," where a majority of peasants were tenant farmers and agricultural laborers, had been awash with agrarian unrest since the early 1930s. Tension between peasants and landowners submerged during the Japanese occupation (1942–early 1945) but resurfaced immediately afterward, aggravated when villagers who had supported the *Hukbalahap,* an anti-Japanese guerrilla movement in central Luzon, were tormented by officials who condemned them as "communists."

The rebellion in 1946 was precipitated by government and landlord repression of former Hukbalahap and members of other peasant organizations. At its peak in 1949–1951, the rebellion had between eleven thousand and fifteen thousand guerrillas. Many top leaders were members of the Communist Party (PKP), which in 1948 decided to support the rebellion. Rebels demanded an end to repression and the implementation of tenancy reforms. As the government began to address these issues in the early 1950s, splits within the movement, especially within the PKP and between the PKP leadership and the guerrillas, became more divisive. By 1954–1955 the rebellion had virtually ended, although small bands of Huks continued to rebel until the 1960s.

Some Huk rebels were among the first members of the New People's Army, formed in 1969. Unlike the Huks, the New People's Army was from the start a creation of another communist party, the CPP (which had formed in 1968 as a breakaway group from the PKP). As the New People's Army expanded, however, the CPP leadership had difficulty maintaining control. Also unlike the Huk movement, the New People's Army spread beyond central Luzon. Indeed, at its zenith, it was strongest in eastern Mindanao and certain islands of the Visayas and parts of northern Luzon. During the 1970s and 1980s, these were the areas in which conflicts over land and tenancy conditions were most intense and where the demise of coconut and sugar industries directly affected millions of rural families. New People's Army members were often peasants and agricultural workers who had attempted to use legal channels to voice their grievances but were driven underground by the military repression of the "martial law" regime, which President Ferdinand Marcos had imposed in 1972. By the end of the Marcos era, in 1986, the New People's Army had about thirty thousand members. The CPP leadership was optimistic of eventually overthrowing the Marcos regime and creating a socialist state. Marcos rule did collapse, but neither the New People's Army nor the CPP played a prominent role in its demise. Rather, Marcos was forced to flee the country in February 1986 by a massive, spontaneous uprising coupled with a mutiny within the armed forces.

As subsequent national governments pursued more constructive solutions to rural discontent and as economic conditions improved, support for the New People's Army withered. Divisions within the New People's Army and the CPP also aggravated the movement's decline. Some units of the New People's Army, however, still operated during the 1990s.

See also *Philippine Independence Wars (1872–1910); Philippine "People Power" Revolution (1986).*

Ben Kerkvliet

BIBLIOGRAPHY

Abinalles, Patrico N., ed. *The Revolution Falters: The Left in Philippine Politics after 1986.* Ithaca, N.Y.: Southeast Asia Program, Cornell University, 1996.

Chapman, William. *Inside the Philippine Revolution: The New People's Army and Its Struggle for Power.* New York: W.W. Norton, 1987.

Kerkvliet, Benedict J. *The Huk Rebellion: A Study of Peasant Revolt in the Philippines.* Berkeley: University of California Press, 1977.

Lachica, Eduardo. *Huk: Philippine Agrarian Society in Revolt.* Manila: Solidaridad Publishing House, 1971.

Pimentel, Benjamin, Jr. *Rebolusyon: A Generation of Struggle in the Philippines.* New York: Monthly Review Press, 1991.

Entrenched American troops take aim at Filipino troops, circa 1899–1900.

PHILIPPINE INDEPENDENCE WARS (1872–1910)

The Philippine wars of independence originated in the economic, political, and social changes occurring in the archipelago during the nineteenth century. Spain's colonial grip weakened following the intrusion into the islands of world commerce, which created a new native elite composed chiefly of Chinese and Spanish *mestizos.* Increasingly educated in Western liberal thought, these people sought greater equality with their Spanish overlords; however, Spain's unwillingness to open the colonial system sufficiently led to stronger protest.

The first major incident in the struggle occurred in 1872, following a mutiny of soldiers and workers at the Cavite arsenal near Manila *(see map, p. 397)*. In the aftermath of its suppression, the government implicated three Filipino secular priests, which pointed to a growing rift between the Spanish friar orders in the Philippines and native clergy. The execution of the three priests triggered growing dissent, known as the Propaganda Movement, among intellectuals residing in Europe and the islands. Led by Jose Rizal, Marcelo del Pilar, and Graciano Lopez-Jaena, the movement for reform intensified when Rizal founded the Ligua Filipina in 1892. For his writings and actions Rizal was banished to the southern Philippines. When war in Cuba began in 1895, a nervous Spanish government brought him back to Manila, executed him on December 30, 1896, and so closed the reformist period.

A militant phase commenced in late August 1896, when the Katipunan, an organization composed mainly of working- and middle-class urban Filipinos, launched the first war of independence, led by Andres Bonifacio and Emilio Jacinto. Open-field warfare between Spain and the fledgling revolutionary government took place between August 1896 and December 1897, mainly in Manila and the surrounding Tagalog-speaking provinces. Emilio Aguinaldo, a landowner from Cavite, took the leadership from Bonifacio, having demonstrated better military and political skills.

With the battle campaign going badly, Aguinaldo agreed to a truce, signed in December 1897, by which he went into exile in Hong Kong. Despite his absence, guerrilla warfare flared around the islands. The beginning of the end for Spain came on May 1, 1898, when, as part of the Spanish-American War, Commodore George Dewey's American fleet defeated the Spanish navy in the battle of Manila Bay. After the return of Aguinaldo to the archipelago, the defeat and surrender of Spanish colonial forces gradually ensued around the archipelago.

Aguinaldo enjoyed considerable insularwide support. On January 23, 1899, he established the First Philippine Republic, following a declaration of independence (on June 12, 1898), the establishment of a congress at Malolos, Bulacan, and the writing of a new constitution. In the meantime, the United States was negotiating with Spain the cession of the archipelago, and by the Treaty of Paris of December 10, 1898, the Philippines became America's colony. War between Aguinaldo's First Philippine Republic and the United States followed in February 1899.

Fighting occurred in two phases: open-field battles from February to November 1899, and guerrilla warfare from then until April 1903. The war was nasty and brutish, with numerous atrocities committed, especially during the guerrilla phase. Some peasant bands, motivated by both nationalistic and millenarian ideals, continued to resist sporadically for several years. One of the last of the peasant leaders, Felipe Salvador, was captured and executed in 1910. All together, several hundred thousand Filipinos died of war injuries and disease, as did more than four thousand Americans.

Although the Philippine struggle for national independence had some political consequences, it did little to change the socioeconomic order in the islands. The indigenous elite emerged with their position intact and even enhanced; on the other hand, while some poor farmers and agricultural workers had participated in the struggle, their lot may have worsened. Filipinos, having begun the first nationalist revolution in Asia, ended the war having disposed of Spain but not having obtained their freedom, which was postponed until 1946. Still, the events of this period have remained the wellspring of Philippine nationalism.

JOHN A. LARKIN

BIBLIOGRAPHY

Agoncillo, Teodoro A. *Filipino Nationalism, 1872–1970.* Quezon City: R. P. Garcia, 1974.

Ileto, Reynaldo Clemeña. *Pasyon and Revolution: Popular Movements in the Philippines, 1840–1910.* Quezon City: Ateneo de Manila University Press, 1979.

May, Glenn Anthony. *Battle for Batangas: A Philippine Province at War.* New Haven, Conn.: Yale University Press, 1991.

Miller, Stuart Creighton. *"Benevolent Assimilation": The American Conquest of the Philippines, 1899–1903.* New Haven, Conn.: Yale University Press, 1982.

PHILIPPINE "PEOPLE POWER" REVOLUTION (1986)

In mid-February 1986 millions of Filipinos demonstrated in the streets of Quezon City and adjacent areas of metropolitan Manila, especially along the major highway known as EDSA, demanding that President Ferdinand Marcos acknowledge defeat in a recent election. The enormous size and mostly spontaneous character of this outburst of opposition to Marcos's rule and support for democratic processes inspired people elsewhere in the Philippines and around the world. By February 25 the demonstrations had forced Marcos, his wife Imelda, his armed forces chief of staff Gen. Fabian Ver, and a large entourage to flee the country. They brought down the authoritarian regime that had dominated the country since 1972 and brought back democratic institutions and a government headed by a new president, Corazon C. Aquino. For having replaced one form of rule with another, many participants, observers, and analysts call this people power uprising a "revolution," although the description continues to be debated.

The immediate cause of the demonstrations was the February 1986 presidential election, which Marcos had called, confident that he and his supporters could orchestrate and manipulate the outcome to assure his victory, as they had done several times before. The longer-term causes were widening and deepening discontent in many quarters of Philippine society with the corrupt and authoritarian ways in which the Marcos regime ruled, with economic conditions that had worsened considerably since the mid-1970s for a majority of Filipinos, and with violent conflict and rebellions in many parts of the country.

In November 1985, when Marcos announced the election, he never expected his many rivals to unite behind Corazon Aquino. She was the widow of Sen. Benigno "Ninoy" Aquino, a prominent opponent to Marcos's rule who had been assassinated in August 1983 by military officers under orders from high-ranking superiors. The assassination made Ninoy Aquino a national martyr and his wife a magnet for those against Marcos and his regime. During the election campaign, support for Aquino mushroomed as her candidacy was transformed into a crusade, appealing to voters on a wide range of levels: emotional, moral, and rational. Marcos and his Kilusang Bagong Lipunan (KBL) party leaders became desperate. On election day, February 7, 1986, and the following days, as votes were tallied, the cheating, intimidation, and other legal violations by the KBL were widespread and often flagrant. People around the country knew of the abuses. Many of the nation's most respected Catholic Church leaders publicly condemned the abuses and demanded that Marcos step aside. Meanwhile, foreign media were broadcasting these developments worldwide. Defiantly, Marcos stayed, and on February 15 the National Assembly, controlled by the KBL, declared him and his vice presidential candidate winners of the election.

For several days prior to February 15 hundreds of thousands of people had been holding vigils at polling stations, outside the National Assembly building, elsewhere in the metropolis, and in several other cities and towns across the country. On February 16 two million people gathered at

Luneta Park in central Manila to hear Aquino again declare firmly that she, not Marcos, had won. She urged people to join a civil disobedience campaign, called "Victory of the People," against the Marcos government and the companies and newspapers supporting it. Vigils, demonstrations, marches, and other public and private expressions of opposition grew during the following days as Aquino traveled around the country to galvanize civil disobedience. She and her advisers also began planning a government to rival Marcos's if the demonstrations failed to force him to leave office.

Splits within the military became another crucial factor leading to Marcos's demise. For months several officers and Minister of Defense Juan Ponce Enrile had been planning ways to overthrow Marcos and form a new government. But while they waited for the right moment to act, officers loyal to Marcos discovered the plot on February 22, 1986. Knowing they might be arrested, Enrile and his allies took refuge in a military base along EDSA highway in Quezon City and were joined by Gen. Fidel Ramos, the chief of the Philippine Constabulary and Integrated National Police. They prepared to fight. Realizing, however, that Marcos's loyal officers could readily defeat them in battle, they used a press conference packed with local and foreign journalists to call on Filipinos to amass around the base and form a human shield to protect them.

Only after national leaders in Aquino's campaign and Aquino herself had endorsed the request did people heed the call. Aquino needed to be persuaded that if the new dynamic brought down Marcos, the military rebels would support her presidency. Within hours thousands, and by the end of the first day millions, of people filled EDSA highway and other avenues for miles on end. They came from metropolitan Manila and from many provinces. Many people were unaffiliated with any political entity; others were with organizations, including numerous religious groups, that had actively opposed Marcos and campaigned for Aquino. The mood was simultaneously festive, tense, fearful, and scintillating. There was no one leader, nor even a single group of leaders, yet there was discipline. By word of mouth and radio reports crowds in one part of the city communicated with others elsewhere, learned what the loyalists and rebel military troops were doing, and realized that the whole world was watching the drama in which they were central players. As armored troop carriers and tanks sent by Marcos came bearing down upon them, they defiantly locked arms to form dense human barricades. Those in front, often women, held out flowers, refreshments, and cigarettes and invited the soldiers to join the struggle.

As the crowds grew and remained firm, calling for Marcos to resign and chanting support for Aquino, more military forces joined the rebel soldiers. Marcos's increasingly tenuous position was made even more so as international bodies, most importantly the U.S. government, urged him to avoid bloodshed and resign peacefully. By February 25, the day he was scheduled to be sworn in as president again, Marcos had lost control of nearly 80 percent of the military and much of the media, and he had virtually no international support. Finally, but not publicly, Marcos agreed to American suggestions that he and his entourage be helicoptered to an American military base in central Luzon that evening. From there they were flown to Hawaii, where Marcos lived the remaining few years of his life.

The People Power Revolution succeeded for a combination of reasons. First, a wide range of opponents to Marcos united behind one candidate who had tremendous popular appeal. Second, people across the country were resolved to make the 1986 election an authentic reflection of voters' sentiments and preferences. Their determination was manifested in a range of activities aimed at making the process as clean and honest as possible, blowing the whistle when violations occurred, and opposing transgressions even after authorities had declared Marcos the winner. Third, the military split in a manner that prevented a coup d'état. To save themselves, the potential coup makers needed the support of the people, which is something they had never anticipated. Fourth, the media kept spotlights on the situation and helped the people communicate with one another. Media attention probably contributed to a fifth factor: the confrontation was virtually nonviolent. Marcos and the military officers who stayed with him refrained from using force against the people. The demonstrators carried no weapons, and the rebel troops decided to rely on the people rather than on their armaments. Last, citizens who supported Marcos were not sufficiently committed to aid him. There were few demonstrations of public support for him between election day and the day he fled the country.

See also *Philippine Huk and New People's Army Rebellions (1946–mid-1950s; late 1960s–late 1980s).*

BEN KERKVLIET

BIBLIOGRAPHY

Bonner, Raymond. *Waltzing with a Dictator: The Marcoses and the Making of American Foreign Policy.* New York: Times Books, 1987.

Crisostomo, Isabelo T. *Cory: Profile of a President.* Quezon City: J. Kriz Publishing, 1986.

Javate-De Dios, Aurora, et al., eds. *Dictatorship and Revolution: Roots of People's Power.* Metro Manila: Conspectus Foundation, 1988.

Kerkvliet, Benedict J., and Resil B. Mojares, eds. *From Marcos to Aquino: Local Perspectives on Political Transition in the Philippines.* Honolulu: University of Hawaii Press, 1991.

Thompson, Mark R. *The Anti-Marcos Struggle: Personalistic Rule and Democratic Transition in the Philippines.* New Haven, Conn.: Yale University Press, 1995.

POLISH PROTEST MOVEMENTS AND SOLIDARITY REVOLUTION (1956–1991)

The year 1956 was a watershed in the "people's democracies," as the Soviet satellites of Eastern Europe were styled *(see map, p. 141)*. Nikita Khrushchev's "Secret Speech" at the twentieth congress of the Communist Party of the Soviet Union in February, detailing some of the abuses of the Stalin era, gave impetus to de-Stalinization, whereas the Soviet military intervention in Hungary in November set its limits. In Poland, June and October were the critical months.

In June 1956 Poznań workers struck over deteriorating living conditions. Their protests were crushed by the army, but political discontent had taken hold in numerous social milieus by then. Students, members of the intelligentsia, and an anti-Stalinist segment of the party apparatus (the so-called revisionists) were clamoring for liberalization. Between the seventh plenum of the Central Committee in July and the eighth in October a new leadership took over the Polish United Workers' Party (PUWP). Wladyslaw Gomulka, removed from the party leadership in 1948 for "nationalist deviation" and later placed under house arrest, was installed as the first secretary of the party. When he spoke in an open-air rally in the city's largest square on October 24, some 300,000 people cheered him as a victim of Stalinism and a symbol of resistance to Soviet pressure.

Soon thereafter, collectivization of agriculture was called off. The primate of Poland, Cardinal Stefan Wyszyński, was allowed to return to Warsaw from his confinement in a provincial monastery. Religion was reintroduced into school curricula. The Catholic intelligentsia of Cracow was given back its journal, *Universal Weekly.* Catholics were invited to send a token representation to parliament, and, with Wyszyński's acquiescence, they accepted the invitation. The Catholic caucus, "Sign," was thus established; over the decades it became a voice of loyal opposition to the regime.

While introducing such measures of institutional pluralism, Gomulka simultaneously demobilized society and reasserted the control of the party apparatus. Press censorship was tightened. In October 1957 the weekly journal of the young intelligentsia, *Simply Stated,* which had spearheaded the drive for de-Stalinization, was ordered to close. For the first time, students went into the streets to protest against the Gomulka regime's policies.

In succeeding years leading revisionists were weeded out of the party leadership; other periodicals were closed or consolidated; workers' councils that had been empowered after October were stripped of their prerogatives. Debating societies, which had proliferated in the country, were driven out of existence by local authorities. The most influential of them—a discussion club of Warsaw intelligentsia called "Crooked Circle"—was ordered to close in February 1962. The remaining few survived as a network, the Clubs of Catholic Intelligentsia.

POLITICS OF DISSENT

Throughout the 1960s the regime was on a collision course with various groups in society. The Catholic episcopate was angered by the administrative obstructions it repeatedly encountered, including the inability to obtain construction permits to build new churches. Conflict with the church peaked in 1966 over celebration of the one thousandth anniversary of Christianity in Poland as well as an exchange of pastoral letters between Polish and German bishops preaching reconciliation.

Conflicts with the intelligentsia occurred over freedom of speech and government censorship of publications. Several people were tried for attempted collaboration with the émigré publishing house Kultura, located in Paris, or with Radio Free Europe. Authors were prosecuted under provisions of the so-called Small Penal Code, a relic of repressive legislation from the Stalinist period that intellectuals argued made a mockery of the law. In 1964 a letter signed by thirty-four prominent intellectuals ("Letter of the 34") was sent to the authorities protesting the damage to the national culture that resulted from these restrictive policies. The year 1964 was also marked by the trial of two young academics who had written an "Open Letter to the Party"—a brilliant Marxist critique of the extant regime in Poland.

Protest letters to the authorities—whether signed by prominent individuals or by the masses—were a common instrument of political opposition in the 1960s and early 1970s. Their content would become widely known throughout the country thanks to Radio Free Europe's Polish-language broadcasts or publication in émigré journals. The last important initiative of this kind dates from 1975, when letters were written protesting against regime-introduced constitutional amendments recognizing the leading role of the Communist Party and the special status of Poland's friendship with the USSR.

By the end of the 1960s the stage had been set for an all-out, obscurantist assault against the students and the intelligentsia—the so-called March events of 1968. After the famous Polish romantic drama "Forefathers' Eve," by Adam Mickiewicz, was banned from the repertoire of the National Theater (for alleged anti-Soviet allusions), the Polish Union of Writers issued a vehement protest. In short order Warsaw students organized a protest rally at Warsaw University for March 8, 1968. An ambitious minister of interior, Mieczyslaw Moczar, used the opportunity to bid for power (unsuccessfully, as it turned out) by unleashing a populist, anti-Semitic campaign against the protesters. Students were brutally beaten by the police, and as their protests spread to campuses all over the country, hundreds were arrested. The student and intellectual protesters received no support from the workers. Official propaganda blamed Zionist influence for the unrest. Many people lost their jobs solely because they were Jewish. Thousands emigrated.

The next surge of antiregime protest involved the workers. Strikes erupted on the Baltic coast in December 1970, protesting a sudden increase in food prices. The army was called in to quell street demonstrations, and several dozen protesters were killed. The country was numbed by the death toll. The intelligentsia, still intimidated by the outcome of the March events, failed to speak up in defense of workers. The party leadership was shaken as well. Gomulka was replaced as first secretary by Edward Gierek. Gierek borrowed heavily from the West in order to improve the living standards of the population, so as to "buy" social and political stability.

HUMAN RIGHTS AND CIVIL SOCIETY

By the mid-1970s the regime had failed to carry out market reforms, and the debts were coming due. A new economic crisis ensued. In June 1976, on the occasion of yet another price increase, massive workers' demonstrations erupted in the city of Radom. Within twenty-four hours the prime minister revoked the increases, while the police arrested hundreds of strikers. They were systematically beaten in police stations and quickly sentenced in rigged trials to long prison terms. This time the intelligentsia did not stand idly by. Within a few weeks prominent individuals from different milieus of the opposition and spanning several generations established the Workers' Defense Committee (KOR) in Warsaw. They were determined to bring legal, financial, and medical assistance to the repressed workers and their families. Members of KOR appealed to the public to support their cause.

With the establishment of KOR in 1976, the strategy of political opposition changed. Instead of petitioning for redress or protesting to the authorities, opposition activists addressed initiatives to their fellow citizens. This strategy began a deliberate construction of civil society, which laid the foundations for the emergence of "Solidarity" a decade later. Wherever possible, the opposition attempted to build cross-class alliances. After 1976 the intelligentsia and the workers challenged the regime in a joint effort.

Uncensored publications proliferated. A movement to establish independent labor unions sprang up. Public lecture series and seminars (the "Flying University") were organized by leading intellectuals, frequently on church premises made available by sympathetic parish priests. And while the regime tried to stem the tide of these activities—by arrests, intimidation by vigilante squads, and occasionally murder—it had to observe a facade of legality. The opposition skillfully invoked the regime's human rights obligations under the Helsinki Agreements. It also appealed to the human rights principles of U.S. foreign policy, freshly articulated under President Jimmy Carter. It sought and found a modicum of safety by publicizing its activities through the Western media. After the election of Cardinal Karol Wojtyla to the papacy in 1978, and John Paul II's pastoral visit to his native country in 1979, a sense of spiritual renewal, transcending Communist Party-imposed controls, began to emerge in Poland.

In August 1980 a strike of shipyard workers on the Baltic coast brought about the birth of the trade union Solidarity. Under the charismatic leadership of Lech Walesa, strikers negotiated a twenty-one-point agreement with the authorities. An independent, self-governing labor union, free of government controls, was established. It was an unprecedented development in a communist people's democracy. Within a few months close to ten million people joined the union—a gigantic protest movement against the regime.

The authorities, under Soviet pressure, tried to undermine and destroy Solidarity. On December 13, 1981, they imposed martial law. Solidarity was banned, thousands of union activists were interned, and numerous strikes were broken by army troops and the riot police. But during the fifteen months of its legal existence, between August 1980 and December 1981, Solidarity had provided intense schooling in participatory democracy for a vast number of Poles. There was free debate within the union, free elections, and an enormous effort of self-organization as Solidarity structures were set up within enterprises, regions, and in the country at large.

NEGOTIATED REVOLUTION

Under martial law Solidarity was driven underground. But the coercive apparatus of the state proved incapable of reviving the economy. In 1988, after yet another wave of strikes and in an atmosphere changed dramatically by the Soviet reformer Mikhail Gorbachev, the leadership of the PUWP decided to enter into negotiations with the still illegal Solidarity. Roundtable talks were held in early spring 1989.

In June 1989 national elections held under provisions agreed upon at the roundtable gave an unprecedented victory to Solidarity. At the time it was not yet clear whether the Soviet Union would relinquish its domination over Eastern

Protesters opposed to the introduction of martial law are dispersed with tear gas.

Europe. So, when the Solidarity-led government was established in September, Communist Party officials still held the so-called power ministries—the ministries of interior and defense—as well as the presidency. The "negotiated revolution" was completed when Lech Walesa was elected president of Poland in December 1990. Communism in Poland had come to an end after almost forty-five years of repeated protests, instability, and repression.

See also *East European Revolutions of 1989; Walesa, Lech.*

JAN T. GROSS

BIBLIOGRAPHY

Boyes, Roger. *The Naked President. A Political Life of Lech Walesa.* London: Secker and Warburg, 1994.

Garton-Ash, Timothy. *The Polish Revolution: Solidarity, 1980–1982.* London: J. Cape, 1983.

Geremek, Bronislaw. *La rupture: La Pologne du communisme a la democracie.* Paris: Seuil, 1991.

Karpiński, Jakub. *Countdown, the Polish Upheavals of 1956, 1968, 1970, 1976, 1980.* New York: Karz-Cohl Publishers, 1982.

Lipski, Jan Józef. *KOR: A History of the Workers' Defense Committee in Poland, 1976–1981.* Berkeley: University of California Press, 1985.

POPULATION

Revolutions have a tremendous impact on the size, marriage rates, fertility, and mortality of the population in the societies in which they occur. But this causal relationship runs in both directions—population change has also been one of the main causes of revolution and rebellion.

POPULATION CHANGE AS A CAUSE OF REVOLUTIONS AND REVOLTS

For most of human history, societies have been dependent on agriculture. Their rate of economic growth was limited by how fast they could clear new land for planting or increase the output of existing land by irrigation, deeper tilling, adding lime or other improvements, and working longer hours at weeding and other labor-intensive tasks. Most preindustrial societies had economic growth rates of well under 1 percent per year. Preindustrial populations, however, were capable of a wider range of growth. In times of good health and good harvests, population could grow by more than 1 percent per year, doubling in the course of two or three generations. In times of high incidence of endemic disease, population growth rates could fall to near zero for many decades. From 1500 to 1640 populations throughout Europe and Asia grew fairly rapidly, doubling in most places; but in the following century smallpox, typhoid, plague, and other diseases led to population decline or stagnation. Starting about 1730 most Eurasian populations again experienced rapid growth.

These cycles of population increase and stagnation, combined with fairly steady but slow economic gains, meant that populations in the monarchies and empires of the world from 1000 A.D. to the present periodically shifted balance in relation to their agrarian base. If the shift was rapid or adverse, it could undermine political stability and lead to revolts and revolutions. One indicator of this relationship is that rebellions and revolutions in Europe, and major rebellions in the Middle East and China, are clustered toward the end of periods of population growth: the mid-seventeenth, nineteenth, and early twentieth centuries.

A shift in the ratio of population to resources affects political stability in several ways. First, if population grows faster than the output of foodstuffs, then the price of food (and the land that produces it) will tend to go up faster than other items. If food output grows faster, however, prices will tend to stagnate or decline. Rising prices make it harder for workers to buy bread and harder for peasants to acquire land. Rising prices can also make it more difficult for kings and emperors to pay their armies and bureaucracies, even if they raise taxes. Finally, a rise in the prices of food and land means that new social groups—if they control land or other expanding sources of income such as foreign trade—will gain wealth and challenge the balance of power among existing elites. This combination of distressed workers and peasants, weakened rulers with fiscal problems, and contentious elites jostling for position is precisely the combination of factors that produces upheavals. A pattern of this sort developed prior to the English Revolution of 1640, the French Revolution of 1789, the Taiping Rebellion of 1850, and many other major state crises.

The reverse shift can also cause political breakdowns. During the Tokugawa regime in Japan, population growth was controlled by infanticide, but rice output continued to grow, causing its value to fall. Because the government and leading aristocrats collected taxes in rice instead of money, this fall was financially ruinous for them. Over the course of the eighteenth and nineteenth centuries, the government of Japan and many leading families fell further and further into debt, while merchants who acted as rice-brokers and handled the commodities trade grew rich. These trends weakened the regime and the traditional social order and helped pave the way for the Meiji Restoration of 1868. Therefore, it is not population growth per se, but a shift in the balance between population and resources that leads prices to rise (or fall), which destabilizes the social and political order.

Two other aspects of population, urbanization and age shifts, also affect political stability. As population becomes concentrated in urban centers, the workers gain a greater ability to disrupt the economy and government. Naturally, if the economy is strong and workers can find employment at good wages, urbanization can promote stability. But if wages and employment are falling and the workers blame the regime, urban crowds can be decisive in overturning governments. In Paris in 1789, 1830, and 1848; in St. Petersburg in 1917; in Tehran in 1979; and in Manila in 1986, urban crowds in greatly enlarged capital cities played a pivotal role. In addition, societies vary greatly in the proportion of their population made up by adolescents and young adults. In rapidly growing societies, the proportion of youth grows even faster, so that young people greatly outnumber older adults. But in stagnant populations, adults over thirty can come to outnumber the youth and young adults (aged 15–29). Because young people are more inclined to take risks and seek change, revolutions almost always occur in societies with a high proportion of youth and young adults, a condition known as a "youth bulge."

In the modern world, economic growth has generally outstripped population growth, even in the developing world. While modern medicine has helped raise modern population growth rates from the preindustrial 1 percent a year to a modern rate of 3 percent or more per year, economic growth rates can range as high as 10 percent per year. A growing economy can accommodate far more rapid population growth than was possible in the preindustrial world. But these higher rates also mean higher risks for countries whose policies discourage economic growth. Rising populations, a youth bulge, and increased urbanization, combined with interrupted or skewed economic growth, have helped pave the way for revolutions and revolts in Africa, the Middle East, Southeast Asia, and Central America in the last quarter of the twentieth century.

THE IMPACT OF REVOLUTION ON POPULATION

Because revolutionary regimes often seek to restructure social life down to the level of the individual household, revolutions can have a dramatic impact on populations. For example, the most rapid increases *and* decreases in fertility have occurred in revolutionary regimes. In Romania under

Nicolae Ceausescu, the fertility rate tripled in a single year (1966–1967) as a result of the regime's decision to ban abortion and severely discourage birth control. In contrast, the government of China implemented a drastic birth-curtailment program—one child for each family—which caused China's fertility to plummet in the 1980s.

Revolutions also affect marriage and mortality, through their impact on people's hopes and fears. Some revolutions have been followed by a sharp increase in marriages and births, as optimism surrounding the new regime encouraged people to start families. In other cases, however, the reverse has occurred: the collapse of the communist regime in the Soviet Union in 1991 was followed by an incredible decrease in marriages and births and a sharp increase in mortality among adult males, due largely to alcohol abuse, industrial accidents, and disease. Evidently, the economic disorder and disappointment following the collapse of the old regime led many older adults who could not adjust to "give up," which weakened their resolve to live and perhaps their immune systems.

Revolutions also have more conventional effects on mortality through civil and international wars and internal upheaval. Several of the mass killings of this century resulted from conflicts or policy decrees following revolutions: the collectivization campaign in the Soviet Union, the deliberate famine in China caused by the Great Leap Forward campaign, the Iran-Iraq war after the Iranian Revolution of 1979, and the "killing fields" of the Cambodian Revolution. Revolutions are often defined as episodes of great institutional change. But they are more than that. They are also often reactions to, and subsequently the shapers of, many aspects of human populations, including size, age, urban concentration, mortality, and fertility.

See also *Economic Development*.

Jack A. Goldstone

BIBLIOGRAPHY

Goldstone, Jack A. "Demography, Development, and Domestic Conflicts." In *The International Order in the Twenty-First Century.* Edited by T. V. Paul and John A. Hall. Cambridge: Cambridge University Press, 1998.

———. *Revolution and Rebellion in the Early Modern World.* Berkeley and Los Angeles: University of California Press, 1991.

Gugler, Joseph. "The Urban Character of Contemporary Revolutions." *Comparative International Development* 17 (1982): 60–73.

Hertzman, Clyde, ed. *Environment and Health in Central and Eastern Europe.* Washington, D.C.: World Bank, 1995.

Moller, H. "Youth as a Force in the Modern World." *Comparative Studies in Society and History* 10 (1968): 238–260.

PORTUGUESE REVOLUTION (1974)

On April 25, 1974, the Armed Forces Movement (MFA) overthrew the dictatorship established by António de Oliveira Salazar in 1932. The coup was led by lower-ranking officers angry about slow promotions, low pay, and a seemingly endless war against liberation movements in Portugal's African colonies. It unleashed social and political forces that transformed Portugal from a dictatorship into a democracy.

After the coup the MFA appointed a Junta of National Salvation (JSN) and named Gen. António de Spínola provisional president of the republic. The JSN quickly dismantled the institutions of the dictatorship. However, a conflict arose between the MFA, whose officers had been radicalized by their contact with the Marxist liberation movements they had been fighting in Africa, and the JSN, composed of moderate senior-ranking officers who preferred an evolutionary path to democracy, decolonization, and economic change.

In June 1974 General Spínola attempted to reduce the MFA's influence but was outmaneuvered by radical officers. The radicals dismissed the moderate first provisional government and appointed the procommunist Col. Vasco Gon çalves as prime minister of the second. In September 1974 General Spínola called for a show of support for the JSN's evolutionary policies in the form of a mass demonstration in Lisbon. Revolutionary forces blockaded Lisbon, preventing Spínola's supporters from assembling. Spínola resigned from the JSN and the presidency on September 30, 1974. He was replaced by Gen. Costa Gomes, nicknamed "The Cork" for his political flexibility.

The resignation of General Spínola allowed the MFA to abolish the JSN, which it replaced with the Council of the Revolution, made up of radical officers, and to proceed with its revolutionary program. In March 1975 the MFA nationalized Portugal's banks and insurance companies, took control of the media, expropriated farms over five hundred hectares, and forced the political parties (Communists, Socialists, Social Democrats, and Christian Democrats), which had been legalized after the coup, to sign two agreements that guaranteed the supremacy of the military in any future regime.

The MFA's revolutionary policies polarized Portugal between the revolutionary south (Lisbon and the Alentejo) and the conservative, rural north. In the south landless farm laborers took over large estates, in Lisbon empty houses were occupied, and in the industrial belt around Lisbon workers took over nationalized factories. During the summer of 1975 small farmers in the north, encouraged by local Catholic

Soldiers and citizens fraternize on the day of the revolution, April 25, 1974.

priests, burned the headquarters of the Communist Party and blockaded roads and rail lines to Lisbon. Fearing civil war, moderate socialist officers of the MFA known as the Group of Nine, led by Maj. Melo Antunes, forced Gonçalves and his procommunist government to resign and installed a provisional government under the moderate socialist Adm. Pinheiro de Azevedo in September 1975.

On November 25, 1975, an army unit commanded by Col. Ramalho Eanes, one of the Group of Nine, crushed an uprising of radical enlisted soldiers, ending the Portuguese Revolution. The constituent assembly, which had been elected on April 25, 1975, produced a new constitution on April 2, 1976, after which elections were held for a new parliament on April 25. The new constitution enshrined a strong tutelary role for the Council of the Revolution and committed Portugal to a democratic and socialist future. Eanes was elected president of the republic on June 27, 1976; the socialist Mário Soares, whose party received the most votes, was appointed prime minister of the first constitutional government.

Although the revolution ended on November 25, 1975, Portugal's evolutionary transition to democracy continued over the next decade. During the 1980s amendments to the constitution abolished the Council of the Revolution, established civilian control over the military, and purged the constitution of its socialist provisions. Subsequent laws allowed the nationalizations of the revolutionary period to be reversed.

See also *Angolan Revolution (1974–1996); Mozambican Revolution (1974–1994).*

WALTER C. OPELLO JR.

BIBLIOGRAPHY

Bruneau, Thomas C. *Politics and Nationhood: Post-Revolutionary Portugal.* New York: Praeger, 1984.

Downs, Charles. *Revolution at the Grassroots: Community Organizations in the Portuguese Revolution.* Albany: State University of New York Press, 1989.

Manuel, Paul C. *Uncertain Outcome: The Politics of the Portuguese Transition to Democracy.* Lanham, Md.: University Press of America, 1995.

Maxwell, Kenneth. *The Making of Portuguese Democracy.* Cambridge: Cambridge University Press, 1995.

Nataf, Daniel. *Democratization and Social Settlements: The Politics of Change in Contemporary Portugal.* Albany: State University of New York Press, 1995.

PROPAGANDA

Propaganda is the deliberate and systematic attempt to shape the way people think and to achieve a response that furthers the goals of the propagandists. It differs from education because, instead of giving people the tools to make up their own minds, it persuades people to think and act in ways that benefit those doing the persuading. For many, the term brings to mind negative images of brainwashed masses being fed lies by oppressive governments for insidious purposes. In fact, we are all subject to propaganda in our daily lives. Advertising, for example, is a common form of propaganda.

The goal of any revolution is power, and an essential part of the revolutionary process is convincing people that the new forms and methods of exercising power are not only appropriate, but also desirable. Propaganda is a critical weapon in this process because, if implemented successfully, it instills in the minds of the recipients beliefs and behaviors desired by the revolutionaries. The American revolutionaries, for example, used propaganda constructively to convince their fellow colonists that the British government was denying them inherent freedoms and that those freedoms were worth their lives.

THE HISTORY OF PROPAGANDA

Propaganda did not always have the pejorative meaning most people associate with it today. In 1622 Pope Gregory XV established the Congregation for the Propagation of Faith and entrusted it with the task of spreading Roman Catholic doctrine abroad. Propaganda became the means by which the converted convinced the unconverted. A turning point in the popular perception of propaganda came during World War I when, to solidify and mobilize the citizenry at home, the combatants—particularly the British—created a body of largely untrue atrocity propaganda. The Bolsheviks and the Nazis learned the lessons of World War I well and used propaganda to mobilize the masses in their own revolutions.

Vladimir Lenin, the Bolshevik leader in the Russian Civil War (1917–1921), believed that the masses were incapable of understanding complex explanations of the nature of the capitalist system and had to be persuaded of the values of the new socialist system through propaganda. Bolshevik success came from an uncanny ability to isolate the Russian people from information that would sabotage the desired message. To create the "new socialist man," the Bolsheviks avoided clever tricks and blatant untruths; instead, they created a sophisticated indoctrination machine that converted acts of government into effective propaganda. Land reform, for example, was a substantive policy of the Bolshevik government, but it also served as a propagandistic gesture designed to gain the support of the peasants. Like the Catholic Church, the Bolsheviks believed that bringing their message to the masses was a necessary and noble task. Their propaganda machine—and the model it provided for other communist governments—was highly successful.

The propaganda machines of the German and Italian fascists in the 1920s and 1930s were not nearly as successful as that of the Bolsheviks. Unlike Bolshevik propagandists, who respected the perceptive power of the people, fascist propagandists were contemptuous of the masses and believed them to be incapable of determining truth from lies. Furthermore, the fascists preferred to practice the art of propaganda in covert ways, avoiding the open propaganda campaigns favored by the Bolsheviks. The fundamental difference between the two groups, however, was that the Germans and Italians, unlike the Russians, had no all-encompassing ideology to be applied to the human experience. What made Bolshevik propaganda effective was its capacity to appeal to people's souls.

TYPES OF PROPAGANDA

There are two kinds of propaganda: agitation and integration. Agitation propaganda seeks to induce people to make the extra effort necessary to achieve goals previously thought unattainable. Integration propaganda helps people reshape their thinking so they can adapt their daily lives to new realities. Both types can be implemented in a variety of ways; speeches, posters, and symbols are but a few examples. One of the most effective tools of the propagandist is the press. What readers believe about a news event is invariably shaped by those who control the news. By focusing on certain issues while ignoring others, those in control are able to limit access to ideas and manipulate the truth to provoke action. In times of revolution, the press becomes an important conduit of propaganda and agitation.

The use of the press by Mao Zedong, leader of the communist revolution in China (1927–1949), is an excellent illustration. When Mao and his followers began to build their power base in the rural areas of China, newspapers and journals formed the core of their system to transmit information quickly. In late 1931 they began publishing *Red China,* which served as the official organ of the area under the communists' control. This publication was followed by others, each targeting a specific audience. Because of their high rate of illiteracy, Chinese peasants were only indirectly the intended audience. Rather, the publications were directed at Communist Party activists who brought the party's message to the peasants. This practice was a very effective use of the propaganda potential of the press because it brought the leadership's message to the masses while reinforcing that message in the minds of lower-ranking party activists.

Mao and the leadership of the Chinese Communist Party used the press productively throughout the revolution. When China went to war with Japan in 1937, the party used the press to arouse people's patriotism and to garner support for the communist army, which was fighting the Japanese in North China. Equally important, Mao and his followers employed the press as a propaganda mouthpiece for their policies and programs and to consolidate their power against their opponents. Through news reports, essays, songs, fiction, short stories, and illustrations, the Chinese communists convinced people that if they worked hard and followed Communist Party guidelines, their lives would be substantially improved. In this revolution, the propagandistic press served as a powerful tool of mass persuasion and an equally powerful tool of nation building.

See also *Art and Representation; Films and Video Documentaries; Ideology; Literature; Media and Communications; Orwell, George.*

PATRICIA STRANAHAN

BIBLIOGRAPHY

Cheek, Timothy. "Redefining Propaganda: Debates on the Role of Journalism in Post-Mao China." *Issues and Studies* 25 (February 1989): 47–74.

Ellul, Jacques. *Propaganda: The Formation of Men's Attitudes.* New York: Alfred A. Knopf, 1968.

Jackall, Robert, ed. *Propaganda.* New York: New York University Press, 1995.

Jowett, Garth S., and Victoria O'Donnell. *Propaganda and Persuasion.* 2d ed. Newbury Park, Calif.: Sage Publications, 1992.

Liu, Alan P. L. *Communications and National Integration in Communist China.* Berkeley: University of California Press, 1971.

Taylor, Philip M. *Munitions of the Mind: A History of Propaganda from the Ancient World to the Present Era.* Manchester, England: Manchester University Press, 1995.

RACE

The idea that human populations can be classified into biologically distinct groups, or "races," has been part of popular perception and scientific debate for at least two centuries. During that time, genetics and biological anthropology have demonstrated the shared physical inheritance of all human beings, confirming the arguments of the critics of racial theorizing. Differences in skin color, hair texture, and body shape—seen as the usual markers of racial membership—have turned out to be minor adaptations which, despite the importance placed on them in certain societies and under particular political regimes, have no connection to intellectual, cultural, or other social aptitudes.

EARLY IDEAS ABOUT RACE

The belief in racial differences is a result of several factors, including European colonial expansion, which placed light-skinned conquerors in a position of domination over darker-skinned Africans and Asians; race-based slavery in the Americas; and the misapplication of certain biological theories associated with the notions of human evolution and the "survival of the fittest." Such theories were popularized by writers such as Herbert Spencer and the Social Darwinists in the later decades of the nineteenth century. They reached their destructive climax in the "race science" of the Nazis (1933–1945) and the apartheid regime in South Africa (1948–1990).

Alexis de Tocqueville, one of the leading nineteenth century theorists of the French Revolution and of political revolutions in general, provided a comprehensive critique of racial theories of history in his correspondence with Arthur de Gobineau, the "father of European racism," over the publication of that writer's influential volume, *Essay on the Inequality of the Human Races* (1853–1855). Stressing the historical naïveté and ethnocentrism of such arguments, Tocqueville pointed out that Julius Caesar, had he had the time and inclination, could have written a similar book to prove that the savages he had conquered in Britain were not of the same "race" as the Romans and were thus destined by nature to rot in obscurity on the periphery of a great empire. The irony of such a comparison was particularly clear in the middle of the nineteenth century when the global industrial and political power of the British Empire was at its height, and when the British themselves were saying similarly derogatory things about other "races."

RACE AND REVOLUTION

Political revolutions are mounted against groups that control the institutions and resources of a state or empire by others who are excluded from control. In societies where racial categorization is an important aspect of stratification, race may become an element in revolutionary movements. This is likely to be particularly significant in slave revolts, civil rights movements, and struggles for national liberation. A central question is whether the racial element adds a distinctive feature to a revolutionary movement and, if so, whether theories of revolutionary change derived from racially homogeneous societies can be used to account for revolutions in which racial divisions are paramount. These questions are well illustrated by the debate between scholars and practitioners of revolution who focus on economic or social class as the primary mobilizing principle in the struggle, versus those who focus on race.

Class-based theories of revolution developed out of Karl Marx's critique of the early phases of the industrial revolution in nineteenth century Britain. Marx gave little salience to race, ethnicity, and nationalism in his writings, seeing them as largely derivative elements masking the fundamental conflict between the capitalist factory owners and the industrial workers.

Subsequent Marxist thinkers have had to respond to the complex manner in which racial and other noneconomic forms of identity have influenced the course of revolutionary struggles. The problem is that there are few cases of racial conflict that do not overlap to a considerable degree with class divisions, making it difficult to disentangle the two forms of conflict. Frantz Fanon, the major theorist of the Algerian Revolution (1954–1962), argued that Marxism had to be "slightly stretched" in the colonial setting. It was not the fact of ownership or possession that distinguished the governing classes in Fanon's mind, but rather the fact that they came from elsewhere and were unlike the original inhabitants.

In Rwanda and Burundi, the conflicts between Hutu and Tutsi that have resulted in several waves of genocidal massacres involve economic differences, but they cannot be reduced simply to those differences. Like most of the agriculturalist Hutu, the majority of Tutsi, who have traditionally lived off a pastoral economy, are also poor, which makes it implausible to characterize the conflict in purely economic terms.

THE CASE OF SOUTH AFRICA

South Africa exemplifies many of the key questions in the debate over the role of race in revolution. During the 1930s, in an attempt to attract white working-class support away from racist and nationalist parties, the South African Communist Party (SACP) developed the slogan, "Workers of the world unite, and fight for a white South Africa!" Later the SACP aligned itself with the African National Congress (ANC), whose strategic aim was to achieve a democratic, nonracial South Africa. Among the disenfranchised African majority, other revolutionary movements competed with the ANC for support, including the Pan African Congress (whose radical slogans included "one settler, one bullet") and the black consciousness movement led, until his murder in police custody, by Steve Biko. These movements stressed racial solidarity and exclusivity as the logical response to the white racism of the apartheid regime.

A revolution against the apartheid system of racial supremacy was predicted in much of the writing on South Africa from the early 1960s, and some observers even saw this as part of a global "race war" that would break out between the industrial and nonindustrial sectors of the world. The remarkable negotiated transition from apartheid to nonracial democracy (1990–1994) constituted a revolutionary transfer of political power and confounded the predictions of most social and political scientists. Among the explanations offered to account for this development include: the integrated nature of the South African industrial economy, which was characterized by a high level of black-white interdependence; external sanctions and financial pressures on the Nationalist government, which raised the costs of elite intransigence and made negotiations more attractive; the skillful political leadership of the ANC and particularly the charismatic authority and moderation of Nelson Mandela; miscalculations and divisions within the Afrikaner political establishment; and the end of the cold war.

The South African experience suggests that although racial divisions can exacerbate revolutionary conflicts, their presence is neither a necessary nor a sufficient condition for a violent outcome.

See also *Class; Colonialism and Anticolonialism; Ethnic Conflict; Fanon, Frantz Omar; Inequality; Injustice; Latin American and Caribbean Slave Revolts (1521–1888); L'Ouverture, François-Dominique Toussaint; Lumumba, Patrice; Mandela, Nelson; Mugabe, Robert Gabriel; Nkrumah, Kwame; Nyerere, Julius Kambarage; Rights; South African Antiapartheid Revolts and Reform (1948–1994); U.S. Civil Rights Movement (1954–1968); U.S. Slave Revolts (1776–1865).*

JOHN STONE

BIBLIOGRAPHY

Adam, Heribert, and Kogila Moodley. *The Opening of the South African Mind.* Berkeley: University of California Press, 1993.

Fanon, Frantz. *The Wretched of the Earth.* New York: Grove Press, 1966.

Gould, Stephen J. *The Mismeasurement of Man.* Harmondsworth, England: Penguin, 1981.

Kuper, Leo. "Theories of Revolution and Race Relations." In *Race, Ethnicity and Social Change.* Edited by John Stone. Belmont, Calif.: Wadsworth, 1977.

Stone, John. *Racial Conflict in Contemporary Society.* Cambridge: Harvard University Press, 1985.

Stone, John, and Stephen Mennell, eds. *Alexis de Tocqueville on Democracy, Revolution and Society.* Chicago: University of Chicago Press, 1980.

RADICALISM

Radicalism is an outlook that demands far-reaching change in political authority, social relations, and the distribution of wealth and income. Generally, radicals are on the fringe of politics, making demands that many think are unrealistic or utopian. But during revolutions, radicals often come into their own, seizing power and implementing these unrealistic policies. In almost all revolutions, radicals themselves are soon swept aside and more moderate, routine politics again takes over. Still, no matter how short their period of dominance, radicals leave an indelible mark on revolutions and on the nations in which those revolutions occur.

THE ROLE OF RADICALISM IN REVOLUTIONARY CHANGE

Most revolutions begin with a diffuse sense of social crisis, a widely shared belief that existing institutions and practices are no longer working in the manner that various social groups have come to expect. At first, states, political elites, and popular groups may seek moderate reforms. If the state adopts reforms that admit new groups to political participation or that solve economic or military problems, and that do so without weakening the state or making powerful enemies, the crisis may be resolved. However, such effective reforms are extremely difficult to design and implement. More commonly, moderate reforms fail to resolve existing problems. Or such reforms anger or burden certain groups, thereby creating social conflicts or exacerbating them. In such cases, a wide and growing range of views on what should be changed, and how, is likely to be expressed. Instead of being an isolated extreme, radical views become part of a broad spectrum of debate. Instead of being unthinkable, they become one pole of a highly contentious debate.

The American historian Crane Brinton has pointed out that radical leaders are unlikely to be the immediate beneficiaries when an existing regime falters. Instead, more moderate leaders, who appeal to a broader audience and promise gradual change, are likely to be the first to take power. Yet the ability of moderate leaders to stay in power is often limited. If a society is facing an extreme crisis (war or counterrevolution), it is difficult for moderate measures to contain the crisis. If moderate measures fail, radical measures come to dominate the debate on needed change. Or moderate leaders, in trying to maintain the support of diverse social groups, may in the end appeal powerfully to none and be outflanked by radical leaders with a committed following among particular segments of society. Radical leaders who are able to mobilize urban crowds are especially effective in forcing revolutions along their desired path. Where radicals are able to paint moderate leaders as ineffective, as clinging to the past instead of forging a better future, as unsympathetic to the needs of the masses, radical leaders can drive the moderates from power. A revolution then enters what Brinton has labeled its radical phase.

It is during the radical phase, rather than in the initial excitement that follows the end of an old regime, that what we tend to think of as revolutionary acts and legislation generally take place. Radicals seek not merely to change but to destroy the institutions of the old regime. Thus, radical policies often include sweeping new laws, the execution of old-regime leaders, and the seizure and redistribution of property. For example, the execution of the king in the English and French Revolutions took place years after the fall of the monarchies, when radical minorities took power. The most radical communist reorganization of Russian society took place in the 1930s under Joseph Stalin, rather than in the early years of the revolution under Vladimir Ilyich Lenin. Radicals are also the ones most likely to initiate a reign of terror or persecution against their perceived foes, for they are most fearful that supporters of the old regime or opponents of change may overthrow them and most impatient to transform society in accord with their vision of a better world.

In some cases, moderate leaders such as Alexander Kerensky in Russia or Francisco Madero in Mexico simply are bypassed or overthrown by more radical leaders. In other cases, leaders who initially appeared moderate in order to appeal to a wide range of supporters reveal themselves as more radical once they take power. Thus the Sandinistas in Nicaragua, Ayatollah Ruhollah Khomeini in Iran, and Fidel Castro in Cuba initially concealed their more radical plans and led a broad revolutionary coalition to power. After consolidating power, they mobilized popular groups to dispense with many of their former allies and took a more narrowly based government down the road of radical change. In either case, it is generally in the few years of the radical phase of revolution that most of the acts that we routinely consider revolutionary occur.

THE PASSING OF THE RADICALS

If the moderate phase of revolution is often ended by a lack of decisive action, the radical phase is often ended by too much. Radical leadership generally demands a high level of mobilization and generates a high level of conflict in society. These levels cannot be indefinitely sustained. Eventually, people seek to settle down to a new routine. Some radical leaders, such as Mao Zedong in China, make a conscious effort to maintain the radical phase of intensive mobilization for change through renewed calls for revolutionary action. But most revolutionary regimes move gradually to seek stability after a few years of radical activity.

The radical phase of a revolution can end in a variety of ways. In some cases, the radicals may provoke such opposition that they themselves are violently overthrown. This was the fate of Maximilien Robespierre and his Jacobins in the French Revolution. Or radicals may fail to win support or institutionalize their gains, and power then slips away to more moderate or conservative groups. This was the fate of the Puritans in the English Revolution, the Sandinistas in Nicaragua, and the followers of Pancho Villa and Emiliano Zapata in the Mexican Revolution. In some cases, the radicals may simply be succeeded by a new generation that seeks to limit and consolidate its gains. This was what happened with the transition from Lenin and Stalin to Nikita Khrushchev and Leonid Brezhnev in the Soviet Union.

The radical phase is thus the main phase of creative destruction of the institutions and habits of the old regime and of the creation of new ones. The radical phase of revolutions is often brief; but without it, much of what we think of as revolution would be unthinkable.

See also *Anarchism*.

JACK A. GOLDSTONE

BIBLIOGRAPHY

Brinton, Crane. *The Anatomy of Revolution*. Rev. ed. New York: Vintage Books, 1965.

Palmer, R. R. *Twelve Who Ruled: The Year of Terror in the French Revolution*. Princeton, N.J.: Princeton University Press, 1958.

Walzer, Michael. *The Revolution of the Saints*. New York: Atheneum, 1974.

Wright, Robin. *In the Name of God: The Khomeini Decade*. New York: Simon and Schuster, 1989.

RATIONALITY

The practical problem of revolution is not leadership but "followership." Lots of people would like to run a revolution, but few people want to run with one. Why are revolutionary entrepreneurs a dime a dozen and revolutionary foot soldiers as precious as gold? The answer is that whereas the majority of people might want a revolution, not every individual in that majority wants to risk his or her life and fortune for a utopia that is probably unattainable and possibly undesirable. Revolutionary resistance to authority is a dangerous and uncertain proposition, and the danger and uncertainty deter all but a few elite, vanguard revolutionaries. Most sympathizers prefer to leave the hard work of making a revolution to others.

THE REVOLUTIONARY'S DILEMMA

The study of the Revolutionary's Dilemma—or the problem of free-riding and nonparticipation in revolution—was sparked by economists and sociologists who drew upon Mancur Olson's idea that the norms of "instrumental rationality" (means-ends calculations), especially in the market-oriented structures of the modern world, promote self-interest and therefore work against collective endeavors like revolutions that require people to take personal risks in the hope of producing a public gain. The theory's famous deduction and prediction is the Five Percent Rule: fewer than 5 percent of the supporters of a revolutionary cause become actively involved in the cause, so that nonrevolutionaries outnumber revolutionaries nineteen to one. Participation in revolution, in other words, is the rare exception and not the general norm. Moreover, rationalists expect that this rule will be correct 95 percent of the time—as good a theory as presently exists in the social sciences.

The evidence is overwhelmingly supportive of the theory. Even successful revolutions—such as the French, Russian, Chinese, Iranian, and east European revolutions—never mobilized more than 5 percent of their potential sympathizers. Rationalist approaches to revolution are therefore worth close scrutiny and careful elaboration.

Rationalists begin by testing the Five Percent Rule with a descriptive map. They observe revolutionary action and inaction, what did and did not happen, and positive and negative cases of revolution, all in some particular context. In other words, they compare the "preference distribution" of a population to a map of the constellation of revolutionary groups (such as peasants, workers). Whether they study one country and look at many potentially revolutionary groups cross-sectionally or one group longitudinally, or study many different countries and look at one group longitudinally or many groups cross-sectionally, rationalists always begin with a group (or groups) rooted in a more or less well-defined historical tradition and linguistic community, which define the group's long-term goals, ideals, meaning, and revolutionary project, that is, the public good that it seeks. Although the group's goals will be important in assessing the intended and unintended consequences of group action, rationalists recognize that revolutionary groups always contain conflicts that have major effects on their collective action.

Second, rationalists produce an explanatory map of mobilizing processes to solve the basic empirical puzzle of the theory: how to account for the 5 percent who did participate in the revolution. The answer is that certain mobilizing processes were operative while others were not. Rationalists ask which of the many plausible rival solutions to the collective-action problem did the work of mobilizing or demobilizing revolutionaries.

SOLUTIONS TO THE REVOLUTIONARY'S DILEMMA

For the researcher, solutions to the revolutionary's collective-action problem vary along two dimensions. The first dimension is deliberative. The revolutionaries may or may not discuss their situation and devise an explicit answer to the dilemma they face. Solutions to the collective-action problem may thus result in either unplanned or planned order for the group. The second dimension is ontological. One might believe that only individuals are involved in the revolutionary's collective-action problem, or one might believe that institutions, structures, and relationships pre-exist individuals and help impose order on the revolutionaries. Solutions to the revolutionary's collective-action problem may thus result in either spontaneous or contingent order.

Combining dimensions produces the classic distinctions of social thought. Market approaches to the Revolutionary's Dilemma assume that their objects of study are individuals who engage in no social planning. Market approaches focus on changes in the private costs and benefits of participation and therefore emphasize unplanned and spontaneous order. Contract approaches also assume individuals, but individuals who collectively plan their revolution. Contract approaches, such as establishing revolutionary governments in exile, thus feature planned but spontaneous order. Community approaches assume that institutions exist and that they are so effective that top-down planning is unnecessary. Community approaches, such as those that study revolutionary-group consciousness, thus highlight unplanned but contingent order. Finally, hierarchy approaches also assume that institutions exist, including institutions created explicitly to make the revolution. Hierarchy approaches, such as building a Leninist party, thus feature planned and contingent order. The result is that there are two approaches to unplanned order, market and community, and two approaches to planned order, contract and hierarchy. Furthermore, there are two spontaneous approaches to the Revolutionary's Dilemma, market and contract, and two contingent approaches, community and hierarchy.

Of these four sets of solutions, market approaches may be thought of as the baseline. They operate by changing the parameters (such as risk propensities) of the classical model of collective action. The other three sets of solutions vary the context in which the baseline model is placed. Community solutions (such as altruism) explore how common belief systems solve Olson's problem; contractual solutions (such as tit-for-tat bargains) study the ways in which mutual agreements produce revolutionary collective action; and hierarchy solutions (such as external patronage of revolutionary organizations) examine how hierarchies structure mobilization.

Third, rationalists recognize that collective-action solutions are merely the possible equilibria or outcomes. Unless the institutional and interpretive context for a particular strategic situation is established, the collective-action problem is indeterminate and "anything goes." Collective-action models therefore need structure. Rationalists provide structure by tracing the causes of the key mobilization processes. This inquiry leads directly to politics. How do competing interests—the regime, revolutionary entrepreneurs, revolutionary followers, and the revolutionaries' allies and opponents—try to shape contexts, structures, and institutions so as to initiate, sustain, and terminate mobilizing processes? The results are generalizations about the origins of the basic properties of revolution—for example, an etiology of the risk propensities of revolutionaries, revolutionary altruism, revolutionary self-government, and external patronage of revolution. These explanations ultimately help us understand how groups are mobilized into revolution.

Finally, rationalists trace the effects of the key mobilization processes. This tracing leads to the intended consequences of group mobilization: new institutions, policies, and programs desired by revolutionaries that help create a new social order. More importantly, it leads to the unintended consequences of group mobilization: the pathologies of revolution. In short, rationalists are interested in determining how the goals and ideals of revolutionaries are fulfilled and frustrated. They look at the gains, successes, and victories as well as the tragedies, comedies, and farces of the revolution. Revolutionary outcomes include, for example, bourgeois, fascist, and communist paths of development. Economic development, national development, state building, and nation building hold many intended and unintended consequences.

In sum, solutions to the collective action problem are the basic building blocks of a rationalist theory of revolution. Showing how those solutions can be attained, and exploring the intended and unintended consequences of those solutions, are the distinctive contributions of rational-choice theories of revolution.

MARK LICHBACH

BIBLIOGRAPHY

Gamson, W. A. *The Strategy of Social Protest.* 2d ed. Belmont, Calif.: Wadsworth, 1990.

Lichbach, Mark I. *The Rebel's Dilemma.* Ann Arbor: University of Michigan Press, 1995.

Moore, W. H. "Rational Rebels: Overcoming the Free-Rider Problem." *Political Research Quarterly* 48 (1995): 417–454.

Olson, Mancur. *The Logic of Collective Action: Public Goods and the Theory of Groups.* Cambridge: Harvard University Press, 1965.

Tullock, G. "The Paradox of Revolution." *Public Choice* 11 (1971): 89–99.

REBELLION AND REVOLT

Irish Catholics of all description—Gaelic Irish and Old English from north and south—rose in the Great Rebellion of 1641 to defend their religious freedom, political autonomy, and, fundamentally, their property. Cromwell's final suppression of the rebellion in 1652 produced the wholesale transfer of land from Catholic to Protestant ownership that animated political struggles for centuries to follow. In the Whiskey Rebellion of 1794, western Pennsylvania frontier communities rose against federal tax collectors in a struggle that tested the new republic's central authority and helped define federal relations for generations to come. Among diversely motivated rebellions of the twentieth century, anticolonial movements and tax revolts continue to occur. Kenya's Mau-Mau Revolt in the early 1950s challenged British imperialism over land, independence, and indigenous cultural practices. In 1978 California citizens launched a property-tax revolt that altered substantially support for public services and, perhaps, initiated an antigovernment movement nationwide.

Although the list of portentous rebellions and revolts could be extended at great length, these cases are sufficient to support four key observations. First, the terms *rebellion* and *revolt* typically are used interchangeably whether in general discourse or analytical studies. Second, either term may be applied to a wide variety of protest events and political movements without apparent contradiction. That is, the general and multipurpose usage is widely accepted. It would be difficult to imagine any convincing criticism of this usage that claimed, for example, "Mau-Mau was a rebellion, not a revolt" or "the Whiskey affair was neither a revolt nor rebellion but a social movement." There is an accepted vagueness of the terms that is unusual even by social science standards. This is easily demonstrated if we imagine someone writing about, say, Ireland's "Great Revolution" and the vigorous denials that the phrase would invite from students of revolution in the case of this relatively more clearly defined concept. Third, to the extent that there is a common denominator in the varied acceptable usages of rebellion and revolt it is the idea that the event in question failed or in some definitive way was "less than" a political transformation, revolution, or major social movement. Rebellion is typically a residual category. Fourth, as a result of this vagueness and inconsistency, revolts are seldom understood in their own right and correctly theorized.

This conventional and problematic usage is often reinforced in standard social science writing that considers the nature of rebellion only insofar as it serves as a contrast with revolution. Thus, Theda Skocpol defines revolutions as basic transformations of state and class structure that are carried through by class-based revolts from below. Revolts here are an undefined, if a necessary, condition of revolutions, but they are not themselves revolutions because they "do not eventuate in structural change." Michael S. Kimmel adopts a similar residual usage in which "social movements and seemingly isolated acts of rebellion" are not revolutions, for lack of broad effects on change. This approach has two fatal flaws. First, however conveniently it may focus the definition of revolution, it offers no substantive conception of rebellion and revolt. Rebellion is defined only as what it is not. Second, the approach is certainly wrong empirically if we look to the abundant social change and pervasive (not isolated) effects of revolts and rebellions in history beginning with the four cases introduced above. Revolts have diverse effects, some of them as far reaching as anything wrought by revolution.

Rebellion and revolt, which I shall continue to use interchangeably, deserve their own conceptualization independent of revolution and various kinds of collective action. In *The Phenomenon of Revolution* Mark N. Hagopian provides a useful beginning by identifying several "false or uninteresting criteria of distinction" that do not inform a useful definition (for example, the success-failure dichotomy, level of violence) and then characterizing revolt as "the angry, violent expression of the refusal of an individual or group to continue in its present condition." This is spare but sound. Rebellion is understood as action and specifically as action that repudiates some former and worsening state of affairs through overt protest. Revolt signifies an abrupt rupture of existing power relations through acts of defiance. In that it differs from milder and covert forms of dispute and noncooperation. Moreover, revolt may respond to varied conditions—Hagopian suggests hunger, rising prices, taxes, military impressment, arbitrary government, wage cuts, withdrawal of privileges—and lend its mobilized energies to social movements, revolutions, or episodic forms of collective action such as riots and demonstrations. The important point here, however, is that rebellion is conceptualized on a dimension independent of the conditions and forms of collective action. Revolt, in essence, is the moment or process in which long suffering turns to spirited opposition—the awareness, as Barrington Moore describes it so cogently, when the existing order of things no longer seems inevitable and change appears as a possibility.

Rebellion conceived generically in its own terms may subsequently be contextualized, described, and related to various forms of collective action. Useful inquiries might, for example, compare revolts over taxation with others centered on price rises, or slave rebellions with peasant uprisings. Important if neglected problems such as the conditions under which obedience turns to revolt are spotlighted in this formulation. Similarly, comparative studies of liberation movements in developing countries can explore the parallels between classical revolutions and modern rebellions. Research on "national revolts" indicates certain key features in common with revolutions—broad peasant and worker mobilization, conventional political objectives, state repression, and links to the international economy—that suggest ways in which it may be necessary to rethink the notion of revolution itself. Far from a lesser (partial, failed) instance of revolution, rebellion conceived in its own right opens new spaces for exploration of collective action.

See also *Coup d'État; Reform.*

John Walton

BIBLIOGRAPHY

Hagopian, Mark N. *The Phenomenon of Revolution.* New York: Dodd, Mead, 1974.

Kimmel, Michael S. *Revolution: A Sociological Interpretation.* Oxford: Polity Press/Blackwell, 1990.

Moore, Barrington, Jr. *Injustice: The Social Bases of Obedience and Revolt.* White Plains, N.Y.: M.E. Sharp, 1978.

Skocpol, Theda. *States and Social Revolutions: A Comparative Analysis of France, Russia, and China.* Cambridge: Cambridge University Press, 1979.

Walton, John. *Reluctant Rebels: Comparative Studies of Revolution and Underdevelopment.* New York: Columbia University Press, 1984.

REFORM

Reform is sometimes considered an alternative to revolution: a peaceful, rather than violent, path to social improvement. The British reform movement of 1828–1832, which extended political participation to Roman Catholics and to the new industrial and middle classes, and the South African reforms of the 1990s, which extended political participation to black South Africans, are often touted as models of how reform can peacefully produce change in situations that otherwise could have led to revolution. Yet reform is also, in many cases, a precipitant of revolution. Quite often, regimes that have fallen to revolution—including tsarist Russia, the French and English monarchies, imperial China, and the Pahlavi shahs in Iran—spent the last decades of their existence implementing various political and economic reforms. Such reforms, as the nineteenth-century French scholar Alexis de Tocqueville noted, did not satisfy people's desire for change. Instead, they seemed to whet the appetite of people for greater changes and to admit the faults and illegitimacy of the existing regime. They thus helped bring on, rather than prevent, revolutions.

SOCIAL CRISIS AND THE NEED FOR REFORM

Both reform and revolution grow from the same roots: a sense of crisis, based on the realization that the existing institutions that control the distribution of wealth and power in a society are no longer working in the way that various groups have come to expect. Whether it is church leaders or state officials who find themselves short of funds; workers or peasants who are unable to provide for their families no matter how hard they work; nobles, merchants, and professionals who find their aspirations for social status and power frustrated by a failure for their positions to correspond with what they believe they deserve; or nationalist leaders, leaders of ethnic or regional groups, intellectuals, or military officers who feel that their society is going to ruin, a wide variety of groups come to demand major changes in the social and political order.

Sometimes, the cause of reforms is a sudden crushing blow. For example, Napoleon's military defeat of Prussia in 1806 helped launch the Prussian reform movement in the ensuing decade; the failed Revolution of 1905 in Russia helped launch the agrarian, economic, and electoral reforms of tsarist minister Peter Stolypin (1906–1911) in the following years; the global economic depression of the 1930s helped launch the New Deal welfare reforms in the United States. At other times, the cumulation of gradual changes renders existing institutions unworkable or obsolete. The steady growth of population and overtaxing of the agricultural economy led the French monarchy in the late eighteenth century, and the Imperial Chinese government in the late nineteenth century, to seek economic and fiscal reforms. Just as revolutions sometimes follow military defeat or economic crisis, while at other times they spring from the gradual escalation of social conflicts, reforms too can stem from a wide range of causes. What is crucial, however, is the sense that a crisis has arrived that can be met only by some significant political or social change.

WHEN REFORMS FAIL

Almost all societies, when faced with demands for change by significant elements of their population, will attempt some sort of reforms. Whether or not such reforms will be successful in meeting the demands for change, however, depends on many factors. These include the resources of the state, the role played by groups that demand reforms, and the conditions of society when reform is being attempted.

A state that has substantial support and resources, that involves broad segments of society in reform to a meaningful degree, and that implements reforms before the problems grow too severe has a good chance of maintaining stability through a period of reform. But a state with weak support and modest resources, or one that implements reforms grudgingly and without meaningful involvement of the groups demanding change or that acts only when the problems and conflicts that underlie the demands for change are so severe they cannot be resolved, is unlikely to stay in power despite making reforms. In the sixteenth century, the Italian writer and adviser to state rulers Niccolò Machiavelli had this advice regarding reform: if reforms are needed, act quickly while you are still strong, and do not wait for overwhelming pressures to arise. By then "you are too late for harsh measures; and mild ones will not help you, for they will be considered as forced from you, and no one will be under any obligations to you for them."

The English monarchy, by the early seventeenth century,

was feeling pressures from all sides, as were its subjects. The church was beset by dissent, the monarchy was financially strapped and in debt, workers had endured decades of falling real wages, and merchants, large farmers, and older noble families scrapped over state and county positions. The king asked Parliament for a number of fiscal reforms, and Parliament in return asked for a number of changes in royal administration. If an agreement had been reached and reforms implemented in the 1620s, perhaps the revolution of the 1640s could have been averted. But the king and Parliament could not agree. The king dismissed Parliament for more than a decade and embarked on a set of fiscal, administrative, and religious reforms decreed by the king and his ministers. The reforms brought the monarchy the worst of all outcomes. Although the new taxes and religious rulings were sufficiently odious to anger many Irish, English, and Scottish subjects, they were not sufficient to build the military strength and war chest that the monarchy needed to cope with the violent religious conflicts that bedeviled Europe in the seventeenth century. When the Scots raised a military protest against the religious reforms of King Charles I, Charles lacked the money or soldiers to meet the challenge, and he was forced to recall Parliament to seek support. But when Parliament assembled, its members made further demands for change and condemned the king's past reforms. With the leaders on both sides agreeing only that a crisis was at hand, and unable to agree on what changes were needed, the conflict over constitutional and religious reform unleashed a revolution that eventually led to the execution of the king and his top ministers.

Similar stories can be told of France in the late eighteenth century, China in the late nineteenth century, and Russia in the early twentieth century. In each case, widespread demands for change were expressed, and the monarchs sought to respond to those demands with reforms. The French monarchy sought to streamline urban administration, make food supplies more dependent on free markets, and restructure the tax system. The Chinese sought to modernize and westernize their army and their educational system. The Russians sought to reform their communal system of village agriculture and to give forums for expressing grievances to the nobility and other leading Russians. But in all cases the reforms were autocratically handed down from above, they often imposed new burdens or strains on the population, and yet they were still insufficient to strengthen the state's finances, to win the allegiance of peasants and workers, or to extend political rights to those groups who felt unfairly denied and excluded. The reforms often antagonized supporters of the regime, while failing to satisfy its opponents.

Moreover, to the extent that modernizing reforms created more teachers, engineers, professionals, intellectuals, and industrial workers, the reforms contributed to increasing the size of new social groups that had little stake in the old regime and were more inclined to seek change than were the old guard. Opposition to the old regime grew, rather than diminished, as a result of the reforms, while the state continued to grow weaker. More severe clashes, and revolutions, thus followed upon the heels of reform.

SUCCESSFUL REFORMS

Successful reforms have several elements in common: they lead to meaningful (not just pro forma) involvement of different groups in political decisions; they strengthen the state sufficiently to meet pending challenges, usually by creating greater efficiency in revenue collection or state administration; and they do not raise the anger of prominent social groups or make enemies of them by imposing new burdens upon them. Examples are the British and Prussian reform movements of the early nineteenth century and the South African reforms of the late twentieth century. In each of these cases, new groups were brought into political power (industrialists in England, professionals and non-noble bureaucrats in Prussia, blacks in South Africa), but the groups who had held power previously (large landowners in England, nobles in Prussia, and whites in South Africa) were not dismissed or excluded. Instead, new power-sharing arrangements broadened the sphere of political life. Instead of a revolutionary seizure and transfer of power, successful reforms generally invoke the image of a sharing of power.

Successful reform movements, however, are somewhat rare. The trick of meeting demands for change while improving conditions for the state and society, and not offending key social groups, is a difficult one to pull off. More often than not, by the time a regime concedes the need to act, social conflicts and deteriorating conditions have advanced so far that most state actions make things worse and destabilize the regime.

Reform then is often a prelude, or even an aggravating factor, in a society's march toward revolution. In some cases, reforms do help a regime respond to demands for change in a way that averts a more serious conflict. But the precise mix of conditions and actions that lead to successful reform is difficult to achieve. More commonly, as Tocqueville remarked, states in trouble that undertake reforms are simply instructing their people in the necessity and methods of dismantling the existing regime.

See also *Radicalism; Rebellion and Revolt.*

Jack A. Goldstone

BIBLIOGRAPHY

McDaniel, Tim. *Autocracy, Modernization, and Revolution in Russia and Iran.* Princeton, N.J.: Princeton University Press, 1991.

Pipes, Richard. *Russia under the Old Regime.* New York: Scribner, 1974.

Spence, Jonathan. *The Search for Modern China.* New York: Norton, 1990.

Tilly, Charles. *Population and Contention in Great Britain, 1758–1834.* Cambridge: Harvard University Press, 1995.

Tocqueville, Alexis de. *The Old Regime and the French Revolution.* Translated by Stuart Gilbert. New York: Anchor, 1955.

RELIGION

One hundred fifty years ago, arguing that religion led people to accept their miseries passively, Karl Marx pronounced religion "the opium of the people." Thirty years ago, a modern scholar, also named Marx, echoed this sentiment in his finding that among American blacks, religious involvement led people away from civil-rights militancy. These two voices are part of a general perspective in nineteenth- and twentieth-century social science that either minimizes the role of religion in large-scale societal transformation or considers it a dangerous hindrance to progress. Many modern states, from the first French Republic to the late Soviet empire, carried out their revolutions by targeting the traditional religion as an enemy to be eliminated and replaced by a new civil religion.

More recent developments have provoked a reappraisal of the part of religion in revolutions, one that suggests religion may be as much a proactive force as a reactive brake. In the 1980s and 1990s, institutional religion provided crucial support for mass and revolutionary movements that succeeded in toppling authoritarian regimes in a variety of settings, from the Philippines of Ferdinand Marcos to the German Democratic Republic and other satellites of the Soviet Union. The rise of fundamentalism in various religious traditions and the dynamic role of clergy in challenging secular states on behalf of oppressed indigenous peoples (for example, the Catholic Church in Guatemala and in Chiapas, Mexico) provide further reason to rethink the conditions and outcomes of religion's involvement with social change.

From a sociological perspective, a religion is a set of deeply held beliefs, symbols, and rituals that provide its adherents with a collective identity and orientation to the world. Its political import is two-edged. By providing rationales for the social order, religion may establish legitimacy for the state. On the other hand, religion can deploy a repertoire of symbols, rhetoric, and even rituals to cast doubt on the legitimacy of the social order and the state, as demonstrated by Martin Luther King Jr. and his church-based civil rights movement. Religious *sects* have long been viewed as levers of change, but classical sociological models failed to recognize that institutional religion could also become in certain circumstances not a hindrance but a stimulant of social transformation, especially of democratization.

FROM LUTHER TO CROMWELL

A watershed event in the history of western religion was the cleric Martin Luther's revolutionary challenge of papal authority in Wittenberg in 1517. Luther's action launched the far-reaching sociocultural and sociopolitical movement of the Protestant Reformation. Quickly diffused throughout Europe by the new medium of the printing press, and particularly successful in northern Europe, Protestantism provided an ideology that challenged the legitimacy of the religious throne of Rome, which was strategically allied at the time to the political throne of Spain.

Two branches of the Protestant movement bear notice. *Calvinism* contributed to the rise of modern capitalism through its emphasis on the spiritual merits of self-disciplined, secular activism. The *Anabaptist* movement, on the other hand, featured a radical rejection of established authority, the equality of all "regenerated" humans converted or graced directly by the spirit, and belief in an imminent, convulsive end of history to be followed by a millennium-long reign of Christ on earth. This radical wing of the Reformation reappeared in new guises in later modern revolutionary movements, including Russia between 1905 and 1914. Anabaptists addressed each other as "brother" and "sister" and in some instances established communal living arrangements with full economic equality. In Münster, proclaimed as the "new Jerusalem" in 1534, Anabaptists banned or burned all books but the Bible, abolished private ownership of money and property, introduced polygamy, and adopted a strict code of Old Testament–based law. Although the Anabaptist rule was short-lived, much of its ideology recurs in later revolutionary groups seeking a radical egalitarian transformation of the social order, including urban-based sects having millenary expectations of the coming end of the world. Even the nineteenth-century socialist dream of the "dictatorship of the proletariat" can trace its ancestry to this early radical orientation. In a forerunner of mass-based nationalist movements, Calvinism and Anabaptism in the Netherlands combined to provide the ideology for the sixteenth-century Dutch-Flemish revolt against Spanish Catholic rule, leading to the establishment of the Dutch republic.

An important group descended from Anabaptism came to prominence in England during the seventeenth century. Puritan sects vigorously opposed England's episcopal church organization in favor of a congregational form with the min-

Long thought to be a conservative force, religion in the late twentieth century became in many places a revolutionary force. In June 1983, when Polish-born Pope John Paul II visited his homeland, citizens made this cross of flowers in a public square. The Catholic Church was a major influence on the Polish anticommunist movement.

istry chosen directly by believers. These sects, influential in the Long Parliament of 1640 to 1660 and in Cromwell's successful but relatively short-lived revolutionary Protectorate (1653–1658), drew Protestant-inclined gentry and merchants disaffected with the monarchy's taxation policies, as well as members of the universities.

TWO MODERN REVOLUTIONS

A fuller measure of Puritan success in linking religious fervor to political outcome obtains in the direct involvement of New England clergymen such as Ezra Stiles (president of Yale), Elisha Williams, Nathaniel Niles, Samuel West, John Cleaveland, and Jonathan Mayhew in the American Revolution. The ideology of the most successful and enduring modern revolution synthesized without conflict the secular, rationalist deism of the Enlightenment—in which God was viewed as being withdrawn from human affairs—with Puritan millennial notions of the collective spiritual rebirth of the "New American Israel." The revolutionary clergy saw the American republic as a redemptive agent of history, fulfilling the eschatological books of Daniel and Revelation and as the twin triumph of religious and civil liberty. The "Great Awakening," experienced most acutely in New England in the 1740s, prepared the American colonists for independence from both the Church of England and the monarchy. The same religious revival and democratic impulse in the urban areas of England and in Wales later gave rise, under the charismatic leadership of John Wesley and George Whitefield, to the evangelical movement that crystallized in Methodism. Politically, according to Elie Halévy's famous thesis *England in 1815* (1913), Methodism warded off a republican revolution in Great Britain by capturing the fervor of the British masses for *individual* rebirth and conversion.

Occurring almost as soon as the American Revolution ended, and sharing the rationalist-scientific beliefs of the

Enlightenment, the French Revolution represented a more conflictual relation of religion and revolution. Attacking traditional religion and the monarchy as the bases of a society based on superstition and status distinction, the revolutionaries required the clergy to take an oath to the new constitution, in effect substituting loyalty to the republic for loyalty to the papacy. In the more extreme moments of the Revolution (the Reign of Terror in 1792–1793), "refractory" priests who did not take the oath, especially in the Paris region, were either expelled or guillotined. Revolutionary leaders also felt the need to replace the old religion with new forms of civil religion to complement the secular ideology of "liberty, equality, fraternity" and to distract citizens from the appeal of Christianity. Maximilien Robespierre encouraged the civil religion envisaged by Rousseau, one having as its cult the Supreme Being and the female deity of Liberty, installed in public places and in former Christian churches, notably Notre Dame. After Robespierre's execution, a more complex secular religion known as theophilanthropy was devised to revitalize revolutionary commitment, complete with elaborate festivals and public rituals, many derived from Masonic rituals, as well as giant rallies that prefigure those of modern mass society. None of the revolutionary cults became widely accepted, however, mainly due to the resistance of women outside Paris.

State policies of "dechristianization" were carried out in other forms in later twentieth-century settings, such as Mexico and Russia in the 1920s. In China, Mao Zedong's Cultural Revolution (1966–1969) sought to substitute the cult of Mao for traditional Confucianism.

CONTEMPORARY SETTINGS: IRAN AND LATIN AMERICA

Under Shah Reza Pahlavi, Iran had in the 1960s and 1970s undergone a "white revolution" of secularization and rapid economic development based on oil exports and Western investment. The process marginalized various urban groups, especially small merchants and migrants forced from the countryside, along with traditional religious authorities. Ayatollahs—learned men of the Shi'ite branch of Islam—spearheaded popular protest against the shah and massive civil disobedience by drawing on Islamic scripture to show the illegitimacy of the regime. They called for an Islamic republic—a new form of Islamic polity—freed from decadent Western influences. Among religious revolutionaries, the charismatic Ayatollah Ruhollah Khomeini stood out. As the head of the revolutionary mass movement dubbed "revolutionary traditionalism," Khomeini capsized the Iranian state in 1979. At the time, the Iranian state faced no financial crisis and no peasant rebellions. The army remained intact during the struggle. Notwithstanding internal dissension after the death of Khomeini in 1989, a long, drawn-out war against Iraq, and American enmity, Iran's religious revolution has retained power and enjoyed broad popular support.

In predominantly Catholic Latin America, the church went through a drastic shake-up in the wake of Vatican II (1962–1965) and the Ecumenical Congress of Bishops in Medellán, Colombia (1968). "Liberation theology," promulgated by progressive theologians in Brazil and Peru, although resisted by conservative members of the episcopate, became an active force in the 1970s, often in interaction rather than confrontation with secular Marxists inspired by Castro's Cuban Revolution. Practitioners of liberation theology established Christian communities among poor and often illiterate people in agrarian and urban areas, drawing on the Gospels to make sense of the everyday world of poverty and inequality. For an ecclesiastical body that had previously either defended the traditional oligarchies or had been the target of left-wing nationalist movements, it was a novel situation for members of the clergy—many of them foreign missionaries—to be in the forefront of social change. In Nicaragua, the Sandinista movement that overthrew the dictatorial regime of Anastasio Somoza in 1979 and carried out vast land and educational reforms had both ordained priests and secular Marxists as cabinet ministers. Similarly, in the wake of French-speaking Quebec's "Quiet Revolution" in the 1960s, several former priests became leaders in the nationalist and social democratic Parti Québecois after its surprise electoral victory in 1976.

Religious motivation and ideology have been a powerful factor in various revolutionary and prerevolutionary settings, both Western and non-Western. In the contemporary period, examples can be found in which religion has opened the door to democracy, as in Nicaragua and Quebec; in others, it has aimed to close the door.

See also *Anabaptism; Chinese Taiping Rebellion (1851–1864); Cromwell, Oliver; French Revolution (1789–1815); French Wars of Religion (1562–1598); German Peasant War (1524–1526); Iranian Islamic Revolution (1979); Islamic Fundamentalism; Khomeini, Ayatollah Ruhollah; King, Martin Luther, Jr.; Liberation Theology; Luther, Martin; Millenarianism; Polish Protests and Solidarity Revolution (1956–1991); Rousseau, Jean-Jacques.*

EDWARD TIRYAKIAN

BIBLIOGRAPHY

Arjomand, Said. *The Turban for the Crown: The Islamic Revolution in Iran.* New York: Oxford University Press, 1988.

Eisenstadt, S. N. *Revolution and the Transformation of Societies.* New York: Free Press, 1979.

Lewy, Guenter. *Religion and Revolution*. New York: Oxford University Press, 1974.

Marx, Gary T. "Religion: Opiate or Inspiration of Civil Rights Militancy Among Negroes?" *American Sociological Review* 32 (February 1967): 64–72.

Ozouf, Mona. *Festivals and the French Revolution*. Cambridge: Harvard University Press, 1988.

Robertson, Roland. "The Development and Modern Implications of the Classical Sociological Perspective on Religion and Revolution." In *Religion, Rebellion, Revolution*. Edited by Bruce Lincoln. New York: St. Martin's Press, 1985.

Stark, Rodney, and Kevin J. Christiano. "Support for the American Left, 1920–1924: The Opiate Thesis Reconsidered." *Journal for the Scientific Study of Religion* 31 (March 1992): 62–75.

Tiryakian, Edward A. "The Wild Cards of Modernity." *Daedalus* 126 (spring 1997): 147–181.

REPUBLICS

Republican government is a Western-inspired concept, both in its most general sense as consensual rule of the citizenry and in its more particular reference to the enactment and enforcement of legislation by elected representatives rather than by the voting populace at large. Since Aristotle, observers have remarked that republics arise out of revolutionary fervor—both economic and political, and often through armed conflict. Implicit in republican revolutions is the notion that previous regimes have been both too narrow and unfair in their exclusion of popular referenda.

ORIGINS AND DEVELOPMENT

Ancient Greek constitutions were usually characterized by several forms of direct involvement of the citizens, their participation in politics limited only by the census requirements (property or capital) set by the various states. But by the fourth century B.C. the Greeks had developed a notion of leagues (for example, the Boeotian, Achaean, and Arcadian Confederacies), to which individual city-states might elect representatives to serve in federal assemblies that established foreign policy for their member populations. In that federal sense of representative government, rather than direct citizen participation, republicanism in Greece antedated Roman republicanism.

The classical complaints against Greek democracy by Plato and Aristotle—the hysteria of a volatile mass, the absence of legal restrictions on majority votes, and the omnipresence of dangerous demagogues—were thought by later Greek and Roman thinkers (Polybius and Cicero among them) to have been addressed by the evolution of Roman republicanism. Various assemblies of representatives elected by popular votes—the most prominent being the Roman Senate—in theory followed written constitutional precedents, represented different constituencies, shared power through checks and balances, and were increasingly immune from direct plebiscites of the people.

Thus the consensus of classical political thought—and later European political philosophy as well—was that republican government was superior to democratic practice largely because republics distanced volatile and uneducated voters from direct involvement in decision making. Such orthodoxy reflects three historical phenomena: the well-recorded gullibility of the Athenian *dêmos* to follow demagogues in their savage propensity to execute and oppress at will; the systematic subjugation of the entire Mediterranean under the Roman republic and its Senate; and the traditional aristocratic prejudices of Greek and Roman philosophers and historians, who feared democratic practices such as ostracism, property confiscation, debt cancellation, and land redistribution, which inevitably subjected the wealthy to the majority vote of the poor.

With the rise of the Roman principate under Augustus and the end of a free and sovereign Senate (A.D. 31), republicanism was relegated to regional and local government, only to disappear altogether for centuries with the fall of the empire in the fifth century A.D. Limitations to divine rule and monarchy returned only slowly in the Middle Ages. By the time of the Renaissance in the fifteenth and sixteenth centuries there were occasional republican city-states in Italy and moves—fueled by the growth of a middling, nonaristocratic class—to check the absolute power of kings among the northern European monarchies. The humanism of the Renaissance, prompted by the rediscovery of Greece and Rome, cast republicanism as the protector among elites of literary, artistic, and individual freedom. And with the eighteenth-century Enlightenment in England and France, the material progress created by Western science and technology was seen as inseparable from the free expression and exchange of ideas, a dynamism best fostered under the aegis of elected government.

Both the American (1776) and French (1789) Revolutions sought to expand classical republicanism beyond mere constitutional questions, but in differing ways—the former by guaranteeing the private citizen individual liberties that were inherently sacrosanct, regardless of legislative or popular assaults, and the latter by extending the notion of political equality to the ideal of economic equivalence. In general, the American paradigm has found more success, since representatives in republican government inevitably tend to be among the wealthier elements of society and rarely wish to interfere in free markets. In addition, the degree of coercion necessary to legislate absolute economic equality is usually felt by the citizenry at large to be antithetical to a free society; and without a bill of rights even elected assemblies can markedly curtail individual freedoms.

CRITICS AND ADVOCATES

Modern communist states such as China and the former Soviet Union purportedly interpreted republicanism solely as the promotion of economic justice. Redistribution of income, the denial of free expression, and confiscation of private property were said to be accomplished through the assent of the people's representatives—even in the absence of free elections. Yet communist expropriation of the term *republic* did not illustrate genuine emphasis on economic or political equality as much as it reflected the propagandistic value obtained through the public avowal of consensual government. In that regard, both the autocratic left and the authoritarian right have adopted the nomenclature "people's republic" or "national republic" for their repressive regimes—clear proof of the global popularity of republicanism that even its veneer can help legitimize totalitarianism.

Despite—or perhaps because of—their separation of civilian and military authority, republics are also lethal war makers. The notion of an entire nation in arms is republican to the core, based on the idea that the citizens' representatives have in their wisdom called the entire populace to defend themselves against autocracy. Yet rarely have true republics fought each other in prolonged conflicts. Established republics are also rarely overthrown; and grassroots revolutions against republican governments are virtually unknown.

Critics on the right who fault republicanism enjoy distinguished company, from Plato and Thomas Hobbes to Friedrich Nietzsche and Georg Hegel. They worry over republics' inherent tendency to champion an empty individualism at the expense of common cultural responsibilities and the ensuing absence of moral censure. In their eyes, republics inevitably spawn an ignorant citizenry seeking from a free society material surfeit and increasing leisure rather than intellectual and spiritual fulfillment. In contrast, the liberal tradition in Western thought has seen few alternatives to republican government and has argued that civic virtue is possible only from shared service to the state. Jean-Jacques Rousseau and Immanuel Kant felt republicanism to be far superior to monarchy; John Locke and Charles de Montesquieu saw it as the best protection of law against despotism. The American federalists and John Stuart Mill sought a middle ground between radical democracy and landed oligarchy. In their view, republicanism alone might combine universal suffrage and free participation in offices with judicial, executive, and legislative checks on popular referenda—in theory, a completely free people guided and occasionally restrained by wiser men.

Critics and advocates can disagree over the moral purposes of republican government but not its unquestioned dynamism and popularity. The revolutionary present-day expansion of Western republican government on the heels of capitalism throughout the world suggests that so far, when given the opportunity, very few people prefer to retain foreign-imposed communism, fascism, or tyranny—or indigenous theocratic, monarchic, or tribal regimes.

See also *Constitutions; Democracy; Liberalism; Rights; States.*

VICTOR DAVIS HANSON

BIBLIOGRAPHY

Everdell, William. *The End of Kings. A History of Republics and Republicanism*. New York: Free Press, 1983.

Larsen, Jakob Aall Otlesen. *Representative Government in Greek and Roman History.* Berkeley: University of California Press, 1955.

Rahe, Paul. *Republics Ancient and Modern. Classical Republicanism and the American Revolution*. Charlotte: University of North Carolina Press, 1992.

RIGHTS

The concept of rights has played a fateful part in political revolutions. Revolutionary movements have used the language of rights and have often gained momentum when the state openly threatened the rights, and even the lives, of opposition political leaders and their supporters. Once in power, however, revolutionaries have suppressed more often than respected the very rights that were one basis of their legitimacy. Rights, in the sense of legitimate claims that individual citizens have against those who rule over them, have seldom flourished at times when zealous revolutionaries have been engaged in remaking the world.

The connection between the idea of rights and the legitimacy of rebellion has a long history in many countries, including England. The Magna Carta, which the English nobility extracted from King John at Runnymede in 1215, contained provisions on rights that, however circumscribed, contained the germs of modern ideas: "We will sell to no man, we will not deny or defer to any man, either justice or right." At the same time, there was a clause in the Magna Carta that if the king failed to carry out his side of the bargain, the barons were empowered to make war on him: a legitimized and conditional right of revolution. Notions of contractual government never disappeared thereafter. They played a key part in events such as the "Glorious Revolution" of 1688, which brought William of Orange to the English throne, and in the Bill of Rights that emerged one year later. They also constituted a key concept in much writing on political philosophy, especially in John Locke's *Two Treatises of Government* (1690).

THE AMERICAN AND FRENCH REVOLUTIONS

The American Revolution was based on an idea of rights. In the Declaration of Independence (1776), the clarion call of rebellion against British rule, Thomas Jefferson gave pride of place to the proposition that all men are "endowed by their Creator with certain unalienable rights, that among these are life, liberty, and the pursuit of happiness." Similarly the French Revolution (1789) was based on a strong assertion of the centrality of rights. As the National Assembly put it on July 9, 1789, on the eve of the revolutionary events: "Every government should have for its only end the preservation of the rights of man." The French Revolution, like the American, not only replaced rule by a hereditary monarch with a republic ruled by elected representatives, but also formally set out the rights of citizens. This cataloguing of rights took the form, in France, of the Declaration of the Rights of Man and of the Citizen of 1789; and, in the United States, of the Bill of Rights that was appended to the Constitution in 1791. Many saw these events as having momentous and beneficial consequences for the whole world. As Tom Paine, who became involved in both revolutions, said in the 1792 edition ofThe Rights of Man, people everywhere were successfully recovering the rights of which they had earlier been deprived by conquest and tyranny: "Government founded on a moral theory, on a system of universal peace, on the indefeasible hereditary Rights of Man, is now revolving from west to east, by a stronger impulse than the government of the sword revolved from east to west."

In the event, the French Revolution descended into the practices that Tom Paine had deplored—conquest abroad and terror at home. In a speech on February 5, 1794, Maximilien Robespierre, the head of the Committee of Public Safety, proclaimed the ascendancy of public over private interests. This upholding of *public* rights was one part of a continental European tradition of thought about the organic nature of the citizen body that was particularly appropriated by revolutionary regimes. Robespierre's central idea, that a virtuous revolutionary leadership must stamp out all opposition, distinguished him from his less zealous and more democratic American contemporaries.

The developments in France, later echoed in many communist revolutions, cast doubt upon the idea that revolutions were the only means of realizing rights. Indeed, the linking of revolution with tyranny and war was to assist the survival of autocratic regimes inside Europe and beyond. In the nineteenth and twentieth centuries many such regimes used antirevolutionary (and later anticommunist) rhetoric to justify their own existence. They exploited popular fears that revolutions, especially those that preached public rather than individual rights, would suppress civil liberties and create a new form of tyranny.

Several of the leaders of the 1848 revolutions in Europe, having absorbed the lessons of the French Revolution of 1789, were notably cautious in their pronouncements, accepting the ideas of individual freedom under law at home and respect for international norms abroad. As French foreign minister Alphonse de Lamartine put it in 1848, France desired to enter into "the family of established governments, as a regular power, and not as a phenomenon destructive of European order."

COLLECTIVE RIGHTS

However, the year 1848 saw an ominous development: the growing emphasis on collective power rather than on individual rights. The "collective" assumed two main forms: nation and class. Ominous denials of minority rights occurred in some of the national revolutions of 1848, notably in Hungary, whose new leaders were not prepared to grant to their Serb minority the same national rights as the Hungarians themselves claimed against the Austrians. The result was open conflict between Hungarians and Serbs.

As for class-based views of revolution, the denial of rights was already evident in *The Communist Manifesto,* by Karl Marx and Friedrich Engels, first published (in German) at the beginning of 1848. The work envisaged the coming triumph of the proletariat over the bourgeoisie but showed little interest in the protection of rights under either form of dominance. The right to revolution was noted in some of Marx's and Engels's writings, but not rights after revolution. Engels wrote in an article entitled "On Authority" (1873) that a revolution "is certainly the most authoritarian thing there is; it is the act whereby one part of the population imposes its will on the other part by means of rifles, bayonets, and cannon . . . and if the victorious party does not want to have fought in vain, it must maintain this rule by means of the terror which its arms inspire in the reactionaries."

The Russian Revolution of 1917 was the first of many successful communist revolutions that, while claiming one basis in rights, left little room for any individual or collective rights as against those of the state and the ruling party. The constitutions of communist states were notable as proclamations of goals, but they largely failed to perform the more normal functions of constitutions as expositions of rules for the control and transfer of political power and as guarantees of the rights of individuals.

However, even communist regimes retained some rudimentary claims to support the rights of citizens, and throughout the first half of the twentieth century, the language of rights was used extensively by opposition movements (both communist and nationalist) in Latin America, Asia, and Africa as a means of legitimizing rebellion and revolution. Thus the declaration of independence of the Democratic Republic of Vietnam, issued by Ho Chi Minh and his mainly communist colleagues on September 2, 1945, shortly after they had seized power in the interlude between Japan's defeat and France's return to Indochina, opened by quoting both the American Declaration of Independence and the French Declaration of the Rights of Man and of the Citizen.

HUMAN RIGHTS SINCE 1945

In the process of building an international coalition against the Axis powers during World War II, the term "human rights" entered common political and diplomatic usage. In October 1945, the preamble and several articles of the United Nations Charter proclaimed the centrality of human rights, for example in Article 55(c), which called for "universal respect for, and observance of, human rights and fundamental freedoms for all without distinction as to race, sex, language, or religion." These were followed by other United Nations documents: the 1948 Universal Declaration of Human Rights and the two 1966 United Nations Covenants (one on political and civil rights, the other on economic and social rights). In Europe the 1975 Helsinki Final Act on Security and Cooperation in Europe, negotiated by thirty-five countries including the United States and the USSR, also put considerable emphasis on human rights.

In many countries, opposition movements, whether seeking revolution or more modest political change, appealed to these internationally recognized rights. Secessionist movements particularly stressed the right of peoples to self-determination, enshrined in Article 1 of the two United Nations covenants of 1966, but in the 1990s a growing body of opinion came to view this provision as a right to democracy rather than to secession or revolution.

Movements against autocracy also used the language of human rights to confirm their legitimacy. In communist Czechoslovakia, the immediate origin of the Charter 77 movement was Czechoslovakia's formal adherence in 1975–1976 to three international agreements dealing with human rights: the 1975 Helsinki Final Act and the two United Nations covenants in this field. On the very day (November 11, 1976) when the Czechoslovak government published the legal texts relating to its ratification of the two United Nations covenants, a few citizens meeting in a kitchen (with the water running to mask their words from microphones) began the discussions that led to Charter 77. Ultimately this movement provided the basis for a new government at the time of the Czechoslovak "Velvet Revolution" in December 1989.

Over many centuries, ideas of rights have contributed to the causation, and sometimes the direction, of many revolutions. What, however, have revolutions contributed to the development of human rights? Revolutions have often produced governments that have been extreme enemies of any notion of rights: the huge numbers of victims of tyranny in Russia, China, and Cambodia in the twentieth century are the most dramatic evidence for this grim proposition. Yet, by a paradox, revolutions have played a part, directly or by provoking a response, in the developments whereby concerns over human rights became a legitimate part of international political discourse. In a momentous change in international opinion, the old idea that a state's internal political system and its treatment of its own subjects are matters for that state alone has gradually been supplanted. The American and French Revolutions established in the public consciousness the idea that rights could be the basis of a new and better international order. In the twentieth century, communist regimes could not wholly reject the idea of human rights, especially after they lost their early messianic momentum, and actually contributed something to the notion of economic and social rights. Above all, however, it was the way in which opponents of communist regimes vigorously used human rights standards that left the idea of rights apparently triumphant over the idea of revolution.

See also *American (U.S.) Revolution (1776–1789); British "Glorious Revolution" (1688–1689); Constitutions; Czechoslovak "Velvet Revolution" and "Divorce" (1989–1993); Democracy; East European Revolutions of 1989; European Revolutions of 1848; French Revolution (1789–1815); Jefferson, Thomas; Liberalism; Locke, John; Marx, Karl, and Friedrich Engels; Paine, Thomas; Russian Revolution of 1917.*

ADAM ROBERTS

BIBLIOGRAPHY

Brownlie, Ian, ed. *Basic Documents on Human Rights.* 3d ed. Oxford: Oxford University Press, 1992.

Crawford, James, ed. *The Rights of Peoples.* Oxford: Oxford University Press, 1988.

Dunn, John. *Modern Revolutions: An Introduction to the Analysis of a Political Phenomenon.* 2d ed. Cambridge: Cambridge University Press, 1989.

Fall, Bernard B., ed. *Ho Chi Minh on Revolution: Selected Writings, 1920–66.* New York: Praeger, 1967.

Lukes, Steven. *Marxism and Morality.* Oxford: Oxford University Press, 1985.

ROBESPIERRE, MAXIMILIEN

The most consistently radical of French revolutionary politicians, Robespierre (1758–1794) was the dominant figure during the Terror of 1793–1794. His downfall marked the end of the Revolution's most extreme and violent phase.

Born into a comfortably off legal family in Arras, northern France, Robespierre won a scholarship to a leading school in Paris, returning home in 1781 to practice law. He defended a handful of poor clients but spent most of his time in polite literary pursuits. His thinking was much influenced, then and later, by the writings of Jean-Jacques Rousseau. After writing radical pamphlets in the spring of 1789, he was elected to the Estates-General. When that body became the National Assembly in June, he became one of the most frequent speakers but was little heeded until 1791. He was even more assiduous in the Jacobin Club, soon the leading political circle in Paris, which proved to be his main power base throughout his revolutionary career. While fellow deputies derided the impracticality of Robespierre's opposition to the death penalty, slavery, and restrictions on popular political participation, his steady devotion to his principles and suspicion of those in power won him the nickname "the Incorruptible." Excluded from election to the subsequent Legislative Assembly by a law he had himself proposed, he was carried shoulder-high from the National Assembly on its last day by the Parisian populace.

During the Legislative Assembly (October 1791–September 1792), he devoted most of his political activity to the Jacobin Club, which his efforts had largely kept alive after its membership had split in July 1791. There he warned in vain of the perils of war against the Austrians, incurring the enmity of war's leading advocates, whom he called Girondins. Welcoming the overthrow of monarchy on August 10, 1792, he was elected to represent Paris in the Convention. In the Convention he argued for the execution of Louis XVI without a trial and was much execrated by the Girondins for his supposed dictatorial ambitions. In fact, he acquiesced only reluctantly in the purge of Girondins from the Convention on June 2, 1793, and later protected their supporters from prosecution.

Elected to the Committee of Public Safety on July 27, Robespierre soon became its main theoretical spokesman, defending the suspension of normal constitutional life until the return of peace and advocating resolute action against traitors. But he was alarmed by the de-Christianization that swept the country over the winter of 1793–1794, and he sought to restore religious practice in May 1794 with a very personal "Cult of the Supreme Being." Concerned lest indiscriminate Terror alienate more people than it punished, in March 1794 he orchestrated the execution of its leading advocates, the so-called Hebertistes. But by then the personal corruption of some who had warned him against terrorist excesses had disgusted him equally, and they too, including the redoubtable Georges Jacques Danton, were executed a few weeks later. Thus began the "great" Parisian Terror, whose necessity Robespierre defended to the last, and whose processes he accelerated with the notorious law of 22 Prairial (June 10), which deprived those accused before the Revolutionary Tribunal of defense counsel. Alarmed that any of them might fall victim to the impossible demands of Robespierre's republic of virtue, his fellow deputies and committee members turned against him. Outlawed on 9 Thermidor (July 28, 1794), Robespierre was guillotined without trial the next day.

In this period etching (1794), Maximilien Robespierre lies mortally wounded on a table in the anteroom of the Committee of Public Safety.

Although no more responsible than many others for the Terror, Robespierre prolonged it unrepentantly and was made a scapegoat by those who survived to dismantle it. His bloody association with the

Terror has always vitiated attempts to commend his earlier humanitarianism, commitment to social justice, and personal probity. He remains deeply controversial, but his admirers and detractors are curiously united in regarding him as the most complete personification of the French Revolution, a classic model (or warning) to all subsequent revolutionaries.

See also *French Revolution (1789–1815); Rousseau, Jean-Jacques; Terrorism.*

WILLIAM DOYLE

BIBLIOGRAPHY

Hampson, Norman. *The Life and Opinions of Maximilien Robespierre.* London: Duckworth, 1974.

Haydon, Colin, and William Doyle, eds. *Robespierre. History, Historiography and Literature.* Cambridge: Cambridge University Press, 1998.

Jordan, David P. *The Revolutionary Career of Maximilien Robespierre.* New York: Free Press, 1985.

Rude, George. *Robespierre. Portrait of a Revolutionary Democrat.* London: Collins, 1975.

Thompson, James M. *Robespierre.* Oxford: Blackwell, 1935.

ROMANIAN REVOLUTION (1989)

More than four decades of communist rule in Romania came to a violent end on December 22, 1989. On that day, the wave of popular rage that had started in the city of Timisoara, 250 miles northwest of the capital, reached its climax in Bucharest and in a matter of hours swept away Nicolae Ceausescu's dictatorship as well as the whole institutional structure of the one-party system.

COLLAPSE OF THE CEAUSESCU REGIME

The events in Romania should be seen within the broader international context *(see map, p. 141)*. After the spectacular collapse of the Berlin Wall on November 9, 1989, and the "Velvet Revolution" in Czechoslovakia, it became clear that the Soviet Union would not intervene to support crumbling communist regimes in eastern Europe. Moreover, the situation in Romania was explosive: the population was desperate, the economy was in shambles, and the dictatorial-personalist regime of Ceausescu and his wife Elena, based primarily on repression exerted by the secret police (the Securitate), was structurally fragile.

The Romanian Revolution actually started on December 15 in Timisoara, where a spontaneously formed crowd opposed the regime's attempt to evict Lászlo Tökés, a defiant pastor of the Reformed (Calvinist) Church, from his parish/residence. Despite the local authorities' threats, the crowd refused to leave the streets, and during the night of December 16–17 the city was virtually taken over by the anticommunist demonstrators. A religiously inspired act of civil disobedience had thus triggered a full-blown political rebellion against one of the most tightly controlled despotisms in the world.

On December 17, on orders from Ceausescu, security and armed forces cracked down on the Timisoara demonstrators. Tens were killed and hundreds wounded, but the revolt continued to gather momentum. Foreign news agencies and Western broadcasters immediately reported about the massacre going on in Romania. Convinced that the Timisoara uprising had been quelled, Ceausescu left Romania for a state visit to Iran. Far from having been defeated, the Timisoara freedom fighters basically took over the city, and the military withdrew into its barracks. Ceausescu's reactions during those hectic days showed how isolated he had become from his country's realities. A prisoner of his own cult, he trusted the Securitate's reassuring reports about the end of the uprising.

Back in Bucharest, Ceausescu made other abysmal blunders: on December 20 he addressed the nation on radio and television, vilifying the Timisoara revolt and calling the protesters "foreign agents" and "hooligans." He praised the secret police and the army and took personal responsibility for the repression, which he described as "legitimate defense of the people's socialist achievements." He threatened any would-be supporters of the Timisoara rebels with ruthless punishment. For many Romanians, revulsion and moral indignation became stronger than fear.

Ceausescu's ultimate error was to organize a huge demonstration of popular support for his rule. The tens of thousands of people herded by the Securitate and party hacks into Bucharest's main public square in front of Communist Party headquarters to acclaim Ceausescu on the morning of December 21 were a highly volatile crowd. Romanian and world television captured the tyrant's confusion and anger as the cheering multitude suddenly began to boo him. Whether the switch from simulated adulation to sincere, contagious abuse was initiated by secret police agents acting on instructions from higher-ups who had realized the imminent end of the regime, we may never know. At any rate, millions of viewers witnessed a large number of people chanting antidictatorial slogans on live television. Ceausescu tried to appease the crowd by promising a rise in the minimum wage, but this was too little and too late. Power had already slipped from the balcony of the Central Committee building to the street.

A sequence of revolutionary events followed: a series of student demonstrations in University Square, which went on through the morning of December 22 in spite of bloody repression; spontaneous anti-Ceausescu marches through the streets of Bucharest, in which hundreds of thousands participated; and the takeover of the television station with the help of army units that had switched sides and joined the popular uprising. The television building became the headquarters of the revolutionary drama, offering gripping reports of the ongoing events. Thus, the Romanian upheaval turned into a "tele-revolution." In spite of the bloody clashes between loyal army units and alleged terrorist commandos, a near-universal sense of hope and relief swept the country.

As soon as the Ceausescus fled the Central Committee building by helicopter, around 11 a.m. on December 22, hundreds of demonstrators seized the party headquarters. Several hours later, Romanian television announced that all the institutions of the old regime had been abolished and that power was held by a newly created body called the National Salvation Front. Its chairman was Ion Iliescu, a former party ideologue known for his refusal to endorse Ceausescu's most egregious measures. The National Salvation Front claimed to be an emanation of the revolutionary movement and pledged to establish full democracy in Romania.

BIRTH PANGS OF DEMOCRACY

By the beginning of 1990, however, disappointment and distrust in the new government had started to set in. Many criticized the Front's decision to become a political party as well as the resurrection among its leaders of former communist cadres.

The December revolution generated a number of mysteries, particularly about the capture and death of the Ceausescus and the provenance of the Front. Rather than a revolutionary tyrannicide, the trial and execution by firing squad of the Ceausescus on Christmas Day was pseudo-judicial. Ceausescu's refusal to plead guilty was linked to his belief that he had been demoted by a conspiracy led by his own military and secret police. Indeed, the Romanian Revolution was a blend of spontaneous revolt from below, conspiracy, and coup d'état.

From the early moments of the revolution, it was obvious that communism per se was dead as a system of government in Romania. But the party bureaucracy continued to hold positions of power. This "second echelon" closed ranks behind Iliescu and the Front, opposing the efforts of the newly formed democratic parties to initiate radical reforms. Not until the election of November 1996, which finally replaced Iliescu, did Romania enter on the path of full democratization.

See also *East European Revolutions of 1989.*

Vladimir Tismaneanu

BIBLIOGRAPHY

Calinescu, Matei, and Vladimir Tismaneanu. "The 1989 Revolution and Romania's Future." In *Romania After Tyranny.* Edited by Daniel N. Nelson. Boulder, Colo.: Westview Press, 1992.

Linz, Juan, and Alfred Stepan. *Problems of Democratic Transition and Consolidation: Southern Europe, South America, and Post-Communist Europe.* Baltimore, Md.: Johns Hopkins University Press, 1996.

Ratesh, Nestor. *Romania: The Entangled Revolution.* New York: Praeger, 1991.

Shafir, Michael. "Ceausescu's Overthrow: Popular Uprising or Moscow-Guided Conspiracy?" *Report on Eastern Europe* (January 19, 1990): 15–19.

Tismaneanu, Vladimir. "The Quasi-Revolution and Its Discontents: Emerging Political Pluralism in Romania." *East European Politics and Societies* 7 (spring 1993): 309–348.

Verdery, Katherine, and Gail Kligman. "Romania After Ceausescu: Post-Communist Communism?" In *Eastern Europe in Revolution.* Edited by Ivo Banac. Ithaca, N.Y.: Cornell University Press, 1992.

ROUSSEAU, JEAN-JACQUES

Perhaps to no other French writer has so much political influence and inspiration been ascribed as to Rousseau (1712–1778). Revered as the champion of democracy, denounced as the theoretician of the totalitarian state, even credited with an important apology of aristocracy, Rousseau produced texts that remain today as emotionally gripping, yet intellectually ambiguous, as when they were published. The principal concepts associated with his name are a "social contract" among citizens, legitimizing government; a "general will," in which all citizens participate; an innate equality of men, which the state must respect; a critique of the ethical value of private property; and a civic mission of educating the citizenry to "virtue."

Rousseau passed abruptly from bohemian obscurity to literary fame when he published the *First Discourse* (1750), on the question of "whether the reestablishment of the arts and sciences has contributed to purifying morals." Rather than the predictable praise of civilization, Rousseau put forth a savage indictment of European society as denatured, effeminate, and degenerate, a set of denunciations that he turned into a posture of moral superiority from which to castigate the monarchy in the name of simple, primitive virtue and to call for violent measures of purification. The *Second Discourse* (1754), on the origins of inequality, consecrated his new identity as the "sage of Europe." In that essay, equating technical progress and artistic refinement with moral decay, he presented an original theory of how the means of production shaped not only man's economic life but his political and private existence as well.

"Man is born free, everywhere he is in chains," Rousseau proclaimed in the *Social Contract* (1762), his major political work. Rousseau attempted to describe what kind of state

Jean-Jacques Rousseau

would be legitimate and how it could be achieved. Rousseau's ideal state constituted a "moral being," a true body politic, absorbing its citizenry like cells in the human body. This unified state would have but a single source of motivation, the general will, and the citizen's virtue would consist of internalizing it: "Each man is virtuous when his private will conforms totally to the General Will" (Oeuvres, *completes,* 1964, 3:254). Aiming to fuse religion, patriotism, and self-interest into one set of beliefs, thus eliminating the fragmentation and contradictions inherent in European societies, Rousseau would substitute adoration of the state for traditional ethical values. Citizens would be obliged to swear a "civil profession of faith," and if someone betrayed that credo, "let him be put to death" (3:468). The tone of his ideal polity was resolutely virile; women were to be strictly relegated to a domestic, subservient mode.

The "common will" was not to be ascertained by elections, or party politics, or other democratic procedures. Rather, it could be voiced only by a superior being, the "legislator," a foreigner to the state who would see to it that the people were "instituted" (a form of political, religious, and social conditioning) to virtue, as Moses had instituted the Jews or Lycurgus the Spartans.

Rousseau applied his ideas to two real European peoples, the Corsicans (in 1764) and the Poles (in 1772), for whom he created constitutions. In both instances his advice was largely consistent with the principles of the social contract, insisting on the necessity for the nation to turn its back to the world and form a self-absorbed entity, totally engrossed in its own exalted devotion to the body politic.

Rousseau's ideas, as well as his posture of virtuous accusation, were assumed and made use of during the French Revolution by leaders of opposing factions. Although he was cited as an authority by monarchists and moderate deputies alike, perhaps his most important disciples were Maximilien Robespierre, Louis-Antoine-Léon Saint-Just, and numerous other Jacobin leaders, who described themselves as the legislator and constantly invoked the authority of Rousseau.

Because of Rousseau's insistence on man's virtually total malleability, his distrust of representative democracy, and his espousal of manipulation in the interests of civic virtue, he has been charged with laying the intellectual groundwork for the modern totalitarian state.

See also *French Revolution (1789–1815); Robespierre, Maximilien.*

Carol Blum

BIBLIOGRAPHY

Cobban, Alfred. *Rousseau and the Modern State.* Hamden, Conn.: Archon, 1964.

Cranston, Maurice. *Jean-Jacques: The Early Life and Work of Jean-Jacques Rousseau, 1712–1754.* Chicago: University of Chicago Press, 1991.

Masters, Roger. *The Political Philosophy of Rousseau.* Princeton, N.J.: Princeton University Press, 1968.

Starobinski, Jean. *Jean-Jacques Rousseau, Transparency and Obstruction.* Chicago: University of Chicago Press, 1988.

Talmon, J. L. *The Origins of Totalitarian Democracy.* New York: Praeger, 1960.

RUSSIAN DECEMBRIST REVOLT (1825)

The so-called Decembrist Revolt, named for the month in which it was carried out, was characteristic of the conspiratorial leftism of the Restoration period all over Europe. As in other contemporary "secret societies"—such as the Greek Etaireia and the Carbonari in Italy—most of the Russian rebels were liberal and radical army officers and veterans of the Napoleonic Wars. Many of the European conspiratorial organizations had evolved from Masonic lodges. Their frustration with the conservative politics of the post-1815 period led the veterans to attempt a series of revolts and coups all across Europe in the decade after Napoleon's defeat, of which the Russian revolt was a curious and quixotic example.

When Tsar Alexander I died on November 19, 1825, he left behind a chaotic situation. Having no children, he should have been succeeded by Constantine, the older of his two brothers. But Constantine had (semisecretly) renounced the throne, and the heir apparent became the unpopular youngest brother, Nicholas. By 1825 dissatisfied Russian army officers had been reacting to the slow death of Alexander's liberal professions for almost a decade. The first real conspiratorial organization was the so-called Union of Salvation, founded early in 1816 to further a vague constitutionalism and to press for the emancipation of the serfs. The original members were Alexander Muraviev, Nikita Muraviev, Prince Sergei Trubetskoi, Ivan Iakushkin, and the Muraviev-Apostol brothers, Matvei and Sergei. These aristocratic and liberal officers were soon joined by a very different sort of man: Pavel Pestel, who was much more radical and has sometimes been characterized by historians as a "despotic visionary." Pestel's father was a middle-class bureaucrat of German origin who had worked his way up in the Russian service to become governor general of Siberia. Like the other Decembrists, Pestel had received an education strongly marked by progressive French thought: Charles de Montesquieu, Jean-Jacques Rousseau, Destutt de Tracy, Cesare Beccaria, and Voltaire.

Pestel's draft constitution for the Union of Salvation, marked by secrecy and centralization, split the organization and led to its demise. The struggle between moderates and radicals continued to divide its successor, the Union of Welfare, which lasted only until 1821. Pestel carried on, founding the Southern Society, whose ruling troika declared the organization's intent "to overthrow the throne by decisive revolutionary means, and if necessary eliminate all those who represent obstacles to the establishment of a republican form of government," a not very subtle declaration of their willingness to commit regicide. Their extreme program was never accepted by the northern moderates, who favored a limited and federal monarchy, with rather heavy property qualifications for voting, rather than Pestel's Jacobin republic. On December 10, 1825, it became known in St. Petersburg that Constantine had definitely renounced the throne and that the army was to take the oath of allegiance to Nicholas. An inept coup attempt ensued on December 14. The northern insurgents—ultimately numbering only a few thousand—were deserted by their designated leader, Trubetskoi. After the insurgents had stood for hours on the Senate Square in St. Petersburg, Nicholas ordered it to be cleared by gunfire. Casualties were heavy, and the tragic and inept rebellion in the north came to an end then and there.

Due to the distances involved, the rebellion in the south took several months to defeat, but it never constituted a serious threat to the government. Numerous death sentences were handed down, but Nicholas commuted all but five. Pestel, the poet Kondratii Ryleev, Sergei Muraviev-Apostol, Mikhail Bestuzhev-Riumin, and Petr Kakhovsky were hanged. One hundred twenty-one others were sent to Siberia, and more than a hundred suffered lesser punishments. Despite the ineptitude of the rebellion, it was of enormous importance in Russian history. The cult of the Decembrists dominated left-wing thinking for generations and became in effect the founding myth of the Russian revolutionary movement.

See also *European Revolutions of 1820.*

Abbott Gleason

BIBLIOGRAPHY

Eidel'man, Natan. *Conspiracy against the Tsar: A Portrait of the Decembrists.* Moscow: State Mutual Book and Periodical Service, 1985.

Lotman, Iu. M. "The Decembrist in Everyday Life." In *The Semiotics of Russian Culture.* Edited by Iu. M. Lotman and B. A. Uspensky. Ann Arbor: University of Michigan Press, 1984.

Mazour, Anatole. *The First Russian Revolution 1825.* Berkeley: University of California Press, 1937. Reprinted by Stanford University Press, 1961.

Raeff, Marc. *The Decembrist Movement.* Englewood Cliffs, N.J.: Prentice-Hall, 1966.

Zetlin, Michael. *The Decembrists.* New York: International Universities Press, 1958.

RUSSIAN REVOLUTION OF 1905

In 1905 ordinary Russians rose in a disconnected series of strikes, demonstrations, and insurrections that transformed the autocratic monarchy of Nicholas II (1894–1917) into a semi-constitutional monarchy. Though no fundamental social changes occurred as a result of the events and power remained essentially in the hands of the monarch and his bureaucracy, the term *revolution* has been applied to the events of 1905 both because of the violence and disorder that threatened the state and the shift in the type of monarchy that ruled Russia. Vladimir Ilyich Lenin's definition of a "revolutionary situation" as the moment when the old ruling classes can no longer govern in the old way and the ruled classes no longer are willing to be ruled in the same way fits neatly the traumatic events of 1905. Labor and peasant unrest joined with upper- and middle-class political discontent briefly in the fall to create a national movement for social and political change, the first on such a scale in Russia's history.

CRISIS AT THE TOP

Autocracy is a form of government in which all power resides in a single person who has no authority above or equal to him or her. In such a system of unlimited executive power the abilities of the ruler are fundamental to the success or failure of the state. Russia's misfortune in 1905 was to be governed by a relatively weak and indecisive man, Nicholas II, who deeply distrusted many of his advisers, appointed people more for their loyalty to him than for their competence, and was determined to prevent any infringement of his autocratic powers. When liberal nobles, middle-class businessmen, or other members of educated society expressed their opinions publicly or organized to defend their interests, the government clamped down on them. What had once been revered as the sacred principle of autocracy appeared to twentieth-century society to be a system of government based on arbitrariness, irresponsibility, and incompetence. Increasingly, the government lost its authority, and the tsar was forced to rely on naked power enforced by his troops.

CRISIS AT THE BOTTOM

Through the 1890s the state-financed industrialization drive brought hundreds of thousands of peasants into the working class, but since the workers lacked legal trade unions or the right to strike, many labor problems escalated into bloody confrontations with the state. The radical intelligentsia, particularly the Social Democrats, formed propaganda circles to teach workers their Marxist vision of class struggle against autocracy and capitalism, led protest marches, and organized strikes. In 1895 there were only sixty-eight strikes in all of Russia; by 1903 there were 550, and they were more violent, better organized, and more likely to result in a victory for labor. In the first years of the twentieth century, general strikes of workers in Baku, Batumi, Tiflis, Rostov, and a number of cities in Ukraine were paralleled by an active student movement and massive peasant uprisings in southern Russia, Tambov, Saratov, and Georgia. Government troops were called out more than 650 times to quell labor conflicts in the first years of the new century.

On January 27 (February 9; Russia's Julian calendar was thirteen days behind the Western Gregorian calendar), 1904, Japan launched a surprise attack on Russia's Pacific fleet lying at Port Arthur in China. After a brief patriotic respite from social conflicts, Russia plunged once again into unrest, as the army suffered repeated defeats in the Far East. On January 9 (22), 1905, 200,000 workers, led by a priest, Father Georgii Gapon, marched peacefully to the tsar's Winter Palace in the capital, St. Petersburg. Soldiers fired on the crowd, killing more than a hundred people. This event, known thereafter as "Bloody Sunday," radicalized the public and dissolved lingering affection for the tsar. In the next few weeks disturbances broke out throughout the country. More than 400,000 workers went on strike in Russia in January 1905 alone.

The tsar limply attempted to placate the opposition with mild reforms, but as further catastrophes in the Pacific war eroded his position, he was forced to make greater concessions. Strikes erupted on May Day. Popular uprisings took place in Warsaw, the Baltic region, and western Georgia (Guria), where social grievances were amplified by national resentments. In June sailors on the Battleship Potemkin mutinied, and in October a general strike throughout Russia linked the labor movement with protests by the liberal middle classes. With the monarchy tottering before this cross-class national opposition, Nicholas II heeded the advice of his able councilor Sergei Witte and issued a constitutional decree, the "October Manifesto," which granted his subjects civil freedoms of speech, conscience, assembly, and association and an elected State Duma with the power to confirm all laws.

The Russian army's disastrous losses in the Far East were a factor precipitating the 1905 revolution, but troops from the Far East, pictured above, were also instrumental in quelling the revolution.

With this act, forced upon him by the people in rebellion, Nicholas limited his own powers and established a kind of "constitutional autocracy." At the same time he also succeeded in fracturing the revolutionary opposition, for the more moderate middle classes and much of the peasantry and working class accepted, at least for a time, the promise that a constitutional order would ameliorate their situation. Part of the working class, however, continued to agitate for more radical social and political change. Soviets (councils) of workers' deputies were elected in St. Petersburg, Moscow, Baku, Tiflis, and other cities. But the tsar, who had concluded peace with Japan in August 1905, could now rely on loyal troops from the Far East. Abandoned by other social groups, the isolated worker leaders were arrested, and when radical workers in Moscow organized a defense of their district in December, tsarist troops brutally suppressed their insurrection. Some 700 were killed and 2,000 wounded. In the next two years special punitive expeditions crushed rebels in various parts of the empire.

The Revolution of 1905 gave Russia a more representative political system and allowed civil society to develop somewhat autonomously from the state. Government was less arbitrary than it had been before 1905, and people of influence had greater access to politics. Workers were permitted to form trade unions, and peasants were encouraged to create their own individual farmsteads out of communal landholdings. Yet power remained in the hands of upper-level bureaucrats and the landed nobility, and the tsar repeatedly undermined his own constitution. On June 3, 1907, he severely limited the franchise so that men with property were given disproportionate representation in the Duma. The 1905 revolution is often called the "dress rehearsal for the revolution of 1917"; its greatest legacy was the deeply divided society that emerged from it.

See also *Russian Revolution of 1917*.

Ronald Grigor Suny

BIBLIOGRAPHY

Ascher, Abraham. *The Revolution of 1905.* 2 vols. Stanford, Calif.: Stanford University Press, 1988, 1992.

Engelstein, Laura. *Moscow, 1905: Working-Class Organization and Political Conflict.* Stanford, Calif.: Stanford University Press, 1982.

Sablinsky, Walter. *The Road to Bloody Sunday: Father Gapon and the St. Petersburg Massacre of 1905.* Princeton, N.J.: Princeton University Press, 1976.

Schwarz, Solomon M. *The Russian Revolution of 1905: The Workers' Movement and the Formation of Bolshevism and Menshevism.* Chicago and London: University of Chicago Press, 1967.

Surh, Gerald D. *1905 in St. Petersburg: Labor, Society, and Revolution.* Stanford, Calif.: Stanford University Press, 1989.

Verner, Andrew M. *The Crisis of Russian Autocracy: Nicholas II and the 1905 Revolution.* Princeton, N.J.: Princeton University Press, 1990.

Weinberg, Robert. *The Revolution of 1905 in Odessa: Blood on the Steps.* Bloomington: Indiana University Press, 1993.

Wynn, Charters. *Workers, Strikes, and Pogroms: The Donbass-Dnepr Bend in Late Imperial Russia, 1870–1905.* Princeton, N.J.: Princeton University Press, 1992.

RUSSIAN REVOLUTION OF 1917

In 1917 the peoples of the Russian Empire experienced two revolutions, first the February/March overthrow of the tsar and second the October/November insurrection against the Provisional Government that had come to power at the beginning of the year. Both of these events, the one labeled democratic by its liberal supporters and bourgeois by the socialists and the second reviled as a "coup d'état" by its opponents and lauded as the "Great October Socialist Revolution" by those who seized power, occurred largely in the capital city of Petrograd (St. Petersburg). But the effects of each of the revolutions were felt outside the capital in a ripple of successive revolutions—a crescendo of peasant revolts that reached its zenith in 1918; nationalist and separatist movements by non-Russian peoples that created independent states on Russia's periphery; and counterrevolutionary reactions by those who lost in February and October that led to the Russian Civil War, which raged into the early 1920s.

THE ROAD TO FEBRUARY

The first revolutionary crisis in 1917 had its origins in a deep social and political polarization in Russian society that intensified in the first decades of the twentieth century. The great majority (more than 80 percent) of the tsar's subjects were peasants, living in relatively poor villages and suffering from land shortages, periodic hunger, high incidence of disease and early mortality, and the burdens of taxation, rents, and military recruitment. Closely related to peasants were the factory workers and artisans, many of whom migrated back to the villages seasonally. They lived in squalid tenements or hovels and worked long hours in dangerous conditions. Though numbering only a few million at the turn of the century, workers were highly concentrated in large factories close to the center of Petersburg, Moscow, and other important cities. The middle and upper classes, as well as the urban population of Russia, were not only materially better off and more literate, educated, and socially mobile than the peasants, but lived under a different code of law and enjoyed privileges that the ordinary villagers did not. Between the top and bottom of Russian society was the intelligentsia, a socially mixed group of educated people who saw as their mission the salvation of the Russian people. Through the nineteenth century politically engaged Russian intellectuals gravitated from liberalism and moderation toward revolutionary socialism, at first oriented toward the peasants and later, by the 1890s, increasingly focused on the urban workers.

Marxism was particularly influential among radical intellectuals in the early years of the twentieth century. It provided a sociological and economic framework for Russian activists, a view of the way the world worked under capitalism, and the European future toward which Russia was headed. Unlike the propeasant socialists or populists, who eventually formed the Socialist Revolutionary Party, the Marxists believed that Russia could not avoid industrialization and capitalism and had to pass through two successive revolutions, a bourgeois-democratic revolution, like those experienced by the Americans in 1776 and the French in 1789, and a proletarian-socialist revolution in which the working people would come to power to build a new social order, socialism. In 1903 the principal Marxist organization, the Russian Social Democratic Workers' Party, split into two rival factions. The moderate Mensheviks were usually more willing to work with other democratic parties, like the populists and liberals, whereas the more radical Bolsheviks, led by Vladimir Ilyich Lenin, generally favored a more rapid transition to the socialist revolution.

Beginning in the late 1880s Russia underwent a rapid industrialization, which increased the number of workers and urban dwellers but in many regions strained the peasants' already precarious situation. Famine struck much of Russia in 1891–1892, in part the result of the state's policy of exporting grain to earn capital for industrial investment. The tsarist government's inability to deal with developing social crises and its reluctance to consider serious political reforms induced a progressive alienation of many intellectuals and political activists away from the autocracy. Tsar Nicholas II (1894–1917) rejected appeals for a government more responsive to educated public opinion as "senseless dreams," and though in 1905 he was forced by mass uprisings to concede a representative assembly (duma) and civil rights to his people, in the next decade he resisted any further encroachments on his autocratic powers.

Many historians, following an initially Marxist approach, have argued that the final crisis of tsarism was in fact caused by the growing contradiction between the social transformations in Russia and the unreformed autocratic state. While the transformations were creating a more industrial, capitalist, and urban society, in which the lower and middle classes insisted on greater political participation, the state sought to monopolize political power and continued to rely for its dwindling support on ever narrower circles in the landed nobility, the Orthodox clergy, and the upper bureaucrats. Autocracy, which acted as a fetter on the further development of capitalism and bourgeois society, eventually had to give way.

Other historians have challenged the pessimistic vision that tsarism was doomed by capitalist industrialization. They noted the rapid economic growth of the 1890s, the new constitutional regime established after 1905, the land reform initiated by Prime Minister Peter Stolypin (1906–1911), and the renewed industrial expansion after 1910. Still other scholars have eschewed social interpretations altogether and emphasized instead the personal weakness of the last tsar, his reliance on his wife, Alexandra, and her adviser, the dissipated "holy man" Gregory Rasputin. A major dispute has divided those who see the revolutionary crisis as already prefigured in the years before World War I (1914–1918) and those who consider the losses in the war to have been a necessary factor in bringing down the autocracy.

Most analysts argue for a refined social interpretation rather than one based on personality and politics alone. In Russia the social divide between the autocracy and society was already wide in the late nineteenth century, and instead of cross-class harmony, industrialization created even greater social polarization. As society withdrew its support from the autocratic state, the top and bottom of society pulled apart, with workers becoming increasingly hostile toward both government and moderate socialist forces. Strikes and political demonstrations increased in the years before the war, reaching the levels of the 1905 revolution. World War I temporarily stirred up a degree of patriotism, but with the devastating defeats of 1915–1916 the gulf between the state and society widened. The war, most importantly, was the moment when millions of peasants were turned into soldiers, given guns, and shown that a wider world existed beyond the edges of the village. These men, who desired nothing more than to return to their farms, would play a decisive role in both 1917 revolutions.

REVOLUTION FROM BELOW

The February/March revolution (the Russian [Julian] calendar was thirteen days behind the Western [Gregorian] calendar) began on February 23 (March 8, International Women's Day) with working-class women demanding bread in the cold, dark streets of Petrograd. They moved from shops to factories, shaming the men to come out and join their strike. Within days hundreds of thousands of Petrograd workers were in the streets, and when Cossacks and ordinary soldiers refused to fire on the crowds, the strike turned into a revolution. The tsar abdicated, as did his brother, Grand Duke Mikhail, and the monarchy came to an end.

On March 1 (14), middle-class members of the Duma formed a Provisional Government, headed by Prince

Tsar Nicholas II (seated in the center) and Tsarina Alexandra (standing directly behind Nicholas) pose with the royal family and entourage.

Georgii Lvov and including leaders of the major liberal party, the Kadets (Constitutional Democrats), the conservative Octobrists, and the proindustrial Progressivists. At the same time, workers and soldiers formed their own representative bodies, the soviets (councils) of workers' and soldiers' deputies, for though their leaders were unwilling to take power on their own, they were suspicious of the intentions of the "bourgeois" members of the Provisional Government. Thus, within days of the women's strike, Russia had not one unchallenged government but "dual power," two competing authorities. One represented the middle and upper classes and the military officers; the other was obeyed by the great mass of workers and soldiers.

In the first political crisis of the revolutionary year it quickly became clear that the Provisional Government held only formal power, and that actual power, the ability to call people out into the streets or to send soldiers to the front or workers back to the factories, belonged to the Petrograd Soviet. The famous "Order Number One" of the Soviet, which called for soldiers to form committees in their units and to obey orders only if they were sanctioned by the Soviet, undercut the authority of officers. In April a serious disagreement broke out between the leaders of the Petrograd Soviet, who favored concluding the war as soon as possible based on a policy of no territorial acquisitions or reparations, and the foreign minister, Paul Miliukov, who insisted on Russia's imperial claims to Constantinople and the Dardanelles. When workers and soldiers poured into the streets, shouting "Down with the Provisional Government," the foreign minister was forced to back down. Within weeks Miliukov resigned, and Lvov called upon the Soviet to appoint several of its members to a broadened "coalition" government.

The moderate socialist leaders of the Soviet, principally Mensheviks and Socialist Revolutionaries, were reluctant to join a "bourgeois" government at first, but their growing sense that anarchy or a renewed threat from antidemocratic forces would overwhelm the fragile government convinced them that they had to join the liberals in power. In the next six months the various coalition governments were unable either to end the world war or to alleviate the social divisions in Russian society. To their political detriment, the moderate socialists were forced to defend the policies of the coalition, and in doing so they progressively lost many of their supporters among the workers and soldiers. The government was unable to meet workers' demands for "workers' control," a policy of allowing workers to supervise the owners and managers of industries, or to satisfy their cries for higher wages at a moment of inflationary spiral. While landlords fought to keep their properties, peasants demanded a radical land reform and often took matters in their own hands, burning the manor houses and redistributing the land among themselves. The Socialist Revolutionary leader, Victor Chernov, was powerless as minister of agriculture to implement programs that might have pleased the peasants.

THE ROAD TO OCTOBER

While the government wavered, the Bolsheviks won majorities in the factory committees and successfully agitated against the war at the fronts. Lenin, who had returned to Russia from exile in Switzerland in April, staked out a radical program for transferring all power to the soviets, ending the war, and moving the revolution rapidly into a socialist phase. The Bolsheviks were the only major party that provided a clear alternative to the government and their moderate socialist allies. As the war exacerbated the economic collapse within the country and radicalized the soldiers, most of whom no longer wanted to fight in a futile conflict, the most radical party in the country, the Bolsheviks, reaped the whirlwind.

To please the Western Allies and contribute to the war effort against the Central Powers, Minister of War Alexander Kerensky launched a disastrous offensive against the enemy in June. As news of Russian defeats reached the capital, workers, sailors, and soldiers demonstrated against the war and the government, even calling on the Petrograd Soviet to take power in its own name. The moderate socialists refused, and at one point the crowd seized Chernov, who had to be rescued by the newly minted Bolshevik Leon Trotsky. In the confusion of the "July Days" (July 3–5 [16–18]), militant elements supporting the Bolsheviks pushed to seize power. Lenin believed that taking power by force was premature at this point and opposed the radical move. When order was restored by troops loyal to the government and soviet, Lenin was forced to go into hiding in Finland. Lvov resigned, and Kerensky formed a new coalition government.

Through the summer of 1917 workers and soldiers increasingly supported the Bolshevik program for a rapid end to the war, "workers' control" of industry, and "All Power to the Soviets!" Liberal and conservative forces became more wary of the lower classes and called for an authoritarian government to restore order. Briefly, the hopes of the Kadets, army officers, and much of the middle and upper classes fell on the ponderous Gen. Lavr Kornilov, who called for discipline, restoration of the death penalty in the rear, and curtailing the powers of the soviets and revolutionary committees. When he marched on Petrograd, believing he had the support of Kerensky, Kornilov met resistance from armed workers and soldiers and was arrested. But in the aftermath of this "mutiny," the lower classes moved swiftly toward the Bolsheviks, electing them the majority party in both the Petrograd and Moscow Soviets by early September.

Preparations began for convening the Second Congress of Soviets, at which, it was believed, a majority of Bolsheviks and their allies, most importantly the Left Socialist Revolutionaries, would proclaim "Soviet Power" and eliminate Kerensky's government. Even before he secretly returned from hiding, Lenin urged his followers to take power immediately and not wait for the congress. He feared that Kerensky would move first against the Bolsheviks. "History will not forgive us," he told his comrades, "if we do not take power now." In the second half of October, the Military-Revolutionary Committee of the Petrograd Soviet, led by Trotsky, began establishing its authority over the garrisons of the city. On the morning of October 24 (November 6), Kerensky made his move to suppress the Bolsheviks and prevent the insurrection that everyone knew was coming. But in the crucial hours the prime minister found his support weak or nonexistent. Even the Cossacks deserted him, and only the Women's Battalion of Death stood between the Soviet forces and the government in the Winter Palace. Though workers did not actively participate in the insurrection, the Bolsheviks found the military muscle to take power. By dawn on October 25 (November 7) the city was in the hands of the Military-Revolutionary Committee, and Lenin went before the Second Congress of Soviets and declared that power had passed to the soviets.

STAYING ALIVE

The October insurrection eliminated the middle and upper classes from political participation. Soviet Power meant that only working people would be eligible to elect people to the new representative councils. When the moderate socialists,

Bystanders scramble for cover as government machine gunners fire at revolutionists in Petrograd during the "July Days" uprising (July 3–5, 1917).

the Mensheviks and Right Socialist Revolutionaries, protested the Bolshevik seizure of power and walked out of the congress, they essentially left the Bolsheviks and Left Socialist Revolutionaries to form a new government. Lenin hoped to have the Bolsheviks form a one-party government, even though the workers, soldiers, and party activists who supported the October Revolution in fact preferred a multiparty government of the left. Within a month, however, the Bolshevik leader was forced to concede significant seats to the Left Socialist Revolutionaries, and until March 1918 Soviet Russia had a left socialist coalition government.

The Bolsheviks came to power in 1917 largely because their program to form a lower-class government, end the war, and give the land to the peasants won significant support by late summer and fall, as society pulled apart and confidence in the Provisional Government evaporated. Yet the new Soviet government remained weak and insecure outside of Petrograd, Moscow, and a few other large cities. In November 1917 elections were held to a Constituent Assembly, a kind of founding congress for the new republic. The Bolsheviks failed to win a majority, taking only 24 percent of the votes cast, while the Right Socialist Revolutionaries emerged with the largest plurality, with 40 percent. But Lenin did not intend to surrender his hard-won position, and after allowing a single day's meeting (January 5 [18], 1918), the Soviet government dispersed the Constituent Assembly, Russia's most freely elected parliamentary body until the early 1990s.

By this act, even more than the seizure of power in October, the Leninists declared war on all those forces that had supported the first revolution of 1917 but not the second. Almost immediately after October, Socialist Revolutionaries attempted an armed attack on the Bolshevik government. Cossacks in southern Russia rallied around Kornilov and other generals to launch what would become a full-fledged civil war. In Transcaucasia, Ukraine, Belorussia, Central Asia, Finland, and the Baltic region, non-Russian nationalist (and often socialist) parties seceded from Russia and formed independent states supported either by the Germans, Turks, or the Western Allies. Lenin's government was opposed by enemies that ranged from reactionary monarchists to liberals, moderate socialists, and peasant anarchists. The Germans occupied Ukraine, Belorussia, and the Baltic region; the Ottoman Turks moved into Transcaucasia; and Britain, France, Japan, and the United States sent armies to Russia to bring her back into the war or overthrow the Bolsheviks.

Against all odds, Lenin and the Bolsheviks managed to defeat their opponents and establish the Soviet state. The Soviet government immediately withdrew Russia from the war and decreed that the peasants should take over and redistribute the land. Lenin and Joseph Stalin, the commissar of nationalities in the Soviet government, decreed national self-determination and full cultural and political rights for the non-Russian peoples of the Soviet state. Even though workers soon found themselves unemployed as the industrial economy nearly shut down and many grew disaffected from the Bolsheviks, most of them still supported Soviet power. Soldiers "voted with their feet" and deserted the fronts, yet most continued to back the Bolsheviks. Peasants were pleased by the Bolshevik land decree that gave them the land outright without compensation to the former owners, and they carried out a radically egalitarian repartition of the land. But when during the Civil War the Bolsheviks, now calling themselves Communists, forced peasants to give up their grain to feed the Red Army and the cities, peasants turned against the Soviets. Caught between the Reds, who had given them the land, and the anti-Bolshevik Whites, who would take it back, peasants chose the Communists as the lesser of the two evils.

Building a centralized party organization, a five-million man Red Army headed by Trotsky, and broad support in the central regions of Russia, the Communists won the Civil War by early 1921. But to win the war and bring the non-Russian territories back into the new state the Communists did not hesitate to use violence and terror. As terrible atrocities occurred on both sides, much of the democratic promise of the revolution of 1917 was lost.

See also *Lenin, Vladimir Ilyich; Russian Revolution of 1905.*

Ronald Grigor Suny

BIBLIOGRAPHY

Acton, Edward, Vladimir Iu. Cherniaev, and William G. Rosenberg, eds. *Critical Companion to the Russian Revolution, 1914–1921.* London: Arnold, 1997.

Figes, Orlando. *A People's Tragedy: A History of the Russian Revolution.* New York: Viking, 1996.

Galili, Ziva. *The Menshevik Leaders in the Russian Revolution: Social Realities and Political Strategies.* Princeton, N.J.: Princeton University Press, 1989.

Hasegawa, Tyoshi. *The February Revolution: Petrograd 1917.* Seattle: University of Washington Press, 1981.

Rabinowitch, Alexander. *The Bolsheviks Come to Power: The Revolution of 1917 in Petrograd.* New York: W.W. Norton, 1976.

Rosenberg, William G. *The Liberals in the Russian Revolution, 1917–1921.* Princeton, N.J.: Princeton University Press, 1974.

Smith, S. A. *Red Petrograd: Revolution in the Factories 1917–18.* Cambridge: Cambridge University Press, 1983.

Steinberg, Mark D., and Vladimir M. Khrustalev. *The Fall of the Romanovs: Political Dreams and Personal Struggles in a Time of Revolution.* New Haven, Conn.: Yale University Press, 1995.

Suny, Ronald, and Arthur Adams, eds. *The Russian Revolution and Bolshevik Victory: Visions and Revisions.* Lexington, Mass.: D.C. Heath, 1990.

Wildman, Allan K. *The End of the Russian Imperial Army.* 2 vols. Princeton, N.J.: Princeton University Press, 1980, 1987.

RUSSIAN-UKRAINIAN COSSACK AND PEASANT REVOLTS (1606–1775)

From the sixteenth through the mid-nineteenth century, most Russians were serfs—peasants or townsmen who owed permanent obligations to their manor lords. But on the southern frontier of the Russian Empire, between the Black and Caspian Seas, lived free military communities of Tatar horsemen known as *cossacks.* Over the centuries, runaway serfs from Lithuania, Poland, and Russia joined the cossack bands. The Russian and Polish states often drew on the cossacks to fight as special detachments in their armies. In addition, as the Polish and Russian Empires expanded, the central authorities aimed to subject the cossack territories to regular conscription, taxation, and bureaucratic rule.

On several occasions, Russian and Ukrainian cossacks revolted in efforts to throw off the control of state officials. These revolts always came after major wars, when the state had been raising its demands for taxes and military service and when the armies were most exhausted. Cossack revolts gained wide support among townsmen, peasants, minor nobles, clergymen, and others with grievances against the central state, the upper nobility, and the bureaucracy. The revolts never aimed to end tsarist rule; rather, they sought to replace the current ruler with the "true" tsar (a minor noble or cossack leader posing as a savior) or to punish and eliminate nobles and officials who were interfering with the tsar's supposed true wishes to provide for the welfare of his people.

The revolt led by Ivan Bolotnikov in 1606–1607 took place in the "Time of Troubles," when the succession to the Russian throne was hotly contested. Bolotnikov supported the claims of the pretender known to history as the False Dmitri. Bolotnikov's revolt attracted not only broad lower-class support but also nobles who supported Dmitri against other claimants to the throne. Bolotnikov gained victory after victory in southern and central Russia, eventually bringing a popular force to the walls of Moscow, where it laid siege to the capital. During the siege, however, Bolotnikov's noble allies decided that it was far too risky to remain allied with a popular rebellion that could later turn against them as well. They defected, sealing the fate of the rebellion.

In 1648 the cossack leader Bogdan Khmelnitsky led a revolt against Polish control of the Ukraine. Khmelnitsky enjoyed great initial success, seizing the city of Lviv before the Polish army regrouped. After several years of war, Khmelnitsky made a pact with the Russian tsar. In return for pledging the cossacks' loyalty to the tsar, Khmelnitsky received Russian support for cossack independence from Poland. The result was, in effect, to deliver the eastern Ukraine from Polish to Russian rule.

Less than thirty years later, another cossack leader, Stenka Razin, waged similarly spectacular campaigns. After repelling Persian efforts to expand northward, Razin turned his armies against Russia. In 1670–1671, peasants and townsmen from across southern Russia joined his campaign against the noble landlords and state bureaucrats who served the tsar. Razin captured several major cities in the southern Volga region before he was defeated and executed. For centuries he remained one of Russia's most dazzling heroic figures, the subject of poetry by Alexander Pushkin and of an opera by Mikhail Glinka.

A smaller cossack uprising, led by Kondrati Bulavin, developed in 1707–1708. Then in 1773–1775 the last great rebellion arose, led by Emilian Pugachev. Pugachev presented himself as the "missing" Tsar Peter III, who had in fact been assassinated by Tsarina Catherine the Great in 1762. Pugachev's revolt was perhaps the most revolutionary of all the cossack and peasant rebellions of the seventeenth and eighteenth centuries. He declared the abolition of serfdom, and—gathering cossacks, peasants, factory workers and miners in the Urals, and conservative clergy—he planned to replace Catherine the Great. Pugachev's revolt spread widely throughout southern and central Russia, but Catherine's professional armies prevailed, and Pugachev's revolt was brutally suppressed.

These rebellions reveal many of the paradoxes of Russian politics. The cossacks' military organization and history of freedom inspired the serfs to join the campaigns. But the cossacks' lack of authority over their popular supporters doomed their efforts to build an alternative state. Successful in raiding and banditry yet generally unable to defeat the professional armies of the Russian state in battle, they overturned Russian authority in vast regions without creating any authority of their own.

JACK A. GOLDSTONE

BIBLIOGRAPHY

Avrich, Paul. *Russian Rebels 1600–1800.* New York: W.W. Norton, 1972.

RWANDAN CIVIL WARS (1959–1994)

Of five Rwandese revolutions during this century, the last four took place in conjunction with military coups and civil wars. However, the peaceful preindependence social revolution was the most radical and provided the template for the others.

Before the arrival of European colonists, King Kugeri IV (1860–1895), a Tutsi, expanded the borders of his kingdom to incorporate Hutu territory in the northwest and centralized authority in Kigali *(see map, p. 66)*. The Belgians, who succeeded the Germans as the colonial power after World War I, completed the process of centralization and fixed the Rwandan border. Classical social institutions were also transformed. For example, *ubuhake,* a form of patron-client relationship and a communal system of social obligation, was superseded by *ubuletwa,* forced labor for someone in political authority; a social institution was converted into an individualistic system of economic exploitation. The practice was also extended to the newly acquired Hutu northwest. As a second example of transforming a traditional practice for the purposes of Belgian colonial exploitation, the practice of granting of land for grazing in the social institution of *igikingi* was privatized, transferring legal ownership of land to an elite group of Tutsis.

However, the most important transformation brought about by the first social revolution was the creation of an ethnic divide within a population that spoke the same language and practiced the same culture. Although the Belgians continued to rule indirectly, they consolidated the economic and political divide that already existed between a small group of aristocratic Tutsis and the rest of the Tutsi and Hutu population. With the introduction of identity cards in 1933–1934, the Hutu/Tutsi divide was ethnicized, universalized, and reified into an ethnic divide between the allegedly superior Tutsis—"Europeans with a black skin"—and the purportedly inferior Hutus. The Tutsis were characterized in terms of distinctive body types of the royal elites. All Tutsis were then seen as tall, thin, and having fine noses, fine lips, and high brows. Those somatic characteristics were identified with a vivacious intelligence, a refinement of feeling, extreme self-control, and calculated good will. This combination of social institutional transformation and racism fostered the monopolization of power and access to education by the Tutsi.

THE FIRST POLITICAL REVOLUTION, 1959–1962

In addition to calling for a political revolution—democratization—the Bahutu Manifesto issued by nine Hutu intellectuals on March 24, 1957, demanded social and economic revolutions—Hutu emancipation from Tutsi oppression and an end to the Tutsi monopoly on power. But hopes for all three revolutions were built on ethnic premises. The manifesto advocated the retention of the identity cards to ensure that a reversal took place. A peasant revolt in 1959 and ethnic riots begun on November 1 of that year translated the Bahutu Manifesto into action. But the actual transformation required an administrative revolution from the top. The Belgians intervened militarily to replace Tutsi administrators and political appointees with Hutus. The gendarmerie and territorial guard were radically altered as newly recruited Hutus soon made up 85 percent of the local armed forces.

As a result, oppression was merely inverted, as the Hutu now dominated the Tutsi. Instead of democracy, a dictatorship began under President Grégoire Kayibanda, leader of the Rwandese Democratic Movement–Party of the Movement and of Hutu Emancipation (MDR-PARMEHUTU) founded in 1959. The dictatorship continued the traditional pattern of governing through a small circle of cohorts from the same region, reinforced by coercion and favoritism. Not only was there a social inversion rather than a social revolution, not only was there no economic or democratic political revolution, but racism became fully integrated and institutionalized in political parties largely divided along ethnic lines. The revolution was consolidated electorally in the parliamentary elections of September 1961, in which PARMEHUTU and its small allied parties won 83 percent of the vote, and legally when the new leadership issued a declaration of independence on July 1, 1962. A centralized Tutsi monarchy had become an equally elitist Hutu-led republic. More significantly, a Tutsi social system that had ingested the beliefs of the European colonists on their racial superiority and right to rule became a Hutu majoritarian state that regarded the Tutsi as foreign invaders who had colonized the state in an earlier period. In addition to the horizontal divide between rulers and ruled, a new divide emerged between the supposedly indigenous population and the alleged foreigners.

The revolution sowed the seeds of its counterrevolution, as an estimated 350,000 Tutsi refugees fled during and immediately after the revolution. More than 10,000 Tutsis were slaughtered in the immediate aftermath of the revolution, from December 1962 to January 1963, exceeding the number killed during the course of the revolution.

Tutsi counterattacks and incursions from the bordering states by the so-called *inyenzi* (cockroaches) became not only more infrequent and ineffective but also counterproductive. An *inyenzi* attack against Bugesera in 1963 resulted in a pogrom in which 6,500 Tutsi were slaughtered. In the violent revolutionary aftermath, an estimated 20,000 Tutsi were executed as traitors. The incursions soon ceased. Nevertheless, the refugees, whose numbers had grown to about 700,000 by the beginning of the 1990s, continued to insist on their right to return even as they reestablished themselves in Tutsi-dominated Burundi to the south, Zaire (now the Democratic Republic of the Congo) on the west, Uganda in the north, and, to a smaller degree, Tanzania to the east.

THE SECOND POLITICAL REVOLUTION, 1973

By 1972 power had been almost totally consolidated in the hands of politicians from Gitarama, Kayibanda's home region. In 1973 Tutsis, who still dominated the Catholic seminaries and educational institutions, were removed. A group of Tutsi attacked an MDR leader. Taking advantage of ethnic riots against the Tutsi, which soon turned against the authoritarian government, Maj. Gen. Juvénal Habyarimana, the defense minister, led a nonviolent coup on July 5, 1973. An original signatory to the Bahutu Manifesto, Habyarimana was one of the few politicians not from Gitarama.

The new constitution of the Second Republic followed the old pattern. Power was centralized in the presidency. Only one party, Habyarimana's own National Revolutionary Movement for Development (MRND), was made legal in 1975. Power shifted to a group of politicians from Habyarimana's region in the Gisenyi and Ruhengeri préfectures. After eliminating his political opponents and allowing Kayibanda to die in prison, Habyarimana was formally elected president on December 24, 1978, beginning a succession of five-year terms.

Tutsis continued to be excluded from political participation, but their persecution stopped. Nevertheless, Habyarimana remained opposed to Tutsi refugee repatriation. Initially, he ran an effective government, opening the country to investment and expanding infrastructure. But the violent authoritarianism of the previous regime continued. Corruption grew with the collapse of the tin markets by 1985 and the coffee markets in the latter half of the decade. By the end of the 1980s political opposition had become vocal.

Even more serious, Tutsi refugees in Uganda had helped Yoweri Museveni achieve power in Uganda in 1986 and had risen to important intelligence and army positions. But in spite of Museveni's support, the local Ugandan population effectively resisted political integration of Tutsi refugees. The refugees determined to return to Rwanda, but negotiations with the Habyarimana government in Rwanda went nowhere. On October 1, 1990, whole (Tutsi) units of the Ugandan army "deserted" and invaded Rwanda as the Rwandese Patriotic Army (RPA), the militant wing of the Rwandese Patriotic Front (RPF).

In spite of initial defeats inflicted by the Rwandan army,

UN Secretary General Boutros Boutros-Ghali stands before a shed containing the remains of scores of people killed during a massacre at Nyarubuye Church, in southeastern Rwanda, in 1994.

assisted by crack units from Zaire and a French expeditionary force, the RPF had advanced to within 25 km. of Kigali by February 1993. After many false starts, broken cease-fire agreements, and periodic organized slaughters of Tutsi civilians, the government finally agreed to the Arusha Peace Accords on August 4, 1993, setting out power sharing, the rule of law, the role of the president, a transition process to democracy, and integration of the armed forces.

THE THIRD POLITICAL REVOLUTION, APRIL 6, 1994

Hutu extremists opposed to the peace accords left the MRND and constituted their own political party, the Coalition for the Defense of the Republic (CDR). The CDR executed a coup and allegedly assassinated Habyarimana on April 6, 1994, for betraying the Hutu cause and agreeing to implement the Arusha Accords. They then assassinated the Hutu moderates in the government, purged human rights workers and other defenders of freedom and democracy, and commenced the long-planned genocide of up to one million Tutsis in a low-tech but highly organized slaughter. The extremists more or less completed that task before their defeat by the RPF. The leadership fled along with 1.5 to 2 million other Hutus, including the army and the militias.

THE FOURTH POLITICAL REVOLUTION, JULY 6, 1994–

The fourth revolution began in July 1994 when the RPF took power. The government was faced with reconstructing an administration from scratch, reconstructing a devastated economy after three and a half years of civil war, resettling a large internally displaced population that at one point reached 900,000, emptying camps in the southwest still controlled by Hutu militants and extremists, holding for trial 120,000 prisoners in inadequate prisons who had been charged with genocidal crimes, and having to do so as a new judicial, police, and prosecutory system was being constructed from virtually nothing.

The Rwandese government also engaged in a barely concealed external war in eastern Zaire to regain control of the refugee camps in Zaire from the Hutu extremists and allow more than a million Hutu refugees to return home from Zaire and Tanzania. Not only did these Hutu refugees have to be reabsorbed, but the 700,000 Tutsi refugees who had been in exile from as long ago as 1959 had to be relocated as Hutus regained their old homes. However, the violence continued, with terrorism in Gisenyi and Ruhengeri, and sometimes overzealous responses by the Tutsi-dominated Rwandese army. And though official racism has been ended, there is still no democracy.

See also *Burundi Civil Wars.*

Howard Adelman

BIBLIOGRAPHY

Adelman, Howard, and Astri Suhrke. *The International Response to Conflict and Genocide: Lessons from the Rwanda Experience; Study 2: Early Warning and Conflict Management.* Volume 2 of the 5-volume *Joint Evaluation of Emergency Assistance to Rwanda.* Copenhagen: DANIDA, 1996.

Braeckman, Colette. *Rwanda. Histoire d'un génocide.* Paris: Editions Fayard, 1994.

Brauman, Rony. *Rwanda. Devant le mal: un génocide en direct.* Paris: Arléa, 1994.

Destexhe, Alain. *Rwanda: essai sur le génocide.* Paris: Ed Complexe, 1994. Translated as *Rwanda and Genocide in the Twentieth Century.* London: Pluto Press, 1995.

Prunier, Gérard. *The Rwandese Crisis (1959–1994): From Cultural Mythology to Genocide.* London: C. Hurst, 1995. Also published as *The Rwanda Crisis: History of a Genocide.* New York: Columbia University Press, 1995.

Reyntjens, Filip. *L'Afrique des Grands Lacs en crise. Rwanda, Burundi: 1988–1994.* Paris: Ed. Karthala, 1994.

Sellström, Tor, et al. *The International Response to Conflict and Genocide: Lessons from the Rwanda Experience; Study 1: Historical Perspective—Some Explanatory Factors.* Volume 1 of the 5-volume *Joint Evaluation of Emergency Assistance to Rwanda.* Copenhagen: DANIDA, 1996.

Waal, Alex de, and Rakiya Omaar, eds. *Rwanda. Death, Despair and Defiance.* Rev. ed. London: African Rights, 1995.

S

SAN MARTÍN, JOSÉ FRANCISCO DE

José Francisco de San Martín (February 25, 1778–August 17, 1850) was born in an Argentine town and joined the Spanish army in 1789. He saw action in Africa, Spain, and France. However, after Napoleon Bonaparte took the Iberian Peninsula, San Martín retired from the Spanish army and returned home in 1812. In Buenos Aires, he built an army out of militia elements and led his army to victories over the Spanish in Chile and Peru, earning for himself the appellation "Liberator."

As South American struggles against Spanish colonial rule intensified in the 1810s, the role of the military became ever more important. Aware that Spanish armies in the Andes and Lima threatened South American freedom, and that a direct attack on the strong Spanish positions in Upper Peru, and especially Buenos Aires, would be dangerous, San Martín began the long but less risky strategy of crossing the Andes to the south and moving on Lima from the Pacific.

His efforts converted the Argentine military into a professional fighting force. Many of his officers would eventually rise to dominate Argentine, Bolivian, and Chilean politics for the next fifty years. The 4,000 soldiers and 1,000 militiamen of his liberating Army of the Andes began marching out of Mendoza to Santiago, Chile, in early 1817. After a grueling Andean crossing, San Martín's forces saw action at Chacabuco (February 12), where they triumphed. Two days later, they entered Santiago. The general quickly prepared for the expedition on Lima, but bogged down by local rivalries in Chile and having to rout Spanish holdouts at Maipú (April 5, 1818), San Martín took several years to muster financial help from Buenos Aires and to secure the help of the English mercenary Lord Thomas Alexander Cochrane to lead a navy.

In 1819 San Martín left local political consolidation in Santiago to one of his generals, Bernardo O'Higgins, and the patriot forces aimed for the South American Spanish bastion of Peru. Lord Cochrane cornered the royalist fleet at Callao; San Martín, with 4,400 Argentine and Chilean soldiers, aimed for Lima. The enemy, however, boasted an army of 23,000. San Martín, ever prudent, sought to avoid the expense and turmoil of open battle. After almost a year of encirclement and only a few skirmishes, San Martín's army entered Lima on July 19, 1821; on July 28 a local council of notables declared Peruvian independence.

José Francisco de San Martín

The Liberator issued a flurry of reforms (ending Indian tribute, freeing the new-born children of slaves, and abolishing press censorship), but consolidating constitutional rule was no easy task. Besides, royalist forces retained control of the highlands. San Martín chose to enlist the support of Gen. Simón Bolívar, now poised in the Ecuadorean port of Guayaquil. There, the two Liberators held a summit in July 1822 to discuss the final phase of the independence struggle. The proceedings of their three meetings remain shrouded in controversy. San Martín trumpeted a constitutional monarchy for the new countries; Bolívar wanted a republic. Bolívar refused to place his larger force under San Martín's command. His resources exhausted and personally dismayed at creole bickering over the constitutional makeup of the fledgling countries and military conspiracies, San Martín returned to Lima in September, where he resigned as Protector of Peru. Shortly thereafter he left for permanent exile in France, leaving the last stage of the wars to his rival, Bolívar.

See also *Bolívar, Simón; Latin American Revolutions for Independence (1808–1898).*

JEREMY ADELMAN

BIBLIOGRAPHY

Lynch, John. *The Spanish American Revolutions, 1808*–1826. New York: W.W. Norton, 1973.

Mitre, Bartolomé. *Historia de San Martín y de la emancipación sudamericana.* 2d ed. 3 vols. Buenos Aires: F. Lajouane, 1890.

Piccirilli, Ricardo. *San Martín y la política de los pueblos.* Buenos Aires: Gure, 1957.

SANDINO, AUGUSTO CÉSAR

Sandino (1895–1934) waged successful rural guerrilla warfare against U.S. troops and surrogate native forces in Nicaragua over a quarter century before the Cuban revolutionary victory of 1959 popularized guerrilla-based insurgency. A poor, self-educated man, Sandino was a fervent nationalist, a spiritualist, and a socialist—in some senses, even a communist. He acquired a distaste for foreign intervention when U.S. marines suppressed Benjamin Zeledón's nationalist rebellion of 1912. Later, as a laborer for multinational corporations in Costa Rica and Mexico, he came to abhor the underside of capitalism.

In the mid-1920s, during a brief interlude in the direct U.S. occupation of Nicaragua (1912–1925, 1926–1932), he joined a Liberal revolt against the pro-United States Conservative government. When Washington reintroduced the marines, Sandino stood alone among Liberal commanders in refusing to negotiate—choosing instead to fight until the invaders left.

After failed attempts at conventional warfare, Sandino improvised rural guerrilla techniques. The ensuing struggle between Sandino's "crazy little army" and the U.S. marines and their surrogate Nicaraguan National Guard would foreshadow aspects of the Vietnam conflict decades later. The United States developed counterinsurgency tactics such as the aerial bombardment of "enemy" population centers, the establishment of rural free-fire zones, and the creation of the equivalent of "protective hamlets." Sandino's forces engaged in hit and run as well as ambush tactics. While the homesick marines saw and referred to Nicaraguans as "Gooks," Sandino cultivated the support of locals who acted as his eyes and ears. The marines, under orders not to bring Sandino back alive should they capture him, were continuously frustrated in that quest.

Augusto César Sandino (with his foot on the bumper) and his staff, June 1929.

As U.S. casualties mounted, the war became unpopular at home. Sandino metamorphosed into an international folk hero through a series of interviews he gave to American reporter Carlton Beals. Published in *The Nation* in 1928, the interviews were subsequently translated and published worldwide. An antiwar movement developed in the United States, which eventually gathered such strength that Congress cut off funding for the Nicaragua war. At the turn of 1932–1933, U.S. troops withdrew, leaving real control of Nicaragua to Anastasio Somoza García, the first native commander of the National Guard. Though Sandino and the nominal civilian government of Nicaragua worked out a peace settlement, Somoza—the first Somoza in a dynastic dictatorship that would last until 1979—ordered the arrest and summary execution of his foe in 1934.

Sandino's immediate legacy to Nicaragua and the world was the U.S. withdrawal and, to a large degree, the forced birth of Franklin Roosevelt's policy of the "Good Neighbor." Later, his name and image became the historical point of reference for the Sandinista Front for National Liberation (FSLN), an organization founded in 1961 to overthrow the Somozas. Though an attempt to implement Sandino's rural guerrilla strategy ironically led to their near obliteration at Pancasán in 1967, the Sandinistas eventually developed techniques of insurgency that would bring their revolution to power for eleven years (1979–1990). Dozens of aged veterans of Sandino's struggle marched proudly in the first victory parade.

See also *Guerrilla Warfare; Nicaraguan Revolution (1979).*

Thomas W. Walker

BIBLIOGRAPHY

Hodges, Donald C. *Sandino's Communism: Spiritual Politics for the Twenty-First Century.* Austin: University of Texas Press, 1992.

Macaulay, Neill. *The Sandino Affair.* Chicago: Quadrangle Books, 1967.

Ramirez, Sergio, and Robert Edgar Conrad, eds. *Sandino: The Testimony of a Nicaraguan Patriot, 1921–1934.* Princeton, N.J.: Princeton University Press, 1990.

Selser, Gregorio. *Sandino, General de Hombres Libres.* Segunda edicion. San Jose: Editorial Universitaria Centroamericana, 1979.

SAUDI ARABIAN WAHHABI MOVEMENT (1744–)

The Wahhabi movement, which began as an Islamic reform movement in the mid-eighteenth century, is notable for its role in the founding of the modern kingdom of Saudi Arabia. It is named for Muhammad Ibn Abd al-Wahhab (c.1703–1792), a sage from Najd in central Arabia, who set out to purify Islam and reinstate what he saw as its original monotheistic beliefs. Al-Wahhab's faith focused on God's oneness *(Tawhid).* He forbade all polytheistic practices including cults of saints, observance of pre-Islamic festivals, worship of humans rather than of God, and prayer accompanied by music and ornamentation. Declaring these practices to be unlawful innovations, he demanded that every Wahhabi believer challenge and purify the existing religious order and the political systems that condoned it, whether Ottoman rule or tribal entities.

In place of the popular religious and political systems, a rightful order was to be established, its fundamentals guaranteed by strict application of the *shari'a,* or holy law. Politically, it was to be a partnership between pious lay rulers of the community *(umara)* and religious sages *(ulama),* whose moral and legal advice the rulers were to follow.

EXPANSION OF THE WAHHABI MOVEMENT

The Wahhabi movement from the beginning was pulled between two conflicting tendencies. Aggression was inherent in their mission. Their fighting forces were composed of large nomadic groups, whose religious zeal and solidarity added to the movement's ruthlessness. The goal, however, was to establish an order based on *shari'a* that would supersede the tribal value system and form a cohesive, morally guided entity.

The history of the Wahhabi movement can be divided into three phases. During the period of expansion and state building, between 1745 and 1818, the Wahhabis were ideologically and organizationally cohesive. After an alliance formed in 1744 between al-Wahhab and Muhammad Ibn Saud, the leader of the Diriyya, in Najd, the Wahhabis were led by a series of strong military rulers. They conquered Riyadh in 1787; the Bani Khalid tribe in the Persian Gulf in 1792; and the Shi'i Muslim center of Karbala in 1803. Finally, between 1803 and 1806 they occupied and purged the holy cities of the Hijaz—Mecca and Medina. The Ottomans responded to these challenges to their authority by commissioning the governor of Egypt, Muhammad Ali, to defeat and destroy the Wahhabis. By 1818, the Egyptian forces had exiled the Wahhabi leader, Abdullah, to Istanbul, where he was beheaded.

As the Ottoman-Egyptian conquerors withdrew to the Hijaz, the Wahhabis were able to establish a second but weaker realm (1821–1891). With their leaders dead, the line of succession was disrupted, and factionalism reemerged within both the ruling Saudi tribal elite and the society. The two important rulers of this phase were Turki, who was assassinated in 1833, and his son Faysal, who was able to maintain some unity during his lifetime. After Faysal's death in 1865, two of his sons, Abdullah and Saud, engaged in a protracted fight, dividing the Wahhabi tribes into two factions. A third faction, of the Banu-Rashid dynasty centered in Jabbal Shammar, emerged as a new, independent Wahhabi chiefdom. With Ottoman support, it took advantage of the Saudi war, subdued the Saudi state into vassalage in the 1870s, conquered Riyadh in 1891, and exiled the Saudi leader, Abd al-Rahman. The last decades of this phase also witnessed a decline in the Wahhabis' influence. The leading sages, while showing remarkable adherence to the law, were unable to bring political unity and cohesion. The Rashidis in effect disregarded the Wahhabi cause and based their chiefdom on commerce and raiding.

The Wahhabi movement got a fresh start, in 1902, when Abd al-Aziz (Ibn Saud), the son of the last Saudi leader, reoccupied Riyadh and reestablished a third Saudi state. By forming an alliance with Great Britain in 1915, Ibn Saud not only neutralized the Ottomans but secured Saudi independence. Territorial expansion, though still a primary goal, was pursued with caution, to avoid creating major territorial disputes. Saud conquered the Gulf region of al-Hassa, which had been under Ottoman control, in 1913. He defeated the Rashidi chiefdom in 1921 and occupied the holy cities in the Hijaz in 1924–1925. This time the Wahhabi occupation was condoned by other Muslim and European states.

THE SAUDI STATE

The need to establish a government led to fissures within the Saud-Wahhabi alliance. Cohesion and enthusiasm had been instilled by the emergence of the *Ikhwan* (Brethren), a Wahhabi revivalist movement among the central Arabian tribes. Since 1912 Ikhwan tribal groups had functioned as a standing army for the Saudis. They had proselytized for the Wahhabi movement and founded new settlements—which signified the turning of the Bedouins from their traditional nomadic ways to a more sedentary life. In the 1920s, however, Ibn Saud sought to establish a centralized state, subdue the tribes, increase his income from trade and pilgrimage dues, and cooperate with other Arab-Muslim states, then under British or French patronage. He sought to turn the Wahhabi principles into a legal and moral code run by the state rather than a blueprint for tribal expansion. The Ikhwan, which resisted this plan, became a liability, and in a series of military clashes in 1929–1930, they were defeated.

After consolidating power, Saud established the Saudi Arabian Kingdom, in September 1932. Wahhabi principles became the unofficial constitution of Saudi Arabia, establishing the norms of law, education, and social behavior. A special "moral police," which enforced proper behavior in public, was enacted. The role of senior sages in advising and justifying government actions—and in being part of the Saudi elite, integrated with the Saudi royal family in marriage and wealth—was maintained. With the sages' approval, the leaders used the country's vast oil money to build a modern infrastructure for education, welfare, urban centers, and businesses under Kings Saud, Faysal Khalid, and Fahd, who still reigns.

The inherent contradiction between opposing sets of Wahhabi principles did not fade away. On November 20, 1979, inspired by the success of the Islamic revolution in Iran, a group of several hundred youths captured the Grand Mosque in Mecca. Led by Juhayman al-Utaybi, they expressed demands similar to those of fundamentalist Muslims in Iran: stop corruption, reinstate the *shari'a* in full, depose unlawful rulers, including the king, and appoint a *mahdi* (savior) to rule. The authorities were able to overpower this group only after several weeks, and they executed its leaders.

In the 1990s economic problems arose. The Saudi government's invitation to foreign, notably Western, forces to secure the kingdom and to liberate Kuwait from Iraqi occupation coincided with a decline in oil revenues. Wahhabi opposition groups protested against pro-Western subservience, unemployment, and unjust administrative appointments. They reiterated the need to topple unlawful rulers, act in Islamic interests rather than state-based interests, and apply the *shari'a*, which would ensure a solid economy and just administration. Although the Wahhabis seemed to have support among professionals, mostly academics and students, the government was able to crack down on the activists, arrest and exile some of them, and sway the religious establishment to condemn them as "rebels." A group of them reappeared in London in 1994, calling themselves the Committee for the Defense of Legitimate Rights, and for a while spread opposition propaganda. Their effect, however has been limited. Still, the Wahhabi movement and its legacy of Islamic puritanism remain as potential challenges to the Saudi state.

See also *Iranian Islamic Revolution (1979); Islamic Fundamentalism; Ottoman Revolts in the Near and Middle East (1803–1922).*

Joseph Kostiner

SCOTTISH REVOLUTION (1559–1568)

As some historians see it, there was a Scottish Revolution that began in 1560 with the triumph of the Protestant party in Scotland, symbolized in the Reformation parliament that brought down the Catholic Church and replaced it with an embryonic Calvinist one in open defiance of the crown. These were indeed traumatic years, with civil war between the Protestants, the Lords of the Congregation of Christ, and the Catholic regent, Mary of Guise. Mary of Guise was the mother of Mary Stuart, also known to history as Mary Queen of Scots.

The civil war was resolved with the death of the regent in June 1560, the intervention of English troops in support of the Protestants that forced the regent's French troops out of Scotland, and the Parliament of that summer, which established the new faith. Yet it is difficult to see these events, dramatic as they were, as truly revolutionary, for nothing was done to remove the Catholic monarch, Mary Stuart. In August 1561 Mary returned without any sort of resistance from her long minority spent in France, the widow of the French king Francis II. She had been queen of Scotland since the death of her father, James V, in 1542.

MARY QUEEN OF SCOTS

It is true that the Catholic Mary Stuart refused to ratify the acts of the Reformation Parliament until in dire straits in early 1567, by which time her regime had tottered through the seismic political shocks of the murder of her favorite, David Rizzio, in March 1566, with the appropriate amount of sexual scandal; the murder of her husband, in which she was regarded—probably correctly—as heavily implicated; and her rush to the arms of James earl of Bothwell. Her removal was no doubt made all the easier because she had given birth to a son in June 1566, thus providing an alternative ruler should one be wanted.

But during the more peaceful years of her personal rule, 1561–1565, the Catholic Mary had also aided the new church rather than the old, helping finance it and ruling through a largely Protestant council. During those years, there was, therefore, no great political or social upheaval or even significant restructuring. There was indeed religious reformation. But it is surely stretching the point too far to call it revolution in Scotland, despite its exceptional beginnings, when Mary herself not only refused to treat it as one but actually went along with it.

It was a different matter in 1567. On the night of February 9–10, 1567, Henry lord Darnley, second husband of Mary Queen of Scots, was strangled when escaping from Kirk o'Field. Four months later, Mary herself, by then married to her third husband, the tough and violently unpopular Bothwell, was defeated in battle at Carberry, south of Edinburgh. Bothwell fled, and Mary, taken to Lochleven Castle, was forced to abdicate in favor of her year-old son James, who was crowned at the end of July. Imprisoned for nearly a year, she escaped in May 1568, enjoying only a brief period of freedom before being once again defeated in battle at Langside near Glasgow.

Mary panicked and fled to England, where she would remain for eighteen years, spending her time complaining, embroidering, and plotting against Queen Elizabeth I. The immediate aftermath of her disasters in Scotland was a brief period of rather low-key civil war between Queen's Men and King's Men that ended with the solution of the summer of 1567 still in place. A Protestant regime, set up under her bastard half-brother James earl of Moray, thus replaced government by a Catholic queen, and the Protestant Elizabeth, though refusing to condemn Mary, did nothing to overturn that new regime.

PROTESTANT RULE

The crisis of 1567–1568 was, therefore, in one sense a confirmation of 1560 rather than a revolution in that the future of Protestantism was now in the firm hands of a Protestant government rather than the unlikely ones of a Catholic queen. This time, however, there was indeed political upheaval. And it is certainly the case that the size of the opposition that Mary's folly had called into being was initially dramatic—to her aristocratic and conciliar opponents were added her officers of state, men who, as direct crown appointees, should have been loyal to her. But by the end of that year, undoubtedly encouraged by the fact that the queen was remote in Lochleven rather than present to remind men of her folly, traditional habits of loyalty to the crown were visibly beginning to reassert themselves. And at Langside she had far more support than she had had at Carberry.

It was Mary's final act of political misjudgment, her flight to England, that left those supporters leaderless and fatally weakened. And if religious upheaval is called reformation, the violent removal of an unsatisfactory ruler in favor of a potentially more effective one is usually termed usurpation, precisely what happened in 1567, although it was usurpation with a somewhat spurious aura of respectability in that Mary had officially abdicated—signing a document to prove it—and was succeeded by her rightful heir. Its only radical aspect was the resistance theory that accompanied it. The great humanist scholar George Buchanan produced a scathing and scurrilous attack on the queen in his *Ane Detectioun of Mary Stuart*. In his treatise *De Iure Regni apud Scotos,* Buchanan invoked an Ancient Constitution that gave "the people" the right to elect and depose kings, which was very much on the lines of the Huguenot resistance theories of the 1570s and as little relevant as they to the practical politics of 1567–1568.

Indeed, perhaps the most revolutionary aspect of these years lay not in domestic but in foreign affairs. Since the late thirteenth century, England had been Scotland's *auld inemie* (old enemy), France, her old ally. During the ebbs and flows of English religion between the 1530s and 1558, the periodic lurches away from Catholicism had introduced a new note of uncertainty into this well-known historical enmity and alliance, as Scottish Protestants looked south for support. That support was crucial in 1560 and decisive in 1567–1568.

ONE CROWN

It would be a grotesque oversimplification to say that the Scots and English immediately began to like one another, or that Scotland lost its image of itself as an important European kingdom, largely sustained because of its ties with France. But the revolution's effect in the longer term was to replace Mary, that deeply suspect heir-presumptive to Elizabeth—as Elizabeth's cousin through her descent from her Tudor grandmother Margaret, mother of James V and aunt of Elizabeth—with an increasingly acceptable one, Mary's son, James VI. And as Elizabeth was still thirty-four in 1567, no one could yet be certain that she would not marry and have an heir. James indeed succeeded her as James I of England, producing in 1603 the greatest irony in Anglo-Scottish history, when long-standing English ambitions to annex Scotland by violence came to an end with the advent of a Scottish king going south to the peaceful acquisition of the English throne.

Scottish politics had their dramatic personal moments but were, by English and European standards, remarkably low key. This was a very low-key revolution, if revolution it was, and it is particularly fitting and somehow typically Scottish that its main effect was not on the world of Scotland within, but on Scotland's place on the world without.

See also *British Civil Wars and Revolution (1638–1660).*

JENNY WORMALD

BIBLIOGRAPHY

Donaldson, Gordon. *All the Queen's Men: Power and Politics in Mary Stewart's Scotland.* London: Batsford, 1983.

———. *Scotland: James V–VII.* Edinburgh: Longman, 1965.

Fraser, Antonia. *Mary Queen of Scots.* London: Weidenfeld and Nicolson, 1969.

Lynch, Michael, ed. *Mary Stewart: Queen in Three Kingdoms.* Oxford: Blackwell, 1988.

Wormald, Jenny. *Mary Queen of Scots: A Study in Failure.* London: Collins and Brown, 1988.

SOCIALISM

Utopian visions of a future perfect order of justice and equality have existed since time immemorial in many civilizations, but modern socialism is a specifically nineteenth-century west European response—on the part of intellectuals and workers alike—to the social ravages of modern industrial capitalism.

EARLY SOCIALISTS

Emerging in the early decades of the nineteenth century, the first socialists were an extraordinarily diverse group of thinkers and activists. In France the pioneers of modern socialism included such disparate figures as the technocratic Compte de Saint-Simon (1760–1825), the agrarian socialist Charles Fourier (1772–1837), and Pierre-Joseph Proudhon (1809–1865), the father of anarchism. In England the industrialist Robert Owen (1771–1858), whom radical socialist theorist Karl Marx later came to admire so greatly, clearly was the most creative and influential socialist of his time. And the origin of German socialism in the 1830s and 1840s is identified with the quasi-religious utopianism of Wilhelm Weitling (1808–1871) and the workers' organization League of the Just.

Although the founders of modern socialism shared an antipathy to capitalism and bourgeois society, they differed sharply on many fundamental issues. While some, such as Saint-Simon and Owen, championed the social benefits of modern science and industry, others, such as Fourier, were inclined to reject not only capitalism but modern industrialism in general. French and German socialists, influenced by the political radicalism of the French Revolution, tended to favor revolutionary methods to achieve socialist ends, whereas English socialism was reformist from the outset—although Owen's ideas were perhaps more profoundly radical than those of most of his continental contemporaries. There also were divisions between religious and secular versions of socialism, with French socialists being almost uniformly secular (as befitted heirs of the French Revolution) while various forms of Christian socialism flourished in Germany and England.

Despite these differences, the early socialists shared certain intellectual proclivities that later earned them the pejorative Marxist label "utopian." The utopian mode of thought tended to be ahistorical, rooted in an Enlightenment-derived faith in an eternal realm of Reason. It was assumed that once that realm was properly understood, social reality could be shaped in accordance with socialist ideals—ideals that corresponded to the dictates of Reason. The early socialists, therefore, placed great emphasis on the will and actions of "men of genius" who were the bearers of Reason—and whose ideas and deeds would appeal to what was assumed to be a naturally good human nature. Once the baneful influences of false institutions and ideologues were removed, people would respond to proper moral examples and social models—such as Fourier's detailed schemes to reorganize society into *phalansteres* (small communal associations) and Owen's "villages of cooperation."

Lacking any conception of history as a process, the early socialists failed to establish any coherent relationship between socialist moral ideals and historical events. Socialism thus appeared as the more or less fortuitous expression of absolute truth, a truth that, as Marx's friend and collaborator Friedrich Engels noted, is "independent of time, space, and of the historical development of man; it is a mere accident when and where it is discovered."

EMERGENCE OF MARXISM

The emergence of Marxism in the 1840s and 1850s marked a major departure from the socialist beliefs of the early nineteenth century. By providing a developmental theory of history, Marxism removed socialism from the realm of the accidental and situated it in a foreseeable future. And on the basis of that conception of history, Marxism distinguished itself from other socialist theories by its acceptance of capitalism as a necessary and progressive stage of historical development. Only capitalism, Marx taught, yields the material basis for socialism through its creation of technologically advanced, large-scale industry. At the same time, capitalism produces the social agent for the socialist future through the creation of its own "gravediggers"—the modern industrial proletariat. Moreover, capitalism prepares the necessary international arena for the future socialist order through the inevitability of its global expansion.

Partly because it took into account the realities of the expanding capitalist system, partly because of its intellectual appeal, Marxism became the dominant socialist ideology in the rapidly growing European labor movements of the late nineteenth century. Although there was no lack of competing socialist ideas—ranging from anarchism and Russian populism to British Fabianism (which favored gradual reform over revolutionary acts)—Marxism was both intellectually and politically the most influential of socialist theories in the three decades prior to World War I (1914–1918).

In view of the central Marxist belief that an advanced capitalist economy—and all of its material, social, and cultural products—is the essential precondition for socialism, it is one of the great ironies of modern history that the first successful Marxist-led socialist revolution took place in backward Russia, a largely precapitalist and agrarian land in 1917. It is further ironic that socialism, which had been intimately joined to democratic movements throughout the nineteenth century, now became associated with political despotism. It also is strange that Marxism, a profoundly internationalist creed, now was employed to promote nationalism and the Stalinist doctrine of "socialism in one country."

But strangest of all was the wholesale transformation of the very meaning of socialism in its inhospitable Russian historical environment. When the term *socialism* was first employed in the 1820s, it conveyed the idea that the laborers who created the new industrial wealth also should be its owners. Marx retained and elaborated on this essential definition, so that socialism in Marxist theory came to be generally understood as a system whereby the immediate producers control the conditions and products of their labor. In Stalinist Russia this radical conception of socialism was abandoned, indeed suppressed, in favor of a definition of socialism that centered on state ownership of productive property, a definition congenial to the conservative bureaucratic masters of the new Soviet order. The notion that socialism essentially meant the nationalization of property soon became a universal twentieth-century belief, accepted not only by communist parties throughout the world but happily embraced by critics of socialism as well.

In recent years much has been heard about the definitive triumph of global capitalism, "the end of history," and the demise of socialism. The obituary may be premature. With the fall of the Soviet Union, socialism, freed from its long and unhappy association with political despotism, may well reappear in its nineteenth-century role as the main democratic alternative to capitalism. Yet to become a viable alternative, socialism must reclaim its original heritage as an ally of political democracy and as a movement expressing the interests and collective will of the great majority of society.

See also *Communism; Marx, Karl, and Friedrich Engels.*

MAURICE MEISNER

BIBLIOGRAPHY

Cole, G. D. H. *A History of Socialist Thought.* 5 vols. London: Macmillan, 1953.
Engels, Friedrich. *Socialism: Utopian and Scientific.* Various editions.
Lichtheim, George. *Marxism: A Historical and Critical Study.* New York: Praeger, 1964.
———. *The Origins of Socialism.* New York: Praeger, 1969.
Marx, Karl, and Friedrich Engels. *The Communist Manifesto, A Modern Edition.* With an introduction by Eric Hobsbawm. London: Verso, 1998.

SOREL, GEORGES

Sorel (1847–1922) was committed, at least in his early years, to the notion of revolution, arising naturally from a general strike, as an energizing agency that would galvanize the industrial proletariat into a genuinely socialist force. Sorel was born in Cherbourg, France, and was educated at the Ecole Polytechnique. In 1870 he became an engineer in the employment of the French government. He retired from his profession at the age of forty-five and devoted the rest of his life to reading and writing.

Sorel began his political writing career as a revolutionary syndicalist, believing that the control of production and distribution should be transferred to groups of industrial workers, but although he was greatly influenced by Marx, he rejected Marx's belief in the historical inevitability of class war and the triumph of the proletariat. There were no inexorable laws for him, only the ceaseless and unflinching pursuit of moral goals that might, through the application of communal energy and will, bring into being a creative, energized, and equal society. His most celebrated works were *The Disintegration of Marxism* (1906), *Reflections on Violence* (1908), and *The Illusions of Progress* (1908).

Sorel adopted an eclectic doctrine, deriving inspiration from the philosopher Henri Bergson, who gave prominence to the *élan vital* (life force) in the development of humanity. Reformist socialists, he came to believe (especially after the Dreyfus affair), were traitors. They shared with the capitalists a belief in progress, and this belief inevitably led to the further decadence of Europe. There was no place for Fabian-style gradualism or parliamentarianism in Sorel's thought. He abhorred compromise and the inevitable gradualness of compromise building. The moral rebirth he sought lay outside progressivism and the social institutions that claim to foster it. Only through action could people discover their virtue. So Sorel advanced instead the myth of the general strike. He used the notion of myth to imply not an illusion but a galvanizing vision. The myth would prove a potent force in persuading the proletariat of its potential for action. But class war would prove to be a creative force in its own right, allowing people to rediscover their Homeric virtues. As Sorel famously put it: "The goal is nothing; the movement is everything." The general strike was an exercise of political will and the imposition of that will upon nature. In its violence, Sorel believed—like Friedrich Nietzsche—the strike was a force for creativity.

By 1910, however, Sorel had abandoned syndicalism and extended his sympathies toward others who sought to use violence to reestablish traditional moral authority, namely those on the extreme right in France and elsewhere, and he became linked to the right-wing patriotic group Action Francaise. Mussolini was later to claim that Sorel had contributed the most to the "discipline, energy and power" of his fascist cohorts. Sorel's hopes for moral regeneration, all but killed by the First World War, were rekindled by the Russian Revolution, and he remained hopeful up to his death that the Soviet Communist Party would be the agent of the moral transformation of society he had sought to bring into being.

Sorel's influence was widespread, linking right-wing Catholics and conservatives, but also pacifists and anarchists. His influence stretched as far as the anticolonialist writers of the modern era, such as Frantz Fanon. More directly, his doctrines inspired revolutionary anarchosyndicalists and fascists in the 1930s: indeed, it has been said that the Spanish Civil War was fought between the supporters of the two branches of Sorel's thought!

See also *Fanon, Frantz Omar.*

Stephen Ingle

BIBLIOGRAPHY

Jennings, Jeremy. *Georges Sorel: The Character and Development of His Thought.* Basingstoke, England: Macmillan, 1985.

Roth, Jack. *The Cult of Violence: Sorel and the Sorelians.* Berkeley: University of California Press, 1980.

Vernon, Richard. *Commitment and Change: Georges Sorel and the Idea of Revolution.* Toronto: University of Toronto Press, 1978.

SOUTH AFRICAN ANTIAPARTHEID REVOLTS AND REFORM (1948–1994)

Few outside observers believed that the transition from apartheid (minority rule by white South Africans) to democracy could occur without a bloody civil war. Many white South Africans expressed ruthless determination to uphold their domination with vicious repression. After centuries of abuse and domination, how could black rage be contained? Yet, despite widespread fears of a "bloodbath," the transition was relatively peaceful.

Some accounts of the transition focus on the leadership of a few wise and charismatic people, such as Nelson Mandela and Cyril Ramaphosa of the African National Congress, and F. W. de Klerk of the National Party. Still, success was not guaranteed by even the most skilled negotiators. Rather, the groundwork was prepared by a multiracial, multiclass antiapartheid movement, which in its struggle to create a democratic state where all South Africans could vote, own land, and marry whomever they wished used strikes, boycotts, sanctions, armed struggle, and persuasion to change the balance of power in South Africa.

The antiapartheid movement began with small-scale, grassroots organizing by different groups whose aims ranged from simple reforms to overturning an entire system of white political, social, psychological, and economic domination and exploitation. Activism grew increasingly well organized, coordinated, and inclusive, attacking the apartheid system on all fronts. Antiapartheid activists also instigated international sanctions against South Africa in order to isolate it culturally, politically, and economically. In this way, antiapartheid movements exploited structural and moral weaknesses in the apartheid regime, eventually making apartheid South Africa ungovernable. Yet, while not the predicted bloodbath, the transition was not entirely peaceful. Thousands of activists were tortured, imprisoned, and killed by the state and in political unrest associated with the struggle, even as negotiations were under way in the early 1990s. Nor was the transition completed with the first democratic elections. Broader goals of bringing healthcare, education, housing, and economic opportunity to the majority population were on the movement's agenda after the political transition in 1994.

EMERGENCE OF APARTHEID AND RESISTANCE

The land that is now South Africa was populated by groups of African people who spoke related though distinct languages for at least twelve centuries before European explorers arrived. White settlement, begun when the Dutch East India Company founded a colony on the Cape in 1652, was the beginning of racial discrimination and African resistance to white domination. Descendants of the Dutch, known as Boers, were joined by other Europeans, including English settlers who in the late 1700s began to take control of portions of the Dutch settlement, pushing Boers further inland. From their earliest settlement, whites sometimes intermarried with the majority population and imported slaves from South Asia and other parts of Africa. Thus, four racial categories were gradually defined, along with systems of control that put people of European descent in dominant political, social, and economic positions. Africans were known by "tribal" names or called black; descendants of unions between Africans and Europeans were called "colored"; and those whose ancestors were from South Asia were known as Indians or Asians.

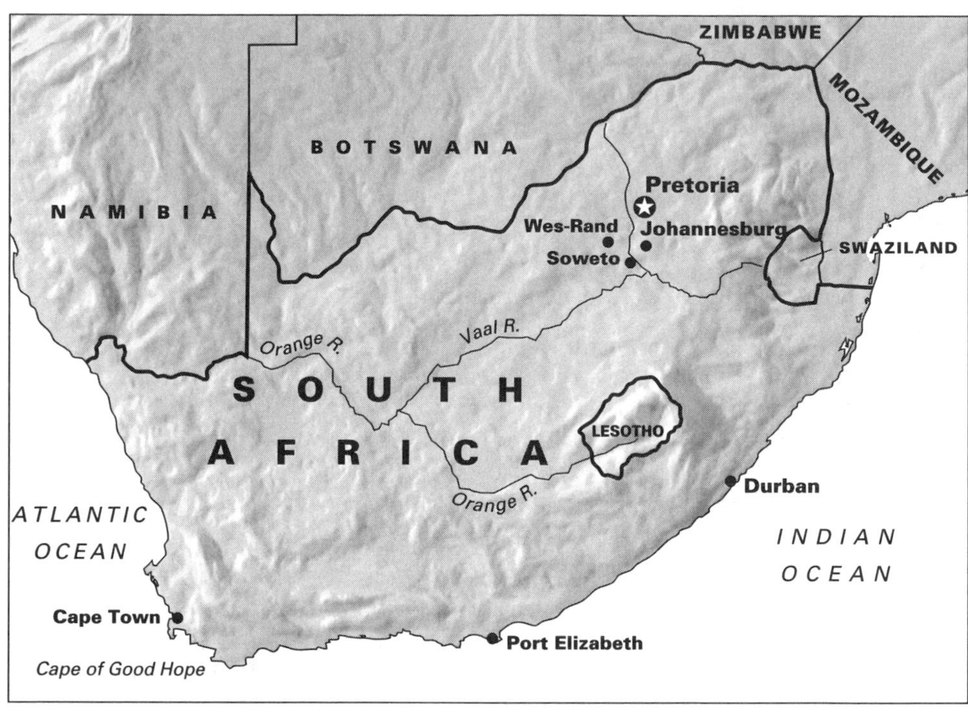

White settlers, both English and Boer, fought hard in the nineteenth century to subdue the African people they met as they moved from the coast to the interior, often exploiting cultural and political differences among African groups, as they waged military campaigns for control of southern Africa. After discovery of diamonds in 1867 and gold in 1886, Britain accelerated its drive for control and won all South Africa in the Boer War (1899–1902).

Boers, whose Dutch-based language, Afrikaans, incorporated words from some European and African languages, felt oppressed by the English. Afrikaners saw themselves a chosen people. Yet, English and Afrikaners cooperated between 1909 and 1913 when they drafted and passed laws to consolidate their political and economic separation from and domination of the rest of South Africa's people. One law, the 1913 Native Land Act, took from native people the right to own land and forced blacks onto economically marginal "native reserves" (only 13 percent of the country's total land), forcing blacks to work as cheap "migrant" labor for white-owned mines, industry, and farms.

These laws spurred local groups to form a national organization in January 1912, the South African Native National Congress (after 1923 known as the African National Congress). Demanding limited reforms at the national level, the ANC pursued a strategy of petitioning the government for inclusion and representation. With no real success to show for its polite pleas, the ANC declined in vitality for two decades, while resistance to work conditions and low wages grew among black industrial, transportation, and mine workers. White mine and industrial workers were also active against discrimination, though white unions and many members of the Communist Party of South Africa (formed in 1921) were notoriously racist, often striking only to improve the wages and working conditions of white workers. Still, with a primarily bourgeois and black-only membership through the mid-1930s, the ANC began organizing more broadly, including making contacts with the Communist Party. During the same period, Afrikaners were also becoming better organized.

Afrikaners gained political power over the English when the Afrikaner-dominated National Party, founded in 1933, won the whites-only elections in 1948. Though whites remained a numerical minority in South Africa, the National Party's main goals were to codify and extend white domination under apartheid and, in particular, to help Afrikaners flourish. Intended to foster "separate development" for each race, apartheid laws were instituted in just a few years. The Mixed Marriages Act of 1949 prohibited marriage between people of different races; the Population Registration Act of 1950 constructed distinct racial categories and required all South Africans to be classified according to race; the Group Areas Act of 1950 organized land by race. In 1953 the

Reservation of Separate Amenities and Bantu Education bills legislated the physical separation of races and ensured that black, Asian, and colored South Africans would receive inferior education. Only white South Africans were allowed to vote. Further, over the next decade the National Party ensured Afrikaners greater economic control: it nationalized some key industries, moved state assets to Afrikaner-controlled banks, and kept minimum wages low while reserving the best jobs and wages for white South Africans.

In the mid-1950s the National Party moved to consolidate the idea of separate development by creating African "homelands" or "Bantustans" where Africans were to become "citizens" of self-governing entities that were supposed to correspond to ten "group" identities. The government also increased forced removals of millions of black people who were on land designated for whites only, and it enforced "pass" laws requiring black people in white-only areas to have papers showing they were employed in the area and were therefore allowed to be there for limited periods. Black, Asian, and colored workers lived in illegal "townships," located outside the urban areas reserved for whites, which in most cases lacked basic amenities such as decent housing, running water, or electricity.

ORGANIZING RESISTANCE, 1948–1963

Resistance to white domination in the 1920s and 1930s had been polite and fragmented by class and race, but over the next decades activists grew increasingly unified and militant. During the mid- and late 1940s, younger members of the ANC found their voice in the ANC Youth League. Their 1944 "Programme for Action" called for an end to discrimination and for the direct representation of African people in government. They urged that ANC strategy move from simply petitioning the government for inclusion to strikes, boycotts, civil disobedience, and any other means to change. In December 1949 these more militant activists, including Nelson Mandela, Walter Sisulu, Oliver Tambo, and others, even communists, were elected to top ANC positions.

In 1950 the Communist Party (banned that year by the Suppression of Communism Act), the Indian Congress, and the ANC organized a May Day work stay-away with thousands of participants. On June 26, 1952, a four-month "national defiance" campaign began, where pass, curfew, and separate amenity laws were ignored. It led to the arrest of more than eight thousand people, including thirty-five top leaders of the ANC who were given short suspended sentences. Boycotts of bus transportation, schools, and commodities were also frequent protest tactics in the 1950s.

In 1955 a Congress of the People, consisting of several antiapartheid organizations, proclaimed a "Freedom Charter." It called for self-government, equal political and economic rights, freedom of movement for all, the end of forced and child labor, equality before the law, the right of workers to organize, education and housing for all, and a peaceful foreign policy. Some antiapartheid activists who rejected the Freedom Charter in favor of a more militant stance formed the Pan African Congress (PAC) in 1959. The PAC criticized the ANC as too reactive and urged the movement to use "positive action" on a mass scale. At a PAC-organized pass law demonstration in Sharpeville on March 21, 1960, South African police killed 69 unarmed protesters and wounded about 200 more people. The government declared a state of emergency and banned several antiapartheid political organizations, notably the ANC and the PAC, detaining many of their leaders. Government repression continued, while armed wings of the ANC, Umkhonto we Sizwe (or MK), and the PAC's Azanian People's Liberation Army began sabotage campaigns.

EXILE, MASS ACTION, AND SANCTIONS: 1963–1990

In July 1963 members of the ANC, including Sisulu and Mandela, were charged with leading guerrilla action and given life in prison. Many who were not imprisoned left the country and organized resistance, including sanctions, from exile. Those who remained worked underground or joined antiapartheid organizations that were not banned.

Black workers became more militant in the 1970s. The large African Mine Workers Union strike of 1946 had been brutally crushed, and for the next twenty-five years African labor was relatively quiescent. The government and white businesses continued to keep wages for African workers down compared with wages for white workers and continued to reserve the best jobs and wages for white workers. But, in part because of import substitution industrialization undertaken to compensate for increasingly biting international sanctions in the 1970s and 1980s, demand for both skilled and unskilled labor increased. African workers, comprising more than 70 percent of the labor force, continued to organize even though their unions were illegal. Strikes, also illegal, grew more frequent in the early 1970s, with a wave of strikes in 1973. Though the government shot some of the striking workers, most strikes, which involved nearly a hundred thousand workers, succeeded in getting some concessions. After the 1973 strike wave, the government attempted to contain worker unrest by co-opting it and simultaneously tried to crush labor by arresting activists. As part of the cooptation strategy, "registered" black unions became legal in 1979. Union activists grew convinced of the importance of linking their struggle to the broader antiapartheid movement, and unions became a focus of antiapartheid organizing. Thus, co-optation failed: a Federation of South African Trade Unions, formed in 1979, and the Congress of South African Trade Unions, formed in 1985, became major players in the antiapartheid movement. The number of strikes grew from 101 in 1979 to 1,025 in 1988.

In the 1970s the black consciousness movement asserted black pride as a militant, nationalist response to apartheid, and young people were energized by its philosophy. On June 16, 1976, about 20,000 students marched in Soweto to protest "Bantu" education, including education in Afrikaans; 1,000 students were killed by police and many more were injured. In August 1977 the police killed Steve Biko, a charismatic black consciousness leader, in detention, and the government banned black consciousness organizations. State repression only bolstered antiapartheid activists' determination, and township dwellers formed "civic" associations to focus their local activism.

In 1983 the government, in an attempt to co-opt internal resistance and to appease international critics, created a new constitution which provided for separate parliamentary chambers for white, colored, and Asian South Africans. While allowing Asians and colored South Africans limited representation, the constitution still denied the black majority the right to vote or hold positions in the national government. The "new dispensation" sparked protest even among colored and Asian South Africans, who for the most part derided the sham reforms as a divide-and-rule strategy. In a response that was explicitly multiracial, about six hundred grassroots civic, student, religious, labor, and peace organizations formed the United Democratic Front (UDF) in August 1983. While the ANC, Communist Party, and PAC were banned and in exile, the UDF became the broadest manifestation of the intensifying resistance.

Hundreds of thousands of students boycotted schools in response to the new constitution. The townships literally became battlefields when in 1984 the South African military joined the police in attempting to subdue township protests. While township dwellers waged rent and utility strikes and workers conducted strikes and "stay-aways," students boycotted school and young protesters fought with stones and gasoline bombs against the military in order to make the townships ungovernable. Antiapartheid activists who feared police informants in their midst sometimes killed suspected traitors and collaborators.

Unable to control the protests, the government declared a state of emergency in 1985. States of emergency were essentially martial law: thousands were detained without trial, press reports were restricted, and both individuals and political organizations were banned. Antiapartheid activists within and outside South Africa continued to be murdered by the police and military. Despite the arrest and detention of tens of thousands of antiapartheid activists in the mid- and late 1980s, the scope of activism grew even more militant. All aspects of life were politicized; even funerals of activists killed in the struggle were mass political events.

With increasing effectiveness, white activists, long part of the antiapartheid struggle, organized the white community. White feminist organizations such as the Black Sash grew. The End Conscription Campaign, formed in 1983, urged white youth not to serve in the South African Defense Force. Each year hundreds of young white men publicly refused to serve in the military in the 1980s, and hundreds of others evaded conscription by applying for conscientious objector status, ignoring their call-up, or joining thousands of whites who left the country for political reasons.

Headquartered in Lusaka, Zambia, the ANC consulted with activists inside South Africa and coordinated an international campaign for sanctions, one of the four pillars of struggle, which included mass action, diplomatic isolation, and armed struggle. ANC guerrillas, who were based in other African countries and received military training there and in Eastern Europe, infiltrated South Africa and conducted hundreds of sabotage attacks in the 1980s, even managing to blow up part of Sasol, the coal-to-oil plant, and one of South Africa's nuclear reactors. Meanwhile, the apartheid government sent the military abroad to kill ANC activists and guerrillas. Still, ANC and PAC guerrillas continued to infiltrate South Africa and sabotage the apartheid infrastructure. In 1988 the ANC made 281 attacks.

Labor organizations and antiapartheid activists over the globe mobilized mass movements and pushed their local and national governments to enact sanctions legislation. The earliest sanctions, including the 1963 United Nations voluntary arms embargo (made mandatory in 1977) and the oil embargo, were joined by more biting economic sanctions as well as by sport, cultural, and diplomatic isolation of the apartheid regime. Sanctions were costly for the regime. Though South Africa partially compensated for sanctions by conducting clandestine trade and industrializing, the former policy was expensive and the latter increased the white minority's dependence on black workers, who in turn used the opportunity to organize. The UN and some private organizations sent aid to antiapartheid organizations in exile and within South Africa.

Even whites who agreed with and benefited from apartheid were interested in accommodation as unrest grew and sanctions became more comprehensive. The National Party came under internal pressure for reform. During the late 1980s the ANC and the National Party made limited, clandestine contact. In September 1989 the slightly more moderate F. W. de Klerk was elected president of South Africa. De Klerk freed ANC leader Sisulu from prison later that year. In February 1990, to defuse international and domestic pressure, de Klerk removed the ban on the ANC, PAC, and Communist Party and freed other political prisoners, including Mandela. Although thousands of ANC activists applied for readmission and returned to South Africa and hundreds of political prisoners were released, many were denied immediate admission and release from prison.

NEGOTIATION 1990–1994

Formal negotiations did not immediately begin. Rather, the relevant parties held talks about the conditions for talks through 1991. The government demanded that the ANC and PAC give up armed struggle; they responded that the government should also renounce violence and release all political prisoners. The government continued attempts to divide and conquer the movement with further arrests, harassment, and the clandestine murder of antiapartheid activists. Further, thousands died as the Inkatha Freedom Party, which ostensibly represented Zulu nationalism but which in reality was partially funded by the apartheid government to foment civil unrest, clashed with the ANC. While government security forces were widely suspected of clandestine murders of antiapartheid activists, the de Klerk government denied any part in fomenting unrest (although its systematic role in the violence would later become public). Thousands died in rural and township violence in 1990 and 1991. In an attempt to halt the political violence, Inkatha, the government, the ANC, and other groups signed a National Peace Accord in September 1991.

In November 1991 nineteen political organizations agreed to hold talks, the Convention for a Democratic South Africa. To keep pressure on the government, antiapartheid organizations continued rent boycotts, strikes, and demonstrations. Negotiators reached a stalemate in May 1992 over the details of writing a new constitution. When formal negotiations stalled, antiapartheid organizations negotiated bilaterally with the government and with each other. Inkatha's leader, Mangosutho Buthelezi, allied with conservative white parties to form a Concerned South Africans Group and attempted to postpone elections.

Negotiations among twenty-six parties and organizations resumed in April 1993 in a multiparty forum. Far right-wing white activists attempted to sabotage the negotiations by killing a popular ANC leader, Chris Hani, and storming the negotiating forum. The Inkatha refused to participate in negotiations, and violence continued between it and the ANC. Antiapartheid activists worked together in committees to envisage the details of everything from education and housing to the environment in postapartheid South Africa. Though it was difficult, the parties who were willing to negotiate wrote an interim constitution, including a new bill of rights, decided on a date for elections, and formed a Transitional Executive Council to run the government from the end of 1993 until the first elections. The Inkatha Freedom Party threatened to boycott elections, but just days before elections were scheduled to occur, it agreed to participate. South Africa's first democratic elections were conducted April 26–29, 1994. The ANC won 62.5 percent of the vote, and President Nelson Mandela was inaugurated on May 10, 1994, to uphold an interim constitution.

See also *Biko, Stephen; Mandela, Nelson; Race.*

Neta Crawford

BIBLIOGRAPHY

Crawford, Neta C., and Audie Klotz, eds. *How Sanctions Work: South Africa.* London: Macmillan, 1998.

Friedman, Steven, and Doreen Atkinson. *South African Review 7: The Small Miracle—South Africa's Negotiated Settlement.* Randberg: Ravan Press, 1994.

Johns, Sheridan, and R. Hunt Davis Jr., eds. *Mandela, Tambo, and the African National Congress: The Struggle against Apartheid, 1948–1990.* New York: Oxford University Press, 1991.

Mandela, Nelson. *The Struggle Is My Life.* New York: Pathfinder Press, 1990.

Manzo, Kathryn A. *Domination, Resistance, and Social Change in South Africa.* Westport, Conn.: Praeger, 1992.

Marx, Anthony W. *Lessons of Struggle: South African Internal Opposition, 1960–1990.* London: Oxford University Press, 1992.

Maylam, Paul. *A History of the African People of South Africa: From the Early Iron Age to the 1970s.* London: Croom Helm, 1986.

Price, Robert M. *The Apartheid State in Crisis: Political Transformation in South Africa, 1975–1990.* London: Oxford University Press, 1991.

Seidman, Gay W. *Manufacturing Militance: Workers' Movements in Brazil and South Africa, 1970–1985.* Berkeley: University of California Press, 1994.

Wilson, Francis, and Mamphela Ramphele. *Uprooting Poverty: The South African Challenge.* Cape Town: David Philip, 1989.

SPANISH CIVIL WAR (1936–1939)

On July 17, 1936, units of the army based in Spanish North Africa rebelled against the liberal democratic Second Republic (founded April 14, 1931). Although there had been a long history of military intervention in Spanish political life, in 1936 the coup was an old instrument being used to a new end: to hold back the modernizing tide of mass political democracy. Like the wealthy landowners and industrialists who backed them, the military rebels were hostile to the economically redistributive, socially leveling, secularizing, and culturally pluralizing intent of the Republic's principal reforms. The junior officers who provided core support for the coup also feared the Republic's military budget cuts would threaten their career prospects.

Weidenfeld and Nicolson Archives. Alex Tait/Equator Graphics, Inc.

On July 18 the rebellion spread to the Spanish mainland. It was successful in the Catholic-conservative, rural Spain of the center and north, where a significant measure of popular support derived from peasant and provincial lower middle class hostility to the Republic's secularization program. But in most of urban industrial Spain (including Bilbao and Asturias in the north), the rebels were defeated by the combined forces of worker militia (formed by trade unions and political parties of the left) and loyal elements in the police. Worker resistance to the coup in Spain was galvanized by the proletarian defeats sustained elsewhere in Europe as fascist or quasi-fascist alliances went into action to hold back democracy (Italy 1922, Portugal 1926, Germany 1933, Austria 1934). But in Spain, with the Republic in control of the country's financial and industrial resources and controlling the bulk of the population, the military looked certain to fail.

Facing defeat, the rebels requested and received planes from Adolf Hitler and Benito Mussolini to transport their crack troops, the Army of Africa (mercenaries commanded by Spanish career officers), across the Strait of Gibraltar (temporarily blockaded by the Republican navy) to mainland Spain. This first act of international intervention by Europe's fascist powers—attracted by the possibility of causing difficulties for France—gave the Spanish rebels their army, allowing them to launch a full-scale war against the Republic.

ESCALATION TO CIVIL WAR

Whereas in the rebel zone the army command assumed supreme military and political control, in the approximately two-thirds of Spain that was Republican, the coup precipitated state collapse. Police and armed forces were dislocated, and the normal functions of government paralyzed. To many in the worker militia, government paralysis was a positive state of affairs. For poor and marginalized social groups in Spain—including many urban and rural workers—the state still had negative connotations: military conscription, indirect taxation, and everyday persecution—particularly for the unionized. Thus for many Spanish workers, resistance to the rebels was also directed against the state and was bound up with building a new social and political order, often on radical anticapitalist economic lines.

In the urban and rural northeast (Barcelona and Aragon)

and Republican parts of the rural south, industry and agriculture were collectivized, and trade union and party committees organized emergency defense and met the needs of the civilian front. Whether the militia, the collectives, and the committees together amounted to a revolution is a subject of historical debate. Thousands of Spanish workers committed their energies, and in many cases gave their lives, to achieve this social transformation. But the social revolution lacked a political leadership or any blueprint for taking power Republic-wide. The radical initiatives remained locally focused and highly fragmented. This fragmentation did not seriously disadvantage the Republicans as long as the enemy also remained "local"—meaning the soldiery of the provincial garrison or (sometimes) the local police. But once German and Italian intervention transformed the nature of the conflict by transporting the Army of Africa to Spain, the Republicans were forced to rethink their resistance strategy.

During August and September 1936, the Army of Africa swept through southern Spain en route for the central capital city of Madrid, strategically butchering and terrorizing the pro-Republican population (especially the rural landless) as it went and seemingly unstoppable against largely untrained militia forces. If the Republic was to survive the rebel onslaught of modern mechanized warfare (courtesy of German and Italian aid), it would need to put an army in the field and mobilize its whole population for total war—something unprecedented in Spanish experience. The revolutionary energy of the politically conscious, organized working class no longer sufficed, as it had in the period of emergency defense. Now everyone had to be brought on board—the politically unmobilized sectors of the population, middle-class sectors and especially their female constituencies—to provide vital industrial and social service labor behind the lines.

The efficient mobilization of the Republic's resources—human and material—was made doubly crucial in view of the regime's international isolation. The Republic was refused military aid by its sister democracies Great Britain and France. Instead, they proposed and established a nonintervention treaty in August 1936 which debarred state and private enterprise in signatory countries from delivering war materiel to Spain. Given that Germany and Italy, though signatories, freely aided the rebels, nonintervention worked solely against the Republic and would do so for the duration of the war. British policy makers knew this. But they believed that the rebels were better able than the Republicans to guarantee the rights of capital and private property in Spain (including substantial British investment), so they turned a blind eye to fascist flouting of nonintervention. British reluctance to act had grave consequences, since an early, resolute message from Britain might have stopped Mussolini and Hitler from intervening so lavishly in Spain.

By the end of October 1936 the rebels were on the outskirts of Madrid. Their arrival had been delayed by a detour to relieve the garrison besieged in Toledo, southeast of Madrid. (This publicity coup clinched for the African Army's Gen. Francisco Franco the position of supreme military and political commander in rebel Spain.) The delay gave the Republicans crucial time to organize the capital city's defenses. The extra time and the Soviet Union's tardy provision of military aid (sent for fear that the threatening Republican collapse would free Nazi firepower for aggression against vulnerable Soviet frontiers) saved the Spanish Republic from certain military defeat in November. Thereafter, Soviet-procured aid, contrary to much received historical wisdom, was barely adequate to offer the Republic scant survival. The battle for Madrid involved intense fighting and vast casualties, especially among the left's volunteer force, the International Brigades, which acted as the Republic's shock troops. As the rebels dug in to besiege the capital, the conflict turned into a war of attrition, which would last until late March 1939.

REBEL AND REPUBLICAN SPAIN

In spite of the different political ideologies and cultural values underpinning rebel and Republican Spain, the war period saw the common continuation and acceleration of a process of mass political mobilization—especially of women and youth. The fascist Falange and Spanish Communist Party organizations fulfilled comparable functions in the two zones, bringing previously unmobilized sectors of the population to the state.

A sharp contrast is often drawn between the "monolithic" political unity of the rebels under Franco and the fragmentation and discord of the Republicans. Rebel unity was in part an appearance produced by dictatorial techniques. But it also had a basis in fact, because the differences between conservative Catholics and fascists or between brands of monarchist took second place to their common and overwhelming opposition to all that the Republic stood for. In Republican Spain, by contrast, political differences were too fundamental to be dissolved by a common anti-Francoism. Moreover, democracy—even if curtailed by wartime imperatives—made the divisions much more visible.

But the reasons for Republican discord also changed during the war. Before May 1937 an unequal struggle was waged between an increasingly marginalized and fragmented revolutionary left—favoring an anticapitalist war effort based on the collectives and committee structures established in the coup's aftermath—and those republicans, socialists, and communists who sought to reestablish the broad, reforming liberal democratic alliance of workers and the middle-class sectors disrupted by the July 1936 military coup. The broad alliance's victory was symbolically sealed in May 1937, when Republican state police defeated workers' social and political protests in the streets of Barcelona and a new government was appointed under the parliamentary socialist Juan Negrín. This outcome reflected as much the balance of social and political forces *inside* Republican Spain as it did the international context and, in particular, Soviet hostility to the revolutionary project.

Thereafter, political divisions and social tensions in Republican Spain were mainly a product of the huge strain of sustaining a war effort under the conditions of chronic shortage imposed by nonintervention. By 1938 the Republic had difficulty delivering the basic requirements of daily life to its civilian population—swelled by constant waves of refugees arriving from rebel-conquered territory. The Republic's political legitimacy eroded as shortages, inflation, population dislocation, starvation, and threatening epidemic disease grew. After the Munich agreement (September 1938) revealed Britain and France's commitment to appeasing the fascist powers, the Soviet Union's always precarious support for the Republic began to dwindle, as Soviet leader Joseph Stalin came to realize that his strategy had failed to win Britain and France over to his goal of a tripartite alliance against expansionist Nazi Germany.

The Munich agreement spurred liberal republican and some socialist leaders, believing in the chimera of a negotiated peace with the rebels, to oppose further Republican resistance. In March 1939 their activities combined with massive war-weariness in Republican territory to spark a complex political and social rebellion against the Negrín government and the Spanish Communist Party—the forces symbolizing continued resistance. The political collapse of the Republican civilian front, rather than outright military defeat, afforded Franco's rebels their victory of April 1, 1939. That collapse was caused primarily by the crippling shortages imposed on the Republic across 1937–1939 by nonintervention. Yet Republican resistance, achieved in spite of British policy, probably delayed other forms of Nazi aggression in Europe, thus allowing Britain crucial time to rearm.

Rebel victory in the war meant the beginning of an ultimately unsuccessful attempt to achieve economic modernization in Spain without the accompanying products of modernity: the mass political democracy and cultural pluralism symbolized by the Republic. Up to 400,000 people went into exile. For the defeated who could not leave, the civil war would continue across the 1940s in the intense forms of institutionalized repression and discrimination through which the Franco regime constructed its power base. More than one million people spent time in prison or labor camps. In addition to 400,000 war deaths, there were, by the most conservative estimates, 100,000 executions between 1939 and 1943. But given that many executions occurred outside the dictatorial legal framework, we will never know the true figure.

See also *Anarchism; Civil Wars; German Nazi Revolution (1933–1945); Hitler, Adolf; Italian Fascist Revolution (1919–1945); Mussolini, Benito; Orwell, George.*

HELEN GRAHAM

BIBLIOGRAPHY

Carr, Raymond. *The Spanish Tragedy: The Civil War in Perspective.* London: Weidenfeld and Nicolson, 1977.

Fraser, Ronald. *Blood of Spain.* London: Allen Lane, 1979.

Graham, Helen, and Jo Labanyi, eds. *Spanish Cultural Studies: An Introduction. The Struggle for Modernity.* Oxford: Oxford University Press, 1995.

Howson, Gerald. *Arms for Spain.* London: John Murray, 1998 forthcoming.

Preston, Paul. *A Concise History of the Spanish Civil War.* London: Fontana, 1996.

———. *Franco: A Biography.* London: Fontana, 1994.

———. *The Politics of Revenge. Fascism and the Military in Twentieth Century Spain.* London: Unwin Hyman, 1990.

Preston, Paul, and Ann L. MacKenzie, eds. *The Republic Besieged: Civil War in Spain 1936–1939.* Edinburgh: University of Edinburgh Press, 1996.

SPANISH *COMUNEROS* REVOLT (1520–1521)

The revolt of the *comuneros* (commoners or townspeople) that engulfed the northern and central sections of the Spanish state of Castile from May 1520 to the battle of Villalar on April 23, 1521, was provoked by festering unhappiness with the government of King Charles I, also known as Charles V, the Holy Roman emperor.

PRECONDITIONS

In no country of western Europe, with the possible exception of England, was the late fifteenth-century change in the fortunes of monarchy so dramatic as in the kingdom of Castile. The joint reign of Ferdinand II of Aragon and Isabella I of Castile (1474–1504)—representing the political unification of Spain—was the longest period of stability and internal peace that Castile had enjoyed since the reign of Alfonso XI (1312–1350). The peace enabled the crown to establish what historians have described as a "new monarchy"—that is, a unified, centralized state under firm royal control. Continuing the practice of their predecessor, Henry IV, of using men with legal training in government positions, Ferdinand and Isabella established a Royal Council, dominated by these jurists, as the centerpiece of their government. On the municipal and regional levels, they extended the system of *corregidores* (magistrates) to all of Castile's principal towns. The *corregidor* presided over meetings of municipal councils and had overall responsibility for local administration.

But the flaws and inconsistencies in royal policy, if not immediately apparent, were nonetheless real and of lasting significance. For example, the 1492 conquest of the Muslim kingdom of Granada eliminated an enemy state but added to Castile's already substantial strategic responsibilities by incorporating a long and vulnerable coastline and a restive population. Protection of the new conquest was one major reason for the crown's increasing financial problems after 1492.

Another problem arose from one of Ferdinand and Isabella's most controversial accomplishments: the expulsion of the Spanish Jews, decreed May 31, 1492. The struggle that resulted first in the separation and then the gradual expulsion of the Jews pitted the crown, which continued to support the Jewish community (the crown was opposed to the expulsion and was forced to act), against city councils strongly influenced by Jews who had converted to Catholicism and who had become hostile to the continued presence of practicing Jews since the Inquisition had begun punishing the latter for Judaizing in the mid-1480s.

But sharp disagreement over the fate of the Jews was not the only issue that divided the crown from its erstwhile supporters among Castile's urban elite. The *corregidores,* once eagerly welcomed by the municipalities, had failed to carry out one of their primary responsibilities: protecting their jurisdictions from encroachment from nearby seigniorial possessions. All over Castile a newly resurgent aristocracy was seizing municipal land while the crown and its representatives looked the other way.

THE DYNASTIC CRISIS

Isabella's death in 1504 exposed an already weakened and unpopular monarchy to a dangerous period of political instability. By the terms of her will Ferdinand was stripped of his title as king of Castile on her death, and the succession was vested in their daughter Juana who, with her husband, the Archduke Philip the Fair, arrived from Flanders to take the throne of Castile in April 1506. Ferdinand remained king of Aragon. When Philip's death on September 25, 1506, undermined Juana's fragile mental health, she had to be removed from office.

Charles of Ghent, the couple's six-year-old son, was now heir to the throne of Castile, where a weak regency government under the leadership of Francisco Jiménez de Cisneros was established. The regency lasted only until 1510, when Ferdinand was named administrator of the kingdom. Ferdinand's death on January 23, 1516, ushered in a second Cisneros regency whose authority was undermined by Charles's insatiable demands for money to finance his lifestyle in Flanders. Charles of Ghent arrived in Spain in the fall of 1517. After meeting with his mother in the palace at Tordesillas and receiving her consent, he assumed power as King Charles I of Spain.

The new king, a boy of seventeen, spoke no Spanish and was dominated by his Flemish advisers. His situation was further complicated by the partial recovery of his mother, whose lucidity was giving rise to uncomfortable rumors that Charles had coerced her into signing away a throne that rightfully was hers.

The inexperienced young ruler also made some serious political mistakes that alienated key sectors of Castilian society. Influential members of the clergy were driven into opposition by the government's attempt to tax their benefices (religious offices) and by Charles's decision to award Spain's most important ecclesiastical benefice—the archbishopric of Toledo—to Guillaume de Croy, a foreigner and the nephew of his all-powerful adviser Grand Chamberlain Guillaume de Croy. Castile's urban dwellers resented the blatant arm-twisting used to force delegates to the national legislature (Cortes) of Castile meeting in Santiago–Coruña to vote in favor of a special subsidy to allow Charles to travel to Germany and assume the post of Holy Roman emperor. Even the aristocracy, arguably the monarchy's most important supporter since the latter part of the reign of Ferdinand and Isabella, was alienated by the appointment of Charles's former tutor Cardinal Adrian of Utrecht as regent instead of one of its own. Thus during the critical first months of the *comunero* revolt the aristocracy did little or nothing to help the floundering regency government.

THE REVOLT

After May 20, 1520, when Charles left Spain, the regency found itself unable to contain the growing opposition to the government. The revolt started gradually in the late spring and summer of 1520, when many of Castile's cities withdrew their support from the government and stopped paying the taxes authorized by the Cortes. After the partial destruction of the city of Medina del Campo by royal troops, the movement gathered strength. The rebel junta of Tordesillas, which first met on September 19, included representatives of thirteen cities from the historical regions of New and Old Castile.

Comunero constitutional ideas were contained in a detailed set of articles drawn up in Valladolid. These articles set forth a contractual framework for the future government of Castile, which would have greatly strengthened the role of the Cortes and made a reformed royal government more responsible to its citizen subjects. But the revolt was destined to fail. For one thing, the great cities of Spain's southern region of Andalusia, especially Seville, never joined the movement. The defection of the Castilian city of Burgos in November 1520 marked the beginning of decline. Even more ominous was the changing attitude of the nobility. Indifferent to the fate of the regency, members were galvanized into action when the *comuneros* began attacking their estates. Charles's appointment of Constable Inigo Fernández de Velasco and Admiral Fredrique Enríquez de Cabrera, the two leading members of Castilian aristocracy, as co-regents, cemented the alliance. The nobility now raised troops from members' estates to put down the revolt. Helped by the appointment of a single military leader—something the *comuneros* had failed to do—the royal army seized Tordesillas and drove out the rebel junta on December 5, 1521. The battle of Villalar on April 23, 1521, was a rout of the demoralized *comunero* army. The revolt was at an end.

POST-*COMUNERO* CASTILE

A subdued and greatly weakened Charles returned to Spain in 1522 to face the task of rebuilding support for the monarchy. Acutely aware that the small force of German mercenaries he brought with him could never keep down a restive kingdom and weakened financially by the costs of repressing the revolt, Charles adopted some of the rebels' demands, especially in marrying his cousin Isabella, the daughter of King Emmanuel of Portugal, and allowing his heirs to be brought up in Castile.

Charles also moved to regain the support of the urban elite who had played such an important part in the opposition movement: he gave them a key role in collecting the taxes authorized by the Cortes. Co-optation of Castile's urban elite meant that the last possible source of effective political opposition to royal government had been removed. The Cortes went along with the drastic overextension of Spain's military responsibilities in Flanders and Italy and approved dramatically increased taxation. Royal power had been reestablished, but the absence of any meaningful political debate meant that the policies that ensured the Spanish military, political, and economic disasters of the seventeenth century were carried to their logical conclusion.

STEPHEN HALICZER

BIBLIOGRAPHY

Haliczer, Stephen. *The Comuneros of Castile: The Forging of a Revolution.* Madison: University of Wisconsin Press, 1981.

Maravall, José Antonio. *Las Comunidades de Castilla: Una primera revolución moderna.* Madrid: Revista de Occidente, 1963.

Pérez, Joseph. *La révolution des "Comunidades" de Castille (1520–21).* Bordeaux: Institut d' Etudes Ibériques, 1970.

Seaver, Henry Latimer. *The Great Revolt in Castile: A Study of the Comunero Movement of 1520–21.* London: Constable, 1928.

SPANISH CONQUEST, AZTEC AND INCA REVOLTS IN THE ERA OF (1500–1571)

The story of the Spanish conquest of the Aztec and Inca empires is often told as a grand tale of courage and war or of terror and disease. A handful of Spanish *conquistadores,* aided by the European diseases they brought to the New World—such as smallpox, which killed hundreds of thousands, possibly millions, of Native Americans—overthrew large and sophisticated empires. However, to tell the story in these terms is too simple. In both the Aztec empire in Mesoamerica and the Inca empire in the Andes region of South America, civil war and rebellions among Native Americans played a major role in the Spaniards' victory. Indeed, one of the key moves of the Spanish conquistadores was to play upon the internal divisions within these empires in order to gain allies for their conquest.

THE FALL OF THE AZTECS

Hernando Cortés landed on the coast of Mexico in 1519. He soon made the conquest of Tenochtitlan, the great capital of the Aztec empire, his main goal. If the Aztec empire had been a united state, such a goal would have been unattainable. But the Aztec empire was not a single, unified structure. Rather, it was a tribute empire, loosely embracing many distinct peoples and preserving some major enemies. Tenochtitlan, dependent for food and raw materials on the tributary states that sent supplies to support its warriors, was vulnerable to any cracks in the tributary system, cracks that the Spanish opened and exploited.

The Aztec empire had been built over the two hundred years prior to the arrival of the Spaniards, as Mexica people from the north migrated into the central valley of Mexico, the site of today's Mexico City. Making alliances and winning battles, the Mexica gradually won from the various cities and peoples of the valley recognition of their overlordship. The Mexica, now calling themselves the Aztecs, built a grand capital, Tenochtitlan, and developed a rich symbolic and ceremonial life that emphasized their domination of the surrounding peoples, including armed raids and the ritual sacrifice of thousands of enemy warriors. For most peoples of the valley, the raids of the Aztec warriors were sufficient to win a grudging consent to Aztec rule and tributary payments. The Aztecs even extended the tribute system to peoples beyond the valley, from the Gulf coast to the Pacific Ocean, although some cities—especially Tlaxcala, located over the hills to the east of the valley—remained independent and resolute enemies of the Aztecs.

Thus when Cortés entered Mexico, he found not only a dominant Aztec empire but a patchwork of independent and tributary states that would gladly take the opportunity to turn on, and even loot, the Aztec empire to which for so many years they had yielded their own men, women, foodstuffs, and luxury goods. At first, the Aztecs welcomed the Spaniards and showered them with gifts, hoping to impress them with the riches and power of their empire. But when the Spaniards repaid their gifts with brutality, the Spanish were driven out of Tenochtitlan with great losses. At this point, Cortés made alliances with the Aztecs' enemies and tributaries. Using horses and cannon to intimidate the tributary cities, and tempting them with offers of cooperation and loot from triumph over the Aztecs, Cortés gained enough allies to be able to place Tenochtitlan under siege. The crucial element for Spanish victory was the turning of the tributary states against the capital; they withdrew their tribute and offered intermittent help to the Spanish invaders. Deprived of its tributary grain, the once-proud capital descended into starvation. Over the next four months, cannon fire, starvation, and disease destroyed and depopulated the magnificent city. When the Spaniards and their allies finally entered, they looted what remained and in 1523 hanged Cuauhtemoc, the last Aztec emperor.

Thus ended the Aztec empire. But even in demoralization and defeat, the Mexica hung on to hopes of a different future. During the siege, the great idols of Tenochtitlan were smuggled out of the city to the north. Although Christianity was imposed upon Mexico, the beliefs and customs of the Mexica were mixed with it, and rebellions against Spanish rule occurred periodically until independence from Spain was won in 1821. Mexico today honors both its Spanish and Mexica heritage. Fittingly, the man who in July 1997 was elected mayor of Mexico City, the new capital that sits on the site of Tenochtitlan, is named Cuauhtemoc Cardenas, honoring the last leader of the Aztecs.

THE COLLAPSE OF THE INCAS

Further to the south, in the Inca empire of the Andes, Spaniards arrived in 1532. There the Spanish commander Francisco Pizarro found an empire that was already thrown into crisis by rebellions and civil wars. Like Cortés before him, Pizarro used the divisions and revolts in the empire to defeat it.

The Inca empire was not a tributary empire like the Aztec; the Incas demanded much more of their subject peoples. The Incas seized land and required that it be tilled to provide for shrines, the state, and royal families; they demanded labor services from craftsmen, farmers, and servants; they even resettled conquered lands with Inca soldiers and forced defeated inhabitants to migrate. Although the Incas also used persuasion, treaties, and ritual to gain adherence, their rule was often demanding, and subject peoples frequently revolted when they perceived weakness in the imperial authorities, especially after the death of a ruler. The Inca emperor's sons were all equally entitled to aspire to the throne, and the emperor's death set off a competition among royal factions for control of the empire. Sometimes the conflicts were settled amicably by negotiation, but at other times they led to civil war. One such civil war, between Washkar and 'Ataw Wallpa, the sons of Emperor Wayna Qhapaq, began in 1527 and was still raging when the Spaniards arrived.

Washkar, whose supporters were mainly in the southern portion of the empire, and 'Ataw Wallpa, whose supporters were mainly in the north, split the empire with their conflict. 'Ataw Wallpa's generals had just captured Washkar and defeated his troops when the Spaniards invited 'Ataw Wallpa to meet with them. The Spaniards, however, ambushed and captured 'Ataw Wallpa. While held by the Spaniards, 'Ataw Wallpa managed to send a message to his generals to execute Washkar. The order was carried out, but soon after, the Spaniards executed 'Ataw Wallpa, leaving the Inca empire without a clear successor. The Spaniards moved to the imperial capital at Cuzco, where they found another son of Wayna Qhapaq, named Manquo 'Inka, who was willing to work with them, and they placed him on the throne as a puppet emperor.

Manquo 'Inka, however, was not widely accepted as the rightful ruler. Several of 'Ataw Wallpa's generals continued to lead armies and hold power in the north, while in the south, recently resettled peoples looked for a chance to reassert their independence. In 1535, when Pizarro departed Cuzco to try to establish order in the north, Manquo 'Inka tried to expel the Spanish garrison from the Inca capital. However, he received little support from the peoples of the Inca empire, and his attack failed. By 1536 what had been a unified empire fragmented into contending parts. While royal factions and their armies continued to battle over the succession to the throne, a series of insurrections against Inca authority broke out throughout the empire. Groups like the Wankas and Cañaris allied with the Spaniards against Inca leaders. In his memoirs, written in 1571, Pedro Pizarro noted that the Spanish could not have won had the Inca empire remained united: "If the land had not been divided by the war between Washkar and 'Ataw Wallpa we could not have entered or conquered it."

Even with these divisions, however, the Spanish did not easily gain control of the broken empire. Various groups of Spaniards quarreled among themselves and with the vice regal authority sent by the King of Spain, leading to civil wars among the Spanish settlers. By the 1560s Peru was in chaos, and many of the native peoples, even those who had earlier supported the Spanish against the Incas, joined a millenarian revolt, called *taki onqoy,* that called on all native peoples to unite against the Spanish invaders.

The crisis was resolved in the 1570s by the viceroy Francisco de Toledo, who finally dismantled the Inca empire and set up a formal bureaucracy to administer the region's resources. Native American communities were broken up and their lands sold; high labor services and taxes in silver were demanded and extracted; and the Spanish and *mestizos* were consolidated into a new ruling class. A half-century after Hernando Cortés landed in Mexico, the divisions and rebellions in the Aztec and Inca empires had helped the Spanish dominate a region extending from central Mexico down the entire Pacific coast to the areas of modern Ecuador, Peru, Bolivia, and Chile.

Jack A. Goldstone

BIBLIOGRAPHY

Clendinnen, Inga. *Aztecs.* Cambridge: Cambridge University Press, 1991.
Patterson, Thomas C. *The Inca Empire.* New York: Berg/St. Martin's Press, 1991.

SPANISH STRUGGLES AGAINST REVOLUTIONARY MOVEMENTS IN SOUTHERN EUROPE (1640–1668)

In the 1640s the Spanish empire ruled by King Philip IV of the royal house of Habsburg faced a series of revolts in peripheral territories in southern Europe. The revolutionary events came in response to Spain's efforts to centralize authority in Madrid according to the practices of the kingdom of Castile, the center of the empire. Revolts in Catalonia, Sicily, and Naples, fueled by popular resentment against Spanish war taxes, sought profound social and political change. Internal divisions undercut all three movements, however, and Spain eventually was able to reassert its control. Portugal's simultaneous revolt against the Spanish crown was, by contrast, successful. Colonial revenues, shrewd diplomacy, nationalist sentiment, and a collaborating nobility all contributed to the recapture of the country's independence from Spain in 1668.

SPAIN'S EMPIRE IN THE SEVENTEENTH CENTURY

In 1640 Philip IV of Spain ruled an empire on which the sun never set. Spain itself was a composite state in which Castile, the largest kingdom, predominated but which also included the kingdom of Aragon. Aragon comprised the kingdom of Valencia, Aragon itself, and the principality of Catalonia. These other realms each had separate constitutional and fiscal arrangements with the crown, a source of constant preoccupation, negotiation, and complaint.

The crown's authority was less constrained in its extensive "conquests" in the Americas and the Philippines, which formed the Spanish empire and provided a large if intermittent flow of precious metals to the metropolis. Philip IV also ruled over the Spanish Habsburg lands in Europe itself: the Spanish Netherlands, the Franche Comté, the Duchy of Milan, Sardinia, and the kingdoms of Naples and Sicily.

The acquisition of Portugal in 1580, following a dynastic crisis, brought another great imperial system under Habsburg control. Portugal's far-flung empire included Macao and Brazil, as well as possessions in India and West Africa. By the 1620s the dominions of the Spanish Habsburgs were truly a global empire, but one already experiencing the strains created by the burdens of war in Europe and the defense of the empire.

Like other societies of the time, the Spanish realms always faced the risk of poor agricultural conditions, food shortages, and price rises, which could set off popular insurrection. Minor insurrections were not a threat to political control as long as the nobility of the various kingdoms remained loyal to the regime. The arrangements between the nobles and the crown, however, were considerably altered between 1622 and 1643 by Philip IV's chief minister, the Count-Duke of Olivares. Olivares launched an extensive reform program designed to centralize control of the disparate parts of the empire, but his plans for creating an integrated military force (the Union of Arms) and equalizing the tax burden throughout the realms were opposed and resented by the peripheral kingdoms, which sought to retain their traditional constitutional arrangements and fiscal independence, as well as their cultural and linguistic distinctiveness. Resistance to Olivares's schemes intensified after the outbreak of open hostilities with France in 1635, as Spain acted to meet its mounting military costs.

THE REVOLTS IN CATALONIA AND PORTUGAL

In 1640 the Spanish army that had been fighting in southern France was billeted in Catalonia. The crown called a meeting of the provincial assembly (the Corts) for the purpose of extracting more war taxes from the province. Fighting broke out between peasants and the billeted troops. Moves to defuse the conflict came too late, and in June a traditional procession of agricultural laborers in Barcelona turned into a riot with social overtones as the homes of the wealthy were sacked and the viceroy himself was killed. Olivares, recognizing that Spain faced a rebellion as complete as that of Holland after 1621, found repression his only course of action. The Catalan nobility may have been willing to come to terms, but the people of Barcelona and rural peasants led by Pau Claris, a cleric who headed the Diputació (a standing committee of the Corts), were intransigent. With the aid of France, delighted to see civil disturbance distracting Spain and hopeful of acquiring a new province across the Pyrenees, the Catalans defeated the royal army in January 1641. The revolt then settled simultaneously into a war against Castile and a civil war that divided Catalan society.

The events of 1640–1641 had effects elsewhere in the Habsburg dominions. Spain's attempt to mobilize support in Portugal for its campaign against the Catalans created resentment among the Portuguese nobility, who had until that point remained aloof from popular anti-Castilian sentiment in Portugal. The local nobility had not joined, for example, in a popular rebellion in Evora in 1637, which Olivares brutally suppressed. Nevertheless, strains were evident. The nobility complained of the absence of king and court, which resided in Madrid. Both they and the merchants of Lisbon watched in despair as the Portuguese empire came under increasing attack from Spain's enemies, particularly the Dutch. Persistent disruptions of Portuguese shipping in the sugar and spice trades, coupled with the loss of Ormuz in the Persian Gulf in 1623, Luanda in Angola in 1641, and northeastern Brazil (1630–1654), all made the attachment to Spain appear suicidal to many elements in Portugal. Moreover, the increasing taxes levied to pay for the defense of the Spanish empire were detested.

By the 1630s, factions had developed among Portuguese nobles involved in the governance of the country in Lisbon and Madrid. Olivares's chief adviser on Portuguese affairs, Diogo Soares, and his brother-in-law, Miguel de Vasconcelos, Spain's chief officer in Lisbon, exercised powerful control of money and offices and were hated by their political opponents. In December 1640, with the Spanish army distracted in Catalonia and the Duke of Bragança, whose family claimed the Portuguese throne, under pressure from Olivares to depart the country, disgruntled nobles staged a palace coup in which Vasconcelos was killed and the Spanish vicereine imprisoned. The local Spanish garrisons were quickly overpowered. The reluctant Duke of Bragança was acclaimed King João IV. To some extent the duke had been pushed into this position by his wife, Luisa de Guzmán, a relative of Olivares and sister of the Spanish Duke of Medina-Sidonia, who had royal ambitions of his own. Word of the rebellion was sent to Portugal's overseas possessions, which almost without exception rallied to the Bragança cause. Popular support was mobilized by calls to national sentiments and messianic prophecies. Within Portugal, however, many nobles continued to take the Habsburg side and departed the country.

Madrid was now faced with provincial revolts on two fronts in Europe, as well as growing obligations overseas. To make matters worse, an ill-formed separatist plot of senior Andalucian nobles, particularly the Duke of Medina-Sidonia, was exposed in 1641 in Castile itself. Through a combination of repression and threat Olivares defused the attempt, but his days were numbered. He fell from power in 1643. His successors, unable to bring the situations in Catalonia and Portugal to rapid resolution, decided to contain the Portuguese rebellion and confront the more serious threat posed by the French in Catalonia.

With the French army providing support for the Catalan insurgents, Spanish forces could do little to penetrate the region militarily. The civil war, however, had divided the clergy, intensified social tensions, encouraged the endemic banditry, and disheartened the mercantile classes, all of which weakened the will of the Catalans to continue the struggle in the face of shortage, hunger, and a great plague in 1650–1654. Moreover, the connection with France came at great cost. The French occupied Roselló and Cerdanya and exacted a heavy tax on the rest of Catalonia to pay for the war. As France became distracted by its own internal revolt of the Fronde, the fortunes of war turned. Spanish armies began a siege of Barcelona in 1651, and the city fell in the following year. The Spanish crown agreed to a general amnesty. Spain also agreed to respect the traditional constitutional arrangements with Catalonia.

UPRISINGS IN THE ITALIAN KINGDOMS

The stress of the revolt in Catalonia and the cost of the war had set off uprisings in the Italian kingdoms. Naples and Sicily were governed by viceroys who ruled in collaboration with the local nobility. The regions had little autonomy, and local institutions were weak. Spain's war with France and the burden of suppressing the Catalan and Portuguese revolts led Philip to impose new demands on the Sicilian and Neapolitan nobility. In response to resistance from the nobles, the crown made concessions of land and fiscal control to encourage the nobility to increase their levels of exaction. Poor agricultural conditions in 1646 made the situation worse. Popular revolt erupted in 1647, first in Palermo (May) and then in Naples (July), fueled in both cases by resentment over taxes on food. The revolt soon spread into the countryside, where peasants sought to regain traditional communal rights.

Both movements were popular uprisings of large urban populations; in Naples, the peasantry participated as well. In general, however, the propertied classes and nobility remained loyal to Spanish rule. In Palermo, internal conflicts and a lack of clear goals made Spanish repression relatively easy. In Naples, a popular figure, Tommaso Aniello ("Masaniello"), emerged as the leader of the urban revolt, which was directed against the symbols of authority and taxation. Cast in the mold of typical "loyalist" movements, that revolt evinced support for the king but sought the repeal of unpopular taxes and the recall of hated imperial officials. Without forces, the viceroy at first acceded to popular demands for the restitution of "ancient" privileges and liberties, but when a Spanish fleet brought troops, he moved to suppress the revolt. Meanwhile, Masaniello had been slain by his own followers, and the popular uprising was now directed by others. Resistance to the Spanish forces now gave the separatist elements a new focus. A republic was declared, and, as in Catalonia, French protection and support were sought. That support was not forthcoming, however, and by April 1648 Spanish rule had been reimposed, although with some concessions on taxes.

THE INDEPENDENCE OF PORTUGAL

By the end of 1652 only Portugal remained in rebellion. The Spanish policy of containment had allowed the new Portuguese king to conduct an active diplomatic campaign and conclude trade and military agreements with Spain's enemies, a situation made possible to some extent by the lure of Portugal's still important colonial trades. Moreover, unlike Catalonia, Portugal could depend on the income from its empire, especially from the Brazilian sugar trade.

The bitter warfare on the Spanish-Portuguese frontier was mostly carried out by small armies razing the countryside and capturing border towns. Distracted by Catalonia and other commitments, Spain found it difficult to field an effective army against the Portuguese. Able commanders were in particularly short supply. Even after peace was concluded with France in 1659, Spain's armies remained hindered by the lack of money, supplies, men, and leaders. Portuguese forces under Marshall Schomberg, a French commander, defeated the Spanish at Amexial in 1663. After another defeat at Villaviçosa in 1665, Spain was forced to recognize the new regime. The crown acknowledged the independence of Portugal in 1668.

Alone among the provincial revolts in the Hispanic world, the Portuguese rebellion succeeded. To some extent, its success was the triumph of traditional political forms, nationalist sentiments, and the benefits of colonialism. Portugal had a pretender to the throne with a legitimate claim. It did not experiment with a "republican" form of government, as did the people of Barcelona and Naples. The independence movement was directed by a segment of the nobility, which was able to force adherence to its position, benefit from the new monarch, and maintain control over the course of thirty years of rebellion. Social tensions did not erupt into class war as they did in Naples and Catalonia, and popular resentments against the Spaniards had been channeled into support of the national monarchy by a protonationalist literature of sermons and propaganda. Finally, Portugal found in its colonial empire the resources to mount a military effort and to attract the support of powerful allies. Although the term "revolution" was applied by contemporaries to the Portuguese rebellion, the event represented a dynastic change along traditional lines. The Catalan and Neapolitan revolts, on the other hand, had overtones of profound social and political change, but they ultimately failed, undercut by the same social divisions that had caused them.

See also *French Frondes (1648–1653); French Peasant Revolts (1594–1648); Spanish* Comuneros *Revolt (1520–1521).*

STUART B. SCHWARTZ

BIBLIOGRAPHY

Elliott, J. H. "Revolts in the Spanish Monarchy." In *Preconditions of Revolution in Early Modern Europe.* Edited by Robert Forster and Jack P. Greene. Baltimore, Md.: Johns Hopkins University Press, 1970.

———. *The Revolt of the Catalans.* Cambridge: Cambridge University Press, 1963.

Lynch, John. *Spain under the Hapsburgs.* New York: Oxford University Press, 1969.

Stradling, R. A. *Philip IV and the Government of Spain, 1621–1665.* Cambridge: Cambridge University Press, 1988.

Villari, Rosario. *The Revolt of Naples.* Cambridge, Mass.: Polity Press, 1993.

SPANISH WAR OF INDEPENDENCE (1808–1813)

The Spanish War of Independence broke out suddenly and spontaneously in May 1808, when French emperor Napoleon Bonaparte replaced the Bourbons with his brother, Joseph. The French crushed a popular uprising in Madrid; resistance then shifted to the provinces. The Spanish War of Independence was not a revolution, but it contained some revolutionary tendencies; it embraced many ideological elements, some reactionary, others liberal or radical.

The first uprisings were mass movements that frightened the Spanish provincial elites and royal administrators, who feared they could turn into revolutions, but few did. Their aims were to drive out the French and restore the old order. The masses were led by their clergy, who rightly feared French anticlericalism. Later, as French military control increased, large revolts gave way to the *guerrilla* (a term coined at the time meaning "the little war"), fought by small bands of peasants who operated outside effective political control. By the end of the war, most of the guerrillas openly opposed all who favored reforms, whether they had collaborated with the French or not, because liberal reforms were associated with the foreign regime. However, the nature of the guerrilla war inadvertently engendered revolutionary conditions and attitudes. Central government collapsed, and Joseph never controlled most of Spain effectively; in the vacuum, the *juntas* (the provincial governments), the popular leaders who emerged in the fighting, and their communities asserted their independence of all authority.

The Spanish War of Independence produced a remarkable political debate on whether it was meant to be revolutionary. By 1810 a stable—if ineffective—government of national resistance had emerged in the besieged coastal city of Cadiz. The deputies to its main body—the Cortez—had been elected by a system that allowed almost every head of household a vote at the lowest, parish level, and which only gradually filtered out popular elements in elections at higher levels. The elections produced a majority of deputies against all reform, especially of the church or local government. Opposed to them was a small but articulate group, "the liberals," that sought substantial reforms in many fields. In 1812 the liberals passed a constitution, but by 1813 Ferdinand VII, the restored king, had easily swept them and their constitution aside. However, the Constitution of Cadiz became a rallying cry and the goal of the revolutions of 1820 in Spain, Naples, and Piedmont.

The liberals in Cadiz planned a constitutional revolution but remained impotent; the guerrillas and most of the *juntas* remained staunchly opposed to their ideas and saw the war as a religious, anti-French crusade. Nevertheless, the breakdown of effective national government in Spain and the creation of a large army to fight the war created conditions of chronic instability, which the restored monarchy failed to deal with effectively. Spain went on to be marked by political unrest and instability for over a century. By engendering social and political anarchy, the War of Independence fostered a revolutionary tradition in a conservative country.

Michael Broers

BIBLIOGRAPHY

Esdaile, Charles J. "Heroes or Villains? The Spanish Guerrillas and the Peninsular War." *History Today* 38 (fall 1988): 29–35.

Esdaile, Charles J. "War and Politics in Spain, 1808–1814." *Historical Journal* 31 (spring 1988): 295–317.

Hamnett, Brian. "Constitutional Theory and Political Reality: Liberalism, Traditionalism and the Spanish Cortes, 1810–1814." *Journal of Modern History* 40 (winter 1977): on demand supplement.

Lovett, Gabriel H. *Napoleon and the Birth of Modern Spain.* 2 vols. New York: New York University Press, 1965.

SRI LANKAN (TAMIL) REVOLT AND CIVIL WAR (1977–)

Sri Lanka, formerly Ceylon, has a multiethnic population: Sinhalese (71 percent), Tamils of recent Indian origin (5.1 percent), indigenous Tamils (12.6 percent), Muslims, Eurasians, and others (about 10 percent). The indigenous Tamils consider the North and East of Sri Lanka their historical and cultural homeland.

Since 1977 a civil war between indigenous Tamils (speakers of Tamil and mainly Hindu) and Sinhalese (speakers of Sinhala and mainly Buddhist) has been carried on in Sri Lanka. In 1997 the official count of deaths in this war was more than fifty thousand. Attempts to reach agreements between the main Tamil antagonist, called the Liberation Tigers of Tamil Eelam (usually abbreviated as Tigers), and successive Sri Lankan governments have been repeatedly scuttled by one or the other party. Although Sinhala parties in power each have attempted a settlement, they have usually joined the Sinhala opposition and taken a noncooperative stance when out of power. Among the Tamils, several groups, many of whom were previously armed partisans against the Sinhala government, have pushed for an amicable settlement since the early 1990s. Among the Tamils the major obstacle to any settlement has been the Tigers.

The point of contention is the demand by the Tamil movement for an independent state that would combine the eastern and northern provinces of the island. Using historical sources and literary tradition, all the protagonists refer to this imagined Tamil state as Eelam. The call for Eelam was precipitated by a number of policies of the Sri Lankan state, whose parliament has always been dominated by Sinhala majorities. The Tamils regarded these policies as ethnically discriminatory, particularly one that concerned the Tamil language and was therefore important to their sense of identity. In 1956 the government of Sri Lanka enacted legislation that made Sinhala the official language, and in 1972 it created a policy, called "standardization," that gave preferential treatment to students from rural areas who took university entrance examinations and those who took the examinations, regardless of urban and rural distinctions, in Sinhala. The Tamils also argue that Sinhala parties never showed an interest in fair negotiation before the war.

On the part of the Sinhalese, these actions were seen as helping the "common man" have greater access to government officials and enhanced mobility onto and up the modern occupational ladder. Because the country had been under the British until 1948, many Sinhala politicians argued for the removal of the privilege that the English language

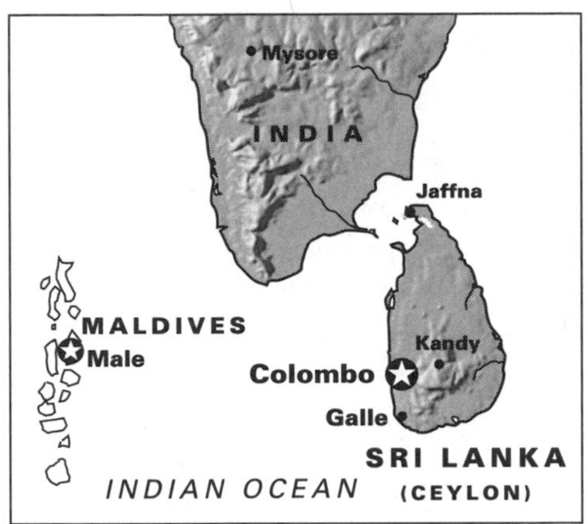

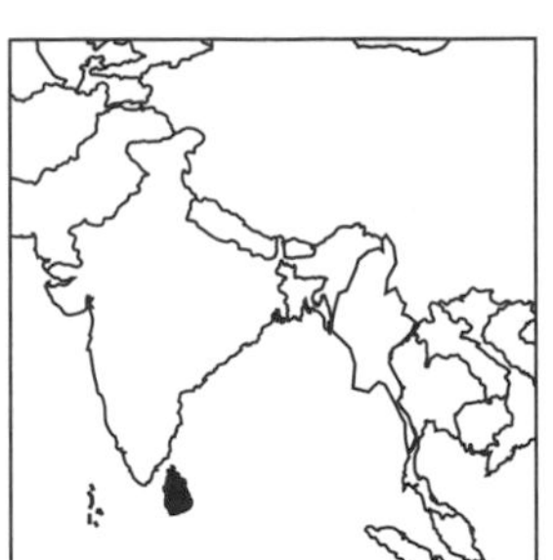

had conferred on some Sri Lankan natives who were mainly urban, members of the upper classes, Christians, and Tamils. Many of these anglophones affected Western traits. The Sinhala call for state intervention on behalf of less-privileged citizens excluded less-privileged Tamils as well.

Tamil perceptions of an ethnically divided electorate had already resulted in the formation of the Federal Party led by S. J. V. Chelvanayakam in 1949. Chelvanayakam argued that a federalist structure of government, replacing the unitary Westminster model derived from British colonial rule, would grant Tamil-majority areas more autonomy. The Sinhala opposition feared that federalism would lead inexorably to an ethnic division of the country.

By 1973 the federalist view was seen as far too conservative by Tamil youth who had been barred from universities by the standardization policy of 1972. Tamils saw educational advancement as the best way to an improved economic and social life. Tamil youth argued that their leaders should shift to a stronger position of violent confrontation. This position was given formal support in 1976 by the newly formed Tamil United Liberation Front, which included Tamil parliamentary parties and trade unions. Violence began to erupt sporadically but became continuous in 1983, when the war reached an important turning point

In 1983 the Tamil Tigers stepped up attacks on army patrols in the Jaffna Peninsula. On one of these occasions, Tamils killed thirteen soldiers, an incident that President Junius Richard Jayawardene called to the public's attention. His speech raised emotions, and very soon Tamil houses and shops in Colombo and elsewhere were attacked. The military delayed intervention, and it was evident that the mob leaders had the names and addresses of Tamil residents in different parts of Colombo: the pogrom appeared to have been premeditated. At this point the conflict became internationalized as governments expressed their concerns.

Since 1983 a number of attempts have been made at negotiation. In 1985 international efforts to bring the contenders together at Thimpu in Bhutan failed disastrously. The offers to negotiate by Jayawardene in December 1986 were quickly withdrawn by him, after pressure from Sinhala activists. A 1987 military attempt to capture the Tigers' territory led India to drop food packages for Tamil victims of the war within Sri Lankan airspace. This action signaled, with impunity, Indian intentions to intervene further. A peace treaty resulting from this threat was concluded between Jayawardene and Rajiv Gandhi of India in July 1987. However, the treaty provoked opposition from both sides: the Sinhala nationalists perceived it as Indian imperial strategy, and the Tamil Tigers objected to Gandhi's pressure to replace their goal of a sovereign Eelam with an autonomous region. The Indian peacekeeping force, which occupied the Jaffna Peninsula, ended up fighting its own bloody war with the Tigers and withdrew in 1990.

Starting in 1983, then, the military engagements escalated. Air attacks prevented the Tigers from scoring more successes, while guerrilla strategy effectively stymied the military efforts of the state. These engagements also produced a refugee population, with its attendant problems. Human rights organizations complained about disappearances through government abduction, and diplomats and foreign governments condemned assassinations of political leaders by the Tigers: Rajiv Gandhi, assassinated May 21, 1991, and President Ranasinghe Premadasa, killed May 1, 1993, constituted the upper echelon of supposed Tiger prey.

Despite the civil war's continuation, a military victory, if achieved, would not produce stability. Several Sinhala leaders supported by Tamil moderates have expressed interest in different political solutions, whereby Tamils could have autonomy short of sovereign independence. But these efforts are opposed by many Sinhala forces, including members of the Buddhist monkhood, that are able to affect public sentiment and influence election results. On the Tamil side, the Tigers have proved to be intransigent and thoroughly mercurial, coming to a negotiating table and then suddenly deserting it. These actions coupled to known and attributed assassinations create a contradictory image of instability and stubborn determination for the Tamil contenders. For these reasons, it is unlikely that the civil war in Sri Lanka will have a solution soon.

Lakshmanan Sabaratnam

BIBLIOGRAPHY

De Silva, Chandra R. "Weightage in University Admissions: Standardization in District Quotas in Sri Lanka." *Modern Ceylon Studies* 5 (1974): 152–178.

Sabaratnam, Lakshmanan. "The Boundaries of the State and the State of Ethnic Boundaries." *Ethnic and Racial Studies* 10 (1987): 291–316.

Spencer, Jonathan, ed. *Sri Lanka: History and the Roots of Conflict.* London: Routledge, 1990.

Tambiah, Stanley J. *Sri Lanka: Ethnic Fratricide and the Dismantling of Democracy.* Chicago: University of Chicago Press, 1991.
Weerawardene, I. D. S. *Ceylon General Elections, 1956.* Colombo: M. D. Gunasena, 1960.
Wilson, Alfred J. *The Break-Up of Sri Lanka.* London: Hurst, 1988.
Wriggins, W. Howard. *Ceylon: Dilemmas of a New Nation.* Princeton, N.J.: Princeton University Press, 1960.

STALIN, JOSEPH

Iossif (Joseph) Vissarionovich Dzhugashvili (1879–1953), who later took the name Stalin (the man of steel), was born of a poor family in Georgia, a part of the Russian Empire. Sent to a Christian Orthodox seminary to be trained as a priest, he instead converted to Marxism and became a revolutionary activist. In 1903 he was one of the relatively few Georgian Marxists who sided with Vladimir Ilyich Lenin's Bolsheviks against the Mensheviks. His activities included carrying out bank robberies to finance the party, and he came to Lenin's attention. Promoted to a leadership position in the party, he became its specialist on ethnic nationalism because of his experience in the diverse, contentious Caucasus. In 1913 he published a pamphlet, "Marxism and the National Question," which later became the guide to ethnic issues in the Soviet Union. In it he called for privileging the bigger linguistic groups, which ultimately meant Russian domination over the many minorities in Russia.

He was arrested and exiled to Siberia in 1913 and emerged in 1917 when the tsar was overthrown. He was one of Lenin's top aides in the Bolshevik Revolution and in the ensuing civil war. In 1922 he became general secretary of the Communist Party and proved to be skillful in filling crucial positions with his own followers. By the time Lenin died in 1924, Stalin was too entrenched to be removed, despite Lenin's explicit warning to the party that Stalin was too brutal and had become too much a Russian nationalist.

In the succession struggle that followed Lenin's death, Stalin had three advantages. First, unlike his three top rivals, including Leon Trotsky, he was not a Jew. Second, he could talk to less educated, more anti-Semitic, newer party members who found Lenin's other close associates too abstract, too intellectual, and too cosmopolitan for their own simpler tastes. Third, he proved to be an adept compromiser who could steer between the many factions in the party and appear as a moderate, practical man rather than as a wild-eyed extremist. But once he had gained absolute power in 1928, he relegated his former rivals to impotence, and then had almost all of them murdered in the 1930s.

In 1929 he set out to create a socialist, industrialized Soviet Union. First, he collectivized the land to make the peasants produce food for less compensation. This resulted in

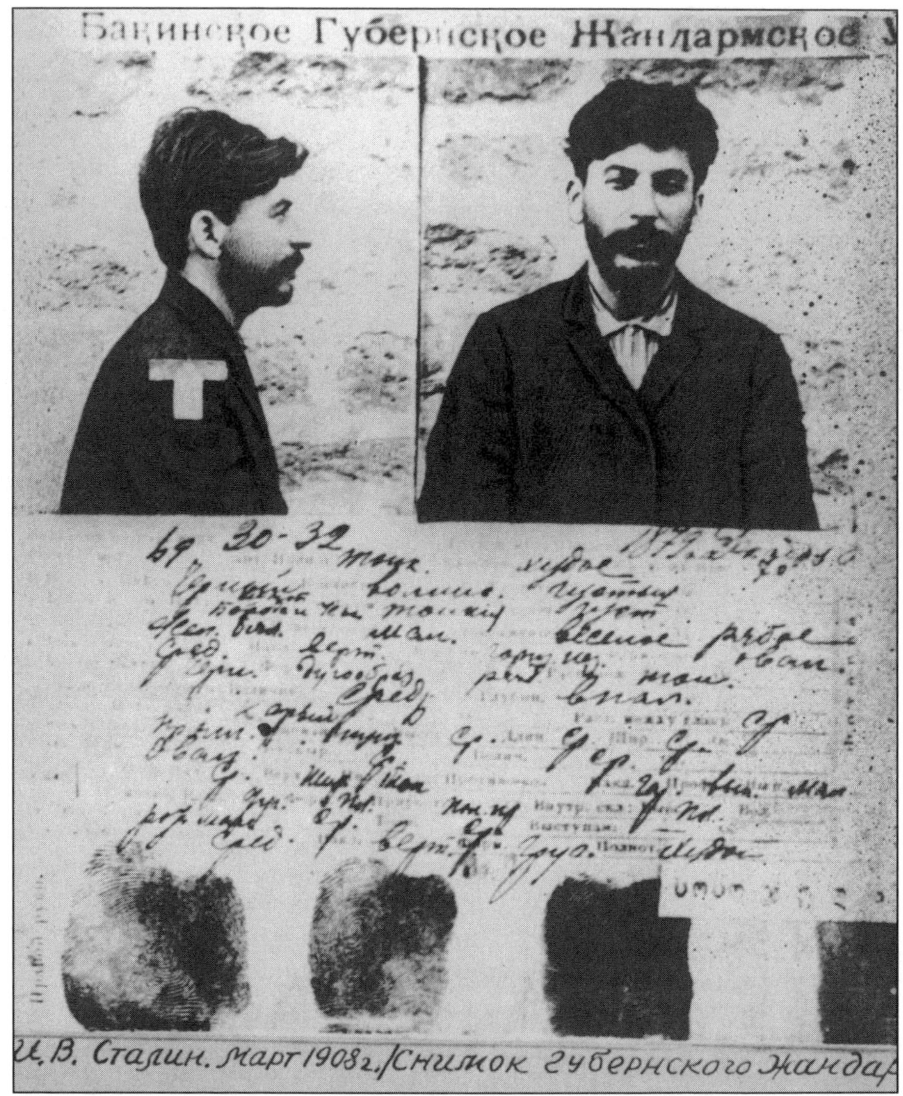

Joseph Stalin was arrested and deported to Siberia on several occasions, the first time in 1901, for his work in propaganda and mass agitation for the Russian Social Democratic Labor Party. This arrest report was made by the tsarist gendarmes in March 1908.

a famine and a war against the peasants, which ultimately killed some ten million. Then, to maintain discipline and absolute obedience to his will, he purged the Communist Party and anyone else suspected of disloyalty to the system. Finally, to ward off any military threat to his power, he destroyed most of his top army officers. By 1939 he had created an industrial, submissive society ruled by terror. Millions were in slave labor camps, and at least twenty million had died.

In 1939 he signed a treaty with Adolf Hitler dividing up Europe, but he was double-crossed when Hitler invaded the USSR in 1941. After suffering enormous losses, Stalin's armies pushed the Germans back, conquered eastern Europe, and occupied Berlin in 1945.

After the victory, Stalin's USSR became one of the world's two superpowers, along with the United States. But in 1946 Stalin resumed the purges and mass persecutions. He was planning to deport all Soviet Jews to Siberia and to execute most of his top aides when he died of a stroke in 1953.

Stalin was revered and praised by revolutionary Marxists all over the world during his lifetime. He was the chief architect of communism whose model was imitated by other communist leaders everywhere. With Hitler and Mao Zedong, he was also one of the greatest mass murderers in history.

See also *Lenin, Vladimir Ilyich; Russian Revolution of 1917; Trotsky, Leon.*

DANIEL CHIROT

BIBLIOGRAPHY

Kersahw, Ian, and Moshe Lewin, eds. *Stalinism and Nazism: Dictatorships in Comparison.* Cambridge: Cambridge University Press, 1997.

Tucker, Robert C. *Stalin as Revolutionary 1879–1929.* New York: W.W. Norton, 1974.

———. *Stalin in Power 1929–1941.* New York: W.W. Norton, 1990.

Volkogonov, Dmitri, *Stalin: Triumph and Tragedy.* New York: Grove, Weidenfeld, 1991.

STATES

The state is best defined in terms of three elements. First, a state is a set of institutions, the most important of which is the means of violence and coercion. The state staffs such institutions with its own personnel; the continuity of personnel over time distinguishes the state from more transient government. Second, these institutions are at the center of a geographically bounded territory, usually referred to as a society. Third, the state monopolizes rule making within its borders, which promotes the creation of a common political culture shared by all citizens. Differently put, the historical record witnesses an increasing merging of nation and state. Sometimes national sentiment is created by the state, but sometimes the national principle can call into existence new states.

Premodern states often took the form of empires, ruling over territories that were home to linguistically and ethnically diverse groups. However, since 1900 the dominant tendency in Europe and Asia has been for states to identify primarily with the particular linguistic/ethnic group that predominates in the society, thus forming nation-states.

It must be stressed that statehood is often an aspiration rather than an actual achievement. For one thing, the search by states for their prime goal, that of security, is normally made difficult by the presence of larger societies—notably those of state competition and of capitalism, between which there are complex relationships—that they cannot control. For another, states have difficulties in dealing with their civil societies. It was once believed that the strength of the state depended on its possession of clear, arbitrary powers. But there is often an irony to state strength. Cooperation with groups in civil society can increase the penetrative powers of the state; this cooperation is likely to place limitations on a state's despotic powers. Thus in the eighteenth century, the absolutist French state may have been autonomous in the sense of being "free from" parliamentary constraint, but it was nonetheless weaker—as the test of warfare showed—than its constitutional rival, Great Britain. For all the importance of coercion, politics based on reciprocal consent is likely to provide the most secure basis for legitimacy.

LINKS TO REVOLUTIONS

Revolutionaries aim to seize the state so as to use its coercive power to transform society—habitually by ignoring and bypassing traditional social institutions. Such revolutionary politics, perhaps curiously, have not been at the center of recent research. Rather, social science has sought to explain the circumstances that make such extraordinary transformations possible. Jack Goldstone's correlation between state breakdown and revolution best helps us understand the circumstances leading to revolution.

The breakdown of a state is a necessary condition for revolution. One important point, highlighted most effectively by Theda Skocpol, is that breakdown is most likely in regimes that have been debilitated by excessive participation or actual defeat in war. This was clearly true of both the Russian and Chinese Revolutions—but not, for particularly interesting reasons, of the Iranian Revolution. A second finding is that states lose effectiveness when different sections of the political elite stalemate one another, refusing to cooperate in a common cause. The classical case here is that of

France during the latter part of the eighteenth century. The fiscal crisis of that state resulted from the landed upper class's exemption from taxation—that is, its effective refusal to reinforce the state that in fact provided the condition for its continued existence.

Some state breakdowns lead to the restoration of traditional authority. The Roman empire was renewed by Diocletian, as was the British state between 1783 and 1848 by "economical reform" and a careful calibration of coercion and inclusion. It is only rational to expect that the collapse of socialist authoritarianism in eastern Europe will not universally lead to the consolidation of democracy. Beyond this, two striking discoveries should be noted.

First, social scientists realize that the form a "social movement" takes results from the regimes with which it interacts. Working classes tend to be militant when a state excludes them from participation in civil society, that is to say, workers take on the state when they are prevented from organizing industrially and arguing with their immediate capitalist opponents. Thus a liberal state with full citizenship sees no working-class revolutionary movement, whereas authoritarian and autocratic regimes see the emergence of Marxist-inspired workers; this principle helps explain the difference in working-class behavior in the United States and tsarist Russia at the end of the nineteenth century. The same principle—that political exclusion breeds militancy—helps Jeffrey Goodwin explain the incidence of revolution in the Third World since 1945. Central American societies share a "mode of production," but only a few witness revolutions. The possibility of participation in a country like Costa Rica diffuses social conflict; its absence in Nicaragua under Anastasio Somoza led to the creation of a revolutionary elite.

Second, total social transformation sometimes occurs through revolution but can also result from the impact of major powers upon those they beat in war. Japan and Germany had liberalism imposed upon them, and thereafter they preferred to advance via trade rather than conquest. More generally, the postwar world has seen the removal, in part at the behest of the United States, of extreme left and extreme right within the nations at the heart of capitalist society, thereby producing centrist politics of great stability.

PROSPECTS

A key part of any future agenda for state-centered theorists interested in revolutions must be that of nationalism. Nationalist state making both creates and grows out of revolutionary movements. Revolution has traditionally been seen as a force on the left, but this perspective fails to help us understand Nazism and leaves us without the tools to comprehend our own world. Revolutions, the nineteenth-century observer Alexis de Tocqueville argued, generally produce stronger, more centralized states. Though these are sometimes liberal states, often they are not, and the Stalinist, Nazi, and postcolonial dictatorships are as much postrevolutionary states as are England, America, and France.

A second point of huge importance concerns the supposed loss of salience of state power in the face of globalizing forces. A good deal of skepticism should be shown to this view. High levels of cooperation and interaction are now present in the North—in part because of agreement between states, in part as the result of American hegemony. But much of the South is still involved in state building, with the politics of revolution accordingly being very likely to continue.

See also *Nationalism*.

JOHN A. HALL

BIBLIOGRAPHY

Goldstone, Jack A. *Revolution and Rebellion in the Early Modern World.* Berkeley: University of California Press, 1991.

Goodwin, Jeffrey. *States and Revolutionary Movements, 1945–1991.* Cambridge: Cambridge University Press, forthcoming.

Skocpol, Theda. *States and Social Revolutions.* Cambridge: Cambridge University Press, 1979.

Tocqueville, Alexis de. *The Old Regime and the French Revolution.* Translated by S. Gilbert. New York: Doubleday, 1955.

STUDENT PROTESTS AND YOUTH MOVEMENTS

With the explosion of campus unrest in the 1960s in places as geographically and culturally disparate as Paris, Berkeley, Tokyo, Prague, and Mexico City, scholars in various disciplines began to focus their attention on students as a potentially revolutionary social group and on generational tensions as potentially revolutionary triggers of collective unrest.

In the decades since the 1960s, that trend has continued. Protest events involving students and youth have continued to grab headlines and to attract the attention of scholars. Now, thanks in part to the scholarship generated by events such as the Iranian upheavals of the 1970s and 1980s and the global unrest of 1989, studies of student protests and youth movements have become significant parts of several academic subfields. Works on student activism as a potentially revolutionary force range from sociological case studies of specific universities as sites of political struggle to forays into intellectual history that treat educated youth as the bottom rung of relatively powerful or virtually powerless intelligentsias. Works on potentially revolutionary youth movements range from analyses of political generations to excursions into the politics of popular culture.

THE BIRTH OF TWO SUBFIELDS

In 1968 it seemed that revolutions led by educated youths might erupt at any moment in many places and were already under way in others. The year marked a crucial turning point in the academic discovery of students and youth movements as subjects for serious inquiry. In the wake of this "discovery" came a growing awareness that both student protests and generationally driven counterculture movements had surprisingly long lineages—at least within certain countries. Before 1968, very little had been published about either subject except within a few unusual settings. (For example, as early as the 1950s, historians connected to the Chinese Communist Party begun to publish studies of the student protests that had occurred during the May Fourth Movement of 1919.) After 1968, however, scholarly books and articles on both topics began to proliferate.

Inspired, concerned, or just confused by the counterculture tides and political demonstrations unfolding around them, social scientists in fields such as sociology and political science began focusing their attention in the late 1960s and early 1970s on previously unexplored questions relating to the economic and social position of students; the psychological forces that might influence youthful acts of rebellion; the kinds of bonds and tensions that can exist between campus-based and factory-based radicals; and the peculiar nature of universities as places that can, through their organizational structures and physical layout, either facilitate or limit the scope of mass mobilization.

Historians also contributed to the publication boom, as they began to look for—and find—past examples of significant student protests and youth movements. Scholars interested in earlier periods in national and world history brought to light many struggles in which students (who were sometimes hardly youths) had taken to the streets in support of radical causes, as well as many revolutionary events in which the youthfulness of the participants may have played an important role. The revolutionary struggles that rocked much of Europe in 1848 and the protests that occurred in Russia at the end of the Tsarist era are just two cases in point.

NEW DEVELOPMENTS AND LINGERING QUESTIONS

The scholarship on student protests and youth movements has become increasingly sophisticated over the past two decades. Instant histories and simplistic models have been replaced by careful case studies and more nuanced paradigms. Scholars have shown increased awareness of the great diversity of the subject. For example, most investigators have ceased to associate the terms "student" and "youth" with the political left—in part because of the role that youthful militants have played in decidedly nonleftist political and counterculture events ranging from the Iranian upheavals of the late 1970s to skinhead rallies in Germany and elsewhere, and in part because of reminders of the part youth groups played in the rise of fascism before World War II. The very striking differences between the Chinese Red Guard activists of the late 1960s, who were inspired by their devotion to Mao Zedong, and the Chinese students demonstrating in Tiananmen Square in 1989, who were inspired in part by a desire to force the government to abandon the last vestiges of Maoism, also illustrated dramatically the need to move beyond simplistic visions of the political orientations of youthful protesters.

The tendency of recent scholars to look for complexity instead of accepting simple models or assertions is encouraging, but in the search for and recognition of complexity some interesting new questions have been raised that deserve careful analysis. For example, while analysts have moved far beyond the once fashionable conservative image of all youthful rebelliousness as the working out of ahistorical and culturally universal Oedipal complexes, they have not come up with very satisfying ways of interpreting, in a fashion sensitive to cultural differences, the psychological dynamics of counterculture movements, which are often framed by participants as rejection of an older generation's values and structures. In addition, although analysts also have moved far beyond the once fashionable radical and utopian image of students as people with an almost magical ability to completely change society, careful studies of the mechanisms through which educated youths have, in specific times and places, been able to forge important and powerful alliances with workers and peasants remain few and far between.

A PROMISING DIRECTION

Recent theoretical work on comparative revolutions and on particular revolutionary events—including some of the events of the 1960s—suggests that several avenues of speculation and investigation might eventually lead to a new understanding of the topic. The most promising trend is the attention being paid by structuralist analysts of revolutions to the radical potential of marginal elites—people who have some of the resources and connections associated with ruling groups and yet are excluded from exercising various sorts of power. Several analysts have emphasized the importance of disillusioned individuals who fall into this broad category, which is difficult to fit into social schemes that use class as the main organizing term.

Young members of dominant classes and students working toward advanced degrees in countries where relatively few people go on to study at this level are quintessential marginal figures of just the sort structuralist analysts seem to have in mind. That is, they have some of the attributes associated with power but lack the kinds of positions that would enable them to exercise it. Case studies of specific revolutions suggest that such connections could be developed in interesting ways and perhaps someday be integrated into comparative models. Those models could in turn be enriched by the findings of the culturally oriented studies of the upheavals of the 1960s, events that pointed toward but in most cases did not bring about social revolution. Because they fell short of revolution, such events have largely been ignored by those who see themselves as specialists in revolutionary processes.

Where should scholars attempting to move in such directions look for promising case studies? China and France might be among the best places to start, because students and youth as generational and social groups have played key roles in major political events in both countries. Focusing on students as a social group, one finds in Chinese history a long-standing tradition of frustrated examination candidates, poised at the edge of full membership in the elite, playing leading roles in many rebellions and insurrections. Focusing on age as a variable, one finds in the May Fourth Movement generational tensions emerging as an important political factor.

Studies of the French Revolution also draw attention to the relevance of youthful members of marginal elites. Many of those who played prominent political roles in and assumed power during this struggle turn out to have been younger than one might expect. For example, in 1793, almost half of the deputies to the National Convention were under forty years old. The Parisian near-revolution of 1968, in which students played such crucial parts, remains in some ways a surprisingly understudied event, but important work has been done that has yet to be integrated as well as it could be into general theories of collective action and revolutionary struggle.

See also *Chinese May Fourth Movement (1919); Chinese Tiananmen Uprising (1989); French Student Revolt (1968).*

JEFFREY N. WASSERSTROM

BIBLIOGRAPHY

Braungart, Richard, and Margaret M. Braungart. "Historical Generations and Citizenship: 200 Years of Youth Movements." *Research in Political Sociology* 6 (1993): 139–174.

DeConde, Alexander, ed. *Student Activism: Town and Gown in Historical Perspective.* New York: Scribners, 1971.

Feuer, Lewis. *The Conflict of Generations.* New York: Basic Books, 1969.

Lipset, Seymour Martin, and Philip Altbach, eds. *Students in Revolt.* Boston: Houghton Mifflin, 1969.

Wasserstrom, Jeffrey N. *Student Protests in Twentieth-Century China: The View from Shanghai.* Stanford, Calif.: Stanford University Press, 1991.

SUDANESE CIVIL WAR (1955–1972; 1982–)

Sudan has experienced civil war since 1955, with a decade of precarious peace from 1972 to 1983. The warring groups are the successive governments of the Arab North, where the population is Muslim, and rebel movements in the South, where the people are indigenous Africans, and the modern elite is predominantly Christian. During the first phase of the war, from 1955 to 1972, the objective of the southern liberation struggle was secession from the North, although the Southern Sudan Liberation Movement and its military wing, the Anyanya, settled in 1972 for regional autonomy. With the resumption of hostilities in 1983, the Sudan People's Liberation Movement and its military wing, the Sudan People's Liberation Army (SPLM/SPLA), stipulated the liberation of the whole country from Arab-Islamic domination. Their goal was to create a "new Sudan" that would be free from any discrimination based on race, ethnicity, religion, sex, or culture. This objective, which threatened the Arab-Muslim identity of Sudan, provoked a radical Islamic fundamentalist reaction from the North. On June 30, 1989, the Islamic revivalists, as the fundamentalists prefer to be known, seized power through a military coup and have since tightened their grip on the country *(see map, p. 159).*

COLONIAL LEGACY

The North-South cleavage, which has been at the core of the civil war, was consolidated and aggravated by the colonial policies of the Anglo-Egyptian Condominium (1898–1956), which was dominated by Britain. The British policy of administering the North and the South separately reinforced Arabism and Islam in the North, encouraged southern development along indigenous African lines, and introduced Christian missionary education and rudiments of Western culture as elements of modernization in the South. Interaction between the two sets of people was strongly discouraged.

While the British administration invested considerably in the political, economic, social, and cultural development of the North, the South remained isolated and undeveloped. The principal objective of colonial rule there was the maintenance of law and order. The separate administration of the North and the South left open the option that the South might eventually be annexed to one of the East African colonies or become an independent state. In 1947, however, only nine years before independence on January 1, 1956, the British suddenly reversed the policy of separate development but failed to put in place any constitutional arrangements that would ensure protection for the South in a united Sudan.

Since independence, the preoccupying concern among the northerners has been to correct the divisive effect of Britain's separatist policies by pursuing the assimilation of the South through Arabization and Islamization, which the South has resisted. Southern resistance first took the form of a mutiny by a battalion in 1955, then of a political call for a federal arrangement, and finally an armed struggle that has destabilized the country.

ATTEMPTS AT MEDIATION

Since the resumption of hostilities in 1983, many attempts have been made at mediation. The most significant of these was undertaken in September 1993 by the member states of the Inter-Governmental Authority on Drought and Desertification (IGADD), an organization whose original aim was to coordinate environmental programs in a region that includes Djibouti, Ethiopia, Eritrea, Kenya, Somalia, Sudan, and Uganda. The organization eventually became the Inter-Governmental Authority for Development (IGAD).

The premise of the IGAD mediators was that the conflict in Sudan was not merely national; rather, it had regional repercussions that affected the neighboring countries. They sought to dig deep into the problem, its root causes, and the ways in which it might be resolved. The resulting Declaration of Principles tried to reconcile the parties' competing perspectives by upholding the right of self-determination while giving national unity high priority. This goal would require creating appropriate conditions to ensure a national consensus. Among these conditions were separation of religion and the state, a system of government based on multiparty democracy, respect for fundamental human rights, and a measure of decentralization through a loose federation or a confederacy. After the interim period, the people of the South would be asked to decide by referendum whether to continue with unity or exercise the right of secession.

The government rejected the declaration with an ideological fervor. Secularism was totally out of the question. For the government, commitment to Shari'a (Islamic law) was a religious and moral obligation to an Islamic mission that colonialism had interrupted. Government officials also saw self-determination as a ploy for partitioning the country and therefore as unacceptable.

In April 1997, however, the government concluded a peace agreement with splinter southern factions. The government ostensibly accepted the principle of self-determination to be exercised through a referendum after an interim period. The conditions attached to this right, such as the nature of the government in the South during the interim period; the structure of authority, which vests the ultimate power in the central government and in the person of the president; the commitment to fight for the unity of the country; the flexibility of the agenda for the referendum—and the stipulation that the right of self-determination be exercised only after a satisfactory degree of stability and socioeconomic development has been achieved—indicate that the agreement may be a tactical ploy for dividing the South, buying time, and consolidating the Islamic agenda during the interim period.

PROSPECTS FOR NATIONAL UNITY

Given the Islamic ideology of the regime and the contrasting vision from the South, the government of the National Islamic Front cannot be expected to concede enough of its religious agenda to satisfy the southern demand for the neutrality of the state on religious matters without undermining the regime's integrity among its Muslim followers. Similarly, it is most unlikely that the South would accommodate itself to the government's vision for peace and unity. Except for the possibility of finding a solution through partition or a framework of loose coexistence, peace within the framework of unity between the Islamic regime in Khartoum and the SPLM/SPLA does not seem likely in the present set of circumstances.

At the same time, the scenarios of the present regime are clearly not sustainable. While any nation-building efforts aimed at making constructive use of religious and cultural values of a people are commendable, imposing one religion and one culture on a heterogeneous society of multiple religions, cultures, ethnicities and races is counterproductive. Prudence dictates that the Sudanese and other interested parties must look for alternatives. Otherwise, Sudan may be headed for more destruction and possible disintegration of the nation.

Francis M. Deng

BIBLIOGRAPHY

Alier, Abel. *Southern Sudan: Too Many Agreements Dishonoured.* Exeter: Ithaca Press, 1990.

Bashir, Mohamed Omar. *The Southern Sudan: Background to Conflict.* London: C. Hurst, 1968.

———. *Southern Sudan: From Conflict to Peace.* London: C. Hurst, 1975.

Deng, Francis Mading. *Africans of Two Worlds: The Dinka in Afro-Arab Sudan.* New Haven, Conn., and London: Yale University Press, 1978.

———. *War of Visions: Conflict of Identities in the Sudan.* Washington, D.C.: Brookings Institution, 1995.

El-Affendi, Abdelwahab. *Turabi's Revolution: Islam and Power in Sudan.* London: Grey Seal, 1991.

Voll, John O., ed. *Sudan: State and Society in Crisis.* Bloomington: Indiana University Press, 1991.

Wai, Dunstan. *The African-Arab Conflict in the Sudan.* New York and London: Africana Publishing Company, 1981.

SUDANESE MAHDIYYA (1881–1898)

The Sudanese Mahdiyya was a religious and political revolt led by Muhammad Ahmad ibn Abdallah (c. 1840–1885), a sufi (mystic) who in 1881 declared himself to be the Mahdi, the expected deliverer of the Muslims. By the time of his death in 1885 he had succeeded in taking control from Egyptian colonial masters of what is today the northern Sudan. Under his successor, the Khalifa Abdallahi, expansion continued, but in 1896–1898, in the final chapter of the European "scramble for Africa," an Anglo-Egyptian army conquered the Mahdist state. Mahdism survives today in the Sudan as an important sect led by the Mahdi's descendants and with millions of followers.

The causes of the Sudanese Mahdist Revolution, and the reasons for its success, are complex. Islamic history provides many examples of similar movements, not least in nineteenth-century Africa and Asia. In the Sudanese case, Egyptian colonial rule, dating from the 1820s, was unpopular; taxation, close administration, interference with the slave trade, imposition of orthodox Muslim institutions, and increasing employment in the colonial government of Christian Europeans were all issues with both political and religious aspects. By declaring himself Mahdi, Muhammad Ahmad created a religious focus for widespread discontent. Pious Muslims, disgruntled tribesmen, and hard-pressed merchants rallied to his cause, and at a time when the Egyptian government was preoccupied in the aftermath of a nationalist revolt and its sequel of British occupation.

Most European-language accounts of the Mahdiyya focus on two events: the fall of Khartoum to the Mahdi (January 1885) and death of Gen. Charles Gordon, the British officer who had been sent to evacuate the Egyptians; and the Anglo-Egyptian campaigns that ended with the battle of Omdurman (September 2, 1898) and destruction of the Mahdist state. The reformist, universalist ideology of the Mahdiyya has received less attention, as have the regime the Mahdi established and the conduct of state affairs under his much-maligned successor, the Khalifa Abdallahi. For all its defects, and despite the war propaganda that informed the views of the outside world, the Mahdist regime was both an Islamic state and an independent Afro-Arab polity of substance and importance.

The changes wrought in the Sudanese state and society during the Mahdiyya had repercussions that continue to this day. The Mahdi's message, and the military power he and the Khalifa Abdallahi wielded, sped a process of detribalization already under way during Egyptian times; the Mahdi is still remembered, even among those who reject his religious message, as the founder of Sudanese independence. In the southern Sudan, the historical memory is clouded by the dislocations of the era and the continuing controversy over the nature of an Islamic state; the national model including Islam as the state religion has largely been rejected by non-Muslim Africans.

The Anglo-Egyptian condominium established on the ruins of the Mahdist state lasted until 1956. Although avowedly anti-Mahdist, the Sudan Government (as the condominium was called) was unable through repression, propaganda, and indeed the whole array of its policies to destroy the Mahdist sect. The Mahdi's son, Abd al-Rahman (1885–1959), became one of the Sudan's two leading political and religious figures; the Mahdi's great-grandson, al-Sadiq al-Mahdi, has twice served as the Sudan's prime minister. Through the Umma Party, the Mahdi family has routinized the revolutionary charisma of the Mahdi himself, while the Mahdist sect has developed along lines familiar in Sudanese sufism.

The Mahdiyya should therefore be seen as one—albeit arguably the most famous and successful—of a series of religious and political revolts that occurred during the eighteenth and nineteenth centuries on the frontiers of the Muslim and non-Muslim worlds. While the future of the Mahdist legacy must be uncertain, parallels with more recent movements are clear; messianism in Islam, as in other religions, has an ancient history and shows no signs of abating.

See also *Egyptian Revolts (1881–1919).*

M.W. DALY

BIBLIOGRAPHY

Hill, Richard L. *Egypt in the Sudan.* London: Royal Institute of International Affairs, 1959.

Holt, P. M. *The Mahdist State in the Sudan 1881–1898. A Study of Its Origins, Development and Overthrow.* 2d ed. Oxford: Clarendon Press, 1970.

SUKARNO

Sukarno (1901–1970), the leader of Indonesia's independence struggle against the Dutch, was born in Surabaya, the Dutch East Indies' largest port city. He attended an elite, Dutch-language high school, where he picked up notions of Indonesian nationalism. The late 1910s was a time of rapid change as the better educated natives were starting to become aware of their common Indonesian and anticolonial identity. As the Dutch Indies were a vast collection of different peoples with distinct languages and many religions, the awareness of a common identity was the requi-

Sukarno

site first step for the creation of an effective independence movement.

In 1926 Sukarno graduated from the Technical College of Bandung with an engineering degree. By then he had become deeply involved in political activity in behalf of the nationalist cause. In 1927 he was one of a small group of intellectuals who formed the Indonesia Nationalist Association (PNI), and he became its chairman. The PNI soon became the main nationalist party in the Indies.

Sukarno's doctrine rested on a vague combination of socialism, Gandhian passive resistance, respect for the many traditional religions of Indonesia, and a faith that somehow these could all be blended with a progressive, secular, Western approach to economic reform. In 1930, to control growing nationalist sentiment, the Dutch imprisoned Sukarno for two years. Then, in 1934, he was exiled by the Dutch to remote outer Indonesian islands. His reputation continued to grow, however, as without him the divided and fractious nationalist movement was repeatedly thwarted by the Dutch.

Sukarno's big chance came when Japan conquered the Dutch East Indies in 1942, during World War II, and set him up as president of a puppet nationalist government. Sukarno declared Indonesia independent on August 17, 1945, three days after Japan's surrender. The Dutch, however, tried to recapture Indonesia, and there followed a bloody war which ended on December 27, 1949, when Indonesian independence was recognized by the Dutch. Sukarno became president of the new nation.

Sukarno tried to steer a moderate path between the many political forces in his country. There were regional rebellions in many of the outer islands, an Islamic movement, and a powerful, growing Communist Party that demanded a genuine socialist revolution. Sukarno's attempt to tie together these various ideological strands proved unworkable. Indonesia's economy decayed as the Dutch left, and his socialist, autarkic policies discouraged both outside and internal investment. To compensate, Sukarno, like many other early nationalist leaders, turned to international affairs to rally his people and rekindle their revolutionary fervor. Internally, he tried to establish a dictatorship under the name of "guided democracy," but he never gained the absolute power he sought.

As Indonesian democracy collapsed into a corrupt, stalemated dictatorship, with Sukarno trying to maintain himself in power by balancing the competing interests of Indonesia's more conservative army and its now enormous Communist Party, he distracted the country by launching a series of foreign adventures and initiatives. He declared that he would destroy neighboring Malaysia because it was a British neocolonialist tool. He took Indonesia out of the United Nations; and he turned increasingly anti-American and procommunist.

By 1965 Sukarno was aging and ill, and his impoverished country was headed toward a civil war between the army and the communists. Sukarno increasingly sided with the communists; when some of them attempted to seize power in 1965, Sukarno was implicated. The army, however, quickly won the battle and annihilated the communists along with hundreds of thousands of their followers.

Sukarno was sidelined and pushed out of power in 1966. He died in semidisgrace in 1970, though more recently he has regained a posthumous status as Indonesia's great anticolonial hero and first president.

See also *Indonesian National Revolution (1945–1950); Indonesian Upheaval (1965–1966).*

DANIEL CHIROT

BIBLIOGRAPHY

Anderson, Benedict R. O'G. *Language and Power: Exploring Political Cultures in Indonesia.* Ithaca, N.Y.: Cornell University Press, 1990.
Legge, J. D. *Sukarno: A Political Biography.* New York: Praeger, 1972.
Mortimer, Rex. *Indonesian Communism Under Sukarno: Ideology and Politics, 1959–1965.* Ithaca, N.Y.: Cornell University Press, 1974.

SUN YAT-SEN

Sun (1866–1925) was the leader of an antimonarchical revolution he could not control and the founder of a republic he could neither command nor fully support. As such, Sun embodied many of the contradictions and complexities that made the early stages of the Chinese revolution long, bloody, and indecisive.

The upwardly and outwardly mobile son of a farming family, Sun had followed the tide of the Chinese diaspora, joining his businessman-elder brother in Hawaii to attend a Christian school. Trained as a medical doctor in the southern coastal city of Guangzhou and in Hong Kong, Sun became a reformer and a nationalist. He tried to win the attention of Qing government reformers, but his Westernizing proposals were unexceptional and his lack of proper literary and examination credentials made him less than persuasive as a peti-

Sun Yat-sen

tioner. Sun led an unsuccessful Guangzhou-based uprising against the Qing dynasty in 1895, pitching him from reform and anonymity to revolution and notoriety. He spent the next sixteen years in exile raising money for the revolutionary cause among overseas Chinese and planning a series of unsuccessful uprisings in China. Sun developed a powerful sense of his own destiny as China's leader, considerable skill as a public speaker, and a broad familiarity with foreign ideas and practices.

Sun's strategy of igniting small revolts in order to fire larger uprisings assumed the imminent collapse of the Qing dynasty. But the decisive blow was not directly delivered by Sun, who was traveling in the United States at the time of the 1911 revolution. Sun's status as a leading revolutionary won him the post of provisional president once he returned to China at the end of 1911. Sun had many assets: a name and face synonymous with revolution, impeccable republican credentials, a plan for national development (the "Three People's Principles" of nationalism, democracy, and people's livelihood), and the support of many revolutionaries. But he lacked military power and soon yielded the presidency to Yuan Shikai, a former Qing official with a modern army based in north China. Sun spent his remaining years trying to win back the post he gave away in 1912 through political campaigns, military expeditions, diplomatic initiatives, and propaganda efforts. In doing so he expanded the political repertoire of the modern Chinese leader.

Sun's many failures and his death in 1925 before he could regain national power make his acknowledged status as a Chinese revolutionary in a league with Hong Xiuquan, Chiang Kai-shek, and Mao Zedong somewhat surprising. Contemporaries accused Sun of stealing credit from more daring colleagues as well as being a politically naive blowhard whose deeds rarely matched his words. But Sun also captured the imagination of Chinese who had shifted their attention from the pattern of China's past to the promise of a brilliant future. Sun spoke of independence for China but also rhapsodized about rail lines, new harbors, paved roads, and a comfortable life in which Chinese would "get rich" (*facai*). Sun called for a disciplined approach to revolution that countenanced sacrificing individual freedom in order to win freedom for the nation and to turn China from a disorganized "plate of sand" into a solid community with an "all-powerful state." His demand for sacrifice and discipline and the alliance of his Nationalist Party with the Communists in 1923 helped pave the way for the rise of Chinese Leninism and Maoist utopianism. Sun also pioneered the role of revolutionary Chinese leader as a potent but unstable mixture of populist rhetoric, statist ambitions, and imperial prerogatives.

See also *Chinese Nationalist Revolution (1919–1927); Chinese Republican Revolution (1911).*

DAVID STRAND

BIBLIOGRAPHY

Bergere, Marie-Claire. *Sun Yat-sen.* Paris: Fayard, 1994.

Schiffrin, Harold Z. *Sun Yat-sen and the Origins of the Chinese Revolution.* Berkeley: University of California Press, 1968.

Wei, Julie Lee, Ramon H. Myers, and Donald G. Gillin, eds. *Prescriptions for Saving China: Selected Writings of Sun Yat-sen.* Translated by Julie Lee Wei, E-su Zen, and Linda Chao. Stanford: Hoover Institution, 1994.

Wilbur, C. Martin. *Sun Yat-sen: Frustrated Patriot.* New York: Columbia University, 1976.

Wong, John Y. *Origins of an Heroic Image: Sun Yat-sen in London, 1896–97.* Oxford: Oxford University Press, 1986.

SWEDISH ROYAL REVOLUTION (1523)

The revolution of 1523, marking the beginning of Sweden's independent existence as a sovereign nation-state, not only freed Sweden from Danish suzerainty, but also established the monarchy under the firm rule of the Vasa dynasty. As a result, Sweden ascended to great-power status in the seventeenth century.

BACKGROUND

The political upheaval of 1523 was not by any means Sweden's first attempt at political independence. Although the three primary Scandinavian kingdoms—Denmark, Norway, and Sweden—already were well defined by the beginning of the High Middle Ages, the ties among the three states were extraordinarily close. The Scandinavian nobility, for example, frequently married across the national frontiers and, as a result, was nearly homogeneous. The natural result of such intimate ties was political union, formalized by the Union of Kalmar in 1397. The union, engineered by the Danish queen and regent Margaret (1353–1412), placed all three kingdoms under the rule of the Danish kings. But elective monarchy remained alive in the Scandinavian kingdoms, at least in principle. Although the Swedish nobility sought at times to elect its own kings, in general Sweden followed Denmark's lead.

Yet serious differences separated Denmark and Sweden. The centralizing policies of the Danish kings—in particular, Erik of Pomerania (ruled 1397–1439) and Christian I (ruled Denmark 1448–1481, Sweden 1457–1464)—provoked a measure of resistance from the Swedish population as a whole. In part, this resistance stemmed from a general desire for greater political autonomy and from hatred of the foreign administrators employed by these kings. Differing commercial and economic priorities played a role as well. Danish hostility toward the German cities of the Hanseatic League (a confederacy of German and Dutch cities that dominated the Baltic trade at the end of the Middle Ages) gave rise to anti-Danish feeling in areas of Sweden (especially Dalarna) heavily dependent on the Hanseatic trade. This dissatisfaction was reflected in the rising frequency of uprisings and minor revolts in the late fifteenth and early sixteenth centuries. The most significant of these revolts—those of Engelbrekt Engelbrektsson and Sten Sture the Elder in the late fifteenth century, and of Sten Sture the Younger in the early sixteenth—enjoyed widespread support from the lower orders but found few noble supporters. The Swedish nobility, on the whole, was disdainful of the humbly born Engelbrektsson and the Stures and saw no advantage in replacing the overlordship of distant Denmark with a home-grown popular tyranny. A successful national revolt would require, then, some element that would unite the interests of the nobility and those of the lower orders, and a champion acceptable to both.

REVOLUTION OF 1523

Both were forthcoming in 1520. Dissatisfaction with Danish rule peaked during the reign of the controversial King Christian II (ruled 1513–1523). Christian II, like the Stures, appears to have aimed at something approaching popular despotism, with a series of reforms canted toward peasant and merchant interests in Denmark. Thus he was unpopular with the nobility of both Denmark and Sweden. In Sweden, in fact, the Estates (legislature) hesitated to accept Christian II as its king, and before 1520 the king was unable to force its recognition of his right to rule. But a dispute between the widely disliked Swedish cleric Gustav Trolle, archbishop of Uppsala, and Sten Sture the Younger, the self-proclaimed regent of Sweden, gave the king the opportunity he needed to assert his authority—and, ultimately, it gave the Swedes the motivation to rise in rebellion.

Trolle's enmity toward Sture compelled the Swedish nobility to coalesce around Sture, and in 1517 it vowed to maintain a common front against Trolle and his protectors. Christian II attempted to resolve the situation and to force his recognition as king of Sweden militarily, attacking Stockholm in 1518 and again in 1520. The first attempt miscarried; the second succeeded, the king defeating Sture's army, killing Sture in the process, and taking Stockholm in the spring. He used the opportunity to compel the Swedish Estates to acknowledge him as hereditary ruler of Sweden; he then set out to eliminate his foremost enemies in the realm. Only a few days after his coronation in Stockholm, the king allowed Trolle to arrest a large number of those who had opposed the bishop. Using Trolle's ecclesiastical office as an excuse, Christian II authorized the trial of a large number of Swedish noblemen and leading citizens of Stockholm, of whom eighty-two were condemned to death and beheaded immediately thereafter. This event—the Stockholm "Bloodbath" of November 8, 1520—eliminated most of Sweden's political leadership, but it also served as a catalyst to unite the nobility and the lower orders in revolt.

One of the few Swedish noblemen to escape the Bloodbath was Gustav Eriksson, scion of the Swedish family of Vasa. Gustav had been one of Sten Sture the Younger's supporters. In 1518, in the wake of Christian II's unsuccessful attempt to take Stockholm, the king had taken the twenty-two-year-old Gustav as hostage to Copenhagen, but he escaped from Denmark to Lübeck (Germany) the following year, and in May 1520 he returned to Sweden. It was not until after the Stockholm Bloodbath, however, that he met with much success in raising support against Christian II. By early 1521 he had managed to scrape together a sizable rebel army. Eriksson was a natural choice as leader: he was charismatic and tireless; he was of noble birth and thus acceptable to the nobility; he was one of the "Sture party" and thus acceptable to the lower orders; and, not least, he was one of the few prominent noblemen to escape the Bloodbath and thus was the focus of the rebel movement by default.

Although the rebel army managed to inflict a stinging defeat on Christian II's forces at Västeras in April 1521, it was not until the Hanseatic cities of Danzig and Lübeck offered substantial military and naval assistance that the rebels were able to make any true progress, wresting command of the sea from the Danes and taking Stockholm. Simultaneously, the Danish nobility's enmity toward Christian II led them in early 1523 to depose their king in favor of his uncle, Frederick of Holstein (King Frederick I, ruled 1523–1533). Constitutional troubles in Denmark precluded the possibility of further attempts to quell the rebellion. The Swedish Estates convened at the town of Strängnäs early in June 1523. With the visible support of the Hanseatic League, the Estates elected Gustav Vasa—who already had been proclaimed regent by the rebel army in August 1521—as King Gustav I Vasa of Sweden.

Paul Douglas Lockhart

BIBLIOGRAPHY

Bergstrom, Rudolf. *Studier till den stora krisen i nordens historia, 1517–1523.* Uppsala: Almqvist och Wiksell, 1943.

Enemark, Poul. *Fra Kalmarbrev til Stockholms Blodbad. Den nordiske trestatsunions epoke, 1397–1521.* Copenhagen: Gyldendal, 1979.

Kumlien, Kjell. "Gustav Vasa och kungavalet i Strängnäs 1523." *Historisk Tidskrift (Svensk)* 80 (1960): 1–31.

Lindqvist, Herman. *Historien om Gustav Vasa och hans soner och döttrar.* Stockholm: Norstedt, 1997.

Roberts, Michael. *The Early Vasas. A History of Sweden, 1523–1611.* Cambridge: Cambridge University Press, 1968.

Sjodin, Lars. *Kalmarunionens slutskede. Gustav Vasas befrielsekrig.* 2 vols. Uppsala: Almqvist och Wiksell, 1943–1947.

SYMBOLISM, RITUALISM, AND DRESS

In times of revolution, symbols, rituals, and dress can be important signs of solidarity, power, opposition to authority, and emotion, denoting humor, rage, piety, or rupture with convention. They also can serve as mechanisms for the diffusion of revolutionary energy.

SYMBOLISM IN EIGHTEENTH CENTURY REVOLUTIONARY MOVEMENTS

Eighteenth century revolutions were filled with evocative symbolism and forms of dress that evoked resistance and built solidarity. American revolutionaries, for example, understood the importance of symbolism. Their liberty trees, boycotts against British luxury goods, and attacks on theaters and stamp men—even the dumping of tea into Boston harbor by "Indians"—were laden with symbolism contrasting British luxury and oppression with colonial simplicity and virtue.

The peak years of the French Revolution saw the first systematic attempts to reshape political culture around new forms of dress, display, religion, and public festivity. Conceiving of revolution as popular sovereignty achieved through mass action, the revolutionaries tried not only to democratize the rights of Frenchmen but also to insist on their social obligation to appear and to act as republicans. Festivals of reason rich with ritual replaced traditional religious ceremonies, and liberty trees—some dangling with effigies of aristocrats—were planted in every commune. Even the bodily image of the royal family was attacked through pornographic libels of the queen. Politicizing the everyday with symbols and costumes widened the range of opportunities for the exercise of revolutionary power.

Nowhere was this process more true than in the changes in dress that accompanied the French Revolution's progress. Most republican politicians affected simple black or brown frock coats without frills. Later, the state commissioned standard revolutionary costumes for high officials. At the height of revolutionary enthusiasm, avid republicans would challenge those who appeared on the streets wearing wigs or silk stockings. Good citizens were to be liberated by the Revolution, but, after 1792, they had to *look* like a republican as well.

Historians like Lynn Hunt and Mona Ozouf have done much to sensitize us to the cultural expressions that grew out of and followed the French Revolution. But can this best-documented of all revolutions be used as a model of the symbolic politics of revolution elsewhere?

There is evidence that the French were not alone in their use of revolutionary symbolism. Although the available documentation about the symbolism of the English Revolution (1688) is not as rich as in the French case, we know that radical religious sects like the Diggers symbolized their assumption of ownership of the common land by digging the wasteland. French Protestants burning down Catholic churches were sure to abuse their statues as well. The American patriots who boycotted English mourning clothes and wore simple leather vests were rejecting the refinements of the mother country as well as its products.

SYMBOLISM AND THE DIFFUSION OF REVOLUTION

Modern anticolonial movements and social revolutions likewise have been deeply imbued with symbolism. Mohandas Karamchand Gandhi and his followers wove and wore the simple khadi cloth that expressed their opposition to imported British garments. From the plain military tunics affected by Joseph Stalin and Mao Zedong to the beards and scruffy appearances of Latin American *guerilleros,* symbolism plays an important role in marking off insurgents from their opponents. Costume has had other important roles as well, notably those of stigmatizing and dehumanizing opponents, as illustrated by the dunce caps placed on the heads of landowners in the Chinese revolution; endowing insurgents with the look of more military prowess than they possess (witness the wooden guns toted by the Chiapas insurgents in 1994 in Mexico); and diffusing solidarity for a movement without obliging noncombatants to take risky action.

Was the eighteenth century revolutionaries' emphasis on physical symbols a function of the low level of literacy of their societies? It is important to remember that eighteenth century America had a very high level of literacy—much higher than that of France. And revolutionary movements in societies with near-universal literacy seem to place no less emphasis on physical symbols than did earlier revolutions. The statue of liberty has been a sufficiently transcultural symbol to embody the hopes of eighteenth-century French revolutionaries, nineteenth-century American immigrants, and twentieth-century Chinese students. In fact, both reading and the mass media have an important role in publicizing and diffusing social movements, as the Chinese students who occupied Tiananmen Square with a goddess of liberty in 1989 well understood. If anything, television has increased the importance of visual symbolism in movements of revolt.

Symbolism is one of the ways by which revolutions are diffused around the world. The French Revolution quickly became "modular" through a set of symbols that told people all over the world that the activity they were engaging in was revolutionary. This process took the form of both the language used to describe enemies as "aristocrats" and "feudatories"—even in societies that had never experienced feudalism and had no real aristocracies—and of the spread of insurrectionary instruments like the barricade to new sites and countries. The physical separation of left and right in the French revolutionary assembly was adopted as the universal plan for legislatures everywhere. The Fascist revolution in Italy and the Nazi revolution in Germany nearly overwhelmed their people with symbols; indeed, the Nazi swastika has become one of the most recognized and reviled symbols in the world today.

Symbols of revolutionary identity and of revolutionary change have always played a key role in mobilizing and energizing populations for action. Whether in largely illiterate nations or in the computer-savvy media age, the power of revolutionary symbols comes from their ability to encapsulate, in graphic form, the anger, aspirations, and commitments of the revolution. The hanging of aristocrats from lamp posts, like the burning of the manor rolls that detailed peasants' feudal obligations, were emotional acts that spoke of vengeance as well as change. The hammer and sickle of communism proclaimed a society where workers and farmers—not emperors with their traditional coats of arms—came first in society. And the flags and banners of many revolutionary regimes—from the tricolor of France to the new flag of Islamic Iran—proclaim to the world new nations founded on new social compacts.

The revolutions in the former Soviet bloc have raised to a new level interest among scholars in the symbolism of revolution. From the use of Catholic symbols by Polish Solidarity militants in the early 1980s, to the symbolism of the "round table" that was used throughout Eastern Europe to legitimize dissidents in 1989, to the role of reburials and theater networks in the Czech Revolution, symbolism has been no less prevalent, if less bloodstained, in modern revolutions than it was in Paris two hundred years ago.

See also *Literature; Media and Communications.*

SIDNEY TARROW

BIBLIOGRAPHY

Esherick, Joseph W., and Jeffrey N. Wasserstrom. "Acting Out Democracy." In *Popular Protest and Political Conflict in Modern China.* 2d ed. Edited by Jeffrey N. Wasserstrom and Elizabeth J. Perry. Boulder, Colo.: Westview Press, 1994.

Hunt, Lynn. *Politics, Culture, and Class in the French Revolution.* Berkeley: University of California Press, 1984.

———. *The Family Romance of the French Revolution.* Berkeley and Los Angeles: University of California Press, 1992.

Kertzer, David. *Ritual, Politics and Power.* New Haven, Conn.: Yale University Press, 1988.

Kubik, Jan. *The Power of Symbols and the Symbols of Power.* University Park: Pennsylvania State University Press, 1994.

Ozouf, Mona. *Festivals and the French Revolution.* Translated by Alan Sheridan. Cambridge: Harvard University Press, 1988.

SYRIAN REVOLUTION (1963)

On March 8, 1963, military officers overthrew Syria's parliamentary system and set up the National Council of the Revolutionary Command. The coup followed a period of instability dating from Syria's independence from France at the end of World War II. Attempts to establish democratic government, including an

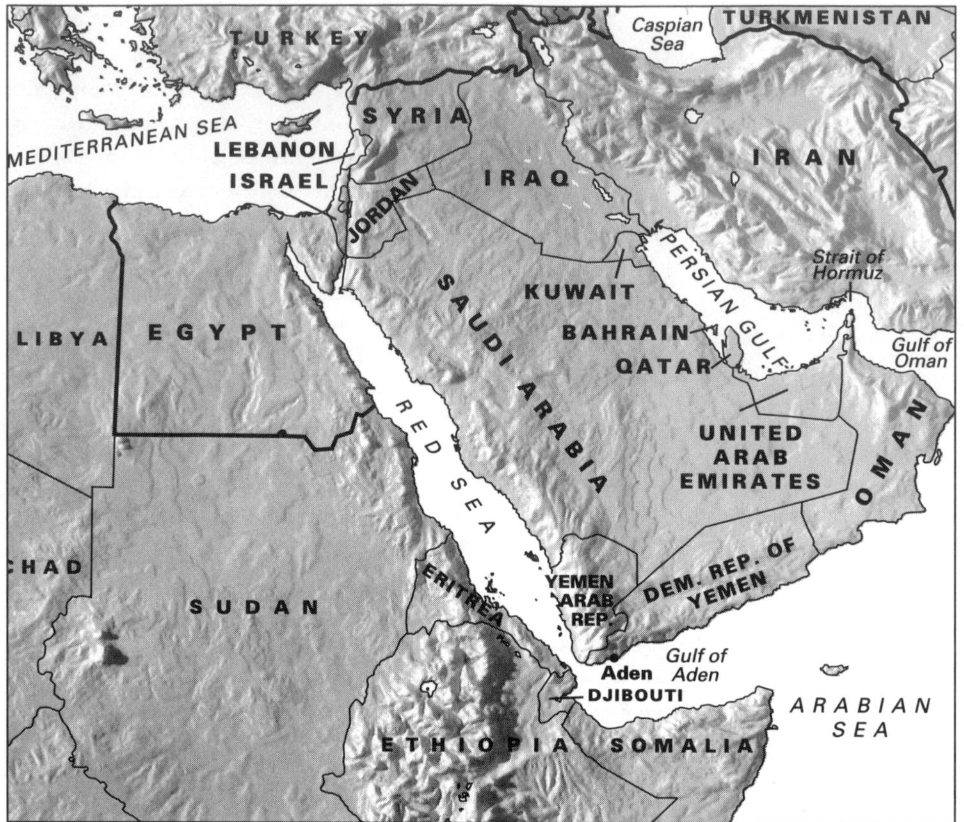

elected government that assumed power in 1943, did not take root and were overshadowed by intermittent military coups, mostly bloodless. The period saw the emergence of the Arab Ba'ath Socialist Party, which became the dominant political organization in Syria and has ruled the nation since 1963. The events of 1963 led seven years later to the capture of power by Hafez al-Assad, an air force general. Assad's assumption of power marked the beginning of a long period of stable but authoritarian government.

The officers in the 1963 coup represented three different political movements. A Nasserist group supported Egyptian president Gamal Abdel Nasser and his program of state-sponsored socialism, which had been introduced into Syria while the two countries were combined as the United Arab Republic (1958–1961). The clandestine Military Committee of the Arab Ba'ath Socialist Party formed the second group. The third group was composed of anti-Nasserists associated with the populist leader Akram Hawrani.

The three factions had jockeyed for position throughout 1962, as the post-UAR government led by liberals Nazim al-Qudsi and Ma'ruf Dawalibi moved to dismantle the public sector and resurrect private ownership. Workers, small farmers, and agricultural laborers resisted privatization, sparking a string of mutinies by Nasserist and Ba'ath officers. Growing criticism of military involvement in politics, combined with signs that the defenders of state-run enterprises had forged an alliance with Islamic activists in the capital, Damascus, finally persuaded the Military Committee of the Ba'ath to join forces with the Nasserists and Hawranists to reinstate a state-dominated socialist order by force.

Overturning the parliamentary system proved easier than establishing a postrevolutionary regime. Nasserist officers quickly began pressing for a revival of the UAR, prompting the Military Committee of the Ba'ath to purge many Nasserists from the armed forces. Proponents of reunification with Egypt organized massive protests in Damascus and Aleppo, which were brutally suppressed. The remaining Nasserist commanders made a desperate attempt to regain power in July 1963 but were beaten back by Ba'ath officers, who took advantage of the situation to capture key positions in the police, the security services, and the armed forces. The Military Committee then extended its influence by transforming the armed forces into an "ideological army" of Ba'ath Party activists drawn largely from the country's minority Alawi, Druze, and Isma'ili communities.

Immediately after seizing power, the leadership of the March 1963 coup nationalized Syria's banks and insurance companies and enacted a new agrarian reform law that imposed strict upper limits on the size of private landholdings. At the same time, the new regime tried to reassure private businesses that comprehensive nationalization was not on the agenda. Following a wave of anti-Ba'ath protests in Syria's northern cities during the spring of 1964, however, radical cadres in the party's branches in Aleppo and Homs sequestered several large, privately owned industrial firms. The radicals then pressured the government to authorize the formation of a national trade union federation and to promulgate a new labor law that would augment the state's role in guaranteeing worker's rights.

These moves set the stage for a series of nationalizations in January 1965, acts that severed the tenuous connection between the primary supporters of the Ba'ath Party (urban workers and farm laborers) and small-scale manufacturers and tradespeople, who were suspicious of the party's economic policies but tended to back its nationalist orientation. Tensions among these social forces erupted into riots and demonstrations in the larger cities that spring, precipitating a power struggle between moderates and doctrinaire socialists over the future course of the Ba'ath revolution. Radical officers loyal to Gen. Salah Jadid, including Gen. Hafez al-Assad, finally ousted the moderates in February 1966.

The new leadership concentrated power in the Regional Command of the Ba'ath Party and authorized that body to appoint the president and cabinet ministers. It also carried out extensive nationalizations of private enterprise and set up a network of state-affiliated popular organizations to supervise the activities of students, women, workers, and farm laborers.

In November 1970 Jadid was in turn overthrown by officers allied to Assad. Calling its action a "corrective movement" designed to reverse the excesses of the radicals, the new Ba'ath leadership took steps to restore private ownership and attract foreign investment. In early 1971 the Regional Command appointed delegates to a People's Assembly that included representatives of four political parties in addition to the Ba'ath Party. The five parties combined to form the ruling National Progressive Front in March 1972.

Assad's rule provided Syria a long period of relative calm following more than two decades of intense political tumult. Assad led Syria to an increasingly important role in regional politics.

See also *Egyptian Revolution (1952); Iraqi Revolution (1958); Nasser, Gamal Abdel.*

Fred H. Lawson

BIBLIOGRAPHY

Hinnebusch, Raymond A. "Syria Under the Ba'ath: Social Ideology, Policy, and Practice." In *Social Legislation in the Contemporary Middle East.* Edited by Laurence O. Michalak and Jeswald W. Salacuse. Berkeley: University of California Institute of International Studies, 1986.

Kerr, Malcolm H. *The Arab Cold War.* London: Oxford University Press, 1971.

Lawson, Fred H. "Political-Economic Trends in Ba'thi Syria: A Reinterpretation." *Orient* 29 (December 1988): 579–594.

Petran, Tabtha. *Syria.* New York: Praeger, 1972.

T

TERRORISM

"The purpose of terrorism is to produce terror," Vladimir Ilyich Lenin, the leader of the Russian Revolution responsible for the Red Terror, once noted dryly. The terrorist aims to produce terror—extreme fear—among his or her opponents. The Latin word *terror* (from *terrere,* to frighten) entered modern Western vocabularies through the French language in the fourteenth century, and the first English usage was recorded in 1528.

A clearly political charge was given to the term *terror* during the French Revolution. After the execution of the Bourbon king Louis XVI by the guillotine on January 21, 1793, the counterrevolution began in earnest. The revolutionaries found themselves threatened by aristocratic emigrants who conspired with foreign rulers to invade the country. At the same time, treason at home in support of this reactionary move was perceived by the leaders of the French Revolution as a danger. In July 1793, after the assassination of Jean-Paul Marat, one of the revolutionary leaders, the French National Assembly, led by the radical Jacobins, created the twelve-man Committee of Public Safety. They declared terror to be the order of the day on September 5, 1793, thereby sanctioning executions of suspected traitors and collaborators. Just a few days earlier, on August 31, the *Messenger of Equality* had suggested that the guillotine was the only means to inspire the terror necessary to consolidate the Revolution.

Originally conceived as an instrument of defense against royalist subversion and the threat of invasion, the Terror of the Committee of Public Safety (of which Maximilien Robespierre was the most prominent member) soon began to target republicans as well. The revolutionary allies to the right of the Jacobins (the "Indulgents," under Georges Jacques Danton) and on the left (the "Hébertists," under Jacques René Hébert) became victims of the wave of terror. Altogether hundreds of thousands of political suspects were arrested throughout France during the Reign of Terror (June 2, 1793–July 27, 1794); seventeen thousand were officially executed, and many others died in prison or without a trial. Those who had originally supported the draconian measures proposed by Robespierre's Committee of Public Safety against counterrevolutionaries began to fear for their own lives and conspired to overthrow him. They could not accuse him of terror, which they had earlier declared to be official state policy; instead, they accused him of *terrorisme,* a word that had an illegal and repulsive ring. On the charge of terrorism, Robespierre and twenty-one of his associates were sent to the guillotine on 9 and 10 Thermidor of the year II (July 27 and 28, 1794). The Revolution was, like the Greek god Kronos, eating its own children. Of the three thousand people executed during the Reign of Terror in Paris, only 20 percent were aristocrats. The main victims were political opponents of the revolutionary dictatorship of the extremist Jacobins.

There have been numerous *reigns of terror* since the French Revolution. Thus the term has become increasingly detached from this specific historical period (1793–1794) and is used to typify regimes that rule by fear caused by unjust mass arrests, arbitrary trials, and executions of victims when individual guilt matters little and political intimidation of the populace matters a great deal. The leaders of the Russian Revolution, who felt threatened after a failed assassination attempt on Lenin on August 30, 1918, established a Marxist "dictatorship of the proletariat" and made a declaration of Red Terror on September 5, 1918, consciously imitating the French revolutionaries who had done so on the same day 125 years before. Up to two hundred thousand people were executed under the Red Terror of the Russian Revolution and in the civil war (1918–1921). Threatened by the so-called White counterrevolutionaries and foreign intervention, and meeting resistance from a war-weary populace, the Bolsheviks could compel political obedience from the public only by terror because they had little else to offer than propaganda. In Communist China, Mao led periodic campaigns of terror to root out capitalist sympathizers or those with connections to the precommunist regime.

Children were urged to denounce their parents, and those convicted of having the wrong "class background" were stripped of jobs and credentials and exiled to re-education camps or to remote villages to work in the fields. In the Iranian Revolution of 1979, radical young Revolutionary Guards arrested or assaulted anyone (especially women) who broke traditional Qur'anic laws, conducted a campaign of violence against more secular Islamic parties, and—with state encouragement—attacked non-Islamic minorities.

PROPAGANDA BY THE DEED

Revolutionary terrorist violence sends a message of fear (to the forces of the status quo) and hope (to the forces of change) and becomes "propaganda by the deed"—a term first used by French anarchists in the 1870s. The basic mechanism of terror, however, was already epitomized in the old Chinese saying, "Kill one, frighten ten thousand." Raymond Aron has correctly observed, "An action of violence is labeled 'terrorist' when the psychological effects are out of proportion to its purely physical result."

The use of atrocities—violence without moral restraints—as a means to scare, intimidate, or paralyze opponents for the purpose of social control has been a tactic of revolutionaries left and right, in and out of power. While assassination serves to eliminate important opponents and genocide (or politicide) is used to destroy whole groups of people, terror stands somewhere in between, but usually closer to murder. Terror is used to intimidate political neutrals and frighten opponents. The arbitrariness with which victims are often selected is meant to send a warning to others who share group characteristics with the victim.

Although terror played no part in the prelude for the French Revolution, subsequent radical revolutionaries with little or no initial mass support have often used terrorism not only to consolidate power but also to achieve it—with mixed success. Agitational terror, while sometimes offering a signal for mass insurrection, tends to provoke massive counterterror except in well-established democracies securely under the rule of law. In the context of revolutions, terror has usually played a bigger part in the consolidation phase of the revolution than in bringing it about.

TERRORISM AND WARFARE

Where revolutionary mass mobilization has led to the taking of state power, this action has often been in the context of war, especially a losing war. Terrorism has mostly been an auxiliary tool, not the main instrument of revolution itself, although some theorists, in particular Mao, gave terrorist tactics a place in the stages of guerrilla warfare. In his *Guerrilla Warfare* (1937), Mao attributed a special role to terrorism in the second stage of a three-stage model of insurrection: (1) organization, consolidation, and preservation of base areas; (2) guerrilla war; and (3) conventional army to destroy the enemy.

Acts of terrorism are in many ways comparable to war crimes—noncombatants are killed, prisoners murdered, and innocent people taken hostage. Terrorists have, in fact, elevated irregular practices that are excesses of war to the level of routine tactics. They do not engage in open combat, as soldiers do. They strike preferably against the unarmed. In other words, the attack on the defenseless is not a side-effect but a deliberate strategy of terrorists. Like war crimes, acts of terrorism distinguish themselves from conventional warfare, and to some extent also from guerrilla warfare, through the disregard of principles of chivalry and humanity contained in humanitarian Law of War.

However, guerrilla forces that rely mainly on terrorist tactics are not likely to obtain many voluntary sympathizers, especially when their terror serves to recruit new fighters for the cause of self-appointed revolutionaries. Acts of terror, including kidnapping for ransom, are also performed to raise "revolutionary taxes," as part (sometimes the only part) of a revolutionary strategy. As an instrument of social change, terror is tyrannical in nature, and claims of its perpetrators that they are using terror to bring about liberation and social justice face a credibility problem. Due to their immoral character, acts or campaigns of terrorism often backfire as popular support and legitimacy shift to the opponent—unless the opponent is also using terror tactics. The propaganda struggle associated with terrorist campaigns has much to do with obtaining the moral high ground in the eyes of observers who might help to shift the power balance in favor of the revolutionaries. Self-legitimation and delegitimation of the opponent are often central elements in the propaganda accompanying terrorist campaigns of violence.

While acts of terrorism are part of most revolutions and counterrevolutions, this tactic has, by itself, been decisive in dislodging an existing regime on few occasions, and then mainly in revolutionary national liberation struggles from colonial rule such as in Algeria or Aden. As an instrument of tyrannical rule, terrorism by revolutionary regimes has been more effective, although its impact is hard to judge because it has never been the only instrument of social control.

See also *French Revolution (1789–1815); Robespierre, Maximilien*.

A. P. SCHMID

BIBLIOGRAPHY

O'Brien, Connor Cruise. *Passion and Cunning: Essays on Nationalism, Terrorism and Revolution*. New York: Simon and Schuster, 1989.

Rubenstein, R. E. *Alchemists of Revolution: Terrorism in the Modern World.* New York: Basic Books, 1987.

Schmid, Alex P., Albert J. Jongman et al. *Political Terrorism: A New Guide to Actors, Authors, Concepts, Data Bases, Theories, and Literature.* Revised, expanded, and updated edition prepared under the auspices of the Center for International Affairs, Harvard University. Amsterdam: North-Holland Publishing, 1988.

THAI REVOLUTION (1932)

The revolution of June 24, 1932, brought to an end the rule of the absolute monarch in Thailand. The change in government was organized by a group of middle-level civilian and military officials, termed collectively the People's Party, and was carried out in a nonviolent manner. A provisional constitution was issued soon after, virtually stripping the monarch of all political power; a permanent document followed by the end of the year that placed the king under constitutional controls. Although the monarchy has gradually recovered its prestige and now wields considerable influence and power in many civil and political institutions, the revolution of 1932 was a defining event in the political consciousness of educated Thai people. The vision of constitutional democracy that motivated the People's Party to move against the throne still inspires Thai reformers campaigning for fuller political participation and democratic rights.

The idea of a constitutional monarchy was not new, having been suggested by young princes and nobles in a petition to the throne as early as 1885. Chulalongkorn, the fifth king in the dynasty, responded by reorganizing the kingdom's administration, education system, and finances. These measures led to an increasingly educated and politically sophisticated bureaucracy. Commoners as well as members of the aristocracy found their way to overseas universities, particularly in England, where they were exposed to Western political philosophies. In 1912 a group of military and civilian officials attempted to seize power. Although it was promptly crushed, the abortive coup d'état intimated growing dissatisfaction and exasperation with the pace of political reform.

In the ensuing years the monarchy was subjected to increasing criticism of its handling of the kingdom's finances and of the domination of the princes in government. Not least of the monarchy's vulnerabilities were the extraterritorial treaties signed in the middle of the nineteenth century with the Western powers, giving countries such as Britain, France, the Netherlands, and the United States consular rights over Siamese citizens, many of whom were of Chinese and Indian descent. The stringent economic conditions forced on the government by the global recession of the

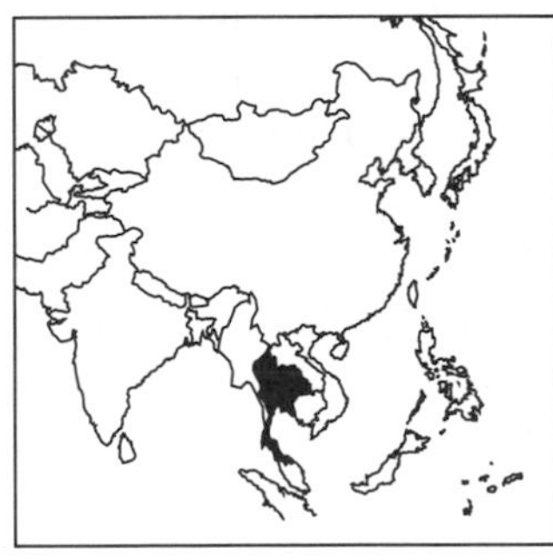

early 1930s finally determined the timing of the challenge to the throne.

Until recently, both Western and Thai historians were content to see the revolution of 1932 as a coup d'état, in other words, as a commoner oligarchy replacing one constituted by royal blood lines. However, new research, some of it in the Thai language and some of it in unpublished dissertations, is revising the conventional interpretation to suggest that the revolution was broadly based in civil society. Thai nationalism "from above," purportedly the creation of an enlightened if increasingly besieged monarch, in fact was a reaction to a vigorous nationalism "from below." A spirited debate about the rights of the governed, such as the rights of women in a society where polygamy had been strategically used to extend the power of princely families, was aired during the 1910s and 1920s in the popular press. This debate put pressure on the monarchy, which, in the end, was forced to agree to the change it feared the most.

Craig J. Reynolds

BIBLIOGRAPHY

Batson, Benjamin A. *The End of the Absolute Monarchy in Siam.* Singapore: Oxford University Press, 1984.

———, ed. *Siam's Political Future: Documents from the End of the Absolute Monarchy.* Ithaca, N.Y.: Cornell University, Southeast Asia Program, 1974.

Nakkarin Mektrairat. *Kanpatiwat sayam pho so 2475.* Bangkok: Social Sciences and Humanities Textbook Project Foundation, 1992.

Thawatt Mokarapong. *History of the Thai Revolution: A Study in Political Behaviour.* Bangkok: Chalermnit, 1972.

Wyatt, David K. *Thailand: A Short History.* New Haven, Conn., and London: Yale University Press, 1984.

TIBETAN REVOLT (1959)

The Tibetan revolt, the culmination of the uncomfortable relationship between the Tibetan government and its Chinese communist conquerors, resulted in the Tibetan government fleeing into exile in India along with hundreds of thousands of ordinary citizens.

After the fall of the Qing dynasty in 1911, Tibet had enjoyed de facto independence. Tibetan leaders felt that their inclusion in the Qing empire had been the result of an alliance between Tibet and the Manchus—the non-Han Chinese rulers—who established the dynasty and did not extend to governments that succeeded the Qing. This stance brought them into conflict with Mao Zedong's highly nationalistic Chinese Communist Party, which was determined to reincorporate lost territories. In October 1950 Chinese communist forces defeated the ill-equipped and poorly prepared forces of Tibet's spiritual and secular ruler, the young Dalai Lama. A seventeen-point agreement, signed in May 1951, declared that Tibet was an integral part of China. The People's Republic of China would take charge of the area's external affairs, while the Tibetan government would maintain internal autonomy; its people's livelihood would be improved; and its existing political system, including the status of the Dalai Lama, would remain intact.

The relationship was characterized by distrust on both sides. Changes made by the Chinese government in the name of improving the Tibetan people's livelihood had the simultaneous result of eroding traditional culture and undermining the position of the traditional elite. Moreover, the Beijing government divided the territories Tibetans regarded as Tibet among several provinces, including Sichuan, Qinghai, Yunnan, and what came to be called the Tibet Autonomous Region (TAR). Whether these changes were done with malice aforethought is less important than the fact that large numbers of Tibetans fervently believed that they were. Preparations for a revolt began. The Chinese government subsequently charged that foreign powers were involved in the plans; plausible evidence indicates that these may have included the governments of India, the United States, and the Republic of China on Taiwan.

In 1958, as part of the disastrous Chinese economic and social experiment known as the Great Leap Forward, sweeping reforms were carried out in ethnically Tibetan areas outside the TAR. Angry refugees flooded from the affected areas into the TAR, recounting scenes of horror and raising the tension level between Han Chinese and Tibetans. When in early March 1959 the Chinese military ignored proper protocol in inviting the Dalai Lama to attend a theatrical performance, the rumor spread that the army intended to kidnap him and then enforce Great Leap Forward-style reforms in supposedly autonomous Tibet. The Tibetan revolt aimed at forestalling these events.

The revolt was suppressed within two weeks. The Chinese government declared that the revolt had abrogated the 1951 agreement, allowing China to begin a much more ambitious reform program inside the TAR. Some have speculated that the Beijing government provoked the revolt with this end in mind. The fleeing of the Dalai Lama and thousands of his supporters was, however, a major embarrassment for the Chinese government.

The Tibetan exile community has been successful in mobilizing international sympathy for its cause, including demands for both complete independence and meaningful autonomy within the Chinese system. In 1989 the Dalai Lama was awarded the Nobel Peace Prize. During the same year, protest movements in Tibet led the Chinese government to declare a state of martial law there, which was lifted one year later. The anniversary of the 1959 revolt, March 8, has become a traditional day of protest within Tibet, as well as a day of commemoration by adherents to the Tibetan cause worldwide.

See also *Chinese Communist Revolution (1921–1949).*

June Teufel Dreyer

BIBLIOGRAPHY

Dalai Lama (Ngawang Lobsang Yishey Tenzing Gyaltso). *My Land and My People.* New York: McGraw-Hill, 1962.

Ginsburgs, George, and Michael Mathos. *Communist China and Tibet: The First Dozen Years.* The Hague: Martinus Nijhoff, 1964.

Goldstein, Melvyn C. *Snow Lion and the Dragon: China, Tibet, and the Dalai Lama.* Berkeley: University of California Press, 1997.

Patterson, George. *Tibet in Revolt.* London: Methuen, 1960.

Shakabpa, Tsepon W. D. *Tibet: A Political History.* New Haven, Conn.: Yale University Press, 1967.

TITO, JOSIP BROZ

Tito (1892–1980) led the partisan resistance movement in Yugoslavia during World War II and was the unquestioned leader of socialist Yugoslavia from the war's end until his death. He also was one of the founders of the movement of nonaligned states, which sought to provide a third force in world politics in the era of cold war rivalry between the United States and the Soviet Union.

Born to a mixed Croatian/Slovenian family in northwest Croatia, Tito had completed his training as a locksmith by the time he was eighteen. In 1913 he entered the Austro-Hungarian army, where during World War I he was wounded and captured by the Russians. In Russia he participated in the Bolshevik Revolution and became a communist. Returning to newly created Yugoslavia in 1920, he rose steadily in the illegal communist party despite spending several years in prison. When Stalinist purges struck down other party leaders, in 1939 he became general secretary. After Hitler's armies invaded the Soviet Union in June 1941, Tito led his underground organization in vigorous resistance to the German occupation of Yugoslavia. Over the course of the war, his partisan movement not only fought the Germans but engaged in a three-way civil war with Croatian fascists and Serbian nationalists. Although later criticized after the war for mistakes of military judgment and other errors, his ability to lead and direct, and his acknowledged position as "the old man" of the movement, permitted him to guide the communist forces to victory in 1945.

Considered in the West as Soviet leader Joseph Stalin's most loyal ally in the years 1945 to 1948, Tito actually took initiatives of which Stalin did not approve, such as agreeing to a federation with Bulgaria. Having won their own revolution, Tito and his colleagues resented the overbearing way in which Russian advisers and functionaries treated them. In 1948, when they expressed these concerns, Stalin expelled Yugoslavia from the Cominform (Communist Information Bureau—the replacement for the disbanded Communist International, or Comintern). Until Stalin's death in 1953, the Soviet bloc pursued a relentless propaganda campaign against Yugoslavia. "Titoism," that is, questioning the leading role of the Soviet Union and Stalin, became a serious crime in Eastern Europe, and many Czechoslovaks, Hungarians, and Bulgarians went to their death as alleged Titoists.

To differentiate Yugoslav communism from the Soviet model, Tito adopted a system of worker self-administration. His willingness to permit somewhat more openness to the West, by letting people emigrate or work abroad, for example, along with the introduction of modest market mechanisms into the Yugoslav economy, permitted Yugoslavia to steer a middle course between East and West until his death in 1980. This policy was exemplified by his early leadership of the nonaligned movement, that is, the effort of states like Indonesia, India, and Egypt to create an alliance of countries committed neither to capitalism nor to communism.

Tito hoped that each of the many ethnic groups in Yugoslavia could retain its national identity while becoming loyal to a larger socialist community. But he was unwilling to open public debate on difficult issues, and he insisted that the party retain control despite rhetoric about self-administration. To try to solve ethnic tensions he did allow the Communist Party to decentralize into eight competing regional units, but this only worsened the problem. His personal, autocratic rule was an important factor in holding Yugoslavia together, but these qualities made it impossible for Yugoslavs to develop a level of civic consciousness sufficient to sustain them when socialism collapsed eleven years after his death.

See also *Yugoslav Communist Collapse and Dissolution (1987–1992); Yugoslav Partisans and Communist Revolution (1941–1948).*

Gale Stokes

BIBLIOGRAPHY

Auty, Phyllis. *Tito: A Biography.* Rev. ed. Hammondsworth: Penguin, 1974.

Dedijer, Vladimir. *Tito.* New York: Simon and Schuster, 1953.

Djilas, Milovan. *Tito: The Story from Inside.* New York: Harcourt Brace Jovanovic, 1980.

Maclean, Fitzroy. *The Heretic: The Life and Times of Josip Broz Tito.* London: Cape, 1949.

TOCQUEVILLE, ALEXIS DE

Although he participated briefly in the early stages of the French Revolution of 1848, Tocqueville (1805–1859) is chiefly important to the study of revolutions as one of the acutest analysts of the origins and significance of the French Revolution of 1789. Insofar as that revolution is a paradigm for the analysis of subsequent ones, his insights have a wider significance.

A nobleman and son of a distinguished Napoleonic administrator who wrote his own history of the French Revolution (having lived through it, unlike several guillotined relatives), Tocqueville embarked on a legal career. His legal research took him to the United States in the early 1830s, ostensibly on an official mission from the French government to study prisons. Out of this visit came his first great masterpiece, *Democracy in America* (1835–1840), which is essential to understanding all his later thought.

Alexis de Tocqueville

In 1839 he entered politics as a deputy. The peak of his public career came after the 1848 revolution, when he served for five months in 1849 as foreign minister. Dismissed by President Louis Napoleon Bonaparte, he protested against Bonaparte's seizure of imperial power in 1851. Tocqueville, excluded in consequence from public life, devoted his remaining years to research and reflection on the Revolution amid whose consequences he had spent his life. The result was *The Old Regime and the French Revolution* (1856), intended as merely the introductory volume to a work he never finished.

Although underpinned by unprecedented archival research, the work is famous for its factual errors. Far more important, however, are its broader insights. The Revolution, Tocqueville argued, was not the radical break that the French had sought and imagined they had achieved in 1789. Nor was it in any sense an accident. The Revolution was merely a phase in the inexorable development of two long-term and interconnected processes. One was the progress of democracy, which Tocqueville had first studied in America. Democracy meant an equalization of ranks, rights, and resources, and was the social pattern of the future. The other was bureaucratic centralization, which throve on democratic uniformity. Both processes were well advanced by 1789. The Revolution's historic destiny was to sweep away the remaining obstacles to their progress in the form of privileges, institutional anomalies, and social distinctions and exceptions of all kinds. The great casualty of the Revolution was liberty, which lost its last institutional underpinnings; and it was in no way surprising that the result should be the dictatorship of Napoleon. The Revolution had left nothing to stand in his way, or in that of his nephew, who had destroyed the revolution of Tocqueville's own lifetime. America, by contrast, had a free press and high levels of public involvement in government; Great Britain retained a powerful aristocracy; and so in both the spirit of liberty remained vigorous. Tocqueville's analysis minimized the religious significance of the Revolution, so central in the perceptions of most of his contemporaries. But his emphasis on the destructive results of hitherto untested Enlightenment ideology is once more fashionable among those revolutionary historians who have turned away from socioeconomic explanations of the Revolution.

See also *European Revolutions of 1848; French Revolution (1789–1815).*

William Doyle

BIBLIOGRAPHY

Brogan, Hugh. *Tocqueville.* London: Collins Fontana, 1973.

Furet, Francois. *Interpreting the French Revolution.* Cambridge: Cambridge University Press, 1982.

Herr, Richard. *Tocqueville and the Old Regime.* Princeton, N.J.: Princeton University Press, 1962.

Palmer, Robert R. *The Two Tocquevilles. Father and Son.* Princeton, N.J.: Princeton University Press, 1987.

Tocqueville, Alexis de. *The Ancien Regime.* Introduction by Norman Hampson. London: Dent, Everyman's Library, 1988.

TROTSKY, LEON

Trotsky (1879–1940), born Lev Davidovich Bronshtein, was a prominent leader and theorist of the Russian revolutionary movement and Marxist socialism and a founder of the Soviet state. During his exile from the Soviet Union, his was a powerful voice in the anti-Stalinist opposition within the international left.

As a student in Odessa and Nikolaev, Trotsky was attracted to the revolutionary politics of social-democracy in the Russian Empire. He began his career as a journalist, pamphleteer, and orator to worker and student groups in 1896. Following his arrest in 1898, he served two years in prison and was sentenced to four additional years of exile in Siberia,

Leon Trotsky

but he escaped to London in 1902. There he met Vladimir Ilyich Lenin and attended the Second Congress of the Russian Social-Democratic Workers' Party in 1903, where he engaged in fierce polemics with Lenin about the character of the Russian revolutionary party. Trotsky prophesied that Lenin's vision of a professional, underground organization carried within it the seeds of future dictatorship.

In fall 1905 he chaired the Petersburg Soviet of Workers' Deputies, the center of revolutionary socialist politics during the brief experiment with quasi-constitutional monarchy. Following the crushing of the 1905 uprising, his arrest, and exile, Trotsky again fled abroad, where he edited social-democratic newspapers and occupied a middle ground between the Bolshevik and Menshevik fractions of the party. During this period he elaborated a theory of permanent revolution, which anticipated a rapid telescoping of the bourgeois-democratic and proletarian-socialist revolutions in the special conditions of Russia's uneven development.

With the outbreak of the First World War, Trotsky became a leader of the internationalist, antiwar wing of social democracy. After the March 1917 revolution in Petrograd, Trotsky returned from exile in America to play a prominent role in the faction (the Interdistrict group) that steered a course between the Bolshevik and Menshevik parties. In July, following his arrest by the Provisional Government, he cast his lot with Lenin's Bolsheviks and became a powerful ally of Lenin during the months before the Bolshevik seizure of power in November 1917; he was elected chairman of the Petrograd Soviet and headed its Military Revolutionary Committee. In the first Bolshevik-dominated Soviet government he served as commissar of foreign relations and negotiated the short-lived peace of Brest-Litovsk. When the Germans resumed their offensive against Soviet Russia, Lenin appointed Trotsky military commissar (1918–1925); he built the Red Army and led the military campaigns of the civil war (1918–1921).

After the war, he withdrew from engagement in military affairs to economic planning and Communist Party politics. When Lenin was incapacitated by a series of strokes, Trotsky became one of the key figures in the succession struggle for leadership of the Soviet state and Communist Party. He criticized the bureaucratization of the once-revolutionary underground party and the concentration of power in an ever narrower circle of party leaders, especially Joseph Stalin. In 1927, however, Stalin defeated his opponents, expelled Trotsky from the party, and exiled him to Kazakhstan. While in Alma-Ata, Trotsky began writing his *History of the Russian Revolution,* a classic of eyewitness-participant history.

From exile in Turkey and later Mexico he waged an untiring campaign against Stalin's policies in the pages of *The Bulletin of the Opposition.* During his final years, he developed his theory of the degeneration of the proletarian revolution and its usurpation by the Thermidorian bureaucracy, which was presiding over counterrevolution. Trotsky still believed that Stalin's dictatorship would be overthrown by a newly assertive working-class movement. He was tried in absentia during the Moscow show trials of the 1930s, accused of spying for foreign powers, and assassinated on orders from Stalin in 1940.

See also *Lenin, Vladimir Ilyich; Russian Revolution of 1917; Stalin, Joseph.*

MARK VON HAGEN

BIBLIOGRAPHY

Deutscher, Isaac. *The Prophet Armed. Trotsky: 1879–1921.* New York: Oxford University Press, 1954.

———. *The Prophet Unarmed. Trotsky: 1921–1929.* New York: Oxford University Press, 1959.

———. *The Prophet Outcast. Trotsky: 1929–1940.* New York: Oxford University Press, 1963.

Knei-Paz, Baruch. *The Social and Political Thought of Leon Trotsky.* Oxford: Oxford University Press, 1978.

Trotsky, Leon. *My Life.* New York: Scribner's, 1930.

TURKISH REVOLUTION (1908–1922)

The "Young Turk" Revolution of 1908 ushered in the second constitutional period (1908–1922) of the Ottoman Empire, an era of war, imperial disintegration, and accelerated social and political change in the Middle East. During the first constitutional period (1876–1878) Sultan Abdülhamid II ascended the Ottoman throne in a palace coup engineered by high functionaries. He proclaimed a constitution in 1876 but suspended it two years later. Popular revolts forced its reinstatement in July 1908. In contrast to the first constitutional period, the revolution of 1908 brought about enduring transformations.

Two distinct political tendencies that had crystallized during the formative period of the constitutionalist movement before 1908 gradually hardened into rival parties in the restored parliament. The Committee of Union and Progress (CUP), which dominated parliament, advocated administrative and economic centralization, whereas the decentralists favored a degree of provincial autonomy and private initiative. Four general elections were held, in 1908, 1912, 1914, and 1919.

The revolutionary governments, hindered by capitulatory treaty obligations to European powers dating from the 1830s, lived with the reality of external economic domination and the need for foreign loans. Constant warfare and territorial loss further thwarted economic development. Nevertheless, the revolution brought to a head transformations that the empire had been undergoing for a century, unleashing profuse intellectual activity and ideological debate. Expanded education for boys and girls and refurbished communications further widened the public sphere. New voices, such as those of women, workers, and intellectuals from outside the Islamic modernist religious establishment, were heard for the first time. The attempt to integrate different social and ethnic groups within a unitary state was paralleled by the growth of ethnolinguistic nationalist movements.

The legacy of the revolutionary period profoundly affected the development of the nation-states of the Middle East. The Turkish Republic created in 1923 assimilated the reformist, statist, and secularist tenets of the Young Turk Revolution, even though it marked a definite break from the Ottoman past in institutional and ideological terms.

BIRTH OF THE YOUNG TURK MOVEMENT

The constitutionalist movement in the Ottoman Empire was founded by a group of intellectuals and bureaucrats in the 1860s. Abdülhamid's termination of the first Ottoman parliament and his institution of a personal rule repressive to his pro-West opponents but popular with the masses defused the movement for a generation. During that time, the sporadic agitation of liberal-minded Ottoman intellectuals living in Europe was ineffective until the expatriates were joined by a wave of liberals from new, clandestine revolutionary groups in the empire's capital, Istanbul. The best known of the underground liberal groups was the Ottoman Union, a revolutionary cell founded in the imperial military medical school in 1889. Fugitives and sympathizers influenced by European positivism recast this revolutionary society in Paris in 1895 as the CUP, shifting the locus of oppositional activity to Europe. The constitutionalist opposition to Abdülhamid, which came to be known as the Young Turk movement, had a broad ethnic, religious, and social base. Differences between proponents of evolutionary and revolutionary change, on the one hand, and of administrative centralization and decentralization, on the other, created divisions among its diverse adherents. The constitutionalists, including the CUP, were active in a number of European cities and in British-controlled Cairo and maintained strong links with secret opposition groups in the empire's capital and provinces. Though the Young Turks tried to oust the reigning sultan, they did not seek to disestablish the Ottoman monarchy. Conspiracies to topple Abdülhamid with coups in 1896 and 1897 failed when uncovered.

The CUP found a following among educated, modernist junior army officers, who, in contrast to the civilians in the movement, benefited from discipline and a hierarchical organization. Other factors made the army units in Macedonia particularly prone to revolt. Those factors included the officers' close links with the CUP in Paris, the secret organizational activity afforded by freemasonic lodges, the example of hostile Balkan revolutionary cells, and the humiliation the army suffered in the course of European interventions in the region. The officers viewed constitutional rule as the means of ensuring the empire's territorial integrity.

THE REVOLUTION OF 1908

Assassination of high-level, proregime emissaries, followed by scattered revolts of military units in the European provinces in July 1908 and an empire-wide telegraphic campaign, broke Abdülhamid's will to resist the constitutionalist movement. On July 24, 1908, the sultan effectively restored the constitution by recalling parliament.

Previously obscure officers, including Majors Enver and Niyazi, who had led the revolts in Macedonia, were lionized in Istanbul by rejoicing crowds. The constitutionalist movement was now identified with the centralist Young Turk groups in Macedonia, which made Salonika on the northern Aegean coast their organizational headquarters and appropriated the CUP name. Young Turk groups outside the empire dissolved, and the ideological forerunners in Europe deferred to young, modernist officers, officials, professionals, and intellectuals in the empire. With a bourgeois world view but low social prestige and no administrative experience, the CUP leaders sought alliances to translate their moral authority into political predominance. Soon, the statesmen of the old regime and a segment of old-guard constitutionalists regrouped as the new decentralist Liberal Party, and provincial notables were locked into alliances and political struggles.

In the summer of 1908 the Young Turks purged the sultan's bureaucracy, dismantled his secret police, and imposed restrictions on his authority. Elections in the fall produced an overwhelmingly pro-CUP parliament in the absence of significant opposition. The cabinet, however, was dominated by statesmen of the old regime, and it was unclear where real power lay. The CUP's attempts to place its loyalists in the cabinet prompted the formation of a parliamentary opposition. Because the CUP was not yet constituted as a political party, its interference in government was sharply criticized by the emergent opposition and its active press.

On April 13, 1909, a counterrevolutionary uprising erupted in Istanbul, instigated by inflammatory articles in a reactionary, antisecular newspaper sympathetic to the opposition. Conservative religious students and officers aggrieved by the purge of the traditional army corps in favor of graduates of the academy rioted and marched on parliament, demanding the replacement of certain ministers and the enforcement of religious laws. The religious rhetoric prevalent on April 13 masked a broader social and political movement that included critics of the CUP's interference in government. The movement was encouraged by the Liberal Party and condoned by Abdülhamid. The revolt was soon repressed, however, with the help of pro-CUP army units stationed in Macedonia, which, under Gen. Mahmud Sevket Pasha, moved to Istanbul as the "Action Army." The assembly reacted by deposing Sultan Abdülhamid in favor of his brother, Sultan Resad (Mehmed V).

THE ASCENDANCE OF THE COMMITTEE OF UNION AND PROGRESS

In August 1909, constitutional amendments increased the parliament's power over the cabinet and the cabinet's power over the sultan. The CUP made sure its members in parliament were well represented in the cabinet and ensured the appointment of favorable prime ministers. Otherwise, it did not operate much like a real political party until it began to encounter opposition from newly formed parties. Aroused by the growth of parliamentary opposition, the CUP forced early elections in 1912. With the opposition organized under a new decentralist party, Liberty and Entente, the elections were preceded by heated campaigns and torrents of press propaganda. Fraudulent tactics—including coercion, secret tallying of votes, and reapportionment of electoral districts—incriminated the victorious CUP, which lost moral authority and stepped down at the behest of the army. Prime Minister Said Pasha resigned, and the sultan dissolved parliament.

The outbreak of the Balkan Wars in the fall of 1912 postponed new elections until 1914. In the first half of this interim period, a nonpartisan cabinet made up of statesmen of the old regime who were sympathetic to the decentralists governed the country. In January 1913 the CUP reclaimed power with a coup, ousting Prime Minister Kamil Pasha at gunpoint and placing Mahmud Sevket at the head of a CUP-dominated government. Mahmud Sevket's assassination in June 1913 only served to consolidate CUP's power.

Between 1908 and 1914 the Ottoman Empire relinquished to Austria-Hungary and the Balkan countries all of its European provinces except Istanbul and its immediate surroundings. It ceded its only remaining African possession, Tripolitania (Libya), to Italy. Simultaneously, the empire dealt with internal revolts against its centralizing policies in the interior of Syria and the Arabian Peninsula. In 1912 an autonomist revolt in predominantly Muslim Albania resulted in independence for that region *(see map, p. 381)*.

In their efforts to arrest secessions and internal revolts, successive Ottoman governments subscribed to different versions of an ideology aimed at integrating various social groups. A parliamentary-democratic, secular model based on equality and elimination of religious communal prerogatives was tried and failed. Growing ethnic and cultural awareness among Arabs, Turks, and other Muslim groups, accompanied by the physical contraction of the Ottoman state to its Muslim core, led eventually to authoritarian rule and the adoption of an Islamic ideology.

Despite internal and external preoccupations, the 1908 revolution brought many changes to the Ottoman state and society. The court system and the bureaucratic structure, particularly the financial administration, were reorganized. A new Provincial Law (1913), precipitated by reform movements in the Arab provinces, strengthened provincial councils. Improved communications, including special attention to education and an explosion of printed materials, engendered ideological debates and literary activity. The empire experienced an unprecedented period of freedom of the press and political association. More and more women appeared in public roles, sponsored and patronized women's journals, and engaged in public debates. The period also saw labor activism and intermittent strikes. Power relations in the countryside changed little, however, as the CUP allied itself with different factions of the provincial elite. The persistence of indebtedness and capitulatory treaty arrangements with European countries hampered the effort to develop the economy.

WORLD WAR I

After unsuccessfully seeking an alliance with Britain and France, the Ottoman government allied itself with Germany in August 1914 and entered the war in November. The CUP ruled during the war with virtually no accountability. Enver Pasha (minister of war), Talat Pasha (interior minister and later prime minister), and Cemal Pasha (minister of the navy) were the most influential representatives of an otherwise diffuse leadership.

The toll of the multifront war, which involved complete mobilization of Ottoman society, was extremely heavy. Epidemics, disruptions in agriculture and manufacturing, supply problems, speculation, forced deportations, and battle casualties ravaged the population. The most significant internal challenge to government authority during the war was the Arab Revolt led by Grand Sharif Hussein of Mecca. In cooperation with Hussein's Arabian tribal forces, the British army by 1918 occupied all of the Ottoman territories south of Anatolia (Asia Minor). In the 1920s those territories were divided between Britain and France. The British mandate covered Iraq, Palestine, and Transjordan; the French, Lebanon and Syria.

Despite the constraints of war, the Ottoman state and society experienced further transformation between 1914 and 1918. In 1914 the government unilaterally abrogated its unfavorable treaty obligations and enforced legislation that favored Muslim producers and merchants, thus strengthening the indigenous Muslim middle class. Aided by German capital and know-how, the military reorganized and modernized. Municipal improvements and infrastructural projects continued in the civilian sector.

The composition of the population in the Anatolian remnants of the empire changed drastically. The influx of Muslim refugees from territories dismembered before the war accelerated. The Armenian population of eastern Anatolia, implicated in secessionist movements and suspected of complicity with the enemy powers, was subjected to deportations and massacres by Ottoman army units and local militias. The huge loss of life at the front forced women to take a greater role in the economy and society.

A new family law in November 1917 subsumed religious codes under a unified civil code that gave women enhanced rights in marriage and divorce. Even though the war was waged under the rhetoric of *jihad* (holy war) and the government embraced Islam as the basis of a unifying ideology, secularizing reforms continued. The ministries of justice and education acquired greater control over schools and courts. Religious foundations came under closer state scrutiny, and in 1916 the chief Muslim religious official was excluded from the cabinet.

WAR OF LIBERATION

The Armistice of Mudros signed by the Ottoman Empire and the victorious Entente Powers on October 30, 1918, imposed severe restrictions on the Ottoman state's sovereignty. Soon after the armistice the strongmen of the CUP fled Istanbul. The party's local organizations, however, remained intact and were responsible for setting afoot a popular resistance movement in unoccupied parts of Anatolia following the Greek occupation of western Anatolia in May 1919. Mustafa Kemal Pasha, later known as Atatürk, a general who had gained renown during the battle of Gallipoli and a CUP supporter who had remained outside of politics, joined the movement soon after the Greek invasion and rose to its leadership in two congresses held in Erzurum and Sivas in eastern Anatolia in 1919. Mustafa Kemal and his followers rallied popular forces and militias to defeat the Greek armies and signed an agreement with France for the evacuation of southeastern Anatolia. The war of liberation sought the recovery of territories not surrendered by treaty and populated predominantly by Turkish and Kurdish-speaking peoples. It rejected neither the monarchy nor the caliphate (the institution through which the Ottoman sultan was recognized as the religious head of Islam).

In 1920 Sultan Vahdeddin agreed to the terms of the Sèvres Treaty, which called for the partition of Anatolia among the Entente Powers and the creation of an independent Armenia and autonomous Kurdistan in eastern Anatolia. With the sultan's government discredited by the treaty, the Kemalists formed a popular assembly in Ankara in April 1920 and declared that the new assembly represented the Turkish nation. Despite that proclamation, the construction of a Turkish nation and the creation of a secular republic had to wait until 1923, when the Lausanne Treaty determined the boundaries and international legal status of the new state, enabling Mustafa Kemal to implement his revolutionary project in the new Turkey.

See also *Arab "Great Revolt" (1916–1918); Atatürk, Kemal; Ottoman Revolts in the Near and Middle East (1803–1922).*

HASAN KAYALI

BIBLIOGRAPHY

Ahmad, Feroz. *The Young Turks: The Committee of Union and Progress in Turkish Politics, 1908–1918.* Oxford: Oxford University Press, 1969.

———. "War and Society under the Young Turks, 1908–1918." *Review* 11 (spring 1988): 265–286.

Hanioglu, Sükrü. *The Young Turks in Opposition.* New York: Oxford University Press, 1995.

Kansu, Aykut. *The Revolution of 1908 in Turkey.* Leiden: Brill, 1997.

Kayali, Hasan. *Arabs and Young Turks: Ottomanism, Arabism, and Islamism in the Ottoman Empire, 1908–1918.* Berkeley: University of California Press, 1997.

Ramsaur, Ernest. *The Young Turks: Prelude to the Revolution of 1908.* Princeton, N.J.: Princeton University Press, 1957.

Zürcher, Erik Jan. *The Unionist Factor: The Role of the Committee of Union and Progress in the Turkish National Movement.* Leiden: Brill, 1984.

TYRANNY

The concept of tyranny as the unjust, unrestrained, and evil exercise of power is ancient. Greek philosophers analyzed tyranny, and in Plato's *Republic* the psychology of the tyrant is discussed at length. Insecure because he is an usurper of legitimate power, feared but able to trust no one because he has harmed so many, the tyrant rules uneasily and is obliged to become increasingly repressive in order to keep power.

Political philosophers from the Renaissance through the Enlightenment used the concept in a similar way. For Niccolò Machiavelli, Caesar was a tyrant; he usurped power in Rome, destroyed the Republic and turned Rome's government into a despotic, abusive instrument of personal rule. Caesar, however, was also a revolutionary who created a new system of government, the Roman Empire. He was no mere petty, thieving despot. But almost two hundred years after Machiavelli, John Locke still interpreted tyranny as simply the exercise of power that transgressed the law and, specifically, used power for personal ends rather than for the benefit of the community. The potentially revolutionary aspect of tyranny was not perceived by Locke, whose definition remained remarkably close to Plato's, written two thousand years earlier.

It was not until the French Revolution that tyranny's association with revolutionary regimes came to be widely understood. The French revolutionary Reign of Terror under Maximilien Robespierre and the tyranny of Napoleon Bonaparte, who consciously imitated Caesar, were implemented in an attempt to change the political and social landscape of France and Europe; they went far beyond the simple exploitation and abuse of power for personal gain. Their abuses, however, pale before the horror of the vast killing machines established by the twentieth century's great tyrants: Adolf Hitler, Joseph Stalin, Mao Zedong, and other modern revolutionary figures whose chief aim was to transform radically the entire world.

Because we continue to use the word "tyrant" in both the modern and old-fashioned way, we risk confusing the Platonic or Lockean tyrant with the revolutionary one. The older type has remained with us; Mobutu Sese Seko of Zaire, the Duvalier family of Haiti, the Somoza family of Nicaragua, Idi Amin of Uganda, and many other dictators have been little more than killers and thieves whose main goal was to loot the societies they ruled for their own benefit and to pay off their supporters. Such tyrants are important for the study of revolutions because they have often given rise to revolutionary movements against their abuses, but they are not, themselves, revolutionary figures.

Quite different have been the modern revolutionary leaders who have claimed to be acting in behalf of a popular general will that demands total change and rejuvenation of the society. Taking power into their hands, they have forced their ideological blueprints onto their societies and, in some cases, much of the world. Hitler's vision was of a racially pure, Aryan Europe that would be rid of polluting races and would enslave the inferior ones. Lenin's vision was of a classless society ruled by egalitarian socialism, but to be achieved by an all-powerful, elite party cadre that knew what the masses really needed. To Lenin's ideal Stalin and Mao added intense Russian and Chinese nationalism and the firm conviction that they alone embodied and understood the masses. Socialism would first make their countries strong and modern, and their countries would serve as a base for spreading revolution throughout the rest of the world. Ho Chi Minh of Vietnam, Pol Pot of Cambodia, Fidel Castro of Cuba, Nicolae Ceausescu of Romania, Enver Hoxha of Albania, and others adopted this same combined goal of bringing about socialism and restoring their nation's greatness. In order to carry out their dreams, they had to force their recalcitrant, weak, and ignorant people into behaving properly and to eliminate all real or potential enemies. In so doing, they all created militarized police states that repressed political expression, jailed and killed their political opponents, and, perhaps not coincidentally, established economic systems that worked inefficiently and wasted vast resources. Some of these revolutionary leaders killed millions of people: Hitler killed ten million, not counting the deaths from military action during World War II; Stalin, well over twenty million; Mao, over thirty million; and Pol Pot, almost two million, over 20 percent of Cambodia's population.

Many other modern nationalistic and religious revolutions have also created tyrannies. When all the political opponents of those in power carrying out revolutionary ends are identified as traitors to the true cause and to the people's general will, then tyranny is highly likely. Saddam Hussein of Iraq is only one of dozens of nationalist revolutionaries who have established ruthless tyrannies that are in part old-fashioned and corrupt, but also modern and revolutionary. The Iranian religious clerics who overthrew the relatively mild, nationalist, modernizing tyranny of the shah of Iran in 1979 replaced that regime with a much more thoroughly intolerant and tyrannical one, just as earlier, Lenin and his communists had replaced a mild tsarist tyranny with a far more effective, brutal, and murderous one in 1917. Revolutionary regimes of any type led by people who are absolutely certain that their vision is the correct one and who think they are entitled, for the sake of the general welfare, to carry out any measures in order to make their ideals triumph will be tyrannical.

One of the greatest ironies of the twentieth century is that major revolutionary ideologies designed to liberate people from the injustices of corrupt, unfair, old-fashioned tyrannies have actually produced even more tyrannical outcomes. Modern "tyrannies of certitude" based on revolutionary social, nationalistic, ethnic, and religious doctrines will continue to proliferate in the twenty-first century. They will present democracies with challenges as severe as those they have presented in the twentieth century.

See also *Cambodian Khmer Rouge Revolution (1967–1979); Castro, Fidel; Dictatorship; Hitler, Adolf; Mao Zedong; Robespierre, Maximilien; Stalin, Joseph; Terrorism*.

DANIEL CHIROT

BIBLIOGRAPHY

Berlin, Isaiah. *Four Essays on Liberty.* London: Oxford University Press, 1969.

Chirot, Daniel. *Modern Tyrants: The Power and Prevalence of Evil in Our Age.* Princeton, N.J.: Princeton University Press, 1996.

McDaniel, Tim. *Autocracy, Modernization, and Revolution in Russia and Iran.* Princeton, N.J.: Princeton University Press, 1991.

Popper, Karl. *The Open Society and Its Enemies.* London: Routledge, 1945.

Skocpol, Theda. *States and Social Revolutions.* Cambridge: Cambridge University Press, 1979.

USSR COLLAPSE AND DISSOLUTION (1989–1991)

Designed to reenergize the socialist system, Mikhail Gorbachev's reforms of the late 1980s resulted in the dissolution of both socialism and the USSR. This shocking double collapse was completely unforeseen. For many people, including the Soviet elite, it took the events of 1989–1991 to reveal the fundamental fragility of the Soviet party-state.

THE PARTY

The USSR entered the 1980s as a revolution in old age. When Yuri Andropov, the former KGB chief, replaced the long enfeebled Leonid Brezhnev as general secretary in 1982, he launched a far-reaching anticorruption campaign. The sixty-eight-year-old Andropov, surrounded on the Politburo by men of the same generation and severely ill, also recognized the need to prepare for an inevitable generational change. He had found his man fortuitously. Along with other members of the top echelon, Andropov had often vacationed at an exclusive sanatorium in Stavropol Province. There, in the late 1960s he met the local party boss, Mikhail Gorbachev, who acted as "host" to visitors from the capital. In 1978 Andropov engineered Gorbachev's transfer to Moscow, and in 1980, his promotion to full membership in the Politburo. Among the infirm Soviet gerontocracy, the party bureaucrat from Stavropol stood out for his relative youth and commitment to socialist ideals. As the head of Andropov's team, Gorbachev was ostentatiously made responsible for a wide range of tasks befitting an heir apparent.

At Andropov's death in 1984, the old guard blocked Gorbachev's ascension. But by the next year, when the near-invalid new general secretary, Konstantin Chernenko, also expired, only two mastodons (Nikolai Tikhonov and Andrei Gromyko) were left, and neither would step aside for the other. After some maneuvering, the septuagenarian Gromyko (Tikhonov was eighty) acknowledged the inevitable and nominated the fifty-four-year-old Gorbachev to lead the country. The mood was captured by the jest: "Who supports Gorbachev in the Kremlin? No one; he walks unaided." But in fact Politburo member Gorbachev found widespread support among other representatives of the new generation in the Central Committee. They were all offspring of Nikita Khrushchev's de-Stalinization, which had been interrupted in 1964 by Khrushchev's ouster. Some two decades later, directing the replacement team that Andropov had assembled, the USSR's third general secretary in three years set about picking up where the erratic Khrushchev had left off.

Gorbachev's program, which came to be called *perestroika* (restructuring), evolved over time and crystallized by 1987. Calling for "openness," or *glasnost,* he sought to outflank party recalcitrants by using the media and appealing directly to the mass of party members and the rest of society. He involved a range of social scientists in policy deliberations and sanctioned the appointment of new editors at influential newspapers and journals. He also launched an international campaign to cajole the United States into mutual disarmament. Various dissidents, including Andrei Sakharov, were released from prison or exile, restrictions were removed on Jewish emigration, and a phased withdrawal from Afghanistan was begun. By "activating" Soviet society and concluding landmark international agreements to reduce military expenditures, Gorbachev hoped to unblock the Soviet economy and allow socialism to realize its unused potential. His was a serious effort aimed above all at mobilizing support for change, though the precise content of that change remained unclear.

The key to conceiving and implementing the reforms was the Communist Party. Gorbachev demanded that the party live up to its vanguard role and "lead" perestroika. Simultaneously, he insisted on democratization, meaning elections to party posts would involve multiple candidates and secret ballots. But the millions of party bureaucrats, accustomed to lifetime appointments and regular promotions for loyalty, had little to gain and everything to lose from the changes. Even

party officials favorably inclined toward "reform" had a difficult time reinventing themselves to appeal to voters, not least because the party was being blamed in open discussions for all the country's accumulated ills. And given that the thrust of the economic reforms was to curb centralized managerial control and permit factory and individual initiative, it was not clear what the vanguard party officials were supposed to "lead" beyond the proliferating public therapy sessions, which invariably pointed fingers at their institution. Unsurprisingly, Gorbachev became frustrated with the party, and the party with him. Keenly aware that Khrushchev had been removed in a conspiracy by the party apparatus, Gorbachev schemed to avoid the same fate.

Signs of deep disaffection in the party emerged into the open at a February 1988 plenary meeting, after which a storm erupted over a letter sent to the editor of an antireform newspaper by a Leningrad school teacher, Nina Andreeva. A special meeting of the Politburo branded the text an antiperestroika manifesto. Yegor Ligachev, the number two man in the Communist Party hierarchy who ran the party's Secretariat, or administrative nerve center, was widely suspected of enhancing and helping publish Andreeva's letter. Gorbachev met with Ligachev privately and exculpated him. Publicly, however, Gorbachev never disavowed the rumors, ceaselessly broadcast in the Soviet and foreign media, that the Secretariat had orchestrated the "attack" on perestroika. The rumors gave Gorbachev a scapegoat for the sluggishness of his reforms: the Ligachev-led "conservatives" were supposedly strangling them. At the same time, he continued to enjoy Ligachev's loyalty, owing to the disingenuous private exculpation and to party discipline. But however adroit, Gorbachev's manipulation did little to transform the behavior of the mass of party bureaucrats, let alone the economy. And it evoked still greater popular anger at the party, his main instrument for change.

Still anxious about a possible repeat of Khrushchev's fate, and aware of the contradictions involved in having the party reform itself, Gorbachev began moving away from the party and toward the soviets (councils). Power had been seized in their name in 1917, yet these grassroots associations of radical democracy, resembling the Jacobin clubs of the French Revolution, had long since atrophied. Beginning in early 1989 they were revived at the local level through competitive elections. At the national level, a new legislative body, the

Congress of Soviets, was introduced. Even though many seats in the new national body were set aside for top-level party officials and most of the people elected to it nominally belonged to the party, a demonstrative shift away from the party's self-assigned monopoly took place. Members of the Politburo did not control or even guide the election proceedings. Not only had the party leadership been marginalized in the congress seating arrangements, but behind the scenes Gorbachev had reorganized the party's all-important Secretariat, essentially eliminating its ability to coordinate the elections or to orchestrate a conspiracy against the general secretary. Thus, well before he permitted the removal of the constitutional clause specifying the party's monopoly, Gorbachev had deliberately severed the levers of the centralized apparatus. His reorganization of the Secretariat completely transformed the political landscape, mostly in ways he did not comprehend.

THE UNION

Oddly enough, almost no one in the Soviet leadership fully understood the USSR's complicated makeup and the party's place therein. After the seizure of power in 1917, a revolutionary government was formed with Vladimir Ilyich Lenin as its head. Lenin held no formal *party* post, and indeed the Communist Party might have been abolished. Instead, the party came to serve as a kind of universal watchdog, a turn of events that took place during the civil war, when tsarist army officers were incorporated into the Red Army and political commissars were appointed to guarantee their loyalty and "correct" politics. This early pattern—installing a trusted party official alongside an expert of questioned loyalty—was haphazardly institutionalized in the government bureaucracy, the media, universities and schools, and just about everywhere else. Eventually, the USSR began to mass produce competent experts who were also party members, yet the original parallelism of party structures alongside administrative structures persisted. Throughout the 1930s and World War II, the state side of the administrative machine greatly expanded, yet the redundant dualism persisted. Why not remove the party and make do with the state? That is more or less what Gorbachev seems to have had in mind in late 1988. He worried about the problems that might follow from the alienation of large masses of Communist Party functionaries, but the more important structural consideration he missed was the party's indispensability to the Union.

Following the February 1917 abdication of the tsar, and in the ensuing vacuum of central authority, many of the Russian Empire's so-called borderlands became de facto independent states. The Red Army, in the name of defending the revolution, forced most of these regions back into some relation with Russia. Joseph Stalin, as commissar for nationalities and general secretary, oversaw the process of forging a new state from the former tsarist territories. He favored their incorporation into the Russian Republic, but the strength of the opposition in the borderlands, particularly Ukraine, forced a compromise: the USSR, a federal state, was officially proclaimed in January 1924. The republics kept their territorial boundaries. They retained (or acquired) parliaments, academies of science, schools in the local languages, and native elites. Notwithstanding purges and deportations, these national states were further consolidated. What kept the federal state from unraveling, of course, was the party's unitary structure. A resolution at the pivotal eighth party congress, in 1919, specified that "all decisions of the Russian Communist Party are unconditionally binding on all branches of the party, regardless of their national composition," so that Ukrainian and other republic Communist Parties "enjoyed the rights of regional committees," and thus were "wholly subordinated" to the Russian Communist Party. Grigorii Zinoviev, a member of Lenin's inner circle, explained the relationship in 1919 as "one single centralized party beside a federation of states"; that relationship held after the formation of the USSR in 1924. Remove the USSR Communist Party, however, and you would be left with a voluntary union of states that could choose to withdraw, as the USSR constitution—unlike that of Yugoslavia—permitted. Gorbachev, by crippling the Secretariat, unintentionally turned loose the Supreme Soviets (the legislatures) of the republics. They began to pass laws superseding those of the (voluntary) Union; Gorbachev responded with condemnations in the USSR Supreme Soviet, which the republics ignored. And although Gorbachev still controlled the executive levers of the USSR state—the KGB, Ministry of the Interior (MVD), and Soviet Army—they were useful only insofar as he was willing to use massive force to pursue political aims.

Contradictions in the USSR's administrative structure were matched by those in the economy. Through the elimination of private property and the market, the USSR had arrived at a "planned economy," which turned out to mean state ownership, state micromanagement, and a fixation on quantity of output. After 1985 various administrative measures to spur growth and raise quality were tried, but they failed. Gorbachev then permitted direct relations among firms and limited entrepreneurial activities by individuals. Legalization of the very market mechanisms whose suppression had been the essence of socialism, however, disrupted planning without improving performance, because the economic problems went far beyond the need for some flexibility and decentralization. By the 1980s, heavy industry accounted for almost 80 percent of the Soviet economy (against 20 percent in the 1920s). On top of this imbalance and the corresponding shortage of consumer goods, most of the heavy industrial factories were well out of date, blithely untouched by the rust-belt shock that had wreaked havoc throughout the postwar capitalist world (where the overall share of heavy industry had been far less). In other words, the USSR economy, with its gigantic assemblage of obsolete manufacturing facilities, required a complete structural overhaul and hence massive new investment, almost none of which was forthcoming in the reforms. On the contrary, the few world-class sectors that might have provided investment capital—defense, for example—were slated for drastic downsizing. In the meantime, the unhinging of the planned economy further loosened the bonds of the Union.

THE ELITE

Eastern Europe in the year 1989 revealed the Soviet reforms for what they entailed: dissolution. Yet even after the fall of communist governments in Eastern Europe, the USSR still existed. Gorbachev had brilliantly, if unwittingly, dismantled the system's political and economic heart, but certain institutions of the Union, above all the military and security police, remained in place. Their removal was effected by Boris Yeltsin.

Yeltsin rose to power as leader of the Russian Republic by taking advantage of Gorbachev's introduction of competitive elections and by forcing through what Gorbachev had made possible yet continued to resist: full sovereignty for the republics and the full-scale introduction of the market. The remarkable rise of Russia inside the USSR broke the back of the all-Union military and security structures, for when it became clear that Gorbachev's reforms had fatally weakened the Union and that Yeltsin had achieved a strong Russian sovereignty rooted in the ballot box, many members of the Union's central elite began to defect. Far from giving up their power, they were trying to preserve it.

The USSR was not brought down by nationalism. Only the central elite, not national movements in the periphery, could bring down the heavily armed empire. They did so by latching on to Yeltsin's drive for Russian sovereignty (against Moscow!). Of course, not everyone was willing or able to walk away from the Union and find refuge in an enhanced Russia. In August 1991 members of Gorbachev's USSR government, fearful of losing their positions, declared a state of emergency while the Soviet president was on vacation, thereby forcing the issue of the dying Union. Yeltsin's defiance in the face of the putsch furthered the split he had fostered in the central Soviet elite, particularly in the military and KGB. The generals who had been weighing the situation were forced to choose between the Union and Russia, and most chose Russia. Yeltsin, for his part, took advantage of the attempted putsch to accelerate the Russian Republic's takeover of the all-Union structures, grabbing, most prominently, the central bank and Ministry of Finance, which paid the salaries of the bureaucrats. By the fall of 1991, only one Union institution, the Soviet presidency, still functioned, but it had been mortally wounded.

In September 1991 negotiations interrupted by the putsch attempt were resumed on some kind of new Union treaty among Gorbachev and the presidents of the eight or so republics that still entertained notions of ties to Moscow. Republic leaders waited on Yeltsin to see what form of association, if any, Russia would support. Earlier, in proclaiming Russian sovereignty, Yeltsin had forced Gorbachev to confront the changes the Soviet leader had wrought but shrank from fully embracing. Now, the Russian president, facing the complete dissolution of the Union that *he* had wrought, seemed to fumble for some way to maintain Russia's links with at least some of the other republics, yet he was apparently unwilling to keep a place for Gorbachev. As the discussions dragged on without resolution, the Ukrainian elite, taking a page out of Russia's book, suddenly declared it would opt for complete independence, subject to a referendum, which was held on December 1 and passed overwhelmingly. A few weeks later, Yeltsin took over Gorbachev's office in the Kremlin. To a stunned world, the hammer and sickle was lowered from the ancient citadel forever.

In retrospect, it is clear that the USSR lost a competition with capitalism that it had willingly assumed in the years after 1917. During the interwar period, when capitalism was closely associated with the horrors of World War I, imperialism, fascism, and the prolonged Great Depression, many people could imagine that the Soviet Union's efforts to achieve a noncapitalist modernity provided a superior and more just sociopolitical order. But after World War II, won in large measure by the USSR, capitalism seemed to become peaceful and enjoyed an economic boom that socialism could not equal. Had the USSR not been locked in a struggle to compete as a superpower, its problems would not have had the same gravity. But to extricate the USSR from its superpower rivalry was not primarily a military issue. Gorbachev achieved disarmament. Yet he kept pursuing his programs of reform because socialism's very identity was at stake. Socialism was a supposedly superior form of social organization. If that was not the case, socialism ought not to exist. Glasnost and perestroika revealed that the USSR had lost not so much the military competition, but the consumer and social justice contest with postwar welfare-state capitalism.

Had Gorbachev understood that the party was not merely unreformable but integral to holding together the Union, and had he understood that his heavy-industrial economy needed not to be made flexible but replaced wholesale, he might have proceeded very differently. But Gorbachev, unlike Chinese leader Deng Xiaoping, was not a realist. Rather, he was a true believer in the Khrushchevian mold. It was the ideals of the October Revolution, the vision of a humane socialism transcending the contradictions of capitalism, that motivated the Soviet leader to exhaust himself trying to democratize the Communist Party and have it live up to its vanguard role. The ideals of October spurred him to continue his quest even after it had become clear that he had put the survival of his country in doubt. It was an irony of history that, when the inevitable generational change occurred in the Soviet leadership, the man who represented the cohort steeped in the chimera of reformed socialism was also one of the most skillful tacticians of the twentieth century. Gorbachev significantly accelerated the USSR's demise. But he and his ideals arose from within the system. Socialism liquidated itself.

See also *East European Revolutions of 1989; Gorbachev, Mikhail.*

STEPHEN KOTKIN

BIBLIOGRAPHY

Black, Joseph, ed. *The USSR Documents Annual, 1987–1991.* 7 vols. Gulf Breeze, Fla.: Academic Press, 1988–1992.

Boldin, Valery. *Ten Years that Shook the World: The Gorbachev Years as Witnessed by His Chief of Staff.* New York: Basic, 1994.

Dunlop, John. *The Rise of Russia and the Fall of the Soviet Empire.* Princeton, N.J.: Princeton University Press, 1993.

Edelhart, Abraham J., and Hershel Edelheit, eds. *The Rise and Fall of the Soviet Union: A Selected Bibliography of Sources in English.* Westport, Conn: Greenwood, 1992.

Gorbachev, Mikhail. *Memoirs.* New York: Doubleday, 1995.

Grachev, Andrei. *Final Days: The Inside Story of the Collapse of the Soviet Union.* Boulder, Colo.: Westview, 1995.

Kotkin, Stephen. *Steeltown, USSR: Soviet Society in the Gorbachev Era.* Berkeley: University of California Press, 1991.

Ligachev, Yegor. *Inside Gorbachev's Kremlin.* New York: Pantheon, 1993.

Medvedev, Zhores. *Yuri Andropov.* New York: W.W. Norton, 1983.

Wieczynski, Joseph, ed. *The Gorbachev Encyclopedia: Gorbachev, the Man and His Times.* Salt Lake City, Utah: Charles Schlacks, 1993.

U.S. CIVIL RIGHTS MOVEMENT (1954–1968)

The civil rights movement stands as the most significant struggle for social change in twentieth-century America. Nearly a century after the Civil War and Reconstruction, the former Confederate states denied blacks equal access to schools, public accommodations, and ballot boxes. For much of that time, black southerners had mounted attempts to improve the quality of their lives despite segregation and disfranchisement. Although white supremacists had largely subverted the legal and political gains extended to blacks following the abolition of slavery, by the 1950s African Americans had stepped up efforts to restore their civil rights and initiate a Second Reconstruction of the South.

ORIGINS

World War II gave black Americans considerable ammunition to wage their fight for first-class citizenship. In June 1941, with the United States poised on the brink of joining the Allied side, civil rights and labor leader A. Philip Randolph threatened to march on Washington with one hundred thousand blacks to protest racial segregation in the military and bias in war-related employment. Seeking to avoid political embarrassment, President Franklin D. Roosevelt agreed to create an investigative body, the Fair Employment Practice Committee, but he postponed integration of the armed forces. A partial victory, this outcome nonetheless fueled black expectations that, by combining conventional political tactics such as voting with pressure exerted through mass demonstrations, African Americans might dismantle Jim Crow, as the systematic discrimination against blacks was called. Their hopes were buoyed by the Supreme Court. Petitioned by the National Association for the Advancement of Colored People (NAACP), the justices ruled in 1944 that white Democratic Party primaries in the South deprived blacks of their constitutional right to vote without racial discrimination, thereby opening the door to increased electoral participation.

The decade following the end of the Second World War brought continued gains for black Americans but illustrated the serious problems facing civil rights advocates. The proportion of black registered voters in the South jumped from 3 percent in 1940 to 20 percent in 1952. At the national level, the administration of Harry S. Truman, Roosevelt's successor, introduced the first comprehensive civil rights bill in Congress since Reconstruction. Although the measure went down to defeat, it established the liberal reform agenda for the next twenty years: it attacked segregation and aimed at extending voting rights. Increased pressure from black voters together with renewed threats of mass demonstrations convinced Truman to bypass a conservative Congress and issue, in 1948, an executive order directing desegregation of the armed forces.

DESEGREGATION AND MASSIVE RESISTANCE

Truman's decree marked the end of civil rights achievements for the rest of his term. Cold war anticommunist hysteria at

Staff members of the National Association for the Advancement of Colored People (NAACP) are at work in the organization's Manhattan headquarters in the 1950s. Although marches and protests made headlines, much of the work of the civil rights movement took place behind the scenes.

home placed liberal civil rights organizations such as the NAACP on the defensive. Communists and left-wing labor unions had been active in mobilizing blacks to pursue economic justice as well as civil rights, but their efforts crumbled under cold war repression. With reformers in retreat and radicals routed, the Supreme Court moved to the forefront of the struggle. Its decision in *Brown v. Board of Education* (1954) validated arguments of NAACP plaintiffs that racial segregation was inherently unequal under the Fourteenth Amendment. As important as the Court's opinion was in raising black morale, it fell far short of producing immediate relief from racial discrimination. The Court in subsequent decisions allowed states to act "with all deliberate speed" in implementing school desegregation, which in practice gave the South opportunity to evade the ruling for more than a decade.

President Dwight Eisenhower compounded the problem by failing to provide moral leadership to persuade the South to comply with the law of the land. Moreover, most southern states embarked on a campaign of counterrevolutionary, massive resistance and adopted measures designed to forestall integration and drive the NAACP out of the region. Only when the situation deteriorated into violence, in obvious defiance of federal authority, did President Eisenhower respond forcefully. In 1957 he dispatched troops to Little Rock, Arkansas, to prevent Gov. Orval Faubus from blocking a court order allowing nine black high school students to enter Central High School.

MONTGOMERY BUS BOYCOTT AND MARTIN LUTHER KING JR.

While the federal government wavered in its commitment to racial equality, African Americans mobilized to gain their civil rights. The Montgomery, Alabama, bus boycott in 1955 helped revolutionize the protest movement. With a strong network of local churches, civic associations, and an NAACP chapter, black activists in Montgomery had been challenging discriminatory seating arrangements on buses and poor treatment by white drivers. When Rosa Parks was arrested on December 1 for failing to give up her seat to a white rider, she inspired a boycott that lasted more than a year. Women played a large part in sustaining the protest, as they would throughout the civil rights movement. Women made up a majority of daily bus riders, and their determination to walk or carpool to work demonstrated both discipline and commitment. Initially, Montgomery blacks merely wanted decent treatment on buses, but when the city failed to compromise, arrested boycott leaders, and ignored racist violence, protesters readjusted their sights to attack segregation itself. Although the boycott showcased the power of community organization and solidarity, it took a Supreme Court decision in November 1956 to outlaw segregated seating practices.

The boycott thrust Rev. Martin Luther King Jr. into the national spotlight. The twenty-six-year-old minister with a doctorate in theology headed the Montgomery Improvement Association, which coordinated the bus challenge. He exhibited great personal courage, deep spiritual faith, and inspirational oratorical powers. Combining the emancipationist teachings of black church traditions with secular doctrines of nonviolence and civil disobedience, Dr. King and his followers applied moral and political pressure to prod both white southerners and national politicians to live up to Judeo-Christian values of brotherhood as well as constitutional principles of equality. To carry on this effort, King established the Southern Christian Leadership Conference (SCLC) in 1957. In the sense that he espoused equal rights and full access to the ballot box, King followed in the footsteps of past reformers; however, his embrace of nonviolent confrontation against all forms of racism had revolutionary potential.

STUDENT ACTIVISM

King also belonged to a larger civil rights coalition, elements of which pushed him in a more militant direction. In addition to the SCLC and the more moderate NAACP and National Urban League, the Congress of Racial Equality (CORE), established in 1942, and the Student Nonviolent Coordinating Committee (SNCC), created in 1960, furnished the most important organizational leadership within the movement. With the guidance of the SCLC executive director, Ella Baker, SNCC grew out of student sit-in struggles. Initiated in Greensboro, North Carolina, black college and high school students, occasionally joined by sympathetic whites, went even further than had Montgomery's bus boycotters. Rather than withholding business, they practiced nonviolent, civil disobedience. Demanding service at segregated white lunch counters, sit-in protesters got arrested when they refused to take no for an answer. The following year, CORE and SNCC launched a series of freedom bus rides throughout the deep South to integrate terminals that should have been desegregated under federal law. The freedom riders encountered retaliatory violence from hostile whites, and many protesters were arrested.

CLIMAX OF THE MOVEMENT

To force the national government to assist heightened civil rights efforts, in 1963 Dr. King orchestrated demonstrations in Birmingham, Alabama. King joined forces with Rev. Fred Shuttlesworth, a local leader, to march against the city's segregated public facilities and protest job discrimination, actions that led to beatings by police and King's arrest. Televised news coverage of racist brutality provided vivid examples of the treatment blacks received in the South under the system of segregation. Outraged by what they saw on their television screens, the majority of northern whites supported strong action by the federal government to combat racial discrimination. Furthermore, white northerners feared that unless something was done to address black demands for equality, protests would escalate and lead to even greater violence. Prompted by these concerns, President John F. Kennedy introduced far-reaching civil rights legislation in Congress aimed at integrating schools and public accommodations. Lawmakers added provisions to combat employment bias, and in 1964 Congress passed the Civil Rights Act, thereby bringing an end to official segregation.

Still, the majority of eligible southern blacks, around 60 percent, remained disfranchised. Consequently, at the beginning of 1965, the SCLC staged protests in Selma, Alabama, for the right to vote. King directed several months of demonstrations, encountering violence similar to what had occurred in Birmingham. Protests reached a climax in March when local and state law enforcement officials assaulted peaceful marchers in route from Selma to the state capital in Montgomery. Spurred to action, President Lyndon B. Johnson persuaded Congress to enact the Voting Rights Law. It abolished discriminatory literacy tests and allowed the federal government to register local blacks, resulting in the majority of black southerners finally regaining the franchise.

DISILLUSIONMENT AND RADICALISM

Although the federal government had passed two powerful antisegregation and enfranchisement measures, it could not assuage radical components of the black freedom coalition. SNCC and CORE had come to distrust white liberals, who they believed were too willing to compromise. Their disenchantment grew stronger after the Democratic National Convention in 1964. Following several months of violence in Mississippi, resulting in the death of three civil rights workers, the Mississippi Freedom Democratic Party (MFDP), an offshoot mainly of SNCC and CORE, challenged the credentials of the all-white state party, which discriminated against black participation. To preserve harmony at the convention, President Johnson pushed through a compromise plan that promised future reform and gave two token seats to the MFDP delegation while allowing the regulars to represent the state. Feeling sold out, the Freedom

Democrats, led by Fannie Lou Hamer, a former sharecropper and SNCC worker, rejected the offer.

Increasingly suspicious of white manipulation of the movement and frustrated by the level of violence against civil rights activists, SNCC and CORE led the way in revising the terms of the struggle. They voiced a black power doctrine that rejected the movement's goals of assimilation, substituting cultural nationalism for integration and retaliatory self-defense for nonviolence. Influenced further by the Nation of Islam's Malcolm X and third-world revolutionaries fighting against colonialism in Africa and Asia, black radicals denounced the United States as an imperialist power and welcomed rioting by black ghetto dwellers, mainly in the North, as rebellions against white American colonizers. Determined to combat rising militancy and the accompanying violence, the Federal Bureau of Investigation infiltrated radical groups, harassed their leaders, and created havoc among their followers. By the end of the 1960s, the civil rights coalition had dissolved.

Throughout this period, Dr. King had become more radical, but without abandoning his core principles. Black power slogans upset him because of their antiwhite connotations, and he remained committed to interracial alliances and nonviolence. Nevertheless, the outbreak of rioting and the persistence of poverty convinced him that racism had become embedded in political and economic institutions despite passage of landmark civil rights acts. By 1967 he had begun to feel that his dream of brotherhood was turning into a nightmare. Making matters worse, the Vietnam War accelerated his despair, and he denounced the American government for fighting an imperialist war against nonwhite people. His direct attacks on the president's domestic and foreign policies caused a break with Johnson. King began to focus on finding ways to redistribute economic wealth to eliminate poverty for poor blacks and whites. Killed by an assassin's bullet on April 4, 1968, he never had a chance to build a new movement uniting race and class issues.

UNFINISHED REVOLUTION

The civil rights movement in the United States contained both reformist and revolutionary elements. It succeeded in restoring to African Americans civil and political rights. In emphasizing individual opportunity, equal protection under law, and voting rights for all citizens regardless of color, the movement affirmed liberal values guiding the reform tradition. Civil rights advocates accomplished many of their goals by invigorating the Constitution, not overthrowing it. Nevertheless, as a struggle for black freedom, the movement revolutionized race relations by destroying the rigid system of white supremacy in the South. Black citizens became political actors as voters and government officials (approximately five thousand held elective office in the South in the mid-1990s compared with seventy-five in 1965); humiliating signposts of official segregation in public spaces were eliminated; and racial etiquette that required blacks to assume a subservient position to whites disappeared. Moreover, the movement transformed African Americans and their communities by demonstrating how ordinary women and men, girls and boys, could join together, assert racial pride, and become effective agents of social change. Problems of racism and poverty that endure do not diminish the outstanding achievements of the civil rights movement; rather, they attest to the fact that the revolution remains unfinished.

See also *King, Martin Luther, Jr.; Race.*

Steven F. Lawson

BIBLIOGRAPHY

Branch, Taylor. *Parting the Waters: America in the King Years 1954–63.* New York: Simon and Schuster, 1988.

Carson, Clayborne. *In Struggle: SNCC and the Black Awakening of the 1960s.* Cambridge, Mass.: Harvard University Press, 1981.

Chafe, William H. *Civilities and Civil Rights: Greensboro, North Carolina, and the Black Freedom Struggle.* New York: Oxford University Press, 1981.

Dittmer, John. *Local People: The Struggle for Civil Rights in Mississippi.* Urbana: University of Illinois Press, 1994.

Garrow, David J. *Bearing the Cross: Martin Luther King, Jr., and the Southern Christian Leadership Conference.* New York: William Morrow, 1986.

King, Mary. *Freedom Song: A Personal Story of the 1960s Civil Rights Movement.* New York: William Morrow, 1987.

Lawson, Steven F. *Running for Freedom: Civil Rights and Black Politics in America Since 1941.* 2d ed. New York: McGraw-Hill, 1997.

Marable, Manning. *Race, Reform and Rebellion: The Second Reconstruction in Black America, 1945–1982.* Jackson: University Press of Mississippi, 1984.

Payne, Charles M. *I've Got the Light of Freedom: The Organizing Tradition and the Mississippi Freedom Struggle.* Berkeley: University of California Press, 1995.

U.S. CIVIL WAR (1861–1865)

The U.S. Civil War was the 1861–1865 conflict between the northern states of the Union and the southern states that seceded to form the Confederacy. The American Civil War was a terrible, blunt fact to the 600,000 Americans who died in it, the owners of the $7 billion worth of Southern property destroyed through it, and the taxpayers who footed the $6 billion in overall costs imposed on the nation. But in political terms, it was a hopeless tangle of ambiguities, not the least of which was the question of whether the war represented a genuinely revolutionary situation in the development of American politics, or more simply a crisis within a constitutional system.

The war was triggered by the attempted secession of seven southern states—Alabama, Florida, Georgia, Louisiana,

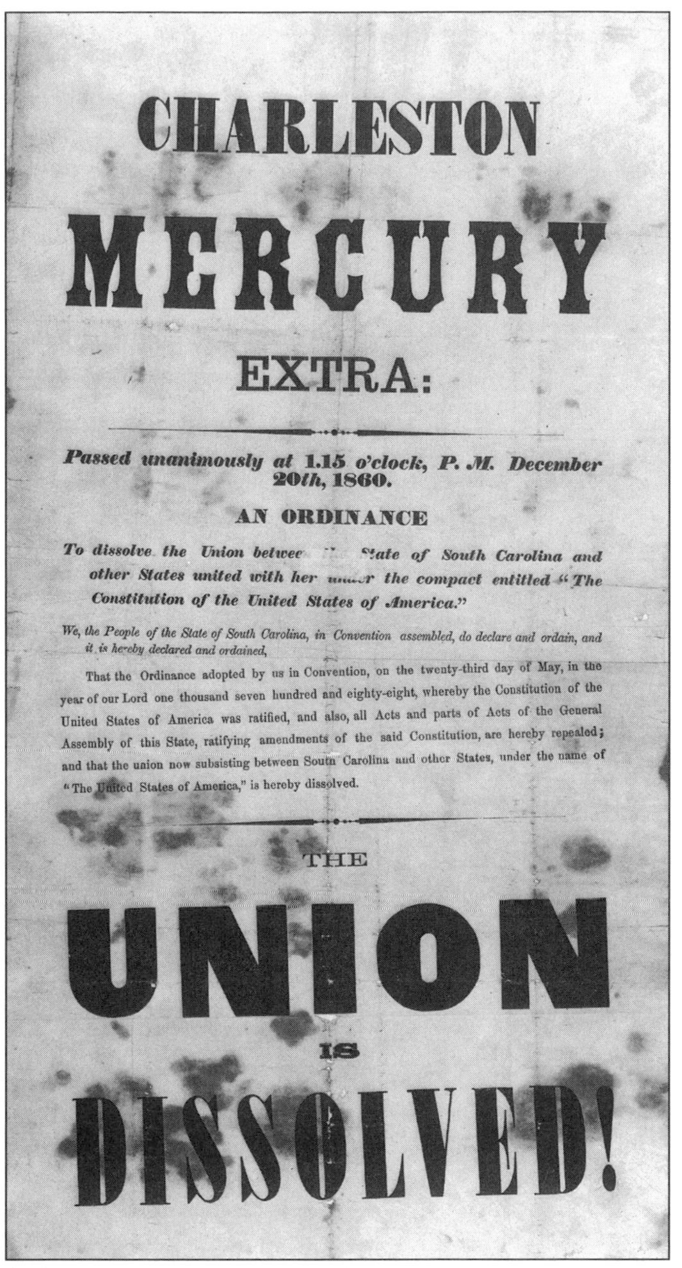

CHARLESTON

MERCURY

EXTRA:

Passed unanimously at 1.15 o'clock, P. M. December 20th, 1860.

AN ORDINANCE

To dissolve the Union betwee[illegible] State of South Carolina and other States united with her [illegible] the compact entitled "The Constitution of the United States of America."

We, the People of the State of South Carolina, in Convention assembled, do declare and ordain, and it is hereby declared and ordained,

That the Ordinance adopted by us in Convention, on the twenty-third day of May, in the year of our Lord one thousand seven hundred and eighty-eight, whereby the Constitution of the United States of America was ratified, and also, all Acts and parts of Acts of the General Assembly of this State, ratifying amendments of the said Constitution, are hereby repealed; and that the union now subsisting between South Carolina and other States, under the name of "The United States of America," is hereby dissolved.

THE

UNION

IS

DISSOLVED!

The *Charleston Mercury* announces the passage of an ordinance by the South Carolina legislature taking the state out of the Union.

Mississippi, South Carolina, and Texas—from the United States between December 1860 and March 1861. These states were soon joined by Arkansas, North Carolina, Tennessee, and Virginia. Yet, in strict terms, it was not the actual secession of the states that caused the war. The Constitution of the United States neither recognized a right of secession belonging to the states of the Union nor expressly stated its impossibility. It was not clear whether secession was a revolutionary repudiation of the Constitution or merely the exercise of an implicit constitutional right to withdraw from the federal Union on the grounds that its original provisions were not being observed, or were in danger of being subverted. President James Buchanan, whose term expired in the midst of the secession crisis, deplored secession but believed that the Constitution gave him no authority as president to prevent it. His successor, Abraham Lincoln—who took office on March 4, 1861—had announced years before his belief that "any people anywhere, being inclined and having the power, have the right to rise up, and shake off the existing government, and form a new one that suits them better." And in his inaugural address as president, Lincoln reaffirmed this belief by acknowledging that "the people" have a "revolutionary right to dismember, or overthrow . . . the existing government . . . whenever they shall grow weary" of it. But Lincoln insisted that the Confederate secession was not a genuine revolution, but only the coup d'état of a radical and unrepresentative Southern elite; and since mere secession from the Union was a constitutional impossibility, the claim of the Southern states to have left the Union was null and void.

Still, Lincoln took no definitive action against the seceders until they actually struck a blow at the United States by directly opening fire on a federal military installation, Fort Sumter, in the harbor of Charleston, South Carolina, on April 12, 1861. This action of the rebel states allowed Lincoln to classify the seceders, who had organized themselves as an independent republic, the Confederate States of America, simply as insurrectionists and for the states and Congress to raise troops to suppress them. All through the war, Lincoln would insist that he was dealing only with a rebel pseudo-government, not a rival American republic. Yet, not even Lincoln was willing to push this logic too far. Confederate prisoners were always treated as prisoners of war rather than insurrectionists, and in the last year of the war, Lincoln was willing to negotiate in a limited fashion with representatives of the Confederate government in hopes of bringing a speedier end to the fighting.

REVOLUTION OR DEFENSE?

This fundamental political problem in defining who-was-who in the Civil War was felt on both sides. In the first flush of secession, it was unclear whether Confederate leaders wanted to regard their movement as a revolutionary repudiation of the old Constitution or a defense of what they regarded as its true intent and principles. Those who were most inclined to see the Confederacy as a revolution argued that the South embodied a radically different cultural system from the northern states, which not only required a political separation but a complete political reconstitution of southern government. English war correspondent William

Howard Russell was astounded at the beginning of the war to hear South Carolinians propose that a member of the British royal family be sent to them as a basis for creating an American monarchy. Or if not a monarchy, then arguments were also made for converting the Confederacy into something more conservative and elitist than democracy. Other Southerners argued that secession had shifted the center of the South's political system toward the glorification of the South's peculiar institution—the enslavement of African-Americans—and so the South (as Confederate vice president Alexander Stephens argued) ought to take a revolutionary attitude toward forming its new government as the first to be self-consciously dedicated to "the great truth that the negro is not equal to the white man."

But the majority of the leaders of the seceding states were uncomfortable with embracing too eagerly the notion that they had created a political revolution. Revolution suggested subversion, and subversion by their slaves was the real revolution that had filled Southern imaginations with horror for generations. For that reason, most Confederates either attempted to redefine revolution in less threatening terms or else surrendered the idea entirely and argued that they were performing a constitutionally legal act. In both cases, Southerners were more likely to insist that their revolution, if it could be called that at all, was a conservative revolution, and the real revolutionaries were Lincoln and the North. On those terms, what appeared as a Confederate revolution was simply a revival or continuation of the original American revolution of the previous century, in which the Confederate States of 1861 were repeating the American Revolution of 1776.

As a result, when the representatives of the seceding states met for the first time in Montgomery, Alabama, in February 1861 to organize the Confederate government, they quickly turned themselves into a provisional congress and wrote a constitution for the Confederate States that paralleled the old federal Constitution in virtually every significant aspect. The preamble recognized that each state was acting in "its sovereign and independent character" in creating the Confederate States' government, but it added that this would create a permanent federal government. No right to secession from the Confederacy was included, nor did the Confederate constitution repeal the old federal constitution's restriction on reopening the African slave trade.

In fact, the body of the Confederate constitution made only the slightest alterations in the procedural provisions of the federal constitution. The Confederacy would be a republic, with a president as its chief executive, a bicameral Congress and an independent judiciary, which was never actually organized due to the exigencies of the war. Perhaps the only noticeable differences concerned the greater overlap of executive and legislative functions in the Confederate constitution. The Confederate president was granted a line-item veto over congressional budgets, and members of the Confederate cabinet were granted privileges of the floor in the Confederate Congress.

THE CONSEQUENCES OF WAR

But the war did hold revolutionary consequences for the South. They were, however, unintentional, and all the more devastating for being so. If the Confederates assumed that their war would be fought in such a way as to leave the sovereign and independent character of the Confederate states untouched, the war quickly taught them otherwise. The Confederate president, Jefferson Davis, warned overconfident Southerners that the war would be a long one and would require a united military effort. He proceeded to enforce that unity by taking over state and private weapons-making facilities for the Confederate government, assuming control of the Southern armies, suspending the writ of habeas corpus to deal with political dissent, and, in 1862, persuading the Confederate Congress to institute forced military conscription of white males.

Not only did these actions represent a departure from what Southern leaders had regarded as the principal reason for secession, but it also plunged the Confederacy into several quasi-revolutionary situations. Pockets of Unionist sentiment in the South—most notably in western Virginia, northern Alabama, and North Carolina—either declared their own secession movements or else organized active resistance to the Confederate government. What was more, the Confederate draft exempted the owners of large-scale plantations on the grounds that their presence was needed to discourage slave revolts, but this only persuaded the non-slaveholding white yeomen who made up the backbone of the Confederate armies that the war was not being fought in their interests, and over the last year of the war, it produced debilitating levels of desertion. And of course the costs of the war for the Confederacy after its loss were staggering financially but also seriously undercut Southern political power in the United States for more than another century. Between the Civil War and the Bicentennial, only one candidate from what had been the old Confederate states—Woodrow Wilson—was elected to the presidency.

In many ways, the Confederacy's identity as a political revolutionary movement seems unconvincingly thin, at least apart from its unintended consequences. But this judgment confines itself too much to political structure and ignores the revolutionary departure the Confederacy represented in the protection it strove to provide for slave labor. Although the

Confederacy sought to maintain the outward forms of the American republic, the explicit sanction of slave labor was not only a distinct march away from the old federal Constitution but also meant a thorough commitment of the Confederacy against free wage labor as the economic basis of Southern capitalist production, and therefore against virtually the whole movement of liberal economic thought in the West in the nineteenth century. To that extent, the South was not only revolutionary but also a revolution against the triumph of nineteenth-century bourgeois liberalism.

LINCOLN AND THE NORTH

The North in the Civil War represents an almost complete inversion of this scenario—instead of a political revolution lurking beneath the surface of apparent continuity, Lincoln and the North pursued policies of political continuity that were often obscured by their potentially revolutionary consequences. Although elected as a Republican in November 1860, Lincoln would always think of himself as "an old Henry Clay Whig." He had always defended the Whig Party message of federally sponsored economic development, national supremacy, and—as a way of drawing a contrast with the Jacksonian Democrats—the submission of the presidency to Congress as the true representative of the people. He looked on himself as a constitutional literalist, even to the point during the 1850s of refusing to join the abolitionists' demand for immediate emancipation of slaves in the states in which slavery was then legal. What he opposed was the extension of slavery into the federally organized western territories.

Even while the war raged, Lincoln still felt sufficiently bound by the Constitution's implicit sanction of slavery to negotiate with slaveholding states for schemes of voluntary, gradual emancipation funded by the federal government, none of which he could persuade any state to adopt. When at last Lincoln did act unilaterally to deal with slavery in the Emancipation Proclamation of January 1, 1863, he limited the freeing of slaves to only those states and counties of the South still resisting federal authority, and even then he justified emancipation not as a personal gesture, based on lofty moral principle, but as a constitutional wartime power based on his obligations as commander in chief.

Lincoln's appeal to the Constitution's wartime powers became the basis for much of what was later interpreted as a revolutionary rebalancing of power within the American republic. Like Jefferson Davis, Lincoln instituted military conscription; his Republican majority in Congress enacted the first direct income tax in American history—a tax that would be judged unconstitutional after the war; his cabinet, and especially Treasury Secretary Salmon Chase, created a national banking system and began substituting paper money for specie as the national currency; his generals arrested political dissidents, broke up protest meetings, and shut down opposition newspapers; and—again like Jefferson Davis—he repeatedly suspended the writ of habeas corpus and stacked the Supreme Court with his own appointees to prevent judicial review of his policies.

But much of the force of these policies was only superficially revolutionary in nature. The Whigs had always made the constitutional war powers of the president the one major exception to executive deference to Congress, and Lincoln was careful to justify every extraordinary measure of his administration under the war-powers rubric. Military conscription in the North was much less pervasive than in the Confederacy; most of it was handled through a state quota system and acted more as an incentive to volunteering than a universal draft. Probably no more than 47,000 Northerners were actually conscripted during the war. Despite the occasional arrests of a high-profile antiadministration critic like Clement Vallandigham, most of the military arrests involved wartime racketeering, desertion, and suspected espionage. And as for emancipation, Lincoln was so sensitive to the provisional nature of his proclamation that in 1865 he rushed through Congress a constitutional amendment abolishing slavery lest the war end and allow his proclamation to be challenged in postwar courts on the grounds that military necessity no longer prevailed.

RECONSTRUCTION

If any Republicans harbored plans for revolutionary changes, it was the Radical faction of the Republican Party, whose spokesmen in Congress—Charles Sumner, Benjamin Wade, Thaddeus Stevens, Zachariah Chandler, and Henry Winter Davis—never ceased to criticize Lincoln as a Milquetoast on the subject of reconstructing the defeated South. The Radicals frankly looked on the war as an opportunity to reconstruct the South as a free-labor economy. But Lincoln, far from sympathizing with revolutionary war aims, was convinced that these would embitter the South and only make it more likely that the old Southern leadership would emerge from defeat with more of a following than ever. He not only offered milder reconstruction terms than Congress but also vetoed alternative congressional plans and used his wartime military authority to set up his own versions of reconstruction in Louisiana and Arkansas.

Like the South, the North experienced far more revolutionary changes as a by-product than a direct consequence of the war. And yet, even here, it has been too easy to exaggerate the revolutionary nature of the war and forget that many of the war's most obvious economic developments—a transcontinental railroad, the explosion of the American financial services sector, federal homestead legislation—were actually aspects of the old Whig domestic policy agenda and would probably have been promoted by Lincoln and the Republicans even if there had been no war.

The most specifically political revolution was the liberation and then enfranchisement of the African-American population; but Lincoln's assassination and the bungled postwar reconstruction in the South soon blunted the possible political influence of black votes through terrorism and restrictive Jim Crow legislation. The Republican Party, which should have expected to create an almost unchallengeable political base in the postwar South through the votes of the ex-slaves, became an almost-invisible minority there after 1877 and remained that way for a century afterward.

If the Civil War was a revolution at any level, it was actually in helping to decide, once and for all, that free-wage labor would be the established labor system of industrial capitalism rather than slave-based or compulsory labor. In a political sense, the Civil War made secession an unthinkable alternative to disharmony and securely located the center of American political identity, if not political authority, at the national level. But many of the war's more localized results were either already in process or less profound than they seem in the war's dramatic light. And in no case did the underlying American republican ideology undergo serious challenge, much less revolution, in either North or South.

See also *Civil Wars*.

Allen C. Guelzo

BIBLIOGRAPHY

Bensel, Richard F. *Yankee Leviathan: The Origins of Central State Authority in America, 1859–1879.* New York: Cambridge University Press, 1990.

Beringer, Richard E., et al. *Why the South Lost the Civil War.* Athens, Ga.: University of Georgia, 1986.

Derosa, Marshall L. *The Confederate Constitution of 1861: An Inquiry into American Constitutionalism.* Columbia, Mo.: University of Missouri Press, 1991.

Faust, Drew Gilpin. *The Creation of Confederate Nationalism: Ideology and Identity in the Civil War South.* Baton Rouge: Louisiana State University Press, 1988.

Fehrenbacher, Don E. "Lincoln and the Constitution." In *Lincoln in Text and Context: Collected Essays.* Stanford, Calif.: Stanford University Press, 1987.

Gallagher, Gary W. *The Confederate War.* Cambridge, Mass.: Harvard University Press, 1997.

Paludan, Philip Shaw. *A People's Contest: The Union and the Civil War, 1861–1865.* New York: Harper and Row, 1988.

Rable, George C. *The Confederate Republic: A Revolution Against Politics.* Chapel Hill: University of North Carolina Press, 1994.

Richardson, Heather Cox. *The Greatest Nation of the Earth: Republican Economic Policies during the Civil War.* Cambridge, Mass.: Harvard University Press, 1997.

Thomas, Emory M. *The Confederate Nation, 1861–1865.* New York: Harper and Row, 1979.

U.S. LABOR REVOLTS (1890–1932)

Conventional wisdom suggests that the United States has been among the most violent societies in the developed world and that its labor history has been punctuated by more violent and destructive conflicts than any other industrial society. Between 1890 and 1932 the United States experienced numerous worker revolts that cost lives, shattered bodies, uprooted families, and destroyed property.

Labor revolts preceded the 1890s, including a nationwide uprising of railroad workers in 1877 that ended only after intervention by regular U.S. army troops. After 1890, however, as the nation rapidly industrialized, industrial conflict and violence intensified. Most business enterprises refused to recognize unions and used strikebreakers to defeat their workers. The use of strikebreakers, who were often protected by police and troops, turned conventional industrial disputes into little civil wars.

RAILWAY AND STEEL STRIKES

Typical of worker revolts in the late nineteenth century were the Homestead steel strike of 1892 and the Pullman boycott and strike of 1894. In the former, Andrew Carnegie and his lieutenant Henry Clay Frick decided that the union that represented the skilled workers at the Homestead steelworks in Homestead, Pennsylvania, diminished company profits. They decided to eliminate the union. Frick fortified the plant, recruited strikebreakers, and hired armed Pinkerton agents to protect them. In response, the Homestead workers armed themselves to thwart the strikebreakers and Pinkertons. In a pitched battle along the shores of the Monongahela River that caused many casualties, the strikers defeated and captured the Pinkertons. The steelworkers and their local sympathizers ruled the town of Homestead as a workers' community. Frick asked the governor of Pennsylvania for help, and the governor sent the state militia to Homestead, where they instituted martial law and removed union members and their allies from local office.

The Pullman strike and boycott of 1894 resembled the Homestead conflict. In this case George Pullman refused to bargain with his workers at the Pullman Palace Car Company or to negotiate with the union that represented them, the American Railway Union (ARU). When members of the ARU voted to strike in solidarity with their brothers and sisters at Pullman, the union's president, Eugene V. Debs, asked union members to refuse to handle Pullman sleeping cars. The boycott of Pullman cars turned the conflict into a battle between the union and the federal government as well as between the workers and Pullman. The boycott tied up the nation's railroads, precipitating what the railroad managers, the newspapers, the public, and political leaders deemed a national crisis. President Grover Cleveland authorized his attorney general to obtain a judicial injunction interdicting all forms of union and strike activity. When a federal judge issued such an injunction, the president sent troops to enforce it. The presence of the regular army caused strike-associated violence to intensify, but it also broke the strike and decimated the ARU. For his part in disobeying the injunction and challenging the authority of the federal government, Debs was sentenced to a term in federal prison.

Homestead and Pullman prefaced a wave of violent labor conflicts that scarred industrial relations in the United States. Workers who were denied a voice at work or saw their jobs and livelihoods imperiled often resorted to violence to redress their grievances and uphold their rights as free and equal citizens.

HARD-ROCK MINING STRIKES AND FOUNDING THE IWW

Between 1892 and 1905 labor conflict and violent rebellion scarred the hard-rock mining regions of the Mountain West. Beginning in the Coeur d'Alenes of northern Idaho in 1892, spreading to Cripple Creek, Colorado, in 1894, returning to the Coeur d'Alenes in 1899, and encompassing nearly all the hard-rock mining regions of Colorado between 1903 and 1905, miners and mineowners waged a bitter industrial war. Armed miners dynamited the property of antiunion companies and intimidated strikebreakers. Mineowners hired armed guards and obtained state militia and sometimes federal troops. In the Coeur d'Alenes in 1892 and 1899, the owners defeated the miners with state and federal troops, who jailed hundreds of strikers in outdoor camps known as "bullpens." Colorado experienced a labor war between 1903 and 1905, which became the object of several federal investigations, served as the backdrop for Jack London's dystopian novel *The Iron Heel,* and brought William D. "Big Bill" Haywood to prominence nationally as a radical labor leader associated with violence. Determined to defeat trade unionists and workers whom he declared to be violent criminals and subversive revolutionaries, the governor of Colorado declared martial law in the mining districts, ordered troops to administer military justice, and financed his operation with funds donated by the mineowners. The military treated scores of union members to summary justice and deported hundreds more across the state's borders in disregard of their constitutional rights.

The labor civil war in Colorado prompted a host of labor radicals, including most leaders of the Western Federation of Miners, to found the Industrial Workers of the World (IWW) in 1905. Committed to organizing all workers regardless of occupation, nationality, race, or gender into "one big union" and equally dedicated to replacing capitalism with a workers' commonwealth, the IWW between 1909 and 1918 waged some of the most notable industrial battles in U.S. history. From McKees Rock, Pennsylvania (1909), to Lawrence, Massachusetts (1912), Paterson, New Jersey (1913), the piney woods of Louisiana and eastern Texas (1910–1913), the iron range of northern Minnesota (1916), and the nation's wheat fields, forests, and copper mines (1917–1918), the IWW waged unrelenting warfare against its capitalist adversaries as well as against local, state, and national governments. Demanding their constitutional rights to free speech, free assembly, and free association, IWW members packed local jails until public authorities conceded some, if not all, of their demands. Because IWW strikes in 1917–1918 during the wheat harvest and in the forests and copper mines threatened the U.S. effort in World War I, the federal government declared the organization's leaders subversives who violated the wartime espionage and sedition statutes. In October 1917 the Justice Department raided the IWW's offices, seized all of its property, and arrested nearly two hundred of its elected and appointed officials. In May 1918 a federal jury in Chicago found more than one hundred IWW leaders guilty of espionage and sedition as charged, and the judge sentenced them to long terms in the federal penitentiary in Leavenworth. The repression of the IWW, however, failed to end labor violence or worker revolts.

COAL STRIKES

The bituminous and anthracite coal industries proved as susceptible to labor violence as the hard-rock mining regions of the West. Coal miners, too, were experienced in using explosives and equally accustomed to a culture of guns and hunting. In southern Appalachia, where mine operators obdurately resisted unionism, worker revolts culminated in 1921–1922 in a West Virginia civil war that featured armed units of union sympathizers, equally numerous and well-armed company forces, and warplanes flown by members of the U.S. Army Air Corps. Even in the heavily unionized Illinois coal fields, the actions of an aggressive antiunion mine owner could precipitate outbursts of raw violence, as happened in "bloody Williamson" county in 1922.

One historian has characterized the years from 1910 through 1915 as "an age of industrial violence." In truth that rubric can be applied to the entire era between 1890 and 1932, when industrial violence and worker revolts scarred every region of the nation.

See also *Workers.*

Melvyn Dubofsky

BIBLIOGRAPHY

Brecher, Jeremy. *Strike!* Boston: South End Press, 1997.

Edwards, P. K. *Strikes in the United States, 1881–1974.* New York: St. Martin's Press, 1981.

Krause, Paul. *The Battle for Homestead, 1880–1892: Politics, Culture, and Steel.* Pittsburgh, Penn.: University of Pittsburgh Press, 1992.

Lukas, J. Anthony. *Big Trouble: A Murder in a Small Western Town Sets Off a Struggle for the Soul of America.* New York: Simon and Schuster, 1997.

Taft, Philip, and Philip Ross. "American Labor Violence: Its Causes, Character, and Outcome." In *Violence in America: Historical and Comparative Perspectives.* Edited by Hugh Davis Graham and Ted Robert Gurr. New York: The New American Library, 1969.

U.S. PREINDEPENDENCE AND PRE-CIVIL WAR REBELLIONS (1675–1850)

Political life in the American countryside before the Civil War was sometimes violent and contentious. Upheavals, often lasting for years and even decades, defined life in many areas, and clubs and guns settled as many disputes as ballots and petitions. These disputes varied greatly over time and place, so much so that it is difficult to generalize about them. Yet four basic problems seem in one way or another to underlie almost all these upheavals: crises of authority caused by disjunctures between the social order and the political structures; disagreement over the origins of property rights resulting in endemic struggles for control of contested lands; fighting between creditors and debtors; and ethnic or religious disputes between yeomen and members of the gentry. Although historians have labeled these episodes of instability "riots" or "regulations" and have generally considered them of secondary importance in the grand schema of the new republic, in fact the unrest helped define the legal and political economy of a nation that would remain overwhelmingly rural until well after the Confederate surrender in 1865. They helped erase any pretension of aristocratic lordship over the countryside and ensure that liberal credit markets were established in American society.

ESTABLISHING AUTHORITY

The first outbreaks of collective violence in the American countryside came in the last third of the seventeenth century, as the colonists struggled with questions of demographic and political change, as well as cultural conflicts. The best known of these upheavals, Bacon's Rebellion, occurred in Virginia in 1675 and 1676. Named after a prominent gentleman, Nathaniel Bacon, who led the rebels, this year-long struggle began with a drive to gain property on the frontier, included several massacres of Native Americans and the burning of Virginia's capital, and concluded only when Bacon died from dysentery and a powerful English fleet arrived in the Chesapeake. Other rebellions in this same period (1660–1710) occurred in Maryland, New Jersey (two), New York, Massachusetts, and South Carolina.

These rebellions have primarily been attributed to a disjuncture between the social and political orders in the new colonies. In Virginia, for example, Bacon and other gentlemen who arrived in North America after 1660 were connected by blood and patronage to some of the most prominent families in England. These newcomers looked down on the men gathered around Gov. William Berkeley, some of whom were people of very humble origins who had risen through the colony's still fluid social order to places of authority.

Although this view of the seventeenth century's instability explains many developments in the period, other factors were clearly at work in most cases. In New Jersey and New England, changes in political structures brought about by the restoration of Charles II to the English throne in 1660 and the resulting threats to established land-tenure systems fomented two rebellions in New Jersey (1667–1674, 1698–1701) and another in Boston in 1689. In New York, conflict between the conquered Dutch majority (subordinated when the city of New Amsterdam was overrun by English forces in 1664) and a heavy-handed Anglo-Dutch elite led to Leisler's Rebellion, an uprising of the non-English-speaking population against the colony's new rulers that coincided with the "Glorious Revolution" in England (1688–1689). In Maryland, the Protestants of the Annapolis area rose against their Catholic rulers in 1689. Ultimately, these rebellions reinforced royal authority and encouraged standardization of legal institutions across provincial America.

The forty years between 1700 and 1740 constituted a type of internal Pax Britannia (British Peace) in provincial society. There was social conflict in some isolated areas, particularly in eastern Connecticut, but in general an increased royal presence, relative economic prosperity, and persistent fear of the French and Native Americans on the colonies' western and northern flanks encouraged peace and unity in the provinces. After 1740, however, demographic pressures and new economic opportunities led to a wave of agrarian violence that stretched on until the Revolution's end.

AGRARIAN UNREST

At the core of these conflicts were disputes over landed property brought on by the migration of excess population into unopened frontier land no more than fifty to one hundred miles from the Atlantic coast. Disputes over the ownership of the so-called Indian lands in eastern Connecticut in the 1710s signaled these changes. But widespread violence did not begin in earnest until the early 1740s, when New Jersey society tore open over the question of property ownership. The colony's location between the major ports of New York and Philadelphia had increased the value of land and resources in the first half of the eighteenth century, and when migrants from the coastal communities began to move into the interior, conflict erupted.

Members of the middle colonies' gentry, constituted in the Board of Proprietors of East New Jersey, claimed hundreds of thousands of these unsettled acres by right of large land grants to English aristocrats from the seventeenth-century Stuart kings of England. Their opponents, largely yeomen farmers of New England and Dutch ancestry, claimed the same land by virtue of squatter's rights and purchase from the Native Americans. The resulting hostility led to twenty years of low-level violence, punctuated by a dramatic upheaval in the mid-1740s that brought New Jersey's royal government to the brink of collapse.

The struggle in New Jersey was only the first of a number of upheavals in the eighteenth century that historians call land riots or agrarian unrest. Migrating New Englanders, primarily from southern Connecticut, began moving into New York east of the Hudson River (including what became Vermont) and Pennsylvania in the 1750s, destabilizing the manorial land-tenure system in the former colony and challenging the Penn family's control of northeast Pennsylvania's Wyoming Valley. Previously peaceful tenants in both areas became unruly as they saw their great landlords successfully challenged, and portions of both colonies descended into armed violence in the 1750s and 1760s.

By the 1760s the interior regions of North and South Carolina had also become the scene of armed violence. Migrants from the north, moving along the Appalachian ridge, had settled lands pried from the Native Americans in the Carolina piedmont and refused to accept the claims to ownership and authority of these lands made by the coastal gentry in both colonies. In North Carolina the situation deteriorated so rapidly and so completely that the government's authority was restored only after a full-fledged battle at the Almanac River in 1771 between the largely yeomen Regulators of the interior and the coastal militia led by the royal governor.

IDENTITY AND IDEOLOGY

Although property issues were at the core of these upheavals, ethnic and religious differences played an important role in the eighteenth-century agrarian disputes. In New York, Vermont, New Jersey, and Pennsylvania, Calvinist New Englanders comprised a large number of the agrarian dissidents. They refused to acknowledge the political or legal authority of the Yorker (New York), Scottish and Anglican (New Jersey), and Quaker (Pennsylvania) gentries and often attacked the great men's German, Dutch, and Scottish clients. In North Carolina, the evangelical Regulators refused to submit to the largely Anglican coastal gentry's authority. Certainly, in all of these cases, the lack of shared cultural terrain encouraged disorder.

These movements and the attitudes that spawned them are complex and often contradictory to the modern eye. Disgruntled yeomen used limited violence to achieve their goals, sought to avoid maiming and killing their opponents, and tended to follow traditional local leaders. Their movements were generally not overtly geared to the overthrow of the existing social orders, and their goals were thus limited. Yet, these farmers and their allies created durable institutions that sustained their movements over long periods of time, denied the royal government's right to establish norms in the society, and most important, perhaps, asserted the validity of nonroyal property titles in the vastness of America. By stressing that labor and possession could establish legal title, they heralded a revolution in the understanding of the nature and origins of property rights, one that would erode the foundations of monarchical society.

The broader political meaning of these movements became apparent in the 1770s as the imperial controversies broadened. In New York, New Jersey, Vermont, and North Carolina, agrarian dissidents appropriated ideologies used by the Whig protest movement and turned them against their local gentry. Agrarian activists became "Sons of Liberty" or "Liberty Boys," and they described their gentlemen opponents as corrupt tyrants determined to destroy an independent yeomanry for their own gain. The arrival of British soldiers in force in 1775 and 1776 dampened these internal social tensions, but it did not end them. Rather, the war postponed the continuing struggle over the political economy of much of North America.

AFTER INDEPENDENCE

The question of what the economic and political character of the new society would be came immediately to the forefront after the Peace of Paris established U.S. independence from Britain in 1783, and again some people in the countryside turned to collective violence to try to find an answer. In the decades following the end of the Revolutionary War, instability in the money supply, disputes over property, and the central government's efforts to collect taxes led to a new wave of agrarian violence in Maine, Massachusetts, Vermont, parts of upstate New York, Pennsylvania, and, later, parts of Ohio, Kentucky, and Missouri.

As early as 1782, instability in the money supply led crowds of debtors to blockade courthouses in central Massachusetts in what became known as Ely's Rebellion. Wartime demand and hyperinflation had encouraged the extension of complex commercial and debt networks across the new state, but the retirement of a large portion of that money supply created an unprecedented debt crisis. At a time when people were still imprisoned for refusal to pay debts, paper money's disappearance threatened thousands of Massachusetts farmers and small merchants with disaster. Those threatened took out their anger on the court system, lawyers, and members of the gentry who seemed to profit from the disaster; the yeomanry seemed unaware that those people were often themselves debtors faced with economic difficulties of their own or simply trying to collect on loans honestly given. The turmoil in the Bay State eventually culminated in Shays's Rebellion, a major upheaval in the central and western region of the state that was put down by a government-armed force raised in the Boston area.

Similar issues underlay other post-Revolutionary rebellions. The Whiskey and Fry's Rebellions and Wyoming Valley controversies in Pennsylvania, the nameless but persistent violence in Maine between squatters and gentlemen proprietors, the continued violence in the New York estates east of the Hudson River, and similar unrest along the frontier from the 1790s to the 1840s—all these episodes were sparked by periodic instability in the money supply, related issues of taxation and authority, and renewed disagreement over the origins of legitimate property title. Perhaps the most enduring of these conflicts was in New York, where the antirenter struggles of the 1840s culminated almost one hundred years of intermittent violence in the large estates east of the Hudson. Taken together, these disputes amounted to a low-intensity struggle over the new society's political economy and, implicitly, the location of sovereignty in the American nation; the agrarians were overwhelmingly localists in their political and economic views, but their opponents were more cosmopolitan.

Labeling the agrarian disputes in the American countryside before 1850 as riots or crowds diminishes their importance and obscures their meaning. The violence itself was admittedly transitory, but the attitudes that informed it—the world views of the agrarians—were more enduring. Their drive for freehold property, inflated economies, and decentralized credit markets eroded the first British empire's foundations and helped define American society's political and economic character. Ultimately, the Homestead Act and the creation of the modern banking structure made their goals a reality. The eighteenth and nineteenth centuries' club-wielding "rioter" was a political forebear of the democratic Americans who emerged in the Jacksonian period and reshaped their world, and our own.

See also *American (U.S.) Revolution (1776–1789); Ethnic Conflict; U.S. Civil War (1861–1865).*

BRENDAN MCCONVILLE

BIBLIOGRAPHY

Bond, Beverley. *The Quit-Rent System in the American Colonies.* New Haven, Conn.: Yale University Press, 1919.

Brown, Richard M., and Don E. Fehrenbacher, eds. *Tradition, Conflict, and Modernization.* New York: Academic Press, 1977.

Gross, Robert A. *In Debt to Shays.* Charlottesville, Va.: University of Virginia Press, 1993.

Kulikoff, Alan. *The Agrarian Origins of American Capitalism.* Charlottesville, Va.: University of Virginia Press, 1992.

Lovejoy, David. *The Glorious Revolution in America.* Middletown, Conn.: Wesleyan University Press, 1972.

McConville, Brendan. *These Daring Disturbers of the Public Peace: The Struggle for Property and Power in Early New Jersey.* Ithaca, N.Y.: Cornell University Press, forthcoming.

Slaughter, Thomas. *The Whiskey Rebellion: Frontier Epilogue to the American Revolution.* New York: Oxford University Press, 1986.

Taylor, Alan. *Liberty Men and Great Proprietors.* Charlotte: University of North Carolina Press, 1991.

U.S. RURAL POST-CIVIL WAR REBELLIONS (1865–1940)

The American countryside was the scene of several farm revolts in the post-Civil War era. Some challenged the existing political order with their militancy, and many of their participants were radicalized at least for a time. The single most important farm revolt in American history took place in the 1890s with historic Populism, but it had been preceded by the Granger movement in the 1870s and followed by the Nonpartisan League of the World War I era and the Farmers' Holiday of the 1930s.

All of these rural insurgencies had regional bases; none had broad support across the nation, which helps explain their limited success. Still, they were noteworthy and helped shape the political culture and agenda in several states, as well as occasionally making a mark on national politics. And as late as the 1980s, hard-pressed farmers looked back to these earlier rural causes, particularly to Populism and the Farmers' Holiday, for inspiration and tactics in their own struggles.

GRANGER MOVEMENT

The first significant rural revolt after the U.S. Civil War was associated with the Granger movement of the 1870s. Initially a social organization, the Grange became involved in a cooperative crusade that drew thousands of farmers to its cause. The Grangers sought to avoid the middleman, who either paid too little or charged too much, and hundreds of Granger cooperatives were formed in the Midwest in the early 1870s. Grangers also turned to politics to advance the interests of farmers. A number of independent or antimonopoly parties were formed and competed against the old parties. Though organizationally distinct from the Grange, they often were referred to as Granger parties and elected legislative candidates in Midwestern states. This insurgency proved short-lived, however, declining in the wake of economic depression and the failure of the Granger cooperative movement.

POPULISM

The 1890s brought one of the greatest rural political uprisings in American history. Known as the Populist revolt, it advocated measures intended to increase farmers' political influence and ensure them a better deal in the marketplace. Although Populism had influence in the South, its strongest electoral base was in the West. In 1890 independent parties contested elections in Kansas, Nebraska, South Dakota, and North Dakota. The launching of these new parties was accompanied by great fanfare and enthusiasm and resulted in the election of seven members of the U.S. House and two U.S. senators, control of the lower house of the legislature in Kansas, and the prospect of future victories in other states.

Enthusiasm for a national third party grew in the wake of the 1890 elections. In 1892 a new national party, the People's Party, was formed and its nominating convention held in Omaha, Nebraska. The Omaha convention produced the famous Omaha Platform, which called for reform of the money system, a government farm program, government ownership of the railroads, direct election of U.S. senators, and the end of poverty in American society. A significant omission was that of women's suffrage, explained by an unwillingness to have such a divisive issue in the platform.

The Populists nominated James Weaver, a former Union Army general and a veteran of earlier third-party struggles, as their presidential candidate. In the fall election, he carried five western states, garnering approximately 8 percent of the total vote. But the Populists' greatest electoral successes then and later came at the state and local levels in the Plains and Mountain states, where they elected U.S. House members, U.S. senators, governors, legislators, and other officials. By the end of the 1890s, however, Populism was a lost cause as an independent third-party movement.

NONPARTISAN LEAGUE

After Populism farmers never again mounted a significant third-party effort on their own because economic organization proved to have greater appeal in the countryside in the twentieth century. Farmers did not abandon politics altogether, however. In North Dakota in the World War I era, they launched an impressive political insurgency. Former Socialists and farm cooperators joined forces in 1915–1916 to organize the new movement.

Taking advantage of the primary law, the Nonpartisan League entered the Republican primary and nominated and then elected its candidates on the GOP ticket. The new movement dominated North Dakota state government for several years and carried out its platform of establishing what continues to be the nation's only state bank, a state mill, and a state grain elevator. Most such enterprises are privately run. The Nonpartisan League also elected U.S. House and Senate members.

Farmers elsewhere found the Nonpartisan League approach appealing. It met with limited success in other states—including Montana, South Dakota, Idaho and Minnesota—but the League's most important achievement outside North Dakota was its role in forming the Minnesota Farmer-Labor Party, the most important state-level third-party effort in twentieth-century American politics. In North Dakota, the league ran out of steam in the early 1920s. It was repudiated at the ballot box in a 1921 recall election, though the same election also brought voter approval for its basic program.

FARMERS' HOLIDAY

When the Great Depression hit the United States in the early 1930s, farmers launched one last major uprising. The farm revolt of the 1930s was dominated by the Farmers' Holiday, the creation of Milo Reno, a former president of the Iowa Farmers Union. Initially, the Holiday called a farm strike in the late summer and early fall of 1932. Omaha, Sioux City, and Sioux Falls were picketed by militant farmers seeking to prevent farm goods from reaching market. The strike did not succeed in raising farm prices but did grab headlines across the nation, focusing attention on the plight of the countryside.

The threat of foreclosures led to attempts to stop or interfere with forced farm sales, called penny auctions and Sears-and-Roebuck sales. Rural activists attended scheduled sales in large numbers, persuading or coercing others from making bids for chattels and occasionally blocking the sale altogether. Sometimes violence marred these episodes, but they helped convince legislatures to pass moratorium laws and insurance companies and banks to delay foreclosure actions. New Deal farm programs, however, stole the thunder of Reno and other rural rebels. Wheat-allotment and corn-hog program checks did not provide farmers with the cost-of-production solution that the Holiday advocated, but they put some money in the pockets of farmers across the region. The farm revolt of the 1930s was at flood tide in 1932 and early 1933, receding in different places at different times but ending everywhere by the end of the decade.

OTHER MOVEMENTS

In addition to these large-scale movements, there were more localized actions to resist innovations from outside. These included vigilante night-rider forays by Kentucky and Tennessee tobacco farmers against the tobacco trust and farmers who sold their crop to the trust in 1905–1909 that resulted in physical intimidation, destruction of crops, and burning of tobacco warehouses. In the ill-fated Green Corn Rebellion of 1917, Oklahoma farmers sought to march on Washington to take the United States out of World War I, but the state militia quickly suppressed the march. There were other episodes as well, such as California's Owen Valley revolt against Los Angeles's domination of the local water supply in the 1920s, which included the dynamiting of the aqueduct that carried water to the city.

But the most important rural revolts in the post-Civil War era involved state and regional movements to get the government to help farmers facing economic crisis. Such efforts stand in sharp contrast to those of right-wing extremist groups of the 1980s and 1990s that essentially declared war on government and society at large.

See also *U.S. Labor Revolts (1890–1932)*.

William C. Pratt

BIBLIOGRAPHY

Dyson, Lowell K. *Farmers' Organizations.* Westport, Conn.: Greenwood Press, 1986.

McMath, Robert, Jr. *American Populism: A Social History, 1877–1898.* New York: Hill and Wang, 1993.

Morlan, Robert L. *Political Prairie Fire: The Nonpartisan League, 1915–1922.* St. Paul: Minnesota Historical Society Press, 1955, 1983.

Shover, John L. *Cornbelt Rebellion: The Farmers' Holiday Association.* Urbana: University of Illinois Press, 1965.

U.S. SLAVE REVOLTS (1776–1865)

At the time of the American Revolution, almost 600,000 residents of the thirteen colonies were enslaved people of African descent. They comprised more than one-fifth of the settler population of the British American mainland. The vast majority of the enslaved population lived in the new states that lay south of Pennsylvania; in those states slaves comprised almost 40 percent of the settler population. By 1860 slavery had been eliminated in the north, but slaves continued to comprise almost 40 percent of the southern population. A nation that proclaimed all men to have been created equal nonetheless held many of its residents in bondage, a contradiction that gave a double meaning to slave revolts in the United States. On the one hand, such revolts were insurrectionary acts against the constituted governments of the states in which they occurred and, by extension, against the United States. On the other hand, by rejecting slavery, they could be understood as attempts to force the young nation to live up to its creed. Thus slave conspiracies and revolts, which existed in all slave societies, took on a special meaning in the United States.

Each slave rebellion had singular causes rooted in the specific society in which it occurred, but certain conditions proved conducive to revolts throughout plantation America. Throughout the hemisphere, uprisings tended to occur where slaves constituted the majority of the population, among slave populations that were predominantly African-born rather than American-born (creole), and where the largest numbers of planters were absentee owners. Those conditions did not prevail in North America after the American Revolution, and, although scholars differ on the best way to count slave rebellions during the national period, they agree that rebellions in the United States were rarer than in the Caribbean and in Brazil. Despite the unfavorable conditions facing potential slave rebels in the United States, however, enslaved people forged several large-scale attempts to win their freedom. Four such events stand out for their scale and for the influence they had on national events.

FOUR MAJOR SLAVE REVOLTS

Gabriel's Conspiracy, the first major slave conspiracy following independence, occurred in Richmond, Virginia, during the summer of 1800. Gabriel, a blacksmith who belonged to a planter named Thomas Henry Prosser, led a movement of Richmond-area creole slaves that was designed to end slavery in the state. The conspirators planned to seize the town and hold Governor James Monroe hostage until white Virginians granted them freedom. The conspiracy was betrayed on August 30, the day the rebellion was to begin, and many alleged conspirators were arrested. Of approximately seventy men who faced trial, twenty-six were executed; eight were convicted but had their sentences commuted to deportation. Gabriel and his followers, inspired by the American and the Haitian Revolutions and by their belief that slavery violated God's laws, failed in their attempt to seize the revolutionary mantel claimed by their masters.

About a decade later a group of slaves living in the recently acquired frontier regions of Louisiana rose in rebellion and marched on New Orleans. With between 150 and 500 rebels, this insufficiently understood rebellion was probably

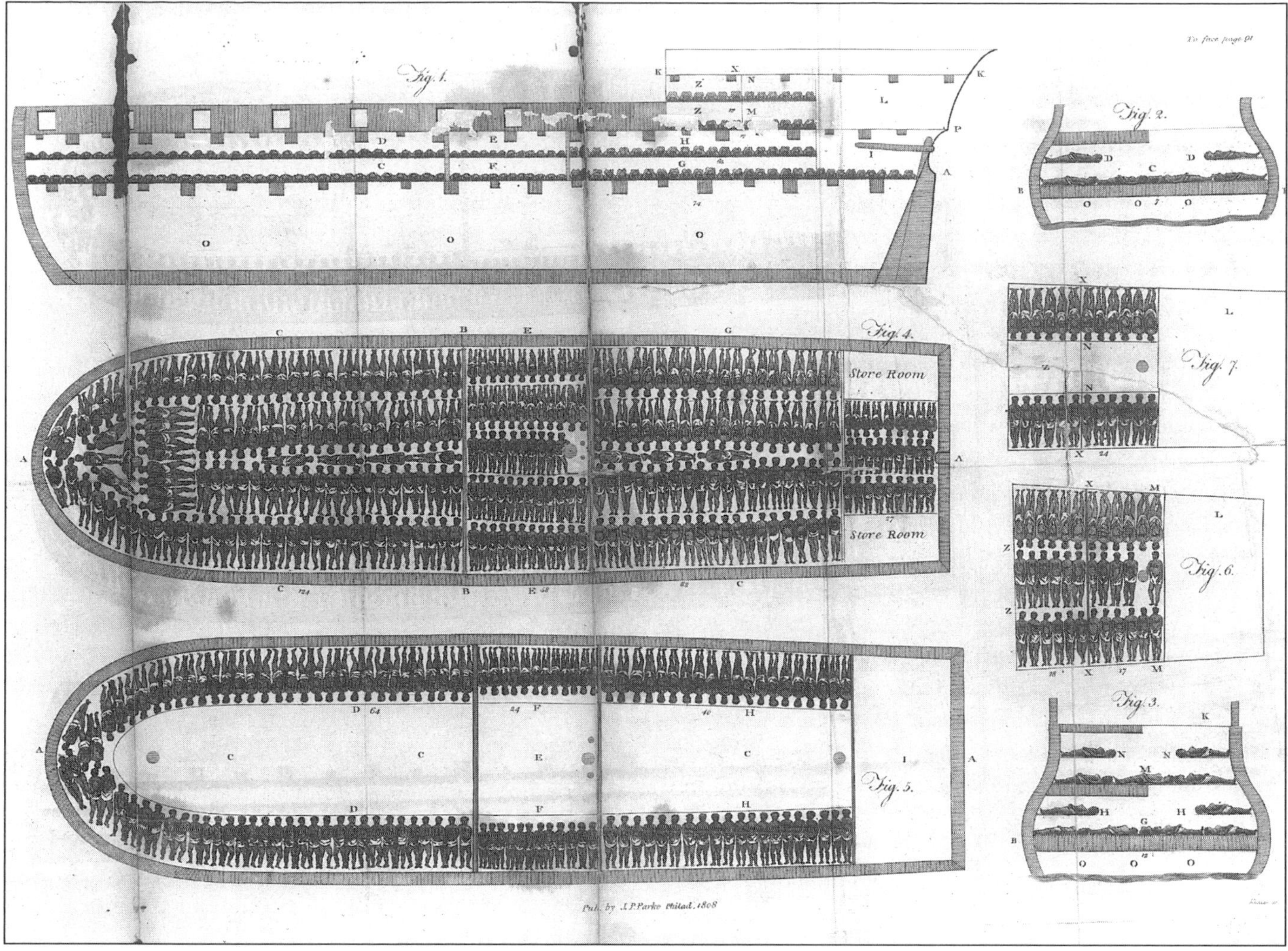

This drawing of a slave ship from 1808 illustrates the conditions under which slaves were transported to the New World.

the largest slave insurrection in the history of the United States. It may have been led by a free mulatto refugee from the Haitian Revolution, suggesting the influence of revolutionary ideas on the rebellion. Before the insurgent slaves reached New Orleans they were met and routed by a combined force of Louisiana militia and U.S. troops under Gen. Wade Hampton. More than sixty slaves were killed in the military encounter, and eighteen more were captured, tried, and executed; two whites are known to have died in the rebellion. An unknown number of enslaved people were killed by whites in a frenzied response to the uprising.

In 1822 a free black carpenter named Denmark Vesey led a complex conspiracy in Charleston, South Carolina. Vesey had been born into slavery but bought his freedom with money won in a lottery. Vesey's conspiracy brought together Gullah-speaking slaves from the rice parishes outside Charleston and assimilated slaves from the city itself. It melded religious traditions from the countryside with the gospel preached in Charleston's African Methodist Episcopal Church. Vesey spoke of his experiences as a mariner in the black republic of Haiti and of congressional debates over the admission of Missouri into the union as a slave state. After taking the city, Vesey and his followers planned to call supporters from the rice parishes to their banner and bring slavery to an end in the state. If they proved unable to hold the city, Vesey planned to seize ships in Charleston's harbor and escape with his followers to Haiti. Like Gabriel's, Vesey's conspiracy was betrayed before the rebellion occurred. White South Carolinians tried more than a hundred alleged conspirators, convicted forty-nine, and hanged thirty-seven. They also closed down Charleston's African Methodist Episcopal Church and, in the wake of the conspiracy, became more convinced of the need to take drastic steps to protect the institution of slavery in the United States.

The most famous slave revolt in the history of the United States was that led by Nat Turner in Southampton County,

Virginia, during the summer of 1831. Turner was a religious visionary who heard God calling him to lead his people in a battle to overthrow slavery. Unlike Gabriel and Vesey, Turner kept his plans secret from all but a small group of followers. On August 21 he and five followers began attacking plantation houses, killing the white inhabitants and recruiting the slaves. Perhaps as many as seventy slaves joined Turner's rebellion and killed at least fifty-seven white Virginians before the Virginia militia dispersed them. Forty-five slaves were tried for participating in Turner's rebellion, and eighteen were hanged. Many more enslaved Virginians were killed in a savage vigilante response to the rebellion. Turner escaped capture for about a month before being arrested and hanged. While awaiting execution he dictated his *Confessions,* which immediately became a bestseller and remains widely read. In it Turner revealed his powerful belief that God had ordained that the slaves should be free.

PATTERNS OF VIOLENT RESISTANCE TO SLAVERY

The prominence of these four insurrectionary events should not obscure the patterns of resistance out of which they arose. Scholars have documented a rich tradition of day-to-day insurgency that ranged from work slowdowns and feigned illness to sabotage of agricultural implements and suicide. Many occurrences of violent resistance did not rise to the level of major rebellions but created the contexts within which the larger slave revolts arose. Such individual acts included fighting back when whipped, secret attempts to poison masters, and isolated violence against masters, overseers, or other white southerners. More significant to the traditions of collective violent resistance that helped fuel slave revolts, however, were the innumerable insurrectionary scares and single-plantation uprisings that occurred throughout the southern states.

It is impossible to know how often enslaved people spoke seriously about organizing slave revolts. Herbert Aptheker, who has made the only systematic attempt to count all such incidents, found hundreds scattered through the southern records, with many scares in every state that had large numbers of slaves. Much of the evidence surrounding these scares is ambiguous, making it difficult to distinguish slave activism from planter fear. Some scholars have argued, in fact, that collectively the events tell more about white anxiety than black resistance. Nonetheless, the frequency of scares shows that southern slaves spoke often of rebellion, that they moved from talk to preliminary organization with some frequency, and that white southerners realized such activity was taking place and feared it.

Those traditions of resistance, although they only rarely culminated in large-scale revolts, kept the possibility of slave revolution alive despite the manifestly unfavorable conditions that existed in the south. They surely helped perpetuate the rhetoric of Christian revolutionary equality that suffused at least three of the four major events, and they help explain why, over the course of the Civil War, about one-fifth of the black men of military age who lived in the United States joined the Union armies to fight against their masters and for freedom. The Civil War broadened American citizenship by enabling black Americans to fight for their natural rights without rebelling against the republic.

See also *Haitian Revolution of Independence (1791–1804); Inequality; Injustice; Latin American and Caribbean Slave Revolts (1521–1888); L'Ouverture, François-Dominique Toussaint; Race; Rights.*

James Sidbury

BIBLIOGRAPHY

Aptheker, Herbert. *American Slave Revolts.* 5th ed. New York: International Publishers, 1987.

Dillon, Merton L. *Slavery Attacked: Southern Slaves and Their Allies, 1619–1865.* Baton Rouge and London: Louisiana State University Press, 1990.

Egerton, Douglas R. *Gabriel's Rebellion: The Virginia Slave Conspiracies of 1800 and 1802.* Chapel Hill: University of North Carolina Press, 1993.

Frey, Sylvia R. *Water From the Rock: Black Resistance in a Revolutionary Age.* Princeton, N.J.: Princeton University Press, 1991.

Genovese, Eugene D. *From Rebellion to Revolution: Afro-American Slave Revolts in the Making of the Modern World.* Baton Rouge: Louisiana State University Press, 1979.

Jordan, Winthrop D. *Tumult and Silence at Second Creek: An Inquiry into a Civil War Slave Conspiracy.* 2d ed. Baton Rouge: Louisiana State University Press, 1996.

Quarles, Benjamin. *The Negro in the American Revolution.* New York: Norton, 1973.

Sidbury, James. *Ploughshares into Swords: Race, Rebellion, and Identity in Gabriel's Virginia, 1730–1810.* Cambridge: Cambridge University Press, 1997.

VENEZUELAN DEMOCRATIC REVOLUTION (1945–1958)

What Venezuelans call their "democratic revolution" between 1945 and 1946 was not a revolution in any conventional sense. It involved a series of political conflicts and irregular changes in government, reflecting socioeconomic changes resulting from petroleum-led development prior to democracy. Although it did not greatly alter the size or power of the state, this development eventually changed Venezuela's form of government from long-standing military rule to democracy, and it encouraged new modes of representation that persist even today.

Venezuela's "real" revolution occurred during the independence wars against Spain (1811–1820) and the decades of disorder that followed. As the central force of Latin America's continental civil war, Simón Bolívar's armies thrust the country into the world spotlight—albeit at a considerable price. Venezuela lost close to 40 percent of its population, suffered enormous damage to its agricultural properties, and saw almost all vestiges of the Spanish colonial bureaucratic system destroyed. From the end of the independence wars and through the federal wars (1858–1869), the country experienced a wrenching social revolution in which the white and privileged classes virtually disappeared, even though the landowning structure of coffee production remained mostly intact. *Caudillismo,* a set of political rules based entirely on force, was the norm, and war remained the means of access to government.

The situation changed in 1899 when military rulers from the Andean region (called the Grupo Tachira) began a half-century of more orderly political domination, culminating in the dictatorial rule of Juan Vincente Gómez (1908–1935), a farmer who had never seen Caracas, the capital, until he was forty-two. Military officers governed Venezuela through World War II—with the support of their powerful neighbor, the United States.

ECONOMIC REVOLUTION

If war was the expression of social revolution, the arrival of the world's biggest oil companies at the turn of the century represented an economic revolution of sorts. By 1928 oil was the most important source of state revenues. Foreign oil companies transformed Venezuela from a relatively insignificant agricultural exporter to the world's leading oil exporter. Oil revenues profoundly changed the state, creating an unprecedented degree of presidential power and a huge increase in the size and jurisdiction of the public sector.

But if oil fortified the state, it also helped to foment the conditions that would eventually change Venezuela's form of government. As rural properties were rapidly sold to foreign oil companies in the "dance of the concessions," the landowning class was permanently destroyed. A new dominant wealthy class and new urban middle and working classes took its place, based on industrial activities linked to the oil sector. Constrained by the conservatism and repressiveness of the government, these new interests pushed for more economic benefits and political rights, and they began the first protests against military rule. Their dissatisfaction was expressed in a national petroleum workers' strike in 1935 and in the formation of two new political parties, the Partido Communista and Accion Democratica. Soon other civilian political parties—for example, the Christian Democratic Party—also appeared. In this respect, petroleum was the single most important factor in shaping the structural conditions for the breakdown of the country's long-standing military rule and the subsequent democratic revolution.

THE BREAKDOWN OF MILITARY RULE

The vast expansion of oil production set the stage, but cannot explain the timing or shape of regime change. Venezuela's new democracy also owed its origins to changes within the military, the growing maturity of political parties, and astute statecraft on the part of the nation's leaders. The transformation of the military was especially important. Venezuela did not have a modern army until the early 1900s; rather, it was ruled by a conglomeration of armed men and

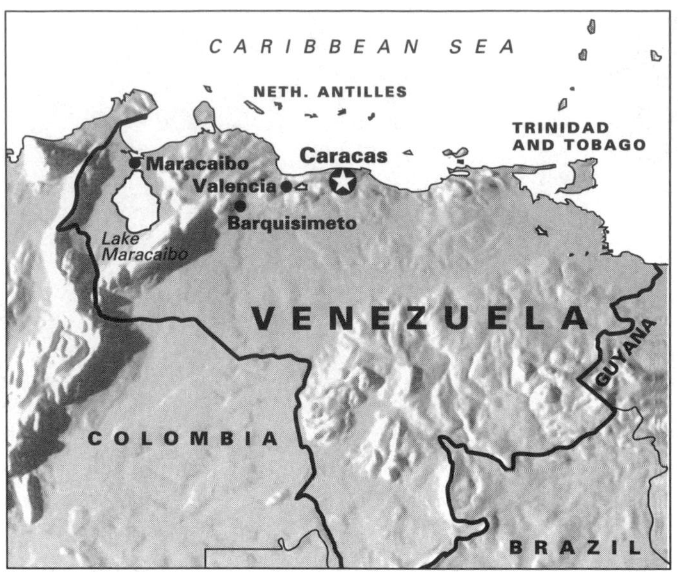

family members loyal to different military leaders. As professionalism grew, it undercut the cronyism of the past. Affected by the democratic idealism and the desire for industrialization that swept the globe during World War II, a secret military society called the Patriotic Military Union began to advocate the end of military rule. In 1945 it led a coup against President (and General) Isaías Medina Angarita and invited Romulo Betancourt, the founder of Accion Democratica, to govern. This government lasted only three years before it too was overthrown by a military coup—provoked in part by the party's efforts to exclude other important political forces. Nevertheless, Accion Democratica's government represented the first civilian rule in Venezuela's history.

When authoritarianism reasserted itself in 1958 under a new leader, Col. Marcos Pérez Jiménez, it did not last long. The coincidence of a political succession crisis within the military and a major economic crisis provided the catalyst for regime change. Rebelling against Pérez Jiménez's extravagant financial policies and corruption, industrialists, labor leaders, and outlawed political party members pressed for reform. They were eventually joined by democratic military officers who fought on the side of the rebels. With the death toll climbing and fears of all-out civil war growing as crowds demanded the end of military rule, Pérez Jiménez fled the country—accompanied by sacks of public monies.

A "PACTED" DEMOCRACY

Civilian rule still might not have been possible had it not been for the statecraft of Accion Democratica's leaders, especially Betancourt. Having learned from the errors of the past, the country's leading political parties negotiated a set of political and economic agreements, called the Pact of Punto Fijo, which established the rules for the new democracy. Based on granting guarantees to the military, leading industrial interests, labor unions, and all parties (except the Communist Party, which was forcefully excluded, despite its role in ending military rule), these pacts set the parameters for the democracy that still exists today. Widely imitated in other transitions to democracy, they brought about both the stability and political reform that was the hallmark of Venezuelan democracy for the next thirty years.

Venezuela's democratic stability has rested heavily on the continued inflow of oil revenues divided among those parties that agreed to the pact. Excluded groups have resorted to low-level, but persistent, guerrilla warfare. The pact and oil money also set the stage for complicity between leading political parties that eventually produced massive corruption and, at the end of the twentieth century, the ongoing erosion of confidence in Venezuela's cherished democracy.

See also *Bolívar, Simón*.

TERRY KARL

BIBLIOGRAPHY

Alexander, Robert. *The Venezuelan Democratic Revolution*. New Brunswick, N.J.: Rutgers University Press, 1964.

Ewell, Judith. *Venezuela: A Century of Change*. Stanford: Stanford University Press, 1984.

Karl, Terry. *The Paradox of Plenty*. Berkeley: University of California Press, 1997.

Martz, John, and David Myers, eds. *Venezuela: The Democratic Experience*. New York: Praeger, 1977.

VIETNAMESE REVOLUTION (1945–1975)

Amid the decolonization winds that swept Asia from the early 1940s, Vietnam became embroiled in a bitter, protracted war with France and then the United States while simultaneously undergoing massive social upheaval. The Vietnamese Revolution began on March 9, 1945, when Japanese army units overthrew the French colonial government that it had permitted to function during most of the Pacific war and allowed Vietnamese nationalists to assume some administrative responsibilities. However, the fledgling regime proved incapable of grappling with a terrible famine already sweeping northern and north-central Vietnam, eventually killing at least one million people, or 10 percent of the population of the region affected. The regime also failed to take advantage of growing disenchantment among the Vietnamese people with established practices and attitudes. Having endured sixty years or more of French rule, and vaguely aware that Japanese fortunes were declining almost everywhere else in Asia, people throughout Vietnam sensed an unparalleled chance to regain national independence and achieve modernity and social justice.

The Indochinese Communist Party (ICP), formed in 1930 but debilitated repeatedly by the colonial authorities, considered the Japanese ouster of the French and escalating Allied battlefield successes as presenting its best opportunity to garner mass support and to prepare to seize power and establish a democratic republic. Its vehicle was the Vietnam Independence League, or Viet Minh, initiated in 1941 as an anticolonial, antifascist united front, but able to attract popular attention only from late 1944. The chief ICP-Viet Minh strategist was Ho Chi Minh, a longtime agent of the Moscow-dominated Communist International (Comintern). But in his new role Ho was applying mass mobilization techniques learned from the Chinese Communist Party and was trying hard to convince the Allies, especially the Americans and some Chinese Nationalist generals, of his sole commitment to liberating his country.

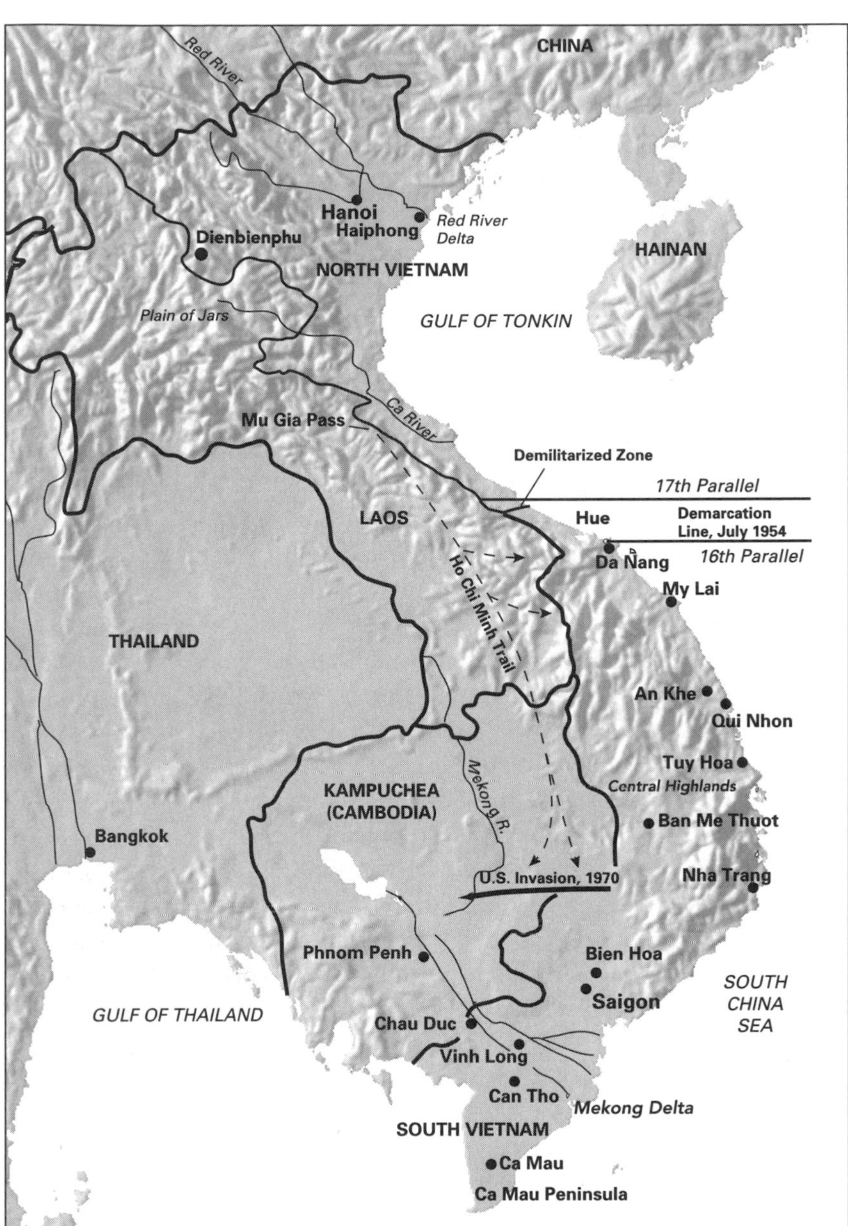

By July 1945 the Viet Minh had established a quasi-government apparatus in six provinces adjacent to China, had begun to receive military training and equipment from the U.S. Office of Strategic Services, and had sent out invitations for Vietnamese luminaries to attend a National People's Congress, scheduled for mid-August. Viet Minh songs, slogans, leaflets, and flags spread throughout the Red River delta in the north and down the central coast of Vietnam. Young men and women of their own volition formed local patriotic associations, printed broadsides, convened meetings, and, where the Japanese army permitted, mounted independence demonstrations. Violent incidents multiplied in some provinces, causing Vietnamese officials and local tax collectors to flee to the towns and cities.

THE OPPORTUNE MOMENT

Within days of Japan's capitulation to the Allies on August 15, Vietnamese crowds were surging through the streets of almost every town and city, occupying administrative bureaus, arming themselves with old French rifles, burning colonial records, arresting alleged traitors, and yelling "independence or death." On August 19 local Viet Minh adherents took control of key facilities, then utilized the telegraph network to convince many provincial officials and civil guard commanders to accept instructions from the new "provisional revolutionary government." Far to the south, in Saigon, a group declaring its allegiance to the Viet Minh took over installations during the night of August 24 and organized a huge, festival-like procession through the city the next day. In the city of Hue, Emperor Bao Dai received a Viet Minh delegation coming from Hanoi, read his abdication edict to a small crowd, and then watched while the royal standard was pulled down slowly and replaced by the yellow star on a red background. In most locations, Japanese army units simply withdrew to their barracks with ample supplies of food to await the arrival of Allied representatives, sometimes donating captured French firearms to eager Vietnamese youths who approached them.

On September 2, before several hundred thousand eager listeners in the Hanoi botanical gardens, Ho Chi Minh read Vietnam's declaration of independence and proclaimed establishment of the Democratic Republic of Vietnam (DRV). In faraway Potsdam, however, the Allies had determined that Chinese Nationalist troops would occupy Indochina north of the sixteenth parallel, and British troops south of that line. The Chinese brought with them anticommunist Vietnamese émigrés but soon decided to accept the DRV as the de facto administration pending negotiations. The British brought French administrators, evicted DRV supporters from government buildings in Saigon, and allowed colonial French soldiers released from Japanese detention to be rearmed. By late September bitter fighting had broken out in Saigon, which spread throughout Cochinchina (the southern third of Vietnam) as well-equipped French regiments arrived from Europe. By January 1946 the British had transferred responsibilities to the French and shifted their troops to other hot spots in Southeast Asia. The United States, having recognized French sovereignty over Indochina, nonetheless continued to issue pious statements about native rights to self-determination.

On March 6, 1946, the Chinese brokered a preliminary accord between France and the DRV in which the DRV agreed to receive fifteen thousand French troops amicably in the north in exchange for formal recognition as a "free state having its own government, parliament, army and finances, and forming a part of the Indochina Federation and French Union." This was the closest that Vietnam came to peaceful decolonization. Within days French officials were interpreting the accord publicly in ways considered entirely unacceptable by the DRV. China, having reached its own agreement with France, withdrew from Indochina like the British and Americans. During the summer of 1946 Ho Chi Minh traveled to Paris to try to resolve differences, but the uncertain French political climate and continued fighting in Cochinchina made a negotiated settlement impossible.

FULL-SCALE CONFLICT

In late November a dispute over customs controls in Haiphong harbor escalated into French naval bombardment of the city, killing as many as six thousand people. Four weeks later, the DRV ordered a nationwide counterattack. Within months, French forces had seized almost all of Vietnam's cities and towns yet were experiencing difficulty pacifying the villages or penetrating the forests. Protracted French discussions with former emperor Bao Dai and diverse noncommunist nationalists produced the State of Vietnam, an avowed alternative to the DRV, although all important decisions continued to be made by the French. In late 1953, aiming to lure DRV general Vo Nguyen Giap into a set piece battle, French commanders committed sixteen thousand troops to the distant valley of Dien Bien Phu. In an unprecedented logistical maneuver, Giap shifted sufficient soldiers, artillery, antiaircraft guns, ammunition, and food 220 kilometers across the mountains of northern Vietnam to be able to isolate, bombard, assault, and finally force the surrender of the entire French garrison in May 1954. Two months later, a new French government took the occasion of an international conference at Geneva to negotiate a cease-fire and troop regroupment formula with a DRV delegation, which was under considerable pressure from Beijing and Moscow to make substantial concessions. French troops withdrew south of the seventeenth parallel, accompanied by almost one million Vietnamese refugees, two-thirds of them Catholic.

Between 1945 and 1954, Vietnam experienced its peak of revolutionary fervor and commitment. Citizens throughout the land joined Viet Minh groups, identified passionately with the DRV flag, anthem, and motto ("Independence, Freedom, Happiness"), and revered the frail, wispy-bearded Ho as national savior. The DRV was transformed from a handful of men issuing edicts to a revolutionary state capable of mobilizing millions of people to achieve explicit anti-imperialist and antifeudal objectives. The People's Army of Vietnam (PAVN) survived early French offensives, patiently constructed combat units from the grassroots upward, expanded the war to Laos and Cambodia, and eventually destroyed the French will to fight.

War and revolution fed upon each other, upsetting the status quo, sparking fear, anticipation, and excitement, idealizing youthful militancy, subjecting every thought and action to the litmus test of patriotism or treason, and making violence commonplace. Local revolutionary committees sometimes ignored DRV directives by seizing the property of landlords, harassing merchants, jailing individuals arbitrarily, extorting heavy financial "contributions" from anyone perceived as having benefited from the colonial system, and prohibiting a range of traditional customs. Particularly flagrant violations of government instructions might result in special investigators being sent to the locality with powers to search, arrest, and punish. However, compliance was achieved more often by persistently explaining to obstreperous local revolutionaries the importance of engaging the vast majority of citizens in united-front activity, while isolating and neutralizing those who refused to go along.

VIETNAM IN THE COLD WAR

The cold war intruded upon the Vietnamese Revolution from 1949, when Chinese communist forces approached the northern frontier, the United States increased its support to France and the nascent Bao Dai regime, and the Vatican promised excommunication for Vietnamese Catholics who continued to pledge allegiance to Ho Chi Minh and the DRV. The ICP stepped up Marxist-Leninist indoctrination efforts dramatically, dispatched personnel to China for Maoist instruction, and in 1951 publicly affirmed leadership over the revolution and the DRV, renaming itself the Vietnam Workers' Party. By this time thousands of intellectuals, students, office clerks, and shopkeepers who had joined Viet Minh groups eagerly in 1945–1946 as patriotic nationalists were gravitating back to French-controlled urban centers, frustrated and disillusioned with the movement's ideological turn. After the 1954 Geneva Accords, many fled south of the seventeenth parallel rather than face Workers' Party and PAVN cadres reentering Hanoi victoriously following eight years of struggle.

As Paris progressively downgraded its Indochina involvement, the United States took up full sponsorship of the fledgling Vietnamese army created by the French, and it bolstered the resolutely anticommunist Ngo Dinh Diem in his endeavors to build a new Republic of Vietnam (RVN) with its capital in Saigon. Diem intended to mount a nationalist revolution that would inoculate his citizens from further communist blandishments, but he proceeded to alienate key religious, political, and intellectual groups one after another, leaving his regime dependent on Catholic refugees, landlords, and Washington for survival. In 1963, dissatisfied at Diem's lack of progress in quelling the renewed communist-led insurgency and politically embarrassed by his violent suppression of Buddhist demonstrators, President John F. Kennedy backed a military coup that resulted in the killing of Diem and his younger brother. By early 1965 President Lyndon B. Johnson felt it necessary to commit American combat forces to South Vietnam, while Hanoi also sent combat regiments down the laboriously crafted Ho Chi Minh Trail to bolster the National Front for the Liberation of South Vietnam (NFLSVN). As the fighting escalated, millions of people were forced to flee the countryside and survive in refugee camps and shantytowns, altering southern society dramatically.

Since 1954 the Workers' Party Politburo had been equally committed to engineering a socialist revolution north of the seventeenth parallel, to include: a violent land redistribution inspired by recent Chinese precedents, the creation of agricultural cooperatives, rapid industrialization with Soviet assistance, a Stalinist command economy, and ruthless suppression of any internal dissent. In particular, the 1954–1956 "land reform" campaigns eliminated landlords as a class but left a legacy of injustice and rancor that hung over northern society for decades. By the early 1960s it was apparent to some Hanoi leaders that socialist expectations far exceeded results, suggesting the need for confidential reassessment. However, Politburo decisions to escalate the armed struggle in the south had the effect of freezing policies in the north for another fifteen years. The impressive revolutionary apparatus and behavioral patterns built up since 1945 were used to recruit, train, and dispatch hundreds of thousands of peasant soldiers to fight and often die far from home, while their families endured American bombings, worked long hours, and lived on bare minimum rations.

The NFLSVN-PAVN Tet Offensive (1968) convinced President Johnson not to stand for reelection and to order a partial bombing halt over northern Vietnam, but diplomatic negotiations stalled over Washington's insistence that PAVN units withdraw from the south. In 1969 President Richard M. Nixon began reducing American troop numbers in the name of "Vietnamization" of the conflict. The January 1973 Paris Peace Accords traded complete withdrawal of U.S. troops for the return of American POWs and the continued functioning of two separate administrations in the south pending further negotiations, which never got off the ground. In early 1975 Hanoi launched a massive military offensive, President Gerald Ford decided not to send U.S. aircraft back over Vietnam to counter it, the RVN collapsed quickly, and PAVN tanks bashed down the gate of Saigon's presidential palace on April 30. Proposals within the Workers' Party to maintain separate northern and southern administrations and economic systems for a transitional period were quashed. In 1976 the unified Socialist Republic of Vietnam was proclaimed, and the Workers' Party renamed itself the Vietnam Communist Party. Revolutionary rhetoric persisted, but the élan and mass momentum were history.

DAVID G. MARR

BIBLIOGRAPHY

Duiker, William J. *The Communist Road to Power in Vietnam.* Boulder, Colo.: Westview Press, 1981.

Kahin, George McTurnan. *Intervention: How America Became Involved in Vietnam.* New York: Knopf, 1986.

Kolko, Gabriel. *Vietnam: Anatomy of a War, 1940–1975.* London: Unwin Paperback, 1987.

Marr, David G. *Vietnam 1945: The Quest for Power.* Berkeley: University of California Press, 1995.

Nguyen Khac Vien. *Tradition and Revolution in Vietnam.* Berkeley: Indochina Resource Center, 1974.

Turley, William S. *The Second Indochina War: A Short Political and Military History, 1954–1975.* Boulder, Colo.: Westview Press, 1986.

Vo Nguyen Giap. *Unforgettable Days.* Hanoi: Foreign Languages Publishing House, 1975.

VIOLENCE

Political revolutions need not include violence, but the more fundamental the political and social change advocated by the forces of revolution, the greater the likelihood that violence will play a role in the revolutionary struggle and the larger that role will be.

THE EXCEPTION OF NONVIOLENT REVOLUTIONS

Revolutions in which the use or threat of violence is *not* an integral part of the revolutionary process are most unusual and generally occur in societies that have high levels of social and cultural cohesion and accepted political mechanisms for implementing and accommodating change. The Jacksonian revolution in American politics of the 1820s is a classic example of nonviolent revolution. The violent European upheavals of the 1830s and 1840s, which were triggered by the same basic aspirations within a similar cultural and socioeconomic milieu, stand in stark contrast to the American case. The primary difference was the accepted legitimacy of the American constitutional process.

Revolutions in which the threat of violence is present but not realized and in which there is no accepted mechanism for peaceful change are almost equally unusual. Such revolutions tend to be the product of transient circumstances, the most common of which is removal of the threat of external military intervention in support of the government. Examples include Norway's throwing off of Swedish rule in 1905 and the "velvet revolutions" of 1989–1991 that brought down the communist regimes of Czechoslovakia, Hungary, and East Germany. In the former case, Swedish military intervention met with no resistance. The economic and political stakes were sufficiently small, however, and the intervention sufficiently unpopular, that the Swedes withdrew. In the velvet revolutions the removal of the threat of military intervention by Soviet leader Mikhail Gorbachev left the tiny Czech, Hungarian, and East German communist ruling elites with no option but to relinquish power peacefully. Their decisions to do so were surely driven, at least in the Hungarian and East German cases, by memories of the violent anticommunist uprisings of 1956.

THE USES OF VIOLENCE

The uses of violence in political revolutions are many and varied. At the most basic level, overt military force may be used to seize power or to suppress revolutionary activity. More subtly, governments may use war as a means of bolstering popular support; the classic examples are the French National Assembly's April 1792 declaration of war on Austria and Chancellor Otto von Bismarck's use of war to achieve German unification (1864–1870). Many attempts to replicate the success of those examples have met with failure, however, such as Greece's attempted annexation of Cyprus in 1974 and Argentina's invasion of the Malvinas (Falkland) Islands in 1982, two cases in which military failure led ultimately to the regime's overthrow.

Attempts to suppress revolution by external military intervention have a checkered history. On the one hand stand the successful suppression of Polish independence in the 1760s and 1830s by Prussia, Austria, and Russia; Russia's use of force against the 1848 uprisings in Habsburg Austria; Austria's prevention of Italian unification during the same period; and Britain's success against communist-led guerrillas in Malaya (1948–1960). On the other hand, we must count the failures of British intervention in North America (1773–1782); Austrian and Prussian intervention in France (1792–1795); Allied intervention in Russia (1918–1919); French and Dutch intervention to maintain control over Vietnam and Indonesia following World War II; and Russia's decade-long war against guerrillas in Afghanistan (1979–1989).

Revolutionary movements too weak to mount a direct military challenge to the ruling authorities may use assassination to eliminate key enemies, to intimidate and demoralize opponents, and to encourage their supporters. They may use kidnapping for the same purposes, as well as to raise funds. Finally, they may use terrorist attacks to delegitimize the government and to provoke reprisals, thereby forcing the uncommitted to choose sides. Authoritarian and revolutionary regimes frequently use widespread incarceration to silence and cow political opposition; this may be combined with the murder and "disappearance" of prisoners, as in the "dirty wars" of the 1970s and 1980s in Latin America. Revolutionary and counterrevolutionary forces alike can use torture to sow terror and demoralization and to obtain information. More subtly, authoritarian regimes may condone or encourage mob violence against unpopular groups, typically ethnic minorities regarded as economically predatory, to provide a "safety valve" for popular frustrations and to bolster the regime's popularity. Examples include pogroms against Jews in tsarist Russia and mob attacks on Chinese-owned shops in Suharto's Indonesia.

Conversely, nonviolent demonstrations can be used to draw a violent official response that will elicit sympathy and bestow moral legitimacy. Classic examples are Mohandas Karamchand Gandhi's tactics of nonviolent noncooperation against British rule in India and those used by the U.S. civil rights movement to secure rights for African-Americans in the South during the 1950s and 1960s. In both cases success depended on the exercise of a degree of restraint by the ruling authorities. In the former case, the promoters of nonviolence were not able to prevent others from pursuing the same political goals by violent means.

THEORIES OF VIOLENCE IN REVOLUTION

The most influential theories of the relationship between violence and revolution emerged from Karl Marx's critique of revolutionary failure in Europe from 1848 to 1871. Vladimir Ilyich Lenin and Leon Trotsky developed that critique into a political program during the Russian Revolution of 1917. The most fully articulated theories of revolutionary war are Mao Zedong's *Guerrilla Warfare* (1937); its subsequent adaptation to Latin American conditions by Ernesto "Che" Guevara; and its development by the Indochinese Communist Party under Ho Chi Minh into a comprehensive, albeit culture-specific, theory of political and military struggle.

Counterrevolutionary theories tend to be more pragmatic. The rural pacification methods developed by French and British military leaders to combat communist-led insurgencies in Indochina and Malaya in the 1940s and 1950s were later applied by the American military in Vietnam and in Latin America. The theories of French colonel Roger Trinquier, developed in imitation of communist methods in Indochina, were applied in an urban setting in the 1957 Battle of Algiers. There, unrestrained force, including the widespread use of torture, exposed and destroyed the Algerian National Liberation Front's underground organization but produced a backlash in national and international public opinion that forced France to grant Algeria independence.

See also *Algerian Revolution (1954–1962); Chinese Communist Revolution (1921–1949); Czechoslovak "Velvet Revolution" and "Divorce" (1989–1993); European Revolutions of 1830; European Revolutions of 1848; Gandhi, Mahatma; Guerrilla Warfare; Guevara, Ernesto "Che"; King, Martin Luther, Jr.; Mao Zedong; Terrorism; U.S. Civil Rights Movement (1954–1968).*

JOHN F. GUILMARTIN JR.

BIBLIOGRAPHY

Atkinson, Alexander. *Social Order and the General Theory of Strategy.* London: Routledge and Kegan Paul, 1981.

Mao Zedong. *Mao Tse-Tung on Guerrilla Warfare.* Translated by Samuel B. Griffith. New York: Praeger, 1961.

Shy, John, and Thomas W. Collier. "Revolutionary War." In *Makers of Modern Strategy from Machiavelli to the Nuclear Age.* Edited by Peter Paret. Princeton, N.J.: Princeton University Press, 1986.

Thompson, Robert. *Defeating Communist Insurgency: The Lessons of Malaya and Vietnam.* New York: Praeger, 1966.

Trinquier, Roger. *Modern Warfare: A French View of Counterinsurgency.* Translated by Daniel Lee. New York: Praeger, 1961.

WALESA, LECH

Walesa (1943–) was a charismatic leader of a social movement known as Solidarity, which attracted millions of adherents in Poland in 1980. He continued to nurture and preserve Solidarity's spirit despite fierce repression until 1989, when he seized and created opportunities that brought the rule of the Communist Party in Poland to an end. Walesa was lionized in the world media for effectively defying the Soviet Union's dominion over Eastern Europe and contributing to the demise of Soviet communism at large. Certainly, he worked in tune with broader historical forces, and he was not alone. But his agency was of great significance.

Walesa was born into a peasant family in central Poland. He completed a vocational education and, after compulsory military service, found employment as an electrician at the Lenin Shipyards in Gdańsk. Three years after his arrival in Gdańsk, food riots broke out in December 1970. Street demonstrations by shipyard workers were brutally repressed, and several dozen protesters were killed by security forces. He was driven into social activism by the memory of these events.

In the late 1970s Walesa ran afoul of the authorities by joining a group of early advocates of independent labor unions on the Baltic coast. He was dismissed from his job, and when the August 1980 strike broke out in the shipyards, he had to "jump over the wall" in order to join it. Walesa at once established himself as a leader of the strike. He had a formidable stage presence when addressing large audiences, and he was a persistent, tough negotiator, with a brilliant sense for public relations. During the two-week-long strike of August, Walesa catapulted himself to worldwide fame.

Solidarity, an independent labor union, was established at the conclusion of the August strike. Within two months a majority of all working men and women in Poland had joined Solidarity. Walesa presided over this vast social movement for the next sixteen months. After the government of Gen. Wojciech Jaruzelski imposed martial law on December 13, 1981, and banned Solidarity, Walesa was held in isolation for over a year. Upon release the security police kept him under close surveillance. But Walesa remained in the public eye—as when he received the Nobel Peace Prize in 1983, for example—and he kept in touch with the clandestine structures of Solidarity.

When a new wave of strikes erupted in the summer of 1988, General Jaruzelski balked at Walesa's demand for relegalization of the labor union. The issue was forced, however, after the leader of government-sponsored labor unions, Alfred Miodowicz, challenged Walesa to a television debate. With the whole country watching the debate, Walesa restored Solidarity to its role of unquestionable mouthpiece for the working people of Poland.

In the spring of 1989 roundtable negotiations between the government and opposition leaders concluded with the relegalization of Solidarity. In return, the union reluctantly agreed to put up candidates in the forthcoming parliamentary elections, thereby lending token legitimacy to the regime. Fearing co-optation, Walesa chose not to run. Electoral support for Solidarity in June 1989 exceeded the most optimistic expectations. In September a Solidarity-sponsored candidate, Tadeusz Mazowiecki, became prime minister. Ironically, the success of Solidarity in ending Communist Party rule in Poland put Walesa on the sidelines.

Walesa grew increasingly impatient with what he perceived to be his former associates' slow pace of reform. But Walesa, as chairman of just a labor union, lacked a suitable base for participating in the process. He engaged in petty quarrels and instigated conflicts until he got himself elected as the country's president in 1990. By then he was perceived as responsible for deep rifts among Solidarity activists-cum-politicians.

The four years of his presidency were uninspiring. The carelessness and internal contradictions of his public pronouncements became proverbial. He played personal favorites; promoted his former chauffeur to the most important position of minister of state in presidential chancellery;

Lech Walesa

and kept changing his entourage in a capricious game of musical chairs. He acquired the reputation of a spoiler, able to undermine any initiative but incapable of constructive collaboration with others. In the end, he brought upon himself the indignity of losing a reelection bid in 1995 to a former second-tier Communist politician, Aleksander Kwaśniewski. Walesa accepted the voters' verdict with dignity.

Following the September 1997 parliamentary elections (in which he was not a candidate for office), he established the Christian Democratic Party of the Third Polish Republic, planning to attract "some of the 52 percent of eligible voters who did not participate in the 1997 elections." Thus, a great, charismatic movement leader and a mediocre, lackluster statesman, Walesa embarked on a new career as a party politician going after hearts and minds of a silent majority.

See also *Polish Protest Movements and Solidarity Revolution (1956–1991)*.

JAN T. GROSS

BIBLIOGRAPHY

Boyes, Roger. *The Naked President. A Political Life of Lech Walesa.* London: Secker and Warburg, 1994.

Walesa, Lech. *The Struggle and the Triumph: An Autobiography.* New York: Arcade, 1992.

WAR

Revolution and war have been closely connected throughout history. Both are violent forms of social competition motivated by specific political aims. In a revolution, the goal is the overthrow of an existing regime and its replacement by a new order based on fundamentally different political principles. In a war, the goal is to defeat the military forces of a rival state and impose a favorable political settlement. Revolutions and wars affect the distribution of power among states, lead to new political alignments, and create new forms of political legitimacy. Not surprisingly, therefore, both are critical to the history of individual nations and are watersheds in the international system.

The relationship between revolution and war is Janus-faced. War is sometimes the midwife of revolution, and revolution is usually a powerful cause of war. The outbreak of war can alter the course of a revolution that is already under way, and revolutions can change the nature of military power and shape the course and outcome of war. Because revolutions cause wars and wars beget revolutions, and because each affects how the other evolves, neither phenomenon can be fully understood in isolation from the other.

DOES WAR CAUSE REVOLUTION?

As a number of scholars have observed, war can be a powerful precipitant of revolution. Charles II's failed expedition to Scotland in 1639–1640 helped trigger the Puritan revolution in England, and France's involvement in the War of American Independence exacerbated the fiscal problems that eventually launched the French Revolution. Russia's defeat in the Russo-Japanese war shook the tsarist regime in 1905, and the protracted bloodletting of World War I eventually toppled the Romanov dynasty and brought the Bolsheviks to power. The German, Austro-Hungarian, and Ottoman Empires were all overthrown after the Allies defeated them in 1918, and the Sino-Japanese War that began in 1931 exposed the weaknesses of the Nationalist government in China and gave the Chinese Communist Party the opportunity it needed.

Why does war cause revolution? Involvement in war strains society enormously and forces governments to extract additional resources from their populations. Discontent is more likely to arise under such circumstances, particularly when the war is long and prospects for victory are slim. Wars also force rulers to place more of their citizenry under arms, thereby reducing their own monopoly over the means of violence and creating greater demands for a share of political power. And defeat in war will cast doubt on the wisdom of the current rulers, call the legitimacy of existing institutions into question, and enhance the appeal of potential challengers. Perhaps most important of all, a losing war will undermine the loyalty and morale of the armed forces, thereby weakening the main defense against armed insurrection and leading in some cases to sudden and catastrophic defections. For all of these reasons, therefore, defeat in war has frequently been seen as a powerful cause of revolution.

Such an inference should be made with some caution, however. Although a number of past wars did trigger major political upheavals, most wars do not. For example, the bloody struggle between Iran and Iraq in the 1980s did not lead to a revolt against either regime, and Saddam Husayn did not face serious opposition following Iraq's costly and ignominious defeat in the 1991 Persian Gulf War. Thus, defeat in war is clearly not a sufficient condition for revolution. Nor is it a necessary condition either, given the number of revolutions that have occurred in states that were not involved in war and that did not face a major external challenge. Mexico had been at peace for decades before the 1910 revolution, and Iran enjoyed an equally benign environment in the years leading to the ouster of the shah. War played no direct role in the origins of the Cuban, Nicaraguan, or American Revolutions either, casting further doubt on the claim that it is inevitably associated with the outbreak of revolution.

DOES REVOLUTION CAUSE WAR?

Although war is at best an erratic cause of revolution, revolutions are a powerful cause of international conflict and war. Revolutions almost always increase the level of security competition among states and raise the probability of war, and they often lead directly to all-out war itself. Thus, the Angolan, Chinese, English, Ethiopian, French, Iranian, Korean, Nicaraguan, and Russian Revolutions all led to major clashes between the new regime and one or more foreign powers, and war also followed the revolutionary unification of Italy in the 1850s, the creation of Israel in 1948, and the Egyptian Revolution of 1952. Although war did not occur after the American, Turkish, Cuban, and Mexican Revolutions, strong pressures for war were present in each case, and these new regimes stood at the brink of war at least once in the immediate aftermath of the revolution.

The close connection between revolution and war is the result of several interrelated and mutually reinforcing causes. Revolutions alter the balance of power among states, creating windows of opportunity that may be difficult for foreign powers to resist. Revolutions also bring to power groups that are strongly opposed to the policies of the old regime. Their ascendance will create new conflicts of interest with other powers, and especially with the allies of the old regime. And revolutionary movements are usually infused with an ideology that depicts opponents as intrinsically hostile, regards victory as inevitable, and tends to see their own struggle as a model for others. Thus, many French radicals saw the European aristocracy as intrinsically hostile to the revolution in France and believed that the outbreak of war in 1792 would spark a wave of sympathetic upheavals throughout Europe. The Bolsheviks generally believed that their triumph in Russia was merely the first step in the inevitable triumph of socialism, and Mao Zedong regarded capitalist imperialism as a paper tiger that was irrevocably hostile but doomed to collapse. In the same way, the Iranian revolutionaries saw the United States as the Great Satan, viewed other great powers with nearly equal suspicion, and believed that their success in Iran would soon lead to similar revolutions elsewhere in the Islamic world.

These ideological beliefs are useful in convincing supporters to risk their lives for the sake of the revolution, but they can be misleading and dangerous when the struggle for power is over. Typical revolutionary ideology tends to make the new rulers more suspicious of others and inclined to export the revolution beyond their borders. These same beliefs will also encourage other states to see the new regime as inherently aggressive and will fuel their own fears that the revolution is likely to spread. The result is a paradoxical combination of insecurity and overconfidence: both sides tend to see the other as hostile and dangerous but also as fragile and vulnerable. These perceptions make the use of force seem especially attractive: force is needed because the other side is an imminent threat, and force will work because the opponent is likely to collapse if challenged.

The enormous uncertainty that normally accompanies a revolution compounds these perceptions. Calculating the balance of power is more difficult after a revolution because no one can know in advance how effective the new system of government will be at mobilizing its society. Existing channels of communication will often be disrupted, and the efforts of counterrevolutionary émigrés or prorevolutionary sympathizers to rally support for their own struggles will further pollute each side's efforts to gauge the intentions and capabilities of the other side. Émigrés who have fled the revolution will portray the new regime as hostile yet vulnerable to persuade other states to aid their efforts to regain power. And foreigners who are sympathetic to the revolution will portray their home countries as ripe for a similar upheaval to entice the new regime to aid their cause. Not only will such testimony fuel each side's sense of fear and overconfidence, but the activities of these opposing groups are also likely to reinforce the impression that each side is actively trying to overthrow the other.

For all these reasons, major revolutions exacerbate preoccupations over security and raise the likelihood of war between states. Ironically, the pressure for war produced by a revolution results from two parallel myths: the belief that the revolution will spread rapidly if it is not strangled in its crib and the belief that such a reversal will be easy to accomplish. Yet as the history of most postrevolutionary wars reveals, the normal result is neither a swift tide of revolutionary contagion nor the quick and easy ouster of the new regime. Instead, the more frequent result is a protracted struggle between the unexpectedly resilient revolutionary regime and its surprisingly impervious opponents.

WAR AND THE CONDUCT OF REVOLUTION

War and revolution are connected in another way as well. The outbreak of war often alters the course of a given revolution, and in ways that the protagonists rarely anticipate. Louis XVI was still on his throne when war was declared in 1792, and the ensuing conflict soon led to the dissolution of the monarchy, to Louis's own execution, and eventually to the Committee on Public Safety and the Reign of Terror. Had war been averted, however, what we now think of as the French Revolution might have been a much more modest affair. In the same way the Iraqi invasion of Iran in 1980 was critical in driving the Islamic revolution in more extreme directions and resulted in the ouster of several secular leaders, the violent repression of potential opponents, and the consolidation of clerical rule. By contrast, the Turkish, American, and Mexican Revolutions yielded more moderate outcomes in part because these states avoided major wars in the years immediately after the revolution. Involvement in war can also affect the course and outcome of a revolution that begins for other reasons.

The pressures of international competition and the omnipresent possibility of war will also shape the subsequent evolution of a revolutionary regime. Although revolutionary states often proclaim ambitious international objectives, the need to survive usually compels them to moderate their behavior—and occasionally their rhetoric—over time. Thus, Soviet Russia gradually recognized that world revolution was not imminent and began to cooperate with capitalist powers when it was in its interest to do so. Similarly, although Iran's revolutionary leaders began by advocating isolation and the export of revolution, they eventually concluded that a failure to develop close relations with other states was counterproductive. As Ayatollah Ruhollah Khomeini later remarked, a policy of isolation would mean defeat in the end, and Iranian foreign minister Ali Akbar Velayati warned that Iran would have no say in decisions on important issues if it did not take part in the world scene. Although revolutionary states often cling to their original ideological visions—for example, the Soviet Union did not publicly abandon the goal of world revolution until the mid-1980s—external pressures encourage both tactical compromises and a gradual lessening of revolutionary fervor.

REVOLUTION AND THE CONDUCT OF WAR

War shapes the course of revolutions, and revolutions can alter the outcome of wars. A revolution may take one or more states out of an existing conflict (as the Russian Revolution of 1917 took Russia out of World War I), thereby altering the distribution of power and forcing other states to rethink their strategies. Revolutions also affect the nature of war itself by creating rapid and unpredictable shifts in the military potential of different societies.

In general, the damage and disorganization a revolution induces tend to weaken a state in the short term. The new authorities will usually lack the capacity to mobilize social resources, and the armed forces will be severely disrupted (if they have not collapsed completely). Weakness at the center will tempt dissident groups to rebel, increasing the challenges the new rulers face and further reducing their ability to deal with external challenges.

Over time, however, revolutions often lead to dramatic increases in state power. By definition, successful revolutionary organizations are good at mobilizing social power and adept at encouraging individual sacrifices, and men like Vladimir Ilyich Lenin, Mao, Khomeini, or Fidel Castro are ruthless and gifted political leaders. Conflicts with a foreign power often allow revolutionary leaders to invoke the power of nationalism, reinforcing their own ideological appeal with more traditional source of allegiance. Revolutionary states usually dismantle old institutions and replace them with new ones, enabling them to mobilize social power in ways that their predecessors could not.

Political revolutions can also spark a more thoroughgoing revolution in military strategy itself. Emergence of mass armies during the war of the French Revolution provided the raw material for Napoleon's various strategic and tactical innovations and provided a crucial ingredient in France's subsequent imperial expansion. Adoption of Leninist forms of social organization accomplished similar tasks in revolutionary China and in Vietnam and made possible the strategy of protracted war that brought both regimes to power and was a lasting legacy to other national liberation movements.

For all of these reasons, triumphant revolutionary armies often emerge from societies that had previously lagged far behind others. France had suffered a series of defeats under the old regime, and the turmoil produced by the Revolution merely increased its impotence in European politics. By 1794, however, the new regime had begun a course of expansion that would culminate in the Napoleonic empire. And tsarist Russia was defeated by Japan in 1905 and by Germany in 1917, but Soviet Russia emerged from World War II as one of two global superpowers. Prerevolutionary China suffered a century of indignities at the hands of foreign powers; under the revolutionary rule of the Chinese Communist Party, however, China reestablished its territorial authority and gradually reemerged as a major force in world politics.

The tendency for revolutions to yield unexpected military repercussions helps explain why they are such a potent cause of conflict and why postrevolutionary wars usually last longer than either side anticipates. The trials of revolution themselves will make the new regime much stronger than its predecessor, but neither side has any way to know that in advance. The unpredictable effects of revolutionary change explain why opposing states enter such wars confident of easy victory, only to find themselves embroiled in a protracted struggle against formidable adversaries.

Much the same problem occurs in reverse, of course, which is why efforts to export a revolution usually fail. States facing a threatening revolutionary regime will take steps to counter the threat, both by mobilizing their own populations and by taking measures to contain the spread of subversive ideas. As a result, efforts to spread a revolution through contagion or subversion rarely succeed. Although successful revolutions almost always create profound fears of contagion, the real threat arises from a revolution's effect on the state's military potential. In other words, the real danger is not contagion but conquest, and policy makers facing a revolutionary regime should in most cases concentrate on containing direct efforts to expand while eschewing any attempt to overthrow the new government by force.

See also *Chinese Communist Revolution (1921–1949); Civil Wars; Cuban Revolution (1956–1970); French Revolution (1789–1815); German Revolution (1918); Hungarian Revolutions (1918–1919); Iranian Islamic Revolution (1979); Italian Risorgimento (1789–1870); Nicaraguan Revolution (1979); Russian Revolution of 1917; Turkish Revolution (1908–1922).*

STEPHEN WALT

BIBLIOGRAPHY

Adelman, Jonathan. *Revolutions, Armies, and War: A Political History.* Boulder, Colo.: Lynne Rienner, 1985.

Armstrong, David. *Revolution and World Order: The Revolutionary State in International Society.* Oxford: Clarendon Press, 1993.

Blanning, T. C. W. *The Origins of the French Revolutionary Wars.* New York: Longman, 1986.

Chorley, Katherine Anne. *Armies and the Art of Revolution.* London: Faber and Faber, 1943.

Shy, John. "Revolutionary War." In *Makers of Modern Strategy.* Edited by Peter Paret. Princeton, N.J.: Princeton University Press, 1987.

Skocpol, Theda. "Social Revolutions and Mass Military Mobilization." *World Politics* 40 (1988).

Walt, Stephen M. *Revolution and War.* Ithaca, N.Y.: Cornell University Press, 1996.

WASHINGTON, GEORGE

Washington (1732–1799) was a Virginia planter who commanded the American Revolutionary Army and later became the first president of the United States. Unlike many modern revolutionary leaders, Washington displayed no traits of asceticism. He was not culturally alienated from England, the mother country, nor did he suffer from a dysfunctional family. He failed to display narcissistic characteristics in an adult life filled with praise and adulation. Solid, steady, and focused, he brought to the national stage extensive military experience as the commander of Virginia's forces from 1755 to 1758 in the Seven Years' War (1756–1763) and seventeen years' legislative service in his colony. His background, as well as his qualities of persistence and tenacity, made him ideally qualified to lead the eight-year struggle for independence against Great Britain (1775–1783).

In June 1775 the Continental Congress appointed Washington, one of its own members, commander in chief of the colonial forces besieging the British troops in Boston following the battles of Lexington and Concord; he was a man the delegates knew and could trust. Ever deferential to Congress even though it was an extralegal body until near the end of the war, Washington believed fervently in civil control of the military, just as he endeavored to strengthen Congress's hand in dealing with the American states after the declaring of independence in 1776.

Washington preferred to engage Britain in a fairly conservative, traditional form of warfare. He feared that a partisan or guerrilla conflict, although tempting because of wilderness condition in much of America, would spawn atrocities and wholesale destruction of cities and towns, leading to the unraveling of American society and institutions. His army steadily improved after suffering reversals in New York City in 1776 and southeastern Pennsylvania the following year. By the summer of 1778 the major fighting had shifted outside Washington's immediate theater of command to the Southern states. An effective organizer and administrator and an inspirational leader, he held his army together and kept the British in the North largely confined to the vicinity of New York City.

George Washington

In 1781, cooperating with American troops in the South, Washington boldly moved most of his own army to Virginia, where, with French military and naval support, he besieged and captured Lord Cornwallis's army, which effectively ended the struggle in America. His generalship throughout showed a mixture of caution and aggressiveness. But keeping his army—the most meaningful symbol of the Revolution during the war—intact was always his first consideration. His own symbolic importance explains his appointment as president of the Constitutional Convention of 1787.

Washington was the preeminent military and political leader of the Revolution. Both as commander in chief and later as first president under the Constitution, he did not seek power but accepted it reluctantly and then voluntarily stepped down from it. As general and as president, he helped mold the new nation by setting lasting military and constitutional precedents.

See also *American (U.S.) Revolution (1776–1789).*

Don Higginbotham

BIBLIOGRAPHY

Cunliffe, Marcus. *George Washington: Man and Monument.* Boston: Little, Brown, 1958.

Freeman, Douglas S. *George Washington: A Biography.* 7 vols. New York, 1948–1957.

Higginbotham, Don. *George Washington and the American Military Tradition.* Athens, Ga.: University of Georgia Press, 1985.

WILLIAM OF ORANGE (KING WILLIAM III OF ENGLAND)

William Henry, prince of Orange, was born at The Hague in November 1650 and died King William III of England in March 1702. He is most famous for leading the revolution of 1688, in which he replaced his Catholic father-in-law James II as ruler of the British Isles. But he was at least as active in Dutch politics and in European warfare and diplomacy as he was in British affairs.

The rulers of the Dutch Republic, in which William grew up, were most often men of merchant families who were rich enough to devote their lives to politics. Since their successful rebellion against Spain in the 1570s they had established a virtually hereditary oligarchy. The "regents," as the rulers were called, controlled local and provincial administration and kept the central government weak. There were nobles, especially among the diplomats and the army officers, but except for the prince of Orange they had little money or influence. The prince not only was the largest landowner in the United Provinces, as captain-general he was the head of the army, and as *stadhouder,* or governor, of the union and many of its individual provinces he was its leading political figure. He provided what little centralization there was in the system.

In 1650 William II attempted a coup against the great city of Amsterdam, failed, and then died eight days before the birth of his son. In 1651 the regents in a constitutional convention called the Great Assembly took away the offices of the House of Orange, and the boy was brought up almost as a private citizen. This too failed. William the Silent, William Henry's great-grandfather, had been the founder of the republic and its great hero; the family still had immense prestige. The regents were unwilling to keep up the army or the frontier fortifications. When France and England attacked the Dutch in 1672, five of the seven provinces were occupied and the regent party collapsed. William Henry, at age twenty-two, was given the offices of his ancestors and called on to save the republic.

He did save it, substantially freeing the republic in two

William of Orange, King William III of England

years while also leading a political revolution to reestablish the position of his family and his party. The oligarchic scheme did not disappear; pro-Orange regents replaced republican ones, and in time Amsterdam learned to work with the prince if not to like him. William Henry, the grandson of Charles I of England, married his cousin, the English princess Mary, in 1677 and from then on was likely to inherit the English throne. At the least, William might make his Dutch position hereditary; if he became king of England, he might unite the two countries, at Dutch expense.

Yet when he went to lead the English Revolution in 1688 he went with the blessing of Amsterdam. During the ten years between wars (1678–1688) the Protestant Dutch had learned to take the French threat seriously. The English did so too, for after 1685 they had in their Catholic king James II a French client. When Louis XIV of France invaded Germany rather than the Dutch Republic in 1688 William seized his opportunity and, in command of a fleet of almost five hundred ships and an army of some forty thousand men, took England in six weeks with very little bloodshed. France fought back in the Nine Years' War (1688–1697), but she had lost momentum and was to lose both that war and its sequel, the War of the Spanish Succession (1702–1713).

Although England became a great military and economic power during his reign, the royal office grew weaker after the death of his Queen Mary II in 1695, and weaker still on William's own death. In the Dutch Republic the very office of *stadhouder* disappeared for two generations. William was the last king of England to lead its armies in battle or to be in full control of its foreign policy. His reign is noted for a substantial increase in civil liberties; for toleration and freedom of the press; for great architecture, including Hampton Court and Kensington Palace; and for the music of Henry Purcell, the science of Isaac Newton, and the philosophy of John Locke.

See also *British "Glorious Revolution" (1688–1689).*

Stephen B. Baxter

BIBLIOGRAPHY

Baxter, Stephen B. *William III and the Defense of European Liberty.* New York: Harcourt, Brace and World, 1966.

Jones, James R. *The Revolution of 1688 in England.* New York: W.W. Norton, 1972.

WILLIAM THE SILENT

William the Silent, prince of Orange (1533–1584), was the unlikely leader of the Netherlands Revolt. The richest noble in the Netherlands after the unexpected death of a relative made him prince of Orange at age eleven, he enjoyed the special favor of Holy Roman Emperor Charles V and, at first, of his son King Philip II of Spain. In 1555 he took a prominent part in the ceremony transferring power from Charles to Philip, and he helped negotiate the Treaty of Cateau-Cambrésis with France in 1559. Orange next served as the king's *stadhouder,* or chief executive officer, in the provinces of Holland, Zeeland, and Utrecht, where he presided over provincial assemblies, controlled military forces, and made official appointments.

Protestantism, a major cause of discord in the Netherlands, was persecuted vigorously by central government officials. Since many Netherlanders wanted to maintain local privileges, they opposed centralized persecutions and plans for ecclesiastical reform and increased taxation. Until 1564 Orange was careful about expressing his concerns. His political enemy, Antoine Perrenot de Granvelle, called him *le taciturne* ("the silent one").

William's religious views may be described as Erasmian: he preferred freedom of conscience. Born to Lutheran parents, he had been raised as a Roman Catholic at the emperor's insistence and continued to practice Catholicism while married to a Protestant. He thought that rulers could not control the faith of their subjects, but when other nobles conspired against the government in 1565, Orange stood aside. Yet when the opposition turned to violent iconoclasm and revolt and the government resorted to brutal repression in 1566–1567, William belatedly broke with Spanish rule.

After the revolt failed, Orange fled to Germany and resigned his stadhouderships. The Council of Troubles, a special court appointed to punish the rebels, issued a summons for him, seized his lands, and kidnapped his son. From exile Orange organized military campaigns to seek personal justice and liberate the Netherlands, but his land forces were poorly coordinated and had little success until the multiple invasions of 1572. Even then, the rebels' military situation remained weak except in Holland and Zeeland.

In October 1572 the States of Holland, an assembly of delegates from the towns and nobility, chose Orange as *stadhouder* without the king's permission. For four years they held out against Spanish invasions and sieges. William had few resources but popular support from urban regents, lower-middle classes, and Calvinists. Although he lobbied for religious toleration, he nevertheless joined the Calvinist Church. He sought foreign help and exploited Spanish atrocities, blunders, financial crises, and troop mutinies. By 1576 Orange could take advantage of the breakdown of Spanish control and the desire for peace to call a meeting of the States-General, which included delegates from seventeen provinces. The delegates agreed to stop fighting each other and to work together against the Spaniards.

The general union did not last, however. Internal stresses surfaced between strongly Catholic southern provinces and militant Calvinists of the north. Orange's proposals for freedom of worship met opposition from both sides. Meanwhile he had to contend with a formidable Spanish commander, Alexander Farnese. The Spaniards declared the prince an outlaw in 1580 and placed a price on his head. William responded with the *Apology,* a masterpiece of self-justification and political propaganda. He recalled the oaths the sovereign had sworn and listed Philip's violations of traditional privileges. Orange's view of the monarchy as a contract between ruler and ruled legitimized resistance when the sovereign failed in his obligations toward his subjects. He pleaded for Protestant worship to be allowed and declared that he was motivated more by patriotism than personal interest.

Yet Orange's vehemence masked his desperation. He thought the revolt would fail without a foreign prince as sovereign to take the place of Philip II. William's choice, the French duke of Anjou, proved a disappointment, and the military situation deteriorated. In 1584 the States of Holland proposed to offer Orange the title count of Holland so that he might hold power independently, but on July 10, 1584, he was murdered by Balthasar Gérard, a Catholic. But William's death did not end the revolt, which continued until 1609, when Spain agreed to the Twelve Years Truce. For the Dutch, William's death raised him to martyrdom as "father of the fatherland."

See also *Netherlands Revolt (1566–1609).*

MAARTEN ULTEE

BIBLIOGRAPHY

Rowen, Herbert H. *The Princes of Orange: The Stadholders in the Dutch Republic.* Cambridge: Cambridge University Press, 1988.

Swart, Koenraad W. *William the Silent and the Revolt of the Netherlands.* London: Historical Association, 1978.

Wansink, Harm, ed. *The Apologie of Prince William of Orange against the Proclamation of the King of Spaine.* Leiden: E.J. Brill, 1969.

WOMAN'S RIGHTS MOVEMENT

In the early nineteenth-century United States, when the Industrial Revolution began, a married woman's position was not that of a citizen, nor did she have a legal existence. She could not vote, sign contracts in her own name, legally inherit property, control her own wages if she worked outside the home, or have legal custody of her children when her husband died or abandoned her. Outside of the exceptional cases of a few elite women, she had no recourse to divorce from a bad marriage. More oppressed than the colonists who threw off England's abusive power over them with the American Revolution, she was like a serf to a lord in feudalism—tied through indenture for life. She was allowed primary schooling and, if her family had the means, even some seminary education, which was mostly ornamental. Universities were closed to her. If she was a slave, her marriage was likely to not be recognized as valid because she was owned by her master, and her children likewise were the master's property.

By 1848, when Karl Marx called to "Working Men of All Countries, Unite!" in the *Communist Manifesto,* women began to organize their own revolution against even more subservient conditions than those of the exploited laborer. Some women had moved out of the home into factories and teaching, the two fields gradually opening to them, giving them the social space necessary to foment the rebellion the influential Abigail Adams had promised a half century before. Men had moved further because they were not only the only legal heads of household, but they conducted the affairs of business and the state.

Elizabeth Cady Stanton decided to address the wrongs against women and called what has become known as the Seneca Falls Convention of 1848, which adopted a Declaration of Woman's Rights that demanded co-education, legal rights for married women, and the most controversial—the political power of suffrage. Within two years, Susan B. Anthony would join her, and together they would forge a movement for women's self-determination for rights already accorded to men decades before.

Susan B. Anthony (seated in the center) and other leaders of the National Woman's Suffrage Association

In the decade of the 1850s, woman's rights leaders worked closely with both the Temperance and Abolitionist Movements. Those fighting against slavery generally supported and encouraged the struggle for women's rights. The Woman's Rights Movement focused on women as a collectivity, demanding change for them in all conditions of life, eagerly searching to get to the roots or radical causes of women's oppression, fighting to establish women's legal existence with property rights and to gain political power for women.

Women's demands took forms that today would not look revolutionary unless they are understood in terms of women's own historical conditions. For example, by 1848 the Industrial Revolution was well under way with factory systems and the labor exploitation associated with them. One consequence was increased alcoholism among men. The religious temperance movement of that time had approached drunkenness as a moral and religious issue, not a social problem. When women took it over from the men in the 1850s, however, their aim was to address wife abuse that often resulted from drunken husbands. Soon women understood that suppressing the sale of alcohol was not sufficient to control men's power over them.

During the Civil War (1861–1865) women suspended their own movement to campaign for the end of slavery. With the war over and constitutional amendments in place that forbade slavery and granted the right to vote to all *men,* women changed their strategies and focus. They would make political power, particularly suffrage, their primary strategy, having learned that they could not trust men to legislate for them.

The Woman's Rights Movement was fighting two fronts at once. Not only were they demanding their rights, but they were also fighting against time. Women's condition, more like that of feudal serfs, was regressed in time—they entered the public sphere of work with lower wages than men, and it would take decades for them to "catch up" to men in education. They did not win the widespread right to a university education until the late nineteenth century.

Just as the Woman's Rights Movement began to grapple with the depth of resistance against women's freedom at home and in public, the movement split. The split is instructive because it highlights the difference between radicals and reformers. By 1870 Susan B. Anthony had organized a National Woman's Suffrage Association, the aim of which was to secure women's right to vote in the U.S. Constitution. This strategy was a direct challenge to the Republican liberals and former abolitionists who had won suffrage for African American men by explicitly excluding women when they, for the first time, added the word "male" to the U.S. Constitution.

To be conciliatory and compromise, another woman's movement leader, Lucy Stone, organized the American Woman Suffrage Association with the goal of gaining suffrage for women state by state, one at a time. In the world of reform, this approach was more popular because it was more acceptable and less confrontational, demanding, and radical than the approach of the national campaign, which was to demand the vote for all U.S. women all at once.

The reform-minded state-by-state "American" approach was hierarchical and was organized on a delegate basis. It was made to appeal to middle- and upper-middle-class women who through their husbands would finance it. The "National," by contrast, was open to all women who paid only minimal dues and attracted women from all classes. The National refused to confine their work to the struggle for suffrage but campaigned for rights of women workers whom the newly emerging labor unions were ignoring and continued to fight on behalf of rights for married women. The American, with their state-by-state strategy, published the *Women's Journal,* while the National published *The Revolution* with the subtitle: "Men their rights and nothing more. Women their rights and nothing less." In an era of reform and reconstruction that had lost its taste for radical change, *The Revolution* lasted two years, while the *Women's Journal* continued for the rest of the century and beyond. Reform prevailed over revolutionary change.

The split in the movement was not bridged until the 1890s. By the time the two organizations reunited, a new generation of reformers had moved in and taken over. They were not there when woman's rights began as a collective movement on behalf of all their sex. Rather, they now fought for individual rights and shifted the reform of the movement to make suffrage more acceptable by placing it in the context of women's traditional roles. "Social housekeeping" was their approach to the vote. With it, individual-rights, reform women promised they would clean up society, just as they kept good, clean homes. By the end of the century, the radical movement that was launched in 1848 was reduced to securing the vote without the political agenda the early reformers had in mind.

The radical woman's rights demand for property rights for married women and the right to divorce by treating marriage as a contract like any other was fully realized only in the 1970s and 1980s as state after state adopted community property laws and no-fault divorce. But women's economic conditions, so severely depressed through systematic discrimination since the beginning of the Industrial Revolution, leave divorced women with a significant decrease in their standard of living compared to men's increased standard of living after divorce. Affirmative action introduced in the 1960s might have had some impact on this historical inequity over time, but it was being systematically withdrawn in the 1990s.

See also *Anthony, Susan B.; Gender; Inequality; Rights.*

KATHLEEN BARRY

BIBLIOGRAPHY

Barry, Kathleen. *Susan B. Anthony: A Biography.* New York: New York University Press, 1988.

Buhle, Mary Jo, and Paul Buhle, eds. *A Concise History of Woman Suffrage: Selections from the Classic Work of Stanton, Anthony, Gage, and Harper.* Urbana: University of Illinois, 1978.

Cott, Nancy F. *The Grounding of Modern Feminism.* New Haven, Conn: Yale University Press, 1987.

Lerner, Gerda. *The Creation of Patriarchy.* New York: Oxford, 1986.

Mankiller, Wilma, et al., eds. *The Reader's Companion to U.S. Women's History.* New York: Houghton Mifflin, 1998.

WORKERS

Nineteenth-century theorists of revolution focused their attention—and pinned their hopes, for they were also champions of revolution—on industrial wage workers. For thinkers from Karl Marx and Friedrich Engels to the twentieth-century French essayist Georges Sorel, the appearance of wage laborers in urban centers throughout the West signaled the emergence of a new social order—industrial capitalism—and the social group whose radical mobilization would topple that order. Unlike anarchists and some socialists (for example, the nineteenth-century French reformer Pierre-Joseph Proudhon) who wrote about the revolutionary potential of skilled craft workers, Marxist militants and philosophers believed that mechanization and centralization of production would create an increasingly unskilled and impoverished class of wage workers, known as the proletariat. They expected that revolutions would be most likely in those nations where industrialization had proceeded the furthest. The concentration of the proletarians in large manufacturing enterprises, their social homogeneity, and their exposure to radical ideas would, according to the theory, furnish the basis for revolutionary consciousness. With intellectuals acting as leaders, strategists, and tacticians, urban wage laborers would become the soldiers of social transformation.

AGRARIAN AND INDUSTRIAL SOCIETIES

The actual history of political and social revolutions has not, by and large, conformed to this theoretical picture. Although societies undergoing industrialization have experienced major political crises, including large-scale popular uprisings, revolutions in the early modern and modern periods have been far more likely to succeed in agrarian societies with only a moderately developed industrial sector. England, for example, as the most advanced capitalist society in the nineteenth century, ought to have been the most ripe for social revolution in the nineteenth century, yet radical working-class movements there never succeeded in threatening the stability of the constitutional monarchy. In most of the great revolutions—France in 1789, Mexico in 1910, Russia in 1917, China from 1921 to 1949—it was peasants, not industrial workers, whose social unrest, combined with weakness in the state's repressive and revenue-gathering institutions, brought about state collapse. In the late twentieth century as well, the forces that mobilized to wrest power from colonial elites or their client states—in Cuba, Algeria, Vietnam, Nicaragua, Zimbabwe, and other cases—have been predominantly rural in origin, even if urban workers and intellectuals took part. Revolutions have often begun with the mobilization of industrial workers, but they have rarely succeeded without peasants.

Moreover, political mobilization among wage earners typically occurred predominantly among skilled craft workers—those who had mastered a trade, often after long apprenticeships—rather than among truly unskilled proletarians. Political radicalism generally found more fertile ground in small workshops than in large industrial enterprises, though the latter proved to be a major site for the emergence of industrial unionism.

This pattern does not mean that urban workers have been irrelevant to revolutions, however. Even when their role has been limited in absolute terms, industrial laborers and the artisans who were their forebears have invariably had a significant impact in proportion to their numbers. As early as the Ciompi revolt in Florence in 1378, in which the wool-carders' guild set up a short-lived revolutionary republic, manufacturing workers have been crucial to political radicalism in urban centers. In the era of nation-states, artisanal laborers during the French Revolution set a durable precedent for worker radicalism during political upheavals. Through street demonstrations and activism in political clubs, these workers, known as *sans-culottes* because they wore trousers rather than the knee breeches favored by the upper elements of Parisian society, repeatedly pushed the National Assembly toward more radical measures. The political activities of the *sans-culottes* culminated in the Terror of 1793–1794 and the establishment in Paris in 1793 of a democratic municipal government known as the Commune.

Throughout the nineteenth century, workers in industrializing Europe were at the center of left-wing politics, and if they were not usually successful in seizing political power, they were routinely influential in placing socialist demands on the agenda. In the 1830s and 1840s mass meetings of working men known as Chartists in England and republican socialist societies in France and Germany denounced property-based electoral laws, which excluded urban (male) laborers from the franchise even as they included rural smallholders. In 1848 the revolutions that swept across Europe placed workers at the center of movements not only to expand suffrage but also to build social citizenship rights into new democratic constitutions. In France and Germany, especially, workers who had received tentative promises of social and political recognition in the wake of republican uprisings set up barricades when the provisional governments, dominated by conservatives and moderates, reneged on those promises. Thousands died when these protests were crushed, setting the stage for periods of military repression and the restoration of monarchy. In the meantime, the victims of 1848 in Paris and in Germany became martyrs for leftists who were forced underground or into exile.

The last revolutionary moment of the nineteenth century was also its largest, at least in numerical terms. Nation building across Europe culminated in the Franco-Prussian War of 1870–1871, resulting in a disastrous defeat for France. This defeat swept away the imperial regime of Napoleon III in France and set off a popular uprising in Paris, whose leaders once again proclaimed the formation of a radical democratic Commune. This revolutionary experiment, like its predecessors, was suppressed in bloody street battles that took tens of thousands of lives. Although Marxist revolutionaries have frequently glorified the Commune of 1871 and its sister communes in other French cities as the birth of a revolutionary industrial proletariat, here again many of the insurgents were craft workers. Workers from newer, more industrialized trades did play a disproportional role, but there is evidence that they saw their insurgency more as a defense of neighborhood autonomy and municipal liberties than as an effort to overthrow capitalism.

RUSSIA AND CHINA

In the twentieth century, revolutionary mobilization moved eastward to Russia and China—notwithstanding a number of abortive uprisings in the West (for example, that of the Spartacus League in Germany) following the First World War. In Russia, revolutionary politics began with the failed Revolution of 1905, in which activists in the emerging labor movement in Moscow and St. Petersburg played a major part. Once again, skilled male workers in artisanal trades such as printing and woodworking predominated, especially in leadership roles; yet there is also evidence of political activism in the more mechanized sector, notably metalworking and textile production.

In the aftermath of the tsar's 1905 liberalizing concessions, both craft- and factory-centered workers' organizations exerted considerable influence on the nascent opposition parties, notably the Mensheviks and Bolsheviks. These relationships heavily influenced the course of revolutionary politics after working-class demonstrations over food rationing and the war effort forced the tsar's abdication in 1917. During the period of dual power that began with the formation of the Soviet of Workers' and Soldiers' Deputies and later the All-Russian Congress of Soviets, demonstrations by workers' groups pushed the latter to take control of the state and armed forces from the Duma (parliament) and the moderate provisional government. The increasing radicalism of Russia's workers was thus crucial to the process that eventually enabled the Bolsheviks to dissolve the Duma and seize power by force in October 1917.

Despite the eventual reliance of the Chinese Communists on rural recruits, workers in China's industrial cities had a similar influence on the course of revolution in the first half of the century and again in the Cultural Revolution of the 1960s. Workers called strikes in support of the May Fourth Movement in 1919 and staged massive work stoppages in the 1920s in Hong Kong and Canton in support of the Nationalist movement led by the Kuomintang. Mao Zedong gained his first experience in labor organization in the ironworks and coal mines of the Wuhan region and turned again to workers throughout China to support his Cultural Revolution. In the Tiananmen uprising of 1989, it was only when workers in Beijing began to join the students that the Communist leadership felt truly threatened. Although never more than a small percentage of China's total work force, industrial workers nevertheless played a significant role in every major upheaval in modern China.

WORKERS AS AGENTS OF CHANGE

The experience of manufacturing workers in revolutions, both in the preindustrial and industrial eras, reveals a recurrent pattern. Workers have played a decisive role not as revolutionary soldiers undermining the stability of the old regime but as agents of radicalization and political dynamism once state elites have yielded some of their control. There are at least three reasons for this pattern, only one of them directly connected to the Marxist picture of revolutionary workers.

First, as Marx and his followers argued, wage earners in large-scale enterprises have been more willing to see themselves in terms of the abstract category "worker" rather than in terms of older, craft-specific collective identities. Without corporate traditions emphasizing communities based on a specific set of skills, industrial workers more readily accepted the notion that political transformation ought to include legal recognition of the general category of wage earners. Yet, at the same time, rather than arrive at this notion spontaneously at work or under the tutelage of an intellectual vanguard, workers usually saw their historical role in this way only when they were integrated into large-scale organizations that specifically highlighted their wage-earning status—as in the national workshops in France in 1848 or the soviets in Russia in 1917—at the expense of narrower, craft-based collective identities. Mass organizations structured along different lines—for example, the Paris National Guard, which during the Commune of 1871 recruited by neighborhood, and unions that in China, the United States, and elsewhere made distinctions by skill level, region, ethnicity, or gender—have often patterned social interactions in such a way that the collective self-understanding most plausible to members has been narrower than, or has cut across, the general identity of "worker." Mobilization of workers as workers has thus been a contingent outcome of the way political organizations structure interactions, not a necessary result of the labor process under capitalism.

The second reason for the radicalizing role of workers in revolution is their location in politically important urban centers. At moments of political uncertainty and crisis, the willingness of organized urban groups to be vocal in pressing their demands, to the point of physically invading the buildings where deliberative bodies meet, has had a powerful effect on the course of revolutionary politics. Even the most seasoned political actors can be swayed by the eruption of an angry crowd into their sedate meeting halls, as has often happened in the history of revolutions. It is no accident that nations whose capital cities are also major industrial centers have been more susceptible to radical revolutionary change than have those whose capitals are dominated by financial, cultural, or administrative institutions.

Third, the cultural resources of urban laborers, as compared with peasants, have made a major difference in the way protest occurs among the two social groups. Although Marx's commonly quoted metaphor likening peasant communities to "sacks of potatoes" drastically overstates the passivity of rural laborers, it does point to one significant aspect of agrarian unrest: it is typically short-term, localistic, and reactive. In the absence of such external organizers as Mao's Red Army and the Vietcong, peasant protest has typically manifested itself as the *jacquerie*—a burst of local insurgency directed at seizure of land, intimidation of the landlord, or destruction of records governing seigneurial rights. Rarely have such insurgencies developed into movements on a large geographic and temporal scale (with some notable exceptions, such as the Taiping Rebellion in China in the mid-nineteenth century). Urban manufacturing workers, on the other hand, typically integrated their short-term claims into broader social agendas and durable organizations, whether fraternal societies in the preindustrial era or unions later on. In addition to the structural influences on patterns of interaction previously noted, this difference owes much to the educational and literacy levels urban laborers have usually attained. The reason urban workers have repeatedly become significant revolutionary actors is not impoverishment and proletarianization; on the contrary, it is the abundance of organizational and conceptual resources at their disposal.

See also *Chinese Communist Revolution (1921–1949); Chinese Cultural Revolution (1966–1969); Communism; European Revolutions of 1848; Intellectuals; Marx, Karl, and Friedrich Engels; Paris Commune (1871); Peasants; Polish Protest Movements and Solidarity Revolution (1956–1991); Russian Revolution of 1905; Russian Revolution of 1917; Sorel, Georges; U.S. Labor Revolts (1890–1932).*

ROGER V. GOULD

BIBLIOGRAPHY

Bonnell, Victoria E. *Roots of Rebellion: Workers' Politics and Organizations in St. Petersburg and Moscow, 1900–1914.* Berkeley: University of California Press, 1983.

Goldstone, Jack A. *Revolution and Rebellion in the Early Modern World.* Berkeley: University of California Press, 1992.

Gould, Roger V. *Insurgent Identities: Class, Community, and Protest in Paris from 1848 to the Commune.* Chicago: University of Chicago Press, 1995.

Perry, Elizabeth J. *Shanghai on Strike: The Politics of Chinese Labor.* Stanford: Stanford University Press, 1993.

Skocpol, Theda. *States and Social Revolutions: A Comparison of France, Russia, and China.* New York: Cambridge University Press, 1979.

YEMENI REVOLUTIONS (1962–1990)

Between the outbreak of revolution in North Yemen in 1962 and the unification of the North with the separate state of South Yemen in 1990, the two Yemeni states underwent a series of political upheavals, involving both collaboration and competition between radical forces in the two parts of Yemen. The two states followed distinctive development paths, until the North prevailed over the South after 1990 *(see map, p. 474)*.

In September 1962 a military coup by radical army officers in North Yemen transformed first North Yemen and then the neighboring state of South Yemen. These upheavals were to have significant international repercussions: they alarmed Saudi Arabia; served throughout much of the 1960s as a focus for rivalry between radical and conservative Arab states; and remained, until the late 1980s, a component of the cold war between pro-American and pro-Soviet forces in the region.

REVOLUTIONS IN NORTH AND SOUTH

The rise of radical Arab nationalism in the Middle East after World War II affected both North Yemen, a state that had won independence from the Turks in 1918, and the South, a colony of the British since 1839, in different ways. In the North, challenges developed to the autocratic *imams,* traditional dynastic rulers, from dissident merchants frustrated with the lack of economic possibilities, army officers, intellectuals of both nationalist and Islamic orientation, and peasant movements. Revolts in 1948 and again in 1955 were crushed. In September 1962, a week after the death of Imam Ahmad, his son Imam al-Badr was overthrown in a military coup by pro-Egyptian Arab nationalist officers. Following the overthrow of the imam, the coup leaders proclaimed the Yemen Arab Republic (YAR).

Mass demonstrations supporting the coup in the main cities of the North—Sana'a, Taiz, and Ibb—and in Aden followed the coup. But the new imam had escaped from Sana'a and rallied tribal opposition to the YAR. For the next eight years North Yemen was ravaged by a civil war, in which government forces, backed by up to seventy thousand troops from Egypt, fought tribal opposition, financed by Saudi Arabia. Only in July 1970 was a compromise reached, under which a coalition government was formed: on the republican side, radical, left-wing forces that had grown among the popular militias and political parties were defeated, and, on the royalist side, the Hamid al-Din family was barred from returning.

In the ensuing two decades the inheritors of the Northern left, now supported by South Yemen, carried out intermittent guerrilla opposition to the Sana'a government. But the Northern government, now a more conventional military regime, survived with the support of Saudi Arabia and the West. The republic endured but was emptied of much of the radical politics present at the beginning.

In the South the growth of nationalist opposition in the 1950s was of a more conventional, anticolonial kind, involving trade unions in Aden and tribal revolts in the interior. Following the revolution in the North in September 1962 a radical guerrilla movement, headed by the National Liberation Front for Occupied South Yemen (NLF), was founded and, with support of the rural population, began armed action in the hinterland in October 1963. The NLF gradually gained the upper hand, not only against the British and their merchant and tribal allies but also against a more moderate nationalist group, the Front for the Liberation of Occupied South Yemen (FLOSY). In November 1967, following the British withdrawal, the NLF came to power and proclaimed the People's Republic of South Yemen, renamed in 1970 the People's Democratic Republic of Yemen. In time the Democratic Republic came to be a close ally of the Soviet Union and the only state run on communist lines in the Arab world.

POSTREVOLUTIONARY CHANGE

Both Yemeni states underwent profound change after their respective revolutions, but in contrasted forms. In the North the post-1962 state introduced few significant changes; beyond the abolition of the monarchy and the suppression of the power of the religious caste of *sada,* supposed descendants of the prophets, the state avoided land reform, the key obstacle to change. Always seeking to compromise with the religious establishment and with the tribal leadership, successive military regimes created a coalition of beneficiaries of state power. Tribal loyalties pervaded state employment. Although the state was officially committed to a generic improvement in the condition of women, legislation on the family, taken from Arab legal codes, had minimal impact outside the urban areas. The main social effect of the post-1962 changes was the increased strength of tribal leaders, who were the beneficiaries of the money and arms supplied to both sides in the civil war. The events of 1962, therefore, revolutionized society more than the state.

In the South, by contrast, the post-1967 regime sought to impose a radical modernization: land was redistributed, industry and services nationalized, and tribal affiliation and organization outlawed. In employment, education, and legislation relating to the family, women's interests were promoted. The 1974 family law, in particular, virtually banned polygamy and made divorce more accessible to women. However, a combination of factional divisions at the top, combined with enduring social and economic problems for the mass of the population, served by the late 1980s to undermine support for the government. It was in this context, and with the ending of Soviet support, that the leadership of the South decided in 1989 to negotiate a unity agreement with the North. In the aftermath of unification, the social achievements of the Southern revolution were rapidly obliterated: land and other property was returned to previous owners, law and practice on women converted to Northern practices, and corruption and tribalism grew apace.

CONFLICTS OVER YEMENI UNITY

That the two Yemens would be reunited, once the oppressors in each part of Yemen had been removed from power, had been an article of faith among nationalists in both North and South. But when the South became independent at the end of 1967, unity became not a policy leading to cooperation but a legitimation for rivalry and for interference in each other's internal affairs. In 1972 and again in 1979 border wars, linked to support for guerrilla opposition inside each other's territory, broke out. Even after unification in 1990 differences between the two leaderships continued, and the military and administrative bodies remained separate. In 1994 the North launched a military attack on the South, in which the latter's forces were defeated. The end of the process that had begun in September 1962 therefore came with the triumph of a now conservative Northern military elite over its opponents in both North and South. Corruption, disorder, and tribalism increasingly pervaded the now united country.

FRED HALLIDAY

BIBLIOGRAPHY

Burrowes, Robert. *The Yemen Arab Republic: The Politics of Development, 1962–1986.* Boulder, Colo.: Westview Press, 1987.

Douglas, J. Leigh. *The Free Yemeni Movement 1935–1962.* Beirut: American University of Beirut Press, 1987.

Halliday, Fred. *Arabia without Sultans.* New York: Random House, 1975.

Kostiner, Joseph. *The Struggle for South Yemen.* London: St. Martin's Press, 1984.

Molyneux, Maxine. "Women's Rights and Political Contingency: The Case of Yemen, 1900–1994." *The Middle East Journal* 49 (summer 1995): 418–431.

Peterson, John. *Yemen. The Search for a Modern State.* Baltimore, Md.: Johns Hopkins University Press, 1982.

Pridham, Brian, ed. *Contemporary Yemen: Politics and Historical Background.* Beckenham, Kent: St. Martin's Press, 1984.

Stookey, Robert. *South Yemen. A Marxist Republic in Arabia.* Boulder, Colo.: Westview Press, 1982.

YUGOSLAV COMMUNIST COLLAPSE AND DISSOLUTION (1987–1992)

By 1990 Yugoslavia's federal institutions and constitutional order had been largely paralyzed by interregional disputes, and support for the regime and multinational state was evaporating. The disintegration of Yugoslavia's ruling Communist Party in January 1990 and the victory of nationalist parties and programs in regional multiparty elections later that year led to the dissolution of the multinational state in 1991, precipitating serial wars within and between several of the successor states from the summer of 1991 to the end of 1995 *(see map, p. 141).*

TITO'S YUGOSLAVIA

Yugoslavia (meaning "land of the South Slavs") was created after World War I, destroyed and divided by Axis invasion in 1941, and re-created on World War II's Balkan battlefields by a communist-led resistance movement, the partisans. Under Josip Broz Tito, head of the Yugoslav Communist Party since 1937 and of the second Yugoslavia until his death in 1980, the partisan leadership skillfully combined a patriotic revolt against Axis occupiers with social revolution to impose its dictatorship and vision of a communist society. A key part of that vision was to do a better job of realizing "the Yugoslav idea" of South Slav union than had the first Yugoslavia, by maintaining the "brotherhood and unity" of the Yugoslav nations as symbolized by the partisans' multinational ranks. The regime's strategy to achieve this goal consisted of two counterbalancing parts. Both would collapse before or during 1990.

The first part sought to minimize internationality disputes through a federal and later almost confederal state structure. Six republics (federal units), whose autonomous powers gradually expanded from cultural to economic and some police and defense matters, provided designated national homelands for Yugoslavia's officially recognized nations: Serbs, Croats, Slovenes, Slavic Muslims, Macedonians, and Montenegrins. Two autonomous provinces within Serbia—Kosovo, with a non-Slavic Albanian majority, and Vojvodina—had more limited powers. A new constitution, adopted in 1974, went further than the previous constitutions by requiring the agreement of all federal units (consensus) for decisions in most of the federal government's remaining areas of competence. It also effectively increased the number of units to eight by giving Kosovo and Vojvodina the powers but not the status of separate republics. Both of these provisions would play major roles in Yugoslavia's collapse and dissolution.

The strategy's second part, providing insurance that disputes never got out of hand, relied on one man and two centralized institutions as ultimate guarantors of Yugoslavia's unity. These were Tito, the Communist Party (after 1952 called the League of Communists of Yugoslavia, or LCY), and the Yugoslav army (whose senior officers were mostly ex-partisan Serbs and Montenegrins fiercely loyal to Tito and "his" Yugoslavia). When the collapse came, only the army would still exist, temporarily, to try to prevent it.

THE PARALYZED FEDERATION AND KOSOVO

Until 1980 this formula for both diversity and unity, and communist Yugoslavia's "different road to socialism" after its break with Soviet leader Joseph Stalin in 1948, seemed to be working. But by the end of the 1980s it was clear that Yugoslavia in its current form could not survive. For different reasons, most Yugoslavs no longer wanted the kind of union that "Tito's Yugoslavia" had become. The question became the form a third Yugoslavia should take, or whether Yugoslavia should cease to exist, and how either of these might be accomplished without widespread violence and even civil war.

Tito died in 1980, just as Yugoslavia's previously robust but fundamentally unhealthy economy and rapidly rising living standards plunged. Yugoslav-wide remedies were needed and proposed, but each would impose more pain on some regions than others. Since consensus rules gave each unit a veto, post-Tito federal governments were paralyzed. By 1985 most Yugoslavs were back to their very low 1960s standards of living. The result was diminishing acceptance of federal institutions, then of the entire nonfunctioning federal system, and finally of the state itself. Declining legitimacy was bound to spur separate, if not yet separatist, nationalisms.

Also in the 1980s, Kosovo was providing the catalyst for a chain reaction in which first Serbs and then Slovenes, Croats, and others came to believe that part or all of their nation was threatened with cultural extinction in part or all of the territory they inhabited. The Albanians of Kosovo, more than 80 percent of the population of Kosovo in 1980 (by 1990 they would be 90 percent), had been in a state of simmering rebellion since the brutal suppression in April 1981 of mass demonstrations demanding full and formal republican status. Blaming alleged Kosovan Albanian intimidation, rather than the province's acute poverty, for the continuing exodus of Slavs from Kosovo, Serbs everywhere grumbled about "genocide" and "ethnic cleansing" in a region they regarded as the cradle of their nation, culture, and state.

SERBIA AND MILOSEVIC

In 1987 Serb bitterness and anger found a focus in Slobodan Milošević, a previously undistinguished party bureaucrat and head of the Serbian Party since May 1986. At a rally of Kosovo Serbs in April, where his "standing up for Serbs" speech met an enthusiastic response, Milošević discovered that Serbian nationalist sentiment could be mobilized in a mass national movement that he could ride to power in Serbia and possibly all of Yugoslavia.

In Serbia the first stage of Milošević's rise was achieved (in October 1987) by a party coup to depose party opponents he accused of being soft on Kosovo and other Serb national interests. Orchestrated mass demonstrations that frightened anti-Milošević party leaders into resignation accomplished the same in Vojvodina and Montenegro. Then he engineered the "reunification" of Serbia, achieved by 1989, through liquidation of Kosovo and Vojvodina's autonomy in all but name.

Milošević had already also promised to defend Serbs outside Serbia (25 percent of Yugoslavia's 8.5 million Serbs, mostly in Croatia and Bosnia) who felt or could be persuaded to feel threatened, as individuals and communities, in increasingly independent republics whose majority nations and leaders they did not trust. If "all Serbs in one state" was truly a precondition for their national survival, as claimed, then Yugoslavia in its confederal form was no longer tolerable.

Two solutions would satisfy Serb insistence on unity in

one state: preferably a partly recentralized Yugoslavia (a "modern federation") governed by a recentralized and genuinely dominant (Communist) Party in which Serbs, as the largest nation and most numerous communists, would have the major say; or, failing that, a "Greater Serbia" that would include most Serbs currently living in Croatia and Bosnia. The second would require major changes in the borders of those republics, whose predictable opposition could easily lead to civil strife and war.

Milošević's tactics in pursuing both possibilities, with the second as a reserve option until the first collapsed in 1990, sparked fears of "yesterday Kosovo, tomorrow us" in non-Serbs. Slovenes were the first to express open and growing alarm that a Serb- and Milošević-dominated Yugoslavia, and the nationalist passions fanned and exploited to achieve it, threatened their small nation's survival. Croatia's Serbs responded to their own minority anxieties with demonstrations decrying "cultural genocide" by the Croatian regime and with calls for a Serb autonomous region closely linked to Serbia. In Bosnia, Serbs (32 percent of the republic population) also demanded autonomy, alarming the Croats (17 percent of the population) and then Bosnian Muslims (43 percent). Encouraged by politicians and would-be politicians copying Milošević by embracing their own nations' equally potent national symbols, vicious circles of reciprocal fear for national survival and competitive nationalist militancy were tearing Yugoslavia apart.

THE CENTER COLLAPSES

By late 1989 deadlock between Serb proposals for a "modern federation" and a joint Slovene-Croat proposal for a loose confederation had blocked any hope of "reuniting" Yugoslavia by amending the federal constitution. However, the party road to the same goal still seemed open.

The year 1990 began with the self-disintegration of the LCY. Milošević had engineered the calling of a special party congress, apparently believing that the four regional delegations he controlled could muster a majority for his bid to recentralize and control the party and reassert its authority. His timing could not have been worse, and not only because of the broad opposition by non-Serbs that his Serb nationalism had engendered. Before the congress assembled, on January 20, a revolutionary wave had swept across the rest of Eastern Europe, toppling communist regimes everywhere except Albania. Slovenia and Croatia's communists had already accepted the principle of multiparty elections. After four days of angry debate and deadlock, focused on Slovene insistence that the congress renounce the communist political monopoly, endorse a multiparty system, and agree to an even looser "confederal" LCY, the Slovenes walked out. Defying Milošević, a rump session endorsed the Croatian view that the congress (and with it the LCY) could not go on without one of its "constituent" parties. After the disintegration of the LCY, only a motley of federal organs with diminishing authority and the army, with its 70 percent Serbian and Montenegrin officer corps, were left to sustain a tattered and discredited "Yugoslav idea" and state.

By the end of 1990 all six republics had held multiparty elections. Four of the six elections produced noncommunist majorities and governments. The winning parties in all, including communists in Serbia (now calling themselves socialists) and Montenegro and the leading Muslim, Serb, and Croat parties in trinational Bosnia, were nationalist in program, appeal, and aims. Prospects for agreement on a "third" Yugoslavia or a formula for peaceful divorce were correspondingly dimmer than before, but some continued to try.

Leaders of the new republican governments and the members of Yugoslavia's collective state presidency met in a series of summits, the first on December 26–27, 1990, and the last on June 6, 1991. Slovenes and Croats stuck to their "confederal model," and Serbs and Montenegrins to their "modern federation." The new presidents of Bosnia and Macedonia, equally fearing a break-up of Yugoslavia and Serb domination, vainly persisted in seeking a compromise.

Serb-Croat tension and violence had been mounting in Serb-majority rural areas in Croatia (Krajina), where the local Serbs, in a series of referendums held since August 1990, had declared autonomy and then union with Serbia. In this context nationalist politicians in charge of Serbia, Croatia, Slovenia, and the principal Muslim, Serb, and Croat parties in Bosnia were painting themselves, whether purposefully or by mismanagement, into corners with policies and promises they could not realize without risking civil war or abandon without causing their own political demise. For nationalist Slovenes and Croats, only secession could save their nations; and for Serbs, whose leaders now accepted the principle of self-determination if it could also be exercised by Croatian and Bosnian Serbs to secede from those states and join Serbia, only unity in Greater Serbia would do.

DISSOLUTION AND WARS OF SUCCESSION

With the federal government and constitution already ignored, the collective state presidency of Yugoslavia, the federation's linchpin, was immobilized and virtually extinguished by two Serb-organized crises within it, in mid-March and mid-May 1991. Slovenia and Croatia's governments interpreted plebiscites in December 1990 and on May 19, 1991, as authority to secede. Both did so on June 25, 1991. Yugoslavia's final dissolution had begun.

A Muslim family stands before its partially destroyed house in Stari Vitez, Bosnia-Herzegovina.

The Yugoslav army made a feeble attempt to maintain the country's borders by trying to take control of Slovenia's border posts with Italy, Austria, and Hungary. Thwarted by determined and skillful Slovene armed resistance in a ten-day miniwar, the army withdrew to a more serious effort to pacify Croatia. By late summer this effort had been transformed into a battle to help Croatian Serb militias hold and expand a "Serb Republic of Krajina" that included nearly 40 percent of Croatia. At the end of the year, an effective cease-fire and introduction of a United Nations Protective Force were negotiated by a UN mediator, Cyrus Vance.

In July the European Community (EC) had tried to hold Yugoslavia together but had succeeded only in winning from the Slovenes and Croats a three-month "moratorium" on implementing their secessions. Implementation proceeded when the moratorium expired. An EC commission declared Yugoslavia to be "in process of dissolution" and invited its republics to apply for recognition as independent states, subject to conditions like the protection of minority rights. On January 15, 1992, the EC recognized Slovenia and Croatia.

Unwilling to stay in a "rump" Yugoslavia in which Serbia would be overwhelmingly dominant, Macedonia declared independence and sought international recognition in December 1991. Bosnia's independence was recognized by the United States and EC in early April, a month after its overwhelming endorsement in a plebiscite boycotted by Bosnian Serbs, who had withdrawn from Bosnia's trinational government to organize their own Bosnian Serb state. Bosnian Croats followed suit, creating another quasi-state (called "Hercegbosna") virtually joined to Croatia. A three-sided civil war and a Serb siege of Sarajevo, the capital, began. The war would last, with brutalities, "ethnic cleansing," and human and material losses that shocked the world, until an uneasy peace was imposed by American diplomats and North Atlantic Treaty Organization (NATO) forces at the end of 1995.

Yugoslavia had died from the serial failure of all of its vital organs (except the army, which later became a Serb army) even before its corpse was dismembered by the secession of four of its six republics. The wars within and between its successor states, aggravated and prolonged by international efforts to stop them that were too little, too late, and usually inappropriate, belong to post-Yugoslav history.

See also *Tito, Josip Broz; Yugoslav Partisans and Communist Revolution (1941–1948).*

Dennison Rusinow

BIBLIOGRAPHY

Cohen, Lenard J. *Broken Bonds.* Boulder, Colo.: Westview Press, 1993.

Glenny, Misha. *The Fall of Yugoslavia.* London: Penguin Books, 1992.

Lampe, John R. *Yugoslavia as History.* Cambridge: Cambridge University Press, 1996.

Ramet, Sabrina Petra, and Ljubisa S. Adamovich, eds. *Beyond Yugoslavia.* Boulder, Colo.: Westview Press, 1995.

Silber, Laura, and Allan Little. *The Death of Yugoslavia.* London: Penguin Books and BBC Worldwide, 1995.

Woodward, Susan L. *Balkan Tragedy.* Washington, D.C.: Brookings Institution, 1995.

Zimmermann, Warren. *Origins of a Catastrophe.* New York: Times Books, 1996.

YUGOSLAV PARTISANS AND COMMUNIST REVOLUTION (1941–1948)

After a whirlwind campaign that utterly crushed the royal Yugoslav state in April 1941, victorious German forces split the country into many parts, including German, Italian, Bulgarian, and Hungarian regions and the Independent State of Croatia. The latter, run by fascists called *ustashe,* attempted to ethnically cleanse Bosnia of Serbs, Jews, Muslims, and others it considered undesirable, while in the quisling Serbian state a resistance movement known as *chetniks* emerged from the remnants of the Yugoslav royal army. Ustashe were primarily Catholic Croats, whereas chetniks were primarily Orthodox Serbs. Into this volatile mix entered the communist resistance movement known as the partisans, led by Josip Broz Tito. At the time the communists took the field (July 1941, after the German invasion of the Soviet Union), the Communist Party of Yugoslavia had only about twelve thousand members, but its leaders had been hardened by long underground experience. Their resistance strategy was to fight, rather than to husband their forces in expectation of eventual Allied victory, as did the chetniks. The partisan leaders also saw their struggle as a revolutionary movement to create a socialist state after the war.

Because the chetniks dominated Serbia, the partisans moved into Bosnia, where Croats disgusted with the ustashe atrocities and Serbs, Muslims, and Jews fleeing those atrocities joined their movement. In 1942 at Bihać, and then in 1943 at Jajce, they created the Anti-Fascist Movement for the Liberation of Yugoslavia as a provisional government. Stalin urged the Yugoslav communists not to be too obvious in their communism, in order not to frighten the British. But Winston Churchill, after sending some missions to Yugoslavia by parachute in 1943 to check on who was fighting the Germans more effectively, switched British support from the chetniks to the partisans. In November 1944, when the Red Army swept through the northeast corner of Yugoslavia, the partisans entered Belgrade.

Under British pressure, the Yugoslav government in exile acquiesced to a temporary coalition arrangement that discarded the monarchy and opened the door to legitimating the communist regime. Enthused by their victory, certain of their revolutionary mission, and with actual power in their hands, the Yugoslav communists jailed their opponents, seized economic assets, and even massacred some thirty thousand people attempting to escape their regime. A controlled election late in 1945 created a new Federal Socialist Republic of Yugoslavia with a Stalinist constitution.

THE BREAK WITH THE USSR

The Yugoslav communists brought at least two broad ideas to their new state. The most important of these was socialism, by which they understood a centrally planned economy on the Soviet model and Stalinist social controls. For the first three postwar years, 1945–1948, they relied on powerful security services, economic planning, and campaign methods of production (such as the youth brigades that built the Zagreb/Belgrade highway) to maintain stability and revive the economy. Their second main idea was “”brotherhood and unity.” Because they adhered to an internationalist ideology, the Yugoslav communists were able to create a broadly Yugoslav movement of all South Slavs that contrasted sharply with the narrow nationalism of the chetniks or ustashe. According to this idea, the many ethnic groups in the country were to retain their national identities while at the same time becoming loyal to socialist Yugoslavia. A federal state organized the various Yugoslav peoples into six republics and two autonomous provinces, which many people considered a significant improvement over the Serb-dominated interwar arrangements.

When in the fall of 1947 Stalin decided to establish the Cominform (Communist Information Bureau) as a counterpoise to the Truman Doctrine and Marshall Plan, he placed its headquarters in Belgrade in recognition of the central place Yugoslavia held in the communist world. But this act hid many tensions. The Yugoslavs were finding Stalin a demanding and overbearing mentor. So-called joint stock companies drained Yugoslav assets, Soviet advisers insisted on meddling in every decision, and, most insulting of all, Stalin denigrated the partisan war effort. When the members of Tito's central committee complained, Stalin accused them of being Trotskyites. “No matter how much each of us loves the land of socialism, the USSR,” the Yugoslavs responded, “he can, in no case, love his own country less.” For this presumption, on June 28, 1948, Stalin expelled Yugoslavia from the Cominform and began a campaign of vilification, economic boycott, and threats that continued until Stalin's death in 1953.

THE SUCCESSES AND FAILURES OF SELF-MANAGEMENT

Shocked and rattled, Tito and his advisers tried briefly to become even more Stalinist than Stalin. But they quickly realized that they could do much better by setting a course between East and West. Criticizing Stalinism as simply a form of state capitalism, they instituted a system of workers self-management that they claimed was more Marxist, more equitable, and more productive than rigid centralized planning. This unique Yugoslav brand of socialism attracted a great deal of attention throughout the world for the next thirty years. By the constitution of 1974 almost every aspect of public life became governed by the principles of self-administration. In some ways, the Yugoslav communists opened up their country, permitting emigration and work abroad, for example, but they could never solve the problem of democracy versus control. In the end, Tito and his comrades always opted for control.

By the time of Tito's death in 1980, self-administration had become a hollow bureaucratic shell, with the actual levers of power resting in the hands of eight feuding republican and provincial parties. When low productivity, overextended credit, and political interference pushed the economy into a nose-dive in the 1980s, the Yugoslav communists had no answers. Worse, their unwillingness to permit any real civil society to emerge left no legacy of democratic culture to sustain the separate republics when the party collapsed in 1991. Even its nationalities policy in the end proved faulty, because it attributed all problems of the past to former bourgeois regimes, fascists, and nationalists and refused to permit difficult issues to receive open discussion and resolution. The party expected socialism to sustain a cooperative nationalities policy, but when socialism collapsed it left a vacuum into which virulent nationalists quickly stepped.

See also *Tito, Josip Broz*.

GALE STOKES

BIBLIOGRAPHY

Banac, Ivo. *With Stalin against Tito: Cominformist Splits in Yugoslav Communism.* Ithaca, N.Y.: Cornell University Press, 1988.

Cohen, Lenard J. *Broken Bonds: Yugoslavia's Disintegration and Balkan Politics in Transition.* 3d. ed. Boulder, Colo.: Westview Press, 1997.

Djilas, Aleksa. *The Contested Country: Yugoslav Unity and Communist Revolution, 1919–1953.* Cambridge, Mass.: Harvard University Press, 1991.

Djilas, Milovan. *Memoirs of a Revolutionary.* Translated by Drenka Willen. New York: Harcourt Brace Jovanovic, 1973.

Roberts, Walter R. *Tito, Mihailović, and the Allies, 1941–1945.* Durham, N.C.: Duke University Press, 1987.

Rusinow, Dennison I. *The Yugoslav Experiment, 1948–1974.* Berkeley: University of California Press for Royal Institute of International Affairs, 1978.

The Soviet-Yugoslav Dispute: Text of the Published Correspondence. London: Oxford University Press for the Royal Institute of International Affairs, 1948.

Tomasevich, Jozo. *The Chetniks.* Stanford, Calif.: Stanford University Press, 1975.

Z

ZANZIBAR REVOLUTION (1964)

In the early morning of Sunday, January 12, 1964, a small group of revolutionary insurgents led by an African of Ugandan descent named John Okello seized a small police armory on the outskirts of Zanzibar Town, capital of the former British colony of Zanzibar *(see map, p. 334)*. Although the revolutionaries appeared to number no more than two or three dozen persons, they enjoyed the element of surprise and encountered only minimal resistance.

Prerevolution Zanzibar was a culturally plural society in which ethnic divisions largely corresponded to divisions of social class. At the top of Zanzibar's social and political structure was a small Arab minority. Arab families derived their wealth principally from ownership of large clove plantations located on the western half of Zanzibar Island. As a well-to-do landed class, Arabs had also risen to positions of prominence in the Zanzibar government, often occupying key positions in the British colonial administration. Much of Zanzibar's middle class consisted of an Asian minority of Indo-Pakistani descent. Asians virtually monopolized the clerical and technical levels of the colonial administration as well as the mercantile and petty manufacturing sectors of the Zanzibar economy.

Zanzibar's African community, which comprised about 75 percent of the total population, was ethnically and socially divided. Africans indigenous to Zanzibar, who commonly identified themselves as "Shirazis" to denote their Persian rather than African origins, were often prosperous landowners in their own right, and many owned clove farms. Africans of mainland descent tended to occupy the bottom tiers of the Zanzibar social structure. They were most commonly employed as squatter-laborers in the farming areas or as dockworkers and household servants in Zanzibar Town.

These cultural-economic divisions were powerfully reflected in Zanzibar's party system. The Arab and Asian minorities tended to support the Zanzibar Nationalist Party (ZNP). The more well-to-do segments of the Shirazi community tended to support the Zanzibar and Pemba People's Party (ZPPP), which was concentrated on Pemba Island, one of the two islands that comprised Zanzibar. The mainland African population and poorer segments of the Shirazi community tended to support the Afro-Shirazi Party (ASP).

The revolution came as no great surprise. A democratic election held approximately six months earlier, in July 1963, had left the country in political turmoil. The most striking feature of that election, held under the careful supervision of the departing colonial authority, was that it had produced a government supported by a minority of the electorate. The two political parties that formed the coalition government—the ZNP and the ZPPP—had gained only about 74,000 of the roughly 160,000 votes cast. But together they had won eighteen of the country's thirty-one constituencies. The losing party, the ASP, had received more than 87,000 votes but won only thirteen seats.

This seemingly anomalous outcome was the result of Zanzibar's single-member district electoral system. The ASP's popular support was densely concentrated in a relatively small number of constituencies that it won by overwhelming majorities. The ZNP, however, had much more widely distributed popular support and was therefore able to win a larger number of constituencies, though with smaller majorities.

The great irony of prerevolutionary politics in Zanzibar lay in the fact that the very conditions that made an ASP electoral victory all but impossible virtually ensured the success of a violent revolution that would install it in power. The newly elected ZNP/ZPPP government, seated in Zanzibar Town, was geographically isolated from the areas where it enjoyed popular support. Zanzibar Town is located on a triangle-shaped isthmus that extends in a westward direction from the center of Zanzibar Island. The constituencies that provided huge majorities for ASP candidates were located in the African quarters of the town, which lay roughly astride the isthmus where it joins the main part of the island. The ASP also had strong support in the adjacent countryside because of the large number of African squatter-laborers working on Arab clove plantations. The pattern of ASP support meant that the newly elected ZNP/ZPPP government was physically cut off from areas of the country where it enjoyed a popular following. Therefore, once Okello's revolutionaries had begun to seize key government installations, they could count on an outpouring of support from nearby throngs of ASP sympathizers.

The period immediately following the overthrow of the ZNP/ZPPP government was one of political confusion. One of Okello's first steps was to form a Revolutionary Council composed of members of his own paramilitary, revolutionary group and the older, more experienced leaders of the ASP. But the factions began to jockey for political power, and within a brief time the more experienced politicians of the ASP had assumed the leadership of the new government. To shore up Zanzibar's new regime, President Abedi Karume, head of the ASP, turned to Tanganyika for assistance, eventually agreeing to the merger of the two countries to form Tanzania in April 1964.

The Zanzibar Revolution had profound consequences. The Arab minority, which had dominated Zanzibar's political life since the mid-nineteenth century, suffered a convulsive loss of social and political status. Many Arabs were killed during the violence that accompanied the revolution, and others fled Zanzibar to take up residence in the countries of the Arab world. Those who remained in the country often found themselves in desperate circumstances. Many in Zanzibar's Asian minority also fled the country, preferring exile in mainland Tanzania to the uncertainties of postrevolutionary Zanzibar. Mainland Africans, long Zanzibar's poorest and most oppressed community, became the country's political and administrative elite, a status reversal most graphically symbolized by Abedi Karume's assumption of the country's presidency.

See also *Nyerere, Julius Kambarage.*

Michael F. Lofchie

BIBLIOGRAPHY

Lofchie, Michael F. *Zanzibar: Background to Revolution.* Princeton, N.J.: Princeton University Press, 1965.

———. "Was Okello's Revolution A Conspiracy?" *Transition (Kampala),* no. 33 (October/November 1967): 36-42.

Okello, John. *Revolution in Zanzibar.* Nairobi: East African Publishing House, 1967.

ZAPATA, EMILIANO

Zapata (1879–1919) led the most radical agrarian movement within the Mexican Revolution from 1910 until his assassination. After death, he became the political and cultural symbol of the rights of Mexico's rural peoples and their demands for land, justice, and local autonomy.

Zapata was born to a modestly prosperous family in the sugar region of Morelos, south of Mexico City. His family owned lands, leased others, raised crops for sustenance and sale, and ran mule trains in the rugged country of southern Mexico. Young Emiliano's skills as a horseman became legendary.

As sugar production became industrialized around 1900, Morelos estates began to invade villagers' lands. Elected mayor of Anenecuilco in 1909, Zapata stood up against the encroaching estates. His defense of community lands made him an outlaw even before Francisco Madero called for revolt against the regime of Porfirio Díaz late in 1910. Zapata and his allies joined Madero, seconding the call for democracy and justice and insisting that justice meant the return of lands to Mexico's villagers. When Díaz fled and Madero became president in 1911, Zapata demanded, unsuccessfully, that village lands be returned immediately.

Zapata broke with Madero in 1911 and produced a "platform" of his group's political demands. This Plan of Ayala demanded a government rooted in autonomous communities and committed to returning land to villagers. When Victoriano Huerta and the military ousted Madero in 1913, Zapata remained in rebellion and joined the Constitutionalist coalition led by Venustiano Carranza. When Huerta fell in 1914, Zapata joined the northern populist Pancho Villa in a revolutionary coalition committed to popular rights and land redistribution. By fall, the radical coalition led by Villa and Zapata ruled the Mexican interior, while Carranza and Gen. Alvaro Obregón clung to opposition in the port of Veracruz.

Early in 1915 Carranza marshaled arms and other supplies from the United States, secured earnings from booming oil and henequen fiber exports in coastal regions he controlled, and adopted—perhaps cynically—Zapata's agrarian platform to revive his fortunes. Meanwhile, the radical coalition was divided between Villa's emphasis on popular concerns in the commercializing northern borderlands and Zapata's program and strategies to serve the peasant villagers of central and southern Mexico. The power of the Constitutionalists rose while the radical coalition split. Obregón defeated Villa in the key battles of the revolution in the summer of 1915.

Emiliano Zapata

Zapata still remained powerful, at times dominant, in his home region of Morelos. As the Constitutionalists began to consolidate the new state, President Carranza returned lands to elite estate owners even while incorporating the promise of land reform in the constitution of 1917. Zapata led a guerrilla struggle in defense of the unfulfilled promise of agrarian justice until he was ambushed and assassinated in 1919 by Carranza's military.

Death did not end Zapata's influence. The demand for land remained strong into the postrevolutionary years. As postrevolutionary governments faced persistent opposition, land distribution—and the invocation of Zapata's legacy—repeatedly proved the key to mobilizing popular support. President Lázaro Cárdenas consolidated the postrevolutionary state in the 1930s with a massive land reform and a political consolidation built on its rural beneficiaries. Zapata and the villagers of Morelos, though defeated in the contest for state power, made land reform essential to the revolutionary settlement in Mexico.

See also *Mexican Revolution (1910–1940)*.

John Tutino

BIBLIOGRAPHY

Brunk, Samuel. *Emiliano Zapata: Revolution and Betrayal in Mexico.* Albuquerque: University of New Mexico Press, 1995.

Warman, Arturo. *"We Come to Object": The Peasants of Morelos and the National State.* Baltimore, Md.: Johns Hopkins University Press, 1980.

Womack, John Jr. *Zapata and the Mexican Revolution.* New York: Alfred A. Knopf, 1968.

ZIMBABWE REVOLT AND REFORM (1966–1980)

The white minority in Rhodesia was removed from power in 1980 after a guerrilla struggle culminating in a negotiated settlement. In 1965 the regime of Ian Smith unilaterally declared independence to preempt British pressures to increase African participation in government, provoking British and international economic sanctions. Africans themselves had been demanding a say in government, voting rights, land redistribution, merit-based job opportunities and promotions, equal pay for equal work, and equal access to government education, health, and agricultural services. But in 1964 the government had banned the two rival nationalist parties, the Zimbabwe African National Union (ZANU), led by Ndabaningi Sithole, and the Zimbabwe African People's Union (ZAPU), led by Joshua Nkomo.

GUERRILLA WARFARE

Both parties established headquarters in Lusaka, Zambia, and continued their earlier efforts to recruit and train guerrilla armies. Important obstacles to guerrilla infiltration in the 1960s were the dangerous Zambezi River crossing and the low population density on the Rhodesian side of the river, disadvantaging the guerrillas by depriving them of food and protection. In 1971 the Front for the Liberation of Mozambique (FRELIMO), the movement fighting for independence in Mozambique, offered the Zimbabwe People's Revolutionary Army (ZIPRA, ZAPU's army) access to its liberated zones near the northeastern Rhodesian border, but internal dissension forced ZAPU to pass up this opportunity. The smaller Zimbabwe African National Liberation Army (ZANLA), linked to the more recently established party, ZANU, became the beneficiary of Frelimo's offer. The long border between Rhodesia and Mozambique, to which

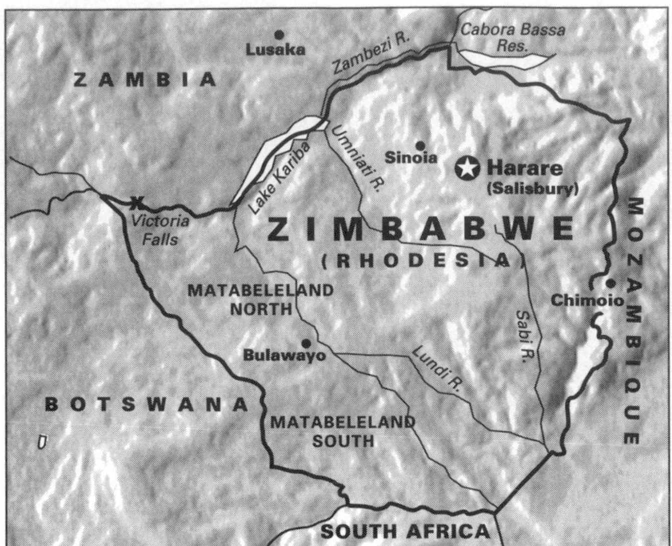

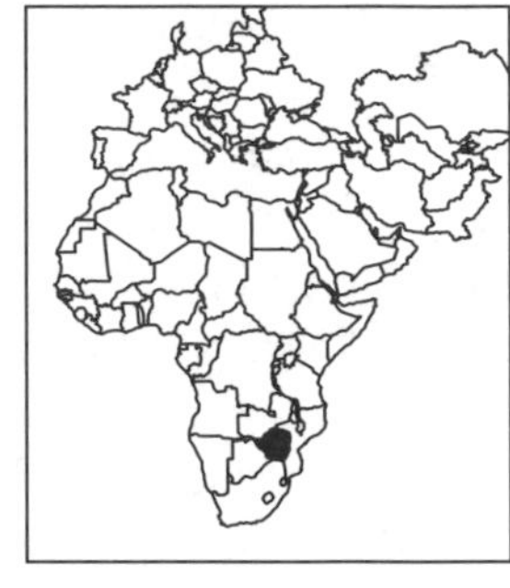

ZANU got access after 1974 when Portugal accepted Mozambique's independence, made guerrilla recruitment and infiltration easier. In contrast, ZIPRA recruits had to pass through Botswana and then be flown to Zambian camps. Consequently, ZANLA became the larger of the two armies, outnumbering ZIPRA both inside and outside the country.

The rivalries between the two parties and armies had many dimensions. Hostility to Nkomo's leadership had precipitated the formation of ZANU in 1963. Party competition later acquired an ethnic cast. Most ZANLA recruits were Shona-speakers, whereas most ZIPRA recruits were speakers of Ndebele and Kalanga, the latter a Shona dialect. ZANLA also became the more active army, raising suspicion that ZAPU was withholding its forces for a showdown with ZANU after independence. ZIPRA's turn to conventional military training in 1979 escalated these fears. ZANU presented itself as the more radical of the two parties, but by the 1970s both proclaimed themselves to be Marxist-Leninist. ZANU and its army were influenced by their Chinese sponsors. ZANLA guerrillas organized rural people into committees to provide logistical support and regularly held nighttime meetings where revolutionary songs and slogans were used as vehicles of political education. ZIPRA's Soviet training may account for its lesser emphasis on political mobilization.

Despite Marxist-Leninist claims, both armies mobilized rural people around indigenous African religious beliefs, and ZANLA often worked successfully through Christian churches. Local struggles for power based on gender, generational, and clan conflicts complicated the guerrillas' quest for civilian support. Similarly, the guerrillas' strategy of attacking government schools and clinics was often resented by local people who had contributed to and benefited from government services, even though they were inferior to the services whites received. African civilians bore the brunt of the war and, according to official statistics, more were killed by guerrillas than by Rhodesian forces. Guerrilla and security force brutality led tens of thousands of rural people to seek safety in the towns and cities.

As the guerrilla struggle expanded, so did the Rhodesian security apparatus and its powers. ZANLA's surprise attack on the town of Sinoia in 1966—for ZANU, the start of the liberation war—led the army to take primary responsibility for internal security from the police. After ZANLA's escalation of the war in 1972–1973, the security forces grew rapidly. With whites outnumbered twenty-two to one, the Rhodesians expanded their forces by recruiting more Africans, by more rigorously conscripting whites, and by introducing and expanding compulsory call-ups for ex-servicemen. By September 1978 the government was relying on martial law. At the war's peak in mid-1979 the government drew on 20,000–25,000 regular and conscripted troops, 36,000 police (regular and conscripted), and 27,000 paramilitary forces. The small all-white air force provided crucial support to ground troops inside the country and in cross-border raids into Mozambique and Zambia after 1976. These sorties aimed at eliminating the growing guerrilla armies before they entered the country and at destroying infrastructure to punish their hosts and to disrupt communications. The quarter-million refugees and tens of thousands of guerrilla recruits in external camps experienced a high death toll from these attacks as well as chronic food shortages and diseases. After 1976 the Rhodesian forces also coerced villagers into protected villages to isolate the guerrillas. This strategy failed and had been abandoned by early 1978.

Neither side was able to win the war. Though ZANLA established a presence throughout the rural areas, even in ZIPRA's ethnic and regional base in Matabeleland, it was unable to establish uncontested control. For their part, the Rhodesian forces were unable to prevent growing numbers of ZANLA guerrillas from infiltrating from Mozambique or prevent them from mobilizing rural people. The war was ended by negotiations, which had coexisted with and often undermined the guerrilla war from its outset.

NEGOTIATIONS

After the collapse of Portugal's southern African empire in 1974, South Africa pressed the Smith regime to accommodate African nationalist demands. The front-line states (Zambia, Botswana, Angola, Mozambique, Tanzania), which hosted or provided transit for the guerrillas, agreed to use their leverage to persuade ZANU, ZAPU, and a smaller party to unite for constitutional talks in exchange for the release of leaders detained in Rhodesia since 1964. To the front-line states, Bishop Abel Muzorewa seemed the only person whom all factions might accept. Imprisoned ZANU and ZAPU leaders had approved his leadership of a new African party formed in 1971 to oppose a constitution on which the Smith and British governments had agreed. However, both ZANU and ZAPU had grown mistrustful of Muzorewa and resented his imposed leadership. Talks held between Smith and the nationalist leaders in August 1975 at Victoria Falls collapsed quickly.

U.S. concerns that superpower rivalries in Angola would spill over into the Rhodesian conflict led to Secretary of State Henry Kissinger's visit to southern Africa in September 1976, followed by a British-chaired constitutional conference in Geneva. The front-line states again exerted pressure on ZANU and ZAPU to attend and to present a united political front. The uneasy alliance was called the Patriotic Front (PF). As an incentive to participate in these talks, Zambia agreed to release ZANU and ZANLA leaders it had detained for their alleged involvement in the assassination of Zambian acting president Herbert Chitepo in March 1975. These negotiations floundered too. An Anglo-American effort to end the war in 1977 was perceived by the Smith regime to favor the guerrillas. When Muzorewa and Sithole returned home, having lost the power struggle among the exiled nationalists, Smith sought to undercut the exiled parties by seeking toward the end of 1977 a constitutional agreement with these two leaders and Chiefs Chirau and Ndiweni, the Shona and Ndebele leaders, respectively, of the Zimbabwe United People's Party (ZUPO).

In March 1978 these four leaders and Smith signed an "internal settlement" that provided for a transitional government headed by an executive council composed of the signatories. A new constitution would be promulgated to allow for universal suffrage. The white regime hoped that an African government would lead the guerrillas to accept an amnesty offer and thus end the war and also would gain international legitimacy and the lifting of economic sanctions. For the exiled movements, a new constitution that granted African parliamentary rule but left power in the hands of a white-controlled bureaucracy and military had to be resisted. African voters in the April 1979 election were caught between government pressures to vote and guerrilla pressures to boycott. Bishop Muzorewa won the majority of African parliamentary seats, thus becoming the first African prime minister of the country, renamed Rhodesia-Zimbabwe. However, he could not stop the war, and only South Africa recognized the new regime.

Britain presided over negotiations at Lancaster House between Prime Minister Muzorewa's delegation, including representatives of Smith's party, and the Patriotic Front. Under pressure from their patrons, the parties agreed in December 1979 to a new constitution, a transitional government headed by a British governor, and a cease-fire. The constitution removed entrenched white power from the bureaucracy and the military but offered the white minority protections—private property rights, reserved parliamentary seats, guaranteed public servants' pensions, and an independent judiciary.

After signing the agreement, the Patriotic Front collapsed. ZANU, renamed ZANU-PF, decided to contest the elections alone. Violating the settlement provisions, ZANU-PF infiltrated thousands of guerrillas into the country from Mozambique after the cease-fire and then directed many of them to campaign in the rural areas. The elections, held in February 1980, were declared "free and fair" despite widespread intimidation, especially by ZANLA. Surprising most observers, ZANU-PF won fifty-seven of the eighty African seats, Nkomo's party twenty, and Muzorewa's party three (despite financial support from South Africa). Smith's party won the twenty seats reserved for whites. ZANU-PF's leader, Robert Mugabe, thus became the new prime minister of Zimbabwe.

See also *Mugabe, Robert Gabriel.*

NORMA KRIGER

BIBLIOGRAPHY

Bhebe, Ngwabi, and Terence Ranger, eds. *Society in Zimbabwe's Liberation War.* Oxford: James Currey, 1996.

———, eds. *Soldiers in Zimbabwe's Liberation War.* Oxford: James Currey, 1995.

Caute, David. *Under the Skin: The Death of White Rhodesia.* Harmondsworth: Penguin, 1983.

Kriger, Norma. *Zimbabwe's Guerrilla War: Peasant Voices.* Cambridge: Cambridge University Press, 1992.

Martin, David, and Phyllis Johnson. *The Struggle for Zimbabwe.* Salisbury: Zimbabwe Publishing House, 1981.

Nkomo, Joshua. *Nkomo. The Story of My Life.* London: Methuen, 1984.

Stiff, Peter. *Selous Scouts. Top Secret War.* Alberton, South Africa: Galago Publishers, 1982.

Tamarkin, M. *The Making of Zimbabwe. Decolonization in Regional and International Politics.* London: Frank Cass, 1990.

CREDITS FOR PHOTOGRAPHS AND OTHER IMAGES

Adams, John / *Library of Congress*

Afghan Revolution (1978–1995) / *UPI / Corbis-Bettmann*

American (U.S.) Revolution (1776–1789) / *National Archives*

Anthony, Susan B. / *Library of Congress*

Art and Representation / The Death of Marat, *Corbis-Bettmann;* The Third of May, 1808, *Francis G. Mayer / Corbis;* Liberty Leading the People, *Corbis-Bettmann;* The Boston Massacre, *Library of Congress;* Guernica, *(c) 1999 Estate of Pablo Picasso / Artists Rights Society (ARS), New York (rights); Corbis-Bettmann (image)*

Atatürk, Kemal / *Library of Congress*

Bolívar, Simón / *Library of Congress*

British "Glorious Revolution" (1688–1689) / *Library of Congress*

Burke, Edmund / *Library of Congress*

Cambodian Khmer Rouge Revolution (1967–1979) / *United Nations Photo*

Castro, Fidel / *National Archives*

Chiang Kai-shek / *Library of Congress*

Chinese Communist Revolution (1921–1949) / *National Archives*

Chinese Republican Revolution (1911) / *Library of Congress*

Communism / *Library of Congress*

Cromwell, Oliver / *Library of Congress*

Dictatorship / *Library of Congress*

East German Revolution and Unification (1989–1990) / *Courtesy German Information Center*

Eritrean Revolution (1962–1991) / *United Nations Photo*

Franklin, Benjamin / *Library of Congress*

French Revolution (1789–1815) / *Library of Congress*

Gandhi, Mahatma / *Library of Congress*

German Nazi Revolution (1933–1945) / *Library of Congress*

Gorbachev, Mikhail / *United Nations Photo*

Grenada "New Jewel" Revolution (1979–1983) / *NJM Photo*

Havel, Václav / *Congressional Quarterly*

Hitler, Adolf / *Library of Congress*

Hungarian Anticommunist Revolution (1989) / *Courtesy Embassy of the Republic of Hungary*

Indian Independence Movement (1885–1947) / *Hulton-Deutsch Collection / Corbis*

Irish Revolution (1916–1923) / *Hulton-Deutsch Collection / Corbis*

Italian Fascist Revolution (1919–1945) / *National Archives*

Jefferson, Thomas / *Library of Congress*

Jinnah, Mohammad Ali / *Courtesy Embassy of Pakistan*

Kenyatta, Jomo / *Library of Congress*

Kim Il Sung / *no credit*

Korean Civil War (1950–1953) / *National Archives*

Lafayette, Gilbert du Motier de / *Library of Congress*

Lenin, Vladimir Ilyich / *Library of Congress*

Locke, John / *Library of Congress*

L'Ouverture, François-Dominique Toussaint / *Library of Congress*

Luxemburg, Rosa / *Hoover Institution Archives*

Mandela, Nelson Rolihlahla / *United Nations Photo*

Mao Zedong / *National Archives*

Marat, Jean-Paul / *Library of Congress*

Martí, José / *Library of Congress*

Marx, Karl, and Friedrich Engels / *both images Library of Congress*

Mexican Revolution (1910–1940) / *National Archives*

Mozambican Revolution (1974–1994) / *United Nations Photo*

Mussolini, Benito / *National Archives*

Nehru, Jawaharlal / *Library of Congress*

Nicaraguan Revolution (1979) / *no credit*

Nkrumah, Kwame / *National Archives*

Nyerere, Julius Kambarage / *Library of Congress*

Paine, Thomas / *Library of Congress*

Philippine Independence Wars (1872–1910) / *National Archives*

Polish Protest Movements and Solidarity Revolution (1956–1991) / *Courtesy Embassy of the Republic of Poland*

Portuguese Revolution (1974) / *Courtesy Embassy of Portugal*
Religion / *Courtesy Embassy of the Republic of Poland*
Robespierre, Maximilien / *Library of Congress*
Rousseau, Jean-Jacques / *Library of Congress*
Russian Revolution of 1905 / *WestStock*
Russian Revolution of 1917 / *both images Library of Congress*
Rwandan Civil Wars (1959-1994) / *United Nations Photo*
San Martín, José Francisco de / *Library of Congress*
Sandino, Augusto César / *National Archives*
Stalin, Joseph / *Library of Congress*
Sukarno / *National Archives*
Sun Yat-sen / *Library of Congress*
Tocqueville, Alexis de / *Library of Congress*
Trotsky, Leon / *National Archives*
U.S. Civil Rights Movement (1954-1968) / *Library of Congress*
U.S. Civil War (1861-1865) / *Library of Congress*
U.S. Slave Revolts (1776-1865) / *Library of Congress*
Walesa, Lech / *Courtesy Embassy of the Republic of Poland*
Washington, George / *Library of Congress*
William of Orange (King William III of England) / *Library of Congress*
Woman's Rights Movement / *Library of Congress*
Yugoslav Communist Collapse and Dissolution (1987-1992) / *United Nations Photo*
Zapata, Emiliano / *Hulton-Deutsch Collection / Corbis*

INDEX

J

X

Y

Z